Western Civilization

▼▼▼▼▼

Volume **II**

Western Civilization

▼▼▼▼▼

Volume **II**

Jackson J. Spielvogel
The Pennsylvania State University

West Publishing Company
St. Paul New York Los Angeles San Francisco

Production Credits

▼ ▼ ▼

Copyediting: Patricia Lewis

Design: David Farr, Imagesmythe Inc. & Tech Arts

Composition: Carlisle Communications, Joan Weber, Coordinator.

Cover Illustration: William Powell Frith, *Many Happy Returns of the Day*; Harrogate Museums and Art Gallery, Bridgeman Art Library, London

▼ ▼ ▼

COPYRIGHT © 1991 by WEST PUBLISHING COMPANY
610 Opperman Drive
P.O. Box 64526
St. Paul, MN 55164–0526

Printed in the United States of America

98 97 96 95 94 93 92   8 7 6 5 4 3 2

Library of Congress Cataloging-in-Publication Data

Spielvogel, Jackson J., 1939–
    Western civilization / Jackson J. Spielvogel.
      p.   cm.
    Includes bibliographical references.
    ISBN 0-314-82894-X (hardcover : comprehensive). — ISBN 0-314-82893-1 (volume I : softcover). — ISBN 0-314-82895-8 (volume II : softcover). — ISBN 0-314-82896-6 (volume A : softcover). — ISBN 0-314-82897-4 (volume B : softcover). — ISBN 0-314-82898-2 (volume C : softcover). — ISBN 0-314-82899-0 (since 1300 : softcover)
    1. Civilization, Occidental—History: I. Title.
CB245.S63 1990
909′.09821—dc20
                     90–21772
                     CIP

Illustration Credits

▼ ▼ ▼

Chapter 15

Page 482 Musées Royaux des Beaux-Arts de Belgique, Bruxelles(Photo by G. Cussac); *485* Musées Royaux des Beaux-Arts de Belgique, Bruxelles (Photo by G. Cussac); *489* National Maritime Museum Greenwich; *491* Francois Dubois D'Amiens, *The St. Bartholomew's Day Massacre*, Musée Cantonal des Beaux-Arts, Lausanne; *494* Derechos Reservados, © Museo del Prado, Madrid; *496* Private Collection; *499* Herzog Anton Ulrich-Museum, Braunschweig; *502* Herzog Anton Ulrich-Museum, Braunschweig; *509* The National Galleries of Scotland, By permission of the Earl of Rosebery; *511* Kunsthistorisches Museum, Vienna; *514*(Left) Scala/Art Resource, N.Y.; (Right) Peter Paul Rubens, *The Landing of Marie de Medicis at Marseilles*, Musée du Louvre, © Photo R. M. N.; *515* Laocoon, El Greco, National Gallery of Art, Washington: Samuel H. Kress Collection; *516* Courtesy of James R. Spencer; *518* The National Portrait Gallery, London.

Chapter 16

Page 522 Hyacinthe Rigaud, *Louis XIV*, Musée du Louvre, © Photo R.M.N.; *525* Reproduced by Courtesy of the Trustees, The National Gallery, London; *527* Hyacinthe Rigaud, *Louis XIV*, Musée du Louvre, © Photo R. M. N.; *531* Courtesy of James R. Spencer; *532* Courtesy of James R. Spencer; *540* The Bettmann Archive; *542* Dumesnil, *Queen Christina of Sweden with Descartes*, Musee du Louvre, © Photo R. M. N.; *547* Courtesy of Jackson Spielvogel; *553* H. v. Schuylenburgh, *Head Office of the Dutch East India Company at Hugly in Bengal, 1665*, Rijksmuseum, Amsterdam; *555* Nicholas Poussin, *Landscape with the Burial of Phocion*, Musée du Louvre, © Photo R. M. N.; *556* Rembrandt, *The Syndics of the Cloth Guild*, Rijksmuseum, Amsterdam.

Chapter 17

Page 562 Bibliothèque Nationale, Paris; *566* Courtesy of the Lilly Library, Indiana University, Bloomington, Indiana; *567* Courtesy of the Lilly Library, Indiana University, Bloomington, Indiana; *569* Deutsches Museum, Munich; *571* Biblioteca Nazionale Centrale, Firenze; *575* National Portrait Gallery, London; *577* Metsys, *Paracelus*, Musée du Louvre, © Photo R. M. N.; *578* Reproduced by Courtesy of the Trustees of the British Museum; *582* Historical Pictures Service, Chicago; *588* Bibliothèque Nationale, Paris; *589* Reproduced by permission of the Trustees of the Science Museum(neg. 4534).

Chapter 18

Page 594 Giraudon/Art Resource, N.Y. Detail from *First Reading of Voltaire's "L'Orphelin de Chine"* at the Salon of Mme Geoffrin, 1725, by Lemmonier; *596* By permission of the Houghton Library, Harvard University; *600* Bibliothèque Nationale, Paris; *606* Allan Ramsay; *Jean-Jaques Rousseau*; National Gallery of Scotland; *608* Giraudon/Art Resource, N.Y. *First Reading of Voltaire's "L'Orphelin de Chine"* at the Salon of Mme

(continued following Index)

About the Author

▼ ▼ ▼

Jackson J. Spielvogel is associate professor of history at The Pennsylvania State University. He received his Ph.D. from The Ohio State University, where he specialized in Reformation history under Harold J. Grimm. His articles and reviews have appeared in such journals as *Moreana, Journal of General Education, Catholic Historical Review, Archiv für Reformationsgeschichte,* and *American Historical Review.* He has also contributed chapters or articles to *The Social History of the Reformation, The Holy Roman Empire: A Dictionary Handbook, Simon Wiesenthal Center Annual of Holocaust Studies,* and *Utopian Studies.* His work has been supported by fellowships from the Fulbright Foundation and the Foundation for Reformation Research. At Penn State, he helped inaugurate the Western civilization courses as well as a popular course on Nazi Germany. His book, *Hitler and Nazi Germany,* was published in 1987. He has won three major university-wide teaching awards. During the year 1988–1989, he held the Penn State Teaching Fellowship, the University's most prestigious teaching award.

To Diane, whose love and support made it all possible

Contents

▼ ▼ ▼ ▼ ▼

Chapter 20

▼ A Revolution in Politics: The Era of the French Revolution and Napoleon   666

Chapter 21

▼ The Industrial Revolution and Its Impact on European Society   702

Chapter 22

▼ Reaction, Revolution, and Romanticism, 1815–1850   732

Chapter 29

▼ The Postwar Western World   1002

Chapter 30

▼ Epilogue–Toward a Global Civilization   1046

Documents

▼▼▼▼▼

Maps

▼ ▼ ▼ ▼ ▼

Chronologies

▼ ▼ ▼ ▼ ▼

Preface

▼ ▼ ▼

We are often reminded how important it is to understand today's world if we are to deal with our growing number of challenges. And yet that understanding will be incomplete if we in the Western world do not comprehend the meaning of Western civilization and the role Western civilization has played in the world. For all of our modern progress, we still greatly reflect our religious traditions, our political systems and theories, our economic and social structures, and our cultural heritage. I have written this history of Western civilization to assist a new generation of students in learning more about the past that has helped create them and the world in which they live.

As a teacher of Western civilization courses at a major university, I have become aware of the tendency of many textbooks to simplify the content of Western civilization courses by emphasizing an intellectual perspective or political perspective or, most recently, a social perspective, often at the expense of sufficient details in a chronological framework. This approach is confusing to students whose high school social studies programs have often neglected a systematic study of Western civilization. I have attempted to write a well-balanced work in which the political, economic, social, religious, intellectual, cultural, and military aspects of Western civilization have been integrated into a chronologically-ordered synthesis. I have been especially aware of the need to integrate the latest research on social history and women's history into each chapter of the book rather than isolating it either in lengthy topical chapters, which confuse the student by interrupting the chronological narrative, or in separate sections that appear at periodic intervals between chapters. If the results of the new social and women's history are to be taken seriously, they must be fully integrated into the basic narrative itself.

Another purpose in writing this history of Western civilization has been to put the story back in history. That story is an exciting one, yet many textbooks, often the product of several authors with different writing styles, fail to capture the imagination of their readers. Narrative history effectively transmits the knowledge of the past and is the form that best aids remembrance. At the same time, I have not overlooked the need for the kind of historical analysis that makes students aware that historians often disagree in their interpretations of the past.

To enliven the past and let readers see for themselves the materials that historians use to create their pictures of the past, I have included primary sources (boxed documents) in each chapter that are keyed to the discussion in the text. The documents include examples of the religious, artistic, intellectual, social, economic, and political aspects of Western life. Such varied sources as a Roman banquet menu, a student fight song in twentieth-century Britain, letters exchanged between a husband on the battle front and his wife in World War I, the Declaration of the Rights of Woman and the Citizen in the French Revolution, and a debate in the Reformation era, all reveal in a vivid fashion what Western civilization meant to the individual men and women who shaped it by their activities.

Each chapter has a lengthy introduction and conclusion to help maintain the continuity of the narrative and to provide a synthesis of important themes. Timelines enable students to see at a glance the major developments of an era, while the more detailed chronologies reinforce the events discussed in the text. An annotated bibliography at the end of each chapter reviews the most recent literature on each period and also gives references to some of the older, "classic" works in each field. Extensive maps and illustrations serve to deepen the readers' understanding of the text. In order to facilitate understanding of cultural movements, illustrations of artistic works discussed in the text are placed next to the discussions.

Because courses in Western civilization at American colleges and universities follow different chronological divisions, a one-volume edition, two two-volume editions, and a three-volume edition of this text are being made available to fit the needs of instructors. Teaching and learning ancillaries include an Instructor's Manual with Test Items (written by the author of the book), a Study Guide, Computerized Test Items, and Map Transparencies.

▼ Acknowledgements

I began to teach at age five in my family's grape arbor. By the age of ten, I wanted to know and understand everything in the world so I set out to memorize our entire set of encyclopedia volumes. At seventeen, as editor of the high school yearbook, I chose "Patterns" as its theme. With that as my early history, followed by twenty rich years of teaching, writing, and family nurturing, it seemed quite natural to accept the challenge of writing a history of Western civilization as I approached that period in life often described as the age of wisdom. Although I see this writing adventure as part of the natural unfolding of my life, I gratefully acknowledge that without the generosity of many others, it would not have been possible.

David Redles gave generously of his time and ideas, especially for chapter 29. Additional research and editorial assistance were provided by Laurie Batitto, Alex Spencer, Stephen Maloney, Shaun Mason, Peter Angelos, and Fred Schooley. I deeply appreciate the valuable technical assistance provided by Dayton Coles. I am thankful to the thousands of students whose questions and responses have caused me to see many aspects of Western civilization in new ways.

My ability to undertake a project of this magnitude was in part due to the outstanding European history teachers that I had both as an undergraduate and graduate student. These included: Kent Forster (modern Europe) and Robert W. Green (early modern Europe) at The Pennsylvania State University; and Franklin Pegues (medieval), Andreas Dorpalen (modern Germany), William McDonald (ancient), and Harold J. Grimm (Renaissance and Reformation) at The Ohio State University. These teachers provided me with profound insights into Western civilization and also taught me by their examples that learning only becomes true understanding when it is accompanied by compassion, gentleness, and openness.

Thanks to West Publishing Company's comprehensive review process, many historians were asked to evaluate my manuscript. I am grateful to the following for the innumerable suggestions that have greatly improved my work:

Roy A. Austensen
Illinois State University

James T. Baker
Western Kentucky University

John F. Battick
University of Maine

Fredric J. Baumgartner
Virginia Polytechnic Institute

Phillip N. Bebb
Ohio University

Leonard R. Berlanstein
University of Virginia

Werner Braatz
University of Wisconsin-Oshkosh

Alfred S. Bradford
University of Missouri

Hugh S. Bonar
California State University

Maryann E. Brink
College of William & Mary

Elizabeth Carney
Clemson University

Marc Cooper
Southwest Missouri State

Richard A. Cosgrove
University of Arizona

Porter Ewing
Los Angeles City College

Steven Fanning
University of Illinois at Chicago

Ellsworth Faris
California State University-Chico

Gary B. Ferngren
Oregon State University

A.Z. Freeman
Robinson College

Frank J. Frost
University of California, Santa Barbara

Richard M. Golden
Clemson University

Amy G. Gordon
Denison University

Hanns Gross
Loyola University

Jeffrey S. Hamilton
Old Dominion University

A.J. Heisserer
University of Oklahoma

Boyd H. Hill, Jr.
University of Colorado at Boulder

Frank L. Holt
University of Houston

Richard A. Jackson
University of Houston

Jenny M. Jochens
Towson State University

William M. Johnston
University of Massachusetts

James M. Kittelson
Ohio State University

Mavis Mate
University of Oregon

Eugene W. Miller, Jr.
The Pennsylvania State University-Hazleton

William M. Murray
University of South Florida

Otto M. Nelson
Texas Tech. University

Donald Ostrowski
Harvard University

James O. Overfield
University of Vermont

Linda J. Piper
University of Georgia

Janet Polasky
University of New Hampshire

Charles A. Povlovich
California State University-Fullerton

Jerome V. Reel, Jr.
Clemson University

Julius R. Ruff
Marquette University

Richard Saller
University of Chicago

Magdalena Sanchez
Texas Christian University

Jack Schanfield
Suffolk County Community College

Roger Schlesinger
Washington State University

Kyle C. Sessions
Illinois State University

Paul W. Strait
Florida State University

James E. Straukamp
Cal. State Univ.-Sacramento

Fred Suppe
Ball State University

Donna L. VanRapphorst
Cuyahoga Community College

Allen M. Ward
University of Connecticut

Walter J. Wussow
University of Wisconsin-Eau Claire

Edwin M. Yamauchi
Miami University

The editors at West Publishing Company have been both helpful and congenial at all times. Their flexible policies allowed the creative freedom that a writer cherishes. I especially wish to thank Clark Baxter, whose faith in my ability to do this project was inspiring. Developmental editor Nancy Crochiere was always helpful with many practical details. My production editor, Tamborah Moore, was a pillar of strength through a very lengthy process. Pat Lewis, my copy editor, taught me much about the fine points of the English language. Kara ZumBahlen and Lynn Reichel provided valuable assistance in obtaining illustrations and permissions for the boxed documents. I appreciate the professional and personal relationships that I have shared with the West "family."

Above all, I thank my family for their support. My daughters Jennifer and Kathryn, my sons Eric and Christian, and my daughter-in-law Liz were patient and tolerant of my time in the study. My wife and best friend Diane provided me with editorial assistance and the loving support that made it possible for me to complete a project of this magnitude. I could not have written the book without her.

JACKSON J. SPIELVOGEL

Western Civilization

▼▼▼▼▼

Volume **II**

Introduction to Western Civilization

▼ ▼ ▼

Civilization, as historians identify it, first emerged between 5000 and 6000 years ago when people began to live in organized communities with distinct political, military, economic, and social structures. Religious, intellectual, and artistic activities also assumed important functions in these early societies. The focus of this book is on Western civilization, a civilization that for most of its history has been identified with the continent of Europe. Its origins, however, go back to the Mediterranean basin, including lands in North Africa and the Near East as well as Europe itself. Moreover, the spread of Europeans abroad led to the development of offshoots of Western civilization in other parts of the world.

Because civilized life includes all of the activities and experiences of people dwelling together in organized communities, the history of a civilization must encompass a series of studies. Examination of a society's economic structure reveals how it grew its food, how it made its goods, how it furnished the services it needed for the life of its people, and how private individuals and public authorities employed the material assets of their community. Although the way private individuals spend their money reflects individual goals, it also affects the larger society of which those individuals are a part. How governing authorities use public resources reveals much about the nature of a society. Huge expenditures on the military sector of a society, for example, decreases the availability of resources for the domestic welfare of its citizens.

From a study of social structure, we learn about the relationships that existed among the various social groups, how the wealth of the community was distributed, and how each social group lived. Political structure reveals how society was governed and which social group or groups controlled power. An investigation of the political structure also discloses the existence of mechanisms for change, or without such mechanisms, how revolutions arose and were justified by their leaders.

Also crucial to the understanding of a civilization is its culture, or the ideas, beliefs, and achievements of its people. This includes what historians now call high culture, which consists of the writings of a society's thinkers and the works of its artists. Frequently, the ideas and achievements of the intellectuals and artists have been used to define the ideals of a civilization. But historians now write as well of a civilization's popular culture, the world of ideas and experiences of the masses who constituted most of the people. Less privileged and less educated, however, they were often unable to express their ideas in writing, and until the recent work of social historians and anthropologists, were often considered less important to the story of a civilization.

The history of a civilization is also explained by how people in a society interpret their relationship to a spiritual reality. The definition of that relationship creates a society's religion and its system of values. In fact, religious values and perspectives have played crucial roles in the development of civilization.

The study of Western civilization, then, requires us to examine the political, economic, social, military, cultural, intellectual, and religious aspects that make up the life of that civilization and show how they are interrelated. In so doing, we need also at times to focus on some of the unique features of Western civilization. Certainly, science played a crucial role in the development of modern Western civilization. Although such societies as those of the Greeks, the Romans, and medieval Europeans were based largely on a belief in the existence of a spiritual order, Western civilization experienced a dramatic departure to a natural or material view of the universe in the seventeenth-century Scientific Revolution. Science and technology have been important in the growth of a modern and largely secular Western civilization, although antecedents to scientific development also existed in Greek, Islamic, and medieval thought and practice. By the twentieth century, science and technology had created the instruments that made possible incredible material and physical benefits as well as a threat of ecological catastrophe and physical annihilation.

For many historians, the concept of political liberty, the fundamental value of every individual, and the creation of a rational outlook, based on a system of logical, analytical thought, have also been viewed as unique aspects of Western civilization. Of course, Western civilization has also witnessed the frightening negation of liberty, individualism, and reason. Racism, violence, world wars, totalitarianism—these, too, must form part of the story. Finally, regardless of our concentration on Western civilization and its characteristics, we need to take into account that Western civilization was influenced by other civilizations and it, in turn, has affected the course of other civilizations.

Chapter 15

Discovery and Crisis in the Sixteenth and Seventeenth Centuries

▼▼▼▼▼

Although the Reformations of the sixteenth century made religion a central focus of people's lives, by the middle of the sixteenth century this renewal of religious passion had been accomplished at a great cost—the breakup of the religious unity of medieval Europe. This religious division (Catholics versus Protestants) was instrumental in beginning a series of wars that dominated much of European history from 1560 to 1650 and, in turn, exacerbated the economic and social crises that were besetting Europe. Wars, revolutions and constitutional crises, economic depression, social disintegration, the witchcraft craze, and demographic crisis all afflicted Europe and have led some historians to speak of the almost hundred years from 1560 to 1650 as an age of crisis in European life.

Periods of crisis, however, are frequently ages of opportunities, nowhere more apparent than in the geographical discoveries that made this an era of European expansion into new worlds. While the discovery of new territories began before the sixteenth century, it was not until the sixteenth and seventeenth centuries that Europeans began to comprehend the significance of their discoveries and to exploit them for their material gain.

▼ An Age of Discovery and Expansion

Nowhere has the dynamic and even ruthless energy of Western civilization been more apparent than in its expansion into the rest of the world. By the sixteenth century, the Atlantic seaboard had become the center of a commercial activity that raised Portugal and Spain and

Columbus Discovers the Americas ▼ | Cortés Conquers Mexico ▼ | French Religious Wars ▼ | Jesuit Church of Il Gesù ▼ | The Thirty Years' War ▼ | Puritan Revolution ▼

·········· 1500 ············· 1540 ············ 1580 ············· 1620 ············· 1660 ··········

▲ El Greco | ▲ William Shakespeare | ▲ Montaigne, *Essays* | ▲ Bank of Amsterdam

later the Dutch Republic, England, and France to prominence. The age of expansion was a crucial factor in the European transition from the agrarian economy of the Middle Ages to a commercial and industrial capitalistic system.

The Motives

For almost a millennium, Catholic Europe had been confined to one area. Its one major attempt to expand beyond those frontiers, the crusades, had largely failed. Of course, Europe had never completely lost contact with the outside world: the goods of Asia and Africa made their way into medieval castles; the works of Muslim philosophers were read in medieval universities; and the Vikings in the ninth and tenth centuries had even made their way to the eastern fringes of North America. But all of these represented limited contacts with non-European civilizations until the end of the fifteenth century, when Europeans embarked upon a remarkable series of overseas journeys. What caused Europeans to undertake such dangerous voyages to the ends of the earth?

Europeans had long had an attraction to the Far East. In the Middle Ages, myths and legends of an exotic Far East of great riches and magic were widespread. Although Muslim control of central Asia cut Europe off from the east, Mongol conquests in the thirteenth century reopened the doors. The most famous medieval travelers to the east were the Polos of Venice. Niccolò and Maffeo, merchants from Venice, accompanied by Niccolò's son Marco, undertook the lengthy journey to the court of the great Mongol ruler Kublai Khan (1259–1294) in 1271. As one of the great Khan's ambassadors, Marco traveled to Japan as well and did not return to Italy until 1295. An account of his experiences, the *Travels*, proved to be the most informative of all the descriptions of Asia by medieval European travelers. Others followed the Polos, but in the fourteenth century

the conquests of the Ottoman Turks and then the overthrow of the Mongols by the first of the Ming Chinese emperors halted Western traffic to the east. The closing of the eastern routes to the Far East now caused a number of people to become interested in the possibility of reaching Asia by sea to gain access to the spices and other precious items of the region.

An economic motive thus looms large in Renaissance European expansion. There were high hopes of finding precious metals and expanding the areas of trade, especially for the spices of the east. The latter continued to come to Europe via Arab middlemen but were outrageously expensive. Many European explorers and conquerors did not hesitate to express their desire for material gain. One Spanish conquistador explained that he and his kind went to the New World to "serve God and His Majesty, to give light to those who were in darkness, and to grow rich, as all men desire to do."[1]

This statement expresses another major reason for the overseas voyages—religious zeal. A crusading mentality was particularly strong in Portugal and Spain where the Muslims had largely been driven out in the Middle Ages. It was said by contemporaries of Prince Henry the Navigator of Portugal (see the next section) that he was motivated by "his great desire to make increase in the faith of our Lord Jesus Christ and to bring him all the souls that should be saved." While most scholars believe the religious motive was secondary to economic considerations, it would be foolish to overlook the genuine desire on the part of both explorers and conquistadores, let alone missionaries, to convert the heathen to Christianity. Hernando Cortés, the conqueror of Mexico, asked his Spanish rulers if it was not their duty to ensure that the native Mexicans "are introduced into and instructed in the holy Catholic faith," and predicted that if "the devotion, trust and hope which they now have in their idols turned so as to repose with the divine power of the true God . . . they would work many miracles."[2] Spiritual and secular affairs were closely intertwined in the sixteenth century. No doubt, grandeur and glory as

Discovery and Crisis in the Sixteenth and Seventeenth Centuries ▼ 483 well as plain intellectual curiosity and spirit of adventure also played some role in European expansion.

If "God, glory, and gold" were the motives, what made the voyages possible? First of all, the expansion of Europe was tied to the growth of centralized monarchies during the Renaissance. While the degree of that centralization is still debated by historians, the reality is that Renaissance expansion was a state enterprise. By the second half of the fifteenth century, European monarchies had increased both their authority and resources and were in a position to turn their energies beyond their borders. That meant the invasion of Italy for France, but for Portugal, a state not strong enough to pursue power in Europe, it meant going abroad. The Spanish scene was more complex since the strength of the Spanish monarchy by the sixteenth century enabled it to pursue power on both the continent and beyond.

At the same time, by the end of the fifteenth century, European states had a level of wealth and technology that enabled them to achieve a regular series of voyages beyond Europe. Although the highly schematic and symbolic medieval maps were of little help to sailors, the portolani or detailed charts made by medieval navigators and mathematicians in the thirteenth and fourteenth centuries, featuring details on coastal contours, distances between ports, and compass readings, proved of great value. By the end of the fifteenth century, cartography had developed to the point that Europeans possessed fairly accurate maps of the known world. Moreover, Europeans had developed remarkably seaworthy ships as well as navigational aids, such as the compass and astrolabe. Much of the geographical knowledge learned in the early phase of expansion was passed on to succeeding generations. Indeed, one of the most immediate results of the age of expansion was an enormous increase in knowledge of the physical proportions of the world.

The Development of a Portuguese Maritime Empire

Portugal took the lead in exploring the coast of Africa under the leadership of Prince Henry the "Navigator" (1394–1460), whose motives were a blend of seeking a Christian kingdom as an ally against the Muslims, acquiring trade opportunities for Portugal, and extending Christianity. Beginning in 1419, Prince Henry founded a school for navigators on the southwestern coast of Portugal and began to send out annual expeditions along the west African coast. After Henry's death in 1460,

there was a hiatus in Portuguese exploration until the 1470s and 1480s. Through regular expeditions, the Portuguese gradually crept down the African coast until Bartholomew Diaz finally rounded the Cape of Good Hope on the southern tip of Africa in 1487. Vasco da Gama surpassed that accomplishment by rounding the cape, skirting the eastern coast of Africa, and cutting across the Indian Ocean to the southwestern coast of India. At the port of Calicut, he took on a cargo of pepper and precious stones and then returned to Portugal, where he made a handsome profit on his valuable goods. Da Gama's successful voyage marked the beginning of an all-water route to India.

After da Gama's return, Portugal sent a larger fleet to the east. Despite opposition from Muslim traders in west India, it managed to return to Portugal with valuable cargo. One contemporary described its contents: "Cinnamon, fresh and dried ginger, much pepper, cloves, nutmegs, mace, musk, porcelains, incense, myrrh, red and white sandalwood, opium, India paper, and a great variety of drugs. . . . I saw many diamonds, rubies, and pearls." By 1501, annual Portuguese fleets to India were making serious inroads into the Mediterranean trade of the Venetians and Turks.

Under the direction of officials known as viceroys, Portugal now created an overseas empire. Most important was Alfonso d'Albuquerque (c. 1462–1515), a tough nobleman who took the lead in establishing a ring of commercial-military bases centered at Goa, an island off the Malabar Coast of India. The Portuguese also reached beyond India by taking the island of Macao at the mouth of the Pearl River in China. The Portuguese empire remained a limited empire of enclaves or trading posts on the coasts of India and China. The Portuguese simply did not possess the power to colonize the Asian regions. Moreover, although they invested heavily in ships and manpower for this empire (hundreds of ships and hundreds of thousands of workers in shipyards and overseas bases), it was very costly. Only one-half of the ships involved in the India trade survived for a second journey. Disease, shipwreck, and battles took a heavy toll of life. Portugal's empire was too large and Portugal too small to maintain it, and by the seventeenth century the Portuguese were being severely challenged in the Far East by the English, Dutch, and French.

Voyages to the New World

Although the Spanish came to overseas discovery and exploration after the initial efforts of Henry the Navigator, their resources enabled them to establish a far grander overseas empire of a quite different nature from the Portuguese.

An important figure in the history of Spanish exploration was an Italian, Cristoforo Colombo, more commonly known as Christopher Columbus (1451–1506). Convinced that the circumference of the earth was less than contemporaries believed and that Asia was larger than people thought, Columbus felt that Asia could be reached by sailing west instead of around Africa. Queen Isabella of Spain was finally persuaded to finance Columbus's exploratory expedition, which reached the Americas in October 1492, exploring the coastline of Cuba and the northern shores of Haiti (Hispaniola). Columbus believed that he had reached Asia and in three subsequent voyages (1493, 1498, 1502) sought in vain to find a route through the outer lands to the Asian mainland. In his four voyages, Columbus reached all the major islands of the Caribbean and Honduras in Central America.

Although Columbus clung to his belief till his death, other explorers soon realized that Columbus had discovered a new frontier altogether. State-sponsored explorers joined the race to the New World. A Venetian seaman, John Cabot, explored the New England coastline of the Americas under a license from King Henry VII of England. Amerigo Vespucci, a Florentine, accompanied several voyages and wrote a series of letters describing the geography of the New World. The publication of these letters led to the use of the name "America" (after Amerigo) for these new lands.

The first two decades of the sixteenth century witnessed numerous overseas voyages that explored the eastern coasts of both North and South America. Perhaps the most dramatic of all these expeditions was the journey of Ferdinand Magellan (1480–1521) in 1519. After passing through the Straits named after him at the bottom of South America, he sailed across the Pacific Ocean and reached the Philippines where he met his death at the hands of the natives. Although only one of his original fleet of five ships survived and returned to Spain, Magellan's name is still associated with the first known circumnavigation of the earth.

The Spanish Empire

The New World was a misnomer since the Western Hemisphere possessed flourishing civilizations populated by millions of people when the Europeans arrived. It was, of course, new to the Europeans who quickly saw

▼ **Two-Masted Ocean-Going Ship.** The Americas were first reached in the fifteenth century by Christopher Columbus, an Italian in the service of the Spanish monarchs. While Columbus believed that he had found a western route to Asia, others realized that he had actually discovered new lands. Explorers such as John Cabot and Amerigo Vespucci rushed to investigate the new world, and numerous overseas voyages to both North and South America were made in the first two decades of the sixteenth century. This detail from a larger work by Pieter Brueghel depicts a two-masted ocean-going ship of the type used in the voyages of sixteenth-century explorers.

opportunities for conquest and exploitation. The Spanish conquistadores were a hardy lot of mostly upper-class individuals motivated by a typical sixteenth-century blend of glory, greed, and religious crusading zeal. Although sanctioned by the Castilian crown, these groups were financed and outfitted privately, not by the government.

Their superior weapons, organizational skills, and determination brought the conquistadores incredible success. Beginning in 1519 with a small band of men, Hernando Cortés took three years to overthrow the mighty

The Spanish Conquistador: Cortés and the Conquest of Mexico
▼▼▼

Hernando Cortés was a Spanish nobleman who came to the New World in 1504 to seek his fortune. Contrary to his superior's orders, Cortés waged an independent campaign of conquest and overthrew the Aztec Empire of Mexico (1519–1521). Cortés wrote a series of five reports to Emperor Charles V to justify his action. The second report includes a description of Tenochtitlán, an Aztec city he had captured. The Spanish conquistador and his men were obviously impressed by this city, awesome in its architecture yet built by people who lacked European technology, such as wheeled vehicles and tools of hard metal.

Cortés's Description of an Aztec City

The great city Tenochtitlán is built in the midst of this salt lake, and it is two leagues from the heart of the city to any point on the mainland. Four causeways lead to it, all made by hand and some twelve feet wide. The city itself is as large as Seville or Córdova. The principal streets are very broad and straight, the majority of them being of beaten earth, but a few and at least half the smaller thoroughfares are waterways along which they pass in their canoes. Moreover, even the principal streets have openings at regular distances so that the water can freely pass from one to another, and these openings which are very broad are spanned by great bridges of huge beams, very stoutly put together, so firm indeed that over many of them ten horsemen can ride at once. Seeing that if the natives intended any treachery against us they would have every opportunity from the way in which the city is built, for by removing the bridges from the entrances and exits they could leave us to die of hunger with no possibility of getting to the mainland, I immediately set to work as soon as we entered the city on the building of four brigs, and in a short space of time had them finished, so that we could ship three hundred men and the horses to the mainland whenever we so desired.

The city has many open squares in which markets are continuously held and the general business of buying and selling proceeds. One square in particular is twice as big as that of Salamanca and completely surrounded by arcades where there are daily more than sixty thousand folk buying and selling. Every kind of merchandise such as may be met with in every land is for sale there, whether of food and victuals, or ornaments of gold and silver, or lead, brass, copper, tin, precious stones, bones, shells, snails and feathers; limestone for building is likewise sold there, stone both rough and polished, bricks burnt and unburnt, wood of all kinds and in all stages of preparation. . . . There is a street of herb-sellers where there are all manner of roots and medicinal plants that are found in the land. There are houses as it were of apothecaries where they sell medicines made from these herbs, both for drinking and for use as ointments and salves. There are barbers' shops where you may have your hair washed and cut. There are other shops where you may obtain food and drink. . . .

Finally, to avoid prolixity in telling all the wonders of this city, I will simply say that the manner of living among the people is very similar to that in Spain, and considering that this is a barbarous nation shut off from a knowledge of the true God or communication with enlightened nations, one may well marvel at the orderliness and good government which is everywhere maintained.

The actual service of Montezuma and those things which call for admiration by their greatness and state would take so long to describe that I assure your Majesty I do not know where to begin with any hope of ending. For as I have already said, what could there be more astonishing than that a barbarous monarch such as he should have reproductions made in gold, silver, precious stones, and feathers of all things to be found in his land, and so perfectly reproduced that there is no goldsmith or silversmith in the world who could better them, nor can one understand what instrument could have been used for fashioning the jewels; as for the featherwork its like is not to be seen in either wax or embroidery, it is so marvellously delicate.

Aztec Empire on mainland Mexico led by the chieftain Montezuma (see the box on p. 486). Between 1531 and 1550, the Spanish gained control of northern Mexico. Between 1531 and 1536, another expedition led by a hardened and somewhat corrupt soldier, Francesco Pizarro (1470–1541), took control of the Inca Empire high in the Peruvian Andes. Although it took another three decades before the western part of Latin America was brought under Spanish control (the Portuguese took over Brazil), already by 1535, the Spanish had created a system of colonial administration that made the New World an extension of the old.

ADMINISTRATION OF THE SPANISH EMPIRE IN THE NEW WORLD Spanish policy toward the Indians of the New World was a combination of confusion, misguided paternalism, and cruel exploitation. Confusion arose over the nature of the Indians. Unsure whether these strange creatures were "full men" or not, Spanish doctors of law debated how to fit them into currently existing European

▼ **Map 15.1** Discoveries and Possessions in the Sixteenth and Early Seventeenth Centuries.

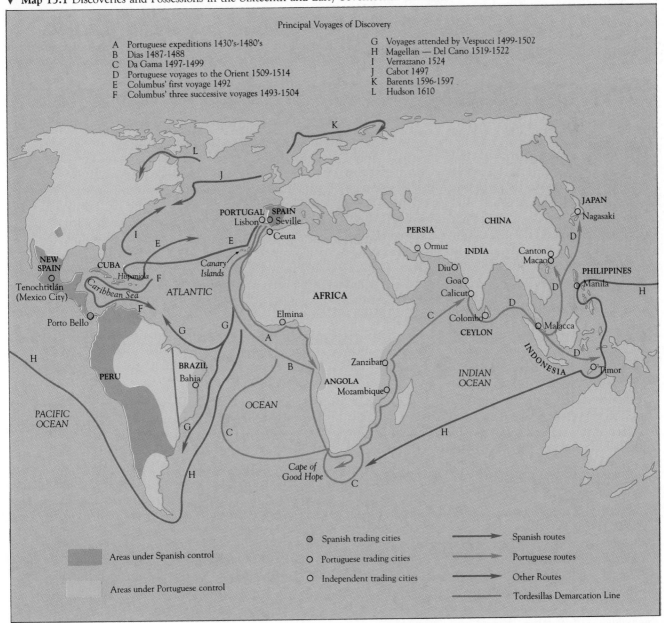

Principal Voyages of Discovery

A Portuguese expeditions 1430's-1480's
B Dias 1487-1488
C Da Gama 1497-1499
D Portuguese voyages to the Orient 1509-1514
E Columbus' first voyage 1492
F Columbus' three successive voyages 1493-1504

G Voyages attended by Vespucci 1499-1502
H Magellan — Del Cano 1519-1522
I Verrazzano 1524
J Cabot 1497
K Barents 1596-1597
L Hudson 1610

Spanish trading cities
Portuguese trading cities
Independent trading cities

Spanish routes
Portuguese routes
Other Routes
Tordesillas Demarcation Line

Areas under Spanish control
Areas under Portuguese control

Las Casas and the Spanish Treatment of the American Natives
▼ ▼ ▼

Bartolomé de Las Casas (1474–1566) was a Dominican monk who participated in the conquest of Cuba and received land and Indians in return for his efforts. But in 1514 he underwent a radical transformation that led him to believe that the Indians had been cruelly mistreated by his fellow Spaniards. He spent the remaining years of his life (he lived to the age of ninety-two) fighting for the Indians. This selection is taken from his most influential work, Brevísima Relación de la Destrucción de las Indias, known to English readers as The Tears of the Indians. This work was particularly responsible for the legend of the Spanish as inherently "cruel and murderous fanatics." Most scholars feel that Las Casas may have exaggerated his account in order to shock his contemporaries into action.

Bartolomé de Las Casas, *The Tears of the Indians*

There is nothing more detestable or more cruel, then the tyranny which the Spaniards use toward the Indians for the getting of pearl. Surely the infernal torments cannot much exceed the anguish that they endure, by reason of that way of cruelty; for they put them under water some four or five ells deep, where they are forced without any liberty of respiration, to gather up the shells wherein the Pearls are; sometimes they come up again with nets full of shells to take breath, but if they stay any while to rest themselves, immediately comes a hangman row'd in a little boat, who as soon as he hath well beaten them, drags them again to their labour. Their food is nothing but filth, and the very same that contains the Pearl, with a small portion of that bread which that Country affords; in the first whereof there is little nourishment; and as for the latter, it is made with great difficulty, besides that they have not enough of that neither for sustenance; they lye upon the ground in fetters, lest they should run away; and many times they are drown'd in this labour, and are never seen again till they swim upon the top of the waves: oftentimes they also are devoured by certain sea monsters, that are frequent in those seas. Consider whether this hard usage of the poor creatures be consistent with the precepts which God commands concerning charity to our neighbour, by those that cast them so undeservedly into the dangers of a cruel death, causing them to perish without any remorse or pity, or allowing them the benefit of the Sacraments, or the knowledge of Religion; it being impossible for them to live any time under the water; and this death is so much the more painful, by reason that by the coarctation of the breast, while the lungs strive to do their office, the vital parts are so afflicted that they die vomiting the blood out of their mouths. Their hair also, which is by nature black, is hereby changed and made of the same color with that of the sea Wolves; their bodies are also so besprinkled with the froth of the sea, that they appear rather like monsters than men.

---

legal patterns. While the conquistadores made decisions based on expediency and their own interests, Queen Isabella declared the natives to be subjects of Castile and instituted the Spanish *encomienda,* a system that permitted the conquering Spaniards to collect tribute from the natives and use them as laborers. In return, the holders of an *encomienda* were supposed to protect the Indians and supervise their spiritual and material needs. In practice, this meant that the settlers were free to implement the paternalistic system of the government as they pleased. Three thousand miles from Spain, Spanish settlers largely ignored their government and brutally used the Indians to pursue their own economic interests. Indians were put to work on plantations and in the lucrative gold and silver mines. Forced labor, starvation, and especially disease took a fearful toll of Indian lives. With little or no natural resistance to European diseases, the Indians of America were ravaged by smallpox, measles, and typhus. These "killers" came with the explorers and the conquistadores. Although scholarly estimates on native population figures vary drastically, a reasonable guess is that 30 to 40 percent of the natives died. On Hispaniola (Haiti) alone, out of an initial population of 100,000 natives when Columbus arrived in 1493, only 300 Indians survived by 1570. In 1542, largely in response to the publications of Bartolomé de Las Casas, a Dominican monk who championed the Indians (see the box above), the government abolished the *encomienda* system and provided more protection for the natives.

The Spanish created a formal administrative system for their new empire. While a board of trade known as the *Casa de Contratación* supervised all economic matters related to the New World, the Council of the Indies became the chief organ of colonial administration. The council suggested the names of colonial officials, oversaw their New World activities, and kept an eye on ecclesiastical affairs in the colonies.

In the New World, the Spanish developed an administrative system based on viceroys. Spanish possessions were initially divided into two major administrative units: New Spain (Mexico, Central America, and the Caribbean islands) with its center in Mexico City and Peru (western South America), governed by a viceroy in Lima. Each viceroy served as the king's chief civil and military officer and was aided by advisory groups called *audiencias*, which also functioned as supreme judicial bodies.

By papal agreement, the Catholic monarchs of Spain were given extensive rights over ecclesiastical affairs in the New World. They could nominate church officials, build churches, collect fees, and supervise the affairs of the various religious orders who sought to Christianize the heathen. Catholic monks had remarkable success in converting and baptizing hundreds of thousands of Indians in the early years of the conquest. Soon after there followed the establishment of dioceses, parishes,

schools, and hospitals—all the trappings of civilized European society.

The Impact of Expansion

European expansion made an enormous impact on both the conquerors and the conquered. The native American civilizations, which had their own unique qualities and a degree of sophistication not much appreciated by Europeans, were virtually destroyed. Ancient social and political structures were ripped up and replaced by European institutions, religion, language, and culture. The Portuguese trading posts in the Far East, on the other hand, had much less impact on native Asian civilizations.

European expansion also affected the conquerors, perhaps most notably in the economic arena. Wherever they went in the New World, Europeans sought to find sources of gold and silver. One Aztec commented that the Spanish conquerors "longed and lusted for gold. Their bodies swelled with greed, and their hunger was ravenous; they hungered like pigs for that gold."[3] Rich silver deposits were found and exploited in Mexico and southern Peru (modern Bolivia). When the mines at Potosí in Peru were opened in 1545, the value of precious metals imported into Europe quadrupled. It has been estimated that between 1503 and 1650 sixteen mil-

▼ **World Map of the Early Sixteenth Century.** Overseas expansion affected not only the inhabitants of the "New World," but also their European conquerors. New sources of gold and silver were discovered and tensions grew between the European states as they competed for trading products. Psychologically, belief in their own superiority was strengthened by the relative ease with which the Europeans dominated the native people. Pictured here is a world map showing the coastlines that had been charted by 1540.

lion kilograms of silver and 185,000 kilograms of gold entered the port of Seville and helped to create a price revolution that affected the Spanish economy.

But gold and silver were only two of the products sent to Europe from the New World. Into Seville flowed sugar, dyes, cotton, vanilla, and hides from livestock raised in the South American pampas. New agricultural products such as potatoes, coffee, corn, and tobacco were also imported. Because of its trading posts in Asia, Portugal soon challenged the Italian states as the chief entry point of the eastern trade in spices, jewels, silk, carpets, ivory, leather, and perfumes, although the Venetians clung tenaciously to the spice trade until they lost out to the Dutch in the seventeenth century. Economic historians believe that the increase in the volume and area of European trade as well as the rise in fluid capital due to this expansion were crucial factors in producing a new era of commercial capitalism that represented the first step toward the world economy that has characterized the modern historical era.

European expansion, which was in part a product of European rivalries, also deepened those rivalries and increased the tensions among European states. Bitter conflicts arose over the cargoes coming from the New World and Asia. Although the Spanish and Portuguese were first in the competition, the Dutch, French, and English soon became involved on a large scale and by the seventeenth century were challenging the Portuguese and Spanish monopolies.

Finally, how does one evaluate the psychological impact of colonization on the colonizers? The relatively easy European success in dominating native peoples reinforced Christian Europe's belief in the inherent superiority of European civilization. The Scientific Revolution of the seventeenth century (see Chapter 17), the Enlightenment of the eighteenth (see Chapter 18), and the imperialism of the nineteenth (see Chapter 26) would all strengthen this Eurocentric perspective that has caused Western civilization so much trouble in its relationship with the rest of the world.

▼ Politics and the Wars of Religion in the Sixteenth Century

The so-called wars of religion were a product of Reformation ideologies that allowed little room for compromise or toleration of differing opinions. By the middle years of the sixteenth century, Calvinism and Catholicism had become highly militant religions dedicated to spreading the word of God as they interpreted it. While

their struggle for the minds and hearts of Europeans is at the heart of the religious wars of the sixteenth century, economic, social, and political forces also played an important role in these conflicts. Of the sixteenth-century religious wars, none was more momentous or shattering than the French civil wars known as the French Wars of Religion.

The French Wars of Religion (1562–1598)

Of all the European countries, France seemed least likely to be the scene of a religious war. The Valois monarchy had proven itself robust and capable in the sixteenth century. Francis I (1515–1547) and Henry II (1547–1559) had been strong rulers aided by royal officials, a permanent mercenary army, the power to tax, and the ability to control the church by nominating French bishops. It soon became apparent, however, that the power of these sixteenth-century monarchs to control France depended upon the forcefulness of their own personalities. When Henry II was killed accidentally in a tournament in 1559 and was succeeded by a series of weak, feeble, and neurotic sons, two of whom were dominated by their mother, Catherine de' Medici, as regent, the forces held in check by the strong monarchy broke loose, beginning a series of intermittent and confused civil wars. Religious, political, economic, and social forces all contributed to these wars.

The religious forces were the most important. The growth of Calvinism led to persecution by Francis I that intensified under Henry II but did little to stop the spread of Calvinism. Huguenots (as the French Calvinists were called) came from all levels of society: artisans and shopkeepers hurt by rising prices and a rigid guild system; merchants and lawyers in provincial towns whose local privileges were tenuous; and members of the nobility. Possibly 40 to 50 percent of the French nobility became Huguenots, including the house of Bourbon, which stood next to the Valois in the royal line of succession and ruled the southern French kingdom of Navarre. The conversion of so many nobles made the Huguenots a potentially dangerous political threat to monarchical power. While the Calvinists constituted only about 7 percent of the population, they were a dedicated, determined, and well-organized minority. Local congregations governed by consistories of ministers and elders sent representatives to district assemblies, which chose delegates for provincial assemblies. The latter sent representatives to a national synod that served as the ultimate authority for all Huguenots in matters of doctrine and discipline. This system of church organization allowed for spontaneity at the local level while guaranteeing the cohesion of a national church. The first national synod met in Paris in 1559 and represented 72 local churches. Only two years later, the national synod represented 2,150 congregations containing 1 to 1.5 million Calvinists. The national synods even mustered troops from local churches or congregations and served as recruiting agents. When civil war came in 1562, the Calvinists were ready for combat.

The Calvinist minority was greatly outnumbered by the Catholic majority. The Valois monarchy was staunchly Catholic, and its control of the Catholic church gave it little incentive to look favorably upon Protestantism. As regent for her sons, the moderate Catholic Catherine de' Medici (1519–1589) looked to religious compromise as a way to defuse the political tensions, but found to her consternation that both sides possessed their share of religious fanatics unwilling to make concessions. The extreme Catholic party—known as the ultra-Catholics—favored strict opposition to the Huguenots and were led by the Guise family. Possessing the loyalty of Paris and large sections of northern and northwestern France through their client-patronage system, they could recruit and pay for large armies and received support abroad from the papacy and Jesuits who favored their noncompromising Catholic position. Ironically, the allegiance of the Catholic Guises to their own dynasty and international Catholicism posed a strong threat to the Catholic Valois monarchy.

The religious issue was not the only factor that contributed to the French civil wars. Towns and provinces, which had long resisted the growing power of monarchical centralization, were only too willing to join a revolt against the monarchy. This was also true of the nobility, and the fact that so many of them were Calvinists created an important base of opposition to the crown. The French Wars of Religion, then, constituted a major constitutional crisis for France. At the same time, they were complicated by foreign intervention. The devout Catholic king of Spain, Philip II, supported the policies of the ultra-Catholic Guise family while Elizabeth I of England supported the Huguenots for political reasons.

The French Wars of Religion temporarily halted the development of the French centralized territorial state. The claim of the ruling dynasty of the state to a person's loyalties was temporarily superseded by loyalty to one's religious belief. The remark of a close friend of the Guises to the Spanish ambassador in 1565 went to the heart of the problem:

Nowadays Catholic princes must not proceed as they once did. At one time friends and enemies were distinguished by the frontiers of provinces and kingdoms, and were called Italians, Germans, French, Spaniards, English, and the like; now we must say Catholics and heretics, and a Catholic prince must consider all Catholics of all countries as his friends, just as the heretics consider all heretics as friends and subjects, whether they are their own vassals or not.[4]

▼ **The St. Bartholomew's Day Massacre.** Although the outbreak of religious war seemed unlikely in France, the collapse of a strong monarchy with the death of Henry II unleashed forces that created a series of civil wars. While religious ideology was the strongest force at work in the outbreak of war, political and social considerations also played a role. Pictured here is the St. Bartholomew's Day massacre of 1572. This contemporary painting of the massacre depicts a number of the incidents of that day when approximately three thousand Huguenots were murdered in Paris.

Francis I	1515–1547
Henry II	1547–1559
Duke of Guise Massacres Huguenot Congregation at Vassy	1562
Charles IX	1560–1574
Saint Bartholomew's Day Massacre	1572
Formation of the Holy League	1576
Henry III	1574–1589
War of the Three Henries	1588–1589
Assassination of Henry III	1589
Coronation of Henry IV	1594
Edict of Nantes	1598

For some people, the unity of France was less important than religious truth. But there also emerged in France a group of politiques who placed politics before religion and believed that no religious truth was worth the ravages of civil war. The politiques ultimately prevailed, but not until both sides were exhausted by bloodshed.

The wars erupted in 1562 when the powerful duke of Guise massacred a peaceful congregation of Huguenots at Vassy. In the decade of the 1560s, the Huguenots held their own. Too small a group to conquer France, their armies were so good at defensive campaigns that they could not be defeated either, even with the infamous Saint Bartholomew's Day massacre.

This massacre of Huguenots on August 24, 1572, occurred at a time when the Catholic and Calvinist parties had apparently been reconciled through the marriage of Henry of Navarre, the Bourbon ruler of Navarre and acknowledged political leader of the Huguenots, to the sister of the reigning Valois king Charles IX (1560–1574). Many Huguenots traveled to Paris for the wedding. But the Guise family persuaded the king that this gathering of Huguenots was a threat to him. The subsequent massacre on the night of August 24 left three thousand Huguenots dead, although not Henry of Navarre who saved his life by promising to turn Catholic. Thousands more were killed in provincial towns. The massacre boomeranged, however, since it discredited the Valois dynasty without ending the conflict.

The fighting continued. The Huguenots rebuilt their strength while the ultra-Catholics formed a Holy League in 1576, vowing to exterminate heresy and seat a true Catholic champion—Henry, duke of Guise—on the

French throne in place of the ruling king, Henry III (1574–1589), who had succeeded his brother Charles IX in 1574. The turning point in the conflict came in the War of the Three Henries in 1588–1589. Henry, duke of Guise, in the pay of Philip II of Spain, seized Paris and forced King Henry III to make him his chief minister. To rid himself of Guise influence, Henry III assassinated the duke of Guise and then joined with Henry of Navarre (who had once again returned to Calvinism), who was next in line to the throne, to crush the Catholic Holy League and retake the city of Paris. Although successful, Henry III in turn was assassinated in 1589 by a monk who was repelled by the spectacle of a Catholic king cooperating with a Protestant. Henry of Navarre now claimed the throne. Realizing, however, that he would never be accepted by Catholic France, Henry took the logical way out and converted once again to Catholicism, issuing his famous aphorism, "Paris is worth a mass." With his coronation in 1594, the Wars of Religion had finally come to an end. It remained only to solve the religious problem, which was accomplished by the Edict of Nantes in 1598. While Catholicism was acknowledged as the official religion of France, the Huguenots were guaranteed their right to worship in selected places in every district and were allowed to retain a number of fortified towns for their protection. In addition, Huguenots were allowed to enjoy all political privileges, including the holding of public offices. Although the Edict of Nantes recognized the rights of the Protestant minority and ostensibly the principle of religious toleration, it did so only out of political necessity, not out of conviction. The French Wars of Religion also demonstrated once again to many Frenchmen the necessity for strong government, laying a foundation for the growth of monarchy in the seventeenth century.

Philip II and the Cause of Militant Catholicism

The greatest advocate of militant Catholicism and the most important political figure in the second half of the sixteenth century was King Philip II of Spain (1556–1598), the son and heir of Charles V (see the box on p. 493). Philip's reign ushered in an age of Spanish greatness, both politically and culturally. A tremendous price was paid, however, for the political and military commitments that Philip made, and we can see in retrospect that the Golden Age of Spain was also the period in which Spain's decline began.

The first major goal of Philip II was to consolidate and secure the lands he had inherited from his father, Charles V. These included Spain, the Netherlands, and

Philip II, the Most Catholic King of Spain

▼ ▼ ▼

After the abdication of Charles V in 1556, his son Philip II became king of Spain at the age of twenty-nine. Modern historical opinions of Philip II have varied widely. Some Protestant historians have viewed him as a moral monster while Catholic apologists have commended him for his sincerity and sense of responsibility. These selections include an assessment of Philip II by a contemporary, the Venetian ambassador to Spain, and a section from a letter by Philip II to his daughters, revealing the more loving side of the king.

Suriano, An Estimate of Philip II

The Catholic king was born in Spain, in the month of May, 1527, and spent a great part of his youth in that kingdom. Here, in accordance with the customs of the country and the wishes of his father and mother, . . . he was treated with all the deference and respect which seemed due to the son of the greatest emperor whom Christendom had ever had, and to the heir to such a number of realms and to such grandeur. As a result of this education, when the king left Spain for the first time and visited Flanders, passing on his way through Italy and Germany, he everywhere made an impression of haughtiness and severity, so that the Italians liked him but little, the Flemings were quite disgusted with him, and the Germans hated him heartily. But when he had been warned by the cardinal of Trent and his aunt, and above all by his father, that this haughtiness was not in place in a prince destined to rule over a number of nations so different in manners and sentiment, he altered his manner so completely that on his second journey, when he went to England, he everywhere exhibited such distinguished mildness and affability that no prince has ever surpassed him in these traits. . . .

In the king's eyes no nation is superior to the Spaniards. It is among them that he lives, it is they that he consults, and it is they that direct his policy; in all this he is acting quite contrary to the habit of his father. He thinks little of the Italians and Flemish and still less of the Germans. Although he may employ the chief men of all the countries over which he rules, he admits none of them to his secret counsels, but utilizes their services only in military affairs, and then perhaps not so much because he really esteems them, as in the hope that he will in this way prevent his enemies from making use of them.

A Letter of Philip II to His Daughters

It is good news for me to learn that you are so well. It seems to me that your little sister is getting her eye teeth pretty early. Perhaps they are in place of the two which I am on the point of losing and which I shall probably no longer have when I get back. But if I had nothing worse to trouble me, that might pass. . . .

I am sending you also some roses and an orange flower, just to let you see that we have them here [Lisbon]. Calabrés brings me bunches of both these flowers every day, and we have had violets for a long time. . . . After this rainy time I imagine that you will be having flowers, too, by the time my sister arrives, or soon after. God keep you as I would have him!

the possessions in Italy and the New World. For Philip this meant a strict conformity to Catholicism, enforced by aggressive use of the Spanish Inquisition, and the establishment of strong, monarchical authority. The latter was not an easy task since Philip inherited a structure of government in which each of the various states and territories of his empire stood in an individual relationship to the king. Even in Spain, there was no really deep sense of nationhood. Philip did manage, however, to expand royal power by making the monarchy less dependent on the traditional landed aristocracy, especially in the higher echelons of government. He enlarged the system of administrative councils first developed by Ferdinand and Isabella and broadened by his father. Although Philip found that his ability to enforce his will was limited by local legal traditions, lack of rapid communication, and an inadequate bureaucracy, he tried to be the center of the whole system and supervised the work of all departments, even down to the smallest details. His meticulousness was tragic for both Philip and Spain. Unwilling to delegate authority, he failed to distinguish between important and trivial matters and fell weeks behind on state correspondence, especially since he was inclined to make marginal notes and even correct spelling. One Spanish official said, "If God used the Escorial [the royal palace where Philip worked] to deliver my death sentence, I would be immortal." Philip's administrative machinery enabled him to do little more than maintain the status quo.

One of Philip's aims was to make Spain a dominant power in Europe. To a great extent, Spain's preeminence depended upon a prosperous economy fueled by its importation of gold and silver from its New World possessions, its agriculture, its commerce, and its industry, especially in textiles, silk, and leather goods. The importation of silver had detrimental effects as well, however, as it helped to lead to a spiraling inflation that disrupted the Spanish economy, eventually hurting both textile production and agriculture. Moreover, the expenses of war, especially after 1580, proved devastating

▼ **Philip II of Spain.** This portrait depicts Philip II of Spain at the age of fifty-two. While Spain entered an era of greatness with Philip's rule, the seeds for its eventual decline were also planted. Philip wished to make Spain a dominant power in Europe and perceived himself as a great defender of Catholicism. His attempts to make Spain a great power led to large financial debts and crushing taxes, and his military actions in defense of Catholicism brought him failure and misfortune in both France and the Netherlands.

to the Spanish economy. American gold and silver never constituted more than 20 percent of the royal revenue, leading the government to impose a crushing burden of direct and indirect taxes, especially on the people of Castile. Even then the government was forced to borrow. Philip repudiated his debts seven times; still two-thirds of state income went to pay interest on the debt by the end of his reign. The attempt to make Spain a great power led to the decline of Spain after Philip's reign.

Crucial to an understanding of Philip II is the importance of Catholicism to the Spanish people and their ruler. Driven by a heritage of crusading fervor, it was not difficult for Spain to see itself as a nation of people divinely chosen to save Catholic Christianity from the Protestant heretics. Philip II, the "Most Catholic King," became the champion of Catholicism throughout Europe. In Philip's mind, church and state were inextricably intertwined, a fact beautifully symbolized in Philip's new palace known as the Escorial, which served as a seat of government, church, and mausoleum for Charles V. Philip's activities on behalf of Catholicism were not done to please the popes, however. Despite his devotion to Catholicism, Philip allowed them little say in the Spanish Catholic church and did not hesitate to disagree with papal religious and political policies.

Philip's role as the champion of Catholicism led to spectacular victories and equally spectacular defeats for the Spanish king. Spain's leadership of a Holy League against Turkish encroachments in the Mediterranean, especially the Muslim attack on the island of Cyprus, led to a stunning victory over the Turkish fleet in the Battle of Lepanto in 1571. But Philip was to experience few other such successes. His intervention in France in the decade of the 1580s on behalf of the ultra-Catholics led only to failure. But the major thrust of his foreign policy lay in the Netherlands and England. Philip's attempt to crush the revolt in the Netherlands and his tortured policy with the English queen Elizabeth led to his greatest misfortunes.

THE REVOLT OF THE NETHERLANDS   One of the richest parts of Philip's empire, the Spanish Netherlands was of great importance to the "Most Catholic King." The Netherlands consisted of seventeen provinces (modern Netherlands and Belgium). The seven northern provinces were largely Germanic in culture and Dutch speaking, while the French- and Flemish-speaking southern provinces were closely tied to France. Situated at the commercial crossroads of northwestern Europe, the Netherlands had become prosperous through commerce and a flourishing textile industry. Because of its location, the Netherlands was open to the religious influences of the age. While both Lutheranism and Anabaptism had been adopted by some inhabitants, by the time of Philip II, Calvinism was also making inroads. There was no real political bond holding these provinces together except for a common ruler, and that ruler was Philip II, a foreigner who was out of touch with the situation in the Netherlands.

Philip II hoped to strengthen his control in the Netherlands, regardless of the traditional privileges of the separate provinces. This was strongly opposed by the nobles who stood to lose the most politically if their jealously guarded privileges and freedoms were weakened. Resentment against Philip was also aroused by the collection of taxes when the residents of the Netherlands realized that these revenues were being used for Spanish interests. Finally, religion became a major catalyst for rebellion when Philip attempted both to reorganize the ecclesiastical structure of the Dutch Catholic church and to crush heresy. Calvinism continued to spread, especially among the nobility and artisans in the towns. Philip's policy of repression served simply to alienate the Calvinists without halting the spread of the movement. Resistance against the king's policies increased, especially from the aristocrats led by William of Nassau, the prince of Orange, also known as William the Silent. Violence erupted in 1566 when Calvinists—especially nobles—began to destroy statues and stained glass windows in Catholic churches. Philip responded by sending the duke of Alva with 10,000 veteran Spanish and Italian troops to crush the rebellion.

The repressive policies of the duke proved counterproductive. The levying of a permanent sales tax alienated many merchants and commoners who now joined the nobles and Calvinists in the struggle against Spanish rule. A special tribunal, known as the Council of Troubles (nicknamed the Council of Blood), inaugurated a reign of terror in which even powerful aristocrats were executed. As a result, the revolt now became organized, especially in the northern provinces where William of Orange and daring Dutch privateers known as the "Sea Beggars" offered growing resistance. In 1573, Philip removed the duke of Alva and shifted to a more conciliatory policy to bring an end to the costly revolt.

William of Orange wished to unify all seventeen provinces, a goal seemingly realized in 1576 with the Pacification of Ghent. This agreement stipulated that all the provinces would stand together under William's leadership, respect religious differences, and demand that Spanish troops be withdrawn. But religious differences proved too strong for any lasting union. When the

Chronology

▼ ▼ ▼

Philip II and Militant Catholicism

Philip II	1556–1598
Battle of Lepanto	1571
Outbreak of Revolt in the Netherlands	1566
Recall of the Duke of Alva	1573
Pacification of Ghent	1576
Union of Arras	1579
The Spanish Armada	1588
Twelve-Year Truce (Spain and Netherlands)	1609
Independence of the United Provinces	1648

duke of Parma, the next Spanish leader, arrived in the Netherlands, he astutely played upon the religious differences of the provinces and split their united front. The southern provinces formed a Catholic union—the Union of Arras—in 1579 and accepted Spanish control. To counter this, William of Orange organized the northern, Dutch-speaking states into a Protestant union—the Union of Utrecht—determined to oppose Spanish rule. The Netherlands was now divided along religious, geographical, and political lines into two hostile camps. Unwilling to rule themselves, the northern provinces sought to place themselves under the French king and then the English queen Elizabeth. Both refused, although Elizabeth further antagonized Philip II by continuing military assistance. The struggle went on after the death of both Philip and Elizabeth until 1609 when a twelve-year truce ended the war, virtually recognizing the independence of the northern provinces. These "United Provinces" soon emerged as the Dutch Republic, although they were not formally recognized as independent by the Spanish until 1648. The southern provinces remained a Spanish possession.

The England of Elizabeth

When Elizabeth Tudor, the daughter of Henry VIII and Anne Boleyn, ascended the throne in 1558, England possessed fewer than four million people. During her reign, England rose to prominence as the relatively small island kingdom became the leader of the Protestant nations of Europe, laid the foundations for a world empire, and experienced a cultural renaissance.

Elizabeth was a complex ruler who was careful to hide her feelings from both private and public sight. While appearing irresolute in avoiding confrontation as long as possible, she was capable of decisive action when it was finally forced upon her. Shrewd, calculating, and self-confident, she moved quickly to solve the difficult and intractable religious problem she inherited from her half-sister, "Bloody" Mary.

Elizabeth's religious policy was based on moderation and compromise. Although she had some deep religious feelings and a sentimental appreciation for religious rites and ceremonies, the changes she had experienced had taught her caution and tolerance. As a ruler, she wished to prevent England from being torn apart over matters of religion. Interests of state and personal choice combined to favor a temperate approach to religious affairs. As the Scottish Calvinist reformer John Knox remarked, "Elizabeth was neither a good Protestant nor yet a resolute Papist." Nor did she care what her subjects believed privately as long as they did not threaten the state's power.

Parliament cooperated with the queen in initiating the Elizabethan religious settlement in 1559. The Catholic legislation of Mary's reign was repealed, and a new Act of Supremacy designated Elizabeth as "the only supreme governor of this realm, as well in all spiritual or ecclesiastical things or causes, as temporal." An Act of Uniformity restored the church service of the Book of Common Prayer from the reign of Edward VI with some revisions to make it more acceptable to Catholics. Elizabeth's religious settlement was basically Protestant but a moderate Protestantism that avoided overly subtle distinctions and extremes. Theologically, it represented a position close to Lutheranism.

The new religious settlement worked, at least to the extent that it smothered religious differences in England in the second half of the sixteenth century. Two groups, however, the Catholics and Puritans, continued to oppose the new religious settlement. The Catholics dwindled to a tiny minority by the end of Elizabeth's reign, a process aided by the identification of Catholicism in English minds with the Spanish King Philip II. The English were made well aware that Elizabeth's immediate heir was Mary, queen of Scots, a Catholic supported by the Spaniards. The attack on England by the Spanish Armada in 1588 sealed the fate of Catholicism and made it virtually a traitorous activity. Potentially more dangerous to Anglicanism in the long run were the Puritans. The term *Puritanism* first appeared in 1564 when it was applied to those Protestants within the Anglican church who, inspired by Calvinist theology, wished to eliminate any trace of popery from the Church of England. Elizabeth managed to contain the Puritans during her reign, but the indefatigible Puritans would dominate the English scene in the first half of the seventeenth century.

Elizabeth proved as adept in government and foreign policy as in religious affairs. She was well served administratively by the principal secretary of state, an office created by Thomas Cromwell (see Chapter 14). The talents of Sir William Cecil and Sir Francis Walsingham, who together held the office for thirty-two years, ensured much of Elizabeth's success in foreign and domestic affairs. Elizabeth also handled Parliament with much skill; it met only thirteen times during her entire reign (see the box on p. 497).

Elizabeth's foreign policy was also dictated by caution, moderation, and expediency. Fearful of other countries' motives, Elizabeth realized that war could be disastrous for her island kingdom and her own rule. While encouraging English piracy and providing clandestine aid to

▼ **Procession of Queen Elizabeth I.** Intelligent and learned, Elizabeth Tudor was familiar with Latin and Greek and spoke several European languages. She repealed the Catholic legislation of her sister Mary in favor of a more moderate Protestant religious settlement. Served by able administrators, Elizabeth ruled for nearly forty-five years and avoided open military action against any real power. Her participation in the revolt of the Netherlands, however, brought England into conflict with Spain. This picture painted near the end of her reign shows the queen on a ceremonial procession.

Queen Elizabeth Addresses Parliament (1601)

▼ ▼ ▼

Queen Elizabeth I ruled England from 1558 to 1603 with a consummate skill that contemporaries considered unusual in a woman. Though shrewd, calculating, and paternalistic, Elizabeth, like other sixteenth-century monarchs, depended for her power upon the favor of her people. This selection is taken from her speech to Parliament in 1601, when she had been forced to retreat on the issue of monopolies after violent protests by members of Parliament. Although the speech was designed to make peace with Parliament, some historians also feel that it was a sincere expression of the existing rapport between the queen and her subjects.

Queen Elizabeth I, "The Golden Speech"

I do assure you there is no prince that loves his subjects better, or whose love can countervail our love. There is no jewel, be it of never so rich a price, which I set before this jewel: I mean your love. For I do esteem it more than any treasure or riches. . . . And, though God has raised me high, yet this I count the glory of my crown, that I have reigned with your loves. This makes me that I do not so much rejoice that God has made me to be a Queen, as to be a Queen over so thankful a people. . . .

Of myself I must say this: I never was any greedy, scraping grasper, nor a strait, fast-holding Prince, nor yet a waster. My heart was never set on any worldly goods, but only for my subjects' good. What you bestow on me, I will not hoard it up, but receive it to bestow on you again. Yea, mine own properties I account yours, to be expended for your good. . . .

I have ever used to set the Last-Judgment Day before mine eyes, and so to rule as I shall be judged to answer before a higher Judge, to whose judgment seat I do appeal, that never thought was cherished in my heart that tended not unto my people's good. And now, if my kingly bounties have been abused, and my grants turned to the hurt of my people, contrary to my will and meaning, and if any in authority under me neglected or perverted what I have committed to them, I hope God will not lay their culps [crimes] and offences to my charge; who, though there were danger in repealing our grants, yet what danger would I not rather incur for your good, than I would suffer them still to continue?

There will never Queen sit in my seat with more zeal to my country, care for my subjects, and that will sooner with willingness venture her life for your good and safety, than myself. For it is my desire to live nor reign no longer than my life and reign shall be for your good. And though you have had and may have many princes more mighty and wise sitting in this seat, yet you never had nor shall have any that will be more careful and loving. . . .

French Huguenots and Dutch Calvinists to weaken France and Spain, she pretended complete aloofness and avoided alliances that would force her into war with any major power. Gradually, however, Elizabeth was drawn into more active involvement in the Netherlands and by 1585 had reluctantly settled upon a policy of active military intervention there. This move accelerated the already mounting friction between Spain and England. After resisting for years the idea of invading England as too impractical, Philip II of Spain was finally persuaded to do so by advisers who assured him that the people of England would rise against their queen when the Spaniards arrived. Moreover, Philip was easily convinced that the revolt in the Netherlands would never be crushed as long as England provided support for it. In any case, a successful invasion of England would mean the overthrow of heresy and the return of England to Catholicism, surely an act in accordance with the will of God. Accordingly, Philip ordered preparations for an Armada that would rendezvous with the army of the duke of Parma in Flanders and escort his troops across the English Channel for the invasion.

The Armada proved to be a disaster. The Spanish fleet that finally set sail had neither the ships nor the manpower that Philip had planned to send. A conversation between a papal emissary and an officer of the Spanish fleet before the Armada departed reveals the fundamental flaw:

"And if you meet the English armada in the Channel, do you expect to win the battle?" "Of course," replied the Spaniard.

"How can you be sure?" [asked the emissary]

"It's very simple. It is well known that we fight in God's cause. So, when we meet the English, God will surely arrange matters so that we can grapple and board them, either by sending some strange freak of weather or, more likely, just by depriving the English of their wits. If we can come to close quarters, Spanish valor and Spanish steel (and the great masses of soldiers we shall have on board) will make our victory certain. But unless God helps us by a miracle the English, who have faster and handier ships than ours, and many more long-range guns, and who know their advantage just as well as we do, will never close with us at all, but stand aloof and knock us to pieces with their culverins, without our being able to do them any serious hurt. So," concluded the captain, and one fancies a grim smile, "we are sailing against England in the confident hope of a miracle."[5]

The hoped-for miracle never materialized. The Spanish fleet, battered by a number of encounters with the English, sailed back to Spain by a northward route around Scotland and Ireland where it was further battered by storms. Although the English and Spanish would continue their war for another sixteen years, the defeat of the Armada guaranteed for the time being that England would remain a Protestant country. Although Spain made up for its losses within a year and a half, the defeat was a psychological blow to the Spaniards.

▼ Economic and Social Crises

The period of European history from 1560 to 1650 witnessed severe economic and social crises as well as political upheaval. Economic uncertainties, intensified by wildly fluctuating boom and bust cycles, were accompanied by social uncertainties and stark contrasts between the living standards of the rich and the poor. Although historians commonly refer to a sixteenth-century price revolution and a seventeenth-century economic crisis, the lack of concrete data has made it difficult to be precise in these areas, leading to numerous historical controversies.

Inflation and Economic Stagnation

Inflation was a major economic problem in the sixteenth and early seventeenth centuries. This so-called price revolution was a Europeanwide phenomenon, although different areas were affected at different times. While the inflation rate was probably a relatively low 2 to 3 percent a year, it was noticeable in a Europe accustomed to stable prices. Foodstuffs were most subject to high prices, especially evident in the price of wheat. An upward surge in wheat prices was first noticed in the Mediterranean area—in Spain, southern France, and

Italy—and reached its peak there in the 1590s. By the 1620s and 1630s, the same price increases for wheat had become obvious in northern Europe.

Although precise data are lacking, economic historians believe that as a result of the price revolution, wages failed to keep up with price increases. Wage earners, especially agricultural laborers and salaried workers in urban areas, began to experience a lower standard of living. At the same time, landed aristocrats who could raise rents managed to prosper. To contemporaries, in fact, the rent increases imposed by the landed nobility were responsible for the problem, as the English Bishop Latimer proclaimed in a sermon preached before King Edward VI in 1549:

> You landlords, you rent-raisers, I may say you step-lords, you have for your possessions yearly too much. For what here before went for twenty or forty pound by year (which is an honest portion to be had gratis in one lordship of another man's sweat and labor), now is let for fifty or an hundred pound by year. Of this "too much" comes this monstrous and portentous dearth made by man . . . that poor men, which live by their labour cannot with the sweat of their face have a living, all kinds of victuals is so dear. . . .[6]

Wealthy commercial and industrial entrepreneurs also benefited from the price revolution because of rising prices, expanding markets, and relatively cheaper labor costs. Some historians regard this profit inflation as a valuable stimulus to investment and the growth of capitalism, helping to explain the economic expansion and prosperity of the sixteenth century. Governments were likewise affected by inflation. They borrowed heavily from bankers and placed new burdens of taxation on their subjects, often creating additional discontent.

The causes of the price revolution are a subject of much historical debate. Already in the 1560s European intellectuals had associated the rise in prices with the great influx of precious metals from the New World. Although this view was accepted for a long time, many economic historians now believe that the increase in population in the sixteenth century played an important role in creating inflationary pressures. A growing population increased the demand for land and food and drove up prices for both.

But the inflation-fueled prosperity of the sixteenth century showed signs of slackening by the beginning of the seventeenth century. Economic contraction began to be evident in some parts of Europe by the 1620s. In the 1630s and 1640s, as imports of silver declined, economic recession intensified, especially in the Mediterranean area. The industrial and financial center of Europe in the age of the Renaissance, Italy was now becoming an economic backwater. Spain's economy was also seriously failing by the decade of the 1640s.

Trade, Industry, Banking, and Agriculture

The flourishing European trade of the sixteenth century revolved around three major areas: the Mediterranean in the south, the Low Countries and the Baltic region in the north, and central Europe, whose inland trade depended on the Rhine and Danube rivers. Because of the expanding overseas trade, however, the Atlantic seaboard began to play an even more important role, linking the Mediterranean, Baltic, and central European trading areas together and making the whole of Europe into a more integrated market that was all the more vulnerable to price shifts. With their cheaper and faster ships, the Dutch came to monopolize both European and world trade, although they were increasingly challenged by the English and French in the seventeenth century.

The commercial expansion of the sixteenth and seventeenth centuries was made easier by new forms of commercial organization, especially the joint-stock trading company. Individuals bought shares in a company and received dividends on their investment while a board of directors ran the company and made the important business decisions. The return on investments could be spectacular. During its first ten years, investors received 30 percent on their money from the Dutch East India Company, which opened the Spice Islands and southeast Asia to Dutch activity. The joint-stock company made it easier to raise large amounts of capital for world trading ventures.

Enormous profits were also being made in shipbuilding and in mining and metallurgy, where technological innovations, such as the use of pumps and new methods of extracting metals from ores, proved highly successful. The mining industry was closely tied to sixteenth-century family banking firms. In exchange for arranging large loans to Charles V, Jacob Fugger was given a monopoly over silver, copper, and mercury mines in the Habsburg possessions of central Europe that produced profits in excess of 50 percent per year. While these close relationships between governments and entrepreneurs could lead to stunning successes, they could also be precarious. The House of Fugger went bankrupt at the end of the sixteenth century when the Habsburgs defaulted on their loans.

By the seventeenth century, the traditional family banking firms were no longer able to provide the multiple services needed for the commercial capitalism of the seventeenth century. New institutions arose to take their place. The city of Amsterdam created the Bank of Amsterdam in 1609 as both a deposit and transfer institution and the Amsterdam Bourse or Exchange where the trading of stocks replaced the exchange of goods. By 1620, the Amsterdam Exchange had become the center of the international business world, just as Amsterdam itself had replaced Antwerp as the greatest commercial and banking center of Europe.

▼ **Jacob Fugger the Rich.** One of the more profitable industries of the sixteenth century was mining, which was closely tied to family banking firms. Jacob Fugger, pictured here with his secretary, was given a monopoly over the silver, copper, and mercury mines in the Habsburg lands in exchange for giving large loans to Charles V. Such dealings could be dangerous, however, as is shown by the fact that the house of Fugger went bankrupt when the Habsburgs defaulted on their loans.

Despite the growth of commercial capitalism, most of the European economy still depended on an agricultural system that had experienced few changes since the thirteenth century. At least 80 to 90 percent of Europeans still worked on the land. Most of the peasants of western Europe were free of serfdom, although many still owed a variety of feudal dues to the nobility. Despite expanding markets and rising prices, increased rents, fees, and higher taxes imposed by the state meant little or no improvement in the lot of the European peasants. In eastern Europe, their position had even worsened as peasants were increasingly tied to the land in a new serfdom enforced by powerful landowners (see Chapter 16).

Population Trends

The sixteenth century was a period of expanding population, possibly related to a warmer climate and increased food supplies. It has been estimated that the population of Europe increased from 60 million in 1500 to 85 million by 1600, the first major recovery of European population since the devastation of the Black Death in the mid-fourteenth century. However, records also indicate a leveling off of the population by 1620 and even a decline by 1650, especially in central and southern Europe. Only the Dutch, English, and, to a lesser degree, the French grew in number in the first half of the seventeenth century. Europe's longtime adversaries, war, famine, and plague, continued to affect population levels. In 1630, for example, northern Italy was hit by the worst outbreak of bubonic plague since the Black Death; Verona and Mantua lost 60 to 70 percent of their populations. Europe's entry into another "little ice age" after the middle of the sixteenth century, when average temperatures fell and glaciers even engulfed small Alpine villages, affected harvests and gave rise to famines. Historians have noted the parallels between population increase and economic prosperity in the sixteenth century and population decline and economic recession in the seventeenth century.

The rise in population was reflected in the growth of cities. In 1500, Paris, Constantinople, and four cities in Italy (Naples, Venice, Milan, Genoa) had populations above 100,000 people. By 1600, Naples had grown to 300,000, while Rome, Palermo, and Messina reached 100,000. Cities along coasts and well-traveled trade routes grew the most, reflecting the close ties between commerce and urban growth. Naples became the largest port in Italy while Seville in Spain, the port of entry for the wealth of the New World, and Lisbon in Portugal had populations over 100,000 by 1600. Across the English Channel, London's domination of the commercial and financial life of England pushed its population to 250,000 by 1600. By that year, Europe's greatest and most populous city was Paris with its 500,000 people.

Seventeenth-century cities visibly reflected the remarkable disparity in wealth during the seventeenth century. The beautiful houses and palaces of rich nobles and wealthy merchants contrasted sharply with the crowded tenements and dirty hovels of the lower classes. Crime, pollution, filth, and lack of sanitation, fresh water, and food were accompanied by the social tensions between landed nobles who moved into the cities and the native wealthy merchants who resented their presence.

▼ Seventeenth-Century Crises: War, Rebellions, and Revolution

Although many Europeans responded to the upheavals of the second half of the sixteenth century with a desire for peace and order, the first fifty years of the seventeenth century continued to be a period of crisis. A devastating war that affected much of Europe, a revolution in England that led to the beheading of a king, and rebellions seemingly everywhere protracted an atmosphere of disorder and violence.

The Thirty Years' War

Religion, especially the struggle between a militant Catholicism and a militant Calvinism, certainly played an important role in the outbreak of the Thirty Years' War, often called the "last of the religious wars." As the war progressed, however, it became increasingly clear that secular, dynastic-nationalist considerations were far more important.

Although much of the fighting in the Thirty Years' War (1618–1648) was done in the Germanic lands of the Holy Roman Empire, the war became a European-wide struggle. In fact, some historians view it as part of a larger conflict between the Bourbon dynasty of France and the Habsburg dynasties of Spain and the Holy Roman Empire for European leadership and date it from 1609 to 1659. A brief look at the motives of the European states and the situation in Germany provides the background necessary to understand the war.

Since the beginning of the sixteenth century, France had worked to break out of what it perceived as its encirclement by the house of Habsburg (see Chapter 14).

The situation had eased in 1556 when Charles V abdicated and divided his empire. His son Philip inherited Spain, the Netherlands, Italy, and the New World while his brother Ferdinand became Holy Roman emperor and received the Habsburg possessions in Austria and eastern Europe. France felt threatened by the Spanish Habsburgs and feared the consolidation of Germany by the Habsburg emperor.

Spain, which viewed the twelve-year truce negotiated with the Dutch in 1609 as only temporary, was determined to regain control of the Netherlands, specifically, the northern Dutch provinces. English and Dutch control of the seas, however, forced the Spanish to seek an alternative route for shipping supplies and men to the Dutch provinces by way of Italy and western Germany. While in retrospect it might be easy to recognize that Spain's economic decline made it foolish to undertake the reconquest of the Dutch, to contemporaries, Spain remained the greatest power in the Christian world.

The Austrian Habsburgs wished to consolidate their holdings in Austria and Bohemia by eliminating Protestantism and establishing stronger central authority. At the same time, as Holy Roman emperors, they remained frustrated by their lack of real authority over the lands of Germany where hundreds of individual states still provided the real basis of political power. It was among these German states that the Thirty Years' War had its immediate beginnings.

The Peace of Augsburg had brought an end to the religious warfare between Catholics and Lutherans in 1555. Religion, however, continued to play a divisive role in German life as Lutherans and Catholics persisted in vying for control of different principalities. In addition, although the treaty had not recognized the rights of Calvinists, a number of German states had adopted Calvinism as their state church. At the beginning of the seventeenth century, the Calvinist ruler of the Palatinate, the Elector Palatine Frederick IV, assumed the leadership in forming a league of German Protestant states called the Protestant Union. To counteract it, a Catholic League of German states was organized by Duke Maximilian of the south German state of Bavaria. What made this division of Germany into two armed camps even more dangerous was the involvement of foreign states. The Protestant Union gained the support of the Dutch, English, and French, while Spain and the Holy Roman emperor aided the Catholic League. By 1609, then, Germany was dividing into two armed camps in anticipation of a religious war.

The religious division was exacerbated by a constitutional issue. The desire of the Habsburg emperors to consolidate their authority in Germany was resisted by the princes who fought for their "German liberties," their constitutional rights and prerogatives as individual rulers. To pursue their policies, the Habsburg emperors looked to Spain for assistance while the princes turned to the enemies of Spain, especially France, for help against the emperor. The divisions in Germany and Europe made it almost inevitable that if war did erupt, it would be widespread and difficult to stop. Events in Bohemia in 1617 and 1618 finally brought the outbreak of the war everyone dreaded.

Historians have traditionally divided the Thirty Years' War into four major phases. The Bohemian phase (1618–1625) began in one of the Habsburgs' own territories. In 1617, the Bohemian Estates (primarily the nobles) accepted the Habsburg Archduke Ferdinand as their king but soon found themselves unhappy with their choice. While many of the nobles were Calvinists, Ferdinand was a devout Catholic who began a process of re-Catholicizing Bohemia and strengthening the royal power. The Protestant nobles rebelled against Ferdinand in May 1618 and proclaimed their resistance by throwing two of the Habsburg governors and a secretary out of the window of the royal castle in Prague, the seat of Bohemian government. The Catholic side claimed that their seemingly miraculous escape from death in the seventy-foot fall from the castle was due to the intercession of the Virgin Mary, while Protestants pointed out that they fell into a manure pile. The Bohemian rebels now seized control of Bohemia, deposed Ferdinand, and elected as his replacement the Protestant ruler of the Palatinate, Elector Frederick V, who was also head of the Protestant Union.

Ferdinand, who in the meantime had been elected as Holy Roman emperor, refused to accept his deposition. Aided by the imposing forces of Maximilian of Bavaria and the Catholic League, the imperial forces defeated Frederick and the Bohemian nobles at the Battle of White Mountain outside Prague on November 8, 1620. Spanish troops meanwhile took advantage of Frederick's predicament by invading the Palatinate and conquering it by the end of 1622. The unfortunate Frederick who had lost two crowns—Bohemia and the Palatinate—fled into exile in Holland. The Spanish took control of the western part of the Palatinate (to gain the access route from Italy to the Netherlands that they had wanted), and Duke Maximilian of Bavaria took the rest of the territory. Reestablished as king of Bohemia, Emperor Ferdinand declared Bohemia a hereditary Habsburg possession, confiscated the land of the Protestant nobles, and established Catholicism as the sole religion. Some

30,000 Protestant families emigrated to Saxony and Hungary. The Spanish renewed their attack on the Dutch, and the forces of Catholicism seemed on the road to victory. But the war was far from over.

The second phase of the war, the Danish phase (1625–1629), began when King Christian IV of Denmark (1588–1648), a Lutheran, intervened on behalf of the Protestant cause by taking an army into northern Germany. Most likely, he also wished to annex territories in northern Germany that would give him control of the southern Baltic. His campaign turned out to be a complete fiasco.

The imperial forces were now led by a brilliant and enigmatic commander, Albrecht von Wallenstein, a Bohemian nobleman who had taken advantage of Ferdinand's victory to become the country's wealthiest landowner. Wallenstein marched the imperial army north, utterly defeated the Danes, and occupied parts of northern Germany, including the Baltic ports of Hamburg, Lübeck, and Bremen. Christian IV's total defeat ended

Danish involvement in the Thirty Years' War and even meant the end of Danish supremacy in the Baltic.

After the success of the imperial armies, the emperor Ferdinand II was at the height of his power and took this opportunity to issue the Edict of Restitution in March 1629. His proclamation prohibited Calvinist worship and restored to the Catholic church all property taken by Protestant princes or cities during the past seventy-five years. But this sudden growth in the power of the Habsburg emperor frightened many German princes who feared for their independent status and reacted by forcing the emperor to dismiss Wallenstein. At the same time, Ferdinand was faced with another intervention by foreign powers as the war entered its third phase.

The Swedish phase (1630–1635) marked the entry of Gustavus Adolphus, king of Sweden (1611–1635), into the war. Gustavus Adolphus was responsible for reviving Sweden and making it into a great Baltic power. The French, disturbed by the Habsburg consolidation of power, provided financial support to Gustavus, a military

▼ **Gustavus Adolphus at the Battle of Lützen.** Both religious and dynastic considerations played roles in the beginning of the Thirty Years' War. Pictured here is Gustavus Adolphus, king of Sweden, leading a cavalry charge just before he was killed in the Battle of Lützen. Beginning the third phase of the war, the Swedes entered the conflict for both political and religious reasons. Gustavus wanted the Baltic to become a Swedish lake. As a Lutheran, he also felt obligated to aid his fellow co-religionists.

▼ **Map 15.2** The Thirty Years' War.

genius who brought a disciplined and well-equipped Swedish army to northern Germany. Gustavus had no desire to see the Habsburgs in northern Germany since he wanted the Baltic Sea to be a Swedish lake. At the same time, Gustavus Adolphus was a devout Lutheran who felt compelled to aid his coreligionists in Germany.

Gustavus's army swept the imperial forces out of northern Germany and moved into the heart of Germany. In desperation, the imperial side recalled Wallenstein, who was given command of the imperial army that met Gustavus Adolphus's troops near Leipzig. At the Battle of Lützen (1632), the Swedish forces prevailed but paid a high price for the victory when the Swedish king was killed in the battle. Although the Swedish forces remained in Germany, they proved much less effective. Despite the loss of Wallenstein,

who was assassinated in 1634 by one of his own captains, the imperial army decisively defeated the Swedes at the Battle of Nördlingen at the end of 1634 and drove them out of southern Germany. This imperial victory guaranteed that southern Germany would remain Catholic. The emperor used this opportunity to make peace with the German princes by agreeing to annul the Edict of Restitution of 1629. But peace failed to come to war-weary Germany. The Swedes wished to continue while the French, under the direction of Cardinal Richelieu, the chief minister of King Louis XIII (see Chapter 16), entered the war directly, beginning the fourth and final phase of the war, the Franco-Swedish phase (1635–1648).

By this time, religious issues were losing their significance as dynastic power politics came to the fore. The

The Protestant Union	1608
The Catholic League	1609
Election of Habsburg Archduke Ferdinand as King of Bohemia	1617
Bohemian Revolt against Ferdinand	1618
The Bohemian Phase	1618–1625
Battle of White Mountain	1620
Spanish Conquest of Palatinate	1622
The Danish Phase	1625–1629
Edict of Restitution	1629
The Swedish Phase	1630–1635
Battle of Lützen	1632
Battle of Nördlingen	1634
The Franco-Swedish Phase	1635–1648
Battle of Rocroi	1643
Peace of Westphalia	1648
Peace of the Pyrenees	1659

Catholic French, after all, were now supporting the Protestant Swedes against the Catholic Habsburgs of Germany and Spain. This phase of the war was fought by Sweden in northern Germany and by France in the Netherlands and along the Rhine in western Germany. The Battle of Rocroi in 1643 proved decisive as the French beat the Spanish and brought an end to Spanish military greatness. The French then moved on to victories over the imperialist-Bavarian armies in southern Germany. By this time all parties were ready for peace, and after five years of protracted negotiations, the war in Germany was officially ended by the Peace of Westphalia in 1648. The war between France and Spain, however, continued until the Peace of the Pyrenees in 1659. By that time, Spain had become a second-class power, and France had emerged as the dominant nation in Europe.

What were the results of this "basically meaningless conflict," as one historian has called it? The Peace of Westphalia ensured that all German states, including the Calvinist ones, were free to determine their own religion. Territorially, France gained parts of western Germany, part of Alsace and the three cities of Metz, Toul, and Verdun, giving the French control of the Franco-German border area. While Sweden and the German states of Brandenburg and Bavaria gained some territory in Germany, the Austrian Habsburgs did not

really lose any, but did see their authority as rulers of Germany further diminished. The over three hundred states that made up the Holy Roman Empire were virtually recognized as independent states, since each received the power to conduct its own foreign policy; this brought an end to the Holy Roman Empire as a political entity and ensured German disunity for another two hundred years. The Peace of Westphalia made it clear that religion and politics were now separate worlds. The pope was completely ignored in all decisions at Westphalia, and political motives became the guiding forces in public affairs as religion was in the process of becoming primarily a matter of personal conviction and individual choice.

Economically and socially, the effects of the Thirty Years' War on Germany are still debated. An older view pictured a ruined German economy and a decline in German population from 21 to 13 million from 1600 to 1650, but more recent opinions have estimated that Germany's population grew from 16 to 17 million while a redistribution of economic activity rather than an overall decline was taking place. Both views contain some truth. Some areas of Germany were completely devastated while others remained relatively untouched and even experienced economic growth. While historians can debate the figures, many people in Germany would have agreed with this comment by Otto von Guericke, a councillor in the city of Magdeburg, which was sacked ten times (see also the box on p. 505):

> Then there was nothing but beating and burning, plundering, torture, and murder. Most especially was every one of the enemy bent on securing much booty. . . . In this frenzied rage, the great and splendid city . . . was now . . . given over to the flames, and thousands of innocent men, women and children, in the midst of a horrible din of heartrending shrieks and cries, were tortured and put to death in so cruel and shameful a manner that no words would suffice to describe . . . . Thus in a single day this noble and famous city, the pride of the whole country, went up in fire and smoke.[7]

The Thirty Years' War was undoubtedly the most destructive conflict Europeans had yet experienced. Unfortunately, it was not the last.

A Military Revolution?

By the seventeenth century, war played an increasingly important role in European affairs. One historian has calculated that between 1562 and 1721 there were

The Face of War in the Seventeenth Century
▼ ▼ ▼

The Thirty Years' War was the most devastating war Europeans had experienced since the Hundred Years' War. Due to the number of nations involved and battles fought, some historians have even called it "the first world war." Destruction was especially severe in Germany. We have a firsthand account of the face of war in Germany from a picaresque novel called Simplicius Simplicissimus, *written by Jakob von Grimmelshausen. The author's experiences as a soldier in the Thirty Years' War give his descriptions of the effect of the war on ordinary people a certain vividness and reality. This selection describes the fate of a peasant farm, an experience all too familiar to thousands of German peasants between 1618 and 1648.*

Jakob von Grimmelshausen,
Simplicius Simplicissimus

The first thing these horsemen did in the nice back rooms of the house was to put in their horses. Then everyone took up a special job, one having to do with death and destruction. Although some began butchering, heating water, and rendering lard, as if to prepare for a banquet, others raced through the house, ransacking upstairs and down; not even the privy chamber was safe, as if the golden fleece of Jason might be hidden there. Still others bundled up big packs of cloth, household goods, and clothes, as if they wanted to hold a rummage sale somewhere. What they did not intend to take along they broke and spoiled. Some ran their swords into the hay and straw, as if there hadn't been hogs enough to stick. Some shook the feathers out of beds and put bacon slabs, hams, and other stuff in the ticking, as if they might sleep better on these. Others knocked down the hearth and broke the windows, as if announcing an everlasting summer. They flattened out copper and pewter dishes and baled the ruined goods. They burned up bedsteads, tables, chairs, and benches, though there were yards and yards of dry firewood outside the kitchen. Jars and crocks, pots and casseroles all were broken, either because they preferred their meat broiled or because they thought they'd eat

only one meal with us. In the barn, the hired girl was handled so roughly that she was unable to walk away, I am ashamed to report. They stretched the hired man out flat on the ground, stuck a wooden wedge in his mouth to keep it open, and emptied a milk bucket full of stinking manure drippings down his throat; they called it a Swedish cocktail. He didn't relish it and made a very wry face. By this means they forced him to take a raiding party to some other place where they carried off men and cattle and brought them to our farm. Among these were my father, mother, and Ursula [sister].

Then they used thumbscrews, which they cleverly made out of their pistols, to torture the peasants, as if they wanted to burn witches. Though he had confessed to nothing as yet, they put one of the captured hayseeds in the bake-oven and lighted a fire in it. They put a rope around someone else's head and tightened it like a tourniquet until blood came out of his mouth, nose, and ears. In short, every soldier had his favorite method of making life miserable for peasants, and every peasant had his own misery. My father was, as I thought, particularly lucky because he confessed with a laugh what others were forced to say in pain and martyrdom. No doubt because he was the head of the household, he was shown special consideration; they put him close to a fire, tied him by his hands and legs, and rubbed damp salt on the bottoms of his feet. Our old nanny goat had to lick it off and this so tickled my knan [father] that he could have burst laughing. This seemed so clever and entertaining to me—I had never seen or heard my knan laugh so long—that I joined him in laughter, to keep him company or perhaps to cover up my ignorance. In the midst of such glee he told them the whereabouts of hidden treasure much richer in gold, pearls, and jewelry than might have been expected on a farm.

I can't say much about the captured wives, hired girls, and daughters because the soldiers didn't let me watch their doings. But I do remember hearing pitiful screams from various dark corners and I guess that my mother and our Ursula had it no better than the rest.

only four years in which all of Europe was at peace. Military power was considered essential to a ruler's reputation and power, intensifying the pressure to build an effective military machine. Although some would disagree, some historians believe that the changes that occurred in the science of warfare between 1560 and 1650 warrant the title of military revolution.

Medieval warfare, with its mounted knights and auxiliary archers, had been transformed in the Renaissance by the employment of massed infantry squares using pikes and halberds in both offensive and defensive actions. The infantry square of pikemen became a crucial element in sixteenth-century armies and helps to explain the success of the Spanish who perfected its use. The utilization of firearms required adjustments to the size of the infantry square while the cavalry began to substitute pistols for lances.

It was Gustavus Adolphus, the king of Sweden, who developed the first standing army of conscripts, notable for the flexibility of its tactics. The infantry brigades of Gustavus's army, six men deep, were composed of equal numbers of musketeers and pikemen. They employed the salvo in which all rows of the infantry fired at once instead of row by row. These salvos of fire, which cut up the massed ranks of the opposing infantry squares, were followed by a pike charge, giving the infantry a primarily offensive deployment. Gustavus also used the cavalry in a more mobile fashion. After shooting a pistol volley, they charged the enemy with their swords. Additional mobility was created by utilizing smaller pieces of artillery that were more easily moved during battle. All of these changes required coordination, careful training, and better discipline, forcing rulers to move away from undisciplined mercenary forces. Naturally, the success of Gustavus Adolphus led to imitation. Perhaps the best example was the New Model Army of Oliver Cromwell (see The Puritan Revolution later in the chapter). His army consisted of infantry (two-thirds musketeers and one-third pikemen), cavalry, mounted infantry known as dragoons, and artillery units. A well-integrated and disciplined army, it was known for its mobility and flexibility.

The military changes from 1560 to 1650 included an increased use of firearms and cannon, greater flexibility and mobility in tactics, and better disciplined and trained armies. These innovations necessitated standing armies, which grew ever larger and more expensive as the seventeenth century progressed. Such armies could only be maintained by levying greater taxes, making war an economic burden and an ever more important part of the early modern European state.

Rebellions

Before, during, and after the Thirty Years' War, a series of rebellions and civil wars stemming from the discontent of both nobles and commoners rocked the domestic stability of many European governments. To strengthen their power, monarchs attempted to extend their authority at the expense of traditional powerful elements who resisted their rulers' efforts. At the same time, to fight their battles, governments increased taxes and created such hardships that common people also rose in opposition. The resulting widespread revolts of subjects against their ruling princes have caused some historians to speak of a general crisis of authority in the first half of the seventeenth century.

Peasant and lower-class revolts occurred in central and southern France in 1593–1597, 1636–1637, and 1639; in Austria in 1595–1597, 1626–1627, and 1632–1636; and in Hungary in 1597, 1604–1607, and 1631–1632. In the decades of the 1640s and 1650s, even greater upheavals occurred. Portugal and Catalonia rebelled against the Spanish government in 1640. The common people in Naples and Sicily revolted against both the government and landed nobility in 1647. Russia, too, was rocked by urban uprisings in 1641, 1645, and 1648. Nobles rebelled in France from 1648 to 1652 to halt the growth of royal power (see Chapter 16). The northern states of Sweden, Denmark, and Holland were also not immune from upheavals involving clergy, nobles, and mercantile groups. Even relatively stable Switzerland had a peasant rebellion in 1656. By far the most famous and wide-ranging struggle, however, was the civil war and rebellion in England, commonly known as the Puritan Revolution. In many ways, it can also be seen as one of the last religious conflicts spawned by the religious Reformation of the sixteenth century.

The Puritan Revolution

The Puritan Revolution or the English Civil War of the seventeenth century is a highly controversial topic. Historians have approached it from a variety of positions, and contradictions abound in its interpretation. At its core was a struggle between king and Parliament, which evolved into an armed conflict to determine the roles king and Parliament should play in governing England. But the struggle over this political issue was complicated by economic problems and most of all by a deep and profound religious controversy.

During the last decade of Elizabeth's reign, serious problems between crown and Parliament began to arise, but did not come to a head, largely out of deference to the aged queen. Two of the Tudor monarchs, Henry VIII and Elizabeth I, had been strong rulers who had worked through Parliament to achieve their goals. Parliament seemed then little more than a rubber stamp for Tudor actions, but all the same the belief emerged that the crown's authority was expressed by means of an act of Parliament and that monarch and Parliament together formed a "balanced polity." With the death of Queen Elizabeth I in 1603, the Tudors became extinct, and the Stuart line of rulers was inaugurated with the accession to the throne of Elizabeth's cousin, King James VI of Scotland (son of Mary, queen of Scots), who became James I of England.

James I (1603–1625) was ill suited to meet the problems that had arisen but been postponed during the last years of Good Queen Bess. Although used to royal power as king of Scotland, he understood little about the laws, institutions, and customs of the English. As he admitted: "When I came into this land, though I were an old king (having governed a kingdom since I was 12 years old), yet I came here a stranger in government though not in blood." All too soon, a serious strain in the relationship between king and Parliament began to develop.

In 1598, King James had written a book called the *True Law of Free Monarchy* in which he defended the divine right of kings, the belief that kings receive their power directly from God and are responsible to no one except God. In the face of James's claims, Parliament responded in its first session in 1603 with its own claims to legislative and financial supremacy. The latter, in fact, proved to be Parliament's trump card in its relationship with the king. The rise in prices and the increased cost of government made the traditional sources of royal revenue used by Queen Elizabeth insufficient for James. And yet Parliament rejected his requests for additional monies because of his strong views on divine-right monarchy.

The king's relationship with the two major dissenting religious groups in England, the Catholics and Calvinists, also proved divisive. James inherited a strong Anglican church structure from the reign of Queen Elizabeth, who had papered over religious differences to create peace. Catholics were optimistic that James would be more sympathetic to them because his mother Mary, queen of Scots, had been a devout Catholic. His failure to appease them by 1605 led to the infamous Gunpowder Plot in which some fanatical Catholics planned to blow up the houses of Parliament while in session. The plot was quickly crushed, but its discovery led to an intensification of the anti-Catholic feeling that

had first been aroused in the late sixteenth century by the Spanish Armada of 1588.

The Puritans were optimistic about James because he had been king of Scotland, long a Calvinist nation with a Presbyterian church organization, modeled after Calvin's church organization in Geneva, in which ministers and elders (also called presbyters) played an important governing role. When the Puritans met with the king in 1604 and requested the elimination of the episcopal system of organization used in the Church of England (in which the bishop or *episcopos* played the major administrative role) in favor of the Presbyterian model, James lost his temper and threatened to "harry them out of the land" if they did not conform to the Anglican church. He realized that the Anglican church, in which the bishops were appointed by the crown, was a major support of monarchical authority. But the Puritans were not easily cowed and added to the rising chorus of opposition to the king. Many of England's lesser landed nobility, the gentry, had become Puritans, and these Puritan gentry formed not only an important and substantial part of the House of Commons, the lower house of Parliament, but also held important positions locally as justices of the peace and sheriffs. It was not wise to alienate them.

The conflict that had begun during the reign of James came to a head during the reign of his son Charles I (1625–1649). Charles was intelligent and perhaps well-meaning, but stubborn and uncompromising and believed as strongly in divine-right monarchy as his father had. From the first stormy session of Parliament, it became apparent that the issues between this king and Parliament would not be easily resolved.

The skirmishing between Charles and Parliament during the first several years of his reign pointed, first of all, to a serious political issue. While the king demanded grants of money to fight the war with Spain begun by his father, Parliament demanded constitutional reforms and especially a redress of grievances before making the grants. In 1628, for example, Parliament passed a Petition of Right that the king was supposed to accept before being granted any taxes. This petition prohibited taxes without Parliament's consent, arbitrary imprisonment, the quartering of soldiers in private houses, and the declaration of martial law in peacetime. Although he initially accepted it, Charles later reneged on the agreement because of its limitations on royal power. In 1629, Charles decided that since he could not work with Parliament, he would not have it meet. From 1629 to 1640, Charles pursued a course of "personal rule," which to outsiders might have appeared as though England was simply following the common European trend in which central representative bodies were fading away while monarchs extended their authority. Successful at first, Charles was forced at last by his need for money to resort to what members of Parliament regarded as illegal taxation. For example, in 1634, Charles extended the tax called Ship Money, which was a levy on seacoast towns to finance coastal defense, to inland towns and counties as well and then used the money to finance other government operations, rather than just defense. Such expedients simply aroused additional opposition from both middle-class merchants and the landed gentry who interpreted the king's actions as an attempt to tax without Parliament's consent.

The king's religious policy also proved disastrous. His marriage to Henrietta Maria, the Catholic sister of King Louis XIII of France, aroused suspicions about the king's own religious inclinations. Even more important, however, the policy of high Anglicanism pursued by William Laud, the archbishop of Canterbury, with the king's approval, struck the Puritans as a return to Catholic popery. Charles's attempt to force them to conform to his religious policies infuriated the Puritans, thousands of whom went to the "howling wildernesses" of America rather than be forced to conform their consciences to the king's supposed pro-popery nonsense.

Grievances mounted, yet Charles might have survived unscathed if he could have avoided calling Parliament, which alone could provide a focus for the many cries of discontent throughout the land. But the foolish attempt of the king and Archbishop Laud to impose the Anglican Book of Common Prayer upon the fanatical Scottish Presbyterian church led to a rebellion of the Scots against the king. Financially strapped and unable to raise troops to defend against the Scots, the king was forced to call Parliament into session. Eleven years of frustration welled up to create a Parliament determined to deal with the king.

In its first session from November 1640 to September 1641, the so-called Long Parliament (since it lasted in one form or another from 1640 to 1660) took a series of steps that placed severe limitations upon royal authority. These included the abolition of arbitrary courts, such as the Star Chamber; the abolition of taxes that the king had collected without Parliament's consent, such as Ship Money; and the passage of the revolutionary Triennial Act, which specified that Parliament must meet at least once every three years, with or without the king's consent. By the end of 1641, one group within Parliament was prepared to go no further, but a group of more radical parliamentarians pushed for more change, including the

elimination of bishops in the Anglican church. When the king tried to take advantage of the split by arresting some members of the more radical faction in Parliament, a large group in Parliament led by John Pym and his fellow Puritans decided that the king had gone too far. England now slipped into civil war (1642).

Some generalizations can be made about the division of English society in the civil war. It is usually argued that support for the Cavaliers (the Royalists) came from the higher nobility, the Anglican clergy, and many peasants, while the Roundheads, as the parliamentary supporters were known, relied upon some of the great nobles, the landed gentry, middle-class merchants, and, above all, the Puritans. Recent studies have shown, however, that local and regional interests often determined sides. The gentry, for example, appear to have divided fairly evenly between the parliamentary and royal parties. What seems most apparent is that religion was the single greatest catalyst, justifying the use of the term Puritan Revolution to describe what perhaps constituted "the last and grandest episode in Europe's age of religious wars." Oliver Cromwell, who eventually emerged as the leader of Parliament's army, stated it in these words: "Religion was not the thing at first contested for, but God brought it to that issue at last, . . . and at last it proved that which was most dear to us."[8] Cromwell neither forgot nor forgave the king's oppression of the Puritans. And in good Calvinist fashion, he and his religious compatriots saw their cause as lawful resistance to an ungodly ruler.

Parliament proved victorious in the first phase of the English Civil War (1642–1646), aided by two significant factors. The Scots came into the war on Parliament's side when Parliament agreed in 1643 to consider a Presbyterian church organization for England. Even more important, however, was the creation of the New Model Army by Oliver Cromwell, the only real military genius of the war. The New Model Army was composed primarily of more extreme Puritans known as the Independents, recruited by Cromwell on the basis that "I think that he that prays and preaches best will fight best." Consequently, Cromwell raised an army of men who had "the fear of God before their eyes," and who, in typical Calvinist fashion, believed they were doing battle for the Lord. It is striking to read in Cromwell's military reports such statements as "Sir, this is none other but the hand of God; and to Him alone belongs the glory." We might also attribute some of the credit to Cromwell himself since his crusaders were well disciplined and trained in the new continental military tactics. Supported by the New Model Army, Parliament ended the first phase of the civil war with the capture of King Charles I in 1646.

A split now occurred in the parliamentary forces. A Presbyterian majority wanted to disband the army and restore Charles I with a Presbyterian state church. The army, composed mostly of Independents, more radical Puritans who favored religious toleration for most Protestant groups and opposed an established Presbyterian church, marched on London in 1647 and began negotiations with the king. Charles took advantage of this division by fleeing and seeking help from the Scots. Enraged by the king's treachery, Cromwell and the army engaged in a second civil war (1648) that ended with Cromwell's victory and the capture of the king. This time Cromwell was determined to achieve a victory for the army's point of view. The Presbyterian members of Parliament were purged, leaving a Rump Parliament of fifty-three members of the House of Commons who then tried and condemned the king on an act of treason and adjudged that "he, the said Charles Stuart, as a tyrant, traitor, murderer, and public enemy to the good people of this nation, shall be put to death by the severing of his head from his body." Charles was executed on January 30, 1649 (see the box on p. 510). The revolution had triumphed, and the monarchy in England had been destroyed, at least for the moment.

After the death of the king, the Rump Parliament abolished the monarchy and the House of Lords and proclaimed England a republic or Commonwealth (1649–1653). This was not an easy period for Cromwell. As commander-in-chief of the army, he had to

(see the box on p. 510)

Chronology
▼ ▼ ▼
The Puritan Revolution

James I	1603–1625
Charles I	1625–1649
Petition of Right	1628
Ship Money Controversy	1634
First Session of the Long Parliament	1640–1641
First Civil War	1642–1646
Second Civil War	1648
Execution of Charles I	1649
Commonwealth	1649–1653
Rule by Military Governors	1655
Death of Cromwell	1658
Restoration of Monarchy—Charles II	1660

crush a Catholic uprising in Ireland, which he did with a brutality that earned him the eternal enmity of the Irish people, as well as an uprising in Scotland on behalf of the son of Charles I. He also faced opposition at home, especially from more radically minded groups who took advantage of the upheaval in England to push their agendas. The Levellers, for example, advocated such advanced ideas as freedom of speech, religious toleration, and a democratic republic. Cromwell, a country gentleman, defender of property and the ruling classes, smashed the radicals by force. At the same time, Cromwell found it difficult to work with the Rump Parliament

▼ **Execution of Charles I.** The Puritan Revolution involved political and economic as well as religious considerations. James I and his son Charles I attempted to assert their divine right to rule while limiting the power of Parliament. Moreover, both failed to deal adequately with the religious problems that divided England. When Charles attempted to arrest radical members of Parliament, a civil war erupted that eventually led to the rise of Oliver Cromwell and the execution of Charles I.

The Execution of a King
▼ ▼ ▼

After winning the civil wars (1642–1648), the Rump Parliament, acting as a "High Court of Justice," condemned King Charles I as a "tyrant, murderer, and public enemy," and ordered that he "be put to death by the severing of his head from his body." This excerpt is taken from a contemporary account of the king's execution, an act that was most uncommon in the seventeenth century.

An Account of the Execution of Charles I

And to the executioner he said, "I shall say but very short prayers, and when I thrust out my hands—"

Then he called to the bishop for his cap, and having put it on, asked the executioner, "Does my hair trouble you?" who desired him to put it all under his cap; which, as he was doing by the help of the bishop and the executioner, he turned to the bishop, and said, "I have a good cause, and a gracious God on my side."

The bishop said, "There is but one stage more, which, though turbulent and troublesome, yet is a very short one. You may consider it will soon carry you a very great way; it will carry you from earth to heaven; and there you shall find to your great joy the prize you hasten to, a crown of glory."

The king adjoins, "I go from a corruptible to an incorruptible crown; where no disturbance can be, no disturbance in the world. . . ."

Then the king asked the executioner, "Is my hair well?"

Then putting off his doublet and being in his waistcoat, he put on his cloak again, and looking upon the block, said to the executioner, "You must set it fast."

The executioner. "It is fast, sir."

King. "It might have been a little higher."

Executioner. "It can be no higher, sir."

King. "When I put out my hands this way, then—"

Then having said a few words to himself, as he stood, with hands and eyes lift up, immediately stooping down he laid his neck upon the block; and the executioner, again putting his hair under his cap, his Majesty, thinking he had been going to strike, bade him, "Stay for the sign."

Executioner. "Yes, I will, as it please your Majesty."

After a very short pause, his Majesty stretching forth his hands, the executioner at one blow severed his head from his body; which being held up and showed to the people, was with his body put into a coffin covered with black velvet and carried into his lodging.

His blood was taken up by divers persons for different ends: by some as trophies of their villainy; by others as relics of a martyr; and in some hath had the same effect, by the blessing of God, which was often found in his sacred touch when living.

---

and finally dispersed it by force. As the members of Parliament departed (April 1653), he shouted after them: "It's you that have forced me to do this, for I have sought the Lord night and day that He would slay me rather than put upon me the doing of this work." With the certainty of one who is convinced he is right, Cromwell had destroyed both king and Parliament.

The army provided a new government when it drew up the Instrument of Government, England's first and last written constitution. Executive power was vested in the Lord Protector (a position held by Cromwell) and legislative power in a Parliament. But the new system also failed to work. Cromwell found it difficult to work with the Parliament, especially when its members debated his authority and advocated once again the cre-

ation of a Presbyterian state church. In 1655, Cromwell dissolved Parliament and divided the country into eleven regions, each ruled by a major general who served virtually as a military governor. To meet the cost of military government, Cromwell levied a 10 percent land tax on all former Royalists. Unable to establish a constitutional basis for a working government, Cromwell had resorted to military force to maintain the rule of the Independents, ironically using even more arbitrary policies than those of Charles I.

Oliver Cromwell died in 1658. After floundering for eighteen months, the military establishment decided that arbitrary rule by the army was no longer feasible and reestablished the monarchy in the person of Charles II, the son of Charles I. The restoration of the Stuart monarchy ended England's time of troubles, but it would not be long before England would experience yet another constitutional crisis (see Chapter 16).

▼ The Witchcraft Craze

Hysteria over witchcraft affected the lives of many Europeans in the sixteenth and seventeenth centuries. Witchcraft trials were prevalent in England, Scotland, Switzerland, Germany, some parts of France and the Low Countries, and even New England in America.

Witchcraft was not a new phenomenon in the sixteenth and seventeenth centuries. Although its practice had been part of traditional village culture for centuries, the medieval church made it both sinister and dangerous when it began to connect witches to the activities of the Devil, thereby transforming witchcraft into a heresy that had to be extirpated. By the thirteenth century, after the creation of the Inquisition, people were being accused of a variety of witchcraft practices and, following the biblical injunction, "Thou shalt not suffer a witch to live," were turned over to secular authorities for burning at the stake or hanging (in England).

The search for scapegoats to explain the disaster of the Black Death in the fourteenth century led to a rise in the persecution of people accused of sorcery. In a papal bull of 1484, Pope Innocent VIII made official the belief of the Catholic church in such pernicious practices:

It has recently come to our ears, not without great pain to us, that in some parts of upper Germany, . . . many persons of both sexes, heedless of their own salvation and forsaking the catholic faith, give themselves over to devils male and female, and by their incantations, charms, and conjurings, . . . ruin and cause to perish the offspring of women, the foal of animals, the products of the earth, the grapes of vines, and the fruits of trees, as well as men and women, cattle and flocks and herds and animals of every kind . . .; that they afflict and torture with dire pains and anguish, both internal and external, these men, women, cattle, flocks, herds, and animals, and hinder men from begetting and women from conceiving, and prevent all consummation of marriage; . . . that, moreover, at the instigation of the enemy of mankind [Satan], they do not fear to commit and perpetrate many other abominable offences and crimes.[9]

To combat these dangers, Innocent sent two Dominican monks, Jacob Sprenger and Heinrich Krämer, to Germany to investigate and root out the witches. Based on their findings, they wrote the *Malleus Maleficarum (The Hammer of the Witches)*, which until the eighteenth century remained the standard handbook on the practices of witchcraft and the methods that could be used to discover and try witches.

What distinguished witchcraft in the sixteenth and seventeenth centuries from these previous developments was the high level of hysteria at which neighbors accused neighbors of witchcraft, leading to widespread trials of witches. Although estimates have varied widely, the

▼ **The Persecution of Witches.** A witchcraft hysteria dominated the daily lives of many Europeans in the sixteenth and seventeenth centuries. The medieval church associated witchcraft with devil worship and the secular authorities approved burning at the stake and hanging as punishments for witchcraft. Pictured here is the witches' sabbat or the infamous gathering where witches supposedly feasted, danced, and participated in orgies.

A Witchcraft Trial in Germany

▼ ▼ ▼

Prosecutions for witchcraft reached their high point in the sixteenth and seventeenth centuries when tens of thousands of people were brought to trial. In this excerpt from the minutes of a trial at Bamberg in 1628, we can see how the trial proceeded and why the accused witch stood little chance of exonerating himself.

The Prosecution of a Witch at Bamberg

On Wednesday, June 28, 1628, was examined without torture Johannes Junius, Burgomaster at Bamberg, on the charge of witchcraft: how and in what fashion he had fallen into that vice. Is fifty-years old . . . . Says he is wholly innocent, knows nothing of the crime, has never in his life renounced God; says that he is wronged before God and the world, would like to hear of a single human being who has seen him at such gatherings [as the witch sabbats].

Confrontation of Dr. Georg Adam Haan. Tells him to his face he will stake his life on it, that he saw him, Junius, a year and a half ago at a witchgathering in the electoral council-room, where they ate and drank. Accused denies the same wholly.

Confronted with Hopffens Elsse. Tells him likewise that he was on Haupts-moor at a witch-dance; but first the holy wafer was desecrated. Junius denies. Hereupon he was told that his accomplices had confessed against him and was given time for thought.

On Friday, June 30, 1628, the aforesaid Junius was again without torture exhorted to confess, but again confessed nothing, whereupon . . . since he would confess nothing, he was put to the torture, and first the *Thumb-screws* were applied. Says he has never denied God his Saviour nor suffered himself to be otherwise baptized [by the devil]; will again stake his life on it; feels no pain in the thumb-screws.

Leg-screws. Will confess absolutely nothing; knows nothing about it. He has never renounced God; will never do such a thing; has never been guilty of this vice; feels likewise no pain.

Strappado. He has never renounced God; God will not forsake him; if he were such a wretch he would not let himself be so tortured; God must show some token of his innocence. He knows nothing about witchcraft.

On July 5, the above named Junius is without torture, but with urgent persuasions, exhorted to confess, and at last begins and confesses:

When in the year 1624 his law-suit at Rothweil cost him some six hundred florins, he had gone out, in the month of August, into his orchard at Friedricsbronnen; and, as he sat there in thought, there had come to him a woman like a grass-maid, who had asked him why he sat there so sorrowful; he had answered that he was not despondent, but she had led him by seductive speeches to yield him to her will. . . . And thereafter this wench had changed into the form of a goat, which bleated and said, "Now you see with whom you have had to do. You must be mine or I will forthwith break your neck." Thereupon he had been frightened, and trembled all over for fear. . . . he was obliged to speak this formula: "I renounce God in Heaven and his host, and will henceforward recognize the Devil as my God."

He was then named Krix. His paramour he had to call Vixen. Those present had congratulated him in Beelzebub's name and said that they were now all alike. . . . At this time his paramour had promised to provide him with money, and from time to time to take him to other witch-gatherings.

Whenever he wished to ride forth [to the witchsabbat] a black dog had come before his bed, which said to him that he must go with him, whereupon he had seated himself upon the dog and the dog had raised himself in the Devil's name and so had fared forth.

---

most recent figures indicate that more than 100,000 people were prosecuted throughout Europe on charges of witchcraft. As more and more people were brought to trial, the fear of witches as well as the fear of being accused of witchcraft escalated to frightening proportions. Approximately 25 percent of the villages in the English county of Essex, for example, had at least one witchcraft trial in the sixteenth and seventeenth centuries. Although larger cities were affected first, the trials also spread to smaller towns and rural areas as the hysteria persisted well into the seventeenth century (see the box above).

From an account of witch persecution in the German city of Trier, we get some glimpse of who the accused were: "Scarcely any of those who were accused escaped punishment. Nor were there spared even the leading men in the city of Trier." Although this statement makes it clear that the witchcraft trials had gone so far that even city officeholders were not immune from persecution, it also implies what is borne out in most witchcraft trials—that the common people were more likely to be accused of witchcraft. Indeed, where lists are given, those mentioned most often are milkmaids, peasant women, and servant girls. In the witchcraft trials of the sixteenth and seventeenth centuries, over 75 percent of those accused were women, most of them single or widowed and many over fifty years old. Moreover, almost all victims belonged to the lower classes, the poor and propertyless.

The accused witches usually confessed to a number of practices. Many of their confessions were extracted by torture, greatly adding to the number and intensity of activities mentioned. But even when people confessed voluntarily, certain practices stand out. Many said that they had sworn allegiance to the devil and attended sabbats or nocturnal gatherings where they feasted, danced, and even copulated with the devil in sexual orgies. More common, however, were admissions of using evil incantations and special ointments and powders to wreak havoc on neighbors by killing their livestock, injuring their children, or raising storms to destroy their crops.

A number of contributing factors have been suggested to explain why the witchcraft craze became so widespread in the sixteenth and seventeenth centuries. Religious uncertainties clearly played some part. Many witchcraft trials occurred in areas where Protestantism had been recently victorious or in regions, such as southwestern Germany, where Protestant-Catholic controversies still raged. As religious passions became inflamed, accusations of being in league with the devil became common on both sides.

Recently, however, historians have emphasized the importance of social conditions, especially the problems of a society in turmoil, in explaining the witchcraft hysteria. At a time when the old communal values that stressed working together for the good of the community were disintegrating before the onslaught of a new economic ethic that emphasized that each person should look out for himself or herself, property owners became more fearful of the growing numbers of poor among them and transformed them psychologically into agents of the devil. Old women were particularly susceptible to suspicion. Many of them, no longer the recipients of the local charity found in traditional society, may even have tried to survive by selling herbs, potions, or secret remedies for healing. When problems arose, and there were many in this crisis-laden period, these same people were the most likely scapegoats at hand.

By the mid-seventeenth century, the witchcraft hysteria began to subside. The destruction of the religious wars had at least forced people to accept a grudging toleration, causing religious passions to subside. Moreover, as governments began to stabilize after the period of crisis, fewer magistrates were willing to accept the unsettling and divisive conditions generated by the trials of witches. Finally, by the end of the seventeenth and beginning of the eighteenth centuries, more and more people were questioning altogether their old attitudes towards religion and found it especially contrary to reason to believe in the old view of a world haunted by evil spirits.

▼ Culture in a Turbulent World

Art and literature passed through two major stylistic stages between the Renaissance and 1650. These changes were closely linked to the religious, political, and intellectual developments of the period.

Art

The artistic Renaissance came to an end when a new movement called Mannerism emerged in Italy in the decades of the 1520s and 1530s. The age of the Reformation had brought a revival of religious values accompanied by much political turmoil. Especially in Italy, the worldly enthusiasm of the Renaissance gave way to anxiety, uncertainty, suffering, and a yearning for spiritual experience. Mannerism reflected this environment in its deliberate attempt to break down the High Renaissance principles of balance, harmony, and moderation. In the *Deposition of Christ* by Jacopo da Pontormo (1494–1557), the rules of proportion are deliberately ignored as elongated figures are used to convey suffering, heightened emotions, and religious ecstasy. A sense of the bizarre is strengthened by the use of strange colors, such as pinkish hues for the color of human skin. Mannerism attempted to substitute a "realistic presentation of emotion" for a "realistic presentation of nature."

Mannerism spread from Italy to other parts of Europe and perhaps reached its apogee in the work of El Greco (1541–1614). Doménikos Theotocópoulos (called "the

Greek"—El Greco) was from Crete, but after studying in Venice and Rome, he moved to Spain in the 1570s where he became a church painter in Toledo. El Greco's use of elongated and contorted figures, portrayed in unusual shades of yellow and green against an eerie background of turbulent grays, reflect well the unresolved tensions created by the religious upheavals of the Reformation.

Mannerism was eventually replaced by a new movement—the Baroque—that dominated the artistic world for another century and a half. The Baroque originated

▼ **Peter Paul Rubens, *The Landing of Marie de' Medici at Marseilles*.** In the realm of Baroque painting, Peter Paul Rubens was an important figure. He played a key role in the spreading of the Baroque style from Italy to other parts of Europe. In *The Landing of Marie de' Medici at Marseilles*, Rubens makes a dramatic use of light and color, bodies in motion, and luxurious nudes to heighten the emotional intensity of the scene.

▼ **Jacopo da Pontormo, *Deposition of Christ*.** The artistic Renaissance came to a close with the rise of Mannerism, which reflected a breakdown of the High Renaissance principles of balance, harmony, and moderation. In Jacopo da Pontormo's *Deposition of Christ*, elongated figures and strange colors ranging from flaming red to icy blue create a world of suffering and strong emotions.

in Italy in the last quarter of the sixteenth century and spread to the rest of Europe. Baroque artists sought to harmonize the classical traditions of Renaissance art with the spiritual dimensions of the sixteenth-century religious revival in a new search for order and unity. The Baroque first appeared in Rome in the Jesuit church of Il Gesù, whose facade was completed in 1575. Although Protestants were also influenced, it was the Catholic reform movement that most wholeheartedly adopted the Baroque, as is evident at Catholic courts, especially those of the Habsburgs in Madrid, Prague, Vienna, and Brussels. Although it was resisted in France, England, and Holland, eventually the Baroque style spread to all of Europe and even Latin America.

In large part, Baroque art and architecture reflected the search for power that was characteristic of much of the seventeenth century (see Chapter 16). Baroque churches and palaces were built with richly ornamented facades, sweeping staircases, and a display and ostentation "exhibited in ornamentation and piling on of material."

The Baroque painting style was known for its use of dramatic effects to heighten emotional intensity, especially evident in the works of Peter Paul Rubens (1577–1640), a prolific artist and an important figure in the spread of the Baroque from Italy to other parts of Europe. In his artistic masterpieces, bodies in violent motion, heavily fleshed nudes, a dramatic use of light and shadow, and rich sensuous pigments converge to show intense emotions. The restless forms and constant movement blend together into a dynamic unity.

Perhaps the greatest figure of the Baroque was the Italian architect and sculptor Gian Lorenzo Bernini (1598–1680), who completed Saint Peter's Basilica and designed the vast colonnade enclosing the piazza in front of it. Action, exuberance, profusion, and dramatic effects mark the work of Bernini in the interior of Saint Peter's, where Bernini's *Throne of St. Peter* hovers in mid-air, held by the hands of the four great doctors of the Catholic church. Above the chair, rays of heavenly

▼ **El Greco,** *Laocöon.* Mannerism reached one of its highest expressions in the work of El Greco. Born in Crete, trained in Venice and Rome, and settling finally in Spain, El Greco worked as a church painter in Toledo. Pictured here is his version of the *Laocöon*, a famous piece of Hellenistic sculpture that had been discovered in Rome in 1506. The elongated, contorted bodies project a world of suffering while the somber background scene of the city of Toledo adds a sense of terror and doom.

▼ **Gian Lorenzo Bernini,** *Throne of St. Peter.* One of the greatest figures of the Baroque period was the Italian sculptor and architect Gian Lorenzo Bernini. Bernini was responsible for the completion of St. Peter's Cathedral and for the designing of the colonnade that surrounds the piazza in front of it. Pictured here is Bernini's *Throne of St. Peter* in the interior of St. Peter's Cathedral.

light drive a mass of clouds and angels toward the spectator. In his most striking sculptural work, the *Ecstasy of St. Theresa,* Bernini depicts a moment of mystical experience in the life of the sixteenth-century Spanish saint; the result is a sensuously real portrayal of physical ecstasy.

Thought: The World of Montaigne

The crises of the century from 1550 to 1650 produced challenges to the optimistic moral and intellectual postulates of the Renaissance. The humanist emphasis on the dignity of man and the role of education in producing moral virtue seemed questionable in view of the often violent and irrational passions of dynastic and religious warfare. Intellectuals and writers began to adopt new approaches in criticizing tradition and authority. The concept of a positive skepticism is closely associated with the work of Michel de Montaigne (1533–1592).

Son of a prosperous French merchant, Montaigne received the kind of classical education advocated by Renaissance humanists. Montaigne served as a lawyer and magistrate in the Parlement of Bordeaux, but the religious wars so disgusted him that he withdrew to his country estate to think and write his *Essays,* the first two books of which were published in 1580. His aim was to "disclose himself," or to use self-knowledge as an instrument to understand the world. Montaigne approached his subjects with an ironic skepticism, questioning inherited tradition and authority with special criticism aimed at moral absolutists. He was especially critical of the Huguenot and ultra-Catholic fanatics of the French Wars of Religion who deluded themselves and took the easy way out of life's complexities by trying to kill each other: "instead of transforming themselves into angels, they transform themselves into beasts."

To counteract fanaticism, Montaigne preached moderation and toleration or the "middle way." In his *Essay on Experience,* he wrote: "It is much easier to go along the sides, where the outer edge serves as a limit and a guide, than by the middle way, wide and open, and to go by art than by nature; but it is also much less noble and less commendable. Greatness of soul is not so much pressing upward and forward as knowing how to set oneself in order."[10] Montaigne also brought his middle way and skeptical mind to bear on other subjects of the day. He wondered, for example, whether "civilized" Europeans were superior to the "savages" of the New World.

Montaigne was secular minded and discussed moral issues without reference to Christian truths. He was, in many ways, out of step with his own age of passionate religious truths and hatreds, but his ideas would be welcomed by many Europeans once Europe passed through this stage of intense intolerance. His maturity, experience, gentleness, and openness all made Montaigne one of the timeless writers of Western civilization.

A Golden Age of Literature: England and Spain

Periods of crisis often produce great writing, and so it was of this age, which was characterized by epic poetry, experimental verse, the first great chivalric novel, and, above all, a golden age of theater. In both England and

William Shakespeare: In Praise of England

▼ ▼ ▼

William Shakespeare is one of the most famous playwrights in the Western world. He was a universal genius, outclassing all others in his psychological insights, depth of characterization, imaginative skills, and versatility. His historical plays reflected the patriotic enthusiasm of the English in the Elizabethan era, as this excerpt from Richard II illustrates.

William Shakespeare, *Richard II*

This royal throne of kings, this sceptered isle,
This earth of majesty, this seat of Mars,
This other Eden, demi-Paradise,
This fortress built by Nature for herself
Against infection and the hand of war,
This happy breed of men, this little world,
This precious stone set in the silver sea,
Which serves it in the office of a wall
Or as a moat defensive to a house
Against the envy of less happier lands—

This blessed plot, this earth, this realm, this England,
This nurse, this teeming womb of royal kings,
Feared by their breed and famous by their birth,
Renowned for their deeds as far from home,
For Christian service and true chivalry,
As is the sepulcher in stubborn Jewry [the Holy
    Sepulcher in Jerusalem]
Of the world's ransom, blessed Mary's Son—
This land of such dear souls, this dear dear land,
Dear for her reputation through the world,
Is now leased out, I die pronouncing it,
Like a tenement or pelting farm.
England, bound in with the triumphant sea,
Whose rocky shore beats back the envious siege
Of watery Neptune, is now bound in with shame,
With inky blots and rotten parchment bonds.
That England, that was wont to conquer others,
Hath made a shameful conquest of itself.
Ah, would the scandal vanish with my life,
How happy then were my ensuing death!

Spain, writing for the stage reached new heights between 1580 and 1640. All of this impressive literature was written in the vernacular. Except for academic fields, such as theology, philosophy, jurisprudence, and the sciences, Latin was no longer a universal literary language.

The golden age of English literature is often called the Elizabethan Era because much of the English cultural flowering of the late sixteenth and early seventeenth centuries occurred during her reign. Elizabethan literature exhibits the exuberance and pride associated with English exploits under Queen Elizabeth (see the box above). Of all the forms of Elizabethan literature, none expressed the energy and intellectual versatility of the era better than drama. Of all the dramatists, none is more famous than William Shakespeare (1564–1614).

Shakespeare was the son of a prosperous glovemaker from Stratford-upon-Avon. When he appeared in London in 1592, Elizabethans were already addicted to the stage. By 1576, two professional theaters run by actors' companies were in existence. Elizabethan theater became a tremendously successful business. In or near London, at least four to six theaters were open six afternoons

a week. London theaters ranged from the Globe, which was a circular unroofed structure holding 3,000, to the Blackfriars, which was roofed and held only 500. In the former, an admission charge of one or two pennies enabled even the lower classes to attend, while the higher prices in the latter ensured an audience of the well-to-do. Elizabethan audiences varied greatly, putting pressure on playwrights to write works that pleased nobles, lawyers, merchants, and even vagabonds. When the Puritans, who had long criticized the wickedness of the London stage, assumed power in 1642, one of their first actions was to close the theaters. They did not reopen until the monarchy was restored, eighteen years later.

William Shakespeare was a "complete man of the theater." Although best known for writing plays, he was also an actor and shareholder in the chief company of the time, the Lord Chamberlain's Company, which played in theaters as diverse as the Globe and the Blackfriars. Shakespeare has long been recognized as a universal genius. A master of the English language, he was instrumental in transforming a language that was still in a period of transition. His technical proficiency, however, was matched by an incredible insight into human

▼ **William Shakespeare.** The golden age of English literature is identified with the Elizabethan era. Drama flourished during this period, and the greatest dramatist of the age was William Shakespeare. An actor and shareholder in a theatrical company as well as a playwright, Shakespeare wrote a number of tragedies, comedies, romances, and histories. Regardless of the kind of play he wrote, Shakespeare always exhibited a keen understanding of the human condition.

psychology. Whether in his tragedies or comedies, Shakespeare exhibited a remarkable understanding of the human condition.

The theater was one of the most creative forms of expression during Spain's golden century. In the course of the sixteenth century, Spanish theater made the transition from religious morality plays to a popular form of dramatic art. The first professional theaters established in Seville and Madrid in the 1570s were run by actors' companies as in England. Soon, every large town had a public playhouse, including Mexico City in the New

World. Touring companies brought the latest Spanish plays to all parts of the Spanish empire.

Beginning in the 1580s, the agenda for playwrights was set by Lope de Vega (1562–1635). Like Shakespeare, he was from a middle-class background. He was an incredibly prolific writer; almost 500 of his 1,500 plays survive. They have been characterized as witty, charming, action-packed, and realistic. Lope de Vega made no apologies for the fact that he wrote his plays to please his audiences. In a treatise on drama written in 1609, he stated that the foremost duty of the playwright was to satisfy public demand. Shakespeare undoubtedly believed the same thing since his livelihood depended on public approval, but Lope de Vega was considerably more cynical about it: he remarked that if anyone thought he had written his plays for fame, "undeceive him and tell him that I wrote them for money."

One of the crowning achievements of the Golden Age of Spanish literature was the work of Miguel de Cervantes (1547–1616), whose *Don Quixote* has been acclaimed as one of the greatest literary works of all time. While satirizing medieval chivalric literature, Cervantes also perfected the chivalric novel and reconciled it with literary realism. In the two main figures of his famous work, Cervantes presented the dual nature of Spanish character. The knight Don Quixote from La Mancha is the visionary who is so involved in his lofty ideals that he is oblivious to the hard realities around him. To him, for example, windmills appear as four-armed giants. In contrast, the knight's fat and earthy squire, Sancho Panza, is the realist who cannot get his master to see the realities in front of him. But after adventures that took them to all parts of Spain, each came to see the value of the other's perspective. We are left with Cervantes's conviction that idealism and realism, visionary dreams and the hard work of reality, are both necessary to the human condition.

The period from 1560 to 1650 witnessed Europe's attempt to adjust to a whole range of change-laden forces. Population contracted as economic expansion gave way to economic recession. The discovery of new trade routes to the Far East and the "accidental" discovery of the Americas led Europeans to plunge outside the medieval world in which they had been enclosed for virtually a thousand years. The conquest of the Americas brought out the worst and some of the best of European civilization. The greedy plundering of resources and the brutal repression, enslavement, and virtual annihilation of millions of native Americans were hardly balanced by attempts to create new institutions, convert the natives to Christianity, and foster the rights of the indigenous peoples.

In the sixteenth century, the discoveries made little impact on Europeans preoccupied with the problems of dynastic expansion and, above all, religious division. It took one hundred years of religious warfare complicated by serious political, economic and social issues—the worst series of wars and civil wars since the collapse of the Roman Empire in the west—before Europeans finally admitted that they would have to tolerate different ways to worship God. That men who were disciples of the

Apostle of Peace would kill each other—often in brutal and painful fashion—aroused skepticism about Christianity itself. As one German writer put it in 1650: "Lutheran, popish, and Calvinistic, we've got all these beliefs here; but there is some doubt about where Christianity has got to."[11] It is surely no accident that the search for a stable, secular order of politics and for order in the universe through natural laws played such important roles in the seventeenth century. The religious wars of the sixteenth and seventeenth centuries opened the door to the secular perspectives that have characterized modern Western civilization.

Notes
▼ ▼ ▼

1. Quoted in J. H. Parry, *The Age of Reconnaissance: Discovery, Exploration and Settlement, 1450 to 1650* (New York, 1963), p. 33.

2. Quoted in Richard B. Reed, "The Expansion of Europe," in Richard DeMolen, ed., *The Meaning of the Renaissance and Reformation* (Boston, 1974), p. 308.

3. Miguel Leon-Portilla, ed., *The Broken Spears: The Aztec Account of the Conquest of Mexico* (Boston, 1969), p. 51.

4. Quoted in E. Harris Harbison, *The Age of Reformation* (Ithaca, N.Y., 1955), p. 109.

5. Quoted in Garrett Mattingly, *The Armada* (Boston, 1959), pp. 216–17.

6. Quoted in H. G. Koenigsberger, *Early Modern Europe: 1500–1789* (London, 1987), pp. 29–30.

7. Quoted in James Harvey Robinson, *Readings in European History* (Boston, 1934), 2: 211–12.

8. Quoted in Maurice Ashley, *The Greatness of Oliver Cromwell* (New York, 1962), p. 65.

9. Quoted in Alan Kors and Edward Peters, eds., *Witchcraft in Europe, 1100–1700* (Philadelphia, 1972), p. 112.

10. *The Complete Essays of Montaigne*, trans. Donald Frame (Stanford, 1958), p. 852.

11. Quoted in Theodore Schieder, *Handbuch der Europäischen Geschichte*, (Stuttgart, 1979), 3: 579.

Suggestions for Further Reading
▼ ▼ ▼

General works on the period from 1560 to 1650 include C. Wilson, *The Transformation of Europe, 1558–1648* (Berkeley, 1976); and H. Kamen, *The Iron Century: Social Change in Europe, 1550–1660* (New York, 1971). For an extremely detailed account of all aspects of life in the Mediterranean basin in the second half of the sixteenth century, see F. Braudel, *The Mediterranean and the Mediterranean World in the Age of Philip II*, trans. S. Reynolds, 2 vols. (New York, 1972–73).

The best general accounts of European discovery and expansion are J. H. Parry, *The Age of Reconnaissance: Discovery, Exploration and Settlement, 1450 to 1650* (New York, 1963); B. Penrose, *Travel and Discovery in the*

Renaissance, 1420–1620 (New York, 1962); and the brief work by J. H. Parry, *The Establishment of the European Hegemony, 1415–1715* (New York, 1961). On the technological aspects of the subject, see C. M. Cipolla, *Guns, Sails, and Empires: Technological Innovation and the Early Phases of European Expansion, 1400–1700* (New York, 1965). On the Portuguese expansion, the fundamental work is C. R. Boxer, *The Portuguese Seaborne Empire: 1415–1825* (New York, 1969); but see also W. B. Diffie and G. D. Winius, *Foundations of the Portuguese Empire, 1415–1580* (Minneapolis, 1979). The story of the discovery and settlement of America is engagingly portrayed in S. E. Morison, *The European*

Discovery of America: The Northern Voyages, A.D. 500–1600 (New York, 1971) and *The Southern Voyages, A.D. 1492–1616* (New York, 1974). On Columbus, see the brief biography by J. S. Collis, *Christopher Columbus* (London, 1976). For a fundamental work on Spanish colonization, see J. H. Parry, *The Spanish Seaborne Empire* (New York, 1966). The standard work on the conquistadores is F. A. Kirkpatrick, *The Spanish Conquistadores* (Cleveland, 1968). Cortés is examined in W. W. Johnson, *Cortés* (Boston, 1975). The impact of expansion on European consciousness is explored in J. H. Elliott, *The Old World and the New, 1492–1650* (Cambridge, 1970). The human and ecological effects of the interaction of New World and Old World cultures is examined thoughtfully in A. W. Crosby, *The Columbian Exchange, Biological and Cultural Consequences of 1492* (Westport, Conn., 1972).

Two works by J. H. M. Salmon provide the best studies on the French Wars of Religion. They are *Society in Crisis: France in the Sixteenth Century* (New York, 1975) and *French Government and Society in the Wars of Religion* (St. Louis, 1976). For specialized studies on different aspects of the French religious wars, see N. M. Sutherland, *The Massacre of St. Bartholomew and the European Conflict, 1559–1572* (New York, 1973); and F. J. Baumgartner, *Radical Reactionaries: The Political Thought of the French Catholic League* (Geneva, 1976). An adequate popular biography of Henry of Navarre can be found in D. Seward, *The First Bourbon: Henry IV, King of France and Navarre* (Boston, 1971).

Two good histories of Spain in the sixteenth century are J. H. Elliott, *Imperial Spain, 1469–1716* (New York, 1964); and J. Lynch, *Spain under the Habsburgs*, vol. 1, *Empire and Absolutism, 1516–1598* (New York, 1964). The best biographies of Philip II are P. Pierson, *Philip II of Spain* (London, 1975); and G. Parker, *Philip II* (Boston and London, 1978). Economic aspects of sixteenth-century Spain are well discussed in the classic account of J. V. Vives, *An Economic History of Spain* (Berkeley, 1969). On the revolt of the Netherlands, see the classic work by P. Geyl, *The Revolt of the Netherlands, 1555–1609* (London, 1962); and the more recent work of G. Parker, *The Dutch Revolt* (London, 1977). The latter has also written an interesting account of how the Spanish army was supplied and maintained in the Low Countries in *The Army of Flanders and the Spanish Road, 1567–1659* (New York, 1972).

Elizabeth's reign can be examined in three good biographies, J. Ridley, *Elizabeth I* (New York, 1988); P. Johnson, *Elizabeth I, A Biography* (New York, 1974); and L. B. Smith, *Elizabeth Tudor: Portrait of a Queen* (London, 1976). The Elizabethan religious settlement has

been examined in C. S. Meyer, *Elizabeth I and the Religious Settlement of 1559* (St. Louis, 1960). The role of the Catholic and Puritan minorities is discussed in A. Morey, *The Catholic Subjects of Elizabeth I* (Totowa, N.J., 1978); and P. Collinson, *The Elizabethan Puritan Movement* (Berkeley, 1967). Works on Elizabethan foreign policy include P. S. Crowson, *Tudor Foreign Policy* (London, 1973); and C. Wilson, *Queen Elizabeth and the Revolt of the Netherlands* (Berkeley, 1970). The classic work on the Armada is the beautifully written *The Armada* by G. Mattingly (Boston, 1959).

The classic study on the Thirty Years' War is C. V. Wedgwood, *The Thirty Years War* (Garden City, N.Y., 1961), but needs to be supplemented by the more recent works by S. H. Steinberg, *The Thirty Years' War and the Conflict for European Hegemony, 1600–1660* (New York, 1966), which emphasizes the wider context of the struggle; and G. Parker, *The Thirty Years War* (London, 1984). The best biography of Wallenstein is G. Mann, *Wallenstein: His Life Narrated*, trans. C. Kessler (New York, 1976). The idea of a military revolution in the sixteenth and seventeenth centuries was first presented forcefully in M. Roberts, *The Military Revolution, 1560–1660* (London, 1956), although it has not gone unchallenged; see G. Parker, *Spain and the Netherlands* (London, 1979), pp. 86–103.

Good general works on the period of the Puritan Revolution include G. E. Aylmer, *Rebellion or Revolution? England, 1640–1660* (New York, 1986); L. Stone, *Causes of the English Revolution, 1529–1642* (New York, 1972); and the brief study by R. Howell, Jr. *The Origins of the English Revolution* (St. Louis, 1975). Biographies of the first two Stuart monarchs include W. L. McElwee, *The Wisest Fool in Christendom: The Reign of King James I and VI* (New York, 1974); and J. Bowle, *Charles I: A Biography* (Boston, 1976). On the war itself, see C. Hill, *God's Englishman: Oliver Cromwell and the English Revolution* (New York, 1970); and R. Ashton, *The English Civil War: Conservatism and Revolution, 1604–1649* (London, 1976). On Oliver Cromwell, see R. Howell, Jr., *Cromwell* (Boston, 1977); and the beautifully written popular account by A. Fraser, *Cromwell: The Lord Protector* (New York, 1974).

The story of the witchcraft craze can be examined in two recent works, J. B. Russell, *A History of Witchcraft* (London, 1980); and B. P. Levack, *The Witch-Hunt in Early Modern Europe* (London, 1987). Although more narrow in scope, also of great value is C. Larner, *Enemies of God: The Witch-hunt in Scotland* (London, 1981).

For a brief, readable guide to mannerism, see L. Murray, *The Late Renaissance and Mannerism* (New York, 1967). For a general survey of baroque culture, see J. S.

Held, *Seventeenth and Eighteenth Century Art: Baroque Painting, Sculpture, Architecture* (New York, 1971). The best biography of Montaigne remains D. M. Frame, *Montaigne: A Biography* (New York, 1965). On the Spanish golden century of literature, see R. O. Jones, *The Golden Age: Prose and Poetry*, which is volume 2 of *The Literary History of Spain* (London, 1971). The literature on Shakespeare is enormous. For a biography, see A. L. Rowse, *The Life of Shakespeare* (New York, 1963). A new way of viewing Shakespeare, showing the influence of the Hermetic tradition, can be found in F. A. Yates, *Shakespeare's Last Plays: A New Approach* (London, 1975).

Chapter 16

Response to Crisis: Absolute and Limited Monarchy in the Seventeenth and Early Eighteenth Centuries (to 1715)

▼▼▼▼▼

The age of crisis from 1560 to 1650 was accompanied by a decline in religious orientation and a growing secularization that affected both the political and intellectual worlds of Europe (on the intellectual effect, see the Scientific Revolution in Chapter 17). Some historians like to speak of the seventeenth century as a turning point in the evolution of Europe to a modern state system. The idea of a united Christian Europe (the practice of a united Christendom had actually been moribund for some time) gave way to the practical realities of a system of secular states in which reason of state took precedence over the salvation of subjects' souls. Of course, these states had emerged and begun their development during the Middle Ages, but medieval ideas about statehood had still been couched in religious terms. By the seventeenth century, Christianity had so weakened its credibility in the religious wars that more and more Europeans could think of politics in secular terms.

One of the responses to the crises of the seventeenth century was a search for order and harmony. As the internal social and political rebellions and revolts died down, it became apparent that the privileged classes of society—the aristocrats—remained in control, although the various states exhibited important differences in political forms. The most general trend saw an extension of monarchical power as a stabilizing force. This development, which historians have called absolutism or absolute monarchy, was most evident in France during the flamboyant reign of

Cardinal Richelieu   Frederick William the Great Elector   Louis XIV   Glorious Revolution   Peter the Great

··········· 1600 ··········· 1625 ··········· 1650 ··········· 1675 ··········· 1700 ···········

Rembrandt   English, French, Dutch Settle North America   Racine   Thomas Hobbes, *Leviathan*   John Locke, *Two Treatises of Civil Government*

Louis XIV. But other states, such as England, responded differently to domestic crisis, and another very different system emerged where monarchs were limited by the power of their representative assemblies. Absolute and limited monarchy were the two poles of seventeenth-century state building.

▼ The Theory of Absolutism

Absolute monarchy or absolutism meant that the sovereign power or ultimate authority in the state rested in the hands of a king who claimed to rule by divine right. But what did sovereignty mean? Late sixteenth-century political theorists believed that sovereign power consisted of the authority to make laws, tax, administer justice, control the state's administrative system, and determine foreign policy. These powers made a ruler sovereign.

One of the chief theorists of divine-right monarchy in the seventeenth century was the French theologian and court preacher Bishop Jacques Bossuet (1627–1704), who expressed his ideas in a book entitled *Politics Drawn from the Very Words of Holy Scripture*. Bossuet argued first that government was divinely ordained so that humans could live in an organized society. Of all forms of government, monarchy, he averred, was the most general, most ancient, most natural, and the best, since God established kings and through them reigned over all the peoples of the world. Since kings received their power from God, their authority was absolute. They were responsible to no one (including parliaments) except God. Nevertheless, Bossuet cautioned, although a king's authority was absolute, his power was not since he was limited by the law of God. Bossuet believed there was a difference between absolute monarchy and arbitrary monarchy. The latter contradicted the rule of law and the sanctity of property and was simply lawless tyranny.

Bossuet's distinction between absolute and arbitrary government was not always easy to maintain. There was also a large gulf between the theory of absolutism as expressed by Bossuet and the practice of absolutism. As we shall see in our survey of seventeenth-century states, a monarch's absolute power was often very limited by practical realities.

▼ Absolutism in Western Europe

An examination of seventeenth-century absolutism must begin with western Europe since France during the reign of Louis XIV (1661–1715) has traditionally been regarded as the best example of the practice of absolute monarchy in the seventeenth century.

France

Although historians have recently challenged the more grandiose assumptions about the absolute power of Louis XIV, there is no doubt that France played a dominant role in European affairs by the end of the seventeenth century. French culture, language, and manners reached into all levels of European society. French diplomacy and wars overwhelmed the political affairs of western and central Europe. The court of Louis XIV seemed to be imitated everywhere in Europe. In his desire to emulate Louis XIV, the elector of Brandenburg, although a happily married German prince, added to his court "a lady who had the title and court functions, though not the pleasures, of being his mistress." Of course, French greatness depended upon a treasury filled by imposing ever-increasing tax burdens on the people while the stability of Louis's reign was magnified by the instability that had preceded it.

FOUNDATIONS OF FRENCH ABSOLUTISM The history of France before the reign of Louis XIV was hardly the story of steady, unbroken progress toward the ideal of absolute monarchy that many historians have tended to portray. The fifty years or so before Louis were a period of struggle by royal and ministerial governments to avoid the breakdown of the state. The line between order and anarchy was often a narrow one. Nevertheless, the French monarchy gradually succeeded in overcoming the threats to its power and establishing a strong monarchical authority that lasted until the French Revolution.

Thirty years of bloody civil war had ceased at the end of the sixteenth century when Henry IV established the Bourbon dynasty (see Chapter 15). Henry began the task of reconstructing a badly shattered France, aided by a forceful group of ministers, including the astute minister of finances, the duke of Sully. The accumulation of debts from the wars and a lack of sufficient revenue constituted the government's most serious problems. Sully took steps to remedy them. Tax collectors, who paid the government a lump sum of the taxes they collected in their districts, were forced to take smaller amounts for themselves. More efficiently administered direct taxes were imposed. The *gabelle*, the much-hated tax on salt, a crucial necessity for preserving food in the seventeenth century, was raised to even higher levels. Furthermore, the sale of government offices was increased by the end of Henry's reign. By 1608, half of the government's debt had been paid, and a reservoir of funds had even been accumulated in the state treasury. Sully's expenditures on roads, land drainage, and agricultural improvements helped to stimulate and improve economic growth.

Another major problem was the government's need to restore the central authority of the monarchical government in France after thirty years of civil war. Henry IV began the process by taking numerous trips through the provinces and exercising more control over the appointment of officials in the town governments. While these steps hardly constituted a "master plan for creating absolute monarchy," they did boost the role of the central government in the life of the country. But monarchical authority was still precarious when the king was unexpectedly assassinated in 1610 and succeeded by his nine-year-old son, Louis XIII. Could the new royal government survive under the regency of Henry's wife, the Italian Marie de' Medici?

At first the issue proved problematic. Marie's policy of bribing the great nobles into submission failed to prevent them from rebelling against her authority, to which she responded—successfully—by giving them more money and new positions of power. Marie's palace clique managed to remain in power until her son, Louis XIII, took personal charge of the government in 1617. Louis's problems seemed only to mount, however, until the king's council fell under the control of the cunning, competent, and clever Cardinal Richelieu in 1624. As leader of the royal council and hence the king's chief minister, Richelieu initiated policies that eventually strengthened the power of the monarchy.

It has usually been assumed that Cardinal Richelieu had a clear plan to create an absolute monarchy and a strong state abroad. In his *Political Testament,* he claimed to have promised the king to "use all my industry and all the authority it has pleased you to give me to ruin the Huguenot party, to humble the pride of the great men, to bring your subjects to their duty and to raise your name abroad to the place that is its due."[1] But recent questions about the *Testament's* authenticity make it more likely that Richelieu's primary aims were to keep himself in power and to extend the central government's authority by any means possible.

One of the dangers to royal authority came from the Huguenots. Richelieu's policy toward them was dictated by political, not religious motives, despite his being a cardinal of the Catholic church. Richelieu realized the potential danger of the fortified cities of the Huguenots to the authority of the king, especially if the Huguenots attracted foreign support as they had in the sixteenth century. Just such a situation occurred in 1627, when the Huguenot city of La Rochelle, with English aid, rebelled against the crown. One year after the rebellion was finally crushed and the city occupied by French troops, Richelieu capitalized on his success by issuing the Peace of Alais (1629), which allowed the Huguenots to keep their religious and civil rights from the Edict of Nantes, but stripped them of their private armies and fortified cities. By eliminating their political and military rights while preserving their religious ones, the Peace of Alais helped transform the Huguenots into more reliable subjects.

Richelieu acted more cautiously in "humbling the pride of the great men," the important French nobility. He understood the influential role played by the nobles in the French state. The dangerous ones were those who asserted their territorial independence when they were excluded from participating in the central government. Proceeding slowly but determinedly, Richelieu developed an efficient network of spies to uncover noble plots and then crushed the conspiracies and executed the conspirators, thereby eliminating a major threat to royal authority. Richelieu even issued edicts against dueling as a remnant of the private warfare reminiscent of medieval nobles. To Richelieu, private warfare was as bad as armed rebellion; both repudiated central state authority.

To reform and strengthen the central administration, initially for financial reasons, Richelieu sent out royal officials called intendants to the provinces to execute the orders of the central government. As the functions of the intendants grew, they came into conflict with provincial governors. Since the intendants were victorious in most of these disputes, they further strengthened the power of the crown. Richelieu proved less capable in financial matters, however. Not only was the basic system of state finances corrupt, but so many people benefited from the system's inefficiency and injustice that the government faced strong resistance when it tried to reform it. The *taille* was increased—in 1643 it was two and a half times what it had been in 1610—and crown lands were mortgaged again. Expenditures, especially the cost of war preparations, soon outstripped the additional revenues, however, and French debt continued its upward spiral under Richelieu.

The general success of Richelieu's domestic policy in strengthening the central role of the monarchy was mirrored by a successful foreign policy. That policy was dictated, first of all, by opposition to Spain, which led in turn to further anti-Habsburg activity in the Holy Roman Empire to France's east. Eventually, the Catholic cardinal of France was led to subsidize Protestant Sweden and then in 1635 to intervene directly with French troops to support the Protestant cause against the Habsburgs (see Chapter 15). Although both Richelieu and Louis XIII died before the Thirty Years' War ended, French policy had proved successful at one level since France emerged as Europe's leading power by 1648.

Richelieu died in 1642, followed five months later by King Louis XIII, who was succeeded by his son Louis XIV, then but four years old. This necessitated a regency under Anne of Austria, wife of the dead king. But she allowed Cardinal Mazarin, the trained successor of Cardinal Richelieu and her lover, to dominate the government. An Italian who had come to France as a papal legate and then become naturalized, Mazarin attempted to carry on Richelieu's policies until his death in 1661.

The most important event during Mazarin's rule was a revolt known as the Fronde, which can be viewed as the last serious attempt to limit the growing power of the crown until the French Revolution. As a foreigner, Mazarin was greatly disliked by all elements of the French population. The nobility, who particularly resented the centralized administrative power being built up at the expense of the provincial nobility, temporarily allied with the members of the Parlement in Paris, the central court of justice, which opposed the new taxes levied by the government to pay the costs of the Thirty Years' War,

and the masses of Paris, who were also dissatisfied with the additional taxes. The first Fronde (1648–1649) broke out in Paris, led by the Parlement of Paris, whose members were nobles of the robe, the service nobility of lawyers and administrators. The first revolt was ended by compromise. The second Fronde, begun in 1650, was led by the nobles of the sword, whose ancestors were medieval nobles. They were interested in overthrowing Mazarin for their own purposes: to secure their positions and increase their own power. The second Fronde was

▼ **Cardinal Richelieu.** A key figure in the emergence of a strong monarchy in France was Cardinal Richelieu, pictured here in a portrait by Philippe de Champagne. Chief minister to Louis XIII, Richelieu strengthened royal authority by eliminating the private armies and fortified cities of the Huguenots and by crushing aristocratic conspiracies. His foreign policy elevated France to the position of Europe's leading power by the close of the Thirty Years' War.

Louis XIV: Kingly Advice

▼ ▼ ▼

Throughout his reign, Louis XIV was always on stage, acting the role of the wise "Grand Monarch." In his Memoirs for the Dauphin, Louis presented a frank collection of precepts for the education of his oldest son and heir to the throne. These Memoirs were begun in 1661, after Louis became a father, and were added to over the next twenty years.

Louis XIV, *Memoirs for the Dauphin*

Kings are often obliged to do things which go against their inclinations and offend their natural goodness. They should love to give pleasure and yet they must often punish and destroy persons on whom by nature they wish to confer benefits. The interest of the state must come first. One must constrain one's inclinations and not put oneself in the position of berating oneself because one could have done better in some important affair but did not because of some private interest, because one was distracted from the attention one should have for the greatness, the good and the power of the state. Often there are troublesome places where is it is difficult to make out what one should do. One's ideas are confused. As long as this lasts, one can refrain form making a decision. But as soon as one has fixed one's mind upon something which seems best to do, it must be acted upon. This is what enabled me to succeed so often in what I have done. The mistakes which I made, and which gave me infinite trouble, were the result of the desire to please or of allowing myself to accept too carelessly the opinions of others. Nothing is more dangerous than weakness of any kind whatsoever. In order to command others, one must raise oneself above them and once one has heard the reports from every side one must come to a decision upon the basis of one's own judgment, without anxiety but always with the concern not to command anything which is of itself unworthy either of one's place in the world or of the greatness of the state. Princes with good intentions and some knowledge of their affairs, either from experience or from study and great diligence in making themselves capable, find numerous cases which instruct them that they must give special care and total application to everything. One must be on guard against oneself, resist one's own tendencies, and always by on guard against one's own natural bent. The craft of a king is great, noble and delightful when one feels worthy of doing well whatever one promises to do. But it is not exempt from troubles, weariness and worries. Sometimes uncertainty causes despair, and when one has spent a reasonable time in examining an affair, one must make a decision and take the step which one believes to be best. When one has the state in view, one works for one's self. The good of the one constitutes the glory of the other. When the former is fortunate, eminent and powerful, he who is the cause thereof becomes glorious and consequently should find more enjoyment than his subjects in all the pleasant things of life for himself and for them. When one has made a mistake, it must be corrected as soon as possible, and no other consideration must stand in the way, not even kindness.

---

crushed by 1652, a task made easier when the nobles began fighting each other instead of Mazarin. With the end of the Fronde, a vast number of Frenchmen concluded that the best hope for stability in France lay in the crown. When Mazarin died in 1661, the greatest of the seventeenth-century monarchs, Louis XIV, took over supreme power.

THE REIGN OF LOUIS XIV (1661–1715) The day after Cardinal Mazarin's death, Louis XIV, at the age of twenty-three, expressed his determination to be a real king and the sole ruler of France:

Up to this moment I have been pleased to entrust the government of my affairs to the late Cardinal. It is now time that I govern them myself. You [secretaries and ministers of state] will assist me with your counsels when I ask for them. I request and order you to seal no orders except by my command, . . . I order you not to sign anything, not even a passport . . . without my command; to render account to me personally each day and to favor no one.[2]

His mother, who was well aware of Louis's proclivity for fun and games and getting into the beds of the maids in the royal palace, laughed aloud at these words. But Louis was quite serious.

Louis proved willing to pay the price of being a strong ruler (see the box on p. 526). He established a conscientious routine from which he seldom deviated, but he did not look upon his duties as drudgery since he judged his royal profession to be "grand, noble, and delightful." Eager for glory, Louis created a grand and majestic spectacle at the court of Versailles (see Daily Life at the Court of Versailles later in the chapter). Consequently, Louis and his court came to set the standard for monarchies and aristocracies all over Europe. Less than fifty years after his death, the great French writer Voltaire used the title "Age of Louis XIV" to describe his history of Europe from 1661 to 1715. Historians have tended to use it ever since.

Although Louis may have believed in the theory of absolute monarchy and consciously fostered the myth of himself as the Sun King, the source of light for all of his people, historians are quick to point out that the realities fell far short of the aspirations. Despite the centralizing efforts of Cardinals Richelieu and Mazarin, France still possessed a bewildering system of overlapping authorities in the seventeenth century. Provinces had their own regional parlements, their own local Estates, their own sets of laws. Members of the high nobility with their huge estates and clients among the lesser nobility still exercised much authority. Both towns and provinces possessed privileges and powers seemingly from time immemorial that they would not easily relinquish. Much of Louis's success rested less on the modernization of administrative machinery, as is frequently claimed, than on his clever and adroit manipulation of the traditional priorities and values of French society.

One of the keys to Louis's power was that he was able to restructure the central policy-making machinery of government because it was part of his own court and household. The royal court was an elaborate structure that served three purposes simultaneously: it was the personal household of the king, the location of central governmental machinery, and the place where powerful subjects came to find favors and offices for themselves and their clients as well as the main arena where rival aristocratic factions jostled for power. The greatest danger to Louis's personal rule came from the very high nobles and princes of the blood (the royal princes) who considered it their natural function to assert the policy-making role of royal ministers. Louis eliminated this threat by removing them from the royal council, the chief administrative body of the king and overseer of the central machinery of government, and enticing them to his court where he could keep them preoccupied with court life and out of politics.

Instead of the high nobility and royal princes, Louis relied for his ministers on nobles who came from relatively new aristocratic families. Such were Michel Le Tellier, secretary of state for war; Hugues de Lionne, secretary for foreign affairs; and Nicholas Fouquet, superintendent of finances. His ministers were expected to be subservient; said Louis, "I had no intention of sharing my authority with them." When Fouquet began to flaunt the enormous wealth and power he had amassed in the King's service, Louis ordered his arrest and imprisoned

▼ **Louis XIV.** Louis XIV was determined to be the sole ruler of France. Louis eliminated the threat of the high nobility by removing them from the royal council and replacing them with relatively new aristocrats whose lives he could dominate. He was successful in converting many Protestants and created a standing army under the rule of the king. His reign was troubled by ever-increasing financial problems. This portrait by Hyacinth Rigaud captures the king's sense of royal dignity and grandeur.

him for life. Fouquet was replaced in the king's council by Colbert, another noble of bourgeois origin. Louis's domination of his ministers and secretaries gave him control of the central policy-making machinery of government and thus authority over the traditional areas of monarchical power: the formulation of foreign policy, the making of war and peace, the assertion of the secular power of crown against any religious authority, and the ability to levy taxes to fulfill these functions.

According to recent historical scholarship, however, Louis had considerably less success with the internal administration of the kingdom. The traditional groups and institutions of French society—the nobles, officials, town councils, guilds, and representative Estates in some provinces—were simply too powerful for the king to have direct control over the lives of his subjects. Louis had three ways to rule the provinces. Officially, he worked through hereditary officeholders, usually aristocrats, who were untrustworthy since they were always inclined to balance the king's wishes against their own interests. The king also had his intendants as direct royal agents, but they also proved unreliable and often provoked disturbances in the provinces by their actions. They were not so much the instruments by which the central government carried out decisions, but simply the "eyes and ears of the ministers" in the provinces. Finally, the king had an informal system of royal patronage, which Louis used successfully. The king and his ministers enlisted the aid of nobles and senior churchmen and their clients by granting them offices and pensions. The control of the central government over the provinces and the people, then, was carried out by the careful bribery of the important people to see that the king's policies were executed. Local officials could still obstruct the execution of policies they disliked, indicating clearly that a so-called absolute monarch was not always that absolute.

The maintenance of religious harmony had long been considered an area of monarchical power. The desire to keep it led Louis into conflict with the French Huguenots and the papacy. Louis XIV did not want to allow Protestants to practice their faith in largely Catholic France. Perhaps he was motivated by religion, but it is more likely that Louis, who believed in the motto, "one king, one law, one faith," felt that the existence of this minority undermined his own political authority. His anti-Protestant policy, aimed at converting the Huguenots to Catholicism, began mildly by offering rewards, but escalated by 1681 to a policy of forced conversions. The most favored method was to quarter French soldiers in Huguenot communities and homes with the freedom

to misbehave so that their hosts would "see the light quickly." This approach did produce thousands of immediate conversions. In October 1685, Louis issued the Edict of Fontainebleau. In addition to revoking the Edict of Nantes, the new edict provided for the destruction of Huguenot churches and the closing of their schools. Although they were forbidden to leave France, it is estimated that 200,000 Huguenots left for shelter in England, the United Provinces, and the German states. Through their exodus, France lost people who had commercial and industrial skills, although some modern scholars have argued this had only a minor impact on the French economy. Perhaps a more important effect of the Huguenot dispersal was the increased hatred of France that the Huguenot émigrés stirred up in their adopted Protestant countries.

Whatever his motives, Louis's anti-Protestant policy was not aimed at currying papal favor. Louis was a defender of Gallicanism, the belief that the monarchy possessed certain rights over the Catholic church in France, irrespective of papal powers. In the 1670s, Louis claimed the *régale* or the right of the French king to appoint the lower clergy and collect the revenues of a diocese when it was vacant. Pope Innocent XI condemned Louis's actions, threatening him with reprisals. Louis responded by calling a special assembly of French clergy and directing them to draw up a Declaration of Gallican Liberties. This document claimed that the pope's authority in France was limited to spiritual matters and that even in spiritual matters, the pope was subject to the decisions of a general council. The pope protested this challenge to papal authority and the possibility of a schism loomed large. But neither side wanted to go that far. After Innocent's death, a compromise was arranged, and by 1693 the Gallican articles had been retracted.

The cost of building Versailles and other palaces, maintaining his court, and pursuing his wars made finances a crucial issue for Louis XIV. He was most fortunate in having the services of Jean-Baptiste Colbert (1619–1683) as controller-general of finances. Colbert sought to increase the wealth and power of France through general adherence to that loose collection of economic policies called mercantilism, which stressed government regulation of economic activities to benefit the state (see Mercantilism later in the chapter). To decrease the need for imports and increase exports, Colbert attempted to expand the quantity and improve the quality of French manufactured goods. He founded new luxury industries, such as the royal tapestry works at Beauvais; invited Venetian glassmakers and Flemish clothmakers to France; drew up instructions regulating the quality of goods produced; oversaw the training of the workers and granted special privileges, including tax exemptions, loans, and subsidies to those who established new industries. To improve communications and the transportation of goods internally, he built roads and canals. To decrease imports directly, he raised tariffs on foreign manufactured goods, especially English and Dutch cloth, and created a merchant marine to facilitate the conveyance of French goods.

Colbert was not really much of an innovator, especially in his financial policies. France still depended on the system of tax farming. Moreover, the sale of offices, which remained a common practice, absorbed huge revenues as officeholders sought to take financial advantage of their positions. As one judge expressed it: "The ministry of the judges, their jurisdiction and distribution of justice are nothing but a shop where the offices they have purchased wholesale are sold at retail." Vast exemptions for clergy and nobility as well as towns and provinces made the collection of revenue highly irrational. Colbert was unable or unwilling to change the basic system, although he attempted to correct the most obvious abuses and eliminate some of the tax exemptions. While Colbert's policies are given much credit for fostering the development of manufacturing, some historians are dubious about the usefulness of many of his mercantilistic policies. Regulations were often evaded, and the imposition of high tariffs brought foreign retaliation. French trading companies entered the scene too late to be really competitive with the British and the Dutch. And above all, Colbert's economic policies, which were geared to making his king more powerful, were ultimately self-defeating. As Colbert collected the finances with which Louis could make war, Louis depleted the treasury faster than Colbert could fill it. At the same time, the burden of taxes fell increasingly upon the peasants who still constituted the overwhelming majority of the French population.

The increase in royal power that Louis pursued as well as his desire for military glory had an effect on the development of the military. During Louis's reign, the French army was transformed from a host of small armies dominated by provincial nobles to a state activity, a standing army subject to the monarch's command. Since the first real standing armies had been organized by Venice and the United Provinces, it was neither new nor a product of absolute monarchy. But French resources enabled Louis to develop one larger than Europe had ever seen.

Under the secretary of war, François le Tellier, the marquis of Louvois, France developed a professional army numbering 100,000 men in peacetime and 400,000 in time of war. Unable to fill the ranks with volunteers, the French resorted to conscription, although this practice created a major problem as unwilling soldiers were eager to desert. But the new standing armies did not exist to be admired. Louis and other monarchs used them to make war an almost incessant activity of the seventeenth and eighteenth centuries.

THE WARS OF LOUIS XIV   Louis XIV had a great proclivity for war. Historians have debated the assertion that Louis pursued war to expand his kingdom to its "natural frontiers"—the Alps, Pyrenees, and Rhine River. But few doubt his desire to achieve the prestige and military glory befitting a Sun King as well as his dynastic ambition, his desire to ensure the domination of his Bourbon dynasty over European affairs. His ends soon outstripped his means, however, as his ambitions roused much of Europe to form coalitions that even he could not overcome.

In 1667, Louis began his first war (called the War of Devolution after a legal term in Louis's preliminary demands) by invading the Spanish Netherlands to his north and Franche-Comté to the east. Despite initial successes, a Triple Alliance of the Dutch, English, and Swedes caused him to sue for peace in 1668 and accept a few towns in the Spanish Netherlands for his efforts. He never forgave the Dutch for arranging the Triple Alliance while Colbert, for economic reasons, became obsessed with defeating the Dutch. In 1672, after isolating the Dutch and paying huge subsidies to Charles II of England to declare war on them, France invaded the United Provinces. Initial successes caused internal dissension in the Netherlands, allowing William III, the prince of Orange, to gain the upper hand and create a new coalition of Brandenburg, Spain, and the Holy Roman emperor. Louis was forced to negotiate and ended the Dutch War by making peace at Nimwegen in 1678. While Dutch territory remained intact, France received Franche-Comté from Spain, serving merely to stimulate Louis's appetite for even more land.

This time, Louis moved eastward against the Holy Roman Empire, which he perceived from his previous war as feeble and unable to resist. The piecemeal and pseudo-legal annexation of the provinces of Alsace and Lorraine was followed by the occupation of the city of Strasbourg, a move that led to widespread protest and the formation of a new coalition. The creation of this League of Augsburg, consisting of Spain, the Holy Roman emperor, the United Provinces, Sweden, and England led to Louis's third war, the War of the League of

Augsburg (1689–1697). This bitterly contested eight-year struggle brought economic depression and famine to France. The Treaty of Ryswick ending the war forced Louis to give up most of his conquests in the empire, although he was allowed to keep Strasbourg and part of Alsace. It was hardly worth the bloodshed and misery he had caused the French people.

Louis's fourth war, the War of the Spanish Succession (1702–1713), was over bigger stakes, the succession to the Spanish throne. Charles II, the sickly and childless Habsburg ruler, left the throne of Spain in his will to a grandson of Louis XIV. When the latter became King Philip V of Spain after Charles's death, the suspicion that Spain and France would eventually be united in the same dynastic family caused the formation of a new coalition, determined to prevent the certain destruction of the European balance of power by a Bourbon hegemony. This coalition of England, Holland, Habsburg Austria, and German states opposed France and Spain in a war that dragged on in Europe and the colonial empires in North America until the Peaces of Utrecht in 1713 and Rastatt in 1714. Although these peace treaties confirmed Philip V as the Spanish ruler, initiating a Spanish Bourbon dynasty that would last into the twentieth century, they also affirmed that the thrones of Spain and France were to remain separated. The Spanish Netherlands, Milan, and Naples were given to Austria while the newly emerging Brandenburg-Prussia gained addi-

▼ **Map 16.1** The Wars of Louis XIV.

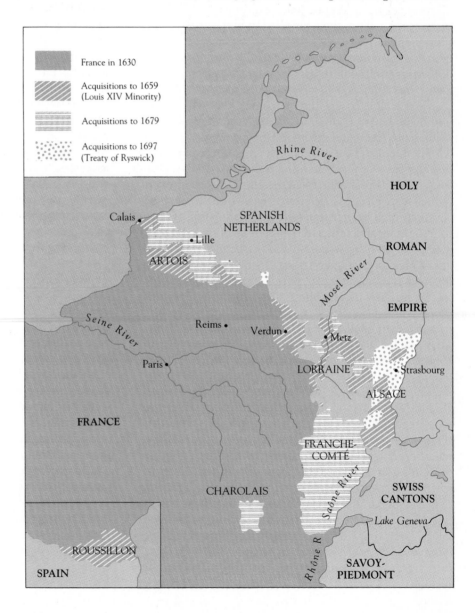

tional territories. The real winner at Utrecht, however, was England, which received Gibraltar as well as the French possessions in America of Newfoundland, Hudson's Bay Territory, and Nova Scotia. While France, by its sheer size and position, remained a great power, England had emerged as a formidable naval power.

Only two years after the treaty, the Sun King was dead, leaving France impoverished and surrounded by enemies. The seventy-six-year-old monarch seemed remorseful when he said to his successor on his deathbed:

> Soon you will be King of a great kingdom. I urge you not to forget your duty to God; remember that you owe everything to Him. Try to remain at peace with your neighbors. I loved war too much. Do not follow me in that or in overspending. Take advice in everything; try to find the best course and follow it. Lighten your people's burden as soon as possible, and do what I have had the misfortune not to do myself.[3]

Did Louis mean it? Did Louis ever realize how tarnished the glory he had sought had become? One of his subjects wrote ten years before the end of his reign: "Even the people . . . who have so much loved you, and have placed such trust in you, begin to lose their love, their trust, and even their respect. . . . They believe you have no pity for their sorrows, that you are devoted only to your power and your glory."[4] In any event, the advice to his successor was probably not remembered; his great-grandson was only five years old.

DAILY LIFE AT THE COURT OF VERSAILLES The court of Louis XIV at Versailles set a standard that was soon

followed by other European rulers. A decision was made in 1669 to convert a hunting lodge at Versailles, located near Paris, into a chateau that made splendor "a permanent and brilliantly organized form of public service." Not until 1688, after untold sums of money had been spent and tens of thousands of workers had labored incessantly, was most of the construction completed on the enormous palace that housed thousands of people.

Versailles served many purposes. It was the residence of the king; a reception hall for state affairs; an office building for the members of the king's government; and home for thousands of royal officials and aristocratic courtiers. Versailles became a symbol for the French absolutist state and the power of the Sun King, Louis XIV. This lavish court was intended to overawe subjects and impress foreign powers as a visible demonstration of France's superiority and wealth. If an age's largest buildings reflect its values, then Versailles is a reminder of the seventeenth-century preoccupation with monarchical authority and magnificence.

Versailles also served a practical political purpose. It became home to the high nobility and princes of the blood (the royal princes), those powerful figures who had aspired to hold the policy-making role of royal ministers. By keeping them involved in the myriad activities that made up daily life at the court of Versailles, Louis excluded them from real power while allowing them to share in the mystique of power as companions of the king.

Life at Versailles became a court ceremony with Louis XIV at the center of it all. The king had little privacy;

▼ **Palace of Versailles.** Between 1669 and 1688, Louis XIV spent untold sums of money in the construction of a new royal residence at Versailles. The palace of Versailles also housed the members of the king's government and served as home for thousands of French nobles. As the largest royal residence in Europe, Versailles impressed foreigners and became a source of envy for other rulers.

only when he visited his wife or mother or mistress or met with ministers was he free of the noble courtiers who swarmed about the palace. Most daily ceremonies were carefully staged, such as those attending Louis's rising from bed, dining, praying, attending mass, and going to bed. A mob of nobles aspired to assist the king in carrying out these solemn activities. It was considered a great honor for a noble to be chosen to hand the king his shirt while dressing. But why did nobles participate in so many ceremonies, some of which were so obviously demeaning? Active involvement in the activities at Versailles was the king's prerequisite for obtaining the offices, titles, and pensions that only he could grant. This policy reduced great nobles and ecclesiastics, the "people of quality," to a plane of equality, allowing Louis to exercise control over them and prevent them from interfering in the real lines of power. To maintain their social prestige, the "people of quality" were expected to adhere to rigid standards of court etiquette appropriate to their rank.

Indeed, court etiquette became so complex that it was virtually a life study. Nobles and royal princes were arranged in an elaborate order of seniority and expected to follow certain rules of precedence. Who could sit down and on what kind of chair was a subject of much debate. Who could sit where at meals with the king was also carefully regulated. On one occasion, when the wife of a minister sat closer to the king than a duchess at dinner, Louis XIV became so angry that he did not eat for the rest of the evening. Another time, Louis reproached his talkative brother for the sin of helping himself to a dish before Louis had touched it with the biting words: "I perceive that you are no better able to control your hands than your tongue."

Besides the daily and occasional ceremonies that made up the regular side of court life at Versailles and the many hours a day Louis spent with his ministers on affairs of state, daily life at Versailles included numerous forms of entertainment. While he was healthy, Louis and his courtiers hunted at least once a week; members of the royal family nearly every day. Walks through the Versailles gardens, boating trips, the performance of tragedies and comedies, ballets, and concerts all provided sources of pleasure (see the box on p. 533). Louis also held an *appartement* three evenings a week when the king was "at home" to his court from seven to ten. The *appartement* was characterized by a formal informality. Relaxed rules of etiquette even allowed people to sit down in the presence of their superiors. The evening's entertainment began with a concert, followed by games of billiards or cards, and ended with a sumptuous buffet.

One form of entertainment—gambling—became an obsession at Versailles. Although a few of the courtiers made a living by their gambling skill, many others were simply amateurs. This did not stop them from playing regularly and losing enormous sums of money. One princess described the scene: "Here in France as soon as people get together they do nothing but play [cards]; they play for frightful sums, and the players seem bereft of their senses. . . . One shouts at the top of his voice, another strikes the table with his fist, a third blasphemes. . . . it is horrible to watch them."[5] Louis did not share the princess's sensibilities; he was not horrified by an activity that kept the Versailles nobles busy and out of mischief.

This obsession with gambling should not surprise us. The lack of really meaningful activities in a world geared to formal and routine ceremonies led inevitably to bore-

▼ **Interior of Versailles: Hall of Mirrors.** Pictured here is the exquisite Hall of Mirrors at Versailles. A number of daily and occasional ceremonies dominated the lives of the residents of Versailles. Rules of etiquette became so complex that they guided every aspect of behavior. Various forms of entertainment were also available to the residents, chief of which was gambling.

Travels with the King

▼ ▼ ▼

The duc de Saint-Simon was one of many noble court-iers who lived at Versailles and had firsthand experi-ence of court life there. In his Memoirs, he left a contro-versial and critical account of Louis XIV and his court. In this selection, he describes the price court ladies paid for the "privilege" of riding with the great king.

Duc de Saint-Simon, Memoirs

The King always traveled with his carriage full of women: His mistresses, his bastard daughters, his daughters-in-law, sometimes Madame [the wife of the king's brother], and the other ladies of the court when there was room. This was the case for hunts, and trips to Fontainebleau, Chantilly, Compiègne, and the like. . . . In his carriage during these trips there was always an abundance and variety of things to eat: meats, pastries, and fruit. Before the carriage had gone a quarter league the King would ask who was hungry. He never ate between meals, not even a fruit, but he enjoyed watching others stuff them-selves. It was mandatory to eat, with appetite and good grace, and to be gay; otherwise, he showed his displeasure by telling the guilty party she was putting on airs and trying to be coy. The same ladies or prin-cesses who had eaten that day at the King's table were obliged to eat again as though they were weak from hunger. What is more, the women were forbidden to mention their personal needs, which in any case they could not have relieved without embarrassment, since there were guards and members of the King's household in front and in back of the carriage, and officers and equerries riding alongside the doors. The dust they kicked up choked everyone in the carriage, but the King, who loved fresh air, insisted that all the windows remain open. He would have been ex-tremely displeased if one of the ladies had pulled a curtain to protect herself from the sun, the wind, or the cold.

He pretended not to notice his passengers' discom-fort, and always traveled very fast, with the usual number of relays. Sickness in the carriage was a de-merit which ruled out further invitations. . . . When the king had to relieve himself he did not hesitate to stop the carriage and get out; but the ladies were not allowed to budge.

---

dom and hence gambling, as well as sexual intrigues, gossip, and backbiting. One participant related that at "the Court the least circumstances made for much talk; all there is futile and of little use." How could it have been otherwise? When people engage for hours in petty quarrels over insignificant matters of precedence, we can be sure that we are witnessing the tragedy of people desperate to find some meaning in their empty lives.

Spain

At the beginning of the seventeenth century, Spain possessed the most populous empire in the world, con-trolling almost all of South America and a number of settlements in Asia and Africa. To most Europeans, Spain still seemed the greatest power of the age, but the reality was quite different. The rich provinces of the Netherlands would soon be lost. The treasury was empty; Philip II went bankrupt in 1596 from excessive expenditures on the Armada while his successor Philip III did the same in 1607 by spending a fortune on his court. The armed forces were out-of-date; the govern-ment inefficient; and the commercial class weak in the midst of a suppressed peasantry, a luxury-loving class of nobles, and an oversupply of priests and monks. Spain continued to play the role of a great power, but appear-ances were deceiving.

During the reign of Philip III (1598–1621), many of Spain's weaknesses became only too apparent. Interested only in court luxury or miracle-working relics, Philip III allowed his first minister, the greedy duke of Lerma, to run the country. The aristocratic Lerma's primary inter-est was amassing power and wealth for himself and his family. While important offices were filled with his rel-atives, crucial problems went unsolved. His most drastic decision was to expel all remaining Moriscos (see Chap-ter 13) from Spain, a spectacular blunder in view of their importance to Spain's economy. The loss of labor and rents in the province of Valencia, for example, brought immediate economic disaster there. During Lerma's mis-rule, the gap between privileged and unprivileged grew wider. Notably absent was a prosperous urban middle

France	
Henry IV	1589–1610
Louis XIII	1610–1642
Cardinal Richelieu as Chief Minister	1624–1642
Peace of Alais	1629
Ministry of Cardinal Mazarin	1642–1661
First Fronde	1648–1649
Second Fronde	1650–1652
Louis XIV	(1642) 1661–1715
War of Devolution	1667–1668
Dutch War	1672–1678
Edict of Fontainebleau	1685
War of the League of Augsburg	1689–1697
War of the Spanish Succession	1702–1713
Spain	
Philip III	1598–1621
Philip IV	1621–1665
Revolts in Catalonia and Portugal	1640
Revolt in Naples	1647
Charles II	1665–1700

man, the count of Olivares. This clever, hard-working, and power-hungry statesman dominated the king's every move and worked to revive the interests of the monarchy. A flurry of domestic reform decrees, aimed at curtailing the power of the church and the landed aristocracy, was soon followed by a political reform program whose purpose was to further centralize the government of all Spain and its possessions in monarchical hands. All of these efforts met with little real success, however, since both the number (estimated at one-fifth of the population) and power of the Spanish aristocracy made them too strong to curtail in any significant fashion. At the same time, most of the efforts of Olivares and Philip were undermined by their desire to pursue Spain's imperial glory and a series of internal revolts.

Participation in the Thirty Years' War led Spain to become involved in the 1620s, 1630s, and 1640s in a series of frightfully expensive military campaigns that produced more economic misery for overtaxed Spanish subjects. Unfortunately for Spain, they also failed to produce victory. As Olivares wrote to King Philip IV, "God wants us to make peace; for He is depriving us visibly and absolutely of all the means of war."[7] At the same time, increasingly heavy financial exactions to fight the wars led to internal revolts, first in Catalonia, the northeastern province, in 1640, then in the same year in Portugal, which had been joined to Spain in 1580 by Philip II, and finally in the Italian dependency of Naples in 1647. Despite years of civil war, the Spanish government regained control of all these territories except for Portugal, which successfully reestablished the monarchy of the old ruling house of Braganza when Duke John was made King John IV in 1640.

The defeats in Europe and the internal revolts of the 1640s ended any illusions about Spain's greatness. The actual extent of Spain's economic difficulties is still a much debated historical topic, but there is no question about Spain's foreign losses. Dutch independence was formally recognized by the Peace of Westphalia in 1648, and the Peace of the Pyrenees with France in 1659 meant the surrender of Artois and the outlying defenses of the Spanish Netherlands as well as certain border regions, such as the Catalan province of Roussillon, which went to France. It did not augur well for the future of Spain that the king who followed Philip IV, Charles II (1665–1700), perhaps unfairly characterized by historians as a "moribund half-wit," was only of interest to the rest of Europe because he had no heirs. The French and Austrians anxiously awaited his death in the hope of placing a member of their royal houses on the Spanish throne. When he died in 1700, the War of the Spanish Succession soon followed.

class, as an astute public official observed in 1600. Spain, he said, had come "to be an extreme contrast of rich and poor, . . . we have rich who loll at ease, or poor who beg, and we lack people of the middling sort, whom neither wealth nor poverty prevents from pursuing the rightful kind of business enjoined by natural law."[6] An apparent factor in this imbalance was the dominant role played by the Catholic church. While maintaining strict orthodoxy by efficient inquisitorial courts, the church prospered and attracted ever-larger numbers of clerics to its ranks. The Castilian Cortes (parliament) was informed in 1626 that Castile alone possessed 9,000 monasteries for men. The existence of so many official celibates offered little help to Spain's declining economy or its declining population.

The early reign of Philip IV (1621–1665) seemed to offer hope for a revival of Spain's energies, especially in the capable hands of his chief minister, Gaspar de Guz-

▼ Absolutism in Central, Eastern, and Northern Europe

During the seventeenth century, a development of great importance for the modern Western world took place in central and eastern Europe, the appearance of three new powers: Prussia, Austria, and Russia.

The German States

The Peace of Westphalia, which officially ended the Thirty Years' War in 1648, left each of the three hundred or more German states comprising the Holy Roman Empire virtually autonomous and sovereign. After 1648, the Holy Roman Empire was largely a diplomatic fiction; as the French intellectual Voltaire said in the eighteenth century, the Holy Roman Empire was neither holy, nor Roman, nor an empire. Properly speaking, there was no German state, but over three hundred "Germanies." Of these states, two emerged in the seventeenth and eighteenth centuries as great European powers.

BRANDENBURG-PRUSSIA For much of the seventeenth century, there was little about the German state of Brandenburg that would lead one to think it would ever be a prosperous and powerful state. Indeed, the German states of Bavaria and Saxony would have seemed better candidates for a brilliant future. The development of Brandenburg as a state was largely the story of the Hohenzollern dynasty, which in 1417 had come to rule the rather insignificant principality in northeastern Germany. In 1609, the Hohenzollerns inherited some lands in the Rhine valley in western Germany; nine years later, they received the duchy of Prussia (or east Prussia). By the seventeenth century, then, the dominions of the house of Hohenzollern, now called Brandenburg-Prussia, consisted of three disconnected masses in western, central, and eastern Germany. Although it would appear that Hohenzollern long-range policy would seek to connect the three lands, the Hohenzollerns' more immediate concern was to establish their power in these diverse territories. Each had its own privileges, customs, and loyalties; only the person of the Hohenzollern ruler connected them. Unlike France, an old kingdom possessing a reasonably common culture based on almost a thousand years of history, Brandenburg-Prussia was an artificial creation, highly vulnerable and dependent upon its ruling dynasty to create a state where one simply did not exist.

The first important Hohenzollern ruler and the one who laid the foundation for the Prussian state was Frederick William the Great Elector (1640–1688), who came to power in the midst of the Thirty Years' War. Realizing that Brandenburg-Prussia as a small, open territory with no natural frontiers for defense was vulnerable to the powerful and unscrupulous neighbors that surrounded it, he came to the conclusion that his only hope for survival was a competent and efficient standing army with which he could force stronger states to take him into their calculations. He was adverse to actually using the army, however, preferring diplomatic maneuver to war to gain his ends. Although largely successful, his emphasis on a standing army also made Brandenburg-Prussia into a basically militaristic state.

In 1648, at the end of the Thirty Years' War in Germany, Frederick William had amassed an army of 8,000 men, sufficiently large to get a hearing at the peace gathering at Westphalia and to receive the territories of Magdeburg and eastern Pomerania. After 1648, he continued to enlarge the army so that by 1678, he possessed a force of 40,000 men that absorbed over 50 percent of the state's revenues. To sustain the army and his own power, Frederick William realized the need for a regular source of income. The Estates of old Brandenburg and the new territories jealously guarded their prerogatives, especially their right to raise taxes. The Great Elector broke the power of the Estates and freed himself to raise money by establishing the General War Commissariat to levy taxes for the army and oversee its growth and training. The Commissariat soon evolved into an agency for civil government as well, collecting the new excise tax in the towns and overseeing the foundation of new industrial and commercial enterprises. Directly responsible to the elector, the new bureaucratic machine became his chief instrument for governing the state. Many of its officials were members of the Prussian landed aristocracy, the Junkers, who also served as officers in the all-important army.

The loyalty of the nobles to Frederick William's policies was derived from the tacit agreement that he made with them. In order to eliminate the power that the members of the nobility could exercise in their provincial Estates-General, Frederick William made a deal with the nobles. In return for a free hand in running the government (in other words, for depriving the provincial Estates of their power), nobles were given almost unlimited power over their peasants, exempted from taxation, and awarded the highest ranks in the army and the Commissariat with the understanding that they would not challenge the elector's political control. As far as the peasants were concerned, the nobles were allowed to appropriate their land and bind them to the soil as serfs.

To build Brandenburg-Prussia's economy, Frederick William followed the fashionable mercantilist policies, using high tariffs, subsidies, and monopolies to manufacturers to stimulate domestic industry and building roads and canals. Wisely, Frederick William invited people from other countries to settle in Brandenburg-Prussia and, in 1685, issued an edict encouraging the dispossessed Huguenots from Louis XIV's France to come to Prussia. Almost 20,000 did. Frederick William continued, however, to favor the interests of the nobility at the expense of the commercial and industrial middle classes in the towns.

In these ways, Frederick William the Great Elector laid the foundations for the Prussian state, although it would be misleading to think that he had a modern conception of that state. He thought nothing of amending his will to give pieces of his supposedly unified state as independent principalities to his younger sons. He was succeeded by his son Frederick III (1688–1713), who, less rigid and militaristic than his father, spent much of the treasury building palaces, creating a university, and imitating the splendors of the court of Louis XIV. He did make one significant contribution to the development of Prussia. In return for aiding the Holy Roman emperor in the War of the Spanish Succession, he received officially the title of king in Prussia. Elector Frederick III was transformed into King Frederick I, and Brandenburg-Prussia became simply Prussia. In the eighteenth century, Prussia emerged as a great power on the European stage.

THE EMERGENCE OF AUSTRIA   The Austrian Habsburgs had long played a significant role in European politics.

They were Holy Roman emperors and had important family connections with the wealthier Habsburgs of Spain. In the seventeenth century, these two bastions of their power collapsed. By the end of the Thirty Years' War, the Habsburg hopes of creating an empire in Germany had been dashed. At the same time, Spain's decline made that relationship less rewarding, and it ended completely at the beginning of the eighteenth century when Spain came into the hands of the French house of Bourbon. In the seventeenth century, then, the house of Austria made an important transition; the German empire was lost, but a new empire was created in eastern and southeastern Europe.

The nucleus of the new Austrian Empire remained the traditional Austrian hereditary possessions: Lower and Upper Austria, Carinthia, Carniola, Styria, and Tyrol. To these had been added the kingdom of Bohemia, which had been reclaimed by the Habsburgs during the Thirty Years' War. Since 1526, the Habsburg ruler had also been king of Hungary, although he exercised little real power except in northwest Hungary. The eastern Hungarian principality of Transylvania remained independent while the central parts of Hungary were controlled by the Ottoman Turks.

Leopold I (1658–1705) encouraged the movement of the Austrian Empire eastward. He was sorely challenged by the revival of Turkish power in the seventeenth century. Having moved into Transylvania, the Turks eventually pushed westward and laid siege to Vienna in 1683. Only a dramatic rescue by a combined army of Austrians, Saxons, Bavarians, and Poles saved the Austrian

▼ **Map 16.2** Brandenburg-Prussia.

▼ **Map 16.3** The Growth of the Austrian Empire.

city. A European army, led by the Austrians, counterattacked and decisively defeated the Turks in 1687. Austria took control of Hungary, Transylvania, Croatia, and Slovenia, thus establishing an Austrian Empire in southeastern Europe. At the end of the War of the Spanish Succession, Austria gained possession of the Spanish Netherlands and received formal recognition of its occupation of the Spanish possessions in Italy, namely Milan, Mantua, Sardinia, and Naples. By the beginning of the eighteenth century, the house of Austria had acquired a new empire of considerable size.

The Austrian monarchy, however, never become a highly centralized, absolutist state, primarily because it contained so many different national groups. The Austrian Empire remained a collection of territories held together by a personal union. The Hapburg emperor was archduke of Austria, king of Bohemia, and king of Hungary. Each of these areas, however, had its own laws, Estates-General, and political life. There was no common sentiment to tie the regions together; only the landed aristocracies everywhere provided a common bond of service to the house of Habsburg, whether as military officers or government bureaucrats. The nobles in the Austrian Empire remained quite strong and were also allowed to impose serfdom on their peasants. By the beginning of the eighteenth century, Austria was a populous empire in central Europe of great potential military strength.

Italy

By 1530, Emperor Charles V had managed to defeat the French armies in Italy and become the arbiter of Italy. Initially, he was content to establish close ties with many native Italian rulers and allow them to rule provided that they recognize his dominant role. But in 1540, he gave the duchy of Milan to his son Philip II and transferred all imperial rights over Italy to the Spanish monarchy.

From the beginning of Philip II's reign in 1559 to 1713, the Spanish presence was felt everywhere in Italy. Only the major states of Florence, the Papal States, and Venice managed to maintain relatively independent policies. At the same time, the influence of the papacy became oppressive in Italy as the machinery of the Catholic Counter-Reformation—the Inquisition, Index, and the Jesuits—was used to stifle any resistance to the Catholic orthodoxy created by the Council of Trent (see Chapter 14). While artistic and intellectual activity continued in post-Renaissance Italy it often exacted a grievous cost. Many a daring intellectual, such as Galilei Galileo and Giordano Bruno (see Chapter 17), found himself imprisoned or executed by the Inquisition.

At the beginning of the eighteenth century, Italy suffered further from the struggles between France and Spain. But it was Austria, not France, that benefited the most from the War of the Spanish Succession. By gaining Milan, Mantua, Sardinia, and Naples, Austria supplanted Spain as the dominant power in Italy. It was a mixed blessing. Austrian rule would eventually galvanize Italians into a desire for freedom from all foreign domination.

From Muscovy to Russia

Beginning in the Middle Ages, Russia had existed only on the fringes of European society, remote and isolated from the western mainstream. But in the seventeenth century, the energetic Peter the Great pushed Russia westward and to the status of a great power.

A new Russian state had emerged in the fifteenth century under the leadership of the principality of Muscovy and its grand dukes (see Chapter 13). In the sixteenth century, Ivan IV the Stern (1533–1584), who was the first ruler to take the title of tsar, expanded the territories of Russia eastward, after finding westward expansion blocked by the powerful Swedish and Polish states. Ivan also extended the autocracy of the tsar by crushing the power of the Russian nobility, known as the boyars.

Ivan's dynasty came to an end in 1598 and was followed by a resurgence of aristocratic power in a period of anarchy known as the Time of Troubles. It was not ended until the Zemsky Sobor or national assembly chose Michael Romanov as the new tsar, beginning a dynasty that lasted until 1917.

In the seventeenth century, Muscovite society was highly stratified. At the top was the tsar, who claimed to be a divinely ordained autocratic ruler, assisted by two consultative bodies, a Duma or council of boyars and the Zemsky Sobor, a parliamentary body of sorts begun in 1550 by Ivan IV to facilitate support for his programs. Russian society was dominated by an upper class of landed aristocrats who, in the course of the seventeenth century, managed to bind their peasants to the land. An abundance of land and a shortage of peasants made serfdom desirable to the landowners, who sustained a highly oppressive system. A law of 1625 stipulated that anyone who killed another's serf simply had to replace him. By the end of the seventeenth century, serfs could even be bought and sold. Only peasants on the personal estates of the tsar (the crown peasants) enjoyed a more favorable position. Townspeople were also stratified and controlled. Artisans were sharply separated from merchants, and many of the latter were not allowed to move from their cities without government permission or to sell their businesses to anyone not of their class. Government restrictions on peasants and merchants, however, led to a series of insurrections. Merchant revolts in Moscow and Novgorod were only ended by mass arrests, deportations, and executions. The most serious peasant revolt erupted in 1670, led by Don Cossacks under the leadership of Stenka Razin. It took the government two years to crush the uprising.

Religious schism added to the turmoil of seventeenth-century Muscovy. Illiteracy and ignorance were not only widespread, but often a matter of pride in a land accustomed to cultural isolation. This chauvinism was encouraged by the Russian Orthodox church, which had become independent of its Greek Orthodox mother church in 1589 when the head of the Russian Orthodox church was recognized as a patriarch in his own right. In the mid-seventeenth century, an attempt was made to reform the Russian church by Patriarch Nikon with the support of Tsar Alexis (1645–1676), the second Romanov ruler. The reforms were not profound; they corrected editions of the Bible and attempted a return to the ritualistic practices of Greek orthodoxy. A group of fundamentalists, however, known as the Old Believers, saw any reform as tampering with the received faith of their fathers and started a serious and persistent schism. The state and ecclesiastical hierarchy took up the struggle against the Old Believers in a sometimes fierce and bloody fashion. Thousands of Old Believers burned themselves in mass holocausts to protest the reforms, but in vain.

In the midst of these political and religious upheavals, seventeenth-century Muscovy was experiencing more frequent contacts with the West while Western ideas also began to penetrate a few Russian circles. When Peter the Great arrived on the scene, Muscovy was already under-

Peter the Great Deals with a Rebellion
▼ ▼ ▼

During his first visit to the West in 1697–1698, Peter received word that the streltsy, an elite military unit stationed in Moscow, had revolted against his authority. Peter hurried home and crushed the revolt in a very savage fashion. This selection is taken from an Austrian account of how Peter dealt with the rebels.

Peter and the Streltsy

How sharp was the pain, how great the indignation, to which the tsar's Majesty was mightily moved, when he knew of the rebellion of the Streltsy, betraying openly a mind panting for vengeance! He was still tarrying at Vienna, quite full of the desire of setting out for Italy; but, fervid as was his curiosity of rambling abroad, it was, nevertheless, speedily extinguished on the announcement of the troubles that had broken out in the bowels of his realm. Going immediately to Lefort . . . , he thus indignantly broke out: "Tell me, Francis, how I can reach Moscow by the shortest way, in a brief space, so that I may wreak vengeance on this great perfidy of my people, with punishments worthy of their abominable crime. Not one of them shall escape with impunity. Around my royal city, which, with their impious efforts, they planned to destroy, I will have gibbets and gallows set upon the walls and ramparts, and each and every one of them will I put to a direful death." Nor did he long delay the plan for his justly excited wrath; he took the quick post, as his ambassador suggested, and in four weeks' time he had got over about three hundred miles without accident, and arrived the 4th of September, 1698,—a monarch for the well deposed, but an avenger for the wicked.

His first anxiety after his arrival was about the rebellion—in what it consisted, what the insurgents meant, who dared to instigate such a crime. And as nobody could answer accurately upon all points, and some pleaded their own ignorance, others the obstinacy of the Streltsy, he began to have suspicions of everybody's loyalty. . . . No day, holy or profane, were the inquisitors idle; every day was deemed fit and lawful for torturing. There were as many scourges as there were accused, and every inquisitor was a butcher. . . . The whole month of October was spent in lacerating the backs of culprits with the knout and with flames; no day were those that were left alive exempt from scourging or scorching; or else they were broken upon the wheel, or driven to the gibbet, or slain with the ax. . . .

To prove to all people how holy and inviolable are those walls of the city which the Streltsy rashly meditated scaling in a sudden assault, beams were run out from all the embrasures in the walls near the gates, in each of which two rebels were hanged. This day beheld about two hundred and fifty die that death. There are few cities fortified with as many palisades as Moscow has given gibbets to her guardian Streltsy.

---

going changes. While neither his aims nor his solutions were new, Peter did accelerate the process with a ruthlessness that accomplished much, but at a great price.

THE REIGN OF PETER THE GREAT (1689–1725) Peter was only four years old when his father died so his sister Sophia acted as regent for him and his feeble-minded brother as joint tsars. At the age of seventeen (in 1689), Peter seized power from his sister. Peter the Great was an unusual character. A towering, strong man, six feet, nine inches tall, Peter was coarse in his tastes and rude in his behavior. He enjoyed a low kind of humor— belching contests, crude jokes, comical funerals—and vicious punishments—floggings, impalings, roastings, and beard burnings (see the box above). At the same time, he was capable of tender feelings, especially toward his family.

Peter gained his initial knowledge of Western ideas in the "German suburb," a section of Moscow where Europeans of different nationalities resided. He received a firsthand view of the West when he made a trip there in 1697–1698 and returned to Russia with a firm determination to westernize or Europeanize Russia. Perhaps too much has been made of Peter's desire to westernize a "backward country." Peter's policy of Europeanization was largely technical. He admired European technology and gadgets and desired to transplant these to Russia. Only this kind of modernization could give him the army and navy he needed to make Russia a great power. His only consistent purpose was to win military victories.

▼ **Peter the Great.** Peter the Great wished to westernize Russia, especially in the realm of technical skills. His foremost goal was the creation of a strong army and navy in order to make Russia a great power. He reorganized the central government and adopted mercantilist economic policies to produce revenue for his military expenditures. Peter achieved his goal of making Russia a great European power, although an aristocratic reaction undid much of his work after his death in 1725.

As could be expected, one of his fist priorities was the reorganization of the army and the creation of a navy. Employing both Russians and Europeans as officers, he conscripted peasants for twenty-five year stints of service to build a standing army of 210,000 men. Peter has also been given credit for forming the first Russian navy.

Peter reorganized the central government, partly along Western lines. What remained of the consultative

bodies disappeared; neither the Duma of boyars nor the Zemsky Sobor was ever summoned. In 1711, Peter created a Senate to supervise the administrative machinery of the state while he was away on military campaigns. In time the Senate became something like a ruling council, but its ineffectiveness caused Peter to borrow the Western institution of "colleges," or boards of administrators entrusted with specific functions, such as foreign affairs, war, and justice. To impose the rule of the central government more effectively throughout the land, Peter divided Russia into eight provinces and, later in 1719, into fifty. Although he hoped to create a "police state," by which he meant a well-ordered community governed in accordance with law, few of his bureaucrats shared his concept of honest service and duty to the state. One of his highest officials even stated: "Would your Majesty like to be a ruler without any subjects? We all steal, only some do it on a bigger scale, and in a more conspicuous way, than others."[8] Peter hoped for a sense of civic duty, but his own forceful personality created an atmosphere of fear that prevented it. He wrote to one administrator, "According to these orders act, act, act. I won't write more, but you will pay with your head if you interpret orders again." But when others were understandably cautious in interpreting his written instructions, he stated: "This is as if a servant, seeing his master drowning, would not save him until he had satisfied himself as to whether it was written down in his contract that he should pull him out of the water."[9] Peter wanted his administrators to be slaves and free men at the same time, and it did not occur to him that the task was impossible.

To satisfy his insatiable need of money for an army and navy that absorbed as much as four-fifths of the state revenue, Peter adopted Western mercantilistic policies to stimulate economic growth. He tried to increase exports and develop new industries while exploiting domestic resources like the iron mines in the Urals. But his military needs were endless, and he came to rely on the old expedient of simply raising taxes, placing additional burdens upon the hapless peasants whose position in Peter's Russia grew ever more oppressed.

Peter also sought to gain state control of the Russian Orthodox church. In 1721, he abolished the position of patriarch and created a body called the Holy Synod to make decisions for the church. At its head stood a procurator, a layman who represented the interests of the tsar and assured Peter of effective domination of the church.

Already after his first trip to the West in 1697–1698, Peter began to introduce Western customs, practices, and manners into Russia. He ordered the preparation of the first Russian book of etiquette to teach Western manners. Among other things, it pointed out that it was not polite to spit on the floor or scratch oneself at dinner. Since westerners did not wear beards or the traditional long-skirted coat, Russian beards had to be shaved and coats shortened, a reform Peter personally enforced at court by shaving off his nobles' beards and cutting their coats at the knees with his own hands. Outside the court, the edicts were enforced by barbers and tailors planted at town gates with orders to cut the beards and cloaks of those who entered or left. Anyone who failed to conform was to be "beaten without mercy." For the nobles, who were already partly westernized, these changes were hardly earth-shattering. But to many others who believed that shaving the beard was a "defacement of the image of God," the attack was actually blasphemous.

One group of Russians benefited greatly from Peter's cultural reforms—women. Having watched women mixing freely with men in Western courts, Peter shattered the seclusion of upper-class Russian women and demanded that they remove the traditional veils that covered their faces. Peter also encouraged gatherings in which both sexes could mix for conversation and dancing, which Peter had learned in the West. Women were also now allowed to marry of their own free will.

The object of Peter's domestic reforms was to make Russia into a great state and military power; an examination of his foreign policy reveals how well he succeeded. His primary goal was to "open a window to the west," meaning an ice-free port easily accessible to Europe. This could only be achieved on the Baltic, but at that time the Baltic coast was controlled by Sweden, the most important power in northern Europe. Desirous of these lands, Peter, with the support of Poland and Denmark, attacked Sweden in the summer of 1700, believing that the young king of Sweden, Charles XII, could easily be defeated. Charles, however, proved to be a brilliant general. He smashed the Danes, flattened the Poles, and, with a well-disciplined force of only 8,000 men, routed the Russian army of 40,000 at the Battle of Narva (1700). The Great Northern War (1701–1721) had begun.

While Charles wasted valuable time in an inconclusive war in Poland, Peter took the opportunity to reorganize his army along Western lines. In 1702, he overran

▼ **Map 16.4** From Muscovy to Russia.

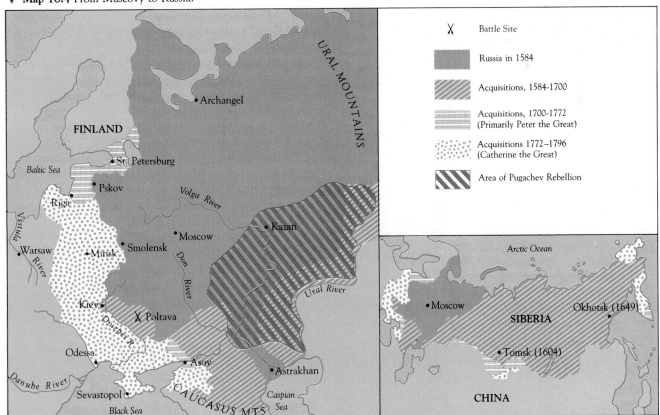

the Swedish Baltic provinces while Charles was preoccupied elsewhere. When the Swedish king turned his attention to Peter again in 1708, he decided to invade Russia and capture Moscow, the capital, but Russian weather and scorched-earth tactics devastated his army. In July 1709, at the Battle of Poltava, Peter's forces defeated Charles's army decisively. Although the war dragged on for another twelve years, the Peace of Nystadt in 1721 gave formal recognition to what Peter had already achieved: the acquisition of Estonia, Livonia, and Karelia. Sweden became a second-rate power while Russia was now the great European state Peter had wanted.

Already in 1703, in these northern lands on the Baltic, Peter had begun the construction of a new city, St. Petersburg, his window on the west and a symbol that Russia was looking westward to Europe. Built on marshland, its construction cost the lives of thousands of peasants. Finished during Peter's lifetime, St. Petersburg remained the Russian capital until 1917.

It is difficult to assess the work of Peter the Great. He modernized and westernized Russia to the extent that it became a great military power and, by his death in 1725, an important member of the European state system. But his policies were also detrimental to Russia. Westernization was a bit of a sham, since Western culture reached only the upper classes while the real object of the reforms, the creation of a strong military, only added more burdens to the masses of the Russian people. The forceful way in which Peter the Great imposed westernization led to a distrust of Europe and Western civilization. Rus-

sia was so strained by Peter the Great that after his death an aristocratic reaction undid much of his work.

Scandinavia

As the economic link between the products of eastern Europe and the West, the Baltic Sea bestowed special importance on the lands surrounding it. In the sixteenth century, Sweden had broken its ties with Denmark and emerged as an independent state (see Chapter 14). Despite their common Lutheran religion, Denmark's and Sweden's territorial ambitions in northern Europe in the seventeenth century kept them in rather constant rivalry.

Under Christian IV (1588–1648), Denmark seemed the likely candidate for expansion, but it met with little success. The system of electing monarchs forced the kings to share their power with the Danish nobility who exercised strict control over the peasants who worked their lands. Danish ambitions for ruling the Baltic were severely curtailed by the losses they sustained in the Thirty Years' War and later in the so-called Northern War (1655–1660) with Sweden. Danish military losses led to a constitutional crisis in which a meeting of Denmark's Estates brought to pass a bloodless revolution in 1660. The power of the nobility was curtailed, a hereditary monarchy reestablished, and a new, absolutist constitution proclaimed in 1665. Under Christian V (1670–1699), a centralized administration was instituted with the nobility as the chief officeholders.

▼ **Queen Christina of Sweden.** In the sixteenth century, Sweden emerged as an independent state and came to play a significant role in European affairs during the seventeenth century. Queen Christina, daughter of Gustavus Adolphus, had little interest in political matters. Focusing more on philosophy and religion, she corresponded with French philosopher René Descartes, who eventually came to reside at her court. Her support of the nobility turned the other estates against her, and only her abdication prevented a peasant revolt against the aristocracy.

Compared to Denmark, Sweden seemed a relatively poor country, and historians have found it difficult to explain why Sweden played such a large role in European affairs in the seventeenth century. Its economy was weak while the monarchy was still locked in conflict with the powerful Swedish nobility. During the reign of Gustavus Adolphus (1611–1632), his wise and dedicated chief minister, Axel Oxenstierna, persuaded the king to adopt a new policy in which the nobility formed a "first estate" occupying the bureaucratic positions of an expanded central government. This created a stable monarchy and freed the king to raise a formidable army and participate in the Thirty Years' War, only to be killed in battle in 1632.

Sweden experienced a severe political crisis after the death of Gustavus Adolphus. His daughter Christina (1633–1654) proved to be far more interested in philosophy and religion than ruling. By favoring the interests of the nobility, she caused the other estates of the Riksdag, Sweden's parliament—the burghers, clergy, and peasants—to protest. Her abdication in favor of her cousin, who became King Charles X (1654–1660), defused a potentially explosive peasant revolt against the nobility.

Charles X reestablished domestic order, but it was his successor, Charles XI (1660–1697), who did the painstaking work of building the Swedish monarchy along the lines of an absolute monarchy. By resuming control of the crown lands and the revenues attached to them from the nobility, Charles managed to weaken the independent power of the nobility. He built up a bureaucracy, subdued both the Riksdag and church, improved the army and navy, and left to his son, Charles XII (1697–1718), a well-organized Swedish state that dominated northern Europe. In 1693, he and his heirs were acclaimed as "absolute, sovereign kings, responsible for their actions to no man on earth."

Charles XII was primarily interested in military affairs. Energetic and regarded as a brilliant general, his grandiose plans and strategies, which involved Sweden in conflicts with Poland, Denmark, and Russia, proved to be Sweden's undoing. By the time he died in 1718, Charles XII had lost much of Sweden's northern empire to Russia, and Sweden's status as a first-class northern power had proved to be short-lived.

The Ottoman Empire

After their conquest of Constantinople in 1453, the Ottoman Turks tried to complete their conquest of the Balkans, where they had been established since the four-

---

Chronology
▼ ▼ ▼
Absolutism in Central, Eastern, and Northern Europe

Brandenburg-Prussia	
Hohenzollerns Established in Brandenburg	1417
Hohenzollerns Acquire Lands along the Rhine	1609
Hohenzollerns Acquire East Prussia	1618
Frederick William the Great Elector	1640–1688
Elector Frederick III (King Frederick I)	1688–1713
The Austrian Empire	
Leopold I	1658–1705
Turkish Siege of Vienna	1683
Russia	
Ivan IV the Stern	1533–1584
Time of Troubles	1598–1613
Michael Romanov	1613–1645
Alexis	1645–1676
Peter the Great	1689–1725
First Trip to the West	1697–1698
Construction of St. Petersburg Begins	1703
Holy Synod	1721
Great Northern War	1701–1721
Battle of Poltava	1709
Denmark	
Christian IV	1588–1648
"Bloodless Revolution"	1660
Christian V	1670–1699
Sweden	
Gustavus Adolphus	1611–1632
Christina	1633–1654
Charles X	1654–1660
Charles XI	1660–1697
Charles XII	1697–1718
The Ottoman Empire	
Suleiman I the Magnificent	1520–1566
Battle of Lepanto	1571
Turkish Defeat at Vienna	1683

teenth century. Although they were successful in taking the Romanian territory of Wallachia in 1476, the resistance of the Hungarians kept them from advancing up the Danube valley. From 1480 to 1520, internal problems and the need to consolidate their eastern frontiers kept the Turks from any further attacks on Europe.

The reign of Sultan Suleiman I the Magnificent (1520–1566), however, brought the Turks back to Europe's attention. Advancing up the Danube, the Turks seized Belgrade in 1521 and Hungary by 1526, although their attempts to conquer Vienna in 1529 were repulsed. At the same time, Turkish power was extended into the western Mediterranean, which they threatened to turn into a Turkish lake until a large Turkish fleet was destroyed by the Spanish at Lepanto in 1571. Despite the defeat, the Turks continued to hold nominal suzerainty over the southern shores of the Mediterranean.

Although Europeans frequently spoke of new Christian crusades against the infidel Turks, by the beginning of the seventeenth century the Ottoman Empire was being treated like another European power by European rulers seeking alliances and trade concessions. The Ottoman Empire possessed a highly effective governmental system, especially when it was led by strong sultans or powerful grand viziers (prime ministers). The splendid capital Constantinople possessed a population far larger than any European city. Nevertheless, Ottoman politics periodically degenerated into bloody intrigues as factions fought each other for influence and the throne. In one particularly gruesome practice, a ruling sultan would murder his brothers to avoid challenges to his rule. Despite the periodic bouts of civil chaos, a well-trained bureaucracy of civil servants continued to administer state affairs efficiently.

▼ **Map 16.5** The Ottoman Empire.

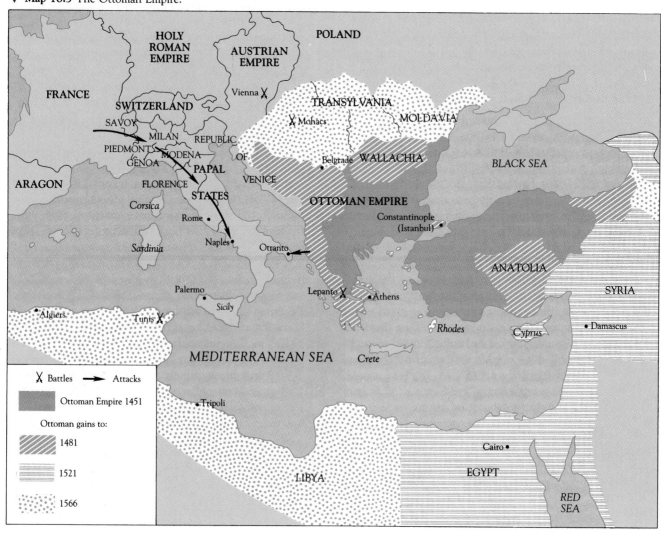

A well-organized military system also added to the strength of the Ottoman Empire. Especially outstanding were the Janissaries, composed of Christian boys who had been taken from their parents, converted to the Muslim faith, and subjected to rigid military discipline to form an elite core of 8,000 troops personally loyal to the sultan. Like other praetorian guards, however, the Janissaries came to play an important role in making and unmaking sultans.

In the first half of the seventeenth century, the Ottoman Empire was a "sleeping giant." Involved in domestic bloodletting and heavily threatened by a challenge from Persia, the Ottomans were content with the status quo in eastern Europe. But under a new line of grand viziers in the second half of the seventeenth century, the Ottoman Empire again took the offensive. By mid-1683, the Ottomans had marched through the Hungarian plain and laid siege to Vienna. Repulsed by a mixed army of Austrians, Poles, Bavarians, and Saxons, the Turks retreated and were pushed out of Hungary by a new European coalition. Although they retained the core of their empire, the Ottoman Turks would never again be a threat to Europe. Although the Ottoman Empire held together for the rest of the seventeenth and eighteenth centuries, it would be faced with new challenges from the ever-growing Austrian Empire in southeastern Europe and the new Russian giant to the north.

The Limits of Absolutism

In recent decades, historical studies of local institutions have challenged the traditional picture of absolute monarchs as powerful rulers whose control of the administrative machinery of state enabled them to dominate the everyday lives of their subjects. The centralization of power was an important element in the growth of the seventeenth-century state, however, and the most successful monarchs were those who managed to restructure the central policy-making machinery of government to give them a certain amount of control over the traditional areas of monarchical power: formulation of foreign policy, making of war and peace, the church, and taxation. Seventeenth-century governments also intervened in economic affairs to strengthen their war-making capacities. In all of these areas, absolute monarchy meant rulers extending their power or at least resisting challenges to their authority.

It is misleading, however, to think that so-called absolute monarchs actually controlled the lives of their subjects. In 1700, government for most people still meant the local institutions that affected their lives: local courts, local tax collectors, and local organizers of armed forces. Kings and ministers might determine policies and issue guidelines, but they still had to function through local agents and had no guarantee whatever that their wishes would be carried out. A mass of urban and provincial privileges, liberties, and exemptions (including from taxation) and a whole host of corporate bodies and interest groups—provincial and national Estates, clerical officials, officeholders who had bought or inherited their positions, and provincial nobles—limited what monarchs could achieve. Really successful rulers were not those who tried to destroy the old system, but those like Louis XIV who knew how to use the old system to their advantage. Above all other considerations stood the landholding nobility. Everywhere in the seventeenth century, the landed aristocracy played an important role in the European monarchical system. As military officers, judges, officeholders, and landowners in control of vast, untaxed estates, their power remained immense. In some places, their strength even severely limited how effectively monarchs could rule.

▼ Limited Monarchy and Republics

Almost everywhere in Europe in the seventeenth century, kings and their ministers were in control of central governments. But not all European states followed the pattern of absolute monarchy. In eastern Europe, the Polish aristocracy controlled a virtually powerless king. In western Europe, two great states—England and the Dutch Republic—successfully resisted the power of hereditary monarchs.

Poland

Poland had played a major role in eastern Europe in the fifteenth century and had ruled over Lithuania and much of the Ukraine by the end of the sixteenth. After the elective throne of Poland had been won by the Swede Sigismund III (1587–1631), Poland had a king who even thought seriously of creating a vast Polish empire that would include at least Russia and possibly Finland and Sweden. Poland not only failed to achieve this goal, but became a weak, decentralized state by the end of the seventeenth century.

It was the elective nature of the Polish monarchy that reduced it to impotence. The *Seym* or Polish diet was a two-chamber assembly in which landowners completely dominated the few townsmen and lawyers who were also members. To be elected to the kingship, prospective monarchs (who were mostly foreigners) made agreements with the *Seym* (in effect with the nobles), by which the latter was to share power in matters of taxation, foreign and military policy, and the appointment of state officials and judges. The power of the *Seym* had disastrous results for central monarchical authority since the real aim of most of its members was to ensure that central authority would not affect local interests. The acceptance of the liberum veto in 1652, whereby the meetings of the *Seym* could be stopped by a single dissenting member, reduced government to virtual chaos.

Poland, then, was basically a confederation of semi-independent estates of landed nobles. By the late seventeenth century, it also became a battleground for foreign powers who found it easy to invade, but difficult to rule. The continuation of Polish weakness into the eighteenth century eventually encouraged its more powerful neighbors—Prussia, Austria, and Russia—to dismember it.

The United Provinces

The seventeenth century has often been called the "Golden Age" of the Dutch Republic as the United Provinces held center stage as one of Europe's great powers. Like France and England, the United Provinces was an Atlantic power, underlining the importance of the shift of political and economic power from the Mediterranean basin to the countries on the Atlantic seaboard. As a result of the sixteenth-century revolt of the Netherlands, the seven northern provinces, which began to call themselves the United Provinces of the Netherlands in 1581, became the core of the modern Dutch state. The new state was officially recognized by the Peace of Westphalia in 1648.

With independence came internal dissension. There were two chief centers of political power in the new state. Each province had an official known as a stadholder who was responsible for leading the army and maintaining order. Beginning with William of Orange and his heirs, the house of Orange occupied the stadholderate in most of the seven provinces and favored the development of a centralized government with themselves as hereditary monarchs. The States General, an assembly of representatives from every province, opposed the Orangist ambitions and advocated a decentralized or republican form of government. A requirement of complete unanimity of the delegates served to weaken the effectiveness of this body, however, causing

the States General to refer all issues back to the provincial assemblies and permitting the latter to retain much power. Moreover, as the largest and richest province, Holland exercised the greatest influence in the States General; in fact, an oligarchy of wealthy merchants and financiers, especially from Amsterdam, tended to control this representative body.

The political rivalry between the monarchical and republican blocs was intensified by religious division within the Calvinist church. Orthodox Calvinists, known as the Counter-Remonstrants, favored a strict interpretation of the Calvinist doctrine of predestination and were supported by the Orangists. The Remonstrants, on the other hand, believed that humans participated to some extent in the process of gaining salvation and favored a generally tolerant position on religious differences. Supported by the republican forces, the latter position ultimately prevailed. Although the Calvinist church remained the official church, other religious groups were tolerated as long as they worshiped in private. Catholics, other Protestants, and even Jewish communities felt relatively free in Holland, especially in Amsterdam. The Dutch were truly unique in the seventeenth century for their religious toleration.

During the first half of the seventeenth century, the Orangist stadholders continued to pursue one fundamental aim—the conversion of the Dutch Netherlands into a monarchy under the house of Orange—but met with little success. Indeed, for twenty-two years after 1650, the seven Dutch provinces became accustomed to their republican existence without a stadholder. But in 1672, burdened with war against both France and England, the United Provinces turned once again to the house of Orange and restored it to the stadholderate in the person of William III (1672–1702). Seventeenth-century Dutch history is remarkable for the relative ease with which the Dutch shifted from one power base to the other in accordance with their external and internal needs. From that year on, William III worked consciously to build up his pseudo-royal power. When he succeeded to the throne of England in 1688 (see England and the Emergence of Constitutional Monarchy later in the chapter), it strengthened his position in the Netherlands as well. However, his death in 1702, without direct heirs, enabled the republican forces to gain control once more. The Dutch Republic would not be seriously threatened again by the monarchical forces.

Underlying Dutch prominence in the seventeenth century was its economic prosperity, fueled by the Dutch role as carriers of European trade. But war proved disastrous to the Dutch Republic. The two Anglo-Dutch wars of the 1650s and 1660s, the war with France and England in the 1670s, and their support of England against France in the War of the Spanish Succession placed heavy burdens on Dutch finances and manpower. English shipping began to challenge what had been Dutch commercial supremacy, and by 1715, the Dutch were experiencing a serious economic decline.

DAILY LIFE IN SEVENTEENTH-CENTURY AMSTERDAM By the beginning of the seventeenth century, Amsterdam had replaced Antwerp as the financial and commercial capital of Europe. In 1570, Amsterdam had 30,000 inhabitants; by 1610, that number had doubled as refugees poured in, especially from the Spanish Netherlands. Intellectuals and Jews drawn by the city's reputation for toleration, as well as merchants and workers attracted by the city's prosperity, added to the number of new inhabitants. This rapid growth caused the city government to approve an "urban expansion plan" in 1613, by which the construction of three large concentric canals expanded the city's territory from 500 to 1,800 acres. Building plots were formed by hammering wooden piles through the mud to the hard sand below, while the canals made it possible for businessmen to use their newly built houses for warehouses. Goods carried by small boats were lifted to the upper stories of these dwellings by block and tackle fastened to the gables of the roofs. Amsterdam's physical expansion was soon matched by its population as the city grew to 100,000 people in 1610 and then to 200,000 by 1660.

The exuberant expansion of Amsterdam in the seventeenth century was based upon the city's new role as the commercial and financial center of Europe (see the box on p. 548). But what had made this possible? For one thing, Amsterdam had an excellent merchant marine. Amsterdam merchants possessed vast fleets of ships, many of which were used for the lucrative North Sea herring catch. Amsterdam ships were also important carriers for the products of other countries. The Dutch invention of the fluyt, a shallow-draft ship of large capacity, enabled them to transport enormous quantities of cereals, timber, and iron. Finally, the Dutch produced large ships for oceanic voyages and, by 1650, owned 50 percent of the merchant ships in Europe.

By making available an enormous variety of goods, Amsterdam merchants induced foreigners to buy and sell in Amsterdam, thus making the city a crossroads for many of Europe's chief products. Amsterdam was, of course, the chief port for the Dutch West and East Indian trading companies (see Overseas Trade and Colonies later in the chapter). Moreover, city industries turned imported raw materials into finished goods, making Amsterdam an important producer of cloth, refined sugar and tobacco products, glass, beer, paper, books, jewelry, and leather goods.

A third factor in Amsterdam's prosperity was its importance as a financial center. Large quantities of capital were available for investment from profits in trade. As a haven for religious minorities, Amsterdam housed a number of wealthy refugees with money to invest. Its financial role was greatly facilitated by the foundation in 1609 of the Exchange Bank of Amsterdam, long the greatest public bank in northern Europe. As an English gentleman noted, the reputation of the bank was "another invitation for People to come, and lodge here what part of their Money they could transport, and knew no way of securing at home."[10] The city also founded the Amsterdam Stock Exchange for trading in commodities. Some of the city's great wealth came from war profits; by 1700, Amsterdam was the principal supplier for military goods in Europe.

Amsterdam's prosperity (it possessed the highest per capita income in Europe) did not prevent it from having enormous social differences. At the bottom of the social ladder was the *grauw* or rabble consisting of beggars, unskilled day laborers, and immigrants attracted by Am-

▼ **View of Amsterdam.** Much of Amsterdam's wealth and prestige as a commercial center was due to its excellent merchant marine. Amsterdam was also a major producer of finished products as well as an important European financial center. As seen in this photograph of Amsterdam, the city's charm stemmed from its small streets crisscrossed by a series of canals.

The Economic Superiority of the Dutch
▼ ▼ ▼

Europeans were astonished by the apparent prosperity of the Dutch in the first half of the seventeenth century. This selection is taken from a treatise entitled Observations Touching Trade and Commerce with the Hollanders, and Other Nations. It was written by an Englishman named John Keymer who believed that the Dutch economy could serve as a guide for the English.

John Keymer, *Observations Touching Trade and Commerce with the Hollanders, and Other Nations*

I have diligently in my travels, observed how the countries herein mentioned [mainly Holland] do grow potent with abundance of all thing to serve themselves and other nations, where nothing groweth; and that their never dried fountains of wealth, by which they raise their estate to such an admirable height, [so] that they are . . . [now] a wonder to the world, [come] from your Majesty's seas and lands.

I thus moved, began to dive into the depth of their policies and circumventing practices, whereby they drain, and still covet to exhaust, the wealth and coin of this kingdom, and so with our own commodities to weaken us, and finally beat us quite out of trading in other countries. I found that they more fully obtained these their purposes by their convenient privileges, and settled constitutions, than England with all the laws, and superabundance of home-bred commodities which God hath vouchsafed your sea and land. . . .

To bring this to pass they have many advantages of us; the one is, by their fashioned ships . . . that are made to hold great bulk of merchandise, and to sail with a few men for profit. For example . . . . [Dutch ships] do serve the merchant better cheap by one hundred pounds [English money] in his freight than we can, by reason he hath but nine or ten mariners, and we near thirty; thus he saveth twenty men's meat and wages in a voyage; and so in all other their ships according to their burden, by which means they are freighted wheresoever they come, to great profit, whilst our ships lie still and decay. . . .

Thus they and others glean this wealth and strength from us to themselves; and these reasons following procure them this advantage to us.

1. The merchants . . . which maketh all things in abundance, by reason of their store-houses continually replenished with all kind of commodities.
2. The liberty of free traffic for strangers to buy and sell in Holland, and other countries and states, as if they were free-born, maketh great intercourse.
3. The small duties levied upon merchants, draws all nations to trade with them.
4. Their fashioned ships continually freighted before ours, by reason of their few mariners and great bulk, serving the merchant cheap.
5. Their forwardness to further all manner of trading.
6. Their wonderful employment of their busses [herring boats] for fishing, and the great returns they make.
7. Their giving free custom inward and outwards, for any new-erected trade, by means whereof they have gotten already almost the sole trade into their hands.

---

sterdam's riches. The upper classes disliked and feared them, which created much ambivalence in the way city authorities treated them. Militia companies made up of upper-class volunteers stood ready to crush lower-class revolts, while wealthy individuals created orphanages and almshouses to care for their needs. Many of the rabble were forcefully recruited as ordinary sailors, especially for dangerous overseas voyages. Above the rabble stood the artisans and manual laborers known as the *kleine man* (little man). These were members of guilds or people who labored for guild members. Since a wife could continue to operate a business after her husband's death, Amsterdam was known for its high number of businesswomen. The *kleine man* lived in an area called the Jordaan, built outside the three new canals. Its closely crowded quarters and small streets crisscrossed by canals created a quaintness and sense of solidarity that appealed to many of Amsterdam's artists.

Above the *kleine man* stood a professional class of lawyers, teachers, bureaucrats, and wealthier guildsmen, but above them were the landed nobles who intermarried with the wealthier burghers and built more elaborate town houses. At the very top of Amsterdam's society stood a small group of very wealthy manufacturers, shipyard owners, and merchants, whose wealth enabled them to control the city government of Amsterdam as well as the Dutch Republic's States General.

In the first half of the seventeenth century, the Calvinist background of the wealthy Amsterdam burghers led them to adopt a simple lifestyle. They wore dark clothes and lived in substantial, but simply furnished houses, known for their narrow and steep stairways. The oft-quoted phrase that "cleanliness is next to Godliness" was literally true for these self-confident Dutch burghers. But in the second half of the seventeenth century, the wealthy burghers began to reject their Calvinist heritage in favor of French styles, a transformation that is especially evident in their more elaborate and colorful clothes.

England and the Emergence of Constitutional Monarchy

The inability of the Puritans to rule England on a long-term basis (see Chapter 15) led to the restoration of the Stuart monarchy in 1660. After eleven years of exile, Charles II (1660–1685) returned to England and entered London amid the acclaim of the people, remarking sardonically, "I never knew that I was so popular in England." The restoration of the monarchy and the House of Lords did not mean, however, that the work of the Puritan Revolution was undone. Parliament kept much of the power it had won: arbitary courts were still abolished; Parliament's role in government was acknowledged; and the necessity for its consent to taxation was accepted.

This did not mean that Charles was content with these limitations on his monarchical authority, but he had lived through the civil wars and eleven years of exile and he was resolved toward moderation. "I am too old to go again on my travels," as he wisely expressed it. Yet Charles utilized adroit and devious political maneuverings to push his own ideas, some of which were clearly out of step with many of the English people.

A serious religious problem disturbed the tranquillity of Charles II's reign. After the restoration of the monarchy, a new Parliament (the Cavalier Parliament) met in 1661 and restored the Anglican church as the official church of England. In addition, laws were passed to force everyone, particularly Catholics and Puritan Dissenters, to conform to the Anglican church and even to exclude these people from holding positions in local government.

Charles was not pleased with this legislation. He was sympathetic to and perhaps even inclined to Catholicism. By the secret Treaty of Dover of 1670 with King Louis XIV of France, Charles had promised, in return for a substantial subsidy, to become Catholic and make England a Catholic commonwealth at the appropriate opportunity. Moreover, Charles's brother James, heir to the throne, did not hide the fact that he was a Catholic. Parliament's suspicions were therefore aroused in 1672 when Charles took the audacious step of issuing a Declaration of Indulgence that suspended the laws that Parliament had passed against Catholics and Puritans. By linking Catholics to Puritan Dissenters, Charles hoped to succeed with his religious policy, but Parliament would have none of it and induced the king to suspend the declaration. Propelled by a strong anti-Catholic sentiment, Parliament then passed a Test Act in 1673, specifying that only Anglicans could hold military and civil offices.

A supposed Catholic plot to assassinate King Charles and place his brother James on the throne, although shown to be imaginary, inflamed Parliament to attempt to pass an Exclusion Bill between 1678 and 1681 that would have barred James from the throne as a professed Catholic. Although these attempts failed, the debate over the bill created two political groupings: the Whigs, who wanted to exclude James and establish a Protestant king with toleration of Dissenters; and the Tories, who supported the king, despite their dislike of James as a Catholic, because they did not believe Parliament should tamper with the lawful succession to the throne. To foil these efforts, Charles dismissed Parliament in 1681, relying on French subsidies to rule alone. When he died in 1685, his Catholic brother came to the throne.

The accession of James II (1685–1688) to the crown virtually guaranteed a new constitutional crisis for England, for the stubborn and uncompromising James II was more reminiscent of his father, Charles I, than his brother. An open and devout Catholic, his attempt to further Catholic interests made religion once more a primary cause of conflict between king and Parliament.

After some initial successes, James took advantage of his newfound popularity to seek advantages for his fellow Catholics. Contrary to the Test Act, he named Catholics to high positions in the government, army, navy, and universities. In 1687, he issued a Declaration of Indulgence, which suspended all laws barring Catholics and Dissenters from office. Parliamentary outcries against

The Bill of Rights

▼ ▼ ▼

In 1688, the English experienced yet another revolution, a rather bloodless one in which the Stuart king James II was replaced by Mary, James's daughter, and her husband, William of Orange. After William and Mary had assumed power, Parliament passed a Bill of Rights that specified the rights of Parliament and laid the foundation for a constitutional monarchy.

The Bill of Rights

Whereas the said late King James II having abdicated the government, and the throne being thereby vacant, his Highness the prince of Orange (whom it hath pleased Almighty God to make the glorious instrument of delivering this kingdom from popery and arbitrary power) did (by the device of the lords spiritual and temporal, and diverse principal persons of the Commons) cause letters to be written to the lords spiritual and temporal, being Protestants, and other letters to the several counties, cities, universities, boroughs, and Cinque Ports, for the choosing of such persons to represent them, as were of right to be sent to parliament, to meet and sit at Westminster upon the two and twentieth day of January, in this year 1689, in order to such an establishment as that their religion, laws, and liberties might not again be in danger of being subverted; upon which letters elections have been accordingly made.

And thereupon the said lords spiritual and temporal and Commons, pursuant to their respective letters and elections, being now assembled in a full and free representation of this nation, taking into their most serious consideration the best means for attaining the ends aforesaid, do in the first place (as their ancestors in like case have usually done), for the vindication and assertion of their ancient rights and liberties, declare:

1. That the pretended power of suspending laws, or the execution of laws, by regal authority, without consent of parliament is illegal.

2. That the pretended power of dispensing with the laws, or the execution of law by regal authority, as it hath been assumed and exercised of late, is illegal.

3. That the commission for erecting the late court of commissioners for ecclesiastical causes, and all other commissions and courts of like nature, are illegal and pernicious.

4. That levying money for or to the use of the crown by pretense of prerogative, without grant of parliament, for longer time or in other manner than the same is or shall be granted, is illegal.

5. That it is the right of the subjects to petition the king, and all commitments and prosecutions for such petitioning are illegal.

6. That the raising or keeping a standing army within the kingdom in time of peace, unless it be with consent of parliament, is against law.

7. That the subjects which are Protestants may have arms for their defense suitable to their conditions, and as allowed by law.

8. That election of members of parliament ought to be free.

9. That the freedom of speech, and debates or proceedings in parliament, ought not to be impeached or questioned in any court or place out of parliament.

10. That excessive bail ought not to be required, nor excessive fines imposed, nor cruel and unusual punishments inflicted.

11. That jurors ought to be duly impaneled and returned, and jurors which pass upon men in trials for high treason ought to be freeholders.

12. That all grants and promises of fines and forfeitures of particular persons before conviction are illegal and void.

13. And that for redress of all grievances, and for the amending, strengthening, and preserving of the laws, parliament ought to be held frequently.

James's policies stopped short of rebellion since members knew that he was an old man and his successors were his Protestant daughters Mary and Anne, born to his first wife. But on June 10, 1688, a son was born to James II's second wife, also a Catholic. Suddenly the specter of a Catholic hereditary monarchy loomed large. A group of seven prominent English noblemen invited William of Orange, husband of James's daughter Mary, to invade

England. An inveterate foe of Louis XIV, William welcomed this opportunity to fight France with England's resources. William and Mary raised an army and invaded England while James, his wife, and infant son fled to France. With almost no bloodshed, England had undergone a "Glorious Revolution," not over the issue of whether there would be a monarchy, but rather over who would be monarch.

The events of late 1688 constituted only the initial stage of the Glorious Revolution. The second, and far more important part, was the Revolution Settlement which confirmed William and Mary as monarchs. In January 1689, a Convention Parliament asserted that James had tried to subvert the constitution "by breaking the original contract between king and people," and declared the throne of England vacant. It then offered the throne to William and Mary, who accepted it along with the provisions of a Declaration of Rights, later enacted into law as a Bill of Rights in 1689 (see the box on p. 550). The Bill of Rights affirmed Parliament's right to make laws and levy taxes and made it impossible for kings to oppose or do without Parliament by stipulating that standing armies could be raised only with the consent of Parliament. Both elections and debates of Parliament had to be free, meaning that the king could not interfere. The rights of citizens to petition the sovereign, keep arms, have a jury trial, and not be subject to excessive bail were also confirmed. The Bill of Rights helped to fashion a system of government based on the rule of law and a freely elected Parliament, thus laying the foundation for a constitutional monarchy.

The Bill of Rights did not settle the religious questions that had played such a large role in England's troubles in the seventeenth century. The Toleration Act of 1689 granted Puritan Dissenters the right of free public worship (Catholics were still excluded), although they did not yet have full civil and political equality since the Test Act was not repealed. Although the Toleration Act did not mean complete religious freedom and equality, it marked a departure in English history since few people would ever again be persecuted for religious reasons.

Many historians have viewed the Glorious Revolution as the end of the seventeenth-century struggle between king and Parliament. By deposing one king and establishing another, Parliament had destroyed the divine-right theory of kingship (William was, after all, king by grace of Parliament, not God) and confirmed its right to participate in the government. Parliament did not have complete control of the government, but it now had an unquestioned right to participate in affairs of state. Over the next century, it would gradually

Chronology

▼ ▼ ▼

Limited Monarchy and Republics

Poland	
Sigismund III	1587–1631
Beginning of Liberum Veto	1652
The United Provinces	
Official Recognition of United Provinces	1648
House of Orange	
William III	1672–1702
England	
Charles II	1660–1685
Cavalier Parliament	1661
Treaty of Dover	1670
Declaration of Indulgence	1672
Test Act	1673
James II	1685–1688
Declaration of Indulgence	1687
Glorious Revolution	1688
Bill of Rights	1689

prove to be the real authority in the English system of constitutional monarchy. This, of course, would not make it a democracy or representative system of government. The members of Parliament, specifically the House of Commons, were elected by a very limited portion of the population, primarily members of the aristocratic landowning class. Indeed, England from 1688 to 1832 was one of the best examples in modern times of rule by an aristocratic oligarchy.

▼ Economic Trends: Mercantilism and European Colonies in the Seventeenth Century

The sixteenth century had witnessed a rising population, severely escalating prices, and a growing economy. The seventeenth century, however, as recent economic studies have demonstrated, was characterized more by economic contraction, if not depression, although variations existed depending on the country or region. Trade, industry, and agriculture all felt the pinch of a depression, which some historians believe bottomed out between 1640 and 1680, while others argue that the decade of the 1690s was still bad, especially in France.

Translated into everyday life, for many people the economic contraction of the seventeenth century meant scarce food, uncertain employment, and high rates of taxation.

Climate, too, played a factor in this economic reversal as Europeans experienced worsening weather patterns. In this "little ice age," extending from the sixteenth well into the eighteenth century, average temperatures fell, winters were colder, summers were wetter, and devastating storms seemed more frequent. Although the exact impact of climatic changes is uncertain, there were numerous reports of crop failures, the worst in 1649, 1660–1661, and the 1690s.

Population was also affected. Based on the birth rate of the seventeenth century, demographers would expect the European population to have doubled every twenty-five years. In reality, Europe experienced either a decline or no steady increase in population, as a result of a variety of factors. Infant mortality rates were high, 30 percent in the first year of life and 50 percent before the age of ten. Epidemics and famines were again common experiences in European life. The last great epidemic of bubonic plague spread across Europe in the middle and late years of the seventeenth century. The Mediterranean region suffered from 1646 to 1657, when the plague killed off 130,000 persons in Naples alone. In 1665, it struck England and devastated London, killing 20 percent of its population. France and Spain experienced outbreaks in the 1690s. The last major outburst of bubonic plague struck Poland, Germany, and Scandinavia between 1708 and 1713.

Mercantilism

Mercantilism is the name historians use to identify a set of economic principles that dominated economic thought in the seventeenth century. Fundamental to mercantilism was the belief that the total volume of trade was unchangeable. Therefore, as Colbert, the French practitioner of mercantilism, stated: "trade causes perpetual conflict, both in war and in peace, among the nations of Europe, as to who should carry off the greatest part. The Dutch, the English and the French are the actors in this conflict."[11] Since one nation could expand its trade and hence its prosperity only at the expense of others, to mercantilists, economic activity was war carried on by peaceful means.

According to the mercantilists, the prosperity of a nation depended upon a plentiful supply of bullion or gold and silver. For this reason, it was desirable to achieve a favorable balance of trade in which goods exported were of greater value than those imported, promoting an influx of gold and silver payments that would increase the quantity of bullion. Furthermore, to encourage exports, governments should stimulate and protect export industries and trade by granting trade monopolies, encouraging investment in new industries through subsidies, importing foreign artisans, and improving transportation systems by building roads, bridges, and canals. By placing high tariffs on foreign goods, they could be kept out of the country and prevented from competing with domestic industries. Colonies were also deemed valuable as sources of raw materials and markets for finished goods.

As a system of economic principles, mercantilism focused on the role of the state, believing that state intervention in some aspects of the economy was desirable for the sake of the national good. Government regulations to ensure the superiority of export goods, the construction of roads and canals, and the granting of subsidies to create trade companies were all predicated on government involvement in economic affairs.

Overseas Trade and Colonies

Mercantilist theory on the role of colonies was matched in practice by Europe's overseas expansion. With the development of colonies and trading posts in the Americas and Far East, Europeans entered into an age of international commerce in the seventeenth century. While some historians speak of a world economy, we should remember that local, regional, and intra-European trade still dominated the scene. At the end of the seventeenth century, for example, English imports totaled 360,000 tons, but only 5,000 tons came from the East Indies. About one-tenth of English and Dutch exports were shipped across the Atlantic; slightly more went to the Far East. What made the transoceanic trade rewarding, however, was not the volume, but the value of its goods. Dutch, English, and French merchants were bringing back products that were still consumed largely by the wealthy, but at the same time were making their way into the lives of artisans and merchants. Pepper and spices from the Indies, West Indian and Brazilian sugar, and Asian coffee and tea were becoming more common for European consumers. The first coffee and tea houses opened in London in the 1650s and spread rapidly to other parts of Europe.

In 1600, much overseas trade was still carried by the Spanish and Portuguese, who alone possessed colonies of any significant size. But war and steady pressure from their Dutch and English rivals eroded Portuguese trade in both the west and east, although Portugal continued to profit from its large colonial empire in Brazil. The Spanish also maintained an enormous South American empire, but Spain's importance as a commercial power declined rapidly in the seventeenth century because of a drop in the output of the silver mines, the poverty of the Spanish monarchy, and the stifling hand of the Spanish aristocracy as well as the pressure of its English rivals.

Although the Dutch became the leading carriers of European products within Europe, they had more severe competition when they moved into Asian and American markets. The Dutch East India Company was formed in 1602 to consolidate the gains made at the expense of the Portuguese and exploit the riches of the Far East. Since the wealthy oligarchy that controlled the company also dominated the Dutch government, this joint-stock company not only had a monopoly on all Asian trade but also possessed the right to make war, sign treaties, establish military and trading bases, and appoint governing officials. Gradually, the Dutch East India Company took control of most of the Portuguese bases in the Far East and opened trade with China and Japan. Its profits were spectacular in the first ten years.

Although the Dutch West India Company was created in 1621 along lines similar to its eastern counterpart, it was less successful. Its efforts were aimed against Portuguese and Spanish trade and possessions, and though it made some inroads in Portuguese Brazil and the Caribbean, they were not enough to compensate for its expenditures. Dutch settlements were also established on the North American continent. The mainland colony of New Netherlands stretched from the mouth of the Hudson as far north as Albany, New York. Present-day names, such as Manhattan, Staten Island, Harlem, and the Catskills remind us that it was the Dutch who

initially settled the Hudson River valley. In the second half of the seventeenth century, rivalry and years of warfare with the English and French brought the decline of the Dutch commercial empire. In 1664, the English seized the colony of New Netherlands and renamed it New York while the Dutch West India Company soon went bankrupt. By the end of the seventeenth century, the Dutch Golden Age was beginning to tarnish.

The Dutch overseas trade and commercial empire faced two major rivals in the seventeenth century—the English and French. The English had founded their own East India Company in 1601 and proceeded to create a colonial empire in the New World along the Atlantic seaboard of North America. The failure of the Virginia Company made it evident that the colonizing of American lands was not necessarily conducive to quick profits. But the desire to escape from religious oppression combined with economic interests did make successful colonization possible, as the Massachusetts Bay Company demonstrated (see the box on p. 554). The Massachusetts colony had 4,000 settlers in its early years, but by 1660 had swelled to 40,000. Although the English had established control over most of the eastern seaboard by the end of the seventeenth century, the North American colonies still remained of minor significance to the English economy.

French commercial companies in the Far East experienced much difficulty. While due in part to a late start, French problems also demonstrated the weakness of a commerce dependent on political rather than economic impetus. The East Indian companies set up by Henry IV and Richelieu all failed. Colbert instituted a new East India Company in 1664 that only barely managed to survive. The French had greater success in North America where in 1663 Canada was made the property of the

▼ **The Dutch East India Company in India.** Pictured here is the Dutch trading post known as Hugly, founded in Bengal in 1610. While being the leading carriers of European products within Europe, the Dutch faced more difficult challenges when they began to deal with Asian and American markets. The Dutch East India Company eventually came to dominate most of the Portuguese bases in the east, but were less successful in the west and ultimately lost ground to the English.

The Pilgrims at Plymouth

▼ ▼ ▼

B *ritish colonization of the eastern seacoast of North America was a slow and often painful process. Unlike the Virginia colony, which had quick profits as its primary aim, the settlers in Massachusetts intended to establish permanent homes. This description of the early colonists at Plymouth is taken from the classic account of Governor William Bradford.*

William Bradford, *History of the Plymouth Settlement*

Having now come to the 25th of March, I will begin the year 1621. . . .

They began now to gather in the small harvest they had, and to prepare their houses for the winter, being well recovered in health and strength, and plentifully provisioned; for while some had been thus employed in affairs away from home, others were occupied in fishing for cod, bass, and other fish, of which they caught a good quantity, every family having their portion. All the summer there was no want. And now, as winter approached, wild fowl began to arrive, of which there were plenty when they came here first, though afterwards, they became more scarce. As well as wild fowl, they got abundance of wild turkeys, besides venison, etc. Each person had about a peck of meal a week, or now, since harvest, Indian corn in that proportion; and afterwards many wrote at length about their plenty to their friends in England—not feigned but true reports. . . .

Soon after this ship's departure, the great Narragansett tribe, in a braving manner, sent a messenger to them with a bundle of arrows tied about with a great snake skin, which their interpreters told them was a threatening challenge. Upon which the Governor, with the advice of the others, sent them a round answer, that if they would rather have war than peace, they might begin when they would; they had done them no wrong, neither did they fear them, nor would they find them unprepared. They sent the snake skin back by another messenger with bullets in it; but they would not receive it, and returned it again. . . .

But this made the settlers more careful to look to themselves. They agreed to enclose their dwellings in a good strong stockade and make flankers in convenient places, with gates to shut. These they locked every night and a watch was kept, and when need required there were also outposts in the daytime. The colonists, at the Captain's and Governor's advice, were divided into four squadrons, and everyone had his quarter appointed, to which to repair at any sudden alarm; and in case of fire, a company with muskets was appointed as a guard, to prevent Indian treachery, whilst the others quenched. This was accomplished very cheerfully, and the town was enclosed by the beginning of March, every family having a pretty garden plot.

---

crown and administered like a French province. But the French failed to provide adequate men or money, allowing their continental wars to take precedence over the conquest of the North American continent. Already in 1713, by the Treaty of Utrecht, the French began to cede some of their American possessions to their English rival.

▼ The World of Seventeenth-Century Culture

The seventeenth century was a remarkably talented one. In addition to the intellectuals responsible for the Scientific Revolution (see Chapter 17), the era was blessed with a number of prominent thinkers, artists, and writers. Some historians have even labeled it a century of genius.

Art

In the second half of the seventeenth century, France replaced Italy as the cultural leader of Europe. Rejecting the Baroque style as overly showy and passionate, the French remained committed to the classical values of the High Renaissance. French late classicism with its emphasis on clarity, simplicity, balance, and harmony of design was, however, a rather "frigid" version of the High Renaissance style. Its triumph reflected the shift in seventeenth-century French society from chaos to order.

The nature of French classicism was evident in the principles of the French Academy of Painting and Sculpture. These included an imitation of the artists of antiquity, an emphasis on geometric shapes and the use of definite lines to clearly delineate objects, a deemphasis on color because of its sensuousness, and the idealization of nature. While French classicism rejected the emotionalism and high drama of the Baroque, the latter's conception of grandeur was continued in the portrayal of noble subjects, especially those from classical antiquity. Nicholas Poussin (1594–1665) exemplified these principles in his paintings. His choice of scenes from classical mythology, the calmness of his vistas, the postures of his figures copied from the sculptures of antiquity, and his use of brown tones all reflect the classical principles of the French Academy.

THE GOLDEN AGE OF DUTCH PAINTING The supremacy of Dutch commerce in the seventeenth century was paralleled by a brilliant flowering of Dutch painting. Since the Dutch possessed no real royal court or rich aristocracy, it was the wealthy patricians and burghers of Dutch urban society who commissioned works of art for their guild halls, town halls, and private dwellings. The interests of this burgher society were reflected in the subject matter of many Dutch paintings: portraits of themselves, group portraits of their military companies and guilds, landscapes, seascapes, genre scenes, still lifes, and the interiors of their residences. Neither classical nor Baroque, Dutch painters were primarily interested in the realistic portrayal of secular, everyday life. To a great extent, they turned away from the religious themes that had dominated art for so long.

The finest example of the Golden Age of Dutch painting was Rembrandt van Rijn (1606–1669). Rembrandt's early career was reminiscent of Rubens since he painted opulent portraits and grandiose scenes in often colorful fashion. Like Rubens, he was prolific and successful; unlike Rubens, he turned away from materialistic success and public approval to follow his own artistic path. In the process, he lost public support and died bankrupt.

Although Rembrandt shared the Dutch preoccupation for realistic portraits, he became more introspective as he grew older. He refused to follow his contemporaries who produced pictures largely secular in subject matter; half of his paintings focused on scenes from biblical tales. Since the Protestant tradition of hostility to religious pictures had discouraged artistic expression, Rembrandt stands out as the one great Protestant painter of the seventeenth century. Rembrandt's religious pictures, however, avoided the monumental subjects, such as the Creation and Last Judgment, that were typical of Catholic artists. Instead, he favored pictures that focused on the individual's relationship with God and depicted people's inward suffering in quiet, evocative scenes.

The Theater: The Triumph of French Neoclassicism

As the great age of theater in England and Spain was drawing to a close around 1630, a new dramatic era began to dawn in France that lasted into the 1680s. Unlike Shakespeare in England and Lope de Vega in Spain, French playwrights wrote more for an elite audience and were forced to depend upon royal patronage.

▼ Nicholas Poussin, *Landscape with the Burial of Phocian.* France became the new cultural leader of Europe in the second half of the seventeenth century. French classicism upheld the values of High Renaissance style, but produced a more static version of it. In Nicholas Poussin's work, we see the emphasis of French classicism on the use of scenes from classical sources and the creation of a sense of grandeur and noble strength in both human figures and landscape.

Louis XIV used theater as he did art and architecture—to attract attention to his monarchy.

French dramatists cultivated a classical style in which the Aristotelian rules for dramatic composition, observing the three unities of time, place, and action, were closely followed. French neoclassicism emphasized the clever, polished, and correct over the emotional and imaginative. Many of the French works of the period derived both their themes and their plots from Greek and Roman sources, especially evident in the works of Jean-Baptiste Racine (1639–1699). In *Phédre,* which has been called his best play, Racine followed closely the plot of the Greek tragedian Euripides' *Hippolytus.* Like the ancient tragedians, Racine, who perfected the French neoclassical tragic style, focused on conflicts, such as between love and honor or inclination and duty, that characterized and revealed the tragic dimensions of life.

Jean-Baptiste Molière (1622–1673) enjoyed the favor of the French court and benefited from the patronage of the Sun King. He wrote, produced, and acted in a series of comedies that often satirized the religious and social world of his time (see the box on p. 557). In *The Misanthrope,* he mocked the corruption of court society, while in *Tartuffe,* he ridiculed the bigotry of the clergy. Molière's satires, however, sometimes got him into trouble. The Paris clergy did not find *Tartuffe* funny and had it banned for five years. Only the protection of Louis XIV saved Molière from more severe harassment.

International Law and Political Thought

The seventeenth-century search for order and harmony, a response to the disorder generated by wars and internal crises, is apparent in the development of international law. This subject had been of much importance to Italian jurists of the Renaissance. Influenced by the revival of Greco-Roman thought and living in Europe's first secular states, they had deliberated upon the problems of diplomatic relations among states.

It was a seventeenth-century Dutch lawyer with a humanist education, Hugo Grotius (1583–1645), who provided a synthesis of previous doctrine on international law. In his work, *On the Law of War and Peace,* which appeared in 1625, he stated that his goal was to treat "of that law that exists between peoples or between the rulers or peoples." International law, Grotius

▼ **Rembrandt von Rijn,** *Syndics of the Cloth Guild.* The Dutch experienced a Golden Age of painting during the seventeenth century. The burghers and patricians of Dutch urban society commissioned works of art, and these quite naturally reflected the worldly interests of burgher society, as this painting by Rembrandt illustrates. Rembrandt eventually abandoned the largely secular matter with which other artists dealt and turned to more introspective religious works.

French Comedy

▼ ▼ ▼

The comedy writer Jean-Baptiste Molière has long been regarded as one of the best playwrights of the age of Louis XIV. Like Shakespeare, Molière was a complete man of the theater. He wrote, directed, produced, and acted in a series of comedies that satirized the social and religious foibles of his age. This selection from The Would-Be Gentleman comes from a scene in Act II in which Molière ridicules the pretensions of the tutors hired by Monsieur Jourdain, a wealthy, but vain and pretentious Parisian merchant.

Jean-Baptiste Molière, *The Would-Be Gentleman*

(Enter a Philosophy Master.)

M. JOURDAIN: Hola, Monsieur Philosopher, you are come in the nick of time with your philosophy. Come, and make peace a little amongst these people here.

PHILOSOPHY MASTER: What's to do? What's the matter, gentlemen?

M. JOURDAIN: They have put themselves into such a passion about the preference of their professions as to call names, and would come to blows.

PHILOSOPHY MASTER: O fie, gentlemen, what need was there of all this fury? Have you not read the learned treatise upon anger, composed by Seneca? Is there anything more base and shameful than this passion which makes a savage beast of a man? And should not reason be master of all our commotions?

DANCING MASTER: How, sir? Why he has just now been abusing us both, in despising character dancing which is my employment, and music which is his profession.

PHILOSOPHY MASTER: A wise man is above all foul language that can be given him, and the grand answer one should make to all affronts is moderation and patience.

FENCING MASTER: They had both the assurance to compare their professions to mine.

PHILOSOPHY MASTER: Should this disturb you? Men should not dispute about vainglory and rank; that which perfectly distinguishes one from another is wisdom and virtue.

DANCING MASTER: I maintained to him that dancing was a science to which one cannot do sufficient honour.

MUSIC MASTER: And I, that music is one of those that all ages have revered.

FENCING MASTER: And I maintained against 'em both that the science of defence is the finest and most necessary of all sciences.

PHILOSOPHY MASTER: And what becomes of philosophy, then? You are all three very impertinent fellows, me-thinks, to speak with this arrogance before me; and impudently to give the name of science to things that one ought not to honour even with the name of art, that can't be comprised but under the name of a pitiful trade of gladiator, ballad-singer, and morris-dancer.

FENCING MASTER: Out, ye dog of a philosopher.

MUSIC MASTER: Hence, ye scoundrel of a pedant.

DANCING MASTER: Begone, ye arrant pedagogue.

(The Philosopher falls upon them, they all three lay him on.)

PHILOSOPHY MASTER: How? Varlets as you are—

M. JOURDAIN: Monsieur Philosopher!

PHILOSOPHY MASTER: Infamous dogs! Rogues! Insolent curs!

M. JOURDAIN: Monsieur Philosopher!

FENCING MASTER: Plague on the animal!

M. JOURDAIN: Gentlemen!

PHILOSOPHY MASTER: Impudent villains!

M. JOURDAIN: Monsieur Philosopher!

DANCING MASTER: Deuce take the pack-saddled ass!

M. JOURDAIN: Gentlemen!

PHILOSOPHY MASTER: Profligate vermin!

M. JOURDAIN: Monsieur Philosopher!

MUSIC MASTER: The devil take the impertinent puppy!

PHILOSOPHY MASTER: Knaves! Ragamuffins! Traitors! Imposters!

M. JOURDAIN: Monsieur Philosopher! Gentlemen! Monsieur Philosopher! Gentlemen!

Monsieur Philosopher!

(The four masters beat each other.)

Nay, beat your hearts out if you will, I shall neither meddle nor make with you, I shan't spoil my gown to part you. I should be a great fool to thrust myself among them, and receive some blow that might do me a mischief.

contended, was derived from the natural law instituted by God that was common to all humanity. Natural law included the human need to live in society, the rationality of human nature, and the central role of the family in human society. While war was undesirable, it was unavoidable. What was needed then, according to Grotius, was a system of rules to govern it, just as there was a rational system that ordered the relationship between states and between rulers and their subjects in peacetime.

Grotius and other theorists on international law seemed to realize that the religious divisions created by the Reformation had destroyed what remained of the medieval tradition of Europe as a *corpus Christianum*, a common community of Christians. They accepted the newfound sovereignty of separate European states, but worried about the morality of living in an international jungle. The doctrine of international law gave European states a "secularized moral code" without restricting their freedom to play the game of power politics.

POLITICAL THOUGHT   The preoccupations with order and power, two significant characteristics of the seventeenth century, were reflected in political thought. Thomas Hobbes was an Englishman who was alarmed by the revolutionary upheavals in seventeenth-century England: "The state of man," he wrote, "can never be without some incommodity or other"; nevertheless, "the greatest, that in any form of government can possibly happen to the people in general, is scarce sensible in respect of the miseries, and horrible calamities, that accompany a civil war, or that dissolute condition of masterless men, without subject to laws, and a coercive power to tie their hands from rapine and revenge." Hobbes's name has since been associated with the state's claim to absolute authority over its subjects, which he elaborated in his major treatise on political thought known as the *Leviathan*, published in 1651.

Hobbes viewed human nature in materialistic and mechanistic terms. He claimed that in the theoretical state of nature, before society was organized, human life was "solitary, poor, nasty, brutish, and short." Humans were guided not by reason and moral ideals, but by animalistic instincts and a ruthless struggle for self-preservation (see the box on p. 559). To save themselves from destroying each other (the "war of every man against every man"), people contracted to form a commonwealth, which Hobbes called "that great Leviathan (or rather, to speak more reverently, that mortal god) to which we owe our peace and defense." This common-

wealth placed its collective power into the hands of a sovereign authority, preferably a single ruler, who served as executor, legislator, and judge. This absolute ruler possessed unlimited power. Subjects may not rebel; if they do, they must be suppressed. If the ruler became incapable of effectively exercising his power, he gave up his sovereignty, and his subjects transferred their loyalty to another ruler who would preserve their peace.

Thomas Hobbes's rational analysis of political authority stunned many of his contemporaries. His acceptance of power politics without recourse to spiritual foundations offended many of them. Later, when the secular nation-state became the standard political unit of Western civilization, Hobbes, like Machiavelli, would be acclaimed as a political theorist of great genius.

Other intellectuals in the seventeenth century viewed the exercise of political power quite differently from Hobbes and argued against the absolute rule of one man. The most famous was another Englishman, John Locke (1623–1704), whose experience of English politics was transformed into a political work called *Two Treatises of Government.*

Like Hobbes, Locke argued from the theoretical condition of the state of nature before human existence became organized socially. But, unlike Hobbes, Locke believed humans lived then in a state of equality and freedom rather than a state of war. In this state of nature, humans had certain inalienable natural rights—to life, liberty, and property. Like Hobbes, Locke did not believe all was well in the state of nature. Since there was no impartial judge in the state of nature, people found it difficult to protect these natural rights. So they made a contract and mutually agreed to establish a government to ensure the protection of their rights. This was a contract of mutual obligations: government would protect the rights of the people while the people would act reasonably toward government. But if a government broke this contract—if a monarch, for example, failed to live up to his obligation to protect the natural rights or claimed absolute authority and made laws without the consent of the community—the people might form a new government. "The community perpetually retains a supreme power," Locke claimed. For Locke, however, the community of people was primarily the landholding aristocracy who were represented in Parliament, not the landless masses. Locke was hardly an advocate of political democracy, but his ideas proved important to both Americans and French in the eighteenth century and were used to support demands for constitutional government, the rule of law, and the protection of rights.

Hobbes and the War of "Every Man against Every Man"

▼ ▼ ▼

The seventeenth-century obsession with order and power was well reflected in the political thought of the Englishman Thomas Hobbes. In his Leviathan, *Hobbes presented the case for the state's claim to absolute authority over its subjects. In this selection from his famous work, he describes human life in its original "state of nature."*

Thomas Hobbes, *Leviathan*

Hereby it is manifest, that during the time men live without a common Power to keep them all in awe, they are in that condition which is called War; and such a War, as is of every man, against every man. For War, consists not of Battle only, or the act of fighting; but in a tract of time, wherein the Will to contend by Battle is sufficiently known: and therefore the notion of Time, is to be considered in the nature of War; as it is in the nature of Weather. For as the nature of Foul weather, lieth not in a shower or two of rain; but in an inclination thereto of many days together; So the nature of War, consists not in actual fighting; but in the known disposition thereto, during all the time there is no assurance to the contrary. All other time is PEACE.

Whatsoever therefore is consequent to a time of War, where every man is Enemy to every man; the same is consequent to the time, wherein men live without other security, than what their own strength, and their own invention shall furnish them withall. In such condition, there is no place for Industry; because the fruit thereof is uncertain: and consequently no Culture of the Earth; no Navigation, nor use of the commodities that may by imported by Sea; no commodious Building; no Instruments of moving, and removing such things as require much force; no Knowledge of the face of the Earth; no account of Time; no Arts; no Letters; no Society; and which is worst of all, continual fear, and anger of violent death; And the life of man, solitary, poor, nasty, brutish, and short.

To many historians, the seventeenth century has assumed extraordinary proportions. The divisive effects of the Reformation had been assimilated and the concept of a united Christendom, held as an ideal since the Middle Ages, had been irrevocably destroyed by the religious wars, making possible the emergence of a system of nation-states in which power politics took on an increasing significance. The growth of international law and political thought focusing on the secular origins of state power reflected the changes that were going on in seventeenth-century society.

Within those states, there slowly emerged some of the machinery that made possible a growing centralization of power. In those states called absolutist, strong monarchs with the assistance of their aristocracies took the lead in providing the leadership for greater centralization. But in England, where the landed aristocracy gained power at the expense of the monarchs, the foundations were laid for a constitutional government in which Parliament provided the focus for the institutions of central-ized power. In all the major European states, a growing concern for power and dynastic expansion led to larger armies and greater conflict. The growth of international law represented an attempt to create a rational system for this conflict, but it did nothing to achieve a peaceful solution to human problems. War remained an endemic feature of Western civilization.

But the search for order and harmony continued, evident in art and literature. At the same time, while it would be misleading to state that Europe had become a secular world, we would have to say that religious preoccupations and values were losing ground to secular considerations. The seventeenth century was a transitional period to a more secular spirit that has characterized modern Western civilization until the present time. No stronger foundation for this spirit could be found than in the new view of the universe that was created by the Scientific Revolution of the seventeenth century, and it is to that story that we must now turn.

Notes
▼ ▼ ▼

1. Quoted in D. H. Pennington, *Europe in the Seventeenth Century*, 2d ed. (London and New York, 1989), p. 313.
2. Quoted in John B. Wolf, *Louis XIV* (New York, 1968), p. 134.
3. Quoted in ibid., p. 618.
4. Quoted in Pennington, *Europe in the Seventeenth Century*, p. 494.
5. Quoted in Wolf, *Louis XIV*, p. 284.
6. Quoted in J. H. Elliott, *Imperial Spain, 1469–1716* (New York, 1963), p. 306.

7. Quoted in ibid., p. 338.
8. Quoted in Vasili Klyuchevsky, *Peter the Great*, trans. Liliana Archibald (New York, 1958), p. 244.
9. Quoted in B. H. Sumner, *Peter the Great and the Emergence of Russia* (New York, 1962), p. 122.
10. Quoted in Violet Barbour, *Capitalism in Amsterdam in the 17th Century* (Ann Arbor, Mich., 1963), p. 46.
11. Quoted in H. G. Koenigsberger, *Early Modern Europe: 1500–1798* (London, 1987), p. 172.

Suggestions for Further Reading
▼ ▼ ▼

In addition to the general works listed in Chapter 15, see also D. H. Pennington, *Europe in the Seventeenth Century*, 2d ed. (London and New York, 1989); and R. S. Dunn, *The Age of Religious Wars, 1559–1715*, 2d ed. (New York, 1979).

For a brief account of seventeenth-century French history, see R. Briggs, *Early Modern France, 1560–1715* (Oxford, 1977). More detailed studies on France during the periods of Henry IV and Cardinals Richelieu and Mazarin are M. Greengrass, *France in the Age of Henri IV: The Struggle for Stability* (London, 1984); R. Bonney, *Political Change in France under Richelieu and Mazarin, 1624–1661* (Oxford, 1978); and J. Bergin, *Cardinal Richelieu: Power and the Pursuit of Wealth* (London, 1985). A solid and very readable biography of Louis XIV is J. B. Wolf, *Louis XIV* (New York, 1968). Also of value are the works by G. R. R. Treasure, *Seventeenth Century France* (Garden City, N.Y., 1967); and P. Goubert, *Louis XIV and Twenty Million Frenchmen*, trans. A. Carter (New York, 1970). A now classic work on life in Louis XIV's France is W. H. Lewis, *The Splendid Century* (Garden City, N.Y., 1953). Well-presented summaries of revisionist views on Louis's monarchical power are R. Mettam, *Power and Faction in Louis XIV's France* (Oxford, 1988); and W. Beik, *Absolutism and Society in Seventeenth-Century France* (Cambridge, 1985). C. W. Cole, *Colbert and a Century of French Mercantilism*, 2 vols. (London, 1939), is still the fundamental study. The effects of the expulsion of the Huguenots are examined in W. C. Scoville, *The Persecution of the Huguenots and*

French Economic Development, 1680–1720 (Berkeley, 1960). A specialized study of Louis's last war is H. Kamen, *The War of the Succession in Spain* (London, 1969).

Good general works on seventeenth-century Spanish history include the relevant sections of J. H. Elliott, *Imperial Spain, 1469–1716* (New York, 1963; rev. ed. 1977); H. Kamen, *Spain 1469–1716: A Society of Conflict* (London, 1983); and R. A. Stradling, *Europe and the Decline of Spain, 1580–1720* (London, 1981). On the last half of the seventeenth century, see the more detailed work by H. Kamen, *Spain in the Later Seventeenth Century, 1665–1700* (London, 1980). The important minister Olivares is examined in J. H. Elliott, *The Count-Duke of Olivares: The Statesman in an Age of Decline* (London, 1986).

An older, but still valuable survey of the German states in the seventeenth century can be found in H. Holborn, *A History of Modern Germany, 1648–1840* (London, 1965). On the creation of an Austrian state, see R. J. W. Evans, *The Making of the Habsburg Monarchy, 1550–1700* (Oxford, 1979). The older work by F. L. Carsten, *The Origins of Prussia* (Oxford, 1954), remains an outstanding study of early Prussian history. On aspects of seventeenth-century Swedish history, see the works by M. Roberts, *Gustavus Adolphus: A History of Sweden, 1611–1632*, 2 vols. (London, 1953–58); and *Sweden's Age of Greatness* (London, 1973). A good biography of the dynamic Charles XII is R. Hatton, *Charles XII of Sweden* (London, 1968). For an introduction to Polish history, see N. Davies, *God's Playground: A History of Poland*, vol. 1, *The Origins to 1795* (Oxford, 1981).

On Russian history before Peter the Great, see the classic work by V. O. Klyuchevsky, *A Course in Russian History: The Seventeenth Century* (Chicago, 1968); and R. Nellie, *Enserfment and Military Change in Muscovy* (Chicago, 1971). Works on Peter the Great include V. O. Klyuchevsky, *Peter the Great*, trans. L. Archibald (New York, 1958); M. S. Anderson, *Peter the Great* (London, 1978); B. H. Sumner, *Peter the Great and the Emergence of Russia* (New York, 1962); and the massive popular biography by R. K. Massie, *Peter the Great* (New York, 1980). For an introduction to Ottoman history, see P. Coles, *The Ottoman Impact on Europe, 1350–1699* (London, 1968). J. Stoye, *The Siege of Vienna* (London, 1964), is a fascinating account of the Turkish empire's last great assault on Europe.

In addition to the works listed in Chapter 15 on the seventeenth century in England, see also J. P. Kenyon, *Stuart England* (London, 1978); and C. Hill, *The Century of Revolution* (Edinburgh, 1961). For a general survey of the post-Cromwellian era, see J. R. Jones, *Country and Court: England, 1658–1714* (London, 1978). A more specialized study is J. R. Jones, *The Revolution of 1688 in England* (London, 1972). On Charles II, see the scholarly biography by R. Hutton, *Charles II* (Oxford, 1989).

On the United Provinces, see two short, but sound introductions, K. H. D. Haley, *The Dutch in the Seventeenth Century* (London, 1972); and C. Wilson, *The Dutch Republic and the Civilisation of the Seventeenth Century* (London, 1968). Works on Amsterdam include J. J. Murray, *Amsterdam in the Age of Rembrandt* (Norman, Okla., 1967); and D. Regin, *Traders, Artists, Burghers: A Cultural History of Amsterdam in the 17th Century* (Assen, 1976). Of much value is S. Schama, *The Embarrassment of Riches: An Interpretation of Dutch Culture in the Golden Age* (New York, 1987).

On the economic side of the seventeenth century, there are the three volumes by F. Braudel, *Civilization and Capitalism in the 15th to 18th Century*, which obviously cover much more than just the seventeenth century: *The Structures of Everyday Life* (London, 1981); *The Wheels of Commerce* (London, 1982); and *The Perspective of the World* (London, 1984). Two single-volume comprehensive surveys are J. de Vries, *The Economy of Europe in an Age of Crisis* (Cambridge, 1976); and H. Kellenbenz, *The Rise of the European Economy: An Economic History of Continental Europe from the Fifteenth to the Eighteenth Century* (London, 1976). On overseas trade and colonial empires, see C. R. Boxer, *The Dutch Seaborne Empire, 1600–1800* (New York, 1965); and R. Davis, *English Overseas Trade, 1500–1700* (London, 1973). Although frequently criticized, the standard work on mercantilism remains E. Hecksher, *Mercantilism*, 2 vols. (London, 1935).

A brief survey of the cultural aspects of the seventeenth century can be found in F. B. Artz, *From the Renaissance to Romanticism* (Chicago, 1962). French theater and literature are examined in M. Turnell, *The Classical Moment* (London, 1964); and A. Adam, *Grandeur and Illusion: French Literature and Society, 1600–1715*, trans. J. Tint (New York, 1972). For an examination of French and Dutch art, see A. Blunt, *Art and Architecture in France, 1500–1700* (London, 1953); J. Rosenberg, S. Silve, and E. H. ter Kuele, *Dutch Art and Architecture, 1600–1800* (London, 1966); and C. White, *Rembrandt and His World* (London, 1964). Locke's political ideas are examined in J. H. Franklin, *John Locke and the Theory of Sovereignty* (London, 1978). On Thomas Hobbes, see D. D. Raphael, *Hobbes* (London, 1977).

Toward a New Heaven and a New Earth: The Scientific Revolution and the Emergence of Modern Science

▼▼▼▼▼

In addition to the constitutional, demographic, political, economic, and international crises of the seventeenth century, we need to add an intellectual one. The Scientific Revolution questioned and ultimately challenged conceptions and beliefs about the nature of the external world and reality that had crystallized into a rather strict orthodoxy by the Late Middle Ages. Derived from the works of ancient Greeks and Romans and grounded in Christian thought, the medieval worldview had become a formidable one. No doubt, the breakdown of Christian unity during the Reformation and the subsequent religious wars had created an environment in which Europeans had become accustomed to challenging both the ecclesiastical and political realms. Should it surprise us that a challenge to intellectual authority soon followed?

The Scientific Revolution brought Europeans a new way of viewing the universe and their place in it. The shift from an earth-centered to a sun-centered cosmos had an emotional as well as an intellectual effect upon those who understood it. Thus the Scientific Revolution, popularized in the eighteenth-century Enlightenment, stands as the major force in the transition to the largely secular, rational, and materialistic perspective that has defined the modern Western mentality since its full acceptance in the nineteenth and twentieth centuries.

In one sense, the Scientific Revolution was not a revolution. It was not characterized by the explosive change and rapid overthrow of traditional authority that we normally associate with the

Copernicus, *On the Revolution*
of the Heavenly Spheres
▼

Galileo,
The Starry Messenger
Kepler's Laws ▼ ▼

Newton, *Principia*
▼

•••••••• 1500 •••••••••• 1550 •••••••••• 1600 •••••••••• 1650 •••••••••• 1700 ••••••••••

▲
Vesalius,
On the Fabric of the Human Body

▲ ▲
Harvey's Theory Descartes,
of Circulation *Discourse on Method*

▲
Cavendish, *Grounds of*
Natural Philosophy

word *revolution*. The Scientific Revolution did overturn centuries of authority, but only in a gradual and piecemeal fashion. Nevertheless, its results were truly revolutionary. While the Renaissance and Reformation might be viewed, as one historian of science has argued, as "a mere internal displacement within the system of medieval Christendom," the Scientific Revolution was the key factor in setting Western civilization along its modern secular and material path.

▼ Background to the Scientific Revolution

To say that the Scientific Revolution brought about a dissolution of the medieval worldview is not to say that the Middle Ages was a period of scientific ignorance. Many educated Europeans took an intense interest in the world around them since it was, after all, "God's handiwork" and therefore an appropriate subject for study. Late medieval scholastic philosophers from Roger Bacon on had advanced mathematical and physical thinking in many ways, but the subjection of these thinkers to a strict theological framework and their unquestioning reliance on a few ancient authorities, especially Aristotle and Galen, limited where they could go. Many "natural philosophers," as medieval scientists were called, preferred refined logical analysis to systematic observations of the natural world. A number of historians have argued, however, that some of the natural philosophers developed ideas that came to fruition in the seventeenth century. These historians have pointed out, for example, that Galileo's development of the science of mechanics was grounded upon the work of fourteenth-century scholastics. And yet, as other scholars have noted, there was still a great contrast between the "the-

oretical" approach of the scholastics and the "practical" experiments of Galileo that enabled him to make his case.

The historical debate over the issue of late medieval influence on the Scientific Revolution reminds us that historians have had a difficult time explaining the causes of the Scientific Revolution. They have pointed out, however, that a number of changes and advances in the fifteenth and sixteenth centuries may have played a major role in helping natural philosophers abandon their old views and develop new ones.

While medieval scholars had made use of Aristotle, Galen, and Ptolemy in Latin translations to develop many of their positions in the fields of physics, medicine, and astronomy, it was the Renaissance humanists who mastered Greek as well as Latin and made available new works of Galen, Ptolemy, and Archimedes as well as Plato and the pre-Socratics. These writings made it apparent that even the unquestioned authorities of the Middle Ages, Aristotle and Galen, had been contradicted by other thinkers. The desire to discover which school of thought was correct stimulated new scientific work that sometimes led to a complete rejection of the classical authorities. We know that Copernicus, for example, founder of the heliocentric theory, had read in Plutarch (discovered by the Renaissance) that Philolaus and a number of other ancients had believed that it was the earth and not the sun that moved.

Renaissance artists have also been credited with making an impact on scientific study. Their desire to imitate nature led them to rely upon a close observation of nature. Their accurate renderings of rocks, plants, animals, and human anatomy established new standards for the study of natural phenomena. At the same time, the "scientific" study of the problems of perspective and correct anatomical proportions led to new insights. "No painter," one Renaissance artist declared, "can paint well without a thorough knowledge of geometry."[1] Renaissance artists were frequently called upon to be practicing mathematicians as well. Leonardo da Vinci devised "war machines" while Albrecht Dürer made designs for the fortifications of cities.

Although these artistic designs for technical innovations were done primarily on paper, mathematicians, military engineers, naval architects, and navigators were being asked to solve such practical problems as how to navigate in unknown seas, how to compute the trajectories of cannon balls for more effective impact, and how to calculate the tonnage of ships accurately. These technical problems served to stimulate scientific activity since all of them required careful observation and accurate measurements. The fifteenth and sixteenth centuries witnessed a proliferation of books dedicated to machines and technology, all of which espoused the belief that innovation in techniques was necessary. The relationship between technology and the Scientific Revolution, however, is not a simple one since many technological experts did not believe in abstract or academic learning. Indeed, many of the technical innovations of the Middle Ages and Renaissance were accomplished by people outside the universities, where the emphasis was on theoretical rather than practical knowledge. In any case, the invention of new instruments and machines, such as the telescope and microscope, often made new scientific discoveries possible. Above all, the printing press had an indirect, but crucial role in spreading innovative ideas quickly and easily.

Mathematics, which played such a fundamental role in the scientific achievements of the sixteenth and seventeenth centuries, was promoted in the Renaissance by the rediscovery of the works of ancient mathematicians and the influence of Plato (see Chapter 13), who had emphasized the importance of mathematics in explaining the universe. While mathematics was applauded as the key to navigation, military science, and geography, the Renaissance also held the widespread belief that mathematics was the key to understanding the nature of things. According to Leonardo da Vinci, since God eternally geometrizes, nature is inherently mathematical: "Proportion is not only found in numbers and measurements but also in sounds, weights, times, positions, and in whatsoever power there may."[2] Moreover, mathematical reasoning was seen as promoting a degree of certainty that was otherwise impossible. In the words of Leonardo da Vinci: "There is no certainty where one can neither apply any of the mathematical sciences nor any of those which are based upon the mathematical sciences."[3] Copernicus, Kepler, Galileo, and Newton were all great mathematicians who believed that the secrets of nature were written in the language of mathematics.

A final factor in the origins of the Scientific Revolution, the role of magic, has been the object of heated scholarly debate. Renaissance magic was the preserve of an intellectual elite from all of Europe (see the box on p. 565). By the end of the sixteenth century, Hermetic and cabalist magic had become fused with alchemical thought into a single intellectual framework. This tradition believed that the world was a living embodiment of divinity. Humans, who it was believed also had that spark of divinity within, could use magic, especially mathematical magic, to understand and dominate the world of nature or employ the powers of nature for beneficial purposes. Was it Hermeticism, then, that inaugurated the shift in consciousness that made the Scientific Revolution possible, since the desire to control and dominate the natural world was a crucial motivating force in the Scientific Revolution? One scholar has argued:

> It is a movement of the will which really originates an intellectual movement. A new centre of interest arises, surrounded by emotional excitement; the mind turns where the will has directed it and new attitudes, new discoveries follow. Behind the emergence of modern science there was a new direction of the will towards the world, its marvels, and mysterious workings, a new longing and determination to understand those workings and to operate with them.[4]

"This time," the author continues, "the return to the occult [Hermetic-cabalist tradition] stimulates the genuine science."[5] Histories of the Scientific Revolution frequently overlook the fact that the great names we associate with the revolution in cosmology—Copernicus, Kepler, Galileo, and Newton—all had a serious interest in Hermetic ideas and the fields of astrology and alchemy. The mention of these names also reminds us of one final consideration in the origins of the Scientific Revolution: it largely resulted from the work of a handful of great intellectuals.

▼ Toward a New Heaven: A Revolution in Astronomy

The greatest achievements in the Scientific Revolution of the sixteenth and seventeenth centuries came in those fields most dominated by the ideas of the Greeks—astronomy, mechanics, and medicine. The cosmological views of the Late Middle Ages had been built upon a synthesis of the ideas of Aristotle, Claudius Ptolemy (the greatest astronomer of antiquity who lived in the second century A.D.), and Christian theology. In the resulting

Magic and Science: The Case of Girolamo Cardano

▼ ▼ ▼

Girolamo Cardano or Jerome Cardan (1501–1576) was a very important figure in the history of mathematics. He also became a physician and professor of medicine at Pavia in 1547. Like many other intellectuals of the sixteenth century, Cardano was a pupil of magic and astrology. In this selection taken from his autobiography, The Book of My Life, Cardano discusses the presence in his life of what we would call paranormal powers, including prescient dreams, extrasensory perception, and intuitive flashes of direct understanding.

Girolamo Cardano, *The Book of My Life*

I am conscious that some influence from without seems to bring a murmuring sound to my ear from precisely that direction or region where some one is discussing me. If this discussion be fair, the sound seems to come to rest on the right side; or, if perchance it approaches from the left, it penetrates to the right and becomes a steady hum. If, however, the talk be contentious, strangely conflicting sounds are heard; when evil is spoken, the noise rests in the left ear, and comes from the quarter exactly whence the voices of my detractors are making disturbance, and, accordingly, may approach from any side of my head. . . . Very often when the discussion about me has taken place in the same city, it has happened that the vibration has scarcely ceased before a messenger has appeared who addresses me in the name of my detractors. But if the conversation has taken place in another state and the messenger should appear, one has but to compute the space of time which had

elapsed between the discussion and the beginning of the messenger's journey, and the moment I heard the voices and the time of the discussion itself will fall out the same. . . .

A few years later, eight perhaps, that is, about 1534, I began to see in my dreams the events shortly to come to pass. If these events were due to happen on the day following the dream, I used to have clear and defined visions of them just after sunrise, so that even on occasion I saw the motion for my admission to the College of Physicians straightway brought to vote, to a decision, and the motion lost. I dreamed, as well, that I was about to obtain my appointment to the professorship at Bologna. This manifestation by dreams ceased in the year just preceding the cessation of the former manifestation, that is, about 1567. . . . And so it had lasted about thirty-three years.

A third peculiarity is an intuitive flash of direct knowledge. This I employed with gradually increasing advantage. It originated about the year 1529; its effectiveness was increased but it could never be rendered infallible, except toward the close of 1573. For a period between the end of August of that year and the beginning of September 1574, and particularly, as it seems to me, now in this year 1575, I have considered it infallible. It is, moreover, a gift which has not deserted me, and it replaces the powers of those two latter faculties which did; it prepares me to meet my adversaries, and for any pressing necessity. Its component parts are an ingeniously exercised employment of the intuitive faculty, and an accompanying lucidity of understanding.

Ptolemaic or geocentric conception, the universe was seen as a series of concentric spheres with a fixed or motionless earth as its center. Composed of material substance, the earth was imperfect and constantly changing. The spheres that surrounded the earth were made of a crystalline, transparent substance and moved in circular orbits around the earth. Circular movement, according to Aristotle, was the most "perfect" kind of motion and hence appropriate for the "perfect" heavenly bodies thought to consist of a nonmaterial, incorruptible "quintessence." These heavenly bodies, pure orbs of light, were embedded in the moving, concentric spheres

and in 1500 numbered ten. Working outward from the earth, eight spheres contained the moon, Mercury, Venus, the sun, Mars, Jupiter, Saturn, and the fixed stars. The ninth sphere imparted to the eighth sphere of the fixed stars its diurnal motion while the tenth sphere was frequently described as the prime mover that moved itself and imparted motion to the other spheres. Beyond the tenth sphere was the Empyrean Heaven—the location of God and all the saved souls. This Christianized Ptolemaic universe, then, was a finite one. It had a fixed end in harmony with Christian thought and expectations.

This medieval, geocentric conception of the universe was one that accorded well with both Christianity and common sense at that time. God and the saved souls were at one end of the universe while humans were at the center. They had been given power over the earth, but their real purpose was to achieve salvation. To ordinary people, this conception of the universe also appeared sensible as they looked up at the night sky. The huge earth could easily be seen as motionless and surrounded by ethereal heavenly bodies circling around it.

This conception, however, did not satisfy professional astronomers who wished to ascertain exactly the paths of the heavenly bodies across the sky. Since observation did not always correspond to the accepted scheme, an elaborate system of devices was developed by astronomers who tried to "save the appearances." They hoped, for example, that epicycles, concentric spheres within spheres as carriers of the planetary bodies, would explain the paths of the planets more precisely while adhering to Aristotle's ideas of circular planetary movement.

Copernicus

Although Nicolaus Copernicus (1473–1543) received a doctorate in canon law and spent the last thirty years of his life as canon of a cathedral, mathematics and astronomy occupied most of his time. He had studied both subjects first at Cracow in his native Poland and later at the Italian universities of Bologna and Padua. Before he left Italy in 1506, he had become aware of ancient views that contradicted the Ptolemaic, earth-centered conception of the universe. Between 1506 and 1530, he completed the manuscript of his famous book, *On the Revolutions of the Heavenly Spheres,* but his own timidity and fear of ridicule from fellow astronomers kept

▼ **Medieval Conception of the Universe.** One of the areas most affected by the Scientific Revolution was astronomy, dominated in the Late Middle Ages by the ideas of Aristotle, Ptolemy, and Christian theology. As this illustration shows, the medieval cosmological view placed earth at the center of the universe, surrounded by a series of concentric spheres. The earth was imperfect and constantly changing while the heavenly bodies that surrounded it were perfect and incorruptible. Beyond the tenth and final sphere was heaven where God and all the saved souls were located.

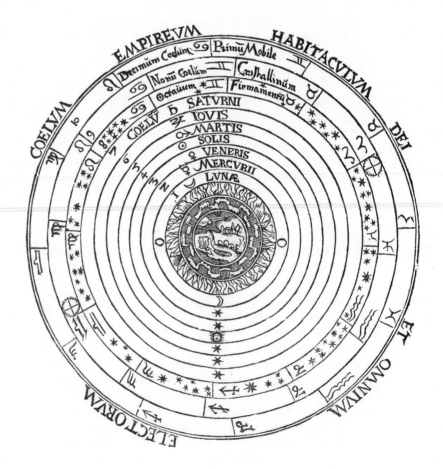

him from publishing it until May 1543, shortly before his death.

Copernicus was not an accomplished observational astronomer and relied for his data on the records of his predecessors. But he was a mathematician who felt that Ptolemy's geocentric system of epicycles, equants, and eccentrics was too complicated and failed to accord with the observed motions of the heavenly bodies (see the box on p. 568). Copernicus hoped that his heliocentric or sun-centered conception would offer a more accurate explanation.

Using elaborate astronomical and mathematical calculations, Copernicus argued that the universe consisted of eight spheres with the sun motionless at the center and the sphere of the fixed stars at rest in the eighth sphere. The planets revolved around the sun in the order of Mercury, Venus, the earth, Mars, Jupiter, and Saturn. The moon, however, revolved around the earth. More-over, according to Copernicus, what appeared to be the movement of the sun and the fixed stars around the earth was really explained by the daily rotation of the earth on its axis and the journey of the earth around the sun each year.

Copernicus, however, was basically conservative. He did not reject Aristotle's principle of the existence of heavenly spheres moving in circular orbits. As a result, when he put forth the calculations to prove his new theory, he retained Ptolemy's epicycles and wound up with a system barely less complicated than that of the Alexandrian astronomer.

Nevertheless, the shift from an earth-centered to a sun-centered system was significant and raised, despite Copernicus's own adherence to Aristotle, serious questions about Aristotle's astronomy and physics. It also seemed to create uncertainty about the human role in the universe as well as God's location. Protestant re-

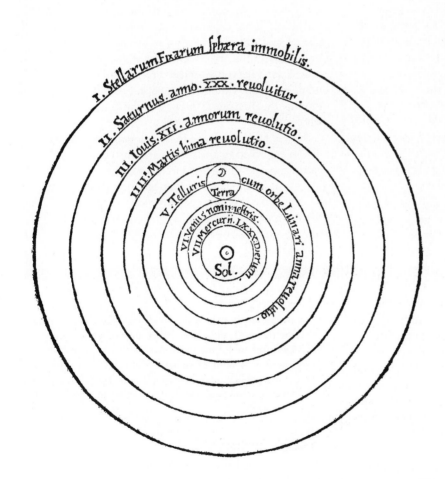

▼ **The Copernican System.** The Copernican system was presented in *On the Revolutions of the Heavenly Spheres*, published shortly before Copernicus's death. As shown in this illustration, Copernicus maintained that the sun was the center of the universe while the planets, including the earth, revolved around it. Moreover, the earth rotated daily on its axis. Copernicus's ideas were condemned by the Catholic church as well as various Protestant reformers.

On the Revolutions of the Heavenly Spheres

▼ ▼ ▼

Nicolaus Copernicus began a revolution in astronomy when he argued that it was the sun and not the earth that was at the center of the universe. Expecting controversy and scorn, Copernicus hesitated to publish the work in which he put forth his heliocentric theory. He finally relented, however, and managed to see a copy of it just before he died.

Nicolaus Copernicus, *On the Revolutions of the Heavenly Spheres*

For a long time, then, I reflected on this confusion in the astronomical traditions concerning the derivation of the motions of the universe's spheres. I began to be annoyed that the movements of the world machine, created for our sake by the best and most systematic Artisan of all, were not understood with greater certainty by the philosophers, who otherwise examined so precisely the most insignificant trifles of this world. For this reason I undertook the task of rereading the works of all the philosophers which I could obtain to learn whether anyone had ever proposed other motions of the universe's spheres than those expounded by the teachers of astronomy in the schools. And in fact first I found in Cicero that Hicetas supposed the earth to move. Later I also discovered in Plutarch that certain others were of this opinion. I have decided to set his words down here, so that they may be available to everybody:

> Some think that the earth remains at rest. But Philolaus the Pythagorean believes that, like the sun and moon, it revolves around the fire in an oblique circle. Heraclides of Pontus and Ecphantus the Pythagorean make the earth move, not in a progressive motion, but like a wheel in a rotation from the west to east about its own center.

Therefore, having obtained the opportunity from these sources, I too began to consider the mobility of the earth. And even though the idea seemed absurd, nevertheless I knew that others before me had been granted the freedom to imagine any circles whatever for the purpose of explaining the heavenly phenomena. Hence I thought that I too would be readily permitted to ascertain whether explanations sounder than those of my predecessors could be found for the revolution of the celestial spheres on the assumption of some motion of the earth.

Having thus assumed the motions which I ascribe to the earth later on in the volume, by long and intense study I finally found that if the motions of the other planets are correlated with the orbiting of the earth, and are computed for the revolution of each planet, not only do their phenomena follow therefrom but also the order and size of all the planets and spheres, and heaven itself is so linked together that in no portion of it can anything be shifted without disrupting the remaining parts and the universe as a whole. . . .

Hence I feel no shame in asserting that this whole region engirdled by the moon, and the center of the earth, traverse this grand circle amid the rest of the planets in an annual revolution around the sun. Near the sun is the center of the universe. Moreover, since the sun remains stationary, whatever appears as a motion of the sun is really due rather to the motion of the earth.

---

formers, adhering to a literal interpretation of Scripture, were the first to attack his ideas. Martin Luther thundered against "the new astrologer who wants to prove that the earth moves and goes round. . . . The fool wants to turn the whole art of astronomy upside down. As Holy Scripture tells us, so did Joshua bid the sun stand still and not the earth." Luther's cohort at Wittenberg, Philip Melanchthon condemned him as well:

> The eyes are witness that the heavens revolve in the space of twenty-four hours. But certain men, either from the love of novelty, or to make a display of ingenuity, have concluded that the earth moves, and they maintain that neither the eighth sphere [of the fixed stars] nor the sun revolves. . . . Now it is a want of honesty and decency to assert such notions publicly, and the example is pernicious. It is the part of a good mind to accept the truth as revealed by God and to acquiesce in it.[6]

The Catholic church remained silent for the time being; it was not until the work of Galileo appeared that Copernicus was denounced. The denunciation came at a time when an increasing number of astronomers were being attracted to Copernicus's ideas.

Brahe and Kepler

The immediate impact of Copernicus, however, was not momentous—no revolution occurred overnight. Nevertheless, although most people were not yet ready to accept the theory of Copernicus, there were growing doubts about the Ptolemaic system. The next step in destroying the geocentric conception and supporting the Copernican system was taken by Johannes Kepler. It has been argued, however, that Kepler's work would not have occurred without the material provided by Tycho Brahe.

While Tycho Brahe (1546–1601) advanced a new model of the solar system based on a compromise between Copernicus and Ptolemy—the sun and planets revolved around the earth while the other planets revolved around the sun—his real fame rests on a less spectacular contribution. A Danish nobleman, Brahe was granted possession of an island near Copenhagen by King Frederick II. Here Brahe built the elaborate Uraniborg castle, which he outfitted with a library, observatories, and instruments he had designed for more precise astronomical observations. For twenty years, Brahe patiently concentrated on building up a detailed record of his observations of the positions and movements of the stars and planets, a series of observations that have been described as the most accurate up to that time. This body of data led him to reject the Aristotelian-Ptolemaic system, but at the same time he was unable to accept Copernicus's suggestion that the earth actually moved. Brahe's last years were spent in Prague as imperial mathematician to Emperor Rudolf II, who took a keen interest in astronomy, astrology, and the entire Hermetic-cabalist tradition. It was in Prague that Brahe took on an assistant by the name of Johannes Kepler.

Johannes Kepler (1571–1630) had been destined by his parents for a career as a Lutheran minister. While studying theology at the university at Tübingen, however, he fell under the influence of Michael Mästlin, Germany's best-known astronomer, and spent much time pursuing his real interests, mathematics and astronomy. He abandoned theology and became a teacher of mathematics and astronomy at Graz in Austria.

Kepler's work illustrates well the narrow line that often separated magic and science in the early Scientific Revolution. An avid astrologer, Kepler possessed a keen interest in Hermetic thought and Neoplatonic mathematical magic. In a book written in 1596, he elaborated upon his theory that the universe was constructed on the basis of geometric figures, such as the pyramid and the cube (see the box on p. 570). Believing that the harmony of the human soul (a divine attribute) was mirrored in the numerical relationships existing between the planets, he focused much of his attention upon discovering the "music of the spheres." Kepler was also a brilliant mathematician and astronomer and, after Brahe's death, succeeded him as imperial mathematician to Rudolf II. There he gained possession of Brahe's detailed astronomical data and, using them, arrived at his three laws of planetary motion. These laws may have confirmed Kepler's interest in the "music of the spheres," but more importantly, they confirmed Copernicus's helio-

▼ **Johannes Kepler.** Abandoning theology in favor of mathematics and astrology, Kepler was a key figure in the rise of the new astronomy. Building upon Tycho Brahe's vast astronomical data, Kepler discovered the three laws of planetary motion that both confirmed and modified the Copernican theory. They also eliminated the Ptolemaic-Aristotelian ideas of uniform circular motion and crystalline spheres moving in circular orbits.

Kepler and the Emerging Scientific Community
▼ ▼ ▼

An important avenue for scientific communication involved the exchange of letters between intellectuals who sought to provide practical assistance to each other as well as encouragement in light of the negative reactions to their innovative work. After receiving a copy of Johannes Kepler's first major work, the Italian Galileo Galilei wrote to Kepler, inaugurating a correspondence between them. This selection contains samples of their letters to each other as well as Kepler's letter to his teacher at Tübingen.

Galileo to Kepler, Padua, August 4, 1597

Your book, highly learned gentleman, which you sent me through Paulus Amberger, reached me not days ago but only a few hours ago, and as this Paulus just informed me of his return to Germany, I should think myself indeed ungrateful if I should not express to you my thanks by this letter. I thank you especially for having deemed me worthy of such a proof of your friendship. . . . So far I have read only the introduction, but have learned from it in some measure your intentions and congratulate myself on the good fortune of having found such a man as a companion in the exploration of truth. For it is deplorable that there are so few who seek the truth and do not pursue a wrong method of philosophizing. But this is not the place to mourn about the misery of our century but to rejoice with you about such beautiful ideas proving the truth. . . . I would certainly dare to approach the public with my ways of thinking if there were more people of your mind. As this is not the case, I shall refrain from doing so. . . . I shall always be at your service. Farewell, and do not neglect to give me further good news of yourself.

Yours in sincere friendship,
Galilaeus Galilaeus
Mathematician at the Academy of Padua

Kepler to Michael Mästlin, Graz, September 1597

. . . Lately I have sent two copies of my little book to Italy. They were received with gladness by a mathematician named Galileo Galilei, as he signs himself. He has also been attached for many years to the Copernican heresy.

Kepler to Galileo, Graz, October 13, 1597

I received your letter of August 4 on September 1. It was a double pleasure to me. First because I became friends with you, the Italian, and second because of the agreement in which we find ourselves concerning Copernican cosmography. As you invite me kindly at the end of your letter to enter into correspondence with you, and I myself feel greatly tempted to do so, I will not let pass the occasion of sending you a letter with the present young nobleman. For I am sure, if your time has allowed it, you have meanwhile obtained a closer knowledge of my book. And so a great desire has taken hold of me, to learn your judgment. For this is my way, to urge all those to whom I have written to express their candid opinion. Believe me, the sharpest criticism of one single understanding man means much more to me than the thoughtless applause of the great masses.

I would, however, have wished that you who have such a keen insight into everything would choose another way to reach your practical aims. By the strength of your personal example you advise us, in a cleverly veiled manner, to go out of the way of general ignorance and warn us against exposing ourselves to the furious attacks of the scholarly crowd. (In this you are following the lead of Plato and Pythagoras, our true masters.) But after the beginning of a tremendous enterprise has been made in our time, and furthered by so many learned mathematicians, and after the statement that the earth moves can no longer be regarded as something new, would it not be better to pull the rolling wagon to its destination with united effort. . . . For it is not only you Italians who do not believe that they move unless they feel it, but we in Germany, too, in no way make ourselves popular with this idea. Yet there are ways in which we protect ourselves against these difficulties. . . . Be of good cheer, Galileo, and appear in public. If I am not mistaken there are only a few among the distinguished mathematicians of Europe who would dissociate themselves from us. So great is the power of truth. If Italy seems less suitable for your publication and if you have to expect difficulties there, perhaps Germany will offer us more freedom. But enough of this. Please let me know, at least privately if you do not want to do so publicly, what you have discovered in favor of Copernicus.

centric theory while modifying it in some ways. Above all, they drove another nail into the coffin of the Aristotelian-Ptolemaic system.

Kepler published his first two laws of planetary motion in 1609. Although at Tübingen he had accepted Copernicus's heliocentric ideas, in his first law he contradicted Copernicus by showing that the orbits of the planets around the sun were not circular but elliptical in shape with the sun at one focus of the ellipse rather than at the center. In his second law, he demonstrated that the speed of a planet is greater when it is closer to the sun and decreases as its distance from the sun increases. This proposition destroyed a fundamental Aristotelian tenet that Copernicus had shared—that the motion of the planets was steady and unchanging. Published ten years later, Kepler's third law established that the square of a planet's period of revolution is proportional to the cube of its average distance from the sun. In other words, planets with larger orbits revolve at a slower average velocity than those with smaller orbits.

Kepler's three laws effectively eliminated the idea of uniform circular motion as well as the idea of crystalline spheres revolving in circular orbits. The basic structure of the traditional Ptolemaic system had been destroyed, and people had been freed to think in new terms of the actual paths of planets revolving around the sun in elliptical orbits. By the end of Kepler's life, the Ptolemaic system was rapidly losing ground to the new ideas. Important questions remained unanswered, however: What were the planets made of? And how does one explain motion in the universe? It was an Italian scientist who achieved the next important breakthrough to a new cosmology by answering the first question and making important strides toward answering the second.

Galileo

Galileo Galilei (1564–1642) was the son of a lesser noble Pisan family. Knowing that his son was obviously gifted, his father encouraged him to study medicine, which at that time was a financially rewarding career. Before long Galileo abandoned medicine for his true love, mathematics, and was soon teaching this subject, first at Pisa and later at Padua, one of the most prestigious universities in Europe.

Galileo was the first European to make systematic observations of the heavens by means of a telescope, thereby inaugurating a new age in astronomy. He had heard of a Flemish lens grinder who had created a "spyglass" that magnified objects seen at a distance and soon constructed his own after reading about it. Instead of

▼ **Galileo's Sketch of the Phases of the Moon.** Galileo Galilei was the first European scientist to use the telescope in making systematic observations of the heavens. Galileo discovered mountains on the moon, sunspots, and the phases of Venus. Pictured here are drawings of the moon from Galileo's notes for one of his books. Galileo was a firm supporter of Copernicus's heliocentric theory, and his defense of this theory brought him into conflict with the Catholic church. Forced to recant his errors in 1633, Galileo spent the remaining eight years of his life in house arrest on his estate.

peering at terrestrial objects, Galileo turned his telescope to the skies and made a remarkable series of discoveries: mountains on the moon, four moons revolving around Jupiter, the phases of Venus, and sun spots. Galileo's observations seemed to destroy yet another aspect of the traditional cosmology in that the universe seemed to be composed of material substance similar to that of the earth rather than ethereal or perfect and unchanging substance.

The Starry Messenger

▼ ▼ ▼

T*he Italian Galileo Galilei was the first European to use a telescope to make systematic observations of the heavens. His observations, as reported in* The Starry Messenger *in 1610, stunned European intellectuals by revealing that the celestial bodies were not perfect and immutable, as had been believed, but were apparently composed of material substance similar to the earth. In this selection, Galileo describes how he devised a telescope and what he saw with it.*

Galileo Galilei, *The Starry Messenger*

About ten months ago a report reached my ears that a certain Fleming had constructed a spyglass by means of which visible objects, though very distant from the eye of the observer, were distinctly seen as if nearby. Of this truly remarkable effect several experiences were related, to which some persons gave credence while others denied them. A few days later the report was confirmed to me in a letter from a noble Frenchman at Paris, Jacques Badovere, which caused me to apply myself wholeheartedly to inquire into the means by which I might arrive at the invention of a similar instrument. This I did shortly afterwards, my basis being the theory of refraction. First I prepared a tube of lead, at the ends of which I fitted two glass lenses, both plane on one side while on the other side one was spherically convex and the other concave. Then placing my eye near the concave lens I perceived objects satisfactorily large and near, for they appeared three times closer and nine times larger than when seen with the naked eye alone. Next I constructed another one, more accurate, which represented objects as enlarged more than sixty times. Finally, sparing neither labor nor expense, I suc-

ceeded in constructing for myself so excellent an instrument that objects seen by means of it appeared nearly one thousand times larger and over thirty times closer than when regarded with our natural vision.

It would be superfluous to enumerate the number and importance of the advantages of such an instrument at sea as well as on land. But forsaking terrestrial observations, I turned to celestial ones, and first I saw the moon from as near at hand as if it were scarcely two terrestrial radii. After that I observed often with wondering delight both the planets and the fixed stars, and since I saw these latter to be very crowded, I began to seek (and eventually found) a method by which I might measure their distances apart. . . .

Now let us review the observations made during the past two months, once more inviting the attention of all who are eager for true philosophy to the first steps of such important contemplations. Let us speak first of that surface of the moon which faces us. For greater clarity I distinguish two parts of this surface, a lighter and a darker; the lighter part seems to surround and to pervade the whole hemisphere, while the darker part discolors the moon's surface like a kind of cloud, and makes it appear covered with spots. . . . From observation of these spots repeated many times I have been led to the opinion and conviction that the surface of the moon is not smooth, uniform, and precisely spherical as a great number of philosophers believe it (and the other heavenly bodies) to be, but is uneven, rough, and full of cavities and prominences, being not unlike the face of the earth, relieved by chains of mountains and deep valleys.

Galileo's revelations, published in the *The Starry Messenger* in 1610, stunned his contemporaries and probably did more to make Europeans aware of the new picture of the universe than the mathematical theories of Copernicus and Kepler (see the box above). The English ambassador in Venice wrote to the chief minister of King James I in 1610:

I send herewith unto His Majesty the strangest piece of news . . . that he has ever yet received from any part of the world; which is the annexed book of the Mathematical Professor at

Padua [Galileo], who by the help of an optical instrument . . . has discovered four new planets rolling about the sphere of Jupiter. . . . So upon the whole subject he has first overthrown all former astronomy. . . . By the next ship your Lordship shall receive from me one of the above instruments [a telescope], as it is bettered by this man.[7]

During a trip to Rome, Galileo was received by cardinals and scholars as a conquering hero. Grand Duke Cosimo II of Florence offered him a new position as his court mathematician, which Galileo readily accepted. But even in the midst of his newfound acclaim, Galileo found himself increasingly suspect by the authorities of the Catholic church.

In *The Starry Messenger*, Galileo had revealed himself as a firm proponent of Copernicus's heliocentric system. Encouraged by the Dominicans, who held strongly to Aristotelian ideas, and Cardinal Robert Bellarmine, head of the Jesuit College in Rome, who like other officials feared any dissension that would weaken Catholicism in its struggle with Protestantism, the Roman Inquisition (or Holy Office) of the Catholic church condemned Copernicanism and ordered Galileo to abandon the Copernican thesis. As one cardinal commented, "the intention of the Holy Spirit is to teach us not how the heavens go, but how to go to heaven." The report of the Inquisition ran: "That the doctrine that the sun was the center of the world and immovable was false and absurd, formally heretical and contrary to Scripture, whereas the doctrine that the earth was not the center of the world but moved, and has further a daily motion, was philosophically false and absurd and theologically at least erroneous."[8] Galileo was told, however, that he could continue to discuss Copernicanism as long as he maintained that it was not a fact but a mathematical supposition. It is apparent from the Inquisition's response that the church attacked the Copernican system because it threatened not only Scripture, but also an entire conception of the universe. The heavens were no longer a spiritual world, but a world of matter. Humans were no longer at the center and God was no longer in a specific place. The new system raised such uncertainties that it seemed prudent simply to condemn it.

Galileo, however, never really accepted his condemnation. In 1632, he published his most famous work, *Dialogue on the Two Chief World Systems: Ptolemaic and Copernican*. Unlike most scholarly treatises, it was written in Italian rather than Latin, making it more widely available to the public, which no doubt alarmed the church authorities. The work took the form of a dialogue between Simplicio, a congenial but somewhat stupid supporter of Aristotle and Ptolemy; Sagredo, an open-minded layman; and Salviati, a proponent of Copernicus's ideas. There is no question who wins the argument, and the *Dialogue* was quickly perceived as a defense of the Copernican system. Galileo was dragged once more before the Inquisition in 1633, found guilty of teaching the condemned Copernican system, and forced to recant his errors. Placed under house arrest on his estate near Florence, he spent the remaining eight years of his life studying mechanics, a field in which he made significant contributions.

One of the problems that fell under the heading of mechanics was the principle of motion. The Aristotelian

conception, which dominated the late medieval world, held that an object remained at rest unless a force was applied against it. If a force was constantly exerted, then the object moved at a constant rate, but if it was removed, then the object stopped. This created some difficulties, especially with a projectile thrown out of a cannon. Late medieval theorists had solved this problem by arguing that the rush of air behind it kept the projectile in motion. The Aristotelian principle of motion also raised problems in the new Copernican system. In the Ptolemaic system, the concentric spheres surrounding the earth were weightless, but in the Copernican system, if a constant force had to be applied to objects to cause movement, then what power or force kept the heavy earth and other planets in motion?

Galileo made two contributions to the problem of motion. First, he demonstrated by experiments that if a uniform force was applied to an object, it would move at an accelerated speed rather than a constant speed. Moreover, Galileo discovered the principle of inertia when he argued that a body in motion continues in motion forever unless deflected by an external force. Thus, a state of uniform motion is just as natural as a state of rest. Before Galileo, natural philosophers had tried to explain motion; now their task was to explain changes in motion. Historians agree that Galileo's work on inertia was important, but differ on whether his work was merely the culmination of the medieval tradition or pointed the way to Newton's law of dynamics.

The condemnation of Galileo by the Inquisition seriously hampered further scientific work in Italy, which had been at the forefront of scientific innovation. Leadership in science now passed to the northern countries, especially England, France, and the Dutch Netherlands. By the 1630s and 1640s, no reasonable astronomer could overlook that Galileo's discoveries combined with Kepler's mathematical laws had made nonsense of the Ptolemaic-Aristotelian world system and clearly established the reasonableness of the Copernican model. Despite Galileo's theories of dynamics, the problem of explaining motion in the universe and tying together the ideas of Copernicus, Galileo, and Kepler had not yet been done. This would be the work of an Englishman who has long been considered the greatest genius of the Scientific Revolution.

Newton

Born in the little English village of Woolsthorpe in 1642, the young Isaac Newton showed little brilliance until he attended Cambridge University and fell under the influence of the mathematician Isaac Barrow. New-

Newton's Rules of Reasoning

▼ ▼ ▼

In 1687, Isaac Newton published his masterpiece, the Mathematical Principles of Natural Philosophy. In this work, Newton demonstrated the mathematical proofs for his universal law of gravitation and completed the new cosmology begun by Copernicus, Kepler, and Galileo. Newton's work demonstrated that the universe was one huge, regulated, and uniform machine operating according to natural laws. He also described the rules of reasoning by which he arrived at his universal law.

Isaac Newton, Rules of Reasoning in Philosophy

Rule 1

We are to admit no more causes of natural things than such as are both true and sufficient to explain their appearances.

To this purpose the philosophers say that Nature does nothing in vain, and more is in vain when less will serve; for Nature is pleased with simplicity, and affects not the pomp of superfluous causes.

Rule 2

Therefore to the same natural effects we must, as far as possible, assign the same causes.

As to respiration in a man and in a beast; the descent of stones in Europe and in America; the light of our culinary fire and of the sun; the reflection of light in the earth, and in the planets.

Rule 3

The qualities of bodies, which admit neither intensification nor remission of degrees, and which are found to belong to all bodies within the reach of our experiments, are to be esteemed the universal qualities of all bodies whatsoever.

For since qualities of bodies are only known to us by experiments, we are to hold for universal all such as universally agree with experiments; and such as are not liable to diminution can never be quite taken away.

Rule 4

In experimental philosophy we are to look upon propositions inferred by general induction from phenomena as accurately or very nearly true, notwithstanding any contrary hypotheses that may be imagined, till such time as other phenomena occur, by which they may either be made more accurate, or liable to exceptions.

This rule we must follow, that the argument of induction may not be evaded by hypotheses.

---

ton experienced his first great burst of creative energy in 1666 when the fear of plague closed Cambridge and forced him to return to Woolsthorpe for eighteen months. There Newton discovered his creative talents: "In those days I was in the prime of my life for invention and minded mathematics and philosophy more than at any time since."[9] During this period he invented the calculus, a mathematical means of calculating rates of change, began his investigations into the composition of light, and inaugurated his work on the law of universal gravitation. Two years after his return to Cambridge, in 1669, he accepted a chair of mathematics at the university. During a second intense period of creativity from 1684 to 1686, he wrote his famous *Principia* (see the box above). After a nervous breakdown in 1693, he sought and received an administrative post as warden of the royal mint and was advanced to master of the mint by 1699, a post he held until his death in 1727. Made president of the Royal Society (see The Scientific Societies later in the chapter) in 1703 and knighted in 1705

for his great achievements, Sir Isaac Newton wound up the only English scientist to be buried in Westminster Abbey.

Although Isaac Newton occupies a very special place in the history of modern science, we need to remember that he, too, remained extremely interested in aspects of the occult world. He left behind hundreds of manuscript pages of his studies of alchemy, and, in fact, his alchemical experiments were a major feature of his life until he moved to London in 1696 to become warden of the royal mint. The British economist John Maynard Keynes said of Newton after examining his manuscripts in 1936:

Newton was not the first of the age of reason. He was the last of the magicians. . . . He looked on the whole universe and all that is in it as a riddle, as a secret which could be read by applying pure thought to certain evidence, certain mystic clues which God had laid about the world to allow a sort of philosopher's treasure hunt to the esoteric brotherhood. He believed that these clues were to be found partly in the evidence of the heavens and in the constitution of elements, . . . but also partly in certain papers and traditions handed down by the brethren in an unknown chain back to the original cryptic revelation in Babylonia.[10]

Although Newton may have considered himself a representative of the Hermetic tradition, he chose, it has been recently argued, for both political and psychological reasons to repress that part of his being, and it is as the "symbol of Western science" that Newton came to be viewed.

Newton's major work, the "hinge point of modern scientific thought," was the *Mathematical Principles of Natural Philosophy*, known simply as the *Principia* by the first word of its Latin title. In this work, the last, highly influential book in Europe to be written in Latin, Newton spelled out the mathematical proofs demonstrating his universal law of gravitation. Newton's work was the culmination of the theories of Copernicus, Kepler, and Galileo. While each had undermined some part of the Ptolemaic-Aristotelian cosmology, no one until Newton had pieced together a coherent synthesis for a new cosmology.

In the first book of the *Principia*, Newton defined the basis concepts of mechanics by elaborating the three laws of motion: the law of inertia that every object continues in a state of rest or uniform motion in a straight line unless deflected by a force; the rate of change of motion of an object is proportional to the force acting upon it; and to every action there is always an equal and opposite reaction. In Book Three, Newton applied his theories of mechanics to the problems of astronomy by demonstrating that these three laws of motion govern the planetary bodies as well as terrestrial objects. Integral to his whole argument was the universal law of gravitation to explain why the planetary bodies did not go off in straight lines but continued in elliptical orbits about the sun. In mathematical terms, Newton explained that every object in the universe was attracted to every other object with a force (that is, gravity) that is directly proportional to the product of their masses and inversely proportional to the square of the distances between them.

The implications of Newton's universal law of gravitation were enormous, even if it took another century before they were widely recognized. Newton had demonstrated that one universal law mathematically proved could explain all motion in the universe. The secrets of the natural world could be known by human investigations. At the same time, the Newtonian synthesis created a new cosmology in which the world was seen

largely in mechanistic terms. The universe was one huge, regulated, and uniform machine that operated according to natural laws in absolute time, space, and motion. Although Newton believed that God was "everywhere present" and acted as the force that moved all bodies on the basis of the laws he had discovered, later generations dropped his spiritual assumptions. Newton's world-machine, conceived as operating absolutely in space, time, and motion, dominated the western worldview until the twentieth century, when the Einsteinian revolution based on a concept of relativity superseded the Newtonian mechanistic concept.

Newton's ideas were soon accepted in England, possibly out of national pride, conviction, and, as has been argued recently, for political reasons (see Science and Society later in the chapter). Natural philosophers on the continent resisted Newton's ideas, and it took much

▼ **Isaac Newton.** Pictured here is a portrait of Isaac Newton by Sir Godfrey Kneller. With a single law, that of universal gravitation, Newton was able to explain all motion in the universe. His great synthesis of the work of his predecessors created a new picture of the universe, one in which the universe was viewed as a great machine operating according to natural laws. Despite his reputation as an eminent scientist, Newton also maintained a keen interest in alchemy.

of the eighteenth century before they were generally accepted everywhere in Europe. They were also reinforced by developments in other fields, especially medicine.

▼ The Breakthrough in Medicine

Although the Scientific Revolution of the sixteenth and seventeenth centuries is associated primarily with the dramatic changes in astronomy and mechanics that precipitated a new perception of the universe, a third field that had been dominated by Greek thought in the Late Middle Ages, that of medicine, also experienced a transformation. Late medieval medicine was dominated not by the teachings of Aristotle, but by those of the Greek physician Galen who had lived in the second century A.D.

Galen's impact on the medieval medical world was pervasive in anatomy, physiology, and disease. Galen had relied on animal, rather than human dissection to arrive at a picture of human anatomy that was quite inaccurate in many instances. Even when Europeans began to practice human dissection in the Late Middle Ages, instruction in anatomy still relied on Galen. While a professor read a text of Galen, an assistant dissected a cadaver for illustrative purposes. Physiology or the functioning of the body was also dominated by Galenic hypotheses, including the belief that there were two separate blood systems. One controlled muscular activities and contained bright red blood moving upward and downward through the arteries; the other governed the digestive functions and contained dark red blood that ebbed and flowed in the veins.

Treatment of disease was highly influenced by Galen's doctrine of four bodily humors: blood, considered warm and moist; yellow bile, warm and dry; phlegm, cold and moist; and black bile, cold and dry. Since disease was supposedly the result of an imbalance of humors that could be discerned from the quantity and color of urine, the examination of a patient's urine became the chief diagnostic tool. Although purging and bleeding to remedy the imbalance were often harmful to patients, the use of traditional herbal medicines frequently proved beneficial.

Three figures are associated with the changes in medicine in the sixteenth and seventeenth centuries: Paracelsus, Andreas Vesalius, and William Harvey. Philippus Aureolus von Hohenheim (1493–1541), who renamed himself Paracelsus (or greater than Celsus, the ancient physician), was born in a small town near Zürich, the son of a country physician who dabbled in astrology. After leaving home at the age of fourteen, Paracelsus traveled widely and may have been awarded a medical degree from the University of Ferrara. He achieved a moment of glory when he was appointed city physician and professor of medicine at Basel in 1527. But this, like so many other appointments, proved short-lived due to his vanity, cantankerous nature, and quick temper. He could never disguise his contempt for universities and physicians who did not agree with his new ideas:

> I am *monarcha medicorum*, monarch of physicians, and I can prove to you what you cannot prove. . . . It was not the constellations that made me a physician: God made me . . . I need not don a coat of mail or a buckler against you, for you are not learned or experienced enough to refute even one word of mine. I wish I could protect my bald head against the flies as effectively as I can defend my monarchy. . . . Let me tell you this: every little hair on my neck knows more than you and all your scribes, and my shoebuckles are more learned than your Galen and Avicenna, and my beard has more experience than all your high colleges.[11]

It was not easy to get along with Paracelsus, and he was forced to wander from one town to another until his death in 1541.

Paracelsus rejected the work of both Aristotle and Galen and attacked the universities as centers of their moribund philosophy. He and his followers hoped to replace the traditional system with a new Christian chemical philosophy that was derived from Neoplatonic, Hermetic, and alchemical foundations and was based upon a new understanding of nature derived from fresh observation and experiment. This chemical philosophy was, in turn, closely connected to a vitalistic universe based on the macrocosm-microcosm analogy. According to this system, a human being was a small replica of the larger world about him. All parts of the universe were represented within each person. As Paracelsus said: "For the sun and the moon and all planets, as well as the stars and the whole chaos, are in man. . . . For what is outside is also inside; and what is not outside man is not inside. The outer and the inner are one thing."[12]

The chemical philosophy of Paracelsus began with his belief that creation had been a "divine chemical separation" in which the four Aristotelian elements—earth, water, air, and fire—were constituted, together with a new triad of elements or "principles," sulfur, mercury, and salt. In accordance with the macrocosmic-microcosmic principle, he believed that the chemical reactions of the universe as a whole were reproduced in human beings on a smaller scale. Disease, then, was not caused by the Galenic imbalance of the four humors, but was due to chemical influences that were localized in specific organs and treated by chemical remedies. Having rejected the humoral theory of Galenic medicine, Paracelsus also rejected the traditional Galenic remedies prepared from herbs. He has since been viewed as the founder of modern chemical medicine.

Although others had used chemical remedies, Paracelsus and his followers differed from them in their careful attention to the proper dosage of their chemically prepared metals and minerals. Gauging the proper amount was especially important in view of the fact that Paracelsus had turned against the Galenic principle that "contraries cure" in favor of the ancient Germanic folk principle that "like cures like." The poison that caused a disease would be its cure if used in proper form and quantity. This use of toxic substances to cure patients was, despite its apparent effectiveness (Paracelsus did have a strong reputation for actually curing his patients), viewed by his opponents as the practice of a "homicide Physician." Later generations came to view Paracelsus more favorably, and historians who have stressed Paracelsus's concept of disease and recognition of "new drugs" for medicine have viewed him as a father of modern medicine. Others have argued that his macrocosmic-microcosmic philosophy and use of "like cures like" drugs make him the forerunner of both homeopathy and the holistic medicine of the postmodern era.

Historians usually associate the name of Paracelsus with the diagnosis and treatment of disease. The new anatomy of the sixteenth century, however, was the work of Andreas Vesalius (1514–1564). His study of medicine at Paris involved him in the works of Galen, the great ancient authority. Especially important to him was a recently discovered text of Galen, *On Anatomical Procedures*, that led Vesalius to emphasize practical research as the principal avenue for understanding human anatomy. After receiving a doctorate in medicine at the University of Padua in 1536, he accepted a position there as professor of surgery. In 1543, he published his masterpiece, *On the Fabric of the Human Body*.

This book was based on his Paduan lectures, in which he deviated from traditional practice by personally dissecting a body to illustrate what he was discussing. Vesalius's anatomical treatise presented a careful examination of the individual organs and general structure of the human body. The book would not have been feasible without either the artistic advances of the Renaissance or technical developments in the art of printing. Together, they made possible the creation of illustrations superior to any hitherto produced.

▼ **Paracelsus.** An extremely arrogant man, Paracelsus was one of the chief figures in the revision of late medieval medicine, which had been dominated by the ideas of the Greek physician Galen. Paracelsus embraced a chemical philosophy in which disease, viewed as the result of chemical influences, could be treated by chemical remedies.

Vesalius's "hands-on" approach to teaching anatomy enabled him to overthrow some of Galen's most glaring errors. He did not hesitate, for example, to correct Galen's assertion that the great blood vessels originated from the liver since his own observations made it apparent that they came from the heart. Nevertheless, Vesalius still clung to a number of Galen's erroneous assertions, including the Greek physician's ideas on the ebb and flow of two kinds of blood in the veins and arteries. It was not until William Harvey's work on the circulation of the blood that this Galenic misperception was corrected.

William Harvey (1578–1657) attended Cambridge University and later Padua where he received a doctorate of medicine in 1602. Appointed physician to St. Bartholomew's Hospital in 1609, he later became physician to King James I and Charles I. His reputation, however, rests upon his book, *On the Motion of the Heart and Blood,* published in 1628.

Although questions had been raised in the sixteenth century about Galen's physiological principles, no major break from his system had occurred. Harvey's work, which was based upon meticulous observations and experiments, led him to demolish the ancient Greek's work. Harvey demonstrated that the heart and not the liver was the beginning point of the circulation of blood in the body, that the same blood flows in both veins and arteries, and, most importantly, that the blood makes a complete circuit as it passes through the body. Although Harvey's work dealt a severe blow to Galen's theories, his ideas did not begin to achieve general recognition until the 1660s, when the capillaries, which explained the passing of the body's blood from the arteries to the veins, were discovered. Harvey's theory of the circulation of the blood laid the foundation for modern physiology.

▼ Women in the Origins of Modern Science

During the Middle Ages, except for members of religious orders, women who sought a life of learning were severely hampered by the traditional attitude that a woman's proper role was as a daughter, wife, and mother. But in the late fourteenth and early fifteenth centuries, new opportunities for elite women emerged as enthusiasm for the new secular learning called humanism encouraged Europe's privileged and learned men to encourage women to read and study classical and Christian

texts. The daughters and sisters of prominent Christian humanists, for example, were known for their learning. In northern Italy, a number of educated families allowed their young women to pursue a life of scholarship. The ideal of a humanist education for some of the daughters of Europe's elite persisted into the seventeenth century, but only for some privileged women.

In the same fashion as they were drawn to humanism, women were also attracted to the Scientific Revolution. Unlike females educated formally in humanist schools, women attracted to science had to obtain a largely informal education. Female contributions to science were even more remarkable when we consider that women

▼ **Vesalius Dissecting a Corpse.** The revision of Galenic anatomy was done in part by Andreas Vesalius, shown here dissecting a corpse. In his lectures on human anatomy, he often dissected a human cadaver to illustrate his point. While correcting many of Galen's faulty conclusions, Vesalius still upheld some of the Greek's mistaken observations, such as the ebb and flow of the two kinds of blood.

were largely excluded from universities and the new scientific societies. This was not quite the handicap that it would be today, however. Since science in the seventeenth century was not the preserve of universities, there was often no real dividing line between popular science and professional science, creating chances for women to enter scientific circles. Aristocratic and princely courts as well as artisan workshops presented two such major opportunities for women.

European nobles had the leisure and resources that gave them easy access to the world of learning. This door was also open to noblewomen who could participate in the informal scientific networks of their fathers and brothers. One of the most prominent female scientists of the seventeenth century, Margaret Cavendish (1623–1673), came from an aristocratic background. Cavendish was not a popularizer of science for women but a participant in the crucial scientific debates of her time. She also corresponded with important people on these issues. Despite her achievements, however, she was excluded from membership in the Royal Society (see The Scientific Societies later in the chapter), although she was once allowed to attend a meeting. She wrote a number of works on scientific matters including *Observations upon Experimental Philosophy* and *Grounds of Natural Philosophy*. In these works she did not hesitate to attack what she considered the defects of the rationalist and empiricist approaches to scientific knowledge and was especially critical of the growing belief that humans through science were the masters of nature: "We have no power at all over natural causes and effects. . . . for man is but a small part, . . . his powers are but particular actions of Nature, and he cannot have a supreme and absolute power."[13]

As an aristocrat, the duchess of Cavendish was a good example of the women in France and England who worked in science. Women interested in science who lived in Germany came from a different background. There the tradition of female participation in craft production enabled some women to become involved in observational science, especially entomology and astronomy. Between 1650 and 1710, women constituted 14 percent of all German astronomers.

A good example of female involvement in the Scientific Revolution stemming from the craft tradition was Maria Sibylla Merian (1647–1717), who had established a reputation as an important entomologist by the beginning of the eighteenth century. Merian's training came from working in her father's workshop where she learned the art of illustration, a training of great importance since her exact observation of insects and plants was only demonstrated through the superb illustrations she made. Her first work was the *Wonderful Metamorphosis and Special Nourishment of Caterpillars*, an illustrated study of caterpillars showing every stage in their development, which she had carefully observed and rendered in her drawings. In 1699, she undertook an expedition into the wilds of the Dutch colony of Surinam to collect and draw samples of plants and insect life. This led to her major scientific work, the *Metamorphosis of the Insects of Surinam*, in which she used sixty illustrations to show the reproductive and developmental cycles of Surinam's insect life.

The craft organization of astronomy also gave women opportunities to become involved in science. Those who did worked in family observatories; hence daughters and wives received training as apprentices to fathers or husbands. The most famous of the female astronomers in Germany was Maria Winkelmann (1670–1720). She was educated by her father and uncle and received advanced training in astronomy from a nearby self-taught astronomer. Her opportunity to be a practicing astronomer came when she married Gottfried Kirch, Germany's foremost astronomer. She became his assistant at the astronomical observatory operated in Berlin by the Academy of Science. She made some original contributions, including a hitherto undiscovered comet as her husband related:

> Early in the morning (about 2:00 A.M.) the sky was clear and starry. Some nights before, I had observed a variable star, and my wife (as I slept) wanted to find and see it for herself. In so doing, she found a comet in the sky. At which time she woke me, and I found that it was indeed a comet . . . I was surprised that I had not seen it the night before.[14]

Moreover, Winkelmann corresponded with the famous scientist Leibniz (who invented the calculus independently of Newton), who was effusive in his praise of her as "a most learned woman who could pass as a rarity." When her husband died in 1710, she submitted herself as a candidate for a position as assistant astronomer for which she was highly qualified. As a woman—with no university degree—she was denied the post by the Berlin Academy, which feared that it would establish a precedent by hiring a woman ("mouths would gape"). Winkelmann managed, nevertheless, to continue her astronomical work a while longer at the private observatory of Baron Friederich von Krosigk in Berlin.

Winkelmann's difficulties with the Berlin Academy reflect the obstacles women faced in being accepted in scientific work, which was considered a male preserve.

Although there were no formal statutes excluding women from membership in the new scientific societies, no woman was invited to join either the Royal Society of England or the French Academy of Sciences until the twentieth century. All of these women scientists were exceptional women since a life devoted to any kind of scholarship was still viewed as being at odds with the domestic duties women were expected to perform.

The nature and value of women had been the subject of an ongoing, centuries-long debate known as the *querelles des femmes*—arguments about women. Male opinions in the debate were largely a carryover from medieval times and were not favorable. Women were portrayed as inherently base, prone to vice, easily swayed, and "sexually insatiable." Hence, men needed to control them. Learned women were viewed as having overcome female liabilities to become like men. One man in praise of a woman scholar remarked that her writings were so good that you "would hardly believe they were done by a woman at all."

In the early modern era, women joined this debate by arguing against the distorted images of women held by men. They argued that women also had rational minds and could grow from education. Further, since most women were pious, chaste, and temperate, there was no need for male authority over them. These female defenders of women in the *querelles des femmes* emphasized education as the key to women's ability to move into the world. How, then, did the era of the Scientific Revolution affect this debate over the nature of women? As an era of intellectual revolution in which traditional authorities were being overthrown, we might expect significant change in men's views of women. But by and large, instead of becoming an instrument for liberation, science was used to find new support for the old, traditional views about a woman's place in the scheme of things. This was done in a variety of ways.

One approach is evident in the work of William Harvey who was renowned for his work on the circulation of the blood. In his 1651 book on human reproduction, he argued that a woman provided "matter" but it was the man who gave it life and form from his semen. Harvey regarded semen as the active agent, and in his view it was so powerful that it was "vivifying, endowed with force and spirit and generative influence." By the end of the century, however, some scientists were arguing that males and females influenced the generative process equally. Likewise, new views on anatomy also appeared, but interestingly enough were used to perpetuate old stereotypes about women.

From the work of Galen until late in the sixteenth century, the male and female genitals had been portrayed as not significantly different. The uterus, for example, had been pictured as an internal and inadequate penis. According to Galen, "All parts that men have, women have too . . . the difference between them lies in only one thing . . . that in women the parts are within the body, whereas in men they are outside."[15] But this perspective was radically reevaluated in the seventeenth century, and the uterus was now presented as a perfect instrument for childbearing. It was not long before this view was used to reinforce the traditional argument that women were designed for their role as bearer of their husband's children.

An important project in the new anatomy of the sixteenth centuries was the attempt to illustrate the human body and skeleton. For Vesalius, the portrayal of physical differences between males and females was limited to external bodily form (the outlines of the body) and the sexual organs. Vesalius saw no difference in skeletons and portrayed them as the same for men and women. It was not until the eighteenth century, in fact, that a new anatomy finally prevailed. Drawings of female skeletons between 1730 and 1790 varied, but females tended to have a larger pelvic area, and, in some instances, female skulls were portrayed as smaller than those of males. Eighteenth-century studies on the anatomy and physiology of sexual differences provided "scientific evidence" to reaffirm the traditional inferiority of women. The larger pelvic area "proved" that women were meant to be childbearers while the larger skull "demonstrated" the superiority of the male mind. Male-dominated science had been used to "prove" male social dominance.

At the same time, during the seventeenth and eighteenth centuries, women even lost the traditional spheres of influence they had possessed, especially in the science-related art of midwifery. Women serving as midwives had traditionally been responsible for birthing. Similar to barber-surgeons or apothecaries (see Chapter 18), midwives had acquired their skills through apprenticeship. But the impact of the Scientific Revolution caused traditional crafts to be upgraded and then even professionalized as males took over. When medical men entered this arena, they also began to use devices and techniques derived from the study of anatomy. These were increasingly used to justify the male takeover of the traditional role of midwives. By the end of the eighteenth century, midwives were simply accessories to the art they had once controlled, except for the poor. Since little money was to be made in serving them, midwives were allowed to continue to practice their traditional art for the lower classes.

Overall the Scientific Revolution reaffirmed traditional ideas about women's nature. Male scientists used

The "Natural" Inferiority of Women
▼ ▼ ▼

Despite the shattering of old views and the emergence of a new worldview in the Scientific Revolution of the seventeenth century, attitudes toward women remained tied to traditional perspectives. In this selection, the philosopher Benedict de Spinoza argues for the "natural" inferiority of women to men.

Benedict de Spinoza, *A Political Treatise*

But, perhaps, someone will ask, whether women are under men's authority by nature or institution? For if it has been by mere institution, then we had no reason compelling us to exclude women from government. But if we consult experience itself, we shall find that the origin of it is in their weakness. For there has never been a case of men and women reigning together, but wherever on the earth men are found, there we see that men rule, and women are ruled, and that on this plan, both sexes live in harmony. But on the other hand, the Amazons, who are reported to have held rule of old, did not suffer men to stop in their country, but reared only their female children, killing the males to whom they gave birth. But if by nature women were equal to men, and were equally distinguished by force of character and ability, in which human power and therefore human right chiefly consist; surely among nations so many and different some would be found, where both sexes rule alike, and others, where men are ruled by women, and so brought up, that they can make less use of their abilities. And since this is nowhere the case, one may assert with perfect propriety, that women have not by nature equal right with men: but that they necessarily give way to men, and that thus it cannot happen, that both sexes should rule alike, much less that men should be ruled by women. But if we further reflect upon human passions, how men, in fact, generally love women merely from the passion of lust, and esteem their cleverness and wisdom in proportion to the excellence of their beauty, and also how very ill-disposed men are to suffer the women they love to show any sort of favour to others, and other facts of this kind, we shall easily see that men and women cannot rule alike without great hurt to peace.

---

the new science to spread the view that women were inferior by nature, subordinate to men, and suited by nature to play a domestic role as nurturing mothers. The widespread distribution of books ensured the continuation of these ideas (see the box above). Jean de La Bruyère, the seventeenth-century French moralist, was typical when he remarked that an educated woman was like a gun that was a collector's item "which one shows to the curious, but which has no use at all, any more than a carousel horse."[16]

▼ Toward a New Earth: Descartes, Rationalism, and a New View of Humankind

The fundamentally new conception of the universe contained in the cosmological revolution of the sixteenth and seventeenth centuries inevitably had an impact on the Western view of humankind. Nowhere is this more evident than in the work of René Descartes (1596–1650), an extremely important figure in Western history. Descartes began by reflecting the doubt and uncertainty that seemed pervasive in the confusion of the seventeenth century and ended with a philosophy that dominated Western thought until the twentieth century.

René Descartes was born into a family of the French lower nobility. After a Jesuit education, he studied law at Poitiers but traveled to Paris to study by himself. As far as can be deduced, he spent much of this period absorbed in the skeptical works of Montaigne. Descartes volunteered for service in 1618 in the army of Maurice of Nassau at the beginning of the Thirty Years' War, but his motives seem to have been guided less by the desire for military action than for travel and leisure time to think. On the night of November 10, 1619, Descartes underwent what one historian has called an experience comparable to the "ecstatic illumination of the mystic." Having perceived in one night the outlines of a new rational-mathematical system, with a sense of divine approval he made a new commitment to mind, mathematics, and a mechanical universe. For the rest of his life, Descartes worked out the details of his vision.

The starting point for Descartes's new system was doubt, as he explained at the beginning of his most famous work, *Discourse on Method,* written in 1637:

▼ **Descartes.** René Descartes was one of the primary figures in the Scientific Revolution. Claiming to use reason as his sole guide to truth, Descartes posited a sharp distinction between mind and matter. The world of matter could be known by the mind, Descartes argued, since the universe was simply a great machine created by God and governed by physical laws.

> From my childhood I have been familiar with letters; and as I was given to believe that by their means a clear and assured knowledge can be acquired of all that is useful in life, I was extremely eager for instruction in them. As soon, however, as I had completed the course of study, at the close of which it is customary to be admitted into the order of the learned, I entirely changed my opinion. For I found myself entangled in so many doubts and errors that, as it seemed to me, the endeavor to instruct myself had served only to disclose to me more and more of my ignorance.[17]

Descartes decided to set aside all that he had learned and begin again. Having rejected the senses, since they easily deceived, one fact seemed to Descartes beyond doubt—his own existence:

> But I immediately became aware that while I was thus disposed to think that all was false, it was absolutely necessary

that I who thus thought should be something; and noting that this truth *I think, therefore I am*, was so steadfast and so assured that the suppositions of the skeptics, to whatever extreme they might all be carried, could not avail to shake it, I concluded that I might without scruple accept it as being the first principle of the philosophy I was seeking.[18]

With this emphasis on the mind, Descartes asserted that he would accept only those things that his reason said were true.

From his first postulate, Descartes deduced two additional principles, the existence of God and the separation of mind and matter. Since he—an imperfect being—had conceived of the idea of perfection, it could only have come from a perfect being, i.e., God:

> And since it is no less contradictory that the more perfect should result from, and depend on, the less perfect than that something should proceed from nothing, it is equally impossible I should receive it from myself. Thus we are committed to the conclusion that it has been placed in me by a nature which is veritably more perfect than I am, and which has indeed within itself all the perfections of which I have any idea, that is to say, in a single word, that is God.[19]

Secondly, Descartes argued that since "the mind cannot be doubted but the body and material world can, the two must be radically different." From this came an absolute dualism between mind and body, or what has also been called Cartesian dualism.

According to Descartes, the universe contains two things, both of which God has created. One is thinking substance, what we call the mind. It is essentially spiritual and not composed of matter. Everything in the universe except the thinking substance or mind is extended substance, what we call matter. The material world is the most fundamental thing in the universe and displays two primary characteristics: extension (it occupies space) and motion (it moves). Using mind or human reason, the path to certain knowledge, and its best instrument, mathematics, humans can understand the material world because it is pure mechanism, a machine that is governed by its own physical laws because it was created by God—the great geometrician.

Descartes's conclusions about the nature of the universe and human beings had important implications. His separation of mind and matter allowed scientists to view matter as dead or inert, as something that was totally separate from themselves and could be investigated independently by reason. The split between mind and body led Westerners to equate their identity with mind and reason rather than with the whole organism. Descartes has rightly been called the father of modern ra-

The Father of Modern Rationalism

▼ ▼ ▼

René Descartes has long been viewed as the founder of modern rationalism and modern philosophy because he believed that human beings could understand the world—itself a mechanical system—by the same rational principles inherent in mathematical thinking. In his Discourse on Method, he elaborated upon his approach to discovering truth.

René Descartes, *Discourse on Method*

In place of the numerous precepts which have gone to constitute logic, I came to believe that the four following rules would be found sufficient, always provided I took the firm and unswerving resolve never in a single instance to fail in observing them.

The first was to accept nothing as true which I did not evidently know to be such, that is to say, scrupulously to avoid precipitance and prejudice, and in the judgments I passed to include nothing additional to what had presented itself to my mind so clearly and so distinctly that I could have no occasion for doubting it.

The second, to divide each of the difficulties I examined into as many parts as may be required for its adequate solution.

The third, to arrange my thoughts in order, beginning with things the simplest and easiest to know, so that I may then ascend little by little, as it were step by step, to the knowledge of the more complex, and in doing so, to assign an order of thought even to those objects which are not of themselves in any such order of precedence.

And the last, in all cases to make enumerations so complete, and reviews so general, that I should be assured of omitting nothing.

Those long chains of reasonings, each step simple and easy, which geometers are wont to employ in arriving even at the most difficult of their demonstrations, have led me to surmise that all the things we human beings are competent to know are interconnected in the same manner, and that none are so remote as to be beyond our reach or so hidden that we cannot discover them—that is, provided we abstain from accepting as true what is not thus related, i.e., keep always to the order required for their deduction one from another. And I had no great difficulty in determining what the objects are with which I should begin, for that I already knew, namely, that it was with the simplest and easiest. Bearing in mind, too, that of all those who in time past have sought for truth in the sciences, the mathematicians alone have been able to find any demonstrations, that is to say, any reasons which are certain and evident, I had no doubt that it must have been by a procedure of this kind that they had obtained them.

---

tionalism (see the box above). His books were placed on the papal Index of Forbidden Books and condemned by many Protestant theologians. The radical Cartesian split between mind and matter, and between mind and body, had devastating implications not only for traditional religious views of the universe, but for how Westerners viewed themselves, a perspective that would not be seriously questioned or challenged until the twentieth century.

▼ The Scientific Method

In the course of the Scientific Revolution, attention was also paid to the problem of establishing the proper means to examine and understand the physical realm. This creation of a scientific method was crucial to the evolution of science in the modern world.

Curiously enough, it was an Englishman with few scientific credentials who attempted to put forth a new method of acquiring knowledge that made an impact on the Royal Society in England in the seventeenth century and other European scientists in the eighteenth century. Francis Bacon (1561–1626), a lawyer and lord chancellor, rejected Copernicus and Kepler and misunderstood Galileo. And yet in his unfinished work, *The Great Instauration* (*The Great Restoration*), he called for his contemporaries "to commence a total reconstruction of sciences, arts, and all human knowledge, raised upon the proper foundations." According to Bacon, two attitudes had held people back from this project. Some men had foolishly continued to rely on the ancients, especially Aristotle: "And for its value and utility it must be plainly avowed that that wisdom which we have derived principally from the Greeks is but like the boyhood of knowledge, and has the characteristic property of boys: it can talk, but it cannot generate; for it is fruitful of controversies but barren of works." Equally harmful was the attitude that it was beyond "the powers of man" to understand what God had created in the world. Bacon did not doubt humans' ability to know the natural world, but believed that they had proceeded incorrectly: "The entire fabric of human reason which we employ in the inquisition of nature is badly put together and built up, and like some magnificent structure without foundation."

Bacon's new foundation—a correct scientific method—was to be built upon inductive principles. Rather than beginning with assumed first principles from which logical conclusions could be deduced, he urged scientists to proceed from the particular to the general. Carefully organized experiments and systematic, thorough observations would lead to the careful development of correct generalizations. Bacon's method—to seek knowledge by experiment and observation—has frequently been criticized for emphasizing the empirical, experimental side while lacking any foundation in mathematics and intuition.

Bacon was clear about what he believed his method could accomplish. His concern was more for practical than for pure science. He stated that "the true and lawful goal of the sciences is none other than this: that human life be endowed with new discoveries and power." He wanted science to contribute to the "mechanical arts" by creating devices that would benefit industry, agriculture, and trade. Bacon was prophetic when he said that "I am laboring to lay the foundation, not of any sect or doctrine, but of human utility and power." And how would this "human power" be used? To "conquer nature in action."[20] The control and domination of nature became a central proposition of modern science and the technology that accompanied it. Only in the twentieth century have some scientists raised the question of whether this assumption might not be at the heart of the twentieth-century ecological crisis.

René Descartes proposed a different approach to scientific methodology by emphasizing deduction and mathematical logic. As Descartes explained in *Discourse on Method,* each step in an argument should be as sharp and well founded as a mathematical proof:

> These long chains of reasonings which geometers are accustomed to using to reach their most difficult demonstrations, had given me cause to imagine that everything which can be encompassed by man's knowledge is linked in the same way, and that provided only that one abstains from accepting any for true which is not true, and that one always keeps the right order for one thing to be deduced from that which precedes

it, there can be nothing so distant that one does not reach it eventually, or so hidden that one cannot discover it.[21]

Descartes believed then that one could start with self-evident truths, comparable to geometrical axioms, and deduce more complex conclusions. His emphasis on deduction and mathematical order complemented Bacon's stress on experiment and induction. It was Sir Isaac Newton who synthesized them into a single scientific methodology by uniting Bacon's empiricism with Descartes's rationalism. The scientific method, of course, was valuable in answering the question "how" something works, and its success in doing this gave others much confidence in the method. It did not attempt to deal with the question of "why" something happens or the purpose and meaning behind the world of nature. This allowed religion still to be important in the seventeenth century.

▼ Science and Religion in the Seventeenth Century

In Galileo's struggle with the inquisitorial Holy Office of the Catholic church, we see the beginning of the conflict between science and religion that has marked the history of modern Western civilization and ultimately led to much grief for the organized religions. Since time immemorial, theology had seemed to be the queen of the sciences. It was natural that the churches would continue to believe that religion was the final measure of everything. To the emerging scientists, however, it often seemed that theologians knew not of what they spoke. These "natural philosophers" then tried to draw lines between the knowledge of religion and the knowledge of "natural philosophy" or nature. Galileo had clearly felt that it was unnecessary to pit science against religion when he wrote that:

> in discussions of physical problems we ought to begin not from the authority of scriptural passages, but from sense-experiences and necessary demonstrations; for the holy Bible and the phenomena of nature proceed alike from the divine word, the former as the dictate of the Holy Ghost and the latter as the observant executrix of God's commands. It is necessary for the Bible, in order to be accommodated to the understanding of every man, to speak many things which appear to differ from the absolute truth so far as the bare meaning of the words is concerned. But Nature, on the other hand, is inexorable and immutable; she never transgresses the laws imposed upon her, or cares a whit whether her abstruse reasons and methods of operation are understandable to men.[22]

To Galileo it made little sense for the church to determine the nature of physical reality on the basis of biblical texts that were subject to radically divergent interpretations. The church, however, decided otherwise in Galileo's case and lent its great authority to one scientific theory, the Ptolemaic-Aristotelian cosmology, no doubt because it fit so well with its own philosophical views of reality. But the church's decision had tremendous consequences, just as the rejection of Darwin's ideas did in the nineteenth century. For educated individuals, it established a dichotomy between scientific investigations and religious beliefs. As the scientific beliefs triumphed, it became almost inevitable that religious beliefs would suffer, leading to a growing secularization in European intellectual life, precisely what the church had hoped to combat by opposing Copernicanism. Many seventeenth-century intellectuals were both religious and scientific and believed that the implications of this split would be tragic. Some believed that the split was largely unnecessary while others felt the need to combine God, humans, and a mechanistic universe into a new philosophical synthesis. Three individuals—Spinoza, Comenius, and Pascal—illustrate some of the wide diversity in the response of European intellectuals to the implications of the cosmological revolution of the seventeenth century.

Benedict de Spinoza (1632–1677) was a Jewish philosopher who grew up in the relatively tolerant atmosphere of Amsterdam. He was excommunicated from the Amsterdam synagogue at the age of twenty-four for rejecting the tenets of Judaism. Ostracized by the local Jewish community and major Christian churches alike, Spinoza lived a quiet, independent life, earning a living by grinding optical lenses and refusing to accept an academic position in philosophy at the University of Heidelberg for fear of compromising his freedom of thought. Spinoza read a great deal of the new scientific literature and was influenced by Descartes.

Although he followed Descartes's rational approach to knowledge, Spinoza was unwilling to accept the implications of Descartes's ideas, especially the separation of mind and matter and the apparent separation of an infinite God from the finite world of matter. God was not simply creator of the universe, he was the universe. All that is is in God and nothing can be apart from God. This philosophy of pantheism (others have labeled it panentheism or monism) was set out in Spinoza's book, *Ethics Demonstrated in the Geometrical Manner*, which was not published until after his death.

To Spinoza, human beings are not "situated in nature as a kingdom within a kingdom," but are as much a part of God or nature or the universal order as other natural objects. The failure to understand God had led to many misconceptions; for one, that nature exists only for one's use:

> As they find in themselves and outside themselves many means which assist them not a little in their search for what is useful, for instance, eyes for seeing, teeth for chewing, herbs and animals for yielding food, the sun for giving light, the sea for breeding fish, they come to look on the whole of nature as a means for obtaining such conveniences.[23]

Furthermore, unable to find any other cause for the existence of these things, they attributed them to a creator-God who must be worshiped to gain their ends: "Hence also it follows, that everyone thought out for himself, according to his abilities, a different way of worshipping God, so that God might love him more than his fellows, and direct the whole course of nature for the satisfaction of his blind cupidity and insatiable avarice." Then, when nature appeared unfriendly in the form of storms, earthquakes, and diseases, "they declared that such things happen, because the gods are angry at some wrong done them by men, or at some fault committed in their worship," rather than realizing "that good and evil fortunes fall to the lot of pious and impious alike."[24] Likewise, human beings made moral condemnations of others since they failed to understand that human emotions, "passions of hatred, anger, envy and so, considered in themselves, follow from the same necessity and efficacy of nature" and "nothing comes to pass in nature in contravention to her universal laws." To explain human emotions, like everything else, we need to analyze them as we would the movements of planets: "I shall, therefore, treat of the nature and strength of my emotions according to the same method as I employed heretofore in my investigations concerning God and the mind. I shall consider human actions and desires in exactly the same manner as though I were concerned with lines, planes, and solids."[25] Everything has a rational explanation of which humans are capable. In using reason, people can find true happiness. Their real freedom comes when they understand the order and necessity of nature and achieve detachment from passing interests.

Spinoza's complex synthesis of God, humans, and the universe was not easily accepted by his contemporaries, and his pantheism was mistakenly condemned as "hideous atheism." Others were upset by his attitude toward morality since he viewed it as found in nature and known by reason, not revealed to people through the Bible. Even Spinoza declared that some would find strange his attempt to treat of human desires "in exactly the same manner as though I were concerned with lines, planes, and solids."

Of the seventeenth-century intellectuals that we might characterize as utopian thinkers, Johann Amos Comenius (1592–1671) perhaps best realized the dangers inherent in the separation of science and religion that was beginning to occur in his century. Comenius used the phrase "pansophia" or universal wisdom to describe the macrocosmic-microcosmic philosophy of Hermeticism: the connection between the inner world of humans and the outer world of nature. Comenius's pansophism was also a utopian fantasy; he dreamed of a revived Christian commonwealth that would begin a universal millennium on earth. By uniting science and religion, pansophism would show the way to a perfected society.

Like other intellectuals influenced by the Hermetic tradition, Comenius favored the establishment of learned societies that would further the goal of working toward a universal reformation of the whole world by the union of science and religion. When the Royal Society was established in England in 1662 (see The Scientific Societies later in the chapter), he hoped that this group would fulfill his goals. He dedicated a new edition of his book, *The Way of Light,* to the Royal Society expressing these hopes. But he also sounded a warning. If the members of the society did not envision ends beyond the cultivation of the natural sciences for themselves alone, their work might turn out to be a "Babylon turned upside down, building not towards heaven, but towards earth."[26] The Royal Society failed to heed his warning, and the separation of science and religion became an established fact of modern Western civilization.

Like Comenius, Blaise Pascal (1623–1662) sought to keep science and religion united; however, his religion was not a utopian Hermeticism but traditional Christianity. Pascal had a brief, but checkered career. He was for a short time a reader of Montaigne and a companion to freethinkers. He was an accomplished scientist and brilliant mathematician, combining the practical by inventing a calculating machine with the abstract by devising a theory of chance or probability and doing work on conic sections. After a profound mystical vision on the night of November 23, 1654, which assured him that God cared for the human soul, he devoted the rest of his life to religious matters. He planned to write an "Apology for the Christian Religion" but died before he could do so. He did leave a set of notes for the larger work, however, which in published form became known as *Pensées* or *The Thoughts.*

In the *Pensées,* Pascal tried to convert rationalists to Christianity by appealing both to their reason and their emotions. Humans were, he argued, frail creatures, often deceived by their senses, misled by reason, and battered by their emotions. And yet they were beings whose very nature involved thinking: "Man is but a reed, the weakest in nature; but he is a thinking reed. . . . Our whole dignity consists, therefore, in thought. By thought we must raise ourselves. . . . Let us endeavour, then, to think well; this is the beginning of morality."[27]

Pascal was determined to show that the Christian religion was not contrary to reason: "If we violate the principles of reason, our religion will be absurd, and it will be laughed at." Christianity, he felt, was the only religion that recognized people's true state of being as both vulnerable and great. To a Christian, a human being was both fallen and at the same time God's special creation. But it was not necessary to emphasize one at the expense of the other—to view humans as only rational or only hopeless. Thus, "Knowledge of God without knowledge of man's wretchedness leads to pride. Knowledge of man's wretchedness without knowledge of God leads to despair. Knowledge of Jesus Christ is the middle course, because by it we discover both God and our wretched state." Pascal even had an answer for skeptics in his famous wager. God is a reasonable bet; it is worthwhile to assume that God exists. If he does, then we win all; if he does not, we lose nothing.

Despite his background as a scientist and mathematician, Pascal refused to rely on the scientist's world of order and rationality to attract people to God: "If we submit everything to reason, there will be no mystery and no supernatural element in our religion." In the new cosmology of the seventeenth century, "finite man," Pascal believed, was lost in the new infinite world, a realization that frightened him: "The eternal silence of those infinite spaces strikes me with terror" (see the box on p. 587). The world of nature, then, could never reveal God: "Because they have failed to contemplate these infinites, men have rashly plunged into the examination of nature, as though they bore some proportion to her. . . . Their assumption is as infinite as their object." A Christian could only rely on a God who through Jesus cared for human beings. In the final analysis, after providing reasonable arguments for Christianity, Pascal came to rest on faith. Reason, he believed, could take people only so far: "The heart has its reasons of which the reason knows nothing." As a Christian, faith was the final step: "The heart feels God, not the reason. This is what constitutes faith: God experienced by the heart, not by the reason."[28]

In retrospect, it is obvious that Pascal failed to achieve his goal. Increasingly, the gap between science and traditional religion grew wider as Europe continued

Pascal: "What Is a Man in the Infinite?"
▼ ▼ ▼

Perhaps no intellectual in the seventeenth century gave greater expression to the uncertainties generated by the cosmological revolution than Blaise Pascal. Himself a scientist, Pascal's mystical vision of God's presence caused him to pursue religious truths with a passion. His work, the Pensées, consisted of notes for a larger, unfinished work justifying the Christian religion. In this selection, Pascal presents his musings on the human place in an infinite world.

Blaise Pascal, *Pensées*

Let man then contemplate the whole of nature in her full and exalted majesty. Let him turn his eyes from the lowly objects which surround him. Let him gaze on that brilliant light set like an eternal lamp to illumine the Universe; let the earth seem to him a dot compared with the vast orbit described by the sun, and let him wonder at the fact that this vast orbit itself is no more than a very small dot compared with that described by the stars in their revolutions around the firmament. But if our vision stops here, let the imagination pass on; it will exhaust its powers of thinking long before nature ceases to supply it with material for thought. All this visible world is no more than an imperceptible speck in nature's ample bosom. No idea approaches it. We may extend our conceptions beyond all imaginable space, yet produce only atoms in comparison with the reality of things. It is an infinite sphere, the center of which is everywhere, the circumference nowhere. In short, it is the greatest perceptible mark of God's almighty power that our imagination should lose itself in that thought.

Returning to himself, let man consider what he is compared with all existence; let him think of himself as lost in his remote corner of nature; and from this little dungeon in which he finds himself lodged—I mean the Universe—let him learn to set a true value on the earth, its kingdoms, and cities, and upon himself. What is a man in the infinite? . . .

For, after all, what is a man in nature? A nothing in comparison with the infinite, an absolute in comparison with nothing, a central point between nothing and all. Infinitely far from understanding these extremes, the end of things and their beginning are hopelessly hidden from him in an impenetrable secret. He is equally incapable of seeing the nothingness from which he came, and the infinite in which he is engulfed. What else then will he perceive but some appearance of the middle of things, in an eternal despair of knowing either their principle or their purpose? All things emerge from nothing and are borne onwards to infinity. Who can follow this marvelous process? The Author of these wonders understands them. None but He can.

---

along its path of secularization. Of course, traditional religions were not eliminated, nor is there any evidence that churches had yet lost their numbers. That would happen later. Nevertheless, more and more of the intellectual, social, and political elites began to act on the basis of secular rather than religious assumptions.

▼ The Spread of Scientific Knowledge

In the course of the seventeenth century, scientific learning and investigation began to increase dramatically. Major universities in Europe established new chairs of science, especially in medicine. Royal and princely patronage of individual scientists became an international phenomenon. The king of Denmark constructed an astronomical observatory for Tycho Brahe; Emperor Rudolf II hired Tycho Brahe and Johannes Kepler as imperial mathematicians; the grand duke of Tuscany appointed Galileo to a similar post. Of greater importance to the work of science, however, was the creation of new learned societies and journals that enabled the new scientists to communicate their ideas to each other and to disseminate them to a wider, literate public.

The Scientific Societies

The first of these scientific societies appeared in Italy and included the Academy of Experiments, founded in Florence in 1657 by two of Galileo's pupils under the patronage of the Medicean grand duke of Tuscany. Its laboratory facilities made possible research carried out along the new experimental lines. This Florentine

Academy was short-lived, however, and came to an end when its Medici supporters discontinued their funding in 1667.

Ultimately of more significance were the scientific societies of England and France. The English Royal Society evolved out of informal gatherings of scientists at London and Oxford in the 1640s, although it did not receive a formal charter from King Charles II until 1662. The French Royal Academy of Sciences also arose out of informal scientific meetings in Paris during the 1650s. In 1666, urged on by his minister Colbert, Louis XIV bestowed upon the group a formal recognition. The French

▼ **Louis XIV and Colbert Visit the Academy of Sciences.** In the seventeenth century, individual scientists received royal and princely patronage and a number of learned societies were established. The Academy of Experiments was established in Florence and the Royal Society was founded in England. In France, Louis XIV, urged on by his minister Colbert, gave formal recognition to the French Academy in 1666. In this illustration, Louis XIV and Colbert are shown visiting the French Royal Academy of Sciences.

Academy received abundant state support and remained under government control; its members were appointed and paid salaries by the state. In contrast, the Royal Society of England received little government encouragement, and its fellows simply co-opted new members.

Early on, both the English and French scientific societies formally emphasized the practical value of scientific research. The Royal Society created a committee to investigate technological improvements for industry while the French Academy collected tools and machines. This concern with the practical benefits of science proved short-lived, however, as both societies came to focus their primary interest on theoretical work in mechanics and astronomy. The construction of observatories at Paris in 1667 and at Greenwich, England, in 1675 greatly facilitated research in astronomy by both groups. The French Academy, however, since it was controlled by the state, was forced by the war minister of France, the marquis de Louvois, to continue its practical work to benefit both the "king and the state." The French example was especially important as a model for the scientific societies established in neighboring Germany. German princes and city governments encouraged the foundation of small-scale scientific societies of their own. Most of them, such as the Scientific Academy created in 1700 by the elector of Brandenburg, as well as the scientific academies established in most European countries in the eighteenth century, were sponsored by governments and were mainly devoted to the betterment of the state. While both the English and French societies made useful contributions to scientific knowledge in the second half of the seventeenth century, their true significance arose from their example that science should proceed as a cooperative venture.

Scientific journals furthered this concept of cooperation. The French *Journal des Savants,* published weekly beginning in 1665, printed results of experiments as well as general scientific knowledge. Its format appealed to both scientists and the educated public interested in the new science. The *Philosophical Transactions* of the Royal Society, however, also initiated in 1665, published papers of its members and learned correspondence and was aimed at practicing scientists. It became a prototype for the scholarly journals of later learned and academic societies and a crucial instrument for circulating news of scientific and academic activities.

Science and Society

The importance of science in the history of modern Western civilization is usually taken for granted. No

PROSPECTUS INTRA CAMERAM STELLATAM.

▼ **The Royal Observatory at Greenwich.** Although both the French and the English scientific societies initially stressed the practical value of scientific research, their interests soon shifted to theoretical work in mechanics and astronomy. To better facilitate their astronomical investigations, both the English and the French constructed observatories, such as the one pictured here, which was built at Greenwich, England, in 1675. The royal astronomer works at the table while his two assistants are shown making observations.

doubt the Industrial Revolution of the late eighteenth and nineteenth centuries provided tangible proof of the effectiveness of science and ensured its victory over Western minds. But how did science become such an integral part of Western culture in the seventeenth and early eighteenth centuries? Recent research has stressed that one cannot simply assert that people perceived that science was a rationally superior system. Two important social factors, however, might help to explain the relatively rapid acceptance of the new science.

It has been argued that the literate mercantile and propertied elites of Europe were soon attracted to a new science that offered new ways to exploit resources for profit. Some of the early scientists made it easier for these groups to accept the new ideas when they showed how they could be applied directly to specific industrial and technological needs. Galileo, for example, consciously sought an alliance between science and the material interests of the educated elite when he assured his listeners that the science of mechanics would be quite useful "when it becomes necessary to build bridges or other structures over water, something occurring mainly in affairs of great importance." At the same time, Galileo stressed that science was fit for the "minds of the wise" and not for "the shallow minds of the common people." This made science part of the high culture of

Europe's wealthy elites at a time when that culture was being increasingly separated from the popular culture of the lower classes (see Chapter 18). This merger of scientists with the literate and propertied elites occurred first in England and later in France and the Low Countries.

It has also been argued that the new scientific conception of the natural world was used by political interests to bolster social stability. One scholar has recently argued that "no single event in the history of early modern Europe more profoundly shaped the integration of the new science into Western culture than did the English Revolution (1640–1660)."[29] Fed by their millenarian expectations that the end of the world would come and usher in a thousand-year reign of the saints, Puritan reformers felt it was important to reform and renew their society. They seized on the new science as a socially useful instrument to accomplish this goal. The Puritan Revolution's role in the acceptance of science, however, stemmed even more from the reaction to the radicalism spawned by the revolutionary ferment. The upheavals of the Puritan Revolution gave rise to groups, such as the Levellers, Diggers, and Ranters, who advocated not only radical political ideas, but also a new radical science based on Paracelsus and the natural magic associated with the Hermetic tradition. The chaplain of the New Model Army said that the radicals wanted "the philosophy of Hermes, revived by the Paracelsian schools." The propertied and educated elites responded vigorously to these challenges to the established order by supporting the new mechanistic science and appealing to the material benefits of science. Hence, the founders of the Royal Society were men who wanted to pursue an experimental science that would remain detached from radical reforms of church and state. Although willing to make changes, they now viewed those changes in terms of an increase in food production and commerce. By the eighteenth century, the Newtonian world-machine had been readily accepted, and Newtonian science would soon be applied to trade and industry by a mercantile and landed elite that believed that they "could retain a social order that primarily rewarded and enriched themselves while still improving the human condition."

The Scientific Revolution represents a major turning point in modern Western civilization. In the Scientific Revolution, the Western world overthrew the medieval, Ptolemaic-Aristotelian worldview and arrived at a new conception of the universe: the sun at the center, the planets as material bodies revolving around the sun in elliptical orbits, and an infinite rather than finite world. With the changes in the conception of "heaven" came changes in the conception of "earth." The work of Bacon and Descartes left Europeans with the separation of mind and matter and the belief that by using only reason they could, in fact, understand and dominate the world of nature. The development of a scientific method furthered the work of scientists while the creation of scientific societies and learned journals spread its results. Although traditional churches stubbornly resisted the new ideas and a few intellectuals pointed to some inherent flaws, nothing was able to halt the replacement of the traditional ways of thinking by new ways of thinking that created a more fundamental break with the past than that represented by the breakup of Christian unity in the Reformation.

The Scientific Revolution forced Europeans to change their conception of themselves. At first, some were appalled and even frightened by its implications. Before humans on earth had been at the center of the universe. Now the earth was only a tiny planet revolving around a sun that was itself only a speck in a boundless universe. Most people remained optimistic despite the apparent blow to human dignity. After all, had Newton not demonstrated that the universe was a great machine governed by natural laws? Newton had found one—the universal law of gravitation. Could others not find other laws? Were there not natural laws governing every aspect of human endeavor that could be found by the new scientific method? Thus, the Scientific Revolution leads us logically to the age of the Enlightenment of the eighteenth century.

Notes

▼ ▼ ▼

1. Quoted in Alan G. R. Smith, *Science and Society in the Sixteenth and Seventeenth Centuries* (London, 1972), p. 59.

2. Edward MacCurdy, *The Notebooks of Leonardo da Vinci* (London, 1948), 1:634.

3. Ibid., p. 636.

4. Frances Yates, *Giordano Bruno and the Hermetic Tradition* (New York, 1964), p. 448.

5. Ibid., p. 450.

6. Quoted in Smith, *Science and Society in the Sixteenth and Seventeenth Centuries*, p. 97.

7. Logan P. Smith, *Life and Letters of Sir Henry Wotton* (Oxford, 1907), 1: 486–87.

8. Quoted in John H. Randall, *The Making of the Modern Mind* (Boston, 1926), p. 234.

9. Quoted in Smith, *Science and Society in the Sixteenth and Seventeenth Centuries*, p. 124.

10. Quoted in Betty J. Dobbs, *The Foundations of Newton's Alchemy* (Cambridge, 1975), pp. 13–14.

11. Jolande Jacobi, ed., *Paracelsus: Selected Writings* (New York, 1965), pp. 5–6.

12. Ibid., p. 21.

13. Quoted in Londa Schiebinger, *The Mind Has No Sex? Women in the Origins of Modern Science* (Cambridge, Mass., 1989), pp. 52–53.

14. Ibid., p. 85.

15. Galen, *On the Usefulness of the Parts of the Body*, trans. Margaret May (Ithaca, N.Y., 1968), 2: 628–29.

16. Quoted in Phyllis Stock, *Better Than Rubies: A History of Women's Education* (New York, 1978), p. 16.

17. René Descartes, *Philosophical Writings*, ed. and trans. Norman K. Smith (New York, 1958), p. 95.

18. Ibid., pp. 118–19.

19. Ibid., p. 120.

20. Francis Bacon, *The Great Instauration*, trans. Jerry Weinberger (Arlington Heights, Ill., 1989), pp. (in order of quotations) 2, 8, 2, 16, 21.

21. Descartes, *Discourse on Method*, in *Philosophical Writings*, p. 75.

22. Stillman Drake, ed. and trans., *Discoveries and Opinions of Galileo* (New York, 1957), p. 182.

23. Benedict de Spinoza, *Ethics*, trans. R. H. M. Elwes (New York, 1955), pp. 75–76.

24. Ibid., p. 76.

25. Benedict de Spinoza, *Letters*, quoted in Randall, *The Making of the Modern Mind*, p. 247.

26. John Amos Comenius, *The Way of Light*, trans. E. T. Campagnac (Liverpool, 1938), p. 51.

27. Blaise Pascal, *The Pensées*, trans. J. M. Cohen (Harmondsworth, 1961), p. 100.

28. Ibid., pp. (in order of quotations) 31, 45, 31, 52–53, 164, 165.

29. Margaret C. Jacob, *The Cultural Meaning of the Scientific Revolution* (New York, 1988), p. 73.

Suggestions for Further Reading
▼ ▼ ▼

Three general surveys of the entire Scientific Revolution are A. G. R. Smith, *Science and Society in the Sixteenth and Seventeenth Centuries* (London, 1972); M. Boas, *The Scientific Renaissance: 1450–1630* (London, 1962); and H. Butterfield, *The Origins of Modern Science* (New York, 1962). A more detailed and technical introduction can be found in A. R. Hall, *The Revolution in Science, 1500–1750* (London, 1983). Also of much value is A. G. Debus, *Man and Nature in the Renaissance* (Cambridge, 1978), which covers the period from the mid-fifteenth through the mid-seventeenth centuries. The importance of mathematics to the Scientific Revolution is brought out in P. L. Rose, *The Italian Renaissance of Mathematics: Studies on Humanists and Mathematicians from Petrarch to Galileo* (Geneva, 1975). On the relationship of magic to the beginnings of the Scientific Revolution, see the pioneering works by F. Yates, *Giordano Bruno and the Hermetic Tradition* (New York, 1969), and *The Rosicrucian Enlightenment* (London, 1975). Some criticism of this approach is provided in R. S. Westman and J. E. McGuire, eds., *Hermeticism and the Scientific Revolution* (Los Angeles, 1977). An important book on magic in the early modern period is

K. Thomas, *Religion and the Decline of Magic* (London, 1971).

A good introduction to the transformation from the late medieval to the early modern worldview is A. Koyré, *From the Closed World to the Infinite Universe* (New York, 1958). Also still of value is the older work by A. Koestler, *The Sleepwalkers: A History of Man's Changing Vision of the Universe* (New York, 1959). On the important figures of the revolution in astronomy, see E. Rosen, *Copernicus and the Scientific Revolution* (New York, 1984); C. Morphet, *Galileo and Copernican Astronomy* (London, 1977); S. Drake, *Galileo* (New York, 1980); M. Casper, *Johannes Kepler*, trans. C. D. Hellman (London, 1959), the standard biography; and F. Manuel, *A Portrait of Isaac Newton* (Cambridge, Mass., 1968), a massive work. On Newton's relationship to alchemy, see the invaluable study by B. J. Dobbs, *The Foundations of Newton's Alchemy* (Cambridge, 1975).

The worldview of Paracelsus and his followers can be examined in W. Pagel, *Paracelsus: An Introduction to Philosophical Medicine in the Era of the Renaissance* (New York, 1958); and A. G. Debus, *The Chemical Philosophy: Paracelsian Science and Medicine in the Sixteenth and*

Seventeenth Centuries, 2 vols. (New York, 1977). The standard biography of Vesalius is C. D. O'Malley, *Andreas Vesalius of Brussels, 1514–1564* (Berkeley, 1964). The work of Harvey is discussed in G. Whitteridge, *William Harvey and the Circulation of the Blood* (London, 1971). A good general account of the development of medicine can be found in W. P. D. Wightman, *The Emergence of Scientific Medicine* (Edinburgh, 1971).

The importance of Francis Bacon in the early development of science is underscored in P. Rossi, *Francis Bacon: From Magic to Science* (Chicago, 1968); and C. Webster, *The Great Instauration: Science, Medicine, and Reform, 1620–1660* (London, 1975). A good introduction to the work of Descartes can be found in A. Kenny, *Descartes* (New York, 1968). The standard biography of Spinoza in English is S. Hampshire, *Spinoza* (New York, 1961).

For a general history of the development of scientific academies, see the older work by M. Ornstein, *The Role of Scientific Societies in the Seventeenth Century* (Chicago, 1928). Individual societies are examined in R. Hahn, *The Anatomy of a Scientific Institution: The Paris Academy of Sciences, 1666–1803* (Berkeley, 1971); and M. Purver, *The Royal Society, Concept and Creation* (London, 1967).

On the subject of women and early modern science, see the comprehensive and highly informative work by L. Schiebinger, *The Mind Has No Sex? Women in the Origins of Modern Science* (Cambridge, Mass., 1989). The social and political context for the triumph of science in the seventeenth and eighteenth centuries is examined in M. Jacobs, *The Cultural Meaning of the Scientific Revolution* (New York, 1988), and *The Newtonians and the English Revolution, 1689–1720* (Ithaca, N.Y., 1976).

Chapter 18

The Eighteenth Century: An Age of Enlightenment

▼▼▼▼▼

T he earth-shattering work of the "natural philosophers" in the Scientific Revolution had affected only a relatively small number of Europe's educated elite. In the eighteenth century, this changed dramatically as a group of intellectuals known as the philosophes popularized the ideas of the Scientific Revolution and used them to undertake a dramatic reexamination of all aspects of life. The widespread impact of the philosophes' ideas on their society has caused historians ever since to call the eighteenth century an age of Enlightenment.

For most of the philosophes, "enlightenment" included the rejection of traditional Christianity. The religious wars and intolerance of the sixteenth and seventeenth centuries had created an environment in which intellectuals had become so disgusted with religious fanaticism that they were open to the new ideas of the Scientific Revolution. While the great scientists of the seventeenth century believed that their work exalted God, the intellectuals of the eighteenth century read their conclusions a different way and increasingly turned their backs on their Christian heritage. Consequently, European intellectual life in the eighteenth century was marked by the emergence of the secularization that has characterized the modern Western mentality. While some historians have argued that this secularism first arose in the Renaissance, it never developed then to the same extent that it did in the eighteenth century. Ironically, at the same time that reason and materialism were beginning to replace faith and worship, a great outburst of religious sensibility manifested itself in music and art. Merely to mention the name of Johann Sebastian Bach is to remind us that the growing secularization of the eighteenth century had not yet captured the hearts and minds of all European intellectuals and artists.

▼ The Enlightenment

In 1784, the German philosopher Immanuel Kant defined the Enlightenment as "man's leaving his self-caused immaturity." Whereas earlier periods had been handicapped by the inability to "use one's intelligence without the guidance of another," Kant proclaimed as the motto of the Enlightenment: "Dare to Know!: Have the courage to use your own intelligence!" The eighteenth-century Enlightenment was a movement of intellectuals who dared to know. They were greatly impressed with the accomplishments of the Scientific Revolution, and when they used the word reason—one of their favorite words—they were advocating the application of the scientific method to the understanding of all life. All institutions and all systems of thought were subject to the rational, scientific way of thinking if people would only free themselves from the shackles of past, worthless traditions, especially religious ones. If Isaac Newton could discover the natural laws regulating the world of nature, they too by using reason could find the laws that governed human society. This belief in turn led them to hope that they could make progress toward a better society than the one they had inherited. Reason, natural law, hope, progress—these were common words in the heady atmosphere of the eighteenth century. But the philosophes were not naive optimists. Many of them realized that the ignorance and suffering of their society were not easily overcome and that progress would be slow and would exact a price.

The Paths to Enlightenment

Many philosophes saw themselves as the heirs of the pagan philosophers of antiquity and the Italian humanists of the Renaissance who had revived the world of classical antiquity. To the philosophes, the Middle Ages had been a period of intellectual darkness, when a society dominated by the dogmatic Catholic church allowed faith to obscure and diminish human reason. Closer to their own period, however, the philosophes were especially influenced by the revolutionary thinkers of the seventeenth century. What were the major intellectual changes, then, that culminated in the intellectual movement of the Enlightenment?

THE POPULARIZATION OF SCIENCE Although the philosophes of the eighteenth century were much influenced by the scientific ideas of the seventeenth century, they did not always acquire this knowledge directly from the original sources. After all, Newton's *Principia* was not an easy book to read or comprehend. The spread of scientific ideas to ever-widening circles of educated Europeans was accomplished not so much by scientists themselves as by popularizers. The greatest of them all, and especially important as the direct link between the Scientific Revolution of the seventeenth century and the philosophes of the eighteenth, was Bernard de Fontenelle (1657–1757), secretary of the French Royal Academy of Science from 1691 to 1741.

Although Fontenelle neither performed any scientific experiments nor made any scientific discoveries, he possessed a deep knowledge of all the scientific work of earlier centuries and his own time. Moreover, he was able to communicate that body of scientific knowledge in a clear and even witty fashion that appealed to his upper-class audiences in a meaningful way. One of his most successful books, the *Plurality of Worlds*, was actually presented in the form of an intimate conversation between a lady aristocrat and her lover who are engaged in conversation under the stars. What are they discussing? "Tell me," she exclaims, "about these stars of yours." Her lover proceeds to tell her of the tremendous advances in cosmology after the foolish errors of their forebears:

> There came on the scene a certain German, one Copernicus, who made short work of all those various circles, all those solid skies, which the ancients had pictured to themselves.

▼ **The Popularization of Science: Fontenelle and the *Plurality of Worlds*.** The ideas of the Scientific Revolution often reached the educated circles of Europe through popularizers, not through the works of the scientists themselves. The most important of the popularizers was Bernard de Fontenelle who, while not a scientist himself, had much knowledge of scientific matters. One of his most popular works, the *Plurality of Worlds*, was set in the form of a dialogue between a lady and her lover.

The former he abolished; the latter, he broke in pieces. Fired with the noble zeal of a true astronomer, he took the earth and spun it very far away from the center of the universe, where it had been installed, and in that center he put the sun, which had a far better title to the honour.[1]

In the course of two evenings under the stars, the lady learned the basic fundamentals of the new mechanistic universe, which, as presented in Fontenelle's summary of Newton, resembled a watch. So too did scores of the educated elite of Europe. What bliss it was to learn the "truth" in such lighthearted fashion.

Thanks to Fontenelle, science was no longer the monopoly of experts, but part of literature. He was especially fond of downplaying the religious backgrounds of the seventeenth-century scientists. Himself a skeptic, Fontenelle portrayed the churches as enemies of scientific progress, adding to the growing skepticism of religion at the end of the seventeenth century.

SKEPTICISM   Although the Reformation had attempted to restore religion as the central focus of people's lives, it was perhaps inevitable that the dogmatic controversies, religious intolerance, and religious warfare engendered by it would open the door to the questioning of religious truths and values. The overthrow of medieval cosmology and the advent of scientific ideas and rational explanations in the seventeenth century likewise affected the belief of educated men and women in the traditional teachings of Christianity. This development of skepticism toward Christian beliefs did not, however, occur in any widespread fashion in the seventeenth century. Even the great scientists, such as Kepler, Galileo, and Newton, had pursued their work in a spirit of exalting God, not undermining Christianity. But as scientific knowledge spread, Christianity was affected ever more detrimentally. Skepticism about religion and the growing secularization of thought were especially evident in the work of Pierre Bayle (1647–1706).

This French precursor of the philosophes was the son of a Huguenot minister who converted briefly to Catholicism before reverting back to Protestantism. He remained a French Protestant while becoming a leading critic of traditional religious attitudes. Bayle attacked superstition, religious intolerance, and dogmatism. In his works, he made two major points. First of all, he argued that Christian religion and morality were not necessarily related:

> Morals and religion, far from being inseparable, are completely independent of each other. A man can be moral

without being religious. An atheist who lives a virtuous life is not a creature of wonder, something outside the natural order, a freak. There is nothing more extraordinary about an atheist living a virtuous life, than there is about a Christian leading a wicked one.[2]

Secondly, the idea of compelling people to believe a particular set of religious ideas (as Louis XIV was doing in Bayle's contemporary France) was wrong. It simply created hypocrites and in itself was contrary to what religion should be about. Individual conscience should determine one's actions. Bayle argued for complete religious toleration, maintaining that a multiplicity of religions would benefit rather than harm the state.

Bayle was one of a select group of intellectuals, including Hobbes and Spinoza (see Chapter 17), who believed that the new rational principles of textual criticism should be applied to the Bible as well as secular documents. In his most famous work, *Historical and Critical Dictionary*, Bayle demonstrated the results of his own efforts by a famous article on the Israelite King David. Undermining the traditional picture of the heroic David, he portrayed him as a sensual, treacherous, cruel, and basically evil man. Bayle's *Dictionary*, while purporting to be a biographical compendium, was primarily an instrument for his attacks on traditional religious practices and heroes. It was well known to eighteenth-century philosophes, and one critic regarded it as the "Bible of the eighteenth century."

THE IMPACT OF TRAVEL LITERATURE   Skepticism about Christianity as well as European culture itself was nourished by travel reports. In the course of the seventeenth century, traders, missionaries, medical men, and navigators began to publish an increasing number of travel books that gave accounts of many different cultures. By the end of the seventeenth century, this travel literature began to make an impact on the minds of educated Europeans. The discovery of highly developed civilizations like those of the Far East with different customs forced Europeans to evaluate their own civilization relative to others. What had seemed to be practices grounded in reason now appeared to be matters of custom. The missionary author of *On the Ceremonies of the Chinese* concluded: "We, too, deceive ourselves, because the prejudices of our childhood prevent us from realizing that the majority of human actions are indifferent in themselves, and that they only derive their significance from the meaning the various races of people arbitrarily attached to them when they were first instituted."[3] This development of cultural relativism was a healthy antidote to European parochialism.

Cultural relativism was accompanied by religious skepticism. As these travel accounts made clear, the Christian perception of God was merely one of many. Some people were devastated by this revelation: "Some complete their demoralization by extensive travel, and lose whatever shreds of religion remained to them. Every day they see a new religion, new customs, new rites."[4]

THE LEGACY OF LOCKE AND NEWTON   The intellectual inspiration for the Enlightenment came primarily from two Englishmen, Isaac Newton and John Locke, acknowledged by the philosophes as two great minds. Newton was frequently singled out for praise as the "greatest and rarest genius that ever rose for the ornament and instruction of the species." Enchanted by the grand design of the Newtonian world-machine, the intellectuals of the Enlightenment were convinced that by following Newton's rules of reasoning they could discover the natural laws that governed politics, economics, justice, religion, and the arts. The world and everything in it was like a giant machine.

In the eyes of the philosophes, only the philosopher John Locke came close to Newton's genius. Although Locke's political ideas had an enormous impact on the Western world in the eighteenth century, it was his theory of knowledge that especially influenced the philosophes. In his *Essay Concerning Human Understanding*, written in 1690, Locke denied Descartes's belief in innate ideas. Instead, argued Locke, every person was born with a *tabula rasa*, a blank mind:

> Let us then suppose the mind to be, as we say, white paper, void of all characters, without any ideas. How comes it to be furnished? Whence comes it by that vast store which the busy and boundless fancy of man has painted on it with an almost endless variety? Whence has it all the materials of reason and knowledge? To this I answer, in one word, from experience. . . . Our observation, employed either about external sensible objects or about the internal operations of our minds perceived and reflected on by ourselves, is that which supplies our understanding with all the materials of thinking.[5]

Our knowledge, then, is derived from our environment, not from heredity; from reason, not from faith. By denying innate ideas, Locke's philosophy implied that people were molded by their environment, by the experiences that they received through their senses from their surrounding world. By changing the environment and subjecting people to proper influences, they could be changed and a new society created. Evil was not innate in human beings, but a product of bad education, rotten institutions, and inherited prejudices. And how should the environment be changed? Newton had already paved the way by showing how reason enabled enlightened people to discover the natural laws to which all institutions should conform. No wonder the philosophes were enamored of Newton and Locke. Taken together, their ideas seemed to offer the hope of a "brave new world" built on reason.

The Philosophes and Their Ideas

The intellectuals of the Enlightenment were known by the French name of philosophes although they were not all French and few were philosophers in the strict sense of the term. They were literary people, professors, journalists, statesmen, economists, political scientists, and, above all, social reformers. They came from both the nobility and the middle class, and a few even stemmed from lower-middle-class origins. Although it was a truly international and cosmopolitan movement, the Enlightenment also enhanced the dominant role being played by French culture; Paris was its recognized capital. Most of the leaders of the Enlightenment were French, although the French philosophes themselves for a long time idolized England as the home of freedom of philosophy. The French philosophes, in turn, affected intellectuals elsewhere and created a movement that touched the entire Western world, including the British colonies in America.

Although the philosophes faced different political circumstances depending upon the country in which they lived, they shared common bonds as part of a truly international movement. Although they were called philosophers, philosophy to them meant only effective criticism. The role of philosophy was to change the world, not just discuss it. As one writer said, the philosophe is one who "applies himself to the study of society with the purpose of making his kind better and happier." To the philosophes, rationalism did not mean the creation of a grandiose system of thought to explain all things. Reason was scientific method, and it meant an appeal to facts, to experience, to reasonableness. A spirit of rational criticism was to be applied to everything, including religion and politics. Traditional religion, in fact, was especially attacked for its miracles and revelations as well as its dogmas and intolerance.

The philosophes aggressively pursued a secular view of life since their focus was not on an afterlife, but on this world and how it could be improved and enjoyed. The philosophes were not simplistic in their appeal to reason, and some even balanced it with the power of passions.

Diderot, one of the most famous of the French philosophes (see Diderot later in the chapter), wrote: "People impute to the passions all of men's pains, and forget that they are also the source of all his pleasures. It is an element of man's constitution of which we can say neither too many favorable, nor too many unfavorable things. . . . It is only the passions, and the great passions, that can raise the soul to great things." Some philosophes attacked Christianity for its antipathy toward beneficent passions, especially human sensuality. To stifle it was to smother a crucial part of human nature.

The philosophes' call for freedom of expression is a reminder that their work was done in an atmosphere of censorship. The philosophes were not free to write whatever they chose. State censors decided what could be published, although standards fluctuated wildly at times, while protests from any number of government bodies could result in the seizure of books and the imprisonment of their authors, publishers, and sellers.

The philosophes found ways to circumvent state censorship. Some published under pseudonyms or anonymously or abroad, especially in Holland. The use of double meanings, such as talking about the Persians when they meant the French, became standard procedure for many. Books were also published and circulated secretly or in manuscript form to avoid censors. As frequently happens with attempted censorship, the government's announcement that a book had been burned often made the book more desirable and more popular.

Although the philosophes constituted a kind of "family circle" bound together by common intellectual bonds, they often disagreed as well. Spanning almost an entire century, the Enlightenment evolved over time with each succeeding generation becoming more radical as it built upon the contributions of the previous one. A few people, however, dominated the landscape completely, and we might best begin our survey of the ideas of the philosophes by looking at the three French giants—Montesquieu, Voltaire, and Diderot.

MONTESQUIEU Charles de Secondat, the baron de Montesquieu (1689–1755), came from the French nobility. He received a classical education and then studied law at the University of Bordeaux. Like almost all of the philosophes, he became interested in science and even conducted experiments on the effect of temperature changes on animal tissues. His own estate, as well as his marriage to a wealthy Protestant heiress, enabled him to live a life dedicated to travel, study, and writing. In his first work published in 1721, the *Persian Letters*, he

The Separation of Powers
▼ ▼ ▼

*T*he Enlightenment affected the "new world" of America as much as it did the "old world" of Europe. American philosophes, such as Benjamin Franklin, James Madison, and Thomas Jefferson, were well aware of the ideas of European Enlightenment thinkers. This selection from Montesquieu's The Spirit of the Laws enunciates the "separation of powers" doctrine. Although Montesquieu had misread the English political system, his ideas were nevertheless incorporated into the American constitution.

Montesquieu, *The Spirit of the Laws*

Of the Constitution of England

In every government there are three sorts of power: the legislative; the executive in respect to things dependent on the law of nations; and the executive in regard to matters that depend on the civil law.

By virtue of the first, the prince or magistrate enacts temporary or perpetual laws, and amends or abrogates those that have been already enacted. By the second, he makes peace or war, sends or receives embassies, establishes the public security, and provides against invasions. By the third, he punishes criminals, or determines the disputes that arise between individuals. The latter we shall call the judiciary power, and the other simply the executive power of the state.

The political liberty of the subject is a tranquility of mind arising from the opinion each person has of his safety. In order to have this liberty, it is requisite the government be so constituted as one man need not be afraid of another.

When the legislative and executive powers are united in the same person, or in the same body of magistrates, there can be no liberty; because apprehensions may arise, lest the same monarch or senate should enact tyrannical laws, to execute them in a tyrannical manner.

Again, there is no liberty, if the judiciary power be not separated from the legislative and executive. Were it joined with the legislative, the life and liberty of the subject would be exposed to arbitrary control; for the judge would be then the legislator. Were it joined to the executive power, the judge might behave with violence and oppression.

There would be an end of everything, were the same man or the same body, whether of the nobles or of the people, to exercise those three powers, that of enacting laws, that of executing the public resolutions, and of trying the causes of individuals.

used the format of two Persians supposedly traveling in Western Europe and sending their impressions back home, to enable him to criticize French institutions, especially the Catholic church and the French monarchy. Much of the program of the French Enlightenment is contained in this work: the attack on traditional religion, the advocacy of religious toleration, the denunciation of slavery, and the use of reason to liberate human beings from their prejudices.

The fame of the *Persian Letters* brought Montesquieu into contact with the leading intellectuals of his age. To enhance his own knowledge, he traveled abroad for a number of years. In England, he was made a member of the Royal Society and initiated into the society of Freemasons. Everywhere he went, he was welcomed as a leading French intellectual. After his return to France, he settled down to manage his estates but still continued to write and visit the salons of Paris (see The Social Environment of the Philosophes later in the chapter).

From this last stage of his life came his famous work, *The Spirit of the Laws,* published in 1748.

This treatise was a comparative study of governments in which Montesquieu attempted to apply the scientific method to the social and political arena to ascertain the "natural laws" governing the social relationships of human beings. It has aptly been called a "pioneering work in political sociology." *The Spirit of the Laws* revealed Montesquieu as a relativist in an age of absolute thinkers. When other philosophes propounded their natural laws, they treated them as applicable everywhere and in every situation. To Montesquieu, the forms of political and social institutions varied since they depended upon conditions unique to different countries. Climate, soil, the size of the state, and the customs and traditions developed over the course of a state's history all determined what kind of government a nation would have.

Montesquieu distinguished three basic kinds of governments: republics, suitable for small states and dependent on civic spirit; despotism, apt for large states and dependent on fear; and monarchy, appropriate for moderate-size states and dependent on the sense of honor of the leading class and respect for law. Montesquieu used England as an example of the last category, and it was his praise and analysis of England's constitution that led to his most far-reaching and lasting contribution to political thought—the importance of checks and balances created by means of a separation of powers (see the box on p. 599). He believed that England's system, with its separate executive, legislative, and judicial powers that served to limit and control each other, provided the greatest freedom and security for a state. In large part Montesquieu misread the English situation

▼ **Voltaire and Frederick II of Prussia.** François-Marie Arouet, better known as Voltaire, achieved his first success as a playwright. A philosophe, Voltaire was well known for his criticism of traditional religion and his support of religious toleration. Voltaire also supported deism, which posited a mechanical universe created by a God who had no direct involvement with his creation. This engraving shows Voltaire with one of his admirers, Frederick II, the king of Prussia.

and insisted on a separation of powers because he wanted the nobility of France (of which he was a member) to play an active role in the running of the French government. The translation of his work into English two years after publication ensured its being read by American philosophes, such as Benjamin Franklin, James Madison, John Adams, Alexander Hamilton, and Thomas Jefferson, who incorporated its principles into the American constitution (see Chapter 20).

VOLTAIRE   The greatest figure of the Enlightenment was François-Marie Arouet, known simply as Voltaire (1694–1778). Son of a prosperous middle-class family from Paris, Voltaire received a classical education typical of Jesuit schools. Although he studied law, he wished to be a writer and achieved his first success as a playwright. By his mid-twenties, Voltaire had been hailed as the successor to Racine (see Chapter 16) for his tragedy *Oedipe* and his epic *Henriade* on his favorite king, Henry IV. His wit and clever repartee made him a darling of the Paris salons but also involved him in a quarrel with a dissolute nobleman that led to Voltaire's imprisonment and voluntary exile to England.

Well received in English literary and social circles, the young playwright was much impressed by England. His *Philosophic Letters on the English*, written in 1733, expressed a deep admiration of English life, especially its respect for merchants, scientists, and literary men, its freedom of the press, its political freedom, and its religious toleration. In judging the English religious situation, he made the famous remark that "If there were just one religion in England, despotism would threaten, if there were two religions, they would cut each other's throats, but there are thirty religions, and they live together peacefully and happily." Although he clearly exaggerated the freedoms England possessed, by indirection Voltaire had managed to criticize many of the ills oppressing France, especially royal absolutism and the lack of religious toleration and freedom of thought. He had left France a playwright; he came back a philosophe.

Upon his return to France, Voltaire's reputation as the author of the *Philosophic Letters* made it necessary for him to live in semiseclusion on the estate at Cirey of Madame de Châtelet, his mistress. Although he was eventually accepted at the court of Louis XV, his alienation of Louis's mistress forced him to go wandering again. After a brief sojourn as a distinguished guest of King Frederick the Great of Prussia (see Chapter 19), he eventually settled on a magnificent estate at Ferney. Located in France near the Swiss border, it gave Voltaire the freedom to write what he wished. By this time,

The Attack on Religious Intolerance
▼ ▼ ▼

Although Voltaire's ideas on religion were in no way original, his lucid prose, biting satire, and clever wit caused his attacks to be widely read and all the more influential. These two selections present different sides of Voltaire's attack on religious intolerance. The first is from his straightforward treatise, The Ignorant Philosopher, while the second is from his only real literary masterpiece, the novel Candide, where he uses humor to make the same fundamental point about religious intolerance.

Voltaire, *The Ignorant Philosopher*

The contagion of fanaticism then still subsists. . . . The author of the Treatise upon Toleration has not mentioned the shocking executions wherein so many unhappy victims perished in the valleys of Piedmont. He has passed over in silence the massacre of six hundred inhabitants of Valtelina, men, women, and children, who were murdered by the Catholics in the month of September, 1620. I will not say it was with the consent and assistance of the archbishop of Milan, Charles Borome, who was made a saint. Some passionate writers have averred this fact, which I am very far from believing; but I say, there is scarce any city or borough in Europe, where blood has not been spilt for religious quarrels; I say, that the human species has been perceptibly diminished, because women and girls were massacred as well as men; I say, that Europe would have had a third larger population, if there had been no theological disputes. In fine, I say, that so far from forgetting these abominable times, we should frequently take a view of them, to inspire an eternal horror for them; and that it is for our age to make reparation by toleration, for this long collection of crimes, which has taken place through the want of toleration, during sixteen barbarous centuries.

Let it not then be said, that there are no traces left of that shocking fanaticism, of the want of toleration; they are still everywhere to be met with, even in those countries that are esteemed the most humane. The Lutheran and Calvinist preachers, were they masters, would, perhaps, be as little inclined to pity, as obdurate, as insolent as they upbraid their antagonists with being.

Voltaire, *Candide*

At last he [Candide] approached a man who had just been addressing a big audience for a whole hour on the subject of charity. The orator peered at him and said:

"What is your business here? Do you support the Good Old Cause?"

"There is no effect without a cause," replied Candide modestly. "All things are necessarily connected and arranged for the best. It was my fate to be driven from Lady Cunégonde's presence and made to run the gauntlet, and now I have to beg my bread until I can earn it. Things could not have happened otherwise."

"Do you believe that the Pope is Antichrist, my friend?" said the minister.

"I have never heard anyone say so," replied Candide; "but whether he is or he isn't, I want some food."

"You don't deserve to eat," said the other. "Be off with you, you villain, you wretch! Don't come near me again or you'll suffer for it."

The minister's wife looked out of the window at that moment, and seeing a man who was not sure that the Pope was Antichrist, emptied over his head a pot full of urine, which shows to what lengths ladies are driven by religious zeal.

---

through his writings, inheritance, and clever investments, Voltaire had become wealthy and now had the leisure to write an almost endless stream of pamphlets, novels, plays, letters, and histories.

Although he touched on all of the themes of importance to the philosophes, he was especially well known for his criticism of traditional religion and his strong attachment to the ideal of religious toleration (see the box above). He lent his prestige and skills as a polemicist to fight cases of intolerance in France. The most famous incident was the Calas affair. Jean Calas was a Protestant from Toulouse who was accused of murdering his own son to stop him from becoming a Catholic. Tortured to confess his guilt, Calas died shortly thereafter. An angry and indignant Voltaire published devastating broadsides that aroused public opinion and forced a retrial in which Calas was exonerated when it was proved that his son had actually committed suicide. The family was paid an indemnity, and Voltaire's appeals for toleration appeared all the more reasonable. In 1763, he penned his *Treatise on Toleration* in which he argued that religious toleration had created no problems for England and Holland and reminded governments that "all men are brothers under God." As he grew older, Voltaire became ever more strident in his denunciations. "Crush the infamous thing," he thundered repeatedly—the infamous thing being religious fanaticism, intolerance, and superstition.

Throughout his life, Voltaire championed not only religious tolerance, but also deism, a religious outlook shared by most other philosophes. Deism was built upon the Newtonian world-machine, which implied the existence of a mechanic (God) who had created the universe. Voltaire said: "In the opinion that there is a God, there are difficulties, but in the contrary opinion there are absurdities." To Voltaire and most other philosophes, God had no direct involvement in the world he had created and which he allowed to run according to its own natural laws. God did not extend grace or answer prayers as Christians liked to believe. Jesus might be a "good fellow," as Voltaire called him, but he was not divine as Christianity claimed. Deism proved to be a halfway house between belief in religion and disbelief and satisfied most philosophes. Voltaire feared atheism, feeling that it posed a threat to social stability among the masses. But deism also proved unsatisfactory. While accepting the idea that God had begun the world-machine and then had withdrawn, allowing it to operate according to its own natural laws, Voltaire expected that everyone would continue to live according to the moral teachings of Christianity. The subsequent history of Western civilization would show that the removal of God from an active role in the world was for many people simply the first step to his total elimination.

DIDEROT   Denis Diderot (1713–1784) was the son of a skilled craftsman from eastern France. He received a Jesuit education and went on to the University of Paris to fulfill his father's hopes that he would be a lawyer or pursue a career in the church. Diderot did neither. Instead he became a free-lance writer so that he could be free to study and read in many subjects and languages. For the rest of his life, Diderot remained dedicated to his independence and was always in love with new ideas. He was especially known for his conversations; as one of his friends remarked: "His discussion was always animated, perfectly sincere, subtle without obscurity, varied in its forms, brilliant in imagination, and fertile in ideas. I have experienced no greater intellectual pleasure."[6]

Diderot was probably the most versatile of all the philosophes. His range of interests was enormous and was reflected in the variety of literature he wrote. His works on the blind and deaf, full of sound psychological observations, led some authors to call him "one of the founders of modern psychology." His profound interest in science led to a work published in 1753 in which he clearly foreshadowed the nineteenth-century theory of organic evolution. His novels ranged from the licentious *The Indiscreet Jewels* to his famous *Rameau's Nephew*, which analyzed an alienated man constantly at war with his society. His plays, such as *The Natural Son* and *The Father of the Family*, represent Diderot's attempt to move away from the traditional neoclassicism of the French theater to a more realistic treatment of the lives of the lower and middle classes. His essays on art created "modern art criticism in France," according to one historian. Diderot's own literary works as well as his essays on drama and art possess a common thread since he was one of the first European writers to see art and literature in social terms. Both, he believed, should serve to teach moral lessons that would improve society. They could, in fact, do this even better than the church: "I am not a Capuchin [monk], yet I would hasten the coming of the day when painting and sculpture, more decent and moral, will think of contributing, together with the other arts, to inspire virtue and purify our manners." Unfortunately, this desire to teach lessons resulted in stilted characters who never came alive on the stage or in his novels.

Diderot's numerous essays reflected typical Enlightened interests. One of his favorite topics was Christianity, which he condemned as fanatical and unreasonable. As he grew older, his literary attacks on Christianity grew more vicious. Of all religions, Christianity, he averred was the worst, "the most absurd and the most atrocious in its dogma" (see the box on p. 603). This progression reflected his own transformation from deism to atheism, ending with an essentially materialistic conception of life: "This world is only a mass of molecules. There is a law of necessity that works without design, without effort, without intelligence, and without progress."

Diderot's most famous contribution to the Enlightenment was the *Encyclopedia, or Classified Dictionary of the Sciences, Arts, and Trades*, a twenty-eight volume compendium of knowledge that he edited and referred to as the "great work of his life." It appeared sporadically since state censors periodically suppressed its publication for "tending to destroy royal authority, to establish the spirit of independence and revolt, . . . and to raise the foundations of error, moral corruption, and irreligion."

Diderot Questions Christian Sexual Standards

▼ ▼ ▼

Denis Diderot was one of the bolder thinkers of the Enlightenment. He moved from outspoken criticism of the Christian religion to outright atheism. Although best remembered for the Encyclopedia, he was the author of many works that he considered too advanced and withheld from publication. In his Supplement to the Voyage of Bouganville, he constructed a dialogue between Orou, a Tahitian who symbolizes the wisdom of a philosophe, and a chaplain who defends Christian sexual mores. The dialogue gave Diderot the opportunity to criticize the practice of sexual chastity and monogamy.

Denis Diderot, *Supplement to the Voyage of Bouganville*

[Orou] "You are young and healthy [speaking to the chaplain] and you have just had a good supper. He who sleeps alone, sleeps badly; at night a man needs a woman at his side. Here is my wife and here are my daughters. Choose whichever one pleases you most, but if you would like to do me a favor, you will give your preference to my youngest girl, who has not yet had any children. . . ."

The chaplain replied that his religion, his holy orders, his moral standards and his sense of decency all prevented him from accepting Orou's invitation.

Orou answered: "I don't know what this thing is that you call religion, but I can only have a low opinion of it because it forbids you to partake of an innocent pleasure to which Nature, the sovereign mistress of us all, invites everybody. It seems to prevent you from bringing one of your fellow creatures into the world, from doing a favor asked of by a father, a mother and their children, from repaying the kindness of a host, and from enriching a nation by giving it an additional citizen. . . . Look at the distress you have caused to appear on the faces of these four women—they are afraid you have noticed some defect in them that arouses your distaste. . . ."

The Chaplain: "You don't understand—it's not that. They are all four of them equally beautiful. But there is my religion! My holy orders!. . . . [God] spoke to our ancestors and gave them laws; he prescribed to them the way in which he wishes to be honored; he ordained that certain actions are good and others he forbade them to do as being evil."

Orou: "I see. And one of these evil actions which he has forbidden is that of a man who goes to bed with a woman or girl. But in that case, why did he make two sexes?"

The Chaplain: "In order that they might come together—but only when certain conditions are satisfied and only after certain initial ceremonies have been performed. By virtue of these ceremonies one man belongs to one woman and only to her; one woman belongs to one man and only to him." Orou: "For their whole lives?"

The Chaplain: "For their whole lives. . . ."

Orou: "I find these strange precepts contrary to nature, and contrary to reason. . . . Furthermore, your laws seem to me to be contrary to the general order of things. For in truth is there anything so senseless as a precept that forbids us to heed the changing impulses that are inherent in our being, or commands that require a degree of constancy which is not possible, that violate the liberty of both male and female by chaining them perpetually to one another? . . . I don't know what your great workman [God] is, but I am very happy that he never spoke to our forefathers, and I hope that he never speaks to our children, for if he does, he may tell them the same foolishness, and they may be foolish enough to believe it. . . ."

These charges by the censors remind us how important the *Encyclopedia* was to the eighteenth century. Its purpose, according to Diderot, was to "change the general way of thinking." It did precisely that in becoming a major weapon of the philosophes' crusade against the old French society. The contributors included many philosophes who expressed their major concerns. They attacked religious superstition and advocated toleration as well as a program for social, legal, and political improve-ments that would lead to a society that was more cosmopolitan, more tolerant, more humane, and more reasonable. In later editions, the price of the *Encyclopedia* was drastically reduced, dramatically increasing its sales and making it available to doctors, clergymen, teachers, lawyers, and even military officers, thus furthering the spread of the ideas of the Enlightenment.

Despite the enormous output and incredible variety of his literary works, Diderot wrote no masterpiece. While important as a suggestive thinker, he was ill suited to systematic thought. As he reflected in old age: "I am not conscious of having made use of half my powers; I have only fiddle-faddled."

TOWARD A NEW "SCIENCE OF MAN"   The Enlightenment belief that Newton's scientific methods could be used to discover the natural laws underlying all areas of human life led to the emergence in the eighteenth century of what the philosophes called a "science of man" or what we would call the social sciences. Philosophes in a number of areas, such as economics and justice, arrived at natural laws that they believed governed human actions. If these "natural laws" seem less than universal to us, it reminds us how much the philosophes were people of their times reacting to the conditions they faced. Nevertheless, their efforts did result in establishing their disciplines on a rational basis and at least laying the foundations for the modern social sciences.

That a "science of man" was possible was a strong belief of the Scottish philosopher David Hume (1711–1776). An important figure in the history of philosophy, Hume has also been called "a pioneering social scientist." In his *Treatise on Human Nature,* which he subtitled "An Attempt to Introduce the Experimental Method of Reasoning into Moral Subjects," Hume argued that observation and reflection, grounded in "systematized common sense," made conceivable a "science of man." Careful examination of the experiences that constituted human life would lead to the knowledge of human nature that would make possible "a science, which will not be inferior in certainty, and will be much superior in utility, to any other of human comprehension."

In Montesquieu's analysis of governmental forms in *The Spirit of the Laws,* we have already seen the beginnings of a comparative method in politics that led toward a science of political sociology. The Physiocrats played a similar role in economics, and they and Adam Smith have been viewed as founders of the modern discipline of economics. The leader of the Physiocrats was François Quesnay (1694–1774), a highly successful French court physician.

Quesnay and the Physiocrats felt that they were the Isaac Newtons of economics and claimed they would discover the natural economic laws that governed human society because they were "susceptible of demonstration as severe and incontestable as those of geometry and algebra." Their first principle was that land constituted the only source of wealth and that wealth itself could be increased only by agriculture since all other economic activities were unproductive and sterile. As Quesnay said, "It is agriculture which furnishes all the material of industry and commerce." To the Physiocrats, agriculture included the exploitation of natural resources, especially mining. Even the state's revenues should come from a single tax on the land rather than the hodgepodge of inequitable taxes and privileges currently in place. In stressing the economic primacy of agricultural production, the Physiocrats were rejecting the mercantilist emphasis on the significance of money—that is, gold and silver—as the primary determinants of wealth (see Chapter 16).

Their second major "natural law" of economics also represented a repudiation of mercantilism, specifically, its emphasis on a controlled economy for the benefit of the state. Instead the Physiocrats stressed that the existence of the natural economic forces of supply and demand made it imperative that individuals should be left free to pursue their own economic self-interest. In doing so, all of society would ultimately benefit. Consequently, they argued that the state should in no way interrupt the free play of natural economic forces by government regulations of the economy, but leave it alone, a doctrine that subsequently became known by its French name, *laissez-faire* (to let alone).

The best statement of laissez-faire was made in 1776 by a Scottish philosopher, Adam Smith (1723–1790), when he published his famous work, *Inquiry into the Nature and Causes of the Wealth of Nations,* known simply as *The Wealth of Nations.* In the process of enunciating three of his basic principles of economics, Smith presented a vigorous attack on mercantilism. First, he condemned the mercantilist use of protective tariffs to protect home industries. A tailor, he argued, does not try to make his own shoes, nor does a shoemaker try to make his own clothes. Following this line of reasoning, if one country can supply another country with a product cheaper than the latter can make it, it is better to purchase than to produce it. Each nation, then, should produce what it did best without the artificial barriers of tariffs. To Adam Smith, free trade was a fundamental economic principle. Smith's second principle was his labor theory of value. Like the Physiocrats, he claimed that gold and silver were not the source of a nation's true wealth; but, unlike the Physiocrats, he did not believe that soil was either. Rather labor—the labor of individual farmers, craftsmen, and merchants—constituted the true wealth of a nation. Finally, like the Physiocrats, Smith believed that the state should not interfere in economic matters; indeed, he gave to government only three basic functions: it should protect society from invasion (army); defend individuals from injustice and oppression (police); and keep up certain public works, such as roads and canals that private individuals could not afford. Thus, in Smith's view the state should be a kind of "passive policeman" that remains out of the lives of individuals.

In the seventeenth century, the mercantilists had elevated the state over the individual. In creating their new human science of economics, the Physiocrats and Adam Smith reversed priorities, emphasizing the economic liberty of the individual and laying the foundation for what became known in the nineteenth century as economic liberalism.

Some philosophes also believed that there were natural laws of justice. They were horrified by the unjust and antiquated laws of their times and sought a new science to make the punishment of crime both effective and civilized. The most notable effort was made by the Italian philosophe, Cesare Beccaria (1738–1794), who wrote *An Essay on Crimes and Punishment* in 1764 proclaiming three fundamental principles of justice.

Beccaria argued first that punishments should fit the crime. The aim of punishment should be "to prevent the criminal from doing further injury to society, and to prevent others from committing the like offence." Therefore, "such punishments . . . ought to be chosen, as will make the strongest and most lasting impressions on the minds of others, with the least torment to the body of the criminal." Second, justice needs to act quickly so that crime and punishment are associated together in people's minds. And finally, Beccaria argued, "Crimes are more effectually prevented by the certainty than the severity of punishment."[7] To Beccaria, severe punishments simply lead to more crimes, since men will do everything to avoid the punishment due the first if it is severe.

Beccaria was opposed to the use of both torture and capital punishment. Torture, he argued, assumes that pain is a test of truth as if truth resides in the body of a mutilated prisoner. Capital punishment was spectacular, but failed to stop others from committing crimes. Imprisonment, the deprivation of freedom, made a far more lasting impression. Moreover, capital punishment was harmful to society because it set an example of barbarism: "Is it not absurd, that the laws, which detest and punish homicide, should, in order to prevent murder, publicly commit murder themselves?"

THE LATER ENLIGHTENMENT By the late 1760s, a new generation of philosophes who had grown up with the worldview of the Enlightenment began to move beyond

Chronology
▼ ▼ ▼
Works of the Philosophes

Montesquieu, *Persian Letters*	1721
Voltaire, *Philosophic Letters on the English*	1733
Hume, *Treatise on Human Nature*	1739–1740
Montesquieu, *The Spirit of the Laws*	1748
Voltaire, *The Age of Louis XIV*	1751
Diderot, *The Encyclopedia*	1751–1765
Rousseau, *The Social Contract, Emile*	1762
Voltaire, *Treatise on Toleration*	1763
Beccaria, *An Essay on Crimes and Punishment*	1764
Holbach, *System of Nature*	1770
Smith, *The Wealth of Nations*	1776
Gibbon, *Decline and Fall of the Roman Empire*	1776–1788
Condorcet, *The Progress of the Human Mind*	1794

their predecessors' beliefs. Baron Paul d'Holbach (1723–1789), a wealthy German aristocrat who settled in Paris, preached a doctrine of strict atheism and materialism. In his *System of Nature* written in 1770, he argued that everything in the universe consisted of matter in motion. Human beings were simply machines; theology, revelation, and God were all products of the human mind and its myth-making capacity and were unnecessary to live moral lives. People needed only reason to live in this world: "Let us persuade men to be just, beneficent, moderate, sociable; not because the gods demand it, but because they must please men. Let us advise them to abstain from vice and crimes; not because they will be punished in the other world, but because they will suffer for it in this."[8] Except for the atheistic Diderot, Holbach shocked almost all of his fellow philosophes with his materialistic determinism and uncompromising atheism. Most intellectuals remained more comfortable with deism and feared the effect of atheism on society.

Marie-Jean de Condorcet (1743–1794), another French philosophe, made an exaggerated claim for optimism that appears utopian in comparison with his predecessors' cautious hopes for gradual progress. Condorcet was a victim of the turmoil of the French Revolution and wrote his chief work, *The Progress of the Human Mind*, while in hiding during the Reign of Terror (see Chapter

20). His survey of human history convinced him that humans had progressed through nine stages of history. Now, with the spread of science and reason, humankind was about to enter the tenth stage, one of perfection, in which people will see that "there is no limit to the perfecting of the powers of man; that human perfectibility is in reality indefinite, that the progress of this perfectibility . . . has no other limit than the duration of the globe upon which nature has placed us." This prophet of humankind's perfection committed suicide shortly after composing this work in order to avoid the guillotine.

No one was more critical of the work of his predecessors than Jean-Jacques Rousseau (1712–1778). He was born in the city of Geneva, the son of a watchmaker. Almost entirely self-educated, he spent a wandering existence as a youth holding various jobs in France and Italy. He went back to school for a while to study music

▼ **Jean-Jacques Rousseau.** By the late 1760s a new generation of philosophes arose who began to move beyond and even to criticize the beliefs of their predecessors. Jean-Jacques Rousseau was perhaps the most critical philosophe of the late Enlightenment. Rousseau considered civilization itself to be an evil and blamed private property for the rise of civilization.

and the classics (he could afford to do so after becoming the paid lover of an older woman). Eventually, he made his way to Paris where he became a friend of Diderot and was introduced into the circles of the philosophes. He never really liked the social life of the cities, however, and especially detested the artificial conventions prevailing in Parisian society. He frequently withdrew into long periods of solitude.

Rousseau's political beliefs were presented in two major works. In his *Discourse on the Origins of the Inequality of Mankind*, Rousseau began with humans in their primitive condition (or state of nature—see Chapter 16) where they were happy. There were no laws, no judges; all people were equal. But what had gone wrong? Civilization had corrupted them, but how had this happened?:

> The first man who, having enclosed a piece of ground, thought of saying, This is mine, and found people simple enough to believe him, was the true founder of civil society. How many crimes, wars, murders; how much misery and horror the human race would have been spared if someone had pulled up the stakes and filled in the ditch, and cried to his fellow men: "Beware of listening to this impostor. You are lost if you forget that the fruits of the earth belong to everyone and that the earth itself belongs to no one!"[9]

Private property was the beginning of inequality and civilization; private property was the cause of crimes, wars, and murders. People adopted laws and governors in order to preserve their property. In so doing, they rushed headlong not to liberty but into chains. "What then is to be done? Must societies be totally abolished? . . . Must we return again to the forest to live among bears?" No, civilized humans could not return to the forests and live like wild animals; they could "no longer subsist on plants or acorns or live without laws and magistrates." Government was an evil, but a necessary one.

In his celebrated treatise *The Social Contract*, published in 1762, Rousseau used the concept of the social contract to try to harmonize the liberty of the individual with the institution of government (see the box on p. 607). An entire society agreed to be governed by its general will. Each individual might have a particular will contrary to the general will, but if the individual put his particular will (self-interest) above the general will, he should be forced to abide by the general will. "This means nothing less than that he will be forced to be free," said Rousseau, because the general will was not only political in nature but also ethical; it represented what the entire community ought to do, that which was its highest good. Thus freedom was achieved in being

A Social Contract

▼ ▼ ▼

Although Jean-Jacques Rousseau was one of the French philosophes, he has also been called "the father of romanticism." His political ideas have proved extremely controversial. While some have hailed him as the prophet of democracy, others have labeled him an apologist for totalitarianism. This selection is taken from one of his most famous books, The Social Contract.

Jean-Jacques Rousseau, *The Social Contract*

Book 1, Chapter 6: The Social Pact

"How to find a form of association which will defend the person and goods of each member with the collective force of all, and under which each individual, while uniting himself with the others, obeys no one but himself, and remains as free as before." This is the fundamental problem to which the social contract holds the solution. . . .

Chapter 7: The Sovereign

Despite their common interest, subjects will not be bound by their commitment unless means are found to guarantee their fidelity.

For every individual as a man may have a private will contrary to, or different from, the general will that he has as a citizen. His private interest may he speak with a very different voice from that of the public interest; his absolute and naturally independent existence may make him regard what he owes to the common cause as a gratuitous contribution, the loss of which would be less painful for others than the payment is onerous for him; and fancying that the artificial person which constitutes the state is a mere rational entity, he might seek to enjoy the rights of a citizen without doing the duties of a subject. The growth of this kind of injustice would bring about the ruin of the body politic.

Hence, in order that the social pact shall not be an empty formula, it is tacitly implied in that commitment—which alone can give force to all others—that whoever refused to obey the general will shall be constrained to do so by the whole body, which means nothing other than that he shall be forced to be free; for this is the condition which, by giving each citizen to the nation, secures him against all personal dependence, it is the condition which shapes both the design and the working of the political machine, and which alone bestows justice on civil contracts—without it, such contracts would be absurd, tyrannical and liable to the grossest abuse.

forced to follow what was best for all people. To Rousseau, since everybody was responsible for framing the general will, the power of legislation could never be delegated to a parliamentary body:

> Thus the people's deputies are not and could not be its representatives; they are merely its agents; and they cannot decide anything finally. Any law which the people has not ratified in person is void; it is not law at all. The English people believes itself to be free; it is gravely mistaken; it is free only during the election of Members of Parliament; as soon as the Members are elected, the people is enslaved; it is nothing.[10]

This is an extreme, idealistic statement, but it is the ultimate statement of participatory democracy. Perhaps Rousseau was thinking of his native city of Geneva, a community small enough that it could conform to these strict rules of absolute democracy. But we do not really know. *The Social Contract* has evoked contradictory interpretations ever since the outbreak of the French Revolution. It was used by the more radical revolutionaries in the second stage of the French Revolution to justify democratic politics, while others have viewed Rousseau's emphasis on a coercive general will ("forced to be free") as leading to a totalitarian system. Rousseau himself said, "Those who boast that they understand the whole of it are cleverer than I am."

Another influential treatise by Rousseau also appeared in 1762. Entitled *Emile*, it is one of the Enlightenment's most important works on education. Written in the form of a novel, the work was really a general treatise "on the education of the natural man." Rousseau began with the premise that the child was an evolving personality, not a small adult. During the years from five to twelve, the child went through a prerational stage with the senses of prime importance. Consequently, the child learned by doing, by a direct observation of nature. From twelve to sixteen, a young person was open to more abstract concepts; this was the time when education in morality would take hold. Seventeen to nineteen was the proper time for training the reasoning faculty and revealing God. Rousseau favored a deistic, but basically profound, spirituality. His fundamental concern was that education should encourage rather than restrict children's natural instincts. Life had taught Rousseau the importance of the promptings of the heart, and what he sought was a balance between heart and mind, between sentiment and reason. This emphasis on heart and sentiment made him a precursor of the intellectual movement called Romanticism that dominated Europe at the beginning of the nineteenth century.

The Social Environment of the Philosophes

The social background of the philosophes varied considerably, from the aristocratic Montesquieu to the lower-middle-class Diderot and Rousseau. The Enlightenment was not the preserve of any one class, although it obviously had its greatest appeal to the aristocracy and upper middle classes of the major cities. The common people, especially the peasants, were little affected by the Enlightenment.

Of great importance to the Enlightenment was the spread of its ideas to the literate elite of European society. While the publication and sale of books and treatises were important to this process, equally important was the salon. Salons came into being in the seventeenth century but rose to new heights in the eighteenth. The salons were the elegant drawing rooms of the wealthy class's great urban houses where invited philosophes and guests gathered together and engaged in witty, sparkling conversations often centered on the new ideas of the philosophes. In France's rigid hierarchical society, the salons were important in bringing together writers and artists with aristocrats, government officials, and wealthy bourgeoisie.

As hostesses of the salons, women found themselves in a position to affect the decisions of kings, sway political opinion, and influence literary and artistic taste. Salons provided havens for people and views unwelcome in the royal court. When the *Encyclopedia* was suppressed by the French authorities, Marie-Thérèse de Geoffrin (1699–1777), the daughter of a valet and a wealthy bourgeois widow, welcomed the encyclopedists to her salon and offered financial assistance to complete the work in secret.

Mme. Geoffrin was not without rivals, however. The marquise du Deffand (1697–1780) had abandoned her husband in the provinces and established herself in Paris where her ornate drawing room attracted many of the Enlightenment's great figures, including Montesquieu, Hume, and Voltaire. In 1754, after she began to go blind, she was joined as a hostess by her illegitimate niece, Julie de Lespinasse (1733–1776). For the next ten years, their salon became the most brilliant in Europe until they quarreled and separated.

Although run by women, the reputation of a salon depended upon the stature of the males a hostess was able to attract (see the box on p. 609). Despite this male domination, however, both French and foreign observers complained that females exerted undue influence in French political affairs. While exaggerated, this perception led to the decline of salons during the French Revolution. The salons were also criticized by some philos-

▼ **The Salon of Madame Geoffrin.** An important factor in the development of the Enlightenment was the spread of Enlightenment ideas to the literate elites of European society. Salons were an important part of this process. Madame Geoffrin, who presided over one of the most well known Parisian salons, is shown here, the third figure from the right in the front row.

The Salon: Can Men and Women Be Friends without Sex?
▼ ▼ ▼

The salon was established in the seventeenth century by aristocratic women who sought conversation with men as intellectual equals without the demands of sexual love. These "precious women," who sought to gain moral prestige over their male suitors by their chastity, dominated the French salon in the early seventeenth century. But in the late seventeenth and eighteenth centuries, the females who organized the salons were well known for their sexual affairs and marriages with the great men invited to their salons. It was now taken for granted "that relations between women and men, however intellectual or artistic they might appear, could not remain platonic." The first two selections are from the novel The Great Cyrus *by Mlle. de Scudéry, who maintained one of the most famous literary salons. She applauded platonic love and scorned marriage. The third selection is from a nostalgic letter of Abbé Galiani to his former salon hostess, Mme. Necker, and describes an eighteenth-century salon.*

Mlle. de Scudéry, *The Great Cyrus*
Among us, love is not a simple passion as it is elsewhere; it is one of the requirements for good breeding. Every man must be in love. Every lady must be loved. No one among us is indifferent. Anyone capable of such hardness of heart would be reproached as for a crime; such liberty is so shameful that those who are not in love at least pretend to be. Custom does not oblige ladies to love but merely to allow themselves to be loved, and they put their pride in making illustrious conquests and in never losing those whom they have brought under their rule; yet they are severe, for the honor of our beauties consists in keeping the slaves they have made by the sheer power of their attractions and not by according favors; so that, by this custom, to be a lover is almost necessarily to be unhappy. . . . Yet it is not forbidden to

reward a lover's perseverance by a totally pure affection . . . whatever can render them more lovable and loving is allowed, provided it does not shock that purity or modesty which, despite their gallantry, is these ladies' supreme virtue.

Mlle. de Scudéry, *The Great Cyrus*
"Then, said Tisandre [to Sapho—the name under which Mlle de Scudéry portrayed herself] "you can hardly regard marriage as desirable." "It is true," replied Sapho, "that I consider it a lengthy slavery." "So you think all men are tyrants?" "I think they may all become so . . . I know of course that there are some very worthy men who deserve all my esteem and could even acquire some friendship from me; but again, as soon as I think of them as husbands, I see them as masters so likely to turn into tyrants that I cannot help hating them there and then and thank the gods for giving me an inclination totally opposed to marriage."

Abbé Galiani, Letter to Madame Necker
Not a Friday passes but I visit you in spirit. I arrive. I find you putting the finishing touches to your clothes. I sit at your feet. . . . Dinner is announced. We come out. The others eat meat. I abstain. I eat a lot of that green Scotch cod which I love. I give myself indigestion while admiring Abbé Morellet's skill at carving a young turkey. We get up from table. Coffee is served. Everyone talks at once. The Abbé Raynal agrees with me that Boston has severed its links with England forever and the same time Creutz and Marmontel agree that Grétry is the Pergolese of France. M. Necker thinks everything is perfect, bows his head, and goes away. That is how I spend my Fridays.

ophes for their superficiality, to which some wealthy men responded by organizing salons exclusively for serious discussion of ideas and for men only. The most famous was that of Baron d'Holbach whose five-hour discussions were, according to Holbach himself, "the most free, the most animated, and most instructive conversation that it was ever possible to hear."

The salon served an important role in making possible conversation and sociability between upper-class men and women as well as spreading the ideas of the Enlightenment. But there were also other means to spread Enlightenment ideas. Coffeehouses, cafes, reading clubs, and public lending libraries created by the state were gathering places to exchange ideas. Secret societies were also developed. The most famous was the Freemasons, established in London in 1717, France and Italy in 1726, and Prussia in 1744, where Frederick II himself was a grand master. It was no secret that the Freemasons were sympathetic to the ideas of the philosophes.

▼ Culture and Society in an Age of Enlightenment

The intellectual adventure fostered by the philosophes was accompanied by both traditional practices and important changes in the eighteenth-century world of culture and society.

Innovations in Art, Music, and Literature

The eighteenth century began with Baroque and neoclassical principles everywhere in evidence (see Chapters 15 and 16). But the philosophes' emphasis on freedom from rules and the need to allow the free play of the artistic imagination underscored the rapid change in the arts in the eighteenth century. Yet some things remained unchanged. Neoclassicism continued to maintain its strong appeal, especially in architecture, and the late eighteenth century even witnessed another classical revival that appealed to the French revolutionary and Napoleonic eras at the end of the century.

ROCOCO   Although the Baroque and neoclassical styles that had dominated the seventeenth century continued into the eighteenth century, by the 1730s a new style affecting decoration and architecture known as Rococo

had spread all over Europe. Though a French invention and enormously popular in Germany, Rococo truly became an international style.

Unlike the Baroque, which stressed grandeur, power, and movement, Rococo emphasized grace, charm, and gentle action. Rococo rejected strict geometrical patterns and had a fondness for curves; it liked to follow the wandering lines of natural objects, such as seashells and flowers. It made much use of interlaced designs colored in gold with delicate contours and graceful curves. Highly secular, its lightness and charm spoke of the pursuit of pleasure, happiness, and love.

Some of Rococo's appeal is evident already in the work of Antoine Watteau (1684–1721), whose lyrical views of aristocratic life, refined, sensual, civilized, with gentlemen and ladies in elegant dress, revealed a world of upper-class pleasure and joy. Underneath that exterior, however, was an element of sadness as the artist revealed the fragility and transitory nature of pleasure, love, and life.

Another aspect of Rococo was the sense of enchantment and exuberance, especially evident in the work of Giovanni Battista Tiepolo (1696–1770). Much of Tiepolo's painting came to adorn the walls and ceilings of churches and palaces. His masterpiece is the ceiling of the Bishop's Palace at Würzburg, a massive scene representing the four continents. Tiepolo's work reminds us that Rococo decorative work could easily be used with Baroque architecture.

The palace of Versailles had made an enormous impact on Europe. "Keeping up with the Bourbons" became important as the Austrian emperor, the Swedish king, German princes and prince-bishops, Italian

▼ Antoine Watteau, *The Pilgrimage to Cythera*. A French invention, the Rococo style spread all over Europe by the 1730s. Rococo emphasized grace and charm over grandeur and power. Antoine Watteau was one of the most gifted painters in eighteenth-century France. His portrayal of aristocratic life reveals a world of elegance, wealth, and pleasure. Yet it is a world also tinged with a sadness created by the realization of the transient nature of life.

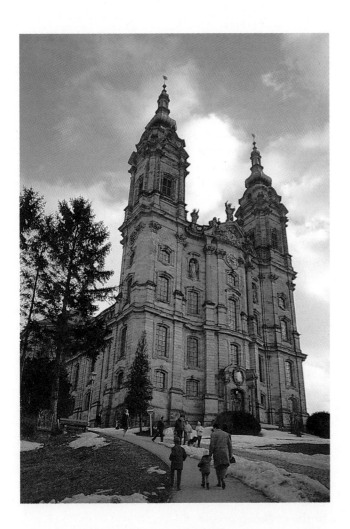

princes, and even a Russian tsar built grandiose palaces. While imitating Versailles's size, they were not so much modeled after the French classical style of Versailles as they were after the seventeenth-century Italian Baroque, as modified by a series of brilliant German and Austrian sculptor-architects. This Baroque-Rococo architectural style of the eighteenth century was conceived as a total work of art in which building, sculptural figures, and wall and ceiling paintings were blended into a harmonious whole. This style was used in both palaces and ecclesiastical buildings, and often the same architects did both. This is evident in the work of one of the greatest architects of the eighteenth century, Balthasar Neumann (1687–1753).

Neumann's two masterpieces are the pilgrimage church of the Vierzehnheiligen (The Fourteen Saints) in southern Germany and the Bishop's Palace known as the Residenz, the residential palace of the Schönborn

▼ **Vierzehnheiligen, Exterior View.** The eighteenth century was marked by a Baroque-Rococo style of architecture, a style in which the building, sculptural figures, and ceiling and wall paintings were blended together to create a harmonious whole. Both palaces and ecclesiastical buildings were constructed in this style, and one of the most prominent architects of the eighteenth century, Balthasar Neumann, used it to design some of the most beautiful buildings of the century. Pictured here is the exterior of his pilgrimage church of the Vierzehnheiligen (The Fourteen Saints), located in southern Germany.

▼ **Vierzehnheiligen, Interior View.** Pictured here is the interior of the Vierzehnheiligen, the pilgrimage church designed by Balthasar Neumann. As this illustration shows, the Baroque-Rococo style of architecture created lavish buildings in which secular and spiritual elements became easily interchangeable. Elaborate detail, blazing light, rich colors, and opulent decoration are blended together to create a work of stunning beauty.

prince-bishop of Würzburg. Secular and spiritual become easily interchangeable as lavish and fanciful ornament, light, bright colors, and elaborate and rich detail greet us in both buildings. An even more stunning example of Rococo is evident in the pilgrimage church of the Wies in southern Bavaria, designed by Domenikus Zimmermann (1685–1766). The pilgrim in search of holiness is struck by an incredible richness of detail. Persuaded by joy rather than fear, the believer is lifted toward heaven on a cloud of rapture.

MUSIC   The eighteenth century was one of the greatest in the history of European music. Important to musicians in that century, as in previous centuries, was patronage, whether it came from princes, well-endowed ecclesiastics, or aristocrats. The many individual princes, archbishops, and bishops, each with his own court, provided the patronage that made Italy and Germany the musical leaders of Europe.

In the first half of the eighteenth century, two composers—Bach and Handel—stand out as musical geniuses. Johann Sebastian Bach (1685–1750) came from a family of musicians. Bach held the post of organist and music director at a number of small German courts before becoming director of church music at the church of St. Thomas in Leipzig in 1723. There Bach composed his Mass in B Minor, his St. Matthew's Passion, and the cantatas and motets that have established his reputation as one of the greatest composers of all time. Like the architect Balthasar Neumann, Bach could move with ease from the religious to the secular. His secular music reflects, in fact, a boisterous spirit; his Coffee Cantata was a dialogue between father and daughter over the daughter's desire to drink the new beverage. Bach had no problem adding religious texts to the secular music he had composed in princely courts to make it church music. Above all for Bach, music was a means to worship God; in his own words, his task in life was to make "well-ordered music in the honor of God."

The other great musical giant of the early eighteenth century, George Frederick Handel (1685–1759) was, like Bach, born in Saxony in Germany and in the same year. Unlike Bach, however, he was profoundly secular in temperament. He began his career by writing operas in the Italian manner and thereafter remained faithful to the Italian Baroque style. In 1712 he moved to England and remained there the rest of his life. Although patronized by the English royal court, Handel wrote music for large public audiences and was not adverse to writing huge, unusual-sounding pieces. The band for his Fireworks Music, for example, was supposed to be accompanied by 101 cannon. Although he wrote much secular music, it is ironic that the worldly Handel is probably best known for his religious music. He had no problem moving from Italian operas to religious oratorios when they proved to be in greater demand from his English public. An oratorio was an extended musical composition on a religious subject, usually taken from a biblical story. Handel's oratorio known as the *Messiah* has been called "one of those rare works that appeal immediately to everyone, and yet is indisputably a masterpiece of the highest order."[11]

To many music historians, Bach and Handel were not great innovators, but great clarifiers who perfected the Baroque musical style with its monumental and elaborate musical structures. Two geniuses of the second half of the eighteenth century—Haydn and Mozart—are viewed as innovators who wrote music called Classical rather than Baroque. Their renown caused the musical center of Europe to shift from Italy to the Austrian Empire.

Franz Joseph Haydn (1732–1809) spent most of his adult life as musical director for the wealthy Hungarian princes, the Esterhazy brothers. Haydn was incredibly prolific, composing 104 symphonies in addition to string quartets, concerti, songs, oratorios, and masses. His visits to England in 1790 and 1794 introduced him to another world where musicians wrote for public concerts rather than princely patrons. This "liberty," as he called it, induced him to write his two great oratorios, *The Creation* and *The Seasons*, both of which were dedicated to the common people.

Wolfgang Amadeus Mozart (1756–1791) was truly a child prodigy who gave his first harpsichord concert at six and wrote his first opera at twelve. He, too, sought a patron, but his discontent with the overly demanding archbishop of Salzburg forced him to move to Vienna where his failure to find a permanent patron made his life miserable. Nevertheless, he wrote music prolifically and passionately: string quartets, sonatas, symphonies, concerti, and operas. *The Marriage of Figaro*, *The Magic Flute*, and *Don Giovanni* are three of the world's greatest operas. Mozart composed with an ease of melody and a blend of grace, precision, and emotion that arguably no one has ever excelled. Haydn remarked to Mozart's father that "your son is the greatest composer known to me either in person or by reputation."

THE DEVELOPMENT OF THE NOVEL   Literary historians credit the eighteenth century with the decisive steps in the development of the novel. The novel was not a completely new literary genre but grew out of the medieval romances and the picaresque stories of the sixteenth century, such as Cervantes's *Don Quixote*. It is the English who are credited with establishing the "modern novel as the chief vehicle" for fiction writing. With no established rules, the novel was open to much experimentation. It also proved especially attractive to women readers and women writers.

Samuel Richardson (1689–1761) was a printer by trade who did not turn to writing until his fifties. His first novel, *Pamela: or, Virtue Rewarded*, focused on a servant girl's resistance to numerous seduction attempts by her master. Finally, by reading the girl's letters describing her feelings about his efforts, the master realizes that she has a good mind as well as body and marries her. Virtue is rewarded. *Pamela* won Richardson a large audience as he appealed to the growing cult of sensibility of the eighteenth century—the taste for the sentimental and emotional. Samuel Johnson, another great English writer of the century and an even greater wit, remarked, "If you were to read Richardson for the story . . . you would hang yourself. But you must read him for the sentiment."

Reacting against the moral seriousness of Richardson, Henry Fielding (1707–1754) wrote novels about people without scruples who survived by their wits. His best work was *The History of Tom Jones, A Foundling*, a lengthy novel about the numerous adventures of a young scoundrel. Fielding presented scenes of English life from the hovels of London to the country houses of the aristocracy. In a number of hilarious episodes, he described characters akin to real types in English society. Although he emphasized action rather than inner feeling, Fielding did his own moralizing by attacking the hypocrisy of his age.

THE WRITING OF HISTORY   The philosophes were responsible for creating a "revolution" in the writing of history. Their secular orientation caused them to eliminate the role of God in history and freed them to concentrate on events themselves and search for causal relationships within a natural world. Earlier, the humanist historians of the Renaissance had also placed their histories in purely secular settings, but not with the same intensity and complete removal of God. While the humanists had deemphasized Christian presuppositions in favor of humans, Voltaire and other philosophe-historians eliminated those presuppositions altogether.

The philosophe-historians also broadened the scope of history from the humanists' preoccupation with politics. Politics still predominated in the work of Enlightenment historians, but they also paid attention to economic, social, intellectual, and cultural developments.

As Voltaire explained in his masterpiece, *The Age of Louis XIV*: "It is not merely the life of Louis XIV that we propose to write; we have a wider aim in view. We shall endeavour to depict for posterity, not the actions of a single man, but the spirit of men in the most enlightened age the world has ever seen."[12] In seeking to describe the "totality of past human experience," Voltaire initiated the modern ideal of social history.

The weaknesses of these philosophe-historians stemmed from their preoccupations as philosophes. Following the ideals of the classics that dominated their minds, the philosophes sought to instruct as well as entertain. Their goal was to help civilize their age, and history could play a role by revealing its lessons according to their vision. Their emphasis on science and reason and their dislike of Christianity made them less than sympathetic to the period we call the Middle Ages. This is particularly noticeable in the other great masterpiece of eighteenth-century historiography, Edward Gibbon's *Decline and Fall of the Roman Empire*. Although Gibbon thought that the decline of Rome had many causes, he could not help blaming Christianity as one of the major ones. Gibbon's work reminds us that history in the eighteenth century was written to prove a point and remained a branch of literature rather than a social science.

High Culture

Historians and cultural anthropologists have grown accustomed to distinguishing between a civilization's high and popular culture. By high culture is usually meant the literary and artistic culture of the educated and wealthy ruling classes; by popular culture is meant the written and unwritten culture of the masses, most of which is passed down orally. By the eighteenth century, European high culture consisted of an ever-expanding and evolving world. There existed a learned culture of theologians, scientists, philosophers, intellectuals, poets, and dramatists, for whom Latin remained a truly international language. Their work was supported by a wealthy and literate lay group, the most important of whom were the landed aristocracy and the wealthier upper classes in the cities. European high culture was noticeably cosmopolitan. In addition to Latin, French had become an international language of the cultural elites. This high culture of Europe's elite was institutionally expressed in the salons, the universities, and the academies.

Especially noticeable in the eighteenth century was an expansion of both the reading public and publishing.

Samuel Johnson and the English Periodical
▼ ▼ ▼

The periodical became a regular feature of upper-class English society in the eighteenth century. Samuel Johnson (1709–1784), one of England's great men of letters, contributed pieces to several of them. This selection is taken from one of Johnson's weekly essays that was published in the Weekly Gazette *under the name of* The Idler.

Samuel Johnson, "Robbery of Time," *The Idler,* no. 14, Saturday, July 15, 1758

When Diogenes received a visit in his tub from Alexander the Great, and was asked, according to the ancient forms of royal courtesy, what petition he had to offer; "I have nothing," said he, "to ask, but that you would remove to the other side, that you may not, by intercepting the sunshine, take from me what you cannot give me."

Such was the demand of Diogenes from the greatest monarch of the earth; which those who have less power than Alexander may, with yet more propriety, apply to themselves. He that does much good may be allowed to do sometimes a little harm. But if the opportunities of beneficence be denied by fortune, innocence should at least be vigilantly preserved.

It is well known that time once past never returns; and that the moment which is lost is lost forever. Time therefore ought, above all other kinds of property, to be free from invasion; and yet there is no man who does not claim the power of wasting that time which is the right of others.

This usurpation is so general that a very small part of the year is spent by choice; scarcely anything is done when it is intended, or obtained when it is desired. Life is continually ravaged by invaders; one steals away an hour, and another a day; one conceals the robbery by hurrying us into business, another by lulling us with amusement; the depredation is continued through a thousand vicissitudes of tumult and tranquillity, till, having lost all, we can lose no more. . . .

If we will have the kindness of others, we must endure their follies. He who cannot persuade himself to withdraw from society must be content to pay a tribute of his time to a multitude of tyrants; to the loiterer, who makes appointments which he never keeps; to the consulter, who asks advice which he never takes; to the boaster, who blusters only to be praised; to the complainer, who whines only to be pitied; to the projector, whose happiness is to entertain his friends with expectations which all but himself know to be vain; to the economist, who tells of bargains and settlements; to the politician, who predicts the fate of battles and breach of alliances; to the usurer, who compares the different funds; and to the talker, who talks only because he loves to be talking.

A recent study of French publishing, for example, reveals that while French publishers issued 300 titles in 1750, about 1,600 were being published yearly in the 1780s. While many of these titles were still geared for small groups of the educated elite, many were also directed to the new reading public of the middle classes, which included women and even urban artisans. The growth of publishing houses made it possible for authors to make money from their works and be less dependent on wealthy patrons. Of course, the increase in publishing does not necessarily mean that the significance and quality of what was being read were improving, as the best-seller in eighteenth-century England, Bishop Sherlock's *Letter from the Lord Bishop of London to the Clergy and People of London on the Occasion of the Late Earthquakes,* would indicate.

An important aspect of the growth of publishing and reading in the eighteenth century was the development of magazines for the general public (see the box above). Great Britain, an important center for the new magazines, saw 25 periodicals published in 1700, 103 in 1760, and 158 in 1780. Although short-lived, the best known was Joseph Addison's and Richard Steele's *Spectator,* begun in 1711. Its goal was "to enliven Morality with wit, and to temper Wit with Morality. . . . To bring Philosophy out of the closets and libraries, schools and colleges, to dwell in clubs and assemblies, at tea-tables and coffeehouses." In keeping with one of the chief intellectual goals of the philosophes, the *Spectator* wished to instruct and entertain at the same time. The *Spectator* with its praise of family, marriage, and courtesy also had a strong appeal to women.

Along with magazines came daily newspapers. The first was printed in London in 1702, but by 1780 thirty-seven other English towns had their own newspapers. Filled with news and special features, they were relatively cheap and were provided free in coffeehouses. Books, too, received wider circulation through the development of public libraries in the cities as well as private circulating libraries, which offered books for rental.

EDUCATION AND UNIVERSITIES   By the eighteenth century, Europe was home to a large number of privately endowed secondary schools, such as the grammar and public school in England, the gymnasium in German-speaking lands, and the collège in France and Spain. In many countries these secondary schools were often dominated by religious orders, especially by the Jesuits who had made education an important part of their philosophy.

These schools tended to be elitist, designed to meet the needs of the children of the upper classes of society. Some scholarships were provided for poor children if they were sponsored by local clerics or nobles. But their lot was not easy, and poor students who completed their studies usually went into the ranks of the lower clergy. Basically then, European secondary schools reinforced the class hierarchy of Europe rather than creating avenues for social mobility. In fact, most of the philosophes reinforced the belief that education should function to keep people in their own social class. Baron d'Holbach said, "Education should teach princes to reign, the ruling classes to distinguish themselves by their merit and virtue, the rich to use their riches well, the poor to live by honest industry."

The curriculum of these secondary schools still largely concentrated on the Greek and Latin classics with little attention paid to mathematics, the sciences, and modern languages. Complaints from philosophe-reformers, as well as from merchants and other middle-class people who wanted their sons to have a more practical education, led to the development of new schools designed to provide a broader education. In England, "dissenting academies," created to educate the non-Anglican segment of the population, offered a broader curriculum than the public and grammar schools. In Germany, the first *Realschule* was opened in Berlin in 1747 and offered modern languages, geography, and bookkeeping to prepare boys for careers in business. New schools of this kind were also created for upper-class girls although they placed most of their emphasis on religion and domestic skills.

The most common complaint about universities, especially from the philosophes, was the old-fashioned curriculum that focused on the classics and Aristotelian philosophy and left out training in the sciences and modern languages. Before the end of the century, this criticism led to reforms that introduced new ideas in the areas of physics, astronomy, and even mathematics into the universities. It is significant, however, that very few of the important scientific discoveries of the eighteenth century occurred in the universities. Most universities, with the exceptions of Edinburgh, Leiden, Vienna, Halle, and Göttingen, produced little intellectual growth and scholarship.

▼ **Library of Göttingen University.** The universities of the seventeenth and eighteenth centuries tended to cling to an old-fashioned curriculum emphasizing the classics and Aristotelian philosophy. Many philosophes argued that the universities should include training in modern languages and science. A reform program was begun before the end of the eighteenth century that allowed new ideas in physics, astronomy, and mathematics to become part of the university curriculum. The University of Göttingen, whose library is pictured here, was one of the universities that placed emphasis on the new physical sciences.

Halle and Göttingen were notable exceptions to this rule, especially in view of the fact that they were new universities. At the University of Halle in Prussia, the philosopher Christian Thomasius (1655–1728) was particularly important in creating a more lively and functional education. He revived theology and philosophy and steered these subjects away from medieval scholasticism. The University of Göttingen in Hanover, founded in 1737, placed its emphasis on the physical sciences. Although a new institution, it had the greatest university library in Europe by the end of the century.

Law, Crime, and Punishment

The legal profession in eighteenth-century Europe was divided into two major branches. Barristers sat atop the legal hierarchy while attorneys constituted a lower group. In England, barristers were usually men of aristocratic background who followed their university studies by apprenticing at the Inns of Court in London. Organized into a corporate group officially recognized by the state, only barristers could appear in court on behalf of their clients. Attorneys, on the other hand, dealt with clients' business outside the courtroom. Becoming an attorney required no university training, but simply a five-year apprenticeship to a regular attorney. Standards were generally lax, and it was not until the end of the century that English attorneys began to become more respectable and gain some prestige.

By the eighteenth century, most European states had developed a hierarchy of courts to deal with civil and criminal cases. With the exception of England, judicial torture remained an important means for obtaining evidence before a trial until the end of the century. Courts used the rack, thumbscrews, and other instruments to obtain confessions in criminal case. Seventeenth century legal reforms, however, led to the gradual demise of judicial torture. France was the last European state to abolish it in 1780.

Most crimes in the eighteenth century fell into four broad categories: violent crimes such as murder; crimes against property; crimes against the government, such as smuggling; and begging or public vagrancy. The eighteenth century seems to have witnessed a decline in crimes of violence while there was a noticeable increase in theft and other crimes against property, especially in the cities. Particularly in rural areas, the unplanned violence of desperate people that had been a prominent feature of the seventeenth century was replaced by "semi-professional vagabonds" who were primarily interested in theft.

Punishments for crimes were often cruel and even spectacular. Public spectacle was a basic part of traditional punishment because of the need to deter potential offenders in an age when a state's police arm was too weak to assure the capture of criminals. Although nobles were executed by simple beheading, lower-class criminals condemned to death were tortured, broken on the wheel, or drawn and quartered (see the box on p. 617). The death penalty was still commonly used in property

▼ **Cruel and Unusual Punishments.** Judicial torture remained a means of obtaining evidence in the eighteenth century. To obtain confessions, courts used the rack and thumbscrews as well as other horrific devices. Punishments for crimes were also often cruel. In this picture, a guilty person is being branded on the hand.

The Punishment of Crime
▼ ▼ ▼

Torture and capital punishment remained common features of European judicial systems well into the eighteenth century. Public spectacles were especially gruesome as this excerpt from the Nocturnal Spectator of Restif de la Bretonne demonstrates.

Restif de la Bretonne, *Nocturnal Spectator*

The Broken Man

I went home by way of rue Saint-Antoine and the Place de Grève. Three murderers had been broken on the wheel there, the day before. I had not expected to see any such spectacle, one that I had never dared to witness. But as I crossed the square I caught sight of a poor wretch, pale, half dead, wracked by the pains of the interrogation inflicted on him twenty hours earlier; he was stumbling down from the Hôtel de Ville supported by the executioner and the confessor. These two men, so completely different, inspired an inexpressible emotion in me! I watched the latter embrace a miserable man consumed by fever, filthy as the dungeons he came from, swarming with vermin! And I said to myself, "O Religion, here is your greatest glory! . . ."

I saw a horrible sight, even though the torture had been mitigated. . . . The wretch had revealed his accomplices. He was garroted before he was put to the wheel. A winch set under the scaffold tightened a noose around the victim's neck and he was strangled; for a long while the confessor and the hangman felt his heart to see whether the artery still pulsed, and the hideous blows were dealt only after it beat no longer. . . . I left, with my hair standing on end in horror.

---

as well as criminal cases. By 1800, the English listed over two hundred crimes that were subject to the death penalty. In addition to executions, European states resorted to forced labor in mines, forts, and navies. England also sent criminals as indentured servants to colonies in the New World and, after the American Revolution, to Australia.

By the end of the eighteenth century, a growing sentiment against executions and torture led to a decline in both corporal and capital punishment. A new type of prison, in which criminals were placed in cells and subjected to discipline and regular work to rehabilitate them, began to replace the public spectacle of barbarous punishments.

Medicine

In the eighteenth century, medicine was practiced by a hierarchy of practitioners. At the top stood the physicians, who were university graduates and enjoyed a high social status. Despite the scientific advances of the seventeenth and eighteenth centuries, however, university medical education was still largely conducted in Latin and was based primarily on Galen's work. New methods emphasizing clinical experience did begin to be introduced at the University of Leiden, which replaced Padua as the foremost medical school of Europe in the first half of the seventeenth century, only to be surpassed in the last half of the seventeenth century by Vienna. A graduate with a doctorate in medicine from a university needed to receive a license before he could be a practicing member of the physicians' elitist corporate body. In England the Royal College of Physicians licensed only one hundred physicians in the early eighteenth century. Only officially licensed physicians could hold regular medical consultations with patients and receive payments, already regarded in the eighteenth century as outrageously high.

Below the physicians were the surgeons, who were still known as barber-surgeons well into the eighteenth century from their original dual occupation. Their primary functions were to bleed patients and perform surgery; the latter was often done in a crude fashion since it was performed without painkillers and in filthy conditions because there was no understanding of bacteria and infection. Bleeding was widely believed to be efficacious as this doctor reported in 1799:

> Bleeding is proper at the beginning of all inflammatory fevers, as pleurisies. . . . It is likewise proper in all topical inflammations, as those of the intestines, womb, bladder, stomach, kidnies, throat, eyes, etc. as also in the asthma, sciatic pains, coughs, head-aches, rheumatisms, the apoplexy, epilepsy, and bloody flux. After falls, blows, bruises, or

any violent hurt received either externally or internally, bleeding is necessary.[13]

The surgeons underwent significant changes in the course of the eighteenth century. In the 1740s, they began to separate themselves from the barbers and organize their own guilds. At the same time, they started to undergo additional training by dissecting corpses and doing a more systematic study of anatomy. As they became more effective, the distinction between physicians and surgeons began to break down, and surgeons came to examine patients in a fashion similar to physicians by the end of the century. Moreover, surgeons also began to be licensed. In England the Royal College of Surgeons required clinical experience before granting the license.

Other medical practitioners, such as apothecaries, midwives, and faith healers, primarily served the common people in the eighteenth century. Although their primary function was to provide herbs and potions as recommended by physicians, apothecaries or pharmacists also acted independently in diagnosing illnesses and selling remedies. In the course of the eighteenth century, midwives were supplanted more and more by male doctors in the delivery of babies. However, the tradition of faith healing, so prominent in medieval medicine, continued to be practiced, especially in the rural areas of Europe.

Hospitals in the eighteenth century seemed more a problem than an aid in dealing with disease and illness. That conditions were bad is evident in this description by the philosophe Denis Diderot, who characterized the Hôtel-Dieu in Paris, France's "biggest, roomiest, and richest" hospital, in these words:

> Imagine a long series of communicating wards filled with sufferers of every kind of disease who are sometimes packed three, four, five or even six into a bed, the living alongside the dead and dying, the air polluted by this mass of unhealthy bodies, passing pestilential germs of their afflictions from one to the other, and the spectacle of suffering and agony on every hand. That is the Hôtel-Dieu.
> The result is that many of these poor wretches come out with diseases they did not have when they went in, and often pass them on to the people they go back to live with. Others are half-cured and spend the rest of their days in an invalidism as hard to bear as the illness itself; and the rest perish, except for the fortunate few whose strong constitutions enable them to survive.[14]

Despite appeals, reform efforts for hospitals in the eighteenth century remained in an infantile stage.

Popular Culture

Popular culture refers to the often unwritten and unofficial culture passed down orally that was fundamental to the lives of most people. The distinguishing characteristic of popular culture is its collective and public nature. Group activity was especially common in the festival, a broad name used to cover a variety of celebrations: family festivals, such as weddings; community festivals in Catholic Europe that celebrated the feastday of the local patron saint; annual festivals, such as Christmas and Easter that go back to medieval Christianity; and Carnival, the most spectacular form of festival, which was celebrated in the Mediterranean world of Spain, Italy, and France as well as in Germany and Austria. All of these festivals shared common characteristics. While having a spiritual function, they were celebrated in a secular fashion. They were special occasions on which people ate, drank, and celebrated to excess. In traditional societies, festival was a time to waste since the rest of the year was a time of thrift; it was a time of play since much of the rest of the year was a time of unrelieved work. As the poet Thomas Gray in 1739 said of Carnival in Turin: "This Carnival lasts only from Christmas to Lent; one half of the remaining part of the year is passed in remembering the last, the other in expecting the future Carnival."[15]

"The example par excellence of the festival" was Carnival, which started in January and lasted until Lent began, traditionally the forty-day period of fasting and purification leading up to Easter. Carnival was a time of great indulgence, just the reverse of Lent when people were expected to abstain from meat, sex, and most recreations. A heavy consumption of food, especially meat and other delicacies, and heavy drinking were the norm: "they drink as if they were never to drink more." Carnival was a time of intense sexual activity as well. Songs with double meanings could be sung publicly at this time of year whereas otherwise they would be considered offensive to the community. A float of Florentine "keymakers," for example, sang this ditty to the ladies: "Our tools are fine, new and useful; We always carry them with us; They are good for anything, If you want to touch them, you can." Finally, it was a time of aggression, a time to release pent-up feelings. Most often this took the form of verbal aggression since people could openly insult other people and were even allowed to criticize their social superiors and authorities. But other acts of violence were also permitted. People pelted each other with apples, eggs, flour, and pig's bladders filled with water.

This limited and sanctioned violence also led to unplanned violence. All contemporaries observed that Carnival was a time when the incidence of murder increased dramatically.

Evident in Carnival was the idea of a "world turned upside down" when the normal order of things was reversed. Peasants became kings, women wore men's clothes, men wore women's clothes, and people were free to express their sexual or violent emotions. Social anthropologists have speculated that the purpose of these traditional "rituals of reversal" was to create their opposite, to strengthen the established order: "By making the low high and the high low, they reaffirm the hierarchical principle."[16] While this may be true, it would be foolish to assume that it always worked. There are numerous examples of Carnival events developing into riots in which public authorities were killed.

The same sense of community evident in festival was also present in the chief gathering places of the common people, the local taverns or cabarets. Taverns were supposedly for travelers but functioned more frequently as a regular gathering place for neighborhood men to talk, play games, conduct small business matters, and, of course, to drink. In some countries, the favorite drinks of poor people, such as gin in England and vodka in Russia, proved devastating as poor people regularly drank themselves into oblivion. Gin was cheap; the classic sign in English taverns, "Drunk for a penny, dead drunk for two pence," was literally true. In England the consumption of gin rose from two to five million gallons from 1714 to 1733 and only declined when complaints finally led to strict laws to restrict sales in the 1750s. Of course, the rich drank too. Samuel Johnson remarked once, "All the decent people in Lichfield got drunk every night and were not the worse thought of." But unlike the poor, the rich drank port and brandy, usually in large quantities.

This difference in drinking habits between rich and poor reminds us of the ever-widening separation between the elite and poor in the eighteenth century. In 1500, popular culture was for everyone; a second culture for the elite, it was the only culture for the rest of society. But between 1500 and 1800, the nobility, clergy, and bourgeoisie had abandoned popular culture to the lower classes. This was, of course, a gradual process, and in abandoning the popular festivals, the upper classes were also abandoning the popular worldview as well. The new scientific outlook had brought a new mental world for the upper classes, and they now viewed such things as witchcraft, faith healing, fortune telling, and

prophecy as the beliefs of "such as are of the weakest judgment and reason, as women, children, and ignorant and superstitious persons."

Despite this growing gulf between elite and common people, there were still some forms of entertainment that occasionally brought them together. Most common were the urban fairs, a product of what some historians now call the "commercialization of leisure," or the attempt by businessmen to turn leisure activities into a good investment. The three fairs in Paris provided entertainment—farcical theater, magic shows, circus performers, or freak shows—as well as food booths and popular wares for purchase. Both the privileged and unprivileged classes were still attracted to boxing matches and horse races as well as the bloodier spectacles of bullbaiting, bearbaiting, and cockfighting.

Popular culture had always included a vast array of traditional songs and stories that were passed down from generation to generation. But popular culture was not entirely based on an oral tradition; there existed a popular literature as well. So-called chapbooks, printed on cheap paper, were short brochures sold by itinerant peddlers to the lower classes. They contained both spiritual and secular material; lives of saints and inspirational stories competed with crude satires and adventure stories. Another kind of popular literature in the eighteenth century was the almanac, which combined the traditional astrological charts and herbal remedies with information on history and how to write letters.

It is apparent from the chapbooks and almanacs that popular culture did not have to remain primarily oral. Its ability to change was dependent upon the growth of literacy. There is still considerable uncertainty about literacy in early modern Europe because of the difficulty in measuring it. Some reasonable estimates based on studies in France indicate that literacy rates for men increased from 29 percent in the late seventeenth century to 47 percent in the late eighteenth century; for women, the increase was from 14 to 27 percent during the same period. Of course, certain groups were more likely to be literate than others. Upper-class elites as well as the upper middle classes in the cities were mostly all literate. However, the figures also indicate dramatic increases for lower-middle-class artisans in urban areas. Recent research in the city of Marseilles, for example, indicates an increase in literacy for male artisans and workers from 28 percent in 1710 to 85 percent in 1789 while rates for women remained at 15 percent. Peasants, who constituted as much as 75 percent of the French population, remained largely illiterate.

The development of literacy was closely connected to primary education. In Catholic Europe, primary education was largely a matter of local community effort, leading to little real growth. Only in the Habsburg Austrian Empire was there created a system of state-supported primary schools (*Volkschulen*). Although attendance was supposedly compulsory, a 1781 census revealed that only one in four school-age children was actually attending.

The emphasis of the Protestant reformers on reading the Bible had led Protestant states to take greater interest in primary education. Some places, especially the Swiss cantons, Scotland, and the German states of Saxony and Prussia, witnessed the emergence of universal primary schools that provided a modicum of education for the masses. An edict of the Prussian king Frederick II (see Chapter 19) in 1763 made the schooling of children compulsory. But effective systems of primary education were hindered by the attitudes of the ruling classes, who feared the consequences of any education beyond teaching the lower classes the virtues of hard work and deference to their superiors. Hannah More, a conservative evangelical educator made clear the philosophy of her charity school for poor children: "My plan of instruction is extremely simple and limited. They learn on weekdays such coarse work as may fit them for servants. I allow of no writing for the poor. My object is to train up the lower classes in habits of industry and piety."

▼ Religion and the Churches

The music of Bach and the pilgrimage and monastic churches of southern Germany and Austria make us cognizant of a curious fact. While much of the great art and music of the time was religious, the thought of the time was antireligious as life became increasingly secularized and men of reason attacked the established churches. And yet most Europeans were still Christians. Except for governments, churches remained the most important institutions in people's lives. Even many of those most critical of the churches accepted that society could not function without religious faith.

The Institutional Church

In the eighteenth century, the established Catholic and Protestant churches were basically conservative institutions that upheld society's hierarchical structure, privileged classes, and traditions. Although churches experienced change because of new state policies, they did not sustain any dramatic internal changes. Whether in Catholic or Protestant countries, the parish church run by priest or pastor remained the center of religious practice. In addition to providing religious services, the parish church kept records of births, deaths, and marriages, provided charity for the poor, supervised whatever primary education there was, and cared for orphans.

CHURCH-STATE RELATIONS Early on, the Protestant Reformation had solved the problem of the relationship between church and state by establishing the principle of state control over the churches. In the eighteenth century, Protestant state churches flourished throughout Europe: Lutheranism in Scandinavia and the north German states; Anglicanism in England; and Calvinism (or Reformed churches) in Scotland, the United Provinces, and some of the Swiss cantons and German states. There were also Protestant minorities in other European countries.

In 1700, the Catholic church still exercised much power in Catholic European states: Spain, Portugal, France, Italy, the Habsburg Empire, Poland, and most of southern Germany. Only Catholics were allowed to hold political office while in some countries, such as France and Austria, Protestants had no civil rights as well. The church continued to possess enormous wealth. In Spain, 3,000 monastic institutions housing 100,000 men and women controlled enormous landed estates.

The Catholic church remained hierarchically structured. In most Catholic countries, the highest clerics, such as bishops, archbishops, abbots, and abbesses, were members of the upper class, especially members of the landed nobility who received enormous revenues from their landed estates and tithes from the faithful. A wide gulf existed between the upper and lower clergy. While the French bishop of Strasbourg, for example, received 100,000 livres a year, parish priests were paid only 500.

In the eighteenth century, the governments of many Catholic states began to seek greater authority over the churches in their countries. This "nationalization" of the Catholic church was not entirely new. Louis XIV had already achieved a certain amount of control over the Catholic church in France in the seventeenth century. Other Catholic rulers now achieved similar results in the eighteenth century. One of the best examples of the changing relations between church and state in Catholic countries can be found in Spain, known above all for its dedication to Catholicism. The Bourbon kings, especially Charles III (1759–1788), continued to appoint Spanish bishops, forbade the publication of papal bulls without royal consent, and established control over the Inquisition by eliminating its more arbitrary features.

For Catholic countries, "nationalization" meant controlling the papacy and in turn the chief papal agents, the Society of Jesus. The Jesuits had proved extremely successful, perhaps too successful for their own good. They had created special enclaves, virtually states-within-states, in the French, Spanish, and Portuguese colonies in the New World. Through their excellent secondary schools, they directed the education of the sons of Catholic aristocrats. As advisers to Catholic rulers, they exercised considerable political influence. The high profile they achieved through their successes led to a wide range of enemies, both religious, from groups within the Catholic church who envied their importance, and political, from government ministers who viewed them as belonging to an international network hostile to the interests of individual states. A series of actions soon undermined Jesuit power. The Portuguese monarch and his adviser Pombal destroyed the powerful Jesuit state in Paraguay and then in 1759 expelled the Jesuits from Portugal and confiscated their property. The Portuguese expulsion was but the beginning of a series of attacks from political interests and enemies of the Jesuits from within the Catholic church itself. In 1764, they were expelled from France and three years later from Spain and the Spanish colonies. In 1773, when Spain and France demanded that the entire society be dissolved, Pope Clement XIV reluctantly complied. The dissolution of the Jesuit order, the pillar of Catholic fanaticism and strength, was yet another victory for Catholic governments determined to win control over their churches.

The end of the Jesuits was paralleled by a decline in papal power. Already by the mid-eighteenth century, the papacy played a minor role in diplomacy and international affairs. The nationalization of the churches by the states meant the loss of the papacy's power to appoint high clerical officials. In addition, a number of aristocratic bishops and archbishops became increasingly less reverent toward papal power. As one bishop remarked: "The Pope has his rights and we have ours."

Another aspect of state control over the Catholic church involved the regulation and suppression of monastic orders. The most radical program was carried out in the Austrian Empire where the Empress Maria Theresa (1745–1780) and later Emperor Joseph II (1780–1790) had already curtailed the Catholic church's power (see Chapter 19). By the Edict on Idle Institutions in 1782, Joseph II suppressed all the contemplative monastic orders, allowing only those that provided charitable or educational services to survive. The number of monks in the Austrian Empire was cut in half while the confiscated monastic properties were used to extend education. Joseph II's attempts to modernize even religious practices by cutting down on pilgrimages and the observation of saints' days backfired, however, for it cost him the support of the peasants who resented this interference in their personal religious life.

TOLERATION AND RELIGIOUS MINORITIES One of the chief battle cries of the philosophes had been a call for religious toleration. Out of political necessity, a certain level of tolerance of different creeds had occurred in the

▼ The Coronation Procession of Louis XV. Although their power had declined significantly, churches continued to play a role in the eighteenth century. This painting by Pierre-Denis Martin shows the procession after the coronation of King Louis XV at Reims cathedral in 1722. Royalty was still conferred by the church through the traditional sacramental ceremony of coronation.

seventeenth century in such places as Germany after the Thirty Years' War and France after the divisive religious wars. But many rulers still found it difficult to accept. Louis XIV had turned back the clock in France at the end of the seventeenth century, insisting on religious uniformity and suppressing the rights of the Huguenots (see Chapter 16). Even devout rulers, such as Maria Theresa of Austria, continued to believe that there was only one path to salvation; it was the true duty of a ruler not to allow subjects to be condemned to hell by being heretics. Catholic minorities in Protestant countries and Protestant minorities in Catholic countries did not enjoy full civil or political rights. Persecution of heretics continued; the last burning of a heretic took place in 1781.

Nevertheless, some progress was made toward the principle of religious toleration. In England, the late seventeenth-century laws against Protestant Dissenters (from the Anglican church) were repealed or enforced loosely or not at all. No ruler was more interested in the philosophes' call for religious toleration than Joseph II of Austria. His Toleration Patent of 1781, while recognizing Catholicism's public practice, granted Lutherans, Calvinists, and Greek Orthodox the right to worship privately. In all other ways, all subjects were now equal: "Non-Catholics are in future admitted under dispensation to buy houses and real property, to practice as master craftsmen, to take up academic appointments and posts in public service, and are not to be required to take the oath in any form contrary to their religious tenets."[17]

TOLERATION AND THE JEWS   The Jews remained the despised religious minority of Europe. The largest number of Jews (known as the Ashkenazic Jews) lived in Eastern Europe. Except in relatively tolerant Poland, Jews were restricted in their movements, forbidden to own land or hold many jobs, forced to pay burdensome special taxes, and also subject to periodic outbursts of popular wrath. The resulting pogroms in which Jewish communities were looted and massacred made Jewish existence precarious and dependent upon the favor of their territorial rulers.

Another major group was the Sephardic Jews who had been expelled from Spain in the fifteenth century. Although many had migrated to Turkish lands, some of them had settled in cities, such as Amsterdam, Venice, London, and Frankfurt, where they were relatively free to participate in the banking and commercial activities that Jews had practiced since the Middle Ages. The highly successful ones came to provide valuable services to rulers, especially in central Europe where they were known as the court Jews. But even these Jews were

insecure since their religion set them apart from the Christian majority and served as a catalyst to social resentment.

Some Enlightenment thinkers in the eighteenth century favored a new acceptance of Jews. They argued that Jews and Muslims were all human and deserved the full rights of citizenship despite their religion. But some philosophes, especially Holbach and Voltaire, made no attempt to hide their hostility and ridiculed Jewish customs. Many Europeans favored the assimilation of the Jews into the mainstream of society, but only by the conversion of Jews to Christianity as the basic solution to the "Jewish problem." This, of course, was not acceptable to most Jews.

The Austrian emperor Joseph II attempted to adopt a new policy toward the Jews, although it too was limited. It freed Jews from nuisance taxes and allowed them more freedom of movement and job opportunities, but they were still restricted from owning land and worshiping in public. At the same time, Joseph II encouraged Jews to learn German and work toward greater assimilation into Austrian society. Joseph's policy was but a small step in the liberation of the Jews as it took a moderate position between toleration and assimilation. The real emancipation of the Jews awaited the French Revolution and nineteenth-century developments.

Popular Religion in the Eighteenth Century

Despite the rise of skepticism and the intellectuals' belief in deism and natural religion, it would appear that religious devotion remained strong in the eighteenth century. Catholic popular piety continued to be strong while within Protestantism the desire for more direct spiritual experience actually led to religious revivalism, especially in Germany and England.

CATHOLIC PIETY   It is difficult to assess precisely the religiosity of Europe's Catholics. The Catholic parish church remained an important center of life for the entire community. How many people went to church regularly cannot be known exactly, but it has been established that 90 to 95 percent of Catholic populations did go to mass on Easter Sunday, one of the church's most special celebrations. Confraternities, which were organizations of lay people dedicated to good works and acts of piety, were especially popular with townspeople. Consecrated to a patron saint, each confraternity honored that saint by holy processions in which members proudly wore their special robes.

Catholic religiosity proved highly selective, however. Despite the Reformation, much popular devotion was still directed to an externalized form of worship focusing on prayers to saints, pilgrimages, and devotion to relics and images. The latter bothered many clergymen who felt that their parishioners were "more superstitious than devout," as one Catholic priest remarked. Many common people continued to fear witches and relied on the intervention of the saints and Virgin Mary to save them from personal disasters caused by the devil. Although more moderate and learned Catholics denounced this behavior as superstitious and wished to make Catholicism more rational, these practices were not confined to the lower classes. When the son of the Emperor Charles VI died shortly after birth, the emperor made a pilgrimage to the shrine of the Virgin Mary at Mariazell in Austria where he placed an image of the Christ child weighing as much as his dead son while praying for another male heir.

Nevertheless, recent research in France has indicated some decline in popular religious practices, especially in the most outward manifestations of faith. Religious phrases, for example, were increasingly dropped from the preambles to wills in the course of the eighteenth century. This was especially true for middle-class businessmen and professionals as well as many urban wage earners. To some historians, this evidence indicates a growing secularization on the eve of the French Revolution and the nineteenth century. Scholars doubt, however, whether this was as widespread in other parts of Europe.

PROTESTANT REVIVALISM   After the initial century of religious fervor that created Protestantism in the sixteenth century, Protestant churches in the seventeenth century had settled down into well-established patterns controlled by state authorities and served by a well-educated clergy. Protestant churches became bureaucratized and bereft of religious enthusiasm. In Germany and England, where rationalism and deism had become influential and moved some theologians to a more "rational" Christianity, the desire of ordinary Protestant churchgoers for greater depths of religious experience led to new and dynamic religious movements.

Pietism in Germany was a response to this desire for a deeper personal devotion to God. Begun in the seventeenth century by a group of German clerics who wished their religion to be more personal and transformative of daily experience, Pietism was spread by the teachings of Count Nikolaus von Zinzendorf (1700–1760). To Zinzendorf and his Moravian Brethren, as his sect was

called, it was the mysticial dimensions—the personal experience of God—in one's life that constituted true religious experience. He was utterly opposed to what he perceived as the rationalistic approach of orthodox Lutheran clergy who were being educated in new "rational" ideas. As Zinzendorf commented, "He who wishes to comprehend God with his mind becomes an atheist." To temper their mysticism, the Moravian Brethren followed a collective discipline akin to that of monasticism. Other Pietists, especially at the University of Halle and in other small German states, downplayed Zinzendorf's mystical element in favor of infusing civil life with Christian spirit and good works. In the eighteenth century, Pietism added an element of liveliness to an orthodox Lutheranism that was threatening to stagnate.

After the civil wars of the seventeenth century, England too had arrived at a respectable, uniform, and complacent state church. While local Anglican parish rectors were under the control of neighboring landholding nobles and reflected their social prejudices, higher members of the clergy—the bishops—were appointed by the crown, most often for political reasons. A pillar of the establishment, the Anglican church seemed to offer little spiritual excitement, especially to the masses of people. The other dissenting Protestant groups—the Puritans, Quakers, Baptists—were relatively subdued while the growth of deism seemed to challenge Christianity itself. The desire for deep spiritual experience seemed unmet until the advent of John Wesley (1703–1791).

An ordained Anglican minister, John Wesley took religion very seriously and experienced a deep spiritual crisis, finally relieved only by the ministrations of a German Pietist. In the process, he underwent a mystical experience: "I felt I did trust in Christ alone for salvation; and an assurance was given me, that He had taken away my sins, even mine, and saved me from the law of sin and death. I felt my heart strangely warmed." To Wesley, "the gift of God's grace" assured him of salvation and led him, despite opposition from the Anglican church, which criticized this emotional mysticism or religious enthusiasm as superstitious nonsense, to become a missionary to the English people, to bring the "glad tidings" of salvation to all people. To Wesley, all could be saved by experiencing God and opening the doors to his grace.

In taking the Gospel to the people, Wesley preached to the masses in open fields, appealing especially to the lower classes neglected by the socially elitist Anglican church. He tried, he said, "to lower religion to the level of the lowest people's capacities." Wesley's charismatic

The Conversion Experience in Wesley's Methodism
▼ ▼ ▼

After his own conversion experience, John Wesley traveled extensively to bring the "glad tidings" of Christ to other people. It has been estimated that he preached over 40,000 sermons, some of them to audiences numbering 20,000 listeners. Wesley gave his message wherever people gathered—in the streets, hospitals, private houses, and even pubs. In this selection from his journal, Wesley describes how emotional and even violent conversion experiences could be.

The Works of the Reverend John Wesley

Sunday, May 20 [1759], being with Mr. B—11 at Everton, I was much fatigued, and did not rise: but Mr. B. did, and observed several fainting and crying out, while Mr. Berridge was preaching: afterwards at Church, I heard many cry out, especially children, whose agonies were amazing: one of the eldest, a girl of ten or twelve years old, was full in my view, in violent contortions of body, and weeping aloud, I think incessantly, during the whole service. . . . The Church was equally crowded in the afternoon, the windows being filled within and without, and even the outside of the pulpit to the very top; so that Mr. B. seemed almost stifled by their breath; yet feeble and sickly as he is, he was continually strengthened, and his voice, for the most part, distinguishable, in the midst of all the outcries. I believe there were present three times more men than women, a great part of whom came from far; thirty of them having set out at two in the morning, from a place thirteen miles off. The text was, *Having a form of godliness, but denying the power thereof.* When the power of religion began to be spoken of, the presence of God really filled the place: and while poor sinners felt the sentence of death in their souls, what sounds of distress did I hear! The greatest number of them who cried or fell, were men: but some women, and several children, felt the power of the same almighty Spirit, and seemed just sinking into hell. This occasioned a mixture of several sounds; some shrieking, some roaring aloud. The most general was a loud breathing, like that of people half strangled and gasping for life: and indeed almost all the cries were like those of human creatures, dying in bitter anguish. Great numbers wept without any noise: others fell down as death: some sinking in silence; some with extreme noise and violent agitation. I stood on the pew-seat, as did a young man in the opposite pew, an able-bodied, fresh, healthy countryman: but in a moment, while he seemed to think of nothing less, down he dropped with a violence inconceivable. The adjoining pews seemed to shake with his fall: I heard afterwards the stamping of his feet; ready to break the boards, as he lay in strong convulsions, at the bottom of the pew. Among several that were struck down in the next pew, was a girl, who was as violently seized as he. . . . Among the children who felt the arrows of the Almighty, I saw a sturdy boy, about eight years old, who roared above his fellows, and seemed in his agony to struggle with the strength of a grown man. His face was as red as scarlet: and almost all on whom God laid his hand, turned either very red or almost black. . . .

The violent struggling of many in the above-mentioned churches, has broken several pews and benches. Yet it is common for people to remain unaffected there, and afterwards to drop down in their way home. Some have been found lying as dead on the road: others, in Mr. B.'s garden; not being able to walk from the Church to his house, though it is not two hundred yards. . . .

preaching often provoked highly charged and even violent conversion experiences (see the box above). Afterward, converts were organized into so-called Methodist societies or chapels in which they could aid each other in doing the good works that Wesley considered a component of salvation. A Central Methodist Conference supervised new lay preachers from Methodist circles. Controlled by Wesley, it enabled him to dominate the evangelical movement he had created. Although Wesley sought to keep Methodism within the Anglican church, after his death it became a separate and independent sect.

John Wesley's Methodism gave lower-class and even some middle-class English people a sense of purpose and community. Emphasizing the virtues of hard work and sobriety, it encouraged patterns of behavior that made people successful and content with spiritual rather than political equality. Indeed, some historians have argued that Methodism insulated the English lower classes from the political radicalism generated in the French revolutionary era of the 1790s. Although this view is an exaggeration, Methodism does represent an important revival of Christianity and proved that the need for spiritual experience had not been expunged by the eighteenth-century search for reason.

One prominent historian of the eighteenth century has appropriately characterized it as a century of change and tradition. Highly influenced by the new worldview created by the Scientific Revolution and especially the ideas of Locke and Newton, the philosophes hoped that they could create a new society by using reason to discover the natural laws that governed it. Like the Christian humanists of the fifteenth and sixteenth centuries,

they believed that education could create better human beings and a better human society. By attacking traditional religion as the enemy and creating the new "sciences of man" in economics, politics, justice, and education, the philosophes laid the foundation for a modern worldview based on rationalism and secularism.

But it was also an age of tradition. While secular thought and rational ideas began to pervade the mental world of the ruling elites, most people in eighteenth-century Europe still lived by seemingly eternal verities and practices—God, religious worship, and farming. The most brilliant architecture and music of the age were religious. And yet, the forces of secularization were too strong to stop. In the midst of intellectual change, economic, political, and social transformations of great purport were taking shape that by the end of the eighteenth century were to lead to both political and industrial revolutions. It is time now to examine the political, economic, and social traditions and changes of the century.

Notes

1. Quoted in Paul Hazard, *The European Mind, 1680–1715* (New York, 1963), pp. 304–5.

2. Quoted in Alan G. R. Smith, *Science and Society in the Sixteenth and Seventeenth Centuries* (London, 1972), pp. 174–75.

3. Quoted in Hazard, *The European Mind*, p. 11.

4. Ibid., p. 12.

5. John Locke, *An Essay Concerning Human Understanding* (New York, 1964), pp. 89–90.

6. Quoted in Frederick Artz, *The Enlightenment in France* (Kent, Ohio, 1968), p. 103.

7. Cesare Beccaria, *An Essay on Crimes and Punishments*, trans. E. D. Ingraham (Philadelphia, 1819), pp. 59–60, 93–94.

8. Baron d'Holbach, *Common Sense*, as quoted in Frank E. Manuel, ed., *The Enlightenment* (Englewood Cliffs, N.J., 1965), p. 62.

9. Jean-Jacques Rousseau, *A Discourse on Inequality*, trans. Maurice Cranston (Harmondsworth, 1984), p. 109.

10. Jean-Jacques Rousseau, *The Social Contract*, trans. Maurice Cranston (Harmondsworth, 1968), p. 141.

11. Kenneth Clark, *Civilisation* (New York, 1969), p. 231.

12. Voltaire, *The Age of Louis XIV*, trans. Martyn P. Pollack (New York, 1961), p. 1.

13. Quoted in Lester S. King, *The Medical World of the Eighteenth Century* (Chicago, 1958), pp. 318–19.

14. Quoted in Rene Sand, *The Advance to Social Medicine* (London, 1952), pp. 86–87.

15. Quoted in Peter Burke, *Popular Culture in Early Modern Europe* (New York, 1978), p. 179.

16. Quotations (in order of appearance) are from ibid., pp. 183, 186, 201.

17. Quoted in C. A. Macartney, *The Habsburg and Hohenzollern Dynasties in the Seventeenth and Eighteenth Centuries* (New York, 1970), p. 157.

Suggestions for Further Reading
▼ ▼ ▼

Two sound, comprehensive surveys of eighteenth-century Europe are I. Woloch, *Eighteenth-Century Europe* (New York, 1982); and M. S. Anderson, *Europe in the Eighteenth Century* (London, 1987).

A good, brief introduction to the Enlightenment can be found in N. Hampson, *A Cultural History of the Enlightenment* (New York, 1968). A more detailed synthesis can be found in P. Gay, *The Enlightenment: An Interpretation,* 2 vols. (New York, 1966–69). Two older works still of value are by P. Hazard, *The European Mind, 1680–1715* (New York, 1963), and *European Thought in the Eighteenth Century* (New York, 1963). For a short, popular survey on the French philosophes, see F. Artz, *The Enlightenment in France* (Kent, Ohio, 1968). Studies on the major Enlightenment intellectuals include R. Shackleton, *Montesquieu, A Critical Biography* (London, 1961); T. Besterman, *Voltaire* (London, 1969); A. Wilson, *Diderot* (New York, 1972); and R. Grimsley, *Jean-Jacques Rousseau* (Cardiff, 1961). Specialized studies on various aspects of the Enlightenment include F. Venturi, *Utopia and Reform in the Enlightenment* (Cambridge, 1971); F. Manuel, *The Eighteenth Century Confronts the Gods* (New York, 1967); M. C. Jacob, *The Radical Enlightenment: Pantheists, Freemasons and Republicans* (London, 1981); H. Chisack, *The Limits of Reform in the Enlightenment: Attitudes toward the Education of the Lower Classes in Eighteenth-Century France* (Princeton, N.J., 1980); and R. Darnton, *The Business of Enlightenment: A Publishing History of the Encyclopédie, 1775–1800* (Cambridge, Mass., 1979). On the role of women in the salon, see P. Quennell, ed., *Affairs of the Mind: The Salon in Europe and America from the 18th to the 20th Century* (Washington, D.C., 1980); and S. I. Spencer, ed., *French Women and the Age of Enlightenment* (Bloomington, Ind., 1984).

Two readable general surveys on the arts and literature are M. Levy, *Rococo to Revolution* (London, 1966); and H. Honour, *Neo-classicism* (Harmondsworth, 1968). On the development of the novel in England, see I. Watt, *The Rise of the Novel: Studies in Defoe, Richardson, and Fielding* (Berkeley, 1957). On one aspect of eighteenth-century education, see C. Bailey, *French Secondary Education, 1763–1790* (Philadelphia, 1978). The development of the attorney and barrister are examined in R. Robson, *The Attorney in Eighteenth Century England* (Cambridge, 1959); and L. Berlanstein, *The Barristers of Toulouse in the Eighteenth Century* (Baltimore, 1975). Different facets of crime and punishment are examined in the important works by M. Foucault, *Discipline and Punish: The Birth of the Prison* (New York, 1977); and J. Langbein, *Torture and the Law of Proof* (Chicago, 1977). On the medical profession, see L. King, *The Medical World of the Eighteenth Century* (Chicago, 1958); and M. Foucault, *The Birth of the Clinic* (New York, 1975).

Important studies on popular culture include P. Burke, *Popular Culture in Early Modern Europe* (New York, 1978); and R. Darnton, *The Great Cat Massacre and Other Episodes in French Cultural History* (New York, 1984). Recreational activities are covered in R. Malcolmson, *Popular Recreation in English Society, 1700–1850* (Cambridge, 1973); and R. Isherwood, *Farce and Fantasy: Popular Entertainment in Eighteenth-Century Paris* (New York, 1986). One approach to the popular literature of the lower classes can be found in B. Capp, *English Almanacs, 1500–1800: Astrology and the Popular Press* (Ithaca, N.Y., 1979).

A good introduction to the religious history of the eighteenth century can be found in G. R. Cragg, *The Church and the Age of Reason, 1648–1789* (London, 1966). A very informative regional study is T. Tacket, *Priest and Parish in Eighteenth-Century France* (Princeton, N.J., 1977). The problem of religious toleration is examined in C. H. O'Brien, *Ideas of Religious Toleration at the Time of Joseph II* (Philadelphia, 1969); and A. Hertzberg, *The French Enlightenment and the Jews* (New York, 1968).

Chapter 19

The Eighteenth Century: European States, International Wars, and Social Change

▼▼▼▼▼

Historians have often defined the eighteenth century chronologically as spanning the years from 1715 to 1789. Politically this makes sense since 1715 marks the end of the age of Louis XIV while 1789 was the year in which the French Revolution erupted. This period has often been portrayed as the final phase of Europe's old order, before the violent upheaval and reordering of society associated with the French Revolution. Europe's old order, still largely agrarian, dominated by kings and landed aristocrats, and grounded in privileges for nobles, clergy, towns, and provinces, seemed to continue a basic pattern that had prevailed in Europe since medieval times. Recent scholarship, however, has tended to undermine the idea of uniformity in the eighteenth century, especially in France and England. Just as a new intellectual order based on rationalism and secularism was emerging from the intellectual revolution of the Scientific Revolution and Enlightenment, demographic, economic, and social patterns were beginning to change in ways that represent the emergence of a modern new order.

In the eighteenth century, the process of centralization that had characterized the growth of states since the Middle Ages continued as most European states enlarged their bureaucratic machinery and consolidated their governments in order to collect the revenues and build the manpower they needed to compete militarily with the other European states. International competition continued to be the favorite pastime of eighteenth-century rulers. Within the European

	Frederick the Great of Prussia ▼	Maria Theresa of Austria ▼	Catherine the Great of Russia ▼	William Pitt the Younger Becomes Prime Minister of Britain ▼

•••••••• 1700 ••••••••••• 1725 ••••••••••• 1750 ••••••••••• 1775 ••••••••••• 1800 •••••••••

	Britain Enters Spanish American Markets ▲	War of Austrian Succession ▲	Seven Years' War ▲	Quaker Criticism of Slave Trade ▲

state system, the nations that would dominate Europe until World War I—Britain, France, Austria, Prussia, and Russia—emerged as the five great powers of Europe. Their rivalries led to major wars, which some have called the first "world wars" since they were fought outside as well as inside Europe. In the midst of this state building and war making, dramatic demographic, economic, and social changes heralded the emergence of a radical transformation in the way Europeans would raise food and produce goods.

▼ The European States

Most European states in the eighteenth century were ruled by monarchs. Although individuals or factional parties often vied for influence over the monarch, few of those involved questioned either the moral or practical superiority of hereditary monarchy as the best form of government, especially in the large and successful states. As Catherine II wrote in 1764, "The Russian Empire is so large that apart from the Autocratic Sovereign every other form of government is harmful to it, because all others are slower in their execution and contain a great multitude of various horrors, which lead to the disintegration of power and strength more than that of one Sovereign."[1] States where hereditary monarchy was not strong, such as in the United Provinces, Sweden, and Poland, suffered decline or even worse. The lack of a strong monarchy led to Poland's partitioning by Austria, Prussia, and Russia in the course of the eighteenth century (see Poland later in the chapter).

The seventeenth-century justification for strong monarchy on the basis of divine right continued into the succeeding century, but in a diminished way as the eighteenth century became increasingly secularized. Although divine-right assumptions died hard, they were

gradually superseded by influential utilitarian arguments. These were well expressed by the Prussian king Frederick II when he attempted to explain the services a monarch must provide for his people:

> These services consisted in the maintenance of the laws; a strict execution of justice; an employment of his whole powers to prevent any corruption of manners; and defending the state against its enemies. It is the duty of this magistrate to pay attention to agriculture; it should be his care that provisions for the nation should be in abundance, and that commerce and industry should be encouraged. He is a perpetual sentinel, who must watch the acts and the conduct of the enemies of the state. . . . If he be the first general, the first minister of the realm, it is not that he should remain the shadow of authority, but that he should fulfill the duties of such titles. He is only the first servant of the state.[2]

This utilitarian argument was reinforced by the praises of the philosophes.

Enlightened Politics?

There is no doubt that Enlightenment thought had some impact on the political development of European states in the eighteenth century. Closely associated with the Enlightenment idea of natural laws was the belief in natural rights, which were thought to be inalienable privileges that ought not to be withheld from any person. These natural rights included equality before the law, freedom of religious worship, freedom of speech and press, and the right to assemble, hold property, and pursue happiness. The American Declaration of Independence summarized the Enlightenment concept of natural rights in its opening paragraph: "We hold these truths to be self-evident, that all men are created equal; that they are endowed by their creator with certain unalienable rights; that among these are life, liberty and the pursuit of happiness."

But how were these natural rights to be established and preserved? Montesquieu had argued for constitutional guarantees achieved by a separation of powers in *The Spirit of the Laws.* Rousseau had advocated a democratic society as the ideal path to maintain people's natural rights. Most philosophes, however, did not trust the "people." "It must please the animals," Voltaire said, "when they see how foolishly men behave." In the opinion of the philosophes, most people needed the direction provided by an enlightened ruler. What, however, made rulers enlightened? They must allow religious toleration, freedom of speech and press, and the rights of private property. They must foster the arts, sciences, and education. Above all, they must not be arbitrary in their rule; they must obey the laws and enforce them fairly for all subjects. To Voltaire, only strong monarchs seemed capable of overcoming vested interests and effecting the reforms society needed. Reforms then should come from above—from the rulers—rather than from below—from the people. The philosophes were only too well aware of the power monarchs possessed and thought it unlikely that they would voluntarily relinquish it. Distrustful of the masses, the philosophes believed that absolute rulers, swayed by enlightened principles, were the best hope of reforming their societies.

The extent to which rulers actually did so is a frequently discussed issue in the political history of the eighteenth century. Many historians once assumed that a new type of monarchy emerged in the later eighteenth century, which they called "enlightened despotism" or "enlightened absolutism." Monarchs such as Frederick II of Prussia, Catherine the Great of Russia, and Joseph II of Austria supposedly followed the advice of the philosophes and ruled by enlightened principles, creating a path to modern nationhood. Recent scholarship, however, has questioned the usefulness of the concept of "enlightened absolutism." We can best determine the extent to which it can be applied by surveying the development of the European states in the eighteenth century and then making a judgment about the "enlightened absolutism" of the later eighteenth century.

The Atlantic Seaboard States

As a result of overseas voyages in the sixteenth century, the European economic axis began to shift from the Mediterranean to the Atlantic seaboard. In the seventeenth century, the English and Dutch expanded as Spain and Portugal declined. By the eighteenth century, Dutch power had waned, and it was left to the English and French to build the commercial empires that presaged the growth of a true global economy.

FRANCE   In the eighteenth century, France experienced an economic revival while the movement of the Enlightenment gained strength. The French monarchy, however, was not overly influenced by the philosophes and resisted reforms while the French aristocracy grew stronger.

Louis XIV had left France with enlarged territories but also an enormous debt, an unhappy populace, and his five-year-old great-grandson as his successor. The governing of France fell into the hands first of the regent, the duke of Orléans, whose good intentions were undermined by his drunken and immoral behavior, and later of Cardinal Fleury, the king's minister. France remained largely at peace as commerce and trade doubled and industry was promoted. Even the budget was balanced, at least for one year in 1738. Louis XV (1715–1774) then decided to rule alone, but his secrecy, deviousness, spendthrift ways, boredom with government affairs, and willingness to allow his mistresses to influence affairs of state undermined the monarchy's prestige. The loss of an empire in the Seven Years' War, accompanied by burdensome taxes, an ever-mounting public debt, more hungry people, and a court life at Versailles that remained frivolous and carefree forced even Louis to realize the growing disgust with his monarchy. "Things will last my time at any rate," he remarked myopically and prophetically.

Perhaps all might not have been in vain if Louis had been succeeded by a competent king. But the new king, the nineteen-year-old grandson who became Louis XVI (1774–1792), was obese, lacking in energy, and unable to stay awake during government business (see the box on p. 631). Unsure of himself, he proved ever indecisive and allowed himself to be swayed by his shallow wife, the Austrian Marie Antoinette. Neither Louis nor Marie Antoinette seemed able to fathom the depths of despair and discontent that soon led to violent revolution (see Chapter 20).

GREAT BRITAIN   The success of the Glorious Revolution in England had prevented absolutism without clearly inaugurating constitutional monarchy. The eighteenth-century British political system was characterized by a sharing of power between king and Parliament, with Parliament gradually gaining the upper hand. (The United Kingdom of Great Britain came into existence in 1707 when the governments of England and Scotland were united; the term *British* came into use to refer to both English and Scots.) The king chose ministers responsible to himself who set policy and guided Parlia-

The French King's Bedtime

▼ ▼ ▼

Louis XIV had used court etiquette to magnify the dignity of kingship. During the reign of Louis XVI (1774–1792), however, court etiquette degenerated to ludicrous depths. This excerpt from the Memoirs of Comtesse de Boigne describes the king's coucher, the formal ceremony in which the king retired for the night.

Comtesse de Boigne, *Memoirs*

The king [Louis XVI] went to his *coucher*. The so-called *coucher* took place every evening at half past nine. The gentlemen of the court assembled in the bedroom of Louis XIV (but Louis XVI did not sleep there). I believe that all those who had been presented at court were permitted to attend.

The king came in from an adjoining room, followed by his domestic staff. His hair was in curlers, and he was not wearing his decorations. Without paying attention to anybody, he stepped behind the handrail surrounding the bed, and the chaplain on duty was given the prayer book and a tall taperstand with two candles by one of the valets. He then joined the king behind the handrail, handed him the book, and held the taperstand during the king's prayer, which was short. The king then went to the part of the room where the courtiers were, and the chaplain gave the taperstand back to the first valet who, in turn, took it over to a person indicated by the king. This person held it as long as the *coucher* lasted. This distinction was very much sought after. . . .

The king had his coat, vest, and finally shirt removed. He was naked to the waist, scratching and rubbing himself as if alone, though he was in the presence of the whole court and often a number of distinguished foreigners.

The first valet handed the nightshirt to the most qualified person. . . . If it was a person with whom the king was on familiar terms, he often played little tricks before donning it, missed it, passed it, and ran away, accompanying this charming nonsense with hearty laughter, making those who were sincerely attached to him suffer. Having donned the nightshirt, he put on his robe and three valets unfastened the belt and the knee buckles of his trousers, which fell down to his feet. Thus attired, hardly able to walk so absurdly encumbered, he began to make the round of the circle.

The duration of this reception was by no means fixed; sometimes it lasted only a few minutes, sometimes almost an hour; it depended on who was there. . . . When the king had enough, he dragged himself backward to an easy chair which had been pushed to the middle of the room and fell heavily into it, raising both legs. Two pages on their knees seized his shoes, took them off, and dropped them on the floor with a thump, which was part of the etiquette. When he heard it, the doorman opened the door and said, "This way, gentlemen." Everybody left, and the ceremony was over. However, the person who held the taperstand was permitted to stay if he had anything special to say to the king. This explains the high price attached to this strange favor.

---

ment; Parliament had the power to make laws, levy taxes, pass the budget, and indirectly influence the king's ministers. The eighteenth-century British Parliament was dominated by a landed aristocracy that historians usually divide into two groups: an upper aristocracy or the peers who sat in the House of Lords and served as lord lieutenants controlling the appointment of the justices of the peace; and the landed gentry, lesser nobles who sat in the House of Commons and served as justices of the peace in the counties. There is much historical debate over whether it makes sense to distinguish between the aristocracies since the two groups had much in common. Both were landowners with similar economic interests, and they frequently intermarried.

Although the British monarchy was faced with a powerful aristocracy that monopolized Parliament and held most of the important governing posts locally (as justices of the peace in the counties) and nationally, it still exercised considerable power. Because the aristocracy was divided by factional struggles based on family rivalries, the kings could use their power of patronage by awarding titles, government posts, and positions in the church and household staff to win supporters among the aristocratic factions.

What enabled the British system of political patronage to work was the structure of parliamentary elections. The deputies to the House of Commons were chosen from the boroughs and counties but not by popular voting and hardly in any equitable fashion. Of the almost five hundred deputies in the House of Commons, about four hundred were chosen from the boroughs. The number of delegates from each borough, however, was determined by past history rather than population so one borough could have six people choosing two representatives while new cities like Manchester had none despite their growing populations. Who could vote also varied wildly, enabling wealthy landed aristocrats to gain support by patronage and bribery, giving rise to a number of "pocket boroughs" controlled by a single person (hence "in his pocket"). The duke of Newcastle, for example, controlled the representatives from seven boroughs. It has been estimated that out of 405 borough deputies, 293 were chosen by fewer than 500 voters. This control of borough deputies was also true of county delegates, two from each of England's forty counties. Although elected by holders of property worth at least forty shillings a year, the members of the leading landed gentry families were elected over and over again. In the Parliament of 1761, for example, over 50 percent of the members of the House of Commons were related to the upper aristocracy. Parliament then was an institution largely dominated by the landed aristocracy, but their factional struggles enabled the monarchy still to exercise some power by its control of patronage.

Since the ministers were responsible for exercising the king's patronage, who became his chief ministers took on great political significance. In 1714, a new dynasty—the Hanoverians—was established when the last Stuart ruler, Queen Anne (1702–1714), died without an heir. The crown was offered to the Protestant rulers of the German state of Hanover. Both George I (1714–1727) and George II (1727–1760) relied on Robert Walpole as their chief or prime minister and the duke of Newcastle as their main dispenser of patronage, putting the latter at the center of British politics. Since the first Hanoverian king did not speak English and neither the first nor the second George had much familiarity with the British system, the chief ministers were allowed to handle Parliament and dispense patronage. Many historians feel that this exercise of ministerial power was an important step in the development of the modern cabinet system in British government.

Robert Walpole served as prime minister from 1721 to 1742 and pursued a peaceful foreign policy to avoid new

▼ **The British House of Commons.** The British political system in the eighteenth century was characterized by a sharing of power between the king and Parliament. Parliament was divided into a House of Lords and a House of Commons. This painting shows the House of Commons in session in 1793 during a debate concerning the possibility of war with France. William Pitt is addressing the House.

land taxes. But new forces were emerging in eighteenth-century Britain as growing trade and industry led an ever-increasing middle class to favor expansion of trade and world empire. The exponents of empire found a spokesman in William Pitt the Elder, who became prime minister in 1757 and furthered imperial ambitions by acquiring Canada and India in the Seven Years' War (see The Seven Years' War later in the chapter).

Despite his successes, however, Pitt the Elder was dismissed by the new king George III (1760–1820) in 1761 and replaced by the king's favorite, Lord Bute. Although characterized as a rather stupid person, George III was not the tyrant he is often portrayed as being. Determined to strengthen monarchical authority, his desire to wield the power of patronage personally led to the ouster of Pitt. At the same time, however, the spread of the ideas of the Enlightenment through a growing number of newspapers and an expanding reading public increased public clamor for the reform of both patronage and the electoral system. The saga of John Wilkes soon enlarged the public outcry.

An ambitious middle-class member of the House of Commons, John Wilkes was an outspoken journalist who publicly criticized the king's ministers. Arrested and soon released, Wilkes was expelled from his seat in Parliament. When he persevered and won another parliamentary seat from the county of Middlesex near London, he was again denied the right to take his place in Parliament. The cause of John Wilkes quickly became identified with liberty, and the slogan "Wilkes and Liberty" was frequently used by his supporters who came from two major social groups: the common people of London, who had no voting rights, and a middle element of voting freeholders, such as guild masters and small merchants in London and the surrounding counties. The cry for liberty soon spilled over into calls for the reform of Parliament and the removal of parliamentary privileges. In 1780, the House of Commons affirmed that "the influence of the crown has increased, is increasing, and ought to be diminished." At the same time, criticism at home was exacerbated by criticism abroad, especially by the American colonists whose discontent with the British system had led to rebellion and separation (see Chapter 20). Although minor reforms of the patronage system were made in 1782, King George III managed to avoid more drastic change by appointing William Pitt the Younger (1759–1806), son of William Pitt the Elder, as prime minister in 1783. Supported by the merchants, industrial classes, and the king, who used patronage to gain support for Pitt in the House of Commons, the latter managed to stay in power through

Chronology
▼ ▼ ▼

The European States: The Atlantic Seaboard States

France	
Louis XV	1715–1774
Louis XVI	1774–1792
Great Britain	
The Stuarts	
Queen Anne	1702–1714
The Hanoverians	
George I	1714–1727
George II	1727–1760
Robert Walpole	1721–1742
William Pitt the Elder	1757–1761
George III	1760–1820
William Pitt the Younger	1783–1801

the French revolutionary and Napoleonic eras. George III, however, remained an uncertain supporter because of periodic bouts of insanity (he once thought a tree in Windsor Park was the king of Prussia). With Pitt's successes, serious reform of the corrupt parliamentary system was avoided for another generation.

THE DUTCH REPUBLIC After its century in the sun, the Dutch Republic or United Netherlands suffered a decline in economic prosperity. Both local and national political affairs were dominated by the municipal oligarchies that governed the Dutch Republic's towns. In the eighteenth century, the struggle continued between these oligarchs (or regents as they were called from their governing positions) and the house of Orange, who as stadholders headed the executive branch of government. The regents sought to reduce the power of the Orangists but soon became divided when Dutch burghers who called themselves the Patriots (artisans, merchants, shopkeepers) began to agitate for democratic reforms that would open up the municipal councils to greater participation than that of the oligarchs. The success of the Patriots, however, led to foreign interference when the Prussian king sent troops to protect his sister, wife of the Orangist stadholder. The Patriots were crushed, and both Orangists and regents reestablished the old system. The intervention by Prussia serves to remind us of the growing power of the central European states.

Absolutism in Central and Eastern Europe

Of the five major European states, three were located in central and eastern Europe and came to play an increasingly important role in European international politics.

PRUSSIA Two able Prussian kings in the eighteenth century, Frederick William I and Frederick II, further developed the two major institutions—the army and the bureaucracy—that were the backbone of Prussia. Frederick William I (1713–1740) promoted the evolution of Prussia's highly efficient civil bureaucracy by establishing the General Directory. Its supervision of military, police, economic, and financial affairs made it the chief administrative agent of the central government. Since Prussia's disjointed territories could hardly have been maintained without a centralized administrative machine, Frederick William strove to maintain a highly efficient bureaucracy of civil service workers. It became a special kind of organization with its own code in which the supreme values were obedience, honor, and service to the king as the highest duty. As Frederick William asserted: "One must serve the king with life and limb, with goods and chattels, with honor and conscience, and surrender everything except salvation. The latter is reserved for God. But everything else must be mine."[3] For his part, Frederick William kept a close personal watch over his officials to ensure the performance of their duties. As the Saxon minister at Berlin related:

> Every day His Majesty gives new proofs of his justice. Walking recently at Potsdam at six in the morning, he saw a post-coach arrive with several passengers who knocked for a long time at the post-house which was still closed. The King, seeing that no one opened the door, joined them in knocking and even knocked in some window-panes. The master of the post then opened the door and scolded the travelers, for no one recognized the King. But His Majesty let himself be known by giving the official some good blows of his cane and drove him from his house and his job after apologizing to the travelers for his laziness. Examples of this sort, of which I could relate several others, make everybody alert and exact.[4]

Close, personal supervision of the bureaucracy became a hallmark of the eighteenth-century Prussian rulers.

Under Frederick William I, the rigid class stratification that had emerged in seventeenth-century Brandenburg-Prussia was continued. The nobility or landed aristocracy known as Junkers, who owned large estates with many serfs, continued to play a dominating role in the Prussian state. The Junkers held a complete monopoly over the officer corps of the Prussian army, which Frederick William assiduously and passionately continued to expand. By the end of his reign, the army had grown from 45,000 to 83,000 men. Though tenth in physical size and thirteenth in population in Europe, Prussia had the fourth largest army after France, Russia, and Austria.

While nobles served as officers, rank-and-file soldiers were usually peasants who served a long number of years. Discipline in the army was extremely rigid and even cruel—so cruel, in fact, that desertion was common. The king advised his generals not to take troops through a forest on maneuvers because it offered too good an opportunity for running away. Frederick William believed that the nobles were naturally the best officers because they were used to commanding peasants on their estates. Moreover, by using nobles as officers, Frederick William ensured a close bond between the nobility and the army and, in turn, the loyalty of the nobility to the absolute monarch.

As officers, the Junker nobility became imbued with a sense of service to the king or state. All the virtues of the Prussian nobility were, in effect, military virtues: duty, obedience, sacrifice. At the same time, because of its size and reputation as one of the best armies in Europe, the Prussian army was the most important institution in the state. "Prussian militarism" became synonymous with the extreme exaltation of military virtues. Indeed, one Prussian minister remarked around 1800 that "Prussia was not a country with an army, but an army with a country which served as headquarters and food magazine."[5]

The remaining classes in Prussia were considerably less important than the nobility. The peasants were born on their lords' estates and spent most of the rest of their lives there or in the army. They had few real rights and even needed their Junker's permission before they could marry. For the middle class, the only opportunity for any social prestige was in the Prussian civil service where the ideal of loyal service to the state became a hallmark of the middle-class official. Frederick William allowed and even encouraged men of nonnoble birth to serve in important administrative posts. When he died in 1740, only three of his eighteen privy councillors were of noble birth.

Frederick the Great (1740–1786) was one of the best educated and most cultured monarchs in the eighteenth century. He was well versed in Enlightenment thought and even invited Voltaire to live at his court for several years. His intellectual interests were despised by his father who forced his intelligent son to prepare for a career in ruling (see the box on p. 635). A believer in the king as the "first servant of the state," Frederick the Great

Frederick the Great and His Father
▼ ▼ ▼

As a young man, the future Frederick the Great was quite different from his strict and austere father, Frederick William I. Possessing a high regard for French culture, poetry, and flute playing, Frederick resisted his father's wishes that he immerse himself in governmental and military affairs. Eventually, Frederick capitulated to his father's will and accepted the need to master affairs of state. These letters, written when Frederick was sixteen, illustrate the difficulties in their relationship.

Frederick to His Father, Frederick William I (September 11, 1728)

I have not ventured for a long time to present myself before my dear papa, partly because I was advised against it, but chiefly because I anticipated an even worse reception than usual and feared to vex my dear papa still further by the favor I have now to ask; so I have preferred to put it in writing.

I beg my dear papa that he will be kindly disposed toward me. I do assure him that after long examination of my conscience I do not find the slightest thing with which to reproach myself; but if, against my wish and will, I have vexed my dear papa, I hereby beg most humbly for forgiveness, and hope that my dear papa will give over the fearful hate which has appeared so plainly in his whole behavior and to which I cannot accustom myself. I have always thought hitherto that I had a kind father, but now I see the contrary. However, I will take courage and hope that my dear papa will think this all over and take me again into his favor. Meantime I assure him that I will never, my life long, willingly fail him, and in spite of his disfavor I am still, with most dutiful and childlike respect, my dear papa's

Most obedient and faithful servant and son,
Frederick

Frederick William to His Son Frederick

A bad, obstinate boy, who does not love his father; for when one does one's best, and especially when one loves one's father, one does what he wishes not only when he is standing by but when he is not there to see. Moreover you know very well that I cannot stand an effeminate fellow who has no manly tastes, who cannot ride or shoot (to his shame be it said!), is untidy about his person, and wears his hair curled like a fool instead of cutting it; and that I have condemned all these things a thousand times, and yet there is no sign of improvement. For the rest, haughty, offish as a country lout, conversing with none but a favored few instead of being affable and popular, grimacing like a fool, and never following my wishes out of love for me but only when forced into it, caring for nothing but to have his own way, and thinking nothing else is of any importance. This is my answer.

Frederick William

became a conscientious ruler who made few innovations in the administration of the state. His diligence in overseeing its operation, however, made the Prussian bureaucracy well known for both its efficiency and honesty.

For a time, Frederick seemed quite willing to follow the philosophes' recommendations for reform. He established a single code of laws for his territories that eliminated the use of torture except in treason and murder cases. He also granted a limited freedom of speech and press as well as complete religious toleration, no difficult task since he had no strong religious convictions anyway. Although Frederick was well aware of the philosophes' condemnation of serfdom, he was too dependent on the Prussian nobility to interfere with it or with the hierarchical structure of Prussian society. In fact, Frederick II was a social conservative who made Prussian society even more aristocratic than it had been before. Frederick reversed his father's policy of allowing commoners to have power in the civil service and reserved the higher positions in the bureaucracy for members of the nobility. The upper ranks of the bureaucracy came close to constituting a hereditary caste over time.

Like his predecessors, Frederick the Great took a great interest in military affairs and enlarged the Prussian army (to 200,000 men). Unlike his predecessors, he had no objection to using it. Frederick did not hesitate to take advantage of a succession crisis in the Habsburg monarchy to seize the Austrian province of Silesia for Prussia. This act led to Austria's bitter hostility to Prussia and Frederick's engagement in two major wars, the War of the Austrian Succession and the Seven Years' War (see Wars and Diplomacy later in the chapter). Although the latter war left his country exhausted, Frederick succeeded in keeping Silesia. After the wars, the first partition of Poland with Austria and Russia in 1772 gave him the Polish territory between Prussia and Brandenburg and created greater unity for the scattered lands of Prussia. By the end of his reign, Prussia was recognized as a great European power.

THE AUSTRIAN EMPIRE   The Austrian Empire had become one of the great European states by the beginning of the eighteenth century. The city of Vienna, center of the Habsburg monarchy, was filled with magnificent palaces and churches built in the Baroque style and became the music capital of Europe. And yet Austria, by its very nature as a sprawling empire composed of many different nationalities, languages, religions, and cultures, found it difficult to provide common laws and administrative centralization for its people.

Empress Maria Theresa (1740–1780), however, stunned by the loss of Austrian Silesia to Prussia in the War of the Austrian Succession, resolved to reform her empire in preparation for the seemingly inevitable next conflict with rival Prussia. Although Maria Theresa was forced to accept the privileges of the Hungarian nobility and the right of her Hungarian subjects to have their own laws, she did abolish the Austrian and Bohemian chancelleries and replaced them with departments of foreign affairs, justice, war, commerce, and internal affairs that functioned for both territories. Maria Theresa also curtailed the role of the diets or provincial assemblies in taxation and local administration. Now clergy

and nobles were forced to pay property and income taxes to royal officials rather than the diets. The Austrian and Bohemian lands were divided into ten provinces and subdivided into districts, all administered by royal officials rather than representatives of the diets. Although the new system was not used in Hungary and the Austrian possessions in Italy and the Netherlands, the rest of the Austrian Empire was becoming more centralized and more bureaucratic. But these administrative reforms were done for practical reasons—to strengthen the power of the Habsburg state—and were accompanied by an enlargement and modernization of the armed forces. Maria Theresa remained staunchly Catholic and conservative and was not open to the wider reform calls of the philosophes. But her successor was.

From 1765 to 1780, Maria Theresa had allowed her son Joseph II to share rule with her, although Joseph felt restrained by his mother's lack of interest in the reform ideas of the Enlightenment that greatly appealed to him. When he achieved sole power in 1780, he was determined to make changes; at the same time, he carried on his mother's chief goal of enhancing Habsburg power within the monarchy and Europe. Joseph II was an earnest man who believed in the need to sweep away anything standing in the path of reason. As Joseph expressed it: "I have made Philosophy the lawmaker of my empire, her logical applications are going to transform Austria."

Joseph's reform program was far-reaching. He abolished serfdom and tried to give the peasants hereditary rights to their holdings. An exponent of the Physiocratic ideas (see Chapter 18), he abandoned economic restraints by eliminating internal trade barriers, ending

▼ **Frederick II.** Frederick II was one of the most cultured and well-educated European monarchs. Not adverse to using the military, Frederick took part in both the War of the Austrian Succession and the Seven Years' War. He is seen here returning from military maneuvers on a white horse, surrounded by his generals. Behind him on a black horse is his son, the future Frederick William II.

monopolies, and removing guild restrictions. A new penal code was instituted that abrogated the death penalty and established the principle of equality of all before the law. Joseph produced drastic religious reforms as well, including complete religious toleration and restrictions on the Catholic church. Altogether, Joseph II issued 6,000 decrees and 11,000 laws in his effort to transform Austria.

Joseph's reform program proved overwhelming for Austria, however. He alienated the nobility by freeing the serfs and alienated the church by his attacks on the monastic establishment. Even the serfs were unhappy, unable to comprehend the drastic changes inherent in Joseph's policies. His attempt to rationalize the administration of the empire by imposing German as the official bureaucratic language alienated the non-German nationalities. As Joseph complained, there were not enough people for the kind of bureaucracy he needed. He realized his failure when he wrote his own epitaph for his gravestone: "Here lies Joseph II who was unfortunate in everything that he undertook." Although his immediate successor, Leopold II (1790–1792), tried to hold the line, he too recognized that he could not rule without the support of the aristocrats and began to retrench. But it was the Emperor Francis II (1792–1835), frightened by the revolutionary terror in France (see Chapter 20), who ensured the undoing of most of Joseph's enlightened efforts.

RUSSIA   Peter the Great was followed by a series of six weak successors who were made and unmade by the palace guard. Only one of these, Elizabeth (1741–1762), Peter's daughter, reigned longer than ten years. She in turn was succeeded by her nephew Peter III (1762), whose German wife Catherine learned Russian and won the favor of the palace guard. Peter was murdered by a faction of nobles, and Catherine II the Great (1762–1796) emerged as autocrat of all the Russias.

Catherine was an intelligent woman who was familiar with the works of the philosophes. Voltaire and Diderot were among her correspondents. It is possible that like Joseph II she wished to reform Russia along the lines of Enlightenment ideas, but she was always shrewd enough to realize that her success depended upon the support of the palace guard and the gentry class from which it stemmed. She could not afford to alienate the Russian nobility.

Initially, Catherine seemed eager to pursue reform. She called for the election of an assembly in 1767 to debate the details of a new law code. In her *Instruction*, written as a guide to the deliberations, Catherine questioned the institution of serfdom, torture, and capital

▼ **Maria Theresa and Her Family.** Maria Theresa governed the vast possessions of the Austrian Empire from 1740 to 1780. In order to prepare for a conflict with Prussia, she attempted to reform her empire by streamlining its administration and restricting the power of local and provincial estates. Administrative reforms enabled Maria Theresa to enlarge and modernize the empire's armed forces.

punishment and even advocated the principle of the equality of all people in the eyes of the law (see the box on p. 638). But one and one-half years of negotiation produced little real change.

In fact, Catherine's subsequent policies had the effect of strengthening the hands of the landholding class at the expense of all others, especially the Russian serfs. In order to reorganize local government, Catherine divided Russia into fifty provinces, each of which in turn was subdivided into districts whose ruling officials were chosen by the nobles. In this way, the local nobility became responsible for the day-to-day governing of Russia. Moreover, the gentry were now formed into corporate groups with special legal privileges, including the right to trial by peers and exemption from personal taxation and corporal punishment. These rights were formalized in 1785 by a Charter of the Nobility.

Catherine's policy of favoring the landed nobility led to even worse conditions for the Russian peasantry. In 1767, serfs were forbidden to appeal to the state against

The Proposals of Catherine II for a New Law Code

▼ ▼ ▼

C atherine II the Great of Russia appeared for a while to be an enlightened ruler. In 1767, she convened a legislative commission to prepare a new code of laws for Russia. In her famous Instruction, *she gave the delegates a detailed guide to the principles they should follow. Although the guidelines were obviously culled from the liberal ideas of the philosophes, the commission itself accomplished nothing, and Catherine's* Instruction *was soon forgotten.*

Catherine II, Proposals for a New Law Code

13. What is the true End of Monarchy? Not to deprive People of their natural Liberty; but to correct their Actions, in order to attain the supreme good.

33. The Laws ought to be so framed, as to secure the Safety of every Citizen as much as possible.

34. The Equality of the Citizens consists in this; that they should all be subject to the same Laws.

38. A Man ought to form in his own Mind an exact and clear Idea of what Liberty is. Liberty is the Right of doing whatsoever the Laws allow: And if any one Citizen could do what the Laws forbid, there would be no more Liberty; because others would have an equal Power of doing the same.

123. The Usage of Torture is contrary to all the Dictates of Nature and Reason; even Mankind itself cries out against it, and demands loudly the total Abolition of it.

180. That Law, therefore, is highly beneficial to the Community where it is established, which ordains that every Man shall be judged by his Peers and Equals. For when the Fate of a Citizen is in Question, all Prejudices arising from the Difference of Rank or Fortune should be stifled; because they ought to have no Influence between the Judges and the Parties accused.

194. No Man ought to be looked upon as guilty, before he has received his judicial Sentence; nor can the Laws deprive him of their Protection, before it is proved that he has forfeited all Right to it. What Right therefore can Power give to any to inflict Punishment upon a Citizen at a Time, when it is yet dubious, whether he is Innocent or guilty?

270. It is highly necessary that the Law should prescribe a Rule to the Lords, for a more judicious Method of raising their Revenues; and oblige them to levy such a Tax, as tends least to separate the Peasant from His House and Family; this would be the Means by which Agriculture would become more extensive, and Population be more increased in the Empire.

---

their masters. Peasant unrest had frequently led to peasant rebellion in the Middle Ages, the Reformation, and seventeenth-century Europe and did so now in eighteenth-century Russia. The attempt of the Russian government to impose restrictions upon free peasants in the border districts of the Russian empire soon led to a full-scale revolt that spread to the Volga valley. It was intensified by the support of the Cossacks, independent tribes of fierce warriors who had at times fought for the Russians against the Turks but who now resisted the government's attempt to absorb them into the empire.

The elements of discontent were welded into a mass revolt by an illiterate Cossack, Emelyan Pugachev. Beginning in 1773, Pugachev's rebellion spread across southern Russia from the Urals to the Volga River. Initially successful, Pugachev won the support of many peasants when he issued a manifesto in July 1774, freeing all peasants from oppressive taxes and military service. Encouraged to seize their landlords' estates by Pugachev, the peasants responded by killing over 1,500 estate owners and their families. The rebellion soon faltered, however, as government forces became more effective. Betrayed by his own subordinates, Pugachev was captured, tortured, and executed. The rebellion collapsed completely, and Catherine responded by even greater repression of the peasantry. Not only was all rural reform dropped, but Catherine denounced and treated as treasonous any suggestion of agrarian reform. Serfdom was expanded into newer parts of the empire while parcels of crown land, on which peasants had received better treatment, were given to nobles to gain their support. There, too, the peasants were reduced to serfdom.

Above all, Catherine proved a worthy successor to Peter the Great in her policies of territorial expansion westward (into Poland) and southward (to the Black Sea). Russia spread southward by defeating the Turks. In the Treaty of Kuchuk-Kainarji in 1774, the Russians gained some land, the privilege of protecting Greek Orthodox Christians in the Ottoman Empire, and the right to sail in Turkish waters. Russian expansion westward occurred at the expense of neighboring Poland. In the three partitions of Poland, Russia gained about 50 percent of Polish territory.

POLAND   Poland was an excellent example of why a strong monarchy was needed in early modern Europe. The failure to develop the machinery of state building because of the excessive powers of the aristocracy proved disastrous. The Polish king was elected by the Polish nobles and forced to accept drastic limitations upon his power, including limited revenues, a small bureaucracy, and a standing army of no more than 20,000 soldiers. For Polish nobles, these limitations eliminated an absolute king; for Poland's powerful neighbors, they were an invitation to meddle in its affairs.

The total destruction of the Polish state in the eighteenth century arose out of the rivalries of its three great neighbors, Austria, Russia, and Prussia. To avoid war,

the leaders of these powers decided to compensate themselves by dividing Poland. A secret memorandum from Maria Theresa to the other two powers demonstrates well the spirit in which these negotiations were undertaken:

> His Majesty the King of Prussia and Her Majesty the Empress of All the Russias have rights and pretensions to certain districts in Poland, as we [Austria], have; in order to prevent any difficulties that might arise in this connection, we declare . . . that whatever the extent of our respective pretensions, the acquisitions . . . should be perfectly equal; that the portion of one should not exceed that of another, and that . . . we should, in the case of need, mutually and in good faith aid each other, in order to facilitate our success.[6]

To maintain the balance of power in central and eastern Europe, the three great powers cynically agreed to the acquisition of roughly equal territories at Poland's expense.

In 1772, Poland lost about 30 percent of its land and 50 percent of its population. Austria gained the agricul-

▼ **Map 19.1** The Partitions of Poland.

Chronology

▼ ▼ ▼

The European States: Absolutism in Central and Eastern Europe

Prussia	
Frederick William I	1713–1740
Frederick II the Great	1740–1786
The Austrian Empire	
Maria Theresa	1740–1780
Joseph II	1780–1790
Leopold I	1790–1792
Francis II	1792–1835
Russia	
Elizabeth	1741–1762
Peter III	1762
Catherine II the Great	1762–1796
Pugachev's Rebellion	1773–1775
Charter of the Nobility	1785
Poland	
First Partition	1772
Second Partition	1793
Third Partition	1795

turally rich district of Galicia, Russia achieved the largest slice of land in eastern Poland, and Prussia acquired West Prussia, the smallest but most valuable territory since it united two of the chief sections of Prussia.

The remaining Polish state was supposedly independent; in truth it was dominated by the Russians who even kept troops on Polish territory. After an effort by the Poles in 1791 to establish a stronger state under a hereditary monarchy, the Russians gained the support of Austria and Prussia and intervened militarily in May 1792. In the following year, a second partition of Polish territory was made by Russia and Prussia. Finally, after a heroic but hopeless rebellion in 1794–1795 under the General Thaddeus Kosciuszko, the remaining Polish state was obliterated by Austria, Prussia, and Russia in the third partition of Poland (1795). Many historians have pointed to Poland's demise as a cogent example of the importance of building a strong, absolutist state to survive in the seventeenth and eighteenth centuries. While true, the partition of Poland also serves to remind us that the cynical politics associated with the name of Machiavelli were becoming Europe's norm. It did not augur well for the future of European civilization.

The Mediterranean World

At the beginning of the eighteenth century, Spain experienced a change of dynasties from the Habsburgs to the Bourbons. Bourbon rule temporarily rejuvenated Spain and at least provided an opportunity to centralize the institutions of the state. Under Philip V (1700–1746), the laws, administrative institutions, and language of Castile were established in the other Spanish kingdoms, making the king of Castile truly the king of Spain. Moreover, French-style ministries replaced the old conciliar system of government, and officials similar to French intendants were introduced into the various Spanish provinces.

Since the Treaty of Utrecht in 1713 had taken the Italian territories and Netherlands away from Spain, the latter now had fewer administrative problems and less drain on its already overtaxed economic resources. In the second half of the eighteenth century, especially during the reign of Charles III (1759–1788), the Catholic church was also brought under control when the king banished the Jesuits and circumscribed the activities of the Inquisition. The landed aristocracy continued to exercise substantial power throughout the eighteenth century, however.

Portugal had experienced decline since the glorious days of empire in the sixteenth century. Nevertheless, during the long ministry of the marquis of Pombal (1699–1782), who served as chief minister to a series of Portuguese kings, the nobility and Catholic church were curtailed and the Portuguese empire temporarily revived. After Pombal was removed from office, the nobility and church regained much of their power.

After the Treaty of Utrecht, Austria had replaced Spain as the dominant force in Italy in the eighteenth century. The duchy of Milan, Sardinia, and the kingdom of Naples were all surrendered to the Habsburg emperors while Sicily was given to the northern Italian state of Savoy, which was slowly emerging as a state with "an appetite for territorial expansion." In 1734, the Bourbons of Spain reestablished control over Naples and Sicily while the remaining independent states of Italy, such as Venice and Genoa, grew increasingly impotent in international affairs.

Scandinavia

In the seventeenth century, Sweden had become the dominant power in northern Europe, but after the Battle of Poltava in 1709, Swedish power declined rapidly. Following the death of the powerful Charles XII in 1718, the Swedish nobility, using the Swedish Diet as its instrument, gained control of public life and reduced the monarchy to puppet status. But the division of the nobility into pro-French and pro-Russian factions eventually enabled King Gustavus III (1771–1792) to reassert the power of the monarchy. Gustavus proved to be one of the "most enlightened monarchs of his age." By decree, he established freedom of religion, speech, and press while instituting a new code of justice that eliminated the use of torture. Moreover, his economic reforms smacked of laissez-faire: he reduced tariffs, abolished tolls, and encouraged trade and agriculture. However, incensed at these reforms and their loss of power, a group of nobles assassinated the king in 1792, although they proved unable to fully restore the rule of the aristocracy.

Denmark also saw an attempt at enlightened reforms by King Christian VII (1766–1808) and his chief minister, John Frederick Struensee. Aristocratic opposition stymied his efforts, however, and led to Struensee's death in 1772.

Enlightened Politics Revisited

The subject of enlightened absolutism revolves around the relationship between "an intellectual movement and the actual practice of government." The ideas of the Enlightenment did have an impact on rulers in the second half of the eighteenth century. Some of the smaller states made the clearest efforts to institute enlightened reforms. Leopold I (1745–1790) of Tuscany, for example, abolished serfdom, encouraged trade and industry, reformed the penal code, abolished the Inquisition, and even toyed with the idea of granting a constitution that would allow his subjects to share governing power. While only Leopold dreamed of challenging the principle of political and social inequality on which all European society was based, almost every European ruler in the second half of the eighteenth century pursued some enlightened reforms, be they reform of laws, the development of secondary education, or religious tolerance.

Few rulers, however, felt compelled to make the state an experimental lab for a set of political principles. Of the three major rulers most closely associated traditionally with enlightened absolutism—Joseph II, Frederick II, and Catherine the Great—only Joseph II sought truly radical changes based on Enlightenment ideas. Both Frederick and Catherine liked to be cast as disciples of the Enlightenment, expressed interest in enlightened re-

Chronology

▼ ▼ ▼

The European States: The Mediterranean World and Scandinavia

Spain	
Philip V, the First Bourbon King	1700–1746
Charles III	1759–1788
Portugal	
Marquis of Pombal	1699–1782
Sweden	
Charles XII	1697–1718
Gustavus III	1771–1792
Denmark	
Christian VII	1766–1808

forms, and even attempted some. But the policies of neither seemed seriously affected by Enlightenment thought. Necessities of state and maintenance of the existing system took precedence over reform. Indeed, many historians feel that Joseph, Frederick, and Catherine were all primarily guided by a concern for the power and well-being of their states and that their policies were not all that different from those of their predecessors. Perhaps their greatest success was in strengthening their administrative systems and creating an ideal of state service that separated the ruler and the ruling dynasty from the state. In the final analysis, however, the heightened state power was used to create armies and wage wars to gain more power. Despite their desire for reforms, enlightened rulers were not able to rise above their predecessors' goals. Nevertheless, in their desire to build stronger state systems, these rulers did pursue such enlightened reforms as legal reform, religious toleration, and the extension of education since these served to create more satisfied subjects and strengthened the state in significant ways.

It would be foolish, however, to overlook the fact that the ability of enlightened rulers to make reforms was also limited by political and social realities. Everywhere in Europe the hereditary aristocracy was still the most powerful class in society. Enlightened reforms were often limited to those administrative and judicial reforms that did not seriously undermine the powerful interests of the European nobility. Although aristocrats might join the populace in opposing monarchical extension of centralizing power, as the chief beneficiaries of a system based on traditional rights and privileges for their class, they were certainly not willing to support a political ideology that trumpeted the principal of equal rights for all.

▼ Wars and Diplomacy

Regardless of the philosophes' denunciations of war as a foolish waste of life and resources in stupid quarrels of no value to humankind, the rivalry among states that led to costly struggles remained unchanged in the European world of the eighteenth century. Although the European state system emerged in the seventeenth century, its implications were more fully realized in the eighteenth century. This system of self-governing, individual states was grounded largely in the amoral and potentially anarchic principle of self-interest. Since international relations were based upon considerations of power, the eighteenth-century concept of a "balance of power" was predicated on how to counterbalance the power of one state by another in order to prevent any one power from dominating the others. This balance of power, however, did not imply a desire for peace. Large armies created to defend a state's security were often used for offensive purposes as well. As Frederick the Great of Prussia remarked, "the fundamental rule of governments is the principle of extending their territories." Nevertheless, there were limits to the use of force in eighteenth-century Europe. No doubt technical considerations restricted the extent of warfare (see European Armies and Warfare later in the chapter), but a lack of the ideological fury that had made the religious wars of the sixteenth and seventeenth centuries so destructive also made compromises easier and the use of diplomacy more regular.

The system of modern diplomacy that had emerged in the Italian Renaissance was more fully developed by the eighteenth century. Parallel to the expansion of standing armies was the development of diplomatic machinery. Virtually every state now possessed a foreign ministry staffed by specialists who employed clerks and maintained archives while ambassadors resided in permanent embassies in the capital cities of the European states. Because most regular ambassadors were aristocrats, they formed a European community of sorts. Nevertheless, their interests remained those of their states, and they were quite prepared to lie if necessary, especially when preparing for war. As Frederick once said, "the safety and greater good of the state demands that treaties should be broken under certain circumstances."

The diplomacy of the eighteenth century still focused primarily on dynastic interests or the desire of ruling families to provide for their dependents and extend their dynastic holdings. But the eighteenth century also saw the emergence of the concept of "reason of state," on the basis of which a ruler such as Frederick II and a minister such as William Pitt the Elder looked beyond dynastic interests to the long-term future of their states.

International rivalry and the continuing centralization of the European states were closely related. The need for taxes to support large armies and navies created its own imperative for more efficient and effective control of power in the hands of bureaucrats who could collect taxes and organize states for the task of winning wars. At the same time, the development of large standing armies ensured that political disputes would periodically be resolved by armed conflict rather than diplomacy.

For a while, however, it seemed that Europe preferred peace. For two and one-half decades after the Peace of Utrecht, European states arranged alliances and met in international congresses that enabled them to maintain an apparent balance of power and keep the peace. There were problems, especially as competition for empire led to serious rivalry among the maritime states. But international cooperation seemed reasonably sure—at least until 1740 when the first of the two major conflicts of the mid-century erupted over the succession to the Austrian throne.

The War of the Austrian Succession (1740–1748)

Unable to produce a male heir to the Austrian throne, the Habsburg emperor Charles VI (1711–1740) so feared the consequences of the succession of his daughter Maria Theresa that he spent much of his reign negotiating the Pragmatic Sanction by which different European powers agreed to recognize his daughter as his legal heir.

Charles, however, failed to count on the faithlessness and duplicity of Europe's rulers. After his death, the Pragmatic Sanction was conveniently pushed aside, especially by Frederick II who had just succeeded to the throne of Prussia. The new Prussian ruler took advantage of the new queen to invade Austrian Silesia. At the same time, the ruler of the south German state of Bavaria seized some Habsburg territory and had himself chosen as the new Holy Roman emperor. The vulnerability of Maria Theresa encouraged France to enter the war against its traditional enemy Austria; in turn, Maria Theresa made an alliance with Great Britain who feared French hegemony over continental affairs. All too quickly, the Austrian succession had produced a world-wide conflagration. The war was fought not only in Europe where Prussia seized Silesia, and France occupied the Austrian Netherlands, but in the Far East where France took Madras in India from the British and in North America where the British captured the French fortress of Louisbourg at the entrance to the St. Lawrence River. By 1748, all parties were exhausted and agreed to stop. The peace treaty of Aix-la-Chapelle guaranteed the return of all occupied territories to their original owners except for Silesia. Prussia's refusal to return Silesia guaranteed another war, at least between the two hostile central European powers of Prussia and Austria.

The Seven Years' War (1756–1763)

Maria Theresa refused to accept the loss of Silesia and prepared for its return by rebuilding her army while working diplomatically to separate Prussia from its chief ally, France. In 1756, Austria achieved what was soon labeled a diplomatic revolution. Bourbon-Habsburg rivalry had been a fact of European diplomacy since the late sixteenth century. But two new rivalries made this old one seem superfluous: Britain and France over colonial empires, and Austria and Prussia over Silesia. France now abandoned Prussia and allied with Austria. Russia, who saw Prussia as a major hindrance to Russian goals in central Europe, joined the new alliance. In turn, Great Britain allied with Prussia. This diplomatic revolution of 1756 now led to another worldwide war.

There were three major areas of conflict: Europe, India, and North America. Europe witnessed the clash of the two major alliances: the British and Prussians against the Austrians, Russians, and French. With his superb army and military prowess, Frederick the Great was able for some time to defeat the Austrian, French, and Russian armies. He won a spectacular victory at the Battle of Rossbach in Saxony (1757) over the combined French-Austrian forces that far outnumbered his own troops.

▼ **Map 19.2** The Seven Years' War.

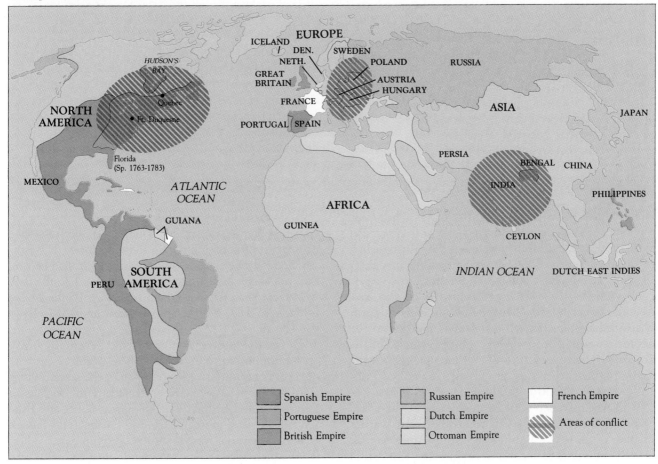

British Victory in India

▼ ▼ ▼

The Seven Years' War was fought in three major areas of the world: Europe, India, and North America. After the War of the Austrian Succession, the French and British continued to maneuver for advantage in India. The success of the British in defeating the French was due to Robert Clive, who, in this excerpt from one of his letters, describes his famous victory at Plassey, north of Calcutta (June 23, 1757). This battle demonstrated the inability of native Indian soldiers to compete with Europeans and signified the beginning of British control in Bengal. Clive claimed to have 1,000 Europeans, 2,000 Sepoys, and eight pieces of cannon available for this battle.

Robert Clive, Account of His Victory at Plassey

At daybreak we discovered the nabob's army moving towards us, consisting, as we since found, of about fifteen thousand horse and thirty-five thousand foot, with upwards of forty pieces of cannon. They approached apace, and by six began to attack with a number of heavy cannon, supported by the whole army, and continued to play on us very briskly for several hours, during which our situation was of the utmost service to us, being lodged in a large grove with good mud banks. To succeed in an attempt on their cannon was next to impossible, as they were planted in a manner round us and at considerable distances from each other. We therefore remained quiet in our post, in expectation of a successful attack upon their camp at night. About noon the enemy drew off their artillery and retired to their camp. . . .

On finding them make no great effort to dislodge us, we proceeded to take possession of one or two more eminences lying very near an angle of their camp, from whence, and an adjacent eminence in their possession, they kept a smart fire of musketry upon us. They made several attempts to bring out their cannon, but our advanced fieldpieces played so warmly and so well upon them that they were always driven back. Their horse exposing themselves a good deal on this occasion, many of them were killed, and among the rest four or five officers of the first distinction; by which the whole army being visibly dispirited and thrown into some confusion, we were encouraged to storm both the eminence and the angle of their camp, which were carried at the same instant, with little or no loss; though the latter was defended (exclusively of blacks) by forty French and two pieces of cannon; and the former by a large body of blacks, both horse and foot. On this a general rout ensued, and we pursued the enemy six miles, passing upwards of forty pieces of cannon they had abandoned, with an infinite number of carts and carriages filled with baggage of all kinds. . . . It is computed there are killed of the enemy about five hundred. Our loss amounted to only twenty-two killed and fifty wounded, and those chiefly blacks.

Under attack from three different directions, however, the forces of Frederick II were gradually worn down and faced utter defeat until they were saved by Russia when the death of Tsarina Elizabeth brought her nephew Peter III to power. A great admirer of Frederick the Great, Peter withdrew Russian troops from the conflict and from the Prussian lands that the Russians had occupied. His withdrawal guaranteed a stalemate and led to the desire for peace. The European conflict was ended by the Peace of Hubertusburg in 1763. All occupied territories were returned while Austria officially recognized Prussia's permanent control of Silesia.

The Anglo-French struggle in the rest of the world had more decisive results. Known as the Great War for Empire, it was fought in India and North America. The French had returned Madras to Britain after the War of the Austrian Succession, but jockeying for power continued as French and British policies were both founded on support of opposing native Indian princes. The British under Robert Clive (1725–1774) ultimately won out, not because they had better forces but because they were more persistent (see the box above). By the Treaty of Paris in 1763, the French withdrew and left India to the British.

By far, the greatest conflicts of the Seven Years' War took place in North America. There were two primary areas of contention. One consisted of the waterways of the Gulf of St. Lawrence, protected by the fortress of Louisbourg and by forts near the Great Lakes and Lake Champlain that protected French Quebec and French traders. The other was the unsettled Ohio River valley. The French began to move down from the Great Lakes and up from their forts on the Mississippi and establish forts from the Appalachians to the Mississippi River. To British settlers in the thirteen colonies, French activity threatened to cut off this vast area for their exploitation. The French were able to gain the support of the Indians; as traders and not settlers, they were viewed by the natives with less hostility than the British.

Despite initial French successes, British fortunes were revived by the efforts of William Pitt the Elder who was convinced that the destruction of the French colonial empire was a necessary prerequisite for the creation of Britain's own colonial empire. Pitt's policy focused on making a minimal effort in Europe while concentrating resources on the colonial war, especially through use of the British navy. Although French troops were greater in number, the ability of the French to use them in the New World was contingent upon naval support. The defeat of French fleets in major naval battles in 1759 gave the British an advantage since the French could no longer easily reinforce their garrisons. A series of British victories soon followed. In 1758, Forts Louisbourg and Duquesne were captured; in 1759, British forces under General Wolfe defeated the French under General Montcalm on the Plains of Abraham outside Quebec. Both generals died in the battle. The British went on to seize Montreal, the Great Lakes area, and the Ohio valley. The French were forced to make peace. By the Treaty of Paris, they ceded Canada and the lands east of the Mississippi to Britain. Their ally Spain transferred

Spanish Florida to British control; in return, the French gave their Louisiana territory to the Spanish. By 1763, Great Britain had become the world's greatest colonial power.

European Armies and Warfare

The professional standing army, initiated in the seventeenth century, became a standard feature of eighteenth-century Europe. Especially noticeable was the increase in the size of armies as the development of absolutist states was paralleled by the growth of ever-larger armies. From 1740 to 1780, the French army grew

Chronology ▼▼▼ The Mid-Century Wars	
War of the Austrian Succession	1740–1748
Peace of Aix-la-Chapelle	1748
The Seven Years' War	1756–1763
Diplomatic Revolution	1756
Battle of Rossbach	1757
British Capture of Forts Duquesne and Louisbourg	1758
Battle of Quebec	1759
Peace of Hubertusburg	1763
Peace of Paris	1763

▼ **The Death of Wolfe.** The Seven Years' War was fought by the great powers of Europe in Europe, India, and North America. Despite initial French successes in North America, the British went on to win the war, and in the Treaty of Paris, the French ceded Canada and their lands east of the Mississippi to Britain. This painting by Benjamin West presents a heroic rendering of the death of General Wolfe, the British commander who defeated the French forces at the Battle of Quebec.

from 190,000 to 300,000 men; the Prussian from 83,000 to 200,000; the Austrian from 108,000 to 282,000; and the Russian from 130,000 to 290,000.

The composition of these armies reflected the hierarchical structure of European society and the great chasm that separated the upper and lower classes. Officers were primarily from the landed aristocracy, which had for centuries regarded military activity as one of its major functions. Prussia made military service compulsory for its nobles and forced the teenaged sons of aristocrats to attend a military academy in Berlin for training as officers. Middle-class individuals were largely kept out of the higher ranks of the officer corps while being admitted to the middle ranks. A prejudice against commoners in the officer corps remained a regular feature of military life in the eighteenth century.

Rank-and-file soldiers came mostly from the lower classes of society. Some states, such as Prussia and Russia, conscripted able-bodied peasants. But many states realized that this was counterproductive since they could not afford to waste agricultural manpower. For that reason, eighteenth-century armies were partially composed of foreign troops, many from Switzerland or the petty German states. Of the great powers, Britain alone had no regular standing army and relied on mercenaries, evident in its use of German troops in America. Most troops in European armies, especially the French and Austrian, were natives who enlisted voluntarily for six-year terms. Some were not exactly volunteers; often vagabonds and the unemployed were pressed into service. Most, however, came from the lower classes—peasants and also artisans from the cities—who saw the military as an opportunity to escape from hard times or personal problems.

The maritime powers, such as Britain and the Dutch Republic, regarded navies as more important than armies. In the second half of the eighteenth century, the British possessed 174 warships manned by 80,000 sailors. Conditions on these ships were often poor. Diseases such as scurvy and yellow fever were rampant, and crews were frequently press-ganged into duty.

The dramatic increase in the size of armies and navies did not necessarily result in more destructive warfare in eighteenth-century Europe. For one thing, warfare was no longer driven by ideological reasons as had been true of the religious wars of the sixteenth and seventeenth century. By their very nature, ideological wars are often violent and destructive. Moreover, since the larger armies depended upon increased taxes, rulers regarded the wanton destruction of civilian life as foolish. Finally,

the costliness of eighteenth-century armies as well as the technology and tactical traditions of the age created a system of warfare based on limited objectives.

Generals were extremely reluctant to risk the destruction of their armies in pitched battles. Clever and elaborate maneuvers, rather than direct confrontation, became the norm. A system of formalities accepted by all sides allowed defeated opponents to withdraw without being captured or destroyed. This mentality also encouraged the construction of vast fortresses to secure major roads and the enormous quantities of supplies needed by eighteenth-century armies. With its own set patterns of tactics, siege warfare often became, as one French critic said disgustingly, "the art of surrendering strongholds honorably after certain conventional formalities."

▼ Economic and Social Change

The economic depression that had characterized the seventeenth century began to end in the early eighteenth century. Rapid population growth, economic expansion in banking and trade, an agricultural revolution (at least in Britain), and the beginnings of a new pattern of industrialization characterized the economic patterns of the eighteenth century.

Growth of the European Population

The cycles of population growth and decline that had characterized Europe since the Middle Ages came to an end in the eighteenth century. Despite regional variations, Europe's population began to grow around 1750 and continued a "slow but irreversible upward movement." It has been estimated that the total European population was around 120 million in 1700, expanded to 140 million by 1750, and then grew to 190 million by 1790; thus, the growth rate in the second half of the century was double that of the first half. Individual states also experienced rapid growth from 1700 to 1790: Russia's population went from 14 million to 28 million; France from 20 to 26 or 27 million; Spain from 6 to 10 million; Brandenburg-Prussia from 1.5 to 5.5 million (over half of this came from territorial acquisition); and Britain from 5 or 6 to 9 million. These increases occurred during the same time that several million Europeans were going abroad as colonists.

Historical demographers are not sure of the causes of this population growth. Enough statistical studies have been done, however, to show that a falling death rate was perhaps most important, especially the decline in infant mortality rates. One study of several French parishes reveals that in the first part of the century the mortality rate for infants under one year was 29 percent and the rate for all children from birth to nineteen years was 51 percent, compared to 20 and 42 percent, respectively, in the 1780s. Although the percentage of decrease seems small, it is statistically significant enough to cause a noticeable increase in population.

But why the decline in the death rate? Historians are not sure. Certainly, it was not from improved health care since little change occurred in that area until the end of the eighteenth century. No doubt, more plentiful food and better transportation of available food supplies led to some improvement in diet and relief from devastating famines. Also of great significance was the lowering of death rates brought by the ending of bubonic plague. The last great outbreak in western Europe occurred in 1720 in southern France. Nevertheless, despite the increase in population, death was still a ubiquitous feature of everyday life. Other diseases, such as typhus, smallpox, influenza, and dysentery, were rampant, especially due to poor hygienic conditions—little bathing, dirty clothes, and no systematic elimination of human wastes. Despite the improved transportation, famine and hunger could still be devastating. As a small textile merchant in Germany wrote in 1770: "And the misery grew so much that poor people could only hope for spring when they could find roots and herbs. And I had to cook that sort of stuff."[7]

Family, Marriage, and Birthrate Patterns

Detailed examination of parish registers has enabled historians to piece together some generalizations about family, marriage, and birthrate patterns in the eighteenth century.

The family, rather than the individual, was still at the heart of Europe's social organization. For the most part, people still thought of the family in traditional terms, as a patriarchal institution with the husband dominating his wife and children. Especially among the upper classes there was still a concern for the family as a "house," an association whose collective interests were more important than those of the individuals who made it up. Parents (especially the fathers) still generally selected marriage partners for their children based on the interests of the family. One French noble responded to his son's request about his upcoming marriage: "Mind your own business."

Generally, lower-class women breast-fed their own children since it provided the best nourishment. Moreover, since there were strong taboos in various parts of Europe against sexual intercourse while one was breast-feeding, mothers might also avoid another immediate pregnancy; if the infant died, they could then have another child. Lower-class women, however, also served as wet nurses for children of the aristocratic and upper middle classes. Mothers from these higher social strata considered breast-feeding undignified and hired wet nurses

▼ **The Practice of Infanticide.** Despite the creation of new foundling homes, infanticide remained one of the solutions to the problem of too many children. This engraving recounts the story of one infanticide in Germany. Top left: the infant is discovered, smothered under a mattress. Bottom left: the mother is taken from prison to be executed. Right: a large crowd observes the execution of the mother for her crime.

instead. Even urban mothers, the wives of artisans, for economic reasons sent their babies to wet nurses in the countryside if they could, making the practice widespread in the eighteenth century.

In the second half of the eighteenth century, traditional attitudes began to alter, especially in western Europe. The impact of Enlightenment thought, such as Rousseau's *Emile,* and the increasing survival of more infants led to new attitudes toward children. Childhood was more and more viewed as a phase in human development. One result was a shift to dressing children in more comfortable clothes appropriate to their age rather than dressing them in clothes modeled after adult styles. Shops for children's clothes appeared for the first time. There were also attacks on primogeniture or the practice of treating the first son as the favorite. All children, it was argued, deserve their parents' attention. Appeals for women to breast-feed their own children rather than use wet nurses soon followed. In England, games and toys specifically for children now appeared. The jigsaw puzzle was invented in the 1760s, and books, such as *Little Pretty Pocket-Book* (1744), aimed to please as well as teach children. These changes, however, were limited mostly to the upper classes of western European society and did not extend to the peasants. For most Europeans,

children were still a source of considerable anxiety. They represented more mouths to feed and in times of economic crisis proved such a liability that infanticide was practiced and foundling homes were overcrowded.

Despite being punishable by death, infanticide remained a solution to the problem of too many children. So many children were being "accidentally" suffocated while in their parents' bed that in Austria in 1784 a law was issued that forbade parents to place children under five years old in bed with them. More common than infanticide was the placement of unwanted children in foundling homes or hospitals, which became a favorite charity of the rich in eighteenth-century Europe. The largest of its kind, located in St. Petersburg, Russia, was founded by members of the nobility. By the end of the century, it was taking in 5,000 new babies a year and caring for 25,000 children at one time.

But severe problems arose as the system became overburdened. One historian has estimated that in the 1770s one-third of all babies born in Paris were taken to foundling institutions by parents or desperate unmarried mothers, creating serious overcrowding. Foundling institutions often proved fatal for infants. Mortality rates ranged from 50 to as high as 90 percent (in a sense making foundling homes a legalized form of infanticide).

▼ **Women at the Foundling Hospital, London.** During the second half of the eighteenth century, traditional attitudes toward children began to change among the upper classes. Nevertheless, children were still a source of much anxiety to most Europeans. Increasingly, parents placed unwanted children in foundling homes built by members of the wealthy classes. This engraving shows babies being brought by their mothers to the gates of a new foundling hospital in London built by Captain Thomas Coram.

Those who survived were usually sent to miserable jobs. The suffering of poor children was one of the blackest pages of eighteenth-century European history.

In most of Europe, newly married couples established their own households independent of their parents. This nuclear family, which had its beginning in the Middle Ages, had become a common European pattern. In order to save what they needed to create their own households, both men and women (outside of the aristocracy) married quite late; the average age for men in northwestern Europe was between twenty-seven and twenty-eight; for women between twenty-five and twenty-seven.

Late marriages imposed limits on the birthrate; in fact, they might be viewed as a natural form of birth control. But was this limitation offset by the number of babies born illegitimately? It would appear from the low illegitimacy rate of 1 percent in some places in France, and 5 percent in some English parishes, that it was not, at least in the first half of the eighteenth century. After 1750, however, illegitimacy appears to have increased. Studies in Germany, for example, show that rates of illegitimacy increased from 2 percent in 1700 to 5 percent in 1760 and to 10 percent in 1800, followed by an even more dramatic increase in the early nineteenth century.

For married couples, the first child usually appeared within one year of marriage, while additional children came at intervals of two or three years, producing an average number of five births per family. It would appear then that the birthrate had the potential of creating a significant increase in population. This possibility was restricted, however, since 40 to 60 percent of European women of childbearing age (between fifteen and forty-four) were not married at any given time. Moreover, by the end of the eighteenth century, especially among the upper classes in France and Britain, birth control techniques were being used to limit the number of children. Figures for the French aristocracy indicate that the average number of children declined from six in the period from 1650–1700 to three from 1700 to 1750 and to two between 1750 and 1780. These figures are even more significant when one considers that aristocrats married at ages younger than the rest of the population. Coitus interruptus remained the most commonly used form of birth control.

Among the working classes, whether peasants or urban workers, the contributions of women and children to the "family economy" were often crucial. In urban areas, both male and female children either helped in the handicraft manufacturing done in the home or were sent out to work as household servants. In rural areas, children worked on the land or helped in the activities of cottage industry. Married women grew vegetables in small plots, tended livestock, and sold eggs, vegetables, and milk. Wives of propertyless agricultural workers labored in the fields or as textile workers, spinning or knitting. In the cities, wives of artisans helped their husbands at their crafts or worked as seamstresses. The wives of unskilled workers labored as laundresses and cleaners for the rich or as peddlers of food or used clothing to the lower classes. But the family economy was often precarious. Bad harvests in the countryside or a downturn in employment in the cities often reduced people to utter poverty and a life of begging (see The Problem of Poverty later in the chapter).

An Agricultural Revolution?

Did improvements in agricultural practices and methods in the eighteenth century lead to an agricultural revolution? The topic is much debated. Some historians have noted the beginning of agrarian changes already in the seventeenth century, especially in the Low Countries. Others, however, have questioned the use of the term, arguing that significant changes occurred only in England and noting that even there the upward trend in agricultural production was not maintained after 1750.

Eighteenth-century agriculture was characterized by increases in food production that can be attributed to four interrelated factors: more land under cultivation, increased yields per acre, healthier and more abundant livestock, and an improved climate. Climatologists believe that the "little ice age" of the seventeenth century declined in the eighteenth, especially evident in the moderate summers that provided more ideal growing conditions.

The increase in the amount of land under cultivation was made possible by abandoning the old open field system in which part of the land was left to lie fallow to renew it. New crops, such as alfalfa, turnips, and clover, which stored nitrogen in their roots and helped to restore the soil's fertility, were planted in England, parts of France, and the Low Countries. The new crops provided winter fodder for livestock, enabling landlords to maintain an ever-larger number of animals; some enterprising landlords also engaged in scientific breeding and produced stronger and more productive strains of animals.

The increase in livestock enlarged the amount of meat in the European diet and affected the food production by making available larger amounts of animal ma-

Propaganda for the New Agriculture
▼ ▼ ▼

Enthusiastic supporters of the new English agricultural practices went to the continent to examine less efficient kinds of farming. One of these Englishmen, Arthur Young, wrote an account of his travels in which he blamed the low yields of French farmers on two causes: the old system of allowing part of the land to lie fallow and the small size of the farms. The latter factor was especially important to English aristocratic landholders who wished to justify the enclosure movement. This selection is taken from Young's account.

Arthur Young, *Travels during the Years 1787, 1788, and 1789 . . . in the Kingdom of France*

The Englishman, in eleven years, gets three bushels more of wheat than the Frenchman. He gets three crops of barley, tares, or beans, which produce nearly twice as many bushels per acre, as what the three French crops of spring corn produce. And he farther gets, at the same time, three crops of turnips and two of clover, the turnips worth 40s. the acre, and the clover 60s. That is 121 for both. What an enormous superiority. More wheat; almost double of the spring corn; and above 20s. per acre per annum in turnips and clover. But farther; the Englishman's land, by means of the manure arising from the consumption of the turnips and clover is in a constant state of improvement, while the Frenchman's farm is stationary.

The great populousness of France, I attribute very much to the division of the lands into small properties, which takes place in that country to a degree of which we have in England but little conception. . . . It has been said to me in France, "Would you leave uncultivated lands wastes, rather than let them be cultivated in small portions, through a fear of population?" I certainly would not: I would, on the contrary, encourage their culture; but I would prohibit the division of small farms, which is as mischievous to cultivation, as it is sure to be distressing to the people. . . . Go to districts where the properties are minutely divided, and you will find (at least I have done it) universally, great distress, and even misery, and probably very bad agriculture. Go to others, where such sub-division has not taken place, and you will find a better cultivation, and infinitely less misery. When you are engaged in this political tour, finish it by seeing England, and I will show you a set of peasants well clothed, well nourished, tolerably drunken from superfluity, well-lodged, and at their ease.

---

nure that helped to fertilize fields and produce better yields per acre. Increased yields were also encouraged by landed aristocrats who shared in the scientific experimentation of the age. Jethro Tull (1674–1741) in England discovered that using a hoe to keep the soil loose allowed air and moisture to reach plants and enabled them to grow better. He also used a drill to plant seeds in rows instead of scattering them by hand, a method that had lost much seed to the birds. The eighteenth century witnessed greater yields of vegetables, including two important American crops, the potato and maize (Indian corn). Both had been brought to Europe from America in the sixteenth century although it was not until after 1700 that they were grown in quantity. The potato became a staple in Germany, the Low Countries, and especially Ireland, where repression by English landlords forced large numbers of poor peasants to survive on small pieces of marginal land. The potato took relatively little effort to produce in large quantities. High in carbohydrates and calories, rich in vitamins A and C, it could be easily stored for winter use.

The new agriculture was considered best suited to large-scale farmers who could make better use of the new techniques. Consequently, a change in landholding accompanied the increase in food production. The end of the open field system led to the demise of the cooperative farming of the village community. Instead, land was enclosed into bigger units by large landowners or yeomen farmers. In England, where small landholders resisted this process, Parliament, dominated by the landed aristocracy, enacted legislation by which agricultural lands could be legally enclosed. As a result of these enclosure acts, England gradually became a land of large estates while many small farmers were forced to become tenant farmers working 100–500 acre farms for land or as paid wage laborers. While some historians have emphasized the advantages of enclosures in enabling large landowners to practice new agricultural techniques and increase food production, the enclosure movement and new agricultural practices also effectively destroyed the traditional patterns of English village life.

In the eighteenth century, it was primarily the English who adopted the new techniques that have been characterized as an agricultural revolution (see the box on p. 650). This early modernization of English agriculture with its noticeable increase in productivity made possible the feeding of an expanding population about to enter a new world of industrialization and urbanization.

Finance and Industry

The decline in the available supply of gold and silver in the seventeenth century had created a chronic shortage of money that undermined the efforts of governments to meet their needs. The creation of new public and private banks and the acceptance of paper notes made possible an expansion of credit in the eighteenth century.

Perhaps the best example of this process can be observed in England where the Bank of England was founded in 1694. Unlike other banks accustomed to receiving deposits and exchanging foreign currencies, the Bank of England also made loans. In return for lending money to the government, the bank was allowed to issue paper "bank notes" backed by its credit. These soon became negotiable and created a paper substitute for gold and silver currency. In addition, the creation of government bonds earning regular interest, backed up by the Bank of England and the London financial community, created the notion of a public or "national debt" distinct from the monarch's personal debts. This process meant that capital could be raised in ever-greater quantities for financing larger armies and other government undertakings.

These new financial institutions and methods were not risk-free, however. In both Britain and France in the early eighteenth century, speculators provided opportunities for people to invest in colonial trading companies. The French company under John Law was also tied to his attempt to create a national bank and paper currency for France. When people went overboard and drove the price of the stock to incredibly high levels, the bubble burst. Law's company and bank went bankrupt, leading to a loss of confidence in paper money that prevented the formation of a French national bank. Consequently, French public finance developed slowly in the eighteenth century.

This was not the case in Britain, however. Despite crises, the development of public confidence in the new financial institutions enabled the British government to borrow large sums of money at relatively low rates of interest, giving it a distinct advantage in the struggle with France. According to a contemporary observer, Britain's public credit was "the permanent miracle of her policy, which has inspired both astonishment and fear in the States of Europe."[8] Despite Britain's growing importance in finance, however, the Dutch Republic remained the leader in Europe's financial life, and Amsterdam continued to be the center of international finance until London replaced it in the nineteenth century. One observer noted in 1769:

If ten or twelve businessmen of Amsterdam of the first rank meet for a banking operation, they can in a moment send circulating throughout Europe over two hundred million florins in paper money, which is preferred to cash. There is no Sovereign who could do as much. . . . This credit is a power which the ten or twelve businessmen will be able to exert over all the States of Europe, in complete independence of any authority.[9]

The decline of Dutch trade, industry, and power meant that Dutch capitalists were inclined to lend money abroad because of fewer opportunities at home. Such investments, of course, did not directly benefit the United Provinces.

The most important product of European industry in the eighteenth century was textiles. Seventy-five percent of Britain's exports in the early eighteenth century were woolen cloth. France, too, was a leader in the production of woolen cloth while other major states emulated both France and Britain by encouraging the development of their own textile industries.

Most textiles were still produced by traditional methods. In cities that were textile centers, master artisans in their guild workshops used timeworn methods to produce their finished goods, while urban craft guilds still attempted to restrict handicraft production to the cities.

But a shift in textile production to the countryside had also begun to occur; it was already evident in Flanders and England by the sixteenth century and was spreading elsewhere by the eighteenth century. In France, not until 1762 did a royal edict strip urban guilds of their manufacturing monopoly and allow rural industries to expand. Industrial production in the countryside was done by the "putting-out" or "domestic" system in which a merchant-capitalist entrepreneur bought the raw materials, mostly wool and flax, and "put them out" to rural workers who spun the raw material into yarn and then wove it into cloth on simple looms. Capitalist-entrepreneurs sold the finished product, made a profit, and used it to manufacture more. This system became known as the "cottage industry," since spinners and weavers did their work on spinning wheels and looms in their own cottages. Cottage industry was truly a family enterprise since women and children could spin while men wove on the looms, enabling rural people to earn incomes that supplemented their pitiful wages as agricultural laborers.

The cottage system utilized traditional methods of manufacturing and in the eighteenth century was expanded to many areas of rural Europe. But significant changes in industrial production also began to occur in the second half of the century, pushed along by the introduction of cotton, originally imported from India. The importation of raw cotton from slave plantations encouraged the production of cotton cloth in Europe where a profitable market developed because of the growing demand for lightweight cotton clothes that were less expensive than linens and woolens. But the traditional methods of the cottage industry proved incapable of keeping up with the growing demand, leading English cloth entrepreneurs to develop new methods and new machines. The flying shuttle sped up the process of weaving on a loom, thereby increasing the need for large quantities of yarn. In response, Richard Arkwright (1732–1792) invented a "water frame," powered by horse or water, which turned out yarn much faster than cottage spinning wheels. This abundance of yarn, in turn, led to the development of mechanized looms, invented in the 1780s but not widely adopted until the early nineteenth century. By that time Britain was in the throes of an industrial revolution, but already at the end of the eighteenth century, rural workers, perceiving that the new machines threatened their traditional livelihood, had begun to call for their destruction (see the box on p. 653).

Mercantile Empires and Worldwide Trade

While bankers and industrialists came to dominate the nineteenth century economically, in the eighteenth century merchants and traders still reigned supreme. Intra-European trade still dominated total trade figures as wheat, timber, and naval stores from the Baltic, wines from France, wool and fruit from Spain, and silk from Italy were exchanged along with a host of other products. But the eighteenth century witnessed only a slight increase in this trade while overseas trade boomed. From 1716 to 1789, total French exports quadrupled while intra-European trade, which constituted 75 percent of these exports in 1716, constituted only 50 percent of the total in 1789. This increase in overseas trade has led some historians to speak of the emergence of a truly global economy in the eighteenth century. By the beginning of that century, Spain, Portugal, and the Dutch Republic, which had earlier monopolized overseas trade, found themselves increasingly overshadowed by France and Britain. The rivalry between these two great western European powers was especially evident in the Americas and the Far East.

COLONIAL EMPIRES   Both the French and British colonial empires in the New World consisted of large parts of

▼ **French Port of Dieppe.** Overseas trade experienced considerable expansion during the eighteenth century. Between 1716 and 1789, total French exports quadrupled while overseas trade expanded from 25 to 50 percent of the total volume of trade. Seen here is the port of Dieppe, typical of several ports along the French coast from which a regular trade was carried on with French colonies in the New World. Rebuilt after it had been bombarded during the War of the League of Augsburg in 1694, Dieppe was a modern town in the eighteenth century.

The Beginnings of Mechanized Industry:
The Attack on New Machines

▼ ▼ ▼

Already by the end of the eighteenth century, mechanization was beginning to bring changes to the traditional cottage industry of textile manufacturing. Rural workers who depended on the extra wages made in their own homes often reacted by attacking the machinery that threatened their livelihoods. This selection is a petition that English wool workers published in their local newspapers asking that machines no longer be used to prepare wool for spinning.

The Leeds Woolen Workers' Petition (1786)

To the Merchants, Clothiers and all such as wish well to the Staple Manufactory of this Nation.

The Humble ADDRESS and PETITION of Thousands, who labour in the Cloth Manufactory.

SHEWETH, That the Scribbling-Machines have thrown thousands of your petitioners out of employ, whereby they are brought into great distress, and are not able to procure a maintenance for their families, and deprived them of the opportunity of bringing up their children to labour: We have therefore to request, that prejudice and self-interest may be laid aside, and that you may pay that attention to the following facts, which the nature of the case requires.

The number of Scribbling-Machines extending about seventeen miles southwest of LEEDS, exceed all belief, being no less than *one hundred and seventy!* and as each machine will do as much work in twelve hours, as ten men can in that time do by hand, (speaking within bounds) and they working night-and day, one machine will do as much work in one day as would otherwise employ twenty men.

As we do not mean to assert any thing but what we can prove to be true, we allow four men to be employed at each machine twelve hours, working night and day, will take eight men in twenty-four hours; so that, upon a moderate computation twelve men are

thrown out of employ for every single machine used in scribbling; and as it may be supposed the number of machines in all the other quarters together, nearly equal those in the South-West, full four thousand men are left to shift for a living how they can, and must of course fall to the Parish, if not time relieved. Allowing one boy to be bound apprentice from each family out of work, eight thousand hands are deprived of the opportunity of getting a livelihood.

We therefore hope, that the feelings of humanity will lead those who have it in their power to prevent the use of those machines, to give every discouragement they can to what has a tendency so prejudicial to their fellow-creatures. . . .

We wish to propose a few queries to those who would plead for the further continuance of these machines:

How are those men, thus thrown out of employ to provide for their families; and what are they to put their children apprentice to, that the rising generation may have something to keep them at work, in order that they may not be like vagabonds strolling about in idleness? Some day, Begin and learn some other business.—Suppose we do, who will maintain our families, whilst we undertake the arduous task; and when we have learned it, how do we know we shall be any better for all our pains; for by the time we have served our second apprenticeship, another machine may arise, which may take away that business also. . . .

But what are our children to do; are they to be brought up in idleness? Indeed as things are, it is no wonder to hear of so many executions; for our parts, though we may be thought illiterate men, our conceptions are, that bringing children up to industry, and keeping them employed, is the way to keep them from falling into those crimes, which an idle habit naturally leads to.

the West Indies and the North American continent. In the former, the British held Barbados, Jamaica, and Bermuda while the French possessed Saint Dominique, Martinique, and Guadeloupe. On these tropical islands both the British and the French had developed plantation economies, worked by African slaves, which produced tobacco, cotton, coffee, and sugar, all products increasingly in demand in Europe.

On the North American continent, the French and British colonies were structured in different ways. French North America (Canada and Louisiana) was run autocratically as a vast trading area, valuable for the acquisition of fur, leather, fish, and timber. However, the inability of the French state to get its people to emigrate to these North American possessions left them thinly populated.

British North America had come to consist of thirteen colonies on the eastern coast of the present United States. They were thickly populated, containing about 1.5 million people by 1750, and were also prosperous. Supposedly run by the British Board of Trade, the Royal Council, and Parliament, these thirteen colonies had legislatures that tended to act independently. Merchants in such port cities as Boston, Philadelphia, New York, and Charleston resented and resisted regulation from the British government.

Both the North American and West Indian colonies of Britain and France were assigned roles in keeping with mercantilist theory. They provided raw materials for the mother country while buying the latter's manufactured goods. Navigation acts regulated what could be taken from and sold to the colonies. Theoretically, the system was supposed to provide a balance of trade favorable to the mother country.

British and French rivalry was also evident in the Spanish and Portuguese colonial empires in Latin America. The decline of Spain and Portugal had led these two states to depend even more on resources from their colonies, and they imposed strict mercantilist rules on them to keep others out. Spain, for example, tried to limit all trade with its colonies to Spanish ships. But the British and French were too powerful to be excluded. The British cajoled the Portuguese into allowing them into the lucrative Brazilian trade. The French, however, were the first to break into the Spanish Latin American market when the French Bourbons became kings of Spain. Britain's entry into Spanish American markets first came in 1713, when Britain was granted the privilege, known as the *asiento,* of transporting 4,500 slaves a year into Spanish Latin America.

The same was true in the Far East as Britain and France competed for trade in India and the East Indies where the valuable products remained tea, spices, cotton, hard woods, and luxury goods. The rivalry between France and Britain was played out by their state-backed national trading companies. In the course of the eighteenth century, the British defeated the French, and by the mid-nineteenth century they had assumed control of the entire Indian subcontinent.

▼ **The Sale of Slaves.** In the eighteenth century, the sale of slaves was one of the more profitable trading enterprises. While the use of slaves in the New World had begun as far back as the sixteenth century, the slave trade was greatly expanded in the eighteenth century due to the need for labor on sugar, tobacco, rice, and cotton plantations. This engraving shows the sale of slaves in the French West Indian possession of Martinique.

GLOBAL TRADE   To justify the term *global economy,* historians have usually pointed to the patterns of trade that interlocked Europe, Africa, the Far East, and the American continents. One such pattern of triangular trade involved British merchant ships, which carried British manufactured goods to Africa, where they were traded for a cargo of slaves, which were then shipped to Virginia and paid for by tobacco, which in turn was shipped back to England where it was processed and then sold in Germany for cash.

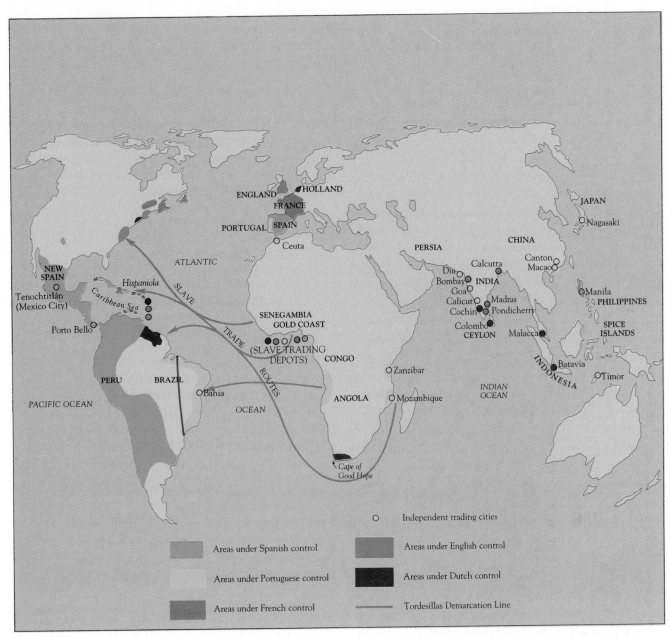

▼ **Map 19.3** The Slave Trade.

Of all the goods traded in the eighteenth century, perhaps the most profitable and certainly the most infamous were African slaves. Of course, the slave trade was not new; the Spanish and Portuguese had introduced black slaves into America in the sixteenth century. But the need for slaves in the lucrative plantation production of sugar, tobacco, rice, and cotton made the eighteenth century the high point of the Atlantic slave trade. It has been estimated that of the total 9,300,000 slaves transported from Africa, almost two-thirds were taken in the eighteenth century. Between 75,000 and 90,000 Afri-

cans were transported annually, 50 percent in British ships, with the rest divided among French, Dutch, Portuguese, Danish, and American ships.

Slaving ships sailed from a European port to the African coast where Europeans had established bases where merchants could trade manufactured goods, rum, and brandy for blacks captured by African middlemen. The captives were then closely packed into cargo ships, 300 to 450 per ship, and chained in holds without sanitary facilities or space in which to stand up for a voyage to America that took at least a hundred days (see the box

The Atlantic Slave Trade
▼ ▼ ▼

One of the most odious practices of early modern Western society was the Atlantic slave trade, which reached its height in the eighteenth century. Blacks were transported in densely packed cargo ships from the western coast of Africa to the Americas to work as slaves in the plantation economy. Not until late in the eighteenth century did a rising chorus of voices raise serious objections to this trade in human beings. This excerpt presents a criticism of the slave trade from an anonymous French writer.

Diary of a Citizen

As soon as the ships have lowered their anchors off the coast of Guinea, the price at which the captains have decided to buy the captives is announced to the Negroes who buy prisoners from various princes and sell them to the Europeans. Presents are sent to the sovereign who rules over that particular part of the coast, and permission to trade is given. Immediately the slaves are brought by inhuman brokers like so many victims dragged to a sacrifice. White men who covet that portion of the human race receive them in a little house they have erected on the shore, where they have entrenched themselves with two pieces of cannon and twenty guards. As soon as the bargain is concluded, the Negro is put in chains and led aboard the vessel, where he meets his fellow sufferers. Here sinister reflections come to his mind; everything shocks and frightens him and his uncertain destiny gives rise to the greatest anxiety. . . .

The vessel sets sail for the Antilles, and the Negroes are chained in a hold of the ship, a kind of lugubrious prison where the light of day does not penetrate, but into which air is introduced by means of a pump. Twice a day some disgusting food is distributed to them. Their consuming sorrow and the sad state to which they are reduced would make them commit suicide if they were not deprived of all the

means for an attempt upon their lives. Without any kind of clothing it would be difficult to conceal from the watchful eyes of the sailors in charge any instrument apt to alleviate their despair. The fear of a revolt, such as sometimes happens on the voyage from Guinea, is the basis of a common concern and produces as many guards as there are men in the crew. The slightest noise or a secret conversation among two Negroes is punished with utmost severity. All in all, the voyage is made in a continuous state of alarm on the part of the white men, who fear a revolt, and in a cruel state of uncertainty on the part of the Negroes, who do not know the fate awaiting them.

When the vessel arrives at a port in the Antilles, they are taken to a warehouse where they are displayed, like any merchandise, to the eyes of buyers. The plantation owner pays according to the age, strength, and health of the Negro he is buying. He has him taken to his plantation, and there he is delivered to an overseer who then and there becomes his tormentor. In order to domesticate him, the Negro is granted a few days of rest in his new place, but soon he is given a hoe and a sickle and made to join a work gang. Then he ceases to wonder about his fate; he understands that only labor is demanded of him. But he does not know yet how excessive this labor will be. As a matter of fact, his work begins at dawn and does not end before nightfall; it is interrupted for only two hours at dinnertime. The food a full-grown Negro is given each week consists of two pounds of salt beef or cod and two pots of tapioca meal. . . . A Negro of twelve or thirteen years or under is given only one pot of meal and one pound of beef or cod. In place of food some planters give their Negroes the liberty of working for themselves every Saturday; others are even less generous and grant them this liberty only on Sundays and holidays.

above). Mortality rates averaged 10 percent except when longer journeys due to storms or adverse winds resulted in even higher death rates.

Once the human cargoes arrived in the New World, they immediately entered the plantation economy, in which the "sugar factories," as the sugar plantations in the Caribbean were called, played an especially valuable

role. By the last two decades of the eighteenth century, the British colony of Jamaica, one of Britain's most important, was producing 50,000 tons of sugar annually with the slave labor of 200,000 blacks. The French colony of Saint Dominique (later Haiti) had 500,000 slaves working on 3,000 plantations at the same time. This colony produced 100,000 tons of sugar a year but at the expense of a high death rate from the brutal treatment of the slaves. It is not surprising that Saint Dominique saw the first successful slave uprising in 1793.

Despite a rising chorus of humanitarian sentiments from the philosophes, the use of black slaves remained acceptable to Western society. By and large, Europeans continued to view blacks as inferior beings fit primarily for slave labor. Not until the Society of Friends or Quakers began to criticize slavery in the 1770s and exclude from their church any member adhering to slave trafficking, did European sentiment against slavery begin to build. Even then it was not until the radical stage of the French Revolution in the 1790s that the French abolished slavery. The British followed suit in 1808. Despite the elimination of the African source, slavery continued in the newly formed United States until the Civil War of the 1860s.

▼ The Social Order of the Eighteenth Century

The pattern of Europe's social organization, first established in the Middle Ages, continued well into the eighteenth century. Social status was still largely determined not by wealth and economic standing but by the division into the traditional "orders" or "estates" determined by heredity and quality. This divinely sanctioned division of society into traditional orders was supported by Christian teaching, which emphasized the need to fulfill the responsibilities of one's estate. Inequality was part of that scheme and could not be eliminated. In the eighteenth century, this emphasis on a fixed order was expressed in secular terms as well. One observer wrote in 1747 that "a reasonable man is always happy if he has what is necessary for him according to his condition [his place in the social order], that is to say, if he has the protection of the laws, and can live as his father lived before him: so that one of the essential things to the good of a nation is being governed in one constant and uniform manner."[10]

Although Enlightenment intellectuals attacked these traditional distinctions, they did not die easily. In the Prussian law code of 1794, marriage between noble males and middle-class females was forbidden without a government dispensation. In cities, sumptuary legislation designated what dress different urban groups should wear so as to keep them separate. Even without government regulation, however, different social groups remained easily distinguished everywhere in Europe by the distinctive, traditional clothes they wore. Such social

conservatism was reinforced by society's ongoing preoccupation with local and regional differences. Local rivalries and local grievances greatly outweighed any loyalty to the larger state. Even local dialects continued to separate people. A French magistrate at Riom was unable to question a young itinerant from a town only fifteen miles away because "the speech of Courpière differs considerably from that of Riom."

Nevertheless, some forces of change were at work in this traditional society. The ideas of the Enlightenment made headway as reformers argued that the idea of an unchanging social order based on privilege was hostile to the progress of society. Moreover, especially in some cities, the old structures were more difficult to maintain as new economic structures, especially the growth of larger industries, brought new social contrasts that destroyed the old order. Despite these forces of change, however, it would take the revolutionary upheavals at the end of the eighteenth century before the old order would finally begin to disintegrate.

The Peasants

Since society was still mostly rural in the eighteenth century, the peasantry constituted the largest social group, making up as much as 85 percent of Europe's population. There were rather wide differences, however, between peasants from area to area. The most important distinction—at least legally—was between the free peasant and the serf. Peasants in Britain, northern Italy, the Low Countries, Spain, most of France, and some areas of western Germany shared freedom despite numerous regional and local differences. Legally free peasants, however, were not exempt from burdens. Some free peasants in Andalusia in Spain, southern Italy, Sicily, and Portugal lived in a poverty more desperate than that of many serfs in Russia and eastern Germany. In France, 40 percent of free peasants owned little or no land whatever by 1789. As the century progressed and new agricultural methods developed, small peasant proprietors were often unable to compete in efficiency with large estates.

Small peasant proprietors or tenant farmers in western Europe were also not free from compulsory services. Most owed tithes, often one-third of their crops. Although tithes were intended for parish priests, in France only 10 percent of the priests received them. Instead they wound up in the hands of towns and aristocratic landowners. Moreover, peasants could still owe a variety of dues and fees. Local aristocrats claimed hunting rights on peasant land and had monopolies over the flour mills, community ovens, and wine and oil presses needed by the peasants. Hunting rights, dues, fees, and tithes were all deeply resented.

Eastern Europe continued to be dominated by large landed estates owned by powerful lords and worked by serfs. Serfdom had come late to the east having largely been imposed in the sixteenth and seventeenth centuries. Peasants in eastern Germany were bound to the lord's estate, had to provide labor services on the lord's land, and could not marry or move without permission and payment of a tax. By the eighteenth century, the landlord also possessed legal jurisdiction, giving him control over the administration of justice. Only in the Habsburg empire had a ruler attempted to improve the lot of the peasants through a series of reforms. In Russia, peasants were not attached to the land but to the landlord and thus existed in a condition approaching slavery. In 1762, landowners were given the right to transfer their serfs from one estate to another. Unlike the rest of Europe and with the exception of the clergy and a small merchant class, eighteenth-century Russia was largely a society of landlords and serfs. Although eastern Europe, especially Poland, Russia, and some Habsburg provinces, experienced revolts by desperate peasants, they were easily crushed.

The local villages in which they dwelt remained the centers of peasants' social lives. Villages, especially in western Europe, maintained public order, provided poor relief, a village church, and sometimes a schoolmaster, collected taxes for the central government, maintained roads and bridges, and established common procedures for sowing, ploughing, and harvesting crops. But villages were often dominated by richer peasants and proved highly resistant to innovations, such as new crops and agricultural practices.

The diet of the peasants in the eighteenth century did not vary much from that of the Middle Ages. Dark bread, made of roughly ground wheat and rye flour, remained the basic staple. It was quite nourishing and high in vitamins, minerals, and even proteins since the bran and germ were not ground out. Peasants drank water, wine, and beer and ate soups and gruel made of grains and vegetables. Especially popular were peas and beans, eaten fresh in summer but dried and used in soups and stews in winter. The new foods of the eighteenth century, potatoes and American corn, added important elements to the peasant diet. Of course, when harvests were bad, hunger and famine became the peasants' lot in life, making them even more susceptible to the ravages of disease.

The Nobility

The nobles, who constituted about 2 or 3 percent of the European population, played a dominating role in society. Being born a noble automatically guaranteed a place at the top of the social order with all of its attendant special privileges and rights. The legal privileges of the nobility included judgment by their peers, immunity from severe punishment, exemption from many forms of taxation, and rights of jurisdiction. Especially in central and eastern Europe, the rights of landlords over their serfs were overwhelming. In Poland until 1768, the nobility even possessed the right of life or death over their serfs. Other aristocratic privileges included the sole right to carry a sword, occupy a special pew in church, and possess a monopoly on hunting rights.

In many countries, nobles were self-conscious about their unique style of life that set them apart from the rest of society. This did not mean, however, that they were unwilling to bend the conventions of that lifestyle if there were profits to be made. For example, nobles by convention were expected to live off the yields of their estates. But although nobles almost everywhere talked about trade as being beneath their dignity, many were not averse to mercantile endeavors. Many were also only too eager to profit from industries based on the exploitation of raw materials found on their estates; as a result, many nobles were involved in mining, metallurgy, and glassmaking. Their diet also set them off from the rest of society. Aristocrats consumed enormous quantities of meat and fish dishes accompanied by cheeses, nuts, and a variety of sweets.

Nobles also played important roles in military and government affairs. Since medieval times, landed aristocrats had functioned as military officers. While monarchs found it impossible to exclude commoners from the ranks of officers, the tradition remained that nobles made the most natural and hence the best officers. Moreover, the eighteenth-century nobility played a significant role in the administrative machinery of state. In some countries, such as Prussia, the entire bureaucracy reflected aristocratic values. Moreover, in most of Europe, the landholding nobility controlled much of the local government in their districts.

The nobility or landowning class was not a homogeneous social group. Landlords in England leased their land to tenant farmers while those in eastern Europe used the labor services of serfs. Nobles in Russia and Prussia served the state while those in Spain and Italy had few official functions. Differences in wealth, education, and political power also led to differences within countries as well. In France, where there were about 350,000 nobles, only 4,000 noble families were allowed access to the court. The gap between rich and poor nobles could be enormous. According to figures for the poll tax in France, the richest nobles were assessed 2,000 livres a year while some nobles, because of their depressed economic state, paid only 6. Both groups were legally nobles. In Poland, where the legal nobility constituted 10 to 15 percent of the population or about 750,000 people, most were poor and owned little or no land. While these nobles had special pews in church and wore special dress, they were often as poor as the peasants. As the century progressed, these poor nobles increasingly sank into the ranks of the unprivileged masses of the population. It has been estimated that the number of European nobles declined by one-third between 1750 and 1815.

Although the nobles clung to their privileged status and struggled to keep others out, almost everywhere the possession of money made it possible to enter the ranks of the nobility. Rights of nobility were frequently attached to certain lands so purchasing the lands made one a noble; the acquisition of government offices also often conferred noble status.

THE ARISTOCRATIC WAY OF LIFE: THE COUNTRY HOUSE

The Comte Charles-Maurice de Talleyrand-Périgord, the arch-survivor of the French revolutionary era, once commented that "no one who did not live before the Revolution" could know the real sweetness of living. Of course, he spoke not for the peasants whose labor maintained the system, but for the landed aristocrats. For them the eighteenth century was a final century of "sweetness" before the Industrial Revolution and bourgeois society diminished their privileged way of life.

In so many ways, the court of Louis XIV had provided a model for other European monarchs who built palaces and encouraged the development of a court society as a center of culture. As at Versailles, these courts were peopled by members of the aristocracy whose income from rents or officeholding enabled them to participate in this lifestyle. This court society, whether in France, Spain, or Germany, manifested common characteristics: participation in intrigues for the king's or prince's favor, serene walks in formal gardens, and duels to maintain one's honor. Hierarchy and status were all important. A complex mixture of family heritage, title, and wealth determined the position one occupied in this society.

The majority of aristocratic landowners, however, remained on their country estates and did not participate in court society; their large houses continued to give witness to their domination of the surrounding countryside. This was especially true in England where the court of the Hanoverian kings (Georges I-III from 1714 to 1820) made little impact on the behavior of upper-class society. English landed aristocrats invested much time, energy, and money in their rural estates, giving the English country house an important role in English social life. One American observer remarked: "Scarcely any persons who hold a leading place in the circles of their society live in London. They have houses in London, in which they stay while Parliament sits, and occasionally visit at other seasons; but their homes are in the country."[11]

After the seventeenth century, the English referred to their country homes, regardless of size, not as chateaus or villas but merely houses. Although there was much variety in country houses, many in the eighteenth century were built in the Georgian style named after the Hanoverian kings. This style was greatly influenced by the classical serenity and sedateness of the sixteenth-century Venetian architect, Andrea Palladio, who had specialized in the design of country villas. The Georgian country house combined elegance with domesticity, and its interior was often characterized as possessing a comfort of home that combined visual delight and usefulness.

The country house also fulfilled a newfound desire for greater privacy. Domestic etiquette militated against unannounced visits, and the rooms were designed to serve specialized purposes while their arrangement ensured more privacy. The central entrance hall contained a large staircase to the upstairs and also led to the common rooms of the downstairs. The entrance hall, whose coats of arms and suits of armor still reflected its medieval ancestry, now also provided the setting for the ceremonial arrival and departure of guests on formal occasions. The lower floors of the country house held a series of common rooms for public activities. The largest was the drawing room (larger houses possessed two), which contained musical instruments and was used for dances or card games, a favorite pastime. Other common rooms included a formal dining room, informal breakfast room, library, study, gallery, billiard room, and a conservatory. The downstairs common rooms were used for dining, entertaining, and leisure. Upstairs rooms consisted of bedrooms for husbands and wives, sons, and daughters. These were used not only for sleeping but also for private activities, such as playing for the children and sewing, writing, and reading for wives. This arrangement reflected the new desire for privacy and to some extent the growing awareness of individuality. "Going upstairs" literally meant leaving the company of others in the downstairs common rooms to be alone in the privacy of the bedroom. This eighteenth-century desire for privacy also meant keeping servants at a distance. They were now housed in their own wing of rooms and alerted to their employers' desire for assistance by a new invention—long-distance cords connected to bells in the servants' quarters.

Although the arrangement of the eighteenth-century Georgian house originally reflected male interests, the influence of women was increasingly evident by the second half of the eighteenth century. Already in the seventeenth century, it had become customary for the sexes to separate after dinner; while the men preoccupied themselves with brandy and cigars in the dining room, women would exit into a "withdrawing room" for their own conversation. In the course of the eighteenth century, the drawing room became a larger, more feminine room with comfortable furniture grouped casually in front of fireplaces to create a cozy atmosphere.

THE ARISTOCRATIC WAY OF LIFE: THE GRAND TOUR   One characteristic of the high culture of the Enlightenment was its cosmopolitanism, reinforced by education in the Latin classics and the use of French as an international language. Travel was another manifestation of the En-

lightenment's cosmopolitanism and interest in new vistas. One important aspect of eighteenth-century travel was the Grand Tour in which the sons of aristocrats completed their educations by making a tour of Europe's major cities. The English aristocracy in particular regarded the Grand Tour as crucial to their education. The great-aunt of Thomas Coke wrote to him upon his completion of school: "Sir, I understand you have left Eton and probably intend to go to one of those Schools of Vice, the Universities. If, however, you choose to travel I will give you 500 pounds [about $12,500] per annum."[12] Coke was no fool and went on the Grand Tour, along with many others. In one peak year alone, 40,000 Englishmen were traveling in Europe.

Travel was not easy in the eighteenth century. Crossing the English Channel could be difficult in rough seas and might take anywhere from three to twelve hours. The trip from France to Italy could be done by sea, where the traveler faced the danger of pirates, or overland by sedan chair over the Alps, where narrow passes made travel an adventure in terror. Inns, especially in Germany, were populated by thieves and the ubiquitous bed bugs. The English were particularly known for spending vast sums of money during their travels, as one observer recounted: "The French usually travel to save money, so that they sometimes leave the places where they sojourn worse off than they found them. The English, on the other hand, come over with plenty of cash, plenty of gear, and servants to wait on them. They throw their money about like lords."[13]

▼ Visit to the Art Collections. The Grand Tour was the final step in the education of young aristocrats and consisted of a visit to Europe's major cities. Young aristocrats were usually accompanied by tutors and spent part of their time studying museum collections and antiquities. Florence was one of their favorite Italian destinations. This painting by Johann Zoffany shows some of the treasures of the Medici collection in the Tribuna of the Uffizi in Florence. This collection in the Uffizi art gallery was visited by all connoisseurs on the Grand Tour. In the center of the room are pieces of classical sculpture while the works of such great European artists as Raphael and Rubens adorn the walls.

Since the trip's purpose was educational, young Englishmen in particular were usually accompanied by a tutor who ensured that his charges spent time looking at museum collections of natural history and antiquities. But tutors were not able to stop young men from also pursuing wine, women, and song. After crossing the Channel, English visitors went to Paris for a cram course on how to act sophisticated. They then went on to Italy, where their favorite destinations were Florence, Venice, and Rome. In Florence, the studious and ambitious studied art in the Uffizi Gallery. The less ambitious followed a less vigorous routine, according to the poet Thomas Gray, since they "get up at twelve o'clock, breakfast till three, dine till five, sleep till six, drinking cooling liquors till eight, go to the bridge till ten, sup till two, and so sleep till twelve again." In Venice, where sophisticated prostitutes had flourished since Renaissance times, the chief attraction for young English males was women. As Samuel Johnson remarked, "If a young man is wild, and must run after women and bad company, it is better this should be done abroad." Rome was another "great object of our pilgrimage," where travelers visited the "modern" sights, such as Saint Peter's and, above all, the ancient ruins. To a generation raised on a classical education, souvenirs of ruins and Piranesi's etchings of classical ruins were required purchases. The accidental rediscovery of the ancient Roman towns of Herculaneum and Pompeii made them a popular eighteenth-century tourist attraction.

The Inhabitants of Towns and Cities

There was a significant difference between the social importance of towns in eastern and western Europe. In eastern Europe, cities were generally smaller and had little real autonomy. In western Europe, they were larger and frequently were accustomed to municipal self-government and municipal privileges that even so-called absolute monarchs had to respect, although in many places the latter had managed to undermine urban governments.

Except in the Dutch Republic, Britain, and parts of Italy, townspeople were still a distinct minority of the total population. At the end of the eighteenth century, about one-sixth of the French population lived in towns of 2,000 or more. The biggest city in Europe was London with its 1,000,000 inhabitants while Paris numbered between 550,000 and 600,000. Altogether, Europe had at least twenty cities in twelve countries with

populations over 100,000, including Naples, Lisbon, Moscow, St. Petersburg, Vienna, Amsterdam, Berlin, Rome, and Madrid.

Although urban dwellers were vastly outnumbered by rural inhabitants, towns played an important role in Western culture. The contrasts between a large city with its education, culture, and material consumption and the surrounding, often poverty-stricken countryside were striking, evident in this British traveler's account of Russia's St. Petersburg in 1741:

> The country about Petersburg has full as wild and desert a look as any in the Indies; you need not go above 200 paces out of the town to find yourself in a wild wood of firs, and such a low, marshy, boggy country that you would think God when he created the rest of the world for the use of mankind had created this for an inaccessible retreat for all sorts of wild beasts.[14]

Peasants often resented the prosperity of towns and their exploitation of the countryside to serve urban interests. Palermo in Sicily used one-third of the island's food production while paying only one-tenth of the taxes. Towns lived off the countryside not by buying, but by using tithes, rents, and dues to acquire peasant produce.

Many cities in western and even central Europe had a long tradition of patrician oligarchies that continued to control their communities by dominating town and city councils. In Zürich half of the seats on the ruling Great Council were controlled by thirteen families while Venice, Frankfurt, Nuremberg, Strasbourg, Amsterdam, and Venice all had closed patrician elites who ran their cities. In some towns in Spain, France, and parts of Germany and Italy, nobles with residences in both town and country dominated their urban societies.

Despite their domination, patricians and nobles constituted only a small minority of the urban population. Just below the patricians stood an upper crust of the middle classes: nonnoble officeholders, financiers and bankers, merchants, wealthy rentiers who lived off their investments, and important professionals, including lawyers. Another large urban group was the petty bourgeoisie or lower middle class made up of master artisans, shopkeepers, and small traders. Below them were the laborers or working classes. Much urban industry was still done in small guild workshops by masters, journeymen, and apprentices. Apprentices who acquired the proper skills became journeymen before entering the ranks of the masters, but increasingly in the eighteenth century guilds became closed oligarchies as membership was restricted to the relatives of masters. Many skilled artisans were then often forced to become low-paid workers. Urban communities also had a large group of unskilled workers who served as servants, maids, and cooks at pitifully low wages. One study of a pre-industrial French city found that two married workers with one child received a family income of 380 livres while needing to spend 336 livres on basic necessities, leaving very little for extra expenses.

Despite an end to the ravages of plague, eighteenth-century cities still experienced high death rates, especially among children, because of unsanitary living conditions, polluted water, and a lack of sewerage facilities. One observer compared the stench of Hamburg to an open sewer that could be smelled for miles around. Overcrowding also exacerbated urban problems as cities continued to grow from an influx of rural immigrants. But cities proved no paradise for them as unskilled workers found few employment opportunities. The result was a serious problem of poverty in the eighteenth century.

THE PROBLEM OF POVERTY   Poverty was a highly visible problem in the eighteenth century both in cities and the countryside (see the box on p. 663). In Venice licensed beggars made up 3 to 5 percent of the population while unlicensed beggars may have constituted as much as 13 to 15 percent. Beggars in Bologna, Italy were estimated at 25 percent of the population while in Mainz figures indicate that 30 percent of the people were beggars or prostitutes. Prostitution was often an alternative to begging. It has been estimated that in France and Britain by the end of the century 10 percent of the people were dependent on charity or begging for food.

Earlier in Europe the poor had been viewed as blessed children of God; the duty of Christians was to assist them. A change of attitude that had begun in the latter part of the sixteenth century became even more apparent in the eighteenth century. Charity to poor beggars, it was argued, simply encouraged their idleness and led them to vice and crime. A French official stated: "Beggary is the apprenticeship of crime; it begins by creating a love of idleness which will always be the greatest political and moral evil. In this state the beggar does not long resist the temptation to steal."[15] While private charitable institutions such as the religious Order of Saint Vincent de Paul and the Sisters of Charity had been founded to help such people, they were soon overwhelmed by the increased numbers of indigent in the eighteenth century.

Although some "enlightened" officials argued that the state needed to become involved in the problem, mixed feelings prevented concerted action. Since the sixteenth century, vagrancy and begging had been considered crimes. In the eighteenth century, French authorities attempted to round up vagrants and beggars and incarcerate them for eighteen months to act as a deter-

▼ **A Market in Turin.** Except in Britain, the Dutch Republic, and parts of Italy, the inhabitants of towns were still a distinct minority in Europe in the eighteenth century. Although towns and cities were dominated by wealthy patrician elites, they were also scene to a remarkable diversity of social groups of varying incomes. This variety is evident in this view of a market square in the Italian city of Turin.

Poverty in France
▼ ▼ ▼

Unlike the British, who had a system of public-supported poor relief, the French responded to poverty with ad hoc policies when conditions became acute. This selection is taken from an intendant's report to the controller-general at Paris describing his suggestions for a program to relieve the grain shortages expected for the winter months.

M. de la Bourdonnaye, Intendant of Bordeaux, to the Controller-General, September 30, 1708

Having searched for the means of helping the people of Agen in this cruel situation and having conferred with His Eminence, the Bishop, it seems to us that three things are absolutely necessary if the people are not to starve during the winter.

Most of the inhabitants do not have seed to plant their fields. However, we decided that we would be going too far if we furnished it, because those who have seed would also apply [for more]. Moreover, we are persuaded that all the inhabitants will make strenuous efforts to find some seed, since they have every reason to expect prices to remain high next year. . . .

But this project will come to nothing if the collectors of the taille continue to be as strict in the exercise of their functions as they have been of late and continue to employ troops [to force collection]. Those inhabitants who have seed grain would sell it to be freed from an oppressive garrison, while those who must buy seed, since they had none left from their harvest and have scraped together a little money for this purchase, would prefer to give up that money [for taxes] when put under police constraint. To avoid this, I feel it is absolutely necessary that you order the receivers-general to reduce their operations during this winter, at least with respect to the poor. . . .

We are planning to import wheat for this region from Languedoc and Quercy, and we are confident that there will be enough. But there are two things to be feared: one is the greed of the merchants. When they see that general misery has put them in control of prices, they will raise them to the point where the calamity is almost as great as if there were no provisions at all. The other fear is that the artisans and the lowest classes, when they find themselves at the mercy of the merchants, will cause disorders and riots. As a protective measure, it would seem wise to establish two small storehouses. . . . Ten thousand ecus [30,000 livres] would be sufficient for each. . . .

A third point demanding our attention is the support of beggars among the poor, as well as of those who have no other resources than their wages. Since there will be very little work, these people will soon be reduced to starvation. We should establish public workshops to provide work as was done in 1693 and 1694. I should choose the most useful kind of work, located where there are the greatest number of poor. In this manner, we should rid ourselves of those who do not want to work and assure the others of a moderate subsistence. For these workshops, we would need about 40,000 livres, or altogether 100,000 livres. The receiver-general of the taille of Agen could advance this sum. The 60,000 livres for the storehouses he would get back very soon. I shall await your orders on all of the above.

Marginal Comments by the Controller-General

Operations for the collection of the taille are to be suspended. The two storehouses are to be established; great care must be taken to put them to good use. The interest on the advances will be paid by the king. His Majesty has agreed to the establishment of the public workshops for the able-bodied poor and is willing to spend up to 40,000 livres on them this winter.

---

rent. They accomplished little, however, since the basic problem was socioeconomic. These people had no work. In the 1770s the French tried to use public works projects, such as road building, to give people jobs, but not enough funds were available to accomplish much. The problem of poverty remained as another serious blemish on the quality of eighteenth-century life.

Everywhere in Europe at the beginning of the eighteenth century, the old order remained strong. Nobles, clerics, towns, provinces all had privileges, some medieval in origin, others the result of the attempt of monarchies in the sixteenth and seventeenth centuries to gain financial support from their subjects. Everywhere in the eighteenth century, monarchs sought to enlarge their bureaucracies to raise taxes to support the new large standing armies that had originated in the seventeenth century. The existence of these armies guaranteed wars. The existence of five great powers, with two of them (France and Britain) in conflict in the Far East and the New World, initiated a new scale of conflict; the Seven Years' War could legitimately be viewed as the first world war. While the wars changed little on the European continent, British victories brought the emergence of Great Britain as the world's greatest naval and colonial power. Everywhere in Europe, increased demands for taxes to

support these conflicts led to attacks on the privileged orders and a desire for change not met by the ruling monarchs.

At the same time, sustained population growth, dramatic changes in finance, trade, and industry, and the growth of poverty created tensions that undermined the traditional foundations of the old order. The inability of that old order to deal meaningfully with these changes led to a revolutionary outburst at the end of the eighteenth century that brought the beginning of the end for that old order.

Notes

▼ ▼ ▼

1. Quoted in Paul Dukes, *The Making of Russian Absolutism, 1613–1801* (London, 1982), pp. 144–45.

2. Frederick II, *Forms of Government*, in Eugen Weber, *The Western Tradition* (Lexington, Mass., 1972), pp. 538, 544.

3. Quoted in Reinhold A. Dorwart, *The Administrative Reforms of Frederick William I of Prussia* (Cambridge, Mass., 1953), p. 36.

4. Quoted in Sidney B. Fay, *The Rise of Brandenburg-Prussia to 1786*, rev. Klaus Epstein (New York, 1964), p. 92.

5. Quoted in Hans Rosenberg, *Bureaucracy, Aristocracy, and Autocracy: The Prussian Experience, 1660–1815* (Cambridge, Mass., 1958), p. 40.

6. Quoted in Herbert Kaplan, *The First Partition of Poland* (New York, 1962), p. 167.

7. Quoted in W. Abel, "Die Landwirtschaft 1648–1800," in *Handbuch der deutschen Wirtschafts-und*

Sozialgeschichte, eds. H. Aubin and W. Zorn (Stuttgart, 1971), 1: 524–25.

8. Quoted in Fernand Braudel, *Civilization and Capitalism* (London, 1981–84), 3: 378.

9. Quoted in ibid., 3: 245.

10. Abbé le Blanc, *Letters on the English and French Nations* (London, 1747), 2: 404–5.

11. Quoted in Witold Rybczynski, *Home: A Short History of an Idea* (New York, 1986), p. 105.

12. Quoted in Peter Gay, *Age of Enlightenment* (New York, 1966), p. 87.

13. Quoted in Paul Hazard, *The European Mind, 1680–1715* (Cleveland, 1963), pp. 6–7.

14. *Oxford Slavonic Papers*, New Series (1982), 15: 76.

15. Quoted in Jeffrey Kaplow, *The Names of Kings: The Parisian Laboring Poor in the Eighteenth Century* (New York, 1972), p. 134.

Suggestions for Further Reading

▼ ▼ ▼

For a good introduction to the political history of the eighteenth century, see the relevant chapters in the general works by Woloch and Anderson listed in Chapter 18. See also G. Treasure, *The Making of Modern Europe, 1648–1780* (London, 1985); W. Doyle, *The Old European Order, 1660–1800* (Oxford, 1978); O. Hufton, *Europe: Privilege and Protest, 1730–1789* (London, 1980); and E. N. Williams, *The Ancien Régime in Europe: Government and Society in the Major States, 1648–1789* (New York, 1970). On the theory of enlightened

absolutism, see L. Krieger, *An Essay on the Theory of Enlightened Despotism* (Chicago, 1970). For a brief study of its practice, see J. Gagliardo, *Enlightened Despotism* (New York, 1967). Good histories of individual states include W. A. Speck, *Stability and Strife: England, 1714–1760* (Cambridge, Mass., 1977); J. B. Owen, *The Eighteenth Century, 1714–1815* (London, 1975), also on England; P. R. Campbell, *The Ancien Régime in France* (Oxford, 1988); E. Wangermann, *The Austrian Achievement, 1700–1800* (London, 1973); R. Vierhaus,

Germany in the Age of Absolutism (Cambridge, 1988); W. N. Hargreaves-Mawdsley, Eighteenth-Century Spain, 1700–1788: A Political, Diplomatic, and Institutional History (London, 1978); S. B. Fay, The Rise of Brandenburg-Prussia to 1786 (New York, 1964); and P. Dukes, The Making of Russian Absolutism, 1613–1801 (London, 1982). Good biographies of some of Europe's monarchs include R. Asprey, Frederick the Great, The Magnificent Enigma (New York, 1986); I. de Madariaga, Russia in the Age of Catherine the Great (New Haven, Conn., 1981); the first volume of a new major work on Joseph II by D. Deales, Joseph II (Cambridge, 1987); and J. Brooke, King George III (London, 1972).

The warfare of this period is examined in J. Childs, Armies and Warfare in Europe, 1648–1789 (Manchester, 1982). On the social composition of European armies, see A. Corvisier, Armies and Society in Europe, 1494–1789 (Bloomington, Ind., 1978). For a study of one army, see C. Duffy, The Army of Frederick the Great (London, 1974). The impact of war on economic life is examined in M. Gutmann, War and Rural Life in the Early Modern Low Countries (Princeton, N.J., 1980).

A good introduction to European population can be found in M. W. Flinn, The European Demographic System, 1500–1820 (Brighton, 1981). Although historians now disagree with many of his conclusions, still worthwhile is the pioneering study of childhood by P. Aries, Centuries of Childhood: A Social History of Family Life (New York, 1965). One of the best works on family and marriage patterns is L. Stone, The Family, Sex, and Marriage in England, 1500–1800 (New York, 1977). An innovative work is A. MacFarlane, Origins of English Individualism: The Family, Property and Social Transition (Oxford, 1978).

A different perspective on economic history can be found in F. Braudel's Capitalism and Material Life, 1400–1800 (New York, 1973). P. G. M. Dickson, The Financial Revolution in England: A Study in the Development of Public Credit, 1688–1756 (London, 1967) is a detailed, specialized study on matters of finance. The subject of mercantile empires and worldwide trade is covered in J. H. Parry, Trade and Dominion: European Overseas Empires in the Eighteenth Century (London,

1971); D. K. Fieldhouse, The Colonial Empires (New York, 1971); and R. Davis, The Rise of the Atlantic Economies (Ithaca, N.Y., 1973). On the problem of slavery, see M. Craton, Sinews of Empire: A Short History of British Slavery (New York, 1974). On England's agricultural revolution, see J. D. Chambers and G. E. Mingay, The Agricultural Revolution, 1750–1880 (London, 1966). Eighteenth-century cottage industry and the beginnings of industrialization are examined in the early chapters of D. Landes, The Unbound Prometheus: Technological Change and Industrial Development in Western Europe from 1750 to the Present (New York, 1969).

For an introduction to the social order of the eighteenth century, see G. Rudé, Europe in the Eighteenth Century: Aristocracy and the Bourgeois Challenge (London, 1972); P. Goubert, The Ancien Régime (New York, 1973); and P. Laslett, The World We Have Lost, 3d ed. (New York, 1984). Two works by J. Blum are valuable on the peasantry, The End of the Old Order in Rural Europe (Princeton, N.J., 1978); and Lord and Peasant in Russia from the Ninth to the Nineteenth Century (Princeton, N.J., 1961). Also of much interest is E. Le Roy Ladurie, The Peasants of Languedoc (Urbana, Ill., 1974). On the European nobility, see the specialized studies of R. Forster, The Nobility of Toulouse in the Eighteenth Century (Baltimore, 1960); R. E. Jones, The Emancipation of the Russian Nobility, 1762–1785 (Princeton, N.J., 1973); and G. E. Mingay, The Gentry: The Rise and Fall of a Ruling Class (London, 1976). Studies of urban communities include F. L. Ford, Strasbourg in Transition, 1648–1789 (Cambridge, Mass., 1958); M. Walker, German Home Towns: Community, State, and General Estate, 1648–1871 (Ithaca, N.Y., 1971); G. Rudé, Hanoverian London, 1714–1808 (Berkeley, 1971); and G. L. Soliday, A Community in Conflict: Frankfurt Society in the Seventeenth and Early Eighteenth Centuries (Hanover, N.H., 1974). On the lower urban classes, see J. Kaplow, The Names of Kings: The Parisian Laboring Poor in the Eighteenth Century (New York, 1972). There is no better work on the problem of poverty than O. Hufton, The Poor of Eighteenth-Century France (Oxford, 1974).

Chapter **20**

A Revolution in Politics: The Era of the French Revolution and Napoleon

▼▼▼▼▼

Historians have long assumed that the modern history of Europe began with two major transformations—the French Revolution and the Industrial Revolution (on the latter, see Chapter 21). Accordingly, the French Revolution has been portrayed as the major turning point in European political and social history when the institutions of the "old regime" were destroyed and a new order was created based on individual rights, representative institutions, and a concept of loyalty to the nation rather than the monarch. This perspective does have certain limitations, however.

Some historians have emphasized that France was only one of a number of areas in the Western world where the assumptions of the old order were challenged. Although they have used the phrase "democratic revolution" to refer to the upheavals of the late eighteenth and early nineteenth centuries, it is probably more appropriate to speak not of a "democratic movement," but of a liberal movement to extend political rights and power to the bourgeoisie "possessing capital," namely, those besides the aristocracy who were literate and had become wealthy through capitalist enterprises in trade, industry, and finance. The years preceding and accompanying the French Revolution included attempts at reform and revolt in the North American colonies, Britain, the Dutch Republic, some Swiss cities, and the Austrian Netherlands. The success of the American and French revolutions makes them the center of attention for this chapter.

American Declaration of Independence ▼

American Independence ▼

Ratification of the American Constitution ▼

•••••••• 1775 •••••••••••• 1785 •••••••••• 1795 •••••••••• 1805 ••••••••••• 1815 ••••••••

▲ Formation of the National Assembly

▲ Reign of Terror

▲ Constitution of 1795

▲ Napoleon Becomes Emperor

▲ Battle of Waterloo

It would be a mistake to assume that all of the decadent privileges that characterized the old European regime were destroyed in 1789. The revolutionary upheaval of the era, especially in France, did create new liberal and national political ideals, summarized in the French revolutionary slogan, "Liberty, Equality, and Fraternity," that transformed France and were then spread to other European countries through the conquests of Napoleon. After Napoleon's defeat, however, the forces of reaction did their best to restore the old order and resist pressures for reform.

▼ The Beginnings of the Revolutionary Era: The American Revolution

The revolutionary era began in North America when the thirteen British colonies along the eastern seaboard revolted against their mother country. Despite their differences, the colonists found ways to create a new government based on liberal principles that made an impact on the "old world" European states.

Reorganization, Resistance, and Rebellion

The immediate causes of the American Revolution stemmed from Britain's response to its victory over France in the Seven Years' War, known as the French and Indian War in America. British imperial policies toward their American colonies changed dramatically after 1763. The western lands of the Ohio and Mississippi valleys, surrendered to the British by the French, appeared to land-hungry Americans as an ideal territory for expansion. The British, however, feared conflict with the numerous Indian tribes settled there and forbade white purchases of land west of the Appalachians; fur-

thermore, they decided to enforce this policy by sending a standing army of 10,000 men to the colonies, a totally unprecedented peacetime act in the eyes of the colonists. It was also expensive. In the course of the French and Indian War (1756–1763), British policymakers realized that the Americans, in return for the British defense of the colonies from the French and their Indian allies, had contributed relatively little to the war's expenses while the British national debt had reached staggering proportions. While Americans were paying an average of one shilling a year in taxes, annual taxes per person in Britain had reached twenty-six shillings. It seemed only fair that the Americans should assume some of the costs of the North American army.

A new regulation of colonial trade appeared to be the most obvious means of obtaining new revenues from the colonies. Although helpful, it failed to raise more than £30,000, only one-tenth of the annual cost of the British army in America. In 1765, Parliament resorted to a Stamp Act, which levied a direct tax on legal documents, newspapers, almanacs, pamphlets, dice, and playing cards. The tax seemed perfectly reasonable to Parliament. It would raise another £60,000 annually and was set at a rate lower than the stamp tax in effect in Britain. The colonists, however, responded with fury. Riots against designated tax collectors and stamp offices were accompanied by boycotts of British goods. British exports to America dropped 14 percent from 1764 to 1765. Reluctantly, Parliament caved in to the pressure and repealed the Stamp Act, not, however, without asserting uncompromisingly its right to make laws "to bind the colonies and the people of America in all cases whatsoever."

The immediate crisis had ended, but the fundamental cause of the dispute had not been resolved. In the course of the eighteenth century, significant differences had arisen between the American and British political worlds. Both peoples shared the same property requirement for voting—voters had to possess a property that could be rented for at least forty shillings a year—but it resulted in a disparity in the number of voters in the two countries. In Britain fewer than one in five adult males had the right to vote. In the colonies, where a radically different economic structure led to an enormous group of independent farmers, the property requirement allowed over 50 percent of adult males to vote.

While both the British and Americans had representative governments, different systems had evolved. Representation in Britain was indirect; the members of Parliament did not speak for local interests but for the entire kingdom. In the colonies direct representation meant that representatives should reside in and own property in the communities electing them; hence, they should represent the interests of their local districts.

This divergence in political systems was paralleled by conflicting conceptions of empire. The British envisioned a single empire with Parliament as the supreme authority throughout; as one parliamentarian argued, "in sovereignty there are no gradations." All the people in the empire, including the American colonists, were consequently represented indirectly by members of Parliament, whether they were from the colonies or not. Colonial assemblies in the British perspective were only committees that made "temporary by-laws"; the real authority to make laws for the empire resided in London.

In view of Britain's "benign neglect" of its colonies, the Americans had been relatively free to develop their own peculiar view of the British Empire. To them, the British Empire was composed of self-regulating parts. While they conceded that as British subjects they owed allegiance to the king and that Parliament had the right to make laws for the peace and prosperity of the whole realm, they argued, nevertheless, that neither king nor Parliament had any right to interfere in the internal affairs of the colonies since they had their own representative assemblies. American colonists were especially defensive about property and believed strongly that no tax could be levied without the consent of an assembly whose members actually represented the people. At the Stamp Act Congress, where moderate representatives from nine colonies reassured the British that they "owe Allegiance to the Crown of Great-Britain" and "all due Subordination to that August Body the Parliament," it was nevertheless argued that the Stamp Act violated the "inherent Rights and Liberties" of Englishmen. No taxes could be imposed upon them "but with their own Consent, given personally, or by their Representatives." And importantly, "the People of these Colonies are not, and from their local Circumstances cannot be, Represented in the House of Commons in Great-Britain."[1]

By the 1760s, the American colonists had developed a sense of a common national identity. It was not unusual for American travelers to Britain in the eighteenth century to see British society as old and decadent compared to the youthfulness and vitality of their own. This sense of superiority made Americans resentful of British actions that seemed to treat them like children. Resentment eventually led to a desire for independence.

The respite gained by the resolution of the Stamp Act crisis proved short-lived. The Townsend Acts of 1767, which attempted to raise new revenues indirectly by imposing tariffs on a number of goods imported to the colonies, simply created another political storm. It, too, was once again resolved by concessions, but the struggle set off by the Tea Act of 1773 finally led to war.

The Tea Act was an attempt to help the financially hard-pressed East India Company by allowing it to go around American wholesalers and sell its tea directly to distributors. Wholesale merchants denounced this tea "monopoly" as the first step in Parliament's subjugation of colonial businesses. Although exaggerated, the argument seemed convincing to Americans grown suspicious of British motives. Some Americans—mistakenly—had even arrived at a sinister interpretation of ultimate British motives. Thomas Jefferson wrote in 1774 that "a series of oppressions, begun at a distinguished period and pursued unalterably through every change of ministers, too plainly proves a deliberate and systematical plan of reducing us to slavery."

In Boston, protest took a destructive turn when 150 Americans dressed as Indians unloaded the East India Company's tea into Boston harbor. Parliament responded vigorously with the Coercive Acts, which the colonists labeled the "Intolerable Acts." These closed the port of Boston until compensation for the destroyed tea was paid, restricted town meetings, and strengthened the power of the royal governor of Massachusetts. Designed to punish radical Massachusetts as an example to the other colonies, the Coercive Acts backfired. Many British politicians continued to believe that most Americans were completely loyal to the empire and that the problems in America came from a small number of radicals. But this was a mistake; colonial assemblies everywhere denounced the British action. The colonies' desire to take collective action led to the First Continental Congress, which met at Philadelphia in September 1774. The more militant members refused to compromise and urged colonists to "take up arms and organize militias." When the British army under General Gage attempted to stop rebel mobilization in Massachusetts,

The Argument for Independence
▼ ▼ ▼

On July 2, 1776, the Second Continental Congress adopted a resolution declaring the independence of the American colonies. Two days later the delegates approved the Declaration of Independence, which gave the reasons for their action. Its principal author was Thomas Jefferson who basically restated John Locke's theory of revolution (see Chapter 16).

The Declaration of Independence

When in the course of human events it becomes necessary for one people to dissolve the political bands which have connected them with another, and to assume among the Powers of the earth, the separate and equal station to which the Laws of Nature and of Nature's God entitle them, a decent respect to the opinions of mankind requires that they should declare the causes which impel them to the separation.

We hold these truths to be self-evident, that all men are created equal, that they are endowed by their Creator with certain unalienable Rights, that among these are Life, Liberty and the pursuit of Happiness. That to secure these rights, Governments are instituted among Men, deriving their just powers from the consent of the governed, That whenever any Form of Government becomes destructive of these ends, it is the Right of the People to alter or to abolish it and to institute new Government, laying its foundation on such principles and organizing its powers in such form, as to them shall seem most likely to effect their Safety and Happiness. Prudence, indeed, will dictate that Governments long established should not be changed for light and transient causes; and accordingly all experience hath shown, that mankind are more disposed to suffer, while evils are sufferable, than to right themselves by abolishing the forms to which they are accustomed. But when a long train of abuses and usurpations, pursuing invariably the same Object evinces a design to reduce them under absolute Despotism, it is their right, it is their duty, to throw off such Government, and to provide new Guards for their future security.—Such has been the patient sufferance of these Colonies; and such is now the necessity which constrains them to alter their former Systems of Government. The history of the present King of Great Britain is a history of repeated injuries and usurpations, all having in direct object the establishment of an absolute Tyranny over these States.

fighting erupted at Lexington and Concord between colonists and redcoats in April 1775.

The War for Independence

Despite the outbreak of hostilities, the colonists did not rush headlong into rebellion and war. It was more than a year after Lexington and Concord before the decision was made to declare their independence from the British Empire. An important factor in mobilizing public pressure for that decision came from *Common Sense*, a pamphlet published in January 1776 by Thomas Paine, a recently arrived English political radical. Within three months, it had sold 120,000 copies. Paine's pamphlet argued that it was ridiculous for "a continent to be perpetually governed by an island." From a practical point of view, Paine also pointed out that other countries, such as France and Spain, which were only too eager to strike at the British Empire, would never provide military aid for the colonies to resist Britain unless they were an independent power. On July 4, 1776, the Second Continental Congress approved a Declaration of Independence written by Thomas Jefferson (see the box above). A stirring political document, the Declaration of Independence affirmed the Enlightenment's natural rights of "life, liberty, and the pursuit of happiness" and declared the colonies to be "free and independent states absolved from all allegiance to the British crown." The war for American independence had formally begun.

The war against Great Britain was a great gamble. Britain was a strong European military power with enormous financial resources; by 1778 Britain had sent 50,000 regular British troops and 30,000 German mercenaries to America. The Second Continental Congress had authorized the formation of a Continental Army under George Washington as commander-in-chief. Washington, who had had political experience in Virginia and military experience in the French and Indian War, was a good choice for the job. As a southerner, he brought balance to an effort that up to now had been led by New Englanders. Nevertheless, compared to the British forces, the Continental Army consisted of undisciplined amateurs whose terms of service were usually very brief. The colonies also had militia units, but they likewise tended to be unreliable. Although 400,000 men served in the Continental Army and the militias during the course of the war, Washington never had more than 20,000 troops available for any single battle. The Americans did possess one advantage, however; they did not always fight the kind of eighteenth-century warfare to which the British were accustomed. Instead, the Americans periodically adopted the guerilla type of warfare that they had learned from their encounters with the Indians. A British officer complained, "Never had the British army so ungenerous an opponent. They send their riflemen five or six at a time, who conceal themselves behind trees, etc. until an opportunity presents itself of taking a shot at our advance sentries, which done they immediately retreat. What an unfair method of carrying on a war."[2]

Complicating the war effort were the internal divisions within the colonies. Fought for independence, the revolutionary war was also a civil war, pitting family members and neighbors against one another. The Loyalists, who may have numbered between 15 to 30 percent of the population, questioned whether British policies justified the rebellion. The Loyalists were strongest in New York and Pennsylvania and tended to be wealthy, older, and politically moderate.

Since probably 50 percent of the colonial population were apathetic at the beginning of the struggle, the patriots, like the Loyalists, constituted a minority of the population. The patriots, however, managed to win over many of the uncommitted, either by persuasion or by force. Committees of Safety harassed and jailed Loyalists, insulted their families, and seized and destroyed their property. There were rich patriots as well; George Washington owned an estate with 15,000 acres and 150 slaves. But the rich patriots joined an extensive coalition that included farmers and artisans. The wide social spectrum in this coalition had an impact on representative governments in the states after the war. The right to vote was often broadened; Pennsylvania, for example, dropped all property qualifications for voting. Fewer wealthy people were chosen for political offices. In the northern states, for example, the number of very wealthy individuals in the assemblies dropped from 36 to 12 percent while the number of people with small holdings increased dramatically from 17 to 62 percent.

Of great importance to the colonies' cause was their support by foreign countries who were eager to gain revenge for their defeats in earlier wars at the hands of the British. The French were particularly generous in sup-

▼ **Washington Reviews His Army.** George Washington was given charge of the Continental Army authorized by the Second Continental Congress. Although inferior to the British forces, the American soldiers did have some advantage in that they followed the guerilla type of warfare used by the native Americans, a style of fighting to which the British were unaccustomed. With the support and aid of other European powers, the Americans finally gained their independence in 1783. This painting shows Washington reviewing the Western Army at Fort Cumberland, Maryland.

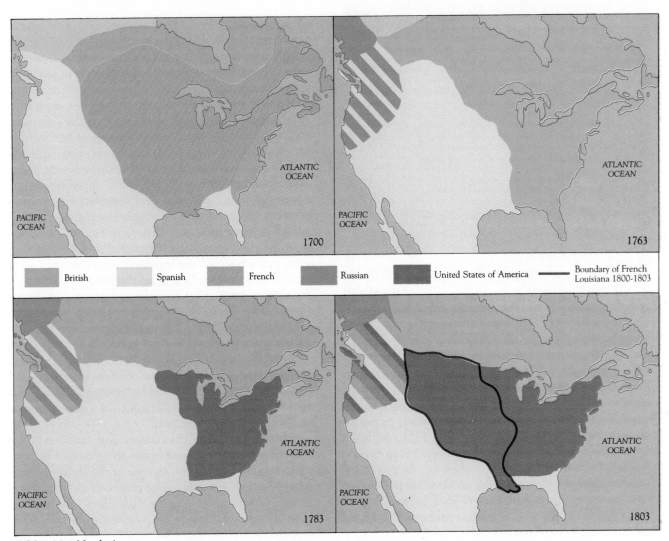

▼ **Map 20.1** North America.

plying arms and money to the rebels from the beginning of the war. French officers and soldiers also served in Washington's army. Uncertain of the military outcome, however, France was at first unwilling to recognize the new republic. The defeat of the British at Saratoga in October 1777 finally led the French to grant diplomatic recognition to the American state. When Spain in 1779 and the Dutch Republic in 1780 entered the war against Great Britain, and Russia formed the League of Armed Neutrality in 1780 to protect neutral shipping from British attacks, the British were faced with war against much of Europe as well as the Americans. Despite having won most of the battles, the British were in danger of losing the war. When the army of General Cornwallis was forced to surrender to a combined American and French army and French fleet under Washington at Yorktown in

1781, the British decided to call it quits. After extensive negotiations, complicated by French and Spanish aims that often conflicted with American desires, the Treaty of Paris was signed in 1783. It recognized the independence of the American colonies and surprisingly granted the Americans control of the western territory from the Appalachians to the Mississippi River. By playing off the mutual fears of the European powers, the Americans had cleverly gained a peace settlement that stunned the Europeans. The Americans were off to a good start but soon showed signs of political disintegration.

Toward a New Nation

Although the thirteen American colonies agreed to "hang together" to gain their independence from the

Stamp Act	1765
Townshend Acts	1767
Tea Act—Boston Tea Party	1773
First Continental Congress	1774
Battle at Lexington and Concord	1775
Second Continental Congress	1775
Declaration of Independence	1776
Battle of Saratoga	1777
Battle of Yorktown	1781
Ratification of the Articles of Confederation	1781
Treaty of Paris	1783
Constitutional Convention	1787
Ratification of the Constitution	1788
Bill of Rights Adopted	1791

British, a fear of concentrated power and concern for their own interests caused them to have little enthusiasm for establishing a united nation with a strong central government. The Articles of Confederation, proposed in 1777 but not completely ratified until 1781, did little to provide for a strong central government. One British official described the scene well when he observed that the American people would stay divided "till the end of time, suspicious and distrustful of each other, divided and subdivided into little commonwealths with no center of union and no common interests."

The Articles of Confederation provided the "United States" with weak central government from 1781 to 1789; some historians view these years as a "critical period" in the history of the new nation. A series of economic, political, and international problems soon led to a movement for a different form of national government. In the summer of 1787, fifty-five delegates attended a convention in Philadelphia that was authorized by the Confederation Congress "for the sole and express purpose of revising the Articles of Confederation." The convention's delegates—wealthy, politically experienced, well educated and nationalistically inclined—rejected revision and decided to devise a new constitution.

The proposed Constitution created a central government distinct from and superior to the governments of the individual states. The national government was given the power to levy taxes, raise a national army, regulate domestic and foreign trade, and create a national currency. While states were not eliminated, their powers were noticeably diminished. Following Montesquieu's principle of a "separation of powers" to provide a system of "checks and balances," the central or federal government was divided into three branches, each with some power to check the functioning of the others. A president, elected by the indirect system of an Electoral College, would serve as the chief executive with the power to execute laws, veto the legislature's acts, make judicial and executive appointments, supervise foreign affairs, and direct military forces. Legislative power was vested in the second branch of government, a bicameral legislature composed of a Senate elected by the state legislatures and a House of Representatives elected directly by the people. The legislative structure was a compromise between delegates from the most and least populous states. Each state, regardless of size, would choose two senators, while the number of representatives to the House would be determined by population. The federal judiciary embodied in a Supreme Court and other courts "as deemed necessary" by Congress, provided the third branch of government. With judges nominated by the executive and approved by the legislative branch, the federal judiciary would enforce the Constitution as the "supreme law of the land."

The constitutional convention had stipulated that the new Constitution would have to be ratified by popularly chosen conventions in nine of the thirteen states before it would take effect. The process of ratification led to fierce debates between the Federalists, who favored the new Constitution, and the Antifederalists, who believed that the Constitution would create another tyranny by destroying the power of the states. One delegate at the Massachusetts convention expressed his fear that "these lawyers, and men of learning, and moneyed men, that talk so finely, and gloss over matters so smoothly, to make us poor illiterate people swallow down the pill, expect to get into Congress themselves." Once they have done so, "they expect to be managers of this Constitution and get all the power and all the money into their own hands." The well-organized Federalists won the debate but certainly not because of a massive outpouring of public support. The public remained largely passive; only one-fourth of the eligible voters bothered to choose the delegates to the state conventions.

The margin of victory for the Federalists had been quite slim. Important to their success had been a promise to add a Bill of Rights to the Constitution as the new government's first piece of business. Accordingly, in March of 1789, the new Congress enacted the first ten amendments to the Constitution, ever since known as the Bill of Rights. These guaranteed freedom of religion, speech, press, petition, and assembly, as well as the right to bear arms, be protected against unreasonable searches and arrests, trial by jury, due process of law, and the protection of property rights. Although many had their origins in English law, others were derived from the natural rights philosophy of the eighteenth-century philosophies and American experience. Is it any wonder that many European intellectuals saw the American Revolution as the embodiment of the Enlightenment's political dreams?

The Impact of the American Revolution on Europe

The year 1789 witnessed two far-reaching events, the beginning of a new United States of America and the eruption of the French Revolution. Was there a connection between the two great revolutions of the last half of the eighteenth century?

There is no doubt that the American Revolution had an important impact on Europeans. Books, newspapers, and magazines provided a newly developing reading public with numerous accounts of American events. To many in Europe, it seemed to portend an era of significant changes, including new arrangements in international politics. The Venetian ambassador to Paris astutely observed in 1783 that "if only the union of the [American] provinces is preserved, it is reasonable to expect that, with the favorable effects of time, and of European arts and sciences, it will become the most formidable power in the world."[3] But the American Revolution also meant far more than that. It proved to many Europeans that the liberal political ideas of the Enlightenment were not merely the vapid utterances of intellectuals. The rights of man, ideas of liberty and equality, popular sovereignty, freedom of religion, thought, and press, and the separation of powers were not merely utopian ideals. The Americans had created a new social contract, embodied it in a written constitution, and made concepts of liberty and representative government a reality. The premises of the Enlightenment seemed confirmed; a new age and a better world could be achieved. As a Swiss philosophe expressed it, "I am tempted to believe that North America is the country where reason and humanity will develop more rapidly than anywhere else."[4]

Returning soldiers were an important source of information about America for Europeans, especially the hundreds of French officers who had served in the American war. One of them, the aristocrat marquis de Lafayette, had volunteered for service in America in order to "strike a blow against England," France's old enemy. Closely associated with Washington, Lafayette returned to France with ideas of individual liberties and notions of republicanism and popular sovereignty. He became a member of the Society of Thirty, a club composed of people from the Paris salons. These "lovers of liberty" were influential in the early stages of the French Revolution. The Declaration of the Rights of Man and Citizen (see The Destruction of the Old Regime later in the chapter) showed unmistakable signs of the influence of the American Declaration of Independence as well as the constitutions of American state governments. Yet, for all of its obvious impact, the American Revolution proved in the long run to be far less important to Europe than the French Revolution. The French Revolution was more complex, more violent, and far more radical with its attempt to reconstruct both a new political and a new social order. The French Revolution provided a model of revolution for Europe and much of the rest of the world; to many it has remained the political movement that truly inaugurated the modern political world.

▼ The French Revolution

Although we associate events like the French Revolution with sudden changes, the causes of such events involve long-range problems as well as immediate, precipitating forces. Revolutions, as has been repeatedly shown, are not necessarily the result of economic collapse and masses of impoverished people hungering for change. In fact, in the fifty years before 1789, France had experienced a period of economic growth due to an expansion of foreign trade and an increase in industrial production. The causes of the French Revolution must be found in a multifaceted examination of French society and its problems in the late eighteenth century.

Background to the French Revolution

Although France experienced an increase in economic growth in the eighteenth century, its wealth was not evenly distributed. The long-range or indirect causes of the French Revolution must first be sought in the condition of French society. Before the Revolution, France was a society grounded in the inequality of rights or the idea of privilege. Its population of 27 million was divided, as it had been since the Middle Ages, into three orders or estates.

The first estate consisted of the clergy and numbered about 130,000 people who owned approximately 10 percent of the land. Clergy were exempt from the *taille*, France's chief tax, although the church had agreed to pay a "voluntary" contribution every five years to the state. Clergy were also radically divided, since the higher clergy, stemming from aristocratic families, shared the interests of the nobility while the parish priests were often poor and from the class of commoners.

The second estate was the nobility, composed of from 120,000 to 350,000 people who nevertheless owned about 25 to 30 percent of the land. Under Louis XV and Louis XVI, the nobility had continued to play an important and even crucial role in French society, holding many of the leading positions in the government, the military, the law courts, and the higher church offices. Much heavy industry in France was controlled by nobles, either through investment or by ownership of mining and metallurgical enterprises. The French nobility was also divided. The nobility of the robe was derived from officeholding, a position that had often opened the doors for commoners to receive noble status. These nobles now dominated the royal law courts and important administrative offices. The nobility of the sword claimed to be descendants of the original medieval nobility. The nobles as a whole sought to expand their power at the expense of the monarchy—to defend liberty by resisting the arbitrary actions of monarchy, as some nobles asserted—and to maintain their monopolistic control over positions in the military, church, and government. In 1781, in reaction to the ambitions of aristocrats newly arrived from the bourgeoisie, the Ségur Law attempted to limit the sale of military officerships to fourth-generation nobles, thus excluding newly enrolled members of the nobility.

Although there were many poor nobles, on the whole the fortunes of the wealthy aristocrats outstripped those of most others in French society. Generally, the nobles tended to marry within their own ranks making the nobility a fairly closed group. Although their privileges varied from region to region, the very possession of privileges remained a hallmark of the nobility. Common to all were tax exemptions, especially from the *taille*.

The third estate, or the commoners of society, constituted the overwhelming majority of the French population. They were divided by vast differences in occupation, level of education, and wealth. The peasants who alone constituted 75 to 80 percent of the total population were by far the largest segment of the third estate. They owned about 35 to 40 percent of the land, although their landholdings varied from area to area and

over half had no or little land on which to survive. Serfdom no longer existed on any large scale in France, but French peasants still had seigneurial obligations to their local landlords. These "relics of feudalism," survivals from an earlier age, had continued and even been reaffirmed in the eighteenth century as a result of aristocratic strength. These obligations included the payment of fees for the use of village facilities, such as the flour mill, community oven, and winepress, as well as tithes to the clergy. The nobility also maintained the right to hunt on peasants' land. Peasants resented these obligations as well as the attempt of noble landowners in the eighteenth century to enclose open fields and divide village common lands since enclosure eliminated the open pastures that poor peasants used for their livestock.

Another part of the third estate consisted of skilled craftsmen, shopkeepers, and other wage earners in the cities. Although the eighteenth century had been a period of rapid urban growth, 90 percent of French towns had fewer than 10,000 inhabitants while only nine cities had more than 50,000. In the eighteenth century, a rise in consumer prices greater than the increase in wages left these urban groups with a noticeable decline in purchasing power. In Paris, for example, income lagged behind food prices and especially behind a 140 percent rise in rents for working people in skilled and unskilled trades. The economic discontent of this segment of the third estate and often simply their struggle for survival led them to play an important role in the Revolution, especially in the city of Paris. Insubordination, one observer noted, "has been visible among the people for some years now and above all among craftsmen." One historian has charted the ups and downs of revolutionary riots in Paris by showing their correlation to changes in bread prices. Sudden increases in the price of bread, which constituted three-fourths of an ordinary person's diet and cost one-third to one-half of his or her income, immediately affected public order. People expected bread prices to be controlled. They grew desperate when prices rose, and their only recourse was mob action to try to change the situation. The towns and cities were also home to large groups of unskilled workers. One magistrate complained that "misery . . . has thrown into the towns people who overburden them with their uselessness, and who find nothing to do, because there is not enough for the people who live there."[5]

About 8 percent or 2.3 million people constituted the bourgeoisie or middle class who owned about 20 to 25 percent of the land. This group included merchants, industrialists, and bankers who controlled the resources of trade, manufacturing, and finance and benefited from the economic prosperity after 1730. The bourgeoisie also included professional people—lawyers, holders of public offices, doctors, and writers. Many members of the bourgeoisie sought security and status in the purchase of land. They had their own set of grievances because they were often excluded from the social and political privileges monopolized by the nobles. These resentments of the middle class were for a long time assumed to be a major cause of the French Revolution. But although these tensions existed, the situation was not simply the case of a unified bourgeoisie against a unified noble class. As is evident, neither group was monolithic. Nobles were separated by vast differences in wealth and importance. A similar gulf separated wealthy financiers from local lawyers in French provincial towns.

Remarkable similarities existed at the upper levels of society between the wealthier bourgeoisie and the nobility. It was still possible for wealthy middle-class individuals to enter the ranks of the nobility by obtaining public offices and entering the nobility of the robe. In fact, between 1774 and 1789, the not insignificant number of 2,500 wealthy bourgeoisie entered the ranks of the nobility. Over the century as a whole, 6,500 new noble families were created. In addition, as we saw in Chapter 19, the aristocrats were also participating in capitalist activities on their landed estates, such as mining, metallurgy, and glassmaking, and even investing in foreign trade. Viewed in terms of economic function, many members of the bourgeoisie and nobility formed a single class. Finally, the new and critical ideas of the Enlightenment proved attractive to both aristocrats and bourgeoisie. Members of both groups shared a common world of liberal political thought. The old view that the French Revolution was the result of the conflict between two rising, rigid orders, the bourgeoisie and nobility, has been enlarged and revised. Both aristocratic and bourgeois elites, long accustomed to a new socioeconomic reality based on wealth and economic achievement, were increasingly frustrated by a monarchical system resting on privileges and on an old and rigid social order based on the concept of estates. The opposition of these elites to the old order led them ultimately to drastic action against the monarchical regime, although they soon split over the problem of how far to proceed in the elimination of traditional privileges. In a real sense, the Revolution had its origins in political grievances.

While the long-range causes of the French Revolution, then, can be found in part in the growing frustration over the inability of the French monarchy to deal with new social realities and problems, other factors were also present. The failure of the French monarchy

was exacerbated by specific problems in the 1780s. Despite economic expansion for fifty years, the French economy experienced periodic crises. Bad harvests in 1787 and 1788 and the beginnings of a manufacturing depression resulted in food shortages, rising prices for food and other necessities, and unemployment in the cities. The number of poor, estimated by some at almost one-third of the population, reached crisis proportions on the eve of the Revolution. An English traveler noted the misery of the poor in the countryside: "All the country girls and women are without shoes or stockings; and the ploughmen at their work have neither sabots nor stockings to their feet. This is a poverty that strikes at the root of national prosperity."[6]

Increased criticism of existing privileges as well as social and political institutions also characterized the eighteenth century. Although the *philosophes* did not advocate revolution, their ideas were widely circulated among the literate bourgeois and noble elites of France. Historians have debated the importance of the ideas of the *philosophes* in precipitating the French Revolution, but there is no doubt that the public statements of revolutionary leaders were often reflections of those ideas.

The French Parlements often frustrated efforts at reform. Responsible for registering royal decrees, these thirteen law courts could block royal edicts by not registering them. Although Louis XIV had forced them into submission, the Parlements had gained new strength in the eighteenth century as they and their noble judges assumed the role of defenders of "liberty" against the arbitrary power of the monarchy. As noble defenders, however, they often pushed their own interests as well, especially by blocking new taxes. This last point reminds us that one of the fundamental problems facing the monarchy was financial.

The immediate cause of the French Revolution was the near collapse of government finances. French governmental expenditures continued to grow due to costly wars and royal extravagance. Since the government responded by borrowing, by 1788 the interest on the debt alone constituted half of the government's spending. The king's finance ministry wrestled with the problem but met with resistance. In 1786, Charles de Calonne, the controller-general of finance, proposed a complete revamping of the fiscal and administrative system of the state. To gain support, Calonne adjourned an Assembly of Notables early in 1787. This gathering of nobles, prelates, and magistrates refused to cooperate, and the government's attempt to go it alone brought further disaster. On the verge of a complete financial collapse, the government was finally forced to call a meeting of the

Estates-General, the French parliamentary body that had not met since 1614. By calling the Estates-General, the government was virtually admitting that the crown could not govern without the assistance of some representative assembly.

The Estates-General consisted of representatives from the three orders of French society. In the elections for the Estates-General, the government had ruled that the Third Estate should get double representation (it did, after all, constitute 97 percent of the population). Consequently, while both the first estate (the clergy) and the second (the nobility) had about 300 delegates each, the commoners had almost 600 representatives. Two-thirds of the latter were people with legal training while three-fourths were from towns with over 2,000 inhabitants, giving the Third Estate a particularly strong legal and urban representation. Of the 282 representatives of the nobility, about 90 were liberal minded, urban oriented, and interested in the enlightened ideas of the century; one-half of them were under forty years of age. The activists of the Third Estate and reform-minded individuals among the first and second estates had common ties in their youthfulness, urban background, and hostility to privilege. The *cahiers de doléances* or statements of grievances, which were drafted during the elections to the Estates-General, advocated a regular constitutional government that would abolish the fiscal privileges of the church and nobility as the major way to regenerate France.

The Estates-General opened at Versailles on May 5, 1789. It was troubled from the start with the problem of whether voting should be by order or by head (each delegate having one vote). The Parlement of Paris, consisting of nobles of the robe, had advocated voting by order according to the form used in 1614. Each order would vote separately; each would have veto power over the other two, thus guaranteeing aristocratic control over reforms. But opposition to the Parlement of Paris's proposal had arisen from a group calling themselves the patriots or "lovers of liberty." Although they claimed to be the nation, they consisted primarily of bourgeoisie and nobles. One group of patriots known as the Society of Thirty drew most of its members from the salons of Paris. They were mostly nobles. Some of them had been directly influenced by the American Revolution, and all had been affected by the ideas of the Enlightenment and favored reforms made in the light of reason and usefulness.

The failure of the government to lead at the opening of the Estates-General created an opportunity for the Third Estate to push its demands for voting by head.

Since it had double representation, with the assistance of liberal nobles and clerics, it could turn the three estates into a single-chamber legislature that would reform France in its own way. One representative, Abbé Sieyès, issued a pamphlet in which he asked, "What is the third estate? Everything. What has it been thus far in the political order? Nothing. What does it demand? To become something." Sieyès's sentiment, however, was not representative of the general feeling in 1789. Most delegates still desired to make changes within a framework of respect for the authority of the king; revival or reform did not mean the overthrow of traditional institutions. When the first estate declared in favor of voting by order, the Third Estate felt compelled to respond in a significant fashion. On June 17, 1789, the Third Estate voted to constitute itself a "National Assembly" and decided to draw up a constitution. This declaration of June 17 stands as the first step in the French Revolution since the Third Estate had no legal right to act as the National Assembly. This revolution, largely the work of the lawyers of the Third Estate, was soon in jeopardy, however, as the king sided with the first estate and threatened to dissolve the Estates-General. Louis XVI now prepared to use force. The revolution of the lawyers appeared doomed.

The intervention of the common people, however, in a series of urban and rural uprisings in July and August of 1789 saved the Third Estate from the king's attempted counterrevolution. From now on, the common people would be used by both revolutionary and counterrevolutionary politicians and mobilized to support their interests. The common people had their own interests as well and would use the name of the Third Estate to wage a war on the rich, claiming the existence of an aristocratic plot to destroy the Estates-General and retain its privileges. This war was not what the deputies of the Third Estate had planned.

The most famous of the urban risings was the fall of the Bastille (see the box on p. 677). The king's attempt to take defensive measures by increasing the number of troops to secure the arsenals in Paris and guard the roads to Versailles served not to intimidate but rather to inflame public opinion. Increased mob activity in Paris led Parisian leaders to form a Permanent Committee to keep order. Needing arms, they organized a popular force to capture the Invalides, a royal armory, and on July 14 attacked the Bastille, another royal armory. But the Bastille had also been a state prison, and though it now contained only seven prisoners, its fall quickly became a popular symbol of triumph over despotism. Paris was abandoned to the insurgents, and Louis XVI was soon

The Fall of the Bastille

▼ ▼ ▼

On July 14, 1789, Parisian crowds in search of weapons attacked and captured the royal armory known as the Bastille. It had also been a state prison, and its fall marked the triumph of "liberty" over despotism. This intervention of the Parisian populace saved the Third Estate from Louis XVI's attempted counterrevolution.

A Parisian Newspaper Account of the Fall of the Bastille

First, the people tried to enter this fortress by the Rue St.—Antoine, this fortress, which no one has ever penetrated against the wishes of this frightful despotism and where the monster still resided. The treacherous governor had put out a flag of peace. So a confident advance was made; a detachment of French Guards, with perhaps five to six thousand armed bourgeois, penetrated the Bastille's outer courtyards, but as soon as some six hundred persons had passed over the first drawbridge, the bridge was raised and artillery fire mowed down several French Guards and some soldiers; the cannon fired on the town, and the people took fright; a large number of individuals were killed or wounded; but then they rallied and took shelter from the fire; . . . meanwhile, they tried to locate some cannon; they attacked from the water's edge through the gardens of the arsenal, and from there made an orderly siege; they advanced from various directions, beneath a ceaseless round of fire. It was a terrible scene. . . . The fighting grew steadily more intense; the citizens had become hardened to the fire; from all directions they clambered onto the roofs or broke into the rooms; as soon as an enemy appeared among the turrets on the tower, he was fixed in the sights of a hundred guns and mown down in an instant; meanwhile cannon fire was hurriedly directed against the second drawbridge, which it pierced, breaking the chains; in vain did the cannon on the tower reply, for most people were sheltered from it; the fury was at its height; people bravely faced death and every danger; women, in their eagerness, helped us to the utmost; even the children, after the discharge of fire from the fortress, ran here and there picking up the bullets and shot; [and so the Bastille fell and the governor, De Launay, was captured]. . . . Serene and blessed liberty, for the first time, has at last been introduced into this abode of horrors, this frightful refuge of monstrous despotism and its crimes.

Meanwhile, they get ready to march; they leave amidst an enormous crowd; the applause, the outbursts of joy, the insults, the oaths hurled at the treacherous prisoners of war; everything is confused; cries of vengeance and of pleasure issue from every heart; the conquerors, glorious and covered in honour, carry their arms and the spoils of the conquered, the flags of victory, the militia mingling with the soldiers of the fatherland, the victory laurels offered them from every side, all this created a frightening and splendid spectacle. On arriving at the square, the people, anxious to avenge themselves, allowed neither De Launay nor the other officers to reach the place of trial; they seized them from the hands of their conquerors, and trampled them underfoot one after the other. De Launay was struck by a thousand blows, his head was cut off and hoisted on the end of a pike with blood streaming down all sides. . . . This glorious day must amaze our enemies, and finally usher in for us the triumph of justice and liberty. In the evening, there were celebrations.

---

informed that the royal troops were unreliable. Louis's acceptance of that reality signaled the collapse of royal authority; Louis XVI could no longer enforce his will. The king then confirmed the appointment of the marquis de Lafayette as commander of a newly created citizens' militia known as the National Guard. The fall of the Bastille had saved the National Assembly.

At the same time, independently of what was going on in Paris, popular revolutions broke out in numerous cities. In Nantes, crowds seized the chief citadels, after which Permanent Committees and National Guards were created to maintain order. This collapse of royal authority in the cities was paralleled by peasant revolutions in the countryside.

A growing resentment of the entire seigneurial system with its fees and obligations, greatly exacerbated by the economic and fiscal activities of the great estate holders—whether noble or bourgeois—in the difficult decade of the 1780s, created the conditions for a popular uprising. The fall of the Bastille and the king's apparent

▼ **Storming of the Bastille.** Fearing that the First and Second Estates would block their desire for reforms, members of the Third Estate voted to constitute themselves a "National Assembly" on June 17, 1789. Louis XVI planned to use force to dissolve the Estates-General, but a number of rural and urban uprisings by the common people prevented this action. The fall of the Bastille, pictured here in an anonymous painting, is perhaps the most famous of the urban risings. The Parisians had attacked the Bastille in an attempt to acquire arms.

capitulation to the demands of the Third Estate now led peasants to take matters into their own hands. From July 19 to August 3, peasant rebellions occurred in five major areas of France. Patterns varied. In some places, peasants simply forced their lay and ecclesiastical lords to renounce dues and tithes; elsewhere they burned charters listing their obligations. The peasants were not acting in blind fury; they knew what they were doing. Many also believed they had the support of the king for their actions. As a contemporary chronicler wrote: "For several weeks, news went from village to village. They announced that the Estates-General was going to abolish tithes, quitrents and dues, that the King agreed but that the peasants had to support the public authorities by going themselves to demand the destruction of titles."[7]

The agrarian revolts served as a backdrop to the Great Fear, a vast panic that spread like wildfire through France between July 20 and August 6. The fear of invasion by foreign troops, aided by a supposed aristocratic plot, encouraged the formation of more citizens' militias and permanent committees. The greatest impact of the agrarian revolts and Great Fear was on the National Assembly meeting in Versailles. We will now examine its attempt to reform France.

The Destruction of the Old Regime

One of the first acts of the National Assembly (sometimes called the Constituent Assembly) was to destroy the relics of feudalism or aristocratic privileges. To some deputies, this was necessary to calm the peasants and restore order in the countryside, although many urban bourgeoisie were willing to abolish feudalism as a matter of principle. On the "night of 4 August," 1789, the National Assembly in an astonishing session voted to abolish seigneurial rights as well as the fiscal privileges of nobles, clergy, towns, and provinces.

On August 26, the assembly provided the ideological foundation for its actions and an educational device for the nation by adopting the Declaration of the Rights of Man and the Citizen (see the box on p. 680). This charter of basic liberties reflected the ideas of the major philosophes of the French Enlightenment and also owed much to the American Declaration of Independence and American state constitutions. The declaration began with a ringing affirmation of "the natural and imprescriptible rights of man" to "liberty, property, security and resistance to oppression." It went on to affirm the

destruction of aristocratic privileges by proclaiming an end to exemptions from taxation, freedom and equal rights for all men, and access to public office based on talent. The monarchy was restricted, and all citizens were to have the right to take part in the legislative process. Freedom of speech and press were coupled with the outlawing of arbitrary arrests.

In the meantime, Louis XVI had remained inactive at Versailles. He did refuse, however, to promulgate the decrees on the abolition of feudalism and the Declaration of Rights. Early in October, a Parisian crowd, initiated by several thousand women but soon taken over and led by Lafayette's National Guard, marched to Versailles and forced the king to accept the constitutional decrees and to change his residence to Paris. It was neither the first nor the last occasion when Parisian crowds would affect national politics. The king was virtually a prisoner in Paris, and the National Assembly, now meet-

▼ **Session of August 4, 1789.** The National Constituent Assembly destroyed many of the aristocratic privileges that still existed in France. During its session of August 4, 1789, the Assembly voted to abolish not only the fiscal privileges of the

nobility, clergy, towns, and provinces, but seigneurial rights as well. As seen in this contemporary rendering of the event, the Third Estate applauded while members of the First and Second Estates offered to give up their privileges.

Declaration of the Rights of Man and the Citizen

▼ ▼ ▼

One of the important documents of the French Revolution, the Declaration of the Rights of Man and the Citizen, was adopted in August 1789 by the National Assembly. The declaration affirmed that "men are born and remain free and equal in rights," that governments must protect these natural rights, and that political power is derived from the people.

Declaration of the Rights of Man and the Citizen

The representatives of the French people, organized as a national assembly, considering that ignorance, neglect, and scorn of the rights of man are the sole causes of public misfortunes and of corruption of governments, have resolved to display in a solemn declaration the natural, inalienable, and sacred rights of man, so that this declaration, constantly in the presence of all members of society, will continually remind them of their rights and their duties. . . . Consequently, the National Assembly recognizes and declares, in the presence and under the auspices of the Supreme Being, the following rights of man and citizen:

1. Men are born and remain free and equal in rights; social distinctions can be established only for the common benefit.

2. The aim of every political association is the conservation of the natural and imprescriptible rights of man; these rights are liberty, property, security, and resistance to oppression.

3. The source of all sovereignty is located in essence in the nation; no body, no individual can exercise authority which does not emanate from it expressly.

4. Liberty consists in being able to do anything that does not harm another person. . . .

6. The law is the expression of the general will; all citizens have the right to concur personally or through their representatives in its formation; it must be the same for all, whether it protects or punishes. All citizens being equal in its eyes are equally admissible to all honors, positions, and public employments, according to their capabilities and without other distinctions than those of their virtues and talents.

7. No man can be accused, arrested, or detained except in cases determined by the law, and according to the forms which it has prescribed. . . .

10. No one may be disturbed because of his opinions, even religious, provided that their public demonstration does not disturb the public order established by law.

11. The free communication of thoughts and opinions is one of the most precious rights of man: every citizen can therefore freely speak, write, and print. . . .

12. The guaranteeing of the rights of man and citizen necessitates a public force; this force is therefore instituted for the advantage of all, and not for the private use of those to whom it is entrusted. . . .

14. Citizens have the right to determine for themselves or through their representatives the need for taxation of the public, to consent to it freely, to investigate its use, and to determine its rate, basis, collection, and duration.

15. Society has the right to demand an accounting of his administration from every public agent.

16. Any society in which guarantees of rights are not assured nor the separation of powers determined has no constitution.

17. Property being an inviolable and sacred right, no one may be deprived of it unless public necessity, legally determined, clearly requires such action, and then only on condition of a just and prior indemnity.

The Declaration of the Rights of Woman and the Female Citizen

▼ ▼ ▼

Olympe de Gouges was a butcher's daughter who wrote plays and pamphlets. She argued that the Declaration of the Rights of Man and the Citizen did not apply to women and composed her own Declaration of the Rights of Woman. She became the principal spokeswoman for the cause of political rights for women in the early stages of the French Revolution.

The Declaration of the Rights of Woman and the Female Citizen (1791)

Mothers, daughters, sisters and representatives of the nation demand to be constituted into a national assembly. Believing that ignorance, omission, or scorn for the rights of woman are the only causes of public misfortunes and of the corruption of governments, the women have resolved to set forth in a solemn declaration the natural, inalienable, and sacred rights of woman in order that this declaration, constantly exposed before all the members of the society, will ceaselessly remind them of their rights and duties. . . .

Consequently, the sex that is as superior in beauty as it is in courage during the sufferings of maternity recognizes and declares in the presence and under the auspices of the Supreme Being, the following Rights of Woman and of Female Citizens.

1. Woman is born free and lives equal to man in her rights. Social distinctions can be based only on the common utility.

2. The purpose of any political association is the conservation of the natural and imprescriptible rights of woman and man; these rights are liberty, property, security, and especially resistance to oppression.

3. The principle of all sovereignty rests essentially with the nation, which is nothing but the union of woman and man; no body and no individual can exercise any authority which does not come expressly from it [the nation].

4. Liberty and justice consist of restoring all that belongs to others; thus, the only limits on the exercise of the natural rights of woman are perpetual male tyranny; these limits are to be reformed by the laws of nature and reason.

6. The law must be the expression of the general will; all female and male citizens must contribute either personally or through their representatives to its formation; it must be the same for all: male and female citizens, being equal in the eyes of the law, must be equally admitted to all honors, positions, and public employment according to their capacity and without other distinctions besides those of their virtues and talents.

7. No woman is an exception; she is accused, arrested, and detained in cases determined by law. Women, like men, obey this rigorous law.

10. No one is to be disquieted for his very basic opinions; woman has the right to mount the scaffold; she must equally have the right to mount the rostrum, provided that her demonstrations do not disturb the legally established public order.

11. The free communication of thoughts and opinions is one of the most precious rights of woman, since that liberty assured the recognition of children by their fathers. . . .

12. The guarantee of the rights of woman and the female citizen implies a major benefit; this guarantee must be instituted for the advantage of all, and not for the particular benefit of those to whom it is entrusted.

14. Female and male citizens have the right to verify, either by themselves or through their representatives, the necessity of the public contribution. This can only apply to women if they are granted an equal share, not only of wealth, but also of public administration, and in the determination of the proportion, the base, the collection, and the duration of the tax.

15. The collectivity of women, joined for tax purposes to the aggregate of men, has the right to demand an accounting of his administration from any public agent.

16. No society has a constitution without the guarantee of rights and the separation of powers; the constitution is null if the majority of individuals comprising the nation have not cooperated in drafting it.

17. Property belongs to both sexes whether united or separate; for each it is an inviolable and sacred right; no one can be deprived of it, since it is the true patrimony of nature, unless the legally determined public need obviously dictates it, and then only with a just and prior indemnity.

▼ **Women Return the King to Paris.** Louis XVI refused to accept either the decrees abolishing feudalism or the Declaration of the Rights of Man and the Citizen. A Parisian crowd, formed under the impetus of several thousand women led by the Marquis de Lafayette's National Guard, marched to Versailles and coerced Louis XVI into accepting the new constitutional decrees and changing his residence to Paris. For the first time, a Parisian crowd had affected national politics. Pictured here is the crowd of women returning in triumph to Paris.

ing in Paris, would also feel the influence of Parisian insurrectionary politics.

Because the Catholic church was viewed as an important pillar of the old order, reforms soon overtook it. Because of the need for money, most of the lands of the church were confiscated, and assignats, a form of paper money, were issued based on the collateral of the newly nationalized church property. The church was also secularized. In July 1790, a new Civil Constitution of the Clergy was put into effect. Both bishops and priests were to be elected by the people and paid by the state. All clergy were also required to swear an oath of allegiance to the Civil Constitution. Since the pope forbade it, only 54 percent of the French parish clergy took the oath while the majority of bishops refused. This was an important development because the Catholic church, still an important institution in the life of the French people, now became an enemy of the Revolution. This has often been viewed as a serious tactical blunder on the part of the National Assembly for it gave counterrevolution a popular base from which to operate.

By 1791, the National Assembly had finally completed a new constitution that established a limited, constitutional monarchy. There was still a monarch (now called king of the French), but he enjoyed few

powers not subject to review by the new Legislative Assembly. The Legislative Assembly, in which sovereign power was vested, was to sit for two years and consist of 745 representatives chosen by an indirect system of election that preserved power in the hands of the more affluent members of society. A differentiation was made between active and passive citizens. While all had the same civil rights, only active citizens (those men over the age of twenty-five paying in taxes the equivalent of three days' unskilled labor) could vote. There were probably 4.3 million active citizens in 1790. These citizens did not elect the members of the Legislative Assembly directly, but voted for electors (those men paying taxes equal in value to ten days' labor). This relatively small group of 50,000 electors chose the deputies. To qualify as a deputy, one had to pay at least a "silver mark" in taxes, an amount equivalent to fifty-four days' labor.

The National Assembly also undertook an administrative restructuring of France. It abolished all the old local and provincial divisions and divided France into eighty-three departments, roughly equal in size and population. In turn, departments were divided into districts and communes, all supervised by elected councils and officials who oversaw financial, administrative, judicial, and ecclesiastical institutions within their domains. Although both bourgeoisie and aristocrats were eligible for offices based on property qualifications, few nobles were elected, leaving local and departmental governments in the hands of the bourgeoisie, especially lawyers of various types.

By 1791, France had moved into a revolutionary reordering of the old regime that had been achieved by a revolutionary consensus that was largely the work of the wealthier bourgeoisie. This consensus, however, faced growing opposition by mid-1791 from clerics against the Civil Constitution of the Clergy, lower classes hurt by the rise in the cost of living resulting from the inflation of the assignats, peasants who remained opposed to dues that had still not been abandoned, and political clubs offering more radical solutions to France's problems. Most famous were the Jacobins. The Jacobins first emerged as a gathering of more radical deputies at the beginning of the Revolution, especially during the events of the night of 4 August. After October 1789, they occupied the former Jacobin convent in Paris. Jacobin clubs also formed in the provinces where they served primarily as discussion groups. Eventually, they joined together in an extensive correspondence network and, by spring 1790, were seeking affiliation with the Parisian club. One year later, there were 900 Jacobin clubs in France associated with its Parisian center. Members were usually the elite of their local societies, but they also included artisans and tradesmen.

In addition, by mid-1791, the government was still facing severe financial difficulties due to massive tax evasion. Despite all of their problems, however, the bourgeois politicians in charge remained relatively unified on the basis of their trust in the king. But Louis XVI disastrously undercut them. Quite upset with the whole turn of revolutionary events, he sought to flee France in June 1791 and almost succeeded before being recognized, captured, and brought back to Paris. While radicals called for the king to be deposed, the members of the National Assembly, fearful of the popular forces in Paris calling for a republic, chose to ignore the king's flight and pretended that he had been kidnapped. In this unsettled situation, with a discredited and seemingly disloyal monarch, the new Legislative Assembly held its first session in October 1791.

The composition of the Legislative Assembly tended to be quite different from that of the National Assembly. The clerics and nobles were largely gone. Most of the representatives were men of property; many were law-yers. Although lacking national reputations, most had gained experience in the new revolutionary politics and prominence in their local areas through the National Guard, the Jacobin clubs, and the many elective offices spawned by the administrative reordering of France. The king made what seemed to be a genuine effort to work with the new Legislative Assembly, but France's relations with the rest of Europe soon led to Louis's downfall.

Over a period of time, some European countries had become concerned about the French example and feared that revolution would spread to their countries. On August 27, 1791, Emperor Leopold of Austria and King Frederick William II of Prussia issued the Declaration of Pillnitz, which invited other European monarchs to take "the most effectual means . . . to put the king of France in a state to strengthen, in the most perfect liberty, the bases of a monarchical government equally becoming to the rights of sovereigns and to the wellbeing of the French Nation."[8] But European monarchs were too suspicious of each other to undertake such a plan, and in any case French enthusiasm for war led the Legislative

▼ **Map 20.2** Reorganization of France by the National Assembly. (*Left:* French Provinces and Regions before 1789; *Right:* French Departments after 1789)

Assembly to declare war on Austria on April 20, 1792. But why take such a step in view of its obvious dangers? Practically everyone in France wanted war. Reactionaries hoped that a preoccupation with war would cool off the Revolution; French defeat, which seemed likely in view of the army's disintegration, might even lead to the restoration of the old regime. Leftists hoped that war would consolidate the Revolution at home and spread it to all of Europe.

The French fared badly in the initial fighting, and loud recriminations were soon heard in Paris. A frantic search for scapegoats began; as one observer noted, "Everywhere you hear the cry that the king is betraying us, the generals are betraying us, that nobody is to be trusted; . . . that Paris will be taken in six weeks by the Austrians . . . we are on a volcano ready to spout flames."[9] Defeats in war coupled with economic shortages in the spring reinvigorated popular groups that had

been dormant since the previous summer and led to renewed political demonstrations, especially against the king. Radical Parisian political groups, declaring themselves an insurrectionary commune, organized a mob attack on the royal palace and Legislative Assembly in August 1792, took the king captive, and forced the Legislative Assembly to suspend the monarchy and call for a National Convention, chosen on the basis of universal male suffrage, to decide on the future form of government. The French Revolution was about to enter a more radical stage as power passed from the assembly to the new Paris Commune composed of many who proudly called themselves the sansculottes, ordinary patriots without fine clothes. While it has become customary to equate the more radical sansculottes with working people or the poor, many were merchants and better-off artisans who were often the elite of their neighborhoods and trades.

▼ **Sansculottes.** The sansculottes identified themselves as ordinary patriots without fine clothes. Composed of workers, merchants, and artisans, and often more radical than the members of the Legislative Assembly, sansculottes were members of the Paris Commune that dominated the political scene before the National Convention of 1792.

The Radical Revolution

Before the National Convention met, the Paris Commune dominated the political scene. Led by the newly appointed minister of justice, Georges Danton, the sansculottes sought revenge on those who had aided the king and resisted the popular will. Thousands of presumed traitors were arrested and then massacred as ordinary Parisian tradesmen and artisans solved the problem of overcrowded prisons by mass executions of their inmates. In September 1792, the newly elected National Convention began its sessions. Although it was called to draft a new constitution, it also acted as the sovereign ruling body of France.

Socially the composition of the National Convention was similar to its predecessors. Dominated by lawyers, professionals, and property owners, it also possessed for the first time a handful of artisans. Two-thirds of the deputies were under forty-five, and almost all had had political experience as a result of the Revolution. Almost all were also intensely distrustful of the king and his activities. It was therefore no surprise that the convention's first major step on September 21 was to abolish the monarchy and establish a republic. But that was about as far as members of the convention could agree, and the National Convention soon split into factions over the fate of the king. The two most important were the Girondins and the Mountain. Both were members of the Jacobin club.

Representing primarily the provinces, the Girondins came to fear the radical mobs in Paris and were disposed to keep the king alive as a hedge against future eventualities. The Mountain, on the other hand, represented the interests of the city of Paris and owed much of its strength to the radical and popular elements in the city, although the members of the Mountain themselves were middle class. The Mountain won out at the beginning of 1793 when they passed a decree condemning Louis XVI to death, although by a very narrow margin. On January 21, 1793, the king was executed and the destruction of the old regime was complete. There could be no turning back. But the execution of the king produced new challenges by creating new enemies for the Revolution both at home and abroad while strengthening those who were already its enemies.

Factional disputes between Girondins and the Mountain were only one part of France's domestic crisis in 1792 and 1793. Within Paris the local government known as the Commune, which possessed a number of leaders from the working classes, favored radical change and put constant pressure on the National Convention,

▼ **Execution of the King.** In 1792, after economic shortages and defeats in war, Louis XVI was taken captive and a National Convention was called to draft a new constitution. The convention abolished the monarchy and established a republic. The National Convention soon split, however, over what to do about the king. The Girondins favored keeping him alive, while the Mountain desired his death. In 1793, the Mountain won out, and on January 21 of that year, Louis XVI was executed.

pushing it to ever more radical positions. As one man warned his fellow deputies, "Never forget that you were sent here by the sansculottes."[10] At the end of May and the beginning of June 1793, the Commune organized a demonstration, invaded the National Convention, and forced the arrest of the Girondins, thus leaving the Mountain in control of the convention. The National Convention itself still did not rule all France. The authority of the convention was repudiated in western France, particularly in the department of the Vendée, by peasants who revolted against the new military draft (see The Levy-in-Mass later in the chapter). The Vendéan rebellion soon escalated into a full-blown counterrevolutionary appeal: "Long live the king and our good priests. We want our king, our priests and the old regime." Some of France's major provincial cities, including Lyons and Marseilles, also began to break away from central authority. Arguing as Marseilles did that "it is time for the anarchy of a few men of blood to stop,"[11] these cities favored a decentralized republic to free themselves of the ascendancy of Paris. In no way did they favor breaking up the "indivisible Republic."

Domestic turmoil was paralleled by a foreign crisis. By the beginning of 1793, after the king had been executed, most of Europe—an informal coalition of Austria, Prussia, Spain, Portugal, Britain, the Dutch Republic, and even Russia—was pitted against France. Carried away by initial successes and their own rhetoric, the French welcomed the struggle. Danton exclaimed to the convention: "They threaten you with kings! You have thrown down your gauntlet to them, and this gauntlet is a king's head, the signal of their coming death."[12] Grossly overextended, the French armies began to experience reverses, and by late spring some members of the anti-French coalition were poised for an invasion of France. If successful, both the Revolution and the revolutionaries would be destroyed and the old regime reestablished. The Revolution had reached a decisive moment.

To meet these crises, the program of the National Convention became one of curbing anarchy and counterrevolution at home while attempting to win the war by a great national mobilization. To administer the government, the convention gave broad powers to an executive committee known as the Committee of Public Safety, which was dominated initially by Danton. Maximilien Robespierre eventually became one of its most important members. For a twelve-month period, from 1793 to 1794, virtually the same twelve members were reelected and gave the country the leadership it needed to weather the domestic and foreign crises of 1793.

THE LEVY-IN-MASS   To meet the foreign crisis and save the republic from its foreign enemies, the Committee of Public Safety decreed a universal mobilization of the nation on August 23, 1793:

> Young men will fight, young men are called to conquer. Married men will forge arms, transport military baggage and guns and will prepare food supplies. Women, who at long last are to take their rightful place in the revolution and follow their true destiny, will forget their futile tasks: their delicate hands will work at making clothes for soldiers; they will make tents and they will extend their tender care to shelters where the defenders of the Patrie will receive the help that their wounds require. Children will make lint of old cloth. It is for them that we are fighting: children, those beings destined to gather all the fruits of the revolution, will raise their pure hands toward the skies. And old men, performing their missions again, as of yore, will be guided to the public squares of the cities where they will kindle the courage of young warriors and preach the doctrines of hate for kings and the unity of the Republic.[13]

In less than a year, the French revolutionary government had raised an army of 650,000; by September 1794, it numbered 1,169,000. The Republic's army was the largest ever seen in European history. It now pushed the allies back across the Rhine and even conquered the Austrian Netherlands. By May 1795, the anti-French coalition of 1793 was breaking up.

Historians have focused on the importance of the French revolutionary army as an important step in the creation of modern nationalism. Previously, wars had been fought between governments or ruling dynasties by relatively small armies of professional soldiers. Although innocent civilians had suffered in those struggles, the new French army was the creation of a "people's" government; its wars were now "people's" wars. The entire nation was to be involved in the war. But when dynastic wars became people's wars, warfare increased in ferocity and lack of restraint. Carnage was appalling at times. The wars of the French revolutionary era opened the door to the total war of the modern world.

THE COMMITTEE OF PUBLIC SAFETY AND THE REIGN OF TERROR   To meet the domestic crisis, the National Convention and the Committee of Public Safety established the "Reign of Terror." Revolutionary courts were instituted to protect the revolutionary Republic from its internal enemies, those "who either by their conduct, their contacts, their words or their writings, showed themselves to be supporters of tyranny or enemies of liberty," or those "who have not constantly manifested their attachment to the revolution."[14] Victims of the Terror ranged from royalists, such as Queen Marie Antoinette, to former revolutionary Girondins, and even to thousands of peasants. Many victims were figures who had opposed the radical activities of the sansculottes. In the course of nine months, 16,000 people were officially killed under the blade of the guillotine, the latter a revolutionary device for the quick and efficient separation of heads from bodies. But the true number of the Terror's victims was probably closer to 30,000. The bulk of the Terror's executions took place in the Vendée and in cities such as Lyons and Marseilles, places that had been in open rebellion against the authority of the National Convention.

Military force in the form of Revolutionary Armies was used to bring recalcitrant cities and districts back under the control of the National Convention. Marseilles fell to a Revolutionary Army in August. Starving Lyons surrendered early in October after two months of bombardment and resistance. Since Lyons was France's second city after Paris and had defied the National Convention during a time when the Republic was in peril, the Committee of Public Safety decided to make an example of it. By April 1794, 1,880 citizens of

Lyons had been executed. When guillotining proved too slow, cannon fire and grape shot were used to blow condemned men into open graves. A German observed:

> . . . whole ranges of houses, always the most handsome, burnt. The churches, convents, and all the dwellings of the former patricians were in ruins. When I came to the guillotine, the blood of those who had been executed a few hours beforehand was still running in the street . . . I said to a group of sansculottes that it would be decent to clear away all this human blood. Why should it be cleared? one of them said to me. It's the blood of aristocrats and rebels. The dogs should lick it up.[15]

In the Vendée, Revolutionary Armies were also brutal in defeating the rebel armies. After destroying one army on December 12, the commander of the Revolutionary Army ordered that no quarter be given: "The road to Laval is strewn with corpses. Women, priests, monks, children, all have been put to death. I have spared nobody." The Terror in the Vendée was the most destructive. Forty-two percent of the death sentences during the Terror were passed in territories affected by the Vendée

rebellion. Perhaps the most notorious act of violence occurred in Nantes where victims were executed by sinking them in barges in the Loire River.

Contrary to popular opinion, the Terror demonstrated no class prejudice. Estimates are that the nobles constituted 8 percent of its victims, the middle classes, 25, the clergy, 6, and the peasant and laboring classes, 60. To the Committee of Public Safety, this bloodletting was only a temporary expedient. Once the war and domestic emergency were over, then would follow "the republic of virtue" in which the Declaration of the Rights of Man and of the Citizen would be fully established. Although theoretically a republic, the French government during the Terror was led by a group of twelve men who ordered the execution of people as enemies of the Republic. But how did they justify this? Saint-Just, one of the younger members of the Committee of Public Safety explained their rationalization in a speech to the convention: "Since the French people has manifested its will, everything opposed to it is outside the sovereign. Whatever is outside the sovereign is an enemy."[16] Clearly, Saint-Just was referring to Rousseau's concept of the general will,

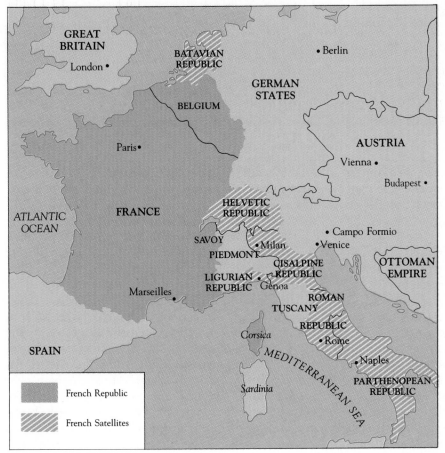

▼ **Map 20.3** French Conquests During the Revolutionary Wars.

Robespierre and Revolutionary Government

▼ ▼ ▼

In its time of troubles, the National Convention, under the direction of the Committee of Public Safety, instituted a Reign of Terror to preserve the Revolution from its internal enemies. In this selection, Maximilien Robespierre, one of the committee's leading members, tries to justify the violence to which these believers in republican liberty resorted.

Robespierre, Speech on Revolutionary Government

The theory of revolutionary government is as new as the Revolution that created it. It is as pointless to seek its origins in the books of the political theorists, who failed to foresee this revolution, as in the laws of the tyrants, who are happy enough to abuse their exercise of authority without seeking out its legal justification. And so this phrase is for the aristocracy a mere subject of terror or a term of slander, for tyrants an outrage and for many an enigma. It behooves us to explain it to all in order that we may rally good citizens, at least, in support of the principles governing the public interest.

It is the function of government to guide the moral and physical energies of the nation toward the purposes for which it was established.

The object of constitutional government is to preserve the Republic; the object of revolutionary government is to establish it.

Revolution is the war waged by liberty against its enemies; a constitution is that which crowns the edifice of freedom once victory has been won and the nation is at peace.

The revolutionary government has to summon extraordinary activity to its aid precisely because it is at war. It is subjected to less binding and less uniform regulations, because the circumstances in which it finds itself are tempestuous and shifting above all because it is compelled to deploy, swiftly and incessantly, new resources to meet new and pressing dangers.

The principal concern of constitutional government is civil liberty; that of revolutionary government, public liberty. Under a constitutional government little more is required than to protect the individual against abuses by the state, whereas revolutionary government is obliged to defend the state itself against the factions that assail it from every quarter.

To good citizens revolutionary government owes the full protection of the state; to the enemies of the people it owes only death.

---

but it is equally apparent that these twelve men, in the name of the Republic, had taken to themselves the right to ascertain the sovereign will of the French people (see the box above) and to kill their enemies as "outside the sovereign."

Along with the Terror, the Committee of Public Safety took other steps to control France. By spring 1793, they were sending "representatives on mission" as agents of the central government to all departments to explain the war emergency measures and to implement the laws dealing with the wartime emergency.

The committee also attempted to provide some economic controls, especially since members of the more radical working class were advocating them. They established a system of requisitions for food supplies to the cities enforced by the forays of Revolutionary Armies into the countryside. The Law of the General Maximum

established price controls on goods declared of first necessity ranging from food and drink to fuel and clothing. The controls failed to work very well since the government lacked the machinery to enforce them.

The National Convention also pursued a policy of dechristianization. The word "saint" was removed from street names, churches were pillaged and closed by Revolutionary Armies, and priests were encouraged to marry. In Paris, the cathedral of Notre Dame was designated a Temple of Reason (see the box on p. 689); in November 1793, a public ceremony dedicated to the worship of reason was held in the former cathedral in which patriotic maidens adorned in white dresses paraded before a temple of reason where the high altar once stood. At the end of the ceremony, a female figure personifying Liberty rose out of the temple. As Robespierre came to realize, dechristianization backfired because

Dechristianization

▼ ▼ ▼

The phenomenon of dechristianization produced some unusual spectacles during the radical stage of the French Revolution. This selection from the minutes of the National Convention describes how the cathedral of Notre Dame was put to new use as a Temple of Reason.

The Temple of Reason

A member puts in the form of a motion the demand of the citizens of Paris that the metropolitan cathedral [Notre Dame] be henceforth the Temple of Reason.

A member requests that the goddess of Reason place herself at the side of the president.

The attorney of the Commune conducts her to the desk. The president and the secretaries give her the fraternal kiss in the midst of applause.

She sits at the side of the president.

A member demands that the National Convention march in a body, in the midst of the People, to the Temple of Reason, to sing the hymn of Liberty there.

This proposal is passed.

The Convention marches with the People to the Temple of Reason in the midst of general enthusiasm and joyful acclamations.

Having entered the Temple of Reason, they sing the following hymn:

Descend, O Liberty, daughter of Nature:
The People have recaptured their immortal power;
Over the pompous remains of age-old imposture
Their hands raise thine altar.
Come, vanquisher of kings, Europe gazes upon you;
Come, vanquish the false gods.
Thou, holy Liberty, come dwell in this temple;
Be the goddess of the French.
Thy countenance rejoices the most savage mountain,
Amid the rocks harvests grow:
Embellished by thy hands, the harshest coast,
Embedded in ice, smiles.
Thou doublest pleasures, virtues, genius;
Under thy holy standards, man is always victorious;
Before knowing thee he does not know life;
He is created by thy glance.
All kings make war on the sovereign People;
Let them henceforth fall at thy feet, O goddess;
Soon on the coffins of the world's tyrants
The world's peoples will swear peace.
Warrior liberators, powerful, brave race,
Armed with a human sword, sanctify terror;
Brought down by your blows, may the last slave
Follow the last king to the grave.

France was still overwhelmingly Catholic. Dechristianization, in fact, created more enemies than friends.

By the Law of 14 Frimaire (passed on December 4, 1793—see the next section for the new calendar), the Committee of Public Safety sought to centralize the administration of France more effectively and to exercise greater control in order to check the excesses of the Reign of Terror. The activities of both the representatives on mission and the Revolutionary Armies were scrutinized more carefully, and the campaign against Christianity was also dampened. Finally, in 1794, the Committee of Public Safety turned against its radical Parisian supporters, executed the leaders of the revolutionary Paris Commune, and turned it into a docile tool. This might have been a good idea for the sake of order, but in suppressing the people who had been its chief supporters, the National Convention alienated an important group. At the same time, the French had been successful against their foreign foes. The military successes meant that there was less need now for the Terror. But the Terror continued since Robespierre, who had become a figure of power and authority, became obsessed with purifying the body politic of all the corrupt. Only then could the Republic of Virtue follow. Many deputies in the National Convention were fearful, however, that they were not safe while Robespierre was free to act. An anti-Robespierre coalition in the National Convention, eager now to destroy Robespierre before he destroyed them, gathered enough votes to condemn him. Robespierre was guillotined on July 28, 1794, beginning a reaction that brought an end to this radical stage of the French Revolution.

The National Convention and its Committee of Public Safety had accomplished a great deal. By creating a

▼ **Robespierre.** While the Committee of Public Safety was originally dominated by Georges Danton, Maximilien Robespierre eventually came to exercise much control over the body. Robespierre and the Committee worked to centralize the administration of France and curb the excesses of the Reign of Terror. However, since Robespierre became obsessed with the idea of purifying the body politic and established a Republic of Virtue, he continued the use of the Terror. Fear of Robespierre led many in the National Convention to condemn him, and on July 28, 1794, Robespierre was executed.

nation-in-arms, they preserved the French Revolution and prevented it from being destroyed by its foreign enemies, who, if they had been successful, would have reestablished the old monarchical order. Domestically, the Revolution had also been saved from the forces of counterrevolution. The committee's tactics, however, provided an example for the use of violence in domestic politics that has continued to bedevil the Western world until this day.

THE REORDERING OF DAILY LIVES: THE REVOLUTIONARY CALENDAR There was no more visible symbol of the French Revolution's attempt to radically reorder the structure of daily life than its adoption of a new repub-

lican calendar on October 5, 1793. In part, this was simply another manifestation of the dechristianization that became popular with some radical leaders in 1793. Years would no longer be numbered from the birth of Christ but from September 22, 1792, the day the French Republic was proclaimed. Thus, at the time the calendar was adopted, the French were already living in year two. The calendar contained twelve months; each month consisted of three ten-day weeks (*décades*) with the tenth day of each week a rest-day (*décadi*). This eliminated Sundays and Sunday worship services and served to end the ordering of French lives by a Christian calendar that emphasized Sundays, saints' days, and church holidays and festivals. The latter were to be replaced by revolutionary festivals. Especially important were the five days (six in leap years) left over in the calendar at the end of the year. These days were to form a half-week of festivals to celebrate the revolutionary virtues—Virtue, Intelligence, Labor, Opinion, and Rewards. The sixth extra day in a leap year would be a special festival day when Frenchmen would "come from all parts of the Republic to celebrate liberty and equality, to cement by their embraces the national fraternity." Of course, ending church holidays also reduced the number of nonworking holidays from fifty-six to thirty-two, a goal long recommended by eighteenth-century economic theorists.

The anti-Christian purpose of the calendar was reinforced in the naming of the months and days of the year. Fabre d'Eglantine, secretary of the National Convention's Committee on Public Instruction, was assigned the task of preparing the new calendar. He made clear the anti-Christian principles that he followed in naming the months and days:

> The priests had assigned to each day of the year the commemoration of some pretended saint. This list of names had no method, and no usefulness; it was a catalogue of lies, dupery, and charlatanism. We have come to the conclusion that, after expelling this crowd of saints from its calendar, the nation ought to put in their places all those things which constitute its real wealth—the worthy objects, not of its cult, but of its culture: the useful products of the ground, the utensils we use in its cultivation, and the domesticated animals, which are doubtless much more precious to the eye of reason than beatified skeletons disinterred from Roman catacombs.[17]

Accordingly, the months were given names that were supposed to evoke the seasons, the temperature, or the state of the vegetation: Vendémiaire (harvest—the first month of thirty days beginning September 22), Brumaire (mist), Frimaire (frost), Nivôse (snow), Pluviôse (rain), Ventôse (wind), Germinal (seeding), Floréal (flowering), Prairial (meadows), Messidor (wheat harvest), Thermidor (heat), and Fructidor (ripening). Names were also devised for each day of the year. The tenth day of each *décade* was named after an agricultural implement; each fifth day after a domestic animal; the rest received names of herbs, flowers, vegetables, minerals, and other natural phenomena. Hence, a typical week would consist of Snowday, Iceday, Honeyday, Waxday, Dogday, Strawday, Petroleumday, Coalday, Resinday, and Flailday. Since France was still largely an agricultural society, Fabre reasoned that his calendar would teach rural economy to French children.

The new calendar faced intense popular opposition, and the revolutionary government relied primarily on coercion to win its acceptance. Property leases were to be dated only by using the new "calendar of liberty." Journalists were commanded to use republican dates in their newspaper articles. But the *décadi* failed to dethrone Sunday as a day of rest, despite penalties for nonobservance and the government's attempt to make it more attractive by holding communal celebrations. One government official reported:

> Sundays and Catholic holidays, even if there are ten in a row, have for some time been celebrated with as much pomp and splendor as before. The same cannot be said of *décadi*, which is observed by only a small handful of citizens. The first to disobey the law are the wives of public officials, who dress up on the holidays of the old calendar and abstain from work more religiously than anyone else.[18]

The government could hardly expect peasants to follow the new calendar when government officials were ignoring it. Napoleon later perceived that the revolutionary calendar was politically unpopular, and he simply abandoned it on January 1, 1806.

In addition to its anti-Christian function, the revolutionary calendar had also served to commemorate the Revolution as a new historical beginning, a radical discontinuity in time. Revolutionary upheavals often project millenarian expectations, the hope that a new age is dawning. The revolutionary dream of a new order presupposed the creation of a new human being freed from the old order and its symbols, a new citizen surrounded by a framework of new habits. Restructuring time itself offered the opportunity to forge new habits and create a lasting new order. The abandonment of the revolutionary calendar in 1806 by Napoleon signaled the abandonment of many of the revolutionary ideals. It would take another eight years and a series of devastating wars before the French people could accept that their brave new world of the Revolution was merely a chimera.

The Role of Women in the French Revolution

There had long been a tradition of laboring women involved in violent mass protests. Women had participated in peasant revolts for centuries and were prominent in the most common form of "crowd action" in the eighteenth century, the food riots, in which people attempted to keep bread prices at a fair level. Women also participated in the first mass protests against the introduction of machines in the late eighteenth century.

From its beginning stages, the French Revolution witnessed female participation in the crowd riots and demonstrations that played such an important role in determining the course of events. While present in the storming of the Bastille on July 14, 1789, women were even more prominent in the "October Days" of the same year. On October 5, after marching to the Hôtel de Ville, the city hall, to demand bread, crowds of Parisian women numbering in the thousands and described by one eyewitness as "detachments of women coming up from every direction, armed with broomsticks, lances, pitchforks, swords, pistols and muskets," set off for Versailles to confront the king and the National Assembly. After meeting with a delegation of these women, Louis XVI promised them provisions for Paris, thinking that this would end the protest. But the women's action had forced the Parisian National Guard under Lafayette to follow their lead and march to Versailles. The crowd now insisted that the royal family return to Paris. On October 6, the king complied. As a goodwill gesture, he brought along wagonloads of flour from the palace stores, escorted by women armed with pikes singing, "We are bringing back the baker, the baker's wife, and the baker's boy" (the king, queen, and their son).

From the "October Days" through 1795, women participated in a variety of activities on behalf of the Revolution. They demonstrated for bread and price controls, issued a "Declaration of the Rights of Woman and the Female Citizen" (see the box on p. 681), joined more violent groups that seized food, petitioned for the right to carry arms ("We are citizens, and we cannot be indifferent to the fate of the fatherland"), and, as spectators at sessions of revolutionary clubs and the National Convention, made the members and deputies aware of their demands. When on Sunday, February 25, 1793, a group of women appealed formally to the National Convention for lower bread prices, the convention reacted by adjourning until Tuesday. The women responded bitterly by accosting the deputies: "We are adjourned until Tuesday; but as for us, we adjourn ourselves until Monday. When our children ask us for milk, we don't adjourn them until the day after tomorrow."[19] In 1793, two women—an actress and a chocolate manufacturer—founded the Society for Revolutionary Republican Women. Composed largely of working-class women, this Parisian group viewed themselves as a "family of sisters" and vowed "to rush to the defense of the Fatherland."

Despite the importance of women to the revolutionary cause, male revolutionaries reacted disdainfully to female participation in political activity. In the radical phase of the Revolution, the Paris Commune outlawed women's clubs and forbade women to be present at its meetings. One of its members explained why:

> It is horrible, it is contrary to all laws of nature for a woman to want to make herself a man. The Council must recall that some time ago these denatured women, these viragos, wandered through the markets with the red cap to sully that badge of liberty and wanted to force all women to take off the modest headdress that is appropriate for them [the bonnet]. . . . Is it the place of women to propose motions? Is it the place of women to place themselves at the head of our armies?[20]

Most men—whether radical or conservative—agreed that women's place was in the home and not in military or political affairs, a position solidified by the classification of women as legal incompetents in Napoleon's Civil Code (see Domestic Policies later in the chapter).

Reaction and the Directory

After the death of Robespierre on July 28, 1794, a reaction set in called the Thermidorean Reaction, named after the month of Thermidor. The Terror came to a halt. The National Convention reduced the power of the Committee of Public Safety, closed the Jacobin club, and made attempts to provide better protection for the National Convention against the Parisian mobs. Churches were allowed to reopen for public worship while a decree of February 21, 1795, gave freedom of worship to all cults. Economic regulation was dropped in favor of laissez-faire policies, another clear indication that moderate forces were again gaining control of the Revolution. In addition, a new constitution was created in August 1795 that reflected this more conservative republicanism or a desire for a stability that did not sacrifice the ideals of 1789.

To avoid the dangers of another single legislative assembly, the Constitution of 1795 established a national legislative assembly consisting of two chambers: a lower house known as the Council of 500 whose function was to initiate legislation and an upper house of 250 mem-

Chronology
▼ ▼ ▼
The French Revolution

1789	
Meeting of Estates-General	May 5
Formation of National Assembly	June 17
Fall of the Bastille	July 14
Great Fear	Summer
Abolition of Feudalism	August 4
Declaration of the Rights of Man and of the Citizen	August 26
March to Versailles; the King's Return to Paris	October 5–6
1790	
Civil Constitution of the Clergy	July 12
1791	
Flight of the King	June 20–21
Declaration of Pillnitz	August 27
1792	
France Declares War on Austria	April 20
Attack on the Royal Palace	August 10
Abolition of Monarchy	September 21
1793	
Execution of the King	January 21
Levy-in-Mass	August 23
1794	
Execution of Robespierre	July 28
1795	
Constitution of 1795 Is Adopted—the Directory	August 22

bers, the Council of Elders, composed of married or widowed members over forty, which accepted or rejected the proposed laws. The 750 members of the two legislative bodies were chosen by electors who had to be owners or renters of property worth between 100 and 200 days' labor, a requirement that limited the number to 30,000, an even smaller base than that provided in the Constitution of 1791. The electors were chosen by the active citizens, now defined as all male taxpayers over twenty-one. The Council of Elders elected five directors from a list presented by the Council of 500 to act as the executive authority or Directory. To ensure some continuity from the old order to the new, the members of the National Convention ruled that two-thirds of the new members of the National Assembly must be chosen from their ranks. This produced disturbances in Paris and an insurrection at the beginning of October that was dispersed after fierce combat by an army contingent under the artillery general Napoleon Bonaparte. This would be the last time the city of Paris would attempt to impose its wishes on the central government. Even more significant and ominous was this use of the army, which made it clear that the Directory from its beginnings had to rely upon the military for survival.

The period of the Revolution under the government of the Directory was an era of stagnation, corruption, and graft, a materialistic reaction to the sufferings and sacrifices that had been demanded in the Reign of Terror and the Republic of Virtue. Speculators made fortunes in property by taking advantage of the government's severe monetary problems. Elaborate fashions, which had gone out of style because of their identification with the nobility, were worn again. Gambling and roulette became popular once more.

The government of the Directory was faced with political enemies from both the left and the right of the political spectrum. On the right, royalists who desired the restoration of the monarchy continued their agitation; some still toyed with violent means. On the left, Jacobin hopes of power were revived by continuing economic problems, especially the total collapse in value of the assignats. Some radicals even went beyond earlier goals, especially Gracchus Babeuf who raised the question "What is the French Revolution? An open war between patricians and plebeians, between rich and poor." Babeuf wanted to abolish private property and eliminate private enterprise. His Conspiracy of Equals was crushed in 1796, and he was executed in 1797.

New elections in 1797 created even more uncertainty and instability. Battered by the left and right, unable to find a definitive solution to the country's economic problems, and still carrying on the wars left from the Committee of Public Safety, the Directory increasingly relied on the military to maintain its power. This led to a coup d'etat in 1799 in which the successful and popular general Napoleon Bonaparte was able to seize power.

▼ The Age of Napoleon (1799–1815)

Napoleon dominated both French and European history from 1799 to 1815. The coup d'etat that brought him to power occurred exactly ten years after the outbreak of the French Revolution. In a sense, Napoleon brought the Revolution to an end in 1799, but Napo-

▼ **Napoleon as a Young Officer.** Napoleon had risen quickly through the military ranks, being promoted to brigadier general at the age of 25. In 1799, Napoleon Bonaparte led a coup d'etat and overthrew the government of the Directory. A new form of the republic was created after Napoleon seized power. In 1804, France returned to a monarchical form of government when Napoleon had himself crowned Emperor Napoleon I. This painting of Napoleon by the Romantic painter Baron Gros presents an idealized, heroic image of the young Napoleon.

leon was also a child of the Revolution; he called himself the son of the Revolution. The French Revolution had made possible his rise first in the military and then to supreme power in France. Even beyond this, Napoleon had once said, "I am the revolution," and he never ceased to remind Frenchmen that they owed to him the preservation of all that was beneficial in the revolutionary program.

The Rise of Napoleon

Napoleon was born in 1769 in Corsica shortly after the island had been annexed to France. The son of a minor noble, Napoleon was sent to France to study in one of the new military schools. When the Revolution

Napoleon and Psychological Warfare
▼ ▼ ▼

In 1796, at the age of twenty-seven, Napoleon Bonaparte was given command of the French army in Italy where he won a series of stunning victories. His use of speed, deception, and surprise to overwhelm his opponents is well known. In this selection from a proclamation to his troops in Italy, Napoleon also appears as a master of psychological warfare.

Napoleon Bonaparte, Proclamation to French Troops in Italy (April 26, 1796)

Soldiers:

In a fortnight you have won six victories, taken twenty-one standards, fifty-five pieces of artillery, several strong positions, and conquered the richest part of Piedmont [in northern Italy]; you have captured 15,000 prisoners and killed or wounded more than 10,000 men. . . . You have won battles without cannon, crossed rivers without bridges, made forced marches without shoes, camped without brandy and often without bread. Soldiers of liberty, only republican troops could have endured what you have endured. Soldiers, you have our thanks! The grateful Patrie [nation] will owe its prosperity to you. . . .

The two armies which but recently attacked you with audacity are fleeing before you in terror; the wicked men who laughed at your misery and rejoiced at the thought of the triumphs of your enemies are confounded and trembling.

But, soldiers, as yet you have done nothing compared with what remains to be done. . . . Undoubtedly the greatest obstacles have been overcome; but you still have battles to fight, cities to capture, rivers to cross. Is there one among you whose courage is abating? No. . . . All of you are consumed with a desire to extend the glory of the French people; all of you long to humiliate those arrogant kings who dare to contemplate placing us in fetters; all of you desire to dictate a glorious peace, one which will indemnify the Patrie for the immense sacrifices it has made; all of you wish to be able to say with pride as you return to your villages, "I was with the victorious army of Italy!"

---

broke out in 1789, Napoleon was a lieutenant and not well regarded by his fellow officers since he was short, spoke with an Italian accent, and had little money. He spent his time pondering military tactics and studying the works of such philosophes as Voltaire and Adam Smith. Although his dream seems to have been to free his native Corsica from French rule, the Revolution and the European war that followed broadened his sights and gave him new opportunities.

Napoleon rose quickly through the ranks. In 1792, he became a captain and in the following year achieved a reputation as an astute artillery commander. In 1794, at the age of only twenty-five, he was made a brigadier general by the Committee of Public Safety. In the next year he defended the National Convention against the Parisian mob and in 1796 was placed in command of the French armies in Italy (see the box above) where he won a series of victories and dictated peace to the Austrians in 1797. He returned to France as a conquering hero and was given command of an army in training to invade England. But Napoleon believed that the French were unready for such an invasion and proposed instead to strike indirectly at Britain by taking Egypt and threatening India, a major source of British wealth. By 1799, Napoleon's army in Egypt had been cut off from supplies because of British control of the seas. Seeing no future in certain defeat, Napoleon did not hesitate to abandon his army and return to Paris where he participated in the coup d'etat that ultimately led to his virtual dictatorship of France. He was only thirty years old at the time.

What kind of man was Napoleon? Usually labeled a genius, he was a person of many talents. Highly temperamental, he was either talkative or silent depending on his mood. A product of the Enlightenment and French Revolution, he believed himself free from conventional ideas and moral scruples. He had an exaggerated faith in his own destiny that grew more pronounced and more mystical as the years passed by (see the box on p. 695). He was a man of remarkable intellectual ability and impressed those he came into contact with as well as himself. Aware of his own special gifts, he was often contemptuous of his fellow human beings. With his ability to comprehend complex problems quickly and make rapid decisions, Napoleon inspired confidence in others.

The Man of Destiny
▼ ▼ ▼

N apoleon possessed an overwhelming sense of his own importance. Among the images he fostered, especially as his successes multiplied and his megalomaniacal tendencies intensified, were those of the man of destiny and the great man who masters luck.

Selections from Napoleon

When a deplorable weakness and ceaseless vacillations become manifest in supreme councils; when, yielding in turn to the influences of opposing parties, making shift from day to day, and marching with uncertain pace, a government has proved the full measure of its impotence; when even the most moderate citizens are forced to admit that the State is no longer governed; when, in fine, the administration adds to its nullity at home the gravest guilt it can acquire in the eyes of a proud nation—I mean its humiliation abroad—then a vague unrest spreads through the social body, the instinct of self-preservation is stirred, and the nation casts a sweeping eye over itself, as if to seek a man who can save it.

This guardian angel a great nation harbors in its bosom at all times; yet sometimes he is late in making his appearance. Indeed, it is not enough for him to exist: he also must be known. He must know himself. Until then, all endeavors are in vain, all schemes collapse. The inertia of the masses protects the nominal government, and despite its ineptitude and weakness the efforts of its enemies fail. But let that impatiently awaited savior give a sudden sign of his existence, and the people's instinct will divine him and call upon him. The obstacles are smoothed before his steps, and a whole great nation, flying to see him pass, will seem to be saying: "Here is the man!"

A consecutive series of great actions never is the result of chance and luck; it always is the product of planning and genius. Great men are rarely known to fail in their most perilous enterprises. . . . Is it because they are lucky that they become great? No, but being great, they have been able to master luck.

Although a consummate opportunist, he was, or at least seemed to be, what many French people were seeking after a decade of unrest.

With the coup d'etat of 1799, a new form of the republic was proclaimed with a constitution that established a bicameral legislative assembly elected indirectly to reduce the role of elections. Executive power in the new government was vested in the hands of three consuls although as Article 42 of the constitution said, "The decision of the First Consul shall suffice." As first consul, Napoleon directly controlled the entire executive authority of government. He had overwhelming influence over the legislature, appointed members of the bureaucracy, controlled the army, and conducted foreign affairs. In 1802, Napoleon was made consul for life and in 1804 returned France to monarchy when he had himself crowned as Emperor Napoleon I. This step undoubtedly satisfied his enormous ego but also stabilized the regime and provided a permanency not possible in the consulate. The revolutionary era that had begun with an attempt to limit arbitrary government had ended with a government far more autocratic than the monarchy of

the old regime. As his reign progressed and the demands of war increased, Napoleon's regime became ever more dictatorial.

Domestic Policies

Napoleon often claimed that he had preserved the gains of the Revolution for the French people. The ideal of republican liberty had, of course, been destroyed by Napoleon's thinly disguised autocracy. But were revolutionary ideals maintained in other ways? An examination of his domestic policies will enable us to judge the truth or falsehood of Napoleon's assertion.

In 1801, Napoleon established peace with the oldest and most implacable enemy of the Revolution, the Catholic church. Napoleon himself was devoid of any personal faith; he was an eighteenth-century rationalist who regarded religion at most as a convenience. In Egypt, he called himself a Muslim; in France, a Catholic. But Napoleon saw the necessity to come to terms with the Catholic church in order to stabilize his regime. In 1800, Napoleon had declared to the clergy of Milan:

"It is my firm intention that the Christian, Catholic, and Roman religion shall be preserved in its entirety, . . . No society can exist without morality; there is no good morality without religion. It is religion alone, therefore, that gives to the State a firm and durable support."[21] Soon after making this statement, Napoleon opened negotiations with Pope Pius VII to reestablish the Catholic church in France.

Both sides gained from the Concordat that Napoleon arranged with the pope in 1801. Although the pope gained the right to depose French bishops, this gave him little real control over the French Catholic church since the state was left with the right to nominate bishops. The Catholic church was also permitted to hold processions again and reopen the seminaries. But Napoleon gained more than the pope. Just by signing the Concordat, the pope acknowledged the accomplishments of the Revolution. Moreover, the pope agreed not to raise the question of the church lands confiscated in the Revolution. Contrary to the pope's wishes, Catholicism was not reestablished as the state religion; Napoleon was only willing to recognize Catholicism as the religion of a majority of the French people. The clergy would be paid by the state, but to avoid the appearance of a state church, Protestant ministers were also put on the state payroll. As a result of the Concordat, the Catholic church was no longer an enemy of the French government. At the same time the agreement reassured those who had acquired church lands during the Revolution that they would not be stripped of them, an assurance that obviously made them supporters of the Napoleonic regime.

Before the Revolution, France did not have a single set of laws, but rather virtually 300 different legal systems. During the Revolution, efforts were made to prepare a codification of laws for the entire nation, but it remained for Napoleon to bring the work to completion in the famous Civil Code. This preserved most of the revolutionary gains by recognizing the principle of the equality of all citizens before the law, the right of the individual to choose his profession, religious toleration, and the abolition of serfdom and feudalism. Property rights continued to be carefully protected while the interests of employers were safeguarded by outlawing trade unions and strikes. The Civil Code clearly reflected the revolutionary aspirations for a uniform legal system, legal equality, and protection of property and individuals.

Napoleon also worked on rationalizing the bureaucratic structure of France by developing a powerful, centralized administrative machine. During the Revolution, the National Assembly had divided France into eighty-three departments and replaced the provincial estates, nobles, and intendants with self-governing assemblies. Napoleon kept the departments but eliminated the locally elected assemblies and instituted new officials, the most important of which were the prefects. As the central government's agents, appointed by the first consul (Napoleon), the prefects were responsible for supervising all aspects of local government. Yet they were not

▼ **Napoleon Creates a New Nobility.** One of Napoleon's domestic policies involved the creation of a new nobility. The new aristocracy was based on merit and talent. The highest officials in the military and civil government were given titles. Service to the state was the primary criterion for the granting of a title. Only twenty-two percent of the nobility of the old regime became part of Napoleon's new aristocracy.

local men and their careers depended on the central government. This centralization of power in the central government represented a radical break with revolutionary practices.

As part of Napoleon's overhaul of the administrative system, tax collection became systematic and efficient (which it had never been under the old regime). Taxes were now collected by professional collectors employed by the state who dealt directly with each individual taxpayer. No tax exemptions due to birth, status, or special arrangement were granted. In principle these changes had been introduced in 1789, but not until Napoleon did they actually work. In 1802, the first consul proclaimed a balanced budget.

Administrative centralization required a bureaucracy of capable officials, and Napoleon worked hard to develop one. Early on, the regime showed its preference for experts and cared little whether that expertise had been acquired in royal or revolutionary bureaucracies. Promotion, whether in civil or military offices, was to be based not on rank or birth but only on demonstrated abilities. This was, of course, what many bourgeoisie had wanted before the Revolution. Napoleon, however, also created a new aristocracy based on merit in the state service. Napoleon created 3,263 nobles between 1808 and 1814; nearly 60 percent were military officers while the remainder came from the upper ranks of the civil service and other state and local officials. Socially, only 22 percent of Napoleon's aristocracy came from the nobility of the old regime; almost 60 percent were bourgeois in origin.

In his domestic policies, then, Napoleon both destroyed and preserved aspects of the Revolution. Liberty had been replaced by an initially benevolent despotism that grew increasingly arbitrary as the demands of war overwhelmed Napoleon and the French. While equality was preserved in the law code and the opening of careers to talent, the creation of a new aristocracy, the strong protection accorded to property rights, and the practices associated with conscription make it clear that a loss of equality accompanied the loss of liberty.

Napoleon's Empire and the European Response

When Napoleon became consul in 1799, France was at war with a second European coalition of Russia, Great Britain, and Austria. Napoleon realized the need for a pause. He remarked to a Prussian diplomat "that the French Revolution is not finished so long as the scourge of war lasts . . . I want peace, as much to settle the present French government, as to save the world from

chaos."[22] The peace he sought was achieved at Amiens in March 1802 and left France with new frontiers and a number of client territories from the North Sea to the Adriatic. But the peace did not last, and war was renewed in 1803 with Britain, who was soon joined by Austria, Russia, and Prussia in the Third Coalition. In a series of battles at Ulm, Austerlitz, Jena, and Eylau from 1805 to 1807, Napoleon's Grand Army defeated the continental members of the coalition, giving Napoleon the opportunity to create a new European order. The Grand Empire was composed of three major parts: the French empire, a series of dependent states, and allied states. The French empire, the inner core of the Grand Empire, consisted of an enlarged France extending to the Rhine in the east and including the western half of Italy north of Rome. Dependent states were kingdoms under the rule of Napoleon's relatives; these came to include Spain, Holland, the kingdom of Italy, the Swiss Republic, the Grand Duchy of Warsaw, and the Confederation of the Rhine, the latter a union of all German states except Austria and Prussia. Allied states were those defeated by Napoleon and forced to join his struggle against Britain and included Prussia, Austria, Russia, and Sweden. Although the internal structure of the Grand Empire varied outside its inner core, Napoleon considered himself leader of the whole: "Europe cannot be at rest except under a single head who will have kings for his officers, who will distribute his kingdom to his lieutenants."

Within his empire, Napoleon demanded obedience, in part because he needed a common front against the British and in part because his growing egotism required obedience to his will. But as a child of the Enlightenment and Revolution, Napoleon also sought acceptance everywhere of certain revolutionary principles, including legal equality, religious toleration, and economic freedom. As he explained to his brother Jerome after he had made him king of the new German state of Westphalia:

What the peoples of Germany desire most impatiently is that talented commoners should have the same right to your esteem and to public employments as the nobles, that any trace of serfdom and of an intermediate hierarchy between the sovereign and the lowest class of the people should be completely abolished. The benefits of the Code Napoléon, the publicity of judicial procedure, the creation of juries must be so many distinguishing marks of your monarchy. . . . What nation would wish to return under the arbitrary Prussian government once it had tasted the benefits of a wise and liberal administration? The peoples of Germany, the peoples of France, of Italy, of Spain all desire equality and liberal ideas. I have guided the affairs of Europe for many years now, and I have had occasion to convince myself that the buzzing of the privileged classes is contrary to the general opinion. Be a constitutional king.[23]

In the inner core and dependent states of his Grand Empire, Napoleon tried to destroy the old order. Nobility and clergy everywhere in these states lost their special privileges. He decreed equality of opportunity with offices open to talent, equality before the law, and religious toleration. This spread of French revolutionary principles was an important factor in the development of liberal traditions in these countries. The nature of these reforms have led some historians to view Napoleon as the last of the enlightened absolutists.

Like Hitler two hundred years later, Napoleon hoped that his Grand Empire would last for centuries; like Hitler's empire, it collapsed almost as rapidly as it had been formed. Two major reasons help to explain this, the survival of Great Britain and the force of nationalism. Britain's survival was primarily due to its seapower. As long as Britain ruled the waves, it was almost invulnerable to military attack. Although Napoleon contemplated an invasion of England and even collected ships for it, he could not overcome the British navy's decisive defeat of a combined French-Spanish fleet at Trafalgar in 1805. Napoleon then turned to his Continental System to defeat Britain. Put into effect between 1806 and 1808, it attempted to prevent British goods from reaching the European continent in order to weaken Britain

▼ **Map 20.4** Napoleon's Empire.

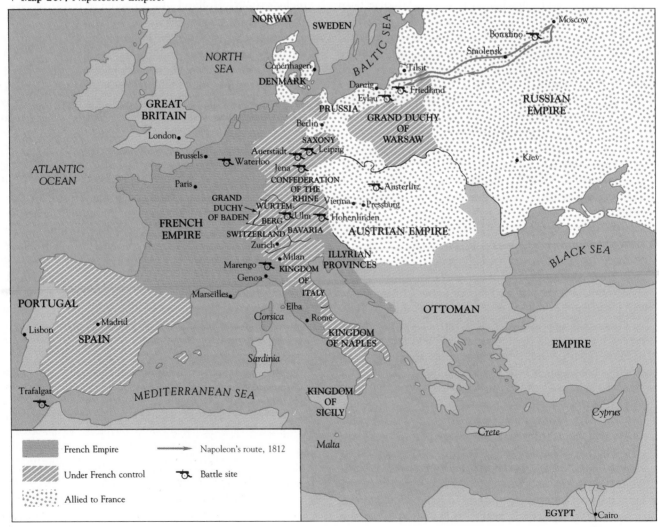

Napoleon as First Consul	1799–1804
Concordat with Catholic Church	1801
Peace of Amiens	1802
Emperor Napoleon I	1804–1815
Battles of Austerlitz; Trafalgar; Ulm	1805
Battle of Jena	1806
Continental System Established	1806
Battle of Eylau	1807
Invasion of Russia	1812
War of Liberation	1813–1814
Exile to Elba	1814
Battle of Waterloo; Exile to Saint Helena	1815
Death of Napoleon	1821

economically and destroy its capacity to wage war. But the Continental System failed. Allied states resented the ever-tightening French economic hegemony; some began to cheat and others to resist, thereby opening the door to British collaboration. New markets in the Levant and in Latin America also provided compensation for the British. Indeed, by 1809–1810 British overseas exports were at near-record highs.

A second important factor in the defeat of Napoleon was nationalism. This political creed had arisen during the French Revolution in the French people's emphasis on brotherhood (*fraternité*) and solidarity against other peoples. Nationalism involved the unique cultural identity of a people based on common language, religion, and national symbols. The spirit of French nationalism had made possible the mass armies of the revolutionary and Napoleonic eras. But Napoleon's spread of the principles of the French Revolution beyond France inadvertently brought a spread of nationalism as well. The French aroused nationalism in two ways: by making themselves hated oppressors and thus arousing the patriotism of others in opposition to French nationalism, and by showing the people of Europe what nationalism was and what a nation in arms could do. It was a lesson not lost on other peoples and rulers. A Spanish uprising against Napoleon's rule, aided by British support, kept a French force of 200,000 pinned down for years.

The beginning of Napoleon's downfall came in 1812 with his invasion of Russia. The latter's defection from the Continental System left Napoleon with little choice. Although aware of the risks in invading such a large country, he also knew that if the Russians were allowed to challenge the Continental System unopposed, others would soon follow suit. Only 30,000 out of his original invading army of 600,000 managed to arrive back in Poland in January 1813. This military disaster then led to a war of liberation all over Europe, culminating in Napoleon's defeat in April 1814. He was allowed to play ruler on the island of Elba, off the coast of Tuscany, while the Bourbon monarchy was restored in the person of Louis XVIII, brother of the executed king. But Napoleon's escape from Elba and return to Paris gave him one last period of rule from March to June 1815. At the Battle of Waterloo, Napoleon's One Hundred Days ended in bloody defeat. Exiled to the forsaken rock of Saint Helena, only his memory would continue to haunt French political life.

The revolutionary era of the late eighteenth century witnessed a dramatic political transformation. Revolutionary upheavals, beginning in North America and continuing in France, produced movements for political liberty and equality. The documents created by these revolutions, the Declaration of Independence and the Declaration of the Rights of Man and the Citizen, embodied the fundamental ideas of the Enlightenment and created a liberal political agenda based on a belief in popular sovereignty—the people are the source of political power—and the principles of liberty and equality. Liberty, frequently limited in practice, meant, in theory, freedom from arbitrary power as well as the freedom to think, write, and worship as one chose. Equality meant equality in rights and equality of opportunity based on talent rather than birth. In practice, equality remained limited; those who owned property had greater opportunities for voting and officeholding while there was certainly no equality between men and women.

The leaders of France's liberal revolution, achieved between 1789 and 1791, were men of property, both bourgeois and noble, but they were assisted by commoners, both sansculottes and peasants. Yet the liberal revolution, despite the hopes of the men of property, was not the end of the Revolution. The decision of the revolutionaries to go to war "revolutionized the Revolution," opening the door to a more radical, democratic, and violent stage. The excesses of the Reign of Terror, however, led to a reaction, first under the Directory and then Napoleon, when men of property willingly forswore liberty to preserve property and the opening of careers to talent. Napoleon, while diminishing freedom by establishing order and centralizing the government, shrewdly preserved equality of rights and the opening of careers to talent and integrated the bourgeoisie and old nobility into a new elite of property owners. For despite the anti-aristocratic revolutionary rhetoric and the loss of their privileges, nobles remained important landowners. While the nobles lost some of their lands during the Revolution, they were still the largest proprietors in the early 1800s. The great gainers from the redistribution of clerical and noble property, however, had been the bourgeoisie, who also gained dramatically when important government and military positions were opened to men of talent. After 1800, an elite group of property owners, both noble and middle class, dominated French society.

The French Revolution created a modern revolutionary concept. No one had foreseen or consciously planned the upheaval that began in 1789, but after 1789 "revolutionaries" knew that the proper use of mass uprisings could produce the overthrow of unwanted governments. The French Revolution became the classical political and social model for revolution. At the same time, the liberal and national political ideals created by the Revolution and spread to Europe by Napoleon's conquests dominated the political landscape of the nineteenth and early twentieth centuries. Until the Communist Revolution in 1917, few would have questioned the belief that it was "the greatest revolution in the history of the world." A new European era had begun and Europe would never again be the same.

Notes

▼ ▼ ▼

1. Quoted in Edmund and Helen Morgan, *The Stamp Act Crisis* (New York, 1963), pp. 142–43.

2. Quoted in Stephan Thernstrom, *A History of the American People* (New York, 1984), 1: 152.

3. Quoted in R. R. Palmer, *The Age of the Democratic Revolutions* (Princeton, N.J., 1959), 1: 239.

4. Quoted in ibid., p. 242.

5. Quoted in O. J. Hufton, "Towards an Understanding of the Poor of Eighteenth Century France," in J. F. Bosher, ed., *French Government and Society: 1500–1850* (London, 1973), p. 152.

6. Arthur Young, *Travels in France during the Years 1787, 1788 and 1789* (Cambridge, 1929), p. 23.

7. Quoted in D. M. G. Sutherland, *France 1789–1815: Revolution and Counter-Revolution* (New York, 1986), p. 74.

8. Quoted in William Doyle, *The Oxford History of the French Revolution* (Oxford, 1989), p. 156.

9. Quoted in ibid., p. 184.

10. Quoted in J. Hardman, ed., *French Revolution Documents* (Oxford, 1973), 2: 23.

11. Quoted in W. Scott, *Terror and Repression in Revolutionary Marseilles* (London, 1973), p. 84.

12. Quoted in H. Morse Stephens, *The Principal Speeches of the Statesmen and Orators of the French Revolution* (Oxford, 1892), 2: 189.

13. Quoted in Leo Gershoy, *The Era of the French Revolution* (Princeton, N.J., 1957), p. 157.

14. Quoted in J. M. Thompson, *French Revolution Documents* (Oxford, 1933), pp. 258–59.

15. Quoted in Doyle, *The Oxford History of the French Revolution*, p. 254.

16. Quoted in R. R. Palmer, *Twelve Who Ruled* (New York, 1965), p. 75.

17. Quoted in J. M. Thompson, *Leaders of the French Revolution* (New York, 1967), pp. 157–58.

18. Quoted in François Furet and Mona Ozouf, *A Critical Dictionary of the French Revolution*, trans. Arthur Goldhammer (Cambridge, Mass., 1989), p. 545.

19. Quoted in Darline Gay Levy, Harriet Branson Applewhite, and Mary Durham Johnson, eds., *Women in Revolutionary Paris, 1789–1795* (Urbana, Ill., 1979), p. 132.

20. Ibid., pp. 219–20.

21. Quoted in Felix Markham, *Napoleon* (New York, 1963), pp. 92–93.

22. Quoted in Doyle, *The Oxford History of the French Revolution*, p. 381.

23. Quoted in J. Christopher Herold, ed., *The Mind of Napoleon* (New York, 1955), pp. 74–75.

Suggestions for Further Reading
▼ ▼ ▼

A well-written, up-to-date introduction to the French Revolution can be found in W. Doyle, *The Oxford History of the French Revolution* (Oxford, 1989). Also valuable is J. F. Bosher, *The French Revolution* (New York, 1988). For the entire revolutionary and Napoleonic eras, the best general survey is D. M. G. Sutherland, *France 1789–1815: Revolution and Counter-Revolution* (New York, 1985). Although controversial, the massive and beautifully written work by S. Schama, *Citizens* (New York, 1989), makes exciting reading. A different approach to the French Revolution can be found in E. Kennedy, *A Cultural History of the French Revolution* (New Haven, Conn., 1989). Two comprehensive reference works are S. F. Scott and B. Rothaus, eds., *Historical Dictionary of the French Revolution*, 2 vols. (Westport, Conn., 1985); and F. Furet and M. Ozouf, *A Critical Dictionary of the French Revolution*, trans. A. Goldhammer (Cambridge, Mass., 1989).

The origins of the French Revolution are examined in the classic work by G. Lefebvre, *The Coming of the French Revolution* (Princeton, N.J., 1947), although his interpretive framework has been superseded by new work. On the latter, see especially W. Doyle, *Origins of the French Revolution* (Oxford, 1988). On the early years of the Revolution, see J. Egret, *The French Pre-Revolution, 1787–88* (Chicago, 1977); M. Kennedy, *The Jacobin Clubs in the French Revolution: The First Years* (Princeton, N.J., 1982); and N. Hampson, *Prelude to Terror* (Oxford, 1988). Important works on the radical stage of the French Revolution include N. Hampson, *The Terror in the French Revolution* (London, 1981); A. Soboul, *The Sans-Culottes* (New York, 1972); R. R. Palmer, *Twelve Who Ruled* (New York, 1965); D. Jordan, *The King's Trial* (Berkeley, 1979); and R. Cobb, *The People's Armies* (London, 1987). For a biography of Robespierre, one of the leading figures of this period, see N. Hampson, *The Life and Opinions of Maximilien Robespierre* (London, 1974). The importance of the revolutionary wars in the radical stage of the Revolution is underscored in T. C. W. Blanning, *The Origins of the French Revolutionary Wars* (London, 1986). Also valuable is J. P. Bertaud, *The Army of the French Revolution: From Citizen-Soldiers to Instruments of Power* (Princeton, N.J., 1988). The importance of the popular revolutionary crowds is examined in the classic work by G. Rudé, *The Crowd in the French Revolution* (Oxford, 1959). On the Directory, see M. Lyons, *France under the Directory* (Cambridge, 1975); and R. B. Rose, *Gracchus Babeuf*

(Stanford, 1978). Interesting regional studies include W. Scott, *Terror and Repression in Revolutionary Marseilles* (London, 1973); and M. Lyons, *Revolution in Toulouse: An Essay on Provincial Terrorism* (Berne, 1978).

The religious history of the French Revolution is covered in J. McManners, *The French Revolution and the Church* (London, 1969). The relationship between religion and counterrevolution is examined in C. Tilly, *The Vendée* (Cambridge, Mass., 1964); and D. M. G. Sutherland, *The Chouans* (Oxford, 1982). On the Great Fear, there is the classic work by G. Lefebvre, *The Great Fear of 1789: Rural Panic in Revolutionary France* (London, 1973). Two recent works that take rather different approaches to the French Revolution are W. H. Sewell, *Work and Revolution in France* (Cambridge, 1980); and P. Higonnet, *Class, Ideology and the Rights of Nobles during the French Revolution* (Oxford, 1981). On the role of women in revolutionary Paris, there is much to be found in the collection of documents edited by D. G. Levy, H. B. Applewhite, and M. D. Johnson, *Women in Revolutionary Paris, 1789–1795* (Urbana, Ill., 1979).

The best, brief biography of Napoleon is F. Markham, *Napoleon* (New York, 1963). Also valuable are J. M. Thompson, *Napoleon Bonaparte* (Oxford, 1963); and P. Geyl, *Napoleon, For and Against* (New Haven, Conn., 1963), a study of biographical writings on the French leader. A good, recent treatment is L. Bergeron, *France under Napoleon* (Princeton, N.J., 1981). On Napoleon's military campaigns, see D. Chandler, *The Campaigns of Napoleon* (London, 1966).

A good, brief survey of the revolutionary era in America can be found in E. S. Morgan, *Birth of the Republic, 1763–1789*, rev. ed. (New York, 1977). The importance of ideology is treated in B. Bailyn, *The Ideological Origins of the American Revolution* (Cambridge, 1966), while G. Wood, *The Creation of the American Republic, 1776–1787* (New York, 1972) examines the transformation of both politics and ideology. A comparative study that puts the American Revolution into a larger context is R. R. Palmer, *The Age of the Democratic Revolutions: A Political History of Europe and America, 1760–1800*, 2 vols. (Princeton, N.J., 1959–64). A more recent comparative study is the stimulating work by P. Higonnet, *Sister Republics: Origins of the French and American Revolutions* (Cambridge, Mass., 1988).

Chapter 21

The Industrial Revolution and Its Impact on European Society

▼▼▼▼▼

The French Revolution dramatically and quickly altered the political structure of France while the Napoleonic conquests spread many of the revolutionary principles in an equally rapid and stunning fashion to other parts of Europe. During the late eighteenth and early nineteenth centuries, another revolution—an industrial one—was transforming the economic and social structure of Europe, although in a less dramatic and rapid fashion.

The use of machinery to produce goods, one of the characteristics of the Industrial Revolution, was not entirely new. Beginning in the Middle Ages, Europeans had developed innovative tools that harnessed the power of wind and water to manufacture articles for consumption. Wind and water power, however, were neither sufficient nor reliable enough to create a self-sustaining system of manufacturing. Most products were still made by hand. The period of the Industrial Revolution witnessed a quantum leap in industrial production. New sources of energy and power, especially coal and steam, replaced wind and water to create labor-saving machines that dramatically decreased the use of human and animal labor and, at the same time, increased the level of productivity. In turn, power machinery called for new ways of organizing human labor in order to maximize the benefits and profits from the new machines; factories replaced shop and home workrooms. During the Industrial Revolution, Europe experienced a shift from a traditional, labor-intensive economy based on agriculture and handicrafts to a more capital-intensive economy

Luddites

Factory
Act

People's
Charter

Chadwick's *Report*
on Cities

▼ ▼ ▼ ▼

•••••••• 1770 •••••••••• 1790 •••••••••• 1810 •••••••••• 1830 •••••••••• 1850 ••••••••

▲ ▲ ▲ ▲ ▲ ▲

Watt's
Steam Engine

Cartwright's
Power Loom

Stephenson's
Rocket

Coke-blast Iron
in Rhineland

Great Exhibition
in Britain

based on manufacturing by machines, specialized labor, and industrial factories.

Although it took decades for the Industrial Revolution to spread, it was truly revolutionary in the way it fundamentally changed Europeans, their society, their relationship to other peoples, and the world itself. The development of large factories encouraged mass movements of people from the countryside to urban areas where impersonal coexistence replaced the traditional intimacy of rural life. Higher levels of productivity led to a search for new sources of raw materials, new consumption patterns, and a revolution in transportation that allowed raw materials and finished products to be moved quickly around the world. The creation of a wealthy industrial middle class and a huge industrial working class (or proletariat) substantially transformed traditional social relationships. Finally, the Industrial Revolution fundamentally altered how the Western world related to nature, ultimately creating an environmental crisis that in the twentieth century has finally been recognized as a danger to human existence itself.

▼ The Industrial Revolution in Great Britain

Although a phenomenon like the Industrial Revolution evolved out of antecedents that occurred over a long period of time, historians generally agree that it had its beginnings in Britain in the 1780s. By 1850, the Industrial Revolution had made Great Britain the wealthiest country in the world; by that time it had also spread to the Continent and the New World. By the end of the nineteenth century, both Germany and the United States would surpass Britain in industrial production.

Origins

A number of factors or conditions coalesced in Britain to produce the first Industrial Revolution. One of these was the agricultural revolution of the eighteenth century. The changes in the methods of farming and stock breeding that characterized this agricultural transformation led to a significant increase in food production. British agriculture could now feed more people at lower prices with less labor. Unlike the rest of Europe, even ordinary British families did not have to use most of their income to buy food, giving them the potential to purchase manufactured goods. At the same time, a rapid growth of population in the second half of the eighteenth century provided a pool of surplus labor for the new factories of the emerging British industry. Rural workers in cottage industries also provided a potential labor force for industrial enterprises.

Britain had a ready supply of capital for investment in the new industrial machines and the factories that were needed to house them. In addition to profits from trade and cottage industry, Britain possessed an effective central bank and well-developed, flexible credit facilities. Nowhere in Europe were people so accustomed to paper instruments to facilitate capital transactions. Many early factory owners were merchants and entrepreneurs who had profited from eighteenth-century cottage industry. Of 110 cotton spinning mills created in the area known as the Midlands between 1769 and 1800, 62 were established by hosiers, drapers, mercers, and others involved in some fashion in the cottage textile industry. But capital alone is only part of the story. Britain had a fair number of individuals who were interested in making profits if the opportunity presented itself (see the box on p. 704). The British were a people, as one historian has said, "fascinated by wealth and commerce, collectively

The Traits of the British Industrial Entrepreneur
▼ ▼ ▼

Richard Arkwright (1732–1792), creator of a spinning frame and founder of cotton factories, was a good example of the successful entrepreneur in the early Industrial Revolution in Britain. In this selection, Edward Baines, who wrote The History of the Cotton Manufacture in Great Britain in 1835, discusses the traits that explain the success of Arkwright and presumably other British entrepreneurs.

Edward Baines, The History of the Cotton Manufacture in Great Britain

Richard Arkwright rose by the force of his natural talents from a very humble condition in society. He was born at Preston on the 23rd of December, 1732, of poor parents: being the youngest of thirteen children, his parents could only afford to give him an education of the humblest kind, and he was scarcely able to write. He was brought up to the trade of a barber at Kirkham and Preston, and established himself in that business at Bolton in the year 1760. Having become possessed of a chemical process for dyeing human hair, which in that day (when wigs were universal) was of considerable value, he travelled about collecting hair, and again disposing of it when dyed. In 1761, he married a wife from Leigh, and the connexions he thus formed in that town are supposed to have afterwards brought him acquainted with Highs's experiments in making spinning machines. He himself manifested a strong bent for experiments in mathematics, which he is stated to have followed with so much devotedness as to have neglected his business

and injured his circumstances. His natural disposition was ardent, enterprising, and stubbornly persevering: his mind was as coarse as it was bold and active, and his manners were rough and unpleasing. . . .

The most marked traits in the character of Arkwright were his wonderful ardour, energy, and perseverance. He commonly laboured in his multifarious concerns from five o'clock in the morning till nine at night; and when considerably more than fifty years of age,—feeling that the defects of his education placed him under great difficulty and inconvenience in conducting his correspondence, and in the general management of his business,—he encroached upon his sleep, in order to gain an hour each day to learn English grammar, and another hour to improve his writing and orthography [spelling]! He was impatient of whatever interfered with his favorite pursuits; and the fact is too strikingly characteristic not to be mentioned, that he separated from his wife not many years after their marriage, because she, convinced that he would starve his family [because of the impractical nature of his schemes], broke some of his experimental models of machinery. Arkwright was a severe economist of time; and, that he might not waste a moment, he generally travelled with four horses, and at a very rapid speed. His concerns in Derbyshire, Lancashire, and Scotland were so extensive and numerous, as to [show] at once his astonishing power of transacting business and his all-grasping spirit. In many of these he had partners, but he generally managed in such a way, that, whoever lost, he himself was a gainer.

and individually." These early industrial entrepreneurs faced considerable financial hazards, however. Fortunes were made and easily lost. The structure of early firms was open and fluid. An individual or family proprietorship was the usual mode of operation, but entrepreneurs also brought in friends to help them. They just as easily jettisoned them. John Marshall, who made money in flax spinning, threw out his partners: "As they could neither of them be of any further use, I released them from the firm and took the whole upon myself."[1]

Britain was richly supplied with important mineral resources, such as coal and iron ore, needed in the manufacturing process. Britain was also a small country, and

the relatively short distances made transportation readily accessible. In addition to nature's provision of abundant rivers, from the mid-seventeenth century onward, both private and public investment poured into the construction of new roads, bridges, and, beginning in the 1750s and 1760s, canals. By 1780, roads, rivers, and canals linked the major industrial centers of the North, the Midlands, London, and the Atlantic. Unlike the continental countries, Britain possessed no internal customs barriers to hinder domestic trade.

Britain's government also played a significant role in the process of industrialization. Parliament added to the favorable business climate by providing a stable government and passing laws that protected private property. Moreover, Britain was remarkable for the freedom it provided for private enterprise. There were fewer restrictions on private entrepreneurs than in any other European state.

Finally, a supply of markets gave British industrialists a ready outlet for their manufactured goods. British exports quadrupled from 1660 to 1760. In the course of its eighteenth-century wars and conquests, Great Britain had developed a vast colonial empire at the expense of its leading continental rivals, the Dutch Republic and France. Britain also possessed a well-developed merchant marine that was able to transport goods to any place in the world. A crucial factor in Britain's successful industrialization was the ability to produce cheaply those articles most in demand abroad. And the best markets abroad were not in Europe, where countries protected their own incipient industries, but in the Americas, Africa, and the Far East, where people wanted sturdy, inexpensive clothes rather than costly, highly finished, luxury items. Britain's machine-produced textiles fulfilled that demand. Nor should we overlook the British domestic market. Britain had the highest standard of living in Europe and a rapidly growing population. As Daniel Defoe noted already in 1728:

For the rest, we see their Houses and Lodgings tolerably furnished, at least stuff'd well with useful and necessary household Goods: Even those we call poor People, Journeymen, working and Pains-staking People do thus; they lye warm, live in Plenty, work hard, and [need] know no Want.

These are the People that carry off the Gross of your Consumption; 'tis for these your Markets are kept open late on Saturday nights; because they usually receive their Week's Wages late . . . in a Word, these are the Life of our whole Commerce, and all by their Multitude: Their Numbers are not Hundreds or Thousands, or Hundreds of Thousands, but Millions; . . . by their Wages they are able to live plentifully, and it is by their expensive, generous, free way of living, that the Home Consumption is rais'd to such a Bulk, as well of our own, as of foreign Production.[2]

It was the demand from both domestic and foreign markets and the inability of the old system to fulfill it that led entrepreneurs to seek and accept the new methods of manufacturing that a series of inventions provided. In so doing, these individuals produced the Industrial Revolution.

Technological Changes and New Forms of Industrial Organization

It was in the cotton textile industry in the 1770s and 1780s that the first major step was taken toward the Industrial Revolution with the creation of the modern factory.

THE COTTON INDUSTRY Already in the eighteenth century, Great Britain had surged ahead in the production of cheap cotton goods using the traditional methods of cottage industry. The development of the flying shuttle had sped the process of weaving on a loom and enabled weavers to double their output. This, however, created short-

▼ **A British Colliery.** While the Industrial Revolution grew out of many prior conditions, it is generally thought to have begun in Britain in the 1780s. Building upon the agricultural revolution of the eighteenth century, rich natural resources, abundant capital for investment, and a supply of markets, Britain was well prepared for industrialization. Britain also had an ample supply of coal. By the 1830s and 1840s, the development of coal mines led to a landscape of coal-mining machinery and smoke-belching chimneys in parts of Britain. Seen here is the Percy Colliery in Northumberland in 1839.

Cotton and woollen textiles
Machinery
Iron

SCOTLAND

Bradford   Leeds

Liverpool

Manchester   Sheffield

Iron
Hardware

Birmingham

Iron
Machinery
Pottery

Iron

Bristol   London

Machinery
Consumer goods

Tin and
copper mining

Cities with over 100,000 people
are labelled

Towns with over 20,000
people are shown:

Exposed coalfields

Industrial areas   ● 50,000

Principal railroads   ◒ 400,000

● 2,400,000

▼ **Map 21.1** England in the Industrial Revolution.

ages of yarn until James Hargreaves's spinning jenny, perfected by 1768, allowed spinners to produce yarn in greater quantities. Richard Arkwright's water frame spinning machine, powered by water or horse, and Samuel Crompton's so-called mule, which combined aspects of the water frame and spinning jenny, increased yarn production even more. Edmund Cartwright's power loom, invented in 1787, allowed the weaving of cloth to catch up with the spinning of yarn. Even then, early power looms were grossly inefficient, enabling cottage,

hand-loom weavers to continue to prosper, at least until the mid-1820s. After that they were gradually replaced by the new machines. In 1813, there were 2,400 power looms in operation in Great Britain, 14,150 in 1820, 100,000 in 1833, and 250,000 by 1850. In the 1820s, there were still 250,000 hand-loom weavers in Britain; by 1860, only 3,000 were left.

The water frame, Crompton's mule, and power looms presented new opportunities to entrepreneurs. It was much more efficient to bring workers to the machines and organize their labor collectively in factories located next to rivers and streams, the sources of power for many of these early machines, than to leave the workers dispersed in their cottages. The concentration of labor in the new factories also brought the laborers and their families to live in the new towns that rapidly grew up around the factories.

The early devices used to speed up the processes of spinning and weaving were the products of weavers and spinners, in effect, of craftsmen tinkerers. But the subsequent expansion of the cotton industry and the ongoing demand for even more cotton goods created additional pressure for new and more complicated technology. The invention that pushed the cotton industry to even greater heights of productivity was the steam engine.

THE STEAM ENGINE   The invention of the steam engine played a major role in the Industrial Revolution. It revolutionized the production of cotton goods and caused the factory system to spread to other areas of production, thereby creating whole new industries. The steam engine secured the triumph of the Industrial Revolution.

As in much of the Industrial Revolution, one kind of change forced other changes. In many ways the steam engine was the result of the need for more efficient pumps to eliminate water seepage from deep mines. Deep coal mines were in turn the result of Britain's need and desire to find new sources of energy to replace wood. By the early eighteenth century, the British were acutely aware of a growing shortage of timber, used in heating, building homes and ships, and in enormous quantities to produce the charcoal utilized in the smelting of iron ore to produce pig iron. The discovery at the beginning of the eighteenth century of new processes for smelting iron ore with coal and coke (see the next section) led to more intensive mining of coal by digging deeper and deeper mines. But as mines were dug below the water table, they filled with water. An early solution to the problem was the use of mechanical pumps powered by horses walking in circles. In one coal mine in Warwickshire, for example, 500 horses were used to lift the water from the mine, bucket by bucket. The need for more efficient pumps led Thomas Newcomen to develop a steam pump or, as it was called, an "atmospheric engine" that was first used in 1712. While better than horses, it still proved inefficient.

In the 1760s, a Scottish engineer, James Watt (1736–1819), was asked to repair a Newcomen engine. Instead he added a separate condenser and steam pump and transformed Newcomen's machine into a genuine steam engine. Power was derived not from air pressure as in Newcomen's atmospheric engine, but from steam itself. Much more efficient, Watt's engine could pump water three times as quickly. Initially, it possessed one major liability, however; as a contemporary noted in 1778: "the vast consumption of fuel in these engines is an immense drawback on the profit of our mines, for every fire-engine of magnitude consumes £3000 worth of coals per annum. This heavy tax amounts almost to a prohibition."[3] As steam engines were made more efficient, however, they also became cheaper to use.

In 1782, James Watt enlarged the possibilities of the steam engine when he developed a rotary engine that could turn a shaft and thus drive machinery. Steam power could now be applied to spinning and weaving cotton, and before long cotton mills using steam engines were multiplying across Britain. By 1850, seven-eighths of the power available to the cotton industry for all of Britain came from steam. Since steam engines were fired by coal, they did not need to be located near rivers; entrepreneurs now had greater flexibility in their choice of location.

The new boost given to cotton textile production by technological changes became readily apparent. In 1760, Britain had imported 2.5 million pounds of raw cotton, which was farmed out to cottage industries. All work was done by hand either in workers' homes or in the small shops of master weavers. In 1787, the British imported 22 million pounds of cotton; most of it was spun on machines, some powered by water in large mills. By 1840, 366 million tons of cotton—now Britain's most important product in value—were imported. By 1840, although there were still some hand-loom weavers, most cotton industry employees worked in factories. The price of yarn was but one-twentieth of what it had been. The cheapest labor in India could not compete in quality or quantity with Britain. British cotton goods sold everywhere in the world. And in Britain itself, cheap cotton cloth made it possible for millions of poor people to wear undergarments, long a preserve of the rich who alone could afford the underwear made with expensive linen

▼ **A Boulton and Watt Steam Engine.** The steam engine was a crucial factor in the growth and spread of the Industrial Revolution. Encouraged by his business partner, Matthew Boulton, James Watt developed the first genuine steam engine. Pictured here is a typical Boulton and Watt engine. Steam pressure in the cylinder on the left drives the beam upwards and sets the fly-wheel in motion. The steam engine was eventually applied to the spinning and weaving of cotton and allowed for greater flexibility in the location of an industry.

cloth. New work clothing that was tough, comfortable to the skin, and yet cheap and easily washable became common. Even the rich liked the colorful patterns of cotton prints and their light weight for summer use.

The steam engine proved invaluable to Britain's Industrial Revolution. In 1800, engines were generating 10,000 horsepower; by 1850, 500,000 in stationary engines and 790,000 in mobile engines, the last largely in locomotives (see A Revolution in Transportation later in the chapter). Unlike horses, the steam engine was a tireless source of power and depended for fuel on a substance—namely, coal—that seemed then to be unlimited in quantity. The popular saying that "Steam is an Englishman" had real significance by 1850. The steam engine also replaced waterpower in such places as flour and sugar mills. Just as the need for more coal had helped lead to the steam engine, so the success of the steam engine led to a need for more coal and an expansion in coal production; between 1815 and 1850, the output of coal quadrupled. In turn, new processes using coal furthered the development of an iron industry.

THE IRON INDUSTRY   The British iron industry was radically transformed during the Industrial Revolution. Britain had large resources of iron ore, but at the beginning of the eighteenth century, the basic process of producing iron had altered little since the Middle Ages and still depended heavily on charcoal. In the early eighteenth century, new methods of smelting iron ore to produce cast iron were devised based on the use of coke derived from coal. A better quality of iron was still not possible, however, until the 1780s when Henry Cort developed a system called puddling, in which coke was used to burn away impurities in pig iron and produce an iron of high quality. A boom then ensued in the British iron industry. In 1740, Britain produced 17,000 tons of iron; in the 1780s, almost 70,000 tons; by the 1840s, over 2 million tons; and by 1852, almost 3 million tons, more than the rest of the world combined.

The development of the iron industry was in many ways a response to the demands for the new machines. The high-quality wrought iron produced by the Cort process made it the most widely used metal until the production of cheaper steel in the 1860s. The growing supply of less costly metal encouraged the growth of machinery in other industries, most noticeably in new means of transportation.

A REVOLUTION IN TRANSPORTATION The eighteenth century had witnessed an expansion of transportation facilities in Britain as entrepreneurs realized the need for more efficient means of moving resources and goods. Turnpike trusts provided new roads, and between 1760 and 1830 a network of canals was built. Both roads and canals were soon overtaken by a new form of transportation that dazzled people by its promises. To many economic historians, railroads were the "most important single factor in promoting European economic progress in the 1830s and 1840s." Again, Britain was the leader in the revolution.

The beginnings of railways can be found in mining operations in Germany as early as 1500 and in British coal mines after 1600 where small handcarts filled with coal were pushed along parallel wooden rails. The rails reduced friction, enabling horses to haul more substantial loads. By 1700, some entrepreneurs began to replace wooden rails with cast-iron rails, and by the early nineteenth century, railways—still dependent on horsepower—were common in British mining and industrial districts. The development of the steam engine brought a radical transformation to railways.

In 1804, Richard Trevithick pioneered the first steam-powered locomotive on an industrial rail-line in south Wales. It pulled ten tons of ore and seventy people at five miles per hour. Better locomotives soon followed.

Those engines built by George Stephenson and his son proved superior, and it was in their workshops in Newcastle upon Tyne that the locomotives for the first modern railways in Britain were built. George Stephenson's *Rocket* was used on the first public railway line, which opened in 1830, extending thirty-two miles from Liverpool to Manchester. *Rocket* sped along at sixteen miles per hour. Within twenty years, locomotives had reached fifty miles per hour, an incredible speed to contemporary passengers. During the same period, new companies were formed to build additional railroads as the infant industry proved to be not only technically but financially successful. In 1840, Britain had almost 2,000 miles of railroads; by 1850, 6,000 miles of railroad track crisscrossed much of the country.

The railroad was an important contribution to the success and maturing of the Industrial Revolution. The demands of railroads for coal and iron furthered the growth of those industries. British supremacy in civil and mechanical engineering, so evident after 1840, was in large part based upon the skills acquired in railway building. The huge capital demands necessary for railway construction encouraged a whole new group of middle-class investors to plough their money into joint-stock companies (see Limitations to Industrialization later in the chapter). Railway construction created new job opportunities, especially for farm laborers and peasants who had long been accustomed to finding work outside their local villages. Perhaps most importantly, a cheaper and faster means of transportation had a rippling effect on the growth of an industrial economy. By reducing the price of goods, larger markets were created; increased sales meant more factories and more machinery, thereby reinforcing the self-sustaining aspect of the Industrial Revolution that marked a fundamental break with the traditional European economy. The great productivity of the Industrial Revolution enabled entrepreneurs to reinvest their profits in new capital equipment, further expanding the productive capacity of the economy. Continuous, even rapid, self-sustaining economic growth came to be seen as a fundamental characteristic of the new industrial economy.

The railroad was the perfect symbol of this aspect of the Industrial Revolution. The ability to transport goods and people at dramatic speeds also provided visible confirmation of a new sense of power. When railway engineers pierced mountains with tunnels and spanned chasms with breathtaking bridges, contemporaries experienced a sense of power over nature not felt before in Western civilization.

THE INDUSTRIAL FACTORY   Initially the product of the new cotton industry, the factory became the chief means of organizing labor for the new machines. As the workplace shifted from the artisan's shop and the peasant's cottage to the factory, the latter was not viewed as just a larger work unit. Employers hired workers who no longer owned the means of production but simply provided the hands to run the machines. Wages formed the basis of their economic relationship, but discipline formed the foundation of their functional relationship.

From its beginning, the factory system demanded a new type of discipline from its employees. For factory owners, the purchase of machinery necessitated its constant use. Workers were forced to work regular hours and in shifts to keep the machines producing at a steady pace for maximum output. This represented a massive adjustment for early factory laborers.

Pre-industrial labor was not accustomed to a "timed" format. Agricultural labor had always functioned on the basis of irregular hours; hectic work at harvest time might be followed by periods of inactivity. Even in the burgeoning cottage industry of the eighteenth century, weavers and spinners who worked at home might fulfill their weekly quotas by working around the clock for two or three days, followed by a leisurely pace until the next week's demands forced another work spurt.

Factory owners, therefore, faced a formidable task. They had to create a system of work discipline in which employees became accustomed to working regular, unvarying hours during which they performed a set number of tasks over and over again as efficiently as possible. One early industrialist said that his aim was "to make such machines of the men as cannot err." Such work, of course, tended to be repetitive and boring, and factory owners resorted to tough methods to accomplish their goals. Factory regulations were minute and detailed (see the box on p. 710). Adult workers were fined for a wide variety of minor infractions, such as being a few minutes late for work, and dismissed for more serious misdoings, especially drunkenness. The latter was viewed as particularly offensive because it set a bad example for younger workers and also courted disaster in the midst of dangerous machinery. Employers found that dismissals and fines worked well for adult employees; in a time when great population growth had produced large masses of unskilled labor, dismissal meant disaster. Children were less likely to understand the implications of dismissal so they were sometimes disciplined more directly—by beating.

The efforts of factory owners in the early Industrial Revolution to impose a new set of values were frequently reinforced by the new evangelical churches. Methodism, in particular, emphasized that people reborn in Christ

▼ **Inside an Early Cotton Factory.**
The development of the factory changed the relationship between workers and employers. Workers were encouraged to adjust to a new system of discipline that forced them to work regular hours and in shifts. Since the early factory workers were not used to such a system, owners often resorted to tough methods to achieve the required discipline. This engraving depicts the inside of an early textile factory.

Discipline in the New Factories
▼ ▼ ▼

*W*orkers in the new factories of the Industrial Revolution had been accustomed to a lifestyle free of overseers. Unlike the cottages, where workers spun thread and wove cloth in their own rhythm and time, the factories demanded a new, rigorous discipline geared to the requirements of the machines. This selection is taken from a set of rules for a factory in Berlin in 1844. They were typical of company rules everywhere the factory system had been established.

The Foundry and Engineering Works of the Royal Overseas Trading Company, Factory Rules

In every large works, and in the co-ordination of any large number of workmen, good order and harmony must be looked upon as the fundamentals of success, and therefore the following rules shall be strictly observed.

1. The normal working day begins at all seasons at 6 A.M. precisely and ends, after the usual break of half an hour for breakfast, an hour for dinner and half an hour for tea, at 7 P.M., and it shall be strictly observed. . . .
Workers arriving 2 minutes late shall lose half an hour's wages; whoever is more than 2 minutes late may not start work until after the next break, or at least shall lose his wages until then. Any disputes about the correct time shall be settled by the clock mounted above the gatekeeper's lodge. . . .

3. No workman, whether employed by time or piece, may leave before the end of the working day, without having first received permission from the overseer and having given his name to the gatekeeper. Omission of these two actions shall lead to a fine of ten silver groschen [pennies] payable to the sick fund.

4. Repeated irregular arrival at work shall lead to dismissal. This shall also apply to those who are found idling by an official or overseer, and refused to obey their order to resume work. . . .

6. No worker may leave his place of work otherwise than for reasons connected with his work.

7. All conversation with fellow-workers is prohibited; if any worker requires information about his work, he must turn to the overseer, or to the particular fellow-worker designated for the purpose.

8. Smoking in the workshops or in the yard is prohibited during working hours; anyone caught smoking shall be fined five silver groschen for the sick fund for every such offence. . . .

10. Natural functions must be performed at the appropriate places, and whoever is found soiling walls, fences, squares, etc., and similarly, whoever is found washing his face and hands in the workshop and not in the places assigned for the purpose, shall be fined five silver groschen for the sick fund. . . .

12. It goes without saying that all overseers and officials of the firm shall be obeyed without question, and shall be treated with due deference. Disobedience will be punished by dismissal.

13. Immediate dismissal shall also be the fate of anyone found drunk in any of the workshops. . . .

14. Every workman is obliged to report to his superiors any acts of dishonesty or embezzlement on the part of his fellow workmen. If he omits to do so, and it is shown after subsequent discovery of a misdemeanour that he knew about it at the time, he shall be liable to be taken to court as an accessory after the fact and the wage due to him shall be retained as punishment.

must forgo immoderation and follow a disciplined path. Laziness and wasteful habits were sinful. The acceptance of hardship in this life paved the way for the joys of the next. Evangelical values paralleled the efforts of the new factory owners to instill their own middle-class values of hard work, discipline, and thrift upon laborers. In one crucial sense the early industrialists proved successful. As the nineteenth century progressed, the second and third generations of workers came to view a regular working week as a natural way of life. It was, of course, an attitude that made possible Britain's incredible economic growth in that century.

The Great Exhibition: Britain in 1851

In 1851, the British organized the world's first industrial fair. It was housed at Kensington in London in the Crystal Palace, an enormous structure made entirely of glass and iron, a tribute to British engineering skills. Covering nineteen acres, the Crystal Palace contained 100,000 exhibits that showed the wide variety of products created by the Industrial Revolution. Six million people visited the fair in six months. While most of them were Britons, who had traveled to London by train, foreign visitors were also prominent. The Great Exhibition displayed Britain's wealth to the world; it was a gigantic symbol of British success. Even trees were brought inside the Crystal Palace as a visible symbol of how the Industrial Revolution had achieved human domination over nature. Prince Albert, Queen Victoria's husband, expressed the sentiments of the age when he described the exhibition as a sign that "man is approaching a more complete fulfilment of that great and sacred mission which he has to perform in this world . . . to conquer nature to his use." Not content with that, however, he also connected British success to divine will: "In promoting [the progress of the human race], we are accomplishing the will of the great and blessed God."[4]

By the year of the Great Exhibition, Great Britain had become the world's first and richest industrial nation. Britain was the "workshop, banker, and trader of the world." It produced one-half of the world's coal and manufactured goods; its cotton industry alone in 1851 was equal in size to the industries of all other European countries combined. The quantity of goods produced was growing at three times the rate it had achieved in 1780. No doubt, Britain's certainty about its mission in the world in the nineteenth century was grounded in its incredible material success story.

▼ The Spread of Industrialization

Beginning first in Great Britain, industrialization spread to the continental countries of Europe and the United States at different times and speeds during the nineteenth century. First to be industrialized on the Continent were Belgium, France, and the German states and in North America, the new nation of the United States. Not until after 1850 did the Industrial Revolution spread to the rest of Europe and other parts of the world.

Limitations to Industrialization

In 1815, Belgium, France, and the German states were still largely agrarian. During the eighteenth century, some of the continental countries had experienced developments similar to that of Britain. They, too, had population growth, made agricultural improvements, expanded their cottage industries, and witnessed growth in

▼ **Opening of the Great Exhibition.** The British organized the world's first industrial fair in 1851. Over 100,000 exhibits were housed within the Crystal Palace, an enormous structure made of glass and iron and covering nineteen acres. The Great Exhibition was a symbol of the success of Great Britain, which had become the world's first and richest industrial nation. Seen here is Queen Victoria at the opening of the Exhibition, surrounded by visitors from all over the world.

foreign trade. But while Britain's economy began to move into new industrial directions in the 1770s and 1780s, continental countries lagged behind because they did not share some of the advantages that had made Britain's Industrial Revolution possible. Lack of good roads and problems with river transit made transportation difficult. Toll stations on important rivers and customs barriers along state boundaries increased the costs and prices of goods. Guild restrictions were also more prevalent, creating restrictions that pioneer industrialists in Britain did not have to face. Finally, adherence to traditional patterns of business life, such as a dislike of competition, a high regard for family security coupled with an unwillingness to take risks in investment, and an excessive worship of thriftiness, left continental entrepreneurs with less enterprising attitudes.

One additional factor also affected most of the Continent between 1790 and 1812: the upheavals associated with the wars of the French revolutionary and Napoleonic eras. Disruption of regular communications between Britain and the Continent made it difficult for continental countries to keep up with the new British technology. Moreover, the wars wreaked havoc with trade, caused much physical destruction and loss of manpower, weakened currencies, and created political and social instability. Napoleon's Continental System helped to ruin a number of hitherto prosperous ports. The elimination of European markets for British textiles did bring a revival to the woolen industry in France and Belgium and stimulated textile manufacturing along the Rhine and in Silesia. After 1815, however, when cheap British goods again flooded European markets, the European textile industry suffered.

In the long run, the revolutionary and Napoleonic wars created an additional hurdle to rapid industrialization by widening the gap between British and continental industrial machinery. By 1815, after Napoleon had finally been defeated and normal communication between Britain and the Continent had been restored, British industrial equipment had grown larger and become more expensive. As a result, self-financed family enterprises were either unable or unwilling to raise the

▼ **Map 21.2** The Industrialization of Continental Europe by 1850.

amount of capital necessary to modernize by investing in the latest equipment. Instead, most entrepreneurs in France, Belgium, and Germany initially chose to invest in used machines and less productive mills. Consequently, industrialization on the Continent faced numerous hurdles, and as it proceeded in earnest after 1815, it did so along lines that were somewhat different from Britain's.

Lack of technical knowledge was a first major obstacle to industrialization. But the continental countries possessed an advantage here; they could simply borrow British techniques and practices. Of course, the British tried to prevent that. Until 1825, British artisans were prohibited from leaving the country; until 1842, the export of important machinery and machine parts, especially for textile production, was forbidden. Nevertheless, the British were not able to control this situation by legislation. Already by 1825, there were at least 2,000 skilled British mechanics on the Continent, and British equipment, whether legally or illegally, was also being sold abroad.

Although many Britons who went abroad to sell their skills were simply skilled mechanics, a number of them were accomplished entrepreneurs who had managerial as well as technical skills. John Cockerill, for example, was an aggressive businessman who established a highly profitable industrial plant at Seraing near Liège in southern Belgium in 1817. Encouraged by the Belgian government, Cockerill thought nothing of pirating the innovations of other British industrialists to further his own factories. Aware of their importance, British technicians abroad were often contentious and arrogant, arousing the anger of continental industrialists. Fritz Harkort, who initiated the engineering industry in Germany, exclaimed once that he could scarcely wait for Germans to be trained "so that the Englishmen could all be whipped out: we must even now tread softly with them, for they're only too quick to speak of quitting if one does so little as not look at them in a friendly fashion."[5]

Gradually, the Continent achieved technological independence as local people learned all the skills they could from their British teachers. By the 1840s, a new generation of skilled mechanics from Belgium and France was spreading their knowledge east and south, playing the same role that the British had earlier. More importantly, however, continental countries, especially France and the German states, began to establish a wide range of technical schools to train engineers and mechanics.

That government played an important role in this regard brings us to a second difference between British and continental industrialization. Governments on much of the Continent were accustomed to play a significant role in economic affairs. Furthering the development of industrialization was a logical extension of that attitude. Hence governments provided for the costs of technical education; awarded grants to inventors and foreign entrepreneurs; exempted foreign industrial equipment from import duties; and, in some places, even financed factories. Of equal, if not greater importance in the long run, governments actively bore much of the cost of building roads and canals, deepening and widening river channels, and constructing railroads. By 1850, a network of iron rails had spread across Europe, although only Germany and Belgium had completed major parts of their systems by that time. Although the real impact of the railroad on European markets was not felt until after 1850, railroad construction itself in the 1830s and 1840s gave great impetus to the metalworking and engineering industries. In fact, by the 1840s, railroad construction had become the "most important single stimulus to industrial growth in western Europe."

Governments on the Continent also worked to further industrialization by tariff protection. After 1815, cheap British goods flooded continental markets. The French responded with high tariffs to protect their fledgling industries. The most systematic exposition for the use of tariffs, however, was made by a German writer, Friedrich List, who emigrated to America and returned to Germany as a United States consul. In his *National System of Political Economy*, written in 1844, List advocated a rapid and large-scale program of industrialization as the surest path to develop a nation's strength. To assure that path to industrialization, he felt that a nation must use protective tariffs. If countries followed the British policy of free trade, then cheaper British goods would inundate national markets and destroy infant industries before they had a chance to grow. Germany, he insisted, could not compete with Britain without protective tariffs.

A third significant difference between British and continental industrialization was the role of the joint-stock investment bank on the Continent. This development mobilized the savings of thousands of small and large investors, creating a supply of capital that could then be ploughed back into industry. Continental banks had been mostly merchant or private banks, but in the 1830s two Belgian banks, the Société Générale and the Banque de Belgique, took a new path. By accepting savings from many depositors, they developed large capital resources that they invested on a large scale in railroads, mining, and heavy industry. These investments were especially important to the Belgian coal industry, which became the largest on the Continent in the 1840s. Shareholders in these joint-stock corporations had limited liability; they could only be held responsible for the amount of their investment.

These new practices emerged in France and German-speaking lands as well in the 1850s with the establishment of the Crédit Mobilier in France, the Darmstadt Bank in Germany, and the Kreditanstalt in Austria. They, too, took in savings of small investors and bought shares in the new industries. The French consul in Leipzig noted their significance: "every town and state [in Germany]," he pointed out, "however small it may be, wants its bank and its Crédit Mobilier." These investments proved invaluable to continental industrialization. By starting with less expensive machines, the British had been able to industrialize largely through the private capital of successful individuals who reinvested their profits. On the Continent advanced industrial machines necessitated large amounts of capital; joint-stock industrial banks provided it.

Centers of Continental Industrialization

The Industrial Revolution on the Continent occurred in three major centers between 1815 and 1850—Belgium, France, and the German states. Here, too, cotton played an important role, although it was not as significant as heavy industry. France was the continental leader in the manufacture of cotton goods but still lagged far behind Great Britain. In 1849, France used 64,000 tons of raw cotton, Belgium, 11,000, and Germany, 20,000, while Britain utilized 286,000 tons. Continental cotton factories were older, used less efficient machines, and had less productive labor. In general, continental technology in the cotton industry was a generation behind Great Britain. But that is not the whole story. With its cheap coal and scarce water, Belgium gravitated toward the use of the steam engine as the major source of power and invested in the new machines. By the mid-1840s, Belgium had the most modern cotton-manufacturing system on the Continent.

Two significant differences characterize the development of cotton manufacturing on the Continent and in Britain. Unlike Britain, where cotton manufacturing was mostly centered in Lancashire and the Glasgow area, cotton mills in France, Germany, and to a lesser degree, Belgium, were dispersed in many regions. Noticeable, too, was the mixture of old and new. The old techniques of the cottage system, such as the use of hand looms, held on much longer. In the French district of

Normandy, for example, in 1849 eighty-three mills were still driven by hand or animal power.

The use of traditional methods alongside the new methods in cotton manufacturing left the continental countries making use of the new steam engine primarily in mining and metallurgy rather than in textile manufacturing. At first, almost all of the steam engines on the Continent came from Britain; not until the 1820s was a domestic machine industry developed.

In Britain, the Industrial Revolution had been built upon the cotton industry; on the Continent, it was the iron and coal of heavy industry that led the way. As in textiles, however, heavy industry on the Continent before 1850 was a mixture of old and new. New techniques, such as coke-smelted iron and puddling furnaces, were combined with the expansion of old-type charcoal blast furnaces. Before 1850, Germany lagged significantly behind both Belgium and France in heavy industry, and most German iron manufacturing remained based on old techniques. Not until the 1840s was coke-blast iron produced in the Rhineland. At that time, no one had yet realized the treasure of coal buried in the Ruhr valley. A German official wrote in 1852, "It is clearly not to be expected that Germany will ever be able to reach the level of production of coal and iron currently attained in England. This is implicit in our far more limited resource endowment." Little did he realize that although continental Europe was about a generation behind Britain in industrial development at mid-century, after 1850 an incredibly rapid growth in continental industry would demonstrate that Britain was not, after all, destined to remain the world's greatest industrial nation.

The Industrial Revolution in the United States

In 1800, society in the United States was agrarian. There were no cities over 100,000, and six out of every seven American workers were farmers. By 1860, however, the population had grown from 5 to 30 million people, larger than Great Britain. Almost half of them lived west of the Appalachian Mountains. There were now thirty-four instead of sixteen states, and nine American cities had over 100,000 in population. Only 50 percent of American workers were farmers. From 1800 to the eve of the Civil War, the United States had experienced an industrial revolution and the urbanization that accompanied it.

The initial application of machinery to production was accomplished—as in continental Europe—by borrowing from Great Britain. A British immigrant, Samuel

Slater, established the first textile factory using water-powered spinning machines in Rhode Island in 1790. By 1813, factories with power looms copied from British versions were being established. Soon thereafter, however, Americans began to equal or surpass British technical inventions. The Harpers Ferry arsenal, for example, built muskets with interchangeable parts. Because all the individual parts of a musket were identical (e.g., all triggers were the same), the final product could be put together quickly and easily; this enabled Americans to avoid the more costly system in which skilled craftsmen fitted together individual parts made separately. The so-called American system reduced costs and revolutionized production by saving labor, important to a society that had few skilled artisans.

Unlike Britain, the United States was a large country. The lack of a good system of internal transportation seemed to limit American economic development by making the transport of goods prohibitively expensive. This was gradually remedied, however. Thousands of miles of roads and canals were built linking east and west. The steamboat facilitated transportation on the Great Lakes, Atlantic coastal waters, and rivers. It was especially important to the Mississippi valley; by 1860, a thousand steamboats plied that river (see the box on p. 716). Most important of all in the development of an American transportation system was the railroad. Beginning with 100 miles in 1830, by 1860 there were over 27,000 miles of railroad track covering the United States. This transportation revolution turned the United States into a single massive market for the manufactured goods of the Northeast, the early center of American industrialization.

Labor for the growing number of factories in this area came primarily from rural New England. The United States did not possess a large number of craftsmen, but it did have a rapidly expanding farm population; its size in the Northeast soon outstripped the available farmland. While some of this excess population, especially men, went West, others, mostly women, found work in the new textile and shoe factories of New England. Indeed, women made up more than 80 percent of the laboring force in the large textile factories. In Massachusetts mill towns, company boarding houses provided rooms for large numbers of young women who worked for several years before marriage. Outside Massachusetts, factory owners sought entire families including children to work in their mills; one mill owner ran this advertisement in a newspaper in Utica, New York: "Wanted: A few sober and industrious families of at least five children each, over the age of eight years, are wanted at the Cotton Factory in Whitestown. Widows with large families would do well to attend this notice." When a decline in rural births threatened to dry up this labor pool in the 1830s and 1840s, European immigrants, especially poor and unskilled Irish, English, Scottish, and Welsh, appeared in large numbers to replace American women and children in the factories.

Women, children, and these immigrants had one thing in common as employees; they were largely unskilled laborers. Unskilled labor pushed American industrialization into a capital-intensive pattern. Factory

▼ **Samuel Slater's Cotton Mill.** While beginning the nineteenth century as an agrarian society, the United States quickly entered the industrial era. Samuel Slater, whose cotton mill at Pawtucket, Rhode Island is pictured here, was the first American to apply machinery to production. Initially, Americans copied from the British, but they soon began to equal or surpass British technical innovations. By the last third of the nineteenth century, American industrial production outstripped that of all Europe.

"S–t–e–a–m–boat a–coming'!"

▼ ▼ ▼

Steamboats and railroads were crucial elements in a transportation revolution that enabled industrialists to expand markets by shipping goods cheaply and efficiently. At the same time, these marvels of technology aroused a sense of power and excitement that was an important aspect of the triumph of industrialization. The American novelist Mark Twain captured this sense of excitement in this selection from Life on the Mississippi.

Mark Twain, *Life on the Mississippi*

After all these years I can picture that old time to myself now, just as it was then: the white town drowsing in the sunshine of a summer's morning; the streets empty, or pretty nearly so; one or two clerks sitting in front of the Water street stores, with their splint-bottomed chairs tilted back against the walls, chins on breasts, hats slouched over their faces, asleep; . . . two or three lonely little freight piles scattered about the "levee"; a pile of "skids" on the slope of the stone-paved wharf, and the fragrant town drunkard asleep in the shadow of them; . . . the great Mississippi, the majestic, the magnificent Mississippi, rolling its mile-wide along, shining in the sun; the dense forest away on the other side; the "point" above the town, and the "point" below, bounding the river-glimpse and turning it into a sort of sea, and withal a very still and brilliant and lonely one. Presently a film of dark smoke appears above on those remote "points"; instantly a negro drayman, famous for his quick eye and prodigious voice, lifts up to cry, "S–t–e–a–m–boat a–coming'!" and the scene changes! The town drunkard stirs, the clerks wake up, a furious clatter of drays follows, every house and store pours out a human contribution, and all in a twinkling the dead town [Hannibal, Missouri] is alive and moving.

Drays, carts, men, boys, all go hurrying from many quarters to a common center, the wharf. Assembled there, the people fasten their eyes upon the coming boat as upon a wonder they are seeing for the first time. And the boat is rather a handsome sight, too. She is long and sharp and trim and pretty; she has two tall, fancy-topped chimneys, with a gilded device of some kind swung between them; a fanciful pilot-house, all glass and "gin-ger bread," perched on top of the "texas" deck behind them; the paddle-boxes are gorgeous with a picture or with gilded rays above the boat's name; the boiler deck, the hurricane deck, and the texas deck are fenced and ornamented with clean white railings; there is a flag gallantly flying from the jack-staff; the furnace doors are open and the fires glaring bravely; the upper decks are black with passengers; the captain stands by the big bell, calm, imposing, the envy of all; great volumes of the blackest smoke are rolling and tumbling out of the chimneys—a husbanded grandeur created with a bit of pitch pine just before arriving at a town; the crew are grouped on the forecastle; the broad stage is run far out over the port bow, and an envied deck-hand stands picturesquely on the end of it with a coil of rope in his hand; the pent steam is screaming through the gauge-cocks; the captain lifts his hand, a bell rings, the wheels stop; then they turn back, churning the water to foam, and the steam is at rest. Then such a scramble as there is to get aboard, and to get ashore, and to take in freight and to discharge freight, all at one and the same time; and such a yelling and cursing as the mates facilitate it all with! Ten minutes later the steamer is under way again, with no flag on the jack-staff and no black smoke issuing from the chimneys. After ten more minutes the town is dead again, and the town drunkard asleep by the skids once more.

owners invested heavily in machines that could produce in quantity at the hands of untrained workers. In Britain, the pace of mechanization was never as rapid because Britain's supply of skilled craftsmen made it more profitable to pursue a labor-intensive economy.

By 1860, the United States was well on its way to being an industrial nation. In the Northeast, the most industrialized section of the country, per capita income was 40 percent higher than the national average. Diets, it has been argued, were better and more varied; machine-made clothing was more abundant. Nevertheless, despite a growing belief in a myth of social mobility based upon equality of economic opportunity, the reality was that the richest 10 percent of the population in the cities held 70 to 80 percent of the wealth compared to 50 percent in 1800. Nevertheless, American historians generally argue that while the rich got richer, the poor, as a result of experiencing an increase in their purchasing power, did not get poorer.

▼ The Social Impact of the Industrial Revolution

Eventually, the Industrial Revolution revolutionized the social life of Europe and the world. Although much of Europe remained bound by its traditional ways, already in the first half of the nineteenth century, the social impact of the Industrial Revolution was being felt and future avenues of growth were becoming apparent. Vast changes in the number of people and where they lived were already dramatically evident.

Population Growth

Population increases had already begun in the eighteenth century, but they became dramatic in the nineteenth century. They were also easier to discern because record keeping became more accurate. Governments in the nineteenth century began to take periodic censuses and systematically collect precise data on births, deaths, and marriages. In Britain, for example, the first census was taken in 1801, and a systematic registration of births, deaths, and marriages was begun in 1836. In 1750, the total European population stood at an estimated 140 million; by 1800, it had increased to 187 million, and by 1850 the population had almost doubled since 1750 to 266 million.

This population explosion cannot be explained by a higher birthrate for birthrates were declining after 1790. Between 1790 and 1850, Germany's birthrate dropped from 40 per thousand to 36.1; Great Britain's from 35.4 to 32.6, and France's from 32.5 to 26.7. The key to the expansion of population was the decline in death rates evident throughout Europe. Historians believe now that two major causes explain this decline. There was a drop in the number of deaths from famines, epidemics, and war. Major epidemic diseases, in particular, such as plague and smallpox declined noticeably, although small-scale epidemics continued. There was also a decline in the ordinary death rate as a general increase in the food supply, already evident in the agricultural revolution of Britain in the late eighteenth century, spread to more areas. More food enabled a greater number of people to be better fed and therefore more resistant to

disease. Famine largely disappeared from western Europe, although there were dramatic exceptions in isolated areas, Ireland being the most significant.

In those areas where industrialization proceeded in the nineteenth century, a change occurred in the composition of the population. By 1850, the proportion of the active population involved in manufacturing, mining, or building had risen to 48 percent in Britain, 37 percent in Belgium, and 27 percent in France. But the actual areas of industrialization in 1850 were minimal, concentrated in northern and central England, northern France, Belgium, and sections of western and eastern Germany. As one author has commented, "they were islands in an agricultural sea."

This minimal industrialization, in light of the growing population, meant severe congestion in the countryside where a growing population divided the same amount of land into ever-smaller plots and also created an ever-larger mass of landless peasants. Overpopulation, especially noticeable in parts of France, northern Spain, southern Germany, Sweden, and Ireland, magnified the already existing problem of rural poverty. In Ireland, it produced the century's greatest catastrophe.

Ireland was one of the most backward and oppressed areas in western Europe. The mostly Catholic peasant population rented land from mostly absentee British Protestant landlords whose primary concern was collecting their rents. Irish peasants lived in mud hovels in desperate poverty. The cultivation of the potato, a nutritious and relatively easy food to grow that produced three times as much food per acre as grain, gave Irish peasants a basic staple that enabled them to survive and even expand in numbers. As only an acre or two of potatoes was sufficient to feed a family, Irish men and women married earlier than elsewhere and started having children earlier as well. This led to significant growth in the population. Between 1781 and 1845, the Irish population doubled from 4 to 8 million. Probably half of this population depended on the potato for survival. In the summer of 1845, the potato crop in Ireland was struck by blight due to a fungus that turned the potato black. Between 1845 and 1851, the Great Famine decimated the Irish population (see the box on p. 718). Over 1 million died of starvation and disease while almost 2 million emigrated to the United States and Britain. Of all the European nations, only Ireland had a declining population in the nineteenth century. But other countries, too, faced problems of dire poverty and declining standards of living as populations exploded. Some historians, in fact, have argued that without industrialization and the improvements it brought in the

The Great Irish Famine
▼ ▼ ▼

*T*he Great Irish Famine was one of the nineteenth century's worst natural catastrophes. Overly dependent on a single crop, the Irish were decimated by the potato blight. In this selection, an Irish nationalist reported what he had witnessed in Galway in 1847.

John Mitchel, *The Last Conquest of Ireland*

In the depth of winter we travelled to Galway, through the very centre of that fertile island, and saw sights that will never wholly leave the eyes that beheld them—cowering wretches, almost naked in the savage weather, prowling in turnip-fields, and endeavouring to grub up roots which had been left, but running to hide as the mail-coach rolled by;—very large fields where small farms had been "consolidated," showing dark bars of fresh mould running through them where the ditches had been levelled;—groups and families, sitting or wandering on the high-road, with failing steps and dim patient eyes, gazing hopelessly into infinite darkness; before them, around them, above them, nothing but darkness and despair;—parties of tall brawny men, once the flower of Meath and Galway, stalking by with a fierce but vacant scowl; as if they knew that all this ought not to be, but knew not whom to blame, saw none whom they could rend in their wrath; . . . . Around those farmhouses which were still inhabited were to be seen hardly any stacks of grain; the poor-rate collector, the rent agent, the county-cess collector had carried it off; and sometimes I could see in front of the cottages little children leaning against a fence when the sun shone out—for they could not stand—their limbs fleshless, their bodies half naked, their faces bloated yet wrinkled, and of a pale greenish hue,—children who would never, it was too plain, grow up to be men and women.

standard of living other countries might have faced "Irish disasters."

The flight of so many Irish to America reminds us that the traditional safety valve for overpopulation has always been emigration. Between 1821 and 1850, the number of emigrants from Europe averaged about 110,000 a year. Most of these emigrants came from places like Ireland and southern Germany, where peasant life had been reduced to marginal existence. Times of agrarian crisis resulted in great waves of emigration. Bad harvests in Europe in 1846–1847 (such as the catastrophe in Ireland) produced massive numbers of emigrants. In addition to the estimated 1,600,000 from Ireland, for example, 935,000 people left Germany between 1847 and 1854. More often than emigration, however, the rural masses sought a solution to their poverty by moving to towns and cities within their own countries to find work. It should not astonish us then that the first half of the nineteenth century was a period of rapid urbanization.

Urbanization

Although it was not until the twentieth century that the Western world became a predominantly urban society, cities and towns had already grown dramatically in the first half of the nineteenth century, a phenomenon related to industrialization. Cities had traditionally been centers for princely courts, government and military offices, churches, and commerce. By 1850, especially in Great Britain and Belgium, they were rapidly becoming places for manufacturing and industry. With the steam engine, entrepreneurs could locate their manufacturing plants in urban centers where they had ready access to transportation facilities and unemployed people from the country looking for work.

In 1800, Great Britain had one major city, London, with a population of 1 million, and six cities between 50,000 and 100,000. Fifty years later, London's population had swelled to 2,363,000 while there were nine cities over 100,000 and eighteen cities with populations between 50,000 and 100,000. All together, these twenty-eight cities accounted for 5.7 million or one-fifth of the total British population. When the populations of cities under 50,000 are added to this total, we realize that over 50 percent of the British population lived in towns and cities by 1850. Britain was forced to become a food importer rather than exporter as the number of people involved in agriculture declined to 20 percent of the population.

Urban populations also grew on the Continent, but less dramatically. Paris had 547,000 inhabitants in 1800, but there were only two other French cities with

100,000: Lyons and Marseilles. In 1851, Paris had grown to 1 million while Lyons and Marseilles were still under 200,000. German and Austrian lands had only three cities with over 100,000 inhabitants (Vienna had 247,000) in 1800; fifty years later, there were only five while Vienna had grown to 440,000. As these figures show, urbanization did not proceed as rapidly here as in Britain; of course, neither had industrialization. Even in Belgium, the most heavily industrialized country on the Continent, almost 50 percent of the male work force was still engaged in agriculture by mid-century.

URBAN LIVING CONDITIONS IN THE EARLY INDUSTRIAL REVOLUTION   The dramatic growth of cities in the first half of the nineteenth century produced miserable living conditions for many of the inhabitants. Of course, this had been true for centuries in European cities, but the rapid urbanization associated with the Industrial Revolution intensified the problems in the first half of the nineteenth century and made these appalling living conditions all the more apparent. City authorities of whatever kind either felt little responsibility for these conditions or more frequently did not have the skills to cope with the complex, new problems produced by such rapidly growing populations. City authorities might also often be factory owners who possessed little or no tradition of public service or public responsibility.

Wealthy, middle-class inhabitants, as usual, insulated themselves as best they could, often living in suburbs or the outer ring of the city where they could have individual houses and gardens. In the inner ring of the city stood the small row houses, some with gardens, of the artisans and lower middle class. Finally, located in the center of most industrial towns were the row houses of the industrial workers. This report on working-class housing in the British city of Birmingham in 1843 gives an idea of the general conditions they faced:

> The courts [of working-class row houses] are extremely numerous; . . . a very large portion of the poorer classes of the inhabitants reside in them. . . . The courts vary in the number of the houses which they contain, from four to twenty, and most of these houses are three stories high, and built, as it is termed, back to back. There is a wash-house, an ash-pit, and a privy at the end, or on one side of the court, and not unfrequently one or more pigsties and heaps of manure. Generally speaking, the privies in the old courts are in a most filthy condition. Many which we have inspected were in a state which renders it impossible for us to conceive how they could be used; they were without doors and overflowing with filth.

The people who lived in such houses were actually the fortunate; the truly unfortunate were those forced to live in cellars. As one reformer asked, "how can a hole underground of from 12 to 15 feet square admit of ventilation so as to fit it for a human habitation?" Rooms were not large and were frequently overcrowded, as this government report of 1838 revealed: "I entered several of the tenements. In one of them, on the ground floor, I found six persons occupying a very small room, two in

▼ **The City of Sheffield.** Cities and towns grew dramatically in the first half of the nineteenth century, largely as a result of industrialization. Cities in Britain expanded substantially. London's population exceeded 2 million by 1850. Countries on the Continent, however, which lagged behind Britain in industrial development, experienced less rapid urban growth. The dominant presence of factories in some British cities in the nineteenth century is evident in this view of Sheffield in 1858.

bed, ill with fever. In the room above this were two more persons in one bed ill with fever." Another report said: "There were 63 families where there were at least five persons to one bed; and there were some in which even six were packed in one bed, lying at the top and bottom—children and adults."[6]

Sanitary conditions in these towns were appalling. Due to the lack of municipal direction, sewers and open drains were common on city streets: "In the centre of this street is a gutter, into which potato parings, the refuse of animal and vegetable matters of all kinds, the dirty water from the washing of clothes and of the houses, are all poured, and there they stagnate and putrefy."[7] Unable to deal with human excrement, cities in the new industrial era smelled horrible and were extraordinarily unhealthy. Towns and cities were fundamentally death traps. As deaths outnumbered births in most large cities in the first half of the nineteenth century, only a constant influx of people from the country kept them alive and growing.

Added to the deterioration of urban life was the adulteration of food. Consumers were defrauded in appalling ways: alum was added to make bread look white and hence more expensive; beer and milk were watered down; and red lead despite its poisonous qualities was substituted for pepper. The government refused to intervene; a parliamentary committee stated that "more benefit is likely to result from the effects of a free competi-tion . . . than can be expected to result from any regulations." It was not until 1875 that an effective Food and Drugs Act was passed in Britain.

Our knowledge of the pathetic conditions in the early industrial cities is largely derived from an abundance of social investigations. Such investigations began in France in the 1820s. In Britain the Poor Law Commissioners produced detailed reports, which culminated in the publication in 1842 of Edwin Chadwick's *Report on the Sanitary Conditions of the Labouring Population*. Chadwick and other reformers were often struck by the physically and morally debilitating effects of urban industrial life on the poor. They observed, for example, that young working-class men were considerably shorter and scrawnier than the sons of middle-class families and much more subject to disease. They were especially alarmed by what they considered the moral consequences of such living conditions: prostitution, crime, and sexual immoralities, all of which they saw as the effect of such squalid lives.

To many of the well-to-do middle classes, this situation presented a clear danger to society. Were not these masses of workers, sunk in crime, disease, and immorality, a potential threat to their own well-being? Might not the masses be organized and used by unscrupulous demagogues to overthrow the established order? One of the most eloquent British reformers of the 1830s and 1840s, James Kay-Shuttleworth, described them as "volcanic

▼ **Slums of Industrial London.**
Industrialization and rapid urban growth produced dreadful living conditions in many nineteenth-century cities. The unskilled laborers suffered most in the area of housing, with five or six people often crowded into one small room. Filled with garbage and human waste, cities often smelled terrible and were extremely unhealthy. This drawing by Gutave Doré shows a London slum district overshadowed by rail viaducts.

elements, by whose explosive violence the structure of society may be destroyed." Another observer spoke more contemptuously in 1850:

> They live precisely like brutes, to gratify . . . the appetites of their uncultivated bodies, and then die, to go they have never thought, cared, or wondered whither. . . . Brought up in the darkness of barbarism, they have no idea that it is possible for them to attain any higher condition; they are not even sentient enough to desire to change their situation. . . . they eat, drink, breed, work and die; and . . . the richer and more intelligent classes are obliged to guard them with police.[8]

Some observers were less arrogant, however, and wondered if the workers could be held responsible for their fate.

One of the best of a new breed of urban reformers was Edwin Chadwick (1800–1890). With a background in law, Chadwick became obsessed with eliminating the poverty and squalor of the metropolitan areas. He became a civil servant and was soon appointed to a number of government investigatory commissions. As secretary of the Poor Law Commission, he initiated a passionate search for detailed facts about the living conditions of the working classes. After three years of investigation, Chadwick summarized the results in his *Report on the Condition of the Labouring Population of Great Britain*. In it he concluded that "the various forms of epidemic, endemic, and other disease" were directly caused by the "atmospheric impurities produced by decomposing animal and vegetable substances, by damp and filth, and close overcrowded dwellings [prevailing] amongst the population in every part of the kingdom." Such conditions, he argued, could be eliminated. As to the means: "The primary and most important measures, and at the same time the most practicable, and within the recognized province of public administration, are drainage, the removal of all refuse of habitations, streets, and roads, and the improvement of the supplies of water."[9] In other words, Chadwick was advocating a system of modern sanitary reforms consisting of efficient sewers and a supply of piped water. Six years after his report and largely due to his efforts, Britain's first Public Health Act created a National Board of Health empowered to form local boards that would establish modern sanitary systems.

New Social Classes: The Industrial Middle Class

The rise of industrial capitalism produced a new middle-class group. The bourgeois or middle class was not new; it had existed since the emergence of cities in the Middle Ages. Originally, the bourgeois was the burgher or town dweller, whether active as a merchant, official, artisan, lawyer, or man of letters, who enjoyed a special set of rights from the charter of his town. As wealthy townspeople bought land, the original meaning of the word *bourgeois* became lost, and the term came to include people involved in commerce, industry, and banking as well as professionals, such as lawyers, teachers, physicians, and government officials at varying levels. At the lower end of the economic scale were master craftsmen and shopkeepers.

Lest we make the industrial middle class too much of an abstraction, we need to look at who the new industrial entrepreneurs actually were. These were the people who constructed the factories, purchased the machines, and figured out where the markets were. Their qualities included resourcefulness, single-mindedness, resolution, initiative, vision, ambition, and often, of course, greed. As Jedediah Strutt, the cotton manufacturer said, "Getting of money . . . is the main business of the life of men."

But this was not an easy task. The early industrial entrepreneurs were called upon to superintend an enormous array of functions that are handled today by teams of managers; they raised capital, determined markets, set company objectives, organized the factory and its labor, and trained supervisors who could act for them. The opportunities for making money were great, but the risks were also tremendous. The cotton trade, for example, which was so important to the early Industrial Revolution, was intensely competitive. A feeling of security came only from constant expansion, requiring that early entrepreneurs reinvest most of their initial profits. Fear of bankruptcy was constant, especially among small firms. Furthermore, most early industrial enterprises were small. Even by the 1840s, in Britain only 10 percent of industrial firms employed more than 5,000 workers. Forty-three percent had fewer than 100 workers. As entrepreneurs went bankrupt, new people could enter the race for profits, especially since the initial outlay was not gigantic. In 1816, only one mill in five in the important industrial city of Manchester was in the hands of its original owners.

The social origins of industrial entrepreneurs were incredibly diverse. Many of the most successful came from a mercantile background. Three London merchants, for example, founded a successful ironworks in Wales that owned eight steam engines and employed 5,000 men. In Britain, land and domestic industry were often interdependent. Joshua Fielden, for example, earned enough from running a family sheep farm while working looms in the farmhouse to acquire sufficient capital to establish a factory. Intelligent, clever, and ambitious apprentices who had learned their trades well could also strike it rich. William Radcliffe's family engaged in agriculture and spinning and weaving at home; he learned quickly how to succeed:

> Availing myself of the improvements that came out while I was in my teens . . . with my little savings and a practical knowledge of every process from the cotton bag to the piece of cloth . . . I was ready to commence business for myself and by the year 1789 I was well established and employed many hands both in spinning and weaving as a master manufacturer.[10]

By 1801, Radcliffe was operating a factory employing 1,000 workers.

Members of dissenting religious minorities were often prominent among the early industrial leaders of Britain. The Darbys and Lloyds who were iron manufacturers, the Barclays and Lloyds who were bankers, and the Trumans and Perkins who were brewers were all Quakers. These were expensive trades and depended upon the financial support that co-religionists in religious minorities provided for each other. Most historians believe that a major reason for the prominence of these religious minorities was that they lacked other opportunities. Legally excluded from many public offices, they directed their ambitions into the new industrial capitalism.

It is interesting to note that in Britain in particular aristocrats also became entrepreneurs. The Lambtons in Northumberland, the Curwens in Cumberland, the Norfolks in Yorkshire, and the Dudleys in Staffordshire all invested in mining enterprises. This close relationship between land and industry helped Britain to assume the leadership role in the early Industrial Revolution.

By 1850, in Britain at least, the kind of traditional entrepreneurship that had created the Industrial Revolution was declining and being replaced by a new business aristocracy. This new generation of entrepreneurs stemmed from the professional and industrial middle classes, especially as sons inherited the successful businesses established by their fathers. It must not be forgotten, however, that even after 1850 a large number of small businesses existed in Britain and some were still created by people from humble backgrounds. Indeed, it was not until the 1890s that the age of large-scale corporate capitalism began (see Chapter 24).

Increasingly, the new industrial entrepreneurs—the bankers and owners of factories and mines—came to amass much wealth and play an important role alongside the traditional landed elites of their societies. The Industrial Revolution began at a time when the pre-industrial agrarian world was still largely dominated by landed elites. As the new bourgeoisie bought great estates and acquired social respectability, they also sought political power, and in the course of the nineteenth century, their wealthiest members would merge with those old elites.

New Social Classes: The Industrial Workers

The industrial middle class sought to reduce the barriers between themselves and the landed elite, but it is clear that they tried at the same time to separate themselves from the laboring classes below them. The working class was actually a mixture of different groups in the first half of the nineteenth century. In the course of the nineteenth century, factory workers would form an industrial proletariat, but in the first half of that century, they by no means constituted a majority of the working class in any major city, even in Britain. According to the 1851 census in Britain, while there were 1.8 million agricultural laborers and 1 million domestic servants, there were only 811,000 workers in the cotton and woolen industries. Even one-third of these were still working in small workshops or in their own homes.

Within the cities, artisans or craftsmen remained the largest group of urban workers during the first half of the nineteenth century. They worked in numerous small industries, such as shoemaking, glovemaking, bookbinding, printing, and bricklaying. Some craftsmen formed a kind of aristocracy of labor, especially those employed in such luxury trades as coachbuilding and clockmaking who earned higher wages than others. Artisans were not factory workers; they were traditionally organized in guilds where they passed on their skills to apprentices. But guilds increasingly lost their power, especially in industrialized countries. Fearful of losing out to the new factories that manufactured goods more cheaply, artisans tended to support movements against industrialization. Industrialists welcomed the decline of skilled craftsmen, as one perceptive old tailor realized in telling his life story:

> It is upwards of 30 years since I first went to work at the tailoring trade in London. . . . I continued working for the honourable trade and belonging to the Society [for tailors] for about 15 years. My weekly earnings then averaged £1 16s. a week while I was at work, and for several years I was seldom out of work . . . no one could have been happier than I was. . . . But then, with my sight defective . . . I could get no employment at the honourable trade, and that was the ruin of me entirely; for working there, of course, I got "scratched"

from the trade society, and so lost all hope of being provided for by them in my helplessness. The workshop . . . was about seven feet square, and so low, that as you [sat] on the floor you could touch the ceiling with the tip of your finger. In this place seven of us worked. [The master] paid little more than half the regular wages, and employed such men as myself— only those who couldn't get anything better to do. . . . I don't think my wages there averaged above 12s a week. . . . I am convinced I lost my eyesight by working in that cheap shop. . . . It is by the ruin of such men as me that these masters are enabled to undersell the better shops. . . . That's the way, sir, the cheap clothes is produced, by making blind beggars of the workmen, like myself, and throwing us on the parish in our old age.[11]

Servants also formed another large group of urban workers, especially in major cities like London and Paris. Many were women from the countryside who became utterly dependent upon their upper- and middle-class employers.

WORKING CONDITIONS FOR THE INDUSTRIAL WORKING CLASS Industrial workers were not the largest working-class group in the first half of the nineteenth century, but they soon would be, and it is appropriate to look at the working conditions they faced. The pathetic living conditions of the industrial working classes were matched by equally wretched working conditions. We have already observed the psychological traumas workers experienced from their employers' efforts to break old pre-industrial work patterns and create a well-disciplined labor force. But what were the physical conditions of the factories?

There is no question that in the early decades of the Industrial Revolution "places of work," as early factories were called, were dreadful. Work hours ranged from twelve to sixteen hours a day, six days a week, with a half hour for lunch and dinner. There was no security of employment and no minimum wage. The worst conditions were in the cotton mills where temperatures were especially debilitating. One report noted that "in the cotton-spinning work, these creatures are kept, fourteen hours in each day, locked up, summer and winter, in a heat of from eighty to eighty-four degrees." Mills were also dirty, dusty, and unhealthy:

Not only is there not a breath of sweet air in these truly infernal scenes, but . . . there is the abominable and pernicious stink of the gas to assist in the murderous effects of the heat. In addition to the noxious effluvia of the gas, mixed with the steam, there are the dust, and what is called cotton-flyings or fuz, which the unfortunate creatures have to inhale; and . . . the notorious fact is that well constitutioned men are rendered old and past labour at forty years of age, and that children are rendered decrepit and deformed, and thousands upon thousands of them slaughtered by consumptions, before they arrive at the age of sixteen.[12]

Thus ran a report on working conditions in the cotton industry in 1824.

Conditions in the coal mines were also harsh. The introduction of steam power into the coal mines meant only that steam-powered engines mechanically lifted coal to the top. Inside the mines, men still bore the burden of digging the coal out while horses, mules, women, and children hauled coal carts on rails to the lift. Dangerous conditions abounded in coal mines; cave-ins, explosions, and gas fumes (called "bad air") were a way of life. The cramped conditions in mines with tunnels not exceeding three or four feet in height, and their constant dampness resulted in deformed bodies and ruined lungs.

Both children and women were employed in large numbers in early factories and mines. Children had been an important part of the family economy in pre-

▼ Women in the Mines. Both women and children were often employed in the early factories and mines of the nineteenth century. However, even though women worked in industry, traditional female working patterns were not greatly altered. Many women continued to work as domestic servants and in agriculture, while the majority of married women continued to work inside their homes.

Child Labor: Discipline in the Textile Mills
▼ ▼ ▼

Child labor was certainly not new, but in the early Industrial Revolution it was exploited more systematically. These selections are taken from the Report of Sadler's Committee, which was commissioned in 1832 to inquire into the condition of child factory workers.

How They Kept the Children Awake

It is a very frequent thing at Mr. Marshall's [at Shrewsbury] where the least children were employed (for there were plenty working at six years of age), for Mr. Horseman to start the mill earlier in the morning than he formerly did; and provided a child should be drowsy, the overlooker walks round the room with a stick in his hand, and he touches that child on the shoulder, and says, "Come here." In a corner of the room there is an iron cistern; it is filled with water; he takes this boy, and takes him up by the legs, and dips him over head in the cistern, and sends him to work for the remainder of the day. . . .

What means were taken to keep the children to their work?—Sometimes they would tap them over the head, or nip them over the nose, or give them a pinch of snuff, or throw water in their faces, or pull them off where they were, and job them about to keep them waking.

The Sadistic Overlooker

Samuel Downe, age 29, factory worker living near Leeds; at the age of about ten began work at Mr. Marshall's mill at Shrewsbury, where the customary hours when work was brisk were generally 5 A.M. to 8 P.M., sometimes from 5:30 A.M. to 8 or 9:

What means were taken to keep the children awake and vigilant, especially at the termination of such a day's labour as you have described?—There was generally a blow or a box, or a tap with a strap, or sometimes the hand.

Have you yourself been strapped?—Yes, most severely, till I could not bear to sit upon a chair without having pillows, and through that I left. I was strapped both on my own legs, and then I was put upon a man's back, and then strapped and buckled with two straps to an iron pillar, and flogged, and all by one overlooker; after that he took a piece of tow, and twisted it in the shape of a cord, and put it in my mouth, and tied it behind my head.

He gagged you?—Yes; and then he ordered me to run round a part of the machinery where he was overlooker, and he stood at one end, and every time I came there he struck me with a stick, which I believe was an ash plant, and which he generally carried in his hand, and sometimes he hit me, and sometimes he did not; and one of the men in the room came and begged me off, and that he let me go, and not beat me any more, and consequently he did.

You have been beaten with extraordinary severity?—Yes, I was beaten so that I had not power to cry at all, or hardly speak at one time. What age were you at that time?—Between 10 and 11.

industrial times, working in the fields or carding and spinning wool at home with the growth of cottage industry. In the Industrial Revolution, however, child labor was exploited more than ever and in a considerably more systematic fashion (see the boxes on pp. 724–725). The owners of cotton factories appreciated certain features of child labor. Children had a particular delicate touch as spinners of cotton. Their smaller size made it easier for them to move under machines to gather loose cotton. Moreover, children were more easily broken to factory work. Above all, children represented a cheap supply of labor. In 1821, 49 percent of the British people were under twenty years of age. Hence children made up a particularly abundant supply of labor, and they were paid only about one-sixth or one-third of what a man was paid. In the cotton factories in 1838, children under eighteen made up 29 percent of the total work force; children as young as seven worked twelve to fifteen hours per day six days a week in cotton mills.

Especially terrible in the early Industrial Revolution was the use of so-called pauper apprentices. These were orphans or children abandoned by their parents who had wound up in the care of local parishes. To save on their upkeep, parish officials found it convenient to apprentice them to factory owners looking for a cheap source of labor. These children worked for long hours, were strictly disciplined, received inadequate food and recreation, and in large numbers frequently became deformed

Child Labor: The Mines
▼ ▼ ▼

After examining conditions in British coal mines, a government official commented that "the hardest labour in the worst room in the worst-conducted factory is less hard, less cruel, and less demoralizing than the labour in the best of coal-mines." Yet it was not until 1842 that legislation was passed eliminating the labor of boys under ten from the mines. This selection is taken from a government report on the mines in Lancashire.

The Black Holes of Worsley

Examination of Thomas Gibson and George Bryan, witnesses from the coal mines at Worsley:

Have you worked from a boy in a coal mine?— (Both) Yes.

What had you to do then?—Thrutching the basket and drawing. It is done by little boys; one draws the basket and the other pushes it behind. Is that hard labour?—Yes, very hard labour.

For how many hours a day did you work?—Nearly nine hours regularly; sometimes twelve; I have worked about thirteen. We used to go in at six in the morning, and took a bit of bread and cheese in our pocket, and stopped two or three minutes; and some days nothing at all to eat.

How was it that sometimes you had nothing to eat?—We were over-burdened. I had only a mother, and she had nothing to give me. I was sometimes half starved. . . .

Do they work in the same way now exactly?—Yes, they do; they have nothing more than a bit of bread and cheese in their pocket, and sometimes can't eat it all, owing to the dust and damp and badness of air; and sometimes it is as hot as an oven; sometimes I have seen it so hot as to melt a candle.

What are the usual wages of a boy of eight?—They used to get 3d or 4d a day. Now a man's wages is divided into eight eighths; and when a boy is eight years old he gets one of those eighths; at eleven, two eighths; at thirteen, three eighths; at fifteen, four eighths; at twenty, man's wages.

What are the wages of a man?—About 15s if he is in full employment, but often not more than 10s, and out of that he has to get his tools and candles. He consumes about four candles in nine hours' work, in some places six; 6d per pound, and twenty-four candles to the pound.

Were you ever beaten as a child?—Yes, many a score of times; both kicks and thumps.

Are many girls employed in the pits?—Yes, a vast of those. They do the same kind of work as the boys till they get above 14 years of age, when they get the wages of half a man, and never get more, and continue at the same work for many years.

Did they ever fight together?—Yes, many days together. Both boys and girls; sometimes they are very loving with one another.

---

from being kept too long in unusual positions. Although economic liberals and some industrialists were against all state intervention in economic matters, Parliament eventually remedied some of the worst ills of child abuse in factories and mines (see Efforts at Change: Reformers and Government later in the chapter). The legislation of the 1830s and 1840s, however, primarily affected child labor in textile factories and mines. It did not touch the use of children in small workshops or the nonfactory trades that were not protected. As these trades were in competition with the new factories, conditions there were often even worse. Pottery works, for example, were not investigated until the 1860s when it was found that 17 percent of the workers were under eleven years of age. One investigator reported what he found:

> The boys were kept in constant motion throughout the day, each carrying from thirty to fifty dozen of moulds into the stoves, and remaining . . . long enough to take the dried earthenware away. The distance thus run by a boy in the course of a day . . . was estimated at seven miles. From the very nature of this exhausting occupation children were rendered pale, weak and unhealthy. In the depth of winter, with the thermometer in the open air sometimes below zero, boys, with little clothing but rags, might be seen running to and fro on errands or to their dinners with the perspiration on their foreheads, "after labouring for hours like little slaves." The

inevitable result of such transitions of temperature were consumption, asthma, and acute inflammation.[13]

Little wonder that child labor legislation included pottery works in 1864.

By 1830, women and children made up two-thirds of the cotton industry's labor. However, as the number of children employed declined under the Factory Act of 1833, their places were taken by women, who came to dominate the labor forces of the early factories. Women made up 50 percent of the labor force in textile (cotton and woolen) factories before 1870. They were mostly unskilled labor and were paid half or less of what men received. Excessive working hours for women were outlawed in 1844, but only in textile factories and mines; not until 1867 were they outlawed in craft workshops.

The employment of children and women in large part represents a continuation of a pre-industrial kinship pattern. Cottage industry had always involved the efforts of the entire family, and it seemed perfectly natural to continue this pattern. Men migrating from the countryside to industrial towns and cities took their wives and children with them into the factory or into the mines. Of 136 employees in Robert Peel's factory at Bury in 1801, 95 belonged to twenty-six families. The impetus for this family work often came from the family itself. The factory owner Jedediah Strutt was opposed to child labor under ten but was forced by parents to take children as young as seven.

The employment of large numbers of women in factories did not produce a significant transformation in female working patterns, as was once assumed. Studies of urban households in France and Britain, for example, have revealed that throughout the nineteenth century traditional types of female labor still predominated in the women's work world. In 1851, fully 40 percent of the female work force in Britain consisted of domestic servants. In France, the largest group of female workers, 40 percent, worked in agriculture. In addition, only 20 percent of female workers labored in Britain's factories, only 10 percent in France. Regional and local studies have also indicated that most of the workers were single women. Few married women worked outside their homes.

The Factory Acts that limited the work hours of children and women also began to break up the traditional kinship pattern of work and led to a new pattern based on a separation of work and home. Men came to be expected to be responsible for the primary work obligations while women assumed daily control of the family and performed low-paying jobs such as laundry work that could be done in the home. Domestic industry made it possible for women to continue their contributions to family survival.

Historians have also reminded us that if the treatment of children in the mines and factories seems particularly cruel and harsh, contemporary treatment of children in general was often brutal. Beatings, for example, had long been regarded, even by dedicated churchmen and churchwomen, as the best way to discipline children.

Standards of Living

One of the most heated debates on the Industrial Revolution concerns the standard of living. Most historians assume that in the long run the Industrial Revolution increased living standards dramatically in the form of higher per capita incomes and greater consumer choices. But did the first generation of industrial workers experience a decline in their living standards and suffer unnecessarily? Some historians have argued that early industrialization required huge profits to be reinvested in new and ever more expensive equipment, thus justifying lower wages and higher profits. Others have questioned that argument, pointing out that initial investments in early machinery were not necessarily large nor did they need to be. What certainly did occur in the first half of the nineteenth century was a widening gap between rich and poor. One estimate, based on income tax returns in Britain, is that the wealthiest 1 percent of the population increased its share of the national product from 25 percent in 1801 to 35 percent in 1848.

Wages, prices, and consumption patterns are some of the criteria used for measuring the standard of living. Between 1780 and 1850, as far as we can determine from the available evidence, both wages and prices fluctuated widely. Most historians believe that during the Napoleonic wars the increase in prices outstripped wages. Between 1815 and 1830, a price fall was accompanied by a slight increase in wages. But from 1830 to the late 1840s, real wages seem to have improved although regional variations make generalizations dangerous.

When we look at consumption patterns, we find that in Britain in 1850 tea, sugar, and coffee were still semiluxuries consumed primarily by the upper and middle classes and better-off artisans. Meat consumption per capita was less in 1840 than in 1780. On the other hand, a mass market had developed in the cheap cotton goods so important to the Industrial Revolution. As a final note on the question of the standard of living, some historians who take a positive view of the early Industrial Revolution have questioned what would have happened to Britain's growing population without the Industrial Revolution. Would it have gone the way of Ireland's in the Great Hunger of the mid-nineteenth century? No one really knows.

No doubt the periodic crises of overproduction that haunted industrialization from its beginnings caused even further economic hardship. Short-term economic depressions brought high unemployment and increased social tensions. Unemployment figures could be astronomical. During one of these economic depressions in 1842, for example, 60 percent of the factory employees in Bolton were laid off. Cyclical depressions were particularly devastating in towns whose prosperity rested on one industry.

Overall we can say that some evidence exists for an increase in real wages for the working classes between 1790 and 1850, especially in the 1840s. But can standards of living be assessed only in terms of prices, wages, and consumption patterns? No doubt those meant little to people who faced dreadful housing, adulterated food, public health hazards, and the psychological traumas associated with a complete change in work habits and way of life. The real gainers in the early Industrial Revolution were the middle and upper classes—and some skilled workers whose jobs were not eliminated by the new machines. But industrial workers themselves would have to wait until the second half of the nineteenth century until they reaped the benefits of industrialization.

Efforts at Change: The Workers

Before long, workers looked to the formation of labor organizations to gain decent wages and working conditions. The British government, reacting against the radicalism of the French revolutionary working classes, had passed a series of Combination Acts in 1799 and 1800 outlawing associations of workmen. The legislation failed to prevent the formation of trade unions, however. Similar to the craft societies of earlier times, these new associations were formed by skilled workers in a number of new industries, including the cotton spinners, ironworkers, coal miners, and shipwrights. These unions served two purposes. One was to preserve their own workers' position by limiting entry into their trade; another was to gain benefits from the employers. These early trade unions had limited goals. They favored a working-class struggle against employers, but only to win improvements for the members of their own trades.

Some trade unions were even willing to strike to gain their goals. Bitter strikes were carried out by hand-loom weavers in Glasgow in 1813, cotton spinners in Manchester in 1818, and miners in Northumberland and Durham in 1810. Such blatant illegal activity caused Parliament to repeal the Combination Acts in 1824, accepting the argument of some members that the acts themselves had so alienated workers that they had formed unions. Unions were now tolerated, but other legislation enabled authorities to keep close watch over their activities.

▼ **Membership Card in an Early Trade Union.** Skilled workers in a number of new industries formed trade unions in an attempt to gain higher wages and better working conditions. The trade union also served to protect the position of its members by limiting entry into the trade. In their attempts to gain benefits for their members, trade unions were even willing to go on strike. Pictured here is a membership card issued to the West of Scotland Power Loom Female Weavers Society in 1833.

In the 1820s and 1830s, the union movement began to focus on the creation of national unions. One of the leaders in this effort was a well-known cotton magnate and social reformer, Robert Owen (1771–1858). Owen came to believe in the creation of voluntary associations that would demonstrate to others the benefits of cooperative rather than competitive living (see Chapter 22 on the utopian socialists). Although Owen's ideas were not directed specifically to trade unionists, his ideas had great appeal to some of their leaders. Under Owen's direction, plans emerged for a Grand National Consolidated Trades Union, which was formed in February 1834. As a national federation of trade unions, its primary purpose was to coordinate a general strike for the eight-hour working day. Rhetoric, however, soon outpaced reality, and by the summer of the same year, the lack of real working-class support led to its total collapse. Afterward, the union movement reverted to trade unions for individual crafts. The largest and most successful was the Amalgamated Society of Engineers, formed in 1850. Its provision of generous unemployment benefits in return for a small weekly payment was precisely the kind of practical gains these trade unions sought. Larger goals would have to wait.

Trade unionism was not the only type of collective action by workers in the early decades of the Industrial Revolution. The Luddites were skilled craftsmen in the Midlands and northern England who in 1812 attacked the machines that they believed threatened their livelihoods. These attacks failed to stop the industrial mechanization of Britain and have been viewed as utterly naive. Some historians, however, have also seen them as an intense eruption of feeling against unrestrained industrial capitalism. The inability of 12,000 troops to find the culprits provides stunning evidence of the local support they received in their areas.

A much more meaningful expression of the attempts of British workers to improve their condition developed in the movement known as Chartism. It was the first "important political movement of working men organized during the nineteenth century." Its aim was to achieve political democracy. A People's Charter was drawn up in 1838 that demanded universal male suffrage, payment of the members of Parliament, and annual sessions of Parliament (see the box on p. 729). Two national petitions incorporating these points, affixed with millions of signatures, were presented to Parliament in 1839 and 1842. Both were rejected by the members of Parliament who were not at all ready for political democracy. As one member said, universal suffrage would be "fatal to all the purposes for which government ex-

ists" and was "utterly incompatible with the very existence of civilization." After 1843, Chartism as a movement had largely played itself out. It had never really posed a serious threat to the British establishment, but it had not been a total failure either. Its true significance stemmed from its ability to arouse and organize millions of working-class men and women, to give them a sense of working-class consciousness that they had not really possessed before. This political education of working people was important to the ultimate acceptance of all the points of the People's Charter in the future.

Efforts at Change: Reformers and Government

Efforts to improve the worst conditions of the industrial factory system also came from outside the ranks of the working classes. From its beginning the Industrial Revolution had been the source of much criticism. Romantic poets like William Wordsworth (see Chapter 22) decried the destruction of the natural world:

I grieve, when on the darker side
Of this great change I look; and there behold
Such outrage done to nature as compels
The indignant power to justify herself.

Reform-minded men, be they factory owners who felt twinges of Christian conscience or social reformers in Parliament, campaigned against the evils of the industrial factory, especially condemning the abuse of children. One hoped for the day "that these little ones should once more see the rising and setting of the sun."

As it became apparent that the increase in wealth generated by the Industrial Revolution was accompanied by ever-increasing numbers of poor people, more and more efforts were made to document and deal with the problems. As reports from civic-minded citizens and parliamentary commissions intensified and demonstrated the extent of poverty, degradation, and suffering, reform efforts began to succeed.

The first success was achieved in a series of Factory Acts passed between 1802 and 1819 that limited labor for children between the ages of nine and sixteen to twelve hours a day; it was forbidden to employ children under nine years old. Moreover, the laws stipulated that children were to receive instruction in reading and arithmetic during working hours. But these acts applied only to cotton mills, not to factories or mines where some of the worst abuses were taking place. Just as important, no provision was made for enforcing the acts through a system of inspection.

The Political Demands of the Chartist Movement

▼ ▼ ▼

In the late 1830s and early 1840s, working-class protest centered on achieving a clear set of political goals, particularly universal male suffrage, as the means to achieve economic and social improvements. This selection is taken from one of the national petitions presented to Parliament by the Chartist movement. Although the petition failed, Chartism helped to arouse and organize millions of workers.

National Petition (1839)

To the Honourable the Commons of the United Kingdom of Great Britain and Ireland, in Parliament assembled, the Petition of the undersigned, their suffering countrymen, HUMBLY SHEWETH,—

The energies of a mighty kingdom have been wasted in building up the power of selfish and ignorant men, and its resources squandered for their aggrandisement. The good of a part has been advanced at the sacrifice of the good of the nation. The few have governed for the interest of the few, while the interests of the many have been sottishly neglected, or insolently . . . trampled upon. . . . We come before your honourable house to tell you, with all humility, that this state of things must not be permitted to continue. That it cannot long continue, without very seriously endangering the stability of the throne, and the peace of the kingdom, and that if, by God's help, and all lawful and constitutional appliances, an end can be put to it, we are fully resolved that it shall speedily come to an end. . . . Required, as we are universally, to support and obey the laws, nature and reason entitle us to demand that in the making of the laws the universal voice shall be implicitly listened to. We perform the duties of freemen; we must have the privileges of freemen. Therefore, we demand universal suffrage. The suffrage, to be exempt from the corruption of the wealthy and the violence of the powerful, must be secret. . . . To public safety, as well as public confidence, frequent elections are essential. Therefore, we demand annual parliaments. With power to choose, and freedom in choosing, the range of our choice must be unrestricted. We are compelled, by the existing laws, to take for our representatives men who are incapable of appreciating our difficulties, or have little sympathy with them; merchants who have retired from trade and no longer feel its harassings; proprietors of land who are alike ignorant of its evils and its cure; lawyers by whom the notoriety of the senate is courted only as a means of obtaining notice in the courts. . . . We demand that in the future election of members of your . . . house, the approbation of the constituency shall be the sole qualification, and that to every representative so chosen, shall be assigned out of the public taxes, a fair and adequate remuneration for the time which he is called upon to devote to the public service. . . . Universal suffrage will, and it alone can, bring true and lasting peace to the nation; we firmly believe that it will also bring prosperity. May it therefore please your honourable house, to take this our petition into your most serious consideration, and to use your utmost endeavours, by all constitutional means, to have a law passed, granting to every male of lawful age, sane mind, and unconvicted of crime, the right of voting for members of parliament, and directing all future elections of members of parliament to be in the way of secret ballot, and ordaining that the duration of parliament, so chosen, shall in no case exceed one year, and abolishing all property qualifications in the members, and providing for their due remuneration while in attendance on their parliamentary duties.

In the reform-minded decades of the 1830s and 1840s, new legislation was passed. The Factory Act of 1833 strengthened earlier labor legislation. All textile factories were now included. Children between nine and thirteen could work only eight hours a day; those between thirteen and eighteen, twelve hours. Inspection was to be enforced. Another piece of legislation in 1833 required that children between nine and thirteen have at least two hours of elementary education during the working day. In 1847, the Ten Hours Act reduced the work day for children between thirteen and eighteen to ten hours. Women were also now included in the ten-hour limitation. It was not until 1842 that a Coal Mines Act eliminated the employment of boys under ten and women in mines. Eventually, men too would benefit from the move to restrict factory hours.

The Industrial Revolution became one of the major forces of change in the nineteenth century as it led Western civilization into the industrial era that has characterized the modern world. Beginning in Britain, its spread to the Continent and the new American nation ensured its growth and domination of the Western world.

The Industrial Revolution seemed to prove to Europeans the underlying assumption of the Scientific Revolution of the seventeenth century—that human beings were capable of dominating nature. By rationally manipulating the material environment for human benefit, people could create new levels of material prosperity and produce machines not dreamed of in their wildest imaginings. Lost in the excitement of the Industrial Revolu-

tion were the voices that pointed to the dehumanization of the work force and the alienation from one's work, one's associates, one's self, and the natural world.

The Industrial Revolution also transformed the social world of Europe. The creation of an industrial proletariat produced a whole new force for change. The development of a wealthy industrial middle class presented a challenge to the long-term hegemony of landed wealth. While that wealth had been threatened by the fortunes of commerce, it had never been overturned. But the new bourgeoisie was more demanding. How, in some places, this new industrial bourgeoisie came to play a larger role in the affairs of state will become evident in the next chapter.

Notes
▼ ▼ ▼

1. Quoted in W. Gorden Rimmer, *Marshall's of Leeds, Flax-Spinners 1788–1886* (Cambridge, 1960), p. 40.

2. Daniel Defoe, *A Plan of the English Commerce* (Oxford, 1928), pp. 76–77.

3. Quoted in David Landes, *The Unbound Prometheus: Technological Change and Industrial Development in Western Europe from 1750 to the Present* (Cambridge, 1969), pp. 99–100.

4. Quoted in Albert Tucker, *A History of English Civilization* (New York, 1972), p. 583.

5. Quoted in Landes, *The Unbound Prometheus*, pp. 149–50.

6. Quotations can be found in E. Royston Pike, *Human Documents of the Industrial Revolution in Britain* (London, 1966), pp. (in order of quotations) 320, 313, 314, 343.

7. Ibid., p. 315.

8. Quoted in A. J. Donajgrodzi, ed., *Social Control in Nineteenth Century Britain* (London, 1977), p. 141.

9. Quoted in Pike, *Human Documents of the Industrial Revolution in Britain*, pp. 343–44.

10. Quoted in Eric J. Evans, *The Forging of the Modern State: Early Industrial Britain, 1783–1870* (London, 1983), p. 113.

11. Henry Mayhew, *London Labour and the London Poor* (London, 1851), 1: 342–43.

12. Quoted in Pike, *Human Documents of the Industrial Revolution in Britain*, pp. 60–61.

13. Quoted in Evans, *The Forging of the Modern State*, p. 124.

Suggestions for Further Reading
▼ ▼ ▼

The well-written work by D. Landes, *The Unbound Prometheus: Technological Change and Industrial Development in Western Europe from 1750 to the Present* (Cambridge, 1969) is still the best introduction to the Industrial Revolution. Although more technical, also of value are C. Trebilcock, *The Industrialization of the Continental Powers, 1780–1914* (London, 1981); and S. Pollard, *Peaceful Conquest: The Industrialization of Europe, 1760–1970* (Oxford, 1981). A volume in the Fontana Economic History of Europe edited by C. M. Cipolla, *The Industrial Revolution* (London, 1973) is also valuable. Although older and dated, T. S. Ashton, *The Industrial Revolution, 1760–1830* (New York, 1948), still provides an interesting introduction to the Industrial Revolution in Britain. Much better, however, are P. Mathias, *The First Industrial Nation: An Economic History of Britain, 1700–1914*, 2d. ed. (New York, 1983); and P. Deane, *The First Industrial Revolution* (Cambridge, 1965). For a discussion of the areas in Europe that lagged behind in the industrialization process, see I. T. Behrend and G. Rankl, *The European Periphery and Industrialization, 1780–1914* (Cambridge, 1982).

Given the importance of Great Britain in the Industrial Revolution, a number of books are available for placing the Industrial Revolution in Britain into a broader context. See E. J. Evans, *The Forging of the Modern State: Early Industrial Britain, 1783–1870* (London, 1983); S. Checkland, *British Public Policy, 1776–1939: An Economic, Social and Political Perspective* (Cambridge, 1983); H. Perkin, *The Origins of Modern English Society, 1780–1880* (London, 1969); and E. J. Hobsbawm, *Industry and Empire* (London, 1968).

The early industrialization of the United States is examined in P. Temin, *Causal Factors in American Economic Growth in the Nineteenth Century* (London, 1975); and D. C. North, *The Economic Growth of the United States, 1790–1860* (New York, 1961), although the latter's stress on the importance of regional specialization to economic growth has been questioned. On the economic ties between Great Britain and the United States, see D. Jeremy, *Transatlantic Industrial Revolution: The Diffusion of Textile Technology between Britain and America, 1790–1830* (Cambridge, Mass., 1981).

A general discussion of population growth in Europe can be found in T. McKeown, *The Modern Rise of Population* (London, 1976), although it has been criticized for its emphasis on nutrition and hygiene as the two major causes of that growth. For an examination of urban growth, see the older but classic work of A. F. Weber, *The Growth of Cities in the Nineteenth Century: A Study in Statistics* (Ithaca, N.Y., 1963); and the more recent work by A. R. Sutcliffe, *Towards the Planned City: Germany, Britain, the United States and France, 1780–1914* (Oxford, 1981). C. Woodham Smith, *The Great Hunger* (New York, 1962) is a well-written account of the great Irish tragedy. Many of the works cited above have much information on the social impact of the Industrial Revolution, but additional material is available in C. Morazé, *The Triumph of the Middle Classes* (London, 1966); F. Crouzet, *The First Industrialists: The Problems of Origins* (Cambridge, 1985), on British entrepreneurs; and E. Gauldie, *Cruel Habitations, A History of Working-Class Housing, 1790–1918* (London, 1974). G. Himmelfarb, *The Idea of Poverty: England in the Early Industrial Age* (New York, 1984) traces the concepts of poverty and poor from the mid-eighteenth century to the mid-nineteenth century. A valuable work on female labor patterns is L. A. Tilly and J. W. Scott, *Women, Work, and Family* (New York, 1978).

Chapter 22

Reaction, Revolution, and Romanticism, 1815–1850

▼▼▼▼▼

The forces of upheaval unleashed during the French revolutionary and Napoleonic eras were temporarily quieted in 1815 as monarchs sought to restore stability by reestablishing much of the old order to a Europe ravaged by war. Kings and landed and bureaucratic elites regained their control over domestic governments while internationally the forces of conservatism attempted to maintain the new status quo; some states even used military force to intervene in the internal affairs of other countries in their desire to crush revolutions.

But the European world had been changed, and it would not readily go back to the old system. New ideologies of change, especially liberalism and nationalism, products of the revolutionary upheaval initiated in France, had become too powerful to be contained forever. Not content with the status quo, the forces of change called forth revolts and revolutions that periodically shook Europe in the 1820s and 1830s and culminated in the widespread revolutions of 1848. Some of the revolutions and revolutionaries were successful; most were not. Although the old order had prevailed in many ways, everywhere it was apparent by 1850 that it would not endure. This perception was reinforced by the changes wrought by the Industrial Revolution. Together the forces unleashed by the dual revolutions—the French Revolution and the Industrial Revolution—made it impossible to return to prerevolutionary Europe. While these two revolutions initiated what historians like to call the modern European world, it will also be apparent

Congress of Vienna ▼	Revolutions in France, Belgium, Poland, Italy ▼	Reform Bill in Britain ▼	Revolutions in France, Germany, Austrian Empire ▼

•••••••• 1810 •••••••••• 1820 •••••••••• 1830 •••••••••• 1840 •••••••••• 1850 •••••••••

▲ Shelley, *Prometheus Unbound*	▲ Beethoven, Ninth Symphony	▲ London Police	▲ Friedrich, *Man and Woman Gazing at the Moon*	▲ Tristan, *Worker's Union*

that much of the old still remained in the midst of the new.

▼ The Conservative Order, 1815–1830

The immediate response to the defeat of Napoleon was the desire to contain revolution and the revolutionary forces by restoring much of the old order. But the triumphant rulers were not naive and realized that they could not return to 1789.

The Peace Settlement

In March 1814, even before Napoleon had been defeated, his four major enemies—Great Britain, Austria, Prussia, and Russia—had agreed to remain united, not only to defeat France but to ensure peace after the war. After Napoleon's defeat, this Quadruple Alliance restored the Bourbon monarchy to France in the person of Louis XVIII and concluded the first Treaty of Paris with the conquered nation. It was a lenient treaty. The Bourbons had not been responsible for France's revolutionary upheaval, and there was little need to burden the government of Louis XVIII unnecessarily. Not only were the French allowed to keep the territories they had acquired by 1792 (some parts of Germany and the Austrian Netherlands), but they paid no indemnity as well. Since the Treaty of Paris did not deal with the problems created by Napoleon's rearrangement of the map of Europe, the great powers agreed to meet at a congress in Vienna in September 1814 to arrange a final peace settlement.

Although all the powers were invited to attend the congress, important decisions were closely guarded by the representatives of the four great powers. The skillful maneuvering of the French representative, the clever Prince Talleyrand, enabled the defeated power, France, to actually participate in some of the decisions. Above all, however, the congress was dominated by the Austrian foreign minister, Prince Klemens von Metternich

(1773–1859). An experienced diplomat, Metternich's public demeanor reflected the conceit and self-assurance of the comments that he recorded in his memoirs in 1819: "There is a wide sweep about my mind. I am always above and beyond the preoccupation of most public men; I cover a ground much vaster than they can see. I cannot keep myself from saying about twenty times a day: 'How right I am, and how wrong they are.'"[1]

Metternich claimed that he was guided at Vienna by the principle of legitimacy. To reestablish peace and stability in Europe, he considered it necessary to restore the legitimate monarchs who would preserve traditional institutions. This had already been done in the restoration of the Bourbons in France, but the principle of legitimacy was in fact largely ignored elsewhere and completely overshadowed by more practical considerations of power. The congress's treatment of Poland, to which Russia, Austria, and Prussia all had claims, illustrates this approach. Prussia and Austria were allowed to keep some Polish territory. A new, nominally independent Polish kingdom, about three-quarters of the size of the duchy of Warsaw, was established with the Romanov dynasty of Russia as its hereditary monarchs. Although the Russian tsar Alexander I (1801–1825) voluntarily granted the new kingdom a constitution guaranteeing its independence, Poland's foreign policy (and Poland) remained under Russian control. Prussia was compensated for its loss of Polish lands by receiving two-fifths of Saxony, the Napoleonic German kingdom of Westphalia, and the left bank of the Rhine. In turn, Austria was compensated for its loss of the Austrian Netherlands by being given control of the northern provinces of Italy called Lombardy and Venetia. In making these territorial rearrangements, the powers at Vienna believed they were following the familiar eighteenth-century practice of maintaining a balance of power or equilibrium among the great powers. Essentially, this meant a balance of political and military forces that guaranteed the independence of the great powers by ensuring that no one country could dominate Europe. To balance Russian gains, Prussia and Austria had been strengthened. According to Metternich, this arrangement had clearly avoided a great danger: "Prussia and Austria are completing their systems of defence; united, the two monarchies form an unconquerable barrier against the enterprises of any conquering prince who might perhaps once again occupy the throne of France or that of Russia."[2]

It was considerations of the balance of power that dictated the allied treatment of France. France had not been overly weakened so that it could remain a great power. Nevertheless, the fear that France might again upset the European peace remained strong enough that the great powers attempted to establish major defensive barriers against possible French expansion. To the north of France, they created a new enlarged kingdom of the Netherlands composed of the former Dutch Republic and the Austrian Netherlands (Belgium) under a new ruler, King William I of the House of Orange. To the southeast, Piedmont (officially styled the kingdom of Sardinia) was enlarged. Prussia was strengthened on France's eastern frontier by giving it control of the territory along the left bank of the Rhine. The British at least expected Prussia to be the major bulwark against French expansion in central Europe, but the Congress of Vienna also created a new league of German states, the Germanic Confederation, to replace the Napoleonic Confederation of the Rhine.

Napoleon's escape from Elba and his One Hundred Days in the midst of the Congress of Vienna, delayed the negotiations but did not significantly alter the overall agreement. It was decided, however, to punish the French people for their enthusiastic response to Napoleon's return. By the second Treaty of Paris, France's borders were returned to those of 1790, and it was forced to pay an indemnity and accept an army of occupation for five years.

The Vienna peace settlement of 1815 has sometimes been criticized for its failure to recognize the liberal and national forces unleashed by the French revolutionary and Napoleonic eras. Containing these revolutionary forces was precisely what the diplomats at Vienna hoped to achieve. Their transfers of territories and peoples to the victors to create a new balance of power, with little or no regard for the wishes of the peoples themselves, was in accord with long-standing traditions of European diplomacy. One could hardly expect Metternich, foreign minister of the Austrian Empire, a dynastic state composed of many different peoples, to espouse a principle of self-determination for European nationalities. Whatever its weaknesses, the Congress of Vienna has received credit for establishing a European order that managed to avoid a general European conflict for almost a century.

The Ideology of Conservatism

The peace arrangements of 1815 were but the beginning of a conservative reaction determined to contain the liberal and nationalist forces unleashed by the French Revolution. Metternich and his kind were representatives of the ideology known as conservatism (see the box on p. 736). As a modern political philosophy, conservatism dates from 1790 when Edmund Burke wrote his *Reflections on the Revolution in France* in reaction to the French Revolution, especially its radical

▼ **The Congress of Vienna.** Following the defeat of Napoleon, the states of Europe met at a congress in Vienna to arrange a final peace settlement. Seen here is a group portrait of the negotiators. Despite the number of states represented at the congress, the most important decisions were reached by the four major enemies of Napoleon—Great Britain, Austria, Prussia, and Russia.

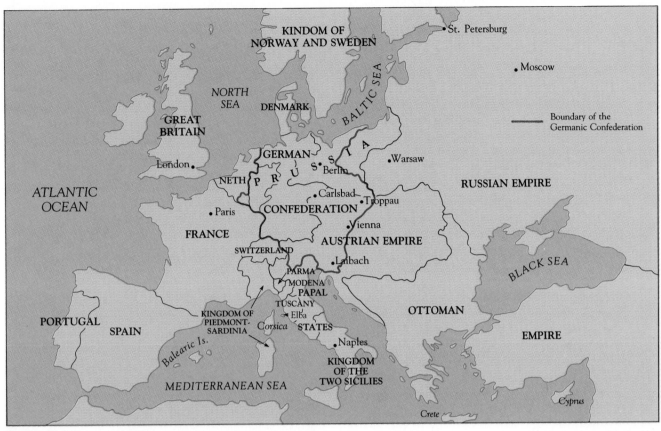

▼ **Map 22.1** Europe in 1815.

republican and democratic ideas. Those people labeled conservatives, however, did not always agree on all principles.

Edmund Burke (1729–1797) enunciated the principles of an evolutionary conservatism. In his *Reflections on the Revolution in France,* Burke maintained that society was a contract, but "the state ought not to be considered as nothing better than a partnership agreement in a trade of pepper and coffee, to be taken up for a temporary interest and to be dissolved by the fancy of the parties." The state was a partnership but one "not only between those who are living, but between those who are living, those who are dead and those who are to be born." No one generation therefore has the right to destroy this partnership; instead, each generation has the duty to preserve and transmit it to the next. Indeed, "changing the state as often as there are floating fancies, . . . no one generation could link with the other." Burke opposed the violent overthrow of a government by revolution, but he did not reject the possibility of change. Sudden change was unacceptable, but that did not eliminate gradual or evolutionary improvements. As Burke

said, "a disposition to preserve and an ability to improve, taken together, would be my standard of a statesman." [3]

Burke's conservatism, however, was not the only kind. The Frenchman Joseph de Maistre (1753–1821) was the most influential spokesman for a counterrevolutionary and authoritarian conservatism. De Maistre espoused an unequivocal restoration of hereditary monarchy. He went beyond Burke's pragmatic justification for monarchy as a social cement needed to hold society together to a defense of monarchy as a divinely sanctioned institution. Only absolute monarchy could guarantee "order in society" and avoid the chaos generated by movements like the French Revolution. De Maistre even took his defense of absolutism to the absurd point of justifying love for and obedience to an unjust ruler: "We find ourselves in a realm whose sovereign has proclaimed his laws. . . . Some appear hard and even unjust." What should we do? "Since we start with the supposition that the master exists and that we must serve him absolutely, is it not better to serve him, whatever his nature, with love than without it?" [4]

The Voice of Conservatism: Metternich of Austria

▼ ▼ ▼

There was no greater symbol of conservatism in the first half of the nineteenth century than Prince Klemens von Metternich of Austria. Metternich played a crucial role at the Congress of Vienna and worked tirelessly for thirty years to repress the "revolutionary seed," as he called it, that had been spread to Europe by the "military despotism of Bonaparte."

Klemens von Metternich, *Memoirs*

We are convinced that society can no longer be saved without strong and vigorous resolutions on the part of the Governments still free in their opinions and actions.

We are also convinced that this may be, if the Governments face the truth, if they free themselves from all illusion, if they join their ranks and take their stand on a line of correct, unambiguous, and frankly announced principles.

By this course the monarchs will fulfil the duties imposed upon them by Him who, by entrusting them with power, has charged them to watch over the maintenance of justice, and the rights of all, to avoid the paths of error, and tread firmly in the way of truth. . . .

If the same elements of destruction which are now throwing society into convulsions have existed in all ages—for every age has seen immoral and ambitious men, hypocrites, men of heated imaginations, wrong motives, and wild projects—yet ours, by the single fact of the liberty of the press, possesses more than any preceding age the means of contact, seduction, and attraction whereby to act on these different classes of men.

We are certainly not alone in questioning if society can exist with the liberty of the press, a scourge unknown to the world before the latter half of the seventeenth century, and restrained until the end of the eighteenth, with scarcely any exceptions but England—a part of Europe separated from the continent by the sea, as well as by her language and by her peculiar manners.

The first principle to be followed by the monarchs, united as they are by the coincidence of their desires and opinions, should be that of maintaining the stability of political institutions against the disorganized excitement which has taken possession of men's minds; the immutability of principles against the madness of their interpretation; and respect for laws actually in force against a desire for their destruction. . . .

The first and greatest concern for the immense majority of every nation is the stability of the laws, and their uninterrupted action—never their change. Therefore, let the Governments govern, let them maintain the groundwork of their institutions, both ancient and modern; for if it is at all times dangerous to touch them, it certainly would not now, in the general confusion, be wise to do so. . . .

Let them maintain religious principles in all their purity, and not allow the faith to be attacked and morality interpreted according to the social contract or the visions of foolish sectarians.

Let them suppress Secret Societies, that gangrene of society. . . .

To every great State determined to survive the storm there still remain many chances of salvation, and a strong union between the States on the principles we have announced will overcome the storm itself.

Despite their differences, most conservatives held to a general body of beliefs. They favored obedience to political authority, believed that organized religion was crucial to social order, hated revolutionary upheavals, and were unwilling to accept either the liberal demands for civil liberties and representative governments or the nationalistic aspirations generated by the French revolutionary era. The community took precedence over individual rights; society must be organized and ordered, and tradition remained the best guide for order. After 1815, the political philosophy of conservatism was supported by hereditary monarchs, government bureaucracies, landowning aristocracies, and revived churches, be they Protestant or Catholic. Although not unopposed, both internationally and domestically the conservative forces appeared dominant after 1815.

The Conservative Domination: The Concert of Europe

The conservative order that European diplomats were constructing at Vienna must have seemed fragile when the French people responded with enthusiasm to Napoleon after his escape from Elba. The great powers' fear of revolution and war led them to develop the Concert of Europe as a means to maintain the new status quo they had constructed. This Concert of Europe grew out of the reaffirmation of the Quadruple Alliance in November 1815. Great Britain, Russia, Prussia, and Austria renewed their commitment against any attempted restoration of Bonapartist power and agreed to meet periodically in conferences to discuss their common interests and examine measures that "will be judged most salutary for the repose and prosperity of peoples, and for the maintenance of peace in Europe."

In accordance with the agreement for periodic meetings, four congresses were held between 1818 and 1822. The first congress, held in 1818 at Aix-la-Chapelle, was by far the most congenial. "Never have I known a prettier little congress," said Metternich. The four great powers agreed to withdraw their army of occupation from France and add France to the Concert of Europe. The Quadruple Alliance became a Quintuple Alliance.

The next congress proved far less pleasant and produced the first fissure in the ranks of the allies. This session at Troppau was called in the autumn of 1820 to deal with the outbreak of revolution in Spain and Italy. The revolt in Spain was directed against Ferdinand VII, the Bourbon king who had been restored to the throne in 1814. In southern Italy, the restoration of another Bourbon, Ferdinand I as king of Naples and Sicily, was accompanied by the return of the nobility and clergy to their privileged positions. Army officers and businessmen led a rebellion that soon spread to the northern Italian kingdom of Piedmont.

Metternich was especially disturbed by the revolts in Italy since he saw them as a threat to Austria's domination of the peninsula. At Troppau, he proposed a protocol that established the principle of intervention. It read:

> States which have undergone a change of Government due to revolution, the results of which threaten other states, *ipso facto* cease to be members of the European Alliance, and remain excluded from it until their situation gives guarantees for legal order and stability. If, owing to such situations, immediate danger threatens other states, the Powers bind themselves, by peaceful means, or if need be by arms, to bring back the guilty state into the bosom of the Great Alliance.[5]

The principle of intervention meant the right of the great powers to send armies into countries where there were revolutions to restore legitimate monarchs to their thrones. Britain refused to agree to the principle, argu-

ing that it had never been the intention of the Quadruple Alliance to interfere in the internal affairs of other states. In Britain's eyes, only revolutionary outbursts threatening the peace of Europe necessitated armed intervention. Ignoring the British response, Austria, Prussia, and Russia met in a third congress at Laibach in January 1821 and authorized the sending of Austrian troops to Naples. These forces crushed the revolt, restored Ferdinand I to the throne, and then moved north to suppress the rebels in Sardinia. At the fourth postwar conference, held at Verona in October 1822, the same three powers authorized France to invade Spain to crush the revolt against Ferdinand VII. In the spring of 1823, French forces restored the Bourbon monarch. By this time, the split between Britain and the more conserva-

▼ **Metternich.** Prince Klemens von Metternich, the foreign minister of Austria, played a major role in the attempt to maintain the new conservative order after 1815. Metternich espoused the principle of intervention, which maintained the right of the great powers to intervene militarily in other countries in order to crush revolutionary movements against legitimate rulers. Metternich was forced to flee abroad during the early stages of the 1848 revolution in the Austrian Empire.

tive powers of central and eastern Europe had become irreversible.

The policy of intervention had succeeded in defeating revolutionary movements in Spain and Italy and in restoring legitimate (and conservative) monarchs to their thrones. It had been done at a price, however. The Concert of Europe had broken down when the British rejected Metternich's principle of intervention. And although the British had failed to thwart allied intervention in Spain and Italy, they were successful in keeping the continental powers from interfering with the revolutions in Latin America.

THE REVOLT OF LATIN AMERICA   While much of North America had been freed of European domination in the eighteenth century by the American Revolution, Latin America remained in the hands of the Spanish and Portuguese. Napoleon's continental wars at the beginning of the nineteenth century, however, soon had repercussions in Latin America. When the Bourbon monarchy of Spain was toppled by Bonaparte, Spanish authority in its colonial empire was weakened. By 1810, the disintegration of royal power in Argentina had led to that nation's

independence. In Venezuela a bitter struggle for independence was led by Simón Bolivar, hailed as the Liberator. His forces freed Colombia in 1819 and Venezuela in 1821. A second liberator was José de San Martin who liberated Chile in 1817 and then, in 1821, moved on to Lima, Peru, the center of Spanish authority. He was soon joined by Bolivar who assumed the task of crushing the last significant Spanish army in 1824. Mexico and the Central American provinces also achieved their freedom, and by 1825, after Portugal had recognized the independence of Brazil, almost all of Latin America had been freed of colonial domination.

In the early 1820s, only one major threat remained to the newly independent Latin American states. Flushed by their success in crushing rebellions in Spain and Italy, the victorious continental powers favored the use of troops to restore Spanish control in Latin America. This time British opposition to intervention prevailed. Eager to gain access to an entire continent for investment and trade, the British proposed joint action with the United States against European interference in Latin America. Distrustful of British motives, President James Monroe acted alone in 1823, guaranteeing the independence of

▼ **Map 22.2** Latin America in the First Half of the Nineteenth Century. (*Left:* Independent Nations by 1828; *Right:* Independent Nations by 1845)

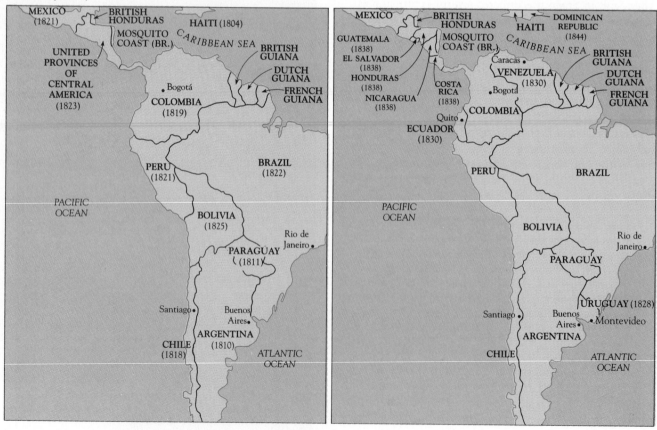

the new Latin American nations and warning against any further European intervention in the New World in the famous Monroe Doctrine. Actually more important to Latin American independence than American words was Britain's navy. It stood between Latin America and any European invasion force, and it was unlikely that any of the continental powers would challenge British naval power.

THE GREEK REVOLT, 1821–1832　The principle of intervention proved to be a double-edged sword. Designed to prevent revolution, it could also be used to support revolution if the great powers found it in their interest to do so. Despite their differences in the congresses, Great Britain, France, and Russia found cause for cooperation.

The Ottoman Empire had long been in control of much of southeastern Europe. By the beginning of the nineteenth century, however, when the Turkish empire was in decline and authority over its outlying territories in southeastern Europe waned, European governments began to take an active interest in its disintegration. This "Eastern Question," as it came to be called, troubled European diplomats throughout the nineteenth century. Russia's proximity to the Ottoman Empire and the religious bonds between the Russians and the Greek Orthodox Christians in Turkish-dominated southeastern Europe naturally gave it special opportunities to enlarge its sphere of influence. Other European powers feared Russian ambitions and had their own interest in the apparent demise of the Ottoman Empire. Austria craved more land in the Balkans, a desire that inevitably meant conflict with Russia, while France and Britain were interested in commercial opportunities and naval bases in the eastern Mediterranean.

In 1821, the Greeks revolted against their Turkish masters. Although subject to Muslim control for four hundred years, they had been allowed to maintain their language and their Greek Orthodox faith. A revival of Greek national sentiment at the beginning of the nineteenth century added to the growing desire for "the liberation of the fatherland from the terrible yoke of Turkish oppression." Initial reaction to the Greek revolt by the European powers was negative since this appeared to be simply another revolt against established authority that should be crushed. But the Greek revolt was soon transformed into a noble cause by an outpouring of European sentiment for the Greeks' struggle. Liberals rallied to the cause of Greek freedom, arguing that Greek democracy was being reborn. Romantic poets and artists (see Romanticism later in the chapter) also publicized the cause of Greek independence.

▼ **The Greek Struggle for Freedom: Eugène Delacroix,** *Greece Expiring on the Ruins of Missolonghi.* The Greek revolt against the Ottoman Empire brought a massive outpouring of European sentiment for the Greeks. Romantic artists and poets were especially eager to publicize the struggle of the Greeks for independence. In this painting, the French painter Delacroix personified Greece as a majestic, defenseless woman appealing for aid against the victorious Turk seen in the background. Delacroix's painting was done soon after the fall of the Greek fortress of Missolonghi to the Turks.

Despite the public ground swell, mutual fears and other interests kept the European powers from intervening until 1827 when a combined British and French fleet went to Greece and defeated a large Turkish fleet. In 1828, Russia declared war on Turkey and invaded its European provinces of Moldavia and Wallachia. By the Treaty of Adrianople in 1829, which ended the Russian-

Congress of Vienna	1814–1815
Reaffirmation of the Quadruple Alliance	1815
Congress of Aix-la-Chapelle	1818
Revolutions in Latin America	1819–1824
Congress of Troppau	1820
Congress of Laibach	1821
Crushing of Revolt in Southern Italy	1821
Greek Revolt against the Turks	1821
Congress of Verona	1822
Crushing of Revolt in Spain	1823
Monroe Doctrine	1823
Treaty of Adrianople	1829
Greek Independence	1830

Turkish war, the Russians received a protectorate over the two provinces. By the same treaty, the Turks agreed to allow Russia, France, and Britain to decide the fate of Greece. In 1830, the three powers declared Greece an independent kingdom, and two years later a new royal dynasty was established in the hands of a son of the Bavarian king.

The Greek revolt made a deep impression on Europeans. It was the first successful revolt against the status quo and represented a victory for both the liberal and national forces that the great powers were trying so hard to repress. But to keep this in perspective, we need to remember that the European powers did not quite see it that way. They had given the Greeks a German king, and the revolution had been successful only because the great powers themselves supported it. Until 1830 the Greek revolt had been the only successful one; the conservative domination was still largely intact.

The Conservative Domination: The European States

Between 1815 and 1830, the conservative domination of Europe evident in the Concert of Europe was also apparent in domestic affairs.

GREAT BRITAIN In 1815, Great Britain was governed by the aristocratic landowning classes that dominated both

houses of Parliament. Suffrage for elections to the House of Commons, controlled by the landed gentry, was restricted and unequal, especially in light of the changing distribution of the British population due to the Industrial Revolution. New, large industrial cities such as Birmingham and Manchester, for example, had no representatives as landowners used pocket and rotten boroughs (see Chapter 19) to control seats in the House of Commons. Although the monarchy was not yet powerless, in practice the power of the crown was largely in the hands of the ruling party in Parliament.

Within Parliament there were two parties, the Tories and Whigs. Although both of them were still dominated by members of the landed classes, the Whigs were beginning to receive support from the new moneyed interests generated by industrialization. Tory ministers largely dominated the government until 1830 and had little desire to change the existing political and electoral system. Tory leadership during the Napoleonic wars made them wary of radicalism and reform movements, an attitude that governed their activities after 1815.

Popular discontent grew apace after 1815 because of severe economic difficulties. The Tory government's response to falling agricultural prices was the Corn Law of 1815, a measure that placed extraordinarily high tariffs on foreign grain. While beneficial to the landowners, subsequent high prices for bread made conditions for the working classes more difficult. Mass protest meetings took a nasty turn when a squadron of cavalry attacked a crowd of 60,000 demonstrators at St. Peter's Fields in Manchester in 1819. The death of eleven people, called the Peterloo Massacre by government detractors, led Parliament to even more repressive measures. The government restricted large public meetings and the circulation of pamphlets and journals among the poor. Before further repression could lead to greater violence, the Tory ministry was broadened by the addition of men who believed that some concessions to change rather than sheer repression might best avoid revolution. By making minor reforms in the 1820s, the Tories managed to avoid meeting the demands for electoral reforms—at least until 1830 (see Reform in Great Britain later in the chapter).

FRANCE In 1814, the Bourbon family was restored to the throne of France in the person of Louis XVIII (1814–1824). Louis was clever enough to realize that the restored monarchy had to accept the constructive work of the revolutionary and Napoleonic eras or face disaster. Consequently, the constitutional Charter of 1814 maintained Napoleon's Concordat with the pope and accepted Napoleon's Civil Code with its recognition of the principle of equality before the law (see Chapter 20). The property rights of those who had purchased confiscated lands during the Revolution were preserved. The Charter of 1814 also established a bicameral (two-house) legislature with a Chamber of Peers chosen by the king and a Chamber of Deputies chosen by an electorate restricted to slightly less than 100,000 wealthy people.

Louis's grudging moderation, however, was opposed by liberals anxious to extend the revolutionary reforms and a group of ultraroyalists who criticized the king's willingness to compromise and retain so many features of the Napoleonic era. The ultras hoped to return to a monarchical system dominated by a privileged landed aristocracy and to restore the Catholic church to its former position of influence.

The initiative passed to the ultraroyalists in 1824 when Louis XVIII died and was succeeded by his brother, the count of Artois, who became Charles X (1824–1830). Charles had been the leader of the ultraroyalists and was determined to restore the old regime as far as possible. In 1825, an indemnity was granted to aristocrats whose lands had been confiscated during the Revolution. Moreover, the king pursued a religious policy that encouraged the church to reestablish control over France's educational system. Public outrage, fed by liberal newspapers, forced the king to compromise in 1827

and even to accept the principle of ministerial responsibility—that the ministers of the king were responsible to the legislature. But in 1829 he violated his commitment. A protest by the deputies led the king to dissolve the legislature in 1830 and call for new elections. France was on the brink of another revolution.

ITALY AND SPAIN   Italy in 1815 was one of the most backward countries in Europe. The typical Italian was a poverty-stricken illiterate peasant who cared little about the change from French to Austrian control of Italy in 1815. A small, educated middle class in the cities of northern Italy, however, who had benefited from Napoleon's changes, objected to the restoration of despotic governments controlled by Austria. Italy was still divided into a number of states; as Metternich contemptuously noted, Italy was only a "geographical expression." The Congress of Vienna had established nine states, including Piedmont in the north ruled by the house of Savoy; the kingdom of the Two Sicilies (Naples and Sicily); the Papal States; a handful of small duchies ruled by relatives of the Austrian emperor; and the important northern provinces of Lombardy and Venetia that were now part of the Austrian Empire.

Italy was largely under Austrian domination while all the states had extremely reactionary governments eager to smother any liberal or nationalist sentiment. The

▼ **The Revolution of 1830.** In 1830, the forces of change began to undo the conservative domination of Europe. In France, the reactionary Charles X was overthrown and replaced by the constitutional monarch Louis-Philippe, a liberal and former revolutionary soldier. In this painting by Gustave Wappers, Louis-Philippe is shown riding to the Hôtel de Ville, preceded by a man holding the French revolutionary tricolor flag, which had not been seen in France since 1815.

crushing of attempts at revolt in the kingdom of the Two Sicilies and Piedmont in 1821 discouraged opposition, although nationalistic secret societies known as the Carbonari—the charcoal burners—continued to conspire and plan for revolution.

In Spain, another Bourbon dynasty had been restored in the person of Ferdinand VII in 1814. Ferdinand (1814–1833) had agreed to observe the liberal constitution of 1812, which allowed for the functioning of an elected parliamentary assembly known as the Cortes. But the king soon reneged on his promises, tore up the constitution, dissolved the Cortes, and persecuted its members. Economic crisis and government despotism, inefficiency, and corruption soon led a combined group of army officers, upper-middle-class merchants, and liberal intellectuals to revolt. The king capitulated in March 1820 and promised once again to restore the constitution and the Cortes.

Metternich's policy of intervention came to Ferdinand's rescue. In April 1823, a French army moved into Spain and forced the revolutionary government to flee Madrid. By August of that year, the king had been restored to his throne. Ignoring French advice to adopt moderate policies, Ferdinand VII tortured to death, imprisoned, or exiled the supporters of a constitutional system. Intervention had succeeded.

CENTRAL EUROPE: THE GERMANIC CONFEDERATION AND THE AUSTRIAN EMPIRE   After 1815 the forces of reaction were particularly successful in central Europe. The Habsburg empire and its chief agent, Prince Klemens von Metternich, played an important role. Metternich boasted: "You see in me the chief Minister of Police in Europe. I keep an eye on everything. My contacts are such that nothing escapes me."[6] Metternich's spies were everywhere, searching for evidence of liberal or nationalist plots. Metternich worried too much in 1815. Although both liberalism and nationalism emerged in Germany and the Austrian Empire, they were initially weak as central Europe tended to remain dominated by aristocratic landowning classes and autocratic, centralized monarchies. Real opposition to the conservative order came from a relatively small group of army officers, merchants, students, teachers, and liberal nobles. Since the Industrial Revolution did not emerge until the 1830s and 1840s, there was no substantial industrial middle class to take on the liberal cause (see Liberalism later in the chapter).

The Vienna settlement in 1815 recognized the existence of thirty-eight sovereign states in what had once been the Holy Roman Empire. Austria and Prussia were the two great powers although their non-German territory was not included in the confederation. The other states varied considerably in size from the large south German kingdom of Bavaria to the small principality of Schaumburg-Lippe. Together these states formed the Germanic Confederation, but the confederation had little real power. It had no real executive, and its only central organ was the federal diet, which needed the consent of all member states to take action, making it virtually powerless. The purpose of the Germanic Confederation was not to govern Germany but to provide a common defense against France or Russia. However, it also came to serve as Metternich's instrument to repress revolutionary movements in Germany.

Initially, Germans who favored the creation of liberal principles and German unity looked to Prussia for leadership. During the Napoleonic era, King Frederick William III (1797–1840), following the advice of his two chief ministers, Baron Heinrich von Stein and Baron Karl von Hardenberg, instituted political and institutional reforms in response to Prussia's defeat at the hands of Napoleon. Hardenberg told the king in 1806: "Your Majesty! We must do from above what the French have done from below." The reforms included the abolition of serfdom, fewer restrictions on the ability of the nobility to go into trade, municipal self-government through town councils, enlargement of primary and secondary schools, and universal military conscription to create a national army. The reforms, however, did not include the creation of a legislative assembly or representative government as Stein and Hardenberg wished. After 1815 Frederick William grew more reactionary and was content to follow Metternich's lead. While reforms had made Prussia strong and efficient, it remained largely an absolutist state with little interest in German unity.

Liberal and national movements in Germany seemed largely limited to university professors and students. The latter began to organize *Burschenschaften* or student societies dedicated to fostering the goal of a free, united Germany (see the box on p. 743). Their ideas and their motto, "Honor, Liberty, Fatherland" were in part inspired by Friedrich Ludwig Jahn, who had organized gymnastic societies during the Napoleonic wars to foster the regeneration of German youth. Jahn was a noisy nationalist who encouraged Germans to pursue their Teutonic heritage and inspired his followers to disrupt the lectures of professors whose views were not nationalistic.

From 1817 to 1819, the *Burschenschaften* pursued a variety of activities that alarmed German governments.

University Students and German Unity
▼ ▼ ▼

In the early nineteenth century, German nationalism was largely supported by university students and professors. Especially important were the Burschenschaften, student societies that espoused the cause of German unity. In this selection, the liberal Heinrich von Gagern explains to his father the purpose of the Burschenschaften.

Heinrich von Gagern, Letter to His Father

It is very hard to explain the spirit of the student movement to you, but I shall try, even though I can only give you a few characteristics. . . . It speaks to the better youth, the man of heart and spirit and love for all that is good, and gives him nourishment and being. For the average student of the past, the university years were a time to enjoy life, and to make a sharp break with his own background in defiance of the philistine world, which seemed to him somehow to foreshadow the tomb. Their pleasures, their organizations, and their talk were determined by their *status* as students, and their university obligation was only to avoid failing the examination and scraping by adequately—bread-and-butter learning. They were satisfied with themselves if they thought they could pass the examination. There are still many of those nowadays, indeed the majority over-all. But at several universities, and especially here, another group —in my eyes a better one—has managed to get the upper hand in the sense that it sets the mood. I prefer really not to call it a mood; rather, it is something that presses hard and tried to spread its ideas. . . .

Those who share in this spirit have then quite another tendency in their student life, Love of Fatherland is their guiding principle. Their purpose is to make a better future for the Fatherland, each as best he can, to spread national consciousness, or to use the much ridiculed and maligned Germanic expression, more folkishness, and to work for better constitutions. . . .

We want more sense of community among the several states of Germany, greater unity in their policies and in their principles of government; no separate policy for each state, but the nearest possible relations with one another; above all, we want Germany to be considered *one* land and the German people *one* people. In the forms of our student comradeship we show how we want to approach this as nearly as possible in the real world. Regional fraternities are forbidden, and we live in a German comradeship, one people in spirit, as we want it for all Germany in reality. We give our selves the freest of constitutions, just as we should like Germany to have the freest possible one, insofar as that is suitable for the German people. We want a constitution for the people that fits in with the spirit of the times and with the people's own level of enlightenment, rather than what each prince gives his people according to what he likes and what serves his private interest. Above all, we want the princes to understand and to follow the principle that they exist for the country and not the country for them. In fact, the prevailing view is that the constitution should not come from the individual states at all. The main principles of the German constitution should apply to all states in common, and should be expressed by the German federal assembly. This constitution should deal not only with the absolute necessities, like fiscal administration and justice, general administration and church and military affairs and so on; this constitution ought to be extended to the education of the young, at least at the upper age levels, and to many other such things.

An aide wrote to Metternich that "of all the evils affecting Germany today, even including the licentiousness of the press, this student nuisance is the greatest, the most urgent and the most threatening."[7] At an assembly held at the Wartburg Castle in 1817, marking the three-hundredth anniversary of Luther's Ninety-Five Theses, the crowd burned books written by conservative authors. When a deranged student assassinated a reactionary playwright, Metternich had the diet of the Germanic Confederation draw up the Karlsbad Decrees of 1819. These closed the *Burschenschaften,* provided for censorship of the press, and placed the universities under close supervision and control. Thereafter, except for a minor flurry of activity from 1830 to 1832, Metternich and the cooperative German rulers maintained the conservative status quo.

The Austrian Empire was a multinational state, a collection of different peoples under the Habsburg emperor who provided a common bond. Eleven peoples of different national origin constituted the empire, including Germans, Czechs, Magyars (Hungarians), Slovaks, Romanians, Slovenes, Poles, Serbians, and Italians. The Germans, though only a quarter of the population, were

▼ **Portrait of Nicholas I.** Tsar Nicholas I was a reactionary ruler who sought to prevent rebellion in Russia by strengthening the government bureaucracy, increasing censorship, and suppressing individual freedom by the use of political police. Nicholas's fear of revolution made him willing to send Russian troops to crush revolutions in other European states. One of his enemies remarked about his facial characteristics: "The sharply retreating forehead and the lower jaw were expressive of iron will and feeble intelligence."

economically the most advanced and played a leading role in governing Austria. Since Austria was predominantly agricultural, the landed nobility continued to be the most important class and held most of the important positions as army officers, diplomats, ministers, and civil servants. Essentially, the Austrian Empire was held together by the dynasty, the imperial civil service, the imperial army, and the Catholic church. But its national groups, especially the Hungarians, with their increasing desire for autonomy acted as forces to break the Austrian Empire apart.

It was Metternich who managed to hold it all together after 1815. His antipathy to liberalism and nationalism was understandably grounded in the realization that these forces threatened to tear the empire apart. The growing liberal belief that each national group had the right to its own system of government could only mean disaster for the multinational Austrian Empire. Metternich however, realized the need for some change and hoped to establish a central parliament with deputies from the different nationalities making up the empire. But he was never permitted to do so by Emperor Francis II (1806–1835) who resisted all change. Thus, the Austrian Empire largely stagnated while the forces of liberalism and nationalism grew. Metternich had not prevented an explosion in Austria; he only postponed it until 1848.

RUSSIA   At the beginning of the nineteenth century, Russia was overwhelmingly rural, agricultural, and autocratic. The Russian tsar was still regarded as a divine-right monarch with unlimited power although the extent of the Russian empire made the claim impractical. Most of the Russian land remained in the control of a class of noble landlords who monopolized the civil service and army officer corps. The land was tilled by serfs, the most exploited lower class in Europe.

In 1801, Alexander I (1801–1825) came to the Russian throne after a group of aristocrats assassinated his detested father, Tsar Paul I (1796–1801). Alexander had been raised in the tradition and ideas of the Enlightenment and gave every appearance of being liberal minded. But his liberalism was always conditioned by the autocratic tradition of the tsars. As one adviser said, "He would have willingly agreed that every man should be free, on the condition that he should voluntarily do only what the Emperor wished."

Initially, however, Alexander seemed willing to make reforms. With the aid of his liberal adviser, Michael Speransky, he relaxed censorship, permitted the sale of foreign books, and reformed the educational system. Substantial changes, however, such as the granting of a constitution and the freeing of the serfs never materialized in the face of opposition from the nobility. Then, too, Alexander himself gradually moved away from his reforming tendencies. No doubt, the struggle against Napoleon contributed to his abandonment of liberal reforms, but after the defeat of Napoleon, Alexander's reactionary tendencies blossomed as he became engrossed in religious mysticism. Now the government reverted to strict and arbitrary censorship. Soon opposition arose to Alexander from a group of secret societies.

One of these groups, known as the Northern Union, was composed of young aristocrats who had served in the Napoleonic wars and had become aware of the world outside Russia as well as intellectuals alienated by the censorship and lack of academic freedom in Russian universities. The Northern Union favored the establishment of a constitutional monarchy and the abolition of serfdom. The sudden death of Alexander in 1825 offered them their opportunity.

Although Alexander's brother Constantine was the legal heir to the throne, he had renounced his claims in favor of his brother Nicholas. As Nicholas was known to be more conservative than Constantine, the military leaders of the Northern Union rebelled against his accession. This so-called Decembrist Revolt was soon crushed by troops loyal to Nicholas and its leaders executed.

The revolt transformed Nicholas I (1825–1855) from a conservative into a reactionary determined to avoid another rebellion. Under Nicholas both the bureaucracy and the secret police were strengthened. Constituting the Third Section of the tsar's chancellery, the political police were given sweeping powers over much of Russian life. They deported suspicious or dangerous persons, maintained close surveillance of foreigners in Russia, and gave regular reports to the tsar on public opinion.

Matching Nicholas's fear of revolution at home was his fear of revolution abroad. There would be no revolution in Russia during the rest of his reign; if he could help it, there would be none in Europe either. Contemporaries called him the Policeman of Europe because of his willingness to use Russian troops to crush revolutions.

▼ The Ideologies of Change

Although the conservative forces were in the ascendancy from 1815 to 1830, powerful movements for change were also at work. These depended on ideas embodied in a series of political philosophies or ideologies that came into their own in the first half of the nineteenth century. They continue to affect the entire world.

Liberalism

One of the most prominent ideologies of the nineteenth century was liberalism. Liberalism owed much to the Enlightenment of the eighteenth century and the American and French revolutions at the end of that century. In addition, liberalism became increasingly important as the Industrial Revolution progressed since the developing industrial middle class largely adopted it as its own. There were divergencies of opinion among people classified as liberals, but all began with a common denominator, a conviction that people should be as free from restraint as possible. This opinion is evident in both economic and political liberalism.

ECONOMIC LIBERALISM   Also called classical economics, economic liberalism is based on the primary tenet of laissez-faire, whose principal exponent had been Adam Smith, author of the *Wealth of Nations* (see Chapter 18). Laissez-faire meant that the state should not interrupt the free play of natural economic forces, especially supply and demand. According to Smith, government should not interfere with the economic liberty of the individual and should restrict itself to only three primary functions: defense of the country, police protection of individuals, and the construction and maintenance of public works too expensive for individuals to undertake. In Smith's view, if individuals were allowed economic liberty, ultimately they would bring about the maximum good for the maximum number and benefit the general welfare of society.

The arguments against government intervention in economic matters were greatly strengthened by Thomas Malthus (1766–1834). In his major work, *Essay on the Principles of Population*, Malthus assailed the ideas of human progress and perfectibility propagated by Enlightenment thinkers. The laws of nature, he argued, made progress impossible. According to Malthus, population, when unchecked, increases in a geometric ratio while the food supply correspondingly increases only in an arithmetic ratio. The result will be severe overpopulation and ultimately starvation for the human race if this growth is not held in check. According to Malthus, two checks operate to hold the population in balance with the food supply. One is the voluntary limiting of the birthrate by moral restraint—by chastity and late marriages. Malthus did not expect much of this voluntary check and postulated yet another, more effective one. Nature, he argued, imposes the second: "unwholesome occupations, severe labor and exposure to the seasons, extreme poverty, bad nursing of children, great towns, excesses of all kinds, the whole train of common disease, and epidemics, wars, plague and famine." Malthus's ideas justified the policies of many industrialists who could not fail to notice his arguments. Misery and poverty were simply the inevitable result of the law of nature; no government or individual should interfere with its operation.

The ideas of Thomas Malthus were further developed by David Ricardo (1772–1823). In his *Principles of Political Economy,* written in 1817, Ricardo developed his famous "iron law of wages." Following Malthus, Ricardo argued that an increase in population means a greater supply of labor; a greater supply of labor causes wages to fall below the subsistence level. The result is misery and starvation, which then reduce the population. Consequently, wages rise above the subsistence level again, which in turn encourages workers to have larger families as the cycle is repeated. According to Ricardo, raising wages arbitrarily would be pointless since it would accomplish little but this vicious cycle. Nature is harsh, but attempting to change the laws of nature through the charity of employers or legislation by the state would merely make the situation worse. An editorial in an 1848 newspaper expressed what some members of the industrial middle class were only too happy to hear: "Suffering and evil are nature's admonitions; they cannot be got rid of; and the impatient attempts of benevolence to banish them from the world by legislation . . . have always been productive of more evil than good."

If economic liberalism was of little comfort to the working classes, it did offer a reward for those laborers who helped themselves. By hard work and thriftiness, an ordinary worker could become a foreman and perhaps even a factory owner. Dr. Samuel Smiles made a fortune with a little book on all the capitalistic virtues. Entitled *Self-Help,* it expounded on how the proverbs of all nations— "No pain no gains," "No sweat no sweet," "A penny saved is a penny gained"—contained the essence of what people must do to be successful entrepreneurs (see the box on p. 747).

POLITICAL LIBERALISM In political as in economic liberalism, liberals stressed that people should be free from restraint. One French liberal proclaimed "The liberty of the individual is the object of all human associations. This liberty is the peaceful enjoyment of private independence, the right to pursue our own ends unimpeded, so long as they do not interfere with the equally legitimate activities of others."

The emphasis on liberty was directly connected to liberal ideas on power. Since power was seen as the ability by people to control the behavior of others, there needed to be limits on the exercise of power so that humans could be free. Politically, liberals came to hold a common set of beliefs. Chief among them was the protection of civil liberties or the basic rights of all people, which included equality before the law, freedom of assembly, speech, and press, and freedom from arbitrary arrest. All of these freedoms should be guaranteed by a written document, such as the American Bill of Rights or the French Declaration of the Rights of Man and the Citizen. In addition to religious toleration for all, most liberals advocated separation of church and state. The right of peaceful opposition to the government in and out of parliament and the making of laws by a representative assembly (legislature) elected by qualified voters constituted two other liberal demands. Many liberals believed, then, in a constitutional monarchy or constitutional state with limits on the powers of government in order to prevent despotism, and in written constitutions that would also help to guarantee these rights.

Many liberals also advocated ministerial responsibility or a system in which ministers of the king were responsible to the legislature rather than to the king, giving the legislative branch a check upon the power of the executive. Liberals in the first half of the nineteenth century also believed in a limited suffrage. While all people were entitled to equal civil rights, they should not have equal political rights. The right to vote and hold office would be open only to men who met certain property qualifications. As a political philosophy, liberalism was tied to middle-class, and especially industrial, middle-class men who favored the extension of voting rights so that they could share power with the landowning classes. They had little desire to let the lower classes share that power. Liberals were not democrats.

Nationalism

Nationalism can be defined as a state of mind rising out of an awareness of being part of a community that has common institutions, traditions, language, and customs. This community is called a "nation," and the primary political loyalty of individuals would be to the nation rather than to a dynasty or city-state or other political unit. Nationalism did not become a popular force for change until the French Revolution, and even then nationalism was not so much political as cultural with its emphasis upon the uniqueness of a particular nationality. People began to undertake the study of their

Self-Help
▼ ▼ ▼

S amuel Smiles (1812–1904) was a writer who made his fortune espousing the belief of middle-class economic liberals that people succeed through "individual industry, energy, and uprightness." This selection is taken from Self-Help, first published in 1859. His most popular book, it was translated into seventeen languages.

Samuel Smiles, *Self-Help*

"Heaven helps those who help themselves," is a well-worn maxim, embodying in a small compass the results of vast human experience. The spirit of self-help is the root of all genuine growth in the individual; and, exhibited in the lives of many, it constitutes the true source of national vigor and strength. Help from without is often enfeebling in its effects, but help from within invariably invigorates. Whatever is done for men or classes, to a certain extent takes away the stimulus and necessity of doing for themselves; and where men are subjected to overguidance and over-government, the inevitable tendency is to render them comparatively helpless. . . .

National progress is the sum of individual industry, energy, and uprightness, as national decay is of individual idleness, selfishness, and vice. What we are accustomed to decry as great social evils, will, for the most part, be found to be only the outgrowth of our own perverted life; and though we may endeavour to cut them down and extirpate them by means of law, they will only spring up again with fresh luxuriance in some other form, unless the individual conditions of

human life and character are radically improved. If this view be correct, then it follows that the highest patriotism and philanthropy consist, not so much in altering laws and modifying institutions, as in helping and stimulating men to elevate and improve themselves by their own free and independent action as individuals. . . .

Many popular books have been written for the purpose of communicating to the public the grand secret of making money. But there is no secret whatever about it, as the proverbs of every nation abundantly testify. . . . "Take care of the pennies and the pounds will take care of themselves."—"A penny saved is a penny gained."—"Diligence is the mother of good-luck."—"No pains no gains."—"No sweat no sweet."—"Sloth, the Key of poverty."—"Work, and thou shalt have." "He who will not work, neither shall he eat."—"The world is his, who has patience and industry."—"It is too late to spare when all is spent."—"Better go to bed supperless than rise in debt."—"The morning hour has gold in its mouth."—"Credit keeps the crown of the causeway." Such are specimens of the proverbial philosophy, embodying the hoarded experience of many generations, as to the best means of thriving in the world. They were current in people's mouths long before books were invented; and like other popular proverbs, they were the first codes of popular morals. Moreover they have stood the test of time and the experience of every day still bears witness to their accuracy, force, and soundness.

language, history, literature, art, and folklore to understand the spirit of their nation.

This cultural idea of nationality usually came before the wish for political unity; cultural nationalism evolved into political nationalism. The latter advocated that governments should coincide with nationalities. Thus, a disunited people such as the Germans wanted national unity in a German nation-state with one central government. Subject peoples, such as the Hungarians, wanted national self-determination or the right to establish their own autonomy rather than be subject to a German minority in a multinational empire.

Nationalism threatened to upset the existing political order, both internationally and nationally, making nationalism fundamentally radical. A united Germany or united Italy would upset the balance of power established in 1815. By the same token, an independent Hungarian state would mean the breakup of the Austrian Empire. Fear of such dramatic change makes it evident why conservatives tried so hard to repress nationalism.

At the same time, in the first half of the nineteenth century, nationalism found a firm ally in liberalism. Most liberals believed that freedom could only be realized by

▼ **Map 22.3** Nationalism in Europe in the Nineteenth Century.

nationalities who ruled themselves. Each people should have its own country; no state should try to dominate others. One British liberal said, "it is in general a necessary condition of free institutions that the boundaries of governments should coincide in the main with those of nationalities." The combination of liberalism with nationalism also gave a cosmopolitan dimension to nationalism. Young Italy, Young Germany, Young Switzerland, all were parts of a wider Young Europe movement (see Italy later in the chapter). Supporting an uprising in

Genoa in 1834 was an invasion army of young Italians, Swiss, Poles, and Germans.

In its German expression, nationalism took a turn that was hardly cosmopolitan and foreshadowed an aggressive kind of nationalism that was popular in the second half of the nineteenth century. An important contribution to German nationalism came from the famous philosopher, Georg Wilhelm Friedrich Hegel (1770–1831). Aspects of Hegel's philosophy of history eventually made their way into German nationalistic thought.

One of these was his emphasis on the nation, which he envisioned as the direct manifestation of the "world-spirit" or "divine idea" operating in history. Since Hegel believed that this spirit of history was progressing toward an ideal of freedom, he implied that individuals could only find their true freedom or meaning by identifying fully with the nation. Moreover, Hegel stressed that the Germanic nation would play a special role as the final "world historical people" in the realization of freedom or the spiritual liberation of humanity. As a philosopher, Hegel did not derive a specific political program from his philosophical system. But others did, and what they stressed was the role of the state and a belief in the peculiar historical destiny of Germany; both became an integral part of German nationalism in the second half of the nineteenth century.

Early Socialism

In the first half of the nineteenth century, the pitiful conditions found in the slums, mines, and factories of the Industrial Revolution gave rise to another ideology for change known as socialism. The term eventually became associated with a Marxist analysis of human society (see Chapter 23), but early socialism was largely the product of political theorists or intellectuals who wanted to introduce equality into social conditions and believed that human cooperation was superior to the competition that characterized early industrial capitalism. To later Marxists, their ideas seemed impractical dreams, and they contemptuously labeled them utopian socialists. The term has remained to this day.

The early socialists accepted the Enlightenment belief that people by nature are not evil and are capable of a higher moral development if they live in a suitable environment. The economic system of their day, which they believed had brought wealth to some and misery to others, was incapable of providing this environment. The utopian socialists were against private property and the competitive spirit of early industrial capitalism. By eliminating them and creating new systems of social organization, they thought that a better environment for humanity could be achieved. Early socialists proposed a variety of ways to accomplish that task.

One approach, set out in the teachings of the Frenchman Henri de Saint-Simon (1760–1825), was the organization of all society into a cooperative community. Two elites, the intellectual leaders and the industrial managers, would use industrial and scientific technology to coordinate society for the benefit of all. In the process, government would vanish, no longer needed in the new society.

Another group of early socialists rejected Saint-Simon's collectivist approach in favor of creating voluntary associations that would demonstrate the advantages of cooperative living. Charles Fourier (1772–1838) offered a concrete scheme for this kind of approach. To Fourier, the competitive industrial system was failing to satisfy human passions or instincts and actually repressed them. He proposed instead the creation of small model communities called phalansteries. These were self-contained cooperatives, each consisting ideally of 1,620 people. Communally housed, the inhabitants of the phalanstery would live and work together for the mutual

▼ Charles Fourier, *Plan of a Phalanstery.* Charles Fourier believed that voluntary associations could be used to encourage cooperative rather than competitive living patterns. This sketch by Fourier is his plan for a phalanstery, a self-contained model community of about 1600 people who would live and work together for the common good of the group. This early socialist scheme of Fourier was attacked by others as an impractical or utopian fantasy.

benefit of its members. Work assignments would be rotated frequently to relieve workers of nonattractive tasks. Unable to gain financial backing for his phalansteries, Fourier's plan remained untested, although his followers did set up a number of communities in the United States.

Robert Owen (1771–1858), the British cotton manufacturer, also believed that humans would reveal their true natural goodness if they lived in a cooperative environment. At New Lanark in Scotland, he was successful in transforming a squalid factory town into a flourishing, healthy community. But when he attempted to create a self-contained cooperative community at New Harmony, Indiana, in the United States in the 1820s, internal bickering within the community eventually destroyed his dream.

The Frenchman Louis Blanc (1813–1882) offered yet another early socialist approach to a better society, based on the idea that government had a responsibility for the welfare of its citizens. In *The Organization of Work*, he maintained that social problems could be solved by government assistance. Denouncing competition as the main cause of the economic evils of his day, he called for the creation of social workshops that would produce goods for current markets. These would be financed by the state and owned and operated by the workers. By the gradual spread of such workshops, he believed, a cooperative rather than competitive foundation could be created for the entire economic life of the nation.

In their plans for the reconstruction of society, utopian socialists included schemes to change the roles of women and the relations between men and women. Saint-Simon's cooperative society included a recognition of equality between men and women, and his movement attracted a group of women who published a newspaper dedicated to the emancipation of women. Fourier's cooperative model communities were supposed to provide the same educational and job opportunities for men and women. Collective living would also entail both male and female responsibilities for child care and housecleaning.

One female utopian socialist, Flora Tristan (1803–1844), even attempted to foster a "utopian synthesis of socialism and feminism." She traveled through France preaching the need for the liberation of women. Her *Worker's Union*, published in 1843, advocated the application of Fourier's ideas to reconstruct both family and work:

> Workers, be sure of it. If you have enough equity and justice to inscribe into your Charter the few points I have just outlined, this declaration of the rights of women will soon pass into custom, from custom into law, and before twenty-five years pass you will then see inscribed in front of the book of laws which will govern French society: THE ABSOLUTE EQUALITY of man and woman. Then, my brothers, and only then, will human unity be constituted.[8]

She envisioned this absolute equality as the only hope to free the working class and transform civilization.

Flora Tristan, like the other utopian socialists, was largely ignored by her contemporaries. Although criticized for their impracticality, the utopian socialists at least laid the groundwork for later attacks on capitalism that would have a far-reaching result. Further industrialization would have to occur before those changes could be realized. In the first half of the nineteenth century, socialism remained merely a fringe movement compared to liberalism and nationalism.

▼ Revolution and Reform, 1830–1850

Beginning in 1830, the forces of change began to break through the conservative domination of Europe, more successfully in some places than in others. Finally, in 1848 a wave of revolutionary fervor moved through Europe, causing liberals and nationalists everywhere to think that they were on the verge of creating a new order.

Another French Revolution

The new elections Charles X had called in 1830 produced another victory for the liberal forces; at this point the king decided to seize the initiative. He believed that concessions had brought the downfall of Louis XVI during the first French Revolution. He was determined not to go in that direction: "I have either got to mount a horse or a death-cart." On July 26, 1830, Charles issued a set of edicts (July Ordinances) that imposed a rigid censorship on the press, dissolved the legislative assembly, and reduced the electorate in preparation for new elections. This unilateral revocation of the Charter of 1814 produced an immediate rebellion—the July Revolution. Barricades went up in Paris as a provisional government led by a group of moderate, propertied liberals was hastily formed and appealed to Louis-Philippe, the duke of Orléans, a cousin of Charles X, to become the constitutional king of France. Charles X fled to Britain; a new monarchy had been born.

THE BOURGEOIS MONARCHY OF LOUIS-PHILIPPE   Louis-Philippe (1830–1848) was soon called the bourgeois monarch since political support for his rule came from the upper middle class. Louis-Philippe even dressed in a conventional business suit rather than a royal uniform. Constitutional changes were also made to favor the interests of the upper bourgeoisie. The Charter of 1814 was reinstated. Financial qualifications for voting were reduced, yet they were sufficiently high that the number of voters only increased from 100,000 to barely 200,000, thus guaranteeing that only the wealthiest people would vote.

The bourgeois monarchy represented the stopping place for political progress to the upper middle class. To the lesser bourgeoisie and the Parisian working class, who had helped to overthrow Charles X in 1830, it was a severe disappointment because they had been completely excluded from political power. The rapid expansion of French industry in the 1830s and 1840s led to the emergence of an industrial working class concentrated in certain urban regions. Terrible working and living conditions and the periodic economic crises that created high levels of unemployment led to worker unrest and sporadic outbursts of violence. In 1831 and 1834, government troops were used to crush working-class disturbances in Lyons, center of the silk industry. These insurrections witnessed an emerging alliance between workers and radical advocates of a republic. The government's response—repression and strict censorship of the press—worked temporarily to curb further overt resistance.

Even in the legislature—the Chamber of Deputies—there were differences of opinion about the bourgeois monarchy and the direction in which it should grow. Two groups rapidly emerged, although both were composed of upper-middle-class representatives. The Party of Movement was led by Adolphe Thiers who wished France to pursue an active foreign policy, adopt the practice of ministerial responsibility, and extend the suffrage, although only in a limited way. Thiers was no democrat. The Party of Resistance was led by François Guizot who believed that France had finally reached the "perfect form" of government and needed no further institutional changes. After 1840, the Party of Resistance dominated

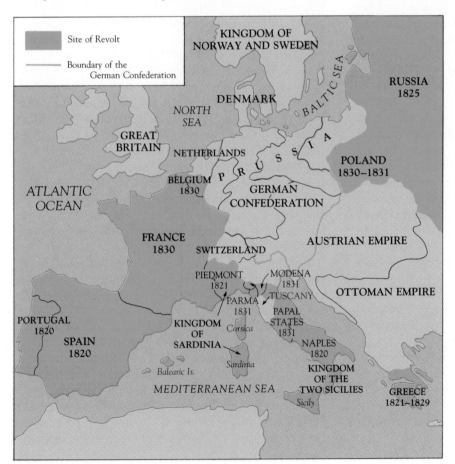

▼ **Map 22.4** European Revolts in the 1820s and 1830s.

the Chamber of Deputies. Guizot cooperated with Louis-Philippe in suppressing ministerial responsibility and pursuing a policy favoring the interests of the wealthier manufacturers and tradesmen. The government's unwillingness to allow any reform of the electoral system or to deal with either republican demands for greater political representation or working-class demands for improved social conditions led to growing frustration and revolutionary stirrings. They finally erupted in 1848.

Revolutionary Outbursts in Belgium, Poland, and Italy

Supporters of liberalism played a primary role in the July Revolution in France, but nationalism was the crucial force in three other revolutionary outbursts in 1830. The Austrian Netherlands or what came to be known as Belgium had been annexed to the Dutch Republic in 1815 to create a larger state to act as a barrier to French aggression. The combination of two states with different languages, traditions, and religions was never really acceptable to the Belgians, nor did they appreciate the absolutist rule of the king, William of Orange, and his Dutch administrators. The success of the July Revolution in France precipitated a student riot that soon turned into an uprising that spread throughout Belgium as the forces of William of Orange proved unable to crush the popular upheaval.

Since the Belgian revolt clearly meant the disruption of the Vienna agreement of 1815, Russia, Prussia, and Austria seemed eager to help King William with armed force. France and Britain opposed this intervention and managed to arrange a conference in December 1830 that created an independent, neutral Belgium under the collective guarantees of the great powers. Leopold of Saxe-Coburg, a minor German prince, was designated to be the new king while a Belgian national congress established a constitutional monarchy for the new state. The cooperation of the great powers had assured the success of the Belgian nationalistic revolution.

The revolutionary scenarios in Poland and Italy were much less successful. The July Revolution in France led Italian secret societies to revolt against reactionary governments in Modena, Parma, and the Papal States. Their only hope for success was to obtain support from the new government of Louis-Philippe in order to counter Austrian intervention. The new French ruler refused. Metternich then sent Austrian troops to the three Italian states, crushed the insurrections, and restored the deposed rulers.

Poland, too, had a nationalist uprising in 1830. Although Poland had been granted a liberal constitution by Tsar Alexander I, Russian interference in Polish affairs grew increasingly burdensome. After the accession of the reactionary Nicholas I to the Russian throne, tension increased until in November 1830 a combined group of junior army officers and university students led a revolt in Warsaw. Leadership of the revolution was soon taken over by Polish landed aristocrats. Their factional divisions and lack of support from the mass of Polish peasants, however, made them incapable of standing up to Russian forces. Hoped-for support from France and Britain, where liberals advocated backing the Polish uprising, failed to materialize as the governments of those countries refused to get involved. By September 1831, the revolt was crushed, and an oppressive Russian military dictatorship was established over Poland.

Reform in Great Britain

In 1830, new parliamentary elections brought the Whigs to power in Britain. At the same time, the successful July Revolution in France served to catalyze change in Britain. The Industrial Revolution had led to an expanding group of industrial leaders who objected to their exclusion from political power by the corrupt British electoral system. The Whigs, though also members of the landed classes, realized that concessions to reform were superior to revolution; the demands of the wealthy industrial middle class could no longer be ignored. In 1830, the Whigs introduced an election reform bill that was enacted in 1832 after an intense struggle (see the box on p. 753).

The Reform Bill gave explicit recognition to the changes wrought in British life by the Industrial Revolution. It disfranchised fifty-six rotten boroughs and enfranchised forty-two new towns and cities and reapportioned others. This gave the new industrial urban communities some voice in government. A property qualification (of £10 annual rent) for voting was retained, however, so the number of voters only increased from 478,000 to 814,000, a figure that still meant that only one in every thirty people was represented in Parliament. Thus, the Reform Bill of 1832 primarily benefited the upper middle class; the lower middle class, artisans, and industrial workers still had no vote. Moreover, the change did not significantly alter the composition of the House of Commons. One political leader noted that the Commons chosen in the first elec-

The Voice of Reform: Macaulay on the Reform Bill of 1832

▼ ▼ ▼

Thomas Babington Macaulay (1800–1859) was a historian and Whig member of Parliament. This selection is an excerpt from his speech given in Parliament in support of the Reform Bill of 1832, which extended the right to vote to the industrial middle classes of Britain. His argument was very simple: it is better to reform than to have a political revolution.

Thomas Babington Macaulay, Speech of March 2, 1831

My hon. friend the member of the University of Oxford tells us that, if we pass this law, England will soon be a Republic. The reformed House of Commons will, according to him, before it has sat ten years, depose the King, and expel the Lords from their House. Sir, if my hon. friend could prove this, he would have succeeded in bringing an argument for democracy infinitely stronger than any that is to be found in the works of Paine. His proposition is, in fact, this—that our monarchical and aristocratical institutions have no hold on the public mind of England; that these institutions are regarded with aversion by a decided majority of the middle class . . . . Now, sir, if I were convinced that the great body of the middle class in England look with aversion on monarchy and aristocracy, I should be forced, much against my will, to come to this conclusion, that monarchical and aristocratical institutions are unsuited to this country. Monarchy and aristocracy, valuable and useful as I think them, are still valuable and useful as means, and not as ends. The end of government is the happiness of the people; and I do not conceive that, in a country like this, the happiness of the people can be promoted by a form of government in which the middle classes place no confidence, and which exists only because the middle classes have no organ by which to make their senti-

ments known. But, sir, I am fully convinced that the middle classes sincerely wish to uphold the royal prerogatives, and the constitutional rights of the Peers. . . .

But let us know our interest and our duty better. Turn where we may—within, around—the voice of great events is proclaiming to us, "Reform, that you may preserve." Now, therefore, while everything at home and abroad forebodes ruin to those who persist in a hopeless struggle against the spirit of the age; now, while the crash of the proudest throne of the Continent is still resounding in our ears; . . . now, while the heart of England is still sound; now, while the old feelings and the old associations retain a power and a charm which may too soon pass away; now, in this your accepted time; now, in this your day of salvation, take counsel, not of prejudice, not of party spirit, not of the ignominious pride of a fatal consistency, but of history, of reason, of the ages which are past, of the signs of this most portentous time. Pronounce in a manner worthy of the expectation with which this great debate has been anticipated, and of the long remembrance which it will leave behind. Renew the youth of the State. Save property divided against itself. Save the multitude, endangered by their own ungovernable passions. Save the aristocracy, endangered by its own unpopular power. Save the greatest, and fairest, and most highly civilised community that ever existed, from calamities which may in a few days sweep away all the rich heritage of so many ages of wisdom and glory. The danger is terrible. The time is short. If this Bill should be rejected, I pray to God that none of those who concur in rejecting it may ever remember their votes with unavailing regret, amidst the wreck of laws, the confusion of ranks, the spoliation of property, and the dissolution of social order.

tion after the Reform Bill seemed "to be very much like every other parliament." Nevertheless, a significant step had been taken. The "monied, manufacturing, and educated elite" had been "hitched" to the landed interest in ruling Britain. At the same time, the Reform Bill established a precedent that would lead to electoral re-

form bills in the second half of the nineteenth century that would extend the right to vote to significantly larger numbers of Britons.

The 1830s and 1840s witnessed considerable reform legislation. The aristocratic landowning class was usually (but not always) the driving force for legislation that halted some of the worst abuses in the industrial system by instituting government regulation of working conditions in the factories and mines. Opposed to such legislation because of their belief in economic liberalism, the industrialists and manufacturers now in Parliament were usually (but not always) the driving forces for legislation that favored the principles of economic liberalism. The Poor Law of 1834 was based on the theory that giving aid to the poor and unemployed only increased their laziness and the number of paupers. The Poor Law of 1834 tried to remedy this by making paupers so wretched they would choose to work. Those unable to support themselves were crowded together in workhouses where living and working conditions were intentionally miserable so that people would be encouraged to find profitable employment.

Another piece of liberal legislation involved the repeal of the Corn Laws. This was primarily the work of the manufacturers Richard Cobden and John Bright who formed the Anti-Corn Law Association in 1838 to help workers by lowering bread prices. But this also aided the industrial middle classes who, as economic liberals, favored the principles of free trade. Repeal came in 1846 when some Tories were converted to free trade principles.

The year 1848, which witnessed revolutions in most of Europe, ended without a major crisis in Britain. On the Continent, middle-class liberals and nationalists took direction of the revolutionary forces. In Britain, however, the middle class had been largely satisfied by the Reform Act of 1832 and the repeal of the Corn Laws in 1846. The British working classes were discontented, but they would have to wait until the second half of the nineteenth century to begin to achieve their goals.

The Growth of the United States

The American Constitution, ratified in 1789, committed the United States to two of the major forces of the first half of the nineteenth century, liberalism and nationalism. Initially, this constitutional commitment to national unity was challenged by divisions over the power of the federal government vis-à-vis the individual states. Bitter conflict erupted between the Federalists and the Republicans. Led by Alexander Hamilton (1757–1804), the Federalists favored a financial program that would establish a strong central government. The Republicans, guided by Thomas Jefferson (1743–1826) and James Madison (1751–1836), feared centralization and its consequences for popular liberties. These divisions were intensified by European rivalries as the

Federalists were pro-British and the Republicans pro-French. The successful conclusion of the War of 1812 brought an end to the Federalists, who had opposed the war, while the surge of national feeling generated by the war served to heal the nation's divisions.

Another strong force for national unity came from the Supreme Court while John Marshall (1755–1835) was chief justice from 1801 to 1835. Marshall made the Supreme Court into an important national institution by asserting the right of the Court to overrule an act of Congress if the Court found it to be in violation of the Constitution. Under Marshall, the Supreme Court contributed further to establishing the supremacy of the national government by curbing the actions of state courts and legislatures.

The election of Andrew Jackson (1767–1845) as president in 1828 opened a new era in American politics. Jacksonian democracy introduced a mass democratic politics. The electorate was expanded by dropping traditional property qualifications; by the 1830s suffrage had been extended to almost all adult white males. During the period from 1815 to 1850, the traditional liberal belief in the improvement of human beings was also given concrete expression. Americans developed detention schools for juvenile delinquents and new penal institutions, both motivated by the liberal belief that the right kind of environment would rehabilitate those in need of it. The abolitionist or national antislavery movement that developed in the 1830s also stemmed from liberal convictions. The American Anti-Slavery Society, established by William Lloyd Garrison (1805–1879) in 1833, already had 250,000 members by 1838.

By 1850, Europeans had become well aware of the growth of the American republic. Between 1830 and 1850, a wide variety of European political writers visited and examined the United States. The general thrust of their collective wisdom was that the United States was emerging as a world power. The French critic Sainte-Beuve wrote in 1847 that: "Russia is still barbarous, but she is great. . . . The other youthful people is America . . . the future of the world is there, between these two great worlds." Sainte-Beuve had the right idea even if he was somewhat premature.

The Revolutions of 1848

Europe had experienced two waves of revolution, one in the early 1820s and another in 1830–1831. And yet, despite successes in France, Belgium, and Greece, the conservative order continued to dominate much of Europe. Revolutions in Spain, Italy, Germany, Russia, and

Poland had all failed. Oftentimes liberal forces depended almost exclusively on junior army officers, liberal nobles, writers, university students, professors, and adventurers. But the forces of liberalism and nationalism, first generated by the French Revolution, continued to grow as the second great revolution—the Industrial Revolution—expanded and brought new groups of people who wanted change. In 1848, these forces of change erupted once more. As usual, revolution in France provided the spark for other countries, and soon most of central and southern Europe was ablaze with revolutionary fires. Tsar Nicholas I of Russia lamented to Queen Victoria in April 1848, "What remains standing in Europe? Great Britain and Russia."

YET ANOTHER FRENCH REVOLUTION   Numerous signs of trouble preceded the revolution. A severe industrial and agricultural depression beginning in 1846 brought untold hardship to the lower middle class, workers, and peasants. One-third of the workers in Paris were unemployed by the end of 1847. Scandals, graft, and corruption were rife while the government's persistent refusal to extend the suffrage angered the disfranchised members of the middle class. Even members of the upper middle class were discontented with the colorless reign of Louis-Philippe.

As Louis-Philippe's government continued to refuse to make changes, opposition grew. Radical republicans and socialists, joined by the upper middle class under the leadership of Adolphe Thiers, agitated for the dismissal of Guizot. Since they were forbidden by law to stage political rallies, they used the political banquet to call for reforms. Almost seventy such banquets were held in France during the winter of 1847–1848; a grand, culminating banquet was planned for Paris on February 22. When the government forbade it, people came anyway; students and workers threw up barricades in Paris. Although Louis-Philippe called out the National Guard, many of its bourgeois members joined the opposition. The king now proposed reform, but unable to form another ministry, he abdicated on February 24 and fled to Britain. A provisional government was established by a group of moderate and radical republicans; the latter even included the socialist Louis Blanc. The provisional government ordered that representatives be elected by universal manhood suffrage for a Constituent Assembly to draw up a new constitution.

The provisional government also established national workshops under the influence of Louis Blanc. As Blanc envisioned them, the workshops were supposed to be co-operative factories run by the workers. In fact, the work-shops became unemployment compensation units or public works, except that they provided little work beyond leaf raking and ditch digging. The cost of the program became increasingly burdensome to the government.

The result was an growing split between the moderate republicans, who had the support of most of France, and the radical republicans, whose main support came from the Parisian working class. In the elections for the National Assembly, 500 seats went to moderate republicans and 300 to avowed monarchists while the radicals gained only 100. From March to June, the number of unemployed enrolled in the national workshops rose from 10,000 to almost 120,000, emptying the treasury and frightening the moderates who responded by closing the workshops on June 21. The workers refused to accept this decision and poured into the streets. Four days of bitter and bloody fighting by government forces crushed the working-class revolt, described by some as a "class struggle, a sort of servile war." Thousands were killed, and 11,000 prisoners were deported to the French colony of Algeria in northern Africa. These "June days" produced a legacy of hate. They had aspects of class warfare as the propertied classes became convinced that they had barely averted an attempt by the working class to destroy the social order. To many Europeans, the "June days" appeared to be a struggle of the bourgeoisie against the working class.

The new constitution, ratified on November 4, 1848, established a republic (Second Republic) with a unicameral (one-house) legislature of 750 elected by universal male suffrage for three years and a president, also elected by universal male suffrage, for four years. In the elections for the presidency held in December 1848, four republicans who had been associated with the early months of the Second Republic were resoundingly defeated by Charles Louis Napoleon Bonaparte.

How could a virtual unknown who had been arrested twice and sent into exile once be chosen president by a landslide? People considered him inept with none of his uncle's ability. And yet the name of Bonaparte had obviously worked its magic. The Napoleonic revival had been going on for years as romanticists glorified his legend. One old veteran said: "Why shouldn't I vote for this gentleman. I, whose nose was frozen near Moscow." Perhaps just as important, the French were tired of revolution, and Louis Napoleon had posed as a defender of order. The large number of rural and urban masses who voted for Napoleon saw him as a man of the people. Since they had been excluded from political life since 1815, what better choice did they have? Within four years President Napoleon had become Emperor Napo-

Revolutionary Excitement: Carl Schurz and the Revolution of 1848 in Germany

▼ ▼ ▼

The excitement with which German liberals and nationalists received the news of the February Revolution in France and their own expectations for Germany are well captured in this selection from the Reminiscences of Carl Schurz (1829–1906). Schurz made his way to America after the failure of the German revolution and eventually became a United States senator.

Carl Schurz, *Reminiscences*

One morning, toward the end of February, 1848, I sat quietly in my attic-chamber, working hard at my tragedy of "Ulrich von Hutten," [a sixteenth-century German humanist and knight] when suddenly a friend rushed breathlessly into the room, exclaiming: "What, you sitting here! Do you not know what has happened?"

"No; what?"

"The French have driven away Louis Philippe and proclaimed the republic."

I threw down my pen—and that was the end of "Ulrich von Hutten." I never touched the manuscript again. We tore down the stairs, into the street, to the market-square, the accustomed meeting-place for all the student societies after their midday dinner. Although it was still forenoon, the market was already crowded with young men talking excitedly. There was no shouting, no noise, only agitated conversation. What did we want there? This probably no one knew. But since the French had driven away Louis Philippe and proclaimed the republic, something of course must happen here, too. . . . We were dominated by a vague feeling as if a great outbreak of elemental forces had begun, as if an earthquake was impending of which we had felt the first shock, and we instinctively crowded together. . . .

The next morning there were the usual lectures to be attended. But how profitless! The voice of the professor sounded like a monotonous drone coming from far away. What he had to say did not seem to concern us. The pen that should have taken notes remained idle. At last we closed with a sigh the notebook and went away, impelled by a feeling that now we had something more important to do—to devote ourselves to the affairs of the fatherland. And this we did by seeking as quickly as possible again the company of our friends, in order to discuss what had happened and what was to come. In these conversations, excited as they were, certain ideas and catchwords worked themselves to the surface, which expressed more or less the feelings of the people. Now had arrived in Germany the day for the establishment of "German Unity," and the founding of a great, powerful national German Empire. In the first line the convocation of a national parliament. Then the demands for civil rights and liberties, free speech, free press, the right of free assembly, equality before the law, a freely elected representation of the people with legislative power, responsibility of ministers, self-government of the communes, the right of the people to carry arms, the formation of a civic guard with elective officers, and so on—in short, that which was called a "constitutional form of government on a broad democratic basis." Republican ideas were at first only sparingly expressed. But the word democracy was soon on all tongues, and many, too, thought it a matter of course that if the princes should try to withhold from the people the rights and liberties demanded, force would take the place of mere petition. Of course the regeneration of the fatherland must, if possible, be accomplished by peaceable means . . . . Like many of my friends, I was dominated by the feeling that at last the great opportunity had arrived for giving to the German people the liberty which was their birthright and to the German fatherland its unity and greatness, and that it was now the first duty of every German to do and to sacrifice everything for this sacred object.

leon (see Chapter 23). The French had once again made their journey from republican chaos to authoritarian order, a pattern that was becoming all too common in French history.

CENTRAL EUROPE   There were rural and urban tensions in central Europe (just as in France) due to an agricultural depression beginning in 1845. But what seems to have caused the upheaval here was news of the revolution in Paris in February 1848 (see the box above). By early March 1848, handicraft workers in Germany were destroying the machines and factories that they blamed for depriving them of their jobs; peasants looted and burned the manor houses of the nobility. Many German rulers promised constitutions, a free press, jury trials and other liberal reforms. In Prussia concessions were also made to appease the revolutionaries. King Frederick William IV (1840–1861) agreed to abolish censorship, establish a new constitution, and work for a united Germany. The latter promise had its counterpart throughout all the German states as governments allowed elections by universal male suffrage for deputies to an all-German parliament. Its purpose was to fulfill a liberal dream—the preparation of a constitution for a new united Germany.

This Frankfurt Assembly was dominated by a university-educated middle class, including civil servants, lawyers, professors, teachers, jurists, and physicians. From its beginning, the assembly claimed to be a government for all Germany, a pretension unacceptable to the German states themselves. Moreover, one especially troublesome problem arose as deliberations over the new Germany ensued. What should be the nature of the new German state? Supporters of a *Grossdeutsch* ("Big German") solution wished to include the German provinces of Austria. The *Kleindeutsch* ("Small German") supporters favored the inclusion only of Prussia and the other German states with the Prussian king as emperor. This, of course, would leave many Germans (in Austria) outside a German state. The problem was solved by the Austrians who withdrew from the assem-

bly, leaving the victory to the *Kleindeutsch* solution. In March 1849, the Frankfurt Assembly elected Frederick William IV of Prussia as "emperor of the Germans." But he contemptuously refused the crown as a "diadem moulded out of the dirt and dregs of revolution, disloyalty and treason." By this time Frederick William IV had regained control of the situation in Prussia and ordered the Prussian delegates home.

The Frankfurt Assembly soon disbanded. Although some members spoke of using force, they had no real means of compelling the German rulers to accept the constitution they had drawn up. The attempt of the German liberals at Frankfurt to create a German state had failed, and leadership for unification would now pass to the Prussian military monarchy (see Chapter 23).

The Austrian Empire also had its social, political, and nationalist grievances and needed only the news of the revolution in Paris to encourage it to erupt in flames in March 1848. The Hungarian liberal gentry under Louis Kossuth agitated for "commonwealth" status; they were willing to keep the Habsburg monarch, but wanted their own legislature. In March, demonstrations in Budapest, Prague, and Vienna led to Metternich's dismissal. The arch-symbol of the conservative order fled abroad. In Vienna, revolutionary forces, carefully guided by the educated and propertied classes, took control of the capital and insisted upon the summoning of a constituent assembly to draw up a liberal constitution. Hungary was granted its wish for its own legislature, a separate national army, and control over its foreign policy and bud-

▼ **Austrian Students in the Revolutionary Civic Guard.** In 1848, revolutionary fervor swept through Europe and toppled governments in France, central Europe, and Italy. In the Austrian Empire, students joined the revolutionary civic guard in taking control of Vienna and forcing the Austrian emperor to call a constituent assembly to draft a liberal constitution. However, divisions between radical and moderate revolutionaries enabled the emperor and his officials to crush the revolution.

The Voice of Italian Nationalism: Giuseppe Mazzini and Young Italy

▼ ▼ ▼

After the failure of the uprisings in Italy in 1830–1831, Giuseppe Mazzini emerged as the leader of the Italian risorgimento—the movement for Italian nationhood. In 1831, he founded an organization known as Young Italy whose goal was the creation of a united Italian republic. This selection is excerpted from the oath that the members of Young Italy were required to take.

Giuseppe Mazzini, The Young Italy Oath

Young Italy is a brotherhood of Italians who believe in a law of Progress and Duty, and are convinced that Italy is destined to become one nation,—convinced also that she possesses sufficient strength within herself to become one, and that the ill success of her former efforts is to be attributed not to the weakness, but to the misdirection of the revolutionary elements within her,—that the secret of force lies in constancy and unity of effort. They join this association in the firm intent of consecrating both thought and action to the great aim of reconstituting Italy as one independent sovereign nation of free men and equals. . . .

Each member will, upon his initiation into the association of Young Italy, pronounce the following form of oath, in the presence of the initiator:

In the name of God and of Italy;

In the name of all the martyrs of the holy Italian cause who have fallen beneath foreign and domestic tyranny;

By the duties which bind me to the land wherein God has placed me, and to the brothers whom God has given me;

By the love—innate in all men—I bear to the country that gave my mother birth, and will be the home of my children. . . .

By the sufferings of the millions,—

I, . . . believing in the mission intrusted by God to Italy, and the duty of every Italian to strive to attempt its fulfillment; convinced that where God has ordained that a nation shall be, He has given the requisite power to create it; that the people are the depositaries of that power, and that in its right direction for the people, and by the people, lies the secret of victory; convinced that virtue consists in action and sacrifice, and strength in union and constancy of purpose: I give my name to Young Italy, an association of men holding the same faith, and swear:

To dedicate myself wholly and forever to the endeavor with them to constitute Italy one free, independent, republican nation; to promote by every means in my power—whether by written or spoken word, or by action—the education of my Italian brothers towards the aim of Young Italy; towards association, the sole means of its accomplishment, and to virtue, which alone can render the conquest lasting; to abstain from enrolling myself in any other association from this time forth; to obey all the instructions, in conformity with the spirit of Young Italy, given me by those who represent with me the union of my Italian brothers; and to keep the secret of these instructions, even at the cost of my life; to assist my brothers of the association both by action and counsel—NOW AND FOREVER.

---

get. Allegiance to the Habsburg dynasty was now Hungary's only tie to the Austrian Empire. In Bohemia, the Czechs began to demand their own government as well.

Although Emperor Ferdinand I and Austrian officials had made concessions to appease the revolutionaries, they awaited an opportunity to reestablish their firm control. As in the German states, they were increasingly encouraged by the divisions between radical and moderate revolutionaries and played upon the middle-class fear of a working-class social revolution. Their first success came in June 1848 when a military force under General Windischgrätz ruthlessly suppressed the Czech rebels in Prague. In October the death of the minister for war at the hands of a Viennese mob gave Windischgrätz the pretext for an attack on Vienna. By the end of the month, radical rebels there had been crushed. In December the feebleminded Ferdinand I agreed to abdicate in favor of his nephew, Francis Joseph I (1848–1916), who worked vigorously to restore the imperial government in Hungary. The Austrian armies, however, were unable to defeat Kossuth's forces, and it was only through the intervention of Nicholas I, who sent a Russian army of 140,000 men to aid the Austrians, that the Hungarian revolution was finally crushed in 1849. The revolutions in Austria had also failed. Autocratic government was restored; emperor and propertied classes remained in control while the numerous nationalities remained subject to the Austrian government.

ITALY   The failure of the revolutionary uprisings in Italy in 1830–1831 had served to discredit the secret societies that had fomented them and encouraged the Italian movement for unification to take a new direction. The leadership of Italy's *risorgimento* ("Resurgence") passed into the hands of Giuseppe Mazzini (1805–1872), a dedicated Italian nationalist who founded an organization known as Young Italy in 1831 (see the box on p.758). With its membership limited to men under forty years old, this group set as its goal the creation of a united Italian republic. In his work, *The Duties of Man,* Mazzini urged Italians to dedicate their lives to the Italian nation: "O my Brother! love your Country. Our Country is our home." And yet to Mazzini love of country represented but one stage towards the higher responsibility of loving humanity: "You are men before you are either citizens or fathers."

Mazzini's dreams seemed on the verge of fulfillment when Italy rose in revolt in 1848. Beginning in Sicily,

rebellions spread northward through the Italian states as ruler after ruler granted a constitution to his people. Citizens in the two provinces of Lombardy and Venetia also rebelled against their Austrian overlords. The Venetians declared a republic in Venice. The king of the northern Italian state of Piedmont, Charles Albert (1831–1849), took up the call and assumed the leadership for a war of liberation from Austrian domination. His invasion of Lombardy proved unsuccessful, however, and by 1849 the Austrians had reestablished complete control over Lombardy and Venetia.

Counterrevolutionary forces also prevailed throughout Italy. French forces helped Pope Pius IX regain control of Rome. Elsewhere Italian rulers managed to regain control on their own. Only Piedmont managed to keep its liberal constitution. Despite the lack of success, revolutionaries in Italy had learned two valuable lessons. Only Piedmont could be relied upon for leadership in the cause of Italian unity and even then, without foreign help, Italy could not succeed in throwing off Austrian domination. Both lessons proved helpful in achieving Italian unification (see Chapter 23).

▼ **Map 22.5** The Revolutions of 1848–1849.

Reaction, Reform, and Revolution: The European States, 1815–1850

Great Britain

Corn Law	1815
Peterloo Massacre	1819
Reform Act	1832
Poor Law	1834
Formation of Anti-Corn Law Association	1838
Repeal of Corn Laws	1846

France

Louis XVIII	1814–1824
Constitutional Charter	1814
Charles X	1824–1830
July Revolution	1830
Louis-Philippe	1830–1848
Abdication of Louis-Philippe; Formation of Provisional Government	1848 (February 22–24)
Formation of National Workshops	1848 (February 26)
June Days: Workers' Revolt in Paris	1848 (June)
Establishment of Second Republic	1848 (November)
Election of Louis Napoleon as French President	1848 (December)

Low Countries

Union of Netherlands and Belgium	1815
Belgian Revolt	1830

Germany

Germanic Confederation Established	1815
Frederick William III of Prussia	1797–1840
Burschenschaften at the Wartburg	1817
Karlsbad Decrees	1819

Frederick William IV of Prussia	1840–1861
Revolution in Germany	1848
Frankfurt Assembly	1848–1849

The Austrian Empire

Emperor Francis II	1806–1835
Emperor Ferdinand I	1835–1848
Revolt in Austrian Empire; Metternich Dismissed	1848 (March)
Austrian Forces under General Windischgrätz Crush Czech Rebels	1848 (June)
Viennese Rebels Crushed	1848 (October)
Abdication of Ferdinand I	1848 (December)
Francis Joseph I	1848–1916
Defeat of Hungarians with Help of Russian Troops	1849

Italy

Crushing of Revolts in Southern Italy and Sardinia	1821
Aborted Revolutions in Modena, Parma, and Papal States	1830
Revolutions in Italy	1848
King Charles Albert of Piedmont	1831—1849
Charles Albert Attacks Austrians	1848
Austrians Reestablish Control in Lombardy and Venetia	1849

Russia

Tsar Paul I	1796–1801
Tsar Alexander I	1801–1825
Decembrist Revolt	1825
Tsar Nicholas I	1825–1855
Polish Uprising	1830
Suppression of Polish Revolt	1831

Throughout Europe in 1848, popular revolts had initiated revolutionary upheavals that had produced the formation of liberal constitutions and liberal governments. But how could so many immediate successes in 1848 be followed by so many disasters only months later? Two reasons stand out. The unity of the revolutionaries had made the revolutions possible, but divisions soon shattered their ranks. Except in France, moderate liberals from the propertied classes failed to extend suffrage to the working classes who had helped to achieve the revolutions. But as radicals pushed for universal male suffrage, liberals everywhere pulled back. Concerned about their property and security, they rallied to the old ruling classes for the sake of order and out of fear of social revolution by the working classes. All too soon, established governments were back in power.

In 1848, nationalities everywhere had also revolted in pursuit of self-government. But here too, frightfully little was achieved as divisions among nationalities proved utterly disastrous. Though the Hungarians demanded autonomy from the Austrians, at the same time they refused the same to their minorities—the Slovenes, Croats, and Serbs. Instead of joining together against the old empire, minorities fought each other. No wonder that one Czech could remark in April 1848: "If the Austrian state had not already existed for so long, it would have been in the interests of Europe, indeed of humanity itself, to endeavour to create it as soon as possible."[9] The Austrians began the successful recovery of the Hungarian provinces when they began to play off Hungary's rebellious minority nationalities against the Hungarians.

▼ The Emergence of an Ordered Society

Everywhere in Europe, the revolutionary upheavals of the late eighteenth and early nineteenth centuries made the ruling elite nervous about social disorder and the potential dangers to their lives and property. At the same time, the influx of large numbers of people from the countryside into rapidly growing cities had led to horrible living conditions, poverty, unemployment, and great social dissatisfaction. The first half of the nineteenth century witnessed a significant increase in crime rates, especially against property, in Britain, France, and Germany. The rise in incidences of pickpocketing, burglary, shoplifting, and embezzlement may in part have reflected the increased desperation of the poor, but it also provoked a severe reaction against crimes of property by middle-class urban inhabitants who feared the threat the urban poor posed to their security and possessions.

Several kinds of organizations already existed to defend the propertied classes from criminals and social misfits. Some European countries, including Prussia, Sardinia, and Spain, had created gendarmes after the French model of 1791. These were essentially military police recruited from ex-soldiers who were employed mainly in the countryside to keep order. During the French revolutionary era, citizen militias (known as the National Guard in France) had also come into existence. Strongly distrusted by reactionary governments, however, they were either disbanded or closely supervised. Finally, military forces were also enlisted for domestic use in times of serious popular disorder.

The Development of New Police Forces

The first major contribution of the nineteenth century to the development of a disciplined or ordered society in Europe was a regular system of police. A number of European states established civilian police forces—a group of well-trained law enforcement officers who were to preserve property and lives, maintain domestic order, investigate crime, and arrest offenders. It was hoped that their very presence would prevent crime. The new police forces were not readily welcomed, especially in countries where the memory of oppressive acts carried out by political and secret police still lingered. The function of the new police—to protect citizens—eventually made them acceptable, and by the end of the nineteenth century many Europeans viewed them approvingly.

This new approach to policing made its first appearance in France in 1828 when Louis-Maurice Debelleyme, the prefect of Paris, proclaimed as his goal: "The essential object of our municipal police is the safety of the inhabitants of Paris. Safety by day and night, free traffic movement, clean streets, the supervision of and precaution against accidents, the maintenance of order in public places, the seeking out of offences and their perpetrators." [10] In March 1829, the new policemen, known as serjents, became visible on Paris streets. They were dressed in blue uniforms to make them easily recognizable by all citizens. They were also lightly armed with a white cane during the day and a saber at night, underscoring the fact that they made up a civilian, not a military body. Initially, there were not many of the new policemen. Paris had 85 by August of 1829 and only 500 in 1850. Before the end of the century, their number had increased to 4,000.

Britain, fearful of the powers exercised by military or secret police in authoritarian continental European states, had long resisted the creation of a professional police force. Instead, Britain depended upon a system of unpaid constables recruited by local authorities. Often these local constables were incapable of keeping order, preventing crimes, or apprehending criminals. Such jobs could also be dangerous and involve incidents like the one reported by a man passing by a local pub in 1827:

> I saw Thomas Franklin [constable of the village of Leighton Buzzard] coming out backwards. John Brandon . . . was opposite and close to the constable. I saw the said John Brandon strike the said constable twice "bang full in the face" the blows knocked the constable down on his back. John Brandon fell down with him. Sarah Adams . . . got on top of the constable and jostled his head against the ground . . . . The constable appeared very much hurt and his face was all over blood.[11]

The failure of the local constables led to a new approach. Between September 1829 and May 1830, 3,000 uniformed policemen appeared on the streets of London. They came to be known as bobbies after Sir Robert Peel, who had introduced the legislation that created the force. The Municipal Corporations Act of 1835 spread the new police into provincial boroughs while counties were permitted to establish police forces in 1839. By 1856, the new police had become obligatory for all local authorities.

As is evident from the first instruction book for the new policemen, the primary goal of the new British police was to prevent crime: "Officers and police constables should endeavour to distinguish themselves by such vigilance and activity as may render it impossible for any one to commit a crime within that portion of the town under their charge."[12] The municipal authorities soon found, however, that the police were also useful for imposing order on working-class urban inhabitants. On Sundays they were called upon to clean up after Saturday night's drinking bouts. As demands for better pay and treatment led to improved working conditions, British policemen began to develop a sense of professionalism (see the box on p. 763).

Police systems were reorganized throughout the Western world during the nineteenth century. Reformers followed first the French and then the British as their models, but local traditions were often important in shaping a nation's system. After the revolutions of 1848 in Germany, a state-financed police force called the *Schutzmannschaft*, modeled after the London police, was created for the city of Berlin. The *Schutzmannschaft* began as a civilian body, but already by 1851 the force had become organized more along military lines and was used for political purposes. Although their work in providing

▼ **The London Police.** Revolutionary upheavals in the late eighteenth and early nineteenth centuries led European ruling elites to seek new ways to create an ordered society. One result was the development of civilian police forces that would be responsible for preserving property, arresting criminals, and maintaining domestic order. This early photograph shows a group of London policemen who came to be known as bobbies after Sir Robert Peel, the man who was responsible for introducing the legislation that initiated the London police force.

The New British Police: "We Are Not Treated as Men"
▼ ▼ ▼

The new British police forces, created first in London in 1829, were generally well established throughout a good part of Britain by the 1840s. As professionalism arose in the ranks of the forces, so too did demands for better pay and treatment. In these two selections, police constables make clear their demands and complaints.

Petition for Higher Pay by a Group of Third-Class Constables (1848)

Men joining the Police service as 3rd Class Constables and having a wife and 3 children to support on joining, are not able properly to do so on the pay of 16/8d. Most of the married men on joining are somewhat in debt, and are unable to extricate themselves on account of rent to pay and articles to buy which are necessary for support of wife and children. We beg leave to state that a married man having a wife and 2 children to support on joining, that it is as much as he can do upon 16/8d per week, and having to remain upon that sum for the first 12 to 18 months.

Complaints from Constables of D Division of the London Metropolitan Police

We are not treated as men but as slaves we englishmen do not like to be terrorised by a set of Irish sergeants who are only lenient to their own countrymen we the D division of Paddington are nearly all ruled by these Irish Sergeants after we have done our night-Duty may we not have the privilege of going to Church or staying at home to Suit our own inclination when we are ordered by the Superintendent to go to church in our uniform on wednesday we do not object to the going to church we like to go but we do not like to be ordered there and when we go on duty Sunday nights we are asked like so many schoolboys have we been to church should we say no let reason be what it may it does not matter we are forthwith ordered from Paddington to Marylebone lane the next night—about 2 hours before we go to Duty that is 2 miles from many of our homes being tired with our walk there and back we must either loiter about the streets or in some public house and there we do not want to go for we cannot spare our trifling wages to spend them there but there is no other choice left—for us to make our time out to go on Duty at proper time on Day we are ordered there for that offence another Man may faultlessly commit—the crime of sitting 4 minutes during the night—then we must be ordered there another to Shew his old clothes before they are given in even we must go to the expense of having them put in repair we have indeed for all these frightful crimes to walk 3 or 4 miles and then be wasting our time that makes our night 3 hours longer than they ought to be another thing we want to know who has the money that is deducted out of our wages for fines and many of us will be obliged to give up the duty unless we can have fair play as to the stationing of us on our beats why cannot we follow round that may all and each of us go over every beat and not for the Sergeants to put their favourites on the good beats and the others kept back their favourites are not the best policemen but those that will spend the most with them at the public house there are a great many of these things to try our temper.

---

welfare services for the city made them more acceptable to the citizens, the Berlin police exercised considerably more power than their British counterparts. Their military nature was reinforced by their weaponry, which included swords, pistols, and brass knuckles. One observer noted that "A German policeman on patrol is armed as if for war."[13]

While the new policemen alleviated some of the fears about the increase in crime, contemporary reformers approached the problem in other ways. Some of them believed that the increase in crime was related to the dramatic increase in poverty. As one commented in 1816: "Poverty, misery are the parents of crime." Relief for the poverty-stricken became a major concern. Strongly influenced by the middle-class belief that unemployment was the result of sheer laziness, European states passed Poor Laws that attempted to force paupers to find work on their own or enter workhouses designed to make people so utterly uncomfortable they would choose to reenter the labor market.

Meanwhile, another group of reformers was arguing that poor laws failed to address the real problem, which was that poverty was a result of the moral degeneracy of the lower-classes, increasingly labeled the "dangerous classes" because of their threat to middle-class society. This belief led one group of secular reformers to form institutes for the instruction of the working classes in the applied sciences in order to make them more productive members of society. The London Mechanics' Institute, established in Britain, and the Society for the Diffusion of Useful Knowledge in the Field of Natural Sciences, Technical Science, and Political Economy, founded in Germany, are but two examples of this approach to the "dangerous classes."

Organized religion took a different approach. British evangelicals created Sunday Schools to improve the morals of working children while in Germany evangelical Protestants established nurseries for orphans and homeless children, women's societies to care for the sick and poor, and prison societies that prepared women to work in prisons. The Catholic church attempted the same kind of work through a revival of its religious orders; dedicated priests and nuns used spiritual instruction and recreation to turn young male workers away from the moral vices of gambling and drinking and female workers from lives of prostitution.

The Reform of Prisons

The increase in crimes led to a rise in arrests. By the 1820s, in most countries the indiscriminate use of capital punishment, even for crimes against property, was being increasingly viewed as ineffective and replaced by imprisonment. Although the British had shipped people convicted for serious offenses to their colonial territory of Australia, that practice began to slow down in the late 1830s when the colonists loudly objected. Incarceration, then, was the only alternative. Prisons served to isolate criminals from society, but a growing number of reformers questioned their purpose and effectiveness, especially when prisoners were subjected to harsh and even humiliating work as punishment. By the 1830s, European governments were seeking ways to reform their penal systems. Motivated by the desire not just to punish, but to rehabilitate and transform criminals into new persons, the British and French in the early 1830s sent missions to the United States to examine how the two different systems then used in American prisons accomplished this goal. At the Auburn Prison in New York, for example, prisoners were separated at night but worked together in the same workshop during the day. At Walnut Street Prison in Philadelphia, prisoners were separated into individual cells.

After examining the American prisons, both the French and British constructed prisons on the Walnut Street model with separate cells that isolated prisoners from one another. At Petite Roquette in France and Pentonville in Britain, prisoners wore leather masks while they exercised and sat in separate stalls when in chapel. Solitary confinement, it was believed, forced prisoners back on their own consciences, led to greater remorse, and increased the possibility that they would change their evil ways. One supporter of the separate-cell system noted how:

> a few months in the solitary cell renders a prisoner strangely impressible. The chaplain can then make the brawny navvy cry like a child; he can work on his feelings in almost any way he pleases; he can, so to speak, photograph his thoughts, wishes and opinions on his patient's mind, and fill his mouth with his own phrases and language.[14]

As prison populations increased, however, solitary confinement proved expensive and less feasible. The French even returned to their custom of sending prisoners to French Guiana to handle the overload.

Prison reform and police forces were geared toward one primary end, the creation of a more disciplined society. Disturbed by the upheavals associated with revolutions and the social discontent wrought by industrialization and urbanization, the ruling elites sought to impose some order upon society. Even many radical working-class activists, who were often the object of police activity, welcomed the domestication and discipline that the new system imposed.

▼ Romanticism

At the end of the eighteenth century, a new intellectual movement was developing to challenge the ideas of the Enlightenment. Although some historians have argued that Romanticism was more a "mood" than a movement, it revolutionized painting, literature, and music in the first half of the nineteenth century. Romanticism was a reaction against the Enlightenment's preoccupation with reason in discovering truth. While the romantics, especially the early romantics, by no means disparaged reason, they tried to balance its use by stressing the importance of feeling, emotion, and imagination as sources of knowing. As one German romantic put it,

"It was my heart that counselled me to do it, and my heart cannot err." Romanticism manifested itself in a remarkable variety of ways, evident in a survey of its major characteristics and some of its major figures.

The Characteristics of Romanticism

Although European in scope, Romanticism had its roots in Germany and can be said to have had its beginnings in the *Sturm und Drang* ("Storm and Stress") literary movement of the 1770s. German poets rejected classicism's adherence to strict discipline and form as artificial and favored more "natural" compositions in which people were moved by inner forces rather than the external events that impinged on them. For romantic writers, this meant an emphasis on emotion and sentiment and the belief that these inner feelings were only understandable to the person experiencing them. An important model for romantics was the tragic figure in *The Sorrows of the Young Werther,* a novel by the great German writer, Johann Wolfgang von Goethe (1749–1832), who later rejected Romanticism in favor of classicism. Werther was a romantic figure who sought freedom in order to fulfill himself. Misunderstood and rejected by society, he continued to believe in his own worth through his inner feelings, but his deep love for a girl who did not love him finally led him to commit suicide.

The romantic preoccupation with sentiment and the suffering that deepens it was easily exaggerated in less talented writers than Goethe. After Goethe's *Sorrows of the Young Werther,* numerous novels and plays appeared whose plots revolved around young maidens tragically carried off at an early age (twenty-three was most common) by disease (usually tuberculosis, at that time a drawn-out disease that was usually fatal) to the sorrow and sadness of their male lovers.

Individualism was another important characteristic of Romanticism. The Enlightenment concern with the universal in human nature, the common qualities of all people, was superseded by the romantics' interest in the uniqueness of each person. This urge to achieve self-realization was aptly portrayed in Goethe's *Faust,* the story of the scholar whose love of life and inability to find truth through the path of reason persuades him to seek fulfillment by turning to occult forces.

The desire of romantics to follow their inner drives to achieve self-realization also led them to rebel against middle-class conventions. Long hair, beards, and outra-

▼ **Neo-Gothic Revival (British Houses of Parliament).** The romantic movement of the first half of the nineteenth century led, among other things, to a revival of medieval Gothic architecture that left European cities bedecked with neo-Gothic buildings. After the Houses of Parliament in London burned down in 1834, they were replaced with the new buildings of neo-Gothic design seen in this photograph.

geous clothes served to reinforce the individualism that young romantics were trying to express. Rejection of contemporary modes of thought could take other directions as well. In his novel *Lucinde,* the German writer and critic, Friedrich Schlegel (1772–1829), presented a portrait of a free and "innocent" girl who followed the demands of her heart by advocating the so-called "natural" practice of free love. But the revolt against convention combined with sentimental suffering could also lead the romantics to disorderly lives and bizarre behavior. Charlotte Stieglitz stabbed herself in the hope that her husband's sorrow would make him a better poet. It failed to work.

Sentiment and individualism came together in the romantics' stress on the heroic. The romantic hero was the solitary genius who was ready to defy the world and sacrifice his life for a great cause. However, in the hands of the British writer, Thomas Carlyle (1795–1881), the romantic hero did not destroy himself in ineffective protests against society, but transformed society instead. In his historical works, Carlyle stressed that the course of history was largely determined by the deeds of such heroes.

Many romantics adhered to a belief in the organic evolution of political and social institutions. States and societies, like individual organisms, they thought, evolved through time. Each people had its own *Geist* or spirit that made it unique. This *Volksgeist* (national spirit) was reflected in governments, culture, traditions, and institutions and was passed on from generation to generation. This perspective inspired romantics to study history because they saw it as a way to understand how a nationality came to be what it was. In the process, the romantics spawned a historical renaissance. Governments supported the publication of collections of documents; historical societies flourished. One period of history—the Middle Ages—was singled out for special attention because it was the age in which European states had begun their existence. It was also seen as an age of faith and religious emotion rather than reason. No doubt, the romantic reverence for history contributed to the age's fascination with nationalism.

This historical mindedness was furthered in many ways. In Germany, the Grimm brothers collected and published their nation's fairy tales, as did Hans Christian Andersen in Denmark. The revival of medieval Gothic architecture left European countrysides adorned with pseudo-medieval castles and cities bedecked with grandiose neo-Gothic cathedrals, city halls, parliamentary buildings, and even railway stations.

Literature, too, reflected this historical consciousness. The novels of Walter Scott (1771–1832) became European best-sellers in the first half of the nineteenth century. Scott had a background in law but was raised on old tales of Scottish history. He first made his mark as a writer of verse romances, but it was his historical novels that brought him even greater attention. *Ivanhoe*, in which he tried to evoke the clash between Saxon and Norman knights in medieval England, became one of his most popular. On the Continent, Alexandre Dumas (1802–1870) likewise gained fame for his historical evocations. Most famous was *The Three Musketeers* with its vivid portrayal of swashbuckling adventurers in seventeenth-century France.

To some historians, the romantic vogue for the past, especially the Middle Ages, represents a nostalgia for a simpler time, for a society envisioned by the romantics themselves as an organic community in which people were secure in knowing their rightful place in life. Many romantics were especially critical of the emerging industrialization and were convinced that it would cause people to become alienated from their inner selves and the natural world around them.

To the historical mindedness of the romantics could be added a love of the exotic and unfamiliar, be it in the past, distant places, or the supernatural. In an exaggerated form, this preoccupation gave rise to so-called Gothic literature, chillingly evident in Mary Shelley's *Frankenstein* and the American Edgar Allen Poe's short stories of horror (see the box on p. 767). Some romantics even sought the unusual in their own lives by seeking extraordinary states of experience in dreams, nightmares, supernatural possession, frenzies, and suicidal depression or in drug-induced, altered states of consciousness by experimenting with cocaine, opium, and hashish.

Romantic Poets and the Love of Nature

To the romantics, poetry ranked above all other literary forms because it was viewed as the direct expression of one's soul. The romantic poets were viewed as seers who could reveal the invisible world to others. Their incredible sense of drama made some of them the most colorful figures of their era, living intense but short lives. Percy Bysshe Shelley (1792–1822), expelled from school for advocating atheism, set out to reform the world. His *Prometheus Unbound*, completed in 1820, is a portrait of the revolt of human beings against the laws and customs that oppress them. He drowned in a storm in the Mediterranean. Lord Byron (1788–1824) dramatized himself as the melancholy romantic hero that he had described in his work, *Childe Harold's Pilgrimage*. He participated in the movement for Greek independence and died in Greece fighting the Turks.

Romantic poetry gave full expression to one of the most important characteristics of Romanticism: love of nature, especially evident in William Wordsworth (1770–1850), the foremost romantic prophet of nature. He spent days wandering through British forests, often hiking as much as forty miles a day. Like other romantics, he was fascinated by the different moods of nature:

From Nature doth emotion come, and moods
Of calmness equally are Nature's gift:
This is her glory; these two attributes
Are sister horns that constitute her strength. [15]

Gothic Literature: Edgar Allan Poe
▼ ▼ ▼

American writers and poets made significant contributions to the movement of Romanticism. Although Edgar Allan Poe (1809–1849) was influenced by the German romantic school of mystery and horror, many literary historians give him the credit for pioneering the modern short story. This selection from the conclusion of "The Fall of the House of Usher" gives a sense of the nature of so-called Gothic literature.

Edgar Allan Poe, "The Fall of the House of Usher"

No sooner had these syllables passed my lips, than—as if a shield of brass had indeed, at the moment, fallen heavily upon a floor of silver—I became aware of a distinct, hollow, metallic, and clangorous, yet apparently muffled, reverberation. Complete unnerved, I leaped to my feet; but the measured rocking movement of Usher was undisturbed. I rushed to the chair in which he sat. His eyes were bent fixedly before him, and throughout his whole countenance there reigned a stony rigidity. But, as I placed my hand upon his shoulder, there came a strong shudder over his whole person; a sickly smile quivered about his lips; and I saw that he spoke in a low, hurried, and gibbering murmur, as if unconscious of my presence. Bending closely over him, I at length drank in the hideous import of his words.

"Not hear it?—yes, I hear it, and *have* heard it. Long-long-long-many minutes, many hours, many days, have I heard it—yet I dared not—oh, pity me, miserable wretch that I am!—I dared not—I *dared* not speak! *We have put her living in the tomb!* Said I not that my senses were acute? I *now* tell you that I heard her first feeble movements in the hollow coffin. I heard them—many, many days ago—yet I dared not—*I dared not speak!* And now—to-night—. . . the rending of her coffin, and the grating of the iron hinges of her prison, and her struggles within the coppered archway of the vault! Oh whither shall I fly? Will she not be here anon? Is she not hurrying to upbraid me for my haste? Have I not heard her footstep on the stair? Do I not distinguish that heavy and horrible beating of her heart? MADMAN!"—here he sprang furiously to his feet, and shrieked out his syllables, as if in the effort he were giving up his soul—"MADMAN! I TELL YOU THAT SHE NOW STANDS WITHOUT THE DOOR!"

As if in the superhuman energy of his utterance there had been found the potency of a spell, the huge antique panels to which the speaker pointed threw slowly back, upon the instant, their ponderous and ebony jaws. It was the work of the rushing gust—but then without those doors there DID stand the lofty and enshrouded figure of the lady Madeline of Usher. There was blood upon her white robes, and the evidence of some bitter struggle upon every portion of her emaciated frame. For a moment she remained trembling and reeling to and fro upon the threshold, then, with a low moaning cry, fell heavily inward upon the person of her brother, and in her violent and now final death-agonies, bore him to the floor a corpse, and a victim to the terrors he had anticipated.

But Wordsworth's admiration of nature went beyond a simple observation of streams and trees. His experience of nature was almost mystical as he claimed to receive "authentic tidings of invisible things":

> One impulse from a vernal wood
> May teach you more of man,
> Of Moral Evil and of good,
> Than all the sages can.[16]

To Wordsworth, nature contained a mysterious force that the poet could perceive and learn from. Nature served as a mirror into which humans could look to learn about themselves. Nature was, in fact, alive and sacred:

> To every natural form, rock, fruit or flower,
> Even the loose stones that cover the high-way,
> I gave a moral life, I saw them feel,
> Or link'd them to some feeling: the great mass
> Lay bedded in a quickening soul, and all
> That I beheld, respired with inward meaning.[17]

Other romantics carried this worship of nature further into pantheism by identifying the great force in nature with God. The romantics would have nothing to do with the deist god of the Enlightenment, the creator of the world-machine, far removed from his creation. As the German romantic poet Friedrich Novalis said, "Anyone seeking God will find him anywhere."

William Blake and the Romantic Attack on Science

▼ ▼ ▼

William Blake (1757–1827) was a British poet, painter, and graphic artist who combined all of these vocations to produce visually stunning books. He was a religious mystic, and much of his poetic and artistic work was an attempt to give visible form to his profound visionary experiences. In this selection from his poem Milton, he expressed his deep distrust of "the Reasoning Power in Man" and materialistic science.

William Blake, Milton

The Negation is the Spectre; the Reasoning Power in
  Man
This is a false body: an Incrustation over my Immortal
Spirit; a Selfhood, which must be put off and
  annihilated away
To cleanse the Face of my Spirit by Self-examination.
To bathe in the Waters of Life; to wash off the Not
  Human
I come in Self-annihilation and the grandeur of
  Inspiration
To cast off Rational Demonstration by Faith in the
  Saviour
To cast off the rotton rags of Memory by Inspiration
To cast off Bacon, Locke and Newton [three English
  forerunners of science] from Albion's [usually
  ancient name of Britain] covering
To take off his filthy garments, & clothe him with
  Imagination
To cast aside from Poetry, all that is not Inspiration
That it no longer shall dare to mock with the aspersion
  of Madness
Cast on the Inspired, by the tame high finisher of paltry
  Blots,

Indefinite, or paltry Rhymes; or paltry Harmonies,
Who creeps into State Government like a catterpiller to
  destroy
To cast off the idiot Questioner who is always
  questioning,
But never capable of answering; who sits with a sly
  grin
Silent plotting when to question, like a thief in a cave;
Who publishes doubt & calls it knowledge; whose
  Science is Despair,
Whose pretence to knowledge is Envy, whose whole
  Science is
To destroy the wisdom of ages to gratify ravenous Envy
That rages round him like a Wolf day & night without
  rest
He smiles with condescension; he talks of Benevolence
  & Virtue
And those who act with Benevolence & Virtue, they
  murder time on time
These are the destroyers of Jerusalem, these are the
  murderers
Of Jesus, who deny the Faith & mock at Eternal Life:
Who pretend to Poetry that they may destroy
  Imagination;
By imitation of Nature's Images drawn from
  Remembrance
These are the Sexual Garments, the Abomination of
  Desolation
Hiding the Human Lineaments as with an Ark &
  Curtains
Which Jesus rent: & now shall wholly purge away with
  Fire
Till Generation is swallowed up in Regeneration.

The worship of nature also led Wordsworth and other romantic poets to a critique of the mechanistic materialism of eighteenth-century science, which, they believed, had reduced nature to a mere object of study, to simply a cold abstraction (see the box above). Against that view of the natural world, Wordsworth offered his own vivid and concrete experience. To him the scientists' dry, mathematical approach left no room for the imagination and even worse none for the human soul. The poet who left to the world "one single moral precept, one single affecting sentiment," Wordsworth said, did more for the world than scientists who were soon forgotten.

Romanticism in Art and Music

Like the literary arts, the visual arts were also deeply affected by Romanticism. Although they varied widely in what they produced, romantic artists shared at least two fundamental characteristics. All artistic expression to them was a reflection of the artist's inner feelings; a painting should mirror the artist's vision of the world and be the instrument of his own imagination. Moreover, romantic artists deliberately rejected the principles of classicism. Beauty was not a timeless thing; its expression depended on one's culture and one's age. The romantics abandoned classical restraint for warmth, emotion, and movement. Through an examination of three painters, we can see how Romanticism influenced the visual arts.

Caspar David Friedrich's (1774–1840) early life experiences left him with a lifelong preoccupation with God and nature. Friedrich painted many landscapes but with an interest that transcended the mere presentation of natural details. His portrayal of mountains shrouded in mist, gnarled trees bathed in moonlight, and the stark ruins of monasteries surrounded by withered trees all conveyed a feeling of mystery and mysticism. For Friedrich, nature was a manifestation of divine life. As in *Man and Woman Gazing at the Moon,* he liked to depict one or two solitary figures gazing upon the grandeur of a natural scene with their backs to the viewer. Not only were his human figures dwarfed by the overwhelming presence of nature, but they expressed the human yearning for infinity, the desire to lose oneself in the universe. To Friedrich, the artistic process depended upon the use of an unrestricted imagination that could only be achieved through inner vision. He advised artists: "Shut your physical eye and look first at your picture with your spiritual eye, then bring to the light of day what you have seen in the darkness."

Another artist who dwelled on nature and made landscape his major subject, although with less spiritual in-

tensity, was the Briton Joseph Malford William Turner (1775–1851). Turner was an incredibly prolific artist who produced over 20,000 paintings, drawings, and watercolors. Turner's concern with nature manifested itself in innumerable landscapes and seascapes, sunrises and sunsets. He, however, did not idealize nature or reproduce it with realistic accuracy. He sought instead to convey its moods by using a skilled interplay of light and color to suggest natural effects. In allowing his objects to melt into their surroundings, he anticipated the Impressionist painters of the last half of the nineteenth century (see Chapter 25).

Eugène Delacroix (1798–1863) was one of the most famous French exponents of the romantic school of painting. Largely self-taught, Delacroix's paintings exhibited two primary characteristics, a fascination with the exotic and a passion for color. Both are visible in his *Women of Algiers.* Significant for its use of light and its patches of interrelated color, this portrayal of the world of harem concubines in exotic north Africa was actually somewhat scandalous to the early nineteenth century. In Delacroix, theatricality and movement combined with a daring use of color. Many of his works reflect his own belief that "a painting should be a feast to the eye."

To many romantics, music was the most romantic of the arts since it enabled the composer to probe deeply into human emotions. One romantic writer noted:

It has been rightly said that the object of music is the awakening of emotion. No other art can so sublimely arouse human sentiments in the innermost heart of man. No other art

▼ Caspar David Friedrich, *Man and Woman Gazing at the Moon.* Romantic artists rejected classical restraint in favor of emotion and sentiment. Moreover, they believed that artistic expression should be a reflection of an artist's inner feelings. The German artist Caspar David Friedrich sought to express in painting his own mystical view of nature. "The divine is everywhere," he once wrote, "even in a grain of sand." In this painting, two solitary wanderers are shown from the back gazing at the moon. Overwhelmed by the all-pervasive presence of nature, the two figures express the human longing for infinity.

can paint to the eyes of the soul the splendours of nature, the delights of contemplation, the character of nations, the tumult of their passions, and the languour of their sufferings as music can.[18]

Although music historians have called the eighteenth century an age of classicism and the nineteenth the era of Romanticism, there was much carryover of classical forms from one century to the next, especially in the use of the sonata, string quartet, and symphony. One of the greatest composers of all time, Ludwig van Beethoven, served as a bridge between classicism and Romanticism.

Beethoven (1770–1827) was born in Bonn (Germany) where he played for a while as an organist at the court of the elector of Cologne. He soon made his way to Vienna, then the musical capital of Europe, where he studied briefly under Mozart. Beginning in 1792, Vienna became his permanent residence although he was barely tolerated by Viennese society because of his unruly manner and repulsive appearance. During his first major period of composing from 1792 to 1802, his work was still largely within the classical framework of the eighteenth century, and his style differed little from that of Mozart and Haydn. But with this Third Symphony, the *Eroica*, originally intended for Napoleon, Beethoven broke through to the elements of Romanticism in his use of uncontrolled rhythms to create dramatic struggle and uplifted resolutions. E. T. A. Hoffman, a contemporary composer and writer, said, "Beethoven's music opens the flood gates of fear, of terror, of horror, of pain, and arouses that longing for the eternal which is the essence of Romanticism. He is thus a pure Romantic composer."[19] Beethoven went on to write a vast quantity of works including symphonies, piano and violin sonatas, concerti, masses, an opera, and a cycle of songs. In the midst of this productivity and growing fame, Beethoven was more and more burdened by his growing deafness, which intensified noticeably after 1800. To the composer Richard Wagner (see Chapter 23), this was a distinct advantage. "Undisturbed by the bustle of life," he wrote, Beethoven "only heard the harmonies of his soul." One of the most moving pieces of music of all time, the chorale finale of his Ninth Symphony, was composed when Beethoven was totally deaf.

The Revival of Religion in the Age of Romanticism

Catholicism experienced a revival after the Napoleonic era. In the eighteenth century, Catholicism had lost its attraction for many of the educated elite as even the European nobility flirted with the ideas of the Enlightenment. The restoration of the nobility, however, brought them to a new appreciation for the Catholic faith as a force for order in society, an appreciation greatly reinforced by the movement of Romanticism. The attraction of romantics to the Middle Ages and their emphasis on emotion led them to their own widespread revival of Christianity. This revival took many forms. Some romantics condemned irreligion as a cause

▼ Eugène Delacroix, *Women of Algiers.* Also characteristic of Romanticism was its love of the exotic and unfamiliar. In his *Women of Algiers,* Delacroix reflected this fascination with the exotic in his portrayal of harem concubines from Morocco. At the same time, Delacroix's painting reflects his preoccupation with light and color.

of civilization's disintegration while others stressed the otherworldly side of Christianity and reawakened a genuine interest in mysticism.

Catholicism particularly benefited from this romantic enthusiasm for religion. Especially among German romantics, there were many conversions to the Catholic faith. One of the most popular expressions of this romantic revival of Catholicism was found in the work of the Frenchman François-René de Chateaubriand (1768–1848). His book, *Genius of Christianity*, published in 1802, was soon labeled the "Bible of Romanticism." His defense of Catholicism was based not upon historical, theological, or even rational grounds, but largely upon romantic sentiment. As a faith, Catholicism echoed the harmony of all things. Its liturgy contained the divine mysteries that mirrored the universe. Its cathedrals brought one into the very presence of God; according to Chateaubriand: "You could not enter a Gothic church without feeling a kind of awe and a vague sentiment of the Divinity . . . every thing in a Gothic church reminds you of the labyrinths of a wood; every thing excites a feeling of religious awe, of mystery, and of the Divinity."[20]

Protestantism also experienced a revival. That revival or Awakening as it was called had already begun in the eighteenth century with the enthusiastic emotional experiences of Methodism in Britain and Pietism in Germany (see Chapter 18). Methodist missionaries from England and Scotland carried their messages of sin and redemption to liberal Protestant churches in France and Switzerland, winning converts to their strongly evangelical message. Germany, too, witnessed a Protestant Awakening as enthusiastic evangelical preachers found that their messages of hellfire and their methods of emotional conversion found a ready response among people alienated by the highly educated establishment clergy of the state churches.

In 1815, a conservative order had been reestablished throughout Europe, and the cooperation of the great powers, embodied in the Concert of Europe, tried to ensure its durability. But the revolutionary waves of the early 1820s and the early 1830s made it clear that the ideologies of liberalism and nationalism, unleashed by the French Revolution and now reinforced by the spread of the Industrial Revolution, were still alive and active. They faced enormous difficulties, however, as failed revolutions in Poland, Russia, Italy, and Germany all testify. At the same time, reform legislation in Britain and successful revolutions in Greece, France, and Belgium demonstrated the continuing strength of these forces of change. In 1848, they erupted once more all across Europe. And once more they failed. But not all was lost. Both liberalism and nationalism would succeed in the second half of the nineteenth century but in ways not foreseen by the idealistic liberals and nationalists who, when they manned the barricades in 1848, were utterly convinced that their time had come.

Notes

▼ ▼ ▼

1. Quoted in Charles Breunig, *The Age of Revolution and Reaction, 1789–1850* (New York, 1970), p. 119.

2. Quoted in M. S. Anderson, *The Ascendancy of Europe, 1815–1914*, 2d ed. (London, 1985), p. 1.

3. Quotations from Burke can be found in Peter Viereck, *Conservatism* (Princeton, N.J., 1956), pp. 27, 114.

4. Quoted in ibid., p. 51.

5. Quoted in René Albrecht-Carrié, *The Concert of Europe* (New York, 1968), p. 48.

6. Quoted in G. de Berthier de Sauvigny, *Metternich and His Times* (London, 1962), p. 105.

7. Quoted in Donald E. Emerson, *Metternich and the Political Police* (The Hague, 1968), p. 110.

8. Quoted in S. Joan Moon, "Feminism and Socialism: The Utopian Synthesis of Flora Tristan," in Marilyn J. Boxer and Jean H. Quataert, eds., *Socialist Women* (New York, 1978), p. 38.

9. Quoted in Stanley Z. Pech, *The Czech Revolution of 1848* (Chapel Hill, N.C., 1969), p. 82.

10. Quoted in Clive Emsley, *Policing and Its Context, 1750–1870* (New York, 1984), p. 58.

11. Quoted in Clive Emsley, *Crime and Society in England, 1750–1900* (London, 1987), p. 173.

12. Quoted in Emsley, *Policing and Its Context, 1750–1870*, p. 66.

13. Quoted in ibid., p. 102.

14. Quoted in Emsley, *Crime and Society in England, 1750–1900*, p. 226.

15. William Wordsworth, *The Prelude* (Harmondsworth, 1971), p. 489.

16. William Wordsworth, "The Tables Turned," *Poems of Wordsworth*, ed. Matthew Arnold (London, 1963). p. 138.
17. Wordsworth, *The Prelude*, p. 109.
18. Quoted in H.G. Schenk, *The Mind of the European Romantics* (Garden City, N.Y., 1969), p. 205.

19. Quoted in Siegbert Prawer, ed., *The Romantic Period in Germany* (London, 1970), p. 285.
20. Quoted in John B. Halsted, ed., *Romanticism* (New York, 1969), p. 156.

Suggestions for Further Reading

▼ ▼ ▼

For a good, up-to-date survey of the entire nineteenth century, see R. Gildea, *Barricades and Borders: Europe 1800–1914* (Oxford, 1987) in the Short Oxford History of the Modern World series. Also valuable is M. S. Anderson, *The Ascendancy of Europe, 1815–1914*, 2d ed. (London, 1985). For surveys of the period covered in this chapter, see C. Breunig, *The Age of Revolution and Reaction, 1789–1850*, 2d ed. (New York, 1979); and J. Droz, *Europe between Revolutions, 1815–1848* (London, 1967). There are also some useful books on individual countries that cover more than the subject of this chapter. These include R. Magraw, *France, 1815–1914: The Bourgeois Century* (London, 1983); H. Seton-Watson, *The Russian Empire, 1801–1917* (Oxford, 1967); H. Holborn, *A History of Modern Germany*, vol. 2, *1648–1840* (New York, 1964); C. A. Macartney, *The Habsburg Empire, 1790–1918* (London, 1971); S. J. Woolf, *A History of Italy, 1700–1860* (London, 1979); and N. Gash, *Aristocracy and People: Britain 1815–1865* (London, 1979).

On the peace settlement of 1814–1815, there is the older work by H. Nicolson, *The Congress of Vienna, 1814–15* (New York, 1946). A concise summary of the international events of the entire nineteenth century can be found in R. Bullen and F. R. Bridge, *The Great Powers and the European States System, 1815–1914* (London, 1980). For the period covered in this chapter, see A. Sked, ed., *Europe's Balance of Power, 1815–1848* London, 1979). On the man whose conservative policies dominated this era, see the brief but good biography by A. Palmer, *Metternich* (New York, 1972). Also useful is D. E. Emerson, *Metternich and the Political Police* (The Hague, 1968). On the revolutions in Europe in 1830, see C. Church, *Europe in 1830: Revolution and Political Change* (Chapel Hill, N.C., 1983). The standard work on the revolution of 1830 in France is D. Pinkney, *The French Revolution of 1830* (Princeton, N.J., 1972), while D. Porch, *Army and Revolution: France 1815–48* (London, 1979), examines republican sentiment in the army. On Great Britain's reform legislation, see M. Brock, *Great Reform Act* (London, 1973); and D. C. Moore, *The Politics of Deference: A Study of the Mid-Nineteenth Century English Political System* (New York, 1976). The Greek revolt is examined in detail in D. Dakin, *The Greek Struggle for Independence, 1821–33* (Berkeley, 1973). Revolt in Russia is covered in M. Raeff, *The Decembrist Movement* (Englewood Cliffs, N.J., 1966). On the role of the political police in the Russia of Nicholas I, see S. Monas, *The Third Section: Police and Society in Russia under Nicholas I* (Cambridge, Mass., 1961).

The best introduction to the revolutions of 1848 is P. Stearns, *1848: The Revolutionary Tide in Europe* (New York, 1974). Good accounts of the revolutions in individual countries include G. Duveau, *1848: The Making of a Revolution* (New York, 1967); R. J. Rath, *The Viennese Revolution of 1848* (Austin, Tex., 1957); I Déak, *The Lawful Revolution: Louis Kossuth and the Hungarians, 1848–49* (New York, 1979); P. Brock, *The Slovak National Awakening* (Toronto, 1976); R. Stadelmann, *Social and Political History of the German 1848 Revolution* (Athens, Ohio, 1975); and P. Ginsborg, *Daniele Manin and the Venetian Revolution of 1848–9* (New York, 1979). An important book on France's relations to the European revolutions of 1848 is L. C. Jennings, *France and Europe in 1848: A Study of French Foreign Affairs in Time of Crisis* (Oxford, 1973).

Good introductions to the major ideologies of the first half of the nineteenth century including both analysis and readings from the major figures can be found in H. Kohn, *Nationalism* (Princeton, N.J., 1955); J. S. Schapiro, *Liberalism: Its Meaning and History* (Princeton, N.J., 1958); and P. Viereck, *Conservatism* (Princeton, N.J., 1956). For a general survey, see R. Stromberg, *An Intellectual History of Modern Europe*, 3d ed. (Englewood Cliffs, N.J., 1981). An excellent work on French utopian socialism is F. Manuel, *The Prophets of Paris* (New York, 1962).

On changes in the treatment of crime and punishment, see M. Foucault, *Discipline and Punish: The Birth of the Prison* (New York, 1977). The new policemen are examined in C. Emsley, *Policing and Its Context, 1750–1870* (New York, 1984). Also useful on crime, policemen, and prisons are J. J. Tobias, *Nineteenth-Century Crime Prevention and Punishment* (Newton Abbott, 1972); G. Wright, *Between the Guillotine and Liberty: Two Centuries of the Crime Problem in France* (New York, 1983); M. Ignatieff, *A Just Measure of Pain: The Penitentiary in the Industrial Revolution, 1750–1850* (New York, 1978); and C. Emsley, *Crime and Society in England, 1750–1900* (London, 1987). The religious approach to solving the problem of the dangerous classes can be studied in T. Laqueur, *Religion and Respectability: Sunday Schools and Working-Class Culture, 1780–1850* (New Haven, Conn., 1976).

G. L. Mosse, *The Culture of Western Europe: The Nineteenth and Twentieth Centuries* (Chicago, 1961), remains a good introduction to the cultural history of Europe. A beautifully illustrated introduction to Romanticism can be found in H. Honour, *Romanticism* (New York, 1979). There is an interesting analysis of the ideas of the romantics in H. G. Schenk, *The Mind of the European Romantics* (Garden City, N.Y., 1969). There is an excellent collection of writings by romantics in J. B. Halsted, ed., *Romanticism* (New York, 1969). On German romanticism, see S. Prawer, ed., *The Romantic Period in Germany* (London, 1970). On Wordsworth and English Romanticism, see J. Wordsworth, *William Wordsworth and the Age of English Romanticism* (New Brunswick, N.J., 1987).

Chapter 23

An Age of Nationalism and Realism, 1850–1871

▼▼▼▼▼

A cross the Continent, the revolutions of 1848 had failed. The forces of liberalism and nationalism appeared to have been decisively defeated as authoritarian governments reestablished their control almost everywhere in Europe by 1850. And yet within twenty-five years, many of the goals sought by the liberals and nationalists during the first half of the nineteenth century seemed to have been achieved. National unity became a reality in Italy and Germany while many European states were governed by constitutional monarchies, even though the constitutional-parliamentary features were frequently facades.

All the same, these goals were not achieved by liberal and nationalist leaders but by a new generation of conservative leaders who were proud of being practitioners of *realpolitik*, a "politics of reality." One reaction to the failure of the revolutions of 1848 had been a new toughness of mind in which people prided themselves on being realistic in their handling of power. The new conservative leaders used armies and power politics to achieve their foreign policy goals. And they did not hesitate to manipulate liberal means to achieve conservative ends at home. Nationalism had failed as a revolutionary movement in 1848–1849; tied to conservatism, national unification was now used to avert revolution.

During the period from 1850 to 1871, international relations changed dramatically. Between 1815 and 1850, the statesmen of Europe, reacting to the upheaval of the French revolutionary and Napoleonic eras, had sought to settle their major

Louis Napoleon Becomes Emperor ▼		Creation of Austro-Hungarian Dual Monarchy ▼	British Reform Act ▼	Unification of Italy ▼	Unification of Germany ▼
•••••••• 1850 ••••••••••• 1855 •••••••••••• 1860 ••••••••••• 1865 ••••••••••• 1870 •••••••••

▲ Marx and Engels, *The Communist Manifesto*   ▲ Flaubert, *Madame Bovary*   ▲ Darwin, *On the Origins of Species*   ▲ Emancipation of the Russian Serfs

differences by diplomacy, fearful that war might once more unleash revolutionary forces. After 1850 a new generation of statesmen was no longer motivated by the fears of 1815 and did not hesitate to use war to achieve their ends. The new attitude eventually had dire consequences for the peace of Europe.

▼ The France of Napoleon III

After 1850 a new generation of conservative leaders came to power in Europe. Foremost among them was Napoleon III (1852–1870) of France who taught his contemporaries how authoritarian governments could use liberal and nationalistic forces to bolster their own power. It was a lesson others quickly learned.

Louis Napoleon: Toward the Second Empire

Even after his election as the president of the French Republic, many of his contemporaries dismissed Napoleon "the Small" as a nonentity whose success was due only to his name. But physical appearances can be deceiving. Louis Napoleon was a clever politician who was especially astute at understanding the popular forces of his day. Some historians think that as a Bonaparte, Louis Napoleon believed it his mission to govern France. Apparently, as he told a friend shortly after the election, the presidency of the Republic was only the beginning of this quest: "We are not at the summit yet. This is only a stop on the way, a terrace where we may rest a moment to gaze at the horizon."

Louis Napoleon was a patient man, however. For three years he persevered in winning the support of the French people while using governmental favors to gain the loyalty of the army and the Catholic church. He faced considerable opposition from the National Assembly, which had a conservative-monarchist majority after elections in May of 1849. When the assembly voted to deprive three million men of the right to vote, Louis Napoleon achieved even more popular favor by posing as the savior of universal male suffrage. When the assembly rejected his proposal to revise the constitution and allow him to stand again for reelection, Louis resorted to a coup d'etat. On December 1, 1851, troops loyal to the president seized the major administrative buildings and arrested opposition leaders. After restoring universal male suffrage, Louis Napoleon asked the French people to restructure the government by electing him president for ten years (see the box on p. 776). By an overwhelming majority, 7.5 million "yes" votes to 640,000 "no" votes, they agreed. A year later, on November 21, 1852, Louis Napoleon returned to the people to ask for the restoration of the Empire. This time 97 percent responded affirmatively, and on December 2, 1852, Louis Napoleon assumed the title of Napoleon III (the first Napoleon had abdicated in favor of his son, Napoleon II, on April 6, 1814). The Second Empire had begun.

The Second Napoleonic Empire

The government of Napoleon III was clearly authoritarian in a Bonapartist sense. Louis Napoleon had asked, "Since France has carried on for fifty years only by virtue of the administrative, military, judicial, religious and financial organization of the Consulate and Empire, why should she not also adopt the political institutions of that period?"[1] As chief of state, Napoleon III controlled the armed forces, police, and civil service. Only he could introduce legislation and declare war. His ministers had no collective responsibility and were answerable only to the emperor. The Legislative Corps gave an appearance of representative government since its members were elected by universal male suffrage for six-year terms. But they could neither initiate legislation nor affect the budget. Moreover, only government candidates were allowed complete freedom to campaign and were supposedly selected from "men enjoying public es-

Louis Napoleon Appeals to the People

▼ ▼ ▼

After his coup d'etat on December 2, 1851, Louis Napoleon asked the French people to approve his actions. By making this appeal, the clever politician was demonstrating how universal male suffrage, considered a democratic and hence revolutionary device, could be used to bolster a basically authoritarian regime. It was a lesson eagerly learned by other conservative rulers in the second half of the nineteenth century. This selection is from Louis Napoleon's proclamation to the French people in 1851.

Louis Napoleon, Proclamation to the People (1851)

Frenchmen! The present situation cannot last much longer. Each passing day increases the danger to the country. The [National] Assembly, which ought to be the firmest supporter of order, has become a center of conspiracies . . . it attacks the authority that I hold directly from the people; it encourages all evil passions; it jeopardizes the peace of France: I have dissolved it and I make the whole people judge between it and me. . . .

I therefore make a loyal appeal to the whole nation, and I say to you: If you wish to continue this state of uneasiness which degrades us and makes our future uncertain, choose another in my place, for I no longer wish an authority which is powerless to do good, makes me responsible for acts I cannot prevent, and chains me to the helm when I see the vessel speeding toward the abyss.

If, on the contrary, you still have confidence in me, give me the means to accomplish the great mission that I hold from you. This mission consists in bringing to a close the era of revolutions by satisfying the legitimate wants of the people and by protecting them against subversive passions. It consists, especially, in creating institutions that may survive men and that may be at length foundations on which something durable can be established.

Persuaded that the instability of authority and the preponderance of a single Assembly are permanent causes of trouble and discord, I submit to you the following fundamental bases of a constitution which the Assemblies will develop later.

1. A responsible chief elected for ten years.
2. Ministers dependent upon the executive power alone.
3. A Council of State composed of the most distinguished men to prepare the laws and discuss them before the legislative body.
4. A legislative body to discuss and vote the laws, elected by universal [male] suffrage. . . .

This system, created by the First Consul [Napoleon I] at the beginning of the century, has already given France calm and prosperity; it will guarantee them to her again.

Such is my profound conviction. If you share it, declare that fact by your votes. If, on the contrary, you prefer a government without force, monarchical or republican, borrowed from I know not what past or from which chimerical future, reply in the negative. . . .

If I do not obtain a majority of your votes, I shall then convoke a new assembly, and I shall resign to it the mandate that I received from you. But if you believe that the cause of which my name is the symbol, that is, France regenerated by the revolution of 1789 and organized by the Emperor, is forever yours, proclaim it by sanctioning the powers that I ask from you. Then France and Europe will be saved from anarchy, obstacles will be removed, rivalries will disappear, for all will respect the decree of Providence in the decision of the people.

teem, concerned more with the interests of the country than with the strife of parties, sympathetic towards the suffering of the labouring classes."[2]

The first five years of Napoleon III's reign were a spectacular success as he reaped the benefits of worldwide economic prosperity, although the government's economic policies also contributed to French economic renewal. In light of the loss of political freedom, Napoleon realized the importance of diverting "the attention of the French from politics to economics." He believed in using the resources of government to encourage the national economy and took many steps to expand industrial growth. He promoted the expansion of credit by backing the formation of new investment banks, which provided long-term loans for industrial, commercial, and agricultural expansion. Government subsidies were used to foster the rapid construction of railroads as well as harbors, roads, and canals. The major French railway lines were completed during Napoleon's reign while industrial expansion was evident in the tripling of iron production. In his concern to reduce tensions and improve the social welfare of the nation, Napoleon provided hospitals and free medicine for the workers, and advocated better housing for the working class.

In the midst of this economic expansion, Napoleon III undertook a vast reconstruction of the city of Paris. Under the direction of Baron Haussmann, the medieval Paris of narrow streets and old city walls was destroyed and replaced by a modern Paris of broad boulevards, spacious buildings, circular plazas, public squares, an underground sewage system, a new public water supply, and gaslights. The new Paris served a military as well as aesthetic purpose. Broad streets made it more difficult for would-be insurrectionists to throw up barricades and easier for troops to move rapidly through the city in the event of revolts.

Napoleon III took a great interest in public opinion. Freedom of speech was, of course, not permitted in the authoritarian empire. Freedom of assembly was limited and newspapers were regularly censored. Nevertheless, Napoleon's desire to know the mood of his people led him to request regular reports on public opinion from his subordinates. In the 1860s, as opposition to some of Napoleon's policies began to mount, his sensitivity to the change in the public mood led him to undertake new policies liberalizing his regime. As a result, historians speak of the "liberal empire" for the latter part of the 1860s.

Opposition to Napoleon came from a variety of sources. His attempt to move toward free trade by lowering tariffs on foreign goods, especially those of the British, angered French manufacturers. Then, too, the financial crash of 1857, a silkworm disease, and the devastation of French vineyards by plant lice, although beyond his control, caused severe damage to the French economy. Retrenchment in government spending proved unpopular as well. To shore up his regime, Napoleon III reached out to the working class by legalizing trade unions and granting them the right to strike. He also began to liberalize the political process.

The Legislative Corps had been closely controlled during the 1850s. In the 1860s, opposition candidates were allowed greater freedom to campaign, and the Leg-

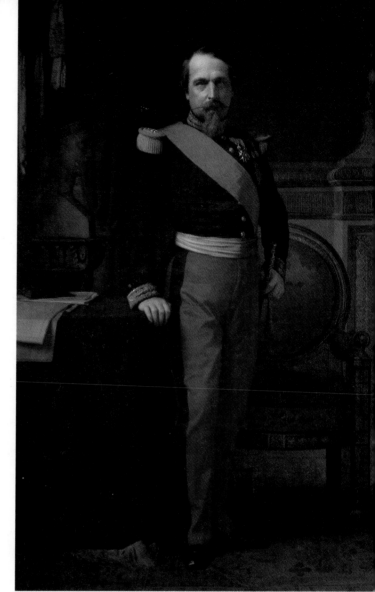

▼ **Emperor Napoleon III.** On December 2, 1852, Louis Napoleon took the title of Napoleon III and then proceeded to create an authoritarian monarchy. As opposition to his policies intensified in the 1860s, Napoleon III began to liberalize his government's policies. However, a disastrous military defeat at the hands of Prussia in 1870–1871 brought the collapse of his regime.

islative Corps was permitted more say in affairs of state, including debate over the budget. Historians do not agree about the ultimate aim and potential of Napoleon's liberalization, although it did serve initially to strengthen the hands of the government. In another plebiscite in May 1870, on whether to accept a new constitution that might have inaugurated a parliamentary regime, the French people gave Napoleon another resounding victory. This triumph was short-lived, however. Foreign policy failures had led to growing criticism, and war with Prussia in 1870 turned out to be the death blow for Napoleon III's regime (see The Franco-Prussian War, 1870–1871 later in the chapter).

Foreign Policy: The Crimean War

As heir to the Napoleonic Empire, Napoleon III was motivated by the desire to free France from the restrictions of the peace settlements of 1814–1815 and to make France the chief arbiter of Europe. Although his foreign policy ultimately led to disaster and his own undoing, Napoleon had initial success in the Crimean War (1854–1856).

The Crimean War was another chapter in the story of the so-called Eastern Question, or who would be the chief beneficiaries of the disintegration of the Turkish or Ottoman Empire. War had erupted between the Russians and Turks in 1853 when the Russians demanded the right to protect Christian shrines in Palestine, a privilege that had already been extended to the French. When the Turks refused, the Russians invaded Turkish Moldavia and Walachia. Failure to resolve the problem by negotiations led the Turks to declare war on Russia on October 4, 1853. In the following year, on March 28, Great Britain and France declared war on Russia.

Why did Britain and France take such a step? The British feared the expansion of Russian power into the eastern Mediterranean as a threat to their own sea power there, although some British statesmen also viewed Russia as the foremost threat to the European balance of power because of its aggressive designs on its neighbors. In his desire to undo the settlement of 1815, Napoleon had no doubt realized that Russia, as the chief supporter of those treaties, was his main obstacle. Although the Russian tsar, Nicholas I, hoped for Austrian support (since Russian troops had saved the Austrian Empire in 1849), the Austrians remained neutral. As the Austrian prime minister remarked, "We will astonish the world by our ingratitude." At least the Russians were, but Austria did not want the Balkans to become a Russian protectorate and very likely had its own designs in the Balkans. Problems among the Balkan Slavs would only serve to inflame the Slavic minorities in the Austrian Empire.

The Crimean War was poorly planned and poorly fought. Britain and France decided on an attack on Russia's Crimean peninsula in the Black Sea. After a long siege and at a terrible cost in manpower for both sides, the main Russian fortress of Sevastopol fell in September 1855, six months after the death of Tsar Nicholas I. His successor, Alexander II, soon sued for peace. By the Treaty of Paris, signed in March 1856, Russia was forced to give up Bessarabia at the mouth of the Danube and accept the neutrality of the Black Sea. In addition, the Danubian principalities of Moldavia and Walachia were placed under the protection of all the great powers.

The Crimean War broke up long-standing European power relationships and effectively destroyed the Concert of Europe. Austria and Russia, the two chief powers maintaining the status quo in the first half of the nineteenth century, were now enemies because of Austria's unwillingness to support Russia in the war. Russia, defeated, humiliated, and weakened by the obvious failure of its serf-armies, withdrew from European affairs for the next two decades to set its house in order and await a better opportunity to undo the Treaty of Paris. Great Britain, disillusioned by its role in the war, also pulled back from continental affairs. Austria, paying the price for its neutrality, was now without friends among the great powers. Not until the 1870s were new combinations formed to replace those that had disappeared, but in the meantime the European international situation remained fluid. Those willing to pursue the "politics of reality" found themselves presented with a situation rife with opportunity. It was this new international situation that made possible the unification of Italy and Germany.

Only Louis Napoleon seemed to have gained in prestige from the Crimean War. His experiences in the war had taught him that he was not the military genius his uncle had been, but he became well aware of the explosive power of the forces of nationalism and determined upon pursuing a foreign policy that would champion the cause of national movements. Some historians have argued that Napoleon believed ardently in the cause of national liberation. Be that as it may, as the liberator of national peoples, Napoleon III envisioned France as the natural leader of free European states. His policy proved to be a disaster as we can observe by examining the movements for unification in Italy and Germany.

▼ National Unification: Italy and Germany

The breakdown of the Concert of Europe opened the way for the Italians and the Germans to establish national states. Their successful unifications transformed the power structure of the Continent. Well into the twentieth century, Europe would still be dealing with the consequences.

The Unification of Italy

The Italians were the first people to benefit from the breakdown of the Concert of Europe. In 1850, Austria was still the dominant power on the Italian peninsula. Austria controlled the prosperous northern provinces of Lombardy and Venetia while Modena and Tuscany were ruled by members of Austria's house of Habsburg. Moreover, the Papal States governed by the pope, the other petty Italian states, and even the Bourbon kingdom of the Two Sicilies looked to the Austrians to maintain the status quo.

Although a minority, Italian liberals and nationalists had tried earnestly to achieve unification in the first half of the nineteenth century. Some had favored the *risorgimento* movement led by Giuseppe Mazzini, which favored a republican Italy; others looked to a confederation of Italian states under the direction of the pope. Neither of those alternatives was feasible after the defeats of 1849. A growing number of advocates of Italian unification now focused on the northern Italian state of Piedmont as their best hope to achieve their goal. As one observed, "To defeat cannons and soldiers, cannons and soldiers are needed. Arms are needed, and not Mazzinian pratings. Piedmont has soldiers and cannons. Therefore I am Piedmontese. By ancient custom, inclination and duty, Piedmont these days is a monarchy. Therefore I am not a republican."[3]

The royal house of Savoy ruled the kingdom of Piedmont, which also included the island of Sardinia. Although soundly defeated by the Austrians in 1848–1849, Piedmont under King Charles Albert had made a valiant effort; it seemed reasonable that it would now assume the leading role in the cause of national unity. It was, however, doubtful that the little state could supply the leadership needed until the new king, Victor Emmanuel II (1849–1878), named Count Camillo di Cavour (1810–1861) as his prime minister in 1852.

Cavour was a liberal-minded nobleman who had made a fortune in agriculture and went on to make even more money in banking, railroads, and shipping. He admired the British, especially their parliamentary system, industrial techniques, and economic liberalism. Cavour was a moderate who favored constitutional government. While he might have wanted Italian unification, he had no preconceived notions about how to obtain it. He was a consummate politician with the ability to persuade others of the rightness of his own convictions. After becoming prime minister in 1852, he pursued a policy of economic expansion, encouraging the building of roads, canals, and railroads and fostering business enterprise by expanding credit and stimulating investment in new industries. The growth in the Piedmontese economy and the subsequent increase in government revenues enabled Cavour to pour money into equipping a large army.

Cavour had no illusions about Piedmont's military strength and was only too well aware that he could not challenge Austrian strength directly. He would need the French. In 1858, Cavour came to an agreement with Napoleon III. The emperor agreed to become an ally of Piedmont in driving the Austrians out of Italy provided that the war could be justified "in the eyes of the public opinion of France and Europe." Once the Austrians were driven out, Italy would be reorganized. Piedmont would be extended into the kingdom of Upper Italy by adding Lombardy, Venetia, Parma, Modena, and part of the Papal States to its territory. In compensation for its efforts, France would receive the Piedmontese provinces of Nice and Savoy. A kingdom of Central Italy would be created for Napoleon III's cousin, Prince Napoleon, who would be married to the younger daughter of King Victor Emmanuel. This agreement between Napoleon and Cavour seemed to assure the French ruler of the opportunity to control Italy. Confident that the Austrians would be driven out of Italy, Cavour provoked the Austrians into invading Piedmont in April 1859, thus fulfilling Napoleon's demand that the war be justified "in the eyes of the public opinion of France and Europe."

In the initial stages of fighting, it was mostly French armies that defeated the Austrians in two major battles. It was also the French who made peace with Austria on July 11, 1859, without informing their Italian ally. Why had Napoleon withdrawn so hastily? For one thing, he realized that, despite two losses, the Austrian army had not yet been defeated; the struggle might be longer and more costly than he had anticipated. Moreover, the Prussians were mobilizing in support of Austria, and Napoleon III had no desire to take on two enemies at once. As a result of Napoleon's peace with Austria, Piedmont received only Lombardy; Austria remained in control of Venetia. Cavour was furious with the French perfidy, but events in northern Italy now turned in his favor. Soon after the war with Austria had begun, some northern Italian states, namely Parma, Modena, Tuscany, and part of the Papal States, had been taken over by nationalists. In plebiscites held in 1860, these states agreed to join Piedmont. Napoleon, in return for Nice and Savoy, agreed to the annexations.

Italian unification might have stopped here since there is little indication that Cavour envisioned uniting all of Italy in the spring of 1860. But the forces of ro-

Garibaldi and Romantic Nationalism

▼ ▼ ▼

Giuseppe Garibaldi was one of the more colorful figures involved in the unification of Italy. Accompanied by only a thousand of his famous "Red Shirts," the Italian soldier of fortune left Genoa on the night of May 5, 1860, for an invasion of the kingdom of the Two Sicilies. The ragged band entered Palermo, the chief city on the island of Sicily, on May 31. This selection is taken from an account by a correspondent for The Times *of* London, *the Hungarian-born Nandor Eber.*

The Times, June 13, 1860

Palermo, May 31—Anyone in search of violent emotions cannot do better than set off at once for Palermo. However blasé he may be, or however milk-and-water his blood, I promise it will be stirred up. He will be carried away by the tide of popular feeling. . . .

In the afternoon Garibaldi made a tour of inspection round the town. I was there, but find it really impossible to give you a faint idea of the manner in which he was received everywhere. It was one of those triumphs which seem to be almost too much for a man. . . . The popular idol, Garibaldi, in his red flannel shirt, with a loose colored handkerchief round his neck, and his worn "wide-awake," [a soft-brimmed felt hat] was walking on foot among those cheering, laughing, crying, mad thousands; and all his few followers could do was to prevent him from being bodily carried off the ground. The people threw themselves forward to kiss his hands, or, at least, to touch the hem of his garment, as if it contained the panacea for all their past and perhaps coming suffering. Children were brought up, and mothers asked on their knees

for his blessing; and all this while the object of this idolatry was calm and smiling as when in the deadliest fire, taking up the children and kissing them, trying to quiet the crowd, stopping at every moment to hear a long complaint of houses burned and property sacked by the retreating soldiers, giving good advice, comforting, and promising that all damages should be paid for. . . .

One might write volumes of horrors on the vandalism already committed, for every one of the hundred ruins has its story of brutality and inhumanity. . . . In these small houses a dense population is crowded together even in ordinary times. A shell falling on one, and crushing and burying the inmates, was sufficient to make people abandon the neighboring one and take refuge a little further on, shutting themselves up in the cellars. When the Royalists retired they set fire to those of the houses which had escaped the shells, and numbers were thus burned alive in their hiding places. . . .

If you can stand the exhalation, try and go inside the ruins, for it is only there that you will see what the thing means and you will not have to search long before you stumble over the remains of a human body, a leg sticking out here, an arm there, a black face staring at you a little further on. You are startled by a rustle. You look round and see half a dozen gorged rats scampering off in all directions, or you see a dog trying to make his escape over the ruins. . . . I only wonder that the sight of these scenes does not convert every man in the town into a tiger and every woman into a fury. But these people have been so long ground down and demoralized that their nature seems to have lost the power of reaction.

mantic republican nationalism forced Cavour to act. Giuseppe Garibaldi (1807–1882) was a dedicated Italian patriot who had supported Mazzini and the republican cause of Young Italy. While in exile in Latin America, he had gained much experience in guerrilla warfare, which he put to good use in the Italian revolutionary struggles of 1848–1849. In 1859, he became involved in the fighting against Austria. Garibaldi was a nuisance to Cavour, and the Piedmontese prime minister diverted his energies by encouraging him to move on to southern

Italy where a revolt had broken out against the Bourbon king of the Two Sicilies. With his thousand Red Shirts, as his volunteers were called because of their distinctive dress, Garibaldi landed in Sicily on May 11, 1860.

Although greatly outnumbered, Garibaldi's daring tactics won the day (see the box above). By the end of July 1860, most of Sicily had been pacified under Garibaldi's control. In August Garibaldi and his forces crossed over to the mainland and began a victorious march up the Italian peninsula. Naples, and with it the kingdom of the Two Sicilies, fell in early September. At this point Cavour reentered the scene. Aware that Garibaldi planned to march on Rome, Cavour feared that such a move would bring war with France as the defender of papal interests. Moreover, Garibaldi and his men favored a democratic republicanism; Cavour did not and acted quickly to preempt Garibaldi. The Piedmontese army invaded the Papal States (although bypassing Rome) and moved into the kingdom of Naples. Ever the patriot, Garibaldi chose to yield to Cavour's fait accompli rather than provoke a civil war and retired to his farm. Plebiscites in the Papal States and the kingdom of the Two Sicilies resulted in overwhelming support for union with Piedmont. On March 17, 1861, a new kingdom of Italy was proclaimed under a centralized government subordinated to the control of Piedmont and King Victor Emmanuel II (1861–1878) of the house of Savoy. Worn out by his efforts, Cavour died three months later.

Despite the proclamation of a new kingdom, the task of unification was not yet complete since Venetia in the north was still held by Austria and Rome was under

▼ **Garibaldi Arrives in Sicily.** The dream of Italian nationalists for a united Italian state finally became a reality by 1870. The northern Italian state of Piedmont played a crucial role in that process. Also important, however, was Giuseppe Garibaldi, a determined Italian patriot. Garibaldi is shown here arriving in Sicily on May 11, 1860, with his band of Red Shirts.

▼ **Map 23.1** The Unification of Italy.

Kingdom of Sardinia: Before 1859

To Kingdom of Sardinia: 1859

To Kingdom of Sardinia: 1860

To Kingdom of Italy: 1866, 1870

papal control, supported by French troops. To attack either one meant war with a major European state, which the Italian army was not prepared to handle. It was the Prussian army that indirectly completed the task of Italian unification. In the Austro-Prussian War of 1866 (see The Austro-Prussian War, 1866 later in the chapter), the new Italian state became an ally of Prussia. Although the Italian army was defeated by the Austrians, Prussia's victory left the Italians with Venetia. In 1870, the Franco-Prussian War (see The Franco-Prussian War, 1870–1871 later in the chapter) resulted in the withdrawal of French troops from Rome. The Italian army then annexed the city on September 20, 1870, and Rome became the new capital of the united Italian state.

The Unification of Germany

After the failure of the Frankfurt Assembly to achieve German unification in 1848–1849, German nationalists focused on Austria and Prussia as the only two states powerful enough to dominate German affairs. Austria had long controlled the existing Germanic Confederation, but Prussian power had grown, strongly reinforced by economic expansion in the 1850s. Industrial growth made rapid strides in Germany, especially within the Zollverein, a German customs union that had been formed in 1834 under Prussian leadership. By eliminating tolls on rivers and roads among member states, the Zollverein had stimulated trade and added to the prosperity of its member states. By 1853, all the German states except Austria had joined the Prussian-dominated customs union. Although Austria attempted to create its own customs union with the south German states, it was

rapidly being excluded from a new Germany based on common economic ties. Prussia benefited the most from this development, as even middle-class liberals began to find some good things in the Prussian state. In 1859, for example, a group of Hanoverian liberals formed the German Nationalverein, which advocated constitutional reforms and a united Germany. It looked openly to Prussia to bring about this unification.

In 1848, Prussia had created a constitution that at least had the appearance of constitutional monarchy as it had established a bicameral legislature with the lower house elected by universal male suffrage. However, the voting population was divided into three classes determined by the amount of taxes they paid, a system that allowed the biggest taxpayers to gain the most seats. Unintentionally this system allowed the rising middle classes, who were growing as a result of continuing industrialization, largely to control the lower house by 1859. Their desire for a real parliamentary system was counteracted, however, by the strength of the king's executive power because royal ministers were responsible to the king alone. Nevertheless, the parliament had been granted important legislative and taxation powers upon which it could build.

In 1861, King Frederick William IV died and was succeeded by his brother William. King William I (1861–1888) had definite ideas about the Prussian army because of his own military training. He and his advisers believed that the army was in dire need of change if Prussia was to remain a great power. Working closely with Albrecht von Roon as minister for war and Helmuth von Moltke as chief of the army general staff, the king planned to double the size of the army, diminish the role of the Landwehr, the popular militia reserves that had first been formed to fight Napoleon in 1806, and institute three years of compulsory military service for all young men.

Middle-class liberals in the parliament, while willing to have reform, feared compulsory military service because they believed the government would use it to inculcate obedience to the monarchy and strengthen the influence of the conservative-military clique in Prussia. The liberals were powerful enough to reject the new military budget submitted to parliament in March 1862. William I, unwilling to rule by military force, in his frustration appointed a new prime minister, Count Otto von Bismarck (1815–1898). Bismarck, regarded even by the king as too conservative, came to determine the course of modern German history. Until 1890, he dominated both German and European politics.

Otto von Bismarck was born into the Junker class, the traditional, landowning aristocracy of Prussia, to which he remained loyal for the rest of his life. "I was born and raised as an aristocrat," he once said. As a university student, Bismarck indulged heartily in wine, women, and song, yet managed to read widely in German history. After earning a law degree, he embarked upon a career in the Prussian civil service but soon tired of bureaucratic, administrative routine and retired to manage his country estates. Comparing the civil servant to a musician in an orchestra, he responded, "But I want to play the tune the way it sounds good to me or not at all . . . . My pride bids me command rather than obey."[4] In 1847, desirous of more excitement and power than he could find in the country, he reentered public life. Four years later, he began to build a base of diplomatic experience as the Prussian delegate to the diet (parliament) of the Germanic Confederation. This, combined with his experience as Prussian ambassador to Russia and later to France, gave him opportunities to acquire a wide knowledge of European affairs and to learn how to assess the character of rulers.

Because Bismarck succeeded in guiding Prussia's unification of Germany, it is often assumed that he had determined upon a course of action that led precisely to that goal. That is hardly the case. Bismarck was a consummate politician and opportunist. He was not a political gambler, but a moderate who waged war only when all other diplomatic alternatives had been exhausted and when he was reasonably sure that all the military and diplomatic advantages were on his side. Nor was he doctrinaire. Although loyal to the Junkers, the Prussian king, and Lutheranism, he was capable of transcending them all in favor of a broader perspective, although there is no doubt that he came to see the German empire, which he had helped to create, as the primary focus of his efforts. Bismarck has often been portrayed as the ultimate realist, the foremost nineteenth-century practitioner of *realpolitik*—the "politics of reality." His ability to manipulate people and power makes that claim justified, but unlike Hitler in the twentieth century, Bismarck also recognized the limitations of power. When he perceived that the advantages to be won from war "no longer justified the risks involved," he became an ardent defender of peace.

In 1862, the immediate problem facing Bismarck was domestic Prussian politics. Bismarck resubmitted the army appropriations bill to parliament along with a passionate appeal to his liberal opponents: "Germany does not look to Prussia's liberalism but to her power. . . . Not by speeches and majorities will the great questions of the day be decided—that was the mistake of 1848–1849—but by iron and blood."[5] His opponents were not impressed and rejected the bill once again. Bismarck went ahead, collected the taxes, and reorganized the

army anyway, blaming the liberals for causing the breakdown of constitutional government. From 1862 to 1866, Bismarck governed Prussia by simply ignoring parliament. Unwilling to revolt and unable to force people not to pay their taxes, parliament did nothing. In the meantime, opposition to his domestic policy determined Bismarck upon an active foreign policy, which led in 1864 to his first war.

THE DANISH WAR, 1864   In the three wars that he waged, Bismarck's victories were as much diplomatic and political as they were military. Before war was declared, Bismarck always saw to it that Prussia would be fighting only one power and that that opponent was isolated diplomatically. He knew enough Prussian history to realize that Frederick the Great had almost been crushed by a mighty coalition in the eighteenth century (see Chapter 19).

The Danish War arose over the duchies of Schleswig and Holstein. In 1863, contrary to international treaty, the Danish government moved to incorporate the two duchies into Denmark. German nationalists were outraged since both duchies had large German populations and were regarded as German states. The diet of the Germanic Confederation urged its member states to send troops against Denmark, but Bismarck did not care to subject Prussian policy to the Austrian-dominated German diet. Instead, he persuaded the Austrians to join Prussia in declaring war on Denmark on February 1, 1864. The Danes were quickly defeated and surrendered Schleswig and Holstein to the victors. Austria and Prussia then agreed to divide the administration of the two duchies; Prussia took Schleswig while Austria administered Holstein. The plan was Bismarck's. By this time Bismarck had come to the realization that the ability of Prussia to expand its power by dominating the northern, largely Protestant part of the Germanic Confederation had to mean the exclusion of Austria from German affairs or, less likely, Austria's willingness to accept Prussian domination of Germany. The joint administration of the two duchies offered plenty of opportunities to create friction with Austria and provide a reason for war if it came to that. While he pursued negotiations with Austria, at the same time he laid the foundations for the isolation of Austria.

THE AUSTRO-PRUSSIAN WAR, 1866   Bismarck had no problem gaining Russia's agreement to remain neutral in the event of an Austro-Prussian war because Prussia had been the only great power to support Russia's repression of a Polish revolt in 1863. A thornier problem was Napoleon III, but Bismarck was able to buy his neutrality by

▼ **Map 23.2** The Unification of Germany

vague promises of territory in the Rhineland in return for France's neutrality in the event of an Austro-Prussian conflict. Finally, Bismarck made an alliance with the new Italian state and promised it Venetia in the event of Austrian defeat.

With the Austrians isolated, Bismarck used the joint occupation of Schleswig-Holstein to goad the Austrians into a war on June 14, 1866. Many Europeans, including Napoleon III, expected a quick Austrian victory, but they overlooked the effectiveness of the Prussian military reforms of the 1860s. The Prussian breech-loading needle gun had a much faster rate of fire than the Austrian muzzle-loader, and a superior network of railroads enabled the Prussians to mass troops quickly. At Königgrätz (or Sadowa) on July 3, the Austrian army was decisively defeated. Looking ahead, Bismarck refused to

create a hostile enemy by burdening Austria with a harsh peace as the Prussian king wanted. Austria lost no territory except Venetia to Italy but was excluded from German affairs. The German states north of the Main River were organized into a North German Confederation controlled by Prussia. The south German states, largely Catholic, remained independent but were coerced into signing military agreements with Prussia. In addition to Schleswig and Holstein, Prussia annexed Hanover, Hesse-Cassel, and the free city of Frankfurt because they had openly sided with Austria.

The Austrian War was a rather decisive turning point in Prussian domestic affairs. After the war, Bismarck asked the Prussian parliament to pass a bill of indemnity, legalizing retroactively the taxes Bismarck had collected illegally since 1862. Most liberals did so, having become enthusiastic supporters of Bismarck's achievements. With his victory over Austria and the creation of the North German Confederation, Bismarck had proven Napoleon III's dictum that nationalism and authoritarian government could be combined. In splitting liberalism and nationalism, the two major forces of change in the early nineteenth century, Bismarck made nationalism itself into an antirevolutionary force.

He showed the same flexibility in the creation of a new constitution for the North German Confederation. Each German state kept its own local government, but the king of Prussia was head of the confederation while the chancellor (Bismarck) was responsible directly to the king. Both the army and foreign policy remained in the hands of the king and his chancellor. Parliament consisted of two bodies: a Bundesrat, or federal council composed of delegates nominated by the states, and a lower house, the Reichstag, elected by universal male suffrage. Like Napoleon, Bismarck believed that the peasants and artisans who made up most of the population were conservative at heart and could be used to overcome the advantages of the liberals. He had not counted on the industrial proletariat whose growth in the years ahead would provide him with some of his most vehement opposition (see Chapter 24).

THE FRANCO-PRUSSIAN WAR, 1870–1871 Bismarck and William I had achieved a major goal by 1866. Prussia now dominated all of northern Germany, and Austria had been excluded from any significant role in German affairs. In effect, Prussian militaristic and counterrevolutionary conservatism had triumphed. At the same time, unsettled business led to new international complications and further change. Bismarck realized that France would never be content with a strong German state to its east because of the potential threat to French security. At the same time, after a series of setbacks, Napoleon III needed a diplomatic triumph to offset his serious domestic problems. The French were not happy with the turn of events in Germany and looked for opportunities to humiliate the Prussians.

After a successful revolution had deposed Queen Isabella II, the throne of Spain was offered to Prince Leopold of Hohenzollern-Sigmaringen, a distant relative of the Hohenzollern king of Prussia. Bismarck welcomed this possibility for the same reason that the French objected to it. By placing Leopold on the throne of Spain, France would be virtually encircled by members of the Hohenzollern dynasty. French objections caused King William I to force his relative to withdraw his candidacy. Bismarck was disappointed with the king's actions, but

at this point the French overreached themselves. Not content with their diplomatic victory, they pushed William I to make a formal apology to France and promise never to allow Leopold to be a candidate again. When Bismarck received a telegraph from the king informing him of the French request, Bismarck edited it to make it appear even more insulting to the French, knowing that the French would probably declare war over the issue (see the box on p. 786). Through diplomacy, Bismarck had already made it virtually certain that no other European power would interfere in a war between France and Prussia. The French reacted as Bismarck expected they would and declared war on Prussia on July 15, 1870. The French prime minister remarked, "We go to war with a light heart."

Unfortunately for the French, a "light heart" was not enough. They had barely started their military reorganization and proved no match for the better led and organized Prussian forces. The south German states honored

▼ **The Unification of Germany: Anton von Werner, *Proclamation of the German Empire*.** Under Prussian leadership, a new German empire was proclaimed on January 18, 1871, in the Hall of Mirrors in the palace at Versailles. King William of Prussia became Emperor William I of the Second German Empire. Otto von Bismarck, the man who had been so instrumental in creating the new German state, is shown here, resplendently attired in his white uniform, standing at the foot of the throne.

Bismarck "Goads" France into War

▼ ▼ ▼

A fter his meeting with the French ambassador at Ems, King William I of Prussia sent a telegraph to Bismarck with a report of their discussions. By editing the telegraph from King William I before he released it to the press, Bismarck made it sound as if the Prussian king had treated the ambassador in a demeaning fashion. Six days later, Napoleon III declared war on Prussia.

The Abeken [Privy Councillor] Text, Ems, July 13, 1870

To the Federal Chancellor, Count Bismarck. His Majesty the King writes to me:

"M. Benedetti intercepted me on the Promenade in order to demand of me most insistently that I should authorize him to telegraph immediately to Paris that I shall obligate myself for all future time never again to give my approval to the candidacy of the Hohenzollerns should it be renewed. I refused to agree to this, the last time somewhat severely, informing him that one dare not and cannot assume such obligations *à tout jamais* [forever]. Naturally, I informed him that I had received no news as yet, and since he had been informed earlier than I by way of Paris and Madrid, he could easily understand why my government was once again out of the matter."

Since then His Majesty has received a dispatch from the Prince [father of the Hohenzollern candidate for the Spanish throne]. As His Majesty has informed Count Benedetti that he was expecting news from the Prince, His Majesty himself, in view of the above-mentioned demand and in consonance with the advice of Count Eulenburg and myself, decided not to receive the French envoy again but to inform him through an adjutant that His Majesty had now received from the Prince confirmation of the news which Benedetti had already received from Paris, and that he had nothing further to say to the Ambassador. His Majesty leaves it to the judgment of Your Excellency whether or not to communicate at once the new demand by Benedetti and its rejection to our ambassadors and to the press.

Bismarck's Edited Version

After the reports of the renunciation by the hereditary Prince of Hohenzollern had been officially transmitted by the Royal Government of Spain to the Imperial Government of France, the French Ambassador presented to His Majesty the King at Ems the demand to authorize him to telegraph to Paris that His Majesty the King would obligate himself for all future time never again to give his approval to the candidacy of the Hohenzollerns should it be renewed.

His Majesty the King thereupon refused to receive the French envoy again and informed him through an adjutant that His Majesty had nothing further to say to the Ambassador.

---

their military alliances with Prussia and joined the war effort against the French. The Prussian armies advanced into France, and at Sedan, on September 2, 1870, an entire French army and Napoleon III himself were captured. Although the Second French Empire collapsed, the war was not yet over. After four months of bitter resistance, Paris finally capitulated on January 28, 1871, and an official peace treaty was signed in May. France had to pay an indemnity of five billion francs (about one billion dollars) and give up the provinces of Alsace and Lorraine to the new German state. The latter demand rankled the French and left them burning for revenge.

Even before the war had ended, the south German states had agreed to enter the North German Confederation. On January 18, 1871, in the Hall of Mirrors in Louis XIV's palace at Versailles, William I was proclaimed kaiser or emperor of the Second German Empire (the first was the medieval Holy Roman Empire). German unity had been achieved by the Prussian monarchy and the Prussian army. In a real sense, Germany had been merged into Prussia, not Prussia into Germany. German liberals also rejoiced. They had dreamed of unity and freedom, but the achievement of unity now seemed much more important. One old liberal proclaimed:

> I cannot shake off the impression of this hour. I am no devotee of Mars; I feel more attached to the goddess of beauty and the mother of graces than to the powerful god of war, but the trophies of war exercise a magic charm even upon the

Chronology

▼ ▼ ▼

The Unification of Germany

King William I of Prussia	1861–1888
Bismarck Becomes Minister-President of Prussia	1862
The Danish War	1864
The Austro-Prussian War	1866
Battle of Königgrätz	1866 (July 3)
The Franco-Prussian War	1870–1871
Battle of Sedan	1870 (September 2)
Fall of Paris	1871 (January 28)
German Empire Is Proclaimed	1871 (January 18)

child of peace. One's view is involuntarily chained and one's spirit goes along with the boundless row of men who acclaim the god of the moment—success.[6]

The Prussian leadership of German unification meant the triumph of authoritarian, militaristic values over liberal, constitutional sentiments in the development of the new German state. With its industrial resources and military might, the new state had become the strongest power on the Continent. A new European balance of power was at hand.

▼ Nationalism and Reform: The National State in Mid-Century

While European affairs were dominated by the unification of Italy and Germany, other states were also undergoing transformations. War, civil war, and changing political alignments served as catalysts for domestic reforms.

The Austrian Empire

After the Habsburgs had crushed the revolutions of 1848–1849, they restored centralized, autocratic government to the empire. What seemed to be the only lasting result of the revolution of 1848 was the act of emancipation of September 7, 1848, that freed the serfs and eliminated all compulsory labor services. Nevertheless, the development of industrialization after 1850, especially in Vienna and the provinces of Bohemia and

Galicia, served to bring some economic and social change to the empire in the form of an urban proletariat, labor unrest, and a new industrial middle class.

In 1851, the revolutionary constitutions were abolished, and a system of centralized autocracy was imposed on the empire. Under the leadership of Alexander von Bach (1813–1893), local privileges were subordinated to a unified system of administration, law, and taxation implemented by German-speaking officials. Hungary was subjected to the rule of military officers while the Catholic church was declared the state church and given control of education. The Bach regime, according to one critic, was composed of "a standing army of soldiers, a sitting army of officials, a kneeling army of priests, and a creeping army of denunciators." Change soon came, however, impelled by severe economic troubles and defeat in war. Failure in war usually had severe internal consequences for European states after 1789, and Austria was no exception. After Austria's defeat in the Italian war in 1859, the Emperor Francis Joseph (1848–1916) attempted to establish an imperial parliament (*Reichsrat*) with a nominated upper house and an elected lower house of representatives. Although the system was supposed to provide representation for the nationalities of the empire, the complicated formula used for elections ensured the election of a German-speaking majority, serving once again to alienate the ethnic minorities, particularly the Hungarians.

Only when military disaster struck again did the Austrians deal with the fiercely nationalistic Hungarians. The result was the negotiated *Ausgleich,* or Compromise, of 1867, which created the dual monarchy of Austria-Hungary. Each part of the empire now had its constitution, its own bicameral legislature, its own governmental machinery for domestic affairs, and its own capital (Vienna for Austria and Budapest for Hungary). Holding the two states together were a single monarch (Francis Joseph was emperor of Austria and king of Hungary) and a common army, foreign policy, and system of finances. In domestic affairs, the Hungarians had become an independent nation. The *Ausgleich* did not, however, satisfy the other nationalities that made up the multinational Austro-Hungarian Empire. The dual monarchy simply enabled the German-speaking Austrians and Hungarian Magyars to dominate the minorities, especially the Slavs, in their respective states. As the Hungarian nationalist Louis Kossuth remarked, "Dualism is the alliance of the conservative, reactionary and any apparently liberal elements in Hungary with those of the Austrian Germans who despise liberty, for the oppres-

▼ **Map 23.3** The Dual Monarchy in 1867.

sion of the other nationalities and races."[7] The nationalities problem remained until the demise of the empire at the end of World War I.

Imperial Russia

The Russian imperial autocracy, based on soldiers, secret police, repression, and censorship, had withstood the revolutionary fervor of 1848 and even served as the "arsenal of autocracy" in crushing revolutions elsewhere in Europe. The defeat in the Crimean War at the hands of the British and French revealed the blatant deficiencies behind the facade of absolute power and made it clear even to staunch conservatives that Russia was falling hopelessly behind the western European powers. Tsar Alexander II (1855–1881), who came to power in the midst of the Crimean War, turned his energies to a se-

rious overhaul of the Russian system. Though called the Liberator because of his great reforms, Alexander II was no liberal but a thoughtful realist who knew reforms could not be postponed. Following the autocratic procedures of his predecessors, he attempted to impose those reforms upon the Russian people.

Serfdom was the most burdensome problem in tsarist Russia. The continuing subjugation of millions of peasants to the land and their landlords was an obviously corrupt and failing system. Reduced to antiquated methods of production based on serf labor, Russian landowners were economically pressed and unable to compete with foreign agriculture. Russian serfs, who formed the backbone of the Russian infantry, were uneducated and consequently increasingly unable to deal with the more complex machines and weapons of war. It was, after all, the failure of the serf-armies in the Crimean War that

Emancipation: Serfs and Slaves

▼ ▼ ▼

*Although overall their histories have been quite differ-
ent, the two great adversaries of the late twentieth
century—the United States and the Soviet Union—shared
a common feature in the 1860s. They were the only states
in the Western world that still had large enslaved populations (the Russian serfs were virtually slaves). The leaders
of both countries issued emancipation proclamations
within two years of each other. The first excerpt is taken
from the Imperial Decree of March 3, 1861, which freed
the Russian serfs. The second excerpt is from Abraham
Lincoln's Emancipation Proclamation, issued on January
1, 1863.*

The Imperial Decree, March 3, 1861

By the grace of God, we, Alexander II, Emperor and
Autocrat of all the Russias, King of Poland, Grand
Duke of Finland, etc., to all our faithful subjects,
make known:

Called by Divine Providence and by the sacred
right of inheritance to the throne of our ancestors, we
took a vow in our innermost heart to respond to the
mission which is intrusted to us as to surround with
our affection and our Imperial solicitude all our faithful subjects of every rank and of every condition, from
the warrior, who nobly bears arms for the defence of
the country to the humble artisan devoted to the
works of industry; from the official in the career of the
high offices of the State to the laborer whose plough
furrows the soil. . . .

We thus came to the conviction that the work of
a serious improvement of the condition of the peasants was a sacred inheritance bequeathed to us by our
ancestors, a mission which, in the course of events,
Divine Providence called upon us to fulfill. . . .

In virtue of the new dispositions above mentioned, the peasants attached to the soil will be invested within a term fixed by the law with all the
rights of free cultivators. . . .

At the same time, they are granted the right of
purchasing their close, and, with the consent of the
proprietors, they may acquire in full property the arable lands and other appurtenances which are allotted to them as a permanent holding. By the acquisition in full property of the quantity of land fixed, the
peasants are free from their obligations towards the
proprietors for land thus purchased, and they enter
definitely into the condition of free peasants—
landholders.

The Emancipation Proclamation, January 1, 1863

Now therefore, I, Abraham Lincoln, President of the
United States, by virtue of the power in me vested as
Commander-in-Chief of the Army and Navy of the
United States in time of actual armed rebellion
against the authority and government of the United
States, and as a fit and necessary war measure for
suppressing such rebellion, do, on this 1st day of January, A.D. 1863, and in accordance with my purpose
to do so, . . . order and designate as the States and
parts of States wherein the people thereof, respectively, are this day in rebellion against the United
States the following, to wit:

Arkansas, Texas, Louisiana, . . . Mississippi, Al-
abama, Florida, Georgia, South Carolina, North
Carolina, and Virginia . . .

And by virtue of the power for the purpose
aforesaid, I do order and declare that all persons held
as slaves within said designated States and parts of
States are, and henceforward shall be free; and that
the Executive Government of the United States,
including the military and naval authorities thereof,
will recognize and maintain the freedom of said
persons.

created the need for change in the first place. Then, too,
peasant dissatisfaction still led to local peasant revolts
that disrupted the countryside. Alexander II seemed to
recognize the inevitable: "The existing order of serfdom," he told a group of Moscow nobles, "cannot remain unchanged. It is better to abolish serfdom from
above than to wait until it is abolished from below."

On March 3, 1861, Alexander issued his emancipation edict (see the box above). Peasants were now free to
own property, marry as they chose, and bring suits in the
law courts. But the system of land redistribution instituted after emancipation was not that favorable to them.
The government provided land for the peasants by
purchasing it from the landlords, but the landowners

▼ **Russian Serfs: A Grandmother and Her Grandchild.**
Serfdom was a costly burden for tsarist Russia. Realizing the
need for change, Tsar Alexander II legally freed the serfs on
March 3, 1861. Nevertheless, Russian peasants remained
economically bound to the land, and emancipation of the serfs
did little to bring any real improvements for the peasants. Most
Russian peasants continued to follow traditional ways of life and
farming.

often chose to keep the best lands. The Russian peasants
soon found that they had inadequate amounts of good
arable land to support themselves, a situation worsened
by the rapidly increasing peasant population in the second half of the nineteenth century.

Nor were the peasants completely free. The state
compensated the landowners for the land given to the
peasants, but the peasants, in turn, were expected to
repay the state in long-term installments. To ensure that
the payments were made, peasants were subjected to the

authority of their *mir* or village commune, which was
collectively responsible for the land payments to the
government. In a very real sense, then, the village commune, not the individual peasants, owned the land the
peasants were purchasing. And since the village communes were responsible for the payments, they were reluctant to allow peasants to leave their land. Emancipation, then, led not to a free, landowning peasantry along
the Western model, but to an unhappy, land-starved
peasantry that largely followed the old ways of agricultural production. Comprehensive reforms that would
have freed the peasants completely and given them access to their own land were unfortunately left until the
early twentieth century.

Alexander II attempted other reforms, however.
In 1864, he instituted a system of zemstvos or local assemblies that provided a moderate degree of self-
government. Representatives to the zemstvos were to be
elected from the noble landowners, townspeople, and
peasants, but the property-based system of voting gave a
distinct advantage to the nobles. Zemstvos were given a
limited power to provide public services, such as education and famine relief, maintain roads and bridges, and
levy taxes to pay for these responsibilities, although government bureaucrats, fearful of such self-government,
often obstructed their efforts. As one official noted, "In
Russia reform can be carried out only by authority. We
have too much disturbance and too much divergence of
interests to expect anything good from the representation of those interests."[8] The hope of liberal nobles and
other social reformers that the zemstvos would be expanded into a national parliament remained unfulfilled.
The legal reforms of 1864, which created a regular system of local and provincial courts and a judicial code
that accepted the principle of equality before the law,
proved successful, however.

Even the autocratic tsar was unable to control the
forces he unleashed by his reform program. Reformers
wanted more and rapid change; conservatives opposed
what they perceived as the tsar's attempts to undermine
the basic institutions of Russian society. By 1870, Russia
was witnessing an increasing number of reform movements. One of the most popular stemmed from the radical writings of Alexander Herzen (1812–1870), a Russian exile living in London, whose slogan of "land and
freedom" epitomized his belief that the Russian peasant
must be the chief instrument for social reform. Following
Herzen's ideas, Russian students and intellectuals created a populist movement that supported a revolutionary
reordering of society based on peasant communal life.
The peasants' lack of interest in their form of revolution,

however, led some revolutionaries to resort to violent means to overthrow tsarist autocracy. One such group of radicals, known as the People's Will, succeeded in as-sassinating Alexander II in 1881. His son and successor, Alexander III, turned against reform and returned to the traditional methods of repression.

Great Britain

Like Russia, Britain also experienced no revolution-ary disturbances during 1848, although for quite differ-ent reasons. The Reform Act of 1832 had opened the door to political representation for the industrial middle

▼ **Map 23.4** Europe in 1871.

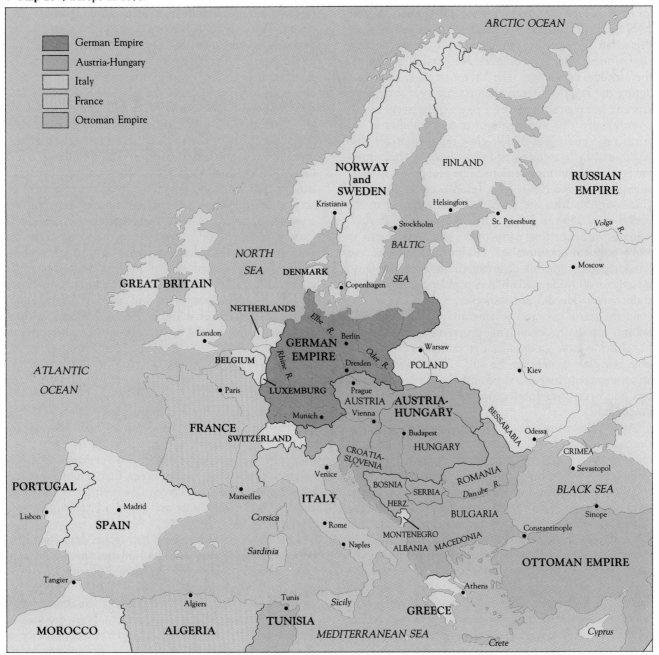

German Empire
Austria-Hungary
Italy
France
Ottoman Empire

class, and in the 1860s the liberal parliamentary system of Britain demonstrated once more its ability to make both social and political reforms that enabled the country to remain stable and prosperous.

One of the reasons for Britain's stability was its continuing economic growth. The British had flaunted their wealth and satisfaction with their achievements to the world in the great Industrial Exhibition in 1851. Now middle-class prosperity was at last coupled with some improvements for the working classes as well. Real wages for laborers increased over 25 percent between 1850 and 1870. The British sense of national pride was well reflected in Queen Victoria (1837–1901), whose self-contentment and sense of moral respectability mirrored the attitudes of her age. The Victorian Age, as Britain during the reign of Queen Victoria has ever since been known, was characterized by a pious complacency.

Politically, this was an era of uneasy stability as the aristocratic and upper-middle-class representatives who dominated Parliament blurred party lines by their internal strife and shifting positions. The one political figure who stood out was Henry John Temple, Lord Palmerston (1784–1865), who was prime minister for most of the period from 1855 to 1865. Although a Whig, Palmerston was without strong party loyalty and found it easy to make political compromises. His primary interest was foreign policy, and his chauvinistic defense of British interests worldwide made him a popular figure with his countrymen. He did not, however, want to move beyond the status quo and became an obstacle to further reform, especially denouncing proposals to expand the franchise to new groups. By extending representation from one class to another, he said, "We should by such an arrangement increase the number of Bribeable Electors and overpower Intelligence and Property by Ignorance and Poverty."

After Palmerston's death in 1865, the movement for the extension of the franchise only intensified. One mass meeting even led to a riot in London's Hyde Park. Although the Whigs (now called the Liberals), who had been responsible for the Reform Act of 1832, talked about passing such reform legislation, it was actually the Tories (now called the Conservatives) who carried it through. The Tory leader in Parliament, Benjamin Disraeli (1804–1881), was apparently motivated by the desire to win over the newly enfranchised groups to the Conservative party, believing that the uneducated classes would defer to their social superiors when they voted. He knew that the Liberals, viewed as the party of reform, would dare not oppose the reform bill. The Reform Act of 1867 was an important step toward the democratization of Britain. It extended the right to vote by lowering the required amount of taxes paid or income earned sufficiently that it by and large enfranchised many male urban workers. The number of voters increased from about one million to slightly over two million. Although Disraeli believed this would benefit the Conservatives, industrial workers helped to produce a huge Liberal victory in 1868.

The extension of the right to vote had an important by-product as it forced the Liberal and Conservative parties to organize carefully in order to manipulate the electorate. Party discipline intensified, and the rivalry between two well-established political parties, the Liberals and Conservatives, became a regular feature of parliamentary life. In large part this was due to the personal and political opposition of the two leaders of these parties, William Gladstone (1809–1898) and Disraeli.

The first Liberal administration of William Gladstone from 1868 to 1874 was responsible for a series of impressive reform acts. In fact, historians have called the first Gladstone ministry the apex of "classical British liberalism." Legislation and government orders opened civil service positions to competitive exams rather than patronage, dropped religious requirements for degrees at Oxford and Cambridge, introduced the secret ballot for voting, and abolished the purchase of military commissions. The Education Act of 1870 attempted to make elementary schools available for all children (see Chapter 25). These reforms were typically liberal. By eliminating abuses and enabling people with talent to compete fairly, they sought to strengthen the nation and its institutions.

The United States: Civil War and Reunion

While the Germans and Italians were fighting Austria and France to achieve national unity, some Americans were hoping to dissolve theirs. During its early existence, the young republic had shown a remarkable ability to resolve peacefully many issues that might have disrupted national unity. Slavery, however, proved to be an issue beyond compromise and led to a bitter and bloody civil war.

Like the North, the South had grown dramatically in population during the first half of the nineteenth century. But its development was quite different. Its cotton economy and social structure were based on the exploitation of enslaved black Africans and their descendants. The importance of cotton is evident from production figures. In 1810, the South produced a raw cotton crop of 178,000 bales worth $10 million. By 1860, it was generating 4.5 million bales of cotton with a value of $249 million. Ninety-three percent of southern cotton in 1850 was produced by a slave population that had grown dramatically in fifty years. Although new slave imports had been barred in 1808, there were 4 million Afro-American slaves in the South by 1860 compared to 1 million in 1800. The cotton economy and a plantation-based slavery were intimately related, and the attempt to maintain them in the course of the first half of the nineteenth century led the South to become increasingly defensive, monolithic, and isolated. At the same time, the growth of an abolitionist movement in the North challenged the southern order and created an "emotional chain reaction" that led to civil war.

The push of Americans westward was a major factor in bringing the issue of slavery to the forefront of American politics. The issue had already arisen in the 1810s as new states were being created by the rush of settlers beyond the Mississippi. The free states of the North feared the creation of a slave state majority in the national government. The debate touched off by the desire of Missouri to obtain statehood as a slave state was only ended by the Missouri Compromise of 1820, which used the latitude 36°30' as a dividing line. All new states north of the line would be admitted as free states; those south of the line as slave states. The Missouri Compromise worked, at least until the addition of vast new territories in the Southwest after the Mexican War (1846–1848). If the line of the Missouri Compromise were extended to the Pacific Ocean, most of the new territory acquired by the United States in its war with Mexico would be open to slavery, a disquieting prospect

▼ **Map 23.5** The United States: The West and Civil War.

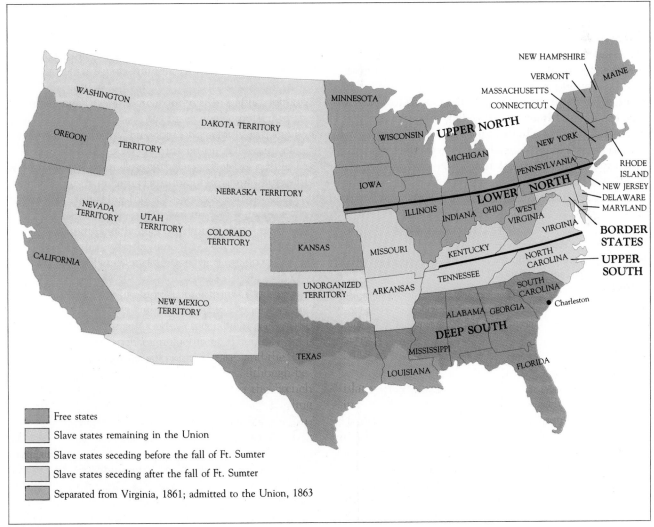

Free states

Slave states remaining in the Union

Slave states seceding before the fall of Ft. Sumter

Slave states seceding after the fall of Ft. Sumter

Separated from Virginia, 1861; admitted to the Union, 1863

to northern free states that feared the growth of southern power in the national government. It was time for another compromise.

The Compromise of 1850, which admitted California as a free state while allowing slavery in Utah and New Mexico if a majority of settlers favored it, was really an armistice, not a compromise. It had merely postponed, not solved this divisive issue. By the 1850s, the slavery question had caused the Whig party to become defunct while the Democrats were splitting along North-South lines. The Kansas-Nebraska Act of 1854, which effectively repealed the Missouri Compromise by allowing slavery in the Kansas-Nebraska territories to be determined by popular sovereignty, created a firestorm in the North and led to the creation of a new one-issue party. The Republicans were united by antislavery and were especially driven by the fear that the "slave power" of the South would attempt to spread the slave system throughout the country.

After 1854, polarization over the issue of slavery intensified. The outbreak of bloody conflict in Kansas between free staters and slave owners demonstrated that the issue was moving beyond the realm of compromise. Six more years of maneuvering only reinforced that point. When Abraham Lincoln, the man who had said in a speech in Illinois in 1858 that "this government cannot endure permanently half slave and half free," was elected president in November 1860, the die was cast. Lincoln carried only 2 of the 1,109 counties in the South; the Republicans were not even on the ballot in ten southern states. On December 20, 1860, a South Carolina convention voted to repeal ratification of the Constitution of the United States. In February 1861, six more southern states did the same, and a rival nation—the Confederate States of America—was formed. In March fighting erupted between North and South.

The American Civil War (1861–1865) was an extraordinarily bloody struggle, a clear foretaste of the total war to come in the twentieth century. Over 600,000 soldiers died, either in battle or from deadly infectious diseases spawned by filthy camp conditions. This figure exceeds the combined American casualties of World War I and World War II. The northern or Union forces enjoyed a formidable advantage in numbers of troops and material resources to fight the war; but to southerners, those assets were not decisive. To them, the Confederacy, after all, did not have to conquer the North, only defend the South from invasion. Many of the most promising young military officers were from the South, whose aristocratic landowning society had a far stronger military tradition than the business-oriented North. Southerners also believed that the dependence of manufacturers in the North and the European countries on southern raw cotton would lead to antiwar sentiment in the North and support abroad for the South.

All these southern calculations meant little in the long run. Over a period of four years, the Union states mobilized their superior assets and gradually wore down the South. As the war dragged on, it had the effect of radicalizing public opinion in the North. What began as a war to save the Union became a war against slavery. On January 1, 1863, Lincoln's Emancipation Proclama-

▼ **The Dead at Antietam.** Nation-building took many forms in the mid-nineteenth century. National unity in the United States dissolved over the issue of slavery and led to a bloody Civil War that restored the Union at a cost of 600,000 American lives. This photograph shows the Southern dead after the Battle of Antietam on September 17, 1862.

tion made most of the nation's slaves "forever free" (see the box on p. 789). The increasingly effective Union blockade of the South combined with a shortage of fighting men made the Confederate cause desperate by the end of 1864. The final push of Union troops under General Ulysses S. Grant forced General Robert E. Lee's army to surrender on April 9, 1865. Although the prob-

lems of reconstruction were ahead, the Union victory confirmed that the United States would be "one nation, indivisible." National unity, not particularism, had prevailed in the United States.

▼ Industrialization and the Marxist Response

Between 1850 and 1871, continental industrialization came of age. The innovations of the British Industrial Revolution—mechanized factory production, the use of coal, the steam engine, and the transportation revolution—all became regular features of economic expansion. Although marred periodically by economic depression (1857–1858) or recession (1866–1867), this was an age of considerable economic prosperity, particularly evident in the growth of domestic and foreign markets.

Industrialization on the Continent

The transformation of textile production from hand looms to power looms had largely been completed in Britain by the 1850s (for cotton) and 1860s (for wool). On the Continent, the period from 1850 to 1870 witnessed increased mechanization of the cotton and textile industries, although continental countries still remained behind Britain. By 1870, hand looms had virtually disappeared in Britain whereas in France there were still 200,000 of them compared to 80,000 power looms; in Germany, there were 125,000 hand looms to 57,000 power looms. However, this period of industrial expansion on the Continent was fueled not so much by textiles but by the growth of railroads, which, as one economic historian has noted, "displaced textiles as the drummer of industrial activity." Between 1850 and 1870, European railroad track mileage increased from 14,500 to almost 70,000. In turn, the railroad stimulated growth in both the iron and coal industries.

Between 1850 and 1870, continental iron industries made the transition from charcoal iron smelting to coke-blast smelting. In Prussia, for example, where charcoal was used to produce 82 percent of iron output in 1842, this figure had declined to 60 percent in 1852, and to only 12.3 percent by 1862. Despite the dramatic increases in the production of pig iron, the continental countries had not yet come close to surpassing British iron production. In 1870, the British iron industry produced one-half of the world's pig iron, four times as much as Germany and five times as much as France. In the middle decades of the nineteenth century, continen-

▼ **Opening of the Suez Canal.** Between 1850 and 1871, continental Europeans built railways, bridges, and canals as part of an ever-spreading process of industrialization. A French diplomat, Ferdinand de Lesseps, was the guiding force behind the construction of the Suez Canal, which provided a link between the Mediterranean and Red seas. Work on the canal began in 1859 and was completed ten years later. As seen here, an elaborate ceremony marked the opening of the canal. A French vessel led the first convoy of ships through the canal.

tal countries also witnessed a rapid conversion to the use of the steam engine in textile, mining, and metallurgical industries.

Although policies varied from country to country, continental governments took a more or less active role in passing laws and initiating actions that were favorable to the expansion of industry and commerce. While some countries exercised direct control over nationalized industries, such as Prussia's development of coal mines in the Saar region, others provided financial assistance to private companies to develop mines, ironworks, dockyards, and railways.

An important factor in the expansion of markets was the elimination of barriers to international trade. Essential international waterways were opened up by the elimination of restrictive tolls. The Danube River in 1857 and the Rhine in 1861, for example, were declared freeways for all ships. The negotiation of trade treaties in the 1860s reduced or eliminated protective tariffs throughout much of Western Europe.

Governments also played a role in first allowing and then encouraging the formation of joint-stock investment banks (see Chapter 21). These banks were crucial to continental industrial development since they mobilized enormous capital resources for investment. In the 1850s and 1860s, they were very important in the promotion of railway construction, although they were not

always a safe investment. During a trip to Spain to examine possibilities for railroad construction, the locomotive manufacturer George Stephenson reported: "I have been a month in the country, but have not seen during the whole of that time enough people of the right sort to fill a single train."[9] His misgivings proved to be well-founded. In 1864, the Spanish banking system, which depended largely on investments in railway shares, collapsed.

During this ongoing process of industrialization between 1850 and 1870, capitalist factory owners remained largely free to hire labor on their own terms based on market forces. Increased mechanization of industry meant further displacement of skilled artisans by semiskilled workers. What the working classes needed were organizations that would fight for improved working conditions and reasonable wages, but the liberal bourgeoisie condemned them as criminal agencies that used strikes and pickets to threaten private property. This did not stop the gradual organization of trade unions in the 1860s, however, as conservative regimes sanctioned the creation of trade unions in order to gain popular support against liberals. Bismarck did so in Prussia in 1863, and Napoleon III did likewise in France in 1864. Even where they did form, however, trade unions tended to represent only a small part of the industrial working class, usually such select groups as engineers, shipbuilders, miners, and printers. Real change for the industrial proletariat would only come with the development of socialist parties and socialist trade unions. These emerged after 1870, but the theory that made them possible had already been developed by midcentury in the work of Karl Marx.

Marx and Marxism

Marxism made its first appearance in 1848 with the publication of a short treatise entitled *The Communist Manifesto*, written by two Germans, Karl Marx (1818–1883) and Friedrich Engels (1820–1895). Karl Marx was born into a relatively prosperous middle-class family in Trier in western Germany. He descended from a long line of Jewish rabbis although his father, a lawyer, had become a Protestant to keep his job. Marx enrolled at the University of Bonn in 1835, but a year later his carefree student ways led his father to send him to the more serious-minded University of Berlin, where he encountered the influence of Hegelian thought (see Chapter 22). After receiving a Ph.D. in philosophy, he planned to teach at a university. Unable to obtain a position because of his professed atheism, Marx decided upon a career in journalism and eventually became the editor of a liberal bourgeois newspaper in Cologne in 1842. After the newspaper was suppressed because of his radical views, Marx moved to Paris. There he met Friedrich Engels, who became his lifelong friend and financial patron.

Engels, the son of a wealthy German cotton manufacturer, had worked in Britain at one of his father's factories in Manchester. There he had acquired a firsthand knowledge of what he came to call the "wage slavery" of the British working classes, which he detailed in a damning indictment of industrial life entitled *The Conditions of the Working Class in England*, written in 1844. Engels would contribute his knowledge of actual working conditions as well as monetary assistance to the financially strapped Marx.

In 1847, Marx and Engels joined a tiny group of primarily German socialist revolutionaries known as the Communist League. By this time, both Marx and Engels were enthusiastic advocates of the radical working-class movement and agreed to draft a statement of their ideas for the league. The resulting *Communist Manifesto*, published in January 1848, appeared on the eve of the revolutions of 1848. One would think from its opening lines that the pamphlet alone had caused this revolutionary upheaval: "A spectre is haunting Europe—the spectre of Communism. All the Powers of Old Europe have entered into a holy alliance to exorcize this spectre: Pope and Czar, Metternich and Guizot, French Radicals and German police spies."[10] In fact, written in German, *The Communist Manifesto* was known to only a few of Marx's friends. Although its closing words—"The proletarians have nothing to lose but their chains. They have a world to win. WORKING MEN OF ALL COUNTRIES, UNITE!"—were clearly intended to rouse the working classes to action, they passed unnoticed in 1848. The work, however, became one of the most influential political treatises in modern European history. At the same time, it contained the substance of the basic economic and political ideas that Marx elaborated upon during the rest of his life.

Engels claimed that Marx's ideas were a synthesis of three major strands of thought: British classical economics, French political and social theory, and German idealist philosophy, namely, that of Hegel. What did each of these contribute to Marx's thought? Much of Marx's economic theory was derived from the British economists, especially the argument that the value of any product depended upon the amount of labor put into it. From this "labor theory of value," Marx developed a doctrine of surplus value. According to Marx, the

worker was given in wages only part of the real value of the product that his toil had created. The difference— the surplus value—was taken by the owners of the factories, the bourgeois capitalists. As workers never received in wages the equivalent of what they made, capitalism was threatened by an accumulation of goods that people could not afford to purchase. This led to economic depressions and depressions led to social revolution.

The influence of French political and social theory on Marx was ultimately derived from his knowledge of the French Revolution and the works of early French socialists. Marx questioned why the great French Revolution had failed to redistribute social wealth, but he did feel

▼ **Karl Marx.** Karl Marx was a radical journalist who joined with Friedrich Engels to write *The Communist Manifesto*, which proclaimed the ideas of a revolutionary socialism. After the failure of the 1848 revolution in Germany, Marx fled to Britain, where he continued to write and become involved in the work of the first International Working Men's Association.

that it had at least demonstrated that there could be a total reconstruction of human society by revolution.

The third influence stemmed from Marx's study of Hegel at the University of Berlin. From Hegel, Marx borrowed the idea of dialectic: everything evolves, and all change in history comes through the conflict of elements antagonistic to one another. But Marx differed from Hegel in one fundamental way. Hegel had said that the course of history was determined by Absolute Spirit or ideas manifested in historical forces. Marx said the course of history was determined by material forces. It is not ideas that determine social conditions but the way in which people make their living. From the "mode of production" or kind of economic system stemmed the class structure; from the class structure came the political and institutional structure of society and the beliefs people held. The state, political institutions, literature, art, and religion are all developed by the dominant class to maintain its position. Ideas did not precede actualities as Hegel would have it, but actualities—the material conditions—preceded the ideas. As Marx said, he found Hegel standing on his head and put him right side up. This dialectical materialism, as others called it, with its sense of inevitability inspired Marxism and raised it not to a level of science, as Marx thought, but to the level of a religious faith.

What, then, was the picture of historical development that Marx and Engels offered in The Communist Manifesto? They began their treatise with the statement that "the history of all hitherto existing society is the history of class struggles." Throughout history, then, oppressor and oppressed have "stood in constant opposition to one another." The agrarian economy of the Middle Ages gave rise to the landholding feudal class, but a change in the mode of production with the development of money, trade, and new production techniques resulted in the emergence of the bourgeoisie: "We see, therefore, how the modern bourgeoisie is itself the product of a long course of development, of a series of revolutions in the modes of production and of exchange." Each class produced an outlook appropriate to its own needs; religion, laws, and morals all reflected the ideology of these classes. As Marx and Engels stated: "What else does the history of ideas prove, than that intellectual production changes in character in proportion as material production is changed? The ruling ideas of each age have ever been the ideas of its ruling class." Likewise, government itself was but the instrument of the ruling class: "The executive of the modern State is but a committee for managing the common affairs of the whole bourgeoisie."[11]

Modern bourgeois society, then, emerged victorious out of the ruins of feudal society, but the class struggle continued: "Our epoch, the epoch of the bourgeoisie, possesses, however, this distinctive feature: it has simplified the class antagonism. Society as a whole is more and more splitting up into two great hostile camps, into two great classes directly facing each other: Bourgeoisie and Proletariat." But in their great struggle, the bourgeoisie would dig its own grave. In order to survive, the bourgeoisie needs constantly expanding markets all over the world. But they will never be sufficient. Because of surplus value, the "epidemic of overproduction" can never be solved, leading to ever more destructive crises or economic depressions. At the same time, the expansion of industrial capitalism will lead to an ever-larger proletariat. As a result of competition, the bourgeoisie will devour each other, and the lower middle class will sink into the ranks of the proletariat. Not only will the proletariat increase in numbers, but it will also become concentrated and organized. As the struggle intensifies, some of the bourgeoisie—"a portion of the bourgeois ideologists who have raised themselves to the level of comprehending theoretically the historical movement as a whole"—will go over to the proletariat and become its leaders, a role Marx and Engels clearly envisioned for themselves. Finally, the struggle between the bourgeoisie and proletariat would break into open revolution, "where the violent overthrow of the bourgeoisie lays the foundation for the sway of the proletariat." The fall of the bourgeoisie "and the victory of the proletariat are equally inevitable."[12] For a while the proletariat would form a dictatorship in order to organize the means of production. However, a classless society would be the end result since classes themselves arose from the economic differences that have been abolished; the state—itself an instrument of the bourgeois interests—would wither away (see the box on p. 799).

After the outbreak of revolution in 1848, Marx returned to Germany where he edited a new newspaper in Cologne, optimistic that the ideas of The Communist Manifesto were beginning to be fulfilled in a "colossal eruption of the revolutionary crater." The counterrevolution ended his hopes, and in August 1849, Marx was forced to return to Britain, where he spent the rest of his life in exile. At first life was not easy for Marx, whose income from Engels and newspaper articles was never sufficient for him and his family. Marx's last years, however, from 1869 to 1883, were quite comfortable due to an annuity from Engels. Marx continued his writing on political economy, especially his famous work, Das Kapital (Capital). He only completed one volume. After his

The Classless Society
▼ ▼ ▼

In The Communist Manifesto, *Karl Marx and Friedrich Engels projected as the final end product of the struggle between the bourgeoisie and the proletariat the creation of a classless society. In this selection, they discuss the steps by which that classless society would be reached. Although Marx had criticized the utopian socialists for their lack of a scientific approach to the labor problem, his solution sounds equally utopian.*

Karl Marx and Friedrich Engels, *The Communist Manifesto*

We have seen above, that the first step in the revolution by the working class, is to raise the proletariat to the position of ruling class. . . . The proletariat will use its political supremacy to wrest, by degrees, all capital from the bourgeoisie, to centralize all instruments of production in the hands of the State, i.e., of the proletariat organized as the ruling class; and to increase the total of productive forces as rapidly as possible.

Of course, in the beginning, this cannot be effected except by means of despotic inroads on the rights of property, and on the conditions of bourgeois production; by means of measures, therefore, which appear economically insufficient and untenable, but which, in the course of the movement, outstrip themselves, necessitate further inroads upon the old social order, and are unavoidable as a means of entirely revolutionizing the mode of production.

These measures will of course be different in different countries.

Nevertheless, in the most advanced countries, the following will be pretty generally applicable:

1. Abolition of property in land and application of all rents of land to public purposes.
2. A heavy progressive or graduated income tax.
3. Abolition of all right of inheritance. . . .
5. Centralization of credit in the hands of the State, by means of a national bank with State capital and an exclusive monopoly.
6. Centralization of the means of communication and transport in the hands of the State.
7. Extension of factories and instruments of production owned by the State . . . .
8. Equal liability of all to labour. Establishment of industrial armies, especially for agriculture.
9. Combination of agriculture with manufacturing industries; gradual abolition of the distinction between town and country, by a more equable distribution of the population over the country.
10. Free education for all children in public schools. Abolition of children's factory labour in its present form. . . .

When, in the course of development, class distinctions have disappeared, and all production has been concentrated in the whole nation, the public power will lose its political character. Political power, properly so called, is merely the organized power of one class for oppressing another. If the proletariat during its contest with the bourgeoisie is compelled, by the force of circumstances, to organize itself as a class, if, by means of a revolution, it makes itself the ruling class, and, as such, sweeps away by force the old conditions of production, then it will, along with these conditions, have swept away the conditions for the existence of class antagonisms and of classes generally, and will thereby have abolished its own supremacy as a class.

In place of the old bourgeois society, with its classes and class antagonisms, we shall have an association, in which the free development of each is the condition for the free development of all.

---

death, the remaining volumes were edited by his friend Engels.

One of the reasons *Capital* was not finished was Marx's own preoccupation with organizing the working-class movement. In *The Communist Manifesto,* Marx had defined the communists as "the most advanced and resolute section of the working-class parties of every country." Their advantage was their ability to understand "the line of march, the conditions, and the ultimate general results of the proletarian movement." Marx saw his role in this light and participated enthusiastically in the activities of the International Working Men's Association. Formed in 1864 by British and French trade unionists, this "First International" served as an umbrella organization for working-class interests. Marx was the dominant personality on the organization's General Council and devoted much time to its activities. He wrote in 1865: "Compared with my work on the book [i.e., *Capital*] the International Association takes up an enormous amount of time, because I am in fact in charge of the whole business."[13] Internal dissension within the ranks of the association soon damaged the organization. In 1871, Marx supported the Paris Commune as a genuine proletarian uprising (see Chapter 24), but British trade unionists did not want to be identified with the crimes of the Parisians. In 1872, Marx essentially ended the association by moving its headquarters to the United States. The First International had failed. Although it would be revived in 1889, the fate of socialism by that time was in the hands of national socialist parties (see Chapter 24).

▼ Cultural Life in an Age of Realism

Between 1850 and 1870, two major intellectual developments stand out: the expansion of scientific knowledge with its rapidly growing impact on the Western worldview; and the shift from Romanticism with its emphasis on the inner world of reality to Realism with its focus on the outer, material world.

A New Age of Science

By the mid-nineteenth century, as theoretical discoveries in science led to an increased number of derived practical benefits, science came to have a greater and greater impact on European life. The Scientific Revolution of the sixteenth and seventeenth centuries had fundamentally transformed the Western worldview and created a modern, rational approach to the study of natural phenomena. Even in the eighteenth century, however, these intellectual developments had remained the preserve of an educated elite and resulted in few practical benefits. Moreover, the technical advances of the early Industrial Revolution had depended little on pure science and much more on the practical experiments of technologically oriented amateur inventors. Advances in industrial technology, however, fed an interest in basic scientific research, which, in turn, in the 1830s and afterward resulted in a rash of basic scientific discoveries that were soon transformed into technological improvements that affected all Europeans.

Important to advances in all the sciences was the development of mathematics, especially mathematical statistics. The development of the steam engine was important in encouraging scientists to work out its theoretical foundations, a preoccupation that led to thermodynamics, the science of the relationship between heat and mechanical energy. The laws of thermodynamics were at the core of nineteenth-century physics. In biology, the Frenchman Louis Pasteur discovered the germ theory of disease, which had enormous practical applications in the development of modern, scientific medical practices (see A Revolution in Health Care later in the chapter). In chemistry, the Russian Dmitri Mendeleyev in the 1860s classified all the material elements then known on the basis of their atomic weights and provided the systematic foundation for the periodic law. The Briton Michael Faraday discovered the phenomenon of electromagnetic induction and put together a primitive generator that laid the foundation for the use of electricity, although it was not until the 1870s that economically efficient generators were built.

The steadily increasing and often dramatic material benefits generated by science and technology led Europeans to a growing faith in the benefits of science. Even ordinary people who did not understand the theoretical concepts of science were impressed by its accomplishments. The popularity of scientific and technological achievement produced a widespread acceptance of the scientific method, based on observation, experiment, and logical analysis, as the only path to objective truth and objective reality. This, in turn, undermined the faith of many people in religious revelation and truth. It is no accident that the nineteenth century was an age of increasing secularization, particularly evident in the growth of materialism or the belief that everything mental, spiritual, or ideal was simply an outgrowth of physical forces. Truth was to be found in the concrete material existence of human beings, not as romanticists imagined in revelations gained by feeling or intuitive flashes. The importance of materialism was strikingly evident in the most important scientific event of the nineteenth century, the development of the theory of organic evolution according to natural selection. On the theories of Charles Darwin could be built a picture of humans as material beings that were simply part of the natural world.

Charles Darwin and the Theory of Organic Evolution

The concept of evolution was not new when Darwin first postulated his theory in 1859. Until the early nineteenth century, most European intellectuals still believed that a divine power had created the world and its species. Humans, of course, occupied a special superior position because the Book of Genesis in the Bible stated: "Let us make man in our image and likeness and let him have dominion over all other things." By the beginning of the nineteenth century, however, people were questioning the biblical account; some had already posited an evolutionary theory. In 1809, the Frenchman Jean-Baptiste Lamarck had presented a theory of evolution that argued that plants and animals were different because of their effort to adjust to their environment. His assumption that they subsequently passed on their acquired characteristics was later rejected. Geologists had also been busy demonstrating that the earth underwent constant change and was far older than had been believed. They argued that it had evolved slowly over millions of years rather than the thousands of years postulated by theological analysis of the biblical account of creation. Despite the growth in evolutionary ideas, however, even by the mid-nineteenth century there was no widely accepted theory of evolution that explained things satisfactorily.

Charles Darwin (1809–1882), like many of the great scientists of the nineteenth century, was a scientific amateur. Born into an upper-middle-class family, he studied theology at Cambridge University while pursuing an intense side interest in geology and biology. In 1831, at the age of twenty-two, his hobby became his vocation when he accepted an appointment as a naturalist to study animals and plants on an official Royal Navy scientific expedition aboard the H.M.S. *Beagle*. Its purpose was to survey and study the land masses of South America and the South Pacific. Darwin's specific job was to study the structure of various forms of plant and animal life. He was able to observe animals on islands virtually untouched by external influence and compare them to animals on the mainland. As a result, Darwin came to discard the notion of a special creation and to believe that animals evolved over time and in response to their environment. When he returned to Britain, he eventually formulated an explanation for evolution in the principle of natural selection. Although he had arrived at his major ideas by 1838, he spent the next twenty years collecting data to demonstrate his theory precisely, finally presenting his ideas in print in 1859 in his celebrated book, *On the Origin of Species by Means of Natural Selection*.

The basic idea of this book was that nature's creatures—all plants and animals—had not been created anew by God, but had evolved over a long period of time from earlier and simpler forms of life, a principle known as organic evolution. Darwin was important in explaining how this natural process worked. He took the first step from Thomas Malthus's theory of population: in every species, "many more individuals of each species are born than can possibly survive." This results in a "struggle for existence." Darwin believed that, "As more individuals are produced than can possibly survive, there must in every case be a struggle for existence, either one individual with another of the same species, or with the individuals of distinct species, or with the physical conditions of life." Those who succeeded in this struggle for existence had adapted better to their environment, a process made possible by the appearance of "variants." Chance variations occurred in the process of inheritance, he thought, that enabled some organisms to be more adaptable to the environment than others, a process that Darwin called natural selection:

> Owing to this struggle [for existence], variations, however slight . . . , if they be in any degree profitable to the individuals of a species, in their infinitely complex relations to other organic beings and to their physical conditions of life, will tend to the preservation of such individuals, and will generally be inherited by the offspring.[14]

Those that were naturally selected for survival ("survival of the fit") survived. The unfit did not and became extinct. The fit who survived, in turn, propagated and passed on the variations that enabled them to survive until, from Darwin's point of view, a new separate species emerged. Darwin did not attempt to explain how variants first occurred and did not arrive at the modern explanation of mutations. This was not crucial to him; he was not concerned with how the fit arrived, but how they survived.

In *On the Origin of Species*, Darwin discussed plant and animal species only. He was not concerned with humans themselves and only later applied his theory of natural selection to humans. In *The Descent of Man*, published in 1871, he argued for the animal origins of human beings: "man is the co-descendant with other mammals of a common progenitor." Humans were not an exception to the rule governing other species (see the box on p. 802).

Although Darwin's ideas were eventually accepted, initially they were highly controversial. Some people objected to what they considered Darwin's debasement of humans; his theory, they claimed, made human beings ordinary products of nature rather than unique beings. The acceptance of Darwinism, one professor of geology at Cambridge declared, would "sink the human race into a lower grade of degradation than any into which it has

Darwin and the Descent of Man
▼ ▼ ▼

Although Darwin published his theory of organic evolution in 1859, it was not until 1871 that his book, The Descent of Man, appeared. In it, Darwin argued that human beings have also evolved from lower forms of life. The theory met with a firestorm of criticism, especially from clergymen. One described Darwin's theory as a "brutal philosophy—to wit, there is no God, and the ape is our Adam."

Charles Darwin, The Descent of Man

The main conclusion here arrived at, and now held by many naturalists who are well competent to form a sound judgment, is that man is descended from some less highly organised form. The grounds upon which this conclusion rests will never be shaken, for the close similarity between man and the lower animals in embryonic development, as well as in innumerable points of structure and constitution, both of high and of the most trifling importance,—the rudiments which he retains, and the abnormal reversions to which he is occasionally liable,—are facts which cannot be disputed. They have long been known, but until recently they told us nothing with respect to the origin of man. Now when viewed by the light of our knowledge of the whole organic world, their meaning is unmistakable. The great principle of evolution stands up clear and firm, when these groups of facts are considered in connection with others, such as the mutual affinities of the members of the same group, their geographical distribution in past and present times, and their geological succession. It is incredible that all these facts should speak falsely. He who is not content to look, like a savage, at the phenomena of nature as disconnected, cannot any longer believe that man is the work of a separate act of creation. He will be forced to admit that the close resemblance of the embryo of man to that, for instance, of a dog—the construction of his skull, limbs and whole frame on the same plan with that of other mammals, independently of the uses to which the parts may be put—the occasional reappearance of various structures, for instance of several muscles, which man does not normally possess . . .—and a crowd of analogous facts—all point in the plainest manner to the conclusion that man is the co-descendant with other mammals of a common progenitor. . . .

Man may be excused for feeling some pride at having risen, though not through his own exertions, to the very summit of the organic scale; and the fact of his having thus risen, instead of having been aboriginally placed there, may give him hope for a still higher destiny in the distant future. But we are not here concerned with hopes or fears, only with the truth as far as our reason permits us to discover it; and I have given the evidence to the best of my ability. We must, however, acknowledge, as it seems to me, that man with all his noble qualities, with sympathy which feels for the most debased, with benevolence which extends not only to other men but to the humblest living creature, with his god-like intellect which has penetrated into the movements and constitution of the solar system—with all these exalted powers—Man still bears in his bodily frame the indelible stamp of his lowly origin.

fallen since its written records tell of its history." Others were disturbed by the implications of life as a struggle for survival, of "nature red in tooth and claw." Was there a place in the Darwinian world for moral values? For those who believed in a rational order in the world, Darwin's theory seemed to eliminate purpose and design from the universe. Gradually, however, Darwin's theory was accepted by scientists and other intellectuals although Darwin was somewhat overly optimistic when he wrote in 1872 that "almost every scientist admits the principle of evolution." In the process of accepting Darwin's ideas, some people even tried to apply them to society, yet another example of science's increasing prestige.

Auguste Comte and Positivism

The impact of the materialistic frame of mind perhaps made it inevitable that a scientific approach would be applied to the realm of human activity. Marx himself presented his view of history as a class struggle grounded in the material conditions of life as a "scientific" work of analysis. The attempt to apply the methods of science systematically to the study of society was perhaps most evident in the work of the Frenchman Auguste Comte (1798–1857). His major work, entitled *System of Positive Philosophy*, was published between 1837 and 1842, but had its real impact after 1850. The title of the work gave rise to the philosophical system called positivism, which maintained that only scientifically established facts and observed phenomena are valid. It rejected idealist philosophies, such as Hegel's, which asserted that ideas constitute the ultimate reality.

Comte maintained that all human knowledge has passed through three major states: the theological, the metaphysical, and the scientific. In the theological era, events were explained as the actions of gods or spirits. The metaphysical age attempted to explain events by attributing them to abstract, transcendental forces. The third and final state, Comte's own age, was the scientific or "positive" age in which events would be explained by general laws discovered by the scientific method—observation, experiment, and logical reasoning. According to Comte, human beings had proceeded through history seeking knowledge first from religion, then philosophy, and now science. His scheme was simplistic but highly attractive to nineteenth-century intellectuals who sought a comprehensive synthesis of all human knowledge.

For the third stage, Comte created a system of "positive" knowledge based upon a hierarchy of all the sciences. Mathematics was the foundation on which the physical sciences, earth sciences, and biological sciences were built. At the top was sociology, the science of human society, which for Comte incorporated economics, anthropology, history, and social psychology. Consequently, some historians call Comte one of the "founders of the modern discipline" of sociology. Comte saw sociology's task as a difficult one. The discovery of the general laws of society would have to be based upon the collection and analysis of data on humans and their social environment. Although his schemes were often complex and dense, Comte played an important role in making science and materialism so popular in the mid-nineteenth century.

Realism in Literature and Art

The belief that the world should be viewed realistically, frequently expressed after 1850, was closely related to the materialistic outlook. Evident in the "politics of reality" of a Bismarck or Cavour, Realism became a movement in the literary and visual arts as well. The word *Realism* was first employed in 1850 to describe a new style of painting and soon spread to literature.

LITERATURE Realism has been more or less a component of literature throughout time, although the literary realists of the mid-nineteenth century were distinguished by their deliberate rejection of Romanticism. The literary realists wanted to deal with ordinary characters from actual life rather than romantic heroes in exotic settings. They also sought to avoid exaggerated and emotional language by using close observation and precise description, an approach that led them to eschew poetry in favor of prose and the novel. Realists often combined their interest in everyday life with a searching examination of social questions. Even then they tried not to preach but to allow their characters to speak for themselves. Although the French were preeminent in literary Realism, it proved to be international in scope.

The leading novelist of the 1850s and 1860s, the Frenchman Gustave Flaubert (1821–1880), perfected the realist novel. His *Madame Bovary* (1857) was a straightforward description of barren and sordid provincial life in France. Emma Bovary, a woman of some vitality, is trapped in a marriage to a drab provincial doctor. Impelled by the images of romantic love she has read about in novels, she seeks the same thing for herself in adulterous love affairs. Unfulfilled, she is ultimately driven to suicide, unrepentant to the end for her lifestyle. Flaubert's hatred of bourgeois society was evident in his portrayal of middle-class hypocrisy and smugness. *Madame Bovary* so offended French middle-class sensibilities that the author was prosecuted—unsuccessfully—for public obscenity.

William Thackeray (1811–1863) wrote the opening manifesto of the realist novel in Britain with his *Vanity Fair* in 1848. Subtitled *A Novel without a Hero*, Thackeray deliberately flaunted the romantic conventions. A novel, Thackeray said, should "convey as strongly as possible the sentiment of reality as opposed to a tragedy or poem, which may be heroical." One of Thackeray's fellow countrymen, Charles Dickens (1812–1870), became extraordinarily successful with his realistic novels focusing on the lower and middle classes in Britain's early industrial age. His descriptions of the urban poor and the brutalization of human life were vividly realistic. But Dickens also demonstrated an interesting facet of Realism—a streak of romantic imagery that permeated his descriptions of the sordid and commonplace. No-

Realism: Charles Dickens and an Image of Hell on Earth
▼ ▼ ▼

*C*harles Dickens was a highly successful English novelist. While he realistically portrayed the material,
social, and psychological milieu of his time, an element of
Romanticism still pervaded his novels. This is evident in
this selection from The Old Curiosity Shop in which his
description of the English mill town of Birmingham takes
on the imagery of Dante's Hell.

Charles Dickens, *The Old Curiosity Shop*

A long suburb of red brick houses,—some with
patches of garden ground, where coal-dust and factory smoke darkened the shrinking leaves, and coarse
rank flowers; and where the struggling vegetation
sickened and sank under the hot breath of kiln and
furnace, making them by its presence seem yet more
blighting and unwholesome than in the town
itself,—a long, flat, straggling suburb passed, they
came by slow degrees upon a cheerless region, where
not a blade of grass was seen to grow; where not a bud
put forth its promise in the spring; where nothing
green could live but on the surface of the stagnant
pools, which here and there lay idly sweltering by the
black roadside.

Advancing more and more into the shadow of this
mournful place, its dark depressing influence stole
upon their spirits, and filled them with a dismal
gloom. On every side, and as far as the eye could see
into the heavy distance, tall chimneys, crowding on
each other, and presenting that endless repetition of
the same dull, ugly form, which is the horror of oppressive dreams, poured out their plague of smoke,
obscured the light, and made foul the melancholy air.
On mounds of ashes by the wayside, sheltered only by
a few rough boards, or rotten pent-house roofs,
strange engines spun and writhed like tortured creatures; clanking their iron chains, shrieking in their
rapid whirl from time to time as though in torment
unendurable, and making the ground tremble with
their agonies. Dismantled houses here and there appeared, tottering to the earth, propped up by frag-
ments of others that had fallen down, unroofed, win-
dowless, blackened, desolate, but yet inhabited.
Men, women, children, wan in their looks and
ragged in attire, tended the engines, fed their tribu-
tary fires, begged upon the road, or scowled half-
naked from the doorless houses. Then came more of
the wrathful monsters, whose like they almost seemed
to be in their wildness and their untamed air, screech-
ing and turning to the right and left, with the same
interminable perspective of brick towers, never ceasing in their black vomit, blasting all things living or
inanimate, shutting out the face of day, and closing
in on all these horrors with a dense dark cloud.

But night-time in this dreadful spot!—night,
when the smoke was changed to fire; when every
chimney spurted up its flame; and places, that had
been dark vaults all day, now shone red-hot, with
figures moving to and fro within their blazing jaws,
and calling to one another with hoarse cries—night,
when the noise of every strange machine was aggra-
vated by the darkness; when the people near them
looked wilder and more savage; when bands of unemployed labourers paraded in the roads, or clustered
by torchlight round their leaders, who told them in
stern language of their wrongs, and urged them on by
frightful cries and threats; when maddened men,
armed with sword and firebrand, spurning the tears
and prayers of women who would restrain them,
rushed forth on errands of terror and destruction, to
work no ruin half so surely as their own—night, when
carts came rumbling by, filled with rude coffins (for
contagious disease and death had been busy with the
living crops); or when orphans cried, and distracted
women shrieked and followed in their wake—night,
when some called for bread, and some for drink to
drown their cares; and some with tears, and some
with staggering feet, and so with bloodshot eyes,
went brooding home—night, which, unlike the night
that Heaven sends on earth, brought with it no
peace, nor quiet, nor signs of blessed sleep—who
shall tell the terrors of the night to that young wandering child!

where is this more evident than in *The Old Curiosity Shop* where his description of an industrial nightmare conjures up the imagery of Dante's Hell (see the box on p. 804).

ART In the first half of the nineteenth century, Romanticism in art had been paralleled by the classical school of painting, but both were superseded by the new mood of the mid-nineteenth century. In art, too, Realism became dominant after 1850, although Romanticism was by no means dead. Realist art demonstrated three major characteristics: a desire to depict the everyday life of ordinary people, whether peasants, workers, or prostitutes; an attempt at photographic realism; and an interest in the natural environment. The French became leaders in realist painting.

Gustave Courbet (1819–1877) was the most famous artist of the realist school. In fact, the word *Realism* was first coined in 1850 to describe one of his paintings. Courbet reveled in a realistic portrayal of everyday life. His subjects were factory workers, peasants, and the wives of saloon keepers. "I have never seen either angels or goddesses, so I am not interested in painting them," he exclaimed. One of his famous works, *The Stonebreakers*, painted in 1849, shows two road workers engaged in the deadening work of breaking stones to build a road. This representation of human misery was a scandal to those who objected to his "cult of ugliness." To Courbet, no subject was too ordinary, too harsh, or too ugly to interest him.

Jean-François Millet (1814–1875) was preoccupied with scenes from rural life, especially peasants laboring in the fields, although his Realism still contained an element of romantic sentimentality. In *The Sower*, a peasant, energetically scattering seeds in a field, becomes a symbol of new life and the symbiotic relationship between humans and nature. Millet, too, was criticized by his contemporaries for crude subject matter and unorthodox technique. One critic wrote that Millet "trowels on top of his dishcloth of a canvas, without oil or turpentine, vast masonries of colored paint so dry that no varnish could quench its thirst." Millet made landscape and country life an important subject matter for French artists.

▼ A Revolution in Health Care

Perhaps no area of everyday life in the nineteenth century was more affected by the application of natural science than the field of medicine. Some improvements had already been made in the development of health services in the eighteenth century, but the nineteenth century was a time of revolutionary breakthroughs in the development of medical science.

The initial tentative steps toward a more scientific basis for medicine arose in Paris hospitals during the first half of the nineteenth century. Clinical observation, consisting of an active physical examination of patients,

▼ **Gustave Courbet, *The Stonebreakers*.** By 1850, Realism began to replace Romanticism as the most important European school of painting. Realism, largely developed by French painters, aimed at a lifelike portrayal of the daily activities of ordinary people. Gustave Courbet was the most famous of the realist artists. As is evident in *The Stonebreakers*, he sought to portray things as they really appear. He shows an old road builder and his young assistant in their tattered clothes, engrossed in their dreary work of breaking stones to construct a road.

▼ **Jean-François Millet, *The Sower*.** Jean-François Millet was another prominent French realist painter. Millet took a special interest in the daily activities of French peasants, although he tended to transform his peasants into heroic figures who dominated their environment. In *The Sower*, for example, the peasant scattering seed into the newly plowed fields, despite his rough clothes, appears as a powerful figure, symbolizing the union of humans with the earth.

was combined with the knowledge gained from detailed autopsies to create a new clinical medicine. Nevertheless, the major breakthrough toward a scientific medicine occurred with the discovery of microorganisms or germs as the agents causing disease. The germ theory of disease was largely the work of Louis Pasteur (1822–1895). Pasteur was not a doctor but a chemist who approached medical problems in a scientific fashion. In 1857, Pasteur went to Paris as director of scientific studies in the École Normale. In his experiments on fermentations, he soon proved that various microorganisms were responsible for the process of fermentation, thus launching the science of bacteriology.

Government and private industry soon perceived the inherent practical value of Pasteur's work. His examina-

tion of a disease threatening the wine industry led to the development in 1863 of a process—subsequently known as pasteurization—for heating a product to destroy the organisms causing spoilage. Additional research on the microorganisms responsible for diseases of the silkworm enabled Pasteur to save the lucrative French silk industry. In 1877, Pasteur turned his attention to human diseases. His desire to do more than simply identify disease-producing organisms led him in 1885 to a preventive vaccination against rabies. In the 1890s, the principle of vaccination was extended to diphtheria, typhoid fever, cholera, and plague, creating a modern immunological science.

Robert Koch (1843–1910) was another important figure in the development of the science of bacteriology. Koch had received a medical degree at the University of Göttingen in Germany. In 1879, his experiments with anthrax led him to discover the bacteria responsible for wound infections. Koch was also responsible for providing specific methodological postulates to determine whether a particular organism was the cause of a disease.

The work of Pasteur and Koch and the many others who followed them in isolating the specific bacteriological causes of numerous diseases had a far-reaching impact. By providing a rational means of treating and preventing infectious diseases, they transformed the medical world. Both the practice of surgery and public health experienced a renaissance.

Surgeons had already experienced a new professionalism by the end of the eighteenth century (see Chapter 18), but the discovery of germs and the introduction of anesthesia created a new environment for surgical operations. Traditionally, surgeons had mainly set broken bones, treated wounds, and amputated limbs, usually shattered in war. One major obstacle to more successful surgery was the inevitable postoperative infection, especially rampant in hospitals.

A Hungarian obstetrician, Ignaz P. Semmelweiss (1818–1865), was the first physician to recognize that a simple hand washing with a chlorine solution before working on patients prevented infection. Rejected by his colleagues for his belief, Semmelweiss was dismissed from the Vienna hospital where he worked and died, a broken man, in an insane asylum. Joseph Lister (1827–1912) has instead been credited with developing the antiseptic principle. Following the work of Pasteur, Lister perceived that bacteria might enter a wound and cause infection. His use of carbolic acid, a newly discovered disinfectant, proved remarkably effective in eliminating infections during surgery. Lister's discoveries dramatically transformed surgery wards as patients no

Anesthesia and Modern Surgery

▼ ▼ ▼

Modern scientific medicine became established in the nineteenth century. Important to the emergence of modern surgery was the development of anesthetic agents that would block the patient's pain and enable surgeons to complete their surgery without the haste that had characterized earlier operations. This document is an eyewitness account of the first successful use of ether anesthesia, which took place at the Massachusetts General Hospital in 1846.

The First Public Demonstration of Ether Anesthesia, October 16, 1846

The day arrived; the time appointed was noted on the dial, when the patient was led into the operating-room, and Dr. Warren and a board of the most eminent surgeons in the State were gathered around the sufferer. "All is ready—the stillness oppressive." It had been announced "that a test of some preparation was to be made for which the astonishing claim had been made that it would render the person operated upon free from pain." These are the words of Dr. Warren that broke the stillness.

Those present were incredulous, and, as Dr. Morton had not arrived at the time appointed and fifteen minutes had passed, Dr. Warren said, with significant meaning, "I presume he is otherwise engaged." This was followed with a "derisive laugh," and Dr. Warren grasped his knife and was about to proceed with the operation. At that moment Dr. Morton entered a side door, when Dr. Warren turned to him and in a strong voice said, "Well, sir, your patient is ready." In a few minutes he was ready for the surgeon's knife, when Dr. Morton said, "Your patient is ready, sir."

Here the most sublime scene ever witnessed in the operating-room was presented, when the patient placed himself voluntarily upon the table, which was to become the altar of future fame. Not that he did so for the purpose of advancing the science of medicine, nor for the good of his fellow-men, for the act itself was purely a personal and selfish one. He was about to assist in solving a new and important problem of therapeutics, whose benefits were to be given to the whole civilized world, yet wholly unconscious of the sublimity of the occasion or the art he was taking.

That was a supreme moment for a most wonderful discovery, and, had the patient died upon the operation, science would have waited long to discover the hypnotic effects of some other remedy of equal potency and safety, and it may be properly questioned whether chloroform would have come into use as it has at the present time.

The heroic bravery of the man who voluntarily placed himself upon the table, a subject for the surgeon's knife, should be recorded and his name enrolled upon parchment, which should be hung upon the walls of the surgical amphitheatre in which the operation was performed. His name was Gilbert Abbott.

The operation was for a congenital tumor on the left side of the neck, extending along the jaw to the maxillary gland and into the mouth, embracing a margin of the tongue. The operation was successful; and when the patient recovered he declared he had suffered no pain. Dr. Warren turned to those present and said, "Gentlemen, this is no humbug."

---

longer succumbed regularly to what was called "hospital gangrene."

The second great barrier to large-scale surgery stemmed from the inability to lessen the pain of the patient. Alcohol and opiates had been used for centuries during surgical operations, but even their use did not allow unhurried operative maneuvers. After experiments with numerous agents, sulfuric ether was first used successfully in an operation at the Massachusetts General Hospital in 1846 (see the box above). Within a year chloroform began to rival ether as an anesthetic agent.

Although the great discoveries of bacteriology came after the emergence of the first public health movement, they significantly furthered its development. Based on a principle of preventive, rather than curative, medicine, the public health movement in urban areas of the 1840s and 1850s was largely a response to the cholera epidemic (see Chapter 24). Robert Koch once called cholera, "our best ally" in furthering public hygiene. The prebacteriological hygiene movement focused on providing clean water, good sewage disposal, and less crowded housing conditions. Bacterial discoveries, however, led to even greater measures of preventive medicine, such as the pasteurization of milk, greater purification of water supplies, immunization against disease, and control of waterborne diseases. The public health movement also resulted in the government hiring medical doctors not just to treat people but to deal with issues of public health.

The new scientific developments also had an important impact on the training of doctors for professional careers in health care. Although there were a few medical schools at the beginning of the nineteenth century, most medical instruction was still done by a system of apprenticeship. In the course of the nineteenth century, virtually every Western country founded new medical schools, but attempts to impose uniform standards on them through certifying bodies met considerable resistance. Entrance requirements were virtually nonexistent, and degrees were granted after several months of lectures. Professional organizations founded around the mid-century, such as the British Medical Association in 1832, the American Medical Association in 1847, and the German Doctors' Society in 1872, attempted to el-

evate professional standards but achieved little until the end of the century. The establishment of the Johns Hopkins University School of Medicine in 1893, with its four-year graded curriculum, clinical training for advanced students, and use of laboratories for teaching purposes, provided a new model for medical training that finally became standard practice in the twentieth century.

During most of the nineteenth century, medical schools in Europe and America were closed to female students. When Harriet Hunt applied to Harvard Medical School, the male students drew up resolutions that prevented her admission:

> Resolved, that no woman of true delicacy would be willing in the presence of men to listen to the discussion of subjects that necessarily come under consideration of the students of medicine.
> Resolved, that we object to having the company of any female forced upon us, who is disposed to unsex herself, and to sacrifice her modesty by appearing with men in the lecture room.[15]

▼ **First Successful Use of Surgical Anesthesia.** Depicted in this scene is an artist's rendering of the first successful operation using ether as an anesthetic agent. The operation took place at the Massachusetts General Hospital in 1846 and was yet another of the many medical advances in the nineteenth century that helped to create modern scientific medicine.

Elizabeth Blackwell (1821–1910) achieved the first major breakthrough for women in medicine. Although she had been admitted to the Geneva College of Medicine in New York by a mistake, Blackwell's perseverance and intelligence won her the respect of her fellow male students. She received her M.D. degree in 1849 and eventually established a clinic in New York City.

European women experienced difficulties similar to those of Elizabeth Blackwell. In Britain, Elizabeth Garret and Sophia Jex-Blake had to struggle for years before they were finally admitted to the practice of medicine. The unwillingness of medical schools to open their doors to women led to the formation of separate medical schools for women. The Female Medical College of Pennsylvania, established in 1850, was the first in the United States while the London School of Medicine for women was founded in 1874. But even after graduation from such institutions, women faced obstacles when they tried to practice as doctors. They were often refused licenses and hospitals often closed their doors to them. In Britain, Parliament finally capitulated to pressure and passed a bill in 1876 allowing women the right to take qualifying examinations. Soon women were entering medical schools in ever-larger numbers. By the 1890s, universities in Great Britain, Sweden, Denmark, Norway, Finland, Russia, and Belgium were admitting women to medical training and practice. Germany and Austria did not do so until after 1900. Even then, medical associations refused to accept women as equals in the medical profession. Women were not given full membership in the American Medical Association until 1915.

Between 1850 and 1871, the national state became the focus of people's loyalty. Wars, both foreign and civil, were fought to create unified nation-states. Political nationalism had emerged during the French revolutionary era and had become a powerful force of change during the first half of the nineteenth century, but its triumph came only after 1850. Tied initially to middle-class liberals, by the end of the nineteenth century it would have great appeal to the broad masses as well. In 1871, however, the political transformations stimulated by the force of nationalism were by no means complete. Significantly large minorities, especially in the polyglot empires controlled by the Austrians, Turks, and Russians, had not achieved the goal of their own national states. Moreover, the nationalism that had triumphed by 1871 was no longer the nationalism that had been closely identified with liberalism. Liberal nationalists had believed that unified nation-states would preserve individual rights and lead to a greater community of European peoples. But the new nationalism of the late nineteenth century, loud and chauvinistic, did not unify peoples, but divided them instead as the new national states became embroiled in bitter competition after 1871.

Europeans, however, were hardly aware of nationalism's dangers in 1871. The spread of industrialization and the wealth of scientific and technological achievements were sources of optimism, not pessimism. After the revolutionary and military upheavals of the mid-century decades, many Europeans undoubtedly believed that they stood on the verge of a new age of progress.

Notes
▼ ▼ ▼

1. Quoted in Robert Gildea, *Barricades and Borders: Europe 1800–1914* (Oxford, 1987), p. 176.

2. Quoted in Maurice Agulhon, *The Republican Experiment, 1848–1852* (Cambridge, 1983), p. 177.

3. Quoted in Raymond Grew, *A Sterner Plan for Italian Unity: The Italian National Society in the Risorgimento* (Princeton, N.J., 1963), p. 10.

4. Quoted in Otto Pflanze, *Bismarck and the Development of Germany: The Period of Unification, 1815–1871* (Princeton, N.J., 1963), p. 60.

5. Louis L. Snyder, ed., *Documents of German History* (New Brunswick, N.J., 1958), p. 202.

6. Quoted in Pflanze, *Bismarck and the Development of Germany*, p. 327.

7. Quoted in György Szabad, *Hungarian Political Trends between the Revolution and the Compromise, 1849–1867* (Budapest, 1977), p. 163.

8. Quoted in George L. Yaney, *The Systematization of Russian Government, 1711–1905* (Champaign, Ill., 1973), p. 241.

9. Quoted in Rondo Cameron, "Crédit Mobilier and the Economic Development of Europe," *Journal of Political Economy* 61 (1953): 470.

10. Karl Marx and Friedrich Engels, *The Communist Manifesto* (Harmondsworth, 1967), p. 79.

11. Ibid., pp. (in order of quotations), 79, 81, 102, 82.

12. Ibid., pp. (in order of quotations), 80, 91, 94.

13. Quoted in David McLellan, *Karl Marx* (New York, 1975), p. 14.

14. Charles Darwin, *On the Origins of Species* (New York, 1872), 1: 77, 79.

15. Quoted in Albert Lyons and R. Joseph Petrucelli, *Medicine: An Illustrated History* (New York, 1978), p. 569.

Suggestions for Further Reading

▼ ▼ ▼

Two general surveys of the mid-century decades are N. Rich, *The Age of Nationalism and Reform, 1850–1890*, 2d ed. (New York, 1979); and J. A. S. Grenville, *Europe Reshaped, 1848–1878* (London, 1976). In addition to the books listed for individual countries in Chapter 22 that also cover the material of this chapter, see H. Holborn, *A History of Modern Germany,* vol. 3, *1840–1945* (New York, 1969); G. Craig, *Germany, 1866–1945* (Oxford, 1981); the two detailed volumes of T. Zeldin, *France, 1848–1945* (Oxford, 1973–77); A. J. May, *The Habsburg Monarchy, 1867–1914* (Cambridge, Mass., 1951); and D. Read, *England, 1868–1914* (London, 1979).

For a good introduction to the French Second Empire, see A. Plessis, *The Rise and Fall of the Second Empire, 1852–1871*, trans. J. Mandelbaum (New York, 1985). Napoleon's role can be examined in W. H. C. Smith, *Napoleon III* (New York, 1972). The Crimean War and its impact are examined in P. W. Schroeder, *Austria, Great Britain and the Crimean War: The Destruction of the European Concert* (Ithaca, N.Y., 1972).

The unification of Italy can best be examined in the works of D. M. Smith, *Victor Emmanuel, Cavour and the Risorgimento* (London, 1971); and *Cavour* (London, 1985). The unification of Germany can be pursued first in two good biographies of Bismarck, E. Crankshaw, *Bismarck* (New York, 1981); and G. O. Kent, *Bismarck and His Times* (Carbondale, Ill., 1978). See also the older, but clear surveys in W. M. Simon, *Germany in the Age of Bismarck* (New York, 1968); and W. N. Medlicott, *Bismarck and Modern Germany* (London, 1965). T. S. Hamerow, *The Social Foundations of German Unification, 1858–1871* (Princeton, N.J., 1969) is good on the political implications of social changes in Germany. Also valuable is O. Pflanze, *Bismarck and the Development of Germany: The Period of Unification, 1815–1871* (Princeton, N.J., 1963). A classic on the role of the Prussian military is G. Craig, *The Politics of the Prussian Army* (New York, 1955). On the position of liberals in the unification of Germany, see J. J. Sheehan, *German Liberalism in the Nineteenth Century* (Chicago, 1978).

A reliable survey on the Austrian-Hungarian *Ausgleich* can be found in G. Szabad, *Hungarian Political Trends between the Revolution and the Compromise, 1849–1867* (Budapest, 1977). On the emancipation of the Russian serfs, see D. Field, *The End of Serfdom: Nobility and Bureaucracy in Russia, 1855–1861* (Cambridge, 1976); and T. Emmons, ed., *Emancipation of the Russian Serfs* (New York, 1970). On the 1867 Reform Act in Britain, see M. Cowling, *1867: Disraeli, Gladstone and Revolution* (London, 1967), while the evolution of British political parties in mid-century is examined in H. J. Hanham, *Elections and Party Management: Politics in the Time of Disraeli and Gladstone,* 2d ed. (London, 1978). On the southern slave economy in the United States, see the opposing views of R. W. Fogel and S. Engerman, *Time on the Cross: The Economics of American Negro Slavery* (Boston, 1974); and G. Wright, *The Political Economy of the Cotton South* (New York, 1978). On the background to the American Civil War, see D. Potter, *The Impending Crisis, 1845–1861* (New York, 1976); and M. Holt, *The Political Crisis of the 1850's* (New York, 1978). A good, brief biography of Lincoln is O. and L. Handlin, *Abraham Lincoln and the Union* (Boston, 1980). A good one-volume survey of the Civil War can be found in P. J. Parish, *The American Civil War* (New York, 1975).

In addition to the general works on economic development listed in Chapters 21 and 23, there are some specialized works on this period that are worthwhile. These include P. O'Brien, *The New Economic History of the Railways* (New York, 1977); W. O. Henderson, *The Rise of German Industrial Power, 1834–1914* (Berkeley, 1975); and F. Crouzet, *The Victorian Economy* (London, 1982). On Marx there is the standard work by D. McLellan, *Karl Marx: His Life and*

Thought (New York, 1974), but it can be supplemented by the interesting and comprehensive work by L. Kolakowski, *Main Currents of Marxism,* 3 vols. (Oxford, 1978).

For an introduction to the intellectual changes of the nineteenth century, see O. Chadwick, *The Secularization of the European Mind in the Nineteenth Century* (Cambridge, 1975). A detailed biography of Darwin can be found in R. W. Clark, *The Survival of Charles Darwin*

(New York, 1984). On Realism, there is a good introduction in L. Nochlin, *Realism* (Harmondsworth, 1971). Also valuable is F. W. J. Hemmings, *Culture and Society in France, 1848–1898* (London, 1971). For an introduction to the transformation of medical practices in the nineteenth century, see the appropriate chapters in E. H. Ackerknecht, *A Short History of Medicine,* rev. ed. (Baltimore, 1982); and A. S. Lyons and R. J. Petrucelli, *Medicine: An Illustrated History* (New York, 1978).

Chapter 24

Society and Politics in the "Age of Progress," 1871–1914

▼▼▼▼▼

During the fifty years before 1914, Europe witnessed a dynamic age of material prosperity. With new industries, new sources of energy, and new goods, a Second Industrial Revolution transformed the human environment, dazzled Europeans, and led them to believe that their material progress meant human progress. Scientific and technological achievements, many naively believed, would improve humanity's condition and solve all human problems. The doctrine of progress became an article of great faith.

This Second Industrial Revolution was also accompanied by political and social transformation. The national state had become the focus of Europeans' lives, and within the nation-state the growth of the middle class had led in many places to the triumph of liberal practices: constitutional states, parliaments, and principles of equality. The period after 1871 also witnessed the growth of political democracy in which universal male suffrage was used to elect parliamentary bodies with cabinets responsible to the legislature.

During the same period, social legislation to benefit the working classes also emerged. While workers turned to socialist parties and labor unions to push for improvements in their working and living conditions, they also used their newly acquired voting rights to push for social legislation that would benefit them. But social welfare measures also came from conservative governments that tried to divert workers away from socialism by making concessions to their demands for a better life.

•••••••• 1870 ••••••••• 1880 •••••••••• 1890 •••••••••• 1900 •••••••••• 1910 ••••••••

First Birth Control Clinic   Germany's Social Welfare Legislation   Separation of Church and State in France   Social Democratic Party Becomes Germany's Largest Party

▼ The Second Industrial Revolution

At the heart of Europe's belief in progress between 1871 and 1914 was the stunning material growth produced by what historians have called the Second Industrial Revolution. The first Industrial Revolution had given rise to textiles, railroads, iron, and coal. In the second revolution, steel, chemicals, electricity, and petroleum led the way to new industrial frontiers.

Technological Innovations and New Products

The first major change in industrial development between 1870 and 1914 was the substitution of steel for iron. The development of a steel industry began in the 1850s when a British engineer, Henry Bessemer, invented a converter furnace. It was not until the end of the 1870s, however, that the process was refined enough to produce large quantities of basic steel at a price cheaper than iron. New methods for rolling and shaping steel made it useful in the construction of lighter, smaller, and faster machines and engines, as well as railways, shipbuilding, and armaments. In 1860, Great Britain, France, Germany, and Belgium produced 125,000 tons of steel; by 1913, the total was 32 million tons. Whereas in the early 1870s Britain had produced twice as much steel as Germany, by 1910, German production was double that of Great Britain. Both had been surpassed by the United States in 1890.

Great Britain also fell behind in the new chemical industry. A change in the method of making soda enabled France and Germany to take the lead in producing the alkalies used in the textile, soap, and paper industries. German laboratories soon overtook the British in the development of new organic chemical compounds, such as artificial dyes. By 1900, German firms had cornered 90 percent of the market for dye stuffs, "imperial Germany's greatest industrial achievement." Germany also led in the development of photographic plates and film.

Electricity was a major new form of energy that proved to be of great value since it could be easily converted into other forms of energy, such as heat, light, and motion, and moved relatively effortlessly through space by means of transmitting wires. It was not until the 1870s that the first commercially practical generators of electrical current were developed. By 1881, Britain had its first public power station. By 1910, hydroelectric power stations and coal-fired steam-generating plants enabled entire districts to be tied into a single power distribution system that provided a common source of power for homes, shops, and industrial enterprises.

Electricity spawned a whole new series of inventions. The creation of the incandescent filament lamp by the American Thomas Edison and the Briton Joseph Swan opened homes and cities to illumination by electric lights. A revolution in communications was fostered when Alexander Graham Bell invented the telephone in 1876 and Guglielmo Marconi sent the first radio waves across the Atlantic in 1901. Although most electricity was initially used for lighting, it was eventually put to use in transportation. The first electric railway was installed in Berlin in 1879. By the 1880s, streetcars and subways had appeared in major European cities. Horse-drawn buses disappeared from London streets by 1911. Electricity also transformed the factory. Conveyor belts, cranes, machines, and machine tools could all be powered by electricity and located anywhere. In the first Industrial Revolution, coal had been the major source of energy. Countries without adequate coal supplies lagged behind in industrialization. Thanks to electricity, they could now enter the industrial age.

The development of the internal combustion engine had a similar effect. The first internal combustion engine, fired by gas and air, was produced in 1878. It proved unsuitable for widespread use as a source of power in transportation until the development of liquid fuels,

▼ An Age of Progress. Between 1871 and 1914, a Second Industrial Revolution led many Europeans to believe that their age was an age of progress in which most human problems could be solved by scientific achievements. This illustration is taken from a special issue of *The Illustrated London News* celebrating the Diamond Jubilee of Queen Victoria in 1897. On the left are scenes from 1837, when Victoria came to the British throne; on the right are scenes from 1897. The vivid contrast was used to underscore the magazine's conclusion: "The most striking . . . evidence of progress during the reign is the ever increasing speed which the discoveries of physical science have forced into everyday life. Steam and electricity have conquered time and space to a greater extent during the last sixty years than all the preceding six hundred years witnessed."

namely, petroleum and its distilled derivatives. An oil-fired engine was made in 1897, and by 1902, the Hamburg-Amerika Line had switched from coal to oil on its new ocean liners. By the beginning of the twentieth century, some naval fleets had been converted to oil burners as well.

The development of the internal combustion engine gave rise to the automobile and airplane. Gottlieb Daimler's creation of a light engine in 1886 was the key to the development of the automobile. In 1900, world production stood at 9,000 cars; by 1906, Americans had overtaken the initial lead of the French. It was an American, Henry Ford, who revolutionized the car industry with the mass production of the Model T. By 1916, Ford's factories were producing 735,000 cars a year. In the meantime an age of air transportation emerged with the Zeppelin airship in 1900. In 1903, at Kitty Hawk, North Carolina, the Wright brothers made the first flight in a fixed-wing, gasoline-engine-powered plane. It took World War I, however, to stimulate the aircraft industry, and it was not until 1919 that the first regular passenger air service was established. Despite the new sources of energy in hydroelectricity, oil, gasoline, and gas, coal remained the primary source of industrial energy at the beginning of the twentieth century.

The Development of Markets

The growth of industrial production depended upon the development of markets for the sale of manufactured goods. The British in particular had actively sought markets abroad for their textiles. In 1820, 60 percent of Britain's cotton cloth was sold outside the country; by 1880, 82 percent was exported. The British were especially active in developing markets in the Far East. In 1814, they sold 1 million yards of cloth to ports east of Suez; by 1870, they were selling 1,402 million yards. But in the second half of the nineteenth century, the British experienced severe competition from Germany and the United States, and even from India and Japan, in their eastern markets.

After 1870, the best markets were already heavily saturated, forcing Europeans to take a renewed look at their domestic markets. As Europeans were the richest consumers in the world, those markets offered abundant possibilities. The dramatic population increases after 1870 (see Chapter 25) were accompanied by a steady rise in national incomes. The leading industrialized nations, Britain and Germany, doubled or tripled their national incomes. Between 1850 and 1900, real wages had increased in Britain by two-thirds and in Germany by one-third. A decline in the cost of food combined with lower prices for manufactured goods because of reduced transportation costs made it easier for Europeans to buy consumer products. In the cities, new methods for retail distribution, in particular the department store (see the box on p. 815), were used to expand sales of a whole

The Department Store and the Beginnings of Mass Consumerism
▼ ▼ ▼

Domestic markets were especially important for the sale of the goods being turned out by Europe's increasing number of industrial plants. New techniques of mass marketing arose to encourage the sale of the new consumer goods. The Parisians pioneered in the development of the department store, and this selection is taken from a contemporary's account of the growth of these stores in the French capital city.

E. Lavasseur, On Parisian Department Stores, 1907

It was in the reign of Louis-Philippe that department stores for fashion goods and dresses, extending to material and other clothing began to be distinguished. The type was already one of the notable developments of the Second Empire; it became one of the most important ones of the Third Republic. These stores have increased in number and several of them have become extremely large. Combining in their different departments all articles of clothing, toilet articles, furniture and many other ranges of goods, it is their special object so to combine all commodities as to attract and satisfy customers who will find conveniently together an assortment of a mass of articles corresponding to all their various needs. They attract customers by permanent display, by free entry into the shops, by periodic exhibitions, by special sales, by fixed prices, and by their ability to deliver the goods purchased to customers' homes, in Paris and to the provinces. Turning themselves into direct intermediaries between the producer and the consumer, even producing sometimes some of their articles in their own workshops, buying at lowest prices because of their large orders and because they are in a position to profit from bargains, working with large sums, and selling to most of their customers for cash only, they can transmit these benefits in lowered selling prices.

They can even decide to sell at a loss, as an advertisement or to get rid of out-of-date fashions. Taking 5–6 percent on 100 million brings them in more than 20 per cent would bring to a firm doing a turnover of 50,000 francs.

The success of these department stores is only possible thanks to the volume of their business and this volume needs considerable capital and a very large turnover. Now capital, having become abundant, is freely combined nowadays in large enterprises, although French capital has the reputation of being more wary of the risks of industry than of State or railway securities. On the other hand, the large urban agglomerations, the ease with which goods can be transported by the railways, the diffusion of some comforts to strata below the middle classes, have all favoured these developments.

As example we may cite some figures relating to these stores, since they were brought to the notice of the public in the *Revue des Deux-Mondes*. . . .

Le Louvre, dating to the time of the extension of the rue de Rivoli under the Second Empire, did in 1893 a business of 120 million at a profit of 6.4 per cent. *Le Bon-Marché*, which was a small shop when Mr. Boucicaut entered it in 1852, already did a business of 20 million at the end of the Empire. During the republic its new buildings were erected; Mme. Boucicaut turned it by her will into a kind of co-operative society, with shares and an ingenious organization; turnover reached 150 million in 1893, leaving a profit of 5 per cent. . . .

According to the tax records of 1891, these stores in Paris, numbering 12, employed 1,708 persons and were rated on their site values at 2,159,000 francs; the largest had then 542 employees. These same stores had, in 1901, 9,784 employees; one of them over 2,000 and another over 1,600; their site value has doubled (4,089,000 francs).

new range of consumer goods made possible by the development of the steel and electrical industries. The desire to own sewing machines, clocks, bicycles, electric lights, and typewriters was rapidly generating a new consumer ethic that has been a crucial part of the modern economy.

Meanwhile, increased competition for foreign markets and the growing importance of domestic demand led to a reaction against free trade. To many industrial and political leaders, protective tariffs guaranteed domestic markets for the products of their own industries. Thus, after a decade of experimentation with free trade in the 1860s, Europeans returned to tariff protection. The Austro-Hungarian Empire was the first in 1874, followed by Russia in 1877, Germany in 1879, Italy in 1887, the United States in 1890, and France in 1892. Only Britain, Denmark, and the Netherlands refused to follow suit.

During this same period, cartels were being formed to decrease competition internally. In a cartel, independent enterprises worked together to control prices and fix production quotas, thereby restraining the kind of competition that led to reduced prices. Cartels were especially strong in Germany, where banks moved to protect their investments by eliminating the "anarchy of competition." German businessmen established cartels in potash, coal, steel, and chemicals. Founded in 1893, the Rhenish-Westphalian Coal Syndicate controlled 98 percent of Germany's coal production by 1904.

The formation of cartels was paralleled by a move toward ever-larger manufacturing plants, especially in the iron and steel, machinery, heavy electrical equipment, and chemical industries. Although evident in Britain, France, and Belgium, it was most pronounced in Germany. Between 1882 and 1907, the number of people working in German factories with over 1,000 employees rose from 205,000 to 879,000. This growth in the size of industrial plants led to pressure for greater efficiency in factory production at the same time that competition led to demands for greater economy. The result was a desire to streamline or rationalize production as much as possible. One way to accomplish this was by cutting labor costs through the mechanization of transport within plants, such as using electric cranes to move materials. More importantly, the development of precision tools enabled manufacturers to produce interchangeable parts, which in turn led to the creation of the assembly line for production. First used in the United States for small arms and clocks, the assembly line had moved to Europe by 1850. In the last half of the nineteenth century, it was primarily used in manufacturing nonmilitary goods, such as sewing machines, typewriters, bicycles, and finally the automobile. Principles of scientific management were also introduced by 1900 to maximize workers' efficiency.

The emergence of protective tariffs and cartels was clearly a response to the growth of the multinational industrial system. Economic competition intensified the political rivalries of the age. The growth of the national state, which had seemed in the mid-nineteenth century to be the answer to old problems, now seemed to be creating new ones.

Economic Patterns

In the fifty years before World War I, the Second Industrial Revolution of Europe played a role in the emergence of basic economic patterns that characterized much of modern European economic life.

EUROPEAN TRENDS   Although we have described the period from 1871 to 1914 as an age of material property, recessions and crises were still very much a part of economic life. Although some historians have questioned the appropriateness of the title Great Depression for the period from 1873 to 1895, Europeans did witness a series of economic crises during those years. Prices, especially those of agricultural products, fell dramatically. Slumps in the business cycle reduced profits although economic recession occurred at different times in different countries. France and Britain, for example, sank into depression in the 1880s while Germany and the United States were recovering from their depression of the 1870s. After 1895, however, until World War I, Europe overall experienced an economic boom and achieved a level of prosperity that encouraged people later to look back to that era as *la belle époque*—a golden age in European civilization.

Between 1870 and 1914, Germany replaced Great Britain as the industrial leader of Europe. Already in the 1890s Germany's superiority was evident in new areas of manufacturing, such as organic chemicals and electrical equipment, and increasingly apparent in its ever-greater share of worldwide trade. Why had industrial leadership passed from Britain to Germany?

Britain's early lead in industrialization gave it an established industrial plant and made it more difficult to shift to the new techniques of the Second Industrial Revolution. As later entrants to the industrial age, the Germans could build the latest and most efficient industrial plant. British entrepreneurs made the situation worse by their tendency to be suspicious of innovations and their reluctance to invest in new plants and industries. As one manufacturer remarked: "One wants to be thoroughly convinced of the superiority of a new method before condemning as useless a large plant that has hitherto done good service."[1] German managers, on the other hand, were accustomed to change, and the formation of large cartels encouraged German banks to provide enormous sums for investment. Then, too, unlike the Germans, the British were not willing to encourage formal scientific and technical education.

The struggle for economic (and political) supremacy between Great Britain and Germany should not cause us to overlook the other great polarization of the age. By 1900, Europe was divided into two economic zones. Great Britain, Belgium, France, the Netherlands, Germany, the western part of the Austro-Hungarian Empire, and northern Italy constituted an advanced industrialized core that had a high standard of living, decent systems of transportation, and relatively healthy and educated peoples. Another part of Europe, the backward and little industrialized area to the south and east, consisting of southern Italy, most of Austria-Hungary, Spain, Portugal, the Balkan kingdoms, and Russia, was still largely agricultural and relegated by the industrial countries to the function of providing food and raw materials. The presence of Romanian oil, Greek olive oil, and Serbian pigs and prunes in western Europe served as reminders of an economic division of Europe that continued well into the twentieth century. Some industrially backward countries of Europe, however, managed to use the export of their produce to boost themselves into the industrial age. Sweden's sale of timber and iron ore abroad, combined with hydroelectric power, gave it the resources to develop paper, steel, and cellulose industries.

SCIENCE AND TECHNOLOGY   Already by 1850, research in the basic sciences was rapidly being translated into new industrial techniques. Between 1870 and 1914, the union of science and technology grew closer. Newer fields of industrial activity, such as organic chemistry and electrical engineering, required more scientific knowledge than the commonsense tinkering once employed by amateur inventors. Companies began to invest capital in laboratory equipment for their own research or hired scientific consultants for advice.

Nowhere was the relationship between science and technology more apparent than in Germany. In 1899, German technical high schools were allowed to award doctorate degrees, and by 1900, they were turning out 3,000 to 4,000 graduates a year. Many of these graduates made their way into industrial firms. Some large firms, such as the Badische Anilin und Soda Fabrike, even established their own schools to train scientists. By

1907, 77 percent of salaried managers in Germany had had the benefit of some kind of higher education.

AGRICULTURAL CRISIS   European agriculture experienced a difficult time after 1870. An abundance of grain and lower costs of transportation caused the prices of farm commodities to plummet. Some countries responded with tariff barriers against lower priced foodstuffs. Where agricultural labor was scarce and hence expensive, as in Britain and Germany, landowners introduced machines for threshing and harvesting. The slump in grain prices also led some countries to specialize in other food products. Denmark, for example, exported eggs, butter, and cheese while sugar beets predominated in Bohemia and northern France, fruit in Mediterranean countries, and wine in Spain and Italy. This age also witnessed the introduction of chemical fertilizers. While large estates could make these adjustments easily, individual small farmers could not afford them and created farm cooperatives that provided capital for making improvements and purchasing tools and fertilizer.

TOWARD A WORLD ECONOMY   The economic developments of the late nineteenth century, combined with the transportation revolution that saw the growth of marine transport and railroads, not only played a role in the new imperialism in the last half of the nineteenth century (see Chapter 25), but also fostered a true world economy. By 1900, Europeans were receiving beef and wool from Argentina and Australia, coffee from Brazil, nitrates from Chile, iron ore from Algeria, and sugar from Java. European capital was also invested abroad to develop railways, mines, electrical power plants, and banks. High rates of return, such as 11.3 percent on Latin American banking shares that were floated in London, provided plenty of incentive. Of course, foreign countries also provided markets for the surplus manufactured goods of Europe. With its capital, industries, and military might, Europe dominated the world economy by the beginning of the twentieth century.

▼ Cities and Social Structure in an Age of Mass Society

The new urban and industrial world created by the rapid economic and social changes of the nineteenth century has led historians to speak of the emergence of a mass society by the late nineteenth century. A mass society meant new forms of expression for the lower classes as they benefited from the extension of voting rights, an improved standard of living, and compulsory elementary education. However, mass society also made possible the development of organizations that manipulated and controlled the populations of the European nation-states. Governments fostered national loyalty and created mass armies by conscription. Big businesses imposed rational systems of discipline and organization upon their working-class employees. A mass press swayed popular opinion by flamboyant journalistic practices. To understand this mass society, we must examine the urban environment in which it lived and the structure of the social classes that made it up.

Transformation of the Urban Environment

By far one of the most important consequences of industrialization and the population explosion of the nineteenth century was urbanization. In the course of the nineteenth century, urban dwellers came to make up an ever-increasing percentage of the European population. In 1800, they constituted 40 percent of the population in Britain, 25 percent in France and Germany,

and only 10 percent in eastern Europe. By 1914, urban inhabitants had increased to 80 percent of the population in Britain, 45 percent in France, 60 percent in Germany, and 30 percent in eastern Europe. The size of cities also expanded dramatically, especially in industrialized countries. In 1800, there were 21 European cities with populations over 100,000; by 1900, there were 147. Between 1800 and 1900, London's population grew from 960,000 to 6,500,000 and Berlin's from 172,000 to 2,700,000. These statistics demonstrate what one observer noted in 1899: "the most remarkable social phenomenon of the present century is the concentration of population in cities."

Urban populations grew faster than the general population primarily because of the vast migration from rural areas to cities. Often this was due to negative factors. People were driven by sheer economic necessity—unemployment, land hunger, and physical want—from the countryside to the cities. Urban centers offered something positive as well, usually mass employment in factories and later in service trades and professions. But

▼ **Map 24.1** The Industrial Regions of Europe by 1914.

▼ **The City at Night.** Industrialization and the population explosion of the nineteenth century fostered the growth of cities. At the same time, technological innovations enabled cities to develop pure water and sewerage systems that dramatically improved living conditions in European cities. Gas lighting and later electricity also transformed the nighttime environment of Europe's cities, as is evident in this painting of Liverpool.

cities also grew faster in the second half of the nineteenth century because health and living conditions in them were improving.

PUBLIC HEALTH AND HOUSING   Throughout the Middle Ages, cities had been important centers of commerce, small industry, church and government offices, and culture, but these medieval cities had also been characterized by filth and disease. Early industrial cities had only magnified the squalor. Well into the mid-nineteenth century, urban death rates outstripped birth rates, and only the influx of large numbers of rural emigrants ensured urban growth. Between 1850 and 1914, however, the environment of the cities improved dramatically as urban reformers and city officials used new technology to improve the urban landscape.

When cholera swept across Europe in the 1830s and 1840s, it proved especially devastating to people living in working-class urban areas. But it also affected middle-class urban dwellers, who often, though incorrectly, believed that dirt caused disease. Consequently, public health and housing became important issues to city dwellers, and they began to put pressure on city governments to clean up the filthy environment.

In the 1840s, a number of urban reformers, such as Edwin Chadwick in England (see Chapter 21) and Rudolf Virchow and Solomon Neumann in Germany, had pointed to filthy living conditions as the primary cause of epidemic diseases and urged sanitary reforms to correct the problem. The efforts of Chadwick led to Britain's first Public Health Act in 1848. The Melun Act in France in 1851 and laws in German states achieved similar purposes. These and later legislative acts created Boards of Health that brought governmental action to bear on public health issues. Urban medical officers and building inspectors were authorized to inspect dwellings for public health hazards. New building regulations made it more difficult for private contractors to build shoddy housing. The Public Health Act of 1875 in Britain, for example, prohibited the construction of new buildings without running water and an internal drainage system. For the first time in Western history, the role of municipal governments had been expanded to include detailed regulations for the improvement of the living conditions of urban dwellers. German municipal administration in particular became a model for other European cities. By 1900, German municipal bureaucracies regularly hired university graduates with specialized medical and scientific knowledge to provide their cities with professional and technocratic management.

Essential to the public health of the modern European city was the ability to bring clean water to it and to expel sewage from it. The accomplishment of those two tasks was a major engineering feat in the last half of the nineteenth century. The problem of fresh water was solved by a system of dams and reservoirs that stored the water and aqueducts and tunnels that carried it from the countryside to the city and into individual dwellings. By the second half of the nineteenth century, regular private baths became accessible to many people as gas heaters in the 1860s and later electric heaters made hot baths possible. Even the shower had appeared by the 1880s. The treatment of sewage was also improved by building mammoth underground pipes that carried raw sewage far from the city for disposal. In the late 1860s, a number of German cities began to construct sewer systems. Frankfurt began its program after a lengthy public campaign enlivened by the slogan "from the toilet to the river in half an hour." London devised a system of five enormous sewers that discharged their loads twelve miles from the city where it was chemically treated. Unfortunately, in many places new underground sewers simply continued to discharge their raw sewage into what soon became highly polluted lakes and rivers. Nevertheless, the development of pure water and sewerage systems dramatically improved the public health of European cities by 1914.

Middle-class reformers who denounced the unsanitary living conditions of the working class also focused on their housing needs. Overcrowded, disease-ridden slums were viewed as dangerous not only to physical health, but to the political and moral health of the entire nation. V. A. Huber, the foremost early German housing reformer, wrote in 1861: "Certainly it would not be too much to say that the home is the communal embodiment of family life. Thus the purity of the dwelling is almost as important for the family as is the cleanliness of the body for the individual."[2] To Huber, good housing was a prerequisite for stable family life, and without stable family life one of the "stabilising elements of society" would be dissolved, much to society's detriment.

Early efforts to attack the housing problem emphasized the middle-class, liberal belief in the efficacy of private enterprise. Reformers such as Huber believed that the construction of model dwellings renting at a reasonable price would force other private landlords to elevate their housing standards. A fine example of this approach was the work of Octavia Hill, granddaughter of a celebrated social reformer (see the box on p. 821). With the financial assistance of a friend, she rehabilitated some old dwellings and constructed new ones to create housing for 3,500 tenants.

Other wealthy reformer-philanthropists took a different approach to the housing problem. In 1887, Lord Leverhulme began construction of a model village called Port Sunlight outside Liverpool for the workers at his soap factory. Port Sunlight offered pleasant living conditions in the belief that good housing would ensure a healthy and happy work force. Yet another approach was the garden city. At the end of the nineteenth century, Ebenezer Howard founded the British garden city movement that advocated the construction of new towns separated from each other by open country that would provide the recreational areas, fresh air, and sense of community that would encourage healthy family life. Letchward Garden City, started in 1903, was the first concrete result of Howard's theory.

As the number and size of cities continued to mushroom, governments by the 1880s came to the conclusion—although reluctantly—that private enterprise could not solve the housing crisis. In 1890, a British Housing Act empowered local town councils to construct cheap housing for the working classes. London and Liverpool were the first communities to take advantage of their new powers. Similar activity had been set in motion in Germany by 1900. In France in 1894 the government took a lesser step by providing easy credit for private contractors to build working-class housing. Everywhere, however, these lukewarm measures failed to do much to meet the real housing needs of the working classes. In Britain, for example, only 5 percent of all dwellings erected between 1890 and 1914 were constructed by municipalities under the Housing Act of 1890. Nevertheless, by the start of World War I, the need for planning had been recognized, and after the war municipal governments moved into housing construction on a large scale. In housing, as in so many other areas of life in the late nineteenth and early twentieth centuries, the liberal principle that the government that governs least governs best had simply proven untrue. More and more, governments were stepping into areas of activity that they would never have touched earlier.

URBAN RECONSTRUCTION   Housing was but one area of urban reconstruction in the fifty years before World War I. As urban populations expanded in the nineteenth

The Housing Venture of Octavia Hill

▼ ▼ ▼

Octavia Hill was a practical-minded British housing reformer who believed that workers and their families were entitled to happy homes. At the same time, she was convinced that the poor needed guidance and encouragement, not charity. In this selection, she describes her housing venture.

Octavia Hill, *Homes of the London Poor*

About four years ago I was put in possession of three houses in one of the worst courts of Marylebone. Six other houses were bought subsequently. All were crowded with inmates.

The first thing to be done was to put them in decent tenantable order. The set last purchased was a row of cottages facing a bit of desolate ground, occupied with wretched, dilapidated cow-sheds, manure heaps, old timber, and rubbish of every description. The houses were in a most deplorable condition—the plaster was dropping from the walls; on one staircase a pail was placed to catch the rain that fell through the roof. All the staircases were perfectly dark; the banisters were gone, having been burnt as firewood by tenants. The grates, with large holes in them, were falling forward into the rooms. The washhouse, full of lumber belonging to the landlord, was locked up; thus the inhabitants had to wash clothes, as well as to cook, eat and sleep in their small rooms. The dust-bin, standing in the front part of the houses, was accessible to the whole neighbourhood, and boys often dragged from it quantities of unseemly objects and spread them over the court. The state of the drainage was in keeping with everything else. The pavement of the backyard was all broken up, and great puddles stood in it, so that the damp crept up the outer walls. . . .

As soon as I entered into possession, each family had an opportunity of doing better: those who would not pay, or who led clearly immoral lives, were ejected. The rooms they vacated were cleansed; the tenants who showed signs of improvement moved into them, and thus, in turn, an opportunity was obtained for having each room distempered and papered. The drains were put in order, a large slate cistern was fixed, the washhouse was cleared of its lumber, and thrown open on stated days to each tenant in turn. The roof, the plaster, the woodwork were repaired; the staircase walls were distempered; new grates were fixed; the layers of paper and rag (black with age) were torn from the windows, and glass was put in; out of 192 panes only eight were found unbroken. The yard and footpath were paved.

The rooms, as a rule, were re-let at the same prices at which they had been let before; but tenants with large families were counselled to take two rooms, and for these much less was charged than if let singly: this plan I continue to pursue. In-coming tenants are not allowed to take a decidedly insufficient quantity of room, and no sub-letting is permitted. . . .

The pecuniary result has been very satisfactory. Five per cent has been paid on all the capital invested. A fund for the repayment of capital is accumulating. A liberal allowance has been made for repairs. . . .

My tenants are mostly of a class far below that of mechanics. They are, indeed, of the very poor. And yet, although the gifts they have received have been next to nothing, none of the families who have passed under my care during the whole four years have continued in what is called "distress," except such as have been unwilling to exert themselves. Those who will not exert the necessary self-control cannot avail themselves of the means of livelihood held out to them. But, for those who are willing, some small assistance in the form of work has, from time to time, been provided—not much, but sufficient to keep them from want or despair.

▼ **The Reconstruction of Paris.** In the second half of the nineteenth century, urban reconstruction projects transformed the appearance of many European cities. Perhaps most famous was the reconstruction of Paris during the reign of Emperor Napoleon III. As can be seen in this illustration, a congested section of old Paris is being torn down to make way for the wide boulevards and open spaces that characterized the new Paris.

century, the older layout in which the city was confined to a compact area enclosed by defensive walls seemed restrictive and utterly useless. In the second half of the nineteenth century, many of the old defensive walls—worthless anyway from a military standpoint—were pulled down, and the areas converted into parks and boulevards. In Vienna, for example, the great boulevards of the Ringstrasse replaced the old medieval walls. While the broad streets served a military purpose—the rapid deployment of troops to crush civil disturbances—they also offered magnificent views of the city hall, the university, and the parliament building, all powerful symbols of middle-class social values.

Like Vienna, many European urban centers were redesigned during the second half of the nineteenth century. The reconstruction of Paris after 1850 by Emperor Napoleon III was perhaps the most famous project and provided a model for other urban centers. The old residential districts located in the central city, many of them working-class slums, were pulled down and replaced with town halls, government office buildings, retail stores, including the new department stores, museums, cafes, and theaters, all of which provided for the shopping and recreational pleasures of the middle classes.

As cities expanded and entire groups of people were displaced from urban centers by reconstruction, city populations spilled over into the neighboring villages and countrysides, which were soon incorporated into the cities. The construction of streetcars and commuter trains by the turn of the century enabled both working-class and middle-class populations to live in their own suburban neighborhoods far removed from their places of work. Cheap, modern transportation essentially separated home and work for many Europeans.

The Social Structure of Mass Society

Historians generally agree that between 1871 and 1914 the average person enjoyed an increasing standard of living. The real wages of British workers, for example, probably doubled between 1871 and 1910. We should not allow this increase in the standard of living to mislead us, however. Great poverty did remain in Western society, and the gap between the rich and poor was enormous by 1914. In the western and central European countries most affected by industrialization, the richest 20 percent of the population received between 50 and 60 percent of the national income. This meant that while the upper and middle classes received almost three-fifths of the wealth, the remaining 80 percent of the population received only two-fifths. It would, however, be equally misleading to portray European society as split simply into rich and poor. Between the small group of the elite at the top and the large number of very poor at the bottom, there existed many different groups of varying wealth.

THE ELITE   At the top of European society stood a wealthy elite, constituting but 5 percent of the population while controlling between 30 and 40 percent of its wealth. This nineteenth-century elite was an amalgamation of the traditional landed aristocracy that had dominated European society for centuries and the wealthy upper middle class. In the course of the nineteenth century, aristocrats coalesced with the most successful industrialists, bankers, and merchants to form a new elite. The growth of big business had created this group of wealthy plutocrats while aristocrats, whose income from landed estates declined, invested in railway shares, public utilities, government bonds, and even businesses, sometimes on their own estates. Gradually, the greatest fortunes shifted into the hands of the upper middle class. In Great Britain, for example, landed aristocrats constituted 73 percent of the country's millionaires in mid-century while the commercial and financial magnates made up 14 percent. By the period 1900–1914, landowners had declined to 27 percent. The wealthiest person in Germany was not an aristocrat, but Bertha Krupp, granddaughter of Alfred Krupp and heiress to the business dynasty left by her father Friedrich, who committed suicide in 1902 over a homosexual scandal.

Increasingly, aristocrats and plutocrats fused as the wealthy upper middle class purchased landed estates to join the aristocrats in the pleasures of country living while the aristocrats bought lavish town houses for part-time urban life. Common bonds were also created when the sons of wealthy middle-class families were admitted to the elite schools dominated by the children of the aristocracy. At Oxford, the landed upper class made up 40 percent of the student body in 1870, but only 15 percent in 1910, while undergraduates from business families went from 7 to 21 percent during the same period. This educated elite, whether aristocratic or middle class in background, assumed leadership roles in government bureaucracies and military hierarchies. Marriage also served to unite the two groups. Daughters of tycoons gained titles while aristocratic heirs gained new sources of cash. Wealth American heiresses were in special demand. When Consuelo Vanderbilt married the duke of Marlborough, the new duchess brought £2 million (approximately $10 million) to her husband.

It would be misleading, however, to assume that the alliance of the wealthy business elite and traditional aristocrats was always harmonious. In Germany class lines were sometimes well drawn, especially if they were complicated by anti-Semitism. Albert Ballin, the wealthy director of the Hamburg-Amerika luxury liners, may have been close to Emperor William II, who entertained him on a regular basis, but the Prussian aristocracy never fully accepted Ballin because of his Jewish origins. Although the upper middle class was allowed into the bureaucracy of the German empire, the diplomatic corps remained the preserve of nobles.

THE MIDDLE CLASSES   The middle classes consisted of a variety of groups. Below the upper middle class was a middle level that included such traditional groups as professionals in law, medicine, and the civil service as well as moderately well-to-do industrialists and merchants. The industrial expansion of the nineteenth century also added new groups to the middle middle class. These included business managers and new professionals, such as the engineers, architects, accountants, and chemists who formed professional associations as the symbols of their newfound importance. Beneath this solid and comfortable middle middle class was a lower middle class of small shopkeepers, traders, manufacturers, and prosperous peasants. Their chief preoccupation was the provision of goods and services for the classes above them.

Standing between the lower middle class and the lower classes were new groups of white-collar workers who were the product of the Second Industrial Revolution. They were the traveling salesmen, bookkeepers, bank tellers, telephone operators, department store salespeople, and secretaries. Although largely propertyless and often little better paid than skilled laborers, these white-collar workers were often committed to middle-class ideals and optimistic about improving their status. Some even achieved professional standing and middle-class status.

The moderately prosperous and successful middle classes shared a certain style of life, one whose values tended to dominate much of nineteenth-century society.

The members of the middle class were especially active in preaching their worldview to their children and to the upper and lower classes of their society. This was especially evident in Victorian Britain, often considered a model of middle-class society. It was the European middle classes who accepted and promulgated the importance of progress and science. They believed in hard work, which they viewed as the primary human good, open to everyone and guaranteed to have positive results. Knowledge was important as a functional instrument for personal gain. They were also regular churchgoers who believed in the good conduct associated with traditional Christian morality. The middle class was concerned with propriety, the right way of doing things, which gave rise to an incessant number of books aimed at the middle-class market with such titles as *The Habits of Good Society* or *Don't: A Manual of Mistakes and Improprieties More or Less Prevalent in Conduct and Speech.*

THE WORKING CLASSES   The working classes of European society constituted almost 80 percent of the European population. Many of them were landholding peasants, agricultural laborers, and sharecroppers, especially in eastern Europe. This was less true, however, in western and central Europe. About 10 percent of the British population worked in agriculture, while in Germany the figure was 25 percent.

Although the experiences of peasants were very different from those of the urban working classes, the two groups were drawing closer together by the end of the nineteenth century. Many prosperous, landowning peasants shared the values of the middle class. Military con-

scription brought peasants into contact with the other groups of mass society while state-run elementary schools forced the children of peasants to speak the national dialect and accept national loyalties.

There was no such thing as a homogeneous urban working class. The elite of the working class included, first of all, skilled artisans in such traditional handicraft trades as cabinetmaking, printing, and the making of jewelry. As the production of more items was mechanized in the course of the nineteenth century, these highly skilled workers found their economic security threatened. Printers, for example, were replaced by automatic typesetting machines operated by semiskilled workers. The Second Industrial Revolution, however, also brought new entrants into the group of highly skilled workers, such as machine-tool specialists, shipbuilders, and metal workers. Many of the skilled workers attempted to pattern themselves after the middle class by seeking good housing and educating their children.

Semiskilled laborers, who included such people as carpenters, bricklayers, and many factory workers, earned wages that were about two-thirds of those of highly skilled workers. At the bottom of the working-class hierarchy stood the largest group of workers, the unskilled laborers. They included day laborers, who worked irregularly for very low wages, and large numbers of domestic servants. One out of every seven employed persons in Great Britain in 1900 was a domestic servant. Most of them were women.

Urban workers did experience a real betterment in the material conditions of their lives after 1871. For one thing, urban improvements meant better living condi-

▼ **Working-Class Housing in London.** Although urban workers experienced some improvements in the material conditions of their lives after 1871, working-class housing remained drab and depressing. This 1912 photograph of working-class housing in the East End of London shows rows of similar-looking buildings on treeless streets. Most often, these buildings had no gardens and no green areas.

tions. A rise in real wages, accompanied by a decline in many consumer costs, especially in the 1880s and 1890s, made it possible for workers to buy more than just food and housing. French workers in 1900, for example, spent 60 percent of their income on food, down from 75 percent in 1870. Workers' budgets now provided money for more clothes and even leisure at the same time that strikes and labor agitation were providing ten-hour days and Saturday afternoons off. The combination of more income and more free time produced whole new patterns of mass leisure (see Chapter 25).

▼ The "Woman Question": Female Experiences

The "woman question" was the term used to identify the debate over the role of women in society. In the nineteenth century, the "woman question" was really a series of "women's questions": Did women have a right to work? Did they have the right to own property? What should be the extent of their political rights? Such questions were important in view of women's position in society. Excluded from citizenship and defined by family and household roles, women remained legally inferior and economically dependent. In the course of the nineteenth century, women struggled to change their status.

Women and Work

During the course of the nineteenth century, considerable controversy erupted over a woman's "right to work." Working-class organizations tended to reinforce the underlying ideology of domesticity; women should remain at home to bear and nurture children and should not be allowed in the industrial work force. Working-class men argued that keeping women out of industrial work would ensure the moral and physical well-being of families. In reality, keeping women out of the industrial work force simply made it easier to exploit them when they needed income to supplement their husbands' wages or to support their families when their husbands were unemployed. The desperate need to work at times forced women to do marginal work at home or labor as pieceworkers in sweatshops. "Sweating" referred to the subcontracting of piecework usually, but not exclusively, in the tailoring trades; it was done at home since it required few skills or equipment. Pieceworkers were poorly paid and worked long hours. The poorest paid jobs for the cheapest goods were called "slop work." In

this description of the room of a London slopper, we see how precarious her position was:

> I then directed my steps to the neighborhood of Drurylane, to see a poor woman who lived in an attic on one of the closest courts in that quarter. On the table was a quarter of an ounce of tea. Observing my eye to rest upon it, she told me it was all she took. "Sugar," she said, "I broke myself of long ago; I couldn't afford it. A cup of tea, a piece of bread, and an onion is generally all I have for my dinner, and sometimes I haven't even an onion, and then I sops my bread."[3]

Excluded from factories and in need of income, many women had no choice but to work for the pitiful wages of the sweated industries.

NEW JOB OPPORTUNITIES The Second Industrial Revolution had an enormous impact on the position of women in the labor market. Although the growth of heavy industry in the mining, metallurgy, engineering, chemicals, and electrical sectors meant fewer jobs for women in manufacturing, the development of larger industrial plants and the expansion of government services created a wide number of service or white-collar jobs. The increased demand for white-collar workers at relatively low wages coupled with a shortage of male workers led employers to hire women. Big businesses and retail shops needed clerks, typists, secretaries, file clerks, and sales clerks. The expansion of government services created opportunities for women to be secretaries and telephone operators and to take jobs in health and social services. Compulsory education necessitated more teachers while the development of modern hospital services opened the way for an increase in nurses.

Many of the new white-collar jobs were by no means exciting. Their work was routine and, except for teaching and nursing, required few skills beyond basic literacy. Although there was little hope for advancement, these jobs had distinct advantages to the daughters of the middle classes and especially the upward-aspiring working classes. For some middle-class women, the new jobs offered freedom from the domestic patterns expected of them. Most of them, however, were filled by working-class females who saw them as an opportunity to escape from the "dirty" work of the lower-class world. Studies in France and Britain indicate that the increase in white-collar jobs did not lead to a rise in the size of the female labor force, but only a shift from industrial jobs to the white-collar sector of the economy.

PROSTITUTION Despite new job opportunities, many lower-class women were forced to become prostitutes to survive. The influx of rural, working-class girls into the cities in search of new opportunities often left them highly vulnerable. Employment was unstable and wages were low. No longer protected by family or village community and church, some girls faced only one grim alternative—prostitution. In Paris, London, and many other large cities with transient populations, thousands of prostitutes plied their trade. One journalist estimated that in 1885 there were 60,000 prostitutes in London. Most prostitutes were active for a short time, usually from late teens through early twenties. Many eventually rejoined the regular work force or married when they could.

In most European countries, prostitution was licensed and regulated by government and municipal authorities. Although the British government provided minimal regulation of prostitution, it did attempt to enforce the Contagious Diseases Acts in the 1870s and 1880s by giving authorities the right to examine prostitutes for venereal disease. Those prostitutes with the disease were confined for some time to special institutions called lock hospitals, where they were given moral instruction. Opposition to the Contagious Diseases Acts by middle-class female reformers, who objected to laws that punished women and not men who suffered from venereal disease, led to the repeal of the acts in 1886.

Marriage, Family, and Children

Many women in the nineteenth century aspired to the ideal of femininity popularized by writers and poets. Alfred Lord Tennyson's *The Princess* expressed it well:

Man for the field and woman for the hearth:
Man for the sword and for the needle she:
Man with the head and woman with the heart:
Man to command and woman to obey;
All else confusion.

Historians have pointed out that this traditional characterization of the sexes, based on gender-defined social roles, was virtually elevated to the status of universal male and female attributes in the nineteenth century, largely due to the impact of the Industrial Revolution on the family. As the chief family wage earners, men worked outside the home while women were left with the care of the family for which they were paid nothing. Of course, the ideal did not always match reality, especially for the lower classes, where the need for supplemental income drove women to do "sweated" work.

For most women, marriage was viewed as the only honorable and available career throughout most of the nineteenth century. While the middle class glorified the ideal of domesticity (see the box on p. 827), for most women marriage was a matter of economic necessity. The lack of meaningful work and the lower wages paid to women made it difficult for single women to earn a living. Since retiring to convents as in the past was no longer an option, many spinsters, who could not find sufficiently remunerative work, entered domestic service as live-in servants. Most women chose instead to marry, which was reflected in the increase in marriage rates and a decline in illegitimacy rates in the course of the nineteenth century.

Birthrates also dropped significantly in the nineteenth century. The most significant development in the modern family was the decline in the number of offspring born to the average woman. The change was not necessarily due to new technology. Although the invention of the vulcanization of rubber in the 1840s made possible the production of condoms and diaphragms, they were not widely used as effective contraceptive devices until the era of World War I. Some historians maintain that the change in attitude that led parents to limit the number of offspring deliberately was more important than the method used. While some historians attribute increased birth control to more widespread use of coitus interruptus, or male withdrawal before ejaculation, others have emphasized female control of family size through abortion and even infanticide or abandonment. That a change in attitude occurred was apparent in the development of a movement to increase awareness of birth control methods. Authorities prosecuted those who spread information about contraception for "depraving public morals," but were unable to stop them. In 1882 in Amsterdam, Dr. Aletta Jacob founded Europe's first birth control clinic. Initially, "family planning" was the suggestion of reformers who thought that the problem of poverty could be solved by reducing the number of children among the lower classes. In fact, the practice spread quickly among the propertied classes, rather than among the impoverished, a good reminder that considerable differences still remained between middle-class and working-class families.

THE MIDDLE-CLASS FAMILY   The family was the central institution of middle-class life. Men provided the family income while women focused on household and child care. The use of domestic servants in many middle-class homes, made possible by an abundant supply of cheap labor, reduced the amount of time middle-class women

Advice to Women: Be Dependent

▼ ▼ ▼

Industrialization had a strong impact on middle-class women as gender-based social roles became the norm. Men worked outside the home to support the family while women provided for the needs of their children and husband at home. In this selection, one woman gives advice to middle-class women on their proper role and behavior.

Elizabeth Poole Sanford, *Woman in Her Social and Domestic Character*

The changes wrought by Time are many. It influences the opinions of men as familiarity does their feelings; it has a tendency to do away with superstition, and to reduce every thing to its real worth.

It is thus that the sentiment for woman has undergone a change. The romantic passion which once almost deified her is on the decline; and it is by intrinsic qualities that she must now inspire respect. She is no longer the queen of song and the star of chivalry. But if there is less of enthusiasm entertained for her, the sentiment is more rational, and, perhaps, equally sincere; for it is in relation to happiness that she is chiefly appreciated.

And in this respect it is, we must confess, that she is most useful and most important. Domestic life is the chief source of her influence; and the greatest debt society can owe to her is domestic comfort: for happiness is almost an element of virtue; and nothing conduces more to improve the character of men than domestic peace. A woman may make a man's home delightful, and may thus increase his motives for virtuous exertion. She may refine and tranquillize his mind,—may turn away his anger or allay his grief. Her smile may be the happy influence to gladden his heart, and to disperse the cloud that gathers on his brow. And in proportion to her endeavors to make those around her happy, she will be esteemed and loved. She will secure by her excellence that interest and that regard which she might formerly claim as the privilege of her sex, and will really merit the deference which was then conceded to her as a matter of course. . . .

Perhaps one of the first secrets of her influence is adaptation to the tastes, and sympathy in the feelings, of those around her. This holds true in lesser as well as in graver points. It is in the former, indeed, that the absence of interest in a companion is frequently most disappointing. Where want of congeniality impairs domestic comfort, the fault is generally chargeable on the female side. It is for woman, not for man, to make the sacrifice, especially in indifferent matters. She must, in a certain degree, be plastic herself if she would mould others. . . .

Nothing is so likely to conciliate the affections of the other sex as a feeling that woman looks to them for support and guidance. In proportion as men are themselves superior, they are accessible to this appeal. On the contrary, they never feel interested in one who seems disposed rather to offer than to ask assistance. There is, indeed, something unfeminine in independence. It is contrary to nature, and therefore it offends. We do not like to see a woman affecting tremors, but still less do we like to see her acting the amazon. A really sensible woman feels her dependence. She does what she can; but she is conscious of inferiority, and therefore grateful for support. She knows that she is the weaker vessel, and that as such she should receive honor. In this view, her weakness is an attraction, not a blemish.

In every thing, therefore, that women attempt, they should show their consciousness of dependence. If they are learners, let them evince a teachable spirit; if they give an opinion, let them do it in an unassuming manner. There is something so unpleasant in female self-sufficiency that it not unfrequently deters instead of persuading, and prevents the adoption of advice which the judgment even approves.

---

had to spend on household work. At the same time, by reducing the number of children in the family, mothers could devote more time to child care and domestic leisure. The idea that leisure should be used for constructive purposes supported and encouraged the cult of middle-class domesticity.

The middle-class family fostered an ideal of togetherness. The Victorians created the family Christmas with its yule log, Christmas tree, songs, and exchange of gifts. In the United States, Fourth of July celebrations changed from drunken revels to family picnics by the 1850s. The education of middle-class females in domes-

▼ **A Middle-Class Family.** Nineteenth-century middle-class moralists considered the family the fundamental pillar of a healthy society. The family was a crucial institution in middle-class life, and togetherness constituted one of the important ideals of the middle-class family. This painting by William P. Frith, entitled *Many Happy Returns of the Day,* shows a family birthday celebration for a little girl in which grandparents, parents, and children take part. The servant at the left holds the presents for the little girl.

tic crafts, singing, and piano playing prepared them for their function of providing a proper environment for home recreation.

The new domestic ideal had an impact on child raising and children's play. Eighteenth-century Enlightenment thought had encouraged a new view of children as unique beings, not small adults, which had carried over into the nineteenth century. They were entitled to a long childhood involved in activities with other children their own age. The early environment in which they were raised, it was thought, would determine how they turned out. And mothers were seen as the most important force in protecting them from the harmful influences of the adult world. New children's games and toys, including mass-produced dolls for girls, appeared in middle-class homes. The middle-class emphasis on the functional value of knowledge was also evident in these games. One advice manual maintained that young children should learn checkers because it "calls forth the resources of the mind in the most gentle, as well as the most successful manner."

Since the sons of the middle-class family were intended to follow careers like their father's, they were isolated and kept in school until the age of sixteen or seventeen. Sport was used in the schools to "toughen" boys up while their leisure activities centered around both national military concerns and character building. This combination was especially evident in the establishment of the Boy Scouts in Britain in 1908. Boy Scouts provided organized recreation for boys between twelve and eighteen in which adventure was combined with the discipline of earning merit badges and ranks in such a way as to instill ideals of patriotism and self-sacrifice. Many men viewed such activities as a corrective to the possible dangers that female domination of the home posed for male development. As one scout leader wrote, "The REAL Boy Scout is not a sissy. [He] adores his mother [but] is not hitched to [her] apron strings." There was little organized recreational activity of this type for girls, although Robert Baden-Powell, the founder of the Boy Scouts, did encourage his sister to establish a girls' division as an afterthought. Its goal is evident from Agnes Baden-Powell's comment that "you do not want to make tomboys of refined girls, yet you want to attract, and thus raise, the slum girl from the gutter. The main object is to give them all the ability to be better mothers and Guides to the next generation."[4] Despite her comment, most organizations of this kind were for middle-class children, although some reformers tried to establish boys' clubs for working-class youths to reform them.

The new ideal of the middle-class woman as nurturing mother and wife who "determined the atmosphere of the household" through her character, not her work, frequently did not correspond to reality. Recent research indicates that in France, Germany, and even mid-Victorian Britain, relatively few families could actually afford to hire a host of servants. More often, middle-class families had one servant, usually a young working-class or country girl not used to middle-class lifestyles. Women, then, were often forced to work quite hard to maintain the expected appearance of the well-ordered household. A German housekeeping manual makes this evident:

> If often happens that even high-ranking ladies help at home with housework, and particularly with kitchen chores, scrubbing, etc., so that, above all the hands have good cause to become very rough, hard, and calloused. When these ladies appear in society, they are extremely upset at having such rough-looking hands. In order to perform the hardest and most ordinary chores . . . and, at the same time, to keep a soft hand like those fine ladies who have no heavier work to do than embroidering and sewing, always keep a piece of fresh bacon, rub your hands with it just before bedtime, and you will fully achieve your goal. You will, as a result, have the inconvenience of having to sleep with gloves on, in order not to soil the bed.[5]

Many middle-class wives, then, were caught in a no-win situation. Often for the sake of the advancement of her husband's career, she was expected to maintain in public the image of the "idle" wife, freed from demeaning physical labor and able to pass her days in ornamental pursuits. In truth, it was frequently the middle-class woman who paid the price for this facade in a life of unpaid work, carefully managing the family budget and participating in housework that could never be done by simply one servant girl. As one historian has argued, the reality of many middle-class women's lives was that "what appears at first glance to be idleness is revealed, on closer examination, to be difficult and tiresome work."

THE WORKING-CLASS FAMILY   Hard work was, of course, standard fare for women in working-class families. Daughters in working-class families were expected to work until they married; even after marriage, they often did piecework at home to help support the family. For the children of the working classes, childhood was over by the age of nine or ten when they became apprentices or were employed in odd jobs.

Between 1890 and 1914, however, family patterns among the working class began to change. High-paying jobs in heavy industry and improvements in the standard of living made it possible for working-class families to depend on the income of husbands and the wages of grown children. By the early twentieth century, some working-class mothers could afford to stay at home, following the pattern of middle-class women. At the same time, new consumer products, such as sewing machines, clocks, bicycles, and cast-iron stoves, created a new mass consumer society whose focus was on higher levels of consumption.

These working-class families also followed the middle classes in limiting the size of their families. Children began to be viewed as dependents rather than wage earners as child labor laws and compulsory education took children out of the work force and into schools. Improvements in public health as well as advances in medicine and a better diet resulted in a decline in infant mortality rates for the lower classes, especially noticeable in the cities after 1890, and made it easier for working-class families to choose to have fewer children. At the same time, strikes and labor agitation (see Trade Unions later in the chapter) led to laws that reduced work hours to ten per day by 1900 and eliminated work on Saturday afternoons, which enabled working-class parents to devote more attention to their children and develop more emotional ties with them. Even working-class fathers became involved in their children's lives.

One observer in the French town of Belleville in the 1890s noted that "the workingman's love for his children borders on being an obsession."[6] Interest in educating children as a way to improve their future also grew.

The Rise of the Feminist Movement

Modern European feminism had its beginnings during the social upheaval of the French Revolution when some women advocated equality for women based on the doctrine of natural rights. Mary Wollstonecraft (1759–1797), who gave expression to this thinking in her book, *Vindication of the Rights of Woman*, is often viewed as the first modern feminist.

In the 1830s, a number of women in the United States and Europe, who worked together in several reform movements, became frustrated by the apparent prejudices against females. They sought improvements for women by focusing on specific goals. Family and marriage law were especially singled out since it was difficult for women to secure divorces and property laws gave husbands almost complete control over the property of their wives. These early efforts were not overly successful, however. For example, women did not gain the right to their own property until 1870 in Britain, 1900 in Germany, and 1907 in France.

Custody and property rights were only a beginning for the women's movement, however. Some middle- and upper-middle-class women gained access to higher education while others sought entry into occupations dominated by men. The first to fall was teaching. As medical training was largely closed to women, they sought alternatives in the development of nursing. A nursing pioneer in Germany was the upper-class spinster Amalie Sieveking (1794–1859), who founded the Female Association for the Care of the Poor and Sick in Hamburg. As she explained: "To me, at least as important were the benefits which [work with the poor] seemed to promise for those of my sisters who would join me in such a work of charity. The higher interests of my sex were close to my heart."[7] Sieveking's work was followed by the more famous British nurse, Florence Nightingale, whose efforts during the Crimean War (1854–1856), combined with those of Clara Barton in the American Civil War (1861–1865), transformed nursing into a profession of trained, middle-class "women in white."

By the 1840s and 1850s, the movement for women's rights had entered the political arena with the call for equal political rights. Many feminists believed that the right to vote was the key to all other reforms to improve

Advice to Women: Be Independent

▼ ▼ ▼

Although a majority of women probably followed the nineteenth-century middle-class ideal of women as keepers of the household and nurturers of husband and children, an increasing number of women fought for the rights of women. This selection is taken from Act III of Henrik Ibsen's A Doll's House *(1879), in which the character Nora Helmer declares her independence from her husband's control.*

Henrik Ibsen: *A Doll's House*

NORA: *(Pause)* Does anything strike you as we sit here?

HELMER: What should strike me?

NORA: We've been married eight years; does it not strike you that this is the first time we two, you and I, man and wife, have talked together seriously?

HELMER: Seriously? What do you mean, *seriously?*

NORA: For eight whole years, and more—ever since the day we first met—we have never exchanged one serious word about serious things. . . .

HELMER: Why, my dearest Nora, what have you to do with serious things?

NORA: There we have it! You have never understood me. I've had great injustice done to me, Torvald; first by father, then by you.

HELMER: What! Your father *and* me? We, who have loved you more than all the world?

NORA *(Shaking her head):* You have never loved me. You just found it amusing to think you were in love with me.

HELMER: Nora! What a thing to say!

NORA: Yes, it's true, Torvald. When I was living at home with father, he told me his opinions and mine were the same. If I had different opinions, I said nothing about them, because he would not have liked it. He used to call me his doll-child and played with me as I played with my dolls. Then I came to live in your house.

HELMER: What a way to speak of our marriage!

NORA *(Undisturbed):* I mean that I passed from father's hands into yours. You arranged everything to your taste and I got the same tastes as you; or pretended to—I don't know which—both, perhaps; sometimes one, sometimes the other. When I look back on it now, I seem to have been living here like a beggar, on hand-outs. I lived by performing tricks for you, Torvald. But that was how you wanted it. You and father have done me a great wrong. It is your fault that my life has come to naught.

HELMER: Why, Nora, how unreasonable and ungrateful! Haven't you been happy here?

NORA: No, never. I thought I was, but I never was.

HELMER: Not—not happy! . . .

NORA: I must stand quite alone if I am ever to know myself and my surroundings; so I cannot stay with you.

HELMER: Nora! Nora!

NORA: I am going at once. I daresay [my friend] Christina will take me in for tonight.

HELMER: You are mad! I shall not allow it! I forbid it!

NORA: It's no use your forbidding me anything now. I shall take with me only what belongs to me; from you I will accept nothing, either now or later.

HELMER: This is madness!

NORA: Tomorrow I shall go home—I mean to what was my home. It will be easier for me to find a job there.

HELMER: On, in your blind inexperience—

NORA: I must try to gain experience, Torvald.

HELMER: Forsake your home, your husband, your children! And you don't consider what the world will say.

NORA: I can't pay attention to that. I only know that I must do it.

HELMER: This is monstrous! Can you forsake your holiest duties?

NORA: What do you consider my holiest duties?

HELMER: Need I tell you that? Your duties to your husband and children.

NORA: I have other duties equally sacred.

HELMER: Impossible! What do you mean?

NORA: My duties toward myself.

HELMER: Before all else you are a wife and a mother.

NORA: That I no longer believe. Before all else I believe I am a human being just as much as you are—or at least that I should try to become one. I know that most people agree with you, Torvald, and that they say so in books. But I can no longer be satisfied with what most people say and what is in books. I must think things out for myself and try to get clear about them.

the position of women. This movement was strongest in Great Britain and the United States, both countries that had been influenced by the natural rights tradition of the Enlightenment. It was not as strong in Germany because of that country's authoritarian structure nor in France where feminists were unable to organize mass rallies in support of women's rights. Suffragists had one basic aim, the right of women to full citizenship in the nation-state (see the box on p. 830).

The British women's movement was the most vocal and active in Europe, but divided over tactics. The liberal Millicent Fawcett (1847–1929) organized a moderate group who believed that women must demonstrate that they would use political power responsibly if they wanted Parliament to grant them the right to vote. Another group, however, favored a more radical approach. Emmeline Pankhurst (1858–1928) and her daughters, Christabel and Sylvia, founded the Women's Social and Political Union in 1903, which enrolled mostly middle- and upper-class women. Pankhurst's organization realized the value of the media and used unusual publicity stunts to call attention to its demands. Derisively labeled suffragettes by male politicians, they pelted government officials with eggs, chained themselves to lampposts, smashed the windows of department stores on fashionable shopping streets, burned railroad cars, and went on hunger strikes in jail. In 1913, Emily Davison accepted martyrdom for the cause when she threw herself in front of the king's horse at the Epsom Derby horse race.

Before World War I, the demands for women's rights were being heard throughout Europe and the United States. Only in Norway and some American states did women actually receive the right to vote before 1914. It would take the dramatic upheaval of World War I before male-dominated governments capitulated on this basic issue (see Chapter 26).

▼ The Socialist Movement

A commonly heard phrase in the second half of the nineteenth century was the "social question," which referred to the debate over class relations and the condition of the poor. The most important response to this "social question" came from the socialist movement.

In 1872, Karl Marx and Friedrich Engels had allowed the International Working Men's Association or First International to wither away (see Chapter 23). A Second International was not formed until 1889, six years after Marx's death. By that time the workingmen's movement had undergone a significant growth and

▼ **The Arrest of Suffragettes.** The nineteenth century witnessed the development of a strong movement for women's rights. For many feminists, the right to vote came to represent the key to making other reforms that would benefit women. In Britain, so-called suffragettes attracted attention to their cause by unusual publicity stunts. This photograph shows the arrest of suffragettes after a demonstration near Buckingham Palace, the London residence of the royal family.

transformation with rise of socialist parties and trade unions, most of which were Marxist in orientation.

The Socialist Parties

The growth of socialist parties after the demise of the First International was rapid and widespread. Most important was the formation of a socialist party in Germany. Ferdinand Lassalle had founded a German Workingman's Association in 1863 that advocated the nonrevolutionary use of political action to make gains for the working classes. After his death, his followers joined with advocates of Marxism to form the German Social Democratic party (SPD) in 1875. Under the direction of its two Marxist leaders, Wilhelm Liebknecht and August Bebel, the SPD espoused revolutionary Marxist rhetoric while organizing itself as a mass political party competing in elections for the Reichstag. Once in the Reichstag, SPD delegates worked to achieve legislation to improve the condition of the working class. As August Bebel explained, "Pure negation would not be accepted by the voters. The masses demand that something should be done for today irrespective of what will happen on the morrow."[8] Despite government efforts to destroy it (see The New Germany later in the chapter), the German Social Democratic party continued to grow. In 1890, it received 1.5 million votes and thirty-five seats in the Reichstag. When it received 4

▼ **The Social Democratic Party in Germany.** The German Social Democratic party was formed in 1875. Although Social Democrats preached revolutionary Marxist rhetoric, they also organized themselves as a mass political organization and competed for seats in the Reichstag, the German parliament. Once in the Reichstag, Social Democrats introduced legislation to benefit the workers. Shown here is a session of the Social Democratic party in Berlin on November 14, 1892.

million votes in the 1912 elections, it became the largest single party in Germany, although it still refused for ideological reasons to participate in a coalition government.

Socialist parties emerged in other European states, although not with the kind of success achieved by the German Social Democrats. France had a variety of socialist parties, including a Marxist one. The leader of French socialism, Jean Jaurès, was an independent socialist who looked to the French revolutionary tradition rather than Marxism to justify revolutionary socialism. In 1905, the French socialist parties succeeded in unifying themselves into a single mostly Marxist-oriented socialist party. Social Democratic parties on the German model were founded in Belgium, Austria, Hungary, Bulgaria, Poland, Romania, and the Netherlands before 1900. A Marxist Social Democratic Labor party had also been organized in Russia by 1898.

As the socialist parties grew, agitation for an international organization that would strengthen their position against international capitalism also grew. In 1889, leaders of the various socialist parties formed the Second International. Significantly, while the First International had been formed by individuals and had been highly centralized, the Second International was created by representatives of national working-class parties and was organized as a loose association of national groups. It was not until 1900 that a permanent executive was established for the organization. While the Second Inter-

national took some coordinated actions—May Day (May 1), for example, was made an international labor day to be marked by strikes and mass labor demonstrations—differences often wreaked havoc at the congresses of the organization. Two issues proved particularly divisive: revisionism and nationalism.

Under the impact of government persecution, the ideology of the German Social Democratic party became increasingly revolutionary. In 1891, the Erfurt Program of the party had reaffirmed an almost pure Marxian platform that accepted the imminent collapse of capitalism and the need for socialist ownership of the means of production. The party's guiding light, August Bebel, confided to another socialist that "Every night I go to sleep with the thought that the last hour of bourgeois society strikes soon." In fact, already at Erfurt, Bebel had said, "I am convinced that the fulfillment of our aims is so close, that there are few in this hall who will not live to see the day."[9] But a severe challenge to this orthodox Marxist position arose in the form of revisionism.

Most prominent among the revisionists was Eduard Bernstein(1850–1932), a member of the German Social Democratic party who had spent years in exile in Britain where he had been influenced by moderate English socialism and the British parliamentary system. In 1899, Bernstein challenged Marxist orthodoxy with a book entitled *Evolutionary Socialism* in which he argued that some of Marx's ideas had turned out to be quite wrong (see the box on p. 833). The capitalist system had not broken down, nor, said Bernstein, did its collapse seem near. Contrary to Marx's assertion, the middle class was not declining but actually growing larger. At the same time, the proletariat was not sinking further down, but its lot was actually improving as workers experienced a higher standard of living. Due to this reality, Bernstein abandoned Marx's emphasis on the class struggle and revolution. The workers, he asserted, must continue to organize in mass political parties and even work together with the other progressive elements in a nation to gain reform. With the extension of the right to vote, workers were in a better position than ever to achieve their aims by democratic channels. Evolution by democratic means, not revolution, would achieve the desired goal of socialism. German and French socialist leaders, as well as the Second International, condemned revisionism as heresy and opportunism. But many socialist parties, including the German Social Democrats, while spouting revolutionary slogans, continued to practice Bernstein's revisionist, gradualist approach.

A second divisive issue for international socialism was nationalism. Karl Marx and Friedrich Engels had said

The Voice of Evolutionary Socialism: Eduard Bernstein

▼ ▼ ▼

The German Marxist Eduard Bernstein was regarded as the foremost late nineteenth-century theorist of Marxist revisionism. In his book, Evolutionary Socialism, *Bernstein argued that Marx had made some fundamental mistakes and that socialists needed to stress cooperation and evolution rather than class conflict and revolution.*

Eduard Bernstein, *Evolutionary Socialism*

It has been maintained in a certain quarter that the practical deductions from my treatises would be the abandonment of the conquest of political power by the proletariat organised politically and economically. That is quite an arbitrary deduction, the accuracy of which I altogether deny.

I set myself against the notion that we have to expect shortly a collapse of the bourgeois economy, and that social democracy should be induced by the prospect of such an imminent, great, social catastrophe to adapt its tactics to that assumption. That I maintain most emphatically.

The adherents of this theory of a catastrophe, base it especially on the conclusions of the *Communist Manifesto*. This is a mistake in every respect.

The theory which the *Communist Manifesto* sets forth of the evolution of modern society was correct as far as it characterised the general tendencies of that evolution. But it was mistaken in several special deductions, above all in the estimate of the time the evolution would take. . . . But it is evident that if social evolution takes a much greater period of time than was assumed, it must also take upon itself forms and lead to forms that were not foreseen and could not be foreseen then.

Social conditions have not developed to such an acute opposition of things and classes as is depicted in the *Manifesto*. It is not only useless, it is the greatest folly to attempt to conceal this from ourselves. The number of members of the possessing classes is to-day not smaller but larger. The enormous increase of social wealth is not accompanied by a decreasing number of large capitalists but by an increasing number of capitalists of all degrees. The middle classes change their character but they do not disappear from the social scale. . . .

In all advanced countries we see the privileges of the capitalist bourgeoisie yielding step by step to democratic organisations. Under the influence of this, and driven by the movement of the working classes which is daily becoming stronger, a social reaction has set in against the exploiting tendencies of capital, a counteraction which, although it still proceeds timidly and feebly, yet does exist, and is always drawing more departments of economic life under its influence. Factory legislation, the democratising of local government, and the extension of its area of work, the freeing of trade unions and systems of co-operative trading from legal restrictions, the consideration of standard conditions of labour in the work undertaken by public authorities—all these characterise this phase of the evolution.

But the more the political organisations of modern nations are democratised the more the needs and opportunities of great political catastrophes are diminished. . . . But is the conquest of political power by the proletariat simply to be by a political catastrophe? Is it to be the appropriation and utilisation of the power of the State by the proletariat exclusively against the whole non-proletarian world? . . .

No one has questioned the necessity for the working classes to gain the control of government. The point at issue is between the theory of a social cataclysm and the question whether, with the given social development in Germany and the present advanced state of its working classes in the towns and the country, a sudden catastrophe would be desirable in the interest of the social democracy. I have denied it and deny it again, because in my judgment a greater security for lasting success lies in a steady advance than in the possibilities offered by a catastrophic crash.

that "the working men have no country" and that "national differences and antagonisms between peoples are daily more and more vanishing, owing to the development of the bourgeoisie."[10] They proved drastically wrong. Congresses of the Second International passed resolutions in 1907 and 1910 advocating joint action by workers of different countries to avert war, but no real machinery was provided to implement them. In truth, socialist parties varied from country to country and remained tied to national concerns and issues. Socialist leaders always worried that in the end national loyalties might outweigh class loyalties among the masses. When World War I came in 1914, not only the working-class masses, but even many of their socialist party leaders, supported the war efforts of their national governments. Nationalism had proved a much more powerful force than socialism, an observation not lost on a young Austrian named Adolf Hitler who fought in World War I.

Trade Unions

Another force working for evolutionary rather than revolutionary socialism and at the same time an expression of a nationalistically oriented socialism was the development of trade unions. Trade unions were not new since they had a history dating back to the Late Middle Ages. The modern trade union, however, was a product of the Industrial Revolution. Initially, European governments tried to suppress the development of trade unions. The Le Chapelier Law in France in 1791 and the Combination Laws of 1799 and 1800 in Great Britain prohibited the formation of trade unions. But prohibitions seemed counterproductive, and European nations found themselves allowing workers to form trade unions while still seeking to prohibit them from such overt action as strikes.

In Great Britain trade unions were legalized with the repeal of the Combination Laws in 1824 and 1825, although the unions did not receive the right to strike. Failure to achieve national trade union organizations over the next two decades led to a reversion to the practice of forming trade unions for skilled workers in specialized crafts, such as the Amalgamated Society of Engineers, formed in 1850. These New Model unions, as they have been called, worked to better their members' wages and improve working conditions by peaceful negotiations with employers. Self-help, in the form of unemployment benefits collected from members' own contributions, was typical of their activity. They avoided political activity and strikes. But New Model unions,

mostly of "elite" skilled craftsmen, were of little help to the masses of unskilled and semiskilled workers in factory industries. Attempts to organize them did not come until the last two decades of the nineteenth century after unions had won the right to strike in the 1870s. Strikes proved necessary to achieve the goals of these workers. A walkout by female workers in the match industry in 1888 and dock workers in London the following year led to the establishment of trade union organizations for both groups. By 1900, there were two million workers in British trade unions, and by the outbreak of World War I, between three and four million workers, less than one-fifth of the total work force, were collectively organized.

Trade unions failed to develop as quickly on the Continent as they had in Britain. In France, the trade union movement was from the beginning closely tied to the socialist ideology. As there were a number of French socialist parties, the socialist trade unions remained badly splintered. Not until 1895 did French unions create a national organization called the General Confederation of Labor. Its decentralization and failure to include some of the more important individual unions, however, left it a weak and ineffective movement.

German trade unions, also closely attached to political parties, were first formed in the 1860s. Although there were liberal trade unions comprised of skilled craftsmen and Catholic or Christian trade unions, the largest German trade unions were those of the socialists. By 1899, even the latter had accepted the practice of collective bargaining with employers. As strikes and collective bargaining achieved successes, German workers were increasingly inclined to forgo revolution for gradual improvements. By 1914, its three million members made the German trade union movement the second largest in Europe after Great Britain's. Almost 85 percent of these three million belonged to socialist unions.

Trade unions in the rest of Europe had varying degrees of success. In the Low Countries, Switzerland, and Austria-Hungary, they followed the German model. Despite local successes, governments prevented them from operating well at a national level. Like the French, the Spanish and Italian trade unions tended toward ideology and divisiveness. Trade unions were prohibited in both Russia and eastern Europe until World War I. Perhaps most successful were the Scandinavian trade unions, which were closely allied with Social Democratic political parties. By the beginning of World War I, they had made considerable progress in bettering both the living and working conditions of the laboring classes.

Anarchism

Despite the revolutionary rhetoric, socialist parties and trade unions gradually became less radical in pursuing their goals. Indeed, this lack of revolutionary fervor drove some people from Marxian socialism into anarchism, a movement that was especially prominent in less industrialized and less democratic countries. The growth of universal male suffrage in Great Britain, France, and Germany had led workers there to believe that they could acquire tangible benefits by elections, not by revolution. These democratic channels were not open in other countries where revolutionary violence seemed the only alternative.

Initially, anarchism was not a violent movement. Early anarchists, such as Pierre-Joseph Proudhon, believed that people were inherently good but corrupted by the state and society. True freedom could only by accomplished by elimination of the state and all existing social institutions. Voluntary cooperation of people in small communities would eliminate the need for the state. Only then could people use their freedom to cooperate toward common ends.

In the second half of the nineteenth century, anarchists in Spain, Portugal, Italy, and Russia advocated radical means to accomplish this goal. The Russian Michael Bakunin, for example, believed that small groups of well-trained, fanatical revolutionaries could perpetrate so much violence that the state and all its institutions would disintegrate. To revolutionary anarchists, that would usher in the anarchist Golden Age. As one Russian anarchist wrote shortly before his execution:

> Slavery, poverty, weakness, and ignorance—the eternal fetters of man—will be broken. Man will be at the center of nature. The earth and its products will serve everyone dutifully. Weapons will cease to be a measure of strength and gold a measure of wealth; the strong will be those who are bold and daring in the conquest of nature, and riches will be the things that are useful. Such a world is called "Anarchy." It will have no castles, no place for masters and slaves. Life will be open to all. Everyone will take what he needs—this is the anarchist ideal. And when it comes about, men will live wisely and well. The masses must take part in the construction of this paradise on earth.[11]

After Bakunin's death in 1876, anarchist revolutionaries used assassinations as their primary instrument of terror. The list of victims of anarchist assassins at the turn of the century included a Russian tsar (1881), a president of the French Republic (1894), the king of Italy (1900), and a president of the United States (1901). Despite anarchist hopes, these states did not collapse.

▼ The National State: Domestic Politics

Throughout much of Europe by 1871, the national state had become the focus of people's loyalties and the arena for political activity. Only in Russia, eastern Europe, Austria-Hungary, and Ireland did national groups still struggle for independence and political unity. Within the major European states, domestic politics focused on five major themes: the achievement of liberal practices (constitutions, parliaments, and individual liberties); the growth of political democracy through universal male suffrage; the organization of mass political parties as a result of a widened electorate; the rise of socialist, working-class parties; and the enactment of social welfare measures to meet the demands of the working classes. These developments varied in expression from place to place. In general, western European states (France and Britain) and, to a lesser degree, Mediterranean states (Spain and Italy) had the greatest success with the growth of parliamentary governments. Central European states (Germany, Austria-Hungary) had the trappings of parliamentary government with their legislative bodies and elections by universal male suffrage, but authoritarian forces, especially powerful monarchies and conservative social groups, remained strong. In eastern Europe, especially Russia, the old system of autocracy was barely touched by the winds of change.

Great Britain

By the end of the first liberal ministry of William Gladstone in 1874, Great Britain had a functioning two-party parliamentary system. For fifty years the Liberals and Conservatives alternated in power at regular intervals. Liberals and Conservatives, however, shared one common feature. Both were dominated by a ruling class comprised of a coalition of aristocratic landowners frequently involved in industrial and financial activities and upper-middle-class businessmen. Three major developments preoccupied British domestic politics until 1914: the growth of political democracy; social welfare legislation for the workers; and the Irish question.

The cause of political democracy was pushed along by the expansion of suffrage. Much advanced by the Re-

▼ **William Gladstone in His Later Years.** The first Liberal ministry of William Gladstone had been responsible for a series of significant liberal reforms. During his second ministry, Gladstone and the Liberals expanded the right to vote by enfranchising agricultural workers. Gladstone had much less political success when he tried to solve the problem of Ireland.

form Act of 1867 (see Chapter 23), the right to vote was further extended during the second ministry of William Gladstone (1880–1885) with the passage of the Reform Act of 1884. It gave the vote to all men who paid regular rents or taxes, thus largely enfranchising the agricultural workers, a group previously excluded. The following year, a Redistribution Act (1885) eliminated historic boroughs and counties and established constituencies with approximately equal populations and one representative each.

Before World War I, the role of the House of Lords, composed of hereditary aristocrats, was also transformed. A Parliamentary Act in 1911 restricted the ability of the House of Lords to impede legislation enacted by the House of Commons. After 1911, the House of Lords became largely a debating society. Also in 1911, the payment of salaries to members of the House of Commons further democratized that institution by at least opening the door to people other than the wealthy. By the beginning of World War I, the British system of gradual reform through parliamentary institutions had become the way of British political life. Political democracy became well entrenched and was soon accompanied by social welfare measures for the working class.

Some social legislation had already been passed during the Conservative ministry of Benjamin Disraeli between 1874 and 1880. In 1875, trade unions had been given the right to strike, and a work week limited to fifty-six hours had been established for factory workers. But there was little other significant reform. While workers were enjoying better wages and living standards, those improvements were relative to the miseries of the first half of the nineteenth century. Considerable suffering still remained. Neither Liberals nor Conservatives were moved to accommodate the working class with significant social reforms until they were forced to do so by the pressure of two new working class organizations: trade unions and the Labor party.

Trade unions began to advocate more radical change of the economic system, calling for "collective ownership and control over production, distribution and exchange." At the same time, there was a movement for laborers among a group of intellectuals known as the Fabian Socialists, which included the playwright George Bernard Shaw, the novelist H. G. Wells, and the social reformers Beatrice and Sidney Webb. The program of the Fabians stressed the need for the workingman to use his right to vote to capture the House of Commons and pass legislation that would benefit the laboring class. Much of the socialism of the Fabians was to be applied at the local level, as in the creation of city-owned water works and power plants. Neither the Fabian socialists nor the British trade unions were Marxist oriented. They did not advocate class struggle and revolution but evolution by democratic means toward a socialist state. In 1900, representatives of the trade unions and Fabian Socialists coalesced to form the Labour party. Initially, they were not too successful, but by 1906 they had managed to elect twenty-nine members to the House of Commons.

The Liberals, who won control of the House of Commons in that year and held the government from 1906 to 1914, perceived that they would have to create a program of social welfare or lose the support of the workers. The policy of reform was especially advanced by David

A Parliamentary Debate on Old Age Pensions

▼ ▼ ▼

After the new British Labour party succeeded in electing twenty-nine of its candidates to the House of Commons in 1906, the ruling Liberals realized the need to provide a program of social legislation if they wished to keep working-class support. In 1908, they introduced a bill providing for old age pensions to be paid by the state to those seventy or older. These excerpts are taken from the parliamentary debate over the bill.

A Labour View on Old Age Pensions

After all, who are these old men and women? Let me appeal to the noble Lord the Member of Marylebone [Lord Robert Cecil]. They are the veterans of industry, people of almost endless toil, who have fought for and won the industrial and commercial supremacy of Great Britain. Is their lot and end to be the Bastille of the everlasting slur of pauperism? We claim these pensions as a right. Ruskin, I think, read you a little homily on the subject—"Even a laborer serves his country with his spade and shovel as the statesman does with his pen, or the soldier with his sword." He has a right to some consideration from the State. Here in a country rich beyond description there are people poverty-stricken beyond description. There can be no earthly excuse for the condition of things which exists in this country today. If it be necessary to have a strong Army and Navy to protect the wealth of the nation, do not let us forget that it is the veterans of industry who have created that wealth; and let us accept this as an installment to bring decency and comfort to our aged men and women.

A Bishop's View on the Subject

We are going forward tonight and saying: "Let us help them [those of seventy years of age], let us give to them something which will ease their later years, and if a few have not deserved well, we will at any rate with large-heartedness forget those who were weak and deal largely and generously with this matter before us, for all these men or women of seventy naturally appeal to the pity and sympathy of our hearts." But when I look beyond and ask whether it is conceivable that we may begin so to hold out the thought that men may be able to receive from the State that which in olden days they won by their own strong labors, self-denial, and thrift, then I am apprehensive lest we should, in attempting to do a good, do a great and grievous wrong, robbing ourselves and our children of that which is the best inheritance, the inheritance of a sturdy, strong, self-reliant manhood, that will take upon itself the responsibilities of life and be equal, therefore, to the responsibilities of Empire. I think none of us can shut our eyes to the fact that there are among us people who are very ready to shirk responsibility, and I, for one, would feel that the whole system and condition of English life had lost its meaning and value if once we should act in such fashion as to remove responsibility, and the sense of responsibility, from the people of this country. We are in this world for responsibility; through responsibility we grow and rise to the height of character which Divine Providence intended us to reach. Let us not, by any action of ours, weaken that which is the best thing we can preserve, the character of the population, for out of that, and out of that alone, will spring the strength and the stability of the nation.

Lloyd George (1863-1945), a brilliant young orator from Wales who had been deeply moved by the misery of Welsh coal miners. The Liberals abandoned the classical principles of laissez-faire and voted for a series of social reforms. The National Insurance Act of 1911 provided benefits for workers in case of sickness and unemployment, to be paid for by compulsory contributions from workers, employers, and the state. Additional legislation provided a small pension for those over seventy (see the box above) and compensation for those injured in accidents while at work. To pay for the new program, Lloyd George increased the tax burden on the wealthy classes. While the benefits of the program and tax increases were both modest, they were the first hesitant steps toward the future British welfare state.

A third problem—the Irish question—proved more difficult to solve. The Irish had long been subject to British rule. An Act of Union had brought the English

▼ **Revolutionary Violence in the Commune.** Defeat in war brought the collapse of Napoleon III's Second Empire in 1871. The authority of the newly-created National Assembly was soon challenged by the Commune, an independent republican government in Paris. The attempt by the National Assembly to crush the Commune led to vicious fighting and brutal reprisals. This photograph shows the execution of 62 hostages by the forces of the Commune.

and Irish parliaments together in 1801, while largely Catholic Ireland had its own official Protestant church—the Church of Ireland. Irish discontent was intense in the nineteenth century. Like other unfree ethnic groups in Europe, the Irish developed a sense of national self-consciousness. They detested the Protestant establishment and the absentee British landlords and their burdensome rents.

William Gladstone was the first British politician to attempt to alleviate Irish discontent. In 1869, Parliament ended the domination of the Church of Ireland by eliminating its official church status and stripping it of half of its property. The Land Law of 1870 accomplished little, however, and as evictions of Irish tenants increased in the 1870s, the Irish peasants responded with terrorist acts. The government reacted in turn with more coercion. In 1881, when Gladstone pushed a Land Act through Parliament that met most of the Irish demands, it was already too late. By this time Irish Catholics wanted only independence. Although Liberals introduced home rule bills that would have given Ireland self-government in 1886 and 1893, they failed to win a majority vote. Only after the Irish representatives in Parliament supported the Liberal reforms against the House of Lords did the Liberals finally enact a Home Rule Act in 1914. But an explosive situation in Ireland itself created more problems. Irish Protestants in northern Ireland, especially in the province of Ulster, wanted no part of an Irish Catholic state. The outbreak of World War I enabled the government to sidestep the poten-

tially explosive issue and to suspend Irish home rule for the duration of the war. Failure to deal decisively with the issue simply led to more problems later.

Between 1815 and 1914, Britain made the shift from classical liberalism to political democracy. The transition was not as smooth as has sometimes been claimed, however. The Irish question, for example, resulted in considerable violence on both sides. The growth of parliamentary democracy also served to make increasing numbers of British aware of the gross financial and social inequalities existing in their country. Especially among the working classes, this awareness led to more determined and even violent action in the form of direct action or strikes in 1911 and 1912. Serious tensions remained in the British system, and World War I would make them all the more obvious.

France

The defeat of the French armies and the capture of Napoleon III at Sedan on September 2–3, 1870, brought the downfall of the Second Empire. Republicans established a provisional government and continued the war with Germany but were forced to surrender by January 28, 1871. Wanting to make peace only with a properly constituted government, the victorious Otto von Bismarck insisted that the French establish a government chosen by universal male suffrage. The French people rejected the republicans who wanted to renew the war and overwhelmingly favored the monarchists who won 400 of the 630 seats in the new National Assembly.

After the National Assembly decided to establish itself at Versailles, radical republicans in Paris, feeling betrayed by the conservative National Assembly, created an independent republican government in Paris known as the Commune on March 26 (see the box on p. 839). Although Karl Marx in London proclaimed the Commune's action as the beginning of the proletarian socialist revolution, the radical lower-middle-class and working-class supporters of the Commune were inspired more by the revolutionary ideals of 1789 and 1848 than by Marxist theory. The National Assembly determined to crush the revolutionary Commune. Vicious fighting in April and May finally ended in a government victory when government troops in the last week of May massacred thousands of the Commune's defenders. Estimates are that 20,000 were shot; another 10,000 were shipped overseas to the French penal colony of New Caledonia. The horrors of the suppression of the Commune left a legacy of hatred that continued to plague French politics

Parisian Violence
▼▼▼

In March 1871, an insurrection erupted in Paris when the National Assembly attempted to disarm the Parisian National Guard. When troops were sent to seize guns that had been moved earlier to the hills of Montmartre, fighting broke out. Georges Clemenceau, the mayor of Montmartre, wrote a description of the day's events. Two generals had been taken prisoner by the National Guard and shot before Clemenceau could arrive to prevent it. This excerpt describes what happened next. Eight days after the events described here, the Parisians established the Commune.

Georges Clemenceau, How the Uprising Began, March 18, 1871

We had hardly turned the corner of the wall when a man ran up and said that the Generals had just been shot. We did not stop to answer him but ran even faster. He did not seem very sure of his facts, anyhow, and seemed to be repeating a rumor rather than something he had seen for himself.

The *Buttes* [hills of Montmartre] were covered with armed National Guards. We made our way into this crowd. My sash called everybody's attention to me, and I at once became the object of the most hostile demonstrations. They reproached me for having conspired with the Government to have the guns taken away, they accused me of betraying the National Guard, they insulted me.

Keeping between Mayer and Sabourdy, who were both fairly well-known in the *arrondissement* [district] and were my only safeguard, I continued on my way without answering.

As we went on, I heard people saying, "It's all over! Justice has been done! The traitors are punished! If anybody doesn't like it, we'll do the same to him! It's too late!" . . . It was no longer possible to doubt the assassination of the Generals, for everyone was repeating the news with somber enthusiasm. . . .

Suddenly there was a great noise, and the mob which filled the courtyard of no. 6 burst into the street, in the grip of a kind of frenzy.

There were chasseurs, soldiers of the line, National Guards, women and children. They were all shrieking like wild beasts, without realizing what they were doing. I observed then that pathological phenomenon which could be called blood lust. A breath of madness seemed to have passed over this mob. From the top of a wall children were waving indescribable trophies, women with streaming hair and all disheveled twisted their bare arms and uttered raucous cries, bereft of any sense. I saw some of them weeping and shouting louder than the others. Men were dancing about and jostling one another in a kind of frenzied fury. It was one of those nervous phenomena so frequent in the Middle Ages, and occasionally occurring still among masses of human beings under the stress of some powerful emotion.

Suddenly a piece of artillery, drawn by four horses, arrived in front of the house. The confusion increased, if that was possible. Men clad in ill-matched uniforms, riding on the horses, swore and shouted. I saw one woman jump onto one of the horses. She was waving her bonnet and yelling, "Down with the traitors!"—a cry the crowd repeated and repeated.

The situation was becoming more and more dangerous for me. The mob looked at me in crazed defiance, shouting its cry of "Down with the traitors!" Several fists were raised.

I could do nothing more in this place. I had not been able to prevent the crime. It remained for me to look after the fate of the prisoners whom I had just seen go by, and to stop any misfortune befalling my prisoners at the Mairie, against whom there was very great hostility.

---

for decades. The split between the middle and working classes, begun in the revolutionary hostilities of 1848–1849, had widened immensely.

Although a majority of the members of the monarchist-dominated National Assembly wished to restore a monarchy to France, inability to agree on who should be king caused the monarchists to miss their opportunity and led to a improvised constitution in 1875 that established a republican form of government as the least divisive compromise. This constitution established a bicameral legislature with an upper house or Senate elected indirectly and a lower house or Chamber of Deputies chosen by universal male suffrage. The powers of the president, chosen by the legislature for seven years as executive of the government, were not completely defined as many expected that his place would soon be taken by a king. But the Constitution of 1875, intended only as a stopgap measure, solidified the republic—the Third Republic—that lasted sixty-five years. New elections in 1876 and 1877 strengthened the hands of the republicans who managed by 1879 to create ministerial responsibility and establish the power of the Chamber of Deputies. The prime minister or premier and his ministers were now responsible not to the president, but to the Chamber of Deputies. France failed, however, to develop a strong parliamentary system on the British model because the existence of a dozen political parties forced a premier to depend upon a coalition of parties to stay in power. The Third Republic was notorious for its changes of government. Between 1875 and 1914, there were no fewer than fifty cabinet changes; during the same period, the British had nine. But figures can be misleading. Despite the numerous changes, the same politicians tended to appear in almost every cabinet. Moreover, since France was by and large a nation of small businessmen and farmers, the numerous political parties appealed to similar constituencies and reflected only minor differences.

Nevertheless, the position of the Third Republic remained precarious after 1875 because monarchists, Catholic clergy, and professional army officers remained its enemies. The government's moderation gradually encouraged more and more middle-class and peasant support. This did not prevent two major crises for the republic in the 1880s and 1890s.

The first of these crises actually served to strengthen the republican government. General Georges Boulanger (1837–1891) was a popular military officer who attracted the public attention of all those discontented with the Third Republic: the monarchists, Bonapartists, aristocrats, and nationalists who favored a war of revenge against Germany. Boulanger appeared as the strong man on horseback, the savior of France. By 1889, just when his strength had grown to the point where many expected a coup d'etat, he lost his nerve and fled France, a completely discredited man. In the long run, the Boulanger crisis served to rally support for the resilient republic.

Perhaps the strongest indication of the fragile nature of the democratic structure of France and an expression of a renewed anti-Semitism in the late nineteenth century was the Dreyfus affair. Alfred Dreyfus, a Jew, was a captain in the French general staff, who was found guilty by a secret military court early in 1895 of selling army secrets and condemned to life imprisonment on Devil's Island. Evidence soon emerged that pointed to his innocence. Another officer, a Catholic aristocrat, was more obviously the traitor, but the army, a stronghold of aristocratic and Catholic officers, refused a new trial. Republican leaders insisted, however, after a wave of immense public outrage. Although the new trial failed to set aside the guilty verdict, the government pardoned Dreyfus in 1899, and in 1906, he was finally fully exonerated.

One result of his whole sorry affair was a change in government. Moderate republicans lost control of the government to radical republicans who were determined to make greater progress toward a more democratic society by breaking the power of the republic's enemies, especially the army and the Catholic church. The army was purged of all high-ranking officers who had anti-republican reputations while a civilian official, the minister for war, was now placed in charge of all promotions to the rank of general. Most of the Catholic religious orders that had controlled many French schools were forced to leave France. Moreover, church and state were officially separated in 1905.

These changes ended the political threat from the right to the Third Republic, which by now commanded the loyalty of most French people. Nevertheless, problems remained. As a nation of small businessmen and farmers, the French fell far behind Great Britain, Germany, and the United States in industrial activity. Moreover, a surge of industrialization after 1896 left the nation with the realization that little had been done to appease the discontent of the French working classes who were suffering from abysmal working conditions. Since only a quarter of the French wage earners worked in industry, there was little pressure for labor legislation from the French parliament. This made the use of strikes more appealing to the working classes. The brutal government repression of labor walkouts in 1911 only further alienated the working classes.

The Mediterranean Powers: Spain and Italy

Both Italy and Spain possessed trappings of constitutional government similar to those of Britain and France, but there were significant differences. In Spain and Italy, the kings could still exercise some power as a result of their control of the army led by conservative generals loyal to the monarch. Although both possessed parliaments, a relatively small conservative social group controlled each country because the middle classes remained relatively small. While each country possessed some industrialized areas, both were still largely agricultural. Workers in both countries were poorly treated, and their desire for change led them to radical movements that were not opposed to the use of violence.

SPAIN Between the 1850s and 1875, Spain had experienced considerable instability as governments proved unable to meet the demands of the most influential groups: the army, the Catholic church, big business, and regional interests. In 1875, a new constitution under King Alfonso XII (1874–1885) established a parliamentary government dominated by two political groups, the Conservatives and Liberals, whose members stemmed from the same small social group of great landowners allied with a few wealthy industrialists. Because suffrage was limited to the propertied classes, Liberals and Conservatives alternated in power but followed basically the same conservative policies.

Spain's defeat in the Spanish-American War in 1898 and the loss of Cuba and the Philippines to the United States increased the discontent with the status quo, which was manifested in a call for political and social reforms from a group of young intellectuals known as the Generation of 1898. In response, both Liberals and Conservatives attempted to enlarge the electorate and win over the masses in support of their policies. Attempted reforms, however, did little to allay the unrest while the growth of industrialization in some areas resulted in more workers being attracted to the radical solutions of socialism and anarchism. Violence erupted in July 1909, when the masses in Barcelona seized the city, destroyed churches and convents, and were then in turn brutally suppressed by military forces. "The army," one astute Spanish politician had said, "will remain for long, perhaps forever, the robust supporter of the social order, and an invincible dyke against the illegal attempts of the proletariat, which will accomplish nothing by violence but the useless shedding of its own blood."[12] The revolt and its repression revealed the strong strain of violence underlying Spanish political life. It also made clear that it was not easy to reform Spain because the Catholic church, large landowners, and the army remained tied to a conservative social order. Dictatorship or revolution seemed the only alternatives available to Spain on the eve of the First World War.

THE NEW ITALIAN STATE Italy had emerged by 1870 as a geographically united state with pretensions to great power status. Its internal weaknesses, however, gave that claim a particularly hollow ring. Newly unified, it had little tradition of centralized government; local loyalties and rivalries remained paramount to most Italians.

Italy suffered a lack of a sense of community due to sectional differences. The south was a conspicuously poverty-stricken area populated by large landowners and an immense number of landless peasants who looked upon the northern Italians as foreigners. In great contrast, the north was becoming industrialized and modern. The attitude of the Catholic church also divided the new nation. Pope Pius IX (1846–1878) refused to accept the loss of his temporal power and declared himself a prisoner in the Vatican. Catholics, who made up most of the population, were forbidden to vote in national elections or participate in the new government. Although ignored by many Italians, the opposition of the Catholic church was an ongoing source of embarrassment to the new government.

Economically, Italy had severe problems as well. Lack of natural resources and a highly illiterate population hindered economic development in most parts of the country. There was, however, considerable industrial growth in the north where hydroelectricity could be used to power electrical, textile, and chemical industries. Between 1896 and 1914, northern Italy experienced rapid industrialization. The growth of industry, in turn, gave rise to a labor movement and the formation of the Italian Socialist party in 1892. Chronic turmoil plagued the relationship between industry and labor. Workers tended to identify with the politics of violence and revolution, while industrialists and landowners favored repressive reaction.

Perhaps all of these problems might have been dealt with more easily if Italy had had a strong national government, but that was not the case. United Italy began as a liberal constitutional monarchy with a Chamber of Deputies elected by a restricted suffrage. Universal male suffrage was granted in 1912. But the ability of the government to function well was weakened by the practice known as *trasformismo* or transformism. This was a system in which old political groups were transformed into new government coalitions by political and economic bribery. The system led to extensive corruption and weak government since it militated against any kind of party coherence and organization. A certain amount of stability was achieved, however, from 1903 to 1914 when Giovanni Giolitti served intermittently as prime minister and emerged as the dominant political figure. His devious means, however, served in the long run to make Italian politics even more corrupt.

Italy also had a problem of imperialistic pretensions. To preserve its status as a great power, it maintained a large army and navy, which it could not really afford, to pursue imperialistic goals. In 1896 Italy became the first European power to lose to an African state, Ethiopia, a disgrace that led later to the costly (but successful) attempt to compensate by conquering Libya in 1911 and 1912.

The New Germany

Despite unification, important divisions remained in German society that could not simply be papered over by the force of nationalism. These divisions were already evident in the new German constitution that provided for a federal system with a bicameral legislature. The Bundesrat or upper house represented the twenty-five states that made up Germany. Individual states, such as Bavaria and Prussia, kept their own kings, their own post offices, and even their own armies in peacetime. The lower house of the German parliament, known as the Reichstag, was elected on the basis of universal male suffrage, but it did not have ministerial responsibility. Ministers of government, the most important of which was the chancellor, were responsible not to the parliament, but to the emperor. The emperor also commanded the armed forces and controlled foreign policy and internal administration. While the creation of a parliament elected by universal male suffrage presented opportunities for the growth of a real political democracy, it failed to develop in Germany before World War I. The army and Bismarck were two major reasons why it did not.

The German (largely Prussian) army viewed itself as the defender of monarchy and aristocracy and sought to escape any control by the Reichstag by operating under a general staff responsible only to the emperor. Prussian military tradition was strong, and military officers took steps to ensure the loyalty of their subordinates to the emperor. While that was easy as long as Junker landowners were officers, the growth of the army made it necessary to turn to the middle class for officers. But extreme care was taken to choose only sons "of honorable bourgeois families in whom the love for King and Fatherland, a warm heart for the soldier's calling, and Christian morality are planted and nurtured."

The policies of Bismarck, who served as chancellor of the new German state until 1890, often served to prevent the growth of more democratic institutions. Although the lack of ministerial responsibility in the constitution meant that Bismarck was not required to achieve a parliamentary majority, he thought it necessary to do so, especially since a Reichstag majority was

necessary for military appropriations bills. Initially, until 1878, Bismarck found this majority by working with the National Liberals, whose admiration for the revered hero of German unification made them willing to work with Bismarck, especially to achieve greater centralization of Germany through common codes of criminal and commercial law. The National Liberals also joined Bismarck in his attack on the Catholic church, the so-called *Kulturkampf* or "struggle for civilization." Like Bismarck, middle-class liberals distrusted Catholic loyalty to the new Germany, especially when the Center party, organized by Catholics in 1870, voted against legislation it considered harmful to the church's interests. Bismarck's strong-arm tactics against Catholic clergy and Catholic institutions proved counterproductive, however, and Bismarck welcomed an opportunity in 1878 to abandon the attack on Catholicism by making an abrupt shift in policy.

In 1878, Bismarck decided to abandon his coalition with the National Liberals and ally himself with the Catholic Center party, the Conservatives (largely the party of the Prussian landowners), and the right wing of the National Liberals. Three factors explain this shift. First, Bismarck realized the failure of *Kulturkampf* and no longer wished to continue a losing cause. Second, Bismarck, contrary to liberal wishes, abandoned free trade and came to support a policy of protective tariffs favored by both the Prussian landowners and upper-middle-class industrialists. The landowners wished to protect their production against the cheap grain being imported from America and Russia while the economic depression that began in 1873 had persuaded German industrialists that British manufactured goods should be kept out by high tariffs. Bismarck's tariff policy received the support of the Catholic Center party, the Conservatives, because they were the party of the landowners, and the right wing of the National Liberals, who were upper-middle-class businessmen.

Bismarck's third reason for abandoning his alliance with the National Liberals stemmed from his desire to persecute the socialists. When the Social Democratic party elected twelve deputies in 1877, Bismarck grew alarmed. He genuinely believed that the socialists' antinationalistic, anticapitalistic, and antimonarchical stance represented a danger to the empire. In 1878, Bismarck got parliament to pass a stringent antisocialist law that outlawed the Social Democratic party and limited socialist meetings and publications, although socialist candidates were still permitted to run for the Reichstag. In addition to repressive measures, Bismarck also attempted to woo workers away from socialism by enacting social welfare legislation. Between 1883 and 1889, the Reichstag passed laws that created sickness, accident, and disability benefits as well as old age pensions paid for by compulsory contributions from workers, employers, and the state. Bismarck's social security system was the most progressive the world had yet seen, although even his system left much to be desired as the Social Democrats pointed out. A full pension, for example, was payable only at age seventy after forty-eight years of contributions. In the event of a male worker's death, no benefits were paid to his widow or children.

Both the repressive and social welfare measures failed to stop the growth of socialism, however. The Social Democratic party continued to grow. In his frustration, Bismarck planned yet more repressive measures in 1890, but before he could carry them out, the new emperor, William II (1888–1918), eager to pursue his own policies, cashiered the aged chancellor.

THE GERMAN EMPIRE UNDER WILLIAM II   The new imperial Germany begun by Bismarck in 1871 continued as an "authoritarian, conservative, military-bureaucratic power state" during the reign of Emperor William II (1888–1918). Unstable and aggressive, the emperor was inclined to tactless remarks, as when he told the soldiers of a Berlin regiment that they must be prepared to shoot their fathers and mothers if he ordered them to do so. A small group of about twenty powerful men joined William in setting government policy.

By 1914, Germany had become the strongest military and industrial power on the Continent. New social configurations had emerged as over 50 percent of German workers had jobs in industry while only 30 percent of the work force was still in agriculture. Urban centers had mushroomed in number and size. The rapid changes in Wilhelmine Germany helped to produce a society torn between modernization and traditionalism.

The growth of industrialization led to even greater expansion for the Social Democratic party. Despite the enactment of new welfare legislation to favor the working classes, William II was no more successful than Bismarck in slowing the growth of the Social Democrats. By 1912, it had become the largest single party in the Reichstag. At the same time, the party increasingly became less revolutionary and more revisionist in its outlook. Nevertheless, its growth frightened the middle and upper classes who blamed labor for their own problems.

With the expansion of industry and cities came demands for more political participation and growing sentiment for reforms that would produce greater democratization. Conservative forces, especially the landowning nobility and representatives of heavy industry, two of the powerful ruling groups in Wilhelmine Germany, tried to block it by supporting William II's activist foreign policy of finding Germany's "place in the sun." Expansionism would divert people from further democratization.

The tensions in German society created by the conflict between modernization and traditionalism were also manifested in a new, radicalized, right-wing politics. A number of nationalist pressure groups arose to support nationalistic goals. Antisocialist and antiliberal, such groups as the Pan-German League stressed strong German nationalism and advocated imperialism as a tool to overcome social divisions and unite all classes. They were also anti-Semitic and denounced Jews as the destroyers of the national community. Traditional conservatives, frightened by the growth of the socialists, often made common cause with these radical right-wing groups, giving them respectability. After Germany's defeat in World War I, Nazism would emerge out of this radical right-wing politics (see Chapter 27).

Austria-Hungary

After the creation of the dual monarchy of Austria-Hungary in 1867, the Austrian part received a constitution that theoretically recognized the equality of the nationalities and established a parliamentary system with the principle of ministerial responsibility. In truth, although ethnic Germans made up only one-third of Austria's population, they dominated the parliament. Moreover, the Emperor Francis Joseph (1848–1916) largely ignored ministerial responsibility by personally appointing and dismissing his ministers and ruling by decree when parliament was not in session.

The problem of the various nationalities remained a difficult one. The German minority that governed Austria felt increasingly threatened by the Czechs, Poles, and other Slavic groups within the empire. The difficulties in dealing with this problem were especially evident from 1879 to 1893 when Count Edward von Taaffe served as prime minister. Taaffe attempted to "muddle through" by relying on a coalition of German conservatives, Czechs, and Poles to maintain a majority in parliament. But his concessions to national minorities, such as allowing the Slavic languages as well as German to be used in education and administration, served to antagonize the German-speaking Austrian bureaucracy and aristocracy, two of the basic pillars of the empire. Opposition to Taaffe's policies brought his downfall in 1893, but no solution to the nationalities problem. While the dissatisfied non-German groups demanded concessions, the ruling Austrian Germans resisted change. The granting of universal male suffrage in 1907 served only to exacerbate the problem when nationalities that had played no role in the government now agitated in the parliament for autonomy. This led prime ministers after 1900 to ignore the parliament and rely increasingly on imperial emergency decrees to govern.

The threat the nationalities posed to the position of the dominant German minority in Austria also produced a backlash in the form of virulent German nationalism. As Austria industrialized in the 1870s and 1880s, two working-class parties came into existence, and both were strongly influenced by nationalism. The Social Democrats, although a Marxist party, supported the Austrian government, fearful that the autonomy of the different nationalities would hinder industrial development and prevent improvements for workers. Even more nationalistic, however, were the Christian Socialists.

The Christian Socialists combined agitation for workers with a virulent anti-Semitism. They were most powerful in Vienna where they were led by Karl Lueger, mayor of Vienna from 1897 to 1910. Imperial Vienna at the turn of the century was a brilliant center of European culture, but it was also the home of an insidious German nationalism that blamed Jews for the corruption of German culture. It was in Vienna from 1907 to 1913 that Adolf Hitler later claimed to have found his worldview, one that was largely based on a violent German nationalism and a rabid anti-Semitism.

Unlike Austria, Hungary had a working parliamentary system, but one controlled by the great Magyar landowners who dominated both the Hungarian peasantry and the other ethnic groups in Hungary. The Hungarians attempted to solve their nationalities problem by systematic Magyarization. The Magyar language was imposed upon all schools and was the only language that could be used by government and military officials.

While subjugating their nationalities, the ruling Magyars developed a movement for complete separation from Austria. When they demanded in 1903 that the Hungarian army be separated from the imperial army, Emperor Francis Joseph (as king of Hungary) responded quickly and forcefully. He threatened to impose universal male suffrage upon Hungary, a move that would challenge Magyar domination of the minorities. Hungarian leaders fell into line, and the new Hungarian parliamentary leader, Count Istvàn Tisza, cooperated in maintaining the dual monarchy. Magyar rule in Hungary, he realized, was inextricably bound up with the Dual Empire; its death would only harm the rule of the Magyar landowning class.

On the eve of World War I, the Austro-Hungarian Empire was as far away as ever from solving its minorities problem. Some imperial leaders even came to believe that only a policy of expansion could unify the nationalities and save the empire. World War I would prove what an illogical and fundamentally stupid idea that was.

Imperial Russia

The assassination of Alexander II in 1881 convinced his son and successor, Alexander III (1881–1894), that reform had been a mistake, and he quickly instituted what he said were "exceptional measures." The powers of the secret police were expanded. Advocates of constitutional monarchy and social reform, along with revolutionary groups, were persecuted. Entire districts of Russia were placed under martial law if the government suspected the inhabitants of treason. The powers of the zemstvos, created by the reforms of Alexander II, were sharply curtailed. When Alexander III died, his weak son and successor, Nicholas II (1894–1917), began his rule with his father's conviction that the absolute power of the tsars should be preserved: "I shall maintain the principle of autocracy just as firmly and unflinchingly as did my unforgettable father."[13] But conditions were changing, especially with the growth of industrialization, and the tsar's approach was not realistic in view of the new circumstances he faced.

THE DRIVE TO INDUSTRIALIZATION Industrialization came late to Russia. It was realized after the fiasco of the Crimean War that Russia could not remain a great power without industrial development. Although it had the natural resources for industry—especially coal, iron, and oil—Russia did not have a very large middle class to provide the necessary capital and skills. Consequently, Russia came to depend on foreign capital for its industrial development. By 1900, over 50 percent of the capital in Russian industrial firms had come from abroad; in mining, 90 percent. The state led the way in subsidizing railway companies to build railroads, an absolute necessity if Russia were to grow industrially. In 1860, 1,250 miles of railroad track had been laid; by 1880, there were 15,500 miles.

Russia's initial industrialization was slowed by economic depression in the 1880s, but another massive surge of industrialism began in the 1890s under the guiding hand of Sergei Witte, the minister for finance from 1892 to 1903. A disciple of the economic nationalist Friedrich List (see Chapter 21), Count Witte saw industrial growth as crucial to Russia's national strength. Believing that railroads were a very powerful weapon in economic development, Witte pushed the government toward a program of massive railroad construction. By 1900, 35,000 miles of railroads, including the 5,000-mile trans-Siberian line between Moscow and Vladivostok on the Pacific Ocean, had been built. As a follower of List, Witte also encouraged a system of protective tariffs to help Russian industry and persuaded the tsar that foreign capital was the only way Russian industrial development could quickly advance. Witte's program made possible the rapid growth of a modern steel and coal industry in the Ukraine, making Russia by 1900, the fourth largest producer of steel behind the United States, Germany, and Great Britain. At the same time, Russia was turning out half of the world's production of oil.

With industrialization came factories, an industrial working class, industrial suburbs around St. Petersburg and Moscow, and the pitiful working and living conditions that were common to the beginnings of industrialization everywhere. Socialist thought and socialist parties were developed, although repression in Russia soon forced them to go underground and become revolutionary. The Marxist Social Democratic party, for example, held its first congress in Minsk in 1898, but the arrest of its leaders caused the next one to be held in Brussels in 1903, attended by Russian emigres. The Social Revolutionaries worked to overthrow the tsarist autocracy and establish peasant socialism. Having no other outlet for opposition to the regime, they advocated political terrorism, attempting to assassinate government officials and members of the ruling dynasty. The growing opposition to the tsarist regime finally exploded into revolution in 1905.

THE REVOLUTION OF 1905   As elsewhere in Europe in the nineteenth century, defeat in war led to political upheaval at home. Like other European powers, Russia pursued imperialistic policies in the late nineteenth century, which led to territorial expansion to the south and east. In the east, Russian designs on northern Korea were countered by Japanese ambitions. Japan made a surprise attack on the Russian Far Eastern fleet at Port Arthur on February 8, 1904. Much to the astonishment of many Europeans who could not believe that an Asian state was militarily superior to a great European power, the Russians were defeated and sued for peace in 1905.

In the midst of the war, the growing discontent of increased numbers of Russians rapidly led to upheaval. A middle class of business and professional people longed

▼ **"Bloody Sunday."** After the defeat of Russia by Japan in 1905, the growing discontent of many Russians led to demonstrations against the tsarist regime. When a peaceful procession of workers outside the Winter Palace in St. Petersburg was fired upon by tsarist troops, a revolution broke out.

for liberal institutions and a liberal political system. Nationalities were dissatisfied with their domination by an ethnic Russian population that constituted only 45 percent of the empire's total population. Peasants were still suffering from lack of land, and laborers felt oppressed by their working and living conditions in Russia's large cities. The breakdown of the transport system caused by the Russo-Japanese War led to food shortages in the major cities of Russia. As a result, on January 9, 1905, a massive procession of workers went to the Winter Palace in St. Petersburg to present a petition of grievances to the tsar (see the box on p. 846). Troops foolishly opened fire on the peaceful demonstration, killing hundreds and launching a revolution. This "Bloody Sunday" incited workers to call strikes and form unions while zemstvos demanded the formation of parliamentary government, ethnic groups revolted, and peasants burned the houses of landowners. After a general strike in October 1905, the government capitulated. Count Witte had advised the tsar to divide his opponents: "It is not on the extremists that the existence and integrity of the state depend. As long as the government has support in the broad strata of society, a peaceful solution to the crisis is still possible."[14] Nicholas II issued the October Manifesto, in which he granted civil liberties and agreed to create a Duma or legislative assembly elected directly by a broad franchise. This satisfied the middle-class moderates who now supported the government's repression of a workers' uprising in Moscow at the end of 1905.

But real constitutional monarchy proved short-lived. Under Peter Stolypin, who served as the tsar's chief ad-

Russian Workers Appeal to the Tsar
▼ ▼ ▼

On January 9, 1905, a massive procession of workers led by an Orthodox priest loyal to the tsar, Father George Gapon, carried a petition to present to the tsar at his imperial palace in St. Petersburg. Although the tsar was not even there, government officials ordered troops to fire on the crowd. "Bloody Sunday," as it was called, precipitated the Revolution of 1905. This selection is an excerpt from the petition that was never presented.

George Gapon and Ivan Vasimov, Petition to the Tsar

Sovereign!

We, the workers and the inhabitants of various social strata of the city of St. Petersburg, our wives, children, and helpless old parents, have come to you, Sovereign, to seek justice and protection. We are impoverished; our employers oppress us, overburden us with work, insult us, consider us inhuman, and treat us as slaves who must suffer a bitter fate in silence. Though we have suffered, they push us deeper and deeper into a gulf of misery, disfranchisement, and ignorance. Despotism and arbitrariness strangle us and we are gasping for breath. Sovereign, we have no strength left. We have reached the limit of endurance. We have reached that terrible moment when death is preferable to the continuance of unbearable sufferings.

And so we left our work and informed our employers that we shall not resume work until they meet our demands. We do not demand much; we only want what is indispensable to life and without which life is nothing but hard labor and eternal suffering. Our first request was that our employers discuss our needs jointly with us. But they refused to do this; they even denied us the right to speak about our needs, saying that the law does not give us such a right. Also unlawful were our requests to reduce the working day to eight hours, to set wages jointly with us; to examine our disputes with lower echelons of factory administration; to increase the wages of unskilled workers and women to one ruble [about $1.00] per day; to abolish overtime work; to provide medical care without insult. . . .

Sovereign, there are thousands of us here; outwardly we resemble human beings, but in reality neither we nor the Russian people as a whole enjoy any human right, have any right to speak, to think, to assemble, to discuss our needs, or to take measures to improve our conditions. They have enslaved us and they did it under the protection of your officials, with their aid and with their cooperation. They imprison and send into exile any one of us who has the courage to speak on behalf of the interests of the working class and of the people. . . . All the workers and the peasants are at the mercy of bureaucratic administrators consisting of embezzlers of public funds and thieves who not only disregard the interests of the people but also scorn these interests. . . . The people are deprived of the opportunity to express their wishes and their demands and to participate in determining taxes and expenditures. The workers are deprived of the opportunity to organize themselves in unions to protect their interests.

Sovereign! Is all this compatible with God's laws, by the grace of which you reign? And is it possible to live under such laws? Wouldn't it be better for all of us if we, the toiling people of all Russia, died? . . . Sovereign, these are the problems that we face and these are the reasons that we have gathered before the walls of your palace. Here we seek our last salvation. Do not refuse to come to the aid of your people.

---

viser from late 1906 until his assassination in 1911, important agrarian reforms dissolved the village ownership of land and opened the door to private ownership by enterprising peasants. Nicholas II, however, was no friend of reform. Already by 1907, the tsar had curtailed the power of the Duma, and after Stolypin's murder he fell back on the army and bureaucracy to rule Russia. World War I would give revolutionary forces another chance to undo the tsarist regime, and this time they would not fail.

The Balkans and the Ottoman Empire

Like the Austro-Hungarian Empire, the Ottoman Empire was severely troubled by the nationalist aspirations of its subject peoples, especially in the Balkans.

The National States: Domestic Politics, 1871–1914

Great Britain

Ministry of Benjamin Disraeli	1874–1880
Trade Unions Receive Right to Strike	1875
Second Ministry of William Gladstone	1880–1885
Irish Land Act	1881
Reform Act	1884
Redistribution Act	1885
Formation of Labor Party	1900
Liberal Ministry	1906–1914
Restriction of Power of the House of Lords	1911
National Insurance Act	1911
Home Rule Act for Ireland	1914

France

Surrender of French Provisional Government to Germany	1871 (January 28)
Paris Commune	1871 (March-May)
Republican Constitution (Third Republic	1875
Boulanger Is Discredited	1889
The Dreyfus Affair	1895–1899

Spain

King Alfonso XII	1874–1885
New Constitution	1875
Defeat in Spanish-American War	1898
Violence in Barcelona	1909

Italy

Foundation of Italian Socialist Party	1892
Defeat by Ethiopia	1896
Ministries of Giovanni Giolitti	1903–1914
Universal Male Suffrage	1912

Germany

Bismarck as Chancellor	1871–1890
Antisocialist Law	1878
Social Welfare Legislation	1883–1889
Emperor William II	1888–1918
Social Democratic Party Becomes Largest Party in Reichstag	1912

Austria-Hungary

Emperor Francis Joseph	1848–1916
Count Edward Taaffe as Prime Minister	1879–1893
Universal Male Suffrage in Austria	1907

Imperial Russia

Tsar Alexander III	1881–1894
Tsar Nicholas II	1894–1917
Count Witte as Minister of Finance	1892–1903
First Congress of Social Democratic Party	1898
Russo-Japanese War	1904–1905
Revolution	1905
Reforms of Peter Stolypin	1906–1911

Corruption and inefficiency had so weakened the Ottoman Empire that only the interference of the great European powers, who were fearful of each other's designs on the Turkish territories, kept it alive.

In the course of the nineteenth century, the Balkan provinces of the empire gradually gained their freedom, although the rivalry in the region between Austria and Russia complicated the process. Serbia had received a large degree of autonomy already in 1829, although it was still a province of the Ottoman Empire until 1878. Greece was made an independent kingdom in 1830 after its successful revolt. By the Treaty of Adrianople in 1829, Russia received a protectorate over the principalities of Moldavia and Walachia, but was forced to give them up after the Crimean War. In 1861, Moldavia and Walachia were merged into the state of Romania. Not until Russia's defeat of Turkey in 1878, however, was Romania recognized as completely independent, as was Serbia at the same time. Although freed from Turkish rule, Montenegro was placed under an Austrian protectorate while Bulgaria achieved autonomous status under Russian protection. Despite these gains, by 1878 the forces of Balkan nationalism were by no means stilled. A series of wars in the region at the beginning of the twentieth century would serve as the prelude to World War I.

The Lesser States of Europe

Switzerland had been an independent, self-governing confederation of cantons since 1648. Although the cantons were divided linguistically (German, French, and Italian) and religiously (Catholic and Protestant), their desire to remain independent and neutral enabled them to compromise and to develop a national tradition. A combination of universal free elementary education, a strong tradition of craftsmanship, and the development of hydroelectricity in the 1880s encouraged the emergence of a modern industrial system. By 1914, the Swiss had achieved a relatively high standard of living and a stable political democracy.

Belgium had achieved its independence in 1830. Growing industrialization led to the emergence of trade unionists and socialists who joined together to form the Belgian Labor party and agitate for electoral reform. The threat of a general strike in 1893 brought the introduction of universal manhood suffrage, but only in a very restricted fashion. Belgium did not achieve full universal suffrage until after World War I. The Netherlands also evolved toward political democracy but did not achieve universal male suffrage until 1917 because of bitter divisions between Catholics and Calvinists.

The Scandinavian nations made remarkable progress toward a modern industrial economy and political democracy between 1871 and 1914. In Sweden, 80 percent of the people were engaged in agriculture in 1850. But the development of Sweden's manufacturing, mining, and handicraft industries transformed the country. By 1910, less than 50 percent of the population still worked the land. Sweden also groped toward democratic institutions and granted universal male suffrage in 1909. Although Norway had been subjected to Swedish rule in 1815, the union was peacefully dissolved in 1905. Norway rapidly developed a highly democratic system and became the first European nation to extend voting rights to women. Denmark resisted political liberalization during most of the nineteenth century and did not achieve political democracy until World War I.

The United States

Four years of bloody civil war had preserved American national unity. The old South had been destroyed; one-fifth of its adult white male population had been killed, and four million black slaves had been freed. Although Reconstruction (1865–1877) was meant to create a new southern order, it largely failed.

For a while at least, a program of radical change was attempted. Slavery was abolished by the Thirteenth Amendment to the Constitution in 1865 while the Fourteenth and Fifteenth Amendments extended citizenship to blacks and guaranteed them the right to vote. Radical Reconstruction in the early 1870s tried to create a new South based on a principle of the equality of black and white people, but it was soon mostly undone. Militia organizations, such as the Ku Klux Klan, used violence to discourage blacks from voting. A new system of sharecropping made blacks once again economically dependent on white landowners. New state laws stripped blacks of their right to vote. By the end of the 1870s, supporters of white supremacy were back in power everywhere in the South.

Between 1860 and World War I, the United States made the shift from an agrarian to a mighty industrial nation. American heavy industry stood unchallenged in 1900. In that year, the Carnegie Steel Company alone produced more steel than Great Britain's entire steel industry. Industrialization also led to urbanization. While established cities, such as New York, Philadelphia, and Boston, grew even larger, other moderate-size cities, such as Pittsburgh, grew by leaps and bounds because of industrialization. While 20 percent of Americans lived in cities in 1860, over 40 percent did in 1900. Four-fifths of the population growth in cities came from migration. Eight to ten million Americans moved from rural areas into the cities, and fourteen million foreigners came from abroad.

By 1900, the United States had become the world's richest nation and greatest industrial power. Yet serious questions remained about the quality of American life. In 1890, the richest 9 percent of Americans owned an incredible 71 percent of all the wealth. Labor unrest over unsafe working conditions, strict work discipline, and periodic cycles of devastating unemployment led workers to organize. By the turn of the century, one national organization, the American Federation of Labor, emerged as labor's dominant voice. Its lack of real power, however, is reflected in its membership figures. In 1900, it constituted but 8.4 percent of the American industrial labor force.

During the so-called Progressive Era after 1900, the reform of many features of American life became a primary issue. Efforts to improve living conditions in the cities included attempts to eliminate corrupt machine politics. At the state level, reforming governors sought to achieve clean government by introducing elements of direct democracy, such as direct primaries for selecting nominees for public office. State governments also enacted economic and social legislation, such as laws that governed hours, wages, and working conditions, especially for women and children. The realization that state laws were ineffective in dealing with nationwide problems, however, led to a progressive movement at the national level.

National progressivism was evident in the administrations of both Theodore Roosevelt and Woodrow Wilson. Under Roosevelt (1901–1909), a Meat Inspection Act and Pure Food and Drug Act provided for a limited degree of federal regulation of corrupt industrial practices. Roosevelt's expressed principle, "We draw the line against misconduct, not against wealth," guaranteed that public protection would have to be within limits tolerable to big corporations. Wilson (1913–1921) was responsible for the creation of a graduated federal income tax and a Federal Reserve System that permitted the federal government to play a role in important economic decisions formerly made by bankers. Like European nations, the United States was moving slowly into policies that extended the functions of the state.

Between 1871 and 1914, the national state began to expand its functions beyond all previous limits. Fearful of the growth of socialism and trade unions, governments attempted to appease the working masses by adopting such social insurance measures as protection against accident, illness, and old age. These social welfare measures were narrow in scope and limited in benefits before 1914. Moreover, they failed to halt the growth of socialism. Nevertheless, they signaled a new direction for state action to benefit the mass of its citizens. The enactment of public health and housing measures, designed to curb the worst ills of urban living, were yet another indication of how state power could be used to benefit the people.

This extension of state functions took place in an atmosphere of increased national loyalty. After 1871, nation-states increasingly sought to solidify the social order and win the active loyalty and support of their citizens by deliberately cultivating national feelings. Yet this policy contained potentially great dangers. Nations had discovered once again that imperialistic adventures and military successes could arouse nationalistic passions and smother domestic political unrest. But they also found—belatedly in 1914—that nationalistic feelings could also lead to intense international rivalries that made war almost inevitable.

Notes

▼ ▼ ▼

1. Quoted in David Landes, *The Unbound Prometheus: Technological Change and Industrial Development in Western Europe from 1750 to the Present* (Cambridge, 1969), p. 353.

2. Quoted in Nicholas Bullock and James Read, *The Movement for Housing Reform in Germany and France, 1840–1914* (Cambridge, 1985), p. 42.

3. Quoted in Barbara Franzoi, ". . . with the wolf always at the door. . . . Women's Work in Domestic Industry and Germany," in Marilyn J. Boxer and Jean H. Quataert, eds., *Connecting Spheres: Women in the Western World, 1500 to the Present* (New York, 1987), p. 151.

4. Quoted in Gary Cross, A *Social History of Leisure since 1600* (State College, Pa., 1990), pp. (in order of quotations) 116, 119.

5. Quoted in Sibylle Meyer, "The Tiresome Work of Conspicuous Leisure: On the Domestic Duties of the Wives of Civil Servants in the German Empire (1871–1918)," in Boxer and Quataert, *Connecting Spheres*, p. 161.

6. Quoted in Lenard R. Berlanstein, *The Working People of Paris, 1871–1914* (Baltimore, 1984), p. 141.

7. Quoted in Catherine M. Prelinger, "Prelude to Consciousness: Amalie Sieveking and the Female

Association for the Care of the Poor and the Sick," in John C. Fout, ed., *German Women in the Nineteenth Century: A Social History* (New York, 1984), p. 119.

8. Quoted in W. L. Guttsman, *The German Social Democratic Party, 1875–1933* (London, 1981), p. 63.

9. Quoted in Leslie Derfler, *Socialism since Marx: A Century of the European Left* (New York, 1973), p. 58.

10. Karl Marx and Friedrich Engels, *The Communist Manifesto* (Harmondsworth, 1967), p. 102.

11. Quoted in Paul Avrich, *The Russian Anarchists* (Princeton, N.J., 1971), p. 67.

12. Quoted in Stanley G. Payne, *Politics and the Military in Modern Spain* (Stanford, 1967), p. 60.

13. Quoted in Shmuel Galai, *The Liberation Movement in Russia, 1900–1905* (Cambridge, 1973), p. 26.

14. Quoted in Geoffrey A. Hosking, *The Russian Constitutional Experiment, 1907–1914* (Cambridge, 1973), p. 5.

Suggestions for Further Reading

▼ ▼ ▼

In addition to the general works on the nineteenth century and individual European countries cited in Chapters 22 and 23, two more specialized works on the subject matter of this chapter are available in N. Stone, *Europe Transformed, 1878–1919* (London, 1983); and F. Gilbert, *The End of the European Era, 1890 to the Present,* 2d ed. (New York, 1979).

The subject of the Second Industrial Revolution is well covered in D. Landes, *The Unbound Prometheus,* cited in Chapter 21. For a fundamental survey of European industrialization, see A. S. Milward and S. B. Saul, *The Development of the Economies of Continental Europe, 1850–1914* (Cambridge, Mass., 1977); while Britain can be examined in A. L. Levine, *Industrial Retardation in Britain, 1880–1914* (New York, 1967); and Germany in W. Henderson, *The Rise of German Industrial Power* (Berkeley, 1975). An examination of the business cycles of the period can be found in A. Lewis, *Growth and Fluctuations, 1870–1913* (London, 1978). For an introduction to the development of mass consumerism in Britain, see W. H. Fraser, *The Coming of the Mass Market, 1850–1914* (Hamden, Conn., 1981). The impact of the new technology on European thought is imaginatively discussed in S. Kern, *The Culture of Time and Space, 1880–1918* (Cambridge, Mass., 1983).

For a good introduction to housing reform on the Continent, see N. Bullock and J. Read, *The Movement for Housing Reform in Germany and France, 1840–1914* (Cambridge, 1985). Working-class housing in Paris during its reconstruction is the subject of A. L. Shapiro, *Housing the Poor of Paris, 1850–1902* (Madison, Wis., 1985). E. Gauldie, *Cruel Habitations* (London, 1974) is a good account of working-class housing in Britain. D. Owen, *The Government of Victorian London, 1855–1889* (Cambridge, Mass., 1982) examines how the city of London confronted urban development. The

reconstruction of Paris is discussed in D. Pinkney, *Napoleon III and the Rebuilding of Paris* (Princeton, N.J., 1958).

An interesting work on aristocratic life is G. D. Philips, *The Diehards: Aristocratic Society and Politics in Edwardian England* (Cambridge, 1979). The argument for the continuing importance of the aristocracy is presented in the provocative book by A. Mayer, *Persistence of the Old Regime: Europe to the Great War* (New York, 1981). On the working classes, see L. Berlanstein, *The Working People of Paris, 1871–1914* (Baltimore, 1984). The transformation of the French peasants into good French citizens is examined in E. Weber, *Peasants into Frenchmen: The Modernization of Rural France, 1870–1914* (Stanford, 1976).

There are good overviews of women's experiences in the nineteenth century in B. S. Anderson and J. P. Zinsser, *A History of Their Own,* vol. 2 (New York, 1988); and M. J. Boxer and J. H. Quataert, eds., *Connecting Spheres: Women in the Western World, 1500 to the Present* (New York, 1987). The world of women's work is examined in L. A. Tilly and J. W. Scott, *Women, Work, and Family* (New York, 1978). Important studies of middle-class women include P. Branca, *Silent Sisterhood: Middle Class Women in the Victorian Home* (London, 1975); and B. G. Smith, *Ladies of the Leisure Class: The Bourgeoises of Northern France in the Nineteenth Century* (Princeton, N.J., 1981). Prostitution is discussed in J. R. Walkowitz, *Prostitution and Victorian Society: Women, Class, and the State* (Cambridge, 1980). The rise of feminism is examined in J. Rendall, *The Origins of Modern Feminism: Women in Britain, France and the United States* (London, 1985). On the family and children, see M. Mitterauer and R. Sieder, *The European Family* (Chicago, 1982); and the controversial E. Shorter, *The Making of the Modern Family* (New York, 1975). The treatment of children is examined in G. Behlmer, *Child Abuse and Moral Reform in England, 1870–1908* (Stanford, 1982).

For an introduction to international socialism, see J. Joll, *The Second International, 1889–1914*, 2d ed. (New York, 1975); and L. Derfler, *Socialism since Marx: A Century of the European Left* (New York, 1973). On the emergence of German social democracy, there is W. L. Guttsman, *The German Social Democratic Party, 1875–1933* (London, 1981); and V. Lidtke, *The Outlawed Party: Social Democracy in Germany, 1878–1890* (Princeton, N.J., 1966). Eduard Bernstein's revisionism is examined in P. Gay, *The Dilemma of Democratic Socialism: Eduard Bernstein's Challenge to Marx* (New York, 1952). On the French socialists, there is a "classic" biography by H. Goldberg, *The Life of Jean Jaurès* (Madison, Wis., 1962). There is a good introduction to anarchism in G. Woodcock, *Anarchism: A History of Libertarian Ideas and Movements* (Cleveland, Ohio, 1962).

The domestic politics of the period can be examined in the general works on individual countries listed in the bibliographies for Chapters 22 and 23. There are also specialized works on aspects of each country's history. The importance of Fabian Socialism in England is discussed in A. H. McBriar, *Fabian Socialism and English Politics, 1884–1918* (Cambridge, 1962); while the beginnings of the Labor party are examined in H. Pelling, *The Origins of the Labour Party*, 2d ed. (Oxford, 1965). On the problem of English industrial decline, see M. J. Wiener, *English Culture and the Decline of the Industrial Spirit, 1850–1980* (Cambridge, 1981). The Irish problem is covered in O. MacDonagh, *States of Mind: A Study of Anglo-Irish Conflict, 1780–1980* (London, 1983). For a detailed examination of French history from 1871 to 1914, see J. M. Mayeur and M. Reberioux, *The Third Republic from Its Origins to the Great War, 1871–1914* (Cambridge, 1984). On the Paris Commune, see R. Tombs, *The War against Paris, 1871* (Cambridge, 1981). On Italy, see C. Seton-Watson, *Italy from Liberalism to Fascism* (London, 1967). An important aspect of Spanish history is examined in S. G. Payne, *Politics and the Military in Modern Spain* (Stanford, 1967). There is a good introduction to the political world of Wilhelmine Germany in J. C. G. Röhl, *Germany without Bismarck* (Berkeley, 1965). An important study on right-wing German politics is G. Eley, *Reshaping the German Right: Radical Nationalism and Political Change after Bismarck* (New Haven, Conn., 1980). K. H. Jarausch, *Students, Society, and Politics in Imperial Germany: The Rise of Academic Illiberalism* (Princeton, N.J., 1982) examines the reaction of universities to the danger of socialism. The best, one-volume biography in English on Emperor William II is M. Balfour, *The Kaiser and His Times* (London, 1964). On the nationalities problem in the Austro-Hungarian Empire, see R. Kann, *The Multinational Empire, Nationalism and National Reform in the Habsburg Monarchy, 1848–1918*, 2 vols. (New York, 1950). On aspects of Russian history, see H. Rogger, *Russia in the Age of Modernization and Revolution, 1881–1917* (London, 1983); and T. H. Von Laue, *Sergei Witte and the Industrialization of Russia* (New York, 1963). On the United States, see D. Cashman, *America in the Gilded Age: From the Death of Lincoln to the Rise of Theodore Roosevelt* (New York, 1984); and J. W. Chambers, *The Tyranny of Change: America in the Progressive Era, 1900–1917* (New York, 1980).

Chapter 25

Imperialism, International Rivalry, and Culture in the "Age of Progress," 1871–1914

▼▼▼▼▼

Many Europeans saw the period between 1871 and 1914 as an age of material and human progress. It was also a time of great tension, however, as imperialist adventures, international rivalries, and cultural uncertainties disturbed the apparent calm. After 1870, Europeans engaged in a great race for colonies that did not end until Africa had been divided among the powers and much of Asia had been incorporated into their spheres of influence. This competition for lands abroad greatly intensified existing antagonisms among European states.

Ultimately, Europeans proved incapable of finding constructive ways to cope with their international rivalries. The development of two large alliance systems—the Triple Alliance and the Triple Entente—may have served to preserve the peace, but at the same time the development of a balance of power based on these alliances led to the creation of mass conscript armies and enormous military establishments that served to exacerbate the tensions among the major powers. These tensions were only finally released when Europeans rushed headlong into the catastrophic carnage of World War I.

The cultural life of Europe between 1871 and 1914 reflected similar dynamic tensions. The advent of mass education created more well-informed citizens, but it also made it easier for governments to stir up the masses by nationalistic appeals through the new mass journalism. At the same time, despite the appearance of progress, European philosophers, writers, and artists were creating modern cultural expressions that ques-

Congress of Berlin ▼   Triple Alliance (Germany, Austria, Italy) ▼   Open Door Policy in China ▼   Boxer Rebellion ▼   Triple Entente (France, Britain, Russia) ▼

•••••••• 1870 ••••••••••• 1880 ••••••••••• 1890 •••••••••• 1900 •••••••••• 1910 ••••••••

▲ Emergence of Mass Newspapers   ▲ Cézanne, *Woman with Coffee Pot*   ▲ Freud, *The Interpretation of Dreams*   ▲ Einstein's Special Theory of Relativity   ▲ Picasso's First Cubist Painting

tioned traditional ideas and values and increasingly provoked a crisis of confidence. Before 1914, many intellectuals had a sense of unease about the direction society was headed, accompanied by a feeling of imminent catastrophe. They proved remarkably prophetic.

▼ The Expansion of Europe

Europeans had begun to explore the world in the fifteenth century, but even as late as 1870 they had not yet completely penetrated North America, South America, and Australia. In Asia and Africa, they had mostly established trading posts. Between 1870 and 1914, however, Western civilization expanded into the rest of the Americas and Australia while all of Africa was divided into European colonies and spheres of influence were created in much of Asia. Two major events explain this remarkable expansion: the migration of many Europeans to other parts of the world due to population growth and the revival of imperialism.

Population Increase and Demographic Transformation

The European population increased dramatically between 1850 and 1910, rising from 270 million to over 460 million by 1910. Between 1850 and 1880, noticeable jumps in the number of inhabitants occurred in Germany, Britain, the Scandinavian countries, the Low Countries, and Russia while France remained static and the Mediterranean countries and Austria-Hungary grew slowly. After 1880, this pattern changed. The rate of population growth remained static in France and relatively slow in the Mediterranean countries and Great Britain. Scandinavia, the Netherlands, Belgium, Germany, and Austria grew faster while eastern Europe, es-

pecially Romania, Bulgaria, Greece, Serbia, and above all Russia, experienced a population explosion (see Table 1).

Between 1850 and 1880, the main cause of population increase was a rising birth rate, at least in western Europe. Industrialization in northwestern Europe created greater employment possibilities, which encouraged earlier marriages and consequently higher birth rates. Death rates remained high during this period. In some areas, especially backward southern and eastern Europe, death rates almost canceled out high birth rates. Large cities had particularly hazardous environments because of the lack of sanitation and overcrowded conditions. In Germany, for example, in 1880, the life expectancy of males in rural Hanover was 43.1, but in the moderate-

Table 1 ▼ European Populations, 1851–1911

	1851	1881	1911
England and Wales	17,928,000	25,974,000	36,070,000
Scotland	2,889,000	3,736,000	4,761,000
Ireland	6,552,000	5,175,000	4,390,000
France	35,783,000	37,406,000	39,192,000
Germany	33,413,000	45,234,000	64,926,000
Belgium	4,530,000	5,520,000	7,424,000
Netherlands	3,309,000	4,013,000	5,858,000
Denmark	1,415,000	1,969,000	2,757,000
Norway	1,490,000	1,819,000	2,392,000
Sweden	3,471,000	4,169,000	5,522,000
Spain	15,455,000	16,622,000	19,927,000
Portugal	3,844,000	4,551,000	5,958,000
Italy	24,351,000	28,460,000	34,671,000
Switzerland	2,393,000	2,846,000	3,753,000
Austria	17,535,000	22,144,000	28,572,000
Hungary	18,192,000	15,739,000	20,886,000
Russia	68,500,000	97,700,000	160,700,000
Romania		4,600,000	7,000,000
Bulgaria		2,800,000	4,338,000
Greece		1,679,000	2,632,000
Serbia		1,700,000	2,912,000

Source: B. R. Mitchell, *European Historical Statistics, 1750–1970* (1975).

▼ **Map 25.1** Population Growth in Europe

1820

NORWAY
SWEDEN
NORTH SEA
DENMARK
Baltic Sea
UNITED KINGDOM
RUSSIA
NETH.
ATLANTIC OCEAN
GERMAN CONFEDERATION
AUSTRIAN EMPIRE
FRANCE
SWITZERLAND
PORTUGAL
SPAIN
Corsica
ITALY
Sardinia
Balearic Is.
Sicily
MEDITERRANEAN SEA

Inhabitants per square mile

<20   20–50   50–100   100+

1900

NORWAY
SWEDEN
NORTH SEA
DENMARK
Baltic Sea
UNITED KINGDOM
RUSSIA
NETH.
BELGIUM
GERMANY
ATLANTIC OCEAN
FRANCE
SWITZERLAND
AUSTRIA-HUNGARY
PORTUGAL
SPAIN
Corsica
ITALY
Sardinia
Balearic Is.
GREECE
Sicily
MEDITERRANEAN SEA

sized industrial town of Düsseldorf, it was 36.7 and in Berlin, 29.9.

After 1880, a noticeable decline in death rates largely explains the increase in population. Although the causes of this decline have been debated, two major factors—medical discoveries and environmental conditions—stand out. Some historians have stressed the importance of improvements in medical science. Smallpox vaccinations, for example, were made compulsory in many European countries by the mid-1850s, although smallpox fatalities accounted for only a small percentage of deaths. More important were such infectious diseases as diarrhea, dysentery, typhoid fever, and cholera, which were spread through contaminated water supplies and improper elimination of sewage. The improvement of the urban environment in the last half of the nineteenth century greatly decreased fatalities from these diseases. Improved nutrition also made a significant difference in the health of the population. The increase in agricultural productivity combined with improvements in transportation facilitated the shipment of food supplies from areas of surplus to regions with poor harvests. Better nutrition and food hygiene were especially instrumental in the decline of infant mortality by 1900. The pasteurization of milk reduced intestinal disorders that had been a major cause of infant deaths.

Although high birth rates continued to be noticeable in economically backward eastern and southern Europe, the general trend for the rest of Europe was a decline in birth rates, especially in France, Scandinavia, the Low Countries, and Great Britain, and to a lesser extent in Germany. Birth rates fell more in cities than in rural areas and more among the upper and middle classes than among the lower classes. This decline in birth rates, coupled with falling death rates, affected the composition of populations. In France, for example, the proportion of the population under fifteen was 22.5 percent in 1910, while in Germany it was 34.1 percent. These figures had great significance in an age of mass armies.

Although marriages still occurred later in western than eastern Europe, the delay in marriage was no longer the chief cause of the falling birth rates. The decline in infant mortality rates meant that couples felt free to have fewer children because there was less need to worry about their early death. Most importantly, however, increased prosperity led to a voluntary limitation of children by birth control as families sought to improve their standard of living. Factory acts in Europe gradually eliminated child labor, which made children less of an asset and more of an economic liability.

Migrations

Although growing agricultural and industrial prosperity supported an increase in European population, it could not do so indefinitely, especially in areas that had little industrialization and a severe problem of rural overpopulation. Some of the excess labor from underdeveloped areas migrated to the industrial regions of Europe. By 1913, over 400,000 Poles were working in the heavily industrialized Ruhr region of western Germany while thousands of Italian laborers had migrated to France. The industrialized regions of Europe, however, were not able to absorb the entire surplus population of heavily agricultural regions like southern Italy, Spain, Hungary, and Romania. A booming American economy after 1898 and cheap shipping fares after 1900 led to mass emigration from southern and eastern Europe to America at the beginning of the twentieth century. In 1880, the average number of annual departures from Europe was around 500,000, but between 1906 and 1910 it increased to 1,300,000, many of them from southern and eastern Europe. Altogether between 1846 and 1932, probably 60 million Europeans left Europe, half of them bound for the United States and most of the rest for Canada or Latin America (see Table 2).

It was not only economic motives that caused people to leave eastern Europe. Migrants from Austria and Hungary, for example, were not the dominant nationalities, the Germans and Magyars, but mostly their oppressed minorities, such as Poles, Slovaks, Serbs, Croats, Romanians, and Jews. Between 1880 and 1914, 3,500,000 Poles from Russia, Austria, and Germany went to the United States. Jews constituted 40 percent of the Russian emigrants to the United States between 1900 and 1913 and almost 12 percent of all emigrants to the United States during the first five years of the twentieth century.

▼ The New Imperialism

Beginning in the 1880s, European states began an intense scramble for overseas territory. This revival of imperialism, or the "new imperialism" as some have called it, led Europeans to carve up Asia and Africa. Imperialism was not a new phenomenon. Since the crusades of the Middle Ages and the overseas expansion between 1500 and 1800, when Europeans established colonies in North and South America and trading posts around Africa and the Indian Ocean, Europeans had shown a marked proclivity for the domination of less technologically oriented, non-European peoples. Nevertheless, the imperialism of the late nineteenth century was different from the earlier European imperialism. It occurred after a period in which Europeans had reacted against imperial expansion. Between 1775 and 1875, Europeans had lost more colonial territory than they acquired as many Europeans had actually come to regard colonies as expensive and useless. The new imperialism was also more rapid and resulted in greater and deeper penetrations into non-European societies. Finally, most of the new imperialism was directed toward the domination of Africa and Asia, two civilizations that had been largely ignored earlier.

Causes of the New Imperialism

Why did Europeans begin their mad scramble for colonies after 1880? Although historians disagree, they have advanced a number of factors to explain the rapid spread of imperialism.

The existence of competitive nation-states after 1870 was undoubtedly a major determinant in the growth of this new imperialism. As European affairs grew tense, heightened competition led European states to acquire colonies abroad that provided ports and coaling stations for their navies. Colonies were also a source of international prestige. Once the scramble for colonies began, failure to enter the race was perceived as a sign of weakness, totally unacceptable to an aspiring great power. Nationalistically oriented intellectuals reinforced these

national aspirations when they argued that nations could not be great without colonies. The German historian Heinrich von Treitschke, for example, maintained that "all great nations in the fullness of their strength have desired to set their mark upon barbarian lands and those who fail to participate in this great rivalry will play a pitiable role in time to come."[1]

Treitschke's comments are a reminder that late nineteenth-century imperialism was closely tied to nationalism, Social Darwinism, and racism. After the unification of Italy and Germany in 1871, nationalism entered a new stage of development. In the first half of the nineteenth century, nationalism had been closely identified with liberals who had pursued both individual rights and national unification and independence. Liberal nationalists maintained that unified, independent nation-states could best preserve individual rights. The new nationalism of the late nineteenth century, tied to conservatism, was loud and chauvinistic. As one exponent expressed it, "a true nationalist places his country above everything"; he believes in the "exclusive pursuit of national policies" and "the steady increase in national power—for a nation declines when it loses military might."

Then, too, imperialism was tied to Social Darwinism and racism (see The Impact of Darwin: Social Darwinism and Racism later in the chapter). Social Darwinists believed that in the struggle between nations, the fit are victorious and survive. Superior races must dominate inferior races by military force to show how strong and virile they are. As the British professor of mathematics,

Table 2 ▼ European Emigration, 1876–1910 (Average Annual Emigration to Non-European Countries per 100,000 Population)

	1876–80	1881–5	1886–90	1891–5	1896–1900	1901–5	1906–10
Europe	94	196	213	185	147	271	322
Ireland	650	1,422	1,322	988	759	743	662
Great Britain	102	174	162	119	88	127	172
Denmark	157	380	401	338	117	292	275
Norway	432	1,105	819	597	312	903	746
Sweden	301	705	759	587	249	496	347
Germany	108	379	207	163	47	50	44
Belgium			86	50	23	57	69
Netherlands	32	136	111	76	25	45	58
France	8	14	49	14	13	12	12
Spain		280	437	434	446	391	758
Portugal	258	356	423	609	417	464	694
Italy	396	542	754	842	974	1,706	1,938
Austria	48	90	114	182	182	355	469
Hungary		92	156	134	205	437	616
Russia	6	13	42	47	32	63	67

Source: Robert Gildea, *Barricades and Borders: Europe, 1800–1914* (Oxford, 1987), p. 283.

Karl Pearson, arrogantly argued in 1900: "The path of progress is strewn with the wrecks of nations; traces are everywhere to be seen of the [slaughtered remains] of inferior races. . . . Yet these dead people are, in very truth, the stepping stones on which mankind has arisen to the higher intellectual and deeper emotional life of today."[2] Others were equally blunt. One Briton wrote: "To the development of the White Man, the Black Man and the Yellow must ever remain inferior, and as the former raised itself higher and yet higher, so did these latter seem to shrink out of humanity and appear nearer and nearer to the brutes."[3]

Some historians have emphasized an economic motivation for imperialism. There was a great demand for natural resources and products not found in Western countries, such as rubber, oil, and tin. Instead of just trading for these products, European investors advocated direct control of the areas where the raw materials were found. The large surpluses of capital that were being accumulated by bankers and industrialists often encouraged them to seek higher rates of profit in underdeveloped areas. All of these factors combined to create an economic imperialism whereby European finance dominated the economic activity of a large part of the world. This economic imperialism, however, was not necessarily the same thing as colonial expansion. Businessmen invested where it was most profitable, not necessarily where their own countries had colonial empires. For example, less than 10 percent of French foreign investments before 1914 went to French colonies; most of the rest went to Latin American and European countries. It should also be remembered that much of the colonial territory that was acquired was mere wasteland from the point of view of industrialized Europe and cost more to administer than it produced economically. Only the search for national prestige could justify such losses.

Followers of Karl Marx were especially eager to argue that imperialism was economically motivated because they associated imperialism with the ultimate demise of the capitalist system. Marx had hinted at this argument, but it was one of his followers, the Russian Vladimir Lenin (see Chapter 26), who in *Imperialism, the Highest Stage of World Capitalism* developed the idea that capitalism led to imperialism. According to Lenin, as the capitalist system concentrated more wealth in ever-fewer hands, it exhausted the possibility of investment at home, thus compelling capitalists to invest abroad, establish colonies, and exploit small, weak nations. The only cure for imperialism, then, was the destruction of capitalism.

Some Europeans took a more religious-humanitarian approach to imperialism when they argued that Europeans had a moral responsibility to civilize ignorant peoples. This notion of the "white man's burden" (see the box on p. 858) helped at least the more idealistic individuals to rationalize imperialism in their own minds. Nevertheless, the belief that the superiority of their civilization obligated them to impose modern industry, cities, and new medicines on supposedly primitive nonwhites—even if the native peoples had to be killed in the process—was yet another form of racism.

The Creation of Empires

Whatever the reasons for the new imperialism, it had a dramatic effect on Africa and Asia as European powers competed for control of these two continents.

AFRICA Europeans controlled relatively little of the African continent before 1880. During the Napoleonic wars, the British had established themselves in south Africa by taking control of Capetown, originally founded by the Dutch. After the wars, the British encouraged settlers to come to what they called Cape Colony where they created a new administrative system that used English as the official language. British policies disgusted the Boers or Afrikaners, as the descendants of the Dutch colonists were called, and led them in 1835 to migrate north on the Great Trek to the region between the Orange and Vaal rivers (later known as the Orange Free State) and north of the Vaal River (the Transvaal). Hostilities between the British and the Boers continued, however. In 1877, the British governor of Cape Colony seized the Transvaal, but a Boer revolt led the British government to recognize Transvaal as the independent South African Republic. These struggles between the British and the Boers did not prevent either white group from massacring and subjugating the Zulu and Xhosa peoples of south Africa.

In the 1880s, British policy in south Africa was largely determined by Cecil Rhodes (1853–1902). Rhodes founded both diamond and gold companies that monopolized production of these precious commodities and enabled him to establish power over a territory north of Transvaal that he named Rhodesia after himself. The imperialist ambitions of Rhodes brought his downfall in 1896 when the British government forced him to resign as prime minister of Rhodesia after he conspired to overthrow the Boer government of the South African Re-

The White Man's Burden
▼ ▼ ▼

One of the justifications for European imperialism was the misguided, arrogant, and racist notion that superior white peoples had the moral responsibility to raise ignorant native peoples to a higher level of civilization. The British poet Rudyard Kipling (1865–1936) captured this notion in his poem, The White Man's Burden.

Rudyard Kipling, *The White Man's Burden*

Take up the White Man's burden—
Send forth the best ye breed—
Go bind your sons to exile
To serve your captives' needs;
To wait in heavy harness,
On fluttered folk and wild—
Your new-caught sullen peoples,
Half-devil and half-child.

Take up the White Man's burden—
In patience to abide,
To veil the threat of terror
And check the show of pride;
By open speech and simple,
An hundred times made plain
To seek another's profit,
And work another's gain.

Take up the White Man's burden—
The savage wars of peace—
Fill full the mouth of Famine
And bid the sickness cease;
And when your goal is nearest
The end for others sought,
Watch sloth and heathen Folly
Bring all your hopes to nought.

Take up the White Man's burden—
No tawdry rule of kings,
But toil of serf and sweeper—
The tale of common things.
The ports ye shall not enter,
The roads ye shall not read,
Go mark them with your living,
And mark them with your dead.

Take up the White Man's burden—
And reap his old reward:
The blame of those ye better,
The hate of those ye guard—
The cry of hosts ye humour
(Ah, slowly!) toward the light:—
'Why brought he us from bondage,
Our loved Egyptian night?'

Take up the White Man's burden—
Ye dare not stoop to less—
Nor call too loud on Freedom
To cloke your weariness;
By all ye cry or whisper,
By all you leave or do,
The silent, sullen peoples
Shall weigh your gods and you.

Take up the White Man's burden—
Have done with childish days—
The lightly proferred laurel,
The easy, ungrudged praise.
Comes now, to search your manhood
Through all the thankless years,
Cold, edged with dear-bought wisdom,
The judgment of your peers!

public without British approval. Although the British government had hoped to avoid war with the Boers, it could not stop extremists on both sides from precipitating such action. The Boer War dragged on from 1899 to 1902 when the Boers were overwhelmed by the larger British army. British policy toward the defeated Boers was remarkably conciliatory. Transvaal and the Orange Free State had representative governments by 1907, and in 1910, a Union of South Africa was created. Like Canada, Australia, and New Zealand, it became a fully self-governing dominion within the British Empire.

Before 1880, the only other European settlements in Africa had been made by the French and Portuguese. The Portuguese had held on to their settlements in An-

The Black Man's Burden
▼ ▼ ▼

The Western justification of imperialism that was based on a sense of moral responsibility, evident in Rudyard Kipling's poem, was often hypocritical. Edward Morel, a British journalist who spent time in the Congo, pointed out the destructive effects of Western imperialism on native Africans in his book, The Black Man's Burden.

Edward Morel, *The Black Man's Burden*

It is [the Africans] who carry the "Black man's burden." They have not withered away before the white man's occupation. Indeed . . . Africa has ultimately absorbed within itself every Caucasian and, for that matter, every Semitic invader, too. In hewing out for himself a fixed abode in Africa, the white man has massacred the African in heaps. The African has survived, and it is well for the white settlers that he has. . . .

What the partial occupation of his soil by the white man has failed to do; what the mapping out of European political "spheres of influence" has failed to do; what the Maxim [machine gun] and the rifle, the slave gang, labour in the bowels of the earth and the lash, have failed to do; what imported measles, small-pox and syphilis have failed to do; whatever the overseas slave trade failed to do; the power of modern capitalistic exploitation, assisted by modern engines of destruction, may yet succeed in accomplishing.

For from the evils of the latter, scientifically applied and enforced, there is no escape for the African. Its destructive effects are not spasmodic: they are permanent. In its permanence resides its fatal consequences. It kills not the body merely, but the soul. It breaks the spirit. It attacks the African at every turn, from every point of vantage. It wrecks his polity, uproots him from the land, invades his family life, destroys his natural pursuits and occupations, claims his whole time, enslaves him in his own home. . . .

In Africa, especially in tropical Africa, which a capitalistic imperialism threatens and has, in part, already devastated, man is incapable of reacting against unnatural conditions. In those regions man is engaged in a perpetual struggle against disease and an exhausting climate, which tells heavily upon child-bearing; and there is no scientific machinery for saving the weaker members of the community. The African of the tropics is capable of tremendous physical labours. But he cannot accommodate himself to the European system of monotonous, uninterrupted labour, with its long and regular hours, involving, moreover, as it frequently does, severance from natural surroundings and nostalgia, the condition of melancholy resulting from separation from home, a malady to which the African is specially prone. Climatic conditions forbid it. When the system is forced upon him, the tropical African droops and dies.

Nor is violent physical opposition to abuse and injustice henceforth possible for the African in any part of Africa. His chances of effective resistance have been steadily dwindling with the increasing perfectibility in the killing power of modern armament. . . .

Thus the African is really helpless against the material gods of the white man, as embodied in the trinity of imperialism, capitalistic exploitation, and militarism. . . .

To reduce all the varied and picturesque and stimulating episodes in savage life to a dull routine of endless toil for uncomprehended ends, to dislocate social ties and disrupt social ties and disrupt social institutions; to stifle nascent desires and crush mental development; to graft upon primitive passions the annihilating evils of scientific slavery, and the bestial imaginings of civilized man, unrestrained by convention or law; in fine, to kill the soul in a people—this is a crime which transcends physical murder.

---

gola on the west coast and Mozambique on the east coast. The French had started the conquest of Algeria in Muslim north Africa in 1830, although it was not until 1879 that French civilian rule was established there. By the next year, 1880, the European scramble for possession of Africa began in earnest. Before 1900, the French had added the huge area of French West Africa and

Tunisia to their African empire. In 1912, they created a protectorate over much of Morocco; the rest was left to Spain.

The British took an active interest in Egypt after the Suez Canal was opened by the French in 1869. Since they believed that the canal was essential to their lifeline to India, the British sought to exercise as much control as possible over the canal area. Egypt was a well-established state with an autonomous Muslim government, but that did not stop the British from landing an expeditionary force in Egypt in 1882. Although they asserted that their occupation was only temporary, they soon established a protectorate over Egypt. From Egypt, the British moved south into Sudan and seized it after narrowly averting a war with France. Not to be undone, Italy joined in the imperialist scramble. The humiliating defeat of the Italians by the Ethiopians in 1896 only led the Italians to try again in 1911 by invading and seizing Turkish Tripoli, which the Italians renamed Libya.

Central Africa was also added to the list of European colonies. Popular interest in the forbiddingly dense tropical jungles of central Africa was first aroused in the 1860s and 1870s by explorers, such as the Scottish missionary David Livingstone and the British-American journalist Henry M. Stanley. But the real driving force for the colonization of central Africa was King Leopold II (1865–1909) of Belgium, who had rushed enthusiastically into pursuit of empire in Africa: "To open to civilization," he said, "the only part of our globe where it has not yet penetrated, to pierce the darkness which envelops whole populations, is a crusade, if I may say so,

▼ **Map 25.2** Africa in 1914.

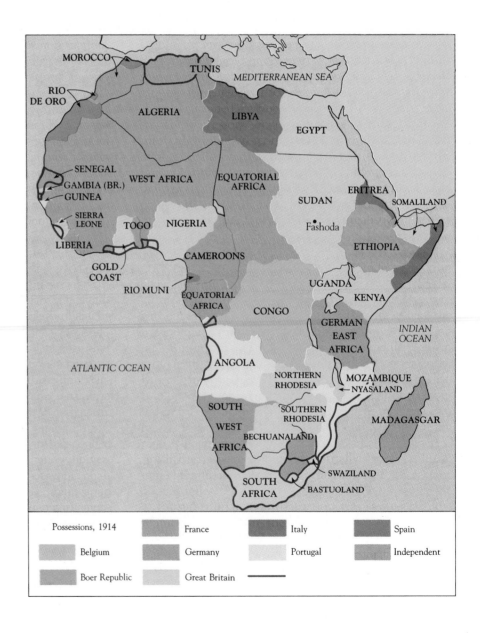

a crusade worthy of this century of progress." Profit, however, was more important to Leopold than progress. In 1876, he created the International Association for the Exploration and Civilization of Central Africa and engaged Henry Stanley to establish Belgian settlements in the Congo. Alarmed by Leopold's actions, the French also moved into the territory north of the Congo River.

Between 1884 and 1900, most of the rest of Africa was carved up by the European powers. Germany also entered the ranks of the imperialist powers at this time. Initially, Bismarck had downplayed the significance of colonies but as domestic political pressures for a German empire increased, Bismarck became a political convert to colonialism. As he expressed it, "All this colonial business is a sham, but we need it for the elections." The Germans established colonies in Southwest Africa, the Cameroons, Togoland, and East Africa.

By 1914, Britain, France, Germany, Belgium, Spain, and Portugal had divided Africa. Only Liberia, founded by emancipated American slaves, and Ethiopia remained free states. Despite the humanitarian rationalizations about the "white man's burden," Africa had been conquered by European states determined to create colonial empires (see the box on p. 859). Any native people who dared to resist (with the exception of the Ethiopians) was simply devastated by the superior military force of the Europeans. At the Battle of Omdurman in 1898, when the native Muslims in the Sudan tried to stop a British expedition armed with the recently developed machine gun, a typical massacre of natives occurred. One observer noted: "It was not a battle but an execution. . . . The bodies were not in heaps—bodies hardly ever are; but they spread evenly over acres and acres. Some lay very composedly with their slippers placed under their heads for a last pillow; some knelt, cut short in the middle of a last prayer. Others were torn to pieces."[4] The battle casualties at Omdurman tell the story of the one-sided conflicts between Europeans and native Africans: 28 British deaths to 11,000 Muslim tribesmen. Military superiority was frequently accompanied by brutality in the handling of blacks. Nor did Europeans hesitate to deceive the natives to gain their way. One south African king, Lo Bengula, informed Queen Victoria about how he had been cheated:

> Some time ago a party of men came to my country, the principal one appearing to be a man called Rudd. They asked me for a place to dig for gold, and said they would give me certain things for the right to do so. I told them to bring what they could give and I would show them what I would give. A document was written and presented to me for signature. I asked what it contained, and was told that in it were my

Chronology
▼ ▼ ▼
The New Imperialism: Africa

Great Trek of the Boers	1835
Opening of the Suez Canal	1869
Leopold of Belgium Establishes Settlements in the Congo	1876
British Seizure of Transvaal	1877
French Complete Conquest of Algeria	1879
British Expeditionary Force in Egypt	1882
Ethiopians Defeat the Italians	1896
Battle of Omdurman in the Sudan	1898
Boer War	1899–1902
Union of South Africa	1910
Italians Seize Tripoli	1911
French Protectorate over Morocco	1912

words and the words of those men. I put my hand to it. About three months afterwards I heard from other sources that I had given by that document the right to all the minerals of my country.[5]

ASIA Although Asia had been open to Western influence since the sixteenth century, not much of its immense territory had fallen under direct European control. The Dutch were established in the East Indies and the Spanish in the Philippines while the French and Portuguese had trading posts on the Indian coast. China, Japan, Korea, and Southeast Asia had largely managed to exclude westerners. The British and the Russians, however, had acquired the most Asian territory.

Britain's interest in the Far East dated back to the seventeenth century, but it was not until the explorations of Australia by Captain James Cook between 1768 and 1771 that Britain took an active interest. By the 1780s, Britain had begun to use Australia as a penal colony to relieve overcrowded British prisons. The availability of land for grazing sheep and the discovery of gold led, however, to an influx of free settlers who slaughtered many of the native inhabitants. In 1850, the British government granted the various Australian colonies virtually complete self-government, and fifty years later, on January 1, 1901, all the colonies were unified into a Commonwealth of Australia. Nearby New Zealand, which the British had declared a colony in 1840, was also granted dominion status in 1907.

The British East India Company (see Chapter 18) had been responsible for subjugating much of India. In 1858, however, after a revolt of the sepoys or native troops of the East India Company's army had been defeated, the British Parliament transferred the company's powers directly to the government in London. In 1876, the title Empress of India was bestowed upon Queen Victoria.

Russian expansion in Asia was a logical outgrowth of its traditional territorial aggrandizement. Russian explorers had penetrated the wilderness of Siberia in the seventeenth century and reached the Pacific coast in 1637. In the eighteenth century, Russians established a claim on Alaska, which was later sold to the United States in 1867. Gradually, Russian settlers moved into cold and forbidding Siberia. Altogether 7 million Russians settled in Siberia between 1800 and 1914; by 1914, 90 percent of the Siberian population were Slavs, not Asiatics.

In the nineteenth century, the Russians also moved south, attracted by warmer lands and the crumbling Ottoman Empire. By 1830, the Russians had established control over the entire northern coast of the Black Sea

▼ **British Tourists in Asia.** After 1870, European states engaged in an intense struggle for overseas territory and did not stop until Africa and Asia had been carved up into colonies or spheres of influence. Western imperialistic attitudes were often based upon an assumption of cultural superiority. Westerners, as is evident in this photograph of British tourists in front of an Indian temple, often seemed to take for granted their superiority over native peoples.

and then pressed on into central Asia, securing the trans-Caspian area by 1881 and Turkestan in 1885. These advances brought the Russians to the borders of Persia and Afghanistan where the British also had interests because of their desire to protect their holdings in India. In 1907, the Russians and British agreed to make Afghanistan a buffer state between Russian Turkestan and British India and divide Persia into two spheres of influence. Halted by the British in their expansion to the south, the Russians moved east in Asia. The Russian occupation of Manchuria and their attempt to move into Korea brought war with the new imperialist power, Japan (see Japan later in the chapter). After losing the Russo-Japanese War in 1905, the Russians agreed to a Japanese protectorate in Korea, and their Asian expansion was brought to a temporary halt.

The thrust of imperialism after 1880 led Westerners to move into new areas of Asia hitherto largely free of Western influence. By the nineteenth century, the ruling Manchu dynasty of the Chinese empire was showing signs of decline. In 1842, the British had obtained (through war) the island of Hong Kong and trading rights in a number of Chinese cities. Other Western nations soon rushed in to gain similar trading privileges. Chinese attempts to resist this encroachment of foreigners led to military defeats and new demands. Only rivalry among the great powers themselves prevented the complete dismemberment of the Chinese empire. Instead, Britain, France, Germany, Russia, the United States, and Japan established spheres of influence and long-term leases of Chinese territory. In 1899, urged along by the American Secretary of State John Hay, they agreed to an "open door" policy in which one country would not restrict the commerce of the other countries in their own spheres of influence.

Japan avoided Western intrusion until 1853–1854 when American naval forces under Commodore Matthew Perry forced the Japanese to grant the United States trading and diplomatic privileges. Japan, however, managed to avoid China's fate. Korea had also largely excluded Westerners. The fate of Korea was determined first by the struggle between China and Japan in 1894–1895 and later between Japan and Russia in 1904–1905. Japan's victories gave it a clear superiority, and in 1910 Japan formally annexed Korea.

In Southeast Asia, Britain established control over Burma and the Malay States while France played an active role in subjugating Indochina. The city of Saigon was occupied in 1858, and four years later Cochin China was taken. In the 1880s, the French extended "protection" over Cambodia, Annam, Tonkin, and Laos and organized them into a Union of French Indochina. Only

Siam (Thailand) remained free as a buffer state because of British-French rivalry.

The Pacific islands were also the scene of great power competition and witnessed the entry of the United States onto the imperialist stage. The Samoan Islands became the first important American colony; the Hawaiian Islands were the next to fall. Soon after Americans had made Pearl Harbor into a naval station in 1887, American settlers gained control of the sugar industry on the islands. When Hawaiian natives tried to reassert their authority, the United States Marines were brought in to "protect" American lives. Hawaii was annexed by the United States in 1898 during the era of American nationalistic fervor generated by the Spanish-American War. The American defeat of Spain encouraged Americans to extend their empire by acquiring Cuba, Puerto Rico, Guam, and the Philippine Islands. Although the Filipinos hoped for independence, the Americans refused to grant it. As President William McKinley said, the United States had the duty "to educate the Filipinos and uplift and Christianize them," a remarkable statement in view of the fact that most of them had been Roman Catholics for centuries. It took three years and 60,000 troops to pacify the Philippines and establish American control. Not until 1946 did the Filipinos receive complete independence.

Native Responses to Imperialism

When Europeans imposed their culture upon peoples they considered inferior, how did the conquered native peoples respond? Initial attempts to expel the foreigners only led to devastating defeats at the hands of Westerners, whose industrial technology gave them modern weapons of war with which to crush the natives. Accustomed to rule by small elites, most native peoples simply accepted their new governors, making Western rule relatively easy. Natives subsequently adjusted to foreign rule in different ways. Traditionalists sought to maintain their cultural traditions while modernizers believed that adoption of Western ways would enable them to reform their societies and subsequently challenge Western rule. Most people probably stood somewhere between these two extremes.

Despite Western domination, movements for change soon arose, led by a few strong-willed figures who usually had the benefit of Western knowledge or good insight into Western ways. These native leaders were especially resentful of Western attitudes of superiority and demanded human dignity for the indigenous people. They also adopted the West's own ideologies for change. Liberalism, with its doctrine of civil rights and political self-determination, and nationalism, with its emphasis on the right of peoples to have their own nations, were used to foster independence movements wherever native people suffered under foreign oppression. Three eventually powerful Asian nations—China, Japan, and India—present different approaches to the question of how native populations responded to foreign rule.

CHINA The humiliation of China by the Western powers led to much antiforeign violence, but this lawlessness was only used as an excuse by Westerners to extort further concessions from the Chinese. A major outburst of violence against foreigners occurred in the Boxer Rebellion in 1900–1901. Boxers was the popular name given to the Chinese who belonged to a secret organization called the Society of Harmonious Fists, whose aim was to push foreigners out of China. The Boxers murdered foreign missionaries, Chinese who had converted to Christianity, railroad workers, foreign businessmen, and even the German envoy to Peking. Response to the killings was immediate and overwhelming. An allied army consisting of British, French, German, Russian, American, and Japanese troops attacked Peking, restored order, and demanded more concessions from the Chinese government. The imperial government was so weakened that the forces of the revolutionary leader Sun Yat-sen (1866–1925), who adopted a program of "nationalism, democracy, and socialism," overthrew the Manchu dynasty in 1912. The new Republic of China remained weak and ineffective, and China's travails were far from over.

JAPAN In the late 1850s and early 1860s, it looked as if Japan would follow China's fate and be carved up into spheres of influence by aggressive Western powers. A remarkably rapid transformation, however, produced a very different result. Before 1868, the shogun, a powerful hereditary military governor assisted by a warrior nobility known as the samurai, exercised real power in Japan. The emperor's functions had become primarily religious. After the shogun's concessions to the Western nations, antiforeign sentiment led to a samurai revolt in 1867 and the restoration of the emperor as the rightful head of the government. The new emperor was the astute, dynamic, young Mutsuhito (1867–1912), who called his reign the Meiji (Enlightened Government) and inaugurated a remarkable transformation of Japan that has since been known as the Meiji Restoration.

Recognizing the obvious military and industrial superiority of the West, the new emperor and his advisers

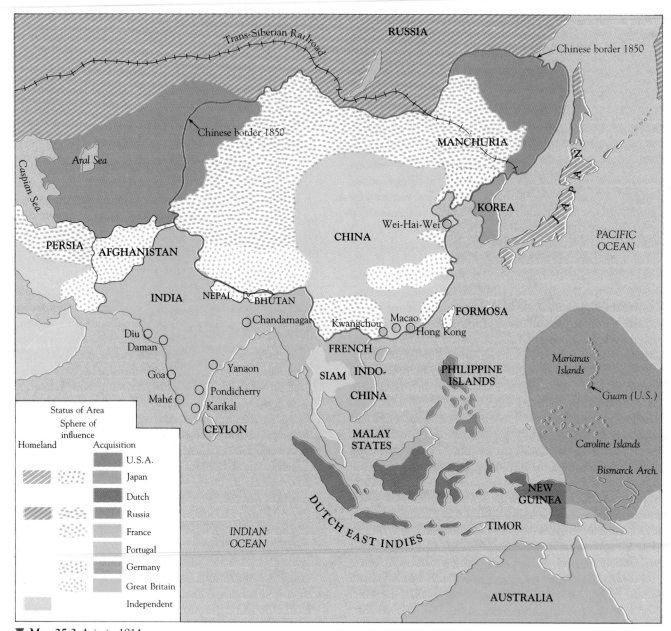

▼ **Map 25.3** Asia in 1914.

decided to modernize Japan by absorbing and adopting Western methods. Thousands of young Japanese were sent abroad to receive Western educations, especially in the social and natural sciences. A German-style army and a British-style navy were adopted. The Japanese copied the industrial and financial methods of the United States and developed a modern commercial and industrial system. A highly centralized administrative system copied from the French replaced the old feudal system. Initially, the Japanese adopted the French principles of social and legal equality, but by 1890 they had created an authoritarian political system that largely rejected democracy.

In its imitation of the West, Japan also developed a powerful military state. Universal military conscription was introduced in 1872, and a modern peacetime army of 240,000 was eventually established. The Japanese avidly pursued the Western imperialistic model. They defeated China in 1894–1895, annexed some Chinese territory, and established their own sphere of influence in China. After they had defeated the Russians in 1905, the Japanese were left in control of Korea. The Japanese had proven that an Eastern power could play the "white man's" imperialistic game and provided a potent example to native peoples in other regions of Asia and Africa.

INDIA   The British had been in control of India since the mid-nineteenth century. After crushing what the natives called the Great Rebellion (the British called it a mutiny), the British ruled India directly. Parliament had overall supervision while a small, all-white civil service directed affairs in India. This meant that 3,500 British officials ruled almost 300 million people.

No doubt, British rule bestowed a number of benefits upon India. The British put an end to the internal wars that had ravaged India for centuries and created a unified state through their centralized bureaucracy. They also brought Western technology—railroads, banks, mines, industry, medical knowledge, and hospitals. The British introduced Western-style secondary schools and colleges where the Indian upper classes were educated so that they could serve as trained subordinates in the government and army.

The Indians, however, had many complaints about British rule. Extreme poverty was a way of life for most Indians; almost two-thirds of the population were malnourished in 1901. British industrialization brought little improvement for the masses. British manufactured goods destroyed native industries while Indian wealth was used to pay British officials and a large army. The system of education served only the elite, upper-class Indians, and it was only conducted in the rulers' English language while 90 percent of the population remained illiterate. Even for the newly educated upper classes who benefited the most from their Western educations, British rule was degrading. The best jobs and the best housing were reserved for Britons. Despite their education, the Indians were never considered equals of the British whose racial attitudes were made quite clear by Lord Kitchener, one of Britain's foremost military commanders of India, when he said: "It is this consciousness of the inherent superiority of the European which has won for us India. However well educated and clever a native may be, and however brave he may prove himself, I believe that no rank we can bestow on him would cause him to be considered an equal of the British officer."[6] Such smug racial attitudes made it difficult for British rule, no matter how beneficent, ever to be ultimately accepted and

led to the rise of an Indian nationalist movement. By 1883, when the Indian National Congress was formed, moderate, educated Indians began to seek some self-government. Within another twenty years, radical demands for complete independence were being expressed. One of the major hurdles to the independence movement, however, came from Indians themselves. The Hindu majority was often bitterly opposed by the Muslim and Sikh religious minorities. These divisions, however, did not stop the movement for national independence.

▼ International Rivalry and the Coming of War

Between 1871 and 1914, Europeans experienced a long period of peace. There were wars (including wars of conquest in the non-Western world), but none involved the great powers. There were, however, a series of crises that might easily have led to general war. Until 1890, Bismarck of Germany exercised a restraining influence on Europeans. He realized that the emergence in 1871 of a unified Germany as the most powerful state on the Continent had upset the balance of power established at Vienna in 1815. Bismarck knew that Germany's success frightened Europeans, and he feared the creation of an anti-German coalition. The preservation of peace would best maintain the new status quo and preserve the new German state. As leader of the powerful German state and an astute diplomat, Bismarck dominated the European international scene until 1890.

The Bismarckian System

Bismarck was well aware that the French constituted Germany's greatest threat. The loss of Alsace-Lorraine to the Germans in the Franco-Prussian War ensured French desire for revenge. Bismarck understood that if France became allied with others, it would pose a real danger to Germany. His first move was to seek the cooperation of the traditionally conservative powers, Austria-Hungary and Russia. By 1873, he had concluded several treaties with them that created the first Three Emperors' League. The three powers agreed to suppress subversive activities at home and consult together if other powers threatened the European peace. The league failed to work very well, however, primarily because of Russian-Austrian rivalry in eastern Europe, specifically, in the Balkans.

The problem in the Balkans was yet another extension of the "Eastern Question" (see Chapter 22). The disintegration of the Turkish or Ottoman Empire had troubled Europeans for some time. Both Russia and Austria had designs on the Balkans. For Russia, the Balkans provided the shortest overland route to Istanbul and the Straits. Austria viewed the Balkans as fertile ground for Austrian expansion, which some Austrian leaders saw as the only way to circumvent the nationalities problem. Both Britain and France feared the extension of Russian power into the Mediterranean and Middle East. Although Germany had no real interests in the Balkans, Bismarck was fearful of the consequences of a war between Russia and Austria over the Balkans and served as a restraining influence on both powers. Events in the Balkans, however, precipitated a new crisis.

In 1876, the Balkan states of Serbia and Montenegro declared war on Turkey. Both were defeated, but Russia, with Austrian approval, attacked and defeated the Turks. By the Treaty of San Stefano in 1878, a large Bulgarian state, extending from the Danube in the north to the Aegean Sea in the south, was created. As Bulgaria was viewed as a Russian satellite, this Russian success caused the other great powers to call for a congress of European powers to discuss a revision of the treaty.

The Congress of Berlin, which met in the summer of 1878, was dominated by Bismarck. The congress effectively demolished the Treaty of San Stefano, much to Russia's humiliation. The new Bulgarian state was considerably reduced while the rest of the territory was returned to Turkish control. The three Balkan states of Serbia, Montenegro, and Romania, until then nominally under Turkish control, were recognized as independent. The other Balkan territories of Bosnia and Herzegovina were placed under Austrian protection; Austria could occupy but not annex them. Although the Germans received no territory, they felt they had at least preserved the peace among the great powers.

The Russians, however, resented the Germans' failure to prevent their diplomatic setback at Berlin. The Three Emperors' League was demolished. Fearful of a possible anti-German alliance between France, Russia, and possibly even Austria, Bismarck made a defensive alliance with Austria in 1879. Both powers agreed to support each other in the event of an attack by Russia. In 1882, this German-Austrian alliance was enlarged with the entrance of Italy, angry with the French over conflicting colonial ambitions in north Africa. The Triple Alliance of 1882 committed the three powers to support the existing political and social order while providing a defensive alliance against France or "two or more great powers not members of the alliance." Although the three powers agreed to a five-year term for the treaty, it was renewed regularly and became a regular feature of European international politics until World War I.

In the midst of his alliance making, Bismarck had not forgotten Russia and sought to reestablish the Three Emperors' League as the "only system offering the maximum stability for the peace of Europe." Austria, Germany, and Russia joined together once more in 1881. Again, however, the Three Emperors' League floundered on the shoals of Austrian-Russian hostility over the Balkans, and the league collapsed in 1886. Bismarck was still eager to maintain a good relationship with Russia, especially to prevent a French-Russian alliance that would threaten Germany with the possibility of a two-front war. In the Reinsurance Treaty of 1887, Germany and Russia pledged to remain neutral if the other became involved in a war with a third power, unless it was an aggressive war by Germany against France or Russia against Austria. At the same time, Bismarck tried to remain on good terms with Great Britain.

The Bismarckian system of alliances, geared to preserving peace and the status quo, had worked. Whether it would have continued to work in the face of Russian, Italian, French, and Austrian desires to change the status quo for their own gains is problematic. Even in Germany there was growing criticism of Bismarck's policy and increased talk about the need for expansion if Germany were to remain a great state. These forces for chauvinistic nationalism were encouraged when William II cashiered Bismarck in 1890 and assumed direction of Germany's foreign policy.

New Directions and New Crises

At the end of the nineteenth century and beginning of the twentieth, diplomatic activity was still largely the preserve of aristocrats who were guided by the eighteenth- and nineteenth-century concepts of balance of power, reason of state, and the concert of Europe. But the manipulation of national interests by the secret negotiations of aristocratic diplomats was increasingly threatened by mass interest in national affairs. The growth of nationalism and mass politics led to an increased emphasis on national competition. Politicians found that an appeal to nationalism carried great weight with the masses of people and could easily be reinforced by the use of mass communications. The growth of literacy after 1870 (see Mass Education later in the chapter) made possible mass-circulation newspapers that fostered jingoistic feelings and encouraged the desire for national prestige. Imperialism, as we have seen, was impelled not only by industrial and commercial interests, but to a great extent by public clamor for national greatness. Driven by popular excitement, diplomats found themselves increasingly directed by events rather than by rational calculations, and they were forced to seek short-term successes regardless of their long-term consequences.

Bismarck's alliances had served to bring the European powers into an interlocking system in which no one state could be certain of much support if it chose to initiate a war of aggression. After 1890, a new European diplomacy unfolded in which Europe became divided into two opposing camps that became more and more inflexible and unwilling to compromise.

After Bismarck's dismissal, Emperor William II embarked upon an activist foreign policy dedicated to enhancing German power by finding, as he put it, Germany's rightful "place in the sun." One of his changes in Bismarck's foreign policy was to drop the Reinsurance Treaty with Russia, which he viewed as being at odds with Germany's alliance with Austria. Although William II tried to remain friendly with Russia, the ending of the alliance achieved what Bismarck had feared: it brought France and Russia together. Long isolated by Bismarck's policies, republican France leapt at the chance to draw closer to tsarist Russia, and in 1894 the two powers concluded a military alliance.

The attitude of the British now became crucial. Secure in its vast empire, the British had long pursued a policy of "splendid isolation" toward the Continent. The British were startled, however, when many Europeans condemned their activity in the Boer War (1899–1902) in south Africa. Fearful of an anti-British continental alliance, they saw the weakness of "splendid isolation" and sought an alliance with a continental power. Initially, neither France nor Russia seemed a logical choice. Britain's traditional enmity with France had only intensified because of their imperialistic rivalries in Africa and Asia. Likewise, British and Russian imperialistic interests had frequently collided.

Germany, therefore, seemed the most likely potential ally. Certainly, there were both Britons and Germans

▼ **The Kaiser and the Krupps.** After 1890, Emperor William of Germany established an activist foreign policy for Germany that tended to increase tensions in Europe. The close connection between the imperialist state and armaments manufacturers is evident in this photograph. Emperor William II is shown visiting the Krupp works in 1912. The Krupp industrial empire was one of the largest in the world.

The Emperor's "Big Mouth"

▼ ▼ ▼

Emperor William II's world policy, which was aimed at finding Germany's "place in the sun," created considerable ill will and unrest among other European states, especially Britain. Moreover, the emperor had the unfortunate tendency to stir up trouble by his often tactless public remarks. In this 1908 interview, for example, William II intended to strengthen Germany's ties with Britain. His words had just the opposite effect and raised a storm of protest in both Britain and Germany.

Daily Telegraph Interview, October 28, 1908

As I have said, his Majesty honoured me with a long conversation, and spoke with impulsive and unusual frankness. "You English," he said, "are mad, mad, mad as March hares. What has come over you that you are so completely given over to suspicions quite unworthy of a great nation? What more can I do than I have done? I declared with all the emphasis at my command, in my speech at Guildhall, that my heart is set upon peace, and that it is one of my dearest wishes to live on the best of terms with England. Have I ever been false to my word? Falsehood and prevarication are alien to my nature. My actions ought to speak for themselves, but you listen not to them but to those who misinterpret and distort them. That is a personal insult which I feel and resent. To be forever misjudged, to have my repeated offers of friendship weighed and scrutinized with jealous, mistrustful eyes, taxes my patience severely. I have said time after time that I am a friend of England, and your Press—or, at least, a considerable section of it—bids the people of England to refuse my proffered hand, and insinuates that the other holds a dagger. How can I convince a nation against its will?"

"I repeat," continued his Majesty, "that I am a friend of England, but you make things difficult for me. My task is not of the easiest. The prevailing sentiment among large sections of the middle and lower classes of my own people is not friendly to England. I am, therefore, so to speak, in a minority in my own land, but it is a minority of the best elements as it is in England with respect to Germany. That is another reason why I resent your refusal to accept my pledged word that I am the friend of England. I strive without ceasing to improve relations, and you retort that I am your arch-enemy. You make it hard for me. Why is it? . . ."

"But, you will say, what of the German Navy? Surely, that is a menace to England! Against whom but England are my squadrons being prepared? If England is not in the minds of those Germans who are bent on creating a powerful fleet, why is Germany asked to consent to such new and heavy burdens of taxation? My answer is clear. Germany is a young and growing Empire. She has a world-wide commerce, which is rapidly expanding, and to which the legitimate ambition of patriotic Germans refuses to assign any bounds. Germany must have a powerful fleet to protect that commerce, and her manifold interests in even the most distant seas. She expects those interests to go on growing, and she must be able to champion them manfully in any quarter of the globe. Germany looks ahead. Her horizons stretch far away. She must be prepared for any eventualities in the Far East. Who can foresee what may take place in the Pacific in the days to come, days not so distant as some believe, but days, at any rate, for which all European Powers with Far Eastern interests ought steadily to prepare? Look at the accomplished rise of Japan; think of the possible national awakening of China; and then judge of the vast problems of the Pacific. Only those Powers which have great navies will be listened to with respect, when the future of the Pacific comes to be solved; and, if for that reason only, Germany must have a powerful fleet. It may even be that England herself will be glad that Germany has a fleet when they speak together on the same side in the great debates of the future."

who believed that their common German heritage (Anglo-Saxons from Germany had settled in Britain in the Early Middle Ages) made them "natural allies." But Britain was not particularly popular in Germany, nor did the British especially like the Germans. Industrial and commercial rivalry had created much ill feeling while William II's imperial posturing and grabbing for colonies made the British suspicious of Germany's ultimate aims (see the box on p. 868). Especially worrisome to the British was the German construction of a large navy, especially the number of battleships advocated by the persistent Admiral von Tirpitz, secretary of the German navy. The British now turned to their traditional enemy, France, and in 1904 concluded the Entente Cordiale by which the two settled all of their outstanding colonial disputes.

German response to the Entente was swift, creating what has been called the First Moroccan Crisis in 1905. The Germans chose to oppose French designs on Morocco in order to humiliate them and drive a wedge between the two new allies—Britain and France. Refusing to compromise, the Germans insisted upon an international conference to settle the problem. Germany's foolish saber rattling had the opposite effect of what had been intended and succeeded only in uniting Russia, France, Great Britain, and even the United States against Germany. The conference at Algeciras, Spain, in January 1906 awarded control of Morocco to France. Germany came out of the conference with nothing.

The First Moroccan Crisis of 1905–1906 had important repercussions. France and Britain drew closer together as both began to view Germany as a real threat to European peace. German leaders, on the other hand, began to speak of sinister plots to encircle Germany and hinder its emergence as a world power. Russia, too, grew more and more suspicious of the Germans and signed an agreement in 1907 with Great Britain. By that year, Europe's division into two major blocs—the Triple Alliance of Germany, Austria-Hungary, and Italy and the Triple Entente, as the loose confederation of Russia, France, and Great Britain was called—grew increasingly rigid at the same time that the problems in the Balkans were heating up.

Three forces were now working against any peaceful resolution of the region's difficult problems. The forces of nationalism continued to grow as Slavic peoples gained their freedom from Turkish overlordship and saw Austrian expansion as the new danger to their national aspirations. At the same time, Austrian and Russian rivalry in the Balkans only intensified. Finally, while Bismarck had labored to make Germany a mediator be-

Three Emperors' League	1873
Serbia and Montenegro Attack the Turks	1876
Treaty of San Stefano	1878
Congress of Berlin	1878
Defensive Alliance: Germany and Austria	1879
Renewal of Three Emperors' League	1881
Triple Alliance: Germany, Austria, and Italy	1882
Collapse of Three Emperors' League	1886
Reinsurance Treaty: Germany and Russia	1887
Military Alliance: Russia and France	1894
Entente Cordiale: France and Britain	1904
First Moroccan Crisis	1905–1906
Triple Entente: France, Britain, and Russia	1907
First Balkan War	1912
Second Balkan War	1913

tween Austria-Hungary and Russia, under Emperor William II, Germany became the chief advocate for maintaining the Ottoman Empire. No longer a mediator but a participant in Balkan affairs, Germany added a potentially dangerous element to the situation. A new series of crises between 1908 and 1913 over the struggle for the control of the remnants of the Ottoman Empire in the Balkans set the stage for World War I.

CRISES IN THE BALKANS, 1908–1913 The Bosnian Crisis of 1908–1909 began a chain of events that eventually went out of control. Since 1878, Bosnia and Herzegovina had been under the protection of Austria, but in 1908, Austria took the drastic step of annexing these two Slavic-speaking territories. Serbia became outraged at this action because it dashed the Serbians' hopes of creating a large Serbian kingdom that would include most of the south Slavs. This was why the Austrians had annexed Bosnia and Herzegovina. To the Austrians, a large Serbia would be a threat to the unity of the Austro-Hungarian Empire with its large Slavic population. The Russians, as protectors of their fellow Slavs and with their own desire to increase their authority in the Balkans, supported the Serbs and opposed the Austrian action. Backed by the Russians, the Serbs prepared for war against Austria. At this point William II intervened and demanded that the Russians accept Austria's annexation of Bosnia and Herzegovina or face war with Germany. Weakened from their defeat in the Russo-Japanese War in 1904–1905, the Russians were afraid to risk war and backed down. Humiliated, the Russians vowed revenge.

European attention returned to the Balkans in 1912 when Serbia, Bulgaria, Montenegro, and Greece organized a Balkan League and defeated the Turks in the First Balkan War. When the victorious allies were unable to agree on how to divide the conquered Turkish provinces of Macedonia and Albania, a second Balkan War erupted in 1913. Greece, Serbia, Romania, and Turkey attacked and defeated Bulgaria. As a result, Bulgaria obtained only a small part of Macedonia, and most of the rest was divided between Serbia and Greece. Yet Serbia's aspirations remained unfulfilled. The two Balkan wars left the inhabitants embittered and created more tensions among the great powers.

One of Serbia's major ambitions had been to acquire Albanian territory that would give it a port on the Adriatic. At the London Conference arranged by Austria at the end of the two Balkan wars, the Austrians had blocked Serbia's wishes by creating an independent Albania. The Germans, as Austrian allies, had supported this move. In their frustration, Serbian nationalists increasingly portrayed the Austrians as evil monsters who were keeping the Serbs from becoming a great nation. As Serbia's chief supporters, the Russians were also upset by the turn of events in the Balkans. A feeling had grown among Russian leaders that they could not back down again in the event of a confrontation with Austria or Germany in the Balkans. One Russian military journal even stated early in 1914: "We are preparing for a war in the west. The whole nation must accustom itself to the idea that we arm ourselves for a war of annihilation against the Germans." Moreover, as a result of the Balkan wars, both Russia and Austria expressed discontent that their supposed friends and allies, Great Britain and Germany, had not done enough to support them.

▼ **Map 25.4a** The Balkans in 1878.

This made the British and Germans more determined to support their allies in order to avoid endangering their alliances with them.

Austria-Hungary had achieved another of its aims, but it was still convinced that Serbia was a mortal threat to its empire and must at some point be crushed. Meanwhile, the French and Russian governments renewed their alliance and promised each other that they would not back down at the next crisis. Britain drew closer to France. By the beginning of 1914, two armed camps viewed each other with suspicion. An American in Europe observed, "The whole of Germany is charged with electricity. Everybody's nerves are tense. It only needs a spark to set the whole thing off." The German ambas-sador to France noted at the same time that "peace remains at the mercy of an accident." The European "age of progress" was about to come to an inglorious and bloody end.

▼ Intellectual and Cultural Developments: Toward the Modern Consciousness

Before 1914, most Europeans continued to believe in the values and ideals that had been generated by the Scientific Revolution and the Enlightenment. Reason,

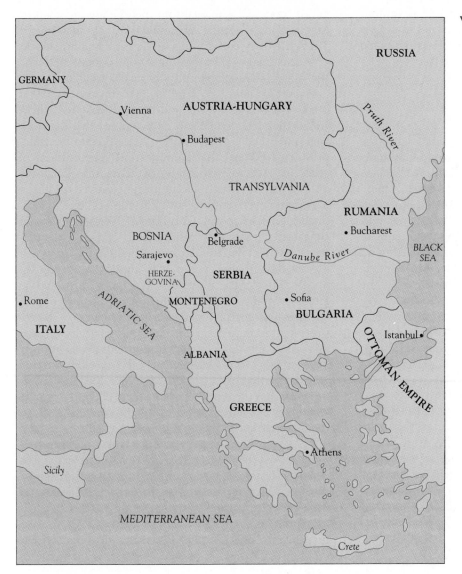

▼ **Map 25.4b.** The Balkans in 1913.

science, and progress were still important words in the European vocabulary. The ability of human beings to improve themselves and achieve a better society seemed to be well demonstrated by a rising standard of living, urban improvements, and mass education. Such products of modern technology as electric lights, phonographs, and automobiles reinforced the popular prestige of science and the belief in the ability of the human mind to comprehend the universe through the use of reason. Between 1870 and 1914, however, a dramatic transformation in the realm of ideas and culture challenged many of these assumptions. A new view of the physical universe, a flight to the irrational, alternative views of human nature, and radically innovative forms of literary and artistic expression shattered old beliefs and opened the way to a modern consciousness. Although the real impact of many of these ideas was not felt until after World War I, they served to provoke a sense of confusion and anxiety before 1914 that would become even more pronounced after the war.

Developments in the Sciences: The Emergence of a New Physics

Science was one of the chief pillars underlying the optimistic and rationalistic view of the world that many Westerners shared in the nineteenth century. Supposedly based on hard facts and cold reason, science offered a certainty of belief in the orderliness of nature that was comforting to many people for whom traditional religious beliefs no longer had much meaning. This faith in science's ability to explain the world was reflected in an introductory paragraph in the University of Chicago's catalog in 1893: "It seems probable that most of the grand underlying principles in the physical sciences have been firmly established and that further advances are to be sought chiefly in the rigorous application of these principles to all the phenomena which come under our notice." Many naively believed that the application of already known scientific laws would give humanity a complete understanding of the physical world and an accurate picture of reality. The new physics dramatically altered that perspective.

Throughout much of the nineteenth century, Westerners adhered to the mechanical conception of the universe postulated by the classical physics of Isaac Newton. In this perspective, the universe was viewed as a giant machine in which time, space, and matter were objective realities that existed independently of those observing them. Matter was thought to be composed of indivisible and solid material bodies called atoms.

These views were first seriously questioned at the end of the nineteenth century. Some scientists had discovered that certain elements such as radium and polonium spontaneously gave off rays or radiation that apparently came from within the atom itself. Atoms were not simply hard, material bodies but small worlds containing such subatomic particles as electrons and protons that behaved in seemingly random and inexplicable fashion. Inquiry into the disintegrative process within atoms became a central theme of the new physics.

Building upon this work, in 1900 a Berlin physicist, Max Planck (1858–1947), disclosed a discovery that he believed was "as important as that of Newton." Planck rejected the belief that a heated body radiates energy in a steady stream but maintained instead that it did so discontinuously, in irregular packets of energy that he called "quanta." The quantum theory raised fundamental questions about the subatomic realm of the atom. By 1900, the old view of atoms as the basic building blocks of the material world was being seriously questioned, and the world of Newtonian physics was in trouble.

Albert Einstein (1879–1955), a German-born patent officer working in Switzerland, pushed these new theories of thermodynamics into new terrain. In 1905, Einstein published a paper entitled "The Electro-dynamics of Moving Bodies" that contained his special theory of relativity. According to relativity theory, space and time are not absolute, but relative to the observer, and both are interwoven into what Einstein called a four-dimensional space-time continuum. Neither space nor time had an existence independent of human experience. As Einstein later explained simply to a journalist: "It was formerly believed that if all material things disappeared out of the universe, time and space would be left. According to the relativity theory, however, time and space disappear together with the things."[7] Moreover, matter and energy reflected the relativity of time and space. Einstein concluded that matter was nothing but another form of energy. His epochal formula $E = mc^2$—that each particle of matter is equivalent to its mass times the square of the velocity of light—was the key theory explaining the vast energies contained within the atom. It led to the atomic age.

Like many geniuses throughout the ages, Einstein soon learned that new ideas are not readily acceptable to people accustomed to old patterns. His work threatened the long-accepted Newtonian celestial mechanics and was not well received initially. When Einstein applied for a position at the University of Bern in 1907, he was immediately rejected. Both Planck's quantum theory and Einstein's theories of relativity were known only to a relatively small group of scientists. A total eclipse of the sun in May 1919, however, which provided calculations derived from the observation of the planet Mercury, confirmed Einstein's general theory of relativity and opened the scientific and intellectual world to his ideas. The 1920s would become the "heroic age" of physics.

Flight to the Irrational

Intellectually, the period from 1871 to 1914 witnessed a combination of contradictory developments. Thanks to the influence of science, confidence in human reason and progress still remained a dominant thread of thought. At the same time, however, a small group of intellectuals attacked optimistic progress, dethroned reason, and glorified the irrational. Although these thinkers and writers were a distinct minority, the destructiveness of World War I made their ideas even more appealing after 1918 when it seemed that they had been proven right.

Friedrich Nietzsche (1844–1900) was one of the intellectuals who glorified the irrational. According to Nietzsche, Western bourgeois society was decadent and incapable of any real cultural creativity, primarily because of an excessive emphasis on the rational faculty at the expense of emotions, passions, and instincts. Reason, claimed Nietzsche, actually played little role in human life because humans were at the mercy of irrational life forces.

Nietzsche believed that Christianity shouldered much of the blame for Western civilization's enfeeblement. The "slave morality" of Christianity, he believed, had obliterated the human impulse for life and had crushed the human will:

> I call Christianity the one great curse, the one enormous and innermost perversion, . . . I call it the one immortal blemish of mankind. . . . Christianity has taken the side of everything weak, base, ill-constituted, it has made an ideal out of opposition to the preservative instincts of strong life. . . . Christianity is called the religion of pity.—Pity stands in antithesis to the basic emotions which enhance the energy of the feeling of life: it has a depressive effect. One loses force when one pities.[8]

According to Nietzsche, Christianity crushed spontaneous human instincts and inculcated weakness and humility.

How, then, could Western society be renewed? Nietzsche first called for the need to recognize that "God is dead." Europeans, said Nietzsche, had killed God, and it

▼ **Friedrich Nietzsche.** Between 1871 and 1914, two contradictory impulses were evident in European intellectual life. Although many thinkers maintained their confidence in human reason and progress, other intellectuals downplayed reason and glorified irrational instincts. Friedrich Nietzsche was a German philosopher who claimed that irrational life forces, not reason, determined the lives of human beings. Nietzsche proclaimed the "death of God" and the arrival of the "Superman."

was no longer possible to believe in some kind of cosmic order. Eliminating God and hence Christian morality had liberated human beings and made it possible to create a higher kind of being Nietzsche called the superman: "I teach you the Superman. Man is something that is to be surpassed."[9] Superior intellectuals must free themselves from the ordinary thinking of the masses, "the slaves, or the populace, or the herd, or whatever name you care to give them." Beyond good and evil, the supermen would create their own values, embrace life passionately, and lead the masses: "It is necessary for higher man to declare war upon the masses." Nietzsche rejected and condemned political democracy, social reform, and universal suffrage.

Another popular revolutionary against reason in the 1890s was Henri Bergson (1859–1941), a French Jewish philosopher whose lectures at the University of Paris made him one of the most important influences in French thought in the early twentieth century. Bergson accepted rational, scientific thought as a practical instrument for providing useful knowledge, but, according to Bergson, it was incapable of arriving at truth or ultimate reality. To him, reality was the "life force" that suffused all things; it could not be divided into analyzable parts. Reality was a whole that could only be grasped intuitively and experienced directly. When we analyze it, we have merely a description, no longer the reality we have experienced.

Georges Sorel (1847–1922), a French political theorist, combined Bergson's and Nietzsche's ideas on the limits of rational thinking with his own passionate interest in revolutionary socialism. Sorel understood the political potential of the nonrational. He criticized Marxism for being an apocalyptical religion, not a scientific system, and advocated violent action as the only sure way to achieve the aims of socialism. To destroy capitalist society, he recommended the use of the general strike, envisioning it as a mythic image that had the power to inspire workers to take violent, heroic action against the capitalist order. Sorel also came to believe in the need for a small elite ruling body for the new socialist society since the masses were incapable of ruling themselves.

Sigmund Freud and the Emergence of Psychoanalysis

The two contradictory trends between 1871 and 1914, the glorification of science and reason and the praise of the irrational, came together in the work of Sigmund Freud. Although poets and mystics had revealed a world of unconscious and irrational behavior, many scientifically oriented intellectuals under the impact of Enlightenment thought continued to believe that human beings responded to conscious motives in a rational fashion. At the end of the nineteenth century and beginning of the twentieth, the Viennese doctor Sigmund Freud put forth a series of theories that undermined optimism about the rational nature of the human mind. Freud's thought, like the new physics and the irrationalism of Nietzsche, added to the uncertainties of the age.

Sigmund Freud (1856–1939) had studied medicine at the University of Vienna where he received a medical degree in 1881. Freud first came to his discovery of the unconscious or subconscious realms of human beings while working with patients who had nervous disorders. He said, "Anyone who wanted to make a living from the treatment of nervous patients must clearly be able to do something to help them. My therapeutic arsenal contained only two weapons: electrotherapy and hypnotism."[10] Freud found electrotherapy worthless, but was fascinated by the results of hypnosis. He found that patients who had been hypnotized often revealed information about their past lives that cured them of hysteria when they were confronted with this information upon awakening. Freud was impressed by what appeared to be an empirically verifiable unconscious level of human existence. He spent the rest of his life studying the unconscious and its relationship to the conscious mind. His major ideas were published in 1900 in *The Interpretation of Dreams*, which contained the basic foundation of what came to be known as psychoanalysis.

According to Freud, human behavior was strongly determined by the unconscious, by past experiences and internal forces of which people were largely oblivious. To explore the contents of the unconscious, Freud relied not only on hypnosis but also on free-thought associations in which the patient spoke freely of thoughts so that the doctor could enter his or her unconscious. Dreams were another entry into the unconscious, but they were dressed in an elaborate code that needed to be deciphered if the contents were to be properly understood.

But why did some experiences whose power continued to influence one's life remain unconscious? According to Freud, this was repression (see the box on p. 876), a process by which painful and unsettling experiences were blotted from conscious awareness but still continued to influence behavior since they had become part of the unconscious. To explain how repression worked, Freud developed an elaborate theory of the inner life of human beings.

According to Freud, a human being's inner life was a battleground of three contending forces: the id, ego, and superego. The id was the center of unconscious drives and was ruled by what Freud termed the pleasure principle. As creatures of desire, human beings directed their energy toward pleasure and away from pain. The id contained all kinds of lustful drives and desires, crude appetites and impulses, loves and hates. The ego was the seat of reason and hence the coordinator of the inner life. It was governed by the reality principle. Although humans were dominated by the pleasure principle, a true pursuit of pleasure was not feasible. The reality principle meant that people rejected pleasure for the sake of life in society; reality thwarted the unlimited pursuit of pleasure. The superego was the locus of conscience and represented the inhibitions and moral values that society in general and parents in particular imposed upon people. The superego served to force the ego to curb the unacceptable pressures of the id.

The human being was thus a battleground between id, ego, and superego. Ego and superego exerted restraining influences on the unconscious id and repressed or kept out of consciousness what they wanted to. The most important repressions, according to Freud, were sexual, and he went on to develop a theory of infantile sexual drives embodied in the Oedipus complex (Electra complex for females) or the infant's craving for exclusive possession of the parent of the opposite sex.

To Freud, the inner life of humans was not a pretty picture. Repression began in childhood, and psychoanalysis was accomplished through a dialogue between psychotherapist and patient in which the therapist probed deeply into memory in order to retrace the chain of repression all the way back to its childhood origins. By making the conscious mind aware of the unconscious and its repressed contents, the patient's psychic conflict was resolved.

Freud, Marx, and Darwin have often been linked together as the three intellectual giants of the nineteenth century. Like the theories of Marx and Darwin, many of Freud's ideas have been shown to be wrong in many details. Like them, nevertheless, he is still regarded as an important figure because of the impact his theories have had. Many historians still accept Freud's judgment of himself: "I have the distinct feeling that I have touched on one of the great secrets of nature."

The Impact of Darwin: Social Darwinism and Racism

In the second half of the nineteenth century, scientific theories were sometimes wrongly applied to achieve other ends. The application of Darwin's principle of organic evolution to the social order came to be known as Social Darwinism. The most popular exponent of Social Darwinism was the British philosopher Herbert Spencer (1820–1893). Using Darwin's terminology, Spencer argued that societies were organisms that evolved through time from a struggle with their environment. Progress came from "the struggle for survival," as the "fit"—the

▼ **Sigmund Freud.** Sigmund Freud was one of the intellectual giants of the nineteenth century. His belief that unconscious forces strongly determined human behavior created the foundation for twentieth-century psychoanalysis.

strong—moved forward while the weak fell by the wayside. As Spencer expressed it in 1896 in his book *Social Statics*:

> Pervading all Nature we may see at work a stern discipline which is a little cruel that it may be very kind. . . . Meanwhile, the well-being of existing humanity and the unfolding of it into this ultimate perfection, are both secured by the same beneficial though severe discipline to which the animate creation at large is subject. It seems hard that an unskillfulness, which with all his efforts he cannot overcome, should entail hunger upon the artisan. It seems hard that a laborer, incapacitated by sickness from competing with his stronger fellows, should have to bear the resulting privations. It seems hard that widows and orphans should be left to struggle for life or death. Nevertheless, when regarded not separately but in connection with the interests of universal

Freud and the Concept of Repression
▼ ▼ ▼

Freud's psychoanalytical theories resulted from his attempt to understand the world of the unconscious. This excerpt is taken from a lecture given in 1909 in which Freud describes how he arrived at his theory of the role of repression. Although Freud valued science and reason, his theories of the unconscious produced a new image of the human being as governed less by reason than by irrational forces.

Sigmund Freud, *Five Lectures on Psychoanalysis*

I did not abandon it [his technique of encouraging patients to reveal forgotten experiences], however, before the observations I made during my use of it afforded me decisive evidence. I found confirmation of the fact that the forgotten memories were not lost. They were in the patient's possession and were ready to emerge in association to what was still known by him; but there was some force that prevented them from becoming conscious and compelled them to remain unconscious. The existence of this force could be assumed with certainty, since one became aware of an effort corresponding to it if, in opposition to it, one tried to introduce the unconscious memories into the patient's consciousness. The force which was maintaining the pathological condition became apparent in the form of resistance on the part of the patient.

It was on this idea of resistance, then, that I based my view of the course of psychical events in hysteria. In order to effect a recovery, it had proved necessary to remove these resistances. Starting out from the mechanism of cure, it now became possible to construct quite definite ideas of the origin of the illness.

The same forces which, in the form of resistance, were now offering opposition to the forgotten material's being made conscious, must formerly have brought about the forgetting and must have pushed the pathogenic experiences in question out of consciousness. I gave the name of "repression" to this hypothetical process, and I considered that it was proved by the undeniable existence of resistance.

The further question could then be raised as to what these forces were and what the determinants were of the repression in which we now recognized the pathogenic mechanism of hysteria. A comparative study of the pathogenic situations which we had come to know through the cathartic procedure made it possible to answer this question. All these experiences had involved the emergence of a wishful impulse which was in sharp contrast to the subject's other wishes and which proved incompatible with the ethical and aesthetic standards of his personality. There had been a short conflict, and the end of this internal struggle was that the idea which had appeared before consciousness as the vehicle of this irreconcilable wish fell a victim to repression, was pushed out of consciousness with all its attached memories, and was forgotten. Thus the incompatibility of the wish in question with the patient's ego was the motive for the repression; the subject's ethical and other standards were the repressing forces. An acceptance of the incompatible wishful impulse or a prolongation of the conflict would have produced a high degree of unpleasure; this unpleasure was avoided by means of repression, which was thus revealed as one of the devices serving to protect the mental personality.

---

humanity, these harsh fatalities are seen to be full of beneficence—the same beneficence which brings to early graves the children of diseased parents, and singles out the intemperate and the debilitated as the victims of an epidemic.[11]

The state, then, should not intervene in this natural process. Some prominent businessmen used Social Darwinism to explain their success in the competitive business world. The strong and fit, the able and energetic

had risen to the top; the stupid and lazy had fallen by the wayside.

Darwin's ideas were also applied to human society in an even more radical way by rabid nationalists and racists. In their pursuit of national greatness, extreme nationalists argued that individual needs must be subordinated to those of the nation and often insisted that nations, too, were engaged in a "struggle for existence" in which only the fittest survived. The German general Friedrich von Bernhardi gave war a Darwinist interpretation in his book, *Germany and the Next War*, published in 1907. He argued that:

> War is a biological necessity of the first importance, a regulative element in the life of mankind which cannot be dispensed with, since without it an unhealthy development will follow, which excludes every advancement of the race, and therefore all real civilization. "War is the father of all things." The sages of antiquity long before Darwin recognized this.[12]

Numerous nationalist organizations preached the same doctrine as Bernhardi. The Nationalist Association of Italy, for example, founded in 1910, declared that "we must teach Italy the value of international struggle. But international struggle is war? Well, then, let there be war! And nationalism will arouse the will for a victorious war, . . . the only way to national redemption."[13]

Although certainly not new to Western society, racism, too, was dramatically revived and strengthened by new biological arguments. Darwinian concepts were used throughout the Western world to justify the new imperialism of the late nineteenth century. Perhaps nowhere was the combination of extreme nationalism and racism more evident and more dangerous than in Germany where racist nationalism was expressed in volkish thought. The concept of the *Volk* (nation, people, or race) had been an underlying idea in German history since the beginning of the nineteenth century. Volkish thought combined a belief in the superiority of German culture with the sense of a universal mission for the German people. One of the chief propagandists for German volkish ideology at the turn of the century was Houston Stewart Chamberlain (1855–1927), a Briton who became a German citizen. His book, *The Foundations of the Nineteenth Century*, published in 1899, made a special impact on Germany. Modern-day Germans, according to Chamberlain, were the only pure successors of the Aryans who were portrayed as the true and original creators of Western culture. The Aryan race, under German leadership, must be prepared to fight for Western civilization and save it from the destructive assaults of such lower races as Jews, Negroes, and Orientals. Increasingly, Jews were singled out by German volkish nationalists as the racial enemy in biological terms and as parasites who wanted to destroy the Aryan race.

ANTI-SEMITISM   Anti-Semitism was not new to European civilization. Since the Middle Ages, Jews had been portrayed as the murderers of Christ and subjected to mob violence; their rights had been restricted, and they had been physically separated from Christians in quarters known as ghettos.

In the nineteenth century, as a result of the ideals of the Enlightenment and the French Revolution, Jews were increasingly granted legal equality in many European countries. The French revolutionary decrees of 1790 and 1791 emancipated the Jews and admitted them to full citizenship. They were not completely accepted, however, and anti-Semitism remained a fact of French life. In 1805, Napoleon consolidated their position as citizens, but followed this in 1808 with an "Infamous Decree" that placed restrictions on Jewish moneylending and on the movement of Jews within France.

This ambivalence toward the Jews was apparent throughout Europe. In Prussia, for example, Jews were emancipated in 1812 but still restricted. They could not hold government offices or take advanced degrees in universities. After the revolutions of 1848, emancipation became a fact of life for Jews throughout western and central Europe. For many Jews, emancipation enabled them to leave the ghetto and become assimilated as hundreds of thousands of Jews entered what had been the closed worlds of parliaments and universities. "A Jew could leave his Jewishness" behind as the career of Benjamin Disraeli, who became prime minister of Great Britain, demonstrated. Many Jews became eminently successful as bankers, lawyers, scientists, scholars, journalists, and stage performers. In 1880, for example, Jews made up 10 percent of the population of the city of Vienna, Austria, but 39 percent of its medical students and 23 percent of its law students.

These achievements represent only one side of the picture, however. When right-wing mobs yelled "Death to the Jews" during the Dreyfus trial, they illustrated the continuing strength of anti-Semitism in France. In Germany and Austria during the 1880s and 1890s, conservatives founded right-wing anti-Semitic parties, such as Adolf Stöcker's Christian Social Workers and Karl Lueger's Christian Socialists. These parties used anti-Semitism to win the votes of traditional lower-middle-class groups who felt threatened by the new economic forces of the times. These German anti-Semitic parties were based on race. In medieval times Jews could convert to Christianity and escape from their religion. To modern racial anti-Semites, Jews were racially stained; this could not be altered by conversion. One could not be both German and Jew. Hermann Ahlwardt, an anti-Semitic member of the German Reichstag, made this clear in a speech to that body: "The Jew is no German. . . . A Jew who was born in Germany does not thereby become a German; he is still a Jew. Therefore it is imperative that we realize that Jewish racial characteristics differ so greatly from ours that a common life of Jews and

The Voice of Zionism: Theodor Herzl and the Jewish State

▼ ▼ ▼

The Austrian Jewish journalist Theodor Herzl wrote The Jewish State in the summer of 1895 in Paris while he was covering the Dreyfus case for his Vienna newspaper. In several weeks, during a period of feverish composition, he set out to analyze the fundamental causes of anti-Semitism and devise a solution to the "Jewish problem." In this selection, he discusses two of his major conclusions.

Theodor Herzl, *The Jewish State*

I do not intend to arouse sympathetic emotions on our behalf. That would be a foolish, futile, and undignified proceeding. I shall content myself with putting the following questions to the Jews: Is it true that, in countries where we live in perceptible numbers, the position of Jewish lawyers, doctors, technicians, teachers, and employees of all descriptions becomes daily more intolerable? True, that the Jewish middle classes are seriously threatened? True, that the passions of the mob are incited against our wealthy people? True, that our poor endure greater sufferings than any other proletariat?

I think that this external pressure makes itself felt everywhere. In our economically upper classes it causes discomfort, in our middle classes continual and grave anxieties, in our lower classes absolute despair.

Everything tends, in fact, to one and the same conclusion, which is clearly enunciated in that classic Berlin phrase: "Juden 'raus!" (Out with the Jews!)

I shall now put the Jewish Question in the curtest possible form: Are we to "get out" now? And if so, to what place?

Or, may we yet remain? And if so, how long?

Let us first settle the point of staying where we are. Can we hope for better days, can we possess our souls in patience, can we wait in pious resignation till the princes and peoples of this earth are more mercifully disposed towards us? I say that we cannot hope for a change in the current of feeling. And why not? Were

we as near to the hearts of princes as are their other subjects, even so they could not protect us. They would only feed popular hatred of Jews by showing us too much favour. By "too much," I really mean less than is claimed as a right by every ordinary citizen, or by every race. The nations in whose midst Jews live are all, either covertly or openly, Anti-Semitic. . . .

The whole plan is in its essence perfectly simple, as it must necessarily be if it is to come within the comprehension of all.

Let the sovereignty be granted us over a portion of the globe large enough to satisfy the rightful requirements of a nation; the rest we shall manage for ourselves.

The creation of a new State is neither ridiculous nor impossible. We have in our day witnessed the process in connection with nations which were not in the bulk of the middle class, but poorer, less educated, and consequently weaker than ourselves. The Governments of all countries scourged by Anti-Semitism will be keenly interested in assisting us to obtain the sovereignty we want. . . .

Palestine is our ever-memorable historic home. The very name of Palestine would attract our people with a force of marvellous potency. Supposing his Majesty the Sultan were to give us Palestine, we could in return undertake to regulate the whole finances of Turkey. We should there form a portion of the rampart of Europe against Asia, an outpost of civilisation as opposed to barbarism. We should as a neutral State remain in contact with all Europe, which would have to guarantee our existence. The sanctuaries of Christendom would be safeguarded by assigning to them an extra-territorial status such as is well known to the law of nations. We should form a guard of honour about these sanctuaries, answering for the fulfillment of this duty with our existence. This guard of honour would be the great symbol of the solution of the Jewish Question after eighteen centuries of Jewish suffering.

Germans under the same laws is quite impossible because the Germans will perish."[14] After 1898, the political strength of the German anti-Semitic parties began to decline.

The worst treatment of Jews in the last two decades of the nineteenth century and the first decade of the twentieth occurred in eastern Europe where 72 percent of the entire world Jewish population lived. In Romania, Jews were not allowed to hold office or vote. Anti-Semitism was a regular part of tsarist Russian life. Russian Jews were admitted to secondary schools and universities only under a quota system and were forced to live in certain regions of the country. Persecutions and pogroms were widespread. Between 1903 and 1906, pogroms took place in almost 700 Russian towns and villages, mostly in the Ukraine region. Hundreds of thousands of Jews decided to emigrate to escape the persecution. Between 1881 and 1899, an average of 23,000 Jews left Russia each year. Many of them went to the United States, although some (probably about 25,000) moved to Palestine, which soon became the focus for a Jewish nationalist movement called Zionism.

The emancipation of the nineteenth century had presented vast opportunities to some Jews, but dilemmas to others. What was the price of citizenship? Did emancipation mean full assimilation and did assimilation mean the disruption of traditional Jewish life? Many paid the price willingly, but others questioned its value and advocated a different answer, a return to Palestine. For many Jews, Palestine had long been the land of their dreams. During the nineteenth century, as nationalist ideas spread and Italians, Poles, Irish, Greeks, and others sought national emancipation so too did the idea of national independence capture the imagination of some Jews. A key figure in the growth of political Zionism was Theodor Herzl (1860–1904). Herzl had received a law degree in Vienna where he became a journalist for a Viennese newspaper. He was shocked into action on behalf of Jews when he covered the Dreyfus trial as a correspondent for his newspaper in Paris. In 1896, he published a book called *The Jewish State* (see the box on p. 878) in which he straightforwardly advocated that "The Jews who wish it will have their state." Financial support for the development of yishuvs or settlements in Palestine came from wealthy Jewish banking families, especially from Baron Edmond James de Rothschild, called "Father of the Yishuv" for his contributions. Rothschild and others like him wanted a refuge in Palestine for persecuted Jews, not a political Jewish state. Even settlements were difficult because Palestine was then part of the Ottoman Empire and Turkish authori-

ties were opposed to Jewish immigration. In 1891, one Jewish essayist pointed to the problems this would create:

> We abroad are accustomed to believe that Erez Israel [the land of Israel] is almost totally desolate at present . . . but in reality it is not so. . . . Arabs, especially those in towns, see and understand our activities and aims in the country but keep quiet and pretend as if they did not know, . . . and they try to exploit us, too, and profit from the new guests while laughing at us in their hearts. But if the time comes and our people make such progress as to displace the people of the country . . . they will not lightly surrender the place.[15]

Despite the warnings, however, the First Zionist Congress, which met in Switzerland in 1897, proclaimed as its aim the creation of a "home in Palestine secured by public law" for the Jewish people. In 1900, 1,000 Jews migrated to Palestine. And although 3,000 Jews went annually to Palestine between 1904 and 1914, the Zionist dream remained just that on the eve of World War I.

The Attack on Christianity and the Response of the Churches

The growth of scientific thinking as well as the forces of modernization presented new challenges to the Christian churches. Although the churches experienced defections among Europe's educated elite, they remained strong at a popular level and in some places even showed remarkable institutional strength.

Industrialization and urbanization had an adverse effect on the churches. The mass migration of people from the countryside to the city meant a change from the close-knit, traditional ties of the village in which the church had been a key force to new urban patterns of social life from which the churches were often excluded. The established Christian churches had a weak hold on workers. For one thing, new churches were rarely built in working-class neighborhoods. Although workers were not atheists, as is sometimes claimed, they tended to develop their own culture in which organized religion played little role.

The political movements of the late nineteenth century were also hostile to the established Christian churches. Beginning during the eighteenth-century Enlightenment and continuing well into the nineteenth century, European governments, especially in predominantly Catholic countries, had imposed controls over church courts, religious orders, and appointments of the clergy. But after the failure of the revolutions of 1848, governments were eager to use the churches' aid in re-establishing order and therefore relaxed these controls. Education was given back to the Catholic church in France, Roman Catholicism was made "the only religion of the Spanish nation," and the jurisdiction of Catholic church courts over marriage was restored in Austria. In France, the murder of the archbishop of Paris by the Paris Commune of 1871 served as an impetus to return people temporarily to organized religion. As the British Catholic Cardinal Manning wrote to the British prime minister, "My belief is that society without Christianity is the Commune. What hope can you give me?"[16]

Eventually, however, the close union of state authorities with established churches produced a backlash in the form of anticlericalism, especially by the liberal nation-states of the late nineteenth century. As one example, in the 1880s the French republican government substituted civic training for religious instruction in order to undermine the Catholic church's control of education. In 1901, Catholic teaching orders were outlawed, and four years later, in 1905, church and state were completely separated.

Science became one of the chief threats to all the Christian churches and even to religion itself in the nineteenth century. Darwin's theory of evolution, accepted by ever-larger numbers of educated Europeans, seemed to contradict the doctrine of divine creation. By suppressing Darwin's books and forbidding the teaching of the evolutionary hypothesis, the churches often caused even more educated people to reject established religions.

The social sciences proved just as dangerous as science to the Christian churches. From their studies of ancient societies, anthropologists concluded that modern religions, including Christianity, were based on early myths, cults, and superstitions. Sociologists placed more and more faith in mechanistic evolution as the key to all social progress and increasingly criticized religion for being detrimental to that progress. Intellectuals such as Nietzsche and psychologists denounced religion as an illusion created by human beings who were afraid of the threatening world around them.

The scientific spirit encouraged a number of biblical scholars to apply critical principles to the Bible, leading to the so-called higher criticism. One of its leading exponents was Ernst Renan (1823–1892), a French Catholic scholar. In his *Life of Jesus*, published in 1863, Renan questioned the historical accuracy of the Bible and presented a radically different picture of Jesus Christ. He saw Christ not as the son of God, but as a human being whose value lay in the example he

provided by his life and teaching. To Renan, Christ's belief in his own divinity was merely the result of hallucinations.

One response of the Christian churches to these attacks was the outright rejection of modern ideas and forces. Protestant fundamentalist sects were especially important in maintaining a literal interpretation of the Bible. The Catholic church under Pope Pius IX (1846–1878) also took a rigid stand against modern ideas. In 1864, Pope Pius issued a papal encyclical called the *Syllabus of Errors* in which he stated that it is "an error to believe that the Roman Pontiff can and ought to reconcile himself to, and agree with, progress, liberalism, and modern civilization." He condemned nationalism, socialism, religious toleration, lay-controlled education, and freedom of speech and press. At the First Vatican Council in 1870, Pius IX championed the doctrine of papal infallibility, which stated that the pope, when speaking *ex cathedra*—that is, officially—on matters of faith and morals, could not err in his pronouncements.

Rejection of the new was not the churches' only response, however. A religious movement called Modernism included an attempt by the churches to reinterpret Christianity in the light of new developments. The modernists viewed the Bible as a book of useful moral ideas, encouraged Christians to become involved in social reforms, and insisted that the churches must provide a greater sense of community. The Catholic church condemned Modernism in 1907 and drove it underground by the beginning of the World War I. In Protestant churches, modernists competed with fundamentalists and had more success.

Yet another response of the Christian churches to modern ideas was compromise, an approach especially evident in the Catholic church during the pontificate of Leo XIII (1878–1903). Pope Leo permitted the teaching of evolution as a hypothesis in Catholic schools and allowed Catholics to take part in the politics of liberal nation-states. In 1892, he urged French Catholics to accept the French Republic. He also responded to the challenges of modernization in the economic and social spheres. In his encyclical *De Rerum Novarum*, issued in 1891, he upheld the individual's right to private property but at the same time criticized "naked" capitalism for the poverty and degradation in which it had left the working classes. Much in socialism, he declared, was Christian in principle, but he condemned Marxian socialism for its materialistic and antireligious foundations. The pope recommended that Catholics form socialist parties and labor unions of their own. Despite his new thoughts, Leo XIII still clung to a conservative, hierarchical social order organized according to corporate groups that would cooperate on the basis of Christian principles. A number of young, radical priests rejected this conservative approach. By accepting class conflict and advocating use of the strike, they hoped to spread the Gospel among poor workers. Jules Lemire organized meetings of Christian democratic priests in France while Romolo Murri founded workers' groups in central Italy after 1900. Before his death in 1903, Pope Leo XIII insisted that these radical priests cease their efforts.

Other steps were taken to win support for Christianity among the working-class poor and to restore religious practice among the urban working classes. These efforts were not strong among mainstream churches because their parish systems were not prepared to cope with the flood of urban immigrants. Sects of evangelical missionaries were more successful, especially the Salvation Army founded in London in 1865 by William Booth, the first "general" of the army. The Salvation Army established food centers, shelters where the homeless could sleep, and "rescue homes" for women, but for a larger purpose as Booth admitted: "it is primarily and mainly for the sake of saving the soul that I seek the salvation of the body."[17] The Salvation Army moved to Paris in the 1880s, but was not well received by French Protestants who considered its revivalist-style meetings vulgar.

Literature and the Arts: Toward Modernism

The revolution in physics and psychology was paralleled by a revolution in literature and the arts. Before 1914, writers and artists were rebelling against the traditional literary and artistic styles that had dominated European cultural life since the Renaissance. The changes that they produced have since been called Modernism.

LITERATURE: NATURALISM AND SYMBOLISM Throughout much of the late nineteenth century, literature was dominated by Naturalism. Naturalists accepted the material world as real and felt that literature should be realistic. By addressing social problems, writers could contribute to an objective understanding of the world. Although Naturalism was a continuation of Realism, it lacked the underlying note of liberal optimism about people and society that had still been prevalent in the 1850s. The Naturalists were pessimistic about Europe's future. They doubted the existence of free will and portrayed characters caught in the grip of forces beyond their control.

The novels of the French writer, Émile Zola (1840–1902), provide a good example of Naturalism. Against a backdrop of the urban slums and coal fields of northern France, Zola showed how alcoholism and different environments affected people's lives. The materialistic science of his age had an important influence on Zola. He had read Darwin's *Origin of Species* and had been impressed by its emphasis on the struggle for survival and the importance of environment and heredity. These themes were central to his *Rougon-Macquart*, a twenty-volume series of novels on the "natural and social history of a family." Zola maintained that the artist must analyze and dissect life as a biologist would a living organism. He said, "I have simply done on living bodies the work of analysis which surgeons perform on corpses."

The last half of the nineteenth century was a golden age for Russian literature. The nineteenth-century realistic novel reached its high point in the works of Leo Tolstoy (1828–1910) and Fyodor Dostoevsky (1821–1881). Tolstoy's greatest work was *War and Peace*, a lengthy novel played out against the historical background of Napoleon's invasion of Russia in 1812. It is realistic in its vivid descriptions of military life and character portrayal. Each person is delineated clearly and analyzed psychologically. Upon a great landscape, Tolstoy imposed a fatalistic view of history that ultimately proved irrelevant in the face of life's enduring values of human love and trust.

Fyodor Dostoevsky combined narrative skill and acute psychological and moral observation with profound insights into human nature. Dostoevsky maintained that the major problem of his age was a loss of spiritual belief. Western people were attempting to gain salvation through the construction of a materialistic paradise built only by human reason and human will. Dostoevsky feared that the failure to incorporate spirit would result in total tyranny. His own life experiences led him to believe that only through suffering and faith could the human soul be purified, views that are evident in his best-known works, *Crime and Punishment* and *The Brothers Karamazov*.

At the turn of the century, a new group of writers, known as the Symbolists, reacted against Realism. Primarily interested in writing poetry, the Symbolists believed that an objective knowledge of the world was impossible. The external world was not real but only a collection of symbols that reflected the true reality of the individual human mind. Art, they believed, should function for its own sake instead of serving, criticizing, or seeking to understand society. In the works of the symbolist poets, W. B. Yeats and Rainer Maria Rilke,

Symbolist Poetry: Art for Art's Sake

▼ ▼ ▼

The Symbolist movement was an important foundation for Modernism. The Symbolists believed that the working of the mind was the proper study of literature. Arthur Rimbaud was one of Symbolism's leading practitioners in France. Although his verses seem to have little real meaning, they were not meant to describe the external world precisely, but to enchant the mind. Art was not meant for the masses, but only for "art's sake." Rimbaud wrote, "By the alchemy of the words, I noted the inexpressible. I fixed giddiness."

Arthur Rimbaud, *The Drunken Boat*

As I floated down impassable rivers,
I felt the boatmen no longer guiding me:
After them came redskins who with war cries
Nailed them naked to the painted poles.

I was oblivious to the crew,
I who bore Flemish wheat and English cotton.
When the racket was finished with my boatmen,
The waters let me drift my own free way.

In the tide's furious pounding,
I, the other winter, emptier than children's minds,
I sailed! And the unmoored peninsulas
Have not suffered more triumphant turmoils.

The tempest blessed my maritime watches.
Lighter than a cork I danced on the waves,
Those eternal rollers of victims,
Ten nights, without regretting the lantern-foolish eye!

Sweeter than the bite of sour apples to a child,
The green water seeped through my wooden hull,
Rinsed me of blue wine stains and vomit,
Broke apart grappling iron and rudder.

And then I bathed myself in the poetry
Of the star-sprayed milk-white sea,
Devouring the azure greens; where, pale
And ravished, a pensive drowned one sometimes floats;

Where, suddenly staining the blueness, frenzies
And slow rhythms in the blazing of day,
Stronger than alcohol, vaster than our lyres,
The russet bitterness of love ferments. . . .

I have dreamed of the green night bedazzled with snow,
A kiss climbing slowly to the eyes of the sea,
The flow of unforgettable sap,
And the yellow-blue waking of singing phosphorous!

Long months I have followed, like maddened cattle,
The surge assaulting the rocks
Without dreaming that the Virgin's luminous feet
Could force a muzzle on the panting ocean!

I have struck against the shares of incredible Floridas
Mixing panther-eyed flowers like human skins!
Rainbows stretched like bridle reins
Under the ocean's horizon, toward sea-green troops!

I have seen the fermenting of monstrous marshes,
Nets where a whole Leviathan rots in the reeds!
The waters collapsing in the middle of the calm,
And horizons plunging toward the abyss!

Glaciers, silver suns, waves of pearl, charcoal skies,
Hideous beaches at the bottom of brown gulfs
Where giant serpents devoured by vermin
Tumble from twisted trees with black perfumes!

I would have liked to show the children those dolphins
On the blue waves, those golden singing fish.
—The froth of flowers lulled my voyagings,
Ineffable winds gave me wings by the moment. . . .

poetry ceased to be part of popular culture because only through a knowledge of the poet's personal language could one hope to understand what the poet was saying (see the box on p. 882). Symbolism began in France and its founder, Stéphane Mallarmé (1842–1898), attempted to summarize its poetic theory in one sentence: "It is not description which can unveil the efficacy and beauty of monuments, seas, or the human face in all their maturity and native state, but rather evocation, allusion, suggestion."

THE ARTS The period from 1871 to 1914 was one of the most fertile in the history of art and witnessed three major movements, Impressionism, Post-Impressionism, and abstract painting.

Since the Renaissance, the task of artists had been to represent reality as accurately as possible. By the late nineteenth century, artists sought new forms of expression. The preamble to modern painting can be found in Impressionism, a movement that originated in France in the 1870s when a group of artists rejected the studios and museums and went out into the countryside to paint nature directly. Camille Pissarro (1830–1903), one of Impressionism's founders, expressed what they sought:

> Precise drawing is dry and hampers the impression of the whole, it destroys all sensations. Do not define too closely the outlines of things; it is the brush stroke of the right value and color which should produce the drawing. . . . The eye should not be fixed on one point, but should take in everything, while observing the reflections which the colors produce on their surroundings. Work at the same time upon sky, water, branches, ground, keeping everything going on an equal basis and unceasingly rework until you have got it. . . . Don't proceed according to rules and principles, but paint what you observe and feel. Paint generously and unhesitatingly, for it is best not to lose the first impression.[18]

Above all, said, Pissarro, "Don't be timid in front of nature: one must be bold, at the risk of being deceived, and making mistakes. One must have only one master—nature; she is the one always to be consulted."

Pissarro's suggestions are visibly portrayed in the work of Claude Monet (1840–1926). He was especially enchanted with water and painted many pictures in which he sought to capture the interplay of light, water, and atmosphere, especially evident in *Impression, Sunrise*. But the Impressionists did not just paint scenes from nature. Streets and cabarets, rivers, and busy boulevards—wherever people congregated for work and leisure—formed their subject matter.

By the 1880s, a new movement known as Post-Impressionism arose in France but soon spread to other European countries. Post-Impressionism retained the Impressionist emphasis upon light and color but revolutionized it even further by paying more attention to structure and form. Post-Impressionists sought to use both color and line to express inner feelings and produce a personal statement of reality rather than an imitation of objects. Impressionist paintings had retained a sense of realism, but the Post-Impressionists shifted from objective reality to subjective reality and, in so doing, began to withdraw from the artist's traditional task of depicting the external world. Post-Impressionists were the real forerunners of modern art.

Paul Cézanne (1839–1906) was one of the most important Post-Impressionists. Initially, he was influenced by the Impressionists but soon rejected their work. In his paintings, such as *Woman with Coffee Pot*, Cézanne sought to express visually the underlying structure and form of everything he painted. The geometric shapes

▼ **Claude Monet, *Impression, Sunrise*.** Impressionism was a movement in painting that originated in France and is often considered the precursor to modern painting. Impressionists rejected "rules and principles" and sought to paint what they observed and felt in order "not to lose the first impression." As is evident in *Impression, Sunrise*, Monet sought to capture his impression of the fleeting moments of sunrise through the simple interplay of light, water, and atmosphere.

▼ **Paul Cézanne, *Woman with Coffee Pot*.** Post-Impressionism began to replace Impressionism in the 1880s, especially in France. Post-Impressionists sought above all to express their inner feelings and capture on canvas their own vision of reality. In *Woman with Coffee Pot*, Paul Cézanne tried to relate the geometric shapes of his central female figure to the geometric shapes of the coffee pot and the rectangles of the door panels.

(cylinders and triangles) of the human form are related to the geometric shapes (cylinders and rectangles) of the other objects in the picture. As Cézanne explained to one young painter: "You must see in nature the cylinder, the sphere, and the cone."

Like Cézanne, Paul Gauguin (1848–1903) was first influenced by the Impressionists, but later turned away from them, calling them superficial. Gauguin sought a deeper reality in the world of the unconscious and primitive life. His rejection of modern civilization and search for paradise in such places as Tahiti resulted in his almost neoprimitive and mystical paintings of Tahitians. As in

The Day of the Gods, Gauguin used shape and large areas of flat color to create intense images.

Another famous Post-Impressionist was the tortured and tragic figure, Vincent van Gogh (1853–1890). For van Gogh, art was a spiritual experience. He was especially interested in color and believed that it could act as its own form of language. Van Gogh maintained that artists should paint what they feel. In his *Starry Night*, he painted a sky alive with whirling stars that overwhelmed the huddled buildings in the village below.

By the beginning of the twentieth century, the belief that the task of art was to represent "reality" had lost much of its meaning. By that time, the new psychology and the new physics had made it evident that many people were not sure what constituted reality anyway. Then, too, the growth of photography gave artists another reason to reject visual realism. First invented in the 1830s, photography became popular and widespread after George Eastman created the first Kodak camera in 1888 for the mass market. What was the point of an artist doing what the camera did better? Unlike the camera, which could only mirror reality, artists could create reality. As in literature, so also in modern art, individual consciousness became the source of meaning. As one artist expressed it: "Each [artist] should follow where the pulse of his own heart leads. . . . Our pounding heart drives us down, deep down to the source of all. What springs from this source, whether it may be called dream, idea or phantasy—must be taken seriously."[19] Between 1905 and 1914, this search for individual expression produced a great variety of painting schools that had their greatest impact after World War I.

Henri Matisse (1869–1954) was the leading figure in a group of painters called the Fauvists—the "wild beasts"—by the critics. Their program, evident in Matisse's 1905 *Portrait with Green Stripe*, was to depict emotions by using colors that were not related to the natural colors of the subject. Criticized for this work, Matisse responded: "I did not create a woman, I made a painting."

By 1905, one of the most important figures in modern art was just beginning his career. Pablo Picasso (1881–1973) was from Spain but settled in Paris in 1904. Picasso was extremely flexible and painted in a remarkable variety of styles. He was instrumental in the development of a new style called cubism that used geometric designs as visual stimuli to recreate reality in the viewer's mind. Picasso's 1907 work *Les Demoiselles d'Avignon* has been called the first cubist painting.

The modern artist's flight from "visual reality" reached a high point in 1910 with the beginning of abstract painting. A Russian who worked in Germany, Vasily Kandinsky (1866–1944), was one of the founders of abstract expressionism. As is evident in his *Painting with White Border* Kandinsky sought to avoid representation altogether. He believed that art should speak directly to the soul. To do so, it must avoid any reference to visual reality and concentrate on color.

Modernism in the arts revolutionized architecture and architectural practices. A new principle known as functionalism motivated this revolution. Functionalism meant that buildings, like the products of machines, should be "functional" or useful, fulfilling the purpose for which they were constructed. Art and engineering were to be unified, and all unnecessary ornamentation was to be stripped away.

The United States was a leader in these pioneering architectural designs. Unprecedented urban growth and the absence of restrictive architectural traditions allowed for new building methods, especially in the relatively "new city" of Chicago. The Chicago school of the

▼ **Vincent Van Gogh, *The Starry Night*.** The Dutch painter Vincent Van Gogh was a major figure among the Post-Impressionists. His career was brief; all of his artistic activity occurred in a ten-year span of time. His originality and power of expression made a strong impact upon his artistic successors. In *The Starry Night*, Van Gogh's subjective vision was given full play as the dynamic swirling forms of the heavens above overwhelmed the village below. The heavens seem alive with a mysterious spiritual force.

▼ **Henri Matisse, *Portrait with a Green Stripe.*** By 1900, art was no longer considered a means of representing reality as artists sought to create reality by examining the depths of their inner consciousness. One group of painters known as the Fauvists sought to express emotions by the use of colors starkly different from the natural colors of the subject. In his *Portrait with a Green Stripe*, Henri Matisse used startling green, black, and purple hues to describe the human face. While recognizable, it is certainly not one that would be encountered in everyday life.

1890s, led by Louis H. Sullivan (1856–1924), used reinforced concrete, steel frames, and electric elevators to build skyscrapers virtually free of external ornamentation. One of Sullivan's most successful pupils was Frank Lloyd Wright (1869–1959), who became known for innovative designs in domestic architecture. Wright's private houses, built chiefly for wealthy patrons, featured geometric structures with long lines, overhanging roofs, and severe planes of brick and stone. The interiors were open spaced and included cathedral ceilings and built-in furniture and lighting fixtures. Wright pioneered the modern American house.

In Europe, the Germans took the lead in modern architectural design. Most outstanding was Walter Gropius (1883–1969), who anticipated much modern building with his Fagus factory building in Alfeld, Germany, built between 1911 and 1914. This unornamented steel box with walls of windows reflected Gropius's belief that "the sensibility of the artist must be combined with the knowledge of the technician to create new forms in architecture and design."

MUSIC   Until the mid-nineteenth century, the classical-Romantic tradition, based on the tonal harmony of the seven-note scale with major and minor keys, dominated the musical world. Richard Wagner (1813–1883) made the first significant departure from this tradition with his "musical dramas." In his operas, such as *Parsifal* and *Tristan and Isolde*, music was combined with poetry and visual effects to produce a total artistic experience. Wagner also experimented with musical moods and even departed from strict tonality in his compositions.

▼ **Pablo Picasso, *Les Demoiselles D'Avignon.*** Pablo Picasso, a major pioneer and activist of modern art, began his career in Paris at the beginning of the twentieth century. Picasso experimented with a remarkable variety of modern styles. His *Les Demoiselles D'Avignon* was the first great example of Cubism, which one art historian has called "the first style of this century to break radically with the past." Geometric shapes replace traditional forms, forcing the viewer to recreate reality in his or her own mind.

At the beginning of the twentieth century, developments in music paralleled those in painting. Expressionism in music was a Russian creation, the product of the composer Igor Stravinsky (1882–1971) and the Ballet Russe, the dancing company of Sergei Diaghilev (1872–1929). Together they revolutionized the world of music with Stravinsky's ballet, *The Rite of Spring*. When it was performed in Paris in 1913, the savage and primitive sounds and beats of the music and dance caused a near riot from an audience outraged at its audacity.

▼ Education and Leisure in an Age of Mass Society

Between 1871 and 1914, Europe witnessed the emergence of a mass society. Trade unions and political parties gave an economic and political voice to many workers. Mass conscription created mass armies and possibilities for warfare on a scale never before imagined. The masses became a major force in Western society as mass education and mass leisure created new forms of popular culture.

Mass Education

Mass education was a product of the "mass society" of the late nineteenth and early twentieth centuries. Being "educated" in the early nineteenth century meant attending a secondary school or possibly even a university.

▼ **Walter Gropius, Fagus Factory Building.** Walter Gropius was one of Europe's pioneers in modern architecture. His Fagus Factory Building in Alfeld, Germany, a simple steel structure with walls of windows, expressed the basic principle of modern architectural functionalism, the belief that buildings should be useful and devoid of all unnecessary ornamentation. Gropius's building established a model for many modern buildings.

Secondary schools, such as the *Gymnasien* in Germany and the public schools (which were really private boarding schools) in Britain, mostly emphasized a classical

▼ **Vasily Kandinsky, *Painting with White Border*.** The attempt of modern artists to reject the principle of visual reality reached its high point with Abstract Expressionism. One of its founders was the Russian Vasily Kandinsky, who sought to eliminate representation altogether by focusing on color and avoiding any resemblance to visual reality. In *Painting with White Border*, Kandinsky used color "to send light into the darkness of men's hearts." He believed that color could, like music, fulfill a spiritual goal of appealing directly to the human being.

education based on the study of Greek and Latin. Secondary and university education were primarily for the elite, the sons of government officials, nobles, or the wealthier middle class. By the 1830s and 1840s, a lesser system of secondary education, such as the *Realschule* in Germany, had come into being for the children of the lower middle class and rich peasants. After 1850, secondary education was expanded as more middle-class families sought employment in public service and the professions or entry into elite scientific and technical schools. Existing secondary schools also placed more emphasis on practical and scientific education by adding foreign languages and natural sciences to their curriculum.

At the beginning of the nineteenth century, European states showed little interest in primary education. In Catholic countries after the upheavals of the French revolutionary era, teaching orders of nuns and lay brothers dominated most primary schools. Only in the German states was there a state-run system for elementary education. In Prussia, primary education had already become compulsory in the eighteenth century.

In 1833, the French government instructed local governments to establish an elementary school for both boys and girls, thus creating a system of state-run, secular schools. Attendance, however, was not required. In the United States, state governments (except in the southern states) had already established both primary and secondary schools. By 1860, 60 percent of the white children in the northeastern United States were enrolled in an educational institution. In England, elementary education was mostly left to the Church of England and to the Nonconformists (Protestants who did not belong to the Church of England). Both Anglican and Nonconformist elementary schools were financed by voluntary subscription.

Although government officials considered primary schools to be guarantors of "social stability," primary school teachers were not highly regarded. Most were from peasant or artisan backgrounds with minimal training. Salaries depended on local community support, and teachers were often forced to supplement their meager incomes with other work. Attendance at primary schools was also irregular. In rural society, children were still expected to work in the fields. In industrializing countries like Britain and France, both employers and parents were eager to maintain the practice of child labor. Even this irregular system of elementary education, however, stimulated a growth in literacy in Europe.

In the decades after 1870, the functions of the state were extended to include the development of mass education in state-run systems. Between 1870 and 1914, most Western governments began to offer at least primary education to both boys and girls between the ages of six and twelve. In most countries it was not optional. Austria had decreed free, compulsory elementary education in 1869. In France, a law of March 29, 1882, made primary education compulsory for all children between six and thirteen. The British Parliament at first was unwilling to go that far but did pass a compromise Education Act in 1870 that provided public support for church schools while subjecting them to government inspection. In 1880, elementary education was made compulsory in Britain, but it was not until 1902 that an act of Parliament brought all elementary schools under county and town control. States also assumed responsibility for better training of teachers by establishing teacher-training schools.

By the beginning of the twentieth century, many European states, especially in northern and western Europe, had provided state-financed primary schools, salaried and trained teachers, and free, compulsory mass elementary education. In 1900, Germany spent 12 percent of its national budget on public education while Britain spent 10 percent and France 8 percent. States in southern and eastern Europe offered much less. Spain, for example, spent only 1.5 percent of its budget on education.

Why did European states make this commitment to mass education? Liberals believed that education was important to personal and social improvement and also sought, as in France, to supplant Catholic education with moral and civic training based on secular values. Even conservatives, however, were attracted to mass education as a means of improving the quality of military recruits and training people in social discipline. In 1875, a German military journal stated: "We in Germany consider education to be one of the principal ways of promoting the strength of the nation and above all military strength."[20]

Another incentive for mass education came from industrialization. In the early Industrial Revolution, unskilled labor was sufficient to meet factory needs, but the new firms of the Second Industrial Revolution demanded skilled labor. Diversification of the economic and social structure provided incentives to learn new skills. Both boys and girls with an elementary education had new possibilities of jobs beyond their villages or small towns, including white-collar jobs in railways, new metro stations, post offices, banking and shipping firms, teaching, and nursing. To industrialists, then, mass education furnished the trained workers they needed.

Nevertheless, the chief motive for mass education was political. On the one hand, the increase in suffrage created the need for a more educated electorate. Even more important, however, mass compulsory education instilled patriotism and nationalized the masses, providing an opportunity for even greater national integration. As people lost their ties to local regions and even to religion, nationalism supplied a new faith. The use of a single national language created greater national unity than did loyalty to a ruler, but in some countries this process was complicated by the existence of large national minorities. In the polyglot empires, such as Austria-Hungary and Russia, ethnic minorities strove to hold on to their languages since these defined their nationalities. In Russian Poland, for example, the attempt by Russian authorities to impose the Russian language on Polish elementary schools led to the creation of underground schools where local clerks, priests, children of local gentry, and, above all, women taught Polish. A Polish primer, written by Konrad Prósszynski in 1872, had sold 750,000 copies by 1906.

A nation's motives for universal elementary education largely determined what was taught in the elementary schools. Obviously, indoctrination in national values took on great importance. At the core of the academic curriculum were reading, writing, arithmetic, national history, especially geared to a patriotic view, geography, literature, and some singing and drawing. The education of boys and girls varied, however. Where possible, the sexes were separated. Girls did less math and no science but concentrated on such domestic skills as sewing, washing, ironing, and cooking, all prerequisites for providing a good home for husband and children. Boys were taught some practical skills, such as carpentry, and even some military drill. Most of the elementary schools also inculcated the middle-class virtues of hard work, thrift, sobriety, cleanliness, and respect for the family. For most students, elementary education led to apprenticeship and a job.

The development of compulsory elementary education created a demand for teachers, and most of them were female. In the United States, for example, females constituted two-thirds of all teachers by the 1880s. Many men viewed the teaching of children as an extension of women's "natural role" as nurturers of children. Moreover, females were paid lower salaries, in itself a considerable incentive for governments to encourage the establishment of teacher-training institutes for women. The first female colleges were really teacher-training schools. In Britain, the women's colleges of Queen's and Bedford were established in the 1840s to provide teacher

▼ A Women's College. Women were largely excluded from male-dominated universities before 1900. Consequently, the demand of women for higher education led to the foundation of women's colleges, most of which were primarily teacher-training schools. This photograph shows a group of women in an astronomy class at Vassar College in the United States in 1878. Maria Mitchell, a famous woman astronomer, was head of the department.

training for middle-class spinsters who needed to work. A pioneer in the development of female education was Barbara Bodichon (1827–1891), who established her own school in which girls were trained not only for domesticity, but also for economic independence. It was not until the beginning of the twentieth century that women were permitted to enter the male-dominated universities. In France, 3 percent of university students in 1902 were women; by 1914, their number had increased to 10 percent of the total.

The most immediate result of mass education was an increase in literacy. Compulsory elementary education and the growth of literacy were directly related. In Germany, Great Britain, France, and the Scandinavian countries, adult illiteracy was virtually eliminated by 1900. Where there was less schooling, the story is very different. Adult illiteracy rates were 79 percent in Serbia, 78 percent in Romania, 72 percent in Bulgaria, and 79 percent in Russia. These were all countries where little had been invested in compulsory mass education. The growth of literacy, in turn, was important in the development of a new mass culture, one of whose prominent features was the emergence of new forms of mass leisure.

Mass Leisure

In the pre-industrial centuries, play or leisure activities had been closely connected to work patterns based on the seasonal or daily cycles typical of agricultural and even artisanal life. The process of industrialization in the nineteenth century had an enormous impact upon that traditional pattern. The factory imposed new work patterns that were determined by the rhythms of machines and clocks and removed work time completely from the family environment of farms and workshops. Work and leisure became opposites as leisure was viewed as what people do for fun after work. In fact, the new leisure hours created by the industrial system—evening hours after work, weekends, and later a week or two in the summer—largely determined the contours of the new mass leisure.

At the same time, the influx of rural people into industrial towns eventually caused the demise of traditional village culture, especially the fairs and festivals that had formed such an important part of that culture. Industrial progress, of course, demanded that such traditional celebrations as Whitsuntide, which had occasioned thirteen days of games and drinking, be eliminated or reduced. In fact, Whitsuntide had been reduced by the 1870s to a single one-day holiday.

New technology and business practices also determined the forms of the new mass leisure. The new technology created novel experiences for leisure, such as the Ferris wheel at amusement parks, while the mechanized urban transportation systems of the 1880s meant that even the working classes were no longer dependent on neighborhood bars, but could make their way to athletic events, amusement parks, and dance halls. Likewise, railroads could take people to the beaches on weekends.

The commercialization of leisure had come first from the upper and middle classes. Their desire for leisure created new forms of tourism, urban entertainment districts, and amusing fads to while away the time. But the increase in real wages after 1860 in the advanced industrial countries opened the way to commercial leisure for

the lower classes. An increase in real wages enabled working classes to enjoy middle-class pleasures, which included not only such unhealthy items as sugar and cigarettes, but also tickets to music halls, amusement parks, and beach excursions.

BACKGROUND TO MASS LEISURE: RATIONAL RECREATION
The new mass leisure did not arrive overnight. Much leisure in the nineteenth century, especially in the middle-class environment, remained a product of the family home. Also important was the development of what social historians have called "rational recreation." After the 1830s, a number of middle-class reformers, fearful of the urban working masses (the "dangerous classes"), believed that there was a need for forms of recreation that would instill in the lower classes the middle-class values of self-control, individualism, family, and, above all, respectability. Some upper- and middle-class reformers hoped as well to create a new sense of community for all classes while improving the individual. One avenue for such activity came from social clubs. In Britain, beginning in the 1850s, Henry Solly's Working Men's Social Clubs joined education with entertainment by providing cards and games and leisure activities for adult men. So, too, did the Young Men's Christian Association (YMCA) established in London in 1844.

The movement for "rational" recreation also led to new urban services, especially public libraries, museums, and public parks. Peel Park, created in Manchester in 1846, provided a model for others. Often the establishment of these new services depended on philanthropy. The wealthy American industrialist Andrew Carnegie explained his generosity: "How a man spends his time at work may be taken for granted but how he spends his hours of recreation is really the key to his progress in all the virtues."[21] To justify the creation of public parks, the British Parliament explained that open places set aside for the pleasure of the "humbler classes, would assist to wean them from low and debasing pleasure."

Historians are divided about the effect these activities had on the working classes. One of the chief purposes of "rational recreation" was to bring social classes together, but this was hardly achieved. Recreational activities continued to divide along class lines. The upper and middle classes continued to go to their own exclusive beach resorts. And when the custom of promenade concerts, which provided live orchestra entertainment, open to all classes of people, was first brought to Britain from Germany, one British observer's comment made clear the class division: "Can an Englishman imagine the inhabitants of the filthy cellars, alleys and courts of our towns, or the peasants of our villages, sitting in Kensington or other gardens, mixed up with the gentry of our metropolis and the officers of our army? The idea seems to us preposterous."[22]

FORMS OF THE NEW MASS LEISURE   The dramatic increase in literacy after 1871 made possible the rise of mass newspapers, such as the *Evening News* (1881) and *Daily Mail* (1896) in London, which sold millions of copies a day. Known as the "yellow press" in the United States, these newspapers shared some common characteristics. They were written in an easily understood style and tended to be extremely sensational. Unlike eighteenth-century newspapers that were full of serious editorials and lengthy political analysis, these tabloids provided lurid details of crimes, jingoistic diatribes, gossip, and sports news. There were other forms of cheap literature as well. Specialty magazines, such as *Family Herald* for the entire family, and women's magazines began in the 1860s. Pulp fiction for adults included the extremely popular westerns with their innumerable variations on conflicts between cowboys and Indians.

Music and dance halls appeared in the last half of the nineteenth century. The first music hall in London was constructed in 1849 for a lower-class audience. As is evident from one Londoner's observation, the music hall was primarily for males:

> [It was a] popular place of Saturday night resort with working men, as at them they can combine the drinking of the Saturday night glass and the smoking of the Saturday night pipe, with the seeing and hearing of a variety of entertainments, ranging from magnificent ballets and marvelous scenic illusions to inferior tumbling, and from well-given operatic selections to the most idiotic of the so-called comic songs of the Jolly Dogs Class.[23]

By the 1880s, there were five hundred music halls in London. Promoters gradually made them more respectable and broadened their fare to entice both women and children to attend the programs. The new dance halls, which were all the rage by 1900, were more strictly oriented toward adults. Contemporaries were often shocked by the sight of young people engaged in sexually suggestive dancing.

The upper and middle classes had created the first market for tourism, but as wages increased and workers were given paid vacations, tourism, too, became another form of mass leisure. Thomas Cook (1808–1892) was a British pioneer of mass tourism. Secretary to a British

▼ **Middle Classes at the Beach.** By the beginning of the twentieth century, changing work and leisure patterns created a new mass leisure. The upper and middle classes created the first market for tourism, although it too became another form of mass leisure as wages increased and workers received paid vacations. This photograph shows primarily the middle classes enjoying a British beach at the beginning of the twentieth century.

temperance group, Cook had accepted responsibility for organizing a railroad trip to temperance gatherings in 1841. This experience led him to offer trips on a regular basis after he found that by renting special trains, lowering prices, and increasing the number of passengers, he could make substantial profits. In 1867, he offered tours to Paris and by the 1880s to Switzerland. Of course, overseas tours were for the rich, but through their savings clubs even British factory workers were able to take weekend excursions by the turn of the century.

By the late nineteenth century, team sports had also developed into yet another important form of mass leisure. Sports were by no means a new activity. Landed elites had long had sporting clubs and activities that enabled them to display their privilege and status. The lower classes also had their sporting contests. In middle-class minds, these were usually associated with drunkenness, gambling, and excessive rowdiness. Attempts by educational and religious reformers in the nineteenth century to "purify" the games of the poor and make them respectable led to the creation of modern sporting contests.

The new team sports of the late nineteenth century exhibited certain characteristics. Unlike the old rural games, they were no longer chaotic and spontaneous activities, but became strictly organized with sets of rules and officials to enforce them. These rules were the products of organized athletic groups, such as the English Football Association (1863) and the American Bowling Congress (1895).

The Fight Song: Sports in the English Public School
▼ ▼ ▼

In the second half of the nineteenth century, organized sports were often placed at the center of the curriculum in English public schools. These sports were not just for leisure, but were intended to instill character, strength, and teamwork. This "fight song" was written by H. B. Tristam for the soccer team at Loretto School.

H. B. Tristam, *Going Strong*

Sing Football the grandest of sports in the world,
And you know it yourself if your pluck's never curled,
If you've gritted your teeth and gone hard to the last,
And sworn that you'll never let anyone past.

Chorus
Keeping close upon the ball—we drive it through them all,

And again we go rushing along, along, along;
O the tackle and the run, and the matches we have won,
From the start to the finish going strong, strong, strong, going strong!

If you live to be a hundred you'll never forget
How they hacked in the scrum, how you payed back the debt;
The joy of the swing when you tackled your man,
The lust of the fray when the battle began.

Long hence when you look with a quivering eye
On the little white tassel you value so high;
You'll think of the matches you've played in and won,
And you'll long for the days that are over and done.

The new sports were not just for leisure or fun, but like other forms of middle-class "rational recreation," they were intended to provide excellent training for people, especially youth. Not only could they develop individual skills, but they could also acquire a sense of teamwork useful for military service. These characteristics were already evident in the British public schools in the 1850s and 1860s when organized sports were placed at the center of the curriculum in such schools as Harrow, Uppingham, and Loretto (see the box above). At Loretto, for example, education was supposed to instill "First—Character. Second—Physique. Third—Intelligence. Fourth—Manners. Fifth—Information."

The new team sports rapidly became professionalized. In Britain, soccer had its Football Association in 1863 and rugby its Rugby Football Union in 1871. In the United States, the first National Association to recognize professional baseball players was formed in 1863. By 1900, the National League and American League had a complete monopoly over professional baseball. The development of urban transportation systems made possible the construction of stadiums where thousands could attend, making mass spectator sports a big business. In 1872, 2,000 people watched the British Soccer Cup finals. By 1885, the crowd had increased to 10,000 and by 1901 to 100,000. Professional teams became objects of

mass adulation by crowds of urbanites who compensated for their lost sense of identity in mass urban areas by developing these new loyalties. Spectator sports even reflected class differences. Upper-class soccer teams in Britain viewed working-class teams as vicious and prone to "money-grubbing, tricks, sensational displays, and utter rottenness."

The sports cult of the late nineteenth century was mostly male oriented. Many men believed that females were not particularly suited for "vigorous physical activity," although it was permissible for middle-class women to indulge in such easy sports as croquet and lawn tennis. Eventually, some athletics crept into women's colleges and girls' public schools in England.

The new forms of popular leisure were standardized forms of amusement that drew mass audiences. Although some argued that they were important for improving people, in truth, they mostly served to provide entertainment and distract people from the realities of their work lives. Much of mass leisure was secular. Churches found that they had to compete with popular amusements for people's attention on Sundays. The new mass leisure also represented a significant change from earlier forms of popular culture. Festivals and fairs had been based on an ethos of active community participation, whereas the new forms of mass leisure were standardized for largely passive mass audiences. Amusement parks and professional sports teams were, after all, big businesses organized to make profits.

Some historians have questioned whether the new mass leisure—standardized, organized for profit, and largely spectator oriented—was a real substitute for the popular culture of previous eras that had involved the active participation of people in the life of their village communities. In view of the multibillion dollar mass entertainment markets of the twentieth century, the question, while worthwhile, may also be largely irrelevant.

What many Europeans liked to call their "age of progress" between 1871 and 1914 was also an era of anxiety. Frenzied imperialist expansion had created vast European empires and spheres of influence around the globe. This feverish competition for colonies, however, had markedly increased the existing antagonisms among the European states. At the same time, the Western treatment of native peoples as racial inferiors caused educated, non-Western elites in these colonies to initiate movements for national independence. Before these movements could be successful, however, the power that Europeans had achieved through their mass armies and technological superiority had to be weakened. The Europeans inadvertently accomplished this task for their colonial subjects by demolishing their own civilization on the battlegrounds of Europe in World War I and World War II.

The cultural revolutions before 1914 had also produced anxiety and a crisis of confidence in European civilization. A brilliant minority of intellectuals had created a modern consciousness that questioned most Europeans' optimistic faith in reason, the rational structure of nature, and the certainty of progress. The devastating experiences of World War I turned this culture of uncertainty into a way of life after 1918.

Notes

1. Quoted in G. H. Nadel and P. Curtis, eds., *Imperialism and Colonialism* (New York, 1964), p. 94.

2. Karl Pearson, *National Life from the Standpoint of Science* (London, 1905), p. 184.

3. Quoted in John Ellis, *The Social History of the Machine Gun* (New York, 1975), p. 80.

4. Quoted in ibid., p. 86.

5. Quoted in Louis L. Snyder, ed., *The Imperialism Reader* (Princeton, N.J., 1962), p. 220.

6. Quoted in K. M. Panikkar, *Asia and Western Dominance* (London, 1959), p. 116.

7. Quoted in Arthur E. E. McKenzie, *The Major Achievements of Science* (New York, 1960), 1: 310.

8. Friedrich Nietzsche, *Twilight of the Idols and The Anti-Christ*, trans. R. J. Hollingdale (New York, 1972), pp. 117–18.

9. Friedrich Nietzsche, *Thus Spake Zarathustra*, in *The Philosophy of Nietzsche* (New York, 1954), p. 6.

10. Sigmund Freud, *Autobiography* (New York, 1935), p. 25.

11. Herbert Spencer, *Social Statics* (New York, 1896), pp. 146–50.

12. Friedrich von Bernhardi, *Germany and the Next War*, trans. Allen H. Powles (New York, 1914), pp. 18–19.

13. Quoted in Edward R. Tannenbaum, *1900: The Generation before the Great War* (Garden City, N.Y., 1976), p. 337.

14. Quoted in Paul Massing, *Rehearsal for Destruction: A Study of Political Anti-Semitism in Imperial Germany* (New York, 1949), p. 147.

15. Quoted in Abba Eban, *Heritage: Civilization and the Jews* (New York, 1984), p. 249.

16. Quoted in Owen Chadwick, *The Secularization of the European Mind in the Nineteenth Century* (Cambridge, 1975), p. 125.

17. William Booth, *In Darkest England and the Way Out* (London, 1890), p. 45.

18. Quoted in John Rewald, *The History of Impressionism* (New York, 1961), pp. 456–58.

19. Paul Klee, *On Modern Art*, trans. Paul Findlay (London, 1948), p. 51.

20. Quoted in Robert Gildea, *Barricades and Borders: Europe, 1800–1914* (Oxford, 1987), p. 249.

21. Quoted in Gary Cross, *A Social History of Leisure since 1600* (State College, Pa., 1990), p. 97.

22. Quoted in Gildea, *Barricades and Borders*, pp. 113–14.

23. Quoted in Cross, *A Social History of Leisure since 1600*, p. 130.

Suggestions for Further Reading
▼ ▼ ▼

Demographic problems are examined in T. McKeown, *The Modern Rise of Population* (New York, 1976). On European emigration, see C. Erickson, *Emigration from Europe, 1815–1914* (Cambridge, 1976). For broad perspectives on imperialism, see the works by T. Smith, *The Pattern of Imperialism* (Cambridge, 1981); and P. Darby, *Three Faces of Imperialism: British and American Approaches to Asia and Africa, 1870–1970* (New Haven, Conn., 1987). Different aspects of imperialism are covered in R. Robinson and J. Gallagher, *Africa and the Victorians*, 2d ed. (New York, 1981); P. Gifford and W. R. Louis, eds., *France and Britain in Africa* (New Haven, Conn., 1971); and W. Baumgart, *Imperialism: The Idea and Reality of British and French Colonial Expansion, 1880–1914* (London, 1982). British-Indian relations are examined in J. M. Brown, *Modern India: The Origins of an Asian Democracy* (New York, 1981).

Two fundamental works on the diplomatic history of the period are W. L. Langer, *European Alliances and Alignments*, 2d ed. (New York, 1966), and *The Diplomacy of Imperialism*, 2d ed. (New York, 1965). Also valuable are S. R. Williamson, *The Politics of Grand Strategy: Britain and France Prepare for War, 1904–1914* (Cambridge, Mass., 1969); G. Kennan, *The Decline of Bismarck's European Order: Franco-Prussian Relations, 1875–1890* (Princeton, N.J., 1979); and the masterful study by P. Kennedy, *The Rise of Anglo-German Antagonism, 1860–1914* (London, 1982).

A well-regarded study of Freud is P. Gay, *Freud: A Life for Our Time* (New York, 1988). Also see R. Clark, *Freud: The Man and the Cause* (New York, 1980). Nietzsche is examined in W. Kaufmann, *Nietzsche: Philosopher, Psychologist, Antichrist* 4th ed. (Princeton, N.J., 1974); and J. P. Stern, *The Mind of Nietzsche* (Oxford, 1980). On the impact of Nietzsche, see R. H. Thomas, *Nietzsche in German Politics and Society, 1890–1918* (Dover, N.H., 1983). On Bergson, see A. E. Pilkington, *Henri Bergson and His Influence* (Cambridge, 1976). The basic study on Sorel is J. J. Roth, *The Cult of Violence: Sorel and the Sorelians* (Berkeley, 1980). The best introduction to social theory is H. S. Hughes, *Consciousness and Society: The Reorientation of European Social Thought, 1890–1930* (New York, 1979). Very valuable on modern art are J. Rewald, *The History of Impressionism* 4th ed. (New York, 1973), and *Post-Impressionism*, 3d ed. (New York, 1962). On literature, see R. Pascal, *From Naturalism to Expressionism: German Literature and Society, 1880–1918*

(New York, 1973). The intellectual climate of Vienna is examined in C. E. Schorske, *Fin de Siècle Vienna: Politics and Culture* (New York, 1980).

The subject of modern anti-Semitism is covered in J. Katz, *From Prejudice to Destruction* (Cambridge, Mass., 1980), which argues that modern anti-Semitism stems from traditional Christian anti-Semitism. European racism is analyzed in G. L. Mosse, *Toward the Final Solution* (New York, 1980); while German anti-Semitism as a political force is examined in P. J. Pulzer, *The Rise of Political Anti-Semitism in Germany and Austria* (New York, 1964). Anti-Semitism in France is the subject of S. Wilson, *Ideology and Experience: Anti-Semitism in France at the Time of the Dreyfus Affair* (Rutherford, N.J., 1982). The problems of Jews in Russia are examined in J. Frankel, *Prophecy and Politics: Socialism, Nationalism and the Russian Jews, 1862–1917* (Cambridge, 1981). On Zionism, see D. Vital, *The Origins of Zionism* (Oxford, 1975).

A good introduction to the challenge scientific movements presented to the established churches is J. W. Burrow, *Evolution and Society: A Study in Victorian Social Theory* (London, 1966). A useful study on the impact of Darwinian thought on religion is J. Moore, *The Post-Darwinian Controversies: A Study of the Protestant Struggle to Come to Terms with Darwin in Great Britain and America, 1870–1900* (Cambridge, 1979). Studies of the popular religion of the period include T. A. Kselman, *Miracles and Prophesies in Nineteenth-Century France* (New Brunswick, N.J., 1983); and J. Sperber, *Popular Catholicism in Nineteenth-Century Germany* (Princeton, N.J., 1984).

On various aspects of education, see M. J. Maynes, *Schooling in Western Europe: A Social History* (Albany, N.Y., 1985); J. S. Hurt, *Elementary Schooling and the Working Classes, 1860–1918* (London, 1979); and J. C. McClelland, *Autocrats and Academics: Education, Culture and Society in Tsarist Russia* (Chicago, 1978). A concise and well-presented survey of leisure patterns is G. Cross, *A Social History of Leisure since 1600* (State College, Pa., 1990). A more specialized study is P. Bailey, *Leisure and Class in Victorian England* (London, 1978). On sport, see T. Mason, *Association Football and English Society, 1863–1915* (Brighton, England, 1980). On the expansion of reading material, see A. J. Lee, *The Origins of the Popular Press in Britain, 1855–1914* (London, 1978).

Chapter 26

The Beginning of the Twentieth-Century Crisis: War and Revolution

▼▼▼▼▼

Worid War I (1914–1918) was one of the dominant events of the twentieth century. It devastated the prewar economic, social, and political order of Europe while its uncertain outcome served to prepare the way for an even more destructive war. Overwhelmed by the size of its battles, the extent of its casualties, and the effects of its impact on all facets of European life, contemporaries referred to it simply as the "Great War."

The Great War was all the more disturbing to Europeans because it came after a period that many believed to have been an age of progress. There had been international crises before 1914, but somehow Europeans had managed to avoid serious and prolonged military confrontations. When smaller European states had gone to war, as in the Balkans in 1912 and 1913, the great European powers had shown the ability to keep the conflict localized. Material prosperity and a fervid belief in scientific and technological progress had convinced many people that Europe stood on the verge of creating the utopia that humans had dreamed of for centuries. The historian Arnold Toynbee expressed what the pre–World War I era had meant to his generation:

> [it was expected] that life throughout the World would become more rational, more humane, and more democratic and that, slowly, but surely, political democracy would produce greater social justice. We had also expected that the progress of science and technology would make mankind richer, and that this increasing wealth would gradually spread from a minority to a majority. We had expected that all this would happen peacefully. In fact we thought that mankind's course was set for an earthly paradise.[1]

Assassination of
Archduke Francis Ferdinand ▼

Battle of
Verdun ▼

United States
Enters the War ▼

Surrender
of Germany ▼

Paris Peace
Conference ▼

•••••••••• 1915 ••••••••••• 1916 •••••••••• 1917 •••••••••• 1918 ••••••••••• 1919 ••••••••

▲ Ministry of Munitions
in Britain

▲ Complete Mobilization for
Total War in Germany

▲ The Bolshevik
Revolution

▲ Civil War in Russia

After 1918, it was no longer possible to maintain naive illusions about the progress of Western civilization. As World War I was followed by the destructiveness of World War II and the mass murder machines of totalitarian regimes, it became all too apparent that instead of a utopia, European civilization had become a nightmare. World War I and the revolutions it spawned can properly be seen as the first stage in the crisis of the twentieth century.

▼ The Road to World War I

On June 28, 1914, the heir to the Austrian throne, the Archduke Francis Ferdinand, was assassinated in the Bosnian city of Sarajevo. Although this event precipitated the confrontation between Austria and Serbia that led to World War I, war was by no means a foregone conclusion. Previous assassinations of European leaders had not usually led to war, and European statesmen had managed before on a number of occasions to localize such conflicts. Although the decisions that European statesmen made during this crisis were crucial in leading to war, there were also long-range, underlying forces that were propelling Europeans toward armed conflict.

Nationalism and Internal Dissent

In the first half of the nineteenth century, liberals had maintained that the organization of European states along national lines would lead to a peaceful Europe based on a sense of international fraternity. They had been very wrong. The system of nation-states that had emerged in Europe in the last half of the nineteenth century led not to cooperation but to competition. Rivalries over colonial and commercial interests intensified during an era of frenzied imperialist expansion while the division of Europe's great powers into two loose alliances (Germany, Austria, and Italy and France, Great Britain, and Russia) only added to the tensions. The series of crises that tested these alliances in the 1900s and early 1910s had left European states with a dangerous lesson. Those governments that had exercised restraint in order to avoid war wound up being publicly humiliated, while those that went to the brink of war to maintain their national interests had often been praised for having preserved national honor. In either case, by 1914, the major European states had come to believe that their allies were important and that their security depended on supporting those allies, even when they took foolish risks.

Diplomacy based on brinkmanship was especially frightening in view of the nature of the European state system. Each nation-state regarded itself as sovereign, subject to no higher interest or authority. Each state was motivated by its own self-interest and success. As Emperor William II of Germany remarked, "In questions of honor and vital interests, you don't consult others." Such attitudes made war an ever-present possibility, particularly since most statesmen considered war an acceptable way to preserve the power of their national states.

The growth of nationalism in the nineteenth century had yet another serious consequence. Not all ethnic groups had achieved the goal of nationhood. Slavic minorities in the Balkans and the polyglot Habsburg empire, for example, still dreamed of creating their own national states. So did the Irish in the British Empire and the Poles in the Russian Empire.

National aspirations, however, were not the only source of internal strife at the beginning of the twentieth century. Socialist labor movements had grown more powerful and were increasingly inclined to use strikes, even violent ones, to achieve their goals. Some conservative leaders, alarmed at the increase in labor strife and class division, even feared that European nations were on the verge of revolution. Did these statesmen opt for war in 1914 because they believed that "prosecuting an active foreign policy," as some Austrian leaders expressed it, would smother "internal troubles"? Some historians have argued that the desire to suppress internal disorder may have encouraged some leaders to take the plunge into war in 1914.

Militarism

The growth of large mass armies after 1900 not only heightened the existing tensions in Europe, but made it inevitable that if war did come it would be highly destructive. Conscription had been established as a regular practice in most Western countries before 1914 (the United States and Britain were major exceptions). European military machines had doubled in size between 1890 and 1914. With its 1.3 million men, the Russian army had grown to be the largest, while the French and Germans were not far behind with 900,000 each. The British, Italian, and Austrian armies numbered between 250,000 and 500,000 soldiers. Most European land armies were filled with peasants, since many young, urban working-class males were unable to pass the physical examinations required for military service.

Militarism, however, involved more than just large armies. As armies grew, so too did the influence of military leaders who drew up vast and complex plans for quickly mobilizing millions of men and enormous quantities of supplies in the event of war. Fearful that changes in these plans would cause chaos in the armed forces, military leaders insisted that their plans could not be altered. In the crises during the summer of 1914, the generals' lack of flexibility forced European political leaders to make decisions for military instead of political reasons.

The Outbreak of War: The Summer of 1914

Militarism, nationalism, and the desire to stifle internal dissent may all have played a role in the coming of World War I, but the decisions made by European leaders in the summer of 1914 directly precipitated the conflict. It was another crisis in the Balkans that forced this predicament upon European statesmen.

As we have seen, states in southeastern Europe had struggled to free themselves of Turkish rule in the course of the nineteenth and early twentieth centuries. But the rivalry between Austria-Hungary and Russia for domination of these new states created serious tensions in the region. The crises of 1908 to 1913 had only intensified the antagonisms. By 1914, Serbia, supported by Russia, was determined to create a large, independent Slavic state in the Balkans, while Austria, which had its own Slavic minorities to contend with, was equally set on preventing that possibility. Many Europeans perceived the inherent dangers in this combination of Serbian am-

▼ **Apprehension of an Assassin.** World War I was precipitated by the assassination of the Archduke Francis Ferdinand, heir to the Austrian throne, on June 28, 1914. His assassin was Gavrillo Princip, an eighteen-year-old Bosnian activist who favored the creation of a pan-Slavic kingdom at Austria's expense. As shown here, he was arrested soon after killing Franz Ferdinand and his wife.

bition bolstered by Russian hatred of Austria and Austrian conviction that Serbia's success meant the end of its empire. The British ambassador to Vienna wrote in 1913:

> Serbia will some day set Europe by the ears, and bring about a universal war on the Continent. . . . I cannot tell you how exasperated people are getting here at the continual worry which that little country causes to Austria under encouragement from Russia. . . . It will be lucky if Europe succeeds in avoiding war as a result of the present crisis. The next time a Serbian crisis arises. . . , I feel sure that Austria-Hungary will refuse to admit of any Russian interference in the dispute and that she will proceed to settle her differences with her little neighbor by herself.[2]

It was against this backdrop of mutual distrust and hatred between Austria-Hungary and Russia, on the one hand, and Austria-Hungary and Serbia, on the other, that the events of the summer of 1914 were played out.

The assassination of the Austrian Archduke Francis Ferdinand and his wife Sophia on June 28, 1914, was carried out by a Bosnian activist who worked for the Black Hand, a Serbian terrorist organization dedicated to the creation of a pan-Slavic kingdom. Although the Austrian government did not know whether the Serbian government had been directly involved in the archduke's assassination, it saw an opportunity to "render Serbia innocuous once and for all by a display of force," as the Austrian foreign minister put it. Fearful of Russian intervention on Serbia's behalf, Austrian leaders sought the backing of their German allies. Emperor William II and his chancellor, Theobald von Bethmann-Hollweg, responded with the infamous "blank check," their assurance that Austria-Hungary could rely on Germany's "full support," even if "matters went to the length of a war between Austria-Hungary and Russia." Much historical debate has focused on this "blank check" extended to the Austrians. Did the Germans realize that an Austrian-Serbian war could lead to a wider war? If so,

▼ Map 26.1 Europe in 1914.

"You Have to Bear the Responsibility for War or Peace"
▼ ▼ ▼

After Austria declared war on Serbia on July 28, 1914, Russian support of Serbia and German support of Austria threatened to escalate the conflict in the Balkans into a wider war. As we can see in these last-minute telegrams between the Russians and Germans, neither side was able to accept the other's line of reasoning.

Communications between Berlin and St. Petersburg on the Eve of World War I

Emperor William II to Tsar Nicholas II, July 28, 10:45 P.M.

I have heard with the greatest anxiety of the impression which is caused by the action of Austria-Hungary against Servia [Serbia]. The inscrupulous agitation which has been going on for years in Servia, has led to the revolting crime of which Archduke Franz Ferdinand has become a victim. The spirit which made the Servians murder their own King and his consort still dominates that country. Doubtless You will agree with me that both of us, You as well as I, and all other sovereigns, have a common interest to insist that all those who are responsible for this horrible murder shall suffer their deserved punishment. . . .

Your most sincere and devoted friend and cousin
(Signed)   Wilhelm

Tsar Nicholas II to Emperor William II, July 29, 1:00 P.M.

I am glad that you are back in Germany. In this serious moment I ask You earnestly to help me. An ignominious war has been declared against a weak country and in Russia the indignation which I full share is tremendous. I fear that very soon I shall be unable to resist the pressure exercised upon me and that I shall be forced to take measures which will lead to war. To prevent a calamity as a European war would be, I urge You in the name of our old friendship to do all in Your power to restrain Your ally from going too far.

(Signed)   Nicolas

Emperor William II to Tsar Nicholas II, July 29, 6:30 P.M.

I have received Your telegram and I share Your desire for the conservation of peace. However: I cannot—as I told You in my first telegram—consider the action of Austria-Hungary as an "ignominious war." Austria-Hungary knows from experience that the promises of Servia as long as they are merely on paper are entirely unreliable. . . . I believe that a direct understanding is possible and desirable between Your Government and Vienna, an understanding which I—as I have already telegraphed you—my Government endeavours to aid with all possible effort. Naturally military measures by Russia, which might be construed as a menace by Austria-Hungary, would accelerate a calamity which both of us desire to avoid and would undermine my position as mediator which—upon Your appeal to my friendship and aid—I willingly accepted.

(Signed)   Wilhelm

Emperor William II to Tsar Nicholas II, July 30, 1:00 A.M.

My Ambassador has instructions to direct the attention of Your Government to the dangers and serious consequences of a mobilisation. I have told You the same in my last telegram. Austria-Hungary has mobilised only against Servia, and only a part of her army. If Russia, as seems to be the case, according to Your advice and that of Your Government, mobilises against Austria-Hungary, the part of the mediator with which You have entrusted me in such friendly manner and which I have accepted upon Your express desire, is threatened if not made impossible. The entire weight of decision now rests upon Your shoulders, You have to bear the responsibility for war or peace.

(Signed)   Wilhelm

German Chancellor to German Ambassador at St. Petersburg, July 31, URGENT

In spite of negotiations still pending and although we have up to this hour made no preparations for mobilisation, Russia has mobilised her entire army and navy, hence also against us. On account of these Russian measures, we have been forced, for the safety of the country, to proclaim the threatening state of war, which does not yet imply mobilisation. Mobilisation, however, is bound to follow if Russia does not stop every measure of war against us and against Austria-Hungary within 12 hours, and notifies us definitely to this effect. Please to communicate this at once to M. Sasonof and wire hour of communication.

did they actually want one? Historians are still seriously divided on the answers to these questions.

Strengthened by German support, Austrian leaders issued an ultimatum to Serbia on July 23. Austrian leaders made their demands so extreme that Serbia had little choice but to reject some of them in order to preserve its sovereignty. Austria then declared war on Serbia on July 28. Although both Germany and Austria had hoped to keep the war limited to Serbia and Austria in order to ensure Austria's success in the Balkans, these hopes soon vanished.

Still smarting from its humiliation in the Bosnian crisis of 1908, Russia was determined to support Serbia's cause. On July 28, Tsar Nicholas II ordered partial mobilization of the Russian army against Austria. At this point, the rigidity of the military war plans played havoc with diplomatic and political decisions. The Russian General Staff informed the Tsar that their mobilization plans were based on a war against both Germany and Austria simultaneously. They could not execute partial mobilization without creating chaos in the army. Consequently, the Russian government ordered full mobilization of the Russian army on July 29, knowing that the Germans would consider this an act of war against them (see the box on p. 900). Germany responded to Russian mobilization with its own ultimatum that the Russians must halt their mobilization within twelve hours. When the Russians ignored it, Germany declared war on Russia on August 1.

At this stage of the conflict, German war plans determined whether or not France would become involved in the war. Under the guidance of General Alfred von Schlieffen, chief of staff from 1891 to 1905, the German General Staff had devised a military plan based on the assumption of a two-front war with France and Russia, since the two powers had formed a military alliance in 1894. The Schlieffen Plan called for a minimal troop deployment against Russia while most of the German army would make a rapid invasion of western France by way of neutral Belgium. After the planned quick defeat of the French, the German army expected to redeploy to the east against Russia. Under the Schlieffen Plan, Germany could not mobilize its troops solely against Russia and therefore declared war on France on August 3 after it had issued an ultimatum to Belgium on August 2 demanding the right of German troops to pass through Belgian territory. On August 4, Great Britain declared war on Germany, officially over this violation of Belgian neutrality, but in fact over the British desire to maintain its world power. As one British diplomat argued, if Germany and Austria were to win the war, "what would be the position of a friendless England?" By August 4, all the great powers of Europe were at war.

▼ The War

Before 1914, many political leaders had become convinced that war involved so many political and economic risks that it was not worth fighting. Others had believed that "rational" diplomats could control any situation and prevent the outbreak of war. At the beginning of August 1914, both of these prewar illusions were shattered, but the new illusions that replaced them soon proved to be equally foolish.

1914–1915: Illusions and Stalemate

Europeans went to war in 1914 with remarkable enthusiasm (see the box on p. 902). Government propaganda had been successful in stirring up national antagonisms before the war. Now in August of 1914, the urgent pleas of governments for defense against aggressors fell on receptive ears in every belligerent nation. Most people seemed genuinely convinced that their na-

▼ **The Excitement of War.** World War I was greeted with incredible enthusiasm. Each of the major belligerents was convinced of the rightness of its nation's cause. Everywhere in Europe, jubilant civilians sent their troops off to war with joyous fervor. Their belief that the soldiers would be home by Christmas proved to be a pathetic illusion.

The Excitement of War

▼ ▼ ▼

The incredible outpouring of patriotic enthusiasm that greeted the declaration of war at the beginning of August 1914 demonstrated the power that nationalistic feeling had attained at the beginning of the twentieth century. Many Europeans seemingly believed that the war had given them a higher purpose, a renewed dedication to the greatness of their nation. This selection is taken from the autobiography of Stefan Zweig, an Austrian writer who captured well the orgiastic celebration of war in Vienna in 1914.

Stefan Zweig, *The World of Yesterday*

The next morning I was in Austria. In every station placards had been put up announcing general mobilization. The trains were filled with fresh recruits, banners were flying, music sounded, and in Vienna I found the entire city in a tumult. . . . There were parades in the street, flags, ribbons, and music burst forth everywhere, young recruits were marching triumphantly, their faces lighting up at the cheering. . . .

And to be truthful, I must acknowledge that there was a majestic, rapturous, and even seductive something in this first outbreak of the people from which one could escape only with difficulty. And in spite of all my hatred and aversion for war, I should not like to have missed the memory of those days. As never before, thousands and hundreds of thousands felt what they should have felt in peace time, that they belonged together. A city of two million, a country of nearly fifty million, in that hour felt that they were participating in world history, in a moment which would never recur, and that each one was called upon to cast his infinitesimal self into the glowing mass, there to be purified of all selfishness. All differences of class, rank, and language were flooded over at that moment by the rushing feeling of fraternity. Strangers spoke to one another in the streets, people who had avoided each other for years shook hands, everywhere one saw excited faces. Each individual experienced an exaltation of his ego, he was no longer the isolated person of former times, he had been incorporated into the mass, he was part of the people, and his person, his hitherto unnoticed person, had been given meaning. . . .

What did the great mass know of war in 1914, after nearly half a century of peace? They did not know war, they had hardly given it a thought. It had become legendary, and distance had made it seem romantic and heroic. They still saw it in the perspective of their school readers and of paintings in museums; brilliant cavalry attacks in glittering uniforms, the fatal shot always straight through the heart, the entire campaign a resounding march of victory—"We'll be home at Christmas," the recruits shouted laughingly to their mothers in August of 1914. . . . A rapid excursion into the romantic, a wild, manly adventure—that is how the war of 1914 was painted in the imagination of the simple man, and the young people were honestly afraid that they might miss this most wonderful and exciting experience of their lives; that is why they hurried and thronged to the colors, and that is why they shouted and sang in the trains that carried them to the slaughter; wildly and feverishly the red wave of blood coursed through the veins of the entire nation.

---

tion's cause was just. Even domestic differences were temporarily shelved in the midst of war fever. Socialists had long derided "imperialist war" as a blow against the common interests that united the working classes of all countries. Nationalism, however, proved more powerful than working-class solidarity in the summer of 1914 as socialist parties everywhere dropped plans for strikes and workers expressed their readiness to fight for their country. The German Social Democrats, for example, decided that it was imperative to "safeguard the culture and independence of our own country."

A new set of illusions fed the enthusiasm for war. Almost everyone in August 1914 believed that the war would be over in a few weeks. People were reminded that all European wars since 1815 had, in fact, ended in a matter of weeks, conveniently overlooking the American Civil War (1861–1865), which was the "real prototype" for World War I. The illusion of a short war was also bolstered by another illusion, the belief that in an age of modern industry war could not be supported for more than a few months without destroying a nation's economy. Both the soldiers who exuberantly boarded the trains for the war front in August 1914 and the jubilant citizens who bombarded them with flowers when they departed believed that the warriors would be home by Christmas.

Then, too, war held a fatal attraction for many people. To some, war was an exhilarating release from humdrum bourgeois existence, from a "world grown old and cold and weary," as one poet wrote. To some, war meant a glorious adventure, as a young German student wrote to his parents: "My dear ones, be proud that you live in such a time and in such a nation and that you . . . have the privilege of sending those you love into so glorious a battle."[3] And finally there were those who believed that the war would have a redemptive effect, that millions would abandon their petty preoccupations with material life, ridding the nation of selfishness and providing a national rebirth based on self-sacrifice, heroism, and nobility. All of these illusions about war died painful deaths on the battlefields of World War I.

German hopes for a quick end to the war rested upon a military gamble. The Schlieffen Plan had called for the

German army to make a vast encircling movement through Belgium into northern France that would sweep around Paris and encircle most of the French army. German troops crossed into Belgium on August 4 and by the first week of September had reached the Marne River, only twenty miles from Paris. The Germans seemed on the verge of success, but an unexpected counterattack by British and French forces under the French commander General Joseph Joffre stopped them at the First Battle of the Marne (September 6–10). The German troops fell back, but the exhausted French army was unable to pursue its advantage. The war quickly turned into a stalemate as neither the Germans nor French could dislodge each other from the trenches they had begun to dig for shelter. Two lines of trenches soon extended from the English Channel to the frontiers of Switzerland. The Western Front had become bogged down in a trench warfare that kept both sides immobilized in virtually the same positions for four years.

In contrast to the West, the war in the East was marked by much more mobility, although the cost in

▼ **Map 26.2** The Western Front, 1914–1918.

lives was equally enormous. At the beginning of the war, the Russian army moved into eastern Germany but was decisively defeated at the Battles of Tannenberg on August 30 and the Masurian Lakes on September 15. These battles established the military reputations of the commanding general, Paul von Hindenburg, and his chief of staff, General Erich Ludendorff. The Russians were no longer a threat to German territory.

The Austrians, Germany's allies, fared less well initially. They had been defeated by the Russians in Galicia and thrown out of Serbia as well. To make matters worse, the Italians betrayed the Germans and Austrians and entered the war on the Allied side by attacking Austria in May 1915. By this time, the Germans had come to the aid of the Austrians. A German-Austrian army defeated and routed the Russian army in Galicia and pushed the Russians back three hundred miles into their own territory. Russian casualties stood at 2.5 million killed, captured, or wounded; the Russians had almost been knocked out of the war. Buoyed by their success, the Germans and Austrians, joined by the Bulgarians in September 1915, attacked and eliminated Serbia from the war.

1916–1917: The Great Slaughter

The successes in the East enabled the Germans to move back to the offensive in the West. The early

▼ **Map 26.3** The Eastern Front, 1914–1918.

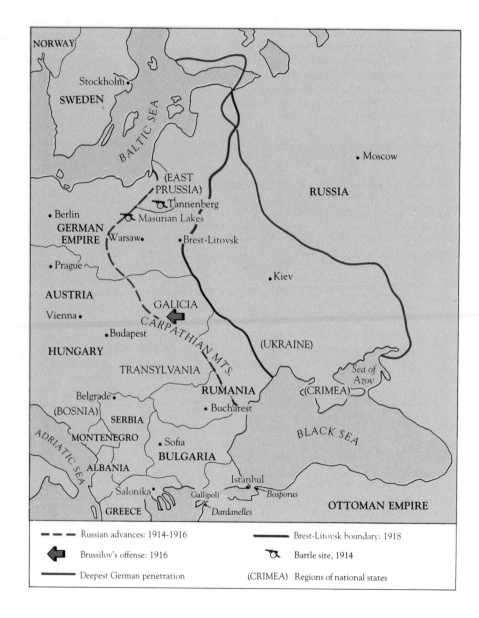

trenches dug in 1914 had by now become elaborate systems of defense. Both lines of trenches were protected by barbed wire entanglements three to five feet high and thirty yards wide, concrete machine-gun nests, and mortar batteries, supported further back by heavy artillery. Troops lived in holes in the ground, separated from each other by a "no man's land."

The unexpected development of trench warfare baffled military leaders who had been trained to fight wars of movement and maneuver. But they were under heavy pressure from public outcries for action. The only plan generals could devise was to attempt a breakthrough by throwing masses of men against enemy lines that had first been battered by artillery barrages. Once the decisive breakthrough had been achieved, they thought, they could then return to the war of movement that they knew best. Periodically, the high command on either side would order an offensive that would begin with an artillery barrage to flatten the enemy's barbed wire and leave the enemy in a state of shock. After "softening up" the enemy in this fashion, a mass of soldiers would climb out of their trenches with fixed bayonets and hope to work their way toward the enemy trenches. The attacks rarely worked, since the machine gun put hordes of men advancing unprotected across open fields at a severe disadvantage. In 1916 and 1917, millions of young men were sacrificed in the search for the elusive breakthrough. In the German offensive at Verdun in 1916, the British campaign on the Somme in 1916, and the French attack in the Champagne in 1917, the senseless-

ness of trench warfare became all too obvious. In ten months at Verdun, 700,000 men lost their lives over a few miles of terrain.

DAILY LIFE IN THE TRENCHES   Warfare in the trenches of the Western Front produced unimaginable horrors (see the box on p. 906). Many participants commented on the fog of confusion that hung over the battlefields. When an attacking force entered "no man's land," the combination of noise, machine-gun fire, bombardment, and terror often caused soldiers to lose their sense of direction; they went forward only because they were carried on by the momentum of the soldiers beside them. Rarely were battles as orderly as they were portrayed on military maps and in civilian newspapers.

Battlefields were hellish landscapes of barbed wire, shell holes, mud, and injured and dying men. The introduction of poison gas in 1915 produced new forms of injuries, as one British writer described:

> I wish those people who write so glibly about this being a holy war could see a case of mustard gas . . . could see the poor things burnt and blistered all over with great mustard-coloured suppurating blisters with blind eyes all sticky . . . and stuck together, and always fighting for breath, with voices a mere whisper, saying that their throats are closing and they know they will choke.[4]

Soldiers in the trenches also lived with the persistent presence of death. Since combat went on for months,

▼ **The Destruction at Verdun.** In 1916, the German high command decided to take the offensive against the French fortifications at Verdun, which was 125 miles east of Paris. The ferocious Battle of Verdun cost 700,000 lives and resulted in an exchange of only a few miles of land. As seen in the photograph, the city of Verdun, subjected to massive artillery shelling, was severely damaged. The population of Verdun dropped from 15,000 to 3,000 in the course of the battle.

The Reality of War: Trench Warfare

▼ ▼ ▼

The romantic illusion about the excitement and adventure of war that filled the minds of so many young men who marched off to battle (see the box on p. 902) quickly disintegrated after a short time in the trenches on the Western Front. This description of trench warfare is taken from the most famous novel that emerged from World War I, Erich Maria Remarque's All Quiet on the Western Front, *written in 1929. Remarque had fought in the trenches in France.*

Erich Maria Remarque, *All Quiet on the Western Front*

We wake up in the middle of the night. The earth booms. Heavy fire is falling on us. We crouch into corners. We distinguish shells of every calibre.

Each man lays hold of his things and looks again every minute to reassure himself that they are still there. The dug-out heaves, the night roars and flashes. We look at each other in the momentary flashes of light, and with pale faces and pressed lips shake our heads.

Every man is aware of the heavy shells tearing down the parapet, rooting up the embankment and demolishing the upper layers of concrete. . . . Already by morning a few of the recruits are green and vomiting. They are too inexperienced. . . .

The bombardment does not diminish. It is falling in the rear too. As far as one can see it spouts fountains of mud and iron. A wide belt is being raked.

The attack does not come, but the bombardment continues. Slowly we become mute. Hardly a man speaks. We cannot make ourselves understood.

Our trench is almost gone. At many places it is only eighteen inches high, it is broken by holes, and craters, and mountains of earth. A shell lands square in front of our post. At once it is dark. We are buried and must dig ourselves out. . . .

Towards morning, while it is still dark, there is some excitement. Through the entrance rushes in a swarm of fleeing rats that try to storm the walls. Torches light up the confusion. Everyone yells and curses and slaughters. The madness and despair of many hours unloads itself in this outburst. Faces are distorted, arms strike out, the beasts scream; we just stop in time to avoid attacking one another. . . .

Suddenly it howls and flashes terrifically, the dug-out cracks in all its joints under a direct hit, fortunately only a light one that the concrete blocks are able to withstand. It rings metallically, the walls reel, rifles, helmets, earth, mud, and dust fly everywhere. Sulphur fumes pour in. . . . The recruit starts to rave again and two others follow suit. One jumps up and rushes out, we have trouble with the other two. I start after the one who escapes and wonder whether to shoot him in the leg—then it shrieks again, I fling myself down and when I stand up the wall of the trench is plastered with smoking splinters, lumps of flesh, and bits of uniform. I scramble back.

The first recruit seems actually to have gone insane. He butts his head against the wall like a goat. We must try tonight to take him to the rear. Meanwhile we bind him, but so that in case of attack he can be released.

Suddenly the nearer explosions cease. The shelling continues but it has lifted and falls behind us, our trench is free. We seize the hand-grenades, pitch them out in front of the dug-out and jump after them. The bombardment has stopped and a heavy barrage now falls behind us. The attack has come.

No one would believe that in this howling waste there could still be men; but steel helmets now appear on all sides out of the trench, and fifty yards from us a machine-gun is already in position and barking.

The wire-entanglements are torn to pieces. Yet they offer some obstacle. We see the storm-troops coming. Our artillery opens fire. Machine-guns rattle, rifles crack. The charge works its way across. Haie and Kropp begin with the hand-grenades. They throw as fast as they can, others pass them, the handles with the strings already pulled. Haie throws seventy-five yards, Kropp sixty, it has been measured, the distance is important. The enemy as they run cannot do much before they are within forty yards.

We recognize the distorted faces, the smooth helmets: they are French. They have already suffered heavily when they reach the remnants of the barbed-wire entanglements. A whole line has gone down before our machine-guns; then we have a lot of stoppages and they come nearer.

I see one of them, his face upturned, fall into a wire cradle. His body collapses, his hands remain suspended as though he were praying. Then his body drops clean away and only his hands with the stumps of his arms, shot off, now hang in the wire.

soldiers had to carry on in the midst of countless bodies of dead men or the remains of men dismembered by artillery barrages. Many soldiers remembered the stench of decomposing bodies and the swarms of rats that grew fat in the trenches.

Soldiers on the Western Front did not spend all of their time on the front line or in combat when they were on the front line. Out of every month an infantryman spent one week in the front-line trenches, one week in the reserve lines, and the remaining two weeks somewhere behind the lines. Daily routine in the trenches was predictable. Thirty minutes before sunrise, troops had to "stand to" or be combat ready to repel any attack. If no attack were forthcoming that day, the day's routine consisted of breakfast followed by inspection, sentry duty, repair work on the trenches, care of personal items, or whiling away the time as best they could. Soldiers often recalled the boredom of life in the dreary, lice-ridden, wet and muddy or dry and dusty trenches.

At many places along the opposing lines of trenches, a "live and let live" system evolved based on the realization that neither side was going to dislodge the other anyway. The "live and let live" system resulted in such unspoken agreements as not to shell the latrines or open fire during breakfast. Some parties even worked out

▼ **Impact of the Machine Gun.** The development of trench warfare on the Western Front stymied military leaders who had expected to fight a war based on movement and maneuver. Their efforts to effect a breakthrough by sending masses of men against enemy lines was the height of folly in view of the machine gun. Masses of men advancing across open land made magnificent targets.

▼ **The Horrors of War.** The slaughter of millions of men in the trenches of World War I created unimaginable horrors for the participants. For the sake of survival, many soldiers learned to harden themselves against the stench of decomposing bodies and the sight of bodies horribly dismembered by artillery barrages.

agreements to make noise before minor raids so that the other side could withdraw to protective bunkers.

On both sides, troops produced their own humorous magazines to help pass the time and fulfill the need to laugh in the midst of their daily madness. The British trench magazine, the *B. E. F. Times*, devoted one of its issues to defining military terms. A typical definition "DUDS—These are of two kinds. A shell on impact failing to explode is called a dud. They are unhappily not as plentiful as the other kind, which often draws a big salary and explodes for no reason. These are plentiful away from the fighting areas."[5] Soldiers' songs also captured a mixture of the sentimental and the frivolous (see the box on p. 908).

The Widening of the War

As another response to the stalemate on the Western Front, both sides sought to gain new allies who might provide a winning advantage. The Turkish or Ottoman Empire had already come into the war on Germany's side in August 1914. Russia, Great Britain, and France declared war on Turkey in November. Although the Allies attempted to open a Balkan front by landing forces at

The Songs of World War I
▼ ▼ ▼

Whether on the march, in bars, in trains, and even in the trenches, the soldiers of World War I spent time singing. The songs sung by soldiers of different nationalities varied considerably. A German favorite, The Watch on the Rhine, focused on heroism and patriotism. British war songs often partook of black humor, as in The Old Barbed Wire. An American favorite was the rousing Over There, written by the professional songwriter George M. Cohan.

From The Watch on the Rhine

There sounds a call like thunder's roar,
Like the crash of swords, like the surge of waves.
To the Rhine, the Rhine, the German Rhine!
Who will the stream's defender be?
　　Dear Fatherland, rest quietly
　　Sure stands and true the Watch,
　　The Watch on the Rhine.

To heaven he gazes.
Spirits of heroes look down.
He vows with proud battle-desire:
O Rhine! You will stay as German as my breast!
　　Dear Fatherland, etc.
Even if my heart breaks in death,
You will never be French.
As you are rich in water
Germany is rich in hero's blood.
　　Dear Fatherland, etc.

So long as a drop of blood still glows,
So long a hand the dagger can draw,
So long an arm the rifle can hold—
Never will an enemy touch your shore.
　　Dear Fatherland, etc.

From The Old Barbed Wire

If you want to find the old battalion,
I know where they are,
I know where they are.

If you want to find a battalion,
I know where they are,
They're hanging on the old barbed wire.
I've seen 'em, I've seen 'em,
Hanging on the old barbed wire,
I've seen 'em,
Hanging on the old barbed wire.

George M. Cohan, Over There

Over There
Over There
Send the word
Send the word
Over There
That the boys are coming
The drums rum-tuming everywhere.
Over There
Say a prayer
Send the word
Send the word
To Beware.
It will be over.
We're coming over
And we won't come back
Till it's over
Over There.

Johnnie get your gun
　　get your gun
　　get your gun
Back in town to run
Home to run Home to run
Hear them calling you and me
Every son of liberty
Hurry right away
Don't delay go today
Make your Daddy glad
To have had such a lad
Tell your sweetheart not to pine
To be proud their boy's in line.

Gallipoli, southwest of Constantinople, in April 1915, the entry of Bulgaria into the war on the side of the Central Powers (as Germany, Austria-Hungary, and Turkey were called) and a disastrous campaign at Gallipoli caused them to withdraw. The Italians, as we have seen, also entered the war on the Allied side after France and Britain promised to further their acquisition of Austrian territory. In the long run, however, Italian military incompetence forced the Allies to come to the assistance of Italy.

By 1917, the war that had originated in Europe had truly become a world conflict. In the Middle East, a British officer who came to be known as Lawrence of Arabia incited Arab princes to revolt in 1917 against their Turkish overlords. In 1918, British forces from Egypt destroyed the rest of the Ottoman Empire in the Middle East. For their Middle East campaigns, the British mobilized forces from India, Australia, and New Zealand. The Allies also took advantage of Germany's preoccupations in Europe and lack of naval strength to seize German colonies in the rest of the world.

ENTRY OF THE UNITED STATES   At first, the United States tried to remain neutral in the Great War, but it became more difficult to do so as the war dragged on. Although there was considerable sentiment for the British side in the conflict, the immediate cause of American involvement grew out of the naval conflict between Germany and Great Britain. Only once did the German and British naval forces engage in direct battle—at the Battle of Jutland on May 31, 1916, when the two fleets fought to a standstill. But Britain used its superior naval power to maximum effect by creating a naval blockade of Germany. Germany retaliated by imposing a counterblockade enforced by the use of unrestricted submarine warfare. At the beginning of 1915, the German government declared the area around the British Isles a war zone and threatened to torpedo any ship caught in it. Strong American protests over the German sinking of passenger liners, especially the British ship Lusitania on May 7, 1915, when over a hundred Americans lost their lives, forced the German government to suspend unrestricted submarine warfare in September 1915 to avoid further antagonizing the Americans.

In January 1917, however, eager to break the deadlock in the war, the Germans decided on another military gamble by returning to unrestricted submarine warfare. German naval officers convinced Emperor William II that the use of unrestricted submarine warfare could starve the British into submission within five months. When the emperor expressed his concern about the

Americans, he was told not to worry. The Americans, the chief of the German Naval Staff said, were "disorganized and undisciplined." The British would starve before the Americans could act. And even if the Americans did intervene, Admiral Holtzendorff assured the emperor, "I give your Majesty my word as an officer, that not one American will land on the continent."

The return to unrestricted submarine warfare brought the United States into the war on April 6, 1917. Although American troops did not arrive in large numbers in Europe until 1918, the entry of the United States into the war in 1917 gave the Allied powers a psychological boost when they needed it. The year 1917 was not a good year for them. Allied offensives on the Western Front were disastrously defeated. The Italian armies were smashed in October, and in November 1917 the Bolshevik Revolution in Russia led to Russia's withdrawal from the war (see The Russian Revolution later in the chapter). The cause of the Central Powers looked favorable, although war weariness in Turkey, Bulgaria, Austria-Hungary, and Germany was beginning to take its toll. The home front was rapidly becoming a cause for as much concern as the war front.

The Home Front: The Impact of Total War

The prolongation of World War I made it a total war that affected the lives of all citizens, however remote they might be from the battlefields. World War I transformed the governments, economics, and societies of the European belligerents in fundamental ways. The need to organize masses of men and matériel for years of combat (Germany alone had 5.5 million men in active units in 1916) led to increased centralization of government powers, economic regimentation, and manipulation of public opinion to keep the war effort going.

TOTAL WAR: POLITICAL CENTRALIZATION AND ECONOMIC REGIMENTATION   As we have seen, the outbreak of World War I was greeted with a rush of patriotism; even socialists joined enthusiastically into the fray. As the war dragged on, governments realized, however, that more than patriotism would be needed. Since the war was expected to be short, little thought had been given to economic problems and long-term wartime needs. Governments had to respond quickly, however, when the war machines failed to achieve their knockout blows and made ever-greater demands for men and matériel.

The extension of government power was a logical outgrowth of these needs. Most European countries had already devised some system of mass conscription or military draft. It was now carried to unprecedented heights as countries mobilized tens of millions of young men for that elusive breakthrough to victory. Even countries that continued to rely on volunteers (Great Britain had the largest volunteer army in modern history—one million men—in 1914 and 1915) were forced to resort to conscription, especially to ensure that skilled laborers did not enlist but remained in factories that were important to the production of munitions. In 1916, despite widespread resistance to this extension of government power, compulsory military service was introduced in Great Britain.

Throughout Europe, wartime governments expanded their powers over their economies. Free-market capitalistic systems were temporarily shelved as governments experimented with price, wage, and rent controls, the rationing of food supplies and materials, the regulation of imports and exports, and the nationalization of transportation systems and industries. Some governments even moved toward compulsory labor employment. In effect, in order to mobilize the entire resources of their nations for the war effort, European nations had moved toward planned economies directed by government agencies. Under total war mobilization, the distinction between soldiers at war and civilians at home was narrowed. In the view of political leaders, all citizens constituted a national army dedicated to victory. As the American president Woodrow Wilson expressed it, the men and women "who remain to till the soil and man the factories are no less a part of the army than the men beneath the battle flags."

Not all European nations made the shift to total war equally well. Germany had the most success in develop-

ing a planned economy. At the beginning of the war, Walter Rathenau, head of the German General Electric Company, was asked by the government to use his business methods to organize a War Raw Materials Board that would allocate strategic raw materials to build the products that were most needed. Rathenau made it possible for the German war machine to be effectively supplied. The Germans were much less successful with the rationing of food, however. Even before the war, Germany had had to import about 20 percent of its food supply. The British blockade of Germany and a decline in farm labor made food shortages inevitable. Daily food rations in Germany were cut from 1,350 calories in 1916 to 1,000 by 1917, barely adequate for survival. As a result of a poor potato harvest in the winter of 1916–1917, turnips became the basic staple for the poor. It has been estimated that 750,000 German civilians died of hunger during World War I.

The German war government was eventually consolidated under military authority. The two popular military heroes of the war, General Paul von Hindenburg, chief of the General Staff, and Erich Ludendorff, deputy chief of staff, came to control the government by 1916 and virtually became the military dictators of Germany. In 1916, Hindenburg and Ludendorff decreed a system of complete mobilization for total war. In the Auxiliary Service Law of December 2, 1916, they required all male noncombatants between the ages of seventeen and sixty to work only in jobs deemed crucial for the war effort.

Germany, of course, had already possessed a rather authoritarian political system before the war began. France and England did not, but even in those countries the power of the central government was dramatically

▼ **The Leaders of Germany.** In the course of the war, the power of central governments was greatly enlarged in order to meet the demands of total war. In Germany, the two military heroes of the war, Paul von Hindenburg and Erich Ludendorf, became the virtual military dictators of Germany by 1916. The two are shown here (Hindenburg on the left) with Emperor William II, whose power declined as the war dragged on.

increased. At first, Great Britain tried to fight the war by continuing its liberal tradition of limited government interference in economic matters. The pressure of circumstances, however, forced the British government to take a more active role in economic matters. The need to ensure an adequate production of munitions led to the creation in July 1915 of a Ministry of Munitions under the dynamic leader, David Lloyd George. The Ministry of Munitions took numerous steps to ensure that private industry would produce war matériel at limited profits. It developed a vast bureaucracy, which expanded from 20 to 65,000 clerks to oversee munitions plants. Beginning in 1915, it was given the power to take over plants manufacturing war goods that did not cooperate with the government. The British government also rationed food supplies and imposed rent controls.

The French were less successful than the British and Germans in establishing a strong war government during much of the war. For one thing, the French faced a difficult obstacle in organizing a total war economy. German occupation of northeastern France cost the nation 75 percent of its coal production and almost 80 percent of its steel-making capacity. Then, too, the relationship between civil and military authorities in France was extraordinarily strained. For the first three years of the war, military and civil authorities struggled over who would oversee the conduct of the war. Not until the end of 1917 did the French war government find a strong leader in Georges Clemenceau. Declaring that "war is too important to be left to generals," Clemenceau established clear civilian control of a total war government.

The three other major belligerents—Russia, Austria-Hungary, and Italy—had much less success than Great Britain, Germany, and France in mobilizing for total war. The autocratic empires of Russia and Austria-Hungary had backward economies that proved incapable of turning out the quantity of war matériel needed to fight a modern war. The Russians, for example, conscripted millions of men but could arm only one-fourth of them. Unarmed Russian soldiers were sent into battle anyway and advised to pick up rifles from their dead colleagues. The multinational nature of the Russian and Austro-Hungarian empires also precluded the kind of internal cohesion necessary to fight a prolonged total war. Italy, too, had neither the public enthusiasm of its people nor the industrial resources to wage a successful total war.

PUBLIC ORDER AND PUBLIC OPINION   As the Great War dragged on and both casualties and privations worsened, internal dissatisfaction replaced the patriotic enthusiasm that had marked the early stages of World War I. By 1916, there were numerous signs that civilian morale was beginning to crack under the pressure of total war.

For one thing, strike activity increased dramatically. The first two years of the war witnessed only a few scattered strikes. By 1916, however, social tranquility was dissipating. In Germany in 1916, 50,000 workers carried out a three-day work stoppage in Berlin to protest the arrest of a radical socialist leader. In both France and Britain, the number of strikes increased significantly. Even worse was the violence that erupted in Ireland when members of the Irish Republican Brotherhood and Citizens Army occupied government buildings in Dublin on Easter Sunday (April 24), 1916. British forces crushed the Easter Rebellion in a week of bloody fighting and then condemned its leaders to death.

Internal opposition to the war came from two major sources in 1916 and 1917, liberals and socialists. Liberals in both Germany and Britain sponsored peace resolutions calling for a negotiated peace without any territorial acquisitions. They were largely ignored. Socialists in Germany and Austria also called for negotiated settlements. By 1917, war morale had so deteriorated that more dramatic protests took place. Mutinies in the Italian and French armies were put down with difficulty. Czech leaders in the Austrian Empire openly called for an independent democratic Czech state. In April 1917, 200,000 workers in Berlin went out on strike for a week to protest the reduction of bread rations. Only the threat of military force and prison brought them back to their jobs. Despite the strains, all of the belligerent countries except Russia survived the war in 1917 and fought on.

War governments also fought back against the growing opposition to the war. Authoritarian regimes, such as those of Germany, Russia, and Austria-Hungary, had always relied on force to subdue their populations. Under the pressures of the war, however, even parliamentary regimes resorted to an expansion of police powers to stifle internal dissent. The British Parliament passed a Defence of the Realm Act (DORA) at the very beginning of the war that allowed the public authorities to arrest dissenters as traitors. The act was later extended to authorize public officials to censor newspapers by deleting objectional material and even to suspend newspaper publication. In France, government authorities had initially been lenient about public opposition to the war. But by 1917, they began to fear that open opposition to the war might weaken the French will to fight. When Georges Clemenceau became premier near the end of 1917, the lenient French policies came to an end, and basic civil liberties were suppressed for the duration of

Daddy, what did YOU do in the Great War?

▼ **British Recruiting Poster.** As the war persisted month after month and year after year, governments found themselves hard pressed to maintain the morale of the civilian populations. Wartime governments resorted to active propaganda campaigns to generate enthusiasm for the war. In this British recruiting poster, the government tried to shame men into volunteering for military service. By 1916, the British were forced to adopt compulsory military service.

the war. When a former premier publicly advocated a negotiated peace, Clemenceau's government had him sentenced to prison for two years for treason. The editor of an antiwar newspaper was even executed on a charge of treason. Clemenceau also punished journalists who wrote negative war reports by having them drafted.

Wartime governments made active use of propaganda to arouse enthusiasm for the war. At the beginning, public officials needed to do little to achieve this goal. The British and French, for example, exaggerated German atrocities in Belgium and found that their citizens were only too willing to believe these accounts. But as the war progressed and morale sagged, governments were forced to devise new techniques to stimulate declining enthusiasm. In one British recruiting poster, for example, a small daughter asked her father, "Daddy, what did YOU do in the Great War?" while her younger brother played with toy soldiers and cannon.

THE SOCIAL IMPACT OF TOTAL WAR   Total war made a significant impact on European society, most visibly by bringing an end to unemployment. The withdrawal of millions of men from the labor market to fight, combined with the heightened demand for wartime products, led to jobs for everyone able to work.

The cause of labor also benefited from the war. The enthusiastic patriotism of workers was soon rewarded with a greater acceptance of trade unions. In order to guarantee worker cooperation, war governments in Britain, France, and Germany not only sought union cooperation but also for the first time allowed trade unions to participate in making important government decisions on labor matters. In return, unions cooperated on wage limits and production schedules. In Britain, for example, the government agreed to limit profits in war industries and gave trade unions representation on the National Labour Advisory Committee while unions in turn agreed to renounce the use of strikes and resort only to arbitration during the course of the war. In Germany, the government pursued a policy of "war socialism" in which trade union representatives were added to labor committees in factories and also to regional farm and labor committees. Two benefits emerged for labor out of these cooperative practices. They opened the way to the collective bargaining practices that became more widespread after World War I and increased the prestige of trade unions, enabling them to attract more members.

World War I also created new roles for women. Since so many men went off to fight at the front, women were called upon to take over jobs and responsibilities that had not been available to them before. These included certain clerical jobs that only small numbers of women had held earlier. In Britain, for example, the number of women who worked in banking rose from 9,500 to almost 64,000 in the course of the war, while the number of women in commerce rose from a half million to almost one million. Overall, the number of women employed in Britain who held new jobs or replaced men rose by 1,345,000. Women were also now employed in jobs that had been considered beyond the "capacity of women." These included such occupations as chimney sweeps, truck drivers, farm laborers, and, above all, factory workers in heavy industry. In France, 684,000 women worked in armaments plants for the first time; in Britain, the figure was 920,000. Thirty-eight percent of the workers in the Krupp Armaments works in Germany in 1918 were women.

Male resistance, however, often made it difficult for women to enter these new jobs, especially in heavy industry. One Englishwoman who worked in a munitions factory recalled her experience: "I could quite see it was hard on the men to have women coming into all their pet jobs and in some cases doing them a good deal better. I sympathized with the way they were torn between not wanting the women to undercut them, and yet hating them to earn as much."[6] While male workers expressed concern that the employment of females at lower wages would depress their own wages, women began to demand equal pay legislation. The French government passed a law in July 1915 that enacted a minimum wage for women homeworkers in textiles, an industry that had grown dramatically because of the need for military uniforms. Later in 1917 the government decreed that men and women should receive equal rates for piecework. Despite the noticeable increase in women's wages that resulted from government regulations, women's industrial wages still were not equal to men's wages by the end of the war.

Even worse, women had achieved little real security about their place in the work force. Both men and women seemed to expect that many of the new jobs for women were only temporary, an expectation quite evident in the British poem, "War Girls," written in 1916:

There's the girl who clips your ticket for the train,
And the girl who speeds the lift from floor to floor,
There's the girl who does a milk-round in the rain,
And the girl who calls for orders at your door.
Strong, sensible, and fit,
They're out to show their grit,
And tackle jobs with energy and knack.
No longer caged and penned up,
They're going to keep their end up
Till the khaki soldier boys come marching back.[7]

At the end of the war, governments moved quickly to remove women from the jobs they had encouraged them to take earlier. By 1919, there were 650,000 unemployed women in Britain while wages for women who were still employed were also lowered. The work benefits for women from World War I seemed to be short-lived.

Nevertheless, in some countries the role played by women in the wartime economies did have a positive impact on the women's movement for social and political emancipation. The most obvious gain was the right to vote that was given to women in Germany and Austria immediately after the war (in Britain already in January 1918). Contemporary media, however, tended to focus on the more noticeable, yet in some ways more superficial, social emancipation of upper- and middle-class women. In ever-larger numbers, these young

▼ **Women Workers in a German Munitions Factory.** World War I created new job opportunities for women. They were now employed in jobs that had earlier been considered beyond their capacity. As seen in this picture, this included factory work in heavy industry. These German women are performing a variety of tasks in a shell factory. Between 1913 and 1917, the total female labor force in metal work increased from five to twenty-eight percent of the total labor force.

women took jobs, had their own apartments, and showed their new independence by smoking in public, wearing shorter dresses, cosmetics, and new hair styles.

In one sense, World War I had been a great social leveler. Death in battle did not distinguish between classes. Although all social classes suffered casualties in battle, two groups were especially hard-hit. Junior officers who led the charges across the "no man's land" that separated the lines of trenches experienced death rates that were three times higher than regular casualty rates. Many of these junior officers were members of the aristocracy (see the box on p. 915). The unskilled workers and peasants who made up the masses of soldiers mowed down by machine guns also suffered heavy casualties. The fortunate ones were the skilled laborers who gained exemptions from military service because they were needed at home to train workers in the war industries.

The burst of patriotic enthusiasm that marked the beginning of the war deceived many into believing that the war was creating a new sense of community that meant the end of the class conflict that had marked European society at the end of the nineteenth and beginning of the twentieth centuries. David Lloyd George, who became the British prime minister in 1916, wrote in September 1914 that "all classes, high and low, are shedding themselves of selfishness. . . . It is bringing a new outlook to all classes. . . . We can see for the first time the fundamental things that matter in life, and that have been obscured from our vision by the . . . growth of prosperity."[8] Lloyd George's optimistic opinion proved to be quite misguided, however. The Great War did not eliminate the class conflict that had characterized pre-1914 Europe, and this became increasingly apparent as the war progressed.

Certainly, the economic impact of the war was felt unevenly. One group of people who especially benefited were the owners of the large industries manufacturing the weapons of war. Despite public outrage, governments rarely limited the enormous profits made by the industrial barons. In fact, in the name of efficiency, wartime governments tended to favor large industries when scarce raw materials were allocated. Small firms considered less essential to the war effort even had to shut down because of a lack of resources.

Growing inflation also caused inequities. The combination of full employment and high demand for scarce consumer goods caused prices to climb. Many skilled workers were able to earn wages that enabled them to keep up with the inflation, but this was not true for unskilled workers and workers in nonessential industries. Only in Great Britain did the wages of workers outstrip prices. Everywhere else in Europe, people experienced a loss of purchasing power.

Many middle-class people were especially hard-hit by inflation. They included both those who lived on fixed incomes, such as retired people on pensions, and professional people, such as clerks, lesser civil servants, teachers, small shopkeepers, and clergymen, who received stable incomes at a time when prices were rising. By the end of the war, many of them were actually doing less well economically than skilled workers. Their discontent would find expression after the war.

▼ War and Revolution

By 1917, total war was creating serious domestic turmoil in all of the European belligerent states. Most countries were able to prop up their regimes and convince their peoples to continue the war for another year. Others, however, were reaching a point of near collapse. In Austria, for example, a government minister warned that "if the monarchs of the Central Powers cannot make peace in the coming months, it will be made for them by their peoples." In 1917, however, Russia was the only belligerent that actually experienced the kind of complete collapse that others were predicting might happen throughout Europe. Out of Russia's collapse came the Russian Revolution, whose impact would be widely felt in Europe for decades to come.

The Russian Revolution

After the Revolution of 1905 had failed to bring any substantial changes to Russia, Tsar Nicholas II fell back on the army and bureaucracy as the basic props for his autocratic regime. Perhaps Russia could have survived this way, as some have argued, but World War I magnified Russia's problems and put the tsarist government to a test that it could not meet.

Russia was unprepared both militarily and technologically for the total war of World War I. Competent military leadership was lacking. Even worse, the tsar, alone of all European monarchs, insisted upon taking personal charge of the armed forces despite his obvious lack of ability and training for such an awesome burden. Russian industry was unable to produce the weapons needed for the army. Ill-led and ill-armed, Russian armies suffered incredible losses. Between 1914 and 1916, two million soldiers had been killed while another four to six million had been wounded or captured. By 1917, the Russian will to fight had vanished.

The Reality of War: War and the Family
▼ ▼ ▼

John Mott was a captain in the British army. He came from an aristocratic family with a strong military tradition. He married Muriel Backhouse in 1907, and they had three sons before he was called up for service in World War I. These excerpts are taken from four of Mott's letters to his wife and a letter informing Mott's wife of her husband's death during the Gallipoli campaign. The human experience of World War I was made up of millions of stories like that of John Mott and his family.

One Family's War

1 July [1915]

My darling Childie,

I hope you got home safely. I have been promised that I shall know the ship we go on tomorrow. But it will be no good writing to Gibraltar as we should get there before the letter. Try Malta as that goes over land. If you get overdrawn go and see Cox. Goodbye Darling. Don't worry I shall come back alright. Your devoted husband John F. Mott

13 July

Mediterranean field force, Mudros
My darling Childie,

This island is very hot indeed but beastly windy. We have absolutely no news from the Front. Troops are pouring out now and I expect we shall be in it next week.

We have all gone through our little bout of diarrhea. I was not too bad and only had pains in my stomach otherwise I am very well indeed.

Everyone is standing the heat very well. The Brigadier has a tent but everybody else is out in the blazing sun.

31 July

My darling Childie,

I got more letters from you today dated 5th, 6th, 7th. I had no idea till I read the letter that they could do all that about writs. I would never have left things in such a muddle, I only hope you can get straight.

Yesterday I left here at 5:30 AM to go to the trenches with the Brigadier. We had an awful day, and I am not at all keen to go into that lot at all events. We sailed over in a trawler and had a long walk in the open under shrapnel fire. It was not very pleasant. Then we got to the communications trenches and had a mile and a half of them to go up. When we got

to the fire trenches the stink was awful. Arms and legs of Turks sticking out of the trench parapets and lying dead all round. In one place the bottom of the trench was made up by dead Turks, but this has been abandoned as the place was too poisonous.

Our battle ships have been shelling very heavily so there may be an attack on. I must write to my mother tonight. All my love and kisses for ever Your loving husband John F. Mott

6 August

My darling Childie,

We are off today just as we stand up, with four days rations. I can't say where we are going but we shall see spots. I shall not get a chance to write again for a bit as we shall be on the move. I expect you have got a map of the place by now and perhaps you will hear where we have gone.

Very good to get away. All my love and kisses for ever

Your loving husband John F. Mott
Best love to all kids and baby

Pte A Thompson
6 Batt Y and L Red Cross Hospital

We landed on the 6th of Aug and took 2 hills and at daybreak on the 7th advanced across an open plain to the left of Salt Lake and got an awful shelling. We came to a small hill which was flat on top and it was about 2 hundred yards further on where the Capt was hit. They gave us it worse than ever when we got on there and I might have been happen 50 yds away when I saw the Capt and about 5 men fall badly hit. I could not say whether it was shrapnel or common shell but I think it was most probably shrapnel as they use that mostly. It was that thick that no one could get to the Capt at the time and I don't think he lived very long, well he could not the way they were hit and was afterwards buried when things had quietened down in the evening and a cross was put on his grave with an inscription and he got as good a burial as could be given out there. Well I think I have told you all I know about Capt Mott. I only wishe I could have given you better news, so I will close with Kind Regards
Yours Obediently,
Pte Thompson

The tsarist government was totally inadequate for the tasks that it faced in 1914. The surge of patriotic enthusiasm that greeted the outbreak of war was soon dissipated by a government that distrusted its own people. When leading industrialists formed committees to improve factory production, a government suspicious of their motives undermined their efforts. Although the middle classes and liberal aristocrats still hoped for a constitutional monarchy, they were sullen over the tsar's revocation of the political concessions made during the Revolution of 1905. Peasant discontent flourished as conditions worsened. The concentration of Russian industry in a few large cities made workers' frustrations all the more evident and dangerous. Even conservative aristocrats were appalled by the incompetent and inefficient bureaucracy that controlled the political and military system. In the meantime, Tsar Nicholas II was increasingly insulated from events by his wife Alexandra.

This German-born princess was a stubborn, willful, and ignorant woman who had fallen under the influence of Rasputin, a Siberian peasant who belonged to a religious sect that indulged in sexual orgies. To the tsarina, Rasputin was a holy man for he alone seemed able to stop the bleeding of her hemophiliac son Alexis. Rasputin's influence made him an important power behind the throne, and he did not hesitate to interfere in government affairs. As the leadership at the top stumbled its way through a series of military and economic disasters, the middle class, aristocrats, peasants, soldiers, and workers grew more and more disenchanted with the tsarist regime. Even conservative aristocrats who supported the monarchy felt the need to do something to reverse the deteriorating situation. For a start, they assassinated Rasputin in December 1916. By then it was too late to save the monarchy, and its fall came quickly at the beginning of March 1917.

THE MARCH REVOLUTION   At the beginning of March, a series of strikes broke out in the capital city of Petrograd (formerly St. Petersburg). Here the actions of working-class women helped to change the course of Russian history. In February of 1917, the government had introduced bread rationing in the capital city after the price of bread had skyrocketed. Many of the women who stood in the lines waiting for bread were also factory workers who had put in twelve-hour days. The number of women working in Petrograd factories had doubled since 1914. The Russian government had become aware of the volatile situation in the capital from a police report:

Mothers of families, exhausted by endless standing in line at stores, distraught over their half-starving and sick children, are today perhaps closer to revolution than [the liberal opposition leaders] and of course they are a great deal more dangerous because they are the combustible material for which only a single spark is needed to burst into flame.[9]

On March 8, a day celebrated since 1910 as International Women's Day, about ten thousand Petrograd women marched through the city demanding "Peace and Bread" and "Down with Autocracy." Soon the women were joined by other workers, and together they called for a general strike that succeeded in shutting down all the factories in the city on March 10. The tsarina wrote to Nicholas II at the battlefront that "This is a hooligan movement. If the weather were very cold they would all probably stay at home." Nicholas ordered the troops to disperse the crowds by shooting them if necessary. Initially, the troops did so, but soon significant numbers of the soldiers joined the demonstrators. The situation was out of the tsar's control. The Duma or legislative body, which the tsar had tried to dissolve, met anyway and on March 12 established a Provisional Government that urged the tsar to abdicate. He did so on March 15.

In just one week, the tsarist regime had fallen apart. It was not really overthrown since there had been no deliberate revolution. Even those who were conscious revolutionaries were caught by surprise at the rapidity of the monarchy's disintegration. Although no particular group had been responsible for the outburst, the moderate Constitutional Democrats were responsible for establishing the Provisional Government. They represented primarily a middle-class and liberal aristocratic minority. Their program consisted of a nineteenth-century liberal agenda: freedom of speech, religion, assembly, and civil liberties. Their determination to carry on the war to preserve Russia's honor was a major blunder since it satisfied neither the workers nor the peasants who above all wanted an end to the war.

The Provisional Government was also faced with another authority, the soviets, or councils of workers' and soldiers' deputies. The soviet of Petrograd had been formed in March 1917; at the same time soviets sprang up spontaneously in army units, factory towns, and rural areas. The soviets represented the more radical interests of the lower classes and were largely composed of socialists of different kinds. Most numerous were the Socialist Revolutionaries, who wished to establish peasant socialism by seizing the great landed estates and creating a rural democracy. Since the beginning of the twentieth century, the Socialist Revolutionaries had come to rely on the use of political terrorism to accomplish their goals. Since 1893, Russia had also had a Marxist Social Democratic party, which had divided in 1903 into two factions known as the Mensheviks and Bolsheviks. The Mensheviks wanted the Social Democrats to be a mass electoral socialist party based on a Western model. Like the Social Democrats of Germany, they were willing to cooperate temporarily in a parliamentary democracy while working toward the ultimate achievement of the socialist state.

The Bolsheviks were a small faction of Russian Social Democrats who had come under the leadership of Vladimir Ulianov, known to the world as V. I. Lenin (1870–1924). Born in 1870 to a middle-class family, Lenin received a legal education and became a lawyer. In 1887, he turned into a dedicated enemy of tsarist Russia when his older brother was executed for planning to assassinate the tsar. Lenin's search for a revolutionary faith led him to Marxism, and in 1894 he moved to St. Petersburg where he organized an illegal group known as the Union for the Liberation of the Working Class. Arrested for this activity, Lenin was shipped to Siberia. After his release, he chose to go into exile in Switzerland and eventually assumed the leadership of the Bolshevik wing of the Russian Social Democratic party.

Under Lenin's direction, the Bolsheviks became a party dedicated to violent revolution. He believed that only a violent revolution could destroy the capitalist system and that a "vanguard" of activists must form a small party of well-disciplined professional revolutionaries to accomplish the task. Between 1900 and 1917, Lenin spent most of his time in Switzerland. When the Provisional Government was formed in March 1917, he believed that an opportunity for the Bolsheviks to seize power had come. In April 1917, with the connivance of the German High Command, who hoped to create disorder in Russia, Lenin, his wife, and a small group of his followers were shipped to Russia in a "sealed train" by way of Finland.

Lenin's arrival in Russia opened a new stage of the Russian Revolution. In his "April Theses," issued on April 20, Lenin presented a blueprint for revolutionary action based on his own version of Marxist theory. According to Lenin, it was not necessary for Russia to experience a bourgeois revolution before it could move toward socialism, as orthodox Marxists had argued. Instead, Russia could move directly into socialism. In the "April Theses," Lenin maintained that the soviets of soldiers, workers, and peasants were ready-made instruments of power. The Bolsheviks must work toward gaining control of these groups and then use them to over-throw the Provisional Government. At the same time, Bolshevik propaganda must seek mass support through promises geared to the needs of the people: an end to the war; redistribution of all land to the peasants; the transfer of factories and industries from capitalists to committees of workers; and the relegation of government power from the Provisional Government to the soviets. Three simple slogans summed up the Bolshevik program: "Peace, Land, Bread," "Worker Control of Production," and "All Power to the Soviets."

In late spring and early summer, while the Bolsheviks set about winning over the masses to their program and gaining a majority in the Petrograd and Moscow soviets, the Provisional Government struggled to gain control of Russia against almost overwhelming obstacles. Although the Provisional Government promised that a constitutional convention called for the fall of 1917 would confiscate and redistribute royal and monastic lands, the offer was meaningless since many peasants had already started seizing lands on their own in March. The military situation was also deteriorating. The Petrograd soviet had issued its Army Order No. 1 in March to all Russian military forces, encouraging them to remove their officers and replace them with committees composed of "the elected representatives of the lower ranks" of the army. Army Order No. 1 led to the collapse of all discipline and created military chaos. When the Provisional Government attempted to initiate a new military offensive in July, the army simply dissolved as masses of peasant soldiers turned their backs on their officers and returned home to join their families in seizing lands.

THE BOLSHEVIK REVOLUTION In July 1917, Lenin and the Bolsheviks attempted to overthrow the Provisional Government. The government was still strong enough to crush the rebellion, however, and Lenin was forced to flee to Finland. But the days of the Provisional Government were numbered. In July 1917, Alexander Kerensky, a Socialist Revolutionary, had become prime minister in the Provisional Government. In September, when General Lavr Kornilov attempted to march on Petrograd and seize power, Kerensky released Bolsheviks from prison and turned to the Petrograd soviet for help. Although General Kornilov's forces never reached Petrograd, Kerensky's action had strengthened the hands of the Petrograd soviet and had shown Lenin how weak the Provisional Government really was.

By the end of October, the Bolsheviks had achieved a slight majority in the Petrograd and Moscow soviets. The number of party members had also grown from

Ten Days That Shook the World: Lenin and the Bolshevik Seizure of Power

▼ ▼ ▼

John Reed was an American journalist who helped to found the American Communist Labor party. Accused of sedition, he fled the United States and went to Russia. In Ten Days That Shook the World, *Reed left an impassioned eyewitness account of the Russian Revolution. It is apparent from his comments that Reed considered Lenin the indispensable hero of the Bolshevik success.*

John Reed, *Ten Days That Shook the World*

It was just 8:40 when a thundering wave of cheers announced the entrance of the presidium, with Lenin—great Lenin—among them. A short, stocky figure, with a big head set down in his shoulders, bald and bulging. Little eyes, a snubbish nose, wide, generous mouth, and heavy chin; clean-shaven now, but already beginning to bristle with the well-known beard of his past and future. Dressed in shabby clothes, his trousers much too long for him. Unimpressive, to be the idol of a mob, loved and revered as perhaps few leaders in history have been. A strange popular leader—a leader purely by virtue of intellect; colourless, humourless, uncompromising and detached; without picturesque idiosyncrasies—but with the power of explaining profound ideas in simple terms, of analysing a concrete situation. And combined with shrewdness, the greatest intellectual audacity. . . .

Now Lenin, gripping the edge of the reading stand, letting his little winking eyes travel over the crowd as he stood there waiting, apparently oblivious to the long-rolling ovation, which lasted several minutes. When it finished, he said simply, "We shall now proceed to construct the Socialist order!" Again that overwhelming human roar.

"The first thing is the adoption of practical measures to realise peace. . . . We shall offer peace to the peoples of all the belligerent countries upon the basis of the Soviet terms—no annexations, no indemnities, and the right of self-determination of peoples. At the same time, according to our promise, we shall publish and repudiate the secret treaties. . . . The question of War and Peace is so clear that I think that I may, without preamble, read the project of a Proclamation to the Peoples of All the Belligerent Countries. . . ."

His great mouth, seeming to smile, opened wide as he spoke; his voice was hoarse—not unpleasantly so, but as if it had hardened that way after years and years of speaking—and went on monotonously, with the effect of being able to go forever. . . . For emphasis he bent forward slightly. No gestures. And before him, a thousand simple faces looking up in intent adoration.

[Reed then reproduces the full text of the Proclamation.]

When the grave thunder of applause had died away, Lenin spoke again: "We propose to the Congress to ratify this declaration. . . . This proposal of peace will meet with resistance on the part of the imperialist governments—we don't fool ourselves on that score. But we hope that revolution will soon break out in all the belligerent countries; that is why we address ourselves especially to the workers of France, England and Germany. . . .

"The revolution of November 6th and 7th," he ended, "has opened the era of the Social Revolution. . . . The labour movement, in the name of peace and Socialism, shall win, and fulfill its destiny. . . ."

There was something quiet and powerful in all this, which stirred the souls of men. It was understandable why people believed when Lenin spoke.

50,000 to 240,000. Lenin had become convinced from reports of unrest abroad that "we are on the threshold of a world proletarian revolution," and he tried to convince his fellow Bolsheviks that the time was ripe for the overthrow of the Provisional Government. Although he faced formidable opposition within the Bolshevik ranks, he managed to gain support for his policy. He was especially fortunate to have the close cooperation of Leon Trotsky (1877–1940), a former Menshevik turned fervid revolutionary. Lenin and Trotsky organized a Military Revolutionary Committee within the Petrograd soviet to plot the overthrow of the government. On the night of November 6–7, Bolshevik forces seized the Winter Palace, seat of the Provisional Government. The

Provisional Government collapsed quickly with little bloodshed.

This coup d'etat had been timed to coincide with a meeting in Petrograd of the all-Russian Congress of Soviets representing local soviets from all over the country. Lenin nominally turned over the sovereignty of the Provisional Government to this Congress of Soviets. Real power, however, passed to a Council of People's Commissars, headed by Lenin (see the box on p. 918). One immediate problem that faced the Bolsheviks was the Constituent Assembly, which had been initiated by the Provisional Government and was scheduled to meet in January 1918. Elections to the assembly by universal male suffrage had produced a defeat for the Bolsheviks, who had only 225 delegates compared to the 420 garnered by the Socialist Revolutionaries. But no matter. Lenin simply broke the Constituent Assembly by force. "To hand over power," he said, "to the Constituent Assembly would again be compromising with malignant bourgeoisie." The Bolsheviks did not want majority rule, but the rule of the proletariat, exercised for them, of course, by the Bolsheviks, soon renamed the Communists.

But the Bolsheviks still had a long way to go. Lenin, ever the opportunist, realized the importance of winning mass support as quickly as possible by fulfilling Bolshevik promises. In his first law, Lenin declared the land nationalized and turned it over to local rural soviets. In effect, this action merely ratified the peasants' seizure of the land and assured the Bolsheviks of peasant support, especially against any attempt by the old landlords to restore their power. The demands of urban workers were also met when Lenin granted control of factories to committees of workers. To Lenin, however, this was merely a temporary expedient.

Lenin had also promised peace and that, he realized, was not an easy task because of the humiliating losses of Russian territory that it would entail. There was no real choice, however. On March 15, 1918, Lenin signed the Treaty of Brest-Litovsk with Germany and gave up eastern Poland, the Ukraine, Finland, and the Baltic provinces. To his critics, Lenin argued that it made no difference since the spread of socialist revolution throughout Europe would make the treaty largely irrelevant. In any case, he had promised peace to the Russian people, but real peace did not come for the country soon sank into civil war.

CIVIL WAR   There was great opposition to the new Bolshevik or Communist regime, not only from groups loyal to the tsar but also from bourgeois and aristocratic liberals and anti-Leninist socialists, including Mensheviks and Socialist Revolutionaries. In addition, thousands of Allied troops were eventually sent to different parts of Russia in the hope of bringing Russia back into the war.

Between 1918 and 1921, the Bolshevik (or Red) Army was forced to fight on many fronts. The first serious threat to the Bolsheviks came from Siberia where a White (anti-Bolshevik) force under Admiral Alexander Kolchak attacked westward and advanced almost to the Volga River before being stopped. Attacks also came from the Ukrainians in the southeast and from the Baltic regions. In mid-1919, White forces under General Anton Denikin, probably the most effective of the White generals, swept through the Ukraine and advanced almost to Moscow. At one point by late 1919, three separate White armies seemed to be closing in on the Bolsheviks, but were eventually pushed back. By 1920, the major White forces had been defeated, and the Ukraine retaken. The next year, the Communist regime regained control over the independent nationalist governments in the Caucasus: Georgia, Russian Armenia, and Azerbaijan.

▼ **Lenin Addresses a Crowd.** V. I. Lenin was the driving force behind the success of the Bolsheviks in seizing power in Russia and creating the Union of Soviet Socialist Republics (USSR). By 1921, after a hard fought Civil War, the Communists managed to retain their control of Russia. Lenin is seen addressing a rally in Moscow in 1917.

How had Lenin and the Bolsheviks triumphed over what seemed at one time to be overwhelming forces? For one thing, the Red Army became a well-disciplined and formidable fighting force, largely due to the organizational genius of Leon Trotsky. As commissar of war, Trotsky reinstated the draft and even recruited and gave commands to former tsarist army officers. Trotsky insisted on rigid discipline; soldiers who deserted or refused to obey orders were summarily executed. The Red Army also had the advantage of interior lines of defense and was able to move its troops rapidly from one battlefront to the other.

The disunity of the anti-Communist forces seriously weakened the efforts of the Whites. Political differences created distrust among the Whites and prevented them from cooperating effectively with each other. Some Whites, such as Admiral Kolchak, insisted on restoring the tsarist regime, while others understood that only a more liberal and democratic program had any chance of success. Since the White forces were forced to operate on the exterior fringes of the Russian empire, it was

difficult enough to achieve military cooperation. Political differences made it virtually impossible.

The lack of a common goal on the part of the Whites was paralleled by a single-minded sense of purpose on the part of the Communists. Inspired by their vision of a new socialist order, the Communists had the advantage of possessing that determination that comes from revolutionary fervor and revolutionary convictions.

The Communists also succeeded in translating their revolutionary faith into practical instruments of power. A policy of "war communism," for example, was used to ensure regular supplies for the Red Army. "War communism" included the nationalization of banks and most industries, the forcible requisition of grain from peasants, and the centralization of state administration under Bolshevik control. Another Bolshevik instrument was "revolutionary terror." Although the old tsarist secret police had been abolished, a new Red secret police—known as the Cheka—replaced it. The Red Terror instituted by the Cheka aimed at nothing less than the destruction of all those who opposed the new re-

▼ **Map 26.4** The Russian Revolution and Civil War.

pitched battles, however, nor did they pursue a common strategy, although they did give material assistance to anti-Bolshevik forces. This intervention by the Allies enabled the Communist government to appeal to patriotic Russians to fight the attempts of foreigners to control their country. Allied interference was never substantial enough to make a military difference in the civil war, but it did serve indirectly to help the Bolshevik cause.

▼ **Trotsky as Leader of the Red Army.** Crucial to the success of the Communists in the Civil War was the Red Army. As commissar of war, Leon Trotsky, who had played an important role in the Bolshevik seizure of power, made the Red Army into a formidable fighting force. He is shown here (at the left) on one of his numerous journeys across Russia during the Civil War.

gime. "Class enemies"—the bourgeoisie—were especially singled out, at least according to a Cheka officer: "The first questions you should put to the accused person are: To what class does he belong, what is his origin, what was his education, and what is his profession? These should determine the fate of the accused." In practice, however, the Cheka promulgated terror against all classes, including the proletariat, if they opposed the new regime. The Red Terror added an element of fear to the Bolshevik regime.

Finally, the intervention of foreign armies enabled the Communists to appeal to the powerful force of Russian patriotism. Although the Allied powers had intervened initially in Russia to encourage the Russians to remain in the war, the end of the war on November 11, 1918, had made that purpose inconsequential. Nevertheless, Allied troops remained, and more were even sent as Allied countries did not hide their anti-Bolshevik feelings. At one point, over 100,000 foreign troops, mostly Japanese, British, American, and French were stationed on Russian soil. These forces rarely engaged in

By 1921, the Communists had succeeded in retaining control of Russia. In the course of the civil war, the Bolshevik regime had also transformed Russia into a bureaucratically centralized state dominated by a single party. It was also a state that was largely hostile to the Allied powers that had sought to assist the Bolsheviks' enemies in the civil war. To most historians, the Russian Revolution is unthinkable without the total war of World War I for only the collapse of Russia made it possible for a radical minority like the Bolsheviks to seize the reins of power. In turn, the Russian Revolution had an impact on the course of World War I.

The Last Year of the War

For Germany, the withdrawal of the Russians from the war in March 1918 offered renewed hope for a favorable end to the war. The victory over Russia persuaded Ludendorff and most German leaders to make one final military gamble—a grand offensive in the west to break the military stalemate. The German attack was launched in March and lasted into July. The German forces succeeded in advancing forty miles to the Marne River, within thirty-five miles of Paris. But an Allied counterattack, led by the French General Ferdinand Foch and supported by the arrival of 140,000 fresh American troops, defeated the Germans at the Second Battle of the Marne on July 18. Ludendorff's gamble had failed. Having used up his reserves, Ludendorff knew that defeat was now inevitable. With the arrival of 2 million more American troops on the Continent, Allied forces began making a steady advance toward Germany.

On September 29, 1918, General Ludendorff informed German leaders that the war was lost. Unwilling to place the burden of defeat on the army, Ludendorff demanded that the government sue for peace at once. When German officials discovered, however, that the Allies were unwilling to make peace with the autocratic imperial government, reforms were instituted to create a liberal government. But these constitutional reforms came too late for the exhausted and angry German people. On November 3, naval units in Kiel mutinied, and within days councils of workers and soldiers, German versions of the Russian soviets, were forming throughout northern Germany and taking over the supervision of civilian and military administrations. William II capitulated to public pressure and left the country on November 9, while the Socialists under Friedrich Ebert announced the establishment of a republic. Two days later, on November 11, 1918, the new German government

agreed to an armistice. The war was over, but the revolutionary forces set in motion by the war were not yet exhausted.

Revolutionary Upheavals in Germany and Austria-Hungary

Like Russia, Germany and Austria-Hungary also experienced political revolution as a result of military defeat. In its early stage, the German November Revolution of 1918 was similar to the Russian Revolution of March 1917. War weariness had led to a popular upheaval that overthrew an autocratic monarchy and created a liberal, democratic republic. As in Russia, liberals and moderate socialists formed a new provisional government while workers' and soldiers' councils competed for ruling power. In Russia, the radical forces represented in these councils went on to overthrow the Provisional Government and establish a socialist state. In Germany, the radicals lost as moderate socialists remained in power in a democratic republic.

In November 1918, when Germany began to disintegrate in a convulsion of mutinies and mass demonstrations, only the Social Democrats were numerous and well organized enough to pick up the pieces. But the German Socialists had divided into two groups during the war. A majority of the Social Democrats still favored parliamentary democracy as a gradual approach to social democracy and the elimination of the capitalist system. A minority of German socialists, however, disgusted with the Social Democrats' support of the war, had formed an Independent Social Democratic Party in 1916. In 1918, the more radical members of the Independent Socialists favored an immediate social revolution carried out by the councils of soldiers, sailors, and workers. Led by Karl Liebknecht and Rosa Luxemburg, these radical, left-wing socialists formed the German Communist party in December 1918. In effect, two parallel governments were established in Germany: the parliamentary republic proclaimed by the majority Social Democrats and the revolutionary socialist republic declared by radicals.

Unlike Russia's Bolsheviks, Germany's radicals failed to achieve control of the government. By ending the war on November 11, the moderate socialists had removed a major source of dissatisfaction. When the radical socialists (now known as Communists) attempted to seize power in Berlin in January 1919, Friedrich Ebert and the moderate socialists called on the regular army and groups of antirevolutionary volunteers known as Free Corps to crush the rebels. The victorious forces brutally murdered Liebknecht and Luxemburg. A similar attempt at Communist revolution in the city of Munich in southern Germany was also crushed by the Free Corps and the regular army. The German republic had been saved, but only because the moderate socialists had relied on the traditional army—in effect, the same conservatives who had dominated the old imperial regime. Moreover, this "second revolution" of January 1919, bloodily crushed by the republican government, created a deep fear of communism among the German middle classes. All too soon, this fear would be cleverly manipulated by a politician named Adolf Hitler.

Austria-Hungary, too, experienced disintegration and revolution. In 1914, when it attacked Serbia, the imperial regime had tried to crush the nationalistic forces that it believed were destroying the empire. By 1918, those same nationalistic forces had brought the complete breakup of the Austro-Hungarian Empire. As war weariness took hold of the empire, ethnic minorities increasingly sought to achieve national independence. This desire was further encouraged by Allied war aims that included calls for the independence of the subject peoples. By the time the war ended, the Austro-Hungarian Empire had been replaced by the independent republics of Austria, Hungary, and Czechoslovakia and the large South Slav monarchical state called Yugoslavia. Other regions clamored to join Italy, Romania, and a reconstituted Poland. Rivalries among the nations that succeeded Austria-Hungary would weaken eastern Europe for the next seventy years. Ethnic pride and national statehood proved far more important to these states than class differences. Only in Hungary was there an attempt at social revolution when Béla Kun established a communist state. It was crushed after a brief five-month existence.

▼ The Peace Settlement

In January 1919, the delegations of twenty-seven victorious Allied nations gathered in Paris to conclude a final settlement of the Great War. Some delegates believed that this conference would avoid the mistakes made at Vienna in 1815 (see Chapter 22) by aristocrats who rearranged the map of Europe to meet the selfish desires of the great powers. Harold Nicolson, one of the British delegates, expressed what he believed this conference would achieve instead: "We were journeying to Paris not merely to liquidate the war, but to found a New Order in Europe. We were preparing not Peace only, but Eternal Peace. There was about us the halo of some divine mission. . . . For we were bent on doing great, permanent and noble things."[10]

National expectations, however, made Nicolson's quest for "eternal peace" a difficult one. Over a period of years, the reasons for fighting World War I had been transformed from selfish national interests to idealistic principles. At the end of 1917, after they had taken over the Russian government, Lenin and the Bolsheviks had publicly revealed the contents of secret wartime treaties found in the archives of the Russian foreign ministry. The Bolshevik action made it clear that European nations had gone to war primarily to achieve territorial gains. But the American president Woodrow Wilson attempted at the beginning of 1918 to shift the discussion of war aims to a higher ground. Wilson outlined "Fourteen Points" to the American Congress that he believed justified the enormous military struggle then being waged. Later, Wilson spelled out additional steps for a truly just and lasting peace. Wilson's proposals included "open covenants of peace, openly arrived at" instead of secret diplomacy; the reduction of national armaments to a "point consistent with domestic safety"; and the self-determination of people so that "all well-defined national aspirations shall be accorded the utmost satisfaction." Wilson characterized World War I as a people's war waged against "absolutism and militarism," two scourges of liberty that could only be eliminated by creating democratic governments and a "general association of nations" that would guarantee the "political independence and territorial integrity to great and small states alike" (see the box on p. 924). As the spokesman for a new world order based on democracy and international cooperation, Wilson was enthusiastically cheered by many Europeans when he arrived in Europe for the peace conference.

Wilson soon found, however, that other states at the Paris Peace Conference were guided by considerably more pragmatic motives. The secret treaties and agreements, for example, that had been made before the war could not be totally ignored, even if they did conflict with the principle of self-determination enunciated by Wilson.

National interests also complicated the deliberations of the Paris Peace Conference. David Lloyd George, prime minister of Great Britain, had won a decisive electoral victory in December of 1918 on a platform of making the Germans pay for this dreadful war. Public opinion had been inflamed during the war by a government propaganda campaign that portrayed the Germans as beasts. With the war over, the influence of that propa-

The Voice of Peacemaking: Woodrow Wilson

▼ ▼ ▼

"We are fighting for the liberty, the self-government, and the undictated development of all peoples. . . ."

When the Allied powers met at Paris in January 1919, it soon became apparent that the victors had differences of opinion on the kind of peace they expected. These excerpts are from the speeches of Woodrow Wilson in which the American president presented his idealistic goals for a peace based on justice and reconciliation.

Woodrow Wilson, May 26, 1917

We are fighting for the liberty, the self-government, and the undictated development of all peoples, and every feature of the settlement that concludes this war must be conceived and executed for that purpose. Wrongs must first be righted and then adequate safeguards must be created to prevent their being committed again. . . .

No people must be forced under sovereignty under which it does not wish to live. No territory must change hands except for the purpose of securing those who inhabit it a fair chance of life and liberty. No indemnities must be insisted on except those that constitute payment for manifest wrongs done. No readjustments of power must be made except such as will tend to secure the future peace of the world and the future welfare and happiness of its peoples.

And then the free peoples of the world must draw together in some common covenant, some genuine and practical cooperation that will in effect combine their force to secure peace and justice in the dealings of nations with one another.

April 6, 1918

We are ready, whenever the final reckoning is made, to be just to the German people, deal fairly with the German power, as with all others. There can be no difference between peoples in the final judgment, if it is indeed to be a righteous judgment. To propose anything but justice, even-handed and dispassionate justice, to Germany at any time, whatever the outcome of the war, would be to renounce and dishonor our own cause. For we ask nothing that we are not willing to accord.

January 3, 1919

Our task at Paris is to organize the friendship of the world, to see to it that all the moral forces that make for right and justice and liberty are united and are given a vital organization to which the peoples of the world will readily and gladly respond. In other words, our task is no less colossal than this, to set up a new international psychology, to have a new atmosphere.

---

ganda continued to be felt as many British believed that only a total victory over Germany could ever compensate for the terrible losses of the war.

France's approach to peace was primarily determined by considerations of national security. To Georges Clemenceau, the feisty premier of France who had led his country to victory, the French people had borne the brunt of German aggression. They deserved revenge and security against future German aggression (see the box on p. 925). The French knew that Germany's larger population (60 million to 40 million) posed a long-term threat to France. Clemenceau wanted a demilitarized Germany, vast German reparations to pay for the costs of the war, and a separate Rhineland as a buffer state between France and Germany, demands that Wilson viewed as vindictive and contrary to the principle of national self-determination.

Yet another consideration affected the negotiations at Paris, namely, the fear that Bolshevik revolution would spread from Russia to other European countries. This concern led the Allies to enlarge and strengthen such eastern European states as Poland, Czechoslovakia, and Romania at the expense of both Germany and Bolshevik Russia.

Although twenty-seven nations were represented at the Paris Peace Conference, the most important decisions were made by Woodrow Wilson, Georges Clemenceau, and David Lloyd George. Italy was considered one of the so-called Big Four powers, but played a much less important role than the other three countries. Germany, of course, was not invited to attend and Russia could not because of its civil war.

In view of the many conflicting demands at Versailles, it was inevitable that the Big Three would quarrel. Wil-

The Voice of Peacemaking: Georges Clemenceau

▼ ▼ ▼

"*For the catastrophe of 1914 the Germans are responsible.*"

The French leader Georges Clemenceau had a vision of peacemaking quite different from that of Woodrow Wilson. The French sought revenge and security. In this selection from his book Grandeur and Misery of Victory, *Clemenceau revealed his fundamental dislike and distrust of Germany.*

Georges Clemenceau, *Grandeur and Misery of Victory*

War and peace, with their strong contrasts, alternate against a common background. For the catastrophe of 1914 the Germans are responsible. Only a professional liar would deny this. . . .

What after all is this war, prepared, undertaken, and waged by the German people, who flung aside every scruple of conscience to let it loose, hoping for a peace of enslavement under the yoke of a militarism, destructive of all human dignity? It is simply the continuance, the recrudescence, of those never-ending acts of violence by which the first savage tribes carried out their depredations with all the resources of barbarism. . . .

I have sometimes penetrated into the sacred cave of the Germanic cult, which is, as every one knows, the *Bierhaus* [beer hall]. A great aisle of massive humanity where there accumulate, amid the fumes of tobacco and beer, the popular rumblings of a nationalism upheld by the sonorous brasses blaring to the heavens the supreme voice of Germany, *Deutschland über alles! Germany above everything!* Men, women, and children, all petrified in reverence before the divine stoneware pot, brows furrowed with irrepressible power, eyes lost in a dream of infinity, mouths twisted by the intensity of will-power, drink in long draughts the celestial hope of vague expectations. These only remain to be realized presently when the chief marked out by Destiny shall have given the word. There you have the ultimate framework of an old but childish race.

---

son was determined to create a League of Nations to prevent future wars. Clemenceau and Lloyd George were equally determined to punish Germany. In the end, only compromise made it possible to achieve a peace settlement. Wilson's wish that the creation of an international peacekeeping organization be the first order of business was granted, and already on January 25, 1919, the conference adopted the principle of a League of Nations. The details of its structure were left for later sessions, and Wilson willingly agreed to make compromises on territorial arrangements to guarantee the establishment of the league, believing that a functioning league could later rectify bad arrangements. Clemenceau also compromised to obtain some guarantees for French security. He renounced France's desire for a separate Rhineland and instead accepted a defensive alliance with Great Britain and the United States. Both states pledged to help France if it were attacked by Germany.

The final peace settlement of Paris consisted of five separate treaties with the defeated nations—Germany, Austria, Hungary, Bulgaria, and Turkey. The Treaty of Versailles with Germany, signed on June 28, 1919, was by far the most important. The Germans considered it a harsh peace, conveniently overlooking that the Treaty of Brest-Litovsk that they had imposed on Bolshevik Russia was even more severe. The Germans were particularly unhappy with Article 231, the so-called War Guilt Clause, which declared Germany (and Austria) responsible for starting the war and ordered Germany to pay reparations for all the damage to which the Allied governments and their people were subjected as a result of the war "imposed upon them by the aggression of Germany and her allies." Reparations were a logical con-

▼ **The Big Four at Paris.** Shown here are the Big Four at the Paris Peace Conference: Lloyd George of Britain, Orlando of Italy, Clemenceau of France, and Wilson of the United States. Although Italy was considered one of the Big Four powers, Britain, France, and the United States (the Big Three) made the major decisions at the peace conference.

sequence of the wartime promises that Allied leaders had made to their people that the Germans would pay for the war effort.

The military and territorial provisions of the treaty also rankled Germans, although they were by no means as harsh as the Germans claimed. Germany had to lower its army to 100,000 men, reduce its navy, and eliminate its air force. German territorial losses included the cession of Alsace and Lorraine to France and sections of Prussia to the new Polish state. German land west and as far as thirty miles east of the Rhine was established as a demilitarized zone and stripped of all armaments or fortifications to serve as a barrier to any future German military moves westward against France. Outraged by the "dictated peace," the new German government vowed to resist rather than accept the treaty, but it had no real alternative. Rejection meant a renewal of the war, and as the army pointed out, that was no longer possible.

The separate peace treaties made with the other Central Powers (Austria, Hungary, Bulgaria, and Turkey) extensively redrew the map of eastern Europe. Many of

▼ **Map 26.5** Europe in 1919.

Lost immediately after World War I

By Russia

By Germany

By Austria-Hungary

By Bulgaria

The Path to War	**1914**	Battle of Verdun	**1916** February 21– December 18
Assassination of Archduke Francis Ferdinand	June 28		
Austria's Ultimatum to Serbia	July 23	Battle of Jutland	May 31
Austrian Declares War on Serbia	July 28	The Somme Offensive	July 1– November 19
Russian Mobilizes	July 29		
German Ultimatum to Russia	July 31		**1917**
Germany Declares War on Russia	August 1	Germany Returns to Unrestricted Submarine Warfare	January
Germany Declares War on France	August 3	United States Enters the War	April 6
German Troops Invade Belgium	August 4	The Champagne Offensive	April 16–29
Great Britain Declares War on Germany	August 4		**1918**
		Last German Offensive	March 21– July 18
The War	**1914**		
Battle of Tannenberg	August 26–30	Second Battle of the Marne	July 18
First Battle of the Marne	September 6–10	Allied Counteroffensive	July 18– November 10
Battle of Masurian Lakes	September 15		
Russia, Great Britain, and France Declare War on Ottoman Empire	November	Armistice between Allies and Germany	November 11
	1915		**1919**
Battle of Gallipoli Begins	April 25	Paris Peace Conference Begins	January 18
Italy Declares War on Austria-Hungary	May 23	Peace of Versailles	June 28
Entry of Bulgaria into the War	October		

these changes merely ratified what the war had already accomplished. The empires that had controlled eastern Europe for centuries had been destroyed or weakened, and a number of new states appeared on the map of Europe.

Both the German and Russian empires lost considerable territory in eastern Europe while the Austro-Hungarian Empire disappeared altogether. New nation-states emerged from the lands of these three empires: Finland, Latvia, Estonia, Lithuania, Poland, Czechoslovakia, Austria, and Hungary. Territorial rearrangements were also made in the Balkans. Romania acquired additional lands from Russia, Hungary, and Bulgaria. Serbia formed the nucleus of a new South Slav state, called Yugoslavia, which combined Serbs, Croats, and Slovenes. Although the Paris Peace Conference was sup-

posedly guided by the principle of self-determination, the mixtures of peoples in eastern Europe made it impossible to draw boundaries along neat ethnic lines. Compromises had to be made, sometimes to satisfy the national interest of the victors. France, for example, had lost Russia as its major ally on Germany's eastern border and wanted to strengthen and expand Poland, Czechoslovakia, Yugoslavia, and Romania as much as possible so that those states could serve as barriers against Germany and Communist Russia. As a result of compromises, virtually every eastern Europe state was left with a minorities problem that could lead to future conflicts. Germans in Poland and Czechoslovakia, Hungarians in Romania, and Turks in Hungary all became sources of later conflict. Moreover, the new map of eastern Europe was based upon the temporary collapse of power in both

Germany and Russia. Since neither country accepted the new eastern frontiers, it seemed only a matter of time before a resurgent Germany or Russia would make changes.

Yet another centuries-old empire—the Ottoman Empire—was dismembered by the peace settlement after the war. To gain Arab support against the Turks during the war, the Western allies had promised to recognize the independence of Arab states in the Middle Eastern lands of the Turkish empire. But the imperialist habits of Western nations died hard. After the war, France took control of Lebanon and Syria while Britain received Iraq and Palestine. Officially, both acquisitions were called mandates. Since Woodrow Wilson had opposed the outright annexation of colonial territories by the Allies, the peace settlement had created a system of mandates whereby a nation officially administered a territory on behalf of the League of Nations. The system of mandates could not hide the fact that the principle of national self-determination at the Paris Peace Conference was largely for Europeans.

The peace settlement negotiated at Paris soon came under attack, not only by the defeated Central Powers, but by others who felt that the peacemakers had been shortsighted. The famous British economist John Maynard Keynes, for example, condemned the preoccupation with frontiers at the expense of economic issues that left Europe "inefficient, unemployed, disorganized." Despite the criticisms, the peace settlement was a sensible one. Self-determination had served reasonably well as a central organizing principle while the establishment of the League of Nations gave some hope that future conflicts could be resolved peacefully. And yet, within twenty years after the signing of the peace treaties, Europe was again engaged in deadly conflict. As some historians have suggested, perhaps the cause of the failure of the peace of 1919 was less in its structure than in its lack of enforcement.

Successful enforcement of the peace necessitated the active involvement of its principal architects, especially in assisting the new German state to develop a peaceful and democratic republic. The failure of the American Senate to ratify the Treaty of Versailles, however, meant that the United States never joined the League of Nations. In addition, the American Senate also rejected Wilson's defensive alliance with Great Britain and France. Already by the end of 1919, America was retreating into isolationism.

This retreat had dire consequences. American withdrawal from the defensive alliance with Britain and France led Britain to withdraw as well. By removing itself from European affairs, the United States forced France to stand alone facing its old enemy, leading the embittered nation to take strong actions against Germany that only intensified German resentment. By the end of 1919, it appeared that the peace of 1919 was already beginning to unravel.

World War I shattered the liberal, rational society of late nineteenth- and early twentieth-century Europe. The incredible destruction and the death of almost 10 million people undermined the whole idea of progress. New propaganda techniques had manipulated entire populations into sustaining their involvement in a meaningless slaughter.

World War I was a total war and involved a mobilization of resources and populations and increased government centralization of power over the lives of its citizens. Civil liberties, such as freedom of the press, speech, assembly, and movement, were circumscribed in the name of national security. Governments' need to plan the production and distribution of goods and to ration consumer goods restricted economic freedom. Although the late nineteenth and early twentieth centuries had witnessed the extension of government authority into such areas as mass education, social welfare legislation, and mass conscription, World War I made the practice of strong central authority a way of life.

Finally, World War I ended the age of European hegemony over world affairs. In 1917, the Russian Revolution laid the foundation for the creation of a new Soviet power, and the United States entered the war. The termination of the European age was not evident to all, however, for it was clouded by two developments—American isolationism and the withdrawal of the Soviets from world affairs while they nurtured the growth of their own socialist system. Although these developments were only temporary, they created a political vacuum in Europe that all too soon was filled by the revival of German power.

Notes

▼ ▼ ▼

1. Arnold Toynbee, *Surviving the Future* (New York, 1971), pp. 106–107.

2. Quoted in Joachim Remak, "1914—The Third Balkan War: Origins Reconsidered," *Journal of Modern History* 43 (1971): 364–65.

3. Quoted in Robert G. L. Waite, *Vanguard of Nazism* (New York, 1969), p. 22.

4. Quoted in J. M. Winter, *The Experience of World War I* (New York, 1989), p. 142.

5. Quoted in ibid., p. 137.

6. Quoted in Gail Braybon, *Women Workers in the First World War: The British Experience* (London, 1981), p. 79.

7. Quoted in Catherine W. Reilly, ed., *Scars upon My Heart: Women's Poetry and Verse of the First World War* (London, 1981), p. 90.

8. Quoted in Robert Paxton, *Europe in the Twentieth Century*, 2d ed. (New York, 1985), p. 110.

9. Quoted in William M. Mandel, *Soviet Women* (Garden City, N.Y., 1975), p. 43.

10. Harold Nicolson, *Peacemaking, 1919* (Boston and New York, 1933), pp. 31–32.

Suggestions for Further Reading

▼ ▼ ▼

The historical literature on the causes of World War I is enormous. A good starting point is the work by J. Joll, *The Origins of the First World War* (London, 1984). Also useful is J. Remak, *The Origins of World War I, 1871–1914* (New York, 1967). The belief that Germany was primarily responsible for the war was argued vigorously by the German scholar F. Fischer, *Germany's Aims in the First World War* (New York, 1967); *World Power or Decline: The Controversy over Germany's Aims in World War I* (New York, 1974); and *War of Illusions: German Policies from 1911 to 1914* (New York, 1975). The role of each great power has been reassessed in a series of books on the causes of World War I. They include V. R. Berghahn, *Germany and the Approach of War in 1914* (London, 1973); Z. S. Steiner, *Britain and the Origins of the First World War* (New York, 1977); R. Bosworth, *Italy and the Approach of the First World War* (New York, 1983); J. F. Keiger, *France and the Origins of the First World War* (New York, 1984); and D. C. B. Lieven, *Russia and the Origins of the First World War* (New York, 1984). The domestic origins of the war are probed in A. Mayer, *The Persistence of the Old Regime* (New York, 1981).

There are two good recent accounts of World War I in B. E. Schmitt and H. C. Vedeler, *The World in the Crucible, 1914–1919* (New York, 1984); and the lavishly illustrated book by J. M. Winter, *The Experience of World War I* (New York, 1989). For an account of the military operations of the war, see the classic work by B. H. Liddell-Hart, *History of the First World War* (Boston,

1970). A good study of the Eastern Front is N. Stone, *The Eastern Front, 1914–1917* (London, 1975). On war as redemption, see R. Stromberg, *Redemption by War: The Intellectuals and 1914* (Lawrence, Kans., 1982). The nature of trench warfare is examined in T. Ashworth, *Trench Warfare, 1914–1918: The Live and Let-Live System* (London, 1980). The use of poison gas is examined in L. F. Haber, *The Poisonous Cloud: Chemical Warfare in the First World War* (Oxford, 1985). On the morale of soldiers in World War I, see J. Keegan, *The Face of Battle* (London, 1975). The war at sea is examined in R. Hough, *The Great War at Sea, 1914–18* (Oxford, 1983). In *The Great War and Modern Memory* (London, 1975), Paul Fussell attempted to show how British writers described their war experiences. Although scholars do not always agree with her conclusions, B. Tuchman's *The Guns of August* (New York, 1962) is a magnificently written account of the opening days of the war. For an interesting perspective on World War I and the beginnings of the modern world, see M. Eksteins, *Rites of Spring, The Great War and the Birth of the Modern Age* (Boston, 1989).

For a good account of the economic consequences for the European states at war, see G. Hardach, *The First World War, 1914–1918* (Princeton, N.J., 1966). On the role of women in World War I, see G. Braybon, *Women Workers in the First World War: The British Experience* (London, 1981); and J. M. Winter and R. M. Wall, eds., *The Upheaval of War: Family, Work and Welfare in Europe, 1914–1918* (Cambridge, 1988). Labor unrest and class conflict are examined in J. J. Becker, *The Great War and the French People* (Leamington Spa, 1985); and B. Waites, *A Class Society at War* (Leamington Spa, 1987).

A good introduction to the Russian Revolution can be found in S. Fitzpatrick, *The Russian Revolution, 1917–1932* (New York, 1982); and R. V. Daniels, *Red October* (New York, 1967). On Lenin, see R. W. Clark, *Lenin* (New York, 1988); and the valuable work by A. B. Ulam, *The Bolsheviks* (New York, 1965). The role of workers in the events of the Russian Revolution is examined in D. Koenker, *Moscow Workers and the 1917 Revolution* (Princeton, N.J., 1981). On Allied intervention in the civil war, see M. Kettle, *Russia and the Allies, 1917–1920* (Minneapolis, 1981). There is now a comprehensive study of the Russian civil war in W. B. Lincoln, *Red Victory: A History of the Russian Civil War* (New York, 1989). On the revolutions in Germany and

Austria-Hungary, see F. L. Carsten, *Revolution in Central Europe* (Berkeley, 1972); and A. J. Ryder, *The German Revolution of 1918* (Cambridge, 1967).

The role of war aims in the shaping of the peace settlement is examined in V. H. Rothwell, *British War Aims and Peace Diplomacy, 1914–1918* (Oxford, 1971); and D. R. Stevenson, *French War Aims against Germany, 1914–1919* (New York, 1982). The fear of Bolshevism as a factor at the Paris Peace Conference is argued in A. Mayer, *The Politics and Diplomacy of Peacemaking: Containment and Counter-Revolution at Versailles, 1918–1919* (New York, 1967).

World War I and the Russian Revolution are also well covered in two good general surveys, R. Paxton, *Europe in the Twentieth Century*, 2d ed. (New York, 1985); and A. Rudhart, *Twentieth Century Europe* (Englewood Cliffs, N.J., 1986).

Chapter 27

The Futile Search for a New Stability: Europe Between the Wars, 1919–1939

▼ ▼ ▼ ▼ ▼

Only twenty years after the Treaty of Versailles, Europeans were again at war. Yet, in the 1920s, many people continued to assume that Europe and the world were about to enter a new era of international peace, economic growth, and political democracy. In all of these areas, the optimistic hopes of the 1920s failed to be realized. After 1919, numerous efforts were made to create conditions for peace. The League of Nations, conceived as a new instrument to provide for collective security, failed to be effective. Attempts to achieve peace by means of treaties that renounced the use of war did not succeed because the treaties lacked any means of enforcement. Having realized that the arms race before World War I had helped lead to war, almost everyone favored disarmament

agreements, but no one could agree on any substantive proposals. These efforts at collective security in the 1920s proved unable to halt aggression in the 1930s.

Internally, Europe was faced with severe economic problems after World War I. The European economy did not begin to recover from the war until 1922, and even then it was beset by serious problems, such as Germany's payment of reparations, Allied war debts to the United States, and, most devastating of all, the Great Depression that began at the end of 1929.

In 1919, there was cause for considerable optimism in regard to political developments, despite the success of the Russian Revolution and the fear that communism would spread to other European states. Overall, political democracy seemed well established in 1919. Four major nations—Great Britain, France, Germany, and

Mussolini and Fascists
Come to Power in Italy
▼

Locarno
Pact
▼

Hitler and Nazis Come
to Power in Germany
▼

Popular Front
in France
▼

Kristallnacht
▼

•••••••••• 1920 •••••••••• 1925 •••••••••• 1930 •••••••••• 1935 •••••••••• 1940 ••••••••••

▲
The Dada Movement
Emerges

▲
Mass Production
of Radios

▲
Heisenberg's
"Uncertainty Principle"

▲
Dali,
The Persistence of Memory

Italy—as well as a host of minor ones maintained democratic forms of government. These democracies, however, were plagued by many problems, and by the 1930s a number of authoritarian regimes had replaced democratic governments.

▼ An Uncertain Peace: The Search for Security

The peace settlement at the end of World War I had tried to fulfill the nineteenth-century dream of nationalism by the creation of boundaries and new states. From its inception, however, this peace settlement had left nations unhappy. Conflicts over disputed border regions between Germany and Poland, Poland and Lithuania, Poland and Czechoslovakia, Austria and Hungary, and Italy and Yugoslavia poisoned mutual relations in eastern Europe for years. Many Germans viewed the Peace of Versailles as a dictated peace and vowed to seek its revision.

The American president Woodrow Wilson had recognized that the peace treaties contained unwise provisions that could serve as new causes for conflicts and had placed many of his hopes for the future in the League of Nations. The league, however, was not particularly effective in maintaining the peace. The failure of the United States to join the league and the subsequent American retreat into isolationism undermined the effectiveness of the league from its beginning. Moreover, the league could only use economic sanctions to halt aggression. The French attempt to strengthen the league's effectiveness as an instrument of collective security by creating some kind of international army was rejected by nations that feared giving up any of their sovereignty to a larger international body.

The weakness of the League of Nations and the failure of both the United States and Great Britain to honor their defensive military alliances with France left France embittered and alone. Before World War I, France's alliance with Russia had served to threaten Germany with the possibility of a two-front war. But Communist Russia was now a hostile power. To compensate, France built a network of alliances in eastern Europe with Poland and the members of the so-called Little Entente (Czechoslovakia, Romania, Yugoslavia). While these alliances looked good on paper as a way to contain Germany and maintain the new status quo, they overlooked the fundamental military weaknesses of those nations. Poland and the Little Entente states were no real substitutes for powerful Russia.

The French Policy of Coercion, 1919–1924

France's search for security between 1919 and 1924 was founded primarily upon a strict enforcement of the Treaty of Versailles. This tough policy toward Germany began with the issue of reparations, or the payments that the Germans were supposed to make to compensate for the "damage done to the civilian population of the Allied and Associated Powers and to their property," as the treaty asserted. Behind reparations lay some straightforward political and economic calculations. The Allied governments needed to raise vast sums of money to reconstruct their war-damaged economies. France, above all, needed to rebuild railroads, bridges, and industrial plants as well as to restore battle-devastated farmlands. Moreover, the Allied governments had war loans to repay. The Allies had received large loans from the United States and expected that after the war the United States would cancel all or part of the debts. The United States refused. To the Allied governments, especially France, reparations from defeated Germany seemed an intelligent and even just way to alleviate postwar financial burdens. From the Allied perspective, shouldn't the Germans, who had caused the war, pay for the damages?

In April 1921, the Allied Reparations Commission settled on a sum of 132 billion marks ($33 billion) for German reparations, payable in annual installments of

2.5 billion (gold) marks. Allied threats to occupy the Ruhr valley, Germany's chief industrial and mining center, led the new German republic to accept the reparations settlement and make its first payment in 1921. By the following year, however, faced with rising inflation and domestic turmoil, the German position on reparations had changed. The German government announced that it was unable to pay more and asked for a moratorium on reparation payments while a commission of experts drew up a more realistic program.

Outraged by what they considered to be Germany's unilateral dissolution of the peace settlement, the French, under Raymond Poincaré and the conservative National Bloc that dominated the government, took a tough stand against Germany. With the cooperation of its Belgian allies, the French government sent troops to

▼ The Effects of Inflation. Germany experienced a number of serious economic problems after the war. The inflationary pressures that had begun in Germany at the end of World War I intensified during the French occupation of the Ruhr. By the early 1920s, the value of the German mark had fallen precipitously. This photograph shows a German housewife using the worthless currency to light a fire in her cooking stove.

occupy the Ruhr valley. French aims were clear. Since the Germans would not pay reparations, the French would collect reparations in kind by operating and using the Ruhr mines and factories. Moreover, the French hoped to hold the occupied Ruhr industries as "productive pledges" that would not be returned to German control until the German government promised to fulfill its reparations responsibilities under the Treaty of Versailles.

Both Germany and France suffered from the French occupation of the Ruhr. The German government adopted a policy of passive resistance to French occupation that was largely financed by printing more paper money. This only intensified the inflationary pressures that had already begun in Germany by the end of the war. The German mark became worthless. Economic disaster fueled political upheavals as Communists staged uprisings in October, and Adolf Hitler's band of Nazis attempted to seize power in Munich in 1923 (see Hitler and Nazi Germany later in the chapter). But the French were hardly victorious. The cost of the French occupation was not offset by the gains; Poincaré's need to raise taxes early in 1924 caused his government to fall in May. Meanwhile, pressure from the United States and Great Britain against the French policy forced the French to agree to a new conference of experts to reassess the reparations problem. By the time the conference did its work in 1924, both France and Germany were opting to pursue a more conciliatory approach toward each other.

The Hopeful Years, 1924–1929

The formation of liberal-socialist governments in both Great Britain and France opened the door to conciliatory approaches to Germany and the reparations problem. At the same time, a new German government led by Gustav Stresemann (1878–1929) ended the policy of passive resistance and committed Germany to carry out the provisions of the Treaty of Versailles while seeking a new settlement of the reparations question.

In August 1924, an international commission produced a new plan for reparations. Named the Dawes Plan after the American banker who chaired the commission, it reduced reparations and stabilized Germany's payments on the basis of its ability to pay. The Dawes Plan also granted an initial $200 million loan for German recovery, which opened the door to heavy American investments in Europe that helped create a new era of European prosperity between 1924 and 1929.

A new era of European diplomacy accompanied the new economic stability. A spirit of international cooperation was fostered by the foreign ministers of Germany and France, Gustav Stresemann and Aristide Briand (1862–1932), who concluded the Treaty of Locarno in 1925. This guaranteed Germany's new western borders with France and Belgium. Britain and Italy agreed to intervene if either Germany or France violated these frontiers. Although Germany's new eastern borders with Poland were conspicuously absent from the agreement, the Locarno pact was viewed by many as the beginning of a new era of European peace. On the day after the pact was concluded, the headlines in the *New York Times* ran "France and Germany Ban War Forever," while the London *Times* declared, "Peace at Last."[1]

Germany's entry into the League of Nations in March 1926 soon reinforced the new spirit of conciliation engendered at Locarno. Two years later, similar optimistic attitudes prevailed in the Kellogg-Briand pact, drafted by the American secretary of state Frank B. Kellogg and the French foreign minister Aristide Briand. Sixty-three nations signed this accord, in which they pledged "to renounce war as an instrument of national policy." Nothing was said, however, about what would be done if anyone violated the treaty.

The spirit of Locarno was based on little real substance. Germany lacked the military power to alter its western borders even if it wanted to. Pious promises to renounce war without mechanisms to enforce them were virtually worthless. And the issue of disarmament soon proved that even the spirit of Locarno could not bring nations to cut back on their weapons. The League of Nations Covenant had suggested the "reduction of national armaments to the lowest point consistent with national safety." Germany, of course, had been disarmed with the expectation that other states would do likewise. Numerous disarmament conferences, however, failed to achieve anything substantial as states proved unwilling to trust their security to anyone but their own military forces. When a World Disarmament Conference finally met in Geneva in 1932, the issue was already dead.

One other hopeful sign of the years between 1924 and 1929 was the new coexistence of the West with Soviet Russia. By the beginning of 1924, Soviet hopes for communist revolutions in Western states had largely dissipated. In turn, these states had realized by then that the Bolshevik regime could no longer be ousted. Weimar Germany had already established full diplomatic relations with Soviet Russia in 1922, and in 1924 Britain, France, Italy, and other small European states did likewise. Nevertheless, Western powers remained highly suspicious of Soviet intentions, especially when the Soviet Union continued to support the propaganda activities of the Comintern, or Communist International, a worldwide organization of pro-Soviet Marxist parties originally formed in 1919 by Lenin to foster world revolution.

The Great Depression

After World War I, most European states began to dismantle the wartime agencies that had regulated their economies in the hope of returning to the liberal ideal of a private-enterprise, market economy largely free of state intervention. But the war had vastly strengthened business cartels and labor unions, and any postwar economy had to include some form of government regulation of these powerful organizations. Moreover, the war had a powerful effect on the postwar international economy. Reparations and war debts, as we have seen, created a cycle of payments from Germany to Britain and France and from France and Great Britain to the United States that came to depend on the American loans to Germany in the second half of the 1920s. Thus, the prosperity between 1924 and 1929 was at best a fragile one, and the dream of returning to the liberal ideal of a self-regulating market economy was merely an illusion. What destroyed the concept altogether was the Great Depression.

Two factors played a major role in the coming of the Great Depression: a downturn in domestic economies and an international financial crisis created by the collapse of the American stock market in 1929. Already in the mid-1920s, prices for agricultural goods were beginning to decline rapidly due to overproduction of basic commodities, such as wheat. In 1925, states in central and eastern Europe began to impose tariffs to close their markets to other countries' goods. An increase in the use of oil and hydroelectricity led to a slump in the coal industry even before 1929.

In addition to these domestic economic troubles, much of the European prosperity between 1924 and 1929 had been built upon American bank loans to Germany. Twenty-three billion marks had been invested in German municipal bonds and German industries since 1924. Already in 1928 and 1929, American investors had begun to pull money out of Germany in order to invest in the booming New York stock market. The crash of the American stock market in October 1929 led panicky American investors to withdraw even more of their funds from Germany and other European markets. The withdrawal of funds seriously weakened the banks of Germany and other central European states. The Credit-Anstalt, Vienna's most prestigious bank, collapsed on May 31, 1931. By that time, trade was slowing down,

The Great Depression: Unemployed and Homeless in Germany

▼ ▼ ▼

In 1932, Germany had six million unemployed workers, many of them wandering about Germany aimlessly, begging for food and seeking shelter in city lodging houses for the homeless. The Great Depression was an important factor in the rise to power of Adolf Hitler and the Nazis. This selection presents a description of unemployed homeless in 1932.

Heinrich Hauser, "With Germany's Unemployed"

An almost unbroken chain of homeless men extends the whole length of the great Hamburg-Berlin highway. . . . All the highways in Germany over which I have traveled this year presented the same aspect. . . .

Most of the hikers paid no attention to me. They walked separately or in small groups, with their eyes on the ground. And they had the queer, stumbling gait of barefooted people, for their shoes were slung over their shoulders. Some of them were guild members,—carpenters . . . milkmen . . . and bricklayers . . . but they were in a minority. Far more numerous were those whom one could assign to no special profession or craft—unskilled young people, for the most part, who had been unable to find a place for themselves in any city or town in Germany, and who had never had a job and never expected to have one. There was something else that had never been seen before—whole families that had piled all their goods into baby carriages and wheelbarrows that they were pushing along as they plodded forward in dumb despair. It was a whole nation on the march.

I saw them—and this was the strongest impression that the year 1932 left with me—I saw them, gathered into groups of fifty or a hundred men, attacking fields of potatoes. I saw them digging up the potatoes and throwing them into sacks while the farmer who owned the field watched them in despair and the local policeman looked on gloomily from the distance. I saw them staggering toward the lights of the city as night fell, with their sacks on their backs. What did it remind me of? Of the War, of the worst periods of starvation in 1917 and 1918, but even then people paid for the potatoes. . . .

I saw that the individual can know what is happening only by personal experience. I know what it is to be a tramp. I know what cold and hunger are. . . . But there are two things that I have only recently experienced—begging and spending the night in a municipal lodging house.

I entered the huge Berlin municipal lodging house in a northern quarter of the city. . . .

Distribution of spoons, distribution of enameled-ware bowls with the words "Property of the City of Berlin" written on their sides. Then the meal itself. A big kettle is carried in. Men with yellow smocks have brought it in and men with yellow smocks ladle out the food. These men, too, are homeless and they have been expressly picked by the establishment and given free food and lodging and a little pocket money in exchange for their work about the house.

Where have I seen this kind of food distribution before? In a prison that I once helped to guard in the winter of 1919 during the German civil war. There was the same hunger then, the same trembling, anxious expectation of rations. Now the men are standing in a long row, dressed in their plain nightshirts that reach to the ground, and the noise of their shuffling feet is like the noise of big wild animals walking up and down the stone floor of their cages before feeding time. The men lean far over the kettle so that the warm steam from the food envelops them and they hold out their bowls as if begging and whisper to the attendant, "Give me a real helping. Give me a little more." A piece of bread is handed out with every bowl.

My next recollection is sitting at a table in another room on a crowded bench that is like a seat in a fourth-class railway carriage. Hundreds of hungry mouths make an enormous noise eating their food. The men sit bent over their food like animals who feel that someone is going to take it away from them. They hold their bowl with their left arm part way around it, so that nobody can take it away, and they also protect it with their other elbow and with their head and mouth, while they move the spoon as fast as they can between their mouth and the bowl.

industrialists were cutting back production, and unemployment was increasing as the ripple effects of international bank failures had a devastating impact on domestic economies.

Economic depression was by no means a new phenomenon in European history. But the depth of the economic downturn after 1929 fully justifies the label Great Depression. During 1932, the worst year of the depression, one British worker in four was unemployed, while 6 million or 40 percent of the German labor force were out of work. Between 1929 and 1932, industrial production plummeted almost 50 percent in the United States and over 40 percent in Germany. The unemployed and homeless filled the streets of the cities throughout the advanced industrial countries (see the box on p. 936).

Governments seemed powerless to deal with the crisis. The classical liberal remedy for depression, a deflationary policy of balanced budgets, which involved cutting costs by lowering wages and raising tariffs to exclude other countries' goods from home markets, only served to worsen the economic crisis and create even greater mass discontent. This, in turn, led to serious political repercussions. Increased government activity in the economy was one reaction, even in countries like the United States that had a strong laissez-faire tradition. Another effect was a renewed interest in Marxist doctrines since Marx had predicted that capitalism would destroy itself through overproduction. Communism took on new popularity, especially with workers and intellectuals. Finally, the Great Depression increased the attractiveness of facile dictatorial solutions, especially from a new movement known as fascism. Everywhere in Europe, democracy seemed on the defensive in the 1930s. We can best understand the full impact of the depression on Europe by examining the domestic scene in Western states between the two world wars.

▼ The Democratic States

According to Woodrow Wilson, World War I had been fought to make the world safe for democracy. In 1919, there seemed to be some justification for his claim. Four major European states and a host of minor ones had functioning political democracies. In a number of states, universal male suffrage had even been replaced by universal suffrage as male politicians rewarded women for their contributions to World War I by granting them the right to vote (except in Italy, France, and Spain where women had to wait until the end of World War II). In the 1920s, Europe seemed to be returning to the political trends of the prewar era—the broadening of parliamentary regimes and the fostering of individual liberties. But it was not an easy process; four years of total war and four years of postwar turmoil made the "return to normalcy" a difficult and troublesome affair.

Great Britain

After World War I, Great Britain went through a period of painful readjustment and serious economic difficulties. During the war, Britain had lost many of the markets for its industrial products, especially to the United States and Japan. The postwar decline of such staple industries as coal, steel, and textiles led to a rise in unemployment, which reached the two-million mark in 1921. The Liberal government of David Lloyd George proved unable either to change this situation or to meet

▼ **The Great Depression: Bread-lines in Paris.** The Great Depression devastated the European economy and led to serious political repercussions. Because of its more balanced economy, France did not feel the effects of the depression as quickly as other European countries. However, by 1931, even France was experiencing lines of unemployed people at free-food centers.

the demands of the working class for better housing and an improved standard of living.

By 1923, British politics experienced a major transformation when the Labour party surged ahead of the Liberals as the second most powerful party in Britain after the Conservatives. In fact, after the elections of November 1923, a Labour-Liberal coalition enabled Ramsay MacDonald (1866–1937) to become the first Labour prime minister of Britain. His tenure, however, was brief and not particularly innovative. Dependent on Liberal support, MacDonald rejected any extreme social or economic experimentation. No doubt, his moderation made the Labour party acceptable to many of the British who had previously feared that a Labour government would nationalize "everything." MacDonald's government lasted only ten months, however, as the Conservative party's charge that MacDonald's government was friendly toward communism proved to be a highly successful campaign tactic.

Under the direction of Stanley Baldwin (1867–1947) as prime minister, the Conservatives guided Britain during an era of renewed prosperity from 1925 to 1929. This prosperity, however, was relatively superficial. British exports in the 1920s never compensated for the overseas investments lost during the war, and even in these so-called prosperous years, unemployment remained at a startling 10 percent level. Coal miners were especially affected by the decline of the antiquated and inefficient British coal mines, which also suffered from a world glut of coal. Attempts by mine owners to lower coal miners' wages only led to a national strike (the General Strike of 1926) by miners and sympathetic trade unions. The Trades Union Congress soon accepted a compromise settlement, but many miners who refused to accept the settlement were eventually forced back to work at lower wages for longer hours.

In 1929, the Conservatives were defeated, and a second Labour government came back into power just as the Great Depression was beginning. Although Labour had now become the largest party in Britain, it still depended on the Liberals for a majority in Parliament. Attempts to deal with the effects of the depression by an increase in unemployment benefits led to budget deficits and a banking crisis. Responding to investors' demands, the Labour government prepared to cut unemployment benefits, a move that split the Labour party and brought the collapse of the Labour government.

The Labour government was replaced in 1931 by the National Government, a coalition of all three parties. Although MacDonald remained as prime minister until 1935, the Conservatives played a leading role in the coalition government, and in 1935, Stanley Baldwin once more replaced MacDonald as prime minister. The National Government claimed credit for bringing Britain out of the worst stages of the depression, primarily by using the traditional policies of balanced budgets and protective tariffs. Historians argue, however, that the general upswing of the business cycle more than anything else helped to revive the British economy. By 1935, industrial production exceeded the predepression level of 1929, and by 1936, unemployment had dropped to 1.6 million after reaching a depression high of 3 million in 1932 (see the box on p. 939).

British politicians largely ignored the new ideas of a Cambridge economist, John Maynard Keynes (1883–1946). In 1936, Keynes published his *General Theory of Employment, Interest, and Money.* Contrary to the traditional view that depressions should be left to work themselves out through the self-regulatory mechanisms of a free economy, Keynes argued that unemployment stemmed not from overproduction but from a decline in demand, and that demand could be increased by public works, financed, if necessary, through deficit spending to stimulate production. These policies, however, could only be accomplished by government intervention in the economy, and Britain's political leaders were unwilling to go that far in the 1930s.

France

After the defeat of Germany and the demobilization of the German army, France had become the strongest power on the European continent. Its biggest problem involved the reconstruction of the devastated areas of northern and eastern France. The conservative National Bloc government, led by Raymond Poincaré (1860–1934), sought to use German reparations for this purpose. Tying French economic stability to German reparations resulted in Poincaré's hard-line policy toward Germany and the Ruhr invasion. When Poincaré's conservative government was forced to raise taxes in 1924 to pay for the cost of the Ruhr fiasco, his National Bloc was voted out of power and replaced by the so-called Cartel of the Left.

The Cartel of the Left was a coalition government formed by two French parties of the left, the Radicals and Socialists. These two leftist parties shared beliefs in antimilitarism, anticlericalism, and the importance of education. But despite their title, the Radicals were a democratic party of small property owners while the Socialists were nominally committed to Marxist socialism. Although they cooperated to win elections, their differ-

The Struggles of a Democracy: Unemployment and Slums in Great Britain

▼ ▼ ▼

During the 1920s and 1930s, Britain struggled with the problems of economic depression. Unemployment was widespread, especially after the onset of the Great Depression. Even after Britain began to recover in the late 1930s, many Britons still lived in wretched conditions. These selections reflect Britain's economic and social problems.

Men without Work: A Report Made to the Pilgrim Trust, 1938

A week's notice may end half a lifetime's service, with no prospects, if he is elderly, but the dole, followed by a still further reduction in his means of livelihood when the old age pension comes. We take as an example a shoe laster from Leicester, who had worked thirty-seven years with one firm. "When I heard the new manager going through and saying: "The whole of this side of this room, this room, and this room is to be stopped, I knew it would be uphill work to get something." He went on to describe to us how he had not been able to bring himself to tell his wife the bad news when he got home, how she had noticed that something was wrong, how confident she had been that he would get work elsewhere, but how he had known that the chances were heavily against him. For months and indeed often for years such men go on looking for work, and the same is true of many casual labourers. There were in the sample old men who have not a remote chance of working again but yet make it a practice to stand every morning at six o'clock at the works gates in the hope that perhaps they may catch the foreman's eye.

George Orwell, "A Woman in the Slums" from The Road to Wigan Pier, 1937

As we moved slowly through the outskirts of the town we passed row after row of little grey slum houses. . . . At the back of one of the houses a young woman was kneeling on the stones, poking a stick up the leaden waste-pipe which ran from the sink inside, and which I suppose was blocked. . . . She had a round pale face, the usual exhausted face of the slum girl who is twenty-five and looks forty, thanks to miscarriages and drudgery; and it wore, for the second in which I saw it, the most desolate, hopeless expression I have ever seen. It struck me then that we are mistaken when we say that "It isn't the same for them as it would be for us," and that people bred in the slums can imagine nothing but the slums. For what I saw in her face was not the ignorant suffering of an animal. She knew well enough what was happening to her—understood as well as I did how dreadful a destiny it was to be kneeling there in the bitter cold, on the slimy stones of a slum backyard, poking a stick up a foul drain-pipe.

---

ences on economic and financial issues made their efforts to solve France's financial problems between 1924 and 1926 largely futile. The failure of the Cartel of the Left led to the return of Raymond Poincaré, whose government from 1926 to 1929 stabilized the French economy during a period of relative prosperity.

France did not feel the effects of the depression as soon as other countries because of its more balanced economy. The French population was almost evenly divided between urban and agricultural pursuits while a slight majority of industrial plants were small enterprises employing five workers or less. Even large industrialists were more conservative and invested little in foreign goods. It was not until 1932 that France began to feel the full effects of the Great Depression, and economic instability soon had political repercussions. During a nineteen-month period in 1932 and 1933, six different cabinets were formed as France faced political chaos. During the same time, French Fascist groups, adhering to far-right policies similar to those of the Fascists in Italy and the Nazis in Germany (see Fascist Italy and Hitler and Nazi Germany later in the chapter), marched through French streets in a number of demonstrations. The February riots of 1934, caused by a number of French Fascist leagues, frightened many into believing that the Fascists intended to seize power. These fears began to drive the leftist parties together despite their other differences and led in 1936 to the formation of the Popular Front.

The first Popular Front government was formed in June 1936 and was a coalition of the Communists, Socialists, and Radicals. The Socialist leader, Léon Blum

(1872–1950), served as prime minister. The Popular Front succeeded in initiating a program for workers that some have called the French New Deal. It consisted of the right of collective bargaining, a forty-hour work week, two-week paid vacations, and minimum wages. The Popular Front's policies, however, failed to solve the problems of the depression. In 1938, French Industrial production was still below the levels of 1929. Although the French Popular Front survived in name until 1938, it was for all intents and purposes dead before then. By 1938, the French were experiencing a serious decline of confidence in their political system that left them unprepared to deal with their aggressive Nazi enemy to the east.

The Scandinavian Example

The Scandinavian democracies were particularly successful in coping with the Great Depression. Socialist parties had grown steadily in the late nineteenth and early twentieth centuries and between the wars came to head the governments of Sweden, Denmark, Norway, and Finland. These Social Democratic governments encouraged the development of rural and industrial cooperative enterprises. Ninety percent of the Danish milk industry, for example, was organized on a cooperative basis by 1933. Privately owned and managed, Scandina-

vian cooperatives seemed to avoid the pitfalls of either communist or purely capitalist economic systems.

Social Democratic governments also greatly expanded social services. Not only did Scandinavian governments increase old age pensions and unemployment insurance, but they also provided such novel forms of assistance as subsidized housing, free prenatal care, maternity allowances, and annual paid vacations for workers. To achieve their social welfare states, the Scandinavian governments required high taxes and large bureaucracies, but these did not prevent both private and cooperative enterprises from prospering. Indeed between 1900 and 1939, Sweden experienced a greater rise in real wages than any other European country.

The United States

After Germany, no Western nation was more affected by the Great Depression than the United States. The full force of the depression had struck the United States by 1932. In that year industrial production fell to 50 percent of what it had been in 1929. By 1933, there were 15 million unemployed. Under these circumstances, the Democrat Franklin Delano Roosevelt (1882–1945) was able to win a landslide electoral victory in 1932.

Roosevelt did not favor either socialism or government ownership of industry to correct America's economic ills. A believer in free enterprise, he realized, however, that capitalism would have to be reformed in order to "save it." Following the example of the American experience during World War I, he and his advisers pursued a policy of active government intervention in the economy that came to be known as the New Deal.

Initially, the New Deal attempted to restore prosperity by creating the National Recovery Administration (NRA), which required government, labor, and industrial leaders to work out regulations for each industry. Declared unconstitutional by the Supreme Court in 1935, the NRA was soon superseded by other efforts collectively known as the Second New Deal. These included a stepped-up program of public works, such as the Works Progress Administration (WPA) established in 1935. This government organization employed between two and three million people who worked at building bridges, roads, post offices, and airports. The Roosevelt administration was also responsible for social legislation that launched the American welfare state. In 1935, the Social Security Act created a system of old age pensions and unemployment insurance. Moreover, the National

Labor Relations Act of 1935 encouraged the rapid growth of labor unions.

No doubt, the New Deal provided some social reform measures that perhaps averted the possibility of social revolution in the United States. It did not, however, solve the unemployment problems of the Great Depression. In May 1937, during what was considered a period of full recovery, American unemployment still stood at 7 million. A recession the following year increased that number to 11 million. Only World War II and the subsequent growth of armaments industries brought American workers back to full employment.

▼ The Retreat from Democracy: The Authoritarian and Totalitarian States

The apparent triumph of liberal democracy in 1919 proved extremely short-lived. By 1939, only two major states, France and Great Britain, and a host of minor ones, the Low Countries, the Scandinavian states, Switzerland, and Czechoslovakia, remained democratic. Italy and Germany had succumbed to the political movement called fascism while Soviet Russia under Stalin moved toward a repressive totalitarian state. A host of other European states, especially in eastern Europe, adopted authoritarian structures of different kinds. The crisis of European civilization, inaugurated in the total war of World War I, seemed only to be worsening with new assaults on individual liberties.

The dictatorial regimes between the wars assumed both old and new forms. Dictatorship was by no means a new phenomenon, but the modern totalitarian state was. The totalitarian regimes, whose best examples can be found in Stalinist Russia and Nazi Germany, extended the functions and power of the central state far beyond what they had been in the past. The immediate origins of totalitarianism can be found in the total warfare of World War I when governments, even in the democratic states, exercised controls over economic, political, and personal freedom in order to achieve victory.

The modern totalitarian state might have begun as an old-fashioned political dictatorship, but it soon moved beyond the ideal of passive obedience expected in a traditional dictatorship or authoritarian monarchy. The new "total states" expected the active loyalty and commitment of citizens to the regime's goals. They used modern mass propaganda techniques and high-speed modern communications to conquer the minds and hearts of their subjects. The total state aimed to control not only the economic, political, and social aspects of life, but the intellectual and cultural as well. But that control also had a purpose: the active involvement of the masses in the achievement of the regime's goals, whether they be war, a socialist state, or a thousand-year Reich.

The modern totalitarian state was to be led by a single leader and a single party. It ruthlessly rejected the liberal ideal of limited government power and constitutional guarantees of individual freedoms. Indeed, individual freedom was to be subordinated to the collective will of the masses, organized and determined for them by a leader or leaders. Modern technology also gave total states unprecedented police controls to enforce their wishes on their subjects.

Totalitarianism is an abstract term, and no state followed all its theoretical implications. The fascist states—Italy and Nazi Germany—as well as Stalin's Communist Russia have all been labeled totalitarian, although their regimes exhibited significant differences and met with varying degrees of success.

At the same time, there were a number of other states in Europe that were not totalitarian but did possess conservative authoritarian governments. These states adopted some of the trappings of totalitarian states, especially their wide police powers, but their greatest concern was not the creation of a mass movement aimed at the establishment of a new kind of society, but rather the defense of the existing social order. Consequently, the authoritarian states tended to limit the participation of the masses and were content with passive obedience rather than active involvement in the goals of the regime.

Fascist Italy

In the early 1920s, in the wake of economic turmoil, political disorder, and the general insecurity and fear stemming from World War I, Benito Mussolini burst upon the Italian scene with a movement that he called the *Fascio di Combattimento* (League of Combat). It was the beginning of the first fascist movement in Europe.

THE BIRTH OF FASCISM   As a new European state after 1870, Italy faced a number of serious problems that were only magnified when Italy became a belligerent in World War I. The war's cost in lives and money was enormous. An estimated 700,000 Italian soldiers died, and the treasury reckoned the cost of war at 148 billion lire, twice the sum of all government expenditures between 1861 and 1913. Italy did gain some territory, namely, Trieste, and a new northern border that included the formerly Austrian South Tyrol area. Italy's demands for Fiume and Dalmatia on the Adriatic coast were rejected, however, which gave rise to the myth that Italy had been cheated of its just rewards by the other victors. The war created untold domestic confusion. Inflation undermined middle-class security. Demobilization of the troops created high unemployment and huge groups of dissatisfied veterans. The government, which continued to be characterized by parliamentary paralysis due to the politicians' reliance on tactical and often unprincipled maneuvering to maintain their grip on power, was unable to deal effectively with these problems.

Benito Mussolini (1883–1945) was an unruly and rebellious child who ultimately received a diploma as an elementary school teacher. After an unsuccessful stint as a teacher, Mussolini became a socialist and gradually became well known in Italian socialist circles. In 1912, he obtained the important position of editor of *Avanti* (*Forward*), the official socialist daily newspaper. After editorially switching his position from ardent neutrality, the socialist position, to intervention in World War I, he was expelled from the socialist party.

In 1919, Mussolini laid the foundations for a new political movement that came to be called fascism after the name of his group, the *Fascio di Combattimento*. Mussolini's small group received little attention and were themselves unclear about their beliefs. In elections held in November 1919, the Fascists won no delegates, and Mussolini reflected bitterly that fascism had "come to a dead end." But political stalemate in Italy's parliamentary system and strong nationalist sentiment saved Mussolini and the Fascists.

The new parliament elected in November quickly proved to be incapable of governing Italy. Three major parties, the socialists, liberals, and popolari (or Christian Democrats, a new Catholic party formed in January 1919), and numerous small ones were unable to form an effective governmental coalition. The socialists, who had now become the largest party, spoke theoretically of the need for revolution, which alarmed conservatives who quickly associated them with bolsheviks or communists. Thousands of industrial and agricultural strikes in 1919 and 1920 created a climate of class warfare and continual violence. Mussolini realized the advantages of capitalizing on the fear created by these conditions and shifted quickly from leftist to rightist politics. The rewards were immediate as Mussolini's Fascist movement began to gain support from middle-class industrialists fearful of working-class agitation and large landowners who objected to the agricultural strikes. Mussolini also perceived that Italians were angry over the failure of Italy to receive more fruits of victory in the form of territorial acquisitions after World War I. Mussolini realized then that anticommunism, antistrike activity, and nationalist rhetoric combined with the use of brute force might help him obtain what he had been unable to achieve in free elections.

In 1920 and 1921, bands of armed Fascists called *squadristi* were formed and turned loose in attacks on socialist offices and newspapers. Strikes by trade unionists and socialist workers and peasant leagues were broken up by force. At the same time, Mussolini entered into a political alliance with the liberals under then Prime Minister Giovanni Giolitti. No doubt, Giolitti and the liberals believed that the Fascists could be used to crush socialism temporarily and then be dropped. In this game of mutual deceit, Mussolini soon proved to be the more skillful player. By allying with the government coalition, he gained respectability and a free hand for his *squadristi* violence. Mussolini's efforts were rewarded with success when the Fascists won thirty-five parliamentary seats, or 7 percent of the total, in the election of May 1921. Mussolini's Fascist movement had gained a new lease on life.

Crucial to Mussolini's plans was the use of violence. By 1921, the black-shirted Fascist squads numbered 200,000 and had become a regular feature of Italian life. World War I veterans and students were especially attracted to the *squadristi* and relished the opportunity to use unrestrained violence. Administering large doses of castor oil to unwilling victims became one of their favorite tactics.

Mussolini and the Fascists believed that these terrorist tactics would eventually achieve political victory. They deliberately created conditions of disorder knowing that fascism would flourish in such an environment. Fascists construed themselves as the party of order and drew the bulk of their support from the middle and upper classes; white-collar workers, professionals and civil servants, landowners, merchants and artisans, and students made up almost 60 percent of the membership of the Fascist party. The middle-class fear of socialism, communist revolution, and disorder made the Fascists attractive.

With the further deterioration of the Italian political situation, Mussolini and the Fascists were emboldened to plan a march on Rome in order to seize power. In a speech in Naples to Fascist blackshirts, Mussolini exclaimed on October 24, 1922: ". . . either we are allowed to govern, or we will seize power by marching on Rome" to "take by the throat the miserable political

The Voice of Italian Fascism
▼ ▼ ▼

Mussolini at first seemed uncertain about how to react to the storm of criticism provoked by the Matteotti murder. Finally, he seized the initiative and in a defiant speech to parliament on January 3, 1925, made clear his intentions to "make the nation fascist."

Mussolini: Speech of January 3, 1925

But, Gentlemen [members of parliament], what butterflies are we chasing?. . . Very well, then. I declare here before this assembly and before the Italian people that I alone take the political, moral, and historical responsibility for all that has happened. . . . If Fascism means nothing but castor oil and the cudgel and not a superb passion of the best Italian youth, it is my fault! If Fascism is a criminal association, if all acts of violence are the result of a given historical, political, and moral climate, mine is the responsibility for it, because it was I who created this historical, political, and moral climate with a propaganda which lasted from the intervention to this day. . . .

It is clear that the Aventine secession [those deputies who withdrew from parliament to protest Matteotti's murder] has had profound repercussions throughout the country. Well, then a moment comes when we must say: Enough! When two irreducible elements clash, the solution is force. There has never been another solution in history and never will be.

Now I dare say the problem will be solved. Fascism, as a Government and Party, is at top efficiency. Gentlemen, you have been laboring under an illusion! You thought Fascism was through because I held it down, that the Party was dead because I chastened it and I was cruel enough to say so. But it will not be necessary [to unleash the Fascists] . . . because the Government is strong enough to break the Aventine secession completely and finally.

Italy wants peace, tranquillity, calm in which to work; we will give it to her, by means of love if possible, by force if necessary. Rest assured that within the next 48 hours the entire situation will be clarified. Everyone must realize that what I am planning to do is not one man's whim, it is not a lust for power, it is not ignoble passion, but solely the expression of a boundless and mighty love of Country. [Loud, prolonged, and repeated applause—cries of Viva Mussolini!]

---

class that governs us."[2] Bold words, but in truth the planned march on Rome was really a calculated bluff to frighten the government into giving them power. The bluff worked, and the government capitulated even before the march occurred. On October 29, 1922, King Victor Emmanuel III (1900–1946) made Mussolini prime minister of Italy. Twenty-four hours later, the Fascist blackshirts were allowed to march into Rome in order to create the "myth" that they had gained power by an armed insurrection after a civil war.

MUSSOLINI AND THE ITALIAN FASCIST STATE   Since the Fascists constituted but a small minority in parliament, the new prime minister was forced to move slowly. Mussolini also had to balance two conflicting interests. The rural Fascists were eager to assume complete power, but the traditional institutions, such as the industrialists, the landowners, the Catholic church, and the military, wanted a period of domestic tranquillity. In the summer of 1923, Mussolini began to prepare for a national election that would consolidate the power of his Fascist government and give him a more secure base from which to govern. In July 1923, parliament enacted the Acerbo Law, which stipulated that any party winning at least 25 percent of the votes in the next national election would automatically be allotted two-thirds of the seats in parliament. The national elections that were subsequently held on April 6, 1924, constituted an enormous victory for the Fascists. They won 65 percent of the votes and garnered 374 seats out of a total of 535 in parliament. Although the elections were conducted in an atmosphere of Fascist fraud, force, and intimidation, the size of the victory indicated the growing popularity of Mussolini and his Fascists.

With this victory, Mussolini moved faster to consolidate his power. A campaign of intimidation of opposition deputies reached its high point with the assassination of the socialist deputy Giacomo Matteotti in June of 1924. Mussolini was severely challenged for his assumed complicity in the murder of Matteotti. The public outcry even caused numerous Italian political leaders to predict in December 1924 that Mussolini would have to resign.

▼ **Mussolini and Hitler.** By 1926, Mussolini and the Italian Fascists had created the institutional framework for the first fascist state in Europe. By the 1930s, Fascist Italy was being increasingly overshadowed by yet another fascist state, Nazi Germany. Benito Mussolini met Adolf Hitler, creator of Germany's fascist dictatorship, at Venice in June 1914.

At the beginning of 1925, yielding to the demands of extremists within his own Fascist party for decisive action and a "second wave" of Fascist change, Mussolini counterattacked. To save himself, Mussolini now pushed to establish a full dictatorship. This may have been Mussolini's ultimate intention anyway, but the Matteotti crisis forced him to make his move at this time. In a speech to parliament on January 3, Mussolini accepted responsibility for all Fascist violence and vowed to establish a new tranquillity (see the box on p. 943).

By 1926, Mussolini had established the institutional framework for his Fascist dictatorship. Press laws gave the government the right to suspend any publications that fostered disrespect for the Catholic church, monarchy, or the state. The prime minister was made "Head of Government" with the power to legislate by decree. A police law empowered the police to arrest and confine anybody for both nonpolitical and political crimes without due process of the law. The government was given the power to dissolve political and cultural associations. In 1926, all antifascist parties were outlawed. A secret police, known as the OVRA, was also established. By the end of 1926, Mussolini ruled Italy as *Il Duce*, the leader.

Mussolini conceived of the Fascist state as totalitarian: "Fascism is totalitarian, and the Fascist State, the synthesis and unity of all values, interprets, develops and gives strength to the whole life of the people."[3] Mussolini did try to create a totalitarian apparatus for police surveillance and for controlling mass communications, but this machinery was not all that effective. Police activities in Italy were never as repressive, efficient, or savage as those of Nazi Germany. Likewise, the Italian Fascists' attempt to exercise control over all forms of mass media, including newspapers, radio, and cinema, in order to use propaganda as an instrument to integrate the masses into the state failed to achieve its major goals. Most commonly, Fascist propaganda was disseminated through simple slogans, such as "Mussolini is always right," plastered on walls all over Italy.

Mussolini and the Fascists also attempted to mold Italians into a single-minded community by pursuing a Fascist educational policy and developing Fascist organizations. In 1939, Giuseppe Bottai, minister of education, proposed a new School Charter whose basic aim was "the will to substitute, both in principle and practice, for the bourgeois schools a people's school, which will really be for everyone and which will really meet the needs of everyone, that is the needs of the State."[4] Bottai hoped to make the educational system an instrument to create the "new Fascist man," but his reforms were never implemented, primarily because the middle class resisted any alterations in the traditional paths of upward mobility.

Since the secondary schools maintained considerable freedom from Fascist control, the regime relied more and more on the activities of Fascist youth organizations known as the Young Fascists to indoctrinate the young people of the nation in Fascist ideals. By 1939, about 6,800,000 children, teenagers, and young adults of both sexes, or 66 percent of the population between eight and eighteen, were enrolled in some kind of Fascist youth group. Activities for these groups included unpopular Saturday afternoon marching drills and calisthenics, seaside and mountain summer camps, and youth contests. An underlying motif for all of these activities was the

Fascist insistence on militarization. Beginning in the 1930s, all male groups were given some kind of premilitary exercises to develop discipline and provide training for war. Results were mixed. Italian teenagers, who liked neither military training nor routine discipline of any kind, simply refused to attend Fascist youth meetings on a regular basis.

The Fascist organizations hoped to create a new Italian, who would be hard-working, physically fit, disciplined, intellectually sharp, and martially inclined; this ideal was symbolized by the phrase, "book and musket—the perfect Fascist." In practice, the Fascists largely reinforced traditional social attitudes in Italy, as is evident in their policies regarding women. The Fascists portrayed the family as the pillar of the state and women as the basic foundation of the family. "Woman into the home" became the Fascist slogan. Women were to be homemakers and baby producers, "their natural and fundamental mission in life," according to Mussolini, for population growth was viewed as an indicator of national strength. To Mussolini, female emancipation was "unfascist." Employment outside the home was an impediment distracting women from conception. "It forms an independence and consequent physical and moral habits contrary to child bearing."[5] A practical consideration also underlay the Fascist attitude toward women. Working women would compete with males for jobs in the depression economy of the 1930s. Eliminating women from the market reduced male unemployment figures.

The Fascists translated their attitude toward women into law by a series of enactments in the 1930s that aimed at encouraging larger families by offering supplementary pay, loans, prizes, and subsidies for families with many offspring. Gold medals were given to mothers of many children. A national holiday of "the Mother and the Child" was held on December 24, at which prizes for fertility were awarded. Also in the 1930s decrees were passed that set quotas on the employment of women, but they were not overly successful in accomplishing their goal.

Despite the instruments of repression, the use of propaganda, and the creation of numerous Fascist organizations, Mussolini never really achieved the degree of totalitarian control accomplished in Hitler's Germany or Stalin's Soviet Union. Mussolini and the Fascist party never really destroyed the old power structure. Some institutions, including the armed forces and monarchy, were never absorbed into the Fascist state and mostly managed to maintain their independence. Mussolini had boasted that he would help workers and peasants, but instead he generally allied himself with the interests of the industrialists and large landowners at the expense of the lower classes.

Even more indicative of Mussolini's compromise with the traditional institutions of Italy was his attempt to gain the support of the Catholic church. In the Lateran Accords of February 1929, Mussolini's regime recognized the sovereign independence of a small enclave of 109 acres within Rome, known as Vatican City, which had remained in the church's possession since unification in 1870; in return, the papacy recognized the Italian state. The Lateran Accords also guaranteed the church a large grant of money and recognized Catholicism as the "sole religion of the state." In return, the Catholic church urged Italians to support the Fascist regime.

In all areas of Italian life under Mussolini and the Fascists, there was a noticeable dichotomy between Fascist ideals and practice. The Italian Fascists promised much but actually delivered considerably less, and they were soon overshadowed by a much more powerful fascist movement to the north.

Hitler and Nazi Germany

In 1923, a small, south German rightist party, known as the Nazis, led by an obscure Austrian rabble-rouser named Adolf Hitler, created a stir with the Beer Hall Putsch, an attempt to seize power in southern Germany in conscious imitation of Mussolini's march on Rome in 1922. Although it failed, the putsch projected Adolf Hitler and the Nazis into national prominence. Within ten years, Hitler and the Nazis had taken over complete power.

WEIMAR GERMANY AND THE RISE OF THE NAZIS After the Imperial Germany of William II had come to an end with Germany's defeat in World War I, a German democratic state known as the Weimar Republic had been established. From its beginnings, the Weimar Republic was plagued by a series of problems. The Republic had no truly outstanding political leaders. Even its more able leaders, such as Friedrich Ebert, who served as president, and Gustav Stresemann, the foreign minister and chancellor, died in the 1920s. When Ebert died in 1925, Paul von Hindenburg, the World War I military hero, was elected president. Hindenburg was a traditional military man, monarchist in sentiment, who at heart was not in favor of the Republic. The young Republic also suffered politically from attempted uprisings and attacks from both the left and right.

Another of the Republic's problems was its inability to change the basic structure of Germany. The government never really controlled the army, which operated as a state within a state. This independence was true of other institutions as well. Hostile judges, teachers, and bureaucrats remained in office and used their positions to undermine democracy from within. At the same time, important groups of landed aristocrats and leaders of powerful business cartels refused to accept the overthrow of the imperial regime and remained hostile to the Weimar Republic.

The Weimar Republic also faced serious economic difficulties. Germany experienced runaway inflation in 1922 and 1923 with serious social effects. Widows, orphans, the retired elderly, army officers, teachers, civil servants, and others who lived on fixed incomes all watched their monthly stipends become worthless or their lifetime savings disappear. Their economic losses increasingly pushed the middle class to the rightist parties that were hostile to the Republic. To make matters worse, after a period of prosperity from 1924 to 1929, Germany faced the Great Depression. Unemployment increased to 3 million in March 1930 and 4.38 million by December of the same year. The depression paved the way for social discontent, fear, and extremist parties. The political, economic, and social problems of the Weimar Republic provided an environment in which Adolf Hitler and the Nazis were able to rise to power.

Born on April 20, 1889, Adolf Hitler was the son of an Austrian customs official. He was a total failure in secondary school and eventually made his way to Vienna to become an artist. Rejected by the Vienna Academy of Fine Arts and supported by an inheritance and orphan's pension, Hitler stayed on in Vienna to live the bohemian lifestyle of an artist. In his autobiography, *Mein Kampf*, Hitler characterized his years in Vienna from 1908 to 1913 as an important formative period in his life: "In this period there took shape within me a world picture and a philosophy which became the granite foundation of all my acts. In addition to what I then created, I have had to learn little, and I have had to alter nothing."[6]

Hitler experienced four major influences in Vienna. Georg von Schönerer, the leader of the Austrian Pan-German movement, was an extreme German nationalist who urged the union of all Germans in one national state. Karl Lueger was mayor of Vienna and leader of the anti-Semitic Christian Social party. Hitler called him "the greatest German mayor of all time" and especially admired his demagogic methods and leadership of a mass party that was formed with the aid of

emotional slogans. Much of Hitler's early anti-Semitism was imbibed from an ex-Catholic monk named Adolf Lanz who called himself Lanz von Liebenfels. Hitler was an avid reader of *Ostara,* a periodical published by Liebenfels in which he propagated his racial beliefs that the German Aryans were exalted beings destined to rule the earth. Liebenfels characterized the Jews and other allegedly inferior races as "animal-men" who must someday be eliminated by sterilization, deportation, forced labor, and even "direct liquidation." Finally, Hitler was also strongly influenced by Richard Wagner's operas, which he attended frequently in Vienna. Hitler absorbed Wagner's ideal of the true artist as a social outcast from the bourgeois world who is subject to his own rhythms. Wagner's music also spoke of a boundless will to power and a need to dominate.

In Vienna, then, Hitler established the basic ideas of an ideology from which he never deviated for the rest of his life. At the core of Hitler's ideas was racism, especially anti-Semitism (see the box on p. 947). His hatred of the Jews lasted to the very end of his life. Hitler had also become an extreme German nationalist who had learned from the mass politics of Vienna how political parties could effectively use propaganda and terror. Finally, in his Viennese years, Hitler also came to a firm belief in the need for struggle, which he saw as the "granite foundation of the world." Hitler emphasized a crude Social Darwinism (see Chapter 23); the world was a brutal place filled with constant struggle in which only the fit survived.

In 1913, Hitler moved to Munich, still without purpose and with no real future in sight. World War I saved him: "Overpowered by stormy enthusiasm, I fell down on my knees and thanked Heaven from an overflowing heart for granting me the good fortune of being permitted to live at this time."[7] As a dispatch runner on the Western Front, Hitler distinguished himself by his brave acts. At the end of the war, finding again that his life had no purpose or meaning, he returned to Munich and decided to enter politics and found, at last, his true profession.

As a Munich politician from 1919 to 1923, Hitler accomplished a great deal. He joined the obscure German Worker's Party, one of a number of right-wing extreme nationalist parties in Munich. By the summer of 1921, Hitler had assumed total control over the party, which he renamed the National Socialist German Workers' Party (NSDAP), or Nazi for short. His idea was that the party's name would distinguish the Nazis from the socialist parties while gaining support from both working-class and nationalist circles. Hitler worked as-

Adolf Hitler's Hatred of the Jews

▼ ▼ ▼

A *believer in Aryan racial supremacy, Adolf Hitler viewed the Jews as the archenemies of the Aryans. Hitler believed that the first task of a true Aryan state would be the elimination of the Jewish threat. This is why Hitler's political career both began and ended with a warning against the Jews. In this excerpt from his autobiography,* Mein Kampf, *Hitler describes how he came to be an anti-Semite when he lived in Vienna in his early twenties.*

Adolf Hitler, *Mein Kampf*

My views with regard to anti-Semitism thus succumbed to the passage of time, and this was my greatest transformation of all. . . .

Once, as I was strolling through the Inner City [of Vienna], I suddenly encountered an apparition in a black caftan and black hair locks. Is this a Jew? was my first thought.

For, to be sure, they had not looked like that in Linz. I observed the man furtively and cautiously, but the longer I stared at this foreign face, scrutinizing feature for feature, the more my first question assumed a new form:

Is this a German?

As always in such cases, I now began to try to relieve my doubts by books. For a few pennies I bought the first anti-Semitic pamphlets of my life. . . .

Yet I could no longer very well doubt that the objects of my study were not Germans of a special religion, but a people in themselves; for since I had begun to concern myself with this question and to take cognizance of the Jews, Vienna appeared to me in a different light than before. Wherever I went, I began to see Jews, and the more I saw, the more sharply they became distinguished in my eyes from the rest of humanity. . . .

In a short time I was made more thoughtful than ever by my slowly rising insight into the type of activity carried on by the Jews in certain fields.

Was there any form of filth or profligacy, particularly in cultural life, without at least one Jew involved in it? . . .

Sometimes I stood there thunderstruck.

I didn't know what to be more amazed at: the agility of their tongues or their virtuosity at lying.

Gradually I began to hate them.

---

siduously to develop the party into a mass political movement with flags, party badges, uniforms, its own newspaper, and its own police force or party militia known as the SA, the *Sturmabteilung,* or Storm Troops. The SA was used to defend the party in meeting halls and to break up the meetings of other parties. It added an element of force and terror to the growing Nazi movement. Hitler's own oratorical skills were largely responsible for attracting an increasing number of followers. By 1923, the party had grown from its early hundreds into a membership of 55,000 with 15,000 SA members.

In its early years, the Nazi party had been only one of many radical right-wing political groups in southern Germany. By 1923, it had become the strongest. When it appeared that the Weimar Republic was on the verge of collapse in the fall of 1923, the Nazis and other right-wing leaders in the south German state of Bavaria decided to march on Berlin to overthrow the Weimar government. When his fellow conspirators reneged, Hitler and the Nazis decided to act on their own by staging an armed uprising in Munich on November 8. The so-called Beer Hall Putsch was quickly crushed. Hitler was arrested, put on trial for treason, and sentenced to prison for five years, a lenient sentence indeed from sympathetic right-wing judges.

THE NAZI SEIZURE OF POWER   The Beer Hall Putsch and Hitler's imprisonment proved to be a major turning point in his career. He now saw clearly the need for a change in tactics. The Nazis could not come to power by overthrowing the Weimar Republic, but would have to use constitutional means to gain power. This implied the formation of a mass political party that would actively compete for votes with the other political parties. Rather than discouraging him, Hitler's trial and imprisonment reinforced his faith in himself and in his mission.

Hitler occupied himself in prison with the writing of *Mein Kampf* (*My Struggle*), an autobiographical account of his movement and its underlying ideology. Extreme

German nationalism, virulent anti-Semitism, and vicious anti-communism are linked together by a Social Darwinian theory of struggle that stresses the right of superior nations to *Lebensraum* (living space) through expansion and the right of superior individuals to secure authoritarian leadership over the masses. The only originality in *Mein Kampf,* as historians have pointed out, is in Hitler's analysis of mass propaganda, mass psychology, and the mass organization of peoples. What is perhaps most remarkable about *Mein Kampf* is its elaboration of a series of ideas that directed Hitler's actions once he took power. That others refused to take Hitler and his ideas seriously was one of his greatest advantages.

When Hitler was released, the Nazi party was in shambles, and he set about to reestablish his sole control over the party and organize it for the lawful takeover of power. Hitler's position on leadership in the party was quite clear. There was to be no discussion of ideas in the party, and the party was to follow the *Führerprinzip,* the leadership principle, which entailed nothing less than a single-minded party under one leader. As Hitler expressed it: "A good National Socialist is one who would let himself be killed for his Führer at any time."[8]

The late 1920s were a period of building and waiting. These were years of relative prosperity for Germany, and, as Hitler perceived, they were not conducive to the growth of extremist parties. He declared, however, that the prosperity would not last and that his time would come. In the meantime, Hitler worked to establish a highly structured party that could compete in elections and attract new recruits when another time of troubles arose. He reorganized the Nazi party on a regional basis and expanded it to all parts of Germany. By 1929, the Nazi party had a national party organization. It also grew from 27,000 members in 1925 to 178,000 by the end of 1929. Especially noticeable was the youthfulness of the regional, district, and branch leaders of the Nazi organization. Many were between the ages of twenty-five and thirty and were fiercely committed to Hitler because he gave them the kind of active politics they sought. Rather than democratic debate, they wanted brawls in beer halls, enthusiastic speeches, and comradeship in the building of a new Germany. One new, young Nazi member expressed his excitement about the party:

> For me this was the start of a completely new life. There was only one thing in the world for me and that was service in the movement. All my thoughts were centred on the movement. I could talk only politics. I was no longer aware of anything else. At the time I was a promising athlete; I was very keen on sport, and it was going to be my career. But I had to give this up too. My only interest was agitation and propaganda.[9]

Such youthful enthusiasm gave the Nazi movement an aura of a "young man's movement" and a sense of dynamism that the other parties could not match. In 1931, almost 40 percent of Nazi party members were under thirty.

By 1929, the Nazi party had also made a significant shift in strategy. Between 1925 and 1927, Hitler and the Nazis had pursued an urban strategy geared toward winning workers from the Socialists and Communists. But failure in the 1928 elections, when the Nazis gained only 2.6 percent of the vote and twelve seats in the Reichstag or German parliament, convinced Hitler of the need for a change. By 1929, the party began to pursue middle-class and lower-middle-class votes in small towns and rural areas, especially in northern, central, and eastern Germany. By the end of 1929, the Nazis had successfully made their shift to the new strategy. The end of 1929 was the beginning of the depression and the beginning of Hitler's real success.

Germany's economic difficulties made possible the Nazi rise to power. Unemployment rose dramatically, from 4.35 million in 1931 to 6 million by the winter of 1932. The economic and psychological impact of the Great Depression made the extremist parties more attractive. Already in the Reichstag elections of September 1930, the Nazis polled 18 percent of the vote and gained 107 seats in the Reichstag, making the Nazi party one of the largest parties.

By 1930, Chancellor Heinrich Brüning (1885–1970) had found it impossible to form a working parliamentary majority in the Reichstag and relied on the use of emergency decrees by President Hindenburg to rule. In a real sense, then, parliamentary democracy was already dying in 1930, three years before Hitler destroyed it.

Hitler's quest for power from late 1930 to early 1933 depended on the political maneuvering around President Hindenburg. Nevertheless, the elections from 1930 through 1932 were indirectly responsible for the Nazi rise to power since they showed the importance of the Nazi party. The party itself grew dramatically during this period, from 289,000 members in September 1930 to 800,000 by 1932. The SA also rose to 500,000 members.

The Nazis proved very effective in developing modern electioneering techniques. They crossed Germany in whirlwind campaigns by car, train, and airplane. His "Hitler Over Germany" campaign by airplane saw Hitler speaking in fifty cities in fifteen days. The Nazis were successful in presenting two fundamentally different approaches to the German voters. In their election campaigns, party members pitched their themes to the needs and fears of different social groups. In working-class districts, for example, the Nazis attacked international high finance, while in middle-class neighborhoods, they exploited fears of a Communist revolution and its threat to private property. At the same time that the Nazis made blatant appeals to class interests, they were denouncing conflicts of interest and maintaining that they stood above classes and parties. Hitler, in particular, claimed to stand above all differences and promised to create a new Germany free of class differences and party infighting. His appeal to national pride, national honor, and traditional militarism struck chords of emotion in his listeners.

Elections, however, proved to have their limits. In the elections of July 1932, the Nazis won 230 seats, making them the largest party in the Reichstag. But four months later, in November, they declined to 196 seats. It became apparent to many Nazis that they would not gain power simply by the ballot box. Hitler saw clearly, however, that the Reichstag after 1930 was not all that important, since the government ruled by decree with the support of President Hindenburg. Increasingly, the right-wing elites of Germany, the industrial magnates, landed aristocrats, military establishment, and higher bureaucrats, came to see Hitler as the man who had the mass support to establish a right-wing, authoritarian regime that would save Germany and their privileged positions from a Communist takeover. Under pressure, President Hindenburg agreed to allow Hitler to become chancellor (on January 30, 1933) and create a new government, but with supposed safeguards. There would be only three Nazis in the cabinet and Franz von Papen (1878–1969), who had served as chancellor and done so

much to win over Hindenburg to the arrangements, would serve as vice-chancellor. To those who reproached von Papen for giving power to Hitler, he responded: "What do you want? I have Hindenburg's trust. Within two months, we will have pushed Hitler so far into a corner that he will squeak."[10]

Within those two months, Hitler basically laid the foundations for the Nazis' complete control over Germany. One of Hitler's important cohorts, Hermann Göring (1893–1946), had been made minister of the interior and hence head of the police of the Prussian state, the largest of the federal states in Germany. He used his power to purge the police of non-Nazis and to establish an auxiliary police force composed of SA members. This action legitimized Nazi terror. On the day after a fire broke out in the Reichstag building (February 27), supposedly set by the Communists, Hitler was also able to convince President Hindenburg to issue a decree that gave the government emergency powers. It suspended all basic rights of citizens for the full duration of the emergency, thus enabling the Nazis to arrest and imprison anyone without redress. Although Hitler promised to return to the "normal order of things" when the Communist danger was past, in reality this decree provided the legal basis for the creation of a police state.

The crowning step of Hitler's "legal seizure" of power came after the Nazis had gained 288 Reichstag seats in the elections of March 5, 1933. Since they still did not possess an absolute majority, on March 23 the Nazis sought the passage of an Enabling Act, which would empower the government to dispense with constitutional forms for four years while it issued laws that would deal with the country's problems. Since it was to be an

▼ **Hitler and the Blood Flag Ritual.** In the development of his mass political movement, Adolf Hitler used ritualistic ceremonies as a means of binding party members to his own person. Hitler is shown here touching the "blood flag," which had supposedly been stained with the blood of Nazis killed during the Beer Hall Putsch, to a SS banner while the SS standard-bearer made a "blood oath" of allegiance: "I vow to remain true to my Führer, Adolf Hitler. I bind myself to carry out all orders conscientiously and without reluctance. Standards and flags shall be sacred to me."

amendment to the Weimar constitution, the Nazis needed and obtained a two-thirds vote to pass it. Only the Social Democrats had the courage to oppose Hitler. The Enabling Act provided the legal basis for Hitler's subsequent acts. He no longer needed either the Reichstag or President Hindenburg. In effect, Hitler became a dictator appointed by the parliamentary body itself.

With their new source of power, the Nazis acted quickly to enforce *Gleichschaltung,* or the coordination of all institutions under Nazi control. The civil service was purged of Jews and democratic elements, concentration camps were established for opponents of the new regime, the autonomy of the federal states was eliminated, trade unions were dissolved and swallowed up by a gigantic Labor Front, and all political parties except the Nazis were abolished. By the end of the summer of 1933, within seven months of being appointed chancellor, Hitler and the Nazis had established the foundations for a totalitarian state.

Why had this seizure of power been so quick and easy? The Nazis were not only ruthless in their use of force, but had also been ready to seize power. The depression had weakened what little faith the Germans had in their democratic state. But negative factors alone cannot explain the Nazi success. To many Germans, the Nazis offered a national awakening. "Germany Awake," one of the many Nazi slogans, had a powerful appeal to a people psychologically crushed by their defeat in World War I. The Nazis presented a strong image of a dynamic new Germany that was above parties and above classes.

By the end of 1933, there were only two sources of potential danger to Hitler's authority: the armed forces and the SA within his own party. The SA spoke of the need for a "second revolution" and the replacement of the regular army by the SA. Neither the army nor Hitler favored such a possibility. Hitler solved both problems simultaneously on June 30, 1934, by a purge of the SA leadership in return for the support of the army in allowing Hitler to succeed Hindenburg when the president died. When Hindenburg died on August 2, 1934, the office of Reich president was abolished, and Hitler became sole ruler of Germany. Public officials and soldiers were all required to take a personal oath of loyalty to Hitler as the "Führer of the German Reich and people." On August 19, 1934, Hitler held a plebiscite in which 85 percent of the German people indicated their approval of the new order. The Third Reich had begun.

THE NAZI STATE, 1933–1939   Having smashed the parliamentary state, Hitler now felt the real task was at hand: to develop the "total state." Hitler's aims had not been simply power for power's sake or a tyranny based on personal power. Hitler had larger ideological goals. The development of an Aryan racial state that would dominate Europe and possibly the world for generations to come required a massive movement in which the German people would be actively involved, not passively cowed by force. Hitler stated:

> We must develop organizations in which an individual's entire life can take place. Then every activity and every need of every individual will be regulated by the collectivity represented by the party. There is no longer any arbitrary will, there are no longer any free realms in which the individual belongs to himself. . . . The time of personal happiness is over.[11]

▼ **The Nazi Mass Spectacle.** Hitler and the Nazis made a clever use of mass spectacles to rally the German people behind the Nazi regime. These mass demonstrations evoked intense enthusiasm, as is evident at the Bückeberg near Hamelin when Hitler arrived for the Harvest Festival in 1937. Almost one million people were present for the celebration.

Propaganda and Mass Meetings in Nazi Germany
▼ ▼ ▼

Propaganda and mass rallies were two of the chief instruments that Hitler used to prepare the German people for the tasks he set before them. In the first selection, taken from Mein Kampf, Hitler explains the psychological importance of mass meetings in creating support for a political movement. In the second excerpt, taken from his speech to a crowd at Nuremberg, he describes the kind of mystical bond he hoped to create through his mass rallies.

Adolf Hitler, Mein Kampf

The mass meeting is also necessary for the reason that in it the individual, who at first, while becoming a supporter of a young movement, feels lonely and easily succumbs to the fear of being alone, for the first time gets the picture of a larger community, which in most people has a strengthening, encouraging effect. . . . When from his little workshop or big factory, in which he feels very small, he steps for the first time into a mass meeting and has thousands and thousands of people of the same opinions around him, when, as a seeker, he is swept away by three or four thousand others into the mighty effect of suggestive intoxication and enthusiasm, when the visible success and agreement of thousands confirm to him the rightness of the new doctrine and for the first time arouse doubt in the truth of his previous conviction—then he himself has succumbed to the magic influ-

ence of what we designate as "mass suggestion." The will, the longing, and also the power of thousands are accumulated in every individual. The man who enters such a meeting doubting and wavering leaves it inwardly reinforced: he has become a link in the community.

Adolf Hitler, Speech at the Nuremberg Party Rally, 1936

Do we not feel once again in this hour the miracle that brought us together? Once you heard the voice of a man, and it struck deep into your hearts; it awakened you, and you followed this voice. Year after year you went after it, though him who had spoken you never even saw. You heard only a voice, and you followed it. When we meet each other here, the wonder of our coming together fills us all. Not everyone of you sees me, and I do not see everyone of you. But I feel you, and you feel me. It is the belief in our people that has made us small men great, that has made us poor men rich, that has made brave and courageous men out of us wavering, spiritless, timid folk; this belief made us see our road when we were astray; it joined us together into one whole! . . . You come, that . . . you may, once in a while, gain the feeling that now we are together; we are with him and he with us, and we are now Germany!

The Nazis pursued the creation of this totalitarian state in a variety of ways.

Mass demonstrations and spectacles were employed to integrate the German nation into a collective fellowship and to mobilize it as an instrument for Hitler's policies (see the box above). These mass demonstrations, especially the Nuremberg party rallies that were held every September and the Harvest Festivals celebrated at the Bückeberg near Hamelin every fall, combined the symbolism of a religious service with the merriment of a popular amusement. They had great appeal and usually evoked mass enthusiasm and excitement. Even foreigners were frequently affected by the passions aroused by these mass demonstrations.

The state apparatus of Hitler's "total state" offers some confusing features. One usually thinks of Nazi Ger-

many as having an all-powerful government that maintained absolute control and order. In truth, Nazi Germany was the scene of almost constant personal and institutional conflict, which resulted in administrative chaos. In matters such as foreign policy, education, and economics, parallel government and party bureaucracies competed with each other over spheres of influence. Incessant struggle characterized relationships within the party, within the state, and between party and state. Why this "authoritarian anarchy," as one observer called it, existed is a source of much controversy. One group of historians has assumed that Hitler's aversion to making decisions resulted in the chaos that subverted his own authority and made him a "weak dictator." Another group believes that Hitler's style of leadership created his regime's administrative chaos, but maintains that Hitler deliberately created this institutional confusion. By fostering rivalry within the party and between party and state, he would be the final decision maker and absolute ruler.

In the economic sphere, Hitler and the Nazis also established control, but industry was not nationalized as the left wing of the Nazi party wanted. Hitler felt that it was irrelevant who owned the means of production so long as the owners recognized their master. Although the regime pursued the use of public works projects and "pump-priming" grants to private construction firms to foster employment and end the depression, there is little doubt that rearmament was a far more important contributor to solving the unemployment problem. Unemployment, which had stood at 6 million in 1932, dropped to 2.6 million in 1934 and less than 500,000 in 1937. The regime claimed full credit for solving Germany's economic woes, and this was an important factor in leading many Germans to accept the new regime, despite its excesses.

The German Labor Front under Robert Ley regulated the world of labor. The Labor Front was a single, state-controlled union. To control all laborers, it used the workbook. Every salaried worker had to have one in order to hold a job. Only by submitting to the policies of the Nazi-controlled Labor Front could a worker obtain and retain a workbook. The Labor Front also sponsored activities to keep the workers happy (see Mass Leisure later in the chapter).

For those who needed coercion, the Nazi total state had its instruments of terror and repression. Until 1934, the SA had been most visible in terrorizing the people, but after the June 30 purge, the SS took over that func-

tion in a much more systematic fashion. Originally created as Hitler's personal bodyguard, the SS, under the direction of Heinrich Himmler (1900–1945), came to control all of the regular and secret police forces. Himmler and the SS functioned on the basis of two principles: terror and ideology. Terror included the instruments of repression and murder: the secret police, criminal police, concentration camps, and later the execution squads and death camps for the extermination of the Jews (see Chapter 28). For Himmler, the SS was a crusading order whose primary goal was to further the Aryan master race. SS members, who constituted a carefully chosen elite, were thoroughly indoctrinated in racial ideology.

Other institutions, such as the Catholic and Protestant churches, primary and secondary schools, and universities, were also brought under the control of the Nazi totalitarian state. Nazi professional organizations and leagues were formed for civil servants, teachers, women, farmers, doctors, and lawyers. These groups were inspired by a sound principle perverted to other ends. Common flags, uniforms, meetings, and indoctrination gave a sense of identity to individuals, a sense of belonging and human warmth, but one that was cultivated to produce inhuman brutality.

Since the early indoctrination of the nation's youth would create the foundation for a strong totalitarian state for the future, youth organizations, the *Hitler Jugend* (Hitler Youth) and its female counterpart, the *Bund deutscher Mädel* (League of German Maidens), were given special attention. The oath required of Hitler Youth members demonstrates the degree of dedication expected of youth in the Nazi state: "In the presence of

▼ **Anti-Semitism in Nazi Germany.** At the core of Hitler's ideology was an intense anti-Semitism. Soon after their seizure of power, Hitler and the Nazis began to translate their anti-Semitic ideas into anti-Semitic policies. This photograph shows one example of Nazi action against the Jews. Two women clean up some of the debris the morning after *Kristallnacht*, the night of shattered glass.

this blood banner, which represents our Führer, I swear to devote all my energies and my strength to the savior of our country, Adolf Hitler. I am willing and ready to give up my life for him, so help me God."

The Nazi total state was intended to be an Aryan racial state. From its beginning, the Nazi party reflected the strong anti-Semitic beliefs of Adolf Hitler. Once in power, it did not take long for the Nazis to translate anti-Semitic ideas into anti-Semitic policies. Already on April 1, 1933, the new Nazi government initiated a two-day boycott of Jewish businesses. A series of laws soon followed that excluded "non-Aryans" (defined as anyone "descended from non-Aryans, especially Jewish parents or grandparents") from the legal professions, civil service, judgeships, the medical profession, teaching positions, cultural and entertainment enterprises, and the press.

In 1935, the Nazis unleashed another stage of anti-Jewish activity when new racial laws were announced in September at the annual party rally in Nuremberg. These "Nuremberg laws" excluded German Jews from German citizenship and forbade marriages and extramarital relations between Jews and German citizens. The "Nuremberg laws" essentially separated Jews from the Germans politically, socially, and legally and were the natural extension of Hitler's stress upon the creation of a pure Aryan race.

Another, considerably more violent phase of anti-Jewish activity took place in 1938 and 1939, initiated on November 9–10, 1938, the infamous *Kristallnacht,* or night of shattered glass. The assassination of a third secretary in the German embassy in Paris became the occasion for a Nazi-led destructive rampage against the Jews in which synagogues were burned, 7,000 Jewish businesses were destroyed, and at least one hundred Jews were killed. Moreover, 20,000 Jewish males were rounded up and sent to concentration camps. *Kristallnacht* also led to further drastic steps. Jews were barred from all public buildings and prohibited from owning, managing, or working in any retail store. Finally, under the direction of the SS, Jews were encouraged to "emigrate from Germany." After the outbreak of World War II, the policy of emigration was replaced by a more gruesome one.

The creation of the Nazi total state also had an impact on women. The Nazi attitude toward women was largely determined by ideological considerations. Women played a crucial role in the Aryan racial state as bearers of the children who would bring about the triumph of the Aryan race. To the Nazis, the differences between men and women were quite natural. Men were

Chronology
▼ ▼ ▼
Fascist Italy and Nazi Germany

Fascist Italy

Creation of *Fascio di Combattimento*	1919
Squadristi Violence	1920–1921
Fascists Win Thirty-five Seats in Parliament	1921
Mussolini Is Made Prime Minister	1922 (October 29)
Acerbo Law	1923
Electoral Victory for Fascists	1924
Establishment of Fascist Dictatorship	1925–1926
Lateran Accords with Catholic Church	1929
Fascist School Charter	1939

Nazi Germany

Hitler as Munich Politician	1919–1923
Beer Hall Putsch	1923
Election of Hindenburg as President	1925
Nazis Win 107 Seats in Reichstag	1930 (September)
Hitler Is Made Chancellor	1933 (January 30)
Reichstag Fire	1933 (February 27)
Enabling Act	1933 (March 23)
Purge of the SA	1934 (June 30)
Hindenburg Dies; Hitler as Sole Ruler	1934 (August 2)
Nuremberg Laws	1935
Kristallnacht	1938 (November 9–10)

warriors and political leaders while women were destined to be wives and mothers. By maintaining this clear distinction, each could best serve to "maintain the whole community."

Nazi ideas determined employment opportunities for women. The Nazis hoped to drive women out of certain areas of the labor market. This included heavy industry or other jobs that might hinder women from bearing healthy children, as well as certain professions, including university teaching, medicine, and law, which were considered inappropriate for women, especially married women. The Nazis encouraged women to pursue professional occupations that had direct practical application, such as social work and nursing. In addition to restrictive legislation against females, the Nazi regime pushed its campaign against working women with such poster slogans as "Get ahold of pots and pans and broom and you'll sooner find a groom!" Nazi policy toward female workers remained inconsistent, however. Especially after the rearmament boom and increased conscription of males for military service produced a labor shortage, the government encouraged women to work, even in areas previously dominated by males.

Authoritarianism in Eastern Europe

Nowhere had the map of Europe been more drastically altered by World War I than in eastern Europe. The new states of Austria, Poland, Czechoslovakia, and Yugoslavia (known as the kingdom of the Serbs, Croats, and Slovenes until 1929) adopted parliamentary systems while the preexisting kingdoms of Romania and Bulgaria gained new parliamentary constitutions in 1920. Greece became a republic in 1924. Hungary's government was parliamentary in form, but controlled by its landed aristocrats. At the beginning of the 1920s, political democracy seemed well established, but almost everywhere in eastern Europe, parliamentary governments soon gave way to authoritarian regimes.

Several problems helped to create this situation. Eastern European states had little tradition of liberalism or parliamentary politics and no substantial middle class to support them. Then, too, these states were largely rural and agrarian in character. While many of the peasants were largely illiterate, much of the land was still dominated by large landowners who feared the growth of agrarian peasant parties with their schemes for land redistribution. Ethnic conflicts also threatened to tear these countries apart. Fearful of land reform, communist agrarian upheaval, and ethnic conflict, powerful landowners, the churches, and even some members of the small middle class looked to authoritarian governments to maintain the old system.

Already in the 1920s, some eastern European states began to move away from political democracy toward authoritarian structures. Poland established an authoritarian regime in 1926 when Marshal Joseph Pilsudski created a military dictatorship. King Alexander I (1921–1934) abolished the constitution and imposed a royal dictatorship on Yugoslavia in 1929. King Boris III

(1918–1943) created an authoritarian regime in Bulgaria in 1923.

During the 1930s, all of the remaining parliamentary regimes (except Czechoslovakia) succumbed to authoritarianism. No doubt, the Great Depression was a crucial factor in this development. The collapse of farm prices worldwide in the late 1920s adversely affected a region so agrarian as eastern Europe. Eastern European states were increasingly attracted to the authoritarian examples of Fascist Italy and Nazi Germany, which in turn gave rise to the growth of their own fascist parties.

Although Admiral Miklós Horthy had ruled Hungary as "regent" since 1919, the appointment of General Julius Gömbös as prime minister in 1932 brought Hungary even closer to Italy and Germany. In Austria, the Christian Socialist chancellor Engelbert Dollfuss used the armed forces to crush the Social Democrats and create his own brand of fascist state, a Christian Corporate State. Romania witnessed the development of a strong fascist movement led by Corneliu Codreanu. Known as the Legion of the Archangel Michael, it possessed its own paramilitary squad called the Iron Guard. As Codreanu's fascist movement grew and became Romania's third largest political party, King Carol II (1930–1940) responded in 1938 by ending parliamentary rule, crushing the leadership of the legion, and imposing authoritarian rule. At the beginning of World War II, General Ian Antonescu seized power and established his own military dictatorship in Romania. In Greece, General John Metaxas imposed a dictatorship in 1936. The new Baltic republics of Lithuania, Latvia, and Estonia also succumbed to dictatorial governments after brief experiments with democracy.

Only Czechoslovakia, with its substantial middle class, liberal tradition, and strong industrial base, maintained its political democracy. Thomas Masaryk, an able and fair leader while serving as president from 1918 to 1935, was able to maintain an uneasy but stable alliance of reformist socialists, agrarians, and Catholics.

The Iberian Peninsula

Parliamentary regimes in both Spain and Portugal also failed to survive. Both countries were largely agrarian, illiterate, and dominated by powerful landlords and Catholic clergy.

Spain's parliamentary monarchy was unable to deal with the social tensions generated by the industrial boom and inflation that accompanied World War I. Supported by King Alfonso XIII (1886–1931), General Miguel Primo de Rivera led a successful military coup in

September 1923 and created a personal dictatorship that lasted until 1930. But a faltering economy because of the Great Depression led to the collapse of de Rivera's regime in January 1930 as well as a widespread lack of support for the monarchy. King Alfonso XIII left Spain in 1931, and a new Spanish Republic was instituted, governed by a coalition of democrats and reformist socialists. Political turmoil ensued as control of the government passed from leftists to rightists until a Popular Front, an antifascist coalition composed of democrats, socialists, and the revolutionary left, took over in 1936. The Popular Front was unacceptable, however, to senior army officers. Led by General Francisco Franco (1892–1975), Spanish military forces revolted against the government and inaugurated a brutal and bloody civil war that lasted three years.

Foreign intervention complicated the Spanish Civil War. Franco's forces were aided by arms, money, and men from the fascist regimes of Italy and Germany while the Popular Front was assisted by 40,000 foreign volunteers and trucks, planes, tanks, and military advisers from the Soviet Union. Gradually, Franco's forces wore down the Popular Front, and after the capture of Madrid on March 28, 1939, the Spanish Civil War finally came to an end.

General Francisco Franco soon established a dictatorship that lasted until his death in 1975. It was not a fascist government. The fascist movement in Spain, known as the Falange and led by José Antonio Primo de Rivera, son of the former dictator, contributed little to Franco's success and played a minor role in the new regime. Franco's regime, which favored large landowners, businessmen, and the Catholic clergy, was yet another example of a traditional, conservative, authoritarian regime.

In 1910, the Portuguese had overthrown their monarchy and established a republic. Severe inflation after World War I, however, undermined support for the republic and helped to intensify political instability. In 1926, a group of army officers seized power, and by the early 1930s, the military junta's finance minister, Antonio Salazar (1889–1970), had become the strong man of the regime. Salazar controlled the Portuguese government for the next forty years.

Soviet Russia

The civil war in Russia had come to an end by the beginning of 1921. It had taken an enormous toll of life, but the Red Terror and the victories of the Red Army had guaranteed the survival of the Communist regime.

During the civil war, Lenin had pursued a policy of "war communism." Under this policy of expedience, the government had nationalized banks, mines, factories, and businesses that employed more than ten workers. The government had also assumed the right to requisition the produce of peasants. War communism worked during the civil war, but once the war was over, peasants began to sabotage the program by hoarding food. Added to this problem was drought, which caused the great famine between 1920 and 1922 that claimed as many as 5 million lives. Industrial collapse paralleled the agricultural disaster. By 1921, industrial output was only 20 percent of its 1913 levels. Russia was exhausted. As Leon Trotsky said, "the collapse of the productive forces surpassed anything of the kind that history had ever seen. The country, and the government with it, were at the very edge of the abyss."[12]

THE NEW ECONOMIC POLICY In March 1921, Lenin pulled Russia back from the abyss by aborting war communism in favor of his New Economic Policy (NEP). Lenin's New Economic Policy was a modified version of the old capitalist system. Forced requisitioning of food from the peasants was halted as peasants were now allowed to sell their produce openly. Retail stores as well as small industries that employed fewer than twenty employees could now operate under private ownership, although heavy industry, banking, and mines remained in the hands of the government. Already by 1922, a revived market and good harvest had brought an end to famine; Soviet agriculture climbed to 75 percent of its prewar level. Industry, especially state-owned heavy industry, fared less well and continued to stagnate. Only coal production had reached prewar levels by 1926. Overall, the NEP had saved Communist Russia from complete economic disaster even though Lenin and other leading Communists intended it to be only a temporary, tactical retreat from the goals of communism.

Between 1922 and 1924, Lenin suffered a series of strokes that finally led to his death on January 21, 1924. Although Communist party rule theoretically rested on a principle of collective leadership, in fact, Lenin had provided an example of one-man rule. Lenin's death inaugurated a struggle for power among the members of the Politburo, the institution that had become the leading organ of the party.

In 1924, the Politburo of seven members was severely divided over the future direction of Soviet Russia. The Left, led by Leon Trotsky, wanted to end the NEP and launch Russia on the path of rapid industrialization, primarily at the expense of the peasantry. This same group wanted to carry the revolution on, believing that the survival of the Russian Revolution ultimately depended on the spread of communism abroad. Another group in the Politburo, called the Right, rejected the cause of world revolution and wanted instead to concentrate on constructing a socialist state in Russia. This group also favored a continuation of Lenin's NEP because it believed that too rapid industrialization would harm the living standards of the Soviet peasantry.

These ideological divisions were underscored by an intense personal rivalry between Leon Trotsky and Joseph Stalin. Trotsky had been a key figure in the success of the Bolshevik Revolution and the Red Army. In 1924, he held the post of commissar of war and was the leading spokesman for the Left in the Politburo. Joseph Stalin (1879–1953) had joined the Bolsheviks in 1903 and had come to Lenin's attention after he had staged a daring bank robbery to obtain funds for the Bolshevik cause. Stalin, who was neither a dynamic speaker nor a forceful writer, was content to hold the dull bureaucratic job of party general secretary while other Politburo members held party positions that enabled them to display their brilliant oratorical abilities. He was a good organizer, and the other members of the Politburo soon found that the position of party secretary was really the most important in the party hierarchy. The general secretary appointed the regional, district, city, and town party secretaries. In 1922, for example, Stalin had made

some 10,000 appointments, many of them trusted followers whose holding of key positions proved valuable in the struggle for power. Although Stalin at first refused to support either the Left or Right in the Politburo, he finally came to favor the goal of "socialism in one country" rather than world revolution.

Stalin used his post as party general secretary to gain complete control of the Communist party. Trotsky was expelled from the party in 1927. Eventually, he made his way to Mexico where he was murdered in 1940, no doubt on Stalin's orders. By 1929, Stalin had succeeded in eliminating the Old Bolsheviks of the revolutionary era from the Politburo and establishing a dictatorship so powerful that the Russian tsars of old would have been envious.

THE STALIN ERA, 1929–1939   The Stalinist era marked the beginning of an economic, social, and political revolution that was more sweeping in its results than the revolutions of 1917. Stalin made a significant shift in economic policy in 1928 when he launched his first five-year plan. Its real goal was nothing less than the transformation of Russia from an agricultural into an industrial country virtually overnight. Instead of consumer goods, the first five-year plan emphasized maximum production of capital goods and armaments and succeeded in quadrupling the production of heavy machinery and doubling oil production. Europe's largest electrical

▼ **Russian Agricultural Workers in the 1930s.** The rapid industrialization of Stalin's Russia was paralleled by the collectivization of agriculture. By 1934, most of Russia's family farms had been collectivized. The process of collectivization included "production meetings" in the fields to encourage higher levels of agricultural production.

The Formation of Collective Farms

▼ ▼ ▼

Accompanying the rapid industrialization of the Soviet Union was the collectivization of agriculture, a feat that involved nothing less than transforming Russia's 26 million family farms into 250,000 collective farms (kolkhozes). This selection provides a firsthand account of how the process worked.

Max Belov, *The History of a Collective Farm*

General collectivization in our village was brought about in the following manner: Two representatives of the [Communist] Party arrived in the village. All the inhabitants were summoned by the ringing of the church bell to a meeting at which the policy of general collectivization was announced. . . . The upshot was that although the meeting lasted two days, from the viewpoint of the Party representatives nothing was accomplished.

After this setback the Party representatives divided the village into two sections and worked each one separately. Two more officials were sent to reinforce the first two. A meeting of our section of the village was held in a stable which had previously belonged to a kulak. The meeting dragged on until dark. Suddenly someone threw a brick at the lamp, and in the dark the peasants began to beat the Party representatives who jumped out the window and escaped from the village barely alive. The following day seven people were arrested. The militia was called in and stayed in the village until the peasants, realizing their helplessness, calmed down. . . .

By the end of 1930 there were two kolkhozes in our village. Though at first these collectives embraced at most only 70 percent of the peasant households, in the months that followed they gradually absorbed more and more of them.

In these kolkhozes the great bulk of the land was held and worked communally, but each peasant household owned a house of some sort, a small plot of ground and perhaps some livestock. All the members of the kolkhoz were required to work on the kolkhoz a certain number of days each month; the rest of the time they were allowed to work on their own holdings. They derived their income partly from what they grew on their garden strips and partly from their work in the kolkhoz.

When the harvest was over, and after the farm had met its obligations to the state and to various special funds (for insurance, seed, etc.) and had sold on the market whatever undesignated produce was left, the remaining produce and the farm's monetary income were divided among the kolkhoz members according to the number of "labor days" each one had contributed to the farm's work. . . . It was in 1930 that the kolkhoz members first received their portions out of the "communal kettle." After they had received their earnings, at the rate of 1 kilogram of grain and 55 kopecks per labor day, one of them remarked, "You will live, but you will be very, very thin."

In the spring of 1931 a tractor worked the fields of the kolkhoz for the first time. The tractor was "capable of plowing every kind of hard soil and virgin sod," as Party representatives told us at the meeting in celebration of its arrival. The peasants did not then know that these "steel horses" would carry away a good part of the harvest in return for their work. . . .

By late 1932 more than 80 percent of the peasant households . . . had been collectivized. . . . That year the peasants harvested a good crop and had hopes that the calculations would work out to their advantage and would help strengthen them economically. These hopes were in vain. The kolkhoz workers received only 200 grams of flour per labor day for the first half of the year; the remaining grain, including the seed fund, was taken by the government. The peasants were told that industrialization of the country, then in full swing, demanded grain and sacrifices from them.

power station was also built during this period. Between 1928 and 1937, during the first two five-year plans, steel production increased from 4 to 18 million tons per year while hard coal output went from 36 to 128 million tons. The annual growth rate of the Soviet Union was between 14 and 20 percent a year, a phenomenal accomplishment. At the same time, new industrial cities, located near iron ore and coal deposits, sprang up overnight in the Urals and Siberia.

The social and political costs of industrialization were enormous. Little provision was made for absorbing the expanded labor force into the cities. While the indus-

The Authoritarian and Totalitarian States

Eastern Europe

Boris III Establishes Authoritarian Regime in Bulgaria	1923
Pilsudski Creates a Military Dictatorship in Poland	1926
Alexander I Creates Royal Dictatorship in Yugoslavia	1929
Gömbös Is Made Prime Minister in Hungary	1932
Dictatorship of General Metaxas in Greece	1936
Carol II Crushes Iron Guard and Imposes Authoritarian Rule in Romania	1938

Spain

Dictatorship of Primo de Rivera	1923–1930
Creation of Spanish Republic	1931
Spanish Civil War	1936–1939

The Soviet Union

New Economic Policy Begins	1921
Death of Lenin	1924
Trotsky Is Expelled from the Communist Party	1927
First Five-Year Plan Begins	1928
Stalin's Dictatorship Is Established	1929
Stalin's Purge	1936–1938

achievement, typified by the Stakhanov cult. Alexei Stakhanov was a coal miner who mined 102 tons of coal in one shift and exceeded the norm by 1,300 percent. He was held up as an example to others.

Rapid industrialization was accompanied by an equally rapid collectivization of agriculture. Almost all of the Bolsheviks had been appalled by one result of Lenin's New Economic Policy, the growth of a class of well-to-do peasant proprietors known as kulaks who employed wage labor. Of the 26 million peasant households in 1929, 2 million were kulaks. It seemed an anomaly to have this capitalist group in the midst of a communist society. To rectify this, Stalin inaugurated a policy of collectivization of agriculture even before he initiated the first five-year plan. Its goal was to eliminate private farms and push people into collective farms (see the box on p. 957). One of its major aims was to stimulate industrial growth through profits from the rural economy.

Initially, Stalin planned to collectivize only the wealthier kulaks, but strong resistance to his plans from peasants who hoarded crops and killed livestock led him to step up the program. By 1930, 10 million peasant households had been collectivized; by 1934, Russia's 26 million family farms had been collectivized into 250,000 units. This was done at tremendous cost, since the hoarding of food and the slaughter of livestock produced widespread famine. Stalin himself is supposed to have told Winston Churchill during World War II that 10 million peasants died in the artificially created famines of 1932 and 1933. The only concession Stalin made to the peasants was that each collective farm worker was allowed to have one tiny, privately owned garden plot.

There were additional costs to Stalin's program of rapid industrialization, however. To achieve his goals, Stalin strengthened the party bureaucracy under his control. Those who resisted were sent into forced labor camps in Siberia. Stalin's desire for sole control of decision making also led to purges of the Old Bolsheviks. Between 1936 and 1938, the most prominent Old Bolsheviks were put on trial and condemned to death. During this same time, Stalin undertook a purge of army officers, diplomats, union officials, party members, intellectuals, and numerous ordinary citizens. Estimates are that 8 million Russians were arrested; millions were sent to Siberian forced labor camps, from which they never returned. The Stalinist blood bath made what some Western intellectuals had hailed as the "New Civilization" much less attractive by the late 1930s.

The Stalin era also reversed much of the permissive social legislation of the early 1920s. Advocating complete equality of rights for women, the Communists had

trial labor force increased by millions between 1932 and 1940, total investment in housing actually declined after 1929, with the result that millions of workers and their families lived in pitiful conditions. Real wages in industry also declined by 43 percent between 1928 and 1940 while strict laws limited workers' freedom of movement. To inspire and pacify the workers, government propaganda stressed the need for sacrifice to create the new socialist state. Soviet labor policy stressed high levels of made divorce and abortion easy to obtain while also encouraging women to work outside the home and liberate themselves sexually. After Stalin came to power, the family was praised as a miniature collective in which parents were responsible for inculcating values of duty, discipline, and hard work. Abortion was outlawed while divorced fathers who did not support their children were fined heavily. The new divorce law of June 1936 imposed fines for repeated divorces. This return of social conservatism was paralleled by official encouragement of Soviet patriotism. Even the tsars were rehabilitated as Russian heroes.

▼ Mass Culture and Mass Leisure between the Wars

Technological innovations continued to have profound effects upon European society. Nowhere is this more evident than in mass culture and mass leisure. The mass distribution of commercialized popular forms of entertainment had a profound effect on European society.

Radio and Movies

A series of technological inventions in the late nineteenth century had prepared the way for a revolution in mass communications. Especially important was Marconi's discovery of "wireless" radio waves. But it was not until June 16, 1920, that a radio broadcast (of a concert by soprano Nellie Melba from London) for a mass audience was attempted. Permanent broadcasting facilities were then constructed in the United States, Europe, and Japan during 1921 and 1922, while mass production of radios (receiving sets) also began. In 1926, when the British Broadcasting Corporation (BBC) was made into a public corporation, there were 2,200,000 radios in Great Britain. By the end of the 1930s there were 9 million. Although broadcasting networks in the United States were privately owned and financed by advertising, those in Europe were usually controlled by the government.

The technical foundation for motion pictures had already been developed in the 1890s when short moving pictures were produced as novelties for music halls. Shortly before World War I, full-length features, such as the Italian film *Quo Vadis* and the American film *Birth of a Nation* became available and made it apparent that cinema had created a new form of mass entertainment. By 1939, about 40 percent of adults in the more advanced industrial countries were attending a movie once

a week. That figure increased to 60 percent by the end of World War II.

Mass forms of communication and entertainment were, of course, not new. But the increased size of audiences and the ability of radio and cinema, unlike the printed word, to provide an immediate mass experience did add new dimensions to mass culture. Of course, radio and movies could be used for political purposes. Hitler had said, "without motor-cars, sound films, and wireless, no victory of National Socialism." Radio seemed to offer great opportunities for reaching the masses, especially when it became apparent that the emotional harangues of an Adolf Hitler had just as much impact on people when heard on radio as in person. The Nazi regime encouraged radio listening by urging manufacturers to produce cheap radios that could be bought on installment plans. The Nazis also erected loudspeaker pillars in the streets to encourage communal radio listening, especially to radio broadcasts of mass meetings.

Film, too, had propaganda potential, a possibility not lost on Joseph Goebbels (1897–1945), the propaganda minister of Nazi Germany. Believing that film constituted one of the "most modern and scientific means of influencing the masses," Goebbels created a special film section in his Propaganda Ministry and encouraged the production of both documentaries and popular feature films that carried the Nazi message. *The Triumph of the Will*, for example, was a documentary of the 1934 Nuremberg party rally that conveyed forcefully to viewers the power of National Socialism. Both Fascist Italy and Nazi Germany controlled and exploited the content of newsreels.

Mass Leisure

Mass leisure activities had developed at the turn of the century, but new work patterns after World War I dramatically expanded the amount of free time available to take advantage of them. By 1920, the eight-hour day had become the norm for many office and factory workers in northern and western Europe.

Professional sporting events for mass audiences became an especially important aspect of mass leisure. Attendance at association football (soccer) games increased dramatically while the creation of the World Cup contest in 1930 added to the nationalistic rivalries that began to surround such mass sporting events. Increased attendance also made the 1920s and 1930s a great era of stadium building. The Germans built a stadium in Berlin for the 1936 Olympics that seated 140,000 people. Strahav Stadium in Prague held

240,000 spectators for gymnastics and track meets. As the popularity of mass spectator sports grew, so too did the amount of money spent on betting.

Travel opportunities also added new dimensions to mass leisure activities. The military use of aircraft during World War I helped to improve planes and make civilian air travel a reality. The first regular international air mail service began in 1919, and regular passenger service soon followed. Although air travel remained the preserve of the wealthy or the adventurous, trains, buses, and private cars made excursions to beaches or holiday resorts more and more popular and affordable. Beaches, such as the one at Brighton in Great Britain, were increasingly mobbed by crowds of people from all social classes.

Mass leisure provided totalitarian regimes with new ways to control their populations. Mussolini's Italy created the *Dopolavoro* (Afterwork) as a vast national recreation agency. The *Dopolavoro* was responsible for establishing clubhouses with libraries, radios, and athletic facilities in virtually every town and village. In some places, they included auditoriums for plays and films and travel agencies that arranged tours, cruises, and resort vacations on the Adriatic at reduced rates. *Dopolavoro* groups introduced many Italians to various facets of mass culture and mass leisure with activities such as band concerts, movies, choral groups, roller skating, and ballroom dancing. Essentially the *Dopolavoro* enabled the Italian government to provide, but also to supervise, recreational activities. By doing so, the state placed new rules and regulations on previously spontaneous activities, thus breaking down old group solidarities and enabling these groups to be guided by the goals of the state.

The Nazi regime adopted a program similar to the *Dopolavoro* in its *Kraft durch Freude* (Strength through Joy). The purpose of the *Kraft durch Freude* was to coordinate the free time of the working class by offering a variety of leisure time activities, including concerts, operas, films, guided tours, and sporting events (see the box on p. 961). Especially popular were the inexpensive vacations, essentially the modern package tour. This could be a cruise to Scandinavia or the Mediterranean or, more likely for workers, a shorter trip to different sites in Germany. Only 130,000 workers took cruises in 1938, compared with the 7 million who took short trips.

More and more, mass culture and mass leisure had the consequence of expanding the homogeneity of national populations, a process that had begun in the nineteenth century with the development of the national state. Local popular culture was increasingly replaced by national and even international culture as new forms of mass production and consumption brought similar styles of clothing and fashion to people throughout Europe.

▼ Cultural and Intellectual Trends in the Interwar Years

The artistic and intellectual innovations of the pre–World War I period, which had shocked many Europe-

▼ **New Patterns of Recreation: The Ford Model T.** Mass leisure activities expanded between the wars as new work patterns increased the free time available to members of the working class. For the middle classes, mass-produced automobiles, such as the American Ford Model T, made possible a new freedom of movement.

Mass Leisure: Strength through Joy
▼ ▼ ▼

I n November 1933, the German Labor Front established an organization called Kraft durch Freude (Strength through Joy), whose purpose was to organize the leisure time of workers in the interests of the Nazi regime. These excerpts are taken from the reports of the Social Democratic party's contact men in Germany and give a fairly accurate account of the attitudes of the German workers toward the Kraft durch Freude (KdF) program.

The SOPADE [Social Democratic Party in Exile] Reports

Central Germany, April 1939
While Beauty of Labor [another Labor Front organization] makes no impressions whatsoever . . . Strength through Joy is not without impact. However, workers' wages are only barely sufficient for essentials and nobody can afford a trip to Madeira, 150 Reichsmarks per person—300 RM with the wife. Even the shorter trips produce so many additional expenses that they often double the cost. But some people like them nonetheless. Anybody who has never made a trip in his life and sees the sea for the first time is much impressed. The effect is: "The Nazis have done some good things after all." The enthusiasm is, however, greater on the first trip. On the second, many are put off by the crowds.

Berlin, February 1938
Strength through Joy is very popular. The events appeal to the yearning of the little man who wants an opportunity to get out and about himself and to take part in the pleasures of the "top people." It is a clever appeal to the petty bourgeois inclinations of the unpolitical workers. For such a man it really means something to have been on a trip to Scandinavia, or even if he only went to the Black Forest or the Harz Mountains, he imagines that he has thereby climbed up a rung on the social ladder.

Bavaria, April 1939
On the group tours there is a sharp social differentiation. The "top people" only go on big trips where there will be a more select clientele. The big mass trips are for the proletariat. People now look for places where there are no KdF visitors. "Not visited by KdF" is now a particular asset for summer vacations. A landlord in a mountain village in Upper Bavaria wrote in his prospectus: "Not visited by KdF tourists." The Labor Front, which was sent the prospectus by someone, took the landlord to court. He had to withdraw the prospectus and was not allowed to receive summer guests. Nevertheless, information about summer Pensions [boardinghouses] which are not used by KdF is becoming more and more widespread.

---

ans, had been the preserve primarily of a small group of avant-garde artists and intellectuals. In the 1920s and 1930s, they became more widespread as artists and intellectuals continued to work out the implications of the ideas developed before 1914. In effect, prewar "outsiders" became "insiders." But what made the prewar avant-garde culture acceptable in the 1920s and the 1930s? Perhaps the most important factor was the impact of World War I.

The optimistic liberal-rationalist clichés that many Europeans had taken for granted before 1914 seemed hopelessly outdated in 1918. Four years of devastating war left many Europeans with a profound sense of despair and disillusionment. World War I indicated to many people that something was dreadfully wrong with West-

ern values. In his *Decline of the West,* the German writer Oswald Spengler (1880–1936) reflected the disillusionment when he emphasized the decadence of Western civilization and posited its collapse. To many people, the experiences of World War I seemed to confirm the prewar avant-garde belief that human beings were really violent and irrational animals who were incapable of creating a sane and rational world. The Great Depression of the late 1920s and early 1930s, as well as the growth of fascist movements based on violence and the degradation of individual rights, only added to the uncertainties generated by World War I. The crisis of confidence in Western civilization indeed ran deep and was well captured in the words of the French poet Paul Valéry in the early 1920s:

The storm has died away, and still we are restless, uneasy, as if the storm were about to break. Almost all the affairs of men remain in a terrible uncertainty. We think of what has disappeared, and we are almost destroyed by what has been destroyed; we do not know what will be born, and we fear the future. . . . Doubt and disorder are in us and with us. There is no thinking man, however shrewd or learned he may be, who can hope to dominate this anxiety, to escape from this impression of darkness. [13]

Political, economic, and social uncertainties were paralleled by intellectual uncertainties, which were quite evident in the cultural and intellectual achievements of the interwar years.

Art and Music

Postwar artistic trends were largely a working out of the implications of prewar developments. Abstract Expressionism, for example, became ever more popular as many pioneering artists of the early twentieth century matured between the two world wars. In addition, prewar fascination with the absurd and the unconscious contents of the mind seemed even more appropriate after the nightmare landscapes of World War I battlefronts. This gave rise to both the Dada movement and Surrealism.

Dadaism attempted to enshrine the purposelessness of life (see the box on p. 964). Revolted by the insanity of life, the Dadaists tried to give it expression by creating anti-art. The 1918 Berlin Dada Manifesto maintained that "Dada is the international expression of our times, the great rebellion of artistic movements." In the hands of Kurt Schwitters (1887–1948), however, Dada represented a form of cultural rebirth that liberated people from conformity. By taking pieces of junk (wire, string, rags, scraps of newspaper, nails, washers) and assembling them into collages, Schwitters believed that he was transforming the refuse of his culture into art. "I am a painter, I nail my pictures together," he once stated.

Perhaps more important as an artistic movement was Surrealism, which sought a reality beyond the material, sensible world and found it in the world of the unconscious through the portrayal of fantasies, dreams, or nightmares. Employing logic to portray the illogical, the Surrealists created disturbing and evocative images. The Spaniard Salvador Dali (1904–1989) became the high priest of Surrealism and in his mature phase became a master of representational Surrealism. In *The Persistence of Memory*, Dali portrayed recognizable objects that have nevertheless been divorced from their normal context. By placing these objects into unrecognizable relationships, Dali created a disturbing world in which the irrational had become tangible.

The move to functionalism in modern architecture also became more widespread in the 1920s and 1930s. Especially important in the spread of functionalism was the Bauhaus school of art, architecture, and design, founded in 1919 at Weimar, Germany, by the Berlin architect Walter Gropius (see Chapter 25). The Bauhaus teaching staff consisted of architects, artists, and designers who worked together to blend the study of fine arts

▼ Salvador Dali, *The Persistence of Memory.* Surrealism was another important artistic movement between the wars. Influenced by the theories of Freudian psychology, surrealists sought to reveal the world of the unconscious, or the "greater reality" that they believed existed beyond the world of physical appearances. Salvador Dali sought to portray the world of dreams by painting recognizable objects in unrecognizable relationships.

(painting and sculpture) with the applied arts (printing, weaving, and furniture making). Gropius urged his followers to foster a new union of arts and crafts to create the buildings and objects of the future.

Important to the development of artistic expression between the wars was the search for a new popular audience. To attract a wider audience, artists and musicians began to involve themselves in the new mass culture. The German Kurt Weill, for example, had been a struggling composer of classical music before he turned to the use of jazz rhythms and other popular musical idioms for *The Threepenny Opera*. Some artists even regarded art as a means to transform society and located their studios in poor, working-class neighborhoods. Walter Gropius envisioned the Bauhaus as a means to "achieve the reunion of all forms and creative work" and thereby create a new civilization. Theater proved especially attractive as postwar artists sought to make an impact on popular audiences. The German director Erwin Piscator began his directing career by offering plays to workers on picket lines. Piscator hoped to reach workers by experimental drama with political messages. Like many other artists, however, he became frustrated by his failure to achieve a mass audience.

The postwar acceptance of modern art forms was by no means universal. Many traditionalists denounced what they considered the degeneracy and decadence in the arts. Nowhere was this more evident than in the totalitarian states of Nazi Germany and the Soviet Union.

In the 1920s, Weimar Germany was one of the chief European centers for modern arts and sciences. Hitler and the Nazis rejected modern art as "degenerate" or "Jewish" art. In an address at the premiere of the Great German Art Exhibition in the newly opened House of German Art in July 1937, Hitler proclaimed:

> The people regarded this art [modern art] as the outcome of an impudent and unashamed arrogance or of a simply shocking lack of skill; it felt that . . . these achievements which might have been produced by untalented children of from eight to ten years old—could never be valued as an expression of our own times or of the German future.[14]

Hitler and the Nazis believed that they had laid the foundation for a new and genuine German art, which would glorify the strong, the healthy, and the heroic—all of which were supposedly attributes of the Aryan race. The new German art was actually the old nineteenth-century genre art with its emphasis on realistic scenes of everyday life.

▼ **Kurt Schwitters,** *Picture with Light Center.* To a great extent, trends in postwar painting were largely a continuation of prewar developments. But the horrors of World War I reinforced prewar preoccupations with the absurd and gave rise to two new movements, Dada and Surrealism. Kurt Schwitters became identified with the Dada movement when he began to create his collages. He wrote in 1928: "Fundamentally, I cannot understand why one is not able to use in a picture, exactly in the same way as commercially made color . . . all the old junk which piles up in closets or the rubbish heaps." Schwitters brought together postage stamps, old handbills, streetcar tickets, newspaper scraps, and pieces of cardboard to form his works of art.

So, too, was the art produced by the school of "socialist realism" in the Soviet Union. After the bold experimentalism of the 1920s, the Stalinist era imposed a stifling uniformity on artistic creativity. Like German painting, Soviet painting was expected to focus on a nineteenth-century pictorial style aimed at realistic presentation. Both the new German art and "socialist re-

The Voice of Dadaism
▼ ▼ ▼

The Dadaists attempted to give expression to what they saw as the meaninglessness and absurdity of life. In this excerpt, Tristan Tzara (1896–1945), a Romanian-French poet and one of the founders of Dadaism, expressed the Dadaist contempt for the Western tradition.

Tristan Tzara, "Lecture on Dada," 1922

I know that you have come here today to hear explanations. Well, don't expect to hear any explanations about Dada. You explain to me why you exist. You haven't the faintest idea. . . .

The acts of life have no beginning or end. Everything happens in a completely idiotic way. That is why everything is alike. Simplicity is called Dada. . . .

The beginnings of Dada were not the beginnings of an art, but of a disgust. Disgust with the magnificence of philosophers who for 3000 years have been explaining everything to us (what for?), disgust with the pretensions of these artists—God's-representatives-on-earth, . . . disgust with a false form of domination and restriction *en masse*, that accentuates rather than appeases man's instinct of domination, disgust with . . . the false prophets who are nothing but a front for the interests of money, pride, disease.

Dada is a state of mind. . . . Dada applies itself to everything, and yet it is nothing, it is the point where the yes and the no and all the opposites meet, not solemnly in the castles of human philosophies, but very simply at street corners, like dogs and grasshoppers.

Like everything in life, Dada is useless.

Dada is without pretension, as life should be.

---

alism" were intended to inculcate social values useful to the ruling regimes.

At the beginning of the twentieth century, a revolution in music parallel to the revolution in art had begun with the work of Igor Stravinsky (see Chapter 25). But Stravinsky still wrote music in a definite key. In 1924, the Viennese composer Arnold Schönberg (1874–1951) released a piano suite in which he used a scale composed of twelve notes independent of any tonal key. His atonal music, which grew out of a quarter century of experimentation, was closely akin to abstract painting. Whereas the latter arranged colors and lines without reference to concrete images, so atonal music organized sounds without making recognizable harmonies. Resistance to modern music was even greater than to modern painting, and it did not begin to win favor until after World War II.

Literature

The interest in the unconscious, evident in Surrealism, was also apparent in the new literary techniques that emerged in the 1920s. One of its most apparent manifestations was in the "stream of consciousness" technique in which the writer presented an interior monologue or a report of the innermost thoughts of each character. The most famous example of this genre was written by the Irish exile James Joyce (1882–1941). His *Ulysses*, published in 1922, told the story of one day in the life of ordinary people in Dublin by following the flow of their inner dialogue. Disconnected ramblings and veiled allusions pervade Joyce's work.

The German writer Hermann Hesse (1877–1962) dealt with the unconscious in a considerably different fashion. His novels reflected the influence of both Carl Jung's psychological theories (see the next section) and Eastern religions and focused among other things on the spiritual loneliness of modern human beings in a mechanized urban society. *Demian* was a psychoanalytic study of incest while *Steppenwolf* mirrored the psychological confusion of modern existence. Hesse's novels made a large impact on German youth in the 1920s. He won the Nobel Prize for literature in 1946.

Intellectual Trends: Physics and Psychology

The prewar revolution in physics initiated by Max Planck and Albert Einstein continued in the interwar period. In fact, Ernest Rutherford (1871–1937), one of the physicists responsible for demonstrating that the atom could be split, dubbed the 1920s the "heroic age of physics." By the early 1940s, seven subatomic particles had been distinguished, and a sufficient understanding of the potential of the atom had been achieved to lay the foundations for the development of the atomic bomb.

The new picture of the universe that was unfolding continued to undermine the old scientific certainties of classical physics. Classical physics had rested on the fundamental belief that all phenomena could be predicted if they could be completely understood; thus, the weather could be accurately predicted if we only knew everything about the wind, sun, and water. In 1927, the German physicist Werner Heisenberg (1901–1976) upset this belief when he posited the "uncertainty principle." In essence, Heisenberg argued that no one could determine the path of an electron because the very act of observing the electron with light affected the electron's location. The "uncertainty principle" was more than an explanation for the path of an electron, however; it was a new worldview. Heisenberg shattered confidence in predictability and dared to propose that uncertainty was at the bottom of all physical laws.

Few nonscientists understood the implications of Heisenberg's work, but another newly emerging scientific field had greater popular impact. The full importance of Sigmund Freud's thought was not felt until after World War I. The 1920s witnessed a worldwide acceptance of his ideas. Freudian terms, such as unconscious, repression, id, ego, and Oedipus complex, entered the popular vocabulary. Popularization of Freud's ideas led to the widespread misconception that an uninhibited sex life was necessary for a healthy mental life. Despite such misconceptions, psychoanalysis did develop into a major profession, especially in the United States. But Freud's

ideas did not go unchallenged, even by his own pupils. One of the most prominent challenges came from Carl Jung.

A disciple of Freud, Carl Jung (1856–1961) came to believe that Freud's theories were too narrow and based on Freud's own personal biases. Jung's study of dreams—his own and others—led him to diverge sharply from Freud. Whereas for Freud the unconscious was the seat of repressed desires or appetites, for Jung, it was an opening to deep spiritual needs and ever-greater vistas for humans. Two concepts were particularly important to his theories: the process of individuation and collective unconscious.

Jung believed that a person's dreams are linked together in some arrangement or pattern, which he called "the process of individuation." Only by examining one's dreams over a long period of time could a person see the pattern. He or she would then be able to understand the process of psychic growth or individuation as the mature personality emerges. The organizing center of the mind from which all this came was the "self," the whole psyche, rather than the ego. The general function of dreams, then, was to bring people back to the center, thereby restoring their psychological balance.

Jung viewed the unconscious as twofold: a "personal unconscious" and a "collective unconscious," which existed at a deeper level of the unconscious. The collective unconscious was the repository of memories that all human beings share and consisted of archetypes, mental forms or images that appear in dreams. The archetypes are not derived from the individual's experience, how-

▼ **Carl Jung.** Although a disciple of Sigmund Freud, Carl Jung broke with his master over the understanding of the nature of the unconscious. In his numerous writings, Jung developed elaborate theories on the individuation process and the concept of a collective unconscious. He is shown here at the age of 85 with one of his followers.

ever, but from the biological, prehistoric, and unconscious development of mind. They are common to all people and have a special energy that creates myths, religions, and philosophies. To Jung, the archetypes proved that mind was only in part personal or individual because their origin was buried so far in the past that they seemed to have no human source. Their function was to bring the original mind of humans into a new, higher state of consciousness.

The devastation wrought by World War I destroyed the liberal optimism of the prewar era. Yet many in the 1920s still hoped that the progress of Western civilization, so seemingly evident before 1914, could somehow be restored. These hopes proved largely unfounded as plans for economic reconstruction gave way to inflation and to an even more devastating Great Depression at the end of the 1920s. Likewise, confidence in political democracy was soon shattered by the rise of authoritarian governments that not only restricted individual freedoms, but in the cases of Italy, Germany, and the Soviet Union, sought even greater control over the lives of their subjects in order to manipulate and guide them to achieve the goals of their totalitarian regimes. For many people, despite the loss of personal freedom, these mass movements at least offered some sense of security in a world that seemed fraught with uncertainties.

But the seeming security of these mass movements gave rise to even greater uncertainties as Europeans, after a brief twenty-year interlude of peace, once again plunged into war, this time on a scale even more horrendous than that of World War I. The twentieth-century crisis, begun in 1914, seemed only to be worsening in 1939.

Notes

▼ ▼ ▼

1. Quoted in Robert Paxton, *Europe in the Twentieth Century*, 2d ed. (San Diego, 1985), p. 237.

2. Quoted in Denis Mack Smith, *Mussolini* (New York, 1982), p. 51.

3. Benito Mussolini, "The Doctrine of Fascism," in Adrian Lyttleton, ed., *Italian Fascisms from Pareto to Gentile* (London, 1973), p. 42.

4. Quoted in Edward Tannenbaum, *The Fascist Experience: Italian Society and Culture, 1922–1945* (New York, 1972), p. 170.

5. Quoted in Alexander De Grand, "Women under Italian Fascism," *Historical Journal* 19 (1976): 958–59.

6. Adolf Hitler, *Mein Kampf*, trans. Ralph Manheim (Boston, 1943), p. 22.

7. Ibid., p. 161.

8. Quoted in Joachim Fest, *Hitler*, trans. Richard and Clara Winston (New York, 1974), p. 241.

9. Quoted in Jeremy Noakes and Geoffrey Pridham, eds., *Nazism, 1919–1945* (Exeter, 1983), 1: 50–51.

10. Quoted in Jackson Spielvogel, *Hitler and Nazi Germany: A History* (Englewood Cliffs, N.J., 1988), p. 67.

11. Quoted in Fest, *Hitler*, p. 418.

12. Irving Howe, ed., *The Basic Writings of Trotsky* (London, 1963), p. 162.

13. Paul Valéry, *Variety*, trans. Malcolm Cowley (New York, 1927), pp. 27–28.

14. Norman H. Baynes, ed., *The Speeches of Adolf Hitler, 1922–1939* (Oxford, 1942), 1: 591.

Suggestions for Further Reading

▼ ▼ ▼

For a general introduction to the interwar period, see R. J. Sontag, *A Broken World, 1919–39* (New York, 1971). On European security issues after the Peace of Paris, see S. Marks, *The Illusion of Peace: Europe's International Relations, 1918–1933* (New York, 1976). The Locarno agreements have been well examined in J. Jacobson, *Locarno Diplomacy* (Princeton, N.J., 1972).

The important role of French diplomacy in the 1920s is examined in J. M. Hughes, *To the Maginot Line: The Politics of French Military Preparations in the 1920s* (Cambridge, Mass., 1971); and J. Néré, *The Foreign Policy of France from 1914 to 1945* (London, 1975). On German foreign policy, see the older but valuable work of H. W. Gatzke, *Stresemann and the Rearmament of*

Germany (Baltimore, Md., 1965). Russian foreign policy is examined in A. B. Ulam, *Expansion and Coexistence: The History of Soviet Foreign Policy, 1917–1943*, 2d ed. (New York, 1974). The best study on the problem of reparations is now M. Trachtenberg, *Reparations in World Politics* (New York, 1980), which paints a more positive view of French policies. S. A. Schuker, *The End of French Predominance in Europe: The Financial Crisis of 1924 and the Adoption of the Dawes Plan* (Chapel Hill, N.C., 1976) demonstrates the importance of economic factors, such as international bankers, in European security problems. The "return to normalcy" after the war is analyzed in C. S. Maier, *Recasting Bourgeois Europe: Stabilization in France, Germany, and Italy in the Decade after World War I* (Princeton, N.J., 1975). Also valuable is D. P. Silverman, *Reconstructing Europe after the Great War* (Cambridge, Mass., 1982). On the Great Depression, see C. P. Kindleberger, *The World in Depression, 1929–39*, rev. ed. (Berkeley, 1986). On Keynes and his new economic theories, see R. Skidelsky, *John Maynard Keynes: A Biography* (New York, 1986).

The best biography of Mussolini is now D. Mack Smith, *Mussolini* (New York, 1982). Two brief, but excellent surveys of Fascist Italy are A. Cassels, *Fascist Italy*, 2d ed. (Arlington Heights, Ill., 1985); and A. De Grand, *Italian Fascism* (Lincoln, Neb., 1982). An excellent reference guide for all aspects of Fascist Italy is P. Cannistraro, ed., *Historical Dictionary of Fascist Italy* (Westport, Conn., 1982). The best work on the rise of Fascism is A. Lyttleton, *Seizure of Power* (New York, 1973), which covers the period from 1919 to 1929. Of the recent regional studies, the best is P. Corner, *Fascism in Ferrara, 1915–1925* (London, 1975). On propaganda and other aspects of cultural life in Fascist Italy, see E. R. Tannenbaum, *The Fascist Experience: Italian Society and Culture, 1922–1945* (New York, 1972).

Two brief but sound surveys of Nazi Germany are J. Spielvogel, *Hitler and Nazi Germany: A History* (Englewood Cliffs, N.J., 1988); and J. Bendersky, *A History of Nazi Germany* (Chicago, 1985). A more detailed examination can be found in K. Bracher, *The German Dictatorship: The Origins, Structure, and Effects of National Socialism* (New York, 1970). The best biographies of Hitler are A. Bullock, *Hitler: A Study in Tyranny* (New York, 1964); and J. Fest, *Hitler*, trans. R. and C. Winston (New York, 1974). A good sociological analysis of the Nazi party can be found in M. Kater, *The Nazi Party: A Social Profile of Members and Leaders, 1919–1945* (Cambridge, Mass., 1983). A good regional study of the Nazi party's rise to power is W. S. Allen's "classic" *The Nazi Seizure of Power: The Experience of a Single German Town*, rev. ed. (New York, 1984). On the SA, see P. Merkl, *The Making of a Stormtrooper* (Princeton, N.J., 1980). The relationship between German big business and Hitler is well covered in H. A. Turner, *German Big Business and the Rise of Hitler* (New York, 1985). On the Nazi administration of the state, see M. Broszat, *The Hitler State: The Foundations and Development of the Internal Structure of the Third Reich* (New York, 1981). A brief perspective on Germany's economic recovery can be found in R. J. Overy, *The Nazi Economic Recovery, 1932–1938* (London, 1982). Basic studies of the SS include R. Koehl, *The Black Corps: The Structure and Power Struggles of the Nazi SS* (Madison, Wis., 1983); and H. Krausnick and M. Broszat, *Anatomy of the SS State* (London, 1970). An insightful book about the responses of ordinary Germans to the Third Reich is D. Peukert, *Inside Nazi Germany: Conformity, Opposition, and Racism in Everyday Life*, trans. R. Deveson (New Haven, Conn., 1987). On women, see J. Stephenson, *Women in Nazi Society* (London, 1975); and C. Koonz, *Mothers in the Fatherland: Women, the Family, and Nazi Politics* (New York, 1987). The Hitler Youth is examined in H. W. Koch, *The Hitler Youth* (New York, 1976). The books on the Holocaust cited in Chapter 28 contain background information on Nazi anti-Jewish policies between 1933 and 1939. The importance of racial ideology in Nazi Germany is evident in R. Proctor, *Racial Hygiene: Medicine Under the Nazis* (Cambridge, Mass., 1988). In addition to these, see K. A. Schleunes, *The Twisted Road to Auschwitz: Nazi Policy towards German Jews, 1933–1939* (Chicago, 1970); and S. Gordon, *Hitler, Germans and the "Jewish Question"* (Princeton, N.J., 1984).

For a general study of other fascist movements, see F. L. Carsten, *The Rise of Fascism*, 2d ed. (Berkeley, 1980). For a general interpretation of fascism, see S. G. Payne, *Fascism: Comparison and Definition* (Madison, Wis., 1980). Starting points for the study of eastern Europe are J. Rothschild, *East Central Europe between the Two World Wars* (New York, 1974); and B. Jelavich, *History of the Balkans*, vol. 2: *The Twentieth Century* (New York, 1983). On Franco, see J. W. D. Trythall, *El Caudillo: A Political Biography* (New York, 1970). On the Spanish Civil War, see S. G. Payne, *The Spanish Revolution* (New York, 1970); and H. Thomas, *The Spanish Civil War*, rev. ed. (New York, 1977).

On Russia in the 1920s, see S. F. Cohen, *Bukharin and the Bolshevik Revolution: A Political Biography, 1888–1938* (New York, 1973). The collectivization of agriculture is examined in R. W. Davies, *The Socialist Offensive: The Collectivization of Soviet Agriculture, 1929–30* (Cambridge,

Mass., 1980); while the impact of that collectivization on the Russian peasants is discussed in R. W. Davies, *The Soviet Collective Farm, 1929–1930* (Cambridge, Mass., 1980). Industrialization is covered in H. Kuromiya, *Stalin's Industrial Revolution: Politics and Workers, 1928–1932* (New York, 1988). Stalin's purges are examined in R. Conquest, *The Great Terror: Stalin's Purge of the Thirties*, rev. ed. (New York, 1973). For a biography of Stalin, see I. Deutscher, *Stalin*, 2d ed. (New York, 1967); and the more recent R. H. McNeal, *Stalin: Man and Ruler* (New York, 1988).

The use of cinema for propaganda purposes is well examined in D. Welch, *Propaganda and the German Cinema* (New York, 1985). The organization of leisure time in Fascist Italy is thoughtfully examined in V. De Grazia, *The Culture of Consent: Mass Organization of Leisure in Fascist Italy* (New York, 1981). On the cultural and intellectual environment of Weimar Germany, see W. Laqueur, *Weimar: A Cultural History* (New York, 1974); and P. Gay, *Weimar Culture: The Outsider as Insider* (New York, 1968). For a study of Carl Jung, see G. Wehr, *Jung: A Biography* (New York, 1987).

Chapter 28

The Deepening of the European Crisis: World War II

▼▼▼▼▼

On February 3, 1933, only four days after he had been appointed chancellor of Germany, Adolf Hitler met secretly with Germany's leading generals. He revealed to them his desire to create a new domestic unity that would enable Germany to rearm and prepare for the conquest of *Lebensraum* ("living space") in the east. Even before he had consolidated his power, Adolf Hitler had a clear vision of his goals. Their implementation meant another European war. World War II was clearly Hitler's war. Although other countries may have helped to make the war possible by not resisting Hitler's Germany earlier, it was Nazi Germany's actions that made World War II inevitable.

World War II was also more, however, than just Hitler's war. This chapter will focus on the European theater of war, but both European and American armies were also involved in fighting around the world. World War II consisted of two conflicts: one provoked by the ambitions of Germany in Europe; the other by the ambitions of Japan in Asia. By 1941, with the involvement of the United States in both wars, the two had merged into one global conflict.

Although World War I has been described as a total war, World War II was even more so, and was fought on a scale unprecedented in history. The entire populations of warring countries were involved: as combatants; as workers in wartime industries; as civilians who suffered invasion, occupation, and aerial bombing; or as victims of persecution and mass extermination. The world had never witnessed such widespread human-made death and destruction.

Hitler Occupies
Demilitarized Rhineland
▼

Munich
Conference
▼

Germany Invades
Soviet Union
▼

German Surrender
at Stalingrad
▼

Germany
Surrenders
▼

•••••••••• 1935 ••••••••••• 1940 ••••••••••• 1943 ••••••••••• 1944 ••••••••••• 1945 •••••••••

▲
Teheran
Conference

▲
Total Mobilization
of German Economy

▲
Atomic Bomb Dropped
on Hiroshima

▲ ▲
Conferences at
Yalta and Potsdam

▼ Prelude to War, 1933–1939

Only twenty years after the war to end war, Europe plunged back into the nightmare of total war. The efforts at collective security in the 1920s—the League of Nations, the attempts at disarmament, the pacts and treaties—all proved meaningless in view of the growth of Nazi Germany and its deliberate scrapping of the postwar settlement in the 1930s. Still weary from the last war, France and Great Britain refused to accept the possibility of another war. The Soviet Union had turned in on itself, while the United States had withdrawn into its traditional isolationism. Finally, the small successor states to Austria-Hungary were too weak to oppose Germany. The power vacuum in the heart of Europe encouraged a revived and militarized Germany to acquire the living space that Hitler claimed Germany needed for its rightful place in the world.

The Role of Hitler

World War II in Europe had its beginnings in the ideas of Adolf Hitler, who believed that only the Aryans were capable of building a great civilization. But to Hitler, the Germans (the leading group of Aryans) were threatened from the east by a large mass of inferior peoples, the Slavs, who had learned to use German weapons and technology. Germany needed more land to support a larger population and be a great power. Hitler was a firm believer in the doctrine of Lebensraum (living space), espoused by Karl Haushofer, a professor of geography at the University of Munich. The doctrine of Lebensraum maintained that a nation's power depended upon the amount and kind of land it occupied. Already in the 1920s, in the second volume of Mein Kampf, Hitler had indicated where a National Socialist regime would find this land: "And so we National Socialists . . . take up where we broke off six hundred years ago. We stop the endless German movement to the south and west, and turn our gaze toward the land in the east. . . .

If we speak of soil in Europe today, we can primarily have in mind only Russia and her vassal border states."[1]

In Hitler's view, the Russian Revolution had created the conditions for Germany's acquisition of land to its east. Imperial Russia had only been strong because of its German leadership. The seizure of power by the Bolsheviks (who, in Hitler's mind, were Jewish) had left Russia weak and vulnerable. Once it had been conquered, the land of Russia could be resettled by German peasants while the Slavic population could be used as slave labor to build the Aryan racial state that would dominate Europe for a thousand years. Hitler's conclusion was apparent: Germany must prepare for its inevitable war with the Soviet Union. Hitler's ideas were by no means secret. He had spelled them out in Mein Kampf, a book readily available to anyone who wished to read it (see the box on p. 972).

Hitler and the Nazis were neither the first Europeans not the first Germans to undertake European conquest and world power. Certainly, a number of elite circles in Germany before World War I had argued that Germany needed to annex lands to its south, east, and west if it wished to compete with the large states and remain a great power. The defeat in World War I destroyed this dream of world power, but the traditional conservative elites in the German military and the Foreign Office supported Hitler's foreign policy until 1937, largely because it accorded with their own desires for German expansion. But, as they realized too late, Nazi policy went far beyond previous German goals. Hitler's desire to create an Aryan racial empire led to slave labor and even mass extermination on a scale that would have been incomprehensible to previous generations of Germans.

Although Hitler had defined his goals, he had no prearranged timetable for achieving them. During his rise to power, he had demonstrated the ability to be both ideologue and opportunist. After 1933, a combination of military and diplomatic situations, organizational chaos in the administration of Germany, and economic pres-

Hitler's Foreign Policy Goals
▼ ▼ ▼

A dolf Hitler was a firm believer in the geopolitical doctrine of Lebensraum, which advocated that nations must find sufficient living space to be strong. This idea was evident in Mein Kampf, but it was explained in even more detail in a treatise that Hitler wrote in 1928. It was not published in his lifetime.

Hitler's Secret Book, 1928

I have already dealt with Germany's various foreign policy possibilities in this book. Nevertheless I shall once more briefly present the possible foreign policy goals so that they may yield a basis for the critical examination of the relations of these individual foreign policy aims to those of other European states.

(1) Germany can renounce setting a foreign policy goal altogether. This means that in reality she can decide for anything and need be committed to nothing at all. . . . [Hitler rejects this alternative.]
(2) Germany desires to effect the sustenance of the German people by peaceful economic means, as up to now. Accordingly even in the future she will participate most decisively in world industry, export and trade. . . . From a folkish standpoint setting this foreign policy aim is calamitous, and it is madness from the point of view of power politics.
(3) Germany establishes the restoration of the borders of the year 1914 as her foreign policy aim. This goal is insufficient from a national standpoint, unsatisfactory from a military point of view, impossible from a folkish standpoint with its eye on the future, and mad from the viewpoint of its consequences. . . .
(4) Germany decides to go over to [her future aim] a clear, far-seeing territorial policy. Thereby she abandons all attempts at world-industry and world-trade and instead concentrates all her strength in order, through the allotment of sufficient living space for the next hundred years to our people, also to prescribe a path of life. Since this territory can be only in the East, the obligation to be a naval power also recedes into the background. Germany tries anew to champion her interests through the formation of a decisive power on land.

This aim is equally in keeping with the highest national as well as folkish requirements. It likewise presupposes great military power means for its execution, but does not necessarily bring Germany into conflict with all European great powers. As surely as France here will remain Germany's enemy, just as little does the nature of such a political aim contain a reason for England, and especially for Italy, to maintain the enmity of the World War.

---

sures, especially after 1936, caused Hitler periodically to take steps that seemed to contradict the foreign policy goals of *Mein Kampf*. But he always returned to his basic ideological plans for racial supremacy and empire. He was certain of one thing: only he had the ability to accomplish these goals, and his fears for his health pushed him to fulfill his mission as quickly as possible. His impatience would become a major cause of his own undoing.

The "Diplomatic Revolution," 1933–1936

Between 1933 and 1936, Hitler and Nazi Germany achieved a "diplomatic revolution" in Europe. When Hitler become chancellor of Germany on January 30, 1933, Germany's position in Europe seemed weak. The Versailles treaty had created a demilitarized zone on Germany's western border that would allow the French to move into the heavily industrialized parts of Germany in the event of war. To Germany's east, the smaller states, such as Poland and Czechoslovakia, had defensive treaties with France. The Versailles treaty had also limited Germany's army to 100,000 troops with no air or naval forces.

The Germans were not without advantages, however. Germany was the second most populous European state after the Soviet Union and still possessed a great industrial capacity. Hitler was also well aware that Great Britain and France, dismayed by the costs and losses of World War I, wanted to avoid another war. Hitler knew that the French posed a threat to an unarmed Germany, but he believed that if he could keep the French from acting unilaterally against Germany in his first years, he could remove the restrictions imposed on Germany by Versailles and restore its strength.

Hitler's ability to rearm Germany and fulfill his expansionist policies depended initially upon his ability to convince others that his intentions were peaceful. Posing as the man of peace in his public speeches, Hitler emphasized that Germany wished only to revise the unfair provisions of Versailles by peaceful means and achieve Germany's rightful place among the European states. During his first two years in office, Hitler pursued a prudent foreign policy without unnecessary risks. His dramatic action in October 1933, when he withdrew Germany from the Geneva Disarmament Conference and the League of Nations, was done primarily for domestic political reasons, to give the Germans the feeling that their country was no longer dominated by other European states.

By the beginning of 1935, Hitler had become convinced that Germany could break some of the provisions of the Treaty of Versailles without serious British and French opposition. Hitler had come to believe, based on their responses to his early actions, that both states wanted to maintain the international status quo, but without using force. Consequently, Hitler decided to announce publicly what had been going on secretly for some time—Germany's military rearmament. On March 9, 1935, Hitler announced the creation of a new air force

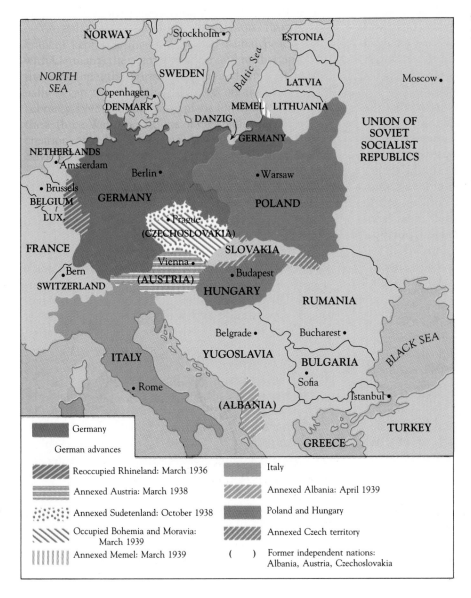

▼ **Map 28.1** Changes in Central Europe, 1936–Summer, 1939.

and, one week later, the introduction of a military draft that would expand Germany's army from 100,000 to 550,000 troops.

Hitler's unilateral repudiation of the Versailles treaty brought a swift reaction as France, Great Britain, and Italy condemned Germany's action and warned against future aggressive steps. But nothing concrete was done. Even worse, Britain subsequently moved toward an open acceptance of Germany's right to rearm when it agreed to the Anglo-German Naval Pact on June 18, 1935. This treaty allowed Germany to build a navy that would be 35 percent of the size of the British navy, with parity in submarines. The British were starting a policy of appeasement, based on the belief that if European states satisfied the reasonable demands of dissatisfied powers, the latter would be content and stability and peace would be achieved in Europe. British appeasement was grounded in large part upon Britain's desire to avoid another war, but it was also fostered by those British statesmen who believed that Nazi Germany offered a powerful bulwark against Soviet Communism.

On March 7, 1936, buoyed by his conviction that the Western democracies had no intention of using force to maintain the Treaty of Versailles, Hitler sent German troops into the demilitarized Rhineland. According to the Versailles treaty, the French had the right to use force against any violation of the demilitarized Rhineland. But France would not act without British support, and the British viewed the occupation of German territory by German troops as another reasonable action by a dissatisfied power. The London *Times* noted that the Germans were only "going into their own back garden." To Hitler, the French and British response only reinforced his growing conviction that they were weak nations unwilling to use force to defend the old order.

Meanwhile, Hitler gained new allies. In October 1935, Benito Mussolini had committed Fascist Italy to imperial expansion by invading Ethiopia. Angered by French and British opposition to his invasion, Mussolini welcomed Hitler's support and began to draw closer to the German dictator he had once called a buffoon. The joint intervention in 1936 of Germany and Italy on behalf of General Francisco Franco in the Spanish Civil War also drew the two nations closer together. In October 1936, Mussolini and Hitler concluded an agreement that recognized their common political and economic interests, and one month later, Mussolini referred publicly to the new Rome-Berlin Axis. Also in November 1936, Germany and Japan (the rising military power in the Far East), concluded the Anti-Comintern Pact and agreed to maintain a common front against communism.

By the end of 1936, Hitler and Nazi Germany had achieved a "diplomatic revolution" in Europe. The Treaty of Versailles had been virtually scrapped and Germany was once more a "World Power," as Hitler proclaimed. Hitler had demonstrated a great deal of diplomatic skill in taking advantage of Europeans' burning desire for peace. He had used the tactic of peaceful revision as skillfully as he had used the tactic of legality in his pursuit of power in Germany. By the end of 1936, Nazi power had increased enough that Hitler could initiate an even more daring foreign policy. As Hitler perceived, if the Western states were so afraid of war that they resisted its use when they were strong and Germany was weak, then they would be even more reluctant to do so now that Germany was strong. Although many Europeans still wanted to believe Hitler's own protestations of peace, his moves had actually made war more possible.

The Path to War, 1937–1939

On November 5, 1937, at a secret conference in Berlin with his military leaders, Adolf Hitler revealed his future aims. Germany's ultimate goal, he assured his audience, must be the conquest of living space in the east. Although this might mean war with France and Great Britain, Germany had no alternative if the basic needs of the German people were to be met. First, however, Germany must deal with Austria and Czechoslovakia and secure its eastern and southern flanks.

By the end of 1937, Hitler was convinced that neither the French nor the British would provide much opposition to his plans. The new British prime minister, Neville Chamberlain (1869–1940), was a strong advocate of appeasement and believed that the survival of the British Empire depended upon an accommodation with Germany. Chamberlain had made it known to Hitler in November 1937 that he would not oppose changes in central Europe provided that they were executed peacefully.

Hitler decided to move first on Austria. Hitler had failed miserably in 1934 when he tried to help the Austrian Nazi party seize power. He was more successful in 1938. By threatening Austria with invasion, Hitler coerced the Austrian chancellor, Kurt von Schuschnigg (1897–1977), into putting Austrian Nazis in charge of the government. The new government promptly invited German troops to enter Austria and assist in maintaining law and order. One day later, on March 13, 1938, after his triumphal return to his native land, Hitler formally annexed Austria to Germany. Great Britain's ready acknowledgment of Hitler's action only increased the German dictator's contempt for Western weakness.

The annexation of Austria improved Germany's strategic position in central Europe and put Germany in position for Hitler's next objective—the destruction of Czechoslovakia. On May 30, 1938, Hitler had already told his generals that it was his "unalterable decision to smash Czechoslovakia by military action in the near future."[2] This goal might have seemed unrealistic since democratic Czechoslovakia was quite prepared to defend itself and was well supported by pacts with France and Soviet Russia. Nevertheless, Hitler believed that France and Britain would not use force to defend Czechoslovakia.

In the meantime, Hitler had stepped up his demands on the Czechs. Initially, the Germans had asked for autonomy for the Sudetenland, the mountainous northwestern border area of Czechoslovakia that was home to three million ethnic Germans. As Hitler knew, the Sudetenland also contained Czechoslovakia's most important frontier defenses and considerable industrial resources as well. But on September 15, 1938, Hitler demanded the cession of the Sudetenland to Germany and expressed his willingness to risk "world war" to achieve his objective. War was not necessary, however, as appeasement triumphed once again. On September 29, at the hastily arranged Munich Conference, the British, French, Germans, and Italians (neither the Czechs nor the Russians were invited) reached an agreement that essentially met all of Hitler's demands. German troops were allowed to occupy the Sudetenland as the Czechs, abandoned by their Western allies, stood by helplessly. The Munich Conference was the high point of Western appeasement of Hitler. When Chamberlain returned to England from Munich, he boasted that the Munich agreement meant "peace in our times." Hitler had promised Chamberlain that he had made his last demand; all other European problems could be settled by negotiation. Like many German politicians, Chamberlain had believed Hitler's assurances (see the box on p. 976).

In fact, Munich confirmed Hitler's perception that the Western democracies were weak and would not fight. Increasingly, Hitler was convinced of his own infallibility, and he had by no means been satisfied at Munich. Already at the end of October 1938, Hitler told his generals to prepare for the final liquidation of the Czechoslovakian state. Using the internal disorder that he had deliberately fostered as a pretext, Hitler occupied the Czech lands (Bohemia and Moravia) while the Slovaks, with Hitler's encouragement, declared their independence of the Czechs and become a puppet state (Slovakia) of Nazi Germany. On the evening of March 15, 1939, Hitler triumphantly declared in Prague that he would be known as the greatest German of them all.

At last, the Western states reacted vigorously to Hitler's threat. After all, the Czechs were not Germans crying for reunion with Germany. Hitler's naked aggression made clear that his promises were utterly worthless. When Hitler began to demand the return of Danzig

▼ **The Munich Conference.** At a conference in Munich at the end of September 1938, the British and French capitulated to Hitler's demands and agreed to the German occupation of Czechoslovakia's Sudetenland area. The Munich Conference represents the high point of the West's appeasement of Hitler. Seen here are the chief participants in the conference: Chamberlain, Daladier (premier of France), Hitler, and Mussolini.

The Munich Conference

▼ ▼ ▼

At the Munich Conference, the leaders of France and Great Britain capitulated to Hitler's demands on Czechoslovakia. While the British prime minister, Neville Chamberlain, defended his actions at Munich as necessary for peace, another British statesman, Winston Churchill, characterized the settlement at Munich as "a disaster of the first magnitude."

Winston Churchill, Speech to the House of Commons, October 5, 1938

I will begin by saying what everybody would like to ignore or forget but which must nevertheless be stated, namely, that we have sustained a total and unmitigated defeat, and that France has suffered even more than we have. . . . The utmost my right honorable Friend the Prime Minister . . . has been able to gain for Czechoslovakia and in the matters which were in dispute has been that the German dictator, instead of snatching his victuals from the table, has been content to have them served to him course by course. . . . And I will say this, that I believe the Czechs, left to themselves and told they were going to get no help from the Western Powers, would have been able to make better terms than they have got. . . .

We are in the presence of a disaster of the first magnitude which has befallen Great Britain and France. Do not let us blind ourselves to that. . . .

And do not suppose that this is the end. This is only the beginning of the reckoning. This is only the first sip, the first foretaste of a bitter cup which will be proffered to us year by year unless by a supreme recovery of moral health and martial vigor, we arise again and take our stand for freedom as in the olden time.

Neville Chamberlain, Speech to the House of Commons, October 6, 1938

That is my answer to those who say that we should have told Germany weeks ago that, if her army crossed the border of Czechoslovakia, we should be at war with her. We had no treaty obligations and no legal obligations to Czechoslovakia. . . . When we were convinced, as we become convinced, that nothing any longer would keep the Sudetenland within the Czechoslovakian State, we urged the Czech Government as strongly as we could to agree to the cession of territory, and to agree promptly. . . . It was a hard decision for anyone who loved his country to take, but to accuse us of having by that advice betrayed the Czechoslovakian State is simply preposterous. What we did was to save her from annihilation and give her a chance of new life as a new State, which involves the loss of territory and fortifications, but may perhaps enable her to enjoy in the future and develop a national existence under a neutrality and security comparable to that which we see in Switzerland today. Therefore, I think the Government deserve the approval of this House for their conduct of affairs in this recent crisis which has saved Czechoslovakia from destruction and Europe from Armageddon.

(which had been made a free city by the Treaty of Versailles to serve as a seaport for Poland) to Germany, Britain recognized the danger and offered to protect Poland in the event of war. At the same time, both France and Britain realized that only the Soviet Union was powerful enough to help contain Nazi aggression, and began political and military negotiations with Joseph Stalin and the Soviets. The West's distrust of Soviet Communism, however, made an alliance unlikely.

Meanwhile, Hitler pressed on in the belief that the West would not really fight over Poland. He ordered his generals to prepare for the invasion of Poland on September 1, 1939. To preclude an alliance between the West and the Soviet Union, which would create the danger of a two-front war, Hitler, ever the opportunist, negotiated his own nonaggression pact with Stalin and shocked the world with its announcement on August 23, 1939. A secret protocol to the treaty created German and Soviet spheres of influence in eastern Europe: Finland, the Baltic states (Estonia, Latvia, and Lithuania), and eastern Poland would go to the Soviet Union while Germany would acquire western Poland. The treaty with the Soviet Union gave Hitler the freedom to attack Poland. He told his generals: "Now Poland is in the position in which I wanted her . . . I am only afraid that at the last moment some swine or other will yet submit to me a plan for mediation."[3] He need not have worried. On September 1, German forces invaded Poland; two days later, Britain and France declared war on Germany. Europe was again at war.

▼ The Course of World War II

Nine days before he attacked Poland, Hitler made clear to his generals what was expected of them: "When starting and waging a war it is not right that matters, but victory. Close your hearts to pity. Act brutally. Eighty million people must obtain what is their right . . . . The wholesale destruction of Poland is the military objective. Speed is the main thing. Pursuit until complete annihilation."[4] Hitler's remarks set the tone for what became the most destructive war in human history.

▼ **Hitler Declares War.** Adolf Hitler believed that Germany's living space must be gained by conquest in the east. This policy meant war. Hitler's nonaggression pact with Soviet Russia on August 23, 1939, paved the way for his invasion of Poland on September 1. On that day, Hitler spoke to the German Reichstag and announced the outbreak of war.

Victory and Stalemate

Using *Blitzkrieg,* or "lightning war," Hitler stunned Europe with the speed and efficiency of the German attack. Armored columns or panzer divisions (a panzer division was a strike force of about three hundred tanks and accompanying forces and supplies) supported by airplanes broke quickly through Polish lines and encircled the bewildered Polish troops. Conventional infantry units then moved in to hold the newly conquered territory. Within four weeks, Poland had surrendered. On September 28, 1939, Germany and the Soviet Union officially divided Poland between them.

Although Hitler's hopes to avoid a war with the West were dashed when France and Britain declared war on

September 3, he was confident that he could control the situation. Expecting another war of attrition and economic blockade, Britain and France refused to go on the offensive. After a winter of waiting (called the "phony war"), Hitler resumed the war on April 9, 1940, with another *Blitzkrieg* against Denmark and Norway. One month later, on May 10, the Germans launched their attack on the Netherlands, Belgium, and France. The main assault through Luxembourg and the Ardennes forest, completely unexpected by the French and British forces, enabled German panzer divisions to break through the weak French defensive positions there and race across northern France, splitting the Allied armies and trapping French troops and the entire British army on the beaches of Dunkirk. Only by heroic efforts did

▼ **German Troops in Paris.** On May 10, 1940, Hitler launched his attack on the Netherlands, Belgium, and France. Overwhelmed by the speed and audacity of the German attack, the French capitulated on June 22. This photograph shows German troops marching in Paris with the Arc de Triomphe in the background.

the British succeed in achieving a gigantic evacuation of 330,000 Allied (mostly British) troops.

On June 5, the Germans launched another offensive into southern France. Five days later, Mussolini, believing that the war was over and eager to grab some of the spoils, declared war on France and invaded from the south. The French capitulated on June 22. German armies occupied about three-fifths of France while the French hero of World War I, Marshal Henri Pétain (1856–1951) established an authoritarian regime (known as Vichy France) over the remainder. Germany was now in control of western and central Europe, but Britain had still not been defeated.

German victories in Denmark and Norway coincided with a change of government in Great Britain. On May 10, 1940, Winston Churchill (1874–1965), a longtime advocate for a hard-line policy toward Nazi Germany, replaced the apostle of appeasement, Neville Chamberlain. Churchill proved to be an inspiring leader who rallied the British people with stirring speeches and stubborn determination. Hitler hoped that the British could be persuaded to make peace so that he could fulfill his long-awaited opportunity to gain living space in the east. The British refused, and Hitler was forced to prepare for an invasion of Britain, a prospect that he faced with little confidence.

As Hitler realized, an amphibious invasion of Britain would only be possible if Germany gained control of the air. At the beginning of August 1940, the *Luftwaffe* (the German air force) launched a major offensive against British air and naval bases, harbors, communication centers, and war industries. The British fought back doggedly, supported by an effective radar system that gave them early warning of German attacks. Moreover, the Ultra intelligence operation, which had broken German military codes, gave the British air force information about the specific targets of German air attacks. Nevertheless, the British air force suffered critical losses by the end of August and was probably saved by Hitler's change of strategy. In September, in retaliation for a British attack on Berlin, Hitler ordered a shift from military targets to massive bombing of British cities to break British morale. The British rebuilt their air strength quickly and were soon inflicting major losses on *Luftwaffe* bombers. By the end of September, Germany had lost the Battle of Britain, and the invasion of Britain had to be postponed.

At this point, Hitler pursued the possibility of a Mediterranean strategy, which would involve capturing Egypt and the Suez Canal and closing the Mediterranean to British ships, thereby shutting off Britain's supply of

▼ **Map 28.2** World War II in Europe and North Africa.

oil. Hitler's commitment to the Mediterranean was never wholehearted, however. His initial plan was to let the Italians defeat the British in North Africa, but this strategy failed when the British routed the Italian army. Although Hitler then sent German troops to the north African theater of war, his primary concern lay elsewhere: he had already reached the decision to fulfill his lifetime obsession with the acquisition of living space in the east.

Already at the end of July 1940, Hitler had told his army leaders to begin preparations for the invasion of the Soviet Union. Although he had no desire for a two-front war, Hitler became convinced that Britain was remaining in the war only because it expected Russian support. If Russia were smashed, Britain's last hope would be eliminated. Moreover, Hitler had convinced himself that the Soviet Union, with its Jewish-Bolshevik leadership and a pitiful army, could be defeated quickly and decisively. Although the invasion of the Soviet Union was scheduled for spring 1941, the attack was delayed because of problems in the Balkans. Hitler had already obtained the political cooperation of Hungary, Bulgaria,

and Romania. Mussolini's disastrous invasion of Greece in October 1940 exposed Hitler's southern flank to British air bases in Greece. To secure his Balkan flank, German troops seized both Yugoslavia and Greece in April. Now reassured, Hitler turned to the east and invaded the Soviet Union on June 22, 1941, in the belief that the Russians could still be decisively defeated before winter set in.

The massive attack stretched out along an 1,800-mile front. German troops advanced rapidly, capturing two million Russian soldiers. By November, one German army group had swept through the Ukraine, while a second was besieging Leningrad; a third approached within twenty-five miles of Moscow, the Russian capital. An early Russian winter and unexpected Russian resistance, however, brought a halt to the German advance. For the first time in the war, German armies had been stopped. A counterattack in December 1941 by a Soviet army supposedly exhausted by Nazi victories brought an ominous ending to the year for the Germans. By that time, another of Hitler's decisions—the declaration of war on the United States—had probably made his defeat inevitable and turned another European conflict into a global war.

THE WAR IN ASIA   The war in Asia arose from the ambitions of Japan, whose rise to the status of world power had been swift. Japan had defeated China in 1895, Russia in 1905, and had taken over many of Germany's eastern and Pacific colonies in World War I. By 1933, the Japanese empire included Korea, Formosa (now Taiwan), Manchuria, and the Marshall, Caroline, and Mariana Islands in the Pacific.

By the early 1930s, Japan was experiencing severe internal tensions. Its population had exploded from 30 million in 1870 to 80 million by 1937. Much of Japan's ability to feed its population and to pay for industrial raw materials depended upon the manufacture of heavy industrial goods (especially ships) and textiles. But in the 1930s, Western nations created tariff barriers to protect their own economies from the effects of the depression. Japan was devastated, both economically and politically.

Although political power had been concentrated in the hands of the emperor and his cabinet, Japan had also experienced a slow growth of political democracy with universal male suffrage in 1924 and the emergence of mass political parties. The economic crises of the 1930s stifled this democratic growth. Right-wing patriotic societies allied themselves with the army and navy to push a program of expansion at the expense of China and Russia, while the navy hoped to make Japan self-sufficient in raw materials by conquering British Malaya and the Dutch East Indies. In 1935, Japan began to build a modern naval fleet, and after 1936 the armed forces exercised much control over the government.

The war in Asia began in July 1937 when Japanese troops invaded northern China. Moreover, Japanese naval expansion brought the Japanese into conflict with the European imperial powers—Britain (in India, Burma, Malaya), France (in Indochina), and the Netherlands (in Indonesia)—as well as with the other rising power in the Pacific, the United States. When the Japanese occupied Indochina in July 1941, the Americans responded by cutting off sales of vital scrap iron and oil to Japan. Japan's military leaders decided to preempt any further American response by attacking the American

▼ **Map 28.3** World War II in Asia and the Pacific.

naval fleet at Pearl Harbor on December 7, 1941. The United States declared war on Japan the next day. Three days later, Hitler declared war on the United States, although he was by no means required to do so by his loose alliance with Japan. This action enabled President Roosevelt to overcome strong American isolationist sentiment and to bring the United States into the European conflict. The simultaneous involvement of the United States in both the European and Asian theaters made World War II a single, truly world war.

The Turning Point of the War, 1942–1943

The entry of the United States into the war created a coalition (the Grand Alliance) that ultimately defeated the Axis powers (Germany, Italy, Japan). Nevertheless, the three major Allies, Britain, the United States, and the Soviet Union, had to overcome mutual suspicions before they could operate as an effective alliance. Two factors aided that process. First, Hitler's declaration of war on the United States made it easier for the United States to accept the British and Russian contention that the defeat of Germany should be the first priority of the United States. For that reason, the United States, under its Lend-Lease program, sent large amounts of military aid, including $50 billion worth of trucks, planes, and other arms, to the British and Soviets. Also important to the alliance was the tacit agreement of the three chief Allies to stress military operations while ignoring political differences and larger strategic issues concerning any postwar settlement. At the beginning of 1943, the Allies agreed to fight until the Axis powers surrendered unconditionally. Although this principle of unconditional surrender might have discouraged dissident Germans and Japanese from overthrowing their governments in order to arrange a negotiated peace, it also had the effect of cementing the Grand Alliance by making it nearly impossible for Hitler to divide his foes.

Defeat, however, was far from Hitler's mind at the beginning of 1942. As Japanese forces advanced into Southeast Asia and the Pacific after crippling the American naval fleet at Pearl Harbor, Hitler and his European allies continued the war in Europe against Britain and the Soviet Union. Until the fall of 1942, it appeared that the Germans might still prevail on the battlefield. Reinforcements in North Africa enabled the Afrika Korps under General Erwin Rommel to break through the British defenses in Egypt and advance toward Alexandria. The Germans were also continuing their success in the Battle of the North Atlantic as their submarines continued to attack Allied ships carrying supplies to

▼ **The Air War.** Air power played a major role in the battles of World War II. Because of his stretched-out supply lines in north Africa, the German general Erwin Rommel was forced to rely heavily on transport aircraft to keep his forces supplied.

Great Britain. In the spring of 1942, a renewed German offensive in Russia led to the capture of the entire Crimea, causing Hitler to boast in August 1942:

> As the next step, we are going to advance south of the Caucasus and then help the rebels in Iran and Iraq against the English. Another thrust will be directed along the Caspian Sea toward Afghanistan and India. Then the English will run out of oil. In two years we'll be on the borders of India. Twenty to thirty elite German divisions will do. Then the British Empire will collapse.[5]

But this would be Hitler's last optimistic outburst. By the fall of 1942, the war had turned against the Germans.

In North Africa, British forces had stopped Rommel's troops at El Alamein in the summer of 1942 and then

A German Soldier at Stalingrad

▼ ▼ ▼

The Russian victory at Stalingrad was a major turning point in World War II. This excerpt comes from the diary of a German soldier who fought and died in the Battle of Stalingrad. His dreams of victory and a return home with medals are soon dashed by the realities of Russian resistance.

Diary of a German Soldier

Today, after we'd had a bath, the company commander told us that if our future operations are as successful, we'll soon reach the Volga, take Stalingrad and then the war will inevitably soon be over. Perhaps we'll be home by Christmas.

July 29. The company commander says the Russian troops are completely broken, and cannot hold out any longer. To reach the Volga and take Stalingrad is not so difficult for us. The Führer knows where the Russians' weak point is. Victory is not far away. . . .

August 10. The Führer's orders were read out to us. He expects victory of us. We are all convinced that they can't stop us.

August 12. This morning outstanding soldiers were presented with decorations. . . . Will I really go back to Elsa without a decoration? I believe that for Stalingrad the Führer will decorate even me. . . .

September 4. We are being sent northward along the front towards Stalingrad. We marched all night and by dawn had reached Voroponovo Station. We can already see the smoking town. It's a happy thought that the end of the war is getting nearer. That's what everyone is saying. . . .

September 8. Two days of non-stop fighting. The Russians are defending themselves with insane stubbornness. Our regiment has lost many men. . . .

September 16. Our battalion, plus tanks, is attacking the [grain storage] elevator, from which smoke is pouring—the grain in it is burning, the Russians seem to have set light to it themselves. Barbarism. The battalion is suffering heavy losses. . . .

October 10. The Russians are so close to us that our planes cannot bomb them. We are preparing for a decisive attack. The Führer has ordered the whole of Stalingrad to be taken as rapidly as possible. . . .

October 22. Our regiment has failed to break into the factory. We have lost many men; every time you move you have to jump over bodies. . . .

November 10. A letter from Elsa today. Everyone expects us home for Christmas. In Germany everyone believes we already hold Stalingrad. How wrong they are. If they could only see what Stalingrad has done to our army. . . .

November 21. The Russians have gone over to the offensive along the whole front. Fierce fighting is going on. So, there it is—the Volga, victory and soon home to our families! We shall obviously be seeing them next in the other world.

November 29. We are encircled. It was announced this morning that the Führer has said: "The army can trust me to do everything necessary to ensure supplies and rapidly break the encirclement."

December 3. We are on hunger rations and waiting for the rescue that the Führer promised. . . .

December 14. Everybody is racked with hunger. Frozen potatoes are the best meal, but to get them out of the ice-covered ground under fire from Russian bullets is not so easy. . . .

December 26. The horses have already been eaten. I would eat a cat; they say its meat is also tasty. The soldiers look like corpses or lunatics, looking for something to put in their mouths. They no longer take cover from Russian shells; they haven't the strength to walk, run away and hide. A curse on this war!

forced them back across the desert. In November 1942, British and American forces invaded French North Africa and forced the German and Italian troops to surrender in May 1943. By that time, new detection devices had enabled the Allies to destroy increasing numbers of German submarines in the shipping war in the Atlantic. On the Eastern Front, the turning point of the war occurred at Stalingrad. After the capture of the Crimea, Hitler's generals wanted him to concentrate on the capture of the Caucasus and its oil fields, but Hitler decided that Stalingrad, a major industrial center on the Volga, should be taken first. Between November 1942 and February 1943, German troops were stopped, then encircled, and finally forced to surrender on February 2, 1943 (see the box on p. 982). The entire German Sixth Army of 300,000 men was lost. By February 1943, German forces in Russia were back to their positions of June 1942. By the spring of 1943, even Hitler knew that the Germans would not defeat the Soviet Union.

The tide of battle in the Far East also turned dramatically in 1942. In the Battle of the Coral Sea on May 7–8, 1942, American naval forces stopped the Japanese advance and temporarily relieved Australia of the threat of invasion. On June 4, at the Battle of Midway Island, American planes destroyed all four of the attacking Japanese aircraft carriers and established American naval superiority in the Pacific. After a series of bitter engagements in the waters near the Solomon Islands from August to November, Japanese fortunes began to fade.

The Last Years of the War

By the beginning of 1943, the tide of battle had turned against Germany, Italy, and Japan. After the Axis forces had surrendered in Tunisia on May 13, 1943, the Allies crossed the Mediterranean and carried the war to Italy, an area that Winston Churchill had called the "soft underbelly" of Europe. After taking Sicily, Allied troops began the invasion of mainland Italy in September. In the meantime, after the ouster and arrest of Benito Mussolini, a new Italian government offered to surrender to Allied forces. But Musso-

lini was liberated by the Germans in a daring raid and then set up as the head of a puppet German state in northern Italy while German troops moved in and occupied much of Italy. The new defensive lines established by the Germans in the hills south of Rome were so effective that the Allied advance up the Italian peninsula was a painstaking affair accompanied by heavy casualties. Rome did not fall to the Allies until June 4, 1944. By that time, the Italian war had assumed a secondary role anyway as the Allies opened their long-awaited "second front" in western Europe.

Since the autumn of 1943, the Allies had been planning a cross-channel invasion of France from Britain. A series of Allied deceptions managed to trick the Germans into believing that the invasion would come on the flat plains of northern France. Instead, the Allies, under the direction of the American general, Dwight D. Eisenhower (1890–1969), landed five assault divisions on the Normandy beaches on June 6 in history's greatest naval invasion. An initially indecisive German response enabled the Allied forces to establish a beachhead. Within three months, they had landed two million men and a half-million vehicles that pushed inland and broke through German defensive lines.

After the breakout, Allied troops moved south and east and liberated Paris by the end of August. Supply problems as well as a last-minute, desperate (and unsuccessful) offensive by German troops in the Battle of the

▼ **Crossing the Rhine.** After landing at Normandy, Allied forces liberated France and prepared to move into Germany. Makeshift bridges enabled the Allies to cross the Rhine in some areas and advance deeper into Germany. By this time, Allied forces had a massive superiority over the Germans in both men and equipment.

Chronology

▼ ▼ ▼

The Course of World War II

Germany and the Soviet Union Divide Poland	October 1939
Blitzkrieg against Denmark and Norway	April 1940
Blitzkrieg against Belgium, Netherlands, and France	May 1940
Churchill Becomes British Prime Minister	May 10, 1940
France Surrenders	June 22, 1940
Battle of Britain	Fall 1940
Nazi Seizure of Yugoslavia and Greece	April 1941
Germany Invades the Soviet Union	June 22, 1941
Japanese Attack on Pearl Harbor	December 7, 1941
Battle of the Coral Sea	May 7–8, 1942
Battle of Midway Island	June 4, 1942
Allied Invasion of North Africa	November 1942
German Surrender at Stalingrad	February 2, 1943
Axis Forces Surrender in North Africa	May 1943
Battle of Kursk	July 5–12, 1943
Invasion of Mainland Italy	September 1943
Allied Invasion of France	June 6, 1944
Hitler Commits Suicide	April 30, 1945
Surrender of Germany	May 7, 1945
Atomic Bomb Dropped on Hiroshima	August 6, 1945
Japan Surrenders	August 14, 1945

greatest tank battle of World War II. The Germans lost eighteen of their best panzer divisions. Soviet forces now began a relentless advance westward. The Soviets had reoccupied the Ukraine by the end of 1943 and lifted the siege of Leningrad and moved into the Baltic states by the beginning of 1944. Advancing along a northern front, Soviet troops occupied Warsaw in January 1945 and entered Berlin in April. Meanwhile, soviet troops swept along a southern front through Hungary, Romania, and Bulgaria.

In January 1945, Adolf Hitler had moved into a bunker fifty-five feet under Berlin to direct the final stages of the war. Hitler continued to arrange his armies on worn-out battle maps as if it still made a difference. In his final political testament, Hitler, consistent to the end in his rabid anti-Semitism, blamed the Jews for the war: "Above all I charge the leaders of the nation and those under them to scrupulous observance of the laws of race and to merciless opposition to the universal poisoner of all peoples, international Jewry."[6] Hitler committed suicide on April 30, two days after Mussolini had been shot by partisan Italian forces. On May 7, German commanders surrendered. The war in Europe was over.

The war in Asia continued. Beginning in 1943, American forces had gone on the offensive and advanced their way, slowly at times, across the Pacific. American forces took an increasing toll of enemy resources, especially at sea and in the air. When President Harry Truman (Roosevelt had died on April 12, 1945) and his advisers become convinced that American troops might suffer heavy casualties in the invasion of the Japanese homeland, they made the decision to drop the newly developed atomic bomb on Hiroshima and Nagasaki. The Japanese surrendered unconditionally on August 14. World War II, in which 17 million men died in battle and perhaps 18 million civilians perished as well (some estimate total losses at 50 million), was finally over.

Bulge slowed the Allied advance. Nevertheless, by March 1945, Allied armies had crossed the Rhine River and advanced further into Germany. At the end of April, Allied forces in northern Germany moved toward the Elbe River where they finally linked up with the Russians.

The Russians had come a long way since the Battle of Stalingrad in 1943. In the summer of 1943, Hitler's generals had urged him to build an East Wall based on river barriers to halt the Russians. Instead, Hitler gambled on taking the offensive by making use of newly developed heavy tanks. German forces were soundly defeated by the Russians at the Battle of Kursk (July 5–12), the

▼ The Nazi New Order

After the German victories in Europe, Nazi propagandists created glowing images of a new European order based on "equal chances" for all nations and an integrated economic community. This was not Hitler's conception of a European New Order. He saw the Europe he had conquered simply as subject to German domination. Only the Germans, he once said, "can really organize Europe."

The Nazi Empire

The Nazi empire stretched across continental Europe from the English Channel in the west to the outskirts of Moscow in the east. In no way was this empire organized systematically or governed efficiently. Some states—Spain, Portugal, Switzerland, Sweden, and Turkey—remained neutral and outside the empire. Germany's allies—Italy, Romania, Bulgaria, Hungary, and Finland—kept their independence, but found themselves increasingly restricted by the Germans as the war progressed. The remainder of Europe was largely organized in one of two ways. Some areas, such as western Poland, were directly annexed by Nazi Germany and made into German provinces. Most of occupied Europe was administered by German military or civilian officials, combined with different degrees of indirect control from collaborationist regimes. Competing lines of authority by different offices in occupied Europe made German occupation inefficient.

Racial considerations played an important role in how conquered peoples were treated. German civil administrations were established in Norway, Denmark, and the Netherlands because the Nazis considered their peoples to be Aryan or racially akin to the Germans and hence worthy of more lenient treatment. "Inferior" Latin peoples, such as the occupied French, were given military administrations. By 1943, however, as Nazi losses continued to multiply, all the occupied territories of northern and western Europe were ruthlessly exploited for material goods and manpower for Germany's war needs.

Because the conquered lands in the east contained the living space for German expansion and were populated in Nazi eyes by racially inferior Slavic peoples, Nazi administration there was considerably more ruthless. Hitler's racial ideology and his plans for an Aryan racial empire were so important to him that he and the Nazis began to implement their racial program soon after the conquest of Poland. Heinrich Himmler, a strong believer in Nazi racial ideology and the leader of the SS, was put in charge of German resettlement plans in the east. Himmler's task was to evacuate the inferior Slavic peoples and replace them with Germans, a policy first applied to the new German provinces created from the lands of western Poland. One million Poles were uprooted and dumped in southern Poland. Hundreds of thousands of ethnic Germans (descendants of Germans who had migrated years ago from Germany to different parts of southern and eastern Europe) were encouraged to colonize the designated areas in Poland. By 1942, two million ethnic Germans had been settled in Poland.

The invasion of the Soviet Union inflated Nazi visions of German colonization in the east. Hitler spoke to his intimate circle of a colossal project of social engineering after the war, in which Poles, Ukrainians, and Russians would become slave labor while German peasants settled on the abandoned lands and Germanized them (see the box on p. 986). Nazis involved in this kind of planning were well aware of the human costs. Himmler told a gathering of SS officers that although the destruction of 30 million Slavs was a prerequisite for German plans in the east, "Whether nations live in prosperity or starve to death interests me only insofar as we need them as slaves for our culture. Otherwise it is of no interest."[7]

Economically, the Nazi New Order meant the ruthless exploitation of conquered Europe's resources. In eastern Europe, economic exploitation was direct and severe. The Germans seized raw materials, machines, and food, leaving only enough to maintain local peoples at a bare subsistence level. Although the Germans adopted legal formalities in their economic exploitation of western Europe, military supplies and important raw materials were taken outright. Nazi policies created drastic shortages of food, clothing, and shelter. Many Europeans suffered severely.

Labor shortages in Germany led to a policy of ruthless mobilization of foreign labor for Germany. After the invasion of Russia, the 4 million Russian prisoners of war captured by the Germans became a chief source of heavy labor, but it was wasted by allowing 3 million of them to die from neglect. In 1942, a special office was created to recruit labor for German farms and industries. By the summer of 1944, 7 million foreign workers were laboring in Germany and constituted 20 percent of Germany's labor force. At the same time, another 7 million workers were supplying forced labor in their own countries on farms, in industries, and even in military camps. Forced labor, however, often proved counterproductive because it created economic chaos in occupied countries and disrupted industrial production that could have helped Germany. Even worse for the Germans, the brutal character of Germany's recruitment policies often led more and more people to resist the Nazi occupation forces.

Resistance Movements

German policies toward conquered peoples quickly led to the emergence of resistance movements throughout Europe, especially in the east, where brutality toward the native peoples produced a strong reaction. In

Hitler's Plans for a New Order in the East
▼ ▼ ▼

H*itler's nightly monologues to his postdinner guests, which were recorded by the Führer's private secretary, Martin Bormann, reveal much about the New Order he wished to create. On the evening of October 17, 1941, he expressed his views on what the Germans would do with their newly conquered territories in the east.*

Hitler's Secret Conversations, October 17, 1941
In comparison with the beauties accumulated in Central Germany, the new territories in the East seem to us like a desert. . . . This Russian desert, we shall populate it. . . . We'll take away its character of an Asiatic steppe, we'll Europeanise it. With this object, we have undertaken the construction of roads that will lead to the southernmost point of the Crimea and to the Caucasus. These roads will be studded along their whole length with German towns, and around these towns our colonists will settle.

As for the two or three million men whom we need to accomplish this task, we'll find them quicker than we think. They'll come from Germany, Scandinavia, the Western countries and America. I shall no longer be here to see all that, but in twenty years the Ukraine will already be a home for twenty million inhabitants besides the natives. In three hundred years, the country will be one of the loveliest gardens in the world.

As for the natives, we'll have to screen them carefully. The Jew, that destroyer, we shall drive out. . . . We shan't settle in the Russian towns, and we'll let them fall to pieces without intervening. And, above all, no remorse on this subject! We're not going to play at children's nurses; we're absolutely without obligations as far as these people are concerned. To struggle against the hovels, chase away the fleas, provide German teachers, bring out newspapers—very little of that for us! We'll confine ourselves, perhaps, to setting up a radio transmitter, under our control. For the rest, let them know just enough to understand our highway signs, so that they won't get themselves run over by our vehicles. . . . There's only one duty: to Germanise this country by the immigration of Germans, and to look upon the natives as Redskins. If these people had defeated us, Heaven have mercy! But we don't hate them. That sentiment is unknown to us. We are guided only by reason. . . .

All those who have the feeling for Europe can join in our work.

In this business I shall go straight ahead, cold-bloodedly. What they may think about me, at this juncture, is to me a matter of complete indifference. I don't see why a German who eats a piece of bread should torment himself with the idea that the soil that produces this bread has been won by the sword.

---

the Ukraine and Baltic states, for example, Germans were hailed as liberators from communist rule, but Hitler's policies of treating Slavic peoples as subhumans only drove those peoples to support and join guerrilla forces.

Resistance movements were formed throughout Europe. Active resisters committed acts of sabotage against German installations, assassinated German officials, spread anti-German newspapers, wrote anti-German sentiments on walls, and spied on German military positions for the Allies. Some anti-Nazi groups from occupied countries, such as the Free French movement under Charles de Gaulle, created governments-in-exile in London. In some countries, resistance groups even grew strong enough to take on the Germans in pitched battles. In Yugoslavia, for example, Josip Broz, known as Tito (1892–1980), led a band of guerrillas against German occupation forces. By 1944, his partisan army numbered 250,000.

After the invasion of Russia in 1941, Communists throughout Europe assumed leadership roles in underground resistance movements. This sometimes led to conflict with other local resistance groups who feared the postwar consequences of Communist power. Charles de Gaulle's Free French movement, for example, thwarted the attempt of French Communists to dominate the major French resistance groups.

Germany, too, had its resistance movements, although the increased control of the SS over everyday life made resistance both dangerous and ineffectual. The White Rose movement involved an attempt by a small group of students and one professor at the University of Munich to distribute pamphlets denouncing the Nazi regime as lawless, criminal, and godless. Its members were caught, arrested, and promptly executed. Likewise, Communist resistance groups were mostly crushed by the Gestapo.

Only one plot against Hitler and the Nazi regime came remotely close to success. It was the work primarily of a group of military officers and conservative politicians who were appalled at Hitler's war mongering and sickened by the wartime atrocities he had encouraged. One of their number, Colonel Count Claus von Stauffenberg (1907–1944), believed that only the elimination of Hitler would bring the overthrow of the Nazi regime. On July 20, 1944, a bomb planted by Stauffenberg in Hitler's East Prussian headquarters exploded, but failed to kill the dictator. The plot was then quickly uncovered and crushed. Five thousand people were executed and Hitler remained in control of Germany.

The Holocaust

There was no more terrifying aspect of the Nazi New Order than the deliberate attempt to exterminate the Jewish people of Europe. Racial struggle was a key element in Hitler's ideology and meant to him a clearly defined conflict of opposites: the Aryans, creators of human cultural development, against the Jews, parasites who were trying to destroy the Aryans. At a meeting of the Nazi party in 1922, Hitler proclaimed: "There can be no compromise—there are only two possibilities: either victory of the Aryan or annihilation of the Aryan and the victory of the Jew."[8] Although Hitler later toned down his anti-Semitic message when his party sought mass electoral victories, anti-Semitism was a recurring theme in Nazism and resulted in a wave of legislative acts against the Jews between 1933 and 1939.

By the beginning of 1939, Nazi policy focused on promoting the "emigration" of German Jews from Germany. At the same time, Hitler had given ominous warnings about the future of European Jewry. When he addressed the German Reichstag on January 30, 1939, he stated:

> I have often been a prophet in life and was generally laughed at. During my struggle for power, the Jews primarily received with laughter my prophecies that I would someday assume the leadership of the state and thereby of the entire Volk and then, among many other things, achieve a solution of the Jewish problem. . . . Today I will be a prophet again: if international finance Jewry within Europe and abroad should succeed once more in plunging the peoples into a world war, then the consequence will be not the Bolshevization of the world and therewith a victory of Jewry, but on the contrary, the destruction of the Jewish race in Europe.[9]

At the time, emigration was still the favored policy. Once the war began in September 1939, the so-called Jewish problem took on new dimensions. For a while there was discussion of the Madagascar Plan, which

▼ **Tito and the Partisan Resistance.** The brutality of German occupation forces quickly led to the emergence of resistance movements in Nazi-occupied Europe. In some places, resistance movements grew strong enough to challenge the Germans to pitched battles. Tito (foreground right), leader of the outlawed Communist party of Yugoslavia, was the leader of a band of partisans who waged guerrilla warfare against German occupation forces. When the odds turned against them, they retreated to hideouts in the rugged mountain areas of Yugoslavia.

aspired to the mass shipment of Jews to the African island of Madagascar. When war contingencies made this plan impractical, an even more drastic policy was conceived.

Heinrich Himmler and the SS organization closely shared Adolf Hitler's racial ideology. The SS was given responsibility for what the Nazis called their Final Solution to the Jewish problem, that is, the annihilation of the Jewish people. Reinhard Heydrich (1904–1942), head of the SS's Security Service, was given administrative responsibility for the Final Solution. After the defeat of Poland, Heydrich ordered the special strike forces (*Einsatzgruppen*) that he had created to round up all Polish Jews and concentrate them in ghettos established in a number of Polish cities.

In June 1941, the *Einsatzgruppen* were given new responsibilities as mobile killing units. These SS death squads followed the regular army's advance into Russia. Their job was to round up Jews in their villages and execute and bury them in mass graves, often giant pits dug by the victims themselves before they were shot. The leader of one these death squads described the mode of operation:

> The unit selected for this task would enter a village or city and order the prominent Jewish citizens to call together all

▼ **The Holocaust: The Extermination Camp at Auschwitz.**
After his initial successes in the east, Hitler set in motion the machinery for the physical annihilation of Europe's Jewish people. Shown here is the arrival at Auschwitz, a major extermination camp, of yet another shipment of Jews. In the background are the chimneys of the crematoria. This photograph was made by a SS guard in 1944.

Jews for the purpose of resettlement. They were requested to hand over their valuables to the leaders of the unit, and shortly before the execution to surrender their outer clothing. The men, women, and children were led to a place of execution which in most cases was located next to a more deeply excavated anti-tank ditch. Then they were shot, kneeling or standing, and the corpses thrown into the ditch.[10]

Such regular killing created morale problems among the SS executioners. During a visit to Minsk in the Soviet Union, SS leader Himmler tried to build morale by pointing out that: "He would not like it if Germans did such a thing gladly. But their conscience was in no way impaired, for they were soldiers who had to carry out every order unconditionally. He alone had responsibility before God and Hitler for everything that was happening, . . . and he was acting from a deep understanding of the necessity for this operation."[11]

Although it has been estimated that as many as one million Jews were killed by the *Einsatzgruppen*, this approach to solving the Jewish problem was soon perceived as inadequate. Instead, the Nazis opted for the systematic annihilation of the European Jewish population in specially built death camps. The plan was basically simple. Jews from countries occupied by Germany (or sympathetic to Germany) would be rounded up, packed like cattle into freight trains, and shipped to Poland, where six extermination centers were built for this purpose. The largest and most infamous was Auschwitz-Birkenau. Technical assistance for the construction of the camps was provided by experts from the T-4 program, which had been responsible for the extermination of 80,000 alleged racially unfit, mental and physical defectives in Germany between 1938 and 1941. Based on their experiences, medical technicians had chosen Zyklon B (the commercial name for hydrogen cyanide) as the most effective gas for quickly killing large numbers of people in gas chambers designed to look like shower rooms to facilitate the cooperation of the victims. After gassing, the corpses would be burned in specially built crematoria.

By the spring of 1942, the death camps were in operation. Although initial priority was given to the elimination of the ghettos in Poland, by the summer of 1942, Jews were also being shipped from France, Belgium, and Holland. In 1943, there were shipments of Jews from the capital cities of Berlin, Vienna, and Prague and from Greece, southern France, Italy, and Denmark. Even as the Allies were making important advances in 1944, Jews were being shipped from Greece and Hungary. These shipments depended on the cooperation of Ger-

The Holocaust: The Camp Commandant and the Camp Victims
▼ ▼ ▼

The systematic annihilation of millions of men, women, and children in extermination camps makes the Holocaust one of the most horrifying events in history. The first document is taken from an account by Rudolf Höss, commandant of the extermination camp at Auschwitz-Birkenau. In the second document, a French doctor explains what happened to the victims at one of the crematoria described by Höss.

Commandant Höss Describes the Equipment

The two large crematoria, Nos. I and II, were built during the winter of 1942–43. . . . They each . . . could cremate c. 2,000 corpses within twenty-four hours. . . . Crematoria I and II both had underground undressing and gassing rooms which could be completely ventilated. The corpses were brought up to the ovens on the floor above by lift. The gas chambers could hold c. 3,000 people.

The firm of Topf had calculated that the two smaller crematoria, III and IV, would each be able to cremate 1,500 corpses within twenty-four hours. However, owing to the wartime shortage of materials, the builders were obliged to economise and so the undressing rooms and gassing rooms were built above ground and the ovens were of a less solid construction. But it soon became apparent that the flimsy construction of these two four-retort ovens was not up to the demands made on it. No. III ceased operating altogether after a short time and later was no longer used. No. IV had to be repeatedly shut down since after a short period in operation of 4–6 weeks, the ovens and chimneys had burnt out. The victims of the gassing were mainly burnt in pits behind crematorium IV.

The largest number of people gassed and cremated within twenty-four hours was somewhat over 9,000.

A French Doctor Describes the Victims

It is mid-day, when a long line of women, children, and old people enter the yard. The senior official in charge . . . climbs on a bench to tell them that they are going to have a bath and that afterwards they will get a drink of hot coffee. They all undress in the yard. . . . The doors are opened and an indescribable jostling begins. The first people to enter the gas chamber begin to draw back. They sense the death which awaits them. The SS men put an end to this pushing and shoving with blows from their rifle butts beating the heads of the horrified women who are desperately hugging their children. The massive oak double doors are shut. For two endless minutes one can hear banging on the walls and screams which are no longer human. And then—not a sound. Five minutes later the doors are opened. The corpses, squashed together and distorted, fall out like a waterfall. . . . The bodies which are still warm pass through the hands of the hairdresser who cuts their hair and the dentist who pulls out their gold teeth . . . One more transport has just been processed through No. IV crematorium.

---

many's Transport Ministry, and despite desperate military needs, the Final Solution had priority in using railroad cars for the transportation of Jews to death camps. Even the military argument that Jews could be used to produce armaments was overridden by the demands of extermination.

A harrowing experience awaited the Jews when they arrived at one of the six death camps. Rudolf Höss, commandant at Auschwitz-Birkenau, described it:

> We had two SS doctors on duty at Auschwitz to examine the incoming transports of prisoners. The prisoners would be marched by one of the doctors who would make spot decisions as they walked by. Those who were fit for work were sent into the camp. Others were sent immediately to the extermination plants. Children of tender years were invariably exterminated since by reason of their youth they were unable to work. . . . at Auschwitz we endeavored to fool the victims into thinking that they were to go through a delousing process. Of course, frequently they realized our true intentions and we sometimes had riots and difficulties due to that fact.[12]

About 30 percent of the arrivals at Auschwitz were sent to a labor camp, while the remainder went to the gas chambers (see the box above). After they had been gassed, the bodies were burned in the crematoria. The victims' goods and even their bodies were used for economic gain. Female hair was cut off, collected, and turned into mattresses or cloth. Some inmates were also subjected to cruel and painful "medical" experiments. The Germans killed between 5 and 6 million Jews, over 3 million of them in the death camps. Virtually 90 percent of the Jewish populations of Poland, the Baltic countries, and Germany were exterminated. Overall, the Holocaust was responsible for the death of nearly two out of every three European Jews.

The Nazis were also responsible for another Holocaust, the death by shooting, starvation, or overwork of at least another 9 to 10 million people. Because the Nazis also considered the Gypsies of Europe (like the Jews) a race containing alien blood, they were systematically rounded up for extermination. About 40 percent of Europe's one million Gypsies were killed in the death camps. The leading elements of the "subhuman" Slavic peoples—the clergy, intelligentsia, civil leaders, judges, and lawyers—were arrested and deliberately killed. Probably an additional 4 million Poles, Ukrainians, and Belorussians lost their lives as slave laborers for Nazi Germany. Finally, probably at least 3–4 million Soviet prisoners of war were killed in captivity.

▼ The Home Front

World War II was even more of a total war than World War I. Fighting was much more widespread and covered most of the world. Economic mobilization was more extensive; so too was the mobilization of women. The number of civilians killed was far higher. Almost 20

million were killed from the strategic bombing of civilian populations, mass extermination policies, and reprisals by invading armies.

The Mobilization of Peoples: Four Examples

The home fronts of the major Western countries varied considerably, based on local circumstances. The British mobilized their resources more thoroughly than their allies or even Germany. By the summer of 1944, 55 percent of the British people were in the armed forces or civilian "war work." The British were especially determined to make use of women. Most women under forty years of age were called upon to do war work of some kind. By 1944, women held almost 50 percent of the civil service positions while the number of women in agriculture doubled as "Land Girls" performed agricultural labor usually undertaken by men.

The government encouraged a "Dig for Victory" campaign to increase food production. Fields normally reserved for athletic events were turned over to citizens to plant gardens in "Grow Your Own Food" campaigns. Even with 1.4 million garden allotments in 1943, Britain still faced a shortage of food as German submarines continued to sink hundreds of British merchant vessels. Food rationing, with its weekly allotments of bacon, sugar, fats, and eggs, intensified during the war as the British became accustomed to a diet dominated by bread and potatoes. For many British people, hours after work were spent in such wartime activities as "Dig for Vic-

▼ **Women in the Factories.** Although only the Soviet Union used women in combat positions, the number of women working in industry increased dramatically in most belligerent countries. British women, dressed in slacks for industrial work, are shown here building the barrage balloons that were used around British cities to defend them against air raid attacks.

tory," the Civil Defence, or Home Guard. The latter had been founded in 1940 to fight off German invaders. Even elderly people were expected to help manufacture airplane parts in their homes.

During the war, the British placed much emphasis on a planned economy. In 1942, the government created a ministry for fuel and power to control the coal industry and a ministry for production to oversee supplies for the armed forces. Although controls and bureaucratic "red tape" became unpopular, especially with businessmen, most British citizens seemed to accept that total war required unusual governmental dominance over people's lives. The British did make substantial gains in manufacturing war materials. Tank production quadrupled between 1940 and 1942. Production of aircraft grew from 8,000 in 1939 to 26,000 in 1943 and 1944, although there was considerable scandal over the inflation of the production figures by building such obsolescent planes as the Whitley bombers. Indeed, some historians have argued that British wartime success helped maintain antiquated enterprises and inefficient industrial practices, contributing to the decline of Britain after the war.

World War II had an enormous impact on the Soviet Union. Known to the Soviets as the Great Patriotic War, the German-Soviet war witnessed the greatest land campaign in history as well as incredible barbarism. To Nazi Germany, it was a war of enslavement and extermination that called for ruthless measures. Two out of every five persons killed in World War II were Soviet citizens.

The shift to a war footing required little administrative adjustment in the Soviet Union. As the central authority, the dictator Joseph Stalin simply created a system of "super-centralization," by which he directed military and political affairs. All civil and military organizations were subjected to the control of the Communist party and Soviet police.

The initial defeats of the Soviet Union led to drastic emergency mobilization measures that affected the civilian population. Leningrad, for example, experienced 900 days of siege, during which its inhabitants faced starvation. As the German army made its rapid advance into Soviet territory, the factories in the western part of the Soviet Union were dismantled and shipped to the interior—to the Urals, western Siberia, and the Volga region. Machines were placed on the bare ground, and walls went up around them as workers began their work. The Kharkov Tank Factory produced its first 25 T-34 tanks only ten weeks after the plant had been rebuilt.

This widespread military, industrial, and economic mobilization created yet another Industrial Revolution for the Soviet Union. Stalin labeled it a "battle of machines," and the Soviets won, producing 78,000 tanks and 98,000 artillery pieces. Fifty-five percent of Soviet national income went for war materials compared to 15 percent in 1940. As a result of the emphasis on military goods, Soviet citizens experienced incredible shortages of both food and housing. Civilian food consumption fell by 40 percent during the war while in the Volga area, the Urals, and Siberia, workers lived in dugouts or dilapidated barracks.

Soviet women played a major role in the war effort. Women and girls were enlisted for work in industries, mines, and railroads. Women constituted between 26 and 35 percent of the laborers in mines and 48 percent in the oil industry. Overall, the number of women working in industry increased almost 60 percent. Soviet women were also expected to dig antitank ditches and work as air-raid wardens. In addition, the Soviet Union was the only country in World War II to use women as combatants. Soviet women functioned as snipers and also as aircrews in bomber squadrons. The female pilots who helped to defeat the Germans at Stalingrad were known as the "Night Witches."

Soviet peasants were asked to bear enormous burdens. They supplied the manpower for 60 percent of the military forces. At the same time, the Soviet peasantry was expected to feed the Red Army and the general population under very difficult circumstances. The German occupation in the early months of the war resulted in the loss of 47 percent of the country's grain-producing regions. Because military needs overshadowed everything else, mechanized farm equipment such as tractors and trucks was requisitioned to carry guns. As a result, women and children were literally harnessed to do the plowing while peasants worked long hours on collective farms for no payment. Although new land was opened in the Urals, Siberia, and Soviet Asia, a shortage of labor hindered the effort to expand agricultural production. In 1943, the Soviet harvest was only 60 percent of its 1940 figure, which meant extreme hardship and poverty for the population. The small private farm plots of Soviet peasants were also subject to compulsory production for the state.

Total mobilization produced victory for the Soviet Union. Stalin and the Communist party had quickly realized after the start of the German invasion that the Soviet people would not fight for communist ideology, but would do battle to preserve "Mother Russia." Government propaganda played on patriotic feelings. In a speech in November 1941, on the anniversary of the Bolshevik Revolution, Stalin rallied the Soviet people by speaking of the country's past heroes, including the famous tsars of Imperial Russia.

The home front in the United States was quite different from those of its two chief wartime allies, largely because the United States faced no threat of war in its own territory. The American home front was disorderly, yet productive in the long run. Although the mobilization of the economy and labor force was slow to develop, eventually the United States became the arsenal of the Allied powers, producing the military equipment they needed. The mobilization of the United States also had a great impact on American social and economic developments.

The American economy was never fully mobilized. In 1941, industries were reluctant to convert to full-time war operations because they feared too much production would flood postwar markets and create another depression. Unemployment did not decrease significantly in the United States until mid-1943, a situation that affected the use of women in industrial jobs. Seventy-one percent of American women over eighteen years of age remained at home, in part due to male attitudes concerning women's traditional place in the home, but also because the services of women were not seriously needed. During the high point of war production in the United States in November 1943, the country was constructing six ships a day and $6 billion worth of war-related goods a month. Within a year many small factories were being shut down because of overproduction.

The mobilization of the American economy produced social problems. The construction of new factories created boom towns where thousands came to work but then faced a shortage of houses, health facilities, and schools. The dramatic expansion of small towns into large cities often brought a breakdown in traditional social mores, especially evident in the growth of teenage prostitution. Economic mobilization also led to considerable internal migration. Sixteen million men and women became members of the armed services, while another 16 million moved around the country. The latter were either wives and sweethearts of servicemen or workers looking for jobs. One million blacks from rural areas in the south, for example, went to urban areas in the north and northwest, especially the Pacific Coast. One social by-product of internal migration was an increase in racial tensions. The migration of blacks brought them to areas where they had not been present before. The one million blacks who joined the armed services, only to be segregated into their own battle units, became deeply resentful. At the same time, the blacks who found industrial jobs were often given the lowest paid, menial tasks.

Japanese-Americans were treated even more shabbily. On the West Coast, 110,000 Japanese-Americans, 65 percent of whom had been born in the United States, were removed to camps encircled by barbed wire and made to take loyalty oaths. Although public officials claimed this policy was necessary for security reasons, no similar treatment of German-Americans or Italian-Americans ever took place. The racism inherent in this treatment of Japanese-Americans was evident when the California governor, Culbert Olson, said: "You know, when I look out at a group of Americans of German or Italian descent, I can tell whether they're loyal or not. I can tell how they think and even perhaps what they are thinking. But it is impossible for me to do this with inscrutable orientals, and particularly the Japanese."[13]

In August 1914, Germans had enthusiastically cheered their soldiers marching off to war. In September 1939, the streets were quiet. Many Germans were apathetic or, even worse for the Nazi regime, had a foreboding of disaster. Hitler was very aware of the importance of the home front. He believed that the collapse of the home front in World War I had caused Germany's defeat, and in his determination to avoid a repetition of that experience, he adopted economic policies that may indeed have cost Germany the war.

To maintain the morale of the home front during the first two years of the war, Hitler refused to cut consumer goods production or increase the production of armaments. *Blitzkrieg* allowed the Germans to win quick victories, after which they could plunder the food and raw materials of conquered countries in order to avoid diverting resources away from the civilian economy. After German defeats on the Russian front and the American entry into the war, the economic situation changed. Early in 1942, Hitler finally ordered a massive increase in armaments production and the size of the army. Hitler's personal architect, Albert Speer, was made minister for armaments and munitions in 1942. By eliminating waste and rationalizing procedures, Speer was able to triple the production of armaments between 1942 and 1943 despite the intense Allied air raids. Speer's urgent plea for a total mobilization of resources for the war effort went unheeded, however. Hitler, fearful of civilian morale problems that would undermine the home front, refused any dramatic cuts in the production of consumer goods. A total mobilization of the economy was not implemented until 1944, when schools, theaters, and

The Bombing of Civilians
▼ ▼ ▼

The home front became a battlefront when civilian populations became the targets of mass bombing raids. Many people believed that mass bombing could effectively weaken the morale of the people and shorten the war. Rarely did it achieve its goal. In these selections, British, German, and Japanese civilians relate their experiences during bombing raids.

London, 1940

Early last evening, the noise was terrible. My husband and Mr. P. were trying to play chess in the kitchen. I was playing draughts with Kenneth in the cupboard. . . . Presently I heard a stifled voice "Mummy! I don't know what's become of my glasses." "I should think they are tied up in my wool." My knitting had disappeared and wool seemed to be everywhere! We heard a whistle, a bang which shook the house, and an explosion. . . . Well, we straightened out, decided draughts and chess were no use under the circumstances, and waited for a lull so we could have a pot of tea.

Hamburg, 1943

As the many fires broke through the roofs of the burning buildings, a column of heated air rose more than two and a half miles high and one and a half miles in diameter. . . . This column was turbulent, and it was fed from its base by in-rushing cooler ground-surface air. One and one and half miles from the fires this draught increased the wind velocity from eleven to thirty-three miles per hour. At the edge of the area the velocities must have been appreciably greater, as trees three feet in diameter were uprooted. In a short time the temperature reached ignition point for all combustibles, and the entire area was ablaze. In such fires complete burn-out occurred; that is, no trace of combustible material remained, and only after two days were the areas cool enough to approach.

Hiroshima, August 6, 1945

I heard the airplane; I looked up at the sky, it was a sunny day, the sky was blue. . . . Then I saw something drop—and pow!—a big explosion knocked me down. Then I was unconscious—I don't know for how long. Then I was conscious but I couldn't see anything. . . . Then I see people moving away and I just follow them. It is not light like it was before, it is more like evening. I look around; houses are all flat! . . . I follow the people to the river. I couldn't hear anything, my ears are blocked up. I am thinking—a bomb has dropped! . . . I didn't know my hands were burned, nor my face. . . . My eyes were swollen and felt closed up.

---

cafes were closed and Speer was finally permitted to use all remaining resources for the production of a few basic military items. By that time, it was in vain. Total war mobilization was too little and too late in July 1944 to save Germany from defeat.

The war produced a reversal in Nazi attitudes toward women. Nazi resistance to female employment declined as the war progressed and more and more men were called up for military service. Nazi magazines now proclaimed: "We see the woman as the eternal mother of our people, but also as the working and fighting comrade of the man."[14] But the number of women working in industry, agriculture, commerce, and domestic service increased only slightly. The total number of employed women in September 1944 was 14.9 million compared to 14.6 in May 1939. Many women, especially those of the middle class, resisted regular employment, particularly in factories. Even the introduction of labor conscription for women in January 1943 failed to achieve much as women found ingenious ways to avoid the regulations.

The Frontline Civilians: The Bombing of Cities

Bombing was used in World War II in a variety of ways: against nonhuman military targets; against enemy troops, in conjunction with land forces; and indiscriminately against civilian populations. The latter made World War II as devastating for civilians as for frontline soldiers (see the box above). A small number of bombing raids in the last year of World War I had given rise to the argument, crystallized in 1930 by the Italian general Giulio Douhet, that the public outcry created by the bombing of civilian populations would be an effective way to coerce governments into making peace. Consequently, European air forces began to develop long-range bombers in the 1930s.

The first sustained use of civilian bombing contradicted Douhet's theory. Beginning in early September 1940, the German *Luftwaffe* subjected London and many other British cities and towns to nightly air raids, making the Blitz (as the British called the German air raids) a national experience. Londoners took the first heavy blows, and it was their maintenance of morale that set the standard for the rest of the British population. One British woman expressed well what many others apparently felt:

> It was a beautiful summer night, so warm it was incredible, and made more beautiful than ever by the red glow from the East, where the docks were burning. We stood and stared for a minute, and I tried to fix the scene in my mind, because one day this will be history, and I shall be one of those who actually saw it. I wasn't frightened any more.[15]

But London morale was helped by the fact that German raids were widely dispersed over a very large city. Smaller communities were more directly affected by the devastation. On November 14, 1940, for example, the *Luftwaffe* destroyed hundreds of shops and a hundred acres of the city center of Coventry. The destruction of smaller cities did produce morale problems as wild rumors of social collapse spread quickly in these communities. Nevertheless, morale was soon restored. War production in these areas, in any case, seems to have been little affected by the raids.

The British failed to learn from their own experience, however, and soon proceeded with the bombing of Germany. Churchill and his advisers believed that destroying German communities would break civilian morale and bring victory. Major bombing raids began in 1942 under the direction of Arthur Harris, the wartime leader of the British air force's Bomber Command, which was rearmed with four-engine heavy bombers capable of taking the war into the center of occupied Europe. On May 31, 1942, Cologne became the first German city to be subjected to an attack by a thousand bombers.

The entry of the Americans into the war produced a new bombing strategy. American planes flew daytime missions aimed at the precision bombing of transportation facilities and war industries, while the British Bomber Command continued nighttime saturation bombing of all German cities with populations over 100,000. Bombing raids added an element of terror to circumstances already made difficult by growing shortages of food, clothing, and fuel. Germans especially feared the incendiary bombs that created firestorms that swept destructive paths through the cities. Four raids on Hamburg in August 1943 produced temperatures of 1,800 degrees Fahrenheit, obliterated half the city's

▼ **Total War: The Destruction of Cologne.** In the 1930s, a number of military theorists had argued that the bombing of civilian populations might be an effective way to coerce nations into making peace. In the course of World War II, Allied bombing raids on German targets became a daily occurrence. Many German cities, as this photograph of Cologne demonstrates, were left in ruins.

buildings, and killed 50,000 civilians. The ferocious bombing of Dresden from February 13 to 15, 1945, created a firestorm that may have killed as many as 100,000 inhabitants and refugees. Even some Allied leaders began to criticize what they saw as the unnecessary terror bombing of German cities. Urban dwellers become accustomed to living in air-raid shelters, usually cellars in businesses or houses. Occupants of shelters could be crushed to death if the shelters were hit directly or die by suffocation from the effects of high-explosive bombs. Not until 1943 did Nazi leaders begin to evacuate women and children to rural areas. This evacuation policy, however, created its own problems since people in country villages were often hostile to the urban newcomers.

Germany suffered enormously from the Allied bombing raids. Millions of buildings were destroyed, and possibly half a million civilians died from the raids. Nevertheless, it is highly unlikely that Allied bombing sapped the morale of the German people. Instead, Germans, whether pro-Nazi or anti-Nazi, fought on stubbornly, often driven simply by a desire to live. Nor did the bombing destroy Germany's industrial capacity. The Allied Strategic Bombing survey revealed that the production of war materials actually increased between 1942 and 1944. Even in 1944 and 1945, Allied raids cut German production of armaments by only 7 percent. Nevertheless, the widespread destruction of transportation systems and fuel supplies made it extremely difficult for the new materials to reach the German military. The destruction of German cities from the air did accomplish one major goal. There would be no stab-in-the-back myth after World War II as there had been after World War I. The loss of the war could not be blamed on the collapse of the home front. Many Germans understood that the home front had been a battlefront, and they had lost on their front just as the soldiers had on theirs.

In Japan, the bombing of civilians reached a new level with the use of the first atomic bomb. Japan was especially vulnerable to air raids because its air force had been virtually destroyed in the course of the war, and its crowded cities were built of flimsy materials. Attacks on Japanese cities by the new American B-29 Superfortresses, the biggest bombers of the war, had begun on November 24, 1944. By the summer of 1945, many of Japan's industries had been destroyed along with one-fourth of its dwellings. After the Japanese government decreed the mobilization of all people between the ages of thirteen and sixty into a People's Volunteer Corps, President Truman and his advisers decided that Japanese fanaticism might mean a million American casualties.

▼ **Hiroshima.** The most devastating destruction of civilians came near the end of World War II when the United States dropped atomic bombs on the Japanese cities of Hiroshima and Nagasaki. This general panoramic view of Hiroshima after the bombing shows the incredible devastation produced by the atomic bomb.

This was the official reason for Truman's decision to drop the atomic bomb on Hiroshima and Nagasaki. The destruction was incredible. Of 76,000 buildings near the hypocenter of the explosion in Hiroshima, 70,000 were flattened, while 140,000 of the city's 400,000 inhabitants died by the end of 1945. By the end of 1950, another 50,000 had perished from the effects of radiation.

▼ The Aftermath of the War: The Emergence of the Cold War

The total victory of the Allies in World War II was not followed by a real peace, but by the beginnings of a new conflict known as the Cold War that dominated European and world politics until the end of the 1980s. The origins of the Cold War stemmed from the military, political, and ideological differences, especially between the Soviet Union and the United States, that became apparent at the Allied war conferences held in the last years of the war. Although Allied leaders were mostly preoccupied with how to end the war, they also were strongly motivated by differing, and often conflicting, visions of postwar Europe.

The Conferences at Teheran, Yalta, and Potsdam

Stalin, Roosevelt, and Churchill, the leaders of the Big Three of the Grand Alliance, met at Teheran (the capital of Iran) in November 1943 to decide the future course of the war. Their major tactical decision concerned the final assault on Germany. Churchill had wanted British and American forces to follow up their north African and Italian campaigns by an indirect attack on Germany through the Balkans. Although an extremely difficult route, this would give the Western Allies a better position in postwar central Europe. Stalin and Roosevelt, however, overruled Churchill and argued successfully for an American-British invasion of the Continent through France, which they scheduled for the spring of 1944. The acceptance of this plan had important consequences. It meant that Soviet and British-American forces would meet in defeated Germany along a north-south dividing line and that, most likely, Eastern Europe would be liberated by Soviet forces. The Allies also agreed to a partition of postwar Germany until denazification could take place, but differences over questions like the frontiers of Poland were carefully set aside. Roosevelt was pleased with the accord with Stalin. Harry Hopkins, one of Roosevelt's advisers at the conference, remarked:

> We really believed in our hearts that this was the dawn of the new day. . . . We were absolutely certain that we had won the first great victory of the peace—and by "we," I mean *all* of us, the whole civilized human race. The Russians had proved that they could be reasonable and farseeing and there wasn't any doubt in the minds of the President or any of us that we could live with them and get along with them peacefully for as far into the future as any of us could imagine.[16]

Winston Churchill was more cautious about future relations with the Soviets. Although overruled at the Teheran Conference, in October of 1944, Churchill met with Stalin in Moscow and was able to pin him down to a more specific determination of postwar spheres of influence. The agreement between Churchill and Stalin, written on a scrap of paper, assigned the various Allies a certain percentage of political influence in a given area on the basis of past historical roles. The Soviet Union received 90 percent influence in Romania and Bulgaria, while Britain obtained 90 percent influence in Greece. Eastern European countries that had a strong tradition of Western ties, such as Yugoslavia and Hungary, were divided "fifty-fifty." Churchill perceived how callous this division of sovereign countries might seem from a distance. He remarked to Stalin, "Might it not be thought rather cynical if it seemed we had disposed of these issues, so fateful to millions of people, in such an offhand manner? Let us burn the paper." Stalin, not worrying what others might think, simply replied, "No, you keep it."[17]

By the time of the conference at Yalta in southern Russia in February 1945, the defeat of Germany was a

▼ **The Victorious Allied Leaders at Yalta.** Even before World War II ended, the leaders of the Big Three of the Grand Alliance, Churchill, Roosevelt, and Stalin (shown from left to right), met in wartime conferences to plan the final assault on Germany and negotiate the outlines of the postwar settlement. At the Yalta meeting (February 5–11, 1945), the three leaders concentrated on postwar issues. The American president, who died two months later, was already a worn-out man at Yalta.

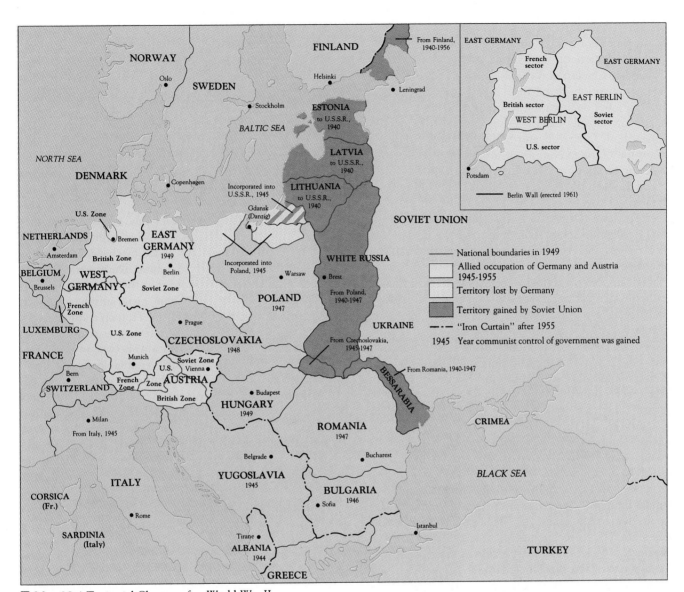

▼ **Map 28.4** Territorial Changes after World War II.

foregone conclusion. The Western powers, which had earlier believed that the Soviets were in a weak position, were now faced with the reality of 11 million Red Army soldiers taking possession of eastern and much of central Europe. Stalin was still operating under the notion of spheres of influence. He was deeply suspicious of the Western powers and desired a buffer to protect the Soviet Union from possible future Western aggression. At the same time, however, Stalin was eager to obtain economically important resources and strategic military positions. Roosevelt by this time was moving away from the notion of spheres of influence to the more Wilsonian ideal of self-determination. He called for "the end of the

system of unilateral action, exclusive alliances, and spheres of influence." The Grand Alliance approved a "Declaration on Liberated Europe." This was a pledge to assist liberated European nations in the creation of "democratic institutions of their own choice." Liberated countries were to hold free elections to determine their political systems.

At Yalta, Roosevelt sought Russian military help against Japan. The atomic bomb was not yet assured, and American military planners feared the possible loss of as many as one million men in amphibious assaults on the Japanese home islands. Roosevelt therefore agreed to Stalin's price for military assistance against Japan: possession of Sakhalin and the Kuril Islands as well as two warm water ports and railroad rights in Manchuria.

The creation of the United Nations was a major American concern at Yalta. Roosevelt hoped to ensure the participation of the Big Three powers in a postwar international organization before difficult issues divided them into hostile camps. After a number of compromises, both Churchill and Stalin accepted Roosevelt's plans for a United Nations organization and set the first meeting for San Francisco in April of 1945.

The issues of Germany and Eastern Europe were treated less decisively. The Big Three reaffirmed that Germany must surrender unconditionally and created four occupation zones. Churchill, over the objections of the Soviets and Americans, insisted that the French be given one occupation zone, carved out of the British and American zones. German reparations were set at $20 billion. A compromise was also worked out in regard to Poland. It was agreed that a provisional government would be established with members of both the Lublin Poles, who were Polish Communists living in exile in the Soviet Union, and the London Poles, who were non-Communists exiled in Britain. Stalin also agreed to free elections in the future to determine a new government. But the issue of free elections in Eastern Europe caused a serious rift between the Soviets and the Americans. The principle was that Eastern European governments would be freely elected, but they were also supposed to be pro-Soviet. As Churchill expressed it: "The Poles will have their future in their owns hands, with the single limitation that they must honestly follow in harmony with their allies, a policy friendly to Russia."[18] This attempt to reconcile two irreconcilable goals was doomed to failure, as soon became evident at the next conference of the Big Three powers.

Even before the conference at Potsdam took place in July 1945, Western relations with the Soviets were deteriorating rapidly. The Grand Alliance had been one of necessity in which ideological incompatibility had been subordinated to the pragmatic concerns of the war. The Allied powers' only common aim was the defeat of Nazism. Once this aim had all but been accomplished, the many differences that antagonized East-West relations came to the surface. Each side committed acts that the other viewed as unbecoming of "allies."

From the perspective of the Soviets, the United States' termination of Lend-Lease aid before the war was over and its failure to respond to the Soviet request for a $6 billion loan for reconstruction exposed the Western desire to keep the Soviet state weak. On the American side, the Soviet Union's failure to fulfill its Yalta pledge on the "Declaration on Liberated Europe" as applied to Eastern Europe set a dangerous precedent. This was evident in Romania as early as February 1945, when the Soviets engineered a coup, ousting the Radescu government and replacing it with the government of Petra Groza, called the "Little Stalin." One month later, the Soviets sabotaged the Polish settlement by arresting the London Poles and their sympathizers and placing the Soviet-backed Lublin Poles in power. To the Americans, the Russians seemed to be asserting control of Eastern European countries under puppet communist regimes.

The Potsdam Conference of July 1945 consequently began under a cloud of mistrust. Roosevelt had died on April 12 and had been succeeded by the somewhat less flexible president, Harry Truman. During the conference, Truman received word that the atomic bomb had been successfully tested. Some historians have argued that this knowledge resulted in Truman's stiffened resolve against the Soviets. Whatever the reasons, there was a new coldness in the relations between the Soviets and Americans. At Potsdam, Truman demanded free elections throughout Eastern Europe. Stalin responded: "A freely elected government in any of these East European countries would be anti-Soviet, and that we cannot allow."[19] After a bitterly fought and devastating war, Stalin sought absolute military security. To him, it could only be gained by the presence of communist states in Eastern Europe. Free elections might result in governments hostile to the Soviets. By the middle of 1945, only an invasion by Western forces could undo developments in Eastern Europe, and after the world's most destructive conflict had ended, few people favored such a policy.

The Soviets did not view their actions as dangerous expansionism but as legitimate security maneuvers. Was it not the West that had attacked the East? When Stalin sought help against the Nazis in the 1930s, had not the West turned a deaf ear? But there was little sympathy from the West for Soviet fears and even less trust in Stalin. When the American secretary of state James Byrnes proposed a twenty-five year disarmament of Germany, the Soviet Union rejected it. In the West, many saw this as proof of Stalin's plans to expand in central Europe and create a communist East German state. When Byrnes responded by announcing that American troops would be needed in Europe for an indefinite time and made moves that foreshadowed the creation of an independent West Germany, the Soviets saw this as a direct threat to Soviet security in Europe.

As the war slowly receded into the past, the reality of conflicting ideologies had reappeared. Many in the West

Emergence of the Cold War: Churchill and Stalin

▼▼▼

Less than a year after the end of World War II, the major Allies that had fought together to destroy Hitler's Germany had divided into two hostile camps. These excerpts, taken from Winston Churchill's speech to an American audience on March 5, 1946, and Joseph Stalin's reply to Churchill only nine days later, reveal the divisions in the Western world that marked the beginning of the Cold War.

Churchill's Speech at Fulton, Missouri, March 5, 1946

From Stettin in the Baltic to Trieste in the Adriatic, an iron curtain has descended across the continent. Behind that line lie all the capitals of the ancient states of central and eastern Europe. Warsaw, Berlin, Prague, Vienna, Budapest, Belgrade, Bucharest, and Sofia, all these famous cities and the populations around them lie in the Soviet sphere and all are subject, in one form or another, not only to Soviet influence but to a very high and increasing measure of control from Moscow. . . .

The Russian-dominated Polish Government has been encouraged to make enormous and wrongful inroads upon Germany, and mass expulsions of millions of Germans on a scale grievous and undreamed of are now taking place. The Communist parties, which were very small in all these eastern states of Europe, have been raised to preeminence and power far beyond their numbers and are seeking everywhere to obtain totalitarian control. Police governments are prevailing in nearly every case, and so far, except in Czechoslovakia, there is no true democracy. . . . Whatever conclusions may be drawn from these facts—and facts they are—this is certainly not the liberated Europe we fought to build up. Nor is it one which contains the essentials of permanent peace.

Stalin's Reply to Churchill, March 14, 1946

In substance, Mr. Churchill now stands in the position of a firebrand of war. And Mr. Churchill is not alone here. He has friends not only in England but also in the United States of America.

In this respect, one is reminded remarkably of Hitler and his friends. Hitler began to set war loose by announcing his racial theory, declaring that only people speaking the German language represent a fully valuable nation. Mr. Churchill begins to set war loose, also by a racial theory, maintaining that only nations speaking the English language are fully valuable nations, called upon to decide the destinies of the entire world.

The German racial theory brought Hitler and his friends to the conclusion that the Germans, as the only fully valuable nation, must rule over other nations. The English racial theory brings Mr. Churchill and his friends to the conclusion that nations speaking the English language, being the only fully valuable nations, should rule over the remaining nations of the world.

---

interpreted Soviet policy as part of a worldwide communist conspiracy. The Soviets, on the other hand, viewed Western, especially American, policy as nothing less than global capitalist expansionism or, in Leninist terms, as nothing less than economic imperialism. Molotov, the Russian foreign minister, referred to the Americans as "insatiable imperialists" and "war-mongering groups of adventurers."[20] In March 1946, in a speech to an American audience, the former British prime minister, Winston Churchill, declared that "an iron curtain" had "descended across the continent," dividing Germany and Europe into two hostile camps. Stalin branded Churchill's speech a "call to war with the Soviet Union" (see the box above). Only months after the world's most devastating conflict had ended, the world seemed once again bitterly divided. Would the twentieth-century crisis of Western civilization never end?

Between 1933 and 1939, Europeans watched as Adolf Hitler rebuilt Germany into a great military power. For Hitler, military power was an absolute prerequisite for the creation of a German racial empire that would dominate Europe and the world for generations to come. If Hitler had been successful, the Nazi New Order, built upon authoritarianism, racial extermination, and the brutal oppression of peoples, would have meant a triumph of barbarism and the end of freedom and equality, which, however imperfectly realized, had become important ideals in Western civilization.

The Nazis lost, but only after tremendous sacrifices and costs. Much of European civilization lay in ruins. Europeans, who had been accustomed to dominating the world at the beginning of the twentieth century, now watched helplessly at mid-century as the two new superpowers created by their two world wars took control of their destinies. Even before the last battles had been fought, the United States and the Soviet Union had arrived at different visions of the postwar European world. No sooner had the war ended than their differences created a new and potentially even more devastating conflict known as the Cold War. Yet even though Europeans seemed merely pawns in the struggle between the two superpowers, they managed to stage a remarkable recovery of their own civilization.

Notes
▼ ▼ ▼

1. Adolf Hitler, *Mein Kampf,* trans. Ralph Manheim (Boston, 1971), p. 654.

2. *Documents on German Foreign Policy* (London, 1956), Series D, 2: 358.

3. Ibid., 7: 204.

4. Quoted in Norman Rich, *Hitler's War Aims* (New York, 1973), 1: 129.

5. Albert Speer, *Spandau,* trans. Richard and Clara Winston (New York, 1976), p. 50.

6. *Nazi Conspiracy and Aggression* (Washington, D.C., 1946), 6: 262.

7. International Military Tribunal, *Trial of the Major War Criminals* (Nuremberg, 1947–49), 22: 480.

8. Adolf Hitler, *My New Order,* ed. Raoul de Roussy de Sales (New York, 1941), pp. 21–22.

9. Quoted in Lucy Dawidowicz, *The War against the Jews* (New York, 1975), p. 106.

10. *Nazi Conspiracy and Aggression,* 5: 341–42.

11. Quoted in Raul Hilberg, *The Destruction of the European Jews,* rev. ed. (New York, 1985), 1: 332–33.

12. *Nazi Conspiracy and Aggression,* 6: 789.

13. Quoted in John Campbell, *The Experience of World War II* (New York, 1989), p. 170.

14. Quoted in Claudia Koonz, "Mothers in the Fatherland: Women in Nazi Germany," in Renate Bridenthal and Claudia Koonz, eds., *Becoming Visible: Women in European History* (Boston, 1977), p. 466.

15. Quoted in Campbell, *The Experience of World War II,* p. 177.

16. Quoted in Robert E. Sherwood, *Roosevelt and Hopkins: An Intimate History* (New York, 1948), p. 870.

17. Quoted in Walter Laqueur, *Europe since Hitler,* rev. ed. (New York, 1982), p. 102.

18. Quoted in Norman Graebner, *Cold War Diplomacy, 1945–1960* (Princeton, N.J., 1962), p. 117.

19. Quoted in ibid.

20. Quoted in Wilfried Loth, *The Division of the World, 1941–1955* (New York, 1988), p. 81.

Suggestions for Further Reading
▼ ▼ ▼

The basic study of Germany's foreign policy from 1933 to 1939 can be found in G. Weinberg, *The Foreign Policy of Hitler's Germany: Diplomatic Revolution in Europe, 1933–36* (Chicago, 1970) and *The Foreign Policy of Hitler's Germany: Starting World War II, 1937–1939* (Chicago, 1980). Additional works on foreign policy include W. Carr, *Arms, Autarchy and Aggression: A Study in German Foreign Policy, 1933–1939* (New York, 1973); and K. Hildebrandt, *The Foreign Policy of the Third Reich,* trans. A. Fothergill (London, 1973). The ideological background of Nazi imperialism is examined in W. Smith, *The Ideological Origins of Nazi Imperialism* (New York, 1986). For a detailed account of the immediate events leading to World War II, see D. C. Watt, *How War Came: The Immediate Origins of the Second World War 1938–1939* (New York, 1989).

Hitler's war aims and the importance of ideology to those aims are examined in N. Rich, *Hitler's War Aims,* vol. 1, *Ideology, the Nazi State and the Course of Expansion* (New York, 1973), and vol. 2, *The Establishment of the New Order* (New York, 1974). General works on World War II include M. K. Dziewanowski, *War at Any Price: World War II in Europe, 1939–1945* (Englewood Cliffs, N.J., 1987); P. Calvocoressi and G. Wint, *Total War: Causes and Courses of the Second World War* (New York, 1979); J. Campbell, *The Experience of World War II* (New York, 1989); and E. Mandel, *The Meaning of the Second World War* (London, 1986). On Hitler as a military leader, see R. Lewin, *Hitler's Mistakes* (New York, 1986). The Eastern Front is covered in J. Erickson, *Stalin's War with Germany*, vol. 1, *The Road to Stalingrad;* vol. 2, *The Road to Berlin* (London, 1973, 1985); A. Seaton, *The Russo-German War, 1941–45* (London, 1971); and O. Bartov, *The Eastern Front, 1941–45: German Troops and the Barbarisation of Warfare* (London, 1986). On the war in Italy, see J. Strawson, *The Italian Campaign* (London, 1987). The second front in Europe is examined in C. D'Este, *Decision in Normandy* (London, 1983). See also S. E. Ambrose, *Eisenhower: The Solider* (London, 1984). On the war at sea, see D. MacIntyre, *Battle of the Atlantic, 1939–1945* (London, 1970).

A standard work on the German New Order in Russia is A. Dallin, *German Rule in Russia, 1941–1945*, rev. ed. (London, 1981). On Poland, see J. T. Gross, *Polish Society under German Occupation* (Princeton, N. J., 1981). On foreign labor, see E. Homze, *Foreign Labor in Nazi Germany* (Princeton, N.J., 1967). Resistance movements in Europe are covered in M. R. D. Foot, *Resistance: An Analysis of European Resistance to Nazism* (London, 1976). A fundamental study on resistance in Germany is P. Hoffmann, *The History of the German Resistance, 1933–1945*, trans. R. Barry (Cambridge, Mass., 1977). On the White Rose, see A. E. Dumbach and J. Newborn, *Shattering the German Night: The Story of the White Rose* (Boston, 1986).

The best studies of the Holocaust include R. Hilberg, *The Destruction of the European Jews*, rev. ed., 3 vols. (New York, 1985); L. Dawidowicz, *The War against the Jews* (New York, 1975); and M. Gilbert, *The Holocaust: The History of the Jews of Europe during the Second World War* (New York, 1985). There is a good overview of the scholarship on the Holocaust in M. Marrus, *The Holocaust in History* (New York, 1987). The role of Hitler in the Holocaust has been well examined in G. Fleming, *Hitler and the Final Solution* (Berkeley, 1984). On the extermination camps, see K. G. Feig, *Hitler's Death Camps: The Sanity of Madness* (New York, 1981). On the problem of what the Allied countries knew about the Holocaust, see D. Wyman, *The Abandonment of the Jews: America and the Holocaust* (New York, 1984); W. Laqueur, *The Terrible Secret* (Boston, 1980); and M. Gilbert, *Auschwitz and the Allies* (New York, 1981). The other holocaust is examined in R. C. Lukas, *Forgotten Holocaust: The Poles under German Occupation, 1939–44* (Lexington, Ky., 1986); and B. Wytwycky, *The Other Holocaust* (Washington, D.C., 1980).

General studies on the impact of total war include J. Costello, *Love, Sex and War: Changing Values, 1939–1945* (London, 1985); A. Marwick, *War and Social Change in the Twentieth Century: A Comparative Study of Britain, France, Germany, Russia and the United States* (London, 1974); A. S. Milward, *War, Economy and Society, 1939–1945* (London, 1977); and M. R. Marrus, *The Unwanted: European Refugees in the Twentieth Century* (New York, 1985). On the home front in Germany, see E. R. Beck, *Under the Bombs: The German Home Front, 1942–1945* (Lexington, Ky., 1986); M. G. Steinert, *Hitler's War and the Germans* (Athens, Ohio, 1977); I. Kershaw, *The "Hitler Myth": Image and Reality in the Third Reich* (Oxford, 1987); J. Stephenson, *The Nazi Organisation of Women* (London, 1981); and L. J. Rupp, *Mobilizing Women for War: German and American Propaganda, 1939–1945* (Princeton, N.J., 1978). On the home front in Britain, see A. Marwick, *The Home Front* (London, 1976). The Soviet Union during the war is examined in M. Harrison, *Soviet Planning in Peace and War, 1938–1945* (Cambridge, 1985). On the American home front, see G. Perrett, *Days of Sadness, Years of Triumph: The American People, 1939–1945* (New York, 1973).

On the destruction of Germany by bombing raids, see H. Rumpf, *The Bombing of Germany* (London, 1963). The German bombing of Britain is covered in T. Harrisson, *Living through the Blitz* (London, 1985). On Hiroshima, see A. Chisholm, *Faces of Hiroshima* (London, 1985).

On the emergence of the Cold War, see W. Loth, *The Division of the World, 1941–1955* (New York, 1988), and the more extensive list of references at the end of Chapter 29. On the wartime summit conferences, see H. Feis, *Churchill, Roosevelt, Stalin: The War They Waged and the Peace They Sought*, 2d ed. (Princeton, N.J., 1967); and D. Clemens, *Yalta* (New York, 1970). The impact of the atomic bomb on Truman's relationship to Stalin is discussed in M. Sherwin, *A World Destroyed: The Atomic Bomb and the Grand Alliance* (New York, 1975).

In 1945, Europe lay in ruins. Some Europeans questioned whether Europe had the will to regain its former prosperity and importance. Winston Churchill wrote: "What is Europe now? A rubble heap, a charnel house, a breeding ground of pestilence and hate."[1] There was ample justification for his pessimism. Almost 40 million people (both soldiers and civilians) had been killed over the last six years. All across Europe, great cities had been reduced to rubble. Millions of Europeans faced starvation as grain harvests were only 50 percent of what they had been in 1939. Transportation systems were paralyzed. In Germany alone, 50 percent of the railroad tracks were not usable. Untold millions of people had been displaced by the war. Eleven million prisoners of war had to be repatriated while fif-

teen million Germans and East Europeans were driven out of countries where they were no longer wanted. Despite the chaos, however, Europe was soon on the road to a remarkable recovery. Already by 1948, Europe's industrial and agricultural output (except in Germany and Italy) had almost reached prewar levels.

World War II, however, had cost Europe more than physical destruction. European supremacy in world affairs had also been destroyed. After 1945, the colonial empires of the European nations rapidly disintegrated while Europe's place in the world radically changed. As the Cold War conflict between the world's two superpowers—the United States and the Soviet Union—intensified, the European nations were divided into two armed camps dependent upon one or the other of these two major powers. The United

Creation of NATO

Creation of Warsaw Pact

Cuban Missile Crisis

Helsinki Agreements

Reunification of Germany

1950 • 1960 • 1970 • 1980 • 1990

De Beauvoir, *The Second Sex*

Beatles Come to America

Student Revolts

John Paul II Becomes Pope

Kiefer, *Departure from Egypt*

States and the Soviet Union, whose rivalry raised the specter of nuclear war, seemed to hold the survival of Europe and the world in their hands. As the danger of nuclear war reached its peak in the Cuban missile crisis in 1962, the immediate possibility of thermonuclear destruction opened the door to a search for compromise. By the end of the 1980s, this trend had accelerated sufficiently that many political observers were speaking of a post–Cold War world.

▼ From Cold War to Post–Cold War: International Relations since 1945

Even before World War II had ended, the two major Allied powers—the United States and the Soviet Union—had begun to disagree on the nature of the postwar European world. Unity had been maintained during the war because of the urgent need to defeat the Axis powers, but once they were defeated, the differences between American and Soviet institutions and ideologies again surged to the front. Stalin had never overcome his fear of capitalist superiority while Western leaders still had serious misgivings about communism.

The Development of the Cold War

There has been considerable historical debate about who was most responsible for the beginning of the Cold War. No doubt, both the United States and the Soviet Union took steps at the end of the war that were unwise or might have been avoided. Both nations, however, were working within a framework conditioned by the past. Ultimately, the rivalry between the two superpowers stemmed from their different historical perspectives and their irreconcilable political ambitions. Intense competition for political and military supremacy had

long been a regular feature of Western civilization. The United States and the Soviet Union were the heirs of that European tradition of power politics, and it should not surprise us that two such different systems would seek to extend their way of life to the rest of the world. Because of its need to feel secure on its western border, the Soviet Union was not prepared to give up the advantages it had gained in Eastern Europe from Germany's defeat. But neither were American leaders willing to give up the power and prestige the United States had gained throughout the world. Suspicious of each other's motives, the United States and Soviet Union soon raised their mutual fears to a level of intense competition. Between 1945 and 1949, a number of events seemed to entangle the two countries in continual conflict.

Eastern Europe was the first area of disagreement. The United States and Great Britain had championed self-determination and democratic freedom for the liberated nations of Eastern Europe. Stalin, however, fearful that the Eastern European nations would return to traditional anti-Soviet attitudes if they were permitted free elections, opposed the West's plans. Having liberated Eastern Europe from the Nazis, the Red Army proceeded to install pro-Soviet governing regimes in Poland, Romania, Bulgaria, and Hungary. Although these pro-Soviet governments ensured Stalin's desire for a buffer zone against the West, to the local populations and their sympathizers in the West, they meant an expansion of Stalin's empire. Only another war could change this situation, and few people advocated another armed conflict.

A civil war in Greece created another arena for confrontation between the superpowers. The Communist People's Liberation Army backed by the Soviet Union and the anticommunist forces supported by the British were fighting each other for control of Greece in 1946. But continued postwar economic problems caused the British to withdraw from the active role they had been playing in both Greece and Turkey. President Harry S. Truman of the United States, alarmed by British weak-

The Truman Doctrine

▼ ▼ ▼

B y 1947, the battlelines had been clearly drawn in the
Cold War. This selection is taken from a speech by
President Harry S. Truman to the American Congress in
which he justified his request for aid to Greece and Turkey.
Truman expressed the urgent need to contain the expan-
sion of communism.

President Harry S. Truman Addresses Congress, March 12, 1947

The peoples of a number of countries of the world
have recently had totalitarian regimes forced upon
them against their will. The Government of the
United States has made frequent protests against coercion and intimidation, in violation of the Yalta
agreement, in Poland, Rumania, and Bulgaria. I must
also state that in a number of other countries there
have been similar developments.

At the present moment in world history nearly
every nation must choose between alternative ways of
life. The choice is too often not a free one.

One way of life is based upon the will of the majority, and is distinguished by free institutions, representative government, free elections, guaranties of
individual liberty, freedom of speech and religion,
and freedom from political oppression.

The second way of life is based upon the will of a
minority forcibly imposed upon the majority. It relies
upon terror and oppression, a controlled press and
radio, fixed elections, and the suppression of personal
freedoms.

I believe that it must be the policy of the United
States to support free peoples who are resisting attempted subjugation by armed minorities or by outside pressures.

I believe that we must assist free people to work
out their own destinies in their own way.

I believe that our help should be primarily through
economic and financial aid which is essential to economic stability and orderly political processes. . . . I
therefore ask the Congress for assistance to Greece
and Turkey in the amount of $400,000,000.

---

ness and the possibility of Soviet expansion into the
eastern Mediterranean, responded with the Truman
Doctrine (see the box above). According to the president, "It must be the policy of the United States to
support free peoples who are resisting attempted subjugation by armed minorities or by outside pressures." This
statement was made to the American Congress in March
1947 when Truman requested $400 million in aid for the
defense of Greece and Turkey. If the Soviets were not
stopped in Greece, the Truman argument ran, then the
United States would have to face the spread of communism throughout the free world. As Dean Acheson, the
American secretary of state explained, "Like apples in a
barrel infected by disease, the corruption of Greece
would infect Iran and all the East . . . likewise Africa
. . . Italy . . . France. . . . Not since Rome and Carth-
age had there been such a polarization of power on this
earth."[2]

The proclamation of the Truman Doctrine was soon
followed in June 1947 by the European Recovery Program, better known as the Marshall Plan. Intended to
rebuild prosperity and stability, this program included
$13 billion for the economic recovery of war-torn Eu-

rope. Underlying it was the belief that communist aggression fed off economic turmoil. From the Soviet perspective, the Marshall Plan was nothing less than
capitalist imperialism, a thinly veiled attempt to buy the
support of the smaller European countries, which in return would be expected to submit to economic exploitation by the United States. A Soviet spokesman described the United States as the "main force in the
imperialist camp," whose ultimate goal was "the
strengthening of imperialism, preparation for a new imperialist war, a struggle against socialism and democracy,
and the support of reactionary and anti-democratic, pro-
fascist regimes and movements." According to the Soviet view, the Marshall Plan aimed at "the construction
of a bloc of states bound by obligations to the USA, and
to guarantee the American loans in return for the relin-
quishing by the European states of their economic and
later also their political independence."[3] The Soviets,
however, were in no position to compete financially with
the United States and could do little to counter the
Marshall Plan.

The fate of Germany also became a source of heated
contention between East and West. Besides denazifica-

tion and a "temporary" partitioning of Germany (and Berlin) into four occupied zones, the Allied powers had agreed on little else with regard to the conquered nation. The Soviets, hardest hit by the war, took reparations from Germany in the form of booty. The technology-starved Soviets dismantled and removed to Russia 380 factories from the western zones of Berlin before transferring their control to the Western powers. By the summer of 1946, 200 chemical, paper, and textile factories in the Soviets' East German zone had likewise been shipped to the Soviet Union. At the same time, the German Communist party was reestablished under the control of Walter Ulbricht (1893–1973) and was soon in charge of the political reconstruction of the Soviet zone in eastern Germany.

Although the foreign ministers of the four occupying powers (the United States, Soviet Union, Britain, and France) kept meeting to arrive at a final peace treaty with Germany, they moved further and further apart. At the same time, the British, French, and Americans gradually began to merge their zones economically and, by February 1948, were making plans for the unification of these three Western sections of Germany and the formal creation of a West German federal government. The Soviets responded with a blockade of West Berlin that allowed neither trucks nor trains to enter the three Western zones of Berlin. The Russians hoped to secure economic control of all Berlin and force the Western powers to stop the creation of a separate West German state.

The Western powers were faced with a dilemma. Direct military confrontation seemed dangerous. American troops were severely outnumbered, and no one wished to risk World War III. Therefore, an attempt to break through the blockade with tanks and trucks was ruled out. The solution was the Berlin Air Lift. At its peak, 13,000 tons of supplies were flown daily to Berlin. The Soviets, also not wanting war, did not interfere and finally lifted the blockade in May 1949. The blockade of Berlin had severely increased tensions between the United States and the Soviet Union and brought the separation of Germany into two states. The West German Federal Republic was formally created in September 1949, and a month later, a separate German Democratic Republic was established in East Germany.

In that same year, the Cold War spread from Europe to the rest of the world. The victory of the Chinese Communists in 1949 in the Chinese civil war created a new Communist regime and only intensified American fears about the spread of communism. The Soviet Union

▼ **Map 29.1** Occupied Germany and Austria.

also detonated its first atomic bomb in 1949, and all too soon both powers were involved in an escalating arms race that resulted in the construction of ever more destructive nuclear weapons. Soon the search for security took the form of mutual deterrence or the belief that an arsenal of nuclear weapons prevented war by assuring that even if one nation launched its nuclear weapons in a preemptive first strike, the other nation would still be able to respond and devastate the attacker.

The search for security in the new world of the Cold War also led to the creation of military alliances. The North Atlantic Treaty Organization (NATO) was formed in April 1949 when Belgium, Luxemburg, the Netherlands, France, Britain, Italy, Denmark, Norway, Portugal, and Iceland signed a treaty with the United States and Canada. All the powers agreed to provide mutual assistance if any one of them was attacked. A few years later West Germany, Greece, and Turkey joined NATO.

The Eastern European states soon followed suit. In 1949, they had already formed the Council for Mutual

Economic Assistance (COMECON) for economic cooperation. But in 1955, Albania, Bulgaria, Czechoslovakia, East Germany, Hungary, Poland, Romania, and the Soviet Union organized a formal military alliance in the Warsaw Pact. Once again, Europe was tragically divided into hostile alliance systems.

A system of military alliances spread to the rest of the world after the United States became involved in the Korean War in 1950. Korea had been liberated from the Japanese in 1945, but was soon divided into two parts. The land north of the thirty-eighth parallel became the Democratic People's Republic (North Korea) and was supported by the Soviet Union. The Republic of Korea (South Korea) received aid from the United States. In 1950, perhaps with Stalin's approval, North Korean forces invaded South Korea. The Americans, perceiving this as yet another example of communist aggression and expansion, gained the support of the United Nations (see The United Nations later in the chapter) and intervened by sending American troops to turn back the invasion. Although the United Nations forces (mostly Americans and South Koreans) under the com-

▼ **Map 29.2** The New European Alliance Systems.

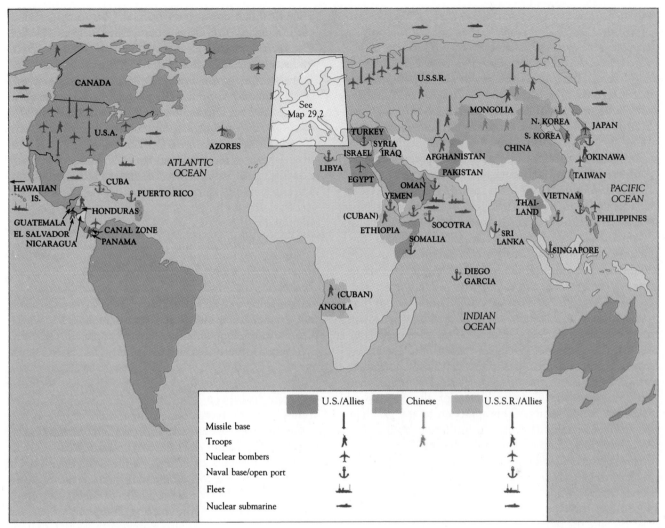

▼ **Map 29.3** The Global Cold War.

mand of General Douglas MacArthur pushed the North Koreans back toward the Chinese border, Mao Zedong (1893–1976), the leader of Communist China, then sent Chinese forces into the fray and forced MacArthur's troops to retreat back to South Korea. Believing that the Chinese were simply the puppets of Moscow, American policymakers created an image of communism as a monolithic force directed by the Soviet Union. After two more years of inconclusive fighting, an uneasy truce was reached in 1953 and the division of Korea reaffirmed. To many Americans, the policy of containing communism had succeeded in Asia, just as it had earlier in Europe.

The Korean experience seemed to confirm American fears of communist expansion and reinforced American determination to contain Soviet power. As President Dwight D. Eisenhower (1890–1969) expressed it: "The freedom we cherish and defend in Europe and in the Americas is no different from the freedom that is imperiled in Asia." As a result, American military alliances were extended around the world. The Central Treaty Organization (CENTO) of Turkey, Iraq, Iran, Pakistan, Britain, and the United States was intended to prevent the Soviet Union from expanding at the expense of its southern neighbors. To stem Soviet aggression in the Far East, the United States, Britain, France, Pakistan, Thailand, the Philippines, Australia, and New Zealand formed the Southeast Asia Treaty Organization (SEATO). By the mid-1950s, the United States found itself allied militarily with forty-two states around the world.

The Cuban Missile Crisis and the Move toward Détente

The Cold War confrontation between the United States and the Soviet Union reached frightening levels in 1962 during the Cuban missile crisis. In 1959, a left-wing revolutionary named Fidel Castro (b. 1927) had overthrown the Cuban dictator Fulgencio Batista and established a Soviet-supported totalitarian regime. After the utter failure of a United States-supported attempt (the "Bay of Pigs" incident) to overthrow Castro's regime in 1961, the Soviet Union decided to place nuclear missiles in Cuba. The United States was not prepared to allow nuclear weapons to be within such close striking distance of the American mainland, despite the fact that it had placed nuclear weapons in Turkey within easy range of the Soviet Union. The Soviet leader, Nikita Khrushchev (see The Soviet Union: From Stalin to Gorbachev later in the chapter), was quick to point out that "your rockets are in Turkey. You are worried by Cuba . . . because it is 90 miles from the American coast. But Turkey is next to us."[4] When American intelligence discovered that a Soviet fleet carrying missiles was heading to Cuba, President John F. Kennedy (1917–1963) decided to blockade Cuba and prevent the fleet from reaching its destination. This approach to the problem had the benefit of delaying confrontation and giving each side time to find a peaceful solution. Khrushchev agreed to turn back the fleet if Kennedy pledged not to invade Cuba. In a conciliatory letter to Kennedy, Khrushchev wrote, "We and you ought not to pull on the ends of the rope in which you have tied the knot of war, because the more the two of us pull, the tighter that knot will be tied. And a moment may come when that knot will be tied too tight that even he who tied it will not have the strength to untie it. . . . Let us not only relax the forces pulling on the ends of the rope, let us take measures to untie that knot. We are ready for this."[5]

The intense feeling that the world might have been annihilated in a few days had a profound influence on both sides. A hotline communications system between Moscow and Washington was installed in 1963 to expedite rapid communications between the two superpowers in a time of crisis. In the same year, the two powers agreed to ban nuclear tests in the atmosphere, a step that at least served to lessen the tensions between the two nations.

By that time, the United States had also been drawn into a new confrontation that had an important impact on the Cold War—the Vietnam War. After Vietnamese forces had defeated their French colonial masters in 1954, Vietnam had been divided. A strongly nationalistic regime in the north under Ho Chi Minh (1890–1969) received Soviet aid, while American sponsors worked to establish a democratic regime in South Vietnam. In 1964, under President Lyndon Johnson (1908–1973), increasing numbers of American troops were sent to Vietnam to keep the Communist regime of the north from uniting the entire country under its control. Although nationalism played a powerful role in this conflict, American policymakers saw the conflict in terms of a domino theory concerning the spread of communism. If the Communists succeeded in Vietnam, the argument was that all the other countries in the Far East freeing themselves from colonial domination would fall (like dominoes) to communism.

Despite their massive superiority in equipment and firepower, American forces failed to prevail over the persistence of the North Vietnamese. The mounting destruction and increasing brutalization of the war, brought into American homes every evening on television, also turned American public opinion against the war. Finally, President Richard Nixon (b. 1913) reached an agreement with North Vietnam in 1973 that allowed the United States to withdraw its forces. Within two years, Vietnam had been forcibly reunited by Communist armies from the North.

Despite the success of the North Vietnamese Communists, the domino theory proved unfounded. A noisy rupture between Communist China and the Soviet Union put an end to the idea of a monolithic communism directed by Moscow. Under President Nixon, American relations with China were resumed. New nations in Southeast Asia also managed to avoid Communist governments. Above all, Vietnam helped to show the limitations of American power. By the end of the Vietnam War, a new era in American-Soviet relations—known as détente—had begun to emerge.

Détente meant a reduction of tensions between the Soviet Union and the United States. An appropriate symbol of détente was the Antiballistic Missiles (ABM) Treaty in 1972. Despite some lessening of tensions after the Cuban missile crisis, both the Soviet Union and the United States had continued to expand their nuclear arsenals. In the 1960s, both nations sought to extend the destructive power of their missiles by arming them with multiple warheads. By 1970, Americans had developed the capacity to arm their inter-continental ballistic missiles (ICBMs) with "multiple independently targeted re-entry vehicles" (MIRVs) that enabled one missile to hit ten different targets. The Soviet Union soon followed suit. Between 1968 and 1972, both sides had also developed antiballistic missiles (ABMs), whose purpose was to hit and destroy incoming missiles. In the 1972 ABM Treaty, the two nations agreed to limit their antiballistic missile systems.

In 1975, the Helsinki Agreements provided yet another example of reduced tensions between the superpowers. Signed by the United States, Canada, and all European nations, these accords recognized all borders in central and eastern Europe that had been established since the end of World War II, thereby acknowledging the Soviet sphere of influence in Eastern Europe. The Helsinki Agreements also committed the signatory powers to recognize and protect the human rights of their citizens.

This protection of human rights became one of the major foreign policy goals of the next American president, Jimmy Carter (b. 1924). Although hopes ran high for détente, the Soviet invasion of Afghanistan in 1979, undertaken to restore a pro-Soviet regime, hardened relations between the United States and the Soviet Union. President Carter canceled American participation in the 1980 Olympic Games held in Moscow and placed an embargo on the shipment of American grain to the Soviet Union.

The early administration of President Ronald Reagan (b. 1911) witnessed a return to the harsh rhetoric, if not all of the harsh practices, of the Cold War. Calling the Soviet Union an "evil empire," Reagan began a military buildup that stimulated a renewed arms race. In 1982, the Reagan administration introduced the nuclear-tipped cruise missile, whose ability to fly at low altitudes made it difficult to detect. President Reagan also became an ardent proponent of the Strategic Defense Initiative (SDI), nicknamed "Star Wars." Its purpose was to create a space shield that could destroy incoming missiles. By providing military support to the Afghan insurgents, the Reagan administration helped to maintain a Vietnam-like war in Afghanistan that the Soviet Union could not win. Like the Vietnam War, the war in Afghanistan demonstrated that the power of a superpower was actually limited in the face of strong nationalist, guerrilla-type opposition.

The accession of Mikhail Gorbachev to power in the Soviet Union (see The Gorbachev Era later in the chapter) in 1985 eventually brought a dramatic end to the Cold War. Gorbachev initiated a plan for arms limitation that led in 1987 to an agreement with the United States to eliminate intermediate-range nuclear weapons (the INF Treaty). Both sides had incentives to dampen the expensive arms race. Gorbachev hoped to make extensive economic and internal reforms while the United

▼ **Gorbachev and Reagan.** The willingness of Mikhail Gorbachev and Ronald Reagan to dampen the arms race was a significant factor in ending the Cold War confrontation between the United States and the Soviet Union. Reagan and Gorbachev are shown standing before St. Basil's Cathedral during Reagan's visit to Moscow in 1988.

States had serious deficit problems. During the Reagan years, the United States had moved from being a creditor nation to the world's biggest debtor nation. By 1990, both countries were becoming aware that their large military budgets made it difficult for them to solve their serious social problems.

The years 1989 and 1990 will surely be remembered as crucial years in the ending of the Cold War. The postwar settlements that had become the norm in central and eastern Europe came unstuck as a mostly peaceful revolutionary upheaval swept through Eastern Europe. Gorbachev's policy of allowing greater autonomy for the Communist regimes of Eastern Europe meant that the Soviet Union would no longer militarily support Communist governments that were faced with internal revolt. The unwillingness of the Soviet regime to use force to maintain the status quo, as it had in Hungary in 1956 and in Czechoslovakia in 1968, opened the door to the overthrow of the Communist regimes (see Eastern Europe: From Soviet Satellites to Sovereign Nations later in the chapter). The reunification of Germany on October 3, 1990, also destroyed one of the most prominent symbols of the Cold War era. Increasingly throughout 1990, the military role of NATO was also being seriously questioned. There is, of course, always the danger that if the Gorbachev revolution fails and right-wing neo-Stalinists take over in the Soviet Union, the Cold War could resume. By the fall of 1990, most of the world's people were hoping instead that a new, truly post–Cold War era had begun. American and Soviet cooperation after the Iraqi invasion of Kuwait in August 1990 seemed to support these hopes.

▼ Europe since 1945: Recovery and Renewal

At the height of Nazi success in 1942, a new era of barbarism seemed to challenge the very existence of European civilization. But Europeans made a remarkable recovery, and within a few years after the defeat of Germany and Italy, economic revival brought a renewed growth to European society. Major differences, however, remained between Western and Eastern Europe.

The Soviet Union: From Stalin to Gorbachev

World War II devastated the Soviet Union. To create a new industrial base, Stalin returned to the method that had proved effective in the 1930s—the acquisition of development capital from Soviet labor. Working hard for little pay, poor housing, and precious few consumer goods, Soviet laborers were expected to produce goods for export with little in return for themselves. The incoming capital from abroad could then be used to purchase machinery and Western technology. The loss of millions of men in the war meant that much of this tremendous work load fell upon Soviet women. Almost 40 percent of heavy manual labor was performed by women.

Although this policy was successful in promoting economic growth in heavy industry, primarily for the benefit of the military, consumer goods were scarce. While the development of thermonuclear weapons in 1953, MIG fighters from 1950 to 1953, and the first space satellite (*Sputnik*) in 1957 elevated the Soviet state's reputation as a world power abroad, domestically the Russian people were shortchanged. Heavy industry grew at a rate three times that of personal consumption. Moreover, the housing shortage was acute. A British military attaché in Moscow reported that "all houses, practically without exception, show lights from every window after dark. This seems to indicate that every room is both a living room by day and a bedroom by night. There is no place in overcrowded Moscow for the luxury of eating and sleeping in separate rooms."[6]

Stalin demanded a dogmatic superpatriotism from all Soviets, but found that contact with Western ways during the war had shaken many people's belief in the superiority of the Soviet system. Returning Russian soldiers brought back stories of the prosperity of the West, and the obvious disparity between the Western and Soviet systems led to a "crisis of faith" for many young Communists. Partly for this reason, Stalin imprisoned

Khrushchev Denounces Stalin
▼ ▼ ▼

Three years after the death of Stalin, the new Soviet premier, Nikita Khrushchev, addressed the Twentieth Congress of the Communist Party and denounced the former Soviet dictator for his crimes. This denunciation was the beginning of a policy of destalinization.

Nikita Khrushchev Addresses the Twentieth Party Congress, February 1956

Comrades, . . . quite a lot has been said about the cult of the individual and about its harmful consequences. . . . The cult of the person of Stalin . . . became at a certain specific stage the source of a whole series of exceedingly serious and grave perversions of Party principles, of Party democracy, of revolutionary legality.

Stalin absolutely did not tolerate collegiality in leadership and in work and . . . practiced brutal violence, not only toward everything which opposed him, but also toward that which seemed to his capricious and despotic character, contrary to his concepts.

Stalin abandoned the method of ideological struggle for that of administrative violence, mass repressions and terror. . . . Arbitrary behavior by one person encouraged and permitted arbitrariness in others. Mass arrests and deportations of many thousands of people, execution without trial and without normal investigation created conditions of insecurity, fear and even desperation.

Stalin showed in a whole series of cases his intolerance, his brutality and his abuse of power. . . . He often chose the path of repression and annihilation, not only against actual enemies, but also against individuals who had not committed any crimes against the Party and the Soviet government. . . .

Many Party, Soviet and economic activists who were branded in 1937–8 as "enemies" were actually never enemies, spies, wreckers and so on, but were always honest communists; they were only so stigmatised, and often, no longer able to bear barbaric tortures, they charged themselves (at the order of the investigative judges-falsifiers) with all kinds of grave and unlikely crimes.

This was the result of the abuse of power by Stalin, who began to use mass terror against the Party cadres. . . . Stalin put the Party and the NKVD [the secret police] up to the use of mass terror when the exploiting classes had been liquidated in our country and when there were no serious reasons for the use of extraordinary mass terror. The terror was directed . . . against the honest workers of the Party and the Soviet state. . . .

Stalin was a very distrustful man, sickly suspicious. . . . Everywhere and in everything he saw "enemies," "two-facers" and "spies." Possessing unlimited power, he indulged in great wilfulness and choked a person morally and physically. A situation was created where one could not express one's own will. When Stalin said that one or another would be arrested, it was necessary to accept on faith that he was an "enemy of the people." What proofs were offered? The confession of the arrested. . . . How is it possible that a person confesses to crimes that he had not committed? Only in one way—because of application of physical methods of pressuring him, tortures, bringing him to a state of unconsciousness, deprivation of his judgement, taking away of his human dignity.

---

many soldiers, who were simply shipped from German concentration camps to Soviet concentration camps. Stalin believed that Western influence was a threat to Communist orthodoxy. In 1946, government decrees subordinated all forms of literary and scientific expression to the political needs of the state. Along with the anti-intellectual campaign came political terror. A new series of purges seemed imminent in 1953 when a number of Jewish doctors were implicated in a spurious plot to kill high-level party officials. Only Stalin's death on March 5, 1953, prevented more bloodletting.

A new collective leadership succeeded Stalin until Nikita Khrushchev (1894–1971) emerged as the chief Soviet policymaker. Khrushchev had been responsible for ending the system of forced-labor camps, a regular feature of Stalinist Russia. At the Twentieth Congress of the Communist Party in 1956, Khrushchev condemned Stalin for his "administrative violence, mass repression, and terror" (see the box on p. 1011).

Once in power, Khrushchev continued and even extended the early policies of the collective leadership that had replaced Stalin. The intellectual thaw continued as Khrushchev stated that "readers should be given the chance to make their own judgments" regarding the acceptability of controversial literature, and that "police measures shouldn't be used."[7] He allowed the publication in 1962 of Alexander Solzhenitsyn's *A Day in the Life of Ivan Denisovich*, a grim portrayal of the horrors of Russia's forced-labor camps. Most importantly, Khrushchev extended the process of destalinization. Khrushchev's revelations about Stalin at the Twentieth Congress created turmoil in Communist ranks everywhere and encouraged rebellions in Soviet satellite countries in Eastern Europe—rebellions that were then crushed by the Red Army (see Eastern Europe: From Soviet Satellites to Sovereign Nations later in the chapter).

Economically, Khrushchev tried to place more emphasis on consumer goods. Likewise, he encouraged the decentralization of agriculture by allowing more local decision making with less interference from Moscow. Khrushchev's attempts to increase agricultural output by growing corn and cultivating vast lands east of the Ural Mountains proved less successful and damaged his reputation within the party. These failures, combined with increased military spending, hurt the Soviet economy. The industrial growth rate, which had soared in the early 1950s, now declined dramatically from 13 percent in 1953 to 7.5 percent in 1964.

Khrushchev's personality also did not endear him to the higher Soviet officials who frowned at his tendency to crack jokes and play the clown. Nor were the higher members of the party bureaucracy pleased when Khrushchev tried to curb their privileges. Foreign policy failures caused additional damage to Khrushchev's reputation among his colleagues. His rash plan to place missiles in Cuba was the final straw. While he was away on vacation in 1964, a special meeting of the Soviet Politburo voted him out of office (because of "ill-health") and forced him into retirement. Although a group of leaders succeeded him, real power came into the hands of Leonid Brezhnev (1906–1982), the "trusted" supporter of Khrushchev who had engineered his downfall.

The Brezhnev years were relatively calm ones for the Soviet Union. Brezhnev benefited from the more relaxed atmosphere associated with détente. The Soviets had reached a rough parity with the United States in nuclear arms and enjoyed a sense of external security that seemed to allow for a relaxation of authoritarian rule. The regime permitted more access to Western styles of music, dress, and art, although dissenters were still punished. Andrei Sakharov, for example, who had played an important role in the development of the Soviet hydrogen bomb, was placed under house arrest for his defense of human rights.

In his economic policies, Brezhnev continued to emphasize heavy industry. Overall industrial growth declined, although the Soviet production of iron, steel, coal, and cement surpassed that of the United States. Two problems bedeviled the Soviet economy. The government's insistence on vigorous central planning led to a huge, complex bureaucracy that discouraged efficiency and reduced productivity. Moreover, the Soviet system, based on guaranteed employment and a lack of incentives, bred apathy, complacency, absenteeism, and drunkenness.

Agricultural problems added to Soviet economic woes. Collective farmers also lacked incentives. Many preferred working their own small private plots to laboring in the collective work brigades. To make matters worse, bad harvests in the mid-1970s, caused by a series of droughts, heavy rains, and early frosts, forced the Soviet government to buy grain from the West, particularly the United States. To their chagrin, the Soviets were increasingly dependent on capitalist countries.

Despite the underlying problems, higher living standards for the Soviet elite—the scientists, managers, and technicians—created a sense of confidence and optimism in the 1970s. This confidence began to wane, however, by the end of the decade, especially when Soviet fears of a growing anti-communist fundamentalist Islamic government in Afghanistan led to the Soviet quagmire in Afghanistan. Brezhnev declined noticeably after 1975 because of frequent illness. Although he was succeeded briefly by two older, ailing members of the Soviet leadership, a new era was about to begin.

THE GORBACHEV ERA   In 1985, Mikhail Gorbachev (b. 1931), a young, vigorous, and progressive politician, took over the reins of Soviet power. Born of the peasantry and educated during the reform years of Khrushchev, Gorbachev seemed intent on taking earlier reforms to their logical conclusions. By the 1980s, Soviet economic problems were obvious. Rigid, centralized planning led to mismanagement and stifled innovation. Although the Soviets still excelled in space exploration, they fell behind the West in high technology, especially in the development and production of computers for private and public use. Most noticeable to the Soviet people was the actual decline in the standard of living. In February 1986, at the Twenty-Seventh Congress of the Communist Party, Gorbachev made clear the need for changes in Soviet society: "The practical actions of the Party and state agencies lag behind the demands of the times and of life itself. . . . Problems grow faster than they are solved. Sluggishness, ossification in the forms, and methods of management decrease the dynamism of work. . . . Stagnation begins to show up in the life of society."[8] Thus, from the start, Gorbachev preached the need for radical reforms.

The cornerstone of Gorbachev's radical reforms was *perestroika* or "restructuring." At first this meant only a reordering of economic policy as Gorbachev called for the beginning of a market economy with limited free enterprise and some private property. But Gorbachev perceived that in the Soviet system, the economic sphere was intimately tied to the social and political spheres. Attempts to reform the economy without political or social reform would be doomed to failure.

One of the most important instruments of *perestroika* was *glasnost* or "openness." Soviet citizens and officials were encouraged to discuss openly the strengths and weaknesses of the Soviet Union. This policy could be seen in *Pravda*, the official newspaper of the Communist party, where increased coverage was given to such disasters as the nuclear accident at Chernobyl in 1986 and collisions of ships in the Black Sea. Soon this type of reporting was extended to include reports of official corruption, sloppy factory work, and protests against government policy. The arts also benefited from the new policy as previously banned works were now published, and motion pictures began to show negative aspects of Soviet life. Music based on Western styles, such as jazz and rock, began to be performed openly.

Political reforms have been equally revolutionary. In June 1987, the principle of two-candidate elections was introduced, whereas before voters were presented with only one candidate. Though multiparty elections have not been introduced as of 1990, their implementation appears almost inevitable. Most dissidents, including Andrei Sakharov, who had spent years in internal exile, were released. The revolutionary nature of Gorbachev's political reforms can perhaps be seen most clearly in Sakharov's rise from dissident to an elected member of the Congress of People's Deputies in March of 1989. As a leader of the dissident deputies, Sakharov called for the end of the Communist monopoly of power, and on the day he died, December 11, 1989, urged the creation of a new noncommunist party.

Gorbachev has also pushed for greater powers for the office of president, previously only a titular post. This is a consequence of the dissociation of the state and the Communist party. Hitherto, the position of first secretary of the party was the most important post in the Soviet Union, but as the Communist party becomes less closely associated with the state, the powers of this office will diminish correspondingly. Increasing the powers of the presidency may well be Gorbachev's way of attempting to secure his political survival if the Communist party does indeed fall.

At the Communist party conference in 1988, Gorbachev called for the creation of a new Soviet parliament. This parliament convened in 1989, the first such meeting in Russia since 1918. Gorbachev consolidated power in 1989 by convincing 110 full and alternate members of the Central Committee of the Communist party to resign "voluntarily." The party congress of July 1990 saw Gorbachev attempting to maintain power against the stiff opposition of party hard-liners such as Yegor Ligachev, who wished to slow or stop reforms, and liberals such as Boris Yeltsin, who wanted more and faster reforms.

Gorbachev made it clear that the Communist monopoly of power in the Soviet Union was ending and that the party must prepare itself accordingly if it hopes to remain a political force in the coming democracy. He emphatically stated that reform must go forward: "There is no way to bring yesterday back. . . . No dictatorship, if someone has this crazy idea in his head, can resolve anything."[9] On July 10, 1990, Gorbachev won reelection as general secretary of the party. On July 12, Boris Yeltsin, the main opposition from the liberals, resigned from the Communist party and announced his intention to form the Democratic Platform into an opposition party, moving the Soviet Union in the direction of a multiparty system.

CRISIS IN THE SOVIET REPUBLICS: ETHNIC VIOLENCE AND INDEPENDENCE MOVEMENTS One of Gorbachev's most serious problems stems from the character of the Soviet Union. The Union of Soviet Socialist Republics is a truly multiethnic country, containing 92 nationalities and 112 recognized languages. Previously, the iron hand of the Communist party, centered in Moscow, kept a lid on the centuries-old ethnic tensions that have periodically erupted. As Gorbachev released this iron grip, tensions resurfaced, a by-product of *glasnost* that Gorbachev had not anticipated. Ethnic groups took advantage of the new openness to protest what they perceived to be ethnically motivated slights. As violence has erupted, the Soviet army, in disrepair since Afghanistan, has had difficulty controlling the situation. In some cases, independence movements and ethnic causes have become linked, as in Azerbaijan where the National Front became the spokesgroup for the Muslim Azerbaijanis in their conflict with Christian Armenians.

The period 1988 to 1990 also witnessed the appearance of nationalist movements throughout the republics of the Soviet Union. Many are motivated by ethnic concerns, with calls for sovereignty of the republics and independence from the Russian-based rule centered in Moscow. These movements sprang up first in Georgia late in 1988 and later in Latvia, Estonia, Moldavia, Uzbekistan, Azerbaijan, and most dramatically in Lithuania.

In December of 1989, the Communist party of Lithuania declared itself independent of the Communist party of the Soviet Union. A leading force in this independence movement was the nationalist Lithuanian Restructuring Movement or "Popular Front for Perestroika," commonly known as *Sajudis*, led by Vytautas Landsbergis. *Sajudis* also favored a more radical policy of independence for Lithuania. Gorbachev made it clear that he supported self-determination, but not secession, which he believed would be detrimental to the Soviet Union. Nevertheless, on March 11, 1990, the Lithuanian Supreme Council unilaterally declared Lithuania independent. Its formal name was now the Lithuanian Republic; the adjectives Soviet and Socialist had been dropped. On March 15, the Soviet Congress of People's Deputies, though recognizing a general right to secede from the Union of Soviet Socialist Republics, declared the Lithuanian declaration null and void; the congress stated that proper procedures must be established and followed before secession will be acceptable. Although Soviet resistance had made immediate independence for Lithuania less likely, Lithuanians seem intent on pursuing their goal.

Eastern Europe: From Soviet Satellites to Sovereign Nations

The political structure of Eastern Europe after World War II was, for the most part, the creation of Joseph Stalin. Communist governments were established by force or subterfuge in most of the countries "liberated" by the Soviet army. The new Communist governments generally fell into two categories, those run by "Little Stalins" and those led by national Communists. The "Little Stalins" ruled as virtual dictators and generally followed the dictates of the Soviets. The national Communists believed in the merits of communism but also cherished national sovereignty and had no desire to follow the wishes of their Soviet "protector" at all times. Nevertheless, whenever they tried to act independently of the Soviet Union, they were forced to retreat. Only at the end of the 1980s did Gorbachev's policies make possible radical changes in Eastern Europe.

POLAND   Stalin had installed a pro-Soviet Communist regime in "liberated" Poland. In 1956, after the circulation of Khrushchev's denunciation of Stalin, protests—especially by workers—erupted in Poland. In response, the Polish Communist party adopted a series of reforms in October 1956 and elected Wladyslaw Gomulka (1905–1982) as first secretary. Gomulka declared that Poland had the right to follow its own socialist path. Fearful of Soviet armed response, however, the Poles compromised. Poland pledged to remain loyal to the Warsaw Pact, while the Soviets agreed to allow Poland to follow its own path to socialism. The Catholic church, an extremely important institution to many Poles, was also permitted to administer its own affairs.

This compromise enabled Poland to achieve a certain stability for the next decade, but economic problems brought the ouster of Gomulka in 1971. His replacement, Edward Gierek, attempted to solve Poland's economic problems by borrowing heavily from the West. But in 1980, when he announced huge increases in food prices in an effort to pay off part of the Western debt, workers' protests erupted once again. This time, however, the revolutionary demands of the workers led directly to the rise of the independent labor movement called Solidarity. Led by Lech Walesa (b. 1943), Solidarity represented 10 million of Poland's 35 million people. Almost instantaneously, Solidarity became a tremendous force for change and a threat to the government's monopoly of power. With the support of the workers, many intellectuals, and the Catholic church, Solidarity was able to win a series of concessions. The Polish government seemed powerless to stop the flow of concessions until December 1981, when it arrested Walesa and other Solidarity leaders, outlawed the union, and imposed military rule under General Wojciech Jaruzelski (b. 1923).

But martial rule did not solve Poland's serious economic problems. In 1988, new demonstrations broke out. After much maneuvering and negotiating with Solidarity, the Polish regime finally consented to elections that led to even greater strength for Solidarity. Bowing to the inevitable, Jaruzelski's regime allowed the

Solidarity-led coalition in the lower house of the new legislature to elect Tadeusz Mazowiecki, a leading member of Solidarity, as prime minister. The Communist monopoly of power in Poland had come to an end after forty-five years. In April 1990, it was decided that a new president would be freely elected by the populace by the end of the year.

YUGOSLAVIA   Most of the initial Communist governments set up by Joseph Stalin after the war were run by "Little Stalins." Yugoslavia, however, was the first to be led by a national Communist and to assert its independence from the Soviet Union. During World War II, Josip Broz, known as Tito, leader of the Communist resistance movement, seemed to be a loyal Stalinist. After the war, however, he moved toward the establishment of an independent Communist state in Yugoslavia. This alienated him from Stalin and created a potential ally for the West in the Cold War. But Tito was not about to be a capitalist pawn either. Communist Yugoslavia became a neutral force in Eastern Europe and the world for the remainder of Tito's rule.

In 1958, the Yugoslav party congress asserted that Yugoslav Communists did not see themselves as deviating from communism, only Stalinism. They considered their way closer to the Marxist-Leninist ideal. This included a more decentralized economic and political system in which workers could manage themselves and local communes could exercise some political power. By the 1970s, however, Tito became concerned that decentralization had gone too far in creating too much power at the local level and encouraging regionalism. As a result, he purged thousands of local Communist leaders who seemed more concerned with local affairs than national concerns.

After Tito's death in 1980, no strong leader emerged as Tito's responsibilities passed to a collective state presidency and the presidium of the League of Communists of Yugoslavia (LCY). At the end of the 1980s, Yugoslavia was caught up in the reform movements sweeping through Eastern Europe. On January 20, 1990, the League of Communists called for an end to authoritarian socialism and proposed the creation of a pluralistic political system with freedom of speech and other civil liberties, free elections, an independent judiciary, and a mixed economy with equal status for private property. But divisions between radical Slovenes who wanted a loose federation and Serbians who wanted to retain the centralized system caused the collapse of the party congress, and hence the Communist party. New parties quickly emerged. In multiparty elections held in the states of Slovenia and Croatia in April and May of 1990 (the first multiparty elections in Yugoslavia in fifty-one years), the Communists fared poorly. Yugoslavia seemed on its way to a pluralistic political system, although ethnic minorities problems could still wreak havoc with a peaceful transition to a new era.

HUNGARY   The developments in Poland in 1956 inspired national Communists in Hungary to seek the same kinds of reforms and independence. Intense debates eventually resulted in the ouster of the ruling Stalinist and the selection of Imry Nagy (1896–1958) as the new Hungarian leader. Internal dissent, however, was not simply directed against the Soviets, but against communism in general, which was viewed as a creation of the Soviets, not the Hungarians. The Stalinist secret police had also bred much terror and hatred. This dissatisfaction, combined with economic difficulties, created a situation ripe for revolt. In order to quell the rising rebellion, Nagy declared Hungary a free nation on November 1, 1956. He promised free elections, and the mood of the country made it clear that this could mean the end of Communist rule in Hungary. But Khrushchev was in no position at home to allow a member of the Communist flock to leave. Just three days after Nagy's declaration, the Red Army attacked Budapest (see the box on p. 1016). The Soviets reestablished control over the country while János Kádár (1912–1989), a cabinet minister who had appeared liberal, replaced Nagy and worked with the Soviets to squash the revolt.

Remaining in power for over thirty years, Kádár enacted the most far-reaching economic reforms in Eastern Europe. In the early 1980s, he legalized small private enterprises, such as retail stores, restaurants, and artisan shops. His economic reforms were termed "Communism with a capitalist facelift." Hungary moved slowly away from its strict adherence to Soviet dominance and even established fairly friendly relations with the West. Multicandidate elections with at least two candidates for each office were held for the first time on June 8, 1985.

As the 1980s progressed, however, the economy sagged, and Kádár fell from power in 1988. By 1989, the Hungarian Communist government was aware of the growing dissatisfaction and began to undertake reforms. The more important new political parties united to form an opposition Round Table, whose negotiations with the Communists led to an agreement that Hungary would become a democratic republic. The Hungarian Communist party changed its name to the Hungarian Socialist party in order to have a greater chance of success in the new elections scheduled for March 25, 1990. The party

Soviet Repression in Eastern Europe: Hungary, 1956
▼ ▼ ▼

Developments in Poland in 1956 inspired the Communist leaders of Hungary to begin to remove their country from Soviet control. But there were limits to Khrushchev's tolerance, and he sent Soviet troops to crush Hungary's movement for independence. The first selection is a statement by the Soviet government justifying the use of Soviet troops, while the second is a brief and tragic final statement from Imry Nagy, the Hungarian leader.

Statement of the Soviet Government, October 30, 1956

The Soviet Government regards it as indispensable to make a statement in connection with the events in Hungary.

The course of the events has shown that the working people of Hungary, who have achieved great progress on the basis of their people's democratic order, correctly raise the question of the necessity of eliminating serious shortcomings in the field of economic building, the further raising of the material well-being of the population, and the struggle against bureaucratic excesses in the state apparatus.

However, this just and progressive movement of the working people was soon joined by forces of black reaction and counterrevolution, which are trying to take advantage of the discontent of part of the working people to undermine the foundations of the people's democratic order in Hungary and to restore the old landlord and capitalist order.

The Soviet Government and all the Soviet people deeply regret that the development of events in Hungary has led to bloodshed. On the request of the Hungarian People's Government the Soviet Government consented to the entry into Budapest of the Soviet Army units to assist the Hungarian People's Army and the Hungarian authorities to establish order in the town.

The Last Message of Imry Nagy, November 4, 1956

This fight is the fight for freedom by the Hungarian people against the Russian intervention, and it is possible that I shall only be able to stay at my post for one or two hours. The whole world will see how the Russian armed forces, contrary to all treaties and conventions, are crushing the resistance of the Hungarian people. They will also see how they are kidnapping the Prime Minister of a country which is a Member of the United Nations, taking him from the capital, and therefore it cannot be doubted at all that this is the most brutal form of intervention. I should like in these last moments to ask the leaders of the revolution, if they can, to leave the country. I ask that all that I have said in my broadcast, and what we have agreed on with the revolutionary leaders during meetings in Parliament, should be put in a memorandum, and the leaders should turn to all the peoples of the world for help and explain that today it is Hungary and tomorrow, or the day after tomorrow, it will be the turn of other countries because the imperialism of Moscow does not know borders, and is only trying to play for time.

---

came in fourth, however, a clear repudiation of communism. By the summer of 1990, Hungary seemed committed to democratic government and the institution of a free market economy.

CZECHOSLOVAKIA The developments in Poland and Hungary in 1956 did not generate similar revolts in Czechoslovakia. The "Little Stalin," Antonin Novotny (1904–1975), placed in power in 1952 by Stalin himself, remained firmly in control. By the late 1960s, however, Novotny had alienated many members of his own party and was particularly resented by Czechoslovakia's writers, such as the playwright Vaclav Havel (b. 1936).

A writers' rebellion late in 1967, in fact, led to Novotny's resignation. In January 1968, Alexander Dubcek (b. 1921) was elected first secretary of the Communist party and soon introduced a number of reforms, including freedom of speech and press, freedom to travel abroad, and a relaxation of secret police activities. Dubcek hoped to create "communism with a human face." A period of euphoria erupted that came to be known as the "Prague Spring."

It proved to be short-lived. This euphoria had led many to call for more far-reaching reforms, including neutrality and withdrawal from the Soviet bloc. To forestall the spreading of this "spring" fever, the Red Army invaded Czechoslovakia in August of 1968 and crushed the reform movement. Gustav Husák (b. 1913), a committed nonreformist, replaced Dubcek, crushed his reforms, and maintained the old order until the end of 1987.

In 1988, dissident movements once again resurfaced. Government attempts to suppress mass demonstrations in Prague and other Czechoslovakian cities in 1988 and 1989 only led to more and larger demonstrations. By November 1989, crowds as large as 500,000, which included many students, were forming in Prague. A new opposition group, the Civic Forum, emerged and was officially recognized on November 17. The Czechoslovakian Federal Assembly now voted to delete the constitutional articles giving the Communists the leading role in politics. In December 1989, as demonstrations continued, the Communist government, lacking any real support, collapsed. President Husák resigned and at the end of December was replaced by Vaclav Havel, the dissident playwright who had played such an important role in bringing the Communist government down. In January 1990, Havel declared amnesty for some 30,000 political prisoners. He also set out on a goodwill tour to various Western countries in which he proved to be an eloquent spokesman for Czech democracy and a new order in Europe.

ROMANIA   By 1948, with Soviet assistance, a Communist People's Democratic Front had assumed complete power in Romania. In 1965, leadership of the Communist government passed into the hands of Nicolae Ceaus-

▼ **President Vaclav Havel of Czechoslovakia and the American Congress, 1990.** The upheaval in Czechoslovakia in 1988 and 1989 brought an end to the Communist government in that country. In December of 1989, Vaclav Havel, a dissident playwright who had been instrumental in bringing the Communist government down, became the new president of Czechoslovakia. During a visit to the United States in February 1990, Havel spoke to the American Congress. His speech received an enthusiastic reception, and he is shown here surrounded by members of Congress after his speech.

escu (1918–1989), who with his wife Elena established a rigid and dictatorial regime. Ceausescu ruled Romania with an iron grip, using a secret police force—the Securitate—as his personal weapon against any dissent. Nevertheless, opposition to his regime grew as Ceausescu rejected the reforms in Eastern Europe promoted by Gorbachev. Economic difficulties also developed from

▼ **Soviet Tanks in Czechoslovakia, 1968.** Alexander Dubcek, the new first secretary of the Communist party, tried to liberalize communist rule in Czechoslovakia in 1968. Feeling threatened by Dubcek's far-reaching reforms, the Soviet Union sent Red Army forces into Czechoslovakia and crushed the reform movement. Shown are Soviet tanks in the capital city of Prague.

Ceausescu's extreme measures to reduce Romania's external debt. Although he was successful in reducing foreign debt, the sharp drop in living standards that resulted from those hardship measures angered many. Despite food shortages and the rationing of bread, flour, and sugar, Ceausescu stated that the exporting of such goods would not cease. Ceausescu's plan for rapid urbanization, especially a rural systematization program that called for the bulldozing of entire villages, further incited the populace.

A small incident became the spark that ignited heretofore suppressed flames of discontent. The ruthless crushing of a demonstration in Timisoara in December 1989 led to other mass demonstrations. After the dictator was booed at a mass rally on December 21, the army refused to support any more repression. Ceausescu and his wife were captured on December 22 and tried and executed on Christmas Day, 1989.

Leadership now passed into the hands of a hastily formed National Salvation Front led by Ion Iliescu (b. 1930), a former Communist who had studied in Moscow with Gorbachev and worked with Ceausescu until they had a falling out. Although the National Salvation Front was the solid victor in elections in the spring of 1990, questions remain about the new government's commitment to democracy, especially since antigovernment demonstrations have been met with Ceausescu-like repression.

BULGARIA In Bulgaria, too, Soviet cooperation after the war enabled the local Communist party to assume control of the country. In 1954, Todor Zhivkov (b. 1911) became the leader of the Bulgarian Communist party and hence leader of the nation. Not until the late 1980s did a number of small opposition groups begin to emerge. In October of 1989, antigovernment demonstrations were held in the capital city of Sofia. On November 10, 1989, Zhivkov was unexpectedly relieved of his post as general secretary of the Communist party, a position he had held for thirty-five years. He was replaced by the minister for foreign affairs, Peter Mladenov (b. 1936), who immediately pledged political and economic reforms with special attention to environmental concerns. In December the central committee recommended the elimination of the constitutional provision according the Communist party the leading role in government. Free elections were slated for the second half of 1990. On February 23, 1990, the Bulgarian Communist party voted to change its name to the Bulgarian Socialist party. Despite antigovernment demonstrations,

the new Socialist party managed to retain control of the government.

EAST GERMANY The ruling Communist government in East Germany, led by Walter Ulbricht, consolidated its position in the early 1950s and became a faithful Soviet

Chronology
▼ ▼ ▼
The Soviet Union and Satellite States in Eastern Europe

Death of Stalin	1953
Workers' Revolt Crushed in East Germany	1953
Zhivkov as Leader of Bulgarian Communist Party	1954
Khrushchev's Denunciation of Stalin	1956
Attempt at Reforms in Poland	1956
Hungarian Revolt is Crushed	1956
Berlin Wall is Built	1961
Breshnev Era	1964–1982
Ceausescu Takes Power in Romania	1965
Soviets Crush "Prague Spring" in Czechoslovakia	1968
Emergence of Solidarity in Poland	1980
Gorbachev Comes to Power in Soviet Union	1985
Multicandidate Elections in Hungary	1985
Collapse of Communist Government in Czechoslovakia	1989
Zhivkov Replaced by Mladenov in Bulgaria	1989
East German Communist Government Collapses	1989
Execution of Ceausescu in Romania	1989
	1990
Lithuania Declares Independence	March 11
East German Elections-Victory of Christian Democrats	March 18
Hungarian Elections	March 25
Multiparty Elections in Yugoslavia	April–May
Union of Currencies-West and East Germany	July 1
Gorbachev Reelected as General Secretary of Communist Party	July 10
Reunification of Germany	October 3

satellite. Industry was nationalized and agriculture collectivized. After a workers' revolt in 1953 was crushed by Soviet tanks, a steady flight of East Germans to West Germany ensued, primarily through the city of Berlin. This exodus of mostly skilled laborers created economic problems and led the East German government to build the infamous Berlin Wall in 1961 separating West from East Berlin, as well as equally fearsome barriers along the entire border with West Germany.

After building the Wall, East Germany succeeded in developing the strongest economy among the Soviet Union's Eastern European satellites. In 1971, Walter Ulbricht was succeeded by Erich Honecker (b. 1912), a party hard-liner who was deeply committed to the ideological battle against détente. Propaganda increased, and the use of the *Stasi,* the secret police, became a hallmark of Honecker's virtual dictatorship. Honecker ruled with an iron fist for the next eighteen years.

In 1988, however, popular unrest, partly fueled by the continual economic slump of the 1980s (which affected most of Eastern Europe) as well as the ongoing oppressiveness of Honecker's regime, caused another mass exodus of East German refugees. Violent repression as well as Honecker's refusal to institute reforms only led to a larger exodus and mass demonstrations against the regime in the summer and fall of 1989. By the beginning of November 1989, the Communist government had fallen into complete disarray. Capitulating to popular pressure on November 9, it opened the entire border with the West. Hundreds of thousands of Germans swarmed across the border, mostly to visit and return.

The Berlin Wall, long the symbol of the Cold War, became the site of a massive celebration. By December, new political parties had emerged, and on March 18, 1990, in East Germany's first free elections ever, the Christian Democrats won almost 50 percent of the vote. The Christian Democrats supported rapid monetary unification followed shortly by political unification with West Germany. On July 1, 1990, the economies of West and East Germany were united with the West German deutsche mark becoming the official currency of the two countries. Political reunification was achieved on October 3, 1990. What had seemed almost impossible at the beginning of 1989 had become a reality by the end of 1990. Developments in Germany reinforced the belief that the Cold War was truly over.

Western Europe: Domestic Politics

With the economic aid of the Marshall Plan, Western European countries recovered relatively rapidly from the devastation of World War II. Between 1950 and the late 1970s, industrial production in Western Europe increased dramatically. The European states had mixed economies that combined private enterprise with varying degrees of public ownership of banks, key industries, public utilities, and transportation systems. Social welfare programs—in the form of health services, housing, and educational opportunities—were also widely extended. Despite adverse economic trends in the 1970s, especially after the dramatic increase in the price of oil in 1973, the economies of the Western European states

▼ **And the Wall Came Tumbling Down.** The Berlin Wall, long a symbol of Europe's Cold War divisions, became the site of massive celebrations after the East German government opened its border with the West. Later, the East German government began to dismantle the wall. This photograph shows children playing on a pile of Berlin Wall rubble in front of the Reichstag building.

De Gaulle Calls for French Autonomy
▼ ▼ ▼

In the 1960s, the French president Charles de Gaulle sought to maintain France's independence from both the Soviet Union and the United States. In this 1966 speech, de Gaulle denounced those who were trying to subordinate France to international organizations.

A Speech of Charles de Gaulle, 1966

It is true that, among our contemporaries, there are many minds . . . who have envisaged that our country renounce its independence under the cover of one or another international group. Having thus handed over to foreign bodies the responsibility for our destiny, our leaders would . . . have nothing more to do than "plead France's case."

Thus some—exulting in the dream of the international—wanted to see our country itself, as they placed themselves, under the obedience of Moscow. Thus others—invoking either the supranational myth, or the danger from the East, or the advantage that the Atlantic West could derive from unifying its economy, or even the imposing utility of world arbitration—maintained that France should allow her policy to be dissolved in a tailor-made Europe, her defense in NATO, her monetary concepts in the Washington Fund, her personality in the United Nations.

Certainly, it is a good thing that such institutions exist, and it is only in our interest to belong to them; but if we had listened to their extreme apostles, these organs in which, as everyone knows, the political protection, military protection, economic power and multiform aid of the United States predominate— these organs would have been for us only a cover for our submission to American hegemony. Thus, France would disappear swept away by illusion.

---

had recovered by the beginning of the 1980s. Western Europeans have been full participants in the technological growth of the age and seem quite capable of standing up to American and Japanese economic competition.

Politically, Western Europe has also become accustomed to political democracy. Even Spain and Portugal, which had maintained their prewar dictatorial regimes until the mid-1970s, established democratic systems in the late 1970s. Overall, Socialist parties, such as the Labour party in Britain and the Social Democrats in West Germany, have fared poorly. Western European Communist parties have declined drastically. During the mid-1970s, a new variety of communism called Eurocommunism briefly emerged as Communist parties tried to work within the democratic system as mass movements committed to better government. But by the 1980s, internal political developments in Western Europe and events within the communist world itself had combined to undermine the Eurocommunist experiment.

FRANCE: FROM DE GAULLE TO MITTERAND The history of France for nearly a quarter century after the war was dominated by one man—Charles de Gaulle (1890–1970). During the war, de Gaulle had assumed leadership of all resistance groups and played an important role in ensuring the establishment of a French provisional government after the war. The creation of the Fourth Republic, with a return to a parliamentary system based on parties that de Gaulle considered weak, led him to withdraw from politics. Eventually, he formed the "French Popular Movement," a decidedly rightist organization. It blamed the parties for France's political mess and called for an even stronger presidency, a goal that de Gaulle finally achieved in 1958.

The fragile political stability of the Fourth Republic had been badly shaken by the Algerian crisis. The French army had suffered defeat in Indochina in 1954 and was determined to defeat Algerian demands for independence. But a strong antiwar movement among French intellectuals and church leaders led to bitter divisions within France that brought the downfall of the Fourth Republic and a call for the return of de Gaulle.

In 1958, de Gaulle immediately drafted a new constitution for the Fifth Republic that greatly enhanced the power of the office of president. As the new president, de Gaulle sought to return France to a position of great power (see the box above). He believed that playing a pivotal role in the Cold War might enhance France's stature. For that reason, he pulled France out of the NATO high command. He increased French prestige among the Third World countries by consenting to Algerian independence despite strenuous opposition from the army. With an eye toward achieving the status of a world power, de Gaulle invested heavily in the nuclear arms race. France exploded its first nuclear bomb in 1960.

Although the cost of the nuclear program increased the defense budget, de Gaulle did not neglect the French economy. Economic decision making was centralized, a reflection of the overall centralization undertaken by the Gaullist government. From 1958 to 1968, the French gross national product experienced an annual increase of 5.5 percent, faster than that of the United States. By the end of de Gaulle's era, France was a major industrial producer and exporter, particularly in such areas as automobiles and armaments.

Despite his successes, de Gaulle did not really achieve his ambitious goals of world power. Although his successors maintained that France was the "third nuclear power" after the United States and the Soviet Union, in truth France was too small for such global ambitions. A tired and discouraged Charles de Gaulle resigned from office in April 1969 and died within a year.

The worsening of France's economic situation in the 1970s brought a shift to the left politically. By 1981, the Socialists had become the dominant party in the National Assembly, and the Socialist leader, François Mitterand (b. 1916), was elected president. His first concern was with France's economic difficulties. In 1982, Mitterand froze prices and wages in the hope of reducing the huge budget deficit and high inflation. Mitterand also passed a number of liberal measures to aid workers: an increased minimum wage, expanded social benefits, a mandatory fifth week of paid vacation for salaried workers, a thirty-nine-hour work week, higher taxes for the rich, and nationalization of major banks. Mitterand's administrative reforms included both centralization (nationalization of banks and industry) and decentralization (granting local governments greater powers). In the 1988 presidential election, Mitterand won a second seven-year term.

WEST GERMANY   As a result of the pressures of the Cold War, the unification of the three Western zones into the West German Federal Republic became a reality in 1949. Konrad Adenauer (1876–1967), the leader of the Christian Democratic Union (CDU) who served as chancellor from 1949 to 1963, became the "founding hero" of the Federal Republic. Adenauer sought respect for Germany by cooperating with the United States and the other Western European nations. The beginning of the Korean War in June of 1950 had unexpected repercussions for West Germany. The fear that South Korea might fall to the Communist forces of the north led many Germans and westerners to worry about the security of West Germany and led to calls for the rearmament of West Germany. Although many people, concerned

▼ **De Gaulle and Adenauer.** While the postwar world was dividing into opposing Cold War camps, old enemies were becoming reconciled. The meeting of French president Charles de Gaulle and the German chancellor Konrad Adenauer in 1962 was an important step in beginning a friendly relationship between France and Germany.

about a revival of German militarism, condemned this proposal, Cold War tensions were decisive. West Germany rearmed in 1955 and became a member of NATO.

Adenauer's chancellorship is largely associated with the resurrection of the West German economy, often referred to as the "economic miracle." It was largely guided by the minister of finance, Ludwig Erhard. Although West Germany had only 75 percent of the population and 52 percent of the territory of prewar Germany, by 1955 the West German gross national product exceeded that of prewar Germany. Real wages doubled from 1950 to 1965 even though work hours were cut by 20 percent.

After the Adenauer era, German voters moved politically from the center-right politics of the Christian Democrats to center-left politics, and in 1969, the Social Democrats became the leading party. By forming a ruling coalition with the small Free Democratic party (FPD), the Social Democrats remained in power until 1982. The first Social Democratic chancellor was Willy Brandt (b. 1913). Brandt was especially successful with his "opening toward the east" (known as *Ostpolitik*), for which he received the Nobel Peace Prize in 1972. On March 19, 1971, Brandt met with Walter Ulbricht, the East German leader, and worked out the details of a Basic Treaty that was signed in 1972. This agreement did not establish full diplomatic relations with East Germany, but did call for "good neighborly" relations. As a result, it led to greater cultural, personal, and economic contacts between West and East Germany. Despite this success, the discovery of an East German spy among Brandt's advisers caused his resignation in 1974.

His successor, Helmut Schmidt (b. 1918), was more of a technocrat than a reform-minded socialist and concentrated primarily on the economic problems largely brought about by high oil prices between 1973 and 1975. Schmidt was successful in eliminating a deficit of 10 billion marks in three years. In 1982, when the coalition of Schmidt's Social Democrats with the Free Democrats fell apart over the reduction of social welfare expenditures, the Free Democrats joined with the Christian Democratic Union of Helmut Kohl (b. 1930) to form a new government. As the two German states approached unification in 1990, Kohl remained in power and became the leading candidate to become the first chancellor of a reunified German state.

Throughout its postwar existence, West Germany has been troubled by its Nazi past. The surviving major Nazi leaders had been tried and condemned as war criminals at the Nuremberg war crimes trials in 1945 and 1946. As part of the denazification of Germany, the victorious Allies continued war crimes trials of lesser officials, but these diminished as the Cold War produced a shift in attitudes. By 1950, German courts had begun to take over the war crimes trials, and the German legal machine has persisted in prosecuting cases. The West German government has also made payments to Israel and to Holocaust survivors and their relatives in order to make some restitution for the crimes of the Nazi era. The German president Richard von Weizsäcker has been especially eloquent in reminding Germans of their responsibility "for the unspeakable sorrow that occurred in the name of Germany."

GREAT BRITAIN   The end of World War II left Britain with massive economic problems. In elections held immediately after the war, the Labour party overwhelmingly defeated Churchill's Conservative party. The Labour party had promised far-reaching reforms, particularly in the area of social welfare, and in a country with a tremendous shortage of consumer goods and housing, its platform was quite appealing. The new Labour government proceeded to enact the reforms that created the modern welfare state. Clement Attlee (1883–1967), the new prime minister, was a pragmatic reformer and certainly not the leftist revolutionary that Churchill had warned against in the election campaign.

The establishment of the British welfare state began with the nationalization of the Bank of England, the coal and steel industries, public transportation, and public utilities, such as electricity and gas. In the area of social welfare, the new government enacted the National Insurance Act and the National Health Service Act in 1946. The insurance act established a comprehensive social security program and nationalized medical insurance, thereby enabling the state to subsidize the unemployed, the sick, and the aged. The health act created a system of socialized medicine that forced doctors and dentists to work with state hospitals, although private practices could be maintained. This was an especially costly measure for the state, but within a few years 90 percent of the medical profession was participating. The British welfare state became the norm for most European states after the war.

The cost of building a welfare state at home forced the British to reduce expenses abroad. This meant the dismantling of the British Empire and the reduction of military aid to such countries as Greece and Turkey. Not a belief in the morality of self-determination, but economic necessity brought an end to the British Empire.

Continuing economic problems, however, brought the Conservatives back into power from 1951 to 1964.

Although they favored private enterprise, the Conservatives accepted the welfare state and even extended it when they undertook an ambitious construction program to improve British housing.

Between 1964 and 1979, Conservatives and Labour alternated in power. Both parties had to face seemingly intractable problems. While separatist movements in Scotland and Wales were overcome, fighting between Catholics and Protestants in Northern Ireland was not so easily settled. Violence increased as the Irish Republican Army (IRA) staged a series of dramatic terrorist acts in response to the suspension of Northern Ireland's parliament in 1972 and the establishment of direct rule by London. The problems in Northern Ireland have not yet been solved. Nor was either party able to deal with Britain's ailing economy. Failure to modernize made British industry less and less competitive. Moreover, Britain was hampered by frequent labor strikes, many of them caused by conflicts between rival labor unions.

In 1979, after Britain's economic problems had seemed to worsen during five years under a Labour government, the Conservatives returned to power under Margaret Thatcher (b. 1925). She became the first woman prime minister in British history. Thatcher pledged to lower taxes, reduce government bureaucracy, limit social welfare, restrict union power, and end inflation. The "Iron Lady," as she was called, did break the power of the labor unions. While she did not eliminate the basic components of the social welfare system, she did use austerity measures to control inflation. "Thatcherism," as her economic policy was termed, improved the British economic situation but at a price. The south of England, for example, prospered, but the old industrial areas of the Midlands and north declined and were beset by high unemployment, poverty, and even violence. Cutbacks in education seriously undermined the quality of British education, long regarded as one of the world's finest.

In the area of foreign policy, Thatcher, like Ronald Reagan in the United States, took a hard-line approach against communism. She oversaw a large military buildup aimed at replacing older technology and reestablishing Britain as a world policeman. In 1982, when Argentina attempted to take control of the Falkland Islands (one of Britain's few remaining colonial outposts) 300 miles off its coast, the British successfully rebuked the Argentines, although at great economic cost and the loss of 255 lives. The Falklands War, however, did generate much popular patriotic support for Thatcher.

Margaret Thatcher dominated British politics in the 1980s. The Labour party, beset by divisions between its moderate and radical wings, offered little effective opposition. Only in 1990 did Labour's fortunes seem to revive when Thatcher's government attempted to replace local property taxes with a flat-rate tax payable by every adult to his or her local authority. While Thatcher argued that this would make local government more responsive to its electors, many argued that this was nothing more than a poll tax that would enable the rich to pay the same rate as the poor. In 1990, after antitax riots broke out, Thatcher's once remarkable popularity fell to all-time lows. At the end of November, a revolt within her own party caused Thatcher to resign as prime minister.

ITALY After the war, Italy faced a period of heavy reconstruction. No other Western country, except Germany, sustained more physical destruction. The monarchy was abolished when 54 percent of Italian voters rejected the royal house, and in June 1946, Italy became a democratic republic.

In the first postwar parliamentary elections held in April 1948, the Christian Democrats, still allied with the Catholic church, emerged as the leading political party. Alcide de Gasperi (1881–1954) became prime minister from 1948 to 1953, an unusually long span of time for an Italian government. Like prefascist governments, postwar Italian coalitions, largely dominated by the Christian Democrats, remained notorious for their instability and short lives. Although the Italian Communist party is one of Italy's three largest parties, it has been largely excluded from all of these government coalitions, although it managed to gain power in a number of provinces and municipalities in the 1960s and 1970s. The Christian Democrats have been able to maintain control by keeping the support of the upper and middle classes and the southern peasantry. In the 1980s, Italian politics continued to be marked by numerous changes of government and prime ministers.

The Marshall Plan helped to stabilize the postwar Italian economy. By 1957, worker income had risen far above 1939 levels. As in other Western welfare states, the Italian economy combined private enterprise with government management, particularly of heavy industry. The major economic problem continued to be the backwardness of southern Italy. In the 1960s millions of Italians from the south migrated to the more prosperous north.

Western Europe: The Move toward Unity

As we have seen, the divisions created by the Cold War led the nations of Western Europe to form the North Atlantic Treaty Organization in 1949. But military unity was not the only kind of unity fostered in Europe after 1945. The destructiveness of two world wars caused many thoughtful Europeans to consider the need for some form of European unity. National feeling was still too powerful, however, for European nations to give up their political sovereignty. Consequently, the desire for unity was forced to focus primarily on the economic arena, not the political.

In 1951, France, West Germany, the Benelux countries (Belgium, Netherlands, and Luxemburg), and Italy formed the European Coal and Steel Community (ECSC). Its purpose was to create a common market for coal and steel products among the six nations by eliminating tariffs and other trade barriers. The success of the ECSC encouraged these six nations to proceed further, and in 1957 they created the European Atomic Energy Community (EURATOM) to further European research on the peaceful uses of nuclear energy.

In the same year, these six nations created the European Economic Community (EEC), also known as the Common Market. The Common Market eliminated customs barriers for the six member nations and created a large free-trade area protected from the rest of the world by a common external tariff. By promoting free trade, the Common Market also encouraged cooperation and standardization in many aspects of the six nations' economies. All the member nations benefited economically. The Common Market was expanded in 1973 when

▼ **Map 29.4** European Economic and Political Developments.

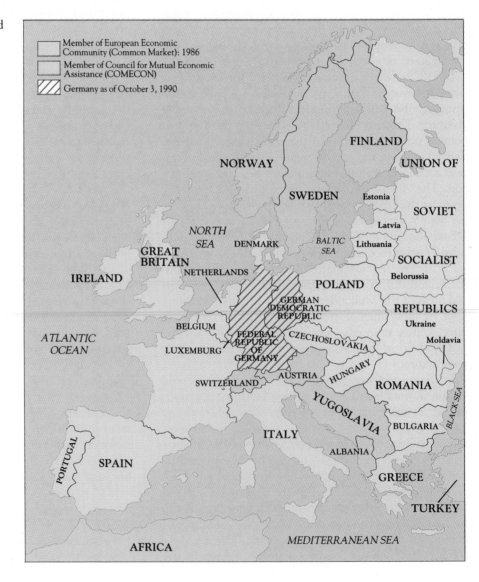

Great Britain, Ireland, and Denmark gained membership in what its members now began to call the European Community (EC). By 1986, three additional members—Spain, Portugal, and Greece—had been added.

The economic integration of the members of the European Community led to cooperative efforts in international and political affairs as well. The foreign ministers of the twelve members consult frequently and provide a common front for negotiations on important issues. Nevertheless, the European Community is still primarily an economic union, not a political one. By 1990, the European Community comprised 320 million people and constituted the world's largest single trading entity, transacting almost one-fourth of the world's commerce. Full economic integration for the European Community is projected by the end of 1992.

▼ Thought and Culture in the Postwar Era: New and Old Directions

Intellectually and culturally, the postwar era has been marked by much diversity. Although many trends represent a continuation of prewar modern developments, new directions have also led some to speak of a postmodern cultural world.

Recent Trends in Art, Music, and Literature

Modern art continued to prevail at exhibitions and museums. For the most part, the United States dominated the art world, much as it did the world of popular culture (see Popular Culture and the Americanization of the World later in the chapter). American art, often vibrantly colored and filled with activity, reflected the energy and exuberance of postwar America. After 1945, New York City became the artistic center of the Western world. The Guggenheim Museum, the Museum of Modern Art, and the Whitney Museum of American art, together with New York's numerous art galleries, promoted modern art and helped determine artistic tastes not only in New York and the United States, but throughout much of the world.

Abstractionism, especially Abstract Expressionism, emerged as the artistic mainstream (see Chapters 25 and 27). American exuberance in Abstract Expressionism is evident in the enormous canvases of Jackson Pollock (1912–1956). In such works as *Lavender Mist* (1950), paint seems to explode, assaulting the viewer with emotion and movement. Pollock's swirling forms and seemingly chaotic patterns broke all conventions of form and structure. His drip paintings, with their total abstraction, were extremely influential with other artists, although the public was initially quite hostile to his work. Pollock also introduced the technique of painting with the canvas laid on the floor or hung on a wall rather than placed on an easel. Significantly, paint itself was more the subject of his work than any preconceived representation.

The early 1960s saw the emergence of Pop Art, which took images of popular culture and transformed them into works of fine art. Andy Warhol (1930–1987), who began his career as an advertising illustrator, was the most famous of the pop artists. Warhol adapted images from commercial art, such as the Campbell soup cans, and photographs of such celebrities as Marilyn Monroe. Derived from mass culture, these works were mass pro-

▼ **Jackson Pollock Does a Painting.** American artists dominated the art world for many decades after the end of World War II. Abstract Expressionism remained at the center of the artistic mainstream. One of its best known practitioners was the American Jackson Pollock, who achieved his ideal of total abstraction by his drip paintings. He is shown here at work in his Long Island studio. Pollock found it easier to cover his large canvases with exploding patterns of color by putting them on the floor.

duced and deliberately "of the moment," expressing the fleeting whims of popular culture.

In the 1980s, styles have emerged that some have referred to as Postmodern. Although as yet ill-defined, Postmodernism tends to move away from the futurism or "cutting edge" qualities of Modernism. Instead it favors "utilizing tradition," whether that includes more

styles of painting or elevating traditional craftsmanship to the level of fine art. Weavers, potters, glassmakers, metalsmiths, and furniture makers have gained respect as artists.

Another response to Modernism can be seen in a return to realism in the arts. Some extreme realists paint or sculpt with such minute attention to realistic detail that their paintings appear to be photographs and their sculptures living human beings. Their subjects are often ordinary individuals, stuck in ordinary lives. These works are often pessimistic and cynical.

Abstract Expressionism, however, continues to proliferate. Anselm Kiefer, born in Germany in 1945, combines aspects of Abstract Expressionism, collage, and German Expressionism to create works that are stark and haunting. His *Departure from Egypt* (1984) is a meditation on Jewish history and its descent into the horrors of Nazism. Kiefer's international stature reflects a movement away from American dominance in the fine arts, a trend that gained momentum in the 1980s.

Classical music also witnessed a continuation of prewar developments. Some composers, the neoclassicists, remained closely tied to nineteenth-century romantic music, although they occasionally used some twentieth-century developments, such as atonality and dissonance. Their style was strongly reminiscent of Stravinsky (see Chapter 25).

The major musical trend since the war, however, has been serialism. Inspired mostly by the twelve tone music of Schönberg (see Chapter 27), serialism is a compositional procedure where an order of succession is set for specific values: pitch (for tones of the tempered scale); loudness (for dynamic levels); and units of time (for rhythm). By predetermining the order of succession, the composer restricts his or her intuitive freedom as the work to some extent creates itself. However, the mechanism the composer initially creates could generate unanticipated musical events, thereby creating new and exciting compositions. Serialist composition diminishes the role of intuition and emotion in favor of intellect and mathematical precision. The first recognized serialist was the Frenchman Olivier Messiaen (b. 1908). Significantly, Messiaen was influenced in part by Indian and Greek music, plain chant, folk music, and birdsongs. Most critics have respected serialism, although the public has been largely indifferent, if not hostile, to it. An offshoot of serialism that has won popular support, but not the same critical favor, is minimalism. Like serialism, this style uses repeated patterns and series and steady pulsation with gradual changes occurring over time. But whereas serialism is often atonal, minimalism is usually tonal and more harmonic.

The most significant new trend in postwar literature has been called the "Theater of the Absurd." This new convention in drama began in France in the 1950s, although its most famous proponent was the Irishman Samuel Beckett (1906–1990), who lived in France. In Beckett's *Waiting for Godot* (1952), it is readily apparent that the action on stage is not realistic. Two men wait incessantly for the appearance of someone, with whom they may or may not have an appointment. No background information on the two men is provided. During the course of the play, nothing seems to be happening. The audience is never told if the action in front of them is a dream, an allegory, or purely symbolic. As in lyric poetry, images in absurdist literature are presented as metaphors for aspects of human existence, involving states of mind and complex feelings. Unlike traditional theater, suspense is not maintained by having the audience wonder, "what is going to happen next?" but simply, "what is happening now?"

The Theater of the Absurd reflected its time. The postwar period was a time of disillusionment with fixed ideological beliefs in politics or religion. The same disillusionment that inspired Sartre's and Camus's existentialism (see The Philosophical Dilemma: Existentialism later in the chapter), with its sense of the world's meaninglessness, underscored the desolate worldview of absurdist drama and literature. This can be seen in Günter Grass's *Tin Drum*, published in 1959, which reflected postwar Germany's preoccupation with the seeming incomprehensibility of Nazi Germany.

The Theater of the Absurd also questioned the ability of language to reflect reality accurately. Beckett's play *Act without Words* contains no dialogue. In another play, Beckett used a beam of light and a buzzing sound as "words" of the discourse. The Czech playwright, Vaclav Havel, in his *Memorandum* (1966), examined the language and mechanics of bureaucracy. The plot revolved around the introduction of an artificial language that is imposed on people in the hope of fostering more efficient communication. Because no one can understand the new language, communication breaks down and, therefore, so do human relationships. The artificial language is finally eliminated, only to be replaced by an equally incomprehensible language imposed from above. The overt critique of Communist bureaucracy and the absurdity of imposing artificial systems with the hope of recreating society along ideological lines did little for Havel's position in Communist Czechoslovakia.

Postwar Science and Technology

Since the Scientific Revolution of the seventeenth century and the Industrial Revolution of the nineteenth century, science and technology have played increasingly important roles in Western civilization. Many of the scientific and technological achievements since

▼ **Anselm Kiefer, *Departure from Egypt*, 1984** Although Western artists experimented with a variety of modern and even postmodern styles in the 1970s and 1980s, Abstract Expressionism continued its popularity. The German artist Anselm Kiefer used the tradition of Abstract Expressionism to create haunting images that reflect the horrors of Germany's Nazi past.

Photo courtesy of the Museum of Contemporary Art. Purchased with funds provided by Douglas S. Cramer, Beatrice and Philip Gersh, Lenore S. and Bernard A. Greenberg, Joan and Fred Nicholas, Robert A. Rowan, Pippa Scott, and an anonymous donor. Photo by Squidds and Nunns.

World War II have revolutionized people's lives. When American astronauts walked on the moon, millions watched the event on their televisions in the privacy of their living rooms.

Before World War II, theoretical science and technology were largely separated. Pure science was the domain of university professors who were quite far removed from the practical technological concerns of technicians and engineers. "Pure" scientists were rarely concerned with the practical usefulness of their research. But during World War II, university scientists were recruited to work for their governments and develop new weapons and practical instruments of war. British physicists played a crucial role in the development of an improved radar system in 1940 that helped to defeat the German air force in the Battle of Britain. German scientists converted coal to gasoline to keep the German war machine moving and created self-propelled rockets as well as jet airplanes to keep Hitler's hopes alive for a miraculous turnaround in the war. The computer, too, was a wartime creation. The British mathematician Alan Turing designed a primitive computer to assist British intelligence in breaking the secret codes of German ciphering machines. The most famous result of wartime scientific research was the creation of the atomic bomb by a team of American and European scientists who worked under the guidance of the physicist J. Robert Oppenheimer. Obviously, most wartime devices were created for destructive purposes, but merely to mention computers and jet airplanes demonstrates that they could easily be adapted for peacetime uses.

The sponsorship of research by governments and the military during World War II created a new model for science that some have labeled "Big Science." Science had become very complex. Only large organizations with teams of scientists, huge laboratories, and complex equipment could undertake such large-scale projects. Such facilities were so expensive, however, that they could only be provided by governments and large corporations. Because of its postwar prosperity, the United States was able to lead in the development of Big Science. Almost 75 percent of all scientific research funds in the United States came from the government in 1965. Unwilling to lag behind, especially in military developments, the Soviet Union was also forced to provide large outlays for scientific and technological research. In fact, the defense establishments of the United States and the Soviet Union generated much of postwar scientific research. One-fourth of trained scientists and engineers after 1945 were utilized in the creation of new weapons systems. Universities found their research agen-

das increasingly determined by government funding for military-related projects.

There was no more stunning example of how Big Science operated than in the space race of the 1960s. The announcement by the Russians in 1957 that they had sent the first space satellite—*Sputnik I*—into orbit around the earth, caused the United States to launch a gigantic project to land a manned spacecraft on the moon within a decade. Massive government funds financed the scientific research and technological advances that achieved this goal in 1969.

The postwar alliance of science and technology led to an accelerated rate of change that became a fact of life in Western society. But the underlying assumption of this alliance—that scientific knowledge gave human beings the ability to manipulate the environment for their benefit—was questioned by some in the 1960s and 1970s who believed that some technological advances had far-reaching side effects damaging to the environment. The chemical fertilizers, for example, that were touted for producing larger crops, wreaked havoc with the ecological balance of streams, rivers, and woodlands. *Small Is Beautiful,* written by the British economist E. F. Schumacher (1911–1977), was a fundamental critique of the dangers of Big Science (see the box on p. 1029). The widespread proliferation of fouled beaches and dying forests and lakes promised to make environmentalism one of the important issues of the 1990s.

After World War II, a number of physicists continued to explore the implications of Einstein's revolution in physics and raised fundamental questions about the nature of reality. To some physicists, quantum and relativity theory described the universe as a complicated web of relations in which there were no isolated building blocks. Thus, the universe was not a "collection of physical objects," but a complicated web of relations between "various parts of a unified whole." Moreover, this web of relations that is the universe also included the human observer. Human beings could not be objective observers of objects detached from themselves because the very act of observation made them participants in the process itself. These speculations implied that the old Newtonian conception of the universe as a machine was an outdated tool for understanding the nature of the universe.

The Philosophical Dilemma: Existentialism

In the twentieth century, philosophy divided itself into two major schools of thought. In Great Britain and the United States, logical positivism (or logical empiri-

Small Is Beautiful: The Limits of Modern Technology
▼ ▼ ▼

Although the alliance of science and technology has produced an amazing array of achievements in the postwar world, some voices have been raised in criticism of the sometimes destructive aspects of Big Science. In 1975, in his book Small Is Beautiful, *the British economist E. F. Schumacher examined the effects modern industrial technology has had on the earth's resources.*

E. F. Schumacher, *Small Is Beautiful*

Is it not evident that our current methods of production are already eating into the very substance of industrial man? To many people this is not at all evident. Now that we have solved the problem of production, they say, have we ever had it so good? Are we not better fed, better clothed, and better housed than ever before—and better educated? Of course we are: most, but by no means all, of us: in the rich countries. But this is not what I mean by "substance." The substance of man cannot be measured by Gross National Product. Perhaps it cannot be measured at all, except for certain symptoms of loss. However, this is not the place to go into the statistics of these symptoms, such as crime, drug addiction, vandalism, mental breakdown, rebellion, and so forth. Statistics never prove anything.

I started by saying that one of the most fateful errors of our age is the belief that the problem of production has been solved. This illusion, I suggested, is mainly due to our inability to recognize that the modern industrial system, with all its intellectual sophistication, consumes the very basis on which it has been erected. To use the language of the economist, it lives on irreplaceable capital which it cheerfully treats as income. I specified three categories of such capital: fossil fuels, the tolerance margins of nature, and the human substance. Even if some readers should refuse to accept all three parts of my argument, I suggest that any one of them suffices to make my case.

And what is my case? Simply that our most important task is to get off our present collision course. And who is there to tackle such a task? I think every one of us. . . . To talk about the future is useful only if it leads to action *now*. And what can we do *now*, while we are still in the position of "never having had it so good"? To say the least . . . we must thoroughly understand the problem and begin to see the possibility of evolving a new life-style, with new methods of production and new patterns of consumption: a life-style designed for permanence. To give only three preliminary examples: in agriculture and horticulture, we can interest ourselves in the perfection of production methods which are biologically sound, build up soil fertility, and produce health, beauty and permanence. Productivity will then look after itself. In industry, we can interest ourselves in the evolution of small-scale technology, relatively nonviolent technology, "technology with a human face," so that people have a chance to enjoy themselves while they are working, instead of working solely for their pay packet and hoping, usually forlornly, for enjoyment solely during their leisure time.

cism) became dominant in university circles. Logical empiricism rejected as senseless the emphasis of traditional philosophy on such issues as God, happiness, and the meaning of freedom. Largely based on the teachings of the Austrian philosopher Ludwig Wittgenstein (1889–1951), logical positivism concentrated on logic and a theory of knowledge. Impressed by the methods and achievements of modern science, it turned to mathematics and linguistics for its models. It was concerned with criticizing what people believe by analyzing what they say and how they know.

On the Continent, the philosophical doctrine of existentialism continued philosophy's traditional concern with moral questions and the immediate problems of life and existence. Although it had antecedents before the twentieth century, existentialism (especially in its atheistic form) was largely born of the desperation caused by two world wars and the breakdown of traditional values. Existentialism reflected the anxieties of the twentieth century and became especially well known after World War II through the works of two Frenchmen, Jean-Paul Sartre (1905–1980) and Albert Camus (1913–1960).

The beginning point of the existentialism of Sartre and Camus was the absence of God in the universe. While the death of God was tragic, it meant that humans had no preordained destiny and were utterly alone

According to Camus, then, the world was absurd and without meaning; humans, too, are without meaning and purpose. Reduced to despair and depression, humans have but one ground of hope—themselves.

While the world might be absurd, Camus argued, it could not be absurd unless people judged it to be so. People are unique in the world, and their kind of being is quite different from that of all others. In the words of Sartre, human "existence precedes essence." Humans are beings who first exist, and then afterward define themselves. They determine what they will be. According to Sartre: "Man is nothing else but what he makes of himself. Such is the first principle of existentialism." People then must take full responsibility for what they are. They create their values and give their lives mean-

▼ **Pope John Paul II.** The travels of Pope John Paul II have helped to strengthen the presence of the Catholic church throughout the world, especially in Third World countries.

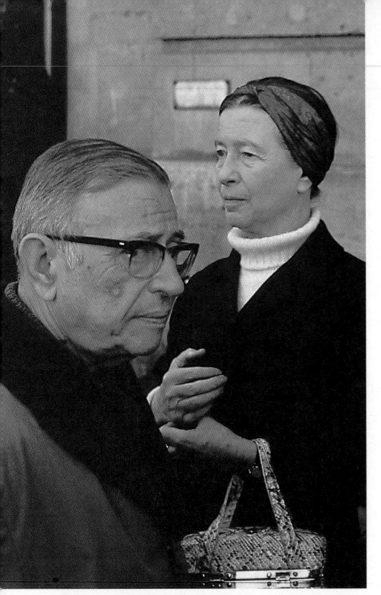

▼ **Sartre and De Beauvoir.** Jean-Paul Sartre and Simone de Beauvoir were two of the leading intellectuals in twentieth-century Europe. Sartre and de Beauvoir had a lifelong relationship that lasted until his death in 1980. Both were actively involved in the existentialist movement. De Beauvoir also played a crucial role in the emergence of the postwar women's liberation movement.

in the universe with no future and no hope. As Camus expressed it:

> A world that can be explained even with bad reasons is a familiar world. But, on the other hand, in a universe suddenly divested of illusions and lights, man feels an alien, a stranger. His exile is without remedy since he is deprived of the memory of a lost home or the hope of a promised land. This divorce between man and his life, the actor and his setting, is properly the feeling of absurdity.[10]

The Pope Denounces the Arms Race

▼ ▼ ▼

Pope John XXIII was a caring man who anguished over the world's social, economic, and political problems. In a papal letter entitled Pacem in Terris (Peace on Earth), *he argued for an end to the arms race.*

Pope John XXIII, *Pacem in Terris,* 1963

It is with deep sorrow that We note the enormous stocks of armaments that have been and still are being made in more economically developed countries, with a vast outlay of intellectual and economic resources. And so it happens that, while the people of these countries are loaded with heavy burdens, other countries as a result are deprived of the collaboration they need in order to make economic and social progress.

The production of arms is allegedly justified on the grounds that in present-day conditions peace cannot be preserved without an equal balance of armaments. And so, if one country increases its armaments, others feel the need to do the same; and if one country is equipped with nuclear weapons, other countries must produce their own, equally destructive.

Consequently, people live in constant fear lest the storm that every moment threatens should break upon them with dreadful violence. And with good reason, for the arms of war are ready at hand. . . . And one must bear in mind that, even though the monstrous power of modern weapons acts as a deterrent, it is to be feared that the mere continuance of nuclear tests, undertaken with war in mind will prove a serious hazard for life on earth.

Justice, then, right reason and humanity urgently demand that the arms race should cease; that the stockpiles which exist in various countries should be reduced equally and simultaneously by the parties concerned; that nuclear weapons should be banned; and that a general agreement should eventually be reached about progressive disarmament and an effective method of control. . . .

All must realize that there is no hope of putting an end to the building up of armaments, nor of reducing the present stocks, nor, still less, of abolishing them altogether, unless the process is complete and thorough and unless it proceeds from inner conviction: unless, that is, everyone sincerely co-operates to banish the fear and anxious expectation of war with which men are oppressed. If this is to come about, the fundamental principle on which our present peace depends must be replaced by another, which declares that the true and solid peace of nations consists not in equality of arms but in mutual trust alone. We believe that this can be brought to pass, and We consider that it is something which reason requires, that it is eminently desirable in itself and that it will prove to be the source of many benefits.

---

ing. And this can only be done by their involvement in life. Only through a person's acts can one determine his or her values. According to Sartre: "I may say that I like so-and-so well enough to sacrifice a certain amount of money for him, but I may say so only if I've done it."

Existentialism, therefore, involved an ethics of action, of involvement in life. But people could not define themselves without their involvement with others. Thus, existentialism's ethical message was just as important as its philosophy of being. Essentially, the message of existentialism was one of authenticity. Individuals true to themselves refused to be depersonalized by their society. As one author noted, "Existentialism is the struggle to discover the human person in a depersonalized age."

The Revival of Religion

Existentialism was one response to the despair generated by the apparent collapse of civilized values in the twentieth century. The revival of religion has been another. Ever since the Enlightenment of the eighteenth century, Christianity and religion had been on the defensive. But a number of religious thinkers and leaders attempted to bring new life to Christianity in the twentieth century. Despite the attempts of the Communist world to build an atheistic society and the West to build a secular society, religion continued to play an important role in the lives of many people.

One expression of this religious revival was the attempt by such theologians as the Lutheran Karl Barth

(1886–1968) to infuse traditional Christian teachings with new life. In his numerous writings, Barth attempted to reinterpret the religious insights of the Reformation era for the modern world. To Barth, the sinful and hence imperfect nature of human beings meant that humans could know religious truth not through reason, but only through the grace of God.

In the Catholic church, attempts at religious renewal came from two charismatic popes—John XXIII and John Paul II. Pope John XXIII (1881–1963) reigned as pope for only a short time (1958–1963), but sparked a dramatic revival of Catholicism when he summoned the twenty-first ecumenical council of the Catholic church. Known as Vatican Council II, it liberalized a number of Catholic practices. The mass was henceforth to be celebrated in the vernacular languages rather than Latin. New avenues of communication with other Christian faiths were also opened for the first time since the Reformation (see the box on p. 1031).

John Paul II (b. 1920), who had been the archbishop of Cracow in Poland before his elevation to the papacy in 1978, was the first non-Italian to be elected pope since the sixteenth century. Although he reasserted traditional Catholic teaching on such issues as papal authority, birth control, and clerical celibacy, John Paul's numerous travels around the world helped strengthen the Catholic church throughout the non-Western world. A strong believer in social justice, the charismatic John Paul II has been a powerful figure in reminding Europeans of their spiritual heritage and the need to temper the pursuit of materialism with spiritual concerns.

▼ The Creation of a New Society

During the postwar era, Western society has witnessed remarkably rapid change. Such products of new technologies as computers, television, jet planes, contraceptive devices, and new surgical techniques have all dramatically and quickly altered the pace and nature of human life.

Social Changes

The rapid changes in postwar society, fueled by scientific advances and rapid economic growth, have led many to view it as a new society. Called a technocratic society by some and the consumer society by others, postwar Western society has been characterized by a changing social structure and new movements for change.

SOCIAL STRUCTURE   The structure of European society was altered after 1945. Especially noticeable were the changes in the middle class. Such traditional middle-class groups as businesspeople and professionals in law, medicine, and the universities were greatly augmented by a new breed of managers and technicians, as large corporations and government agencies employed increasing numbers of white-collar supervisory and administrative personnel. Whether in Eastern or Western Europe, the new managers and experts were not very different from each other. Everywhere their positions depended upon specialized skills acquired from some form of higher education. Everywhere they focused on the practical and efficient administration of their organizations. Since their positions usually depended upon their skills, they took steps to ensure that their own children would be educated.

Changes have also occurred among the traditional lower classes. Especially noticeable was the dramatic shift of people from rural to urban areas. After 1945, the number of peasants in most European countries dropped by 50 percent. While the size of the industrial working class stabilized or declined, making up slightly less than 50 percent of laborers in highly industrialized countries, there was a dramatic increase in the number of white-collar service employees. At the same time, a substantial increase in their real wages enabled the working classes to aspire to the consumption patterns of the middle class, leading to what some observers have called the "consumer society." Buying on the installment plan, which was introduced in the 1930s, became widespread in the 1950s and gave workers a chance to imitate the middle class by buying such products as televisions, washing machines, refrigerators, vacuum cleaners, and stereos. But the most visible symbol of mass consumerism was the automobile. Before World War II, cars were reserved mostly for the European upper classes. In 1948, there were 5 million cars in all of Europe, but by 1957, the number had tripled. By the 1960s, there were almost 45 million cars.

Rising incomes, combined with decreased working hours, created an even greater market for mass leisure activities. Between 1900 and 1980, the work week was reduced from sixty hours to forty hours. All aspects of popular culture—music, sports, media—became commercialized (see Popular Culture later in the chapter). Another very visible symbol of mass consumerism was the growth of mass travel and tourism. Before World War II, mostly the upper and middle classes enjoyed travel for pleasure. After the war, the combination of more vacation time and automobiles made it possible for many

1968: The Year of Student Revolts
▼ ▼ ▼

The outburst of student upheavals in the late 1960s reached its high point in 1968. These two very different selections illustrate some of the issues that prompted university students to occupy campus buildings and demand reforms.

A Student Manifesto in Search of a Real and Human Educational Alternative (University of British Columbia), June 1968

Today we as students are witnessing a deepening crisis within our society. We are intensely aware, in a way perhaps not possible for the older generation, that humanity stands on the edge of a new era. Because we are young, we have insights into the present and visions of the future that our parents do not have. Tasks of an immense gravity wait solution in our generation. We have inherited these tasks from our parents. We do not blame them so much for that . . . but we do blame them for being unwilling to admit that there are problems or for saying that it is we who have visited these problems on ourselves because of our perversity, ungratefulness and unwillingness to listen to "reason."

   Much of the burden of solving the problems of the new era rests on the university. We have been taught to look to it for leadership. While we know that part of the reason for the university is to render direct services to the community, we are alarmed at its servility to industry and government as to what and how

it teaches. We are scandalized that the university fails to realize its role in renewing and vivifying those intellectual and moral energies necessary to create a new society—one in which a sense of personal dignity and human community can be preserved.

Student Inscriptions on the Walls of Paris, May and June 1968

The dream is the reality.
May 1968. World revolution is the order of the day.
I decree a state of permanent happiness.
To be free in 1968 is to take part.
Take the trip every day of your life.
Make love, not war.
No exams.
The mind travels farther than the heart but it doesn't go as far.
Run, comrade, the old are behind you!
Don't make a revolution in the image of your confused and hide-bound university.
Exam = servility, social promotion, hierarchic society.
Love each other.
SEX. It's good, said Mao, but not too often.
Alcohol kills. Take LSD.
Are you consumers or participants?
Professors, you are as old as your culture; your modernism is only the modernization of the police.
Live in the present.
Revolution, I love you.
Long live direct democracy!

members of the middle class and even workers to go to beaches, ski resorts, and mountain retreats. Moreover, as packaged tours with their lower travel rates and low-budget rooms became widely available, possibilities for travel abroad to other continents increased.

EDUCATION AND STUDENT REVOLT   Before World War II, higher education had largely remained the preserve of Europe's wealthier classes. Even in 1950, for example, only 3 or 4 percent of West European young people were enrolled in some form of higher education. Moreover, European higher education still largely centered on the liberal arts, pure science, and preparation for the professions of law and medicine.

Much of this changed after World War II as European universities experienced an influx of more students from the middle and even lower classes. The curriculum also expanded as such applied disciplines as computer science and business administration were introduced. Enrollments grew dramatically; in France, 4.5 percent of young people went to a university in 1950. By 1965, the figure had increased to 14.5 percent. Enrollments in European universities more than tripled between 1940 and 1960.

But there were problems. Overcrowded classrooms and lack of attention from professors led to student discontent. Moreover, despite changes in the curriculum, students often felt that the universities were not providing a really modern education. This discontent led to an outburst of student revolts in the late 1960s (see the box on p. 1033). In part, these protests were an extension of the large-scale disruptions in American universities in the mid-1960s, which were often sparked by student opposition to the Vietnam War. Perhaps the most famous student revolt occurred in France in 1968. It erupted at the University of Nanterre outside Paris but soon spread to the Sorbonne, the main campus of the University of Paris. French students demanded curriculum changes and a greater voice in the administration of the university. Students took over buildings and then expanded the scale of their protests when they invited workers to support them. Half of France's work force went on strike in May 1968. After the Gaullist government instituted a hefty wage hike, the workers returned to work and the police repressed the remaining student protesters.

The high point of the student protest movement was reached in 1968, although scattered incidents lasted into the early 1970s. There were several reasons for the student radicalism. Some students were genuinely motivated by the desire to reform the university. Others were protesting the Vietnam War, which they viewed as a product of Western imperialism. They also attacked other aspects of Western society, such as its materialism, and expressed concern about becoming cogs in the large and impersonal bureaucratic jungles of the modern world. For many students, the calls for democratic decision making within the universities were a reflection of their deeper concerns about the direction of Western society. Although student revolts fizzled out in the

1970s, the larger issues they raised have been increasingly revived in the late 1980s.

New (and Old) Patterns: Women in the Postwar World

After World War II, the trend toward earlier marriage continued. In Sweden, the average age of first marriage dropped from twenty-six in the 1940s to twenty-three in 1970. Although birthrates rose immediately after World War II, they have mostly declined since the war as both contraceptive devices and abortion have become widely available. It is estimated that mothers need to average 2.1 children in order to ensure a natural replacement of a country's population. In many European countries, the population stopped growing in the 1960s, and the trend has worsened since then. By 1990, fertility rates were down drastically; among the twelve nations of the European Community, the average number of children per mother was 1.58. No doubt, the trend toward early marriage and smaller families contributed to the changes in the character of women's employment in both Europe and the United States as women experienced considerably more years when they were not involved in rearing children.

The most important development was the increased number of married women in the work force. At the beginning of the twentieth century, even working-class wives tended to stay at home if they could afford to do so. In the postwar period, this was no longer the case. In the United States, for example, in 1900, married women made up about 15 percent of the female labor force; by

▼ **Student Revolts in Paris, 1968.** The discontent of university students exploded in the late 1960s in a series of student revolts. Perhaps best known was the student revolt in Paris in 1968. This photograph depicts one of the many violent confrontations between helmeted anti-riot policemen and rioting students.

1970, their number had increased to 62 percent. The percentage of married women in the female labor force in Sweden increased from 47 to 66 percent between 1963 and 1975. Figures for the Soviet Union and its satellites were even higher. In 1970, 92.5 percent of all women in the Soviet Union held jobs compared to around 50 percent in France and West Germany. The industrial development of the Soviet Union relied on female labor.

But the increased number of women in the work force has not changed some old patterns. Working-class women in particular still earn salaries lower than those of men for equal work. Women still tend to enter traditionally female jobs. As one Swedish woman guidance counselor remarked in 1975: "Every girl now thinks in terms of a job. This is progress. They want children, but they don't pin their hopes on marriage. They don't intend to be housewives for some future husband. But there has been no change in their vocational choices."[11] A 1980 study of twenty-five European nations revealed that women still made up over 80 percent of the typists, nurses, tailors, and dressmakers in their countries. Many European women also still faced the double burden of earning income on one hand and raising a family and maintaining the household on the other. Such inequalities led increasing numbers of women to rebel.

THE FEMINIST MOVEMENT: THE SEARCH FOR LIBERATION
The participation of women in World War I and II helped them achieve one of the major aims of the nineteenth-century feminist movement—the right to vote. Already after World War I, many governments acknowledged the contributions of women to the war effort by granting them the right to vote. Sweden, Great Britain, Germany, Poland, Hungary, Austria, and Czechoslovakia did so in 1918, followed by the United States in 1920. Women in France and Italy did not obtain the right to vote until 1945. After World War II, European women tended to fall back into the traditional roles expected of them, and little was heard of feminist concerns. But by the late 1960s, women began to assert their rights again and speak as feminists. Along with the student upheavals of the late 1960s came renewed interest in feminism, or the women's liberation movement as it was now called. Increasingly women protested that the acquisition of political and legal equality had not brought true equality with men:

> We are economically oppressed: in jobs we do full work for half pay, in the home we do unpaid work full time. We are commercially exploited by advertisement, television and the

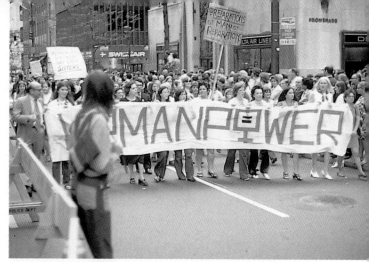

▼ WOMANPOWER. In the late 1960s, as women began once again to assert their rights, a revived women's liberation movement emerged. Feminists in the women's liberation movement maintained that women themselves must alter the conditions of their lives. This sign in a women's liberation parade shows that some women believed that it was time for "womanpower."

> press; legally we often have only the status of children. We are brought up to feel inadequate, educated to narrower horizons than men. This is our specific oppression as women. It is as women that we are, therefore, organizing.[12]

These were the words of a British Women's Liberation Workshop in 1969.

Of great importance to the emergence of the postwar women's liberation movement was the work of Simone de Beauvoir (1908–1986). Born into a Catholic middle-class family and educated at the Sorbonne in Paris, she supported herself as a teacher and later as a novelist and writer. She established a lifelong relationship (but not marriage) with Jean-Paul Sartre. Her involvement in the existentialist movement—the leading intellectual movement of its time—led to her involvement in political causes. De Beauvoir believed that she lived a "liberated" life for a twentieth-century European woman, but for all her freedom, she still came to perceive that as a woman she faced limits that men did not. In 1949, she published her highly influential work, *The Second Sex,* in which she argued that as a result of male-dominated societies, women had been defined by their differences from men and consequently received second-class status: "What peculiarly signalizes the situation of woman is that she—a free and autonomous being like all human creatures—nevertheless finds herself living in a world where men compel her to assume the status of the Other."[13] De Beauvoir took an active role in the French women's movement of the 1970s, and her book was a

The Voice of the Women's Liberation Movement
▼ ▼ ▼

Simone de Beauvoir was an important figure in the emergence of the postwar women's liberation movement. This excerpt is taken from her influential book, The Second Sex, in which she argued that women have been forced into a position subordinate to men.

Simone de Beauvoir, *The Second Sex*

Now, woman has always been man's dependent, if not his slave; the two sexes have never shared the world in equality. And even today woman is heavily handicapped, though her situation is beginning to change. Almost nowhere is her legal status the same as man's, and frequently it is much to her disadvantage. Even when her rights are legally recognized in the abstract, long-standing custom prevents their full expression in the mores. In the economic sphere men and women can almost be said to make up two castes; other things being equal, the former hold the better jobs, get higher wages, and have more opportunity for success than their new competitors. In industry and politics men have a great many more positions and they monopolize the most important posts. In addition to all this, they enjoy a traditional prestige that the education of children tends in every way to support, for the present enshrines the past—and in the past all history has been made by men. At the present time, when women are beginning to take part in the affairs of the world, it is still a world that belongs to men—they have no doubt of it at all and women have scarcely any. To decline to be the Other, to refuse to be a party to a deal—this would be for women to renounce all the advantages conferred upon them by their alliance with the superior caste. Man-the-sovereign will provide woman-the-liege with material protection and will undertake the moral justification of her existence; thus she can evade at once both economic risk and the metaphysical risk of a liberty in which ends and aims must be contrived without assistance. Indeed, along with the ethical urge of each individual to affirm his subjective existence, there is also the temptation to forgo liberty and become a thing. This is an inauspicious road, for he who takes it—passive, lost, ruined—becomes henceforth the creature of another's will, frustrated in his transcendence and deprived of every value. But it is an easy road; on it one avoids the strain involved in undertaking an authentic existence. When man makes of woman the *Other*, he may, then, expect her to manifest deep-seated tendencies toward complicity. Thus, woman may fail to lay claim to the status of subject because she lacks definite resources, because she feels the necessary bond that ties her to man regardless of reciprocity, and because she is often very well pleased with her role as the *Other*.

Now, what peculiarly signalizes the situation of woman is that she—a free and autonomous being like all human creatures—nevertheless finds herself living in a world where men compel her to assume the status of the Other.

---

major influence on both the American and European women's movements (see the box above).

Feminists in the women's liberation movement came to believe that women themselves must transform the fundamental conditions of their lives. They did so in a variety of ways. First, in the 1960s and 1970s, they formed numerous "consciousness-raising" groups to further awareness of women's issues. Women also sought and gained a measure of control over their own bodies by seeking to overturn the illegality of both contraception and abortion. In the 1960s and 1970s, hundreds of thousands of European women worked to repeal the laws that outlawed contraception and abortion and began to meet with success. A French law in 1968 permitted the sale of contraceptive devices. In 1979, another French law legalized abortion. Even in Catholic countries, where the church remained strongly opposed to abortion, legislation allowing contraception and abortion was passed in the 1970s and 1980s. In the 1980s, the women's liberation movement concentrated on developing new cultural attitudes through the new academic field of "women's studies" and affecting the political and natural environment by allying with the antinuclear and ecological movements.

Popular Culture

Popular culture in the twentieth century, especially since World War II, has played an important role in helping Western people define themselves. If on one level popular culture is but the history of the superficial and transient whims of mass taste, on another level "it is a history of how modern society has created images of itself and expressed its fantasies, its fears, its ambitions."[14]

The history of popular culture is also the history of the economic system that supports it, for it is this system that manufactures, distributes, and sells the images that people consume as popular culture. As popular culture and its economic support system become increasingly intertwined, industries of leisure emerge. As one historian of popular culture has argued, "industrial societies turn the provision of leisure into a commercial activity, in which their citizens are sold entertainment, recreation, pleasure, and appearance as commodities that differ from the goods at the drugstore only in the way they are used."[15] Modern popular culture therefore is inextricably tied to the mass consumer society in which it has emerged. This consumer-oriented aspect of popular culture delineates it clearly from the folk culture of preceding centuries, for folk culture is something people make while popular culture is something people buy.

POPULAR CULTURE AND THE AMERICANIZATION OF THE WORLD   The United States has been the most influential force in shaping popular culture in the West and, to a lesser degree, the entire world. Through movies, music, advertising, and television, the United States has spread its particular form of consumerism and the American Dream to millions around the world. Already in 1923 the New York *Morning Post* noted that "the film is to America what the flag was once to Britain. By its means Uncle Sam may hope some day . . . to Americanize the world."[16] In movies, television, and popular music, the impact of American popular culture on the Western world is apparent.

In the years immediately following the war, motion pictures continued to be the primary vehicle for the diffusion of American popular culture. The emergence of *film noir*—films with a darker outlook—was a characteristic of the period. The heroes, often private detectives, were not the typical good guys in white hats of the past, but characters who had a nasty side and often broke the law themselves. They were troubled individuals, sometimes by the war, more often by women. Women in *film noir* were usually portrayed as independent and highly sexual and were often linked to betrayal and murder. This darker side of male-female relationships stood in contrast to the light screwball comedies that had proliferated in the 1930s.

In the 1950s, Cold War tensions and the "bomb" found expression in a rash of spy movies and nuclear war films. In the 1960s, the film industry sagged as television prospered. In the late 1960s, youth-oriented films, such as *The Graduate* and *Easy Rider,* appealed to the eighteen to twenty-five year olds to whom Hollywood increasingly geared its films. Also popular were films that presented antiestablishment figures as heroes, such as *Bonnie and Clyde.* This was a clear reflection of the antiestablishment sentiment that was pervasive at this time in both the United States and Europe. These films mixed the reality of historical figures with contemporary social sentiment. From the mid-1970s throughout the 1980s, Hollywood concentrated on "blockbusting," the practice of spending huge sums on a few, big star films, often with tremendous special effects. All this was done to ensure huge box office hits. In this way one film could make or break a studio's year.

Although American films dominated both European and American markets (40 percent of Hollywood's income in the 1960s came from the European market), the existence of a profitable art-house circuit in America and Europe enabled European filmmakers to make films whose themes and avant-garde methods were quite different from those of Hollywood. Italy and Sweden, for example, developed a tradition of "national cinema" that reflected "specific cultural traits in a mode in which they could be successfully exported." The 1957 film *The Seventh Seal,* by the Swedish director Ingmar Bergman, was a good example of the successful European art film. Bergman's films caused him to be viewed as "an artist of comparable stature to a novelist or playwright." So too were François Truffaut in France and Federico Fellini in Italy; such directors gloried in experimenting with subject matter and technique and produced films dealing with more complex and daring themes than Hollywood would attempt.

Although developed in the 1930s, television did not become readily available until the late 1940s. By 1954, there were 32 million sets in the United States as television became the centerpiece of middle-class life. It has been said that television was perfect for the suburban home, the "nuclear family's bunker," as it was "a piece of furniture that did something." Early television borrowed heavily from radio. Like radio, it was based in New York.

In 1951, however, when the two most popular shows were "I Love Lucy" and "Dragnet," both based in Hollywood, television studios relocated to the West Coast.

In the 1960s, as television spread around the world, American networks unloaded their products on Europe and the Third World at extraordinarily low prices. For instance, the British Broadcasting Corporation (BBC) could buy American programs for one-tenth the cost per viewer of producing its own. The establishment of quota systems prevented American television from completely inundating these countries. Nevertheless, American shows have remained popular in Europe with the result that many Europeans base their understanding of American life on such programs as "Dallas" and "Dynasty."

Unlike the United States, television and radio in Europe have largely been controlled by the state. The BBC model strongly influenced German broadcasting after the war. In France, de Gaulle saw state control of television as an important counterbalance to the opposition French press. In the Communist countries of Eastern Europe and the Soviet Union, state control was even more pervasive. In the 1980s, however, there has been an increasing trend toward commercial television in Western Europe. As communism began to loosen its grip in Eastern Europe, calls for freedom of press and speech have been extended to mass media. In July of 1990, Gorbachev announced that independent television and radio productions would be allowed in the Soviet Union for the first time.

The United States has dominated popular music since the end of World War II. Jazz, blues, rhythm and blues, rap, and rock and roll have been by far the most popular music forms in the Western world—and much of the non-Western world—during this time. All of them originated in the United States, and all are rooted in African-American musical innovations. These forms later spread to the rest of the world, inspiring local artists who then transformed the music in their own way. Often these transformed models then returned to the United States to inspire American artists. This was certainly the case with rock and roll. Through the 1950s, American figures such as Chuck Berry, Little Richard, and Elvis Presley inspired the Beatles and other British performers, who then led an "invasion" of the United States in the 1960s, creating a sensation and in part sparking new rockers in America. Rock music itself developed in the 1950s. In 1952, white disc jockeys began playing rhythm and blues and traditional blues music performed by African-Americans to young white audiences. The music was popular with this audience, and record companies began recording watered-down white cover versions of this music. It was not until such individuals as Elvis Presley mixed white "folkabilly" with rhythm and blues that rock and roll became popular with the larger white audience.

The period from 1967 to 1973 was probably the true golden age of rock. During this brief period, much experimentation in rock music took place, as it did in society in general. Straightforward rock and roll competed with a new hybrid blues rock, created in part by British performers such as the Rolling Stones, who were in turn inspired by African-American blues artists. Many musicians also experimented with non-Western musical sounds, such as Indian sitars. The one-world philosophy of the 1960s was expressed musically in this way. The popular music of the 1960s was also noted for

▼ **The Beatles in Concert.** Popular music has played a significant role in the impact of American popular culture on the postwar Western world. Although rock and roll originated in the United States, it also inspired musical groups in Europe as well. This was certainly true of Britain's Beatles, who created a sensation among young people when they came to the United States in the 1960s. Shown here are the Beatles during a performance on "The Ed Sullivan Show."

its social conscience. It was against the Vietnam War and materialism and promoted "peace and love" as alternatives to the prevailing "establishment" culture.

The same migration of a musical form from the United States to Britain and back to the United States occurred when the early punk movement in New York, which failed to make an immediate impact in the United States, spread to Britain in the mid-1970s. The more influential British punk movement of 1976–1979 was also fueled by an economic crisis that had resulted in large numbers of unemployed and undereducated young people. However, the punk movement was not simply a proletarian movement. Many of its supporters, performers, and promoters were British art school graduates who applied a leftist political philosophy and avant-garde experimentation to the movement. Punk rockers rejected most social conventions and preached anarchy and rebellion. They often wore tattered clothes and clothespins in their cheeks, symbolizing their rejection of a materialistic and degenerate culture. Musically, punk was extremely primitive in structure and performance, with noise and distortion elevated to art. Pure punk was short-lived, partly because its intense energy quickly burned out (as did many of its performers) and partly because, as ex-punk Mick Hucknall stated, "the biggest mistake of the punks was that they rejected music." However, offshoots of punk proliferated through the 1980s and continue to influence the rock and roll scene.

The social consciousness of popular music, so prevalent in the 1960s, also began to reappear in the late 1980s. Benefit concerts such as Live Aid, a high-technology affair staged simultaneously in London and Philadelphia, were held for the benefit of famine victims in Africa. At the same time, non-Western musical forms and sounds, heavy on rhythm and exotic tunings, began to influence Western pop music. The increasingly shrinking world, brought on by advancements in mass media technology, has led to a reemergence of the one-world philosophy of the 1960s. Some see this melding of world cultures as a positive step toward world unity, while others warn that it could lead to the watering down of cultural diversity and therefore the loss of unique forms of art.

SPORTS In the postwar years, sports have become a major product of both popular culture and the leisure industry. The development of satellite television and various electronic breakthroughs helped make sports a global phenomenon. Olympic Games could now be broadcast across the globe from anywhere in the world. Sports became a cheap form of entertainment for the consumer as fans did not have to leave their homes to enjoy athletic competitions. In fact, some sports organizations initially resisted television fearing that it would hurt ticket sales. However, the tremendous revenues possible from television contracts overcame this hesitation.

Television has also helped some sports, such as American football, to expand. Long a poor cousin of baseball, the suitability of American football to television programming and technology made it a perfect "telesport." By the mid-1960s, the National Football League had an exclusive contract with CBS for $14 million. By the end of the 1980s, football's television contract passed the $1 billion mark. As sports television revenue has escalated, many sports now receive the bulk of their yearly revenue from television contracts. The Olympics, for example, are now funded primarily by American television. These contracts are paid for by advertising sponsors, mostly for products to be consumed along with the sport: beer, soda, and snack foods. The 1984 Los Angeles Olympic Games were dubbed "the Corporate Games" and were the most financially successful in history. Whereas other Olympic contests have left massive debts, the Los Angeles Olympic Games turned a profit.

Sports have become big politics as well as big business. The politicization of sports has been one of the most significant trends in sports during the second half of the twentieth century. Football (soccer) remains the dominant world sport and has become more than ever a vehicle for nationalist sentiment and expression. The World Cup is the most watched event on television. Although the sport can be a positive outlet for national and local pride, all too often it has been marred by violence as nationalistic energies have overcome rational behavior. Events in Britain in particular have been marred by fan violence as extreme hooligans have rioted at matches.

The most telling example of the potent mix of politics and sport continues to be the Olympic Games. When the Soviets entered Olympic competition in 1952, the Olympics began to take on Cold War implications and became known as the "war without weapons." The Soviets saw the Olympics as a way to stimulate nationalist spirit, as well as to promote the Communist system as the best path for social progress. The Soviets have led the Olympics in terms of total medals won since 1956. The nature of the Olympics, with their daily medal count by nation and elaborate ceremonies and rituals such as the playing of the national anthem of the winning athletes and the parade of nations, virtually ensured the politicization of the games originally intended to foster international cooperation through friendly competition.

The political nature of the games found expression in other ways as well. In 1956, six nations withdrew from the games to protest the Soviet crushing of the Hungarian uprising. In 1972, twenty-seven African nations threatened to pull out of the Munich Olympics because of apartheid in South Africa. Also at the Munich Games, the Palestinian terrorist group Black September seized eleven Israeli athletes as hostages, all of whom died in a confrontation at an airport. The United States led a boycott of the 1980 Moscow Games to protest the Soviet invasion of Afghanistan, and the Soviets responded by boycotting the Los Angeles Games in 1984.

POPULAR CULTURE: TOWARD A NEW GLOBALISM   Media critic and theorist Marshall McLuhan predicted in the 1960s that advancements in mass communications technology, such as satellites and electronics, would eventually lead to a shrinking of the world, a lessening of cultural distinctions, and a breaking down of cultural barriers, all of which would in time transform the world into a single "global village." McLuhan was quite optimistic about these developments, and his ideas became quite popular at the time. Many critics have since argued that McLuhan was too utopian about the benefits of technological progress and maintain that the mass media that these technological breakthroughs created are still controlled by a small number of multinational corporations that "colonize the rest of the world, sometimes benignly, sometimes not." They argue that this has allowed Western popular culture to disrupt the traditional cultures of Third World countries and inculcate new patterns of behavior as well as new desires and new dissatisfactions.

Cultural contacts, however, often move in two directions. While the world has been "Americanized" to a great extent, formerly unfamiliar ways of life and styles of music have also come into the world of the West. This has expanded the horizons of Westerners and led to the creation of new cultural hybrids in music, philosophy, and religion. There is some truth in the "global village" image, for increasingly in the late 1980s the one-world vision of the late 1960s has reemerged in popular culture. This was evident in the benefit concerts, for example, as well as in the increasing concern for such global issues as the destruction of the rain forests in South America. This emergence of a global culture has been part of the new globalism in the postwar world.

▼ A New Globalism

In large part, the new globalism that has come to characterize the postwar world has been a product of Western expansion. For better or worse, non-Western peoples have been forced to modernize. This has basically meant that these peoples have had to adjust to the continuing imposition of Western institutions, technology, and even attitudes upon their societies. The work of combining Western and non-Western ways to construct modern states began with the process of decolonization after World War II.

Decolonization

World War I had initiated nationalistic movements against colonial rule, but World War II greatly accelerated this process. The colonial empires of the Western nations in the Far East had already been overrun by the Japanese during the war. Moreover, colonial soldiers who had fought on behalf of the Allies were well aware that Allied war aims included the principle of self-determination for the peoples of the world. Equally important to the process of decolonization after the war, the power of the European states had been destroyed by the exhaustive struggles of World War II. The greatest colonial empire builder, Great Britain, no longer had the energy or wealth to maintain its colonial empire after the war and quickly sought to let its colonies go. Given the combination of circumstances, a rush of decolonization swept through the world. Between 1947 and 1962, almost every colony gained independence and achieved statehood. While some colonial powers willingly relinquished their control, others, especially the French, had to be driven out by national wars of liberation. Decolonization created a new world as the non-Western states ended the long-held ascendancy of the Western nations.

In Asia, the United States began the process of decolonization in 1946 when it granted independence to the Philippines. Britain soon followed suit with its oldest and largest nonwhite possession—India. The conflict between India's Hindu and Muslim populations was solved by forming two states, a mostly Hindu India and a predominantly Muslim Pakistan in 1947. In 1948, Britain granted independence to Ceylon (modern Sri Lanka) and Burma. When the Dutch failed to reestablish control over the Dutch East Indies, Indonesia emerged as an independent nation in 1949. The French effort to remain in Indochina led to a bitter defeat in

▼ **Map 29.5** Asia After World War II.

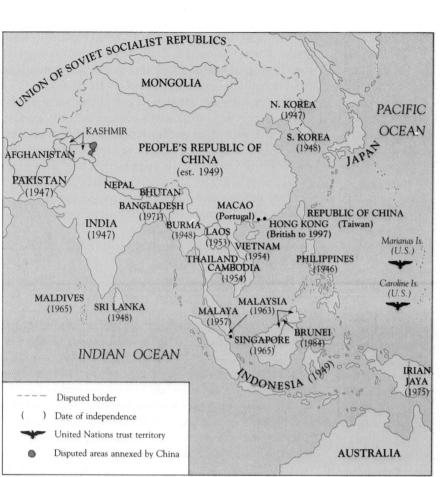

1954 by the forces of Ho Chi Minh, the Communist and nationalist leader of the Vietnamese. In the midst of the decolonization of Asia, a civil war between the Nationalist Chinese under Chiang Kai-Shek (1887–1975) and the Communists under Mao Zedong was being vigorously fought. Mao's victory in 1949 led to the creation of a powerful Communist state in Asia.

In the Middle East and northern Africa, Arab nationalism was a powerful factor in ending colonial empires. Although some Arab states had already become independent before the end of World War II, they were joined by other free Arab states, not without considerable bloodshed and complications, however. When the British left Palestine in 1947, the United Nations voted to create both an Arab and a Jewish state. When the Arabs attempted to destroy the new Israeli state, Israel's victories secured its existence. But the problem of the Palestinian refugees, supported by existing Arab states, created an Arab-Israeli conflict that has lasted to this day. In northern Africa, Arab nationalists in Algeria fought a bitter war of liberation with their French masters until Charles de Gaulle accepted the inevitable and granted Algerian independence in 1962.

Decolonization in Africa south of the Sahara took place less turbulently. Ghana proclaimed its independence in 1957, and by 1960, almost all French and British possessions in Africa had gained their freedom. In 1960, the Belgians freed the Congo (modern Zaire). The Portuguese held on stubbornly but were also driven out of Africa by 1975. Nevertheless, the continuing economic presence of European states in black Africa led radicals to accuse Europeans of "neocolonial" attitudes.

Although expectations ran high in the new states, they soon found themselves beset with problems of extreme poverty and antagonistic tribal groups that had little loyalty to the new nations. Under the new globalism, the world's nations soon divided into three levels. The "First World" consisted of the advanced industrial countries, basically by the 1960s Japan and the states of Western Europe and North America. The "Second World" comprised the Soviet Union and its satellites while most of the rest of the world's nations are known collectively as the "Third World." Their status as "backward" nations led many Third World countries to modernize by pursuing Western technology and industrialization. The gulf between the "developed" and "less developed" nations of the world, however, offers a major challenge to global stability in the decade ahead.

The United Nations

The United Nations has been one of the most visible symbols of the new postwar globalism. It was founded in 1945 in San Francisco when Allied representatives worked out a plan for the new organization. President Roosevelt had been especially anxious to create a new international organization to help maintain the peace after the war. At the Yalta Conference in February 1945, Stalin had agreed to join. In the original charter of the organization, its members pledged:

> to save succeeding generations from the scourge of war, which twice in our lifetime has brought untold sorrow to mankind, and to reaffirm faith in fundamental human rights, in the dignity and worth of the human person, in the equal rights of men and women and of nations large and small, and . . . to promote social progress and better standards of life in larger freedom.[17]

The United Nations, then, has two chief goals: peace and human dignity.

The General Assembly of the United Nations is composed of representatives of all members and is empowered to discuss any question of importance to the organization and to recommend action to be taken. The day-to-day administrative business of the United Nations is supervised by the secretary-general, whose offices are located at the permanent headquarters in New York City. The most important organ of the United Nations is the Security Council. It is composed of five permanent members—the United States, the Soviet Union, Great Britain, France, and China—and ten members chosen by the General Assembly. The Security Council decides what actions the United Nations should take to settle international disputes, but since each of the permanent members can veto the council's decision, a stalemate has frequently resulted.

A number of specialized agencies function under the auspices of the United Nations. These include the United Nations Educational, Scientific, and Cultural Organization (UNESCO), the World Health Organization (WHO), and the United Nations International Children's Emergency Fund (UNICEF). All of these have been successful in providing assistance for the world's economic and social problems. The United Nations has also performed a valuable service in organizing international conferences on such important issues as population growth and the environment.

The United Nations has also managed to provide peacekeeping military forces drawn from neutral member states to settle conflicts. Until recently, however, the fundamental weakness of the United Nations has been that throughout its history it has been subject to the whims of the two superpowers, whose rivalry in the Cold

▼ **Map 29.6** The Middle East After World War II.

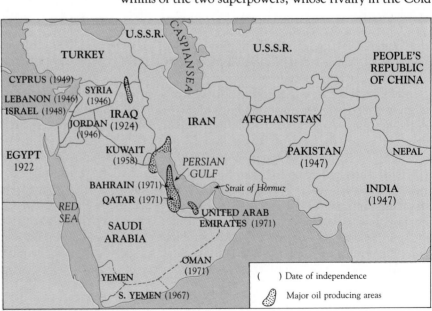

War was often played out at the organization's expense. The United Nations had little success, for example, in reducing the arms race between the United States and the Soviet Union. Nevertheless, the United Nations remains important in keeping alive a vision of international order and peace.

At the end of World War II, a new conflict erupted in the Western world as the two new superpowers, the United States and the Soviet Union, competed for political domination. Europeans, whether they wanted to or not, were forced to become supporters of one side or the other. But this ideological division also spread to the rest of the world as the United States fought in Korea and Vietnam to prevent the spread of communism,

while the Soviet Union used its armies to prop up pro-Soviet regimes in Eastern Europe and Afghanistan.

But at the end of the 1980s, profound changes in the Soviet Union, initiated by Mikhail Gorbachev, brought an apparent end to the Cold War. The rapid collapse of Communist governments in Eastern Europe was clearly due to Gorbachev's reversal of Soviet postwar policy as he decided not to interfere in the internal turmoils of the Soviet satellites. Almost everywhere in Eastern Europe, Communist regimes gave way to popular demands for political reforms and restructuring.

In addition to the Cold War conflict, the postwar era has also been characterized by a new globalism, evident in popular culture as well as political, economic, and social developments around the world. World War II had

▼ **Map 29.7** Africa After World War II.

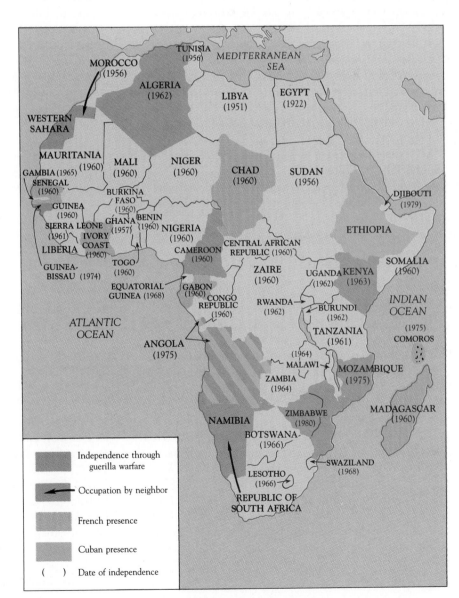

been a truly global conflict that ushered in a new global era. After the war, the colonial empires of the European states were largely dissolved, and the liberated territories of Africa, Asia, and the Middle East emerged as sovereign states. By the late 1980s, the approximately 160 sovereign states of the world had become an emerging global community. But the differences among the members of this global community are immense. An enormous economic gulf separates the "advanced industrial nations" from the "less developed" countries. More and more, however, the world's states have become aware of the fragile interdependence that connects them all.

Notes
▼ ▼ ▼

1. Quoted in Walter Laqueur, *Europe since Hitler*, rev. ed. (New York, 1982), p. 118.

2. Quoted in Joseph M. Jones, *The Fifteen Weeks (February 21–June 5, 1947)*, 2d ed. (New York, 1964), pp. 140–41.

3. Quoted in Wilfried Loth, *The Division of the World, 1941–1955* (New York, 1988), pp. 160–61.

4. Quoted in Peter Lane, *Europe since 1945: An Introduction* (Totowa, N.J., 1985), p. 248.

5. Quoted in Robert F. Kennedy, *Thirteen Days: A Memoir of the Cuban Missile Crisis* (New York, 1969), pp. 89–90.

6. R. Hilton, *Military Attaché in Moscow* (London, 1949), p. 41.

7. Nikita Khrushchev, *Khrushchev Remembers*, trans. Strobe Talbott (Boston, 1970), p. 77.

8. Mikhail Gorbachev, "Report to the 27th Party Congress," February 25, 1986, in *Current Soviet Policies 9* (1986): 10.

9. *Philadelphia Inquirer*, July 11, 1990, p. 1a.

10. Quoted in Henry Grosshans, *The Search for Modern Europe* (Boston, 1970), p. 421.

11. Quoted in Hilda Scott, *Sweden's 'Right to be Human'—Sex-Role Equality: The Goal and the Reality* (London, 1982), p. 125.

12. Quoted in Marsha Rowe et al., *Spare Rib Reader* (Harmondsworth, 1982), p. 574.

13. Simone de Beauvoir, *The Second Sex*, trans. H. M. Parshley (New York, 1961), p. xxviii.

14. Richard Maltby, ed., *Passing Parade: A History of Popular Culture in the Twentieth Century* (New York, 1989), p. 8.

15. Ibid.

16. Quoted in ibid., p. 11.

17. "The Charter of the United Nations," *Yearbook of the United Nations* (New York, 1983), p. 1325.

Suggestions for Further Reading
▼ ▼ ▼

Three introductory surveys on postwar Europe are P. Lane, *Europe Since 1945: An Introduction* (Totowa, N.J., 1985); J. R. Wegs, *Europe Since 1945: A Concise History*, 2d ed. (New York, 1984); and W. Laqueur, *Europe Since Hitler*, rev. ed. (New York, 1982). There is a detailed literature on the Cold War. Two general accounts are R. B. Levering, *The Cold War, 1945–1972* (Arlington Heights, Ill., 1982); and B. A. Weisberger, *Cold War, Cold Peace: The United States and Russia Since 1945* (New York, 1984). The following works maintain that the Soviet Union was chiefly responsible for the Cold War: H. Feis, *From Trust to Terror: The Onset of the Cold War, 1945–1950* (New York, 1970); and A. Ulam, *The Rivals: America and Russia Since World War II* (New York, 1971). Revisionist studies on the Cold War have emphasized the responsibility of the United States for the Cold War, especially its global aspects. These works include J. and G. Kolko, *The Limits of Power: The World and United States Foreign Policy, 1945–1954* (New York, 1972); W. LaFeber, *America, Russia and the Cold War, 1945–1966*, 2d ed. (New York, 1972); and M. Sherwin, *A World Destroyed: The Atomic Bomb and the Grand Alliance* (New York, 1975). For a critique of the revisionist studies, see R. L. Maddox, *The New Left and the Origins of the Cold War* (Princeton, N. J., 1973). There is a detailed analysis of American-Soviet relations in the 1970s and 1980s in R. Garthoff, *Détente and Confrontation: American-Soviet Relations From Nixon to Reagan* (Washington, D. C., 1985). On the end of the Cold War, see B. Denitch, *The End of the Cold War* (Minneapolis, Minn., 1990); W. G. Hyland, *The Cold War is Over* (New York, 1990); and W. Laqueur, *Soviet Union 2000: Reform or Revolution?* (New York, 1990). For important studies of Soviet foreign policy, see A. B. Ulam, *Expansion and Coexistence: Soviet Foreign Policy 1917–1973*, 2d ed. (New York, 1974), and *Dangerous Relations: The Soviet Union in World Politics,*

1970–1982 (New York, 1983). The effects of the Cold War on Germany are examined in J. H. Backer, *The Decision to Divide Germany: American Foreign Policy in Transition* (Durham, N. Car., 1978). On atomic diplomacy in the Cold War, see G. F. Herken, *The Winning Weapon: The Atomic Bomb in the Cold War, 1945–1950* (New York, 1981). For a good introduction to the arms race, see E. M. Bottome, *The Balance of Terror: A Guide to the Arms Race,* rev. ed. (Boston, 1986). On the Cuban Missile Crisis, see R. A. Chayes, *The Cuban Missile Crisis* (New York, 1974). For a good account of the Vietnam War, see S. Karnow, *Vietnam: A History* (New York, 1983).

For a general view of Soviet society, see D. K. Shipler, *Russia: Broken Idols, Solemn Dreams* (New York, 1983). On the Khrushchev years, see E. Crankshaw, *Khrushchev: A Career* (New York, 1966). Recent problems in the Soviet Union are analyzed in A. Brown and M. Kaser, *Soviet Policy for the 1980s* (London, 1983). For a general study of the Soviet satellites in Eastern Europe, see A. Brown and J. Gary, *Culture and Political Changes in Communist States* (London, 1977); and S. Fischer-Galati, *Eastern Europe in the 1980s* (London, 1981). On the Soviet Union's actions against Czechoslovakia in 1968, see J. Valenta, *Intervention in Czechoslovakia in 1968* (Baltimore, 1979). The unique path of Yugoslavia is examined in L. J. Cohen and P. Warwick, *Political Cohesion in a Fragile Mosaic: The Yugoslav Experience* (Boulder, Colo., 1983). On Romania, see L. S. Graham, *Rumania: A Developing Socialist State* (Boulder, Colo., 1978). On Hungary, see B. Kovrig, *The Hungarian People's Republic* (Baltimore, 1970). The Solidarity movement in Poland is examined in T. G. Ash, *The Polish Revolution: Solidarity* (New York, 1984). On East Germany, see C. B. Scharf, *Politics and Change in East Germany* (Boulder, Colo., 1984).

The rebuilding of postwar Europe is examined in A. S. Milward, *The Reconstruction of Western Europe, 1945–51* (Berkeley, 1984). On the building of common institutions in Western Europe, see J. Lodge, *Institutions and Policies of the European Community* (New York, 1983). For a survey of West Germany, see M. Balfour, *West Germany: A Contemporary History* (London, 1983). France under de Gaulle is examined in P. Williams and M. Harrison, *Politics and Society in de Gaulle's Republic* (New York, 1971). On Britain, see C. J. Bartlett, *A History of Post-War Britain* (London, 1977); and A. Sampson, *The Changing Anatomy of Britain* (New York, 1982). On Italy, see J. LaPalombara, *Democracy, Italian Style* (New Haven, Conn., 1987).

For a general view of postwar thought, see R. N. Stromberg, *European Intellectual History Since 1789,* 4th ed. (Englewood Cliffs, N. J. 1986). Also valuable is D. LaCapra and S. L. Kaplan, eds., *Modern European Intellectual History: Reappraisals and New Perspectives* (Ithaca, N. Y., 1982). A physicist's view of science is contained in J. Ziman, *The Force of Knowledge: The Scientific Dimension of Society* (Cambridge, 1976). A physicist's view of a new conception of reality is D. Bohm, *Wholeness and the Implicate Order* (Boston, 1980). The space race is examined in W. A. McDougall, *The Heavens and the Earth: A Political History of the Space Age* (New York, 1984). For background on logical positivism, see A. Janik and S. Toulmin, *Wittgenstein's Vienna* (New York, 1973). A classic work on existentialism is W. Barrett, *Irrational Man* (Garden City, New York, 1962).

For a survey of contemporary Western society, see A. Sampson, *The New Europeans* (New York, 1968). The changing role of women is examined in E. Sullerot, *Women, Society and Change* (New York, 1971); and A. Cherlin, *Marriage, Divorce, Remarriage* (Cambridge, Mass., 1981). On the women's liberation movement, see D. Bouchier, *The Feminist Challenge: The Movement for Women's Liberation in Britain and the United States* (New York, 1983). The student revolts of the late 1960s are put into a broader context in L. S. Feuer, *The Conflict of Generations* (New York, 1969). There is an excellent survey of twentieth-century popular culture in R. Maltby, ed., *Passing Parade: A History of Popular Culture in the Twentieth Century* (Oxford, 1989). Also valuable is D. Horne, *The Public Culture: The Triumph of Industrialism* (London, 1986). On film and the media, see L. May, *Screening Out the Past: The Birth of Mass Culture and the Motion Picture Industry* (New York, 1980); E. A. Rhodes, *A History of the Cinema from the Silents to the Seventies* (Harmondsworth, 1978); and F. Wheen, *Television* (London, 1985). On popular music, see P. Eberly, *Music in the Air* (New York, 1982). Sport is examined in A. Guttmann, *From Ritual to Record: The Nature of Modern Sports* (New York, 1978); and R. Mandell, *Sport: A Cultural History* (New York, 1984). On the "global village" idea, see M. McLuhan, *Understanding Media: The Extensions of Man* (London, 1964).

On decolonization after World War II, see R. von Albertini, *Decolonization* (New York, 1971); A. Mazrui and M. Tidy, *Nationalism and New States in Africa* (London, 1984); J. Talbott, *The War without a Name: France in Algeria, 1954–1962* (New York, 1980); D. K. Shipler, *Arab and Jew: Wounded Spirits in a Promised Land* (New York, 1986). On the problems of the Third World, see P. Harrison, *Inside the Third World,* 2d ed. (New York, 1984). On the United Nations, see H. G. Nicholas, *The United Nations as a Political Institution* (New York, 1967).

Chapter 30

Epilogue: Toward A Global Civilization

▼▼▼▼▼

I ncreasingly, more and more people are becoming aware of the political and economic interdependence of the world's nations as well as the global nature of our contemporary problems. On the threshold of the twenty-first century, human beings are coming to understand that destructive forces generated in one part of the world soon affect the entire world. Nuclear proliferation makes nuclear war an ever-present possibility; nuclear war would mean radioactive fallout for the entire planet. Smokestack pollution in one nation can produce acid rain in another. Oil spills and dumping of wastes in the ocean have an impact on the shores of many nations. The consumption of drugs in the world's wealthy nations affects the stability of both wealthy and less developed nations. As food,

water, energy, and natural resources crises proliferate, solutions by one nation often affect other nations. The new globalism includes the recognition that the challenges that seem to threaten human existence at the end of the twentieth century are global challenges. As a Soviet physicist and an American engineer jointly concluded: "The emergence of global problems and the recognition of their importance is perhaps the greatest accomplishment of contemporary thought."[1]

▼ The Emergence of New Global Visions

The authors of a report on the impact of population growth in South Asia concluded that the only way to avoid disaster in that region was to build a new global economic order:

In summary, the only feasible solution to the world food situation requires:

1. A global approach to the problem. . . .
3. A balanced economic development for all regions. . . .
5. Worldwide diversification of industry, leading to a truly global economic system.

Only a proper combination of these measures can lead to a solution. Omission of any one measure will surely lead to disaster. But the strains on the global food production capacity would be lessened if the eating habits in the affluent part of the world would change, becoming less wasteful.[2]

At the same time, some Western political thinkers have argued that we need to let go of practices that have evolved over the course of Western civilization, but no longer serve much purpose. Above all, war has been singled out as an issue that the current generation must seek to change. According to the Soviet and American editors of *Breakthrough-Emerging New Thinking*: "War, indiscriminate and brutal, which destroys the fragile civil processes it is designed to protect, wastes and ravages everything in its path, and twice in our century has decimated a generation of young men. . . . War is the issue for this generation, and global thinking is the challenge."[3]

As the heirs of Western civilization have become aware that the problems humans face are global—not national—they have responded to this challenge in several ways. One approach has been to develop grass-roots social movements, including environmental, women's and men's liberation, human potential, appropriate-technology, and nonviolence movements. Hazel Henderson, a British-born economist, has been especially active in founding public interest groups. She believes that citizen groups can be an important force for greater global unity and justice. In *Creating Alternative Futures*, she explained: "These aroused citizens are by no means all mindless young technophobes or radicals. Well-dressed, clean-shaven, middle-class businessmen and their suburban wives comprise the major forces in California fighting against nuclear power. Hundreds of thousands of middle-class mothers are bringing massive pressure to ban commercials and violent programs from children's television."[4] "Think globally, act locally" is frequently the slogan of these grass-roots groups.

Related to the emergence of these social movements is the growth of nongovernmental organizations (NGOs). The American educator Elise Boulding has been especially active in encouraging and publicizing the existence of these groups. According to Boulding,

NGOs are an important instrument in the cultivation of global perspectives:

Since NGOs by definition are identified with interests that transcend national boundaries, we expect all NGOs to define problems in global terms, to take account of human interests and needs as they are found in all parts of the planet. Because they have neither armies nor large bureaucracies at their command, we assume that they will utilize the power of shared values and concerns, rather than the power of political dominance to carry out aims. . . . Since they are emergent structures, we may also assume that they will reflect new perceptions of planetary society, and of appropriate social roles for individuals and groups. In short, we might look to them for new definitions of problems based on global frames of reference, and new ways of thinking and working.[5]

NGOs are often represented at the United Nations and include professional, business, and cooperative organizations; foundations; religious, peace, and disarmament groups; youth and women's organizations; environmental and human rights groups; and research institutes. The number of international NGOs increased from 176 in 1910 to 18,000 in 1988.

Some international NGOs have sections in both NATO and Warsaw Pact states, a reminder that the Communist countries are participating in the new global thinking. While this new sociopolitical thought began to emerge in the Soviet Union in the 1970s, it was Mikhail Gorbachev who implemented it in the 1980s in his policies for *glasnost* (openness) and *perestroika* (restructuring). In his book *Perestroika*, Gorbachev stated:

Thereby, an altogether different situation has emerged. A way of thinking and a way of acting, based on the use of force in world politics, have formed over centuries, even millennia. It seems they have taken root as something unshakable. Today, they have lost all reasonable grounds. . . . For the first time in history, basing international politics on moral and ethical norms that are common to all humankind, as well as humanizing interstate relations, has become a vital requirement. . . .

There is a great thirst for mutual understanding and mutual communication in the world. It is felt among politicians, it is gaining momentum . . . . among the public at large. And if the Russian word "perestroika" has easily entered the international lexicon, this is due to more than just interest in what is going on in the Soviet Union. Now the whole world needs restructuring, . . . a fundamental change.

People feel and understand this. They have to find their bearings, to understand the problems besetting mankind, to realize how they should live in the future. The restructuring is a must for a world overflowing with nuclear weapons; for a world ridden with serious economic and ecological problems; for a world laden with poverty, backwardness and disease; for a human race now facing the urgent need of ensuring its own survival.[6]

Gorbachev's thinking was clearly based on the recognition of an interdependent world.

Another source for global thinking in the West has come from the Western tradition's own spiritual perspective. As might be expected, a number of religious leaders have urged the West not to overlook its spiritual heritage as it searches for solutions to its problems. Somewhat more surprisingly, some secular figures, including Vaclav Havel, the president of Czechoslovakia, have also found inspiration in the West's spiritual tradition. In a speech to the American Congress on February 21, 1990, Havel declared:

> For this reason, the salvation of this human world lies nowhere else than in the human heart, in the human power to reflect, in human meekness and in human responsibility.
>
> Without a global revolution in the sphere of human consciousness, nothing will change for the better in the sphere of our being as humans, and the catastrophe toward which this world is headed—be it ecological, social, demographic or a general breakdown of civilization—will be unavoidable. . . .
>
> In other words, we still don't know how to put morality ahead of politics, science and economics. We are still incapable of understanding that the only genuine backbone of all our actions, if they are to be moral, is responsibility.
>
> Responsibility to something higher than my family, my country, my company, my success—responsibility to the order of being where all our actions are indelibly recorded and where and only where they will be properly judged.
>
> The interpreter or mediator between us and this higher authority is what is traditionally referred to as human conscience.[7]

Many lessons can be learned from the history of Western civilization, but one of them is especially clear. Lack of involvement in the affairs of one's society leads to powerlessness. An understanding of our Western heritage and its lessons might well give us the wisdom not to continue to repeat the mistakes of the past. For we are all creators of history and upon us depends the future of Western and indeed world civilization.

▼ **The Earth.** For many people in the West as in the rest of the world, the view of Earth from outer space fostered an important image of global unity. The American astronaut Russell Schweickart wrote: "From where you see it, the thing is a whole, and it is so beautiful." In a similar reaction, Yuri Gagarin, a Soviet cosmonaut, remarked: "What strikes me, is not only the beauty of the continents . . . but their closeness to one another . . . their essential unity."

Notes

▼ ▼ ▼

1. Sergei Kapitza and Martin Hellman, "A Message to the Scientific Community," in Anatoly Gromyko and Martin Hellman, eds., *Breakthrough—Emerging New Thinking: Soviet and Western Scholars Issue a Challenge to Build a World beyond War* (New York, 1988), p. xii.

2. Mihajlo Mesarovic and Eduard Pestel, *Mankind at the Turning Point: The Second Report to the Club of Rome* (New York, 1974), p. 127.

3. Gromyko and Hellman, eds., *Breakthrough*, p. 2.

4. Hazel Henderson, *Creating Alternative Futures* (New York, 1978), p. 356.

5. Elise Boulding, *Women in the Twentieth Century World* (New York, 1977), pp. 186–187.

6. Mikhail Gorbachev, *Perestroika* (New York, 1987), pp. 141, 253–254.

7. Vaclav Havel, *The Washington Post,* February 22, 1990, p. A28d.

Index

▼ ▼ ▼

Illustration Credits (*continued*)

▼ ▼ ▼

the British Museum; **867** © Ullstein Bilderdienst; **873** The Bettmann Archive; **875** Bild-Archiv der Osterreichischen Nationalbibliothek, Vienna; Photo by Lichtbildwerkstatte Alpenland; **883** Scala/Art Resource, N.Y.; **884** Paul Cezanne, *Femme a la cafetiere*, Paris, Musee d'Orsay, © Photo R. M. N.; **885** Vincent Van Gogh, *The Starry Night*, (1889), Oil on canvas, 29 x 36¼'', Collection, The Museum of Modern Art, New York; Acquired through the Lillie P. Bliss Bequest; **886** (Top Left) Henri Matisse, *Madame Matisse* (1905), Statens Museum for Kunst, Kopenhagen (R. 171), Photo: Hans Peterson © 1991 Succession H. Matisse/A.R.S., N.Y.; (Bottom Right) Pablo Picasso, *Les Demoiselles d'Avignon*, Paris (Begun May reworked July 1907), Oil on canvas, 8' x 7'8'', Collection, the Museum of Modern Art, New York, Acquired through the Lillie P. Bliss Bequest; **887** (Bottom Left) Vasily Kadinsky, *Painting with White Border*, May 1913; Collection, the Solomon R. Guggenheim Museum, New York; (Top Right) © Peter Aaron/ESTO; **889** Courtesy, Vassar College Library; **891** The Mansell Collection.

Chapter 26

Page 896 Bilderdienst Suddeutscher Verlag, Munich; **898** The Bettmann Archive; **901** Librairie Larousse, Paris; **905** Librairie Larousse, Paris; **907**(Left) © Roger-Viollet; (Right) Bilderdienst Suddeutscher Verlag, Munich; **910** The Bettmann Archive; **912** The Trustees of the Imperial War Museum; **913** © Ullstein Bilderdienst; **919** Brown Brothers; **921** Bettmann/Hulton; **926** Bettmann/Hulton.

Chapter 27

Page 932 Paulman, 10 November, 1938, Photo © Bildarchiv Preussischer Kulturbesitz, Berlin; **934** UPI/Bettmann; **937** © Roger-Viollet; **944** AP/Wide World Photos; **949** Hugo Jaeger, Life Magazine, © Time Warner Inc.; **950** Hugo Jaeger, Life Magazine, © Time Warner Inc.; **952** Paulman, 10 November, 1938, Photo © Bildarchiv Preussischer Kulturbesitz,

Berlin; **956** AP/Wide World Photos; **960** Courtesy of the Ford Motor Company; **962** Salvador Dali, *The Persistence of Memory*, 1931, Oil on canvas, 9½ × 13", Collection, The Museum of Modern Art, New York, Given Anonymously; **963** Kurt Schwitters, *Picture with White Center*, 1919, Collage of cut and pasted papers and oil on cardboard, 33¼ × 25⅞", Collection, The Museum of Modern Art, New York, Purchase; **965** AP/Wide World Photos.

Chapter 28

Page 970 © Topham/The Image Works; **975** The Bettmann Archive; **977** National Archives(#306-NT-1222E); **978** AP/Wide World Photos; **981** © Topham/The Image Works; **983** National Archives(#111-C-273); **987** The Trustees of the Imperial War Museum; **988** AP/Wide World Photos; **990** Popperfoto; **944** National Archives(#239-RC-18-1); **995** AP/Wide World Photos; **996** E.T. Archive.

Chapter 29

Page 1002 AP/Wide World Phots; **1009** AP/Wide World Photos; **1017**(Bottom Left) Bettmann/Hulton; (Top Right) AP/Wide World Photos; **1019** Reuters/Bettmann; **1021** AP/Wide World Photos; **1026**(Left) Hans Namuth, Photo Researchers, Inc; (Right) The Museum of Contemporary Art. Purchased with funds provided by Douglas S. Cramer, Beatrice and Philip Gersh, Lenore S. and Bernard A. Greenberg, Joan and Fred Nicholas, Robert A. Rowan, Pippa Scott, and an anonymous donor; Photo by Squidds and Nunns; **1030** (Left) Barbey/Magnum Photos, Inc.; (Right) AP/Wide World Photos; **1034** AP/Wide World Photos; **1035** Michael Ginsberg/Magnum Photos, Inc.; **1038** AP/Wide World Photos.

Chapter 30

Page 1046 Courtesy of NASA; **1048** Courtesy of NASA.